RETAILING

RETAILING

Fourth Edition

DALE M. LEWISON
University of Akron

Macmillan Publishing Company
New York
Collier Macmillan Canada, Inc.
Toronto
Maxwell Macmillan International Publishing Group
New York Oxford Singapore Sydney

Cover photo: © 1989 Mort Tucker Photography, Inc.

Editors: Michele Rhoades and David B. Boelio
Production Editor: Linda H. Bayma
Art Coordinator: Ruth A. Kimpel
Photo Editors: Chris Migdol and Gail Meese
Text Designer: Anne Daly
Cover Designer: Russ Maselli
Production Buyer: Pamela D. Bennett

This book was set in New Caledonia.

Printed in the United States of America

Text photos: All photos copyrighted by individuals or companies listed. Tim Cairns—Cobalt Productions/Macmillan, pp. 122 (top right, bottom left and right), 309, 629; Larry Hamill/Macmillan, pp. 48, 252, 263, 275, 280, 300, 304, 364, 371, 374, 375, 380, 396, 410, 420, 440, 442, 447, 456, 479, 481, 492, 503, 561, 569, 603, 622, 657; Amy Morgan, pp. 2, 21, 24, 43, 106, 203, 277, 282, 285, 286, 299, 300, 302, 305, 306, 370, 373, 378, 401, 402, 439, 446, 562, 634, 637, 668; Michael Pogony—Photographic Communications/Macmillan, p. 122 (top left).

Macmillan Publishing Company
866 Third Avenue, New York, New York 10022

Collier Macmillan Canada, Inc.

Library of Congress Cataloging-in-Publication Data
Lewison, Dale M.
Retailing / Dale M. Lewison.—4th ed.
p. cm.
Includes bibliographical references and indexes.
ISBN 0-02-370521-3
1. Retailing. I. Title.
HF5429.L487 1991
658.8′7—dc20 90-49925
CIP

Printing: 1 2 3 4 5 6 7 8 9 **Year:** 1 2 3 4

RETAILING IN THE 90'S INSERTS

"Merchandise Displays"
Page One: (top) HTI/Space Design International; (bottom) Stores Magazine
Page Two: (top) HTI/Space Design International; (middle) Sears, Roebuck and Company; (bottom) Stores Magazine

"Superstore Building"
Page One: Stores Magazine
Page Two: (top) Stores Magazine; (middle) Shop Ko; (bottom) Staples

"Retail Technologies"
Page One: Symbol Tech., Bohemia, NY
Page Two: (top left and right) Symbol Tech., Bohemia, NY; (bottom) Zebra Technologies Corporation/COMSTOCK Inc./Russ Kinne

"Storefronts"
Page One: (left) Michael L. Abramson; (right) Richard Vogel/Gamma Liaison
Page Two: (top) Stores Magazine; (middle) Architects Collab.; (bottom) Sears, Roebuck and Company

"Store Atmospherics"
Page One: (top) Jesse Gerstein; (bottom) © The Sharper Image
Page Two: HTI/Space Design International

"Recreation and Entertainment"
Page One: Stores Magazine
Page Two: (left and top right) Stores Magazine; (bottom right) Hickory Ridge Mall, Memphis, TN

"Central Courts and Facility Restorations"
Page One: (top) Mort Tucker Photography, Inc. Associates/Nesnadny & Schwartz/ Convention & Visitors Bureau of Greater Cleveland; (bottom) C. Bruce Forster
Page Two: (top) Tower City Development, Cleveland, OH; (bottom) Jennie Jones/Tower City Development, Cleveland, OH

"Handling Merchandise"
Page One: (top left and bottom) Bill Barley—Superstock; (top right) Art Montes De Oca
Page Two: (top) Jim Pickerell—F.P.G.; (bottom) Tom Tracy—F.P.G.

"Institutional Advertising"
Page One: Benetton
Page Two: (top left) Sears, Roebuck and Company; (top right) Saks Fifth Avenue; (bottom) NBO

"Product Advertising"
(top left) K mart Corporation; (top right) Rax Restaurants, Inc., Greg Stroube Studios, photographer; Joy Bullivant, food stylist; Louis London, advertising agency; (bottom left) Nugent, Wenckus, Inc. Photographics; (bottom right) Pier Imports

"Cooperative Advertising"
(top) Oshkosh B'Gosh/Sears, Roebuck and Company; (bottom) Saks/Prestige Fragrances, Ltd.

"Service Retailing"
Page One: Margeotes, Fertitta & Weiss
Page Two: (top) Professional Carpet Services; (bottom) Chemical Bank/photo by Steven Wilkes
Page Three: (top) Great Scott Advertising; (bottom) Hinkley & Slade, Houston
Page Four: (top) Reprinted from Marketing News, October 9, 1989, page 2, published by the American Marketing Association; (bottom) EVANS/Los Angeles

MACMILLAN SERIES IN COLLEGE MARKETING

BAGOZZI	*Principles of Marketing Management*
BEISEL	*Contemporary Retailing*
BERMAN AND EVANS	*Retail Management,* Fourth Edition
BOWERSOX, CLOSS, AND HELFERICH	*Logistical Management,* Third Edition
CHAPMAN AND BRADLEY	*Dynamic Retailing,* Second Edition
COHEN	*The Practice of Marketing Management,* Second Edition
DOUGLAS	*Writing for Public Relations*
ETZEL AND WOODSIDE	*Cases in Retailing Strategy*
EVANS AND BERMAN	*Marketing,* Fourth Edition
EVANS AND BERMAN	*Principles of Marketing,* Second Edition
GALLOWAY, EVANS, AND BERMAN	*Paintco III: A Computerized Marketing Simulation*
GREER	*Cases in Marketing,* Fifth Edition
HAIR, ANDERSON, AND TATHAM	*Multivariate Data Analysis,* Second Edition
HARTLEY	*Sales Management*
HISE AND MCDANIEL	*Cases in Marketing Strategy*
HISRICH AND PETERS	*Marketing Decisions for New and Mature Products,* Second Edition
HORTON	*Buyer Behavior*
JOHNSON AND WOOD	*Contemporary Logistics,* Fourth Edition
KATZENSTEIN AND SACHS	*Direct Marketing*
KINCAID	*Promotion: Products, Services, and Ideas,* Second Edition
LEWISON	*Retailing,* Fourth Edition
LEWISON	*Essentials of Retailing*
LEWISON AND HAWES	*Cases in Retail Management*
LILL	*Selling: The Profession*
MORRIS	*Industrial and Organizational Marketing*
MOWEN	*Consumer Behavior,* Second Edition
O'CONNOR	*Personal Selling*
OLSZEWSKI	*Product Pursuit*
ONKVISIT AND SHAW	*International Marketing*
RISCH	*Retail Merchandising,* Second Edition
RUNYON	*Advertising,* Second Edition
RUNYON AND STEWART	*Consumer Behavior,* Third Edition
SCHEUING	*New Product Management*
SEITEL	*Practice of Public Relations,* Fourth Edition
SOLDOW AND THOMAS	*Professional Selling: An Interpersonal Perspective*
TULL AND HAWKINS	*Marketing Research,* Fifth Edition
TULL AND KAHLE	*Marketing Management*
WEEKS, PERENCHIO, MILLER, AND METCALF	*Merchandising Mathematics*
WEILBACHER	*Cases in Advertising*
WEILBACHER	*Marketing Management Cases,* Fourth Edition
WOOD AND JOHNSON	*Contemporary Transportation,* Third Edition

PREFACE

Goal for the Text

Courses in retailing have never been more popular than they are today. The demand for practical, job-oriented courses that enhance students' chances of finding entry-level management positions is clear, and certainly helps to explain the increase in course offerings and growing enrollments.

With the growing emphasis on job-oriented skills, though, comes the need to "balance" the material presented. Students as well as the business community view retailing as a practical, operations-oriented discipline. Accordingly, operations-oriented policies, methods, and procedures must be an integral part of a retailing course. Academic credibility requires, however, that course materials be couched within a conceptual, theoretical framework. To meet these dual needs, the goal for this fourth edition of *Retailing* has been to strike a balance between academic credibility and the basic, operations-oriented needs of the job-seeking student.

Plan for the Text

The organization and plan for *Retailing*, Fourth Edition, combined with many features from previous editions and several new features, accomplish this text goal. The book is organized into six parts, divided into 20 chapters, that provide comprehensive yet manageable learning modules. The book covers all major topics: consumers; retail site location; designing, staffing, and organizing the retail store; developing the retail offering and getting the merchandise into the store; developing and controlling the merchandise plan; setting and adjusting retail prices; promotional activities; the importance of environmental influences in retail business; and retail financial statements and operations control. All chapters have been thoroughly updated and reviewed to include the most recent developments in the field and to reinforce the decision-making approach.

The fourth edition involves several significant changes and improvements that will help in achieving the book's goals. They include:

- Reduction of the textbook from 24 chapters to a more manageable 20 chapters. The lighter structure was achieved by careful editing and by combining six compatible chapters.
- Reorganization of the chapter sequence. The first 17 chapters are devoted to the basics of retailing within a tactical management perspective; the remaining 3 chapters deal with strategic management issues. The new organization will permit greater flexibility in course design.

- Repositioning of the material on retail careers within Appendix B. The career dimension can be covered at any point in the course deemed appropriate by the professor.
- A new chapter, "Retailing Dynamics—Future Trends and Directions." This chapter examines which consumer demographic and lifestyle trends are impacting retail operations and how retail organizations are adapting to their changing environment.
- A new chapter section on business ethics in Chapter 4, "The Legal and Ethical Aspects of Retailing." Ethical issues and concerns are reinforced throughout the text with boxed inserts, student projects, and case problems.
- Expanded coverage of retailing technologies in Chapter 5, "Retail Information Systems and Technologies." New technologies and their applications are interjected throughout the text with additional text discussions, chapter graphics, boxed inserts, and student projects.
- Greater emphasis on global retailing in terms of expanded text coverage, boxed inserts, and case situations.
- New chapter organization. The student learning process is enhanced through the expanded use of learning aids, study guides, and application manuals.
- Addition of end-of-chapter tactical cases, supported by supplementary cases in Appendix A.
- A new text design and revised art program. Key concepts and processes are presented in both verbal and graphic form, complementing and reinforcing the student learning process. Several photo essays highlight contemporary retailing issues.

Learning Aids

- Chapter-opening outlines that preview the important topics covered in each chapter help students organize their reading of the chapter.
- Learning objectives guide students' reading and help them identify important ideas for review and application.
- Opening chapter vignettes spark students' interest and establish the tone of the chapter's subject matter.
- "The World of Retailing," a series of boxed inserts, highlights such key issues as business ethics, retail technologies, and international retailing.
- "Retail Strategies and Tactics," a series of boxed inserts, focuses students' attention on key decision-making and problem-solving examples.
- Brief, end-of-chapter summaries reflect the chapter objectives and streamline students' review of major concepts.
- The end-of-chapter Student Study Guide provides students with a convenient means of reviewing the chapter, preparing for tests, and obtaining greater understanding of the materials. The guide consists of Key Terms and Concepts, Review Questions, and a Review Exam.
- The end-of-chapter Student Applications Manual provides the student with investigative projects that expand student skills through field studies, library searches, and survey assignments. Short, pragmatic tactical cases that provide problem-solving opportunities and practice in applying analytical skills and improving presentation skills are also included.
- Key terms and concepts, including both technical and nontechnical terms, are conveniently defined in a glossary at the end of the book.

Ancillaries and Supplements

Instructor's Manual: The Instructor's Manual contains complete lecture outlines, answers to review questions, review exams, project investigations, and solutions to both tactical and supplementary cases.

Transparency Masters: Transparency Masters of key text illustrations and lecture organization are available to all adopters.

Test Bank: Updated and revised 2,000-item test banks (paper and computerized) are available to all adopters.

Supplementary Lecture Series: Fifty nontext, supplementary lectures, consisting of a lecture outline and a colored or shaded transparency, are available to all adopters.

Video: A videotape and video instructor's manual are available to all adopters. The videotape contains a variety of corporate cases covering different retailing subjects. The video instructor's manual includes information on the video and suggestions for integration of the video into your course curriculum.

ACKNOWLEDGMENTS

This book would not have been possible without the valuable support of many people. Therefore, I wish to thank the following professors for reviewing the manuscript: Robert Dornoff, University of Cincinnati; Peter Doukas, Westchester Community College; Joanne Ezkstein, Macomb Community College; Myrna Glenny, Fashion Institute of Design and Merchandising; Marianne Knue, University of Cincinnati; Robert Miller, Central Michigan University; James Ogden, Kutztown University; C. William Roe, Nicholls State University; and Anthony Urbaniak, Northern State University.

Also, I wish to extend my appreciation for the helpful suggestions of reviewers in the earlier stages of manuscript preparation: Dave Snyder, Pennsylvania State University; Lewis J. Neisner, SUNY at Buffalo; John B. Gifford, Miami University; Dr. Robert Solomon, Stephen F. Austin State University; John J. Porter, West Virginia University; William Piper, University of Wisconsin; Rebecca Kaminsky Shidel, Bauder Fashion College; Morton Cooper, Cleveland State University; Paul Gulbicki, Middlesex Community College; Del Clayton, Spalding University; Jean Shanneyfelt, Edison State Community College; and Ethel Fishman, Fashion Institute of Technology. With such qualitative input from so many knowledgeable people in the field of retailing, I believe this book can fulfill students' needs for a basic understanding of both the theoretical and the practical applications of retailing.

For his support and encouragement, special appreciation goes to Russell Peterson, Dean of the College of Business Administration at the University of Akron. Special thanks to my colleagues and the staff of the Marketing Department at the University of Akron; Pat Johnson, who oversaw all the original production of this revision; to my graduate assistant Amy Morgan for her research efforts; and to Jim Connell, Nannette Wellendorf, and Ilena Vaneria for their numerous contributions.

Additionally, I wish to thank the editors of Macmillan Publishing for their support in this project, specifically David Boelio and Michele Rhoades. Finally, I am indebted to my students, who, through their questions and comments, guide me in the teaching of the basics of retailing.

BRIEF CONTENTS

CONTENTS

RETAILING

OUTLINE

OBJECTIVES

- Appreciate the complexities of operating a retail business.
- Understand the role of the retailer as a key link in the chain that connects the producer/wholesaler with the final consumer.
- Distinguish retailers and their activities from other marketing institutions.
- Delineate the marketing channel of distribution and discern the relationships between the retailer and other channel participants.
- Describe the importance of retailing within our nation's economy.
- Discuss the retailer's problem of striking a balance between the customer's merchandising needs and the retailer's performance needs.
- Explain which merchandising factors play a role in offering the right product . . . in the right quantities . . . in the right place . . . at the right time . . . at the right price . . . by the right appeal.
- Identify the role of operating and financial ratios in establishing performance standards for retailers.

PART I

THE NATURE OF RETAILING

CHAPTER 1

RETAILING—THE WINDS OF CHANGE

Retailing is a dynamic activity. Hence, retailers must be adaptive organizations to survive; status quo is never good enough to accommodate the ebb and flow of market upheaval. In today's retailing environment, the winds of change are blowing stronger than ever before. Several writers have described this dynamic nature of retailing:

- *The word "retail" has been around for more than five centuries, and the concept is as old as commerce itself. But the patterns and systems of retailing undergo massive transformations from time to time. Today is one such time for many markets around the world. New technology, more sophisticated consumer preferences and habits, less restrictive government regulations . . . all these influences are transforming the retail scene from Tokyo to Tulsa, shifting the balance of power between manufacturers and retailers, and driving retailers to restructure their strategies.*[1]
- *The days when the retail giants—Sears, K mart, J.C. Penney—could open a store, stock the shelves, offer reasonable pricing and service, and wait for the customers to roll in, ended in the 70s . . . . The atmosphere of the 80s was more competitive as chains such as The Limited and Toys 'R' Us spawned myriad technological and management systems and controls to cut operating costs, speed deliveries, increase turns and ensure in-stock positions. These controls were focused on corporate results, and not on what it takes to generate profits in the first place—people. This tried-and-true, operations-and-control focus won't cut the retail mustard in the 1990s.*[2]
- *Technology, demographics, consumer attitudes, and the advent of a global economy are all conspiring to rewrite the rules for success. Without question, the decade ahead will be a dramatic one for retailers. . . . At the core of the change is a shift in attitude and expectations of consumers and the power they have within the economic system. In the aggregate, people are much more informed . . . . Success in the next decade, then, will depend upon the level of understanding retailers have about the new values, expectations, and needs of the customer.*[3]

Many retailing experts see the 1990s as the "decade of the customer," a decade in which retail organizations must become totally customer focused if they are to survive until the turn of the century.[4] Retail survival depends on "continuous innovation both in marketing to consumers and in better managing the business internally. Winner retailers . . . create value for customers by sustaining a corporate climate that values better performance above everything else."[5] Customer satisfaction will be not only a corporate goal but a daily operational requirement. In this and the following chapters, we examine the retail merchandising, financial, operational, and organizational dimensions in "creating total customer responsiveness" within today's chaotic retail environment.[6]

WHAT IS RETAILING?

The Retailer as a Marketing Institution

The many definitions of retailing share the same basic concept: **Retailing** is the business activity of selling goods or services to the final consumer. A **retailer** is any business establishment that directs its marketing efforts toward the final consumer for the purpose of selling goods or services. The key words in this definition are *the final consumer*. A business selling the same product to two different buyers may in one instance perform a retailing activity but in the other *not* perform a retailing activity. As an example, assume you buy a chandelier to hang in your dining room. In this case, the lighting company has made a retail sale. On the other hand, assume a home builder walks into the same store, purchases the same chandelier, and installs it in a home he or she is building. In this case, the lighting company has not made a retail sale, because the chandelier was not sold to the final consumer (user) of the product. Thus, a sale is a retail sale only when the ultimate consumer purchases the product. What distinguishes a retail sale from other types of sales is the buyer's *reason* for buying. If the buyer purchases the product for personal use, the sale is considered a retail sale. If

Retailers overcome the assortment gap by buying from many different suppliers.

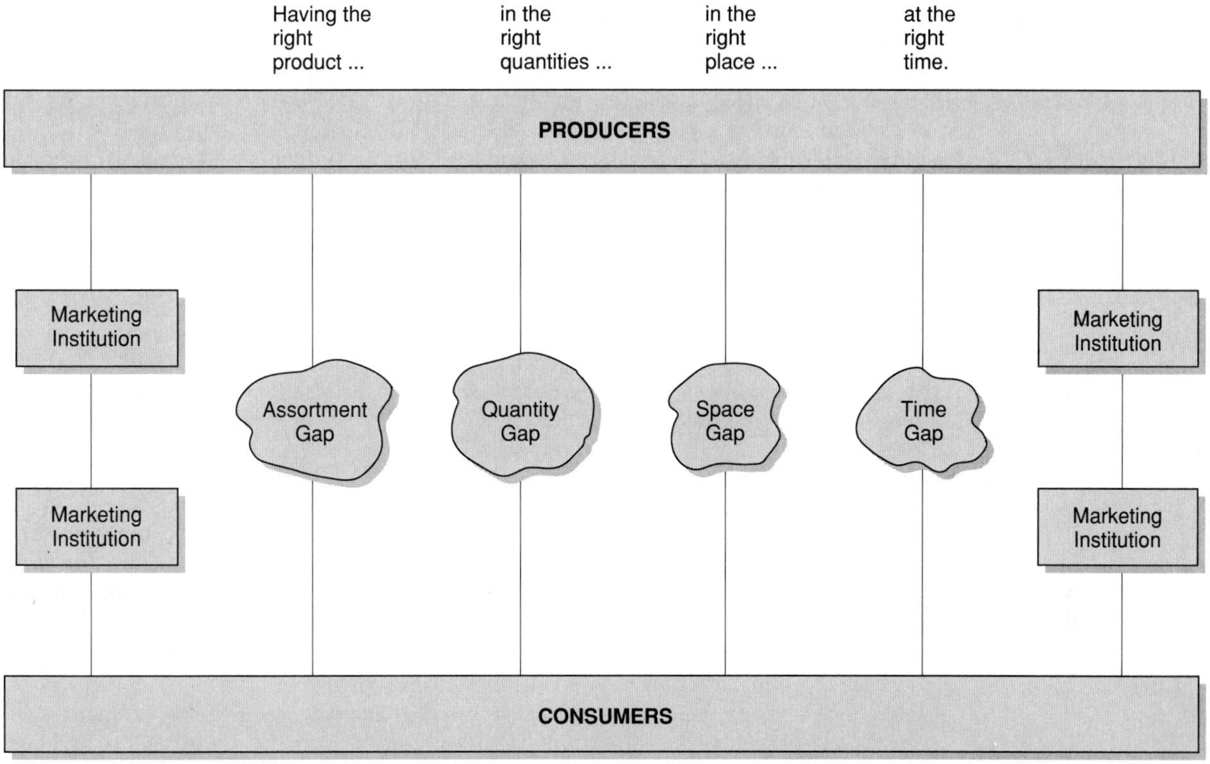

FIGURE 1–1
The retailer as a producer/consumer linkage

the buyer purchases the product for resale at a profit or to use in a business, the sale is *not* a retail sale; instead, it is a *business* sale. According to the U.S. Bureau of the Census in its *Census of Retailing*, a retailer is any business establishment that makes both retail and business (nonretail) sales but is classified as a retailer when its retail sales exceed 50 percent of its total sales.

The Retailer as a Producer/Consumer Linkage

As marketing institutions, retailers act as links between producers and consumers by directing their efforts at overcoming a series of discrepancies between what is ideal for the producer's production process and what consumers need in their consumption activities. The producer/consumer discrepancies are identified as assortment, quantity, space, and time gaps (see Figure 1–1).

The *assortment gap* is the discrepancy that occurs because producers need to produce and sell a limited line of identical or nearly identical products while consumers want to choose from a wide selection of products. This limited assortment production on the part of producers stems from their need to realize the economies of scale associated with the mass production process. Retailers help bridge the assortment gap by buying the limited product line offering of several producers/wholesalers, creating product selection by combining these lines, and offering the combined product lines for sale to consumers. Hence, by engaging in this *accumulation* and *assorting process*, retailers are able to collect and merchandise product groupings that create greater customer satisfaction.

A *quantity gap* develops from economies of scale in production that require producers to produce and sell in large and often bulky quantities. Consumers, on the other hand, need to buy in small, individual units because of low rates of consumption, limited storage space and transportation capabilities, and restricted funds available for making purchases at any given time. To overcome this discrepancy in selling and buying quantities, retailers buy in large quantities from producers/wholesalers, perform "break-in-bulk" functions, and sell smaller quantities to other intermediaries (i.e., case lots) and consumers (i.e., individual units). This *allocation process* is vital for meeting the quantity demands of the marketplace.

Points of production and points of consumption are likely to be characterized by spatial separation. Retailers assist in bridging the *space gap* by creating place utility. By buying products from many producers in several areas and transporting them to a place that is centrally and conveniently located with respect to consumers, retailers create *place utility*. Neighborhood, community, and regional shopping centers, as well as the central business districts (CBDs) of major metro areas, that offer coffee, designer clothing, and diamonds are all good examples of places retailers use to enhance the place utility of the producers' product offerings.

A *time gap* occurs when producers must produce on a continuous, long-run basis (i.e., staple products) or at certain appropriate times (i.e., seasonal products) while consumers want to consume products at times that may or may not coincide with producers' requirements. An additional "in-transit" time gap arises from the time required to overcome the distance between points of production and those of consumption. This time gap is bridged in part when retailers add *time utility* by purchasing products as they are produced and transporting and storing them at various places until consumers need them. Finally, retailers add time utility by extending credit. Consumers who have the opportunity to "buy now and pay later" are able to realize immediate gratification of their needs rather than having to postpone need gratification.

This chapter examines the nature of retailers and their contribution to having the right product . . . in the right quantities . . . in the right place . . . at the right time (see Figure 1–1).

The Retail Level within the Marketing Channel

Retailers are referred to as *middlemen* or *intermediaries*. Both terms suggest that retailers occupy a position "in the middle of" or "between" two other levels. In fact, retailers occupy a middle position between the consumption level and the wholesale or production level of the marketing channel of distribution. They purchase, receive, and store products from producers and wholesalers to provide consumers with convenient locations for buying products.

As Figure 1–2 shows, retailers are part of a chain called a **marketing channel**—a team of marketing institutions that direct a flow of goods or services from the producer to the final consumer. Generally the team consists of a producer, one or more wholesalers, and many retailers. Operationally retailers are distinguished from wholesalers and producers in the following ways:

1. Retailers sell in smaller quantities (individual units) on a frequent basis, while wholesalers and producers sell in much larger quantities (case and truck load lots) on a less frequent basis.
2. Retailers' places of business are open to the general consuming public, but producers and wholesalers normally do not make over-the-counter sales to the general public (factory and wholesaler outlets are exceptions).
3. Retailers charge higher per-unit prices than do producers and wholesalers (loss leaders are a notable exception).

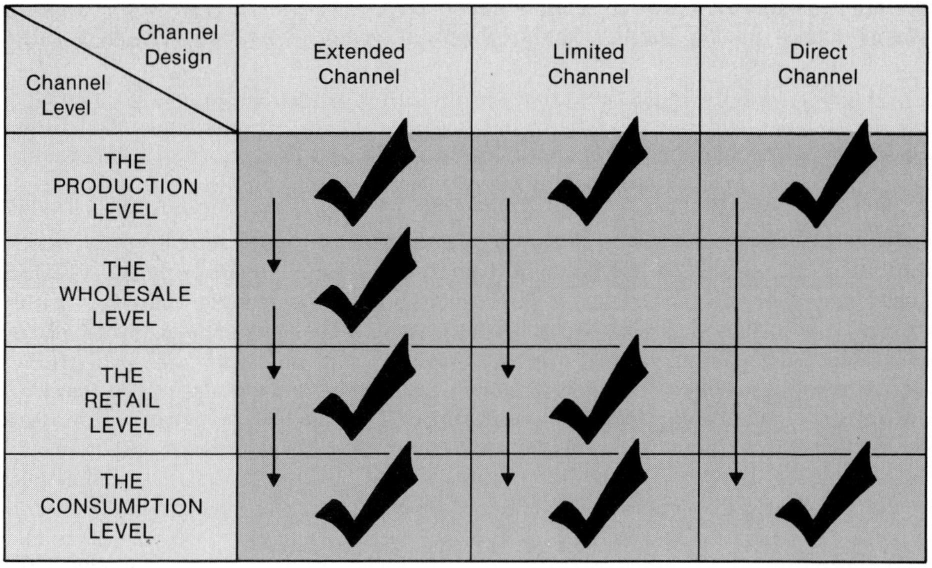

Channel Level \ Channel Design	Extended Channel	Limited Channel	Direct Channel
THE PRODUCTION LEVEL	✔	✔	✔
THE WHOLESALE LEVEL	✔		
THE RETAIL LEVEL	✔	✔	
THE CONSUMPTION LEVEL	✔	✔	✔

FIGURE 1–2
Alternative channel structures

4. Retailers tend to use a one-price policy, while producers and wholesalers typically use variable prices based on some form of discounting structure.
5. Retailers rely on consumers to make the initial contact by visiting the store or placing mail or telephone orders, while producers and wholesalers employ outside sales representatives to make initial sales contacts (at-home retailing is a notable exception).
6. Retailers place greater emphasis than do producers and wholesalers on the external and internal atmospherics of their physical facilities and fixtures as major merchandising tools.

The marketing channel can be described as a multilevel structure made up of channel teams whose interactions coordinate channel flows through channel teamwork. To facilitate our understanding of the marketing channel, we will examine each of the major components of this system: (1) channel levels, (2) channel teams, (3) channel interactions, (4) channel flows, and (5) channel teamwork.

Channel Levels

Marketing channels can be characterized by a number of structural designs defined by the inclusion or exclusion of various intermediaries. The producer has a number of alternative channel structures through which to reach consumers. As Figure 1–2 illustrates, there are three basic alternative channel structures: extended, limited, and direct.

The first alternative is to use an **extended channel** by marketing through both wholesalers and retailers. In this case, producers rely on wholesalers to reach retailers, which in turn stock their products and sell them to final consumers. Because there usually are fewer wholesalers than retailers in a marketing channel, this option allows the producer to spend less time and money cultivating the necessary channel contacts to reach the ultimate consumers.

The second alternative for a producer is the **limited channel**, that is, to use only retailers, thereby eliminating the wholesaler. A growing number of producers of products such as automobiles, furniture, appliances, and other big-ticket items are using the limited channel. Manufacturers of "perishable" products such as clothing (which goes out of style quickly) and fresh and frozen foods (which spoil rapidly) also frequently use a limited channel.

The third alternative is the **direct channel**. In this case, the producer eliminates both the retailer and the wholesaler and markets directly to final consumers using door-to-door, television, magazine, or direct-mail selling techniques. John Deere & Co. and E. I. duPont de Nemours & Co. are two examples of manufacturers engaged in direct-channel operations via catalog retailing; brand enhancement and positive public relations are additional benefits of this direct-marketing effort.[7] Examples of products distributed door to door are Electrolux vacuum cleaners, Avon cosmetics, and Fuller brushes. Another direct marketer is Hartmarx Corp., the venerable manufacturer of high-end men's suits (e.g., Hart, Schaffner & Marx and Hickey-Freeman), which owns and operates a far-flung network of retail stores.[8]

Although a producer may choose not to use another team member in the channel, it can never eliminate the functions that must be performed at each channel level. In other words, *it can eliminate the retailer but not the retail level and the retail functions*. Thus, producers that sell directly to consumers have taken over, but not eliminated, retailer operations at the retail level. Such producers become both wholesalers and retailers.

Channel Teams

Channel teams include both full- and limited-member institutions supported by facilitating nonmember institutions. Membership in the marketing channel team is based on the nature of an institution's transactional involvements and whether members assume title to the goods involved in the transaction. A *full-member institution* is a wholesaler or retailer that is directly involved in the purchase and/or sale of products and takes title to the products involved in the transaction. Merchant wholesalers and nearly all retailers have full membership in the channel team. *Limited-member institutions* are marketing intermediaries that are directly involved in purchase/sales transactions and do not take title to the products involved. Agent wholesalers hold limited team membership, as do retailers engaged in consignment selling. A number of organizations provide a wide range of support functions; these *facilitating nonmember institutions* assist the team effort by providing specialized advertising, research, transportation, storage, financial, risk-taking, and/or consulting services. These facilitators neither take title to the goods involved in a transaction nor directly participate in the sale and/or purchase of those goods.

Channel Interactions

Interactions among participants within the marketing channel of distribution can take several forms. As intermediaries, wholesalers and retailers must successfully complete a number of tasks for each other and their clientele to perform distribution and transactional functions most efficiently and effectively. These interactive tasks include buying, selling, breaking bulk, creating assortments, stocking, delivering, extending credit, informing, consulting, and transferring titles and payments (see Figure 1–3).

Channel Flows

A marketing channel can be likened to a pipeline, or conduit, that guides the movement of entire marketing programs among channel participants. Although the flow of physical goods is the channel flow most commonly recognized by the general public, other types of flows are equally important to delivering a successful marketing effort. The five major types of channel flow are as follows:

1. **Physical flow**—the actual movement of a physical product from one channel participant to another

Store Wars: Direct Channels for Fashion Apparel

Many top fashion apparel manufacturers are engaged in marketing their products directly to the consuming public. Anne Klein, Ralph Lauren, Liz Claiborne, Adrienne Vittadini, Esprit, and Escade are among those that are establishing direct channels of distribution by opening company stores. Traditionally, apparel companies have restricted their retail venture to selling distressed merchandise in factory outlet stores; today the new stores are conspicuous competitors in major shopping malls and upscale specialty clusters (e.g., Rodeo Drive). As more and more department stores have either faltered under the weight of unsuccessful takeover activities or pursued the promotion-oriented strategy of a perennial sales atmosphere, fashion apparel producers have had to explore new and different distribution alternatives to ensure adequate market exposure for their entire collections of product lines. While department and specialty stores remain the principal distribution channels for these fashion houses, a state of "undeclared war" has erupted in this highly competitive retail environment.

Major benefits to be realized by the apparel producers in establishing their own retail outlets include the opportunities to:

- Test new fashion concepts, thereby reducing the amount of guesswork involved in identifying fashion trends
- Experiment with different pricing levels and tactics to learn their impact on sales and profits
- Try various merchandise display techniques and enhance the visual presentation that is so essential in fashion merchandising
- Offer a complete variety and assortment of products (collections) and counter department stores' practice of offering an "edited selection of many different designer labels" (often referred to as "cherry picking" —selecting only the best lines)
- Control the amount and timing of markdown activities and avoid department stores' demands for markdown insurance
- Realize a higher profit margin by eliminating an intermediary (e.g., department store)
- Counter some retailers' product strategy of replacing designer labels with private store labels

Source: Based on Teri Agins, "Apparel Makers Increasingly Market Their Clothes Directly to Consumers," *The Wall Street Journal*, February 7, 1990, B-SA, and Teri Agins, "Clothing Makers Don Retailers' Garb," *The Wall Street Journal* July 13, 1984, B-1.

RETAIL STRATEGIES AND TACTICS

2. **Ownership flow**—transferring title (right of ownership and usage) from one channel participant to another
3. **Information flow**—the two-way communication of useful data among channel participants
4. **Payment flow**—the transfer of monies from one channel participant to another as compensation for services rendered and/or goods delivered
5. **Promotion flow**—the flow of persuasive communication directed at influencing the decisions of consumers (consumer promotion) and other channel participants (trade promotion)

The nature and degree of involvement with each of these flows for any given channel participant will vary depending on the channel structure. In most channel structures, however, retailers are directly involved in each flow and play a key role in successful channel flow management.

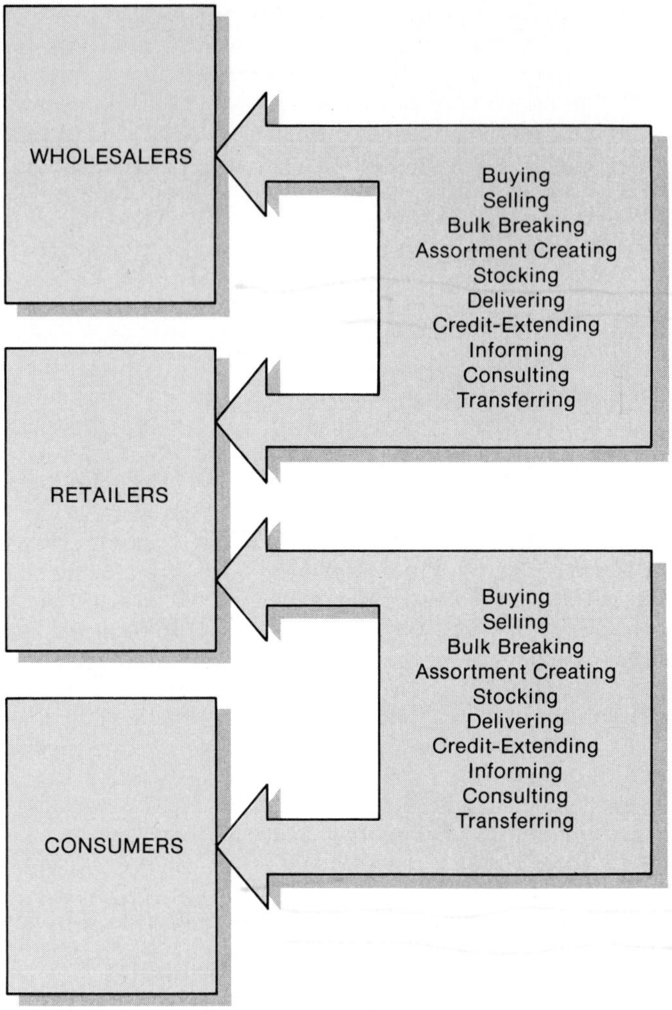

FIGURE 1–3
Interactive tasks performed by the channel team

Channel Teamwork

As a social interactive system, the marketing channel is subject to the behavioral processes inherent in all such systems. The behavior of each channel participant affects all the other participants, hence the need for channel teamwork. Good teamwork results in a cooperative spirit and a coordinated effort; poor teamwork generates channel disruptions and conflict. From the retailer's perspective, good relationships with customers require that the retailer "pay attention not only to them and to employees, but also to every link in the distribution chain."[9] To ensure good teamwork, the channel of distribution must be integrated. **Channel integration** is the process of incorporating all channel members into one channel system and uniting them under one leadership and one set of goals.

Channel integration ends the segregation of intermediary operations and their functional tasks. As Figure 1–4 shows, channel integration can take the form of a highly integrated vertical marketing system or a modestly integrated conventional marketing channel. A **vertical marketing system** is *"a professionally managed and centrally programmed network, pre-engineered to achieve operating economies and maximum market impact."*[10] The advantage of this type of system is that it allows the channel team to achieve technological, managerial, and promotional leverages through integrating

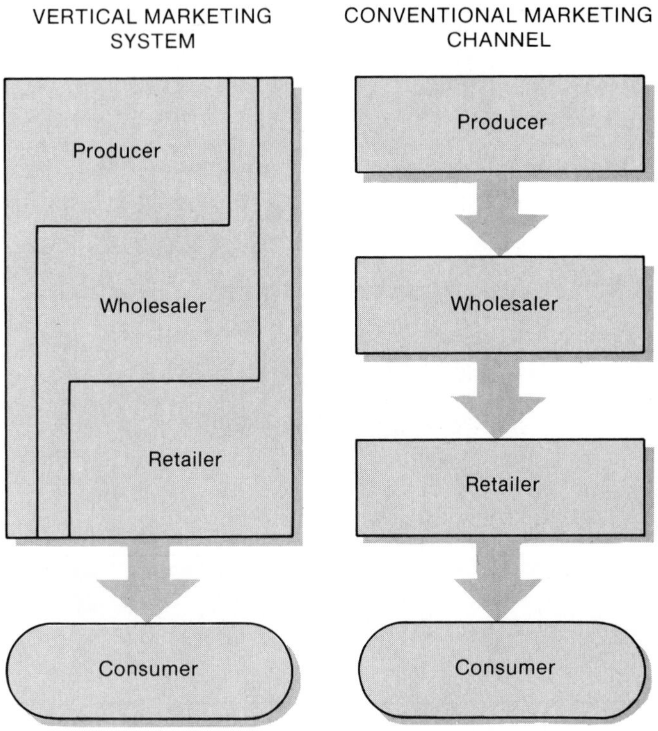

FIGURE 1–4
Forms of channel integration

and synchronizing the five channel flows.[11] A vertical marketing system can be established using persuasive administrative powers, legally binding contractual agreements, and partial or total ownership of channel members.

In a vertical marketing system, each channel member assumes the functions and tasks that will best support the entire channel system. As a team member, the retailer operates within the retail level of distribution and provides most of the teamwork at that level. Some retailers, however, engage in operations at the wholesale and even the production level of the marketing channel. Sears, Roebuck & Co., for example, conducts extensive operations at both the wholesale and production levels of the channel. Sears buys a large portion of its products from manufacturers in which it has part ownership. Also, individual stores obtain most of their merchandise from Sears' wholesale distribution facilities.

A conventional marketing channel is a loosely aligned, independently owned and operated channel team. The chief advantage of this arrangement is the freedom each member has in conducting business. The disadvantages of conventional channels include (1) the failure to achieve economies of scale, (2) the instability of the arrangement as a result of the ease of channel entry and exit, and (3) the limited levels of cooperation and coordination due to the greater autonomy of participating members.

THE IMPORTANCE OF RETAILING

Retailing has a profound effect on our society. The large number of establishments engaging in retail activities, the huge number of people those establishments employ, and the tremendous sales volume they generate indicate the importance of retailing on the U.S. economy.

Retail establishments (individual operating units) outnumber the combined total of the other two major members of the distribution channel, manufacturers and wholesalers. As Figure 1–5 shows, 1,441,000 retail establishments operate within the

FIGURE 1–5
Number of establishments within the channel of distribution (source: U.S. Department of Commerce, *Statistical Abstract of the United States,* 109th ed. [Washington, D.C.: U.S. Government Printing Office, 1989], 523)

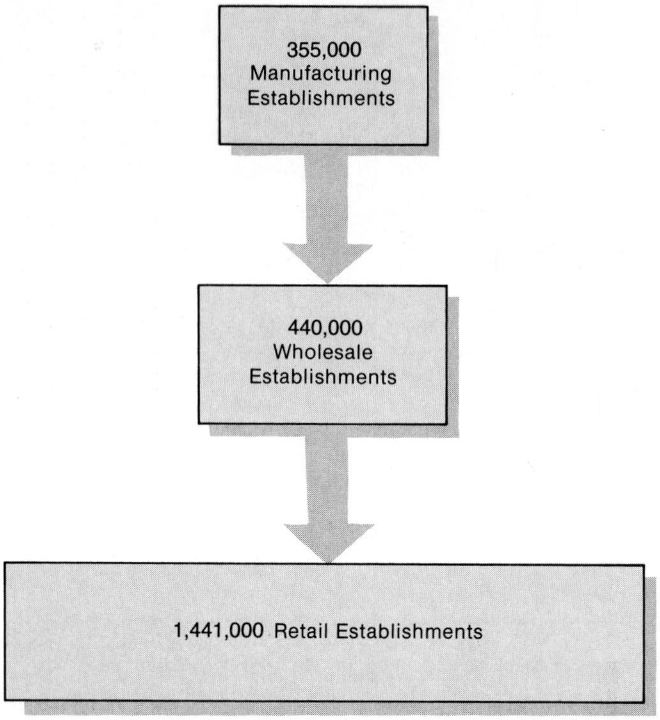

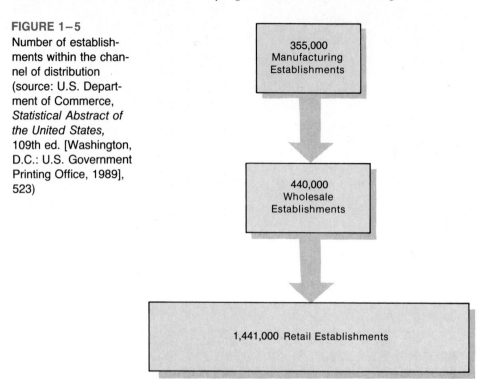

U.S. economy, compared with 355,000 manufacturers and 440,000 wholesalers. In relative terms, there are approximately 4.1 retail establishments for each manufacturing establishment and 3.3 retailers for every wholesaler.

Retailing's significance for the nation's economic welfare is reflected by the status of the retail industry as an employer of U.S. workers. Figure 1–6 portrays employment figures by industry. Retailing is the third largest employer, exceeded only by the manufacturing and service sectors. Retailers provide employment for approximately one out of every six workers.

Total retail sales, as well as per capita retail sales, have netted steady gains over the last 19 years (see Figure 1–7). Total retail sales in 1987 were about $1,510 billion, compared to total retail sales of $375.2 billion in 1970. Per capita retail sales increased from $1,834 to $6,206 during the same period. These figures increase in significance when one considers that retail sales account for approximately 45 percent of personal income.

Figure 1–8 shows retail store sales by type of business in 1989. The dominance of our stomachs and our love for the automobile was readily apparent in our spending. Combined food and drink sales accounted for 30.6 percent of total retail sales, and automotive-related expenditures exceeded 38 percent.

THE PROBLEM OF RETAILING

The retailer's problem is how to maintain a proper balance between the ability of the firm's merchandising programs to meet the needs of targeted consumers satisfactorily and the ability of the firm's administrative plans to meet the retailer's need to operate effectively and efficiently. Just as the scales of justice must balance the rights and responsibilities of two disputing parties, the "scale of retailing" must weigh the product and service needs of the customer against the operational and financial needs of the retailer. A successful retail business strikes a balance between the customer's merchandising needs and the retailer's performance standards (see Figure 1–9). In

Merchandise Displays...
creating effective product presentations.

Retail displays are in-store presentations of merchandise designed to maximize product exposure, enhance product appearance, stimulate product interest, exhibit product information, facilitate sales transactions, ensure product security, provide product storage, remind customers to buy, and generate impulse sales. In addition, displays are an essential ingredient in creating store atmospherics and directing customer traffic.

The Resource

Number employed	Industry	Percentage employed
3,208,000	Agriculture, Forestry	2.8%
818,000	Mining	0.8%
7,456,000	Construction	6.6%
20,935,000	Manufacturing	18.6%
7,880,000	Transportation, Communications, Public Utilities	7.0%
4,580,000	Wholesale Trade	4.1%
18,812,000	Retail Trade	16.7%
7,763,000	Finance, Insurance and Real Estate	6.9%
35,743,000	Services	31.8%
5,246,000	Public Administration	4.7%

FIGURE 1–6
Employment by industry, 1987 (source: U.S. Department of Commerce, *Statistical Abstract of the United States,* 109th ed. [Washington, D.C.: U.S. Government Printing Office, 1989], 391)

other words, a successful retail management team consists of both "out-front" merchandisers and "behind-the-scenes" operations managers, a problem that lies at the heart of the marketing concept. As one author states, some managers "are better at the glitz-and-glamour side of the business than at the ledger-and-eyeshade part."[12]

The Marketing Concept

The **marketing concept** is the philosophy that the overall goal of every business organization is to satisfy consumer needs and still make a profit. Before the general acceptance of the marketing concept, the role of marketing in most businesses was

FIGURE 1–7
Total and per capita retail sales, 1970–1987 (in current dollars)

Year	Total Retail Sales ($ Billions)	Annual Percentage Change (%)	Per Capita Retail Sales ($)
1970	375.2	6.4	1.839
1971	414.2	10.4	2.002
1972	458.5	10.7	2.191
1973	511.9	11.6	2.422
1974	542.0	5.9	2.541
1975	588.1	8.5	2.730
1976	656.4	11.6	3.017
1977	722.5	10.1	3.288
1978	804.2	11.3	3.621
1979	896.8	11.5	3.993
1980	957.3	6.8	4.212
1981	1,038.7	8.5	4.523
1982	1,069.3	2.9	4.609
1983	1,168.4	9.3	4.987
1984	1,282.6	9.8	5.424
1985	1,367.3	6.6	5.727
1986	1,437.5	5.1	5.962
1987	1,510.5	5.1	6.206

Source: U.S. Department of Commerce, *Statistical Abstract of the United States,* 109th ed. (Washington, D.C.: U.S. Government Printing Office, 1989), 754.

either "to sell what we have produced" or "to sell what we have bought." A firm that adopts the marketing concept, however, strives to sell what the customer wants. "It is the willingness to recognize and understand the consumer's needs and wants and a willingness to adjust any of the marketing mix elements [product, price, place, and promotion] . . . to satisfy those needs and wants."[13] The marketing concept, then, stresses keying supply to demand rather than keying demand to supply. In an attempt to regain lost market share, Sears has divided some of its stores into "ministores" or "power formats" that focus on a particular merchandise category. Brand Central is one such ministore; it focuses on famous-maker appliances and electronics. By adding brand names to its mix, Sears has forced managers to "focus more on what customers really want rather than on what Sears wants to sell them."[14]

The other, equally important objective according to the marketing concept is profit. Without profit, the firm cannot stay in business to satisfy anyone's needs. Retailers that adopt the marketing concept are neither exclusively customer driven nor profit driven; rather, they seek a workable balance between these two important goals.

For the retailer—more so than for any other marketing institution—adoption of the marketing concept is an immediate problem. Because the retailer deals with consumers on a day-to-day basis, it is more directly affected than wholesalers and producers by the need to deliver consumer satisfaction at a profit. The retailer is the first to reap the benefits of consumer satisfaction but also the first to bear the brunt of consumer dissatisfaction. As Stanley Marcus of Neiman Marcus Co. states, "Satisfaction means that customers come back."[15] Research indicates that most dissatisfied customers never complain to the company; instead, 60 to 90 percent simply switch stores or brands.

In summary, a high level of customer satisfaction is an integral part of the retailer's program of "relationship marketing";[16] it "helps retailers to satisfy current retail customers, do more business with existing customers, and attract new customers."[17] Because it costs five times as much to attract a new customer as it does to retain an existing one, it makes sense for a retailer to try to ensure customer satisfaction.[18]

!!!

Satisfying the customer at a profit is not a simple task, however. By definition, the solution to the marketing concept—and to the problem of retailing—demands the solution of two other problems: the right merchandising blend and the right performance standards.

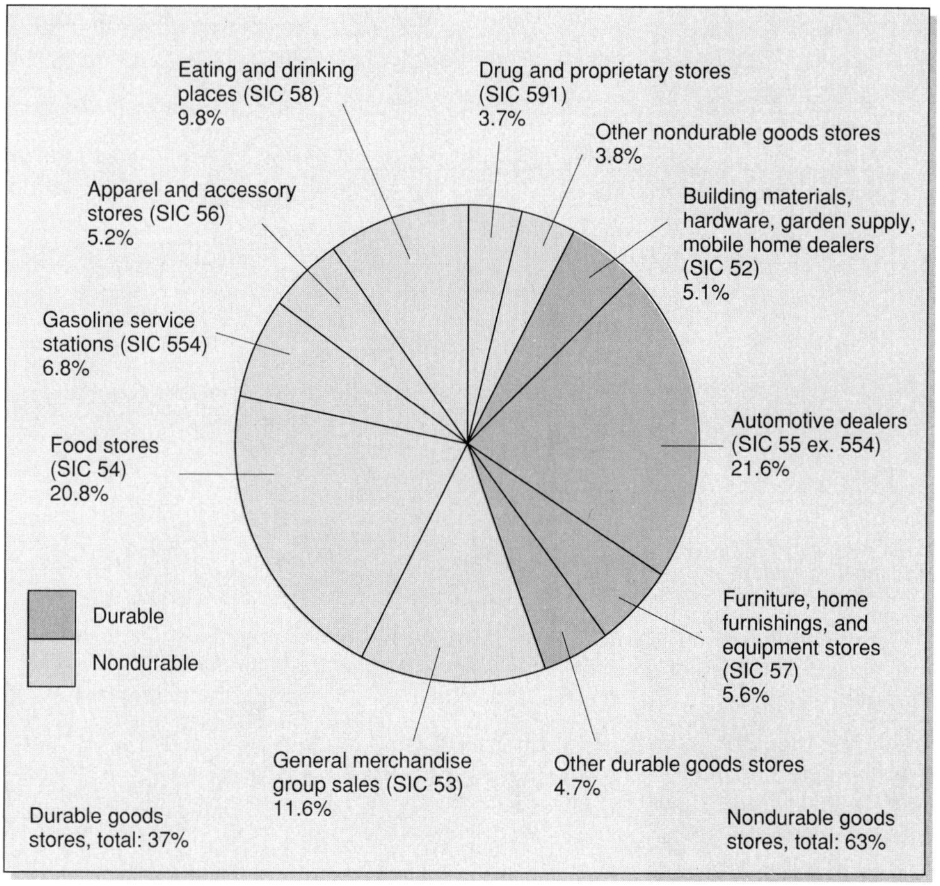

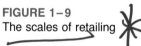

FIGURE 1–8
Estimated sales of all retail stores, by type of business, as a percentage of total retail sales, 1989 (source: U.S. Department of Commerce, *Statistical Abstract of the United States,* 109th ed. [Washington, D.C.: U.S. Government Printing Office, 1989], 754)

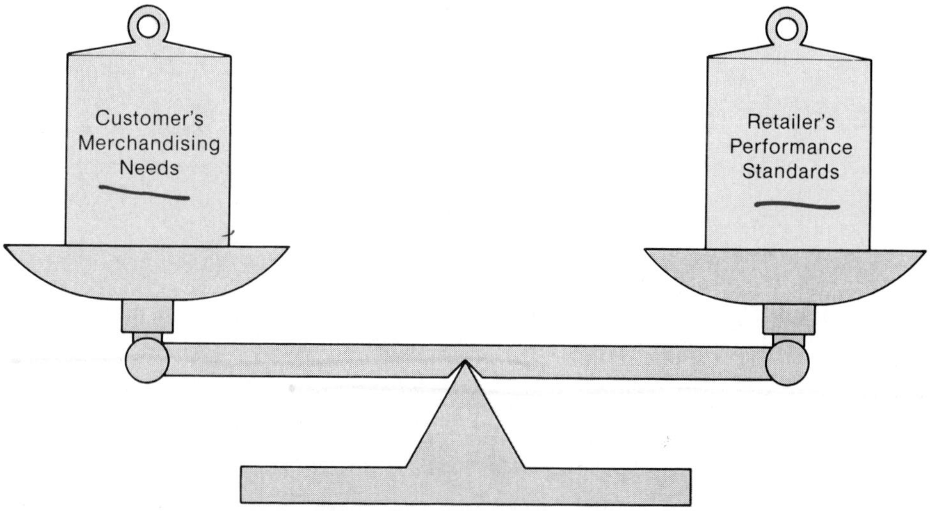

FIGURE 1–9
The scales of retailing

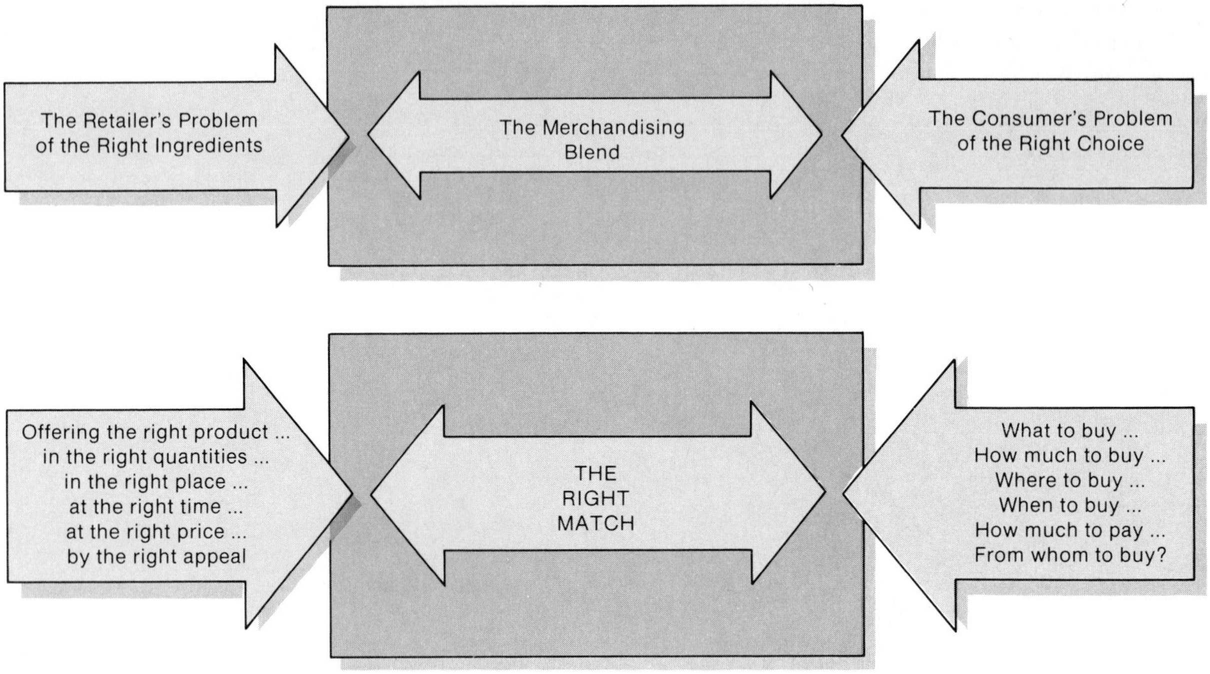

FIGURE 1–10
The problem of the right merchandising blend

THE RIGHT MERCHANDISING BLEND

The right **merchandising blend** matches the ingredients of the retailer's merchandising program with the decisions the consumer faces in making the right choice. Figure 1–10 illustrates this problem. The right blend includes the following six ingredients:

- Offering the right product
- In the right quantities
- In the right place
- At the right time
- At the right price
- By the right appeal

The right blend thus is the one that satisfies both customer and retailer. The right choice is the set of decisions that best satisfies the consumer's needs before, during, and after the purchase decision.

The Right Product

What makes a product "right" is a unique composite of three product elements—merchandising utilities, intrinsic qualities, and augmenting extras. Figure 1–11 portrays the concept of the **right product**.

Merchandising Utilities

The merchandising utilities associated with each product provide the foundation for building the right product offering. A **product's merchandising utilities** are benefits the consumer seeks in buying, using, and possessing the product. Millard Drexler, president of The Gap, describes his product's merchandising utilities as "well-made, classic clothing that doesn't cost a fortune and doesn't render you a fashion failure within a month. . . . We want to provide the basic pieces for anyone's closet."[19] In other words,

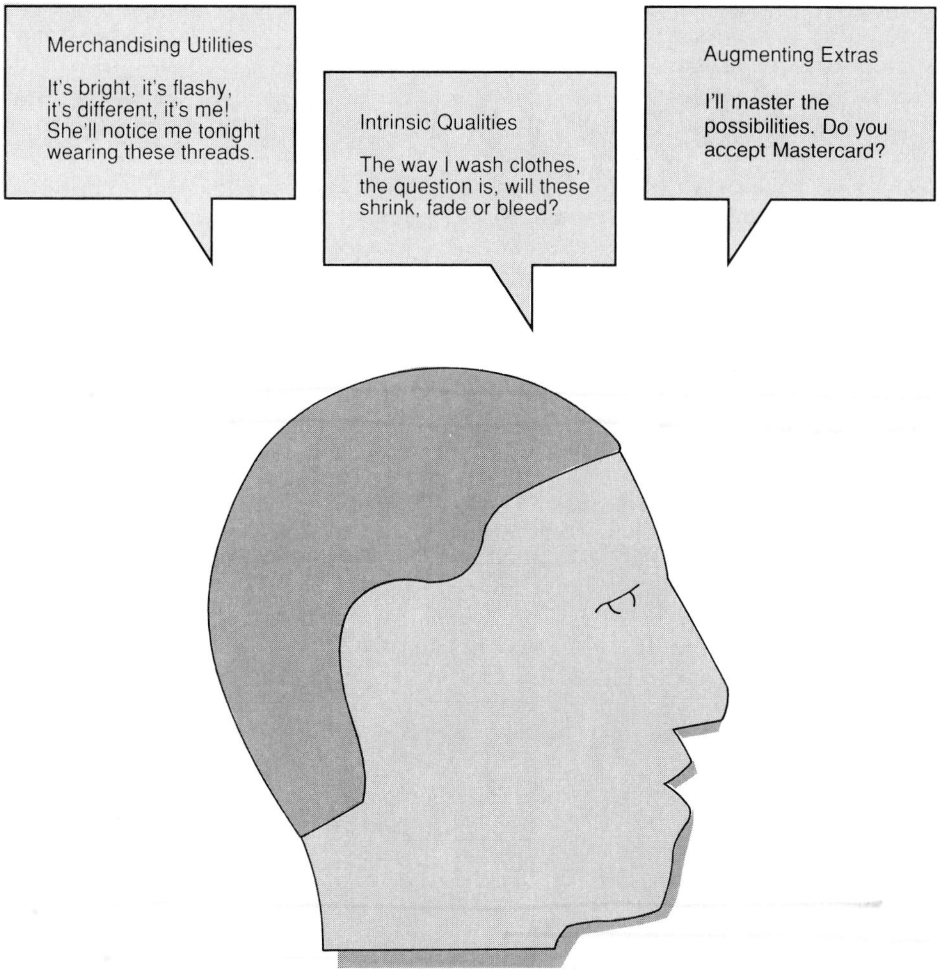

FIGURE 1–11
Elements of the right product

a product's merchandising utilities are satisfactions that are either *perceived* (a woman feels her new suit makes her look more distinguished), *real* (other people think she looks more distinguished in her new suit), *functional* (the new suit has a comfortable fit), or *psychological* (she believes the new suit makes her look thinner). We must then ask what the retailer is really selling. Is it deodorant or security, cosmetics or hope, club membership or acceptance? To enhance the customer's perceived, real, functional, and psychological benefits of its upscaled merchandise, K mart "hired actress Jaclyn Smith and decorator Martha Stewart to design and promote better-quality apparel and merchandise."[20] One writer notes, "Without a unique point of view, general merchandise becomes a commodity."[21] In the current "skin-thirsty environment," many consumers perceive anything (i.e., skin cream) with aloe, vitamin E, or sunscreen as a definite product benefit.[22] From the merchandising utilities perspective, the retailer is selling the expected benefits of security, hope, and acceptance.

Intrinsic Qualities

The tangible aspects of a product are also important in the consumer's evaluation of what makes a product right. **Intrinsic qualities** are the inherent physical attributes, such as product form, features, materials, and workmanship, that satisfy consumer needs. The intrinsic qualities of a product are important because they determine whether the product is capable of doing what it is supposed to do and looking the way it is supposed to look. These qualities determine the product's utility. In today's health-conscious world, a product's intrinsic qualities may be determined by what is lacking (e.g., fat, sodium, and cholesterol) rather than by a tangible attribute. Kraft markets a wide variety of low-fat, fat-free, and low-cholesterol products (e.g., salad dressings, ice cream, yogurt, and cheese) in an attempt to ensure that its products do what they should do—help the consumer lose or maintain weight and live a healthier life.[23] Intrinsic qualities strongly influence the consumer's perception of a product's quality, suitability, and durability. Some aspects that determine a product's intrinsic qualities are style, design, shape, weight, color, and material.

Augmenting Extras

Augmenting extras are auxiliary product dimensions that provide supplementary benefits to the customer. Warranties, delivery, installation, packaging, instructions, and alterations are some of the major extras that can greatly enhance the customer's satisfaction with the product. The type and extent of the benefits such extras provide depend on the customer's buying and usage behavior. For example, the additional benefit of convenience can be provided by offering home delivery and packages with handles. "One of the hottest trends of the past few years is actually a revival of a very old service—home delivery."[24] The resurgence of this augmenting extra is a result of (1) time-constrained consumers with extensive career commitments; (2) the "me" baby boom generation, which has become accustomed to instant gratification; and (3) increased competitive actions of retailers looking for ways to differentiate themselves.[25] A customer's need for additional security and reassurance when making a purchase decision can be augmented by warranties, maintenance contracts, and liberal return policies.

The Right Quantity

The **right quantity** is the exact match between the consumer's buying and using needs and the retailer's buying and selling needs. Consumer factors the retailer must consider in determining the right quantity are the number of units and the size of units. For some consumers, a single unit is the right quantity: one tube of toothpaste, one pack of cigarettes, or one can of Coke. For other consumers, multiple-unit quantities are the right quantity: two tubes of toothpaste, a carton of cigarettes, or a six-pack of Coke. A single tube of toothpaste might be the right quantity if the retailer knows that its customers are not concerned about price, are unmarried, have only one bathroom, or shop frequently. However, a retailer whose customers are price sensitive, married, have more than one bathroom, or shop infrequently should offer larger quantities at a price saving per unit. With the growing acceptance of office supply superstores, other retailers are adjusting the concept of what is the right quantity for stationery items. While dozens are larger quantities than most customers need, multipacks (three) and convenience packs (six) are consistent with customer needs.[26] Because more of today's parents are working couples, they tend to buy duplicates. These time-pressed consumers may buy two high chairs, walkers, and cribs: "one for the home and one for the sitter's house or the grandparent's home, so they don't have to travel with it."[27]

Products come in many sizes: small, medium, large, and extra-large; short, regular, and long; king, queen, and regular; individual and family. Retailers know that the "size" labels they carry affect the kind of clientele they attract and the sales they make. A shrewd clothing retailer, for example, knows that the right size for Bill is "extra large" but the right size for Mary is one for the "full-figured woman." K mart has added a new line of Jordache clothing for larger-size women. Spiegel's upscaled *For You* catalog for larger-size women is a successful market introduction. The Limited, Inc. has two specialty store formats that target women who need special-size apparel: Lane Bryant and Sizes Unlimited. In Japan, American retailers have had to rethink the size categories. Talbots, Inc., a retailer of classic American clothing, has had to downsize. "Japanese women are tiny compared with the average American woman . . . so Talbots plans to carry only petite-size clothing. . . . Williams-Sonoma [a retailer of gourmet cookware] found itself in a similar size-related predicament . . . it learned to carry only smaller cookware that fit smaller Japanese stoves."[28] The right size, then, is the size that fits the customer's needs, both physically and psychologically. And even though the sizes consumers desire usually are predictable, without proper inventory control retailers can lose many sales by stocking the wrong sizes.

The retailer's decision about quantity is in many ways more critical than the consumer's. A retailer that does not purchase enough merchandise risks stockouts and therefore lost sales. Purchasing too much merchandise causes overstocking and subsequently higher inventory carrying costs—and very likely reduced profit margins if markdowns are necessary. Buying the proper quantity therefore leads to both customer satisfaction and higher retail profits.

The Right Place

A retailer trying to determine the **right place** should consider the following place factors: (1) market area, (2) market coverage, and (3) store layout and design.

Market Areas

A market is a geographic area where buyers and sellers meet to exchange money for products and services. The right market for retailers is the area containing enough people to allow them to satisfy consumer needs at a profit. The retailer's market can range from one block to several hundred miles. To find the "right" market area, the retailer must consider (1) regional markets, (2) local markets, (3) trading areas, and (4) site.

Regional Markets. For the retailer, the **regional market** may be the entire nation or the right part of the country. Chain retailers, however, must evaluate different parts of the country to determine where to locate new stores. Many chain retailers face the decision of whether to expand into or increase their representation within various parts of the United States. "Many geographic areas are targets for continued expansion, even though more than sufficient retail store space exists—the Sunbelt and especially the Southeast are overstored and overcentered. The East and West Coasts are in balance, neither overstored nor understored. Areas of understoring include Michigan, Illinois, parts of Massachusetts, and New Jersey."[29] In essence, everyone was focusing on the Sunbelt in the last decade—hence, the need to rebuild and refurbish the Rustbelt. The Sunbelt has been an unlikely but successful market for an unlikely Rustbelt retail format; Burlington Coat Factory's perennial success has been due to its ability to sell cold-weather coats in southern markets. The company credits its success to a low level of competition in this product category and to its strategy of catering to middle-class customers who travel to northern destinations.[30]

Local Markets. With respect to **local markets**, retailers must determine the right town and the right part of town. For some retailers, the right town is one with a minimum population of 100,000. Large megastore merchandisers, such as Sam's Warehouse Clubs, or hypermarket retailing formats, such as Meijer and Carrefour, need a large population base to develop the sales volume they need to operate their stores profitably. Smaller retailers, on the other hand, are less concerned with total population and more interested in the size and demographic composition of a *segment* of the population. In some cases, a smaller town might be a preferred local or second-tier market if it represents a better competitive environment.[31] The local market strategy of Family Dollar Stores (a general-merchandise discounter) and Food Lion (a supermarket) is to locate in small, rural towns with minimal price competition.

The right part of town for some retailers is the central city; for others, it is the suburbs. An office supply store probably would not succeed in a residential suburb, and a garden center likely would not flourish downtown. Some retailers cater to upper- and middle-income consumers who cluster in suburbs; others target lower-income consumers who live in or near the inner city. When it acquired the Zayre discount store chain, Ames Department Stores, Inc. rechristened all of the suburban Zayre stores with the Ames name; however, it retained the Zayre logo on all urban locations. "Zayre's biggest strength was it never lost the loyalty of inner-city shoppers. To keep them Ames is devising a separate merchandising strategy geared to ethnic tastes."[32]

Trading Areas. Once the right local market has been chosen, the retailer must determine the **trading area**—the right shopping area or the right shopping center. Some retailers go it alone, relying on their own abilities to draw customers. A convenience food store located near a residential neighborhood is an example. Other retailers depend on the drawing power of a cluster of stores. They believe that by grouping together in shopping centers or associating with anchor stores (such as department stores, discount houses, and supermarkets), they can create the "right" place. For Bob Evans, a family restaurant chain in 11 eastern and midwestern states, the right trading area is incorporated into its "I-75 strategy." This plan calls for locating restaurants on a major interstate highway and within the immediate vicinity of a large shopping center or mall with a minimum of 50,000 residents living within a five-mile radius of the proposed location.[33]

Site. For the freestanding retailer, the right **site** allows the store to intercept customers on their way to work or on their way home; is readily accessible to consumers from the standpoints of approaching, entering, and exiting; and is visible to passing consumer traffic. Within a shopping mall, the right site may be on the ground floor, at one end of the mall, or away from shoppers who are incompatible with the operation. Place des Antiquaires, New York City's glitzy underground art and antique mall, has proven to be something less than the right place for subway-weary New Yorkers, who find the underground location a big drawback.[34]

Market Coverage

The right place may be every place, a few places, or a single place. As part of the "right place" decision, retailers must decide whether they want intensive, selective, or exclusive market coverage (see Figure 1–12).

Intensive Market Coverage. A retailer that wants **intensive market coverage** selects and uses as many retail outlets as are justified to obtain "blanket" coverage of an entire market area. Generally convenience-goods retailers use an intensive market strategy. (Convenience goods are products and services consumers want to purchase with a minimum of effort; examples are snack foods and soft drinks.) Because the retailer that employs an intensive coverage strategy must try to serve *all* customers within a given market area, the right place is *every* place. The ultimate intensive market coverage is to offer home delivery. Domino's pizza has become the second largest chain in the pizza industry by offering home delivery convenience under the theme "one call does it all." Its success has forced number-one Pizza Hut to adopt a similar strategy in many of the latter's markets.

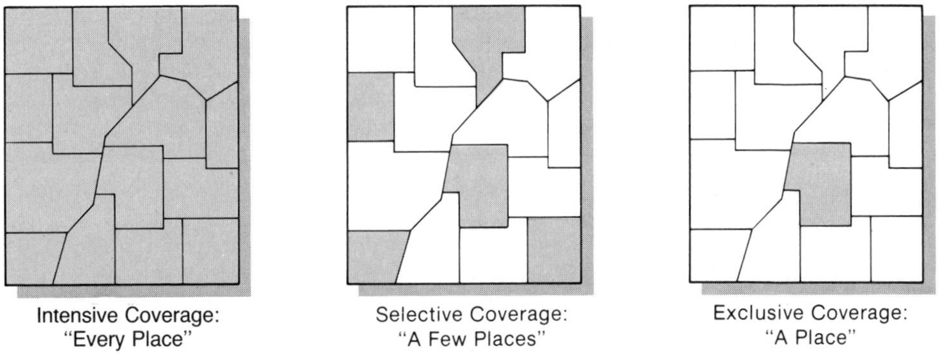

FIGURE 1–12
Market area coverage and the right place

Selective Market Coverage. When a retailer sells shopping goods, the logical strategy is to pursue **selective market coverage**. (Shopping goods are products that consumers want to compare for style, price, or quality before making a purchase decision; examples are clothing, furniture, and appliances.) For these products, a retailer should choose enough locations to ensure adequate coverage of selected target markets. The number of outlets the retailer establishes in the selective coverage strategy should equal the number of market segments served. Generally speaking, many chain retailers, such as apparel stores and department stores, follow a selective market coverage strategy by locating an outlet in each of the major shopping malls within a given city or metro area. In this case, the right place is the *select* place.

Exclusive Market Coverage. In an **exclusive market coverage** strategy, the retailer elects to use one location to serve either an entire market area or some major segment of that market. An exclusive coverage strategy is ideal for retailers of specialty goods. (Specialty goods are goods that consumers are willing to put forth considerable effort to obtain.) Specialty-goods manufacturers often enter into exclusive arrangements with certain retailers. The advantages to manufacturers are more intense selling efforts on the part of their retailers and an exclusive, high-quality image for their products. The exclusive retailer also enjoys several advantages, including (1) an enhanced store image because of the exclusive merchandise and (2) no *direct* competition for the *brands* of merchandise carried. For these retailers, the right place is *a* place. Many specialty stores dealing in well-known, prestigious products such as Mercedes-Benz, Jaguar, and Steuben Glass use this form of market coverage.

Store Layout and Design

Store layout and design are two essential elements in creating the right shopping atmosphere for the chosen target market. The retailer should consider floor locations, shelf position, in-store location, and display location.

Floor Location. In some department stores, the right place for a product, department, display, event, or activity may be the basement, the first floor, or the top floor. Customers often think of the basement as the "bargain basement," the first floor as the "main floor," and the top floor as the "exclusive floor." The right floor is the one that is most consistent with where customers think things should be and where the retailer can provide the level of service customers expect.

Shelf Position. Retail merchandisers and marketers generally agree that the best place to shelve merchandise is at eye level. **Eye-level merchandising** is especially important when the retailer wants to attract new or additional sales. For example, in a supermarket Campbell often places several popular varieties of its soups, such as tomato, chicken noodle, and vegetable beef, at *non-eye-level* positions. These soups are in great demand, and customers will seek them out. New varieties and slower-selling ones, however, often are positioned at eye level to generate additional sales.

In-store Location. The right place within a store for a product, customer service, or display is the one that best conforms to customer in-store traffic patterns. The right place therefore might be either in front, in back, along the sides, or in the center. The in-store layout of most supermarkets, for example, is based on the "ring of perishables" principle. Food retailers know that consumers purchase their perishables (eggs, milk, butter, meat, vegetables, etc.) every week. Supermarket retailers have learned that by placing perishables in a ring around the store (sides and back), they can draw customers into other sections of the store. Supermarkets using this technique greatly increase the chance that customers will pass by and purchase other products in the store's total merchandise offering (i.e., make impulse purchases). Wellpet, a pet care specialty chain in Oregon and northern California, uses a similar strategy in its stores: a wood veneer pathway guides customers through the store, thereby increasing their exposure to the firm's total product line.

Another strategy some retailers use is the "attractors and interceptors" strategy. Many department stores place merchandise such as men's suits, better women's wear, and other big-ticket items in the back of the store to act as attractors, drawing customers through the entire length of the store. In the process, customers are intercepted by departments carrying complementary product lines such as shirts, scarves, and jewelry.

Display Location. Retailers use displays to draw attention to their product offerings. Whether at the end of an aisle, at the checkout stand, or in a freestanding location near high-traffic areas, the right place is the "visible" place for these special displays. Some retailers are increasingly recognizing that their selling space is valuable real estate and an important asset in their negotiations with vendors. For example, most major supermarket chains are now demanding that manufacturers pay "slotting allowances" (fees for displaying new product lines) and other charges. Stores are "looking to make money not just by selling products to consumers, but by renting shelf space to manufacturers."[35] Within the display itself, "right is also right": The best position within a display is the right side. The right-side bias is based on the belief that most consumers view a display from right to left. So right is "right" because it is the first place consumers look.

The Right Time

The **right time** to sell is when consumers are willing to buy. Because time affects various types of consumers differently, retailers must develop retailing strategies that coincide with consumer buying times.[36] With two-income families approaching 50 percent, time has become a scarce commodity. The perception that time is scarce is resulting in "time-buying" behavior: While people can try to earn more money, they cannot get more time, so they must use time differently. By trading dollars for timesaving goods and services and shopping in time-efficient stores, consumers are doing just that.[37] Sonic Industries, Inc., a fast-food franchiser scattered across 21 Sunbelt states, operates outlets with 24 drive-through stalls serviced by carhops; the average waiting time for an order at a Sonic outlet is under four minutes.[38]

> A treasure hunt, that's how off-price retailers have usually described their marketing strategy. . . . [T]he discount shopper is still primarily a woman, and these days she rarely has time to go treasure hunting. Ten years ago shoppers spent two hours in an off-price store. . . . Today the average is 40 minutes.[39]

End-of-aisle and within-the-aisle displays call special attention to selected product offerings.

To survive in today's time-compressed world, retailers need to get their customers in and out quickly and efficiently. People are willing to buy time to make life simpler. Some particular times that retailers consider in developing time strategies are (1) calendar times, (2) seasonal times, (3) life times, and (4) personal times.

Within a display, "Right is right." Why?

Calendar Times

In the category of calendar times, the retailer considers times of the day, times of the week, times of the month, and times of the year. Since consumers' behavior is largely geared toward these times, any one of them can be an opportune time for the retailer.

Whether morning, noon, afternoon, or evening, many retailers have businesses with daily peak periods. Restaurants, for example, have definite "right times" of the day: breakfast, lunch, and dinner times. For most restaurants, these are the only times for sales and profits. As examples, "Bennigan's, a unit of Pillsbury Co., puts stopwatches on its restaurants' tables and promises to serve in 15 minutes or [the meal is] free. Pizza Hut offers a second pizza free if the first takes more than five minutes."[40] In essence, the lunch hour has become the third rush hour. Evenings are "most times" for motion picture theaters. By reducing prices for the afternoon matinee, however, the theater manager can make afternoons a "sometimes" for some moviegoers. Morning and afternoon rush hours are the right times for some retailers that want to intercept consumers going to and from work.

Certain days of the week are better times to sell some products than other days. Sunday is the right time of the week for some consumers because they have free time to shop. On the other hand, Sunday may be the wrong time for other consumers because for them it is "God's time" or is an illegal time in their area (i.e., Sunday closing laws are in effect). With the aid of electronic shelf labels, retailers are experimenting with offering different prices at different times of the day or week to build customer traffic. This new technology may assist retailers in changing shopping habits to buying patterns that are more conducive to their operating capabilities.[41]

Paydays and bill-paying days are two examples of times of the month of which every retailer should be aware. Paydays are usually once, twice, or four times a month, and they could very well be the most important times for the retailer regardless of when they occur. With money in their pockets, consumers are more susceptible to advertising, new merchandise, and old merchandise clearance sales. Bill-paying days are the right time to collect on past credit sales. However, they usually are poor times for making sales.

Holiday seasons often represent the "best times" of the year for retailers. Christmas, Easter, Thanksgiving, Memorial Day, Labor Day, and New Year's Eve are "special times" for consumers and provide unique opportunities to retailers. For many retailers, back-to-school time is second only to Christmas in its potential to generate sales. Christmas is the only time of the year for Toy Liquidator's "Christmas-only" store concept; this closeout store concept of the Wisconsin Toy Company involves leasing vacant stores in strip centers from November 1 through Christmas.[42]

Seasonal Times

Consumers' buying patterns change with the seasons—not only spring, summer, fall, and winter but perhaps football, basketball, and baseball seasons; planting, growing, and harvesting seasons; or even opera, social, and theater seasons. Most retailers know which times are best for selling seasonal goods in their geographic and cultural regions. They also know that the best part of the season is the beginning, when they can sell goods at full markup. In addition, they know that during the middle and latter parts of the season consumers are thinking about the next season, and therefore retailers must mark down prices on certain merchandise.

Life Times

In everyone's life there are special times—births, weddings, graduations, and many more—that are rare times for the retailer to make a special effort to sell merchandise. They are also the right time for the retailer because consumers are in one of their most susceptible buying moods. At these times, the retailer can generate additional sales by "trading up" the consumer, that is, inducing him or her to buy a higher-quality, higher-price, or markup product or add features and extras to the selection.

Personal Times

Every consumer experiences working times, leisure times, and maintenance times. Every retailer should be sensitive to the merchandising times of the weekday, the weekend, the workday, and the day off. A building materials firm that caters to the home handyman, for example, makes most sales on Friday and Saturday.

For the retailer, all of the times just discussed can be either good or bad times, fast or slow times, profitable or unprofitable times. In summary, a right time is any time that helps the retailer either avoid losing sales or create new sales that ordinarily would not be possible.

The Right Price

The **right price** is the amount consumers are willing to pay and retailers are willing to accept in exchange for merchandise and services. Consumers experience various forms of prices in the marketplace. They encounter odd prices, even prices, prices with coupons, sticker prices, bid prices, bargain prices, status prices, sales prices, manufacturers' suggested list prices, and retailers' prices, among others. Like consumers, retailers face different forms of prices. There are markup prices, markdown prices, price lines, base prices, unit prices, package prices, promotional prices, regular prices, loss-leader prices, illegal prices, and prices that include accessories.

In developing a pricing strategy, the retailer must price merchandise low enough to generate sales but high enough to cover costs and make a fair profit.[43] At the same time, the retailer must consider pricing products in a manner consistent with consumers' expectations. Tiffany & Co., the high-end New York jeweler, is seeking to further enhance its exclusivity by pursuing a pricing strategy than can best be described as "everyday high prices."[44] The right price is one that is satisfactory to the customer not only before the sale but after it. One of the better means for ensuring price satisfaction after the sale is to offer "everyday low prices." The companies "that have been most successful in retailing over the past 5 to 10 years have been Toys 'R' Us, Wal-Mart, and Circuit City, and basically they all have everyday low pricing."[45] A consumer who is willing to pay a "premium" price for a product generally expects premium performance. If the product does not display this expected level of performance, the consumer might never buy products from the same retailer again. Because retailers depend heavily on repeat business, failure to meet consumers' performance expectations would be disastrous.

Finally, the right price must be competitive—if not with all competitors, then at least with those in the same trading area or those with similar operations. Competitive pricing means setting a price that is about the same as that found in similar stores within the same trading area. To ensure price competitiveness, many retailers promise to match the lowest advertised price a shopper can find. "Retailers have gone into the business of selling price insurance . . . an insurance policy that shoppers won't feel foolish."[46]

The Right Appeal

The **right appeal** presents the **right message** to the **right audience** through the **right media.** Even if the product, place, and price are right, the retailer will not succeed unless it can effectively communicate its offering to its target market. The retailer must inform and persuade consumers that its product mix precisely meets their particular needs. In making the right appeal, the retailer's problem is how to identify the target

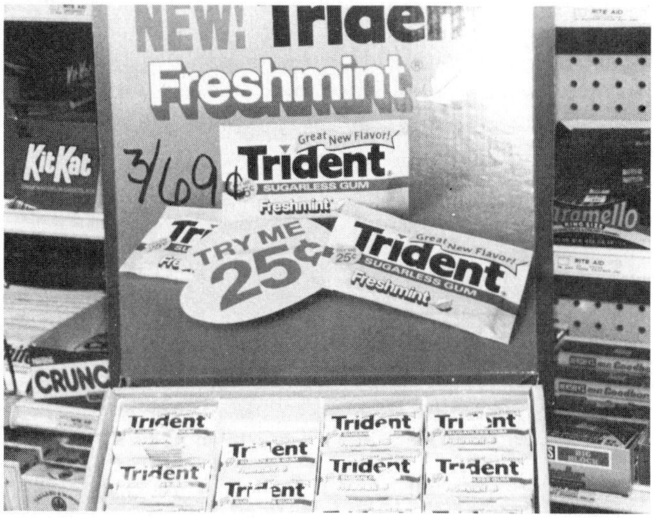

Trial prices, odd prices, and sales prices are all part of the retailer's product strategy.

audience, create the appropriate message, and select the best medium of communication.

The Right Message

The right message is the right thing to say (the right message *content*) presented in the right *manner*. The right message content emphasizes what consumers are most concerned about and explains how the retailer's offerings can address those concerns. For example, homemakers deciding among supermarkets may be more concerned with what they buy and how much they pay (e.g., selection and value) than from whom, where, and when they buy. In this case, the best message emphasizes the *what* and *how much*. When deciding among furriers, however, the same individuals may be more concerned with what and from whom they buy (e.g., quality and status) and less concerned with where and when they buy and how much they pay. An average image "haunts retailers J.C. Penney Co. and Sears, both of which have seen their middle-income customers defect to discount outlets or trendier specialty stores. Both chains are scrambling to revitalize sales by trying to project an image that's a step up from vanilla. They are stocking more national brand goods and running slicker, more stylish ads to herald the change."[47] Brooks Brothers, the "paragon of pinstripes," sells only private-label merchandise to the image-conscious, moneyed consumer at selected locations within upscale shopping malls and avenues.[48] In these situations, the retailer should emphasize the *what* and *from whom*.

The retailer must determine which purchase factors are most important to the consumer's buying decision and emphasize those appeals in the message. After gathering consumer information, a retailer may decide to make a **product appeal,** emphasizing the rightness of its products for consumers; a **patronage appeal,** emphasizing the rightness of the store, location, and hours; or a **price appeal**. The retailer may also make a combined appeal if it thinks several "right choice" elements are important to the consumer.

In structuring the message content, the retailer must also choose between direct action and indirect action. **Direct-action messages** urge the consumer to come to the store now to either take advantage of a sale or redeem a coupon. **Indirect-action messages,** on the other hand, have long-run goals. They attempt to change consumers' attitudes toward the retailer by cultivating its image as the "right" place to buy (e.g., "When you think of fine furniture, think of us"). Direct-action messages usually result in immediate sales but normally do not encourage regular patronage. Indirect-action messages encourage regular patronage, but the retailer must invest considerable time and money to develop it.

The retailer must not only present the right message content; it must also present it in the right manner by choosing either a logical or an emotional approach. Using the **logical approach,** the retailer makes a factual presentation about its offering and then shows consumers why buying from that source is the "right" choice. For example, a retailer might say, "Compare prices, and you'll see why you should shop with us." A retailer that uses an **emotional approach** speaks not to what consumers think, but to what they feel (pride, fear, etc.). For example, retailers create emotional messages that appeal to consumers' sense of loyalty ("Shop your local hometown merchants"), sense of security ("We sell only brand-name merchandise"), sense of tradition and stability ("Serving you from the same location for 25 years"), or sense of belonging ("Shop with us, where only the discriminating shop"). The Metropolitan Museum of Art in New York City operates several retail outlets that sell a wide variety of high-quality reproductions of art objects found in the museum. "Marketing the Met's collection is a natural. People feel secure that anything that's been in a museum has good taste. . . . No one ever went broke playing to the basic insecurity of American shoppers. After all, anything in the Met has been endorsed by generations of art critics."[49]

The Right Audience

The right message must be directed to the right audience. In seeking to determine the right audience, the retailer can make one of two choices: Pursue the mass-market audience or pursue one or more target-market audiences.

A retailer that decides to appeal to all consumers within a market area should use a broad appeal to the mass market. By using a broad appeal, the retailer hopes to attract a few customers from all segments of the market. The message must be general enough to appeal to a wide range of consumers and their needs but specific enough to stimulate them to action.

The retailer may decide to appeal to a select group of customers within a market area. The process of dividing a market into smaller subsets is called *market segmentation*, and the market segment to which the retailer directs its appeal is the *target market*. Any market can be segmented along the lines of demographic characteristics, patronage motives, and psychographic profiles. We discuss market segmentation and target marketing in depth throughout the remainder of this text.

The Right Media

The means by which a retailer communicates its product offering to consumers is just as important as the content. Typically a retailer has several choices in reaching an audience: newspapers, television, radio, magazines, telephone, direct mail, window displays, outdoor signs, in-store demonstrations, and personal sales representatives. The right medium for the retailer effectively and economically reaches the largest portion of the mass or target audience.

Having discussed the elements of the right merchandising blend, let us now examine the other half of the equation for a successful retail organization: the **right performance standards**.

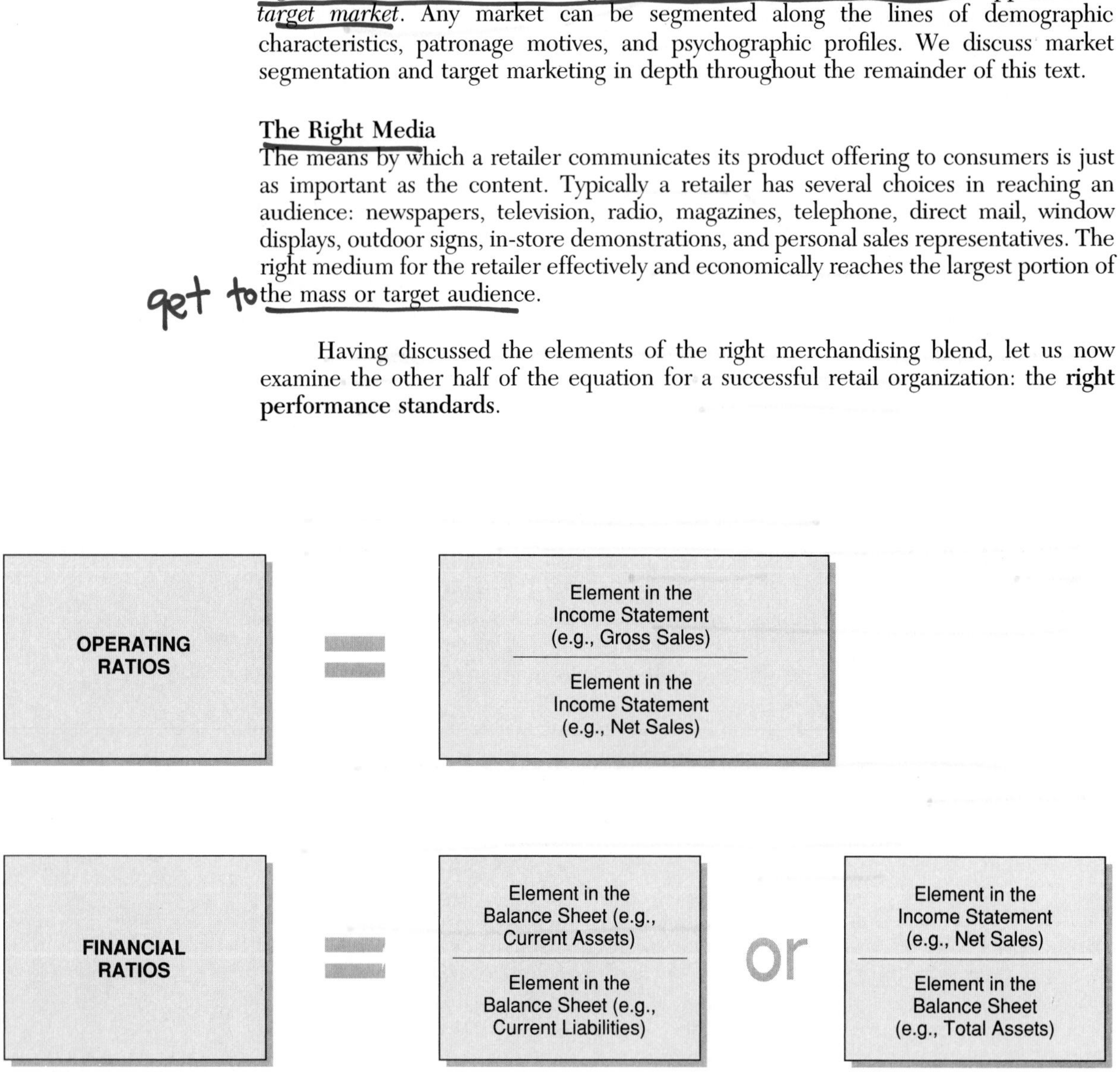

FIGURE 1–13
Computing performance standards

RETAIL STRATEGIES AND TACTICS

Goldblatt's Department Store—An Old Merchandising Blend for a New Consumer Market

To escape Chapter 11 and rebuild the business, Chicago's Goldblatt's department stores returned to their immigrant heritage. While blacks and Hispanics have replaced Poles and Bohemians as the immigrant customer base, what constitutes the right merchandise blend is the same today as it was at the turn of the century. In its most basic form, Goldblatt's merchandising strategy can be described as follows:

- *Offer the right product:* Basic personal and household necessities—coats to flatwear, dresses to lamps
- *In the right quantities:* Smaller quantities that are tolerable and affordable
- *In the right place:* Down-at-the-heels inner-city neighborhoods that are the castoffs of mainstream retailing
- *At the right time:* Schedule promotion to coincide with customers' cash flow—first of the month, when patrons receive pay, social security, unemployment, and welfare checks
- *At the right price:* Bottom prices and sale prices low enough to move inventory within 30 days—the "incredible bargain store"
- *By the right appeal:* Monthly sales advertising circulars delivered directly to neighborhood doorsteps; spartan yet colorful store decors and Spanish-speaking clerks who will make customers feel comfortable

By being the "poor man's" Marshall's for inner-city markets, Goldblatt's has pursued a market-niching strategy that affords the firm some competitive protection while generating a respectable ($50 million) business.

Source: Based on Steve Weiner, "Poor Customer, Rich Profits," *Forbes,* March 6, 1984, 145–146.

THE RIGHT PERFORMANCE STANDARDS

Retailers must have some means by which to judge their operational and financial performances. Several operating and financial ratios can aid in their judgment. These ratios concisely express the relationships among elements in the income statement and the balance sheet. Because these ratios have gained wide acceptance within the general business community as well as within specific retail trades, they have become trade standards by which retailers can judge their individual performances against national and trade norms. These standard ratios are published annually by private firms such as Dun & Bradstreet and trade organizations such as the National Retail Federation, Inc. Within individual retail organizations managers can make comparisons between current ratios and past ratios. The availability of these external and internal standards helps retailers make meaningful judgments about their operating efficiency and financial ability. Ratio analysis provides a "snapshot" of the relative health of the retailer's operating and financial condition and serves as a control to identify conditions that deviate from established norms.

Operating Ratios

Retailers compute some ratios to gain insight into their operating performance. Retailers use **operating ratios** to compute relationships among elements in the income statement. Ratio computations simply divide one element of the income statement (e.g., operating profit) by another element (e.g., net sales—see Figure 1–13). A standard practice is to convert ratios into percentages by multiplying the results by 100. Of particular concern to most retailers are operating ratios involving net sales (i.e., operating profit divided by net sales). Operating ratios are discussed in Chapter 7.

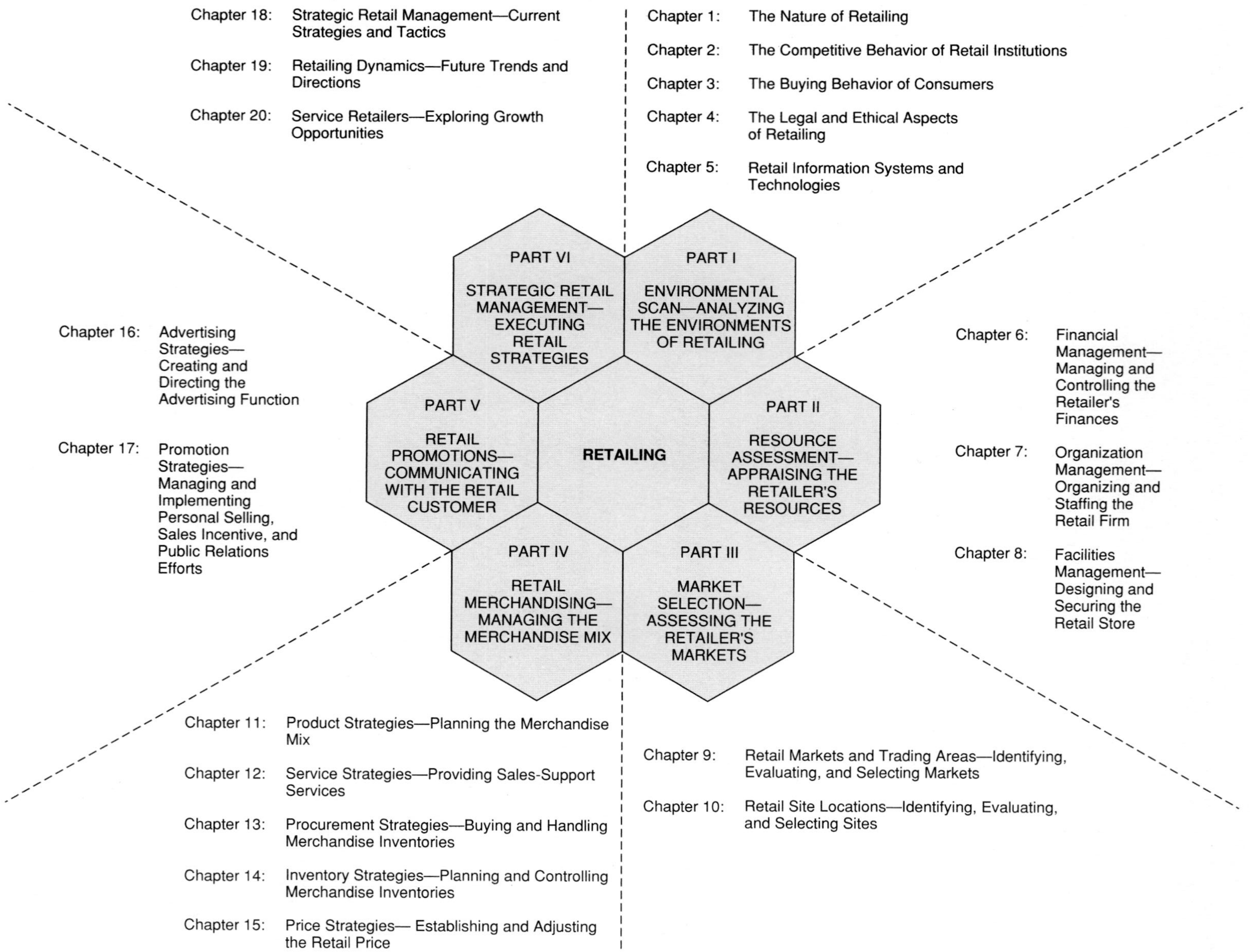
Chapter 18: Strategic Retail Management—Current Strategies and Tactics
Chapter 19: Retailing Dynamics—Future Trends and Directions
Chapter 20: Service Retailers—Exploring Growth Opportunities
Chapter 1: The Nature of Retailing
Chapter 2: The Competitive Behavior of Retail Institutions
Chapter 3: The Buying Behavior of Consumers
Chapter 4: The Legal and Ethical Aspects of Retailing
Chapter 5: Retail Information Systems and Technologies
Chapter 16: Advertising Strategies—Creating and Directing the Advertising Function
Chapter 17: Promotion Strategies—Managing and Implementing Personal Selling, Sales Incentive, and Public Relations Efforts
PART VI
STRATEGIC RETAIL MANAGEMENT—EXECUTING RETAIL STRATEGIES
PART I
ENVIRONMENTAL SCAN—ANALYZING THE ENVIRONMENTS OF RETAILING
PART V
RETAIL PROMOTIONS—COMMUNICATING WITH THE RETAIL CUSTOMER
RETAILING
PART II
RESOURCE ASSESSMENT—APPRAISING THE RETAILER'S RESOURCES
PART IV
RETAIL MERCHANDISING—MANAGING THE MERCHANDISE MIX
PART III
MARKET SELECTION—ASSESSING THE RETAILER'S MARKETS
Chapter 6: Financial Management—Managing and Controlling the Retailer's Finances
Chapter 7: Organization Management—Organizing and Staffing the Retail Firm
Chapter 8: Facilities Management—Designing and Securing the Retail Store
Chapter 11: Product Strategies—Planning the Merchandise Mix
Chapter 12: Service Strategies—Providing Sales-Support Services
Chapter 13: Procurement Strategies—Buying and Handling Merchandise Inventories
Chapter 14: Inventory Strategies—Planning and Controlling Merchandise Inventories
Chapter 15: Price Strategies— Establishing and Adjusting the Retail Price
Chapter 9: Retail Markets and Trading Areas—Identifying, Evaluating, and Selecting Markets
Chapter 10: Retail Site Locations—Identifying, Evaluating, and Selecting Sites

FIGURE 1–14
The retailing plan—Overview of the text organization and content

Financial Ratios

Financial ratios identify relationships among elements of a balance sheet or between a balance sheet element and an element in the income statement (see Figure 1–13). The most widely used financial ratios are those reported by Dun & Bradstreet. These key performance measurements help the retailer make meaningful comparisons between its financial performance and the national median performance of similar retailers. These ratios are also useful in establishing realistic financial objectives.

The ratios of retailing are used as basic reference points and not as absolute guidelines for judging financial performance levels for a given retail firm. Chapter 7 provides more in-depth coverage of financial ratios in the discussion of managing the firm's resources.

THE RETAILING PLAN—OVERVIEW OF THE TEXT ORGANIZATION AND CONTENT

The retailing plan describes the organizational structure of this text and addresses the operational questions of why, what, when, where, and how specific retail business activities are to be accomplished. The retailing process can be viewed as a cyclical activity involving six stages or parts. Figure 1–14 illustrates the six-part structure of this text and the content (chapters) covered in each part.

Part I, "Environmental Scan," analyzes the uncontrollable environments surrounding each retail operation. This chapter reviewed the general nature of retailing. The remaining chapters in Part I deal with the competitive environment facing each retail institution (Chapter 2), the buying behavior of retail consumers (Chapter 3), the legal and ethical conditions facing each retailer (Chapter 4), and the systems and technologies used in gathering and analyzing retail information (Chapter 5).

Management of resources is an essential element of any retailing plan. The management of financial resources (Chapter 6), human resources (Chapter 7), and physical resources (Chapter 8) is the focus of Part II, "Resource Assessment."

Part III, "Market Selection," examines the geographical dimensions of retailing. Identifying, evaluating, and selecting regional/local markets and trading areas (Chapter 9) and retail site locations (Chapter 10) are the focus in this third stage of the retail plan.

Part IV, "Retail Merchandising," deals with managing the merchandise mix. Chapter 11 focuses on developing the merchandise mix; Chapter 12 discusses how the retailer's service offering supports the merchandise mix; Chapter 13 outlines the buying and handling of merchandise inventories; Chapter 14 discusses how to plan and control merchandise inventories; and Chapter 15 examines pricing strategies.

Part V, "Retail Promotions," explores the advertising function (Chapter 16) and the roles of personal selling, sales incentives, and public relations (Chapter 17).

Part VI, "Strategic Retail Management," examines retail management strategies (Chapter 18) and the dynamics of retail trends (Chapter 19). Chapter 20 explores the growth opportunities currently being enjoyed by service retailers.

Review Figure 1–14 again. It will help you to organize the vast subject matter called retailing.

SUMMARY

Retailing is the business activity of selling goods and services to the final consumer. A retailer is a business organization that makes most of its sales to the ultimate consumer. As an institutional link between producer and consumer, retailers play an essential role in overcoming the assortment, quantity, space, and time gaps that separate consumers from producers. Retailers are members of the marketing channel of distribution; hence, they are involved with directing the goods and services flows between producers and consumers. Retailing is an important part of the nation's fiber and one of the major threads in the country's economic system.

The basic task of retailing is to balance the product and service needs of the consuming public with the operational and financial needs of the retail organization—in other words, find the right merchandising blend to ensure the right performance standards. Elements of the retailer's right merchandising blend are offering the right products in the right quantities, in the right place, at the right time, at the right price, by the right appeal. Performance standards can be expressed in terms of operating ratios and financial ratios.

STUDENT STUDY GUIDE

Key Terms and Concepts

accumulation process (p. 2)
allocation process (p. 4)
assorting process (p. 2)
assortment gap (p. 2)
augmenting extras (p. 16)
channel integration (p. 8)
conventional marketing channel (p. 9)
direct-action message (p. 25)
direct channel (p. 6)
emotional approach (p. 25)
exclusive market coverage (p. 19)
extended channel (p. 5)
eye-level merchandising (p. 19)
facilitating nonmember institutions (p. 6)
financial ratios (p. 29)
full-member institution (p. 6)
indirect-action message (p. 25)
information flow (p. 7)
intensive market coverage (p. 18)
intrinsic qualities (p. 15)
limited channel (p. 5)
limited-member institution (p. 6)
local market (p. 17)
logical approach (p. 25)
market (p. 17)
marketing channel (p. 4)
marketing concept (p. 11)
merchandising blend (p. 14)
merchandising utilities (p. 14)
operating ratios (p. 26)
ownership flow (p. 7)
patronage appeal (p. 25)
payment flow (p. 7)
physical flow (p. 6)
place utility (p. 4)
price appeal (p. 25)
product appeal (p. 25)
promotion flow (p. 7)
quantity gap (p. 4)
regional market (p. 17)
retailer (p. 2)
retailing (p. 2)
right appeal (p. 23)
right audience (p. 26)
right media (p. 26)
right message (p. 25)
right performance standards (p. 26)
right place (p. 17)
right price (p. 23)
right product (p. 14)
right quantity (p. 16)
right time (p. 20)
selective market coverage (p. 19)
site (p. 18)
space gap (p. 4)
time gap (p. 4)
time utility (p. 4)
trading area (p. 18)
vertical marketing system (p. 8)

Review Questions

1. What is retailing? How do retailers differ from other members of the marketing channel of distribution, wholesalers and producers?
2. Characterize the five types of channel flows that must be effectively managed to ensure successful retailing operations.
3. Why is channel teamwork important? How is it achieved?
4. Explain the role of retailing in our national economy.
5. Define the marketing concept. How does it relate to the problem of retailing?
6. Describe the match between retailers' decisions about the right merchandising blend and consumers' decisions about the right shopping choices.
7. Profile the three elements that comprise the retailer's right product decision.
8. What quantity is the right quantity? Provide an original example for each factor the retailer considers in determining the right quantity.
9. Outline the geographic dimensions of regional and local markets, trading areas, and site locations.
10. Compare and contrast intensive, selective, and exclusive market coverage.
11. Identify the four types of time categories. Provide two examples of merchandising strategies for each category that retailers use to meet the needs associated with different consumer buying times.
12. When is a retail price right for both the consumer and the retailer?
13. The right appeal equals the right message plus the right audience plus the right media. Briefly characterize each element of this equation.

Review Exam

True or False

_____ 1. If a buyer purchases a product from a retailer to resell the product at a profit or to use it in a business, the sale is still considered a retail sale.

_____ 2. Retailers differ from wholesalers in that retailers tend to use variable prices, while wholesalers tend to use a one-pricing policy based on some form of discounting structure.

_____ 3. The marketing concept stresses matching supply to demand rather than matching demand to supply.

_____ 4. A product's merchandising utilities are benefits the customer seeks in buying, using, and possessing the product.

_____ 5. Exclusive market coverage is most appropriate when merchandising specialty goods.

_____ 6. Customer satisfaction is the most important factor in determining the right price.

_____ 7. The retailer's problem in making the right appeal consists of how to identify the target audience, how to create the appropriate message, and how to select the best medium of communication.

Multiple Choice

_____ 1. The marketing channel alternative in which the producer elects to market directly to the retailer and thereby eliminate the independent wholesaler from the channel team is the _____ channel.
a. Limited
b. Extended
c. Selected
d. Direct
e. Extensive

_____ 2. The _____ flow is the flow of persuasive communication directed at influencing the decisions of consumers and other channel participants.
a. Information
b. Ownership
c. Promotion
d. Payment
e. Network

_____ 3. The advantages of the _____ marketing system is that it allows the channel team to achieve technological, managerial, and promotional leverages through integrating and synchronizing the five channel flows.
a. Conventional
b. Historical
c. Traditional
d. Vertical
e. None of the above

_____ 4. Which of the following is *not* one of the ingredients of the "right blend?"
a. The right product
b. The right appeal
c. The right time
d. The right profit
e. The right price

_____ 5. The best part of any selling season is the _____ season when retailers can sell goods at full markup.
a. Post-period
b. Beginning
c. Middle
d. End
e. Aftermath

_____ 6. If the retailer elects to emphasize the rightness of its store facilities, location, and operating hours, it is attempting to make a(n)
a. Patronage appeal
b. Product appeal
c. Price appeal
d. Combined appeal
e. Emotional appeal

_____ 7. Operating and financial ratios are beneficial to retailers because they can
a. Be used for historical comparisons
b. Be used to determine operating efficiency and financial stability
c. Provide a "snapshot" of the retailer's operating and financial health
d. Serve as a control to identify deviations from established norms
e. Do all of the above

STUDENT APPLICATIONS MANUAL

Investigative Projects: Practice and Applications

1. In 1987, Sears unveiled its McKids sportswear line of popular-priced clothes. The line incorporates subtle and overt use of the fast-food company's logo and special line identifiers and bears McKids labels and hang tags. Sportswear, nightwear, shoes, and accessory lines are included in the total McKids product mix. Is this a

case of *offering the right product in the right place?* Investigate this issue by (1) surveying children and parents for their perceptions of the idea; (2) reviewing trade literature to discover the opinions of the industry; and (3) visiting your local Sears store to ascertain how well Sears is merchandising the product line. Explain and support your answer to the above question.

2. Benetton Sportswear Shops have expanded rapidly throughout the United States and the world. In the 1980s, the number of U.S. stores jumped from 250 to 758, an impressive growth rate for the Italian manufacturer of colorful knitwear and cotton apparel. One of the "right place" strategies this prestigious specialty retailer uses is to cluster several retail shops in one upscaled trading area on the theory that the more there are, the larger the total market they will create. Do you agree with this strategy? Identify and explain some of the possible pros and cons of such a strategy.
3. Stop N Go, a Houston-based chain of convenience stores, offered the traditional product mix—beer, soft drinks, snacks, fill-in groceries, and gasoline. In an attempt at greater market impact, Stop N Go pursued a low-price strategy designed to make the chain competitive with supermarkets for convenience goods. The strategy failed due to unacceptably low profit margins. Are there any other nonprice strategies that might be more conducive to the convenience-store format? Develop a mini-strategic plan for Stop N Go that would allow this firm to have greater market impact without a negative profit performance.

Tactical Cases: Problems and Decisions

■ CASE 1–1
Lands' End: Maintaining the Competitive Edge*

Lands' End, the Dodgeville, Wisconsin, apparel company, is one of the nation's most successful catalog marketers. It has achieved a continuous record of increasing sales ($540 million) and earnings ($28 million) by selling well-tailored, classic apparel to the well-heeled, preppy consumer. In an ever-expanding sea of apparel catalogs (over 500), Lands' End has managed to create a high level of name recognition and brand identity. The catalog marketer's general line of casual clothing is directed at consumers whose favorite uniform is a rugby shirt, Khaki pants, and penny loafers. Quality merchandise, competitive prices, superior service, and a certain mystique are the company's trademarks.

The Lands' End catalog is supported by a carefully conceived merchandising program. Each catalog is informative and easy to use; it furnishes the customer with extensive product information (e.g., material, construction, workmanship, price, color, and size) and provides easy instructions for ordering merchandise. Reader involvement with each catalog is heightened by entertaining travel and recreation essays (e.g., backpacking in the Grand Canyon). Service support includes (1) a toll-free number for ordering merchandise or obtaining information; (2) free cloth swatches for customer inspection; (3) a quick response order system that fills 90 percent of all orders within 24 hours; (4) guaranteed satisfaction backed by an extensive personal service and quality control staff; and (5) customer size, color, and wardrobe coordination service.

A customer profile of Lands' End customers revealed the following:

- Ninety percent of its customers have some college education—more than double the national average.
- Patrons are five times more likely to have some post-graduate education than the general public.
- Seventy percent of its customers are in managerial or professional positions.
- Seventy-five percent of its female customers work outside the home.
- Sixty-five percent of its customers have annual incomes exceeding $35,000—twice as many as the population as a whole.
- Customers have a higher than average participation rate in a wide variety of sporting and traveling activities.

Despite the high level of effectiveness and efficiency of the firm's operational and merchandising programs, however, both sales growth and earnings are starting to slide. A number of difficult problems have emerged in the last several years, including:

- Skyrocketing costs for catalog paper and printing, together with increased postage costs
- Increased price competition (25 percent or higher discounts) from department and specialty stores, cutting into the pricing edge enjoyed by mail-order houses
- Increased competition from Eddie Bauer, Inc., a catalog house that also operates retail outlets and specializes in outdoor and sports apparel (Chicago's Spiegel, Inc. is the new owner)
- Increased competition from the growing number (16.5 percent annually) of specialty catalogs that target selective consumer groups with highly tailored merchandise mixes
- A tired and stale merchandise mix that is somewhat vulnerable to competitive actions of general merchandisers and niche retailers

ASSIGNMENT

Review Lands' End's current merchandising tactics. What adjustment in the merchandising blend would you recommend to correct or neutralize the five problems identified in the case? Are there any major strategic changes that might be effective in strengthening the firm's position with current customers while attracting a new and different customer base?

*This case was prepared by Dale M. Lewison and Jon M. Hawes, The University of Akron.

Sources: Brian Bremner and Keith H. Hammonds, "Lands' End Looks a Bit Frayed at the Edges," *Business Week,* March 19, 1990, 42; Ronit Addis, "Big Picture Strategy," *Forbes,* January 9, 1989, 70–72; "Four of the Trendsetters," *Chain Store Age Executive,* January 1990, 33–35; and Rayna Skolnik, "Selling via Catalog," *Stores,* October 1989, 47–50.

■ CASE 1–2
What Happened to the Department Store? —Seeking New Strategies and Tactics*

☼ ☼ ☼

What's Happening to Department Stores

Jeb Brown,
Senior Staff Writer,
New York

At the turn of the century, department stores had positioned themselves for absolute dominance of the retail market. Through mergers and integration, these retail organizations became large conglomerate corporations capable of dominating many supply markets. As a dominant retail force, department stores established the competitive position by which all other retailers were judged. Their dominance continued into the post–World War II period and through the 1960s. However, by the early 1970s, department stores were being outflanked by savvy competitors whose specialty and/or value-discount business formats were delivering more and better goods for the money. While total retail sales continue to increase, the conventional department store market share is decreasing. In addition, specialty stores have passed department stores in profitability and discounters have drawn about even with department store operations.

Many conventional department stores have become so aggressive in price promotions, that it is almost impossible to distinguish them from discounters. By employing this suicidal pricing practice, department stores can expect the continuing loss of consumer confidence, the steady declining of operating profits, and an ever-stiffening of competitive actions. So, what's happening to department stores? One answer is that they have forgotten the other five "rights" of merchandising (product, quantity, place, time, and appeal) in their never ending quest for cheaper prices.

Retail Weekly January 10, 1991

☼ ☼ ☼

One more trade article lamenting the downturn in department store fortunes, Stan Morris thought. It seemed he had read basically the same article five times in the last couple of months. As an associate at Retail Associates International, a consulting organization specializing in strategic retail planning, Stan had a vested interest in department stores' futures. He was one of the firm's principal resident experts in department store strategies and tactics. What troubled Stan was that everyone knew that department stores had entered the late maturity stage of the retail life cycle; however, these armchair experts offered only a very few concrete suggestions for reviving the industry. Perhaps that was why Stan had been so busy lately; if everyone had a workable answer for the revival of the department store business, Stan might have been out of work.

It was time for Stan to prepare the firm's annual report on the state of the department store industry. Given the fact that each of Retail Associates International's 24 department store clients paid an annual fee of $20,000 for this report and the right to access the firm's extensive research files on all aspects of retailing, Stan had to be able to identify the specific causes for the woes of department store retailing. More important, some constructive strategies and tactics for overcoming past problems and promoting the growth and revitalization of the industry were essential to the report's credibility. One comment in the article Stan had just read rang true: Department stores needed to place less emphasis on price promotions and pay greater attention to the other five merchandising "rights."

ASSIGNMENT

Assume that you have a summer internship with Retail Associates International. Stan Morris has asked you to conduct a library search to find trade and other articles that

1. Identify specific merchandising and operational problems within the department store industry
2. Identify specific merchandising and/or operating strategies and tactics that might help overcome the problems of department store retailing.

Prepare a well-organized written report to Stan Morris on your findings. You might want to think of future employment opportunities and make your own recommendations, fully supported by a complete rationale.

*This case was prepared by Dale M. Lewison and Jon M. Hawes, The University of Akron.

ENDNOTES

1. Bruce Hirobayashi, "Retailing—Winds of Change," *AIM,* 1989, 9.
2. Robert F. Lusch, "Retail Control Systems for the 1990's," *Retailing Issues Letter,* vol. 2, no. 5 (Arthur Andersen & Co. in conjunction with the Center for Retailing Studies, Texas A&M University, January 1990), 1.
3. Jeffrey J. Hallett, "Retailing in the 1990's: Love Your Customers or Lose Them," *Retail Control* (February 1990): 8.
4. Stephen Phillips, Amy Dunkin, James B. Treece, and Keith H. Hammonds, "King Customer," *Business Week,* March 12, 1990, 88.
5. George A. Rieder, "Mythbusters: Key to Creating a Climate for Innovation and Risk-taking," *Retailing Issues Letter,* vol. 2, no. 2. (Arthur Andersen & Co. in conjunction with the Center for Retailing Studies, Texas A&M University, May 1989), 1.
6. See Tom Peters, *Thriving on Chaos* (New York: Knopf, 1987).
7. Steve Weiner, "But Will They Ever Know Zytel from Lycra?", *Forbes,* June 26, 1989, 152.
8. Brian Bremner, "Hartmarx Is Suddenly Looking Threadbare," *Business Week,* January 29, 1990, 40.
9. Patricia Sellers, "Getting Customers to Love You," *Fortune,* March 13, 1989, 44.
10. Bert C. McCammon, Jr., "Perspectives for Distribution Programming," in *Vertical Marketing Systems,* ed. Louis P. Bucklin (Glenview, Ill.: Scott, Foresman, 1970), 43.
11. Ibid.
12. Amy Dunkin and Leah J. Nathans, "A Wholesale Makeover of Retail?", *Business Week,* October 23, 1989, 138.
13. Franklin S. Houston, "The Marketing Concept: What It Is and What It Is Not," *Journal of Marketing* 50 (April 1986): 86.
14. Paul Glastris and Lynn Adkins, "A Season of Hope for Sears," *U.S. News & World Reports,* 11 Dec. 1989, 52–53.
15. Joe Agnew, "Marcus on Marketing: Profits Are By-products of Rendering Satisfactory Customer Service," *Marketing News,* April 10, 1987, 16.
16. Gerald McMahon, "Grocers Need Shopper Data Base to Build Strong Relationships," *Marketing News,* March 12, 1990, 26.
17. Larry G. Gulledge, "Simplify Complexity of Satisfying Customers," *Marketing News,* June 8, 1990, 6.
18. See John C. Szabo, "Service = Survival," *Nation's Business* (March 1989): 17.
19. Susan Caminiti, "How The Gap Keeps Ahead of The Pack," *Fortune,* February 12, 1990, 129.
20. David Woodruff, "Will K mart Ever Be a Silk Purse?", *Business Week,* January 22, 1990, 46.
21. Muriel J. Adams, "Robots in the Future?" *Stores* (April 1988): 40.
22. See Renee M. Covino, "Health Craze Puts H&BA in Good Shape," *Discount Merchandiser,* September 1989, 34.
23. Lois Therrien, "Kraft Is Looking for Fat Growth from Fat-Free Foods," *Business Week,* March 26, 1990, 100.
24. "Home Delivery: An Old Idea Born Again," *Mere-trends* (Winter 1987): 4–5.
25. Ibid.
26. Ela Schwartz, "Keeping Up with Stationery Trends," *Discount Merchandiser,* February 1990, 44.
27. Jennifer Pellet, "Bumper Crop for Babies," *Discount Merchandiser,* September 1989, 47.
28. Pat Sloan and Judith Graham, "International Intriguing," *Advertising Age,* January 29, 1990, S-2.
29. Joan E. Primo and Howard L. Green, "To Mall or Not to Mall: Where Retail Opportunities Lie," *Marketing News,* February 10, 1988, 10.
30. Jay L. Johnson, "Burlington Coat Factory's Formula: Stamina," *Discount Merchandiser,* February 1990, 38–39.
31. See "Wal-Mart Puts Indiana in High Gear," *Chain Store Age Executive,* March 1990, 27–31.
32. Christopher Tucher, "How America Is Digesting Its 'Whale,'" *Business Week,* September 11, 1989, 62.
33. Joe Agnew, "Breakfast Only Image Shed as Bob Evans Flees the Farm," *Marketing News,* June 5, 1987, 13.
34. Alexander Peers, "Art Mall Tries to Be More Than a Still Life," *The Wall Street Journal,* March 28, 1990, B-1.
35. Lois Therrien, "Want Shelf Space at Supermarket? Ante Up," *Business Week,* August 7, 1990, 60.
36. See Easwar S. Iver, "Unplanned Purchasing: Knowledge of Shopping Environment and Time Pressure," *Journal of Retailing* 65 (Spring 1989): 40–57.
37. Leonard L. Berry, "Market to the Perception," *American Demographics,* February 1990, 32.
38. Seth Lubove, "People Talk Thin but Eat Fat," *Forbes,* April 2, 1990, 56.
39. Ellen Paris, "A Touch of Class," *Forbes,* February 5, 1990, 148.
40. Robert Johnson and Dae Tononarive, "Eatery Chains Pour on Speed at Lunchtime," *The Wall Street Journal,* February 1, 1988, 1.
41. Warren Thayer, "Electronic Shelf Labels: How They Stack Up," *Progressive Grocer,* January 1990, 62.
42. Ela Schwartz, "Capitalizing on Overlooked Toys," *Discount Merchandiser,* February 1990, 56.
43. See David Stipp, "Ames Suspends Payout Pending Return to Profit," *The Wall Street Journal,* March 20, 1990, A-4.
44. See Jeffrey A. Trachtenberg, "Cocktails at Tiffany," *Forbes,* February 6, 1989, 128–130.
45. See Amy Dunkin, David Woodruff, and Dean Foust, "Little Prices Are Looking Good to Buy Retailers," *Business Week,* July 3, 1989, 42.
46. Francine Schwadel, "Who Wins with Price-Matching

Plans?", *The Wall Street Journal*, January 16, 1989, B-1.
47. Kathleen Deveny, "Middle-Price Brands Come under Siege," *The Wall Street Journal*, March 20, 1990, B-1.
48. Mark Maremont, "Marks & Spencer Pays a Premium for Pinstripes," *Business Week*, April 18, 1988, 67.
49. Joshua Levine, "Art Chic," *Forbes*, August 21, 1989, 96.

OUTLINE

OBJECTIVES

- Identify and discuss the four major types of retail competition.
- Recognize the different types of retailing institutions that comprise the retailing community.
- Identify the organizational and operational traits that characterize each type of retailer.
- Discuss the principal product, price, place, and promotional strategies each type of retailer uses.
- Explain the relative advantages and disadvantages for each type of retailer.
- Identify and discuss the theories of retail institutional change that explain the evolution of retailing and predict future developments.

PART I

THE COMPETITIVE BEHAVIOR OF RETAIL INSTITUTIONS

CHAPTER 2

THE 24-HOUR-A-DAY WAR

A century ago, department stores positioned themselves for absolute domination of the retail market. Through mergers and integration into large department store conglomerates, these full-line retailers were also threatening to control many supply markets.[1] Today department stores are struggling to survive—survive not only the turmoil of mergers, acquisitions, and liquidations[2] but also that tremendously increased competition from a wide range of alternative retail formats.[3] Because this venerable institution has staying power as a retailing concept, department stores will not disappear.[4] Nevertheless, retailing is a very competitive industry; one author describes it as a "24-hour-a-day war." Survival and growth require the retailer to "create a differential advantage over competitors, and give consumers a reason to shop at their stores."[5] Retail success is built on multidimensional market strategies: "Merchandise quality, selection, assortment, and services typically have been used in conjunction with prices to build store traffic and loyalty."[6]

One of the most dramatic developments in today's world of retailing is the myriad of store types available to consumers. This chapter surveys the broad spectrum of competitive retail business formats. Specifically it reviews (1) the types of retail competition, (2) the methods of classifying retail institutions, (3) the strategies and tactics of competing retail business formats, and (4) the changing and adapting character of retail competition.

THE NATURE OF RETAIL COMPETITION

Retailers compete with one another on the basis of their product, place, price, service, and promotion strategies. These strategies are directed at securing the attention and patronage of ultimate consumers and serve as the focus for retail competitive actions. As *Business Week* describes, "power retailers" are highly competitive organizations that succeed by sharply defining their customer base and fully understanding what their target customer wants. What the customer wants is assurance that the retailer is on the cutting edge and there is good reason to visit it frequently.[7] In assessing the competitive structure a particular retailer faces, we must examine two dimensions of competition: the types of competition and the levels of competition.

Types of Competition

Retail competition is more complex than competition between two similar stores. Figure 2–1 shows the four types of retail competition: intratype, intertype, vertical, and systems competition.

Intratype competition involves competition between two or more retailers that use the same business format. For example, a regional shopping mall often contains several small independent women's apparel shops competing with one another.

Intertype competition is competition between two or more retailers that use different business formats to sell the same type of merchandise. A supermarket

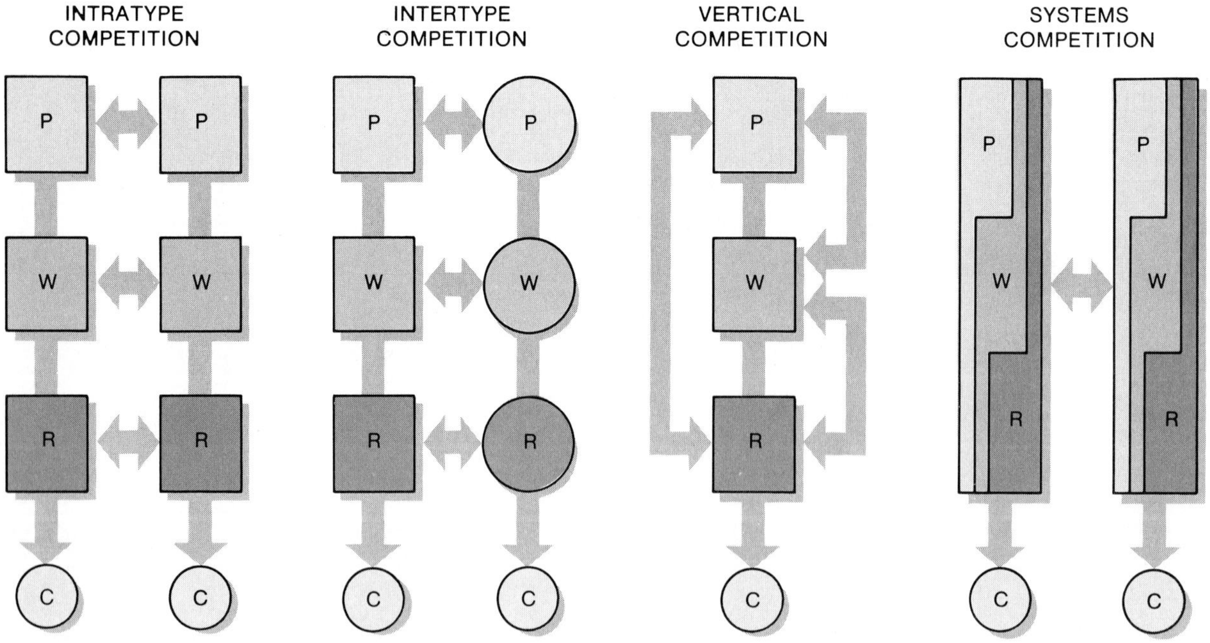

FIGURE 2–1
Types of competition

(Safeway) and a discount store (Wal-Mart) attempting to sell Crest toothpaste to the same customer are engaging in intertype competition.

Vertical competition is the competition between a retailer and a wholesaler or producer that is attempting to make retail sales to the retailer's customers. For example, if a retailer stocks and sells a product line that the manufacturer also offers through a catalog operation, the retailer and the manufacturer are engaged in vertical competition. Many manufacturers sell their goods directly to consumers through their own outlets located in factory outlet malls (e.g., Bass Shoes, Calvin Klein Sportswear). "Taking a cue from the successful designer stand-alone shops of ready-to-wear manufacturers, upscale tabletop resources have followed suit in an effort to increase prestige and consumer awareness. . . . Names like Lenox, Waterford, Wedgewood . . . Buccellati, Baccarat, and Stuben [are] selling their products direct to the consumer in high fashion, studio-type settings."[8]

Finally, **systems competition** is competition between two or more vertical marketing systems. The competition among McDonald's, Burger King, and Wendy's is among three highly integrated marketing systems at all levels of the distribution channel.

Levels of Competition

The level of competition a retailer faces in any market area is a function of the number, size, and quality of competitors within that area. Ideally the retailer that faces a few small competitors is better off than one that must compete against a large number of small competitors or a few large competitors. The number and size of competitors can be determined with reasonable accuracy; Figure 2–2 shows the number (existing units) and size (sales volume) of the top 50 retail chains. The quality of each competitor, however, is difficult to measure and analyze. The aggressiveness and effectiveness of competitors are important determinants of the level of competition for a market area. In the following pages, we examine the competitiveness and effectiveness of various types of retailers in detail.

COMPETITIVE STRATEGIES OF RETAILERS

Retailers can be classified on the basis of their ownership, merchandise, size, affiliation, contractual, location, service, organizational, and operational characteristics. The diversity and complexity of business formats within the retailing industry preclude developing a mutually exclusive classification that clearly differentiates each type of retailer. For example, specialty and department stores can be distinguished on the basis of their respective merchandise mix; however, each might also be classified as a chain, affiliated, or integrated operation.

Figure 2–3 outlines the characteristics that classify retail institutions. In this section, we discuss the competitive strategies of various retail institutions from the perspective of eleven general types of retail institutions. Figure 2–4 illustrates the eleven competitive retail formats we will review in this chapter.

Specialty Store Retailing

The merchandising and operating strategies of the specialty retailer are directed at serving the needs of a more closely targeted and homogeneous market segment. The specialty retailer attempts to serve all consumers in one or a limited number of market segments. To accomplish this targeting effect, **specialty store** retailers "specialize" in the merchandise they offer consumers; they become "focused merchandisers." While all specialty stores offer a focused merchandise selection, the size, scope, and nature of their operations vary significantly. As Figure 2–5 shows, the specialty store concept exhibits a wide range of merchandising and operating strategies. Specialty retailers vary

FIGURE 2–2
The top 50 retail chains
(source: Reprinted by permission from *Chain Store Age Executive* [August 1989]: 22–29. Copyright © Lebhar-Friedman, Inc., 425 Park Avenue, New York, New York 10022.)

Rank Chain	1988 Sales ($000)	1988 Profits as Percentage of Sales	Number of Stores
1. Sears, Roebuck & Co.[a]	30,256,000	0.6	1,649
2. K mart	27,301,400	2.9	2,307
3. Wal-Mart	20,649,001	4.0	1,381
4. Kroger	19,050,000	0.1	2,206
5. American	18,478,354	0.5	1,285
6. J. C. Penney[a]	14,833,000	4.5	1,789
7. Safeway	13,612,300	0.2	1,261
8. Dayton Hudson	12,204,000	2.4	618
9. May	11,525,000	4.4	3,091
10. A & P	10,067,776	1.3	1,241
11. Winn-Dixie	9,007,700	1.3	1,246
12. Campeau/Federated-Allied-Ralphs	8,388,000	8.9[b]	394
13. F. W. Woolworth	8,088,000	3.6	7,739
14. Melville	6,780,359	5.2	6,540
15. Albertson's	6,773,061	2.4	497
16. Supermarkets General	5,962,200	N/A	268
17. R. H. Macy	5,729,000	N/A	149
18. Walgreen	4,883,520	2.6	1,416
19. Publix	4,848,000	2.1	353
20. Montgomery Ward	4,747,400	2.9	324
21. Stop & Shop	4,624,000	N/A	114
22. The Price Club	4,162,400	2.3	39
23. The Limited	4,070,777	5.8	3,381
24. Toys 'R' Us	4,000,192	6.7	522
25. Vons	3,916,600	N/A	350
26. Southland Corp.	3,820,200	N/A	7,414
27. Food Lion	3,815,400	2.9	567
28. Ahold USA	3,514,000	4.2	329
29. Ames	3,362,865	1.4	850
30. Tandy	3,260,688	9.7	7,336
31. Service Merchandise	3,092,817	2.5	317
32. Meijer	3,000,000	N/A	52
33. Giant Food	2,987,154	3.3	145
34. Eckerd	2,900,000	N/A	1,600
35. Grand Union	2,872,000	0.8	300
36. Rite Aid[a]	2,868,297	5.0	2,270
37. Super Valu[b]	2,769,019	2.6	156
38. Circle K	2,656,700	2.3	4,536
39. Batus[b]	2,643,327	6.7[b]	108
40. Carter Hawley Hale[a]	2,617,100	0.4	112
41. Dillards	2,558,395	4.4	146
42. Lowe's[a]	2,516,879	2.7	296
43. Revco	2,409,262	N/P	1,886
44. Thrifty Corp.	2,400,000	2.8	230
45. U.S. Shoe[a]	2,343,045	0.6	2,512
46. Nordstrom	2,327,946	5.3	58
47. H. E. Butt	2,300,000	N/A	150
48. Mercantile	2,265,500	6.4	80
49. Best Products	2,088,317	0.2	194
50. Fred Meyer	2,073,544	1.8	112

N/A = Not available.
N/P = No profit.
[a]Before extraordinary items or changes in accounting principles.
[b]Operating income.

A. By ownership of establishment
   1. Single-unit independent stores
   2. Multiunit retail organizations
      a) chain stores
      b) branch stores
   3. Manufacturer-owned retail outlets
   4. Consumers' cooperative stores
   5. Farmer-owned establishments
   6. Company-owned stores (industrial stores) or commissaries
   7. Government operated stores (post exchanges, state liquor stores)
   8. Public utility company stores (for sale of major appliances)
B. By kind of business (merchandise handled)
   1. General merchandise group
      a) department stores
      b) dry goods, general merchandise stores
      c) general stores
      d) variety stores
   2. Single-line stores (e.g., grocery, apparel, furniture)
   3. Specialty stores (e.g., meat markets, lingerie shops, floor coverings stores)
C. By size of establishment
   1. By number of employees
   2. By annual sales volume
D. By degree of vertical integration
   1. Nonintegrated (retailing functions only)
   2. Integrated with wholesaling functions
   3. Integrated with manufacturing or other form-utility creation
E. By type of relationship with other business organizations
   1. Unaffiliated
   2. Voluntarily affiliated with other retailers
      a) through wholesaler-sponsored voluntary chains
      b) through retailer cooperation
   3. Affiliated with manufacturers by dealers franchises
F. By method of consumer contact
   1. Regular store
      a) leased department
   2. Mail order
      a) by catalog selling
      b) by advertising in regular media
      c) by membership club plans
   3. Household contacts
      a) by house-to-house canvassing
      b) by regular delivery route service
      c) by party plan selling
G. By type of location
   1. Urban
      a) central business district
      b) secondary business district
      c) string street location
      d) neighborhood location
      e) controlled (planned) shopping center
      f) public market calls
   2. Small city
      a) downtown
      b) neighborhood
   3. Rural stores
   4. Roadside stands
H. By type of service rendered
   1. Full service
   2. Limited service (cash-and-carry)
   3. Self-service
I. By legal form of organization
   1. Proprietorship
   2. Partnership
   3. Corporation
   4. Special types
J. By management organization or operational technique
   1. Undifferentiated
   2. Departmentalized

Source: T. N. Beckman, W. R. Davidson, and W. W. Talarzyk, *Marketing,* 9th ed. (New York: Ronald Press, 1973), 239.

FIGURE 2–3
Classifying retail institutions

according to (1) the type, selection, and quality of merchandise; (2) the range of price lines; and (3) the size, design, and location of stores.

Some specialists offer personal merchandise for individual consumers and their homes; others focus on consumer recreational and entertainment activities or consumers' needs for various accessory items (see Figure 2–5a). Figure 2–6 identifies the nation's top specialty store chains as defined by sales volume. Of the top 50 specialty

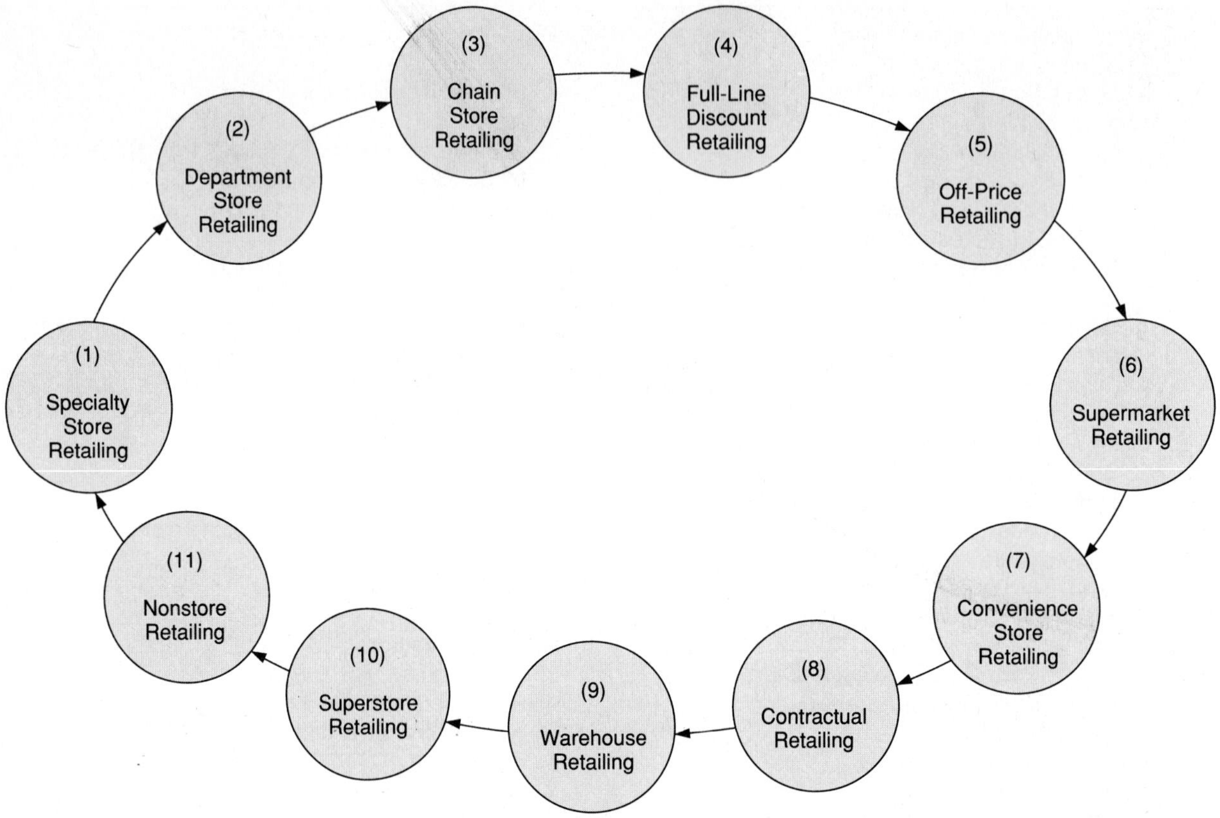

FIGURE 2–4
Competitive retail formats

stores, 18 are apparel outlets, 7 specialize in consumer electronics, 5 are shoe stores, 4 merchandise toys, 3 sell books, and 3 sell jewelry. The remaining members of the top 50 are furniture, home furnishings, textiles, hard goods, records, optical, and software chains.

The available selection of merchandise the retailing specialist offers ranges from the very narrowly defined product line of the classification retailer (e.g., one that carries specific product lines such as dress shirts and/or ties with men's apparel) to the wider selection of products merchandised by the category specialists (e.g., broadly related product lines such as men's apparel). Classification retailers, such as **super specialists** and **niche specialists,** use "focus formats" wherein they direct their efforts at meeting the product needs for a specific customer segment. Category retailers, such as **category killers** and **mini-department specialists,** are "power formats" that use their size, merchandising muscle, and operational efficiency to dominate the market for a product category or at least assume a market leader position within the product category (see Figure 2–5b). Some selected examples of each of these merchandising strategies are:

- *Super specialist*—Sock Appeal, Little Piggie, Ltd., Sock Market, Leg Room, and Sock Express offer a single, narrowly defined classification of merchandise (socks and hosiery) with an extensive assortment of brands, sizes, colors, materials, styles, and prices.[9]
- *Niche specialist*—Kids Mart (F. W. Woolworth Co.), McKids (Sears and McDon-

Specialty retailers offer a focused assortment of goods and services targeted at selected consumer segments.

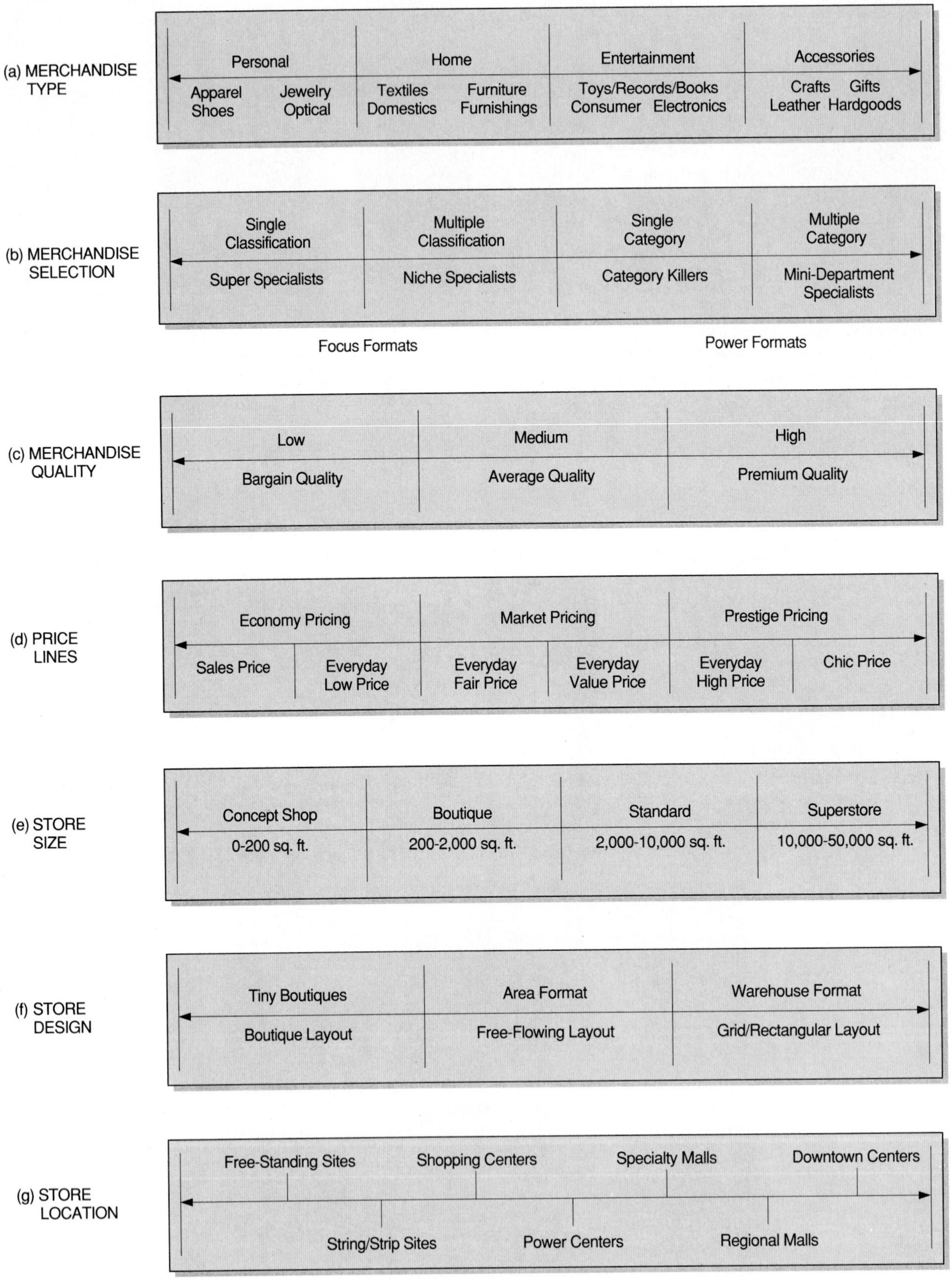
(a) MERCHANDISE TYPE
Personal
Apparel
Shoes
Jewelry
Optical
Home
Textiles
Domestics
Furniture
Furnishings
Entertainment
Toys/Records/Books
Consumer Electronics
Accessories
Crafts Gifts
Leather Hardgoods
(b) MERCHANDISE SELECTION
Single Classification
Super Specialists
Multiple Classification
Niche Specialists
Single Category
Category Killers
Multiple Category
Mini-Department Specialists
Focus Formats
Power Formats
(c) MERCHANDISE QUALITY
Low
Bargain Quality
Medium
Average Quality
High
Premium Quality
(d) PRICE LINES
Economy Pricing
Sales Price
Everyday Low Price
Market Pricing
Everyday Fair Price
Everyday Value Price
Prestige Pricing
Everyday High Price
Chic Price
(e) STORE SIZE
Concept Shop
0-200 sq. ft.
Boutique
200-2,000 sq. ft.
Standard
2,000-10,000 sq. ft.
Superstore
10,000-50,000 sq. ft.
(f) STORE DESIGN
Tiny Boutiques
Boutique Layout
Area Format
Free-Flowing Layout
Warehouse Format
Grid/Rectangular Layout
(g) STORE LOCATION
Free-Standing Sites
Shopping Centers
Specialty Malls
Downtown Centers
String/Strip Sites
Power Centers
Regional Malls

FIGURE 2–5
Profile of the specialty store retailer

ald's), The Kids Store (Montgomery Ward), Benetton 012 (Benetton), GapKids (The Gap), Little Folks Shop (F. W. Woolworth Co.), Esprit Kids (Esprit), Limited Too (The Limited), and Mother and Child (Laura Ashley) target the children's apparel market with carefully selected merchandise and appropriately designed stores. This growth market is the result of the baby boomlet spawned by the baby boomers during the late 1980s; it is expected to continue throughout the 1990s.[10]

- *Category killers*—Silk Greenhouse (silk plants and flowers)[11], Blockbusters (video rental and sales)[12], Today's Man (off-price men's suits)[13], Sports Authority (sporting goods and apparel)[14], Office Club (office supplies and equipment)[15], and Soft Warehouse (computer hardware and software)[16] want to be the Toys 'R' Us of their industries; that is, they want to achieve merchandise dominance in their respective categories by creating narrowly focused, jumbo-size stores.
- *Mini-department specialist*—The Limited's new superstore format allows the retailer to offer its traditional merchandise lines and showcase its new sportswear and career wear lines, intimate apparel, coats, and suits together with a major presentation of accessories. These mini-departments of merchandise are further enhanced in some stores with children's and men's apparel boutiques.[17] This line extension strategy is the next logical developmental step for The Limited in its effort to retain its crown as "king" of specialty store retailing.

Specialty retailing covers the entire merchandise quality continuum (see Figure 2–5c). At the low end of the continuum are one-price clothing stores (One Price Clothing Co., Bargain Town, Only $1, Everything's A $1.00, The Five Dollar Clothing Store, One Price Shops, and Ten Below). These specialty apparel retailers offer mostly bargain-quality merchandise at bargain prices.[18] Premium-quality merchandise is well characterized by the English tailor of conservative Saville Row and the avant-garde men's shops on London's Floral Street.[19]

As Figure 2–5d illustrates, retailer specialists use the complete complement of pricing alternatives: (1) economy prices in terms of sales promotion pricing and everyday low prices; (2) market pricing, which stresses fairness and value (that is, an acceptable relationship between price and merchandise quality); and (3) prestige pricing in the form of everyday high prices to top-of-the-line chic prices. In this case, the psychological value delivered by the store and/or product image is as important a price determinant as is a more functional assessment of product worth.

Specialty stores range in size from small concept (lifestyle) shops of fewer than 200 square feet that depend on other retailers for customer traffic generation to huge superstores of 10,000 to 50,000 square feet—destination stores that can attract and hold their own clients (see Figure 2–5e). Store designs range from upscale, exclusive, tiny boutiques with luxurious and intimate environments to the spartan yet efficient environs of the warehouse format designed to get customers in and out of the store (see Figure 2–5f). While some specialty retailers opt for free-standing, isolated locations, most specialists prefer clustering together to enhance their customer drawing power and create comparison shopping and one-stopping opportunities (see Figure 2–5g).

Department Store Retailing

Despite the restructuring and repositioning that took place in the 1980s, the department store of the 1990s is being defined in a broader context. During the last decade, department stores eliminated many of the departments that made them traditional department stores. "No longer can consumers pick up a new outfit or accessory, and then stroll to the next aisle or floor to shop for a new refrigerator, record album, book, or sewing notions. . . . The result is that the line between department stores and specialty stores has blurred. . . ."[20]

Traditionally, the **department store** is defined as a large retailing institution that carries a wide variety of merchandise lines with a reasonably good selection within each

FIGURE 2–6
The top 50 specialty store chains

Rank	Company Chain (Headquarters)	Type	Sales ($000,000s)	Units
1.	The Limited	Apparel	4,071	3,381
2.	Toys 'R' Us[a]	Toys	4,000	358
3.	Radio Shack[b]	Consumer electronics	3,000	1,812
4.	Kinney	Shoe	2,574	2,660
5.	Marshall's	Apparel	1,753	309
6.	Circuit City	Consumer electronics	1,721	122
7.	T. J. Maxx	Apparel	1,485	308
8.	Gap, Inc.[c]	Apparel	1,252	900
9.	Petrie Stores	Apparel	1,218	1,584
10.	U. S. Shoe[d]	Apparel	1,151	1,758
11.	Volume Shoe	Shoe	1,132	2,602
12.	Zale[e]	Jewelry	923	1,293
13.	Levitz	Furniture	921	108
14.	Waldenbooks	Books	920	1,218
15.	Highland Superstores	Consumer electronics	911	84
16.	Silo Electronics	Consumer electronics	825	206
17.	Child World	Toys	807	163
18.	Kay Bee	Toys	780	727
19.	Lechmere	Hard goods	769	27
20.	Wohl Shoe[f]	Shoe	755	1,832
21.	Herman's	Sporting goods	730	250
22.	Charming Shoppes	Apparel	725	926
23.	B. Dalton	Books	665	800
24.	Burlington Coat[g]	Apparel	639	134
25.	Ross Stores	Apparel	634	140
26.	Musicland	Records	603	682
27.	Thom McAn	Shoe	521	952
28.	Best Buy	Consumer electronics	507	41
29.	Edison Bros. Shoe	Shoe	460	1,116
30.	Edison Apparel	Apparel	459	1,231
31.	Hartmarx Specialty[h]	Apparel	450	258

line. In 1979, a breakdown of department store merchandise resulted in an even split between hard goods and soft goods. By 1989, department stores had become largely soft-goods retailers—80 percent soft goods and 20 percent hard goods.[21] The reduction in hard goods certainly calls into question the traditional description of the department store as a "wide-variety retailer." This decline in variety has led many retail watchers to categorize department stores as large-space specialty stores, multidepartment soft-goods stores, apparel supermarkets, and specialty department stores. Given this evolution, the National Retail Federation, Inc. has broadened its definition of *department store* to include both the traditional full-line institutions and the limited-line, departmentalized retailers that have "a fashion orientation, full markup policy, and operating in stores large enough to be shopping center anchors."[22] Today's definition of *department store* would include specialized department stores such as Neiman Marcus, Lord & Taylor, Saks Fifth Avenue, and Nordstrom, together with traditional department store chains such as the May Company, Dillards, Dayton Hudson, Macy's, and the popular-priced department stores of Sears and J.C. Penney.

Regardless of the number and nature of individual departments, the department store is distinguished by its organizational structure, specifically the high degree of

FIGURE 2–6
continued

Rank	Company Chain (Headquarters)	Type	Sales ($000,000s)	Units
32.	Bealls/Palais Royal	Apparel	450	165
33.	Kay Jewelers	Jewelry	420	462
34.	Pier One[i]	Home furnishings	415	450
35.	Lenscrafters[j]	Optical	414	296
36.	Lionel	Toys	409	84
37.	Pic n' Save	Apparel	402	158
38.	Tower Records	Entertainment software	400	66
39.	C. R. Anthony	Apparel	397	247
40.	Brooks Fashion	Apparel	395	586
41.	Talbots	Apparel	392	137
42.	Gordon Jewelry[k]	Jewelry	390	615
43.	Hit or Miss	Apparel	375	506
44.	Tandy Brand Names[b]	Consumer electronics	365	292
45.	Heilig-Meyers[i]	Furniture	352	277
46.	Barnes & Noble	Books	350	50
47.	Egghead Software[l]	Software	342	196
48.	House of Fabrics	Textile	338	658
49.	Loehmann's	Apparel	334	71
50.	Wherehouse Entertainment[m]	Consumer electronics	330	229

[a]Includes revenues from international toy stores and Kids 'R' Us. Store count is for domestic toy stores only.
[b]Estimates for fiscal year ended June 30, 1989.
[c]Includes Gap Kids, Banana Republic, and Hemisphere stores.
[d]Includes Casual Corner, Ups N Downs, Petite Sophisticate, Caren Charles, among other chains.
[e]For fiscal year ended March 30, 1989.
[f]Includes leased departments.
[g]Burlington Coat and Dress Barn—for 12-month period ended January 28, 1989.
[h]Hartmarx Specialty and Kuppenheimer—for fiscal year ended November 30, 1988.
[i]For fiscal year ended February 28, 1989.
[j]Includes Canadian stores.
[k]For fiscal year ended August 31, 1989.
[l]For fiscal year ended April 30, 1989, includes direct sales as well as retail sales.
[m]For fiscal year ended February 26, 1989.

Source: David P. Schulz, "The Top 100 Stores," *Stores,* (August 1989): 11–17. Copyright © National Retail Federation, Inc., New York, New York.

"departmentalization." From an operational standpoint, most of the basic functions of buying, selling, promoting, and servicing are conducted entirely, or at least in part, at the department level. Accounting and control procedures also are organized on a departmental basis. The advantages of this type of organization are that it allows both *functional* (buying, selling, etc.) and *merchandise* (apparel, shoes, etc.) specialization while permitting the economies of scale associated with a large retailing operation.

Some department store organizations are local independents (see Figure 2–7, page 50); others are part of a national chain (e.g., Sears and J.C. Penney) or an ownership group (e.g., see Figure 2–8, pages 52–53).

The product strategy of department stores is to offer a wide selection of brand-name and designer-label merchandise within those product classifications stocked by the store. To differentiate themselves from competitors, department stores are becoming more focused in their merchandising approach (see Figure 2–9, page 54): "They are defining the economic level of the customer they want to attract, the fashion attitude of this segment, and making preparations to satisfy the various lifestyle needs of these customers."[23] May Co. has targeted a loyal middle-class clientele by focusing on national brands at promotional prices instead of designer goods at prestige prices. A

There are many different ways to classify retailers, and some classifications overlap.

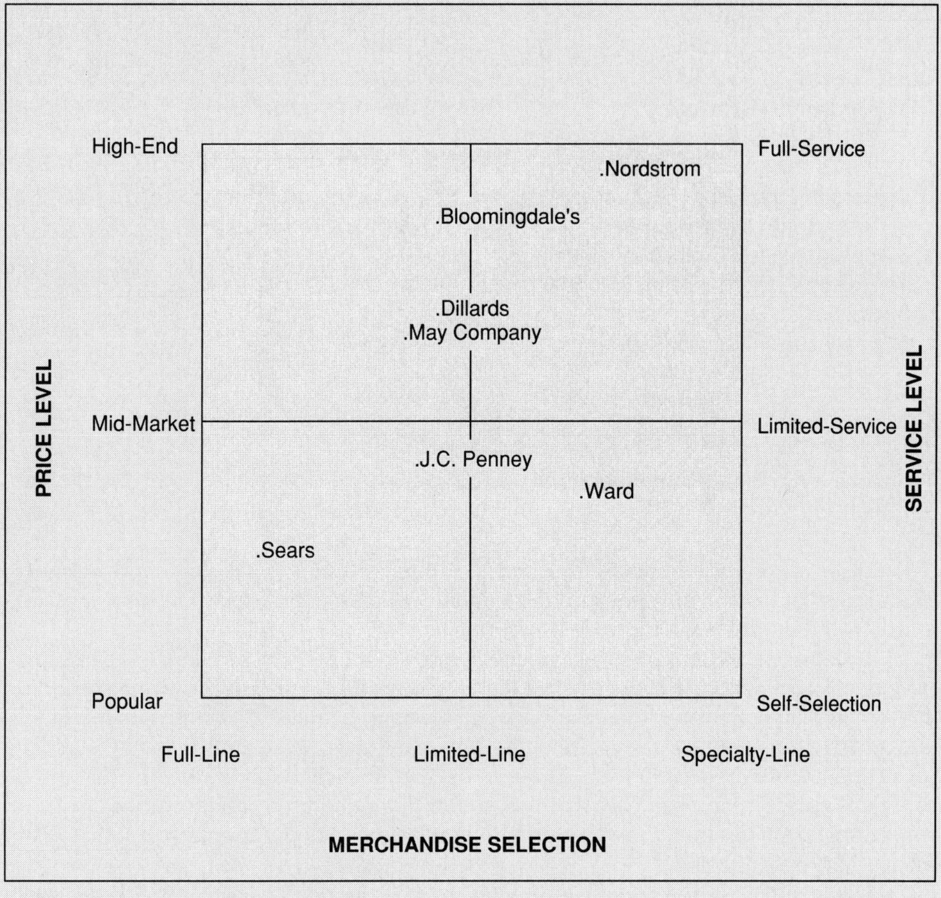

Department Store Retailing Finds a Market Position

The competitive strategies of department stores involve various combinations of merchandise selections at different price levels and supported by varying levels of service. Department store merchandise selection strategies range from full-line outlets that offer both hard and soft goods (e.g., Sears) to specialty department stores offering only soft goods (e.g., Nordstrom). Popular-priced department store chains like J.C. Penney and Montgomery Ward compete with the mid-market prices offered by Dillards and The May Company, which in turn compete with the high-end prices of Bloomingdale's and Nordstrom. While Sears and Ward offer self-selection with personal assistance in some departments, Nordstrom has built a national reputation as a provider of exceptional service. As the dynamics of the marketplace continue to change in the 1990s, department store chains will need to constantly adapt their merchandise, service, and pricing strategies. What repositioning strategies might each of the above department stores consider for the year 2000?

FIGURE 2–7
The top 10 independent department store organizations

Rank	Organization (Location)	Sales Volume ($ Millions)	Number of Units
1.	Nordstrom (Seattle)	2,327.9	58
2.	Woodward & Lothrop (Washington, D.C.)	901	31
3.	Kohl's (Menomonee Falls, Wis.)[a]	730	66
4.	Carson Pirie Scott (Chicago)[b]	700	33
5.	P. A. Bergner (Milwaukee)[b]	468.2	32
6.	Strawbridge & Clothier (Philadelphia)	460	13
7.	Maison Blanche (Baton Rouge)	439	21
8.	Boscov's (Reading, Pa.)	405.7	15
9.	Jacobson's (Jackson, Mich.)	357	22
10.	McRae's (Jackson, Miss.)	351	28

[a]Includes acquisition of MainStreet stores, November 1988.
[b]Prior to acquisition of Carson Pirie Scott by P. A. Bergner.

Source: David P. Schulz, "Mervyn's Takes No. 1 Spot," *Stores,* (July 1989): 11–14. Copyright © National Retail Federation, Inc., New York, New York.

chic image is not what May Co. is about.[24] While Saks targets the high-end business, Macy's aims at fashion customers in the middle "by being a little more fashion-forward, a little trendier while staying very promotional."[25]

Because of the competition from off-price retailers, "many department stores have developed private-label programs that enable them to offer exclusive merchandise and receive higher profits than for brand name merchandise."[26] While private labels add an extra dimension to the merchandise mix, they are not the cure for what ails some department store organizations.[27] As one retail expert suggests, it is still a broad variety of branded-label merchandise that will allow "a real differentiation from smaller specialty stores, discounts, and so-called popular-price department stores that offer primarily private labels."[28]

Department stores usually are high-margin operations. Because of the high operating expenses (30 to 40 percent of sales) stemming from the stores' organizational structure, service offerings, physical facilities, and high-risk merchandise, margins between merchandise costs and retail selling prices must be substantial to ensure a fair profit. Department stores normally appeal to middle- and upper-income consumers. To attract such a diverse group of consumers, some department stores have multiple pricing points. "Promotional" prices are directed at the lower- to middle-income consumer; "regular" prices appeal to those who want neither the lowest- nor the highest-priced merchandise; and "prestige" prices are aimed at the upper-income consumer who desires the best. These good, better, and best price lines not only allow the department store to project a broad price appeal; they also help consumers make price and quality comparisons. While upscale department stores such as Bloomingdale's and Nieman Marcus focus on the middle and upper pricing points, Dillards directs most of its efforts at the middle-price lines.

Department stores typically occupy high-rent locations within major commercial centers. The place strategy of most department stores has been to locate in an "anchor" (end) position at one or more major suburban shopping centers. The exterior and interior motifs of the average department store are designed to create a prestige image. Externally the architectural form might communicate bigness, success, uniqueness, strength, security, elegance, or any number of store images. Internally the store's layout, fixtures, and decor create consumer buying moods by appealing to all of the sensory modes of sight, sound, smell, taste, and touch.

The department store's principal promotional appeals are product selection and quality, service offerings, and shopping atmosphere. Each of these appeals is directed toward enhancing a unique image for the department store:

> A well-honed identity helps persuade customers that they are getting their money's worth even if the department store is higher priced than some of its rivals. Bloomingdale's is renowned as a yuppie emporium where trendiness makes up for higher prices. Macy's aims for the shopper on a budget who is interested in wide assortment and name brands. A reputation for quality merchandise, hassle-free returns, and more personal service may still draw a value-conscious crowd.[29]

Both product and institutional advertising are an integral part of the department store's strategy to favorably influence potential consumers. Although advertisements feature several carefully selected products, every department store advertising campaign subtly communicates the message that "this is the place to shop." Department stores often create the "big event" by developing shopping themes consistent with the customer's moods and needs, the seasons or current events, the merchandise, and the store's environment. For example, Bloomingdale's likes to stage multi-million-dollar extravaganzas honoring individual countries' crafts.

Chain Store Retailing

A **chain store** is a retail organization that operates multiple outlets, offers a standardized merchandise mix, and uses a centralized form of ownership and control. Technically, any retail organization that operates more than one unit can be classified as a chain. However, the *Census of Business* defines chains as retail organizations that operate 11 or more units. A workable compromise is to refer to chain organizations as *small chains* (two to ten units) and *large chains* (11 or more units). Another criterion for classifying a conglomeration of stores as a chain is that each unit in the chain must *sell similar lines of merchandise*. A third criterion is whether there is a *central form of ownership and control*. With central ownership, the parent organization has control over all operating and merchandising aspects of the entire chain of stores.

Technically, a chain store organization can be a multiunit operation of specialty stores, discount outlets, department stores, or food markets. However, this discussion will focus on the nation's three national mass merchandising chains—Sears, Roebuck, J. C. Penney, and Montgomery Ward. While Sears is the seventh largest company in the United States, with sales exceeding $53 billion,[30] "America's Big Store" is in big trouble: "The era of the general merchant has passed. Real growth now comes from powerful niche players."[31] Trendier specialty retailers and superdiscounters have siphoned off consumers and market share during the past decade.[32]

In response to competitive threats, each of "the big three" is struggling to alter its image. J. C. Penney is attempting to "recast itself from a dowdy general merchandiser into a moderately priced fashion specialist."[33] It has shed many of its hard lines (e.g., home electronics and sports equipment) in favor of apparel lines and soft home furnishings.[34]

Montgomery Ward is pursuing a transformation from "a dusty, broad-line general merchant into an operator of stores with narrowly focused formats. Today its remodeled stores group specialty 'boutiques' selling brand-name electronics, apparel, jewelry, and home and auto accessories under one roof."[35]

Like its counterparts, Sears is streamlining its stores into a collection of specialty departments; a two-concept strategy forms the basis for coping with competitors (see Figure 2–10). Concept one is a "superstore within a store" wherein a merchandise combination of private labels and national brands is merchandised within a boutique layout. Brand Central (appliances and home electronics) and Kids and More (children's apparel) are two such "power formats" that Sears is counting on to make a major

FIGURE 2–8
Major department store ownership groups

Chain and Division(s)	Sales Volume ($ Millions)	Number of Units
Amfac Corporation		
Liberty House (Honolulu)[a]	320	9
Steinbach's (White Plains, N.Y.)	203	29
Campeau Corporation		
Bloomingdale's (New York)	4,518	17
Lazarus (Cincinnati)	944.7	43
Rich's (Atlanta)[b]	850.5	26
Burdine's (Miami)	835.4	30
Jordan Marsh New England (Boston)	725.7	26
Abraham & Straus (Brooklyn, N.Y.)	721.2	14
Stern's (Paramus, N.J.)	704	27
Maas Bros. (Tampa)	627.7	38
The Bon (Seattle)	586.9	39
Carter Hawley Hale		
The Broadway (Los Angeles)[c]	1,125	43
Emporium-Capwell (San Francisco)[c]	730	22
Thalhimer's (Richmond, Va.)[c]	385	25
Weinstock's (Sacramento)[c]	245	12
The Broadway Southwest (Phoenix)[c]	220	11
Crown American Corporation		
Hess's (Allentown, Pa.)	613.8	72
Dayton Hudson		
Mervyn's (Hayward, Cal.)	3,411	213
Dayton Hudson (Minneapolis)	7,738	37
Marshall Field's (Chicago)	1,024	25
Dillard		
Dillards (Forth Worth)	760	42
Dillards (San Antonio)	525	31
Dillards (St. Louis)	520	27
Dillards (Little Rock)	440	27
Dillards (Phoenix)	315	19
Dillards–Edward J. DeBartolo		
Higbee's (Cleveland)	328	12
Equitable of Iowa		
Younkers (Des Moines)	313.4	36
L. J. Hooker Retail Group		
Parisian (Birmingham)	263	17
B. Altman (New York)	229	6
Bonwit Teller (New York)	175	16

merchandise classification statement that will appeal to the consuming public and counteract specialty competitors. Concept two expresses Sears' commitment to specialty store retailing. It involves establishing free-standing specialty stores, each with an individual identity and image. McKids (a licensing agreement with McDonald's), Eye Care Centers of America, and Pinstripe Petites are three examples of Sears' specialty format.

FIGURE 2–8
continued

Chain and Division(s)	Sales Volume ($ Millions)	Number of Units
May Department Stores		
Lord & Taylor (New York)	963	47
May California (Los Angeles)	900	34
Foley's (Houston)	804	34
Hecht's (Washington, D.C.)	759	22
Robinson's (Los Angeles)	720	29
Kaufmann's (Pittsburgh)	516	14
Famous-Barr (St. Louis)	502	17
May Co. (Cleveland)[d]	424	16
G. Fox (Hartford, Conn.)	369	10
Filene's (Boston)	357	18
L. S. Ayres (Indianapolis)	315	14
May D & F (Denver)	267	13
Meier & Frank (Portland)	254	8
Sibley's (Rochester)	182	10
Mercantile Stores		
McAlpin (Cincinnati)	390	9
Gayfer's (Mobile, Ala.)	375	12
Castner-Knott (Nashville)	275	11
Jones Store (Kansas City)	260	9
Joslin's (Denver)	235	11
Gayfer's (Montgomery, Ala.)	195	6
Bacon's/Roots (Louisville)	180	7
J. B. White (Augusta, Ga.)	160	7
Lion (Toledo)	120	3
Hennessey's (Billings, Mont.)	72	5
Kevin Donohue		
Miller & Rhoads (Richmond)	125	15
R. H. Macy & Co.		
Macy's Northeast (New York)[c]	3,315	46
Macy's California[c]	6,040	28
Macy's South (Atlanta)[c]	785	25
Bullocks (Los Angeles)[c]	755	22
I. Magnin (San Francisco)[c]	350	25
Neiman Marcus Group		
Neiman Marcus (Dallas)[c]	1,029	22
Bergdorf Goodman (New York)[c]	160	1

[a]Includes results of resort shops.
[b]Includes results of Goldsmith's.
[c]For the 52-week period ended January 28, 1989.
[d]Includes operations of O'Neil, Akron, Ohio.

Source: Adapted from David P. Schulz, "Mervyn's Takes No. 1 Spot," *Stores* (July 1989): 11–14. Copyright © National Retail Federation, Inc., New York, New York.

FIGURE 2–9
Market segmentation through store departmentalization

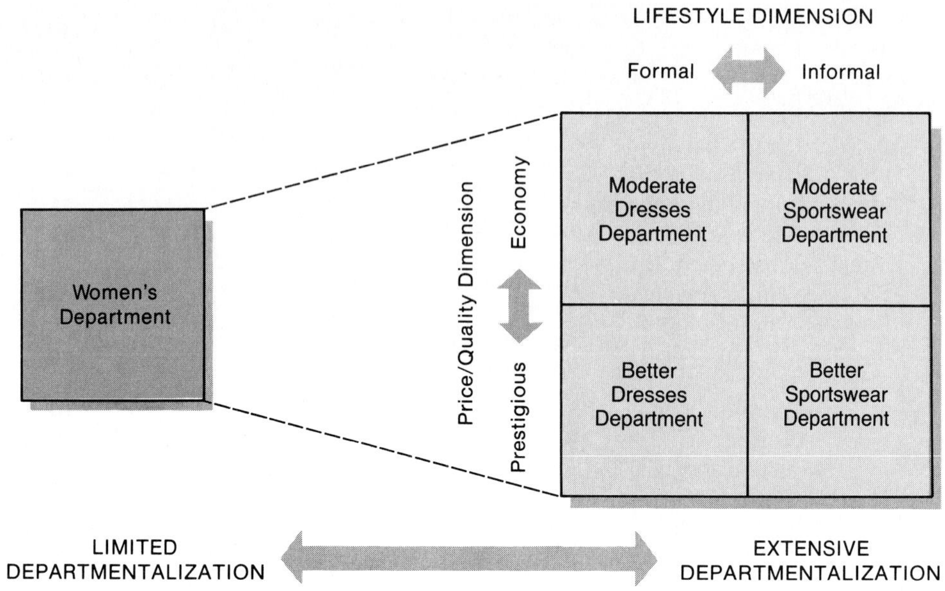

FIGURE 2–10
Sears—A specialty retailer or a general merchant

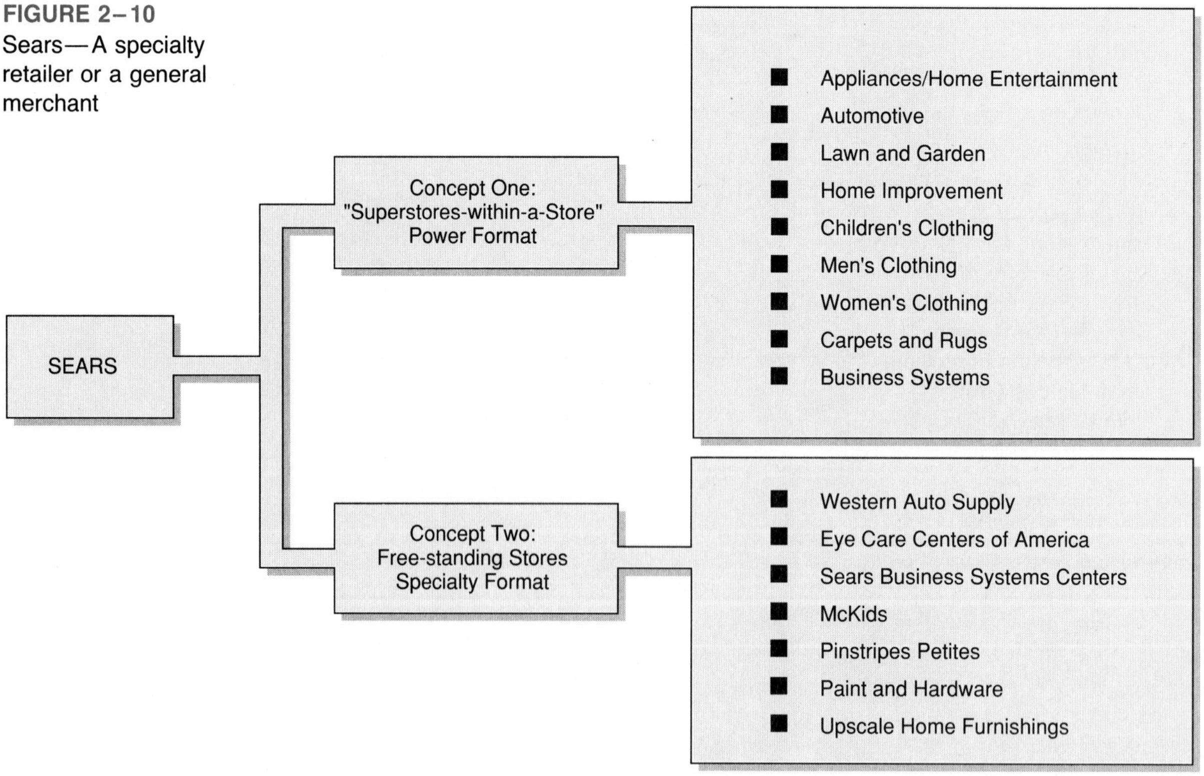

Economies of scale are an important part of the chain's central buying policies. By buying in large quantities, often directly from manufacturers, chain stores receive substantial quantity discounts. Large-quantity purchases also reduce the cost of merchandise, because the chains can take advantage of lower transportation rates on carload and truckload shipments. An additional benefit associated with large-scale purchases are *promotional allowances* (payments chains receive from suppliers to help defray the cost of advertising the suppliers' products). The net result of the chain's centralized buying policies is that it can acquire merchandise at the lowest costs in the retailing industry.

Several advantages accrue to chain store operations. First, by operating a large number of stores within a particular market, chains can exert substantial control over their stores and achieve economies of scale through a centralized distribution system. The result is high inventory turnover rates and few stockouts and overstocks. Second, chains can spread risk over many different stores in many different markets. Third, chain organizations derive benefits from vertically integrating their channels of distribution. Sears, for example, obtains approximately 50 percent of its merchandise from manufacturers in which it has equity interest (partial ownership). Finally, chain operations enjoy a high level of consumer recognition. The use of a standardized sign and architectural motif reinforces consumers' awareness of the chain and what it has to offer.

Chain stores usually promote both their store image and their individual products. Generally chains promote the standardized nature of their operations and therefore the consistency (product quality, customer service, etc.) of their product offerings from store to store. Chains also commonly promote their convenience and large number of locations to their customers. Many chains stress the reliability of buying from a large national or regional firm. Finally, with multiple locations within a given market, chain stores can effectively use the most expensive media (television) and exposure time (prime time).

Full-Line Discount Retailing

The **full-line discount store** is a retailing institution that sells a wide variety of merchandise (full-line) at less than traditional retail prices. Targeted to meet the needs of the economy-minded consumer, the discount store uses mass-merchandising techniques that enable it to use discount prices as its major consumer appeal. The discount store sells name-brand (national or manufacturers' brands) and private-label merchandise at prices that consumers easily recognize as below traditional prices. The full-line discounter carries a fairly complete variety of hard and/or soft goods. In its drive for high turnover, the typical discounter stocks only the most popular brands, styles, models, sizes, and colors, along with its own private labels. In general, the product strategy of the full-line store is to carry many product lines but limit the amount of selection within each line. K mart, Wal-Mart, and Target head the list of the nation's top 15 full-line discount store chains (see Figure 2–11).

A few nationally well-known brands in key product line areas are an integral part of the discounter's product strategy. In selling national brands, the discounter takes advantage of consumers' knowledge of the going prices for various products. Thus, it sells most of its merchandise to the price-conscious shopper. Also, selling national brands below suggested manufacturers' retail prices greatly enhances the store's discount image. This image helps the discounter convince the general public that its large selection of private labels are also a good value. To purge K mart of its "polyester palace" image, K mart has added "more expensive merchandise to low-priced lines and recruited a covey of celebrities to hawk the goods."[36] To enhance the image of its private labels, K mart has secured the endorsement of race car driver Mario Andretti

FIGURE 2–11
The top 15 full-line discount store chains

Company	1988 Sales (000 Omitted)	Stores
1. K mart, Troy, Michigan	$22,940,000	2145
2. Wal-Mart, Bentonville, Ark.	16,820,000	1259
3. Target, Minneapolis	6,331,000	341
4. Ames Dept. Stores, Rocky Hill, Conn.	3,362,865	850
5. Meijer, Grand Rapids, Mich.	3,000,000	52
6. Bradlees, Braintree, Mass.	2,106,747	130
7. Fred Meyer, Portland, Ore.	2,073,544	112
8. Hills Dept. Stores, Canton, Mass.	1,670,866	167
9. Caldor, Norwalk, Conn.	1,574,000	119
10. Rose's, Henderson, N.C.	1,439,279	250
11. Venture Stores, O'Fallon, Mo.	1,282,000	73
12. Shopko Stores, Green Bay, Wis.	1,300,870	87
13. Jamesway, Secaucus, N.J.	782,504	121
14. Fedco, Santa Fe Springs, Calif.	685,000	12
15. Pamida, Omaha	568,000	165

Source: Reprinted by permission from *Chain Store Age Executive* (August 1989): 39. Copyright © Lebhar-Friedman, Inc., 425 Park Avenue, New York, New York 10022.

(automotive products), golfer Fuzzy Zoeller (sporting equipment), author Martha Stewart (household goods), and actress Jaclyn Smith (dressier women's apparel).

The discounter's service offering is limited to services necessary to run the operation. Traditionally cash-and-carry businesses, most major discount chains now offer credit services. Sales personnel are used in departments (jewelry, cameras, etc.) that absolutely need them. Store personnel also include those who staff information booths, return and credit approval counters, and checkouts.

The pricing strategy of the conventional discount store promotes the highest possible turnover rate. A high rate of stock turns is the key to success and profitability for the discount retailer. Although the amount of the discount varies greatly from one product line to another, it is always large enough for the majority of the consuming public to recognize it as a discount.

Conventional discounters select suburban locations convenient to the large, middle-class consumer market; discount houses frequently serve as anchors for community shopping centers and, in some rare cases, as the major anchors of a regional shopping center. An exception to this strategy is Wal-Mart, which became one of the nation's largest retailers by following a place strategy of locating discount stores in small-town America. The typical discounter operates out of a modern one-story building ranging in area from 20,000 to 150,000 square feet. The store size depends on the local market size. Many discount stores create a carnival-like environment through their store decor and special sales events. Centralized checkout areas are a prominent part of all discount operations. Some leased departments and high-ticket item departments have localized checkouts.

Most discount stores are aggressive advertisers. They use a broad message appeal highlighting variety, selection, and especially price. Newspapers are the discounter's principal medium, but use of television and radio advertising is increasing. Another key promotional strategy discounters use to inform and persuade the consumer is the point-of-purchase display. Bargain tables, bins, and stacks greet consumers as they enter, check out, and exit. End-of-aisle and main-aisle displays intercept shoppers as they travel through the store. In an attempt to create a more upscale shopping atmosphere and enhance customer shopping opportunities, K mart is enlarging and refurbishing many of its stores to include "wider aisles, bolder displays, and taller, deeper shelves. The idea of the spacious new design is to keep merchandise out where customers can get it instead of in the stockroom."[37] In-store loudspeaker announcements of unadvertised specials are used to draw customers throughout the store.

Off-Price Retailing

Off-price retailers are specialty retailers that sell soft goods and/or hard goods at price levels (20 to 60 percent) below regular retail prices. There are two general types of off-price operation: (1) **factory outlet** stores, or *direct manufacturers' outlets* (e.g., Levi Strauss, Manhattan's Brand Name Fashion Outlet, Burlington Coat Factory Warehouse, and Bass Shoes), which sell their own seconds, overruns, and packaways from the previous season, and (2) **independents** (e.g., Loehmann's, T. J. Maxx, Marshall's, and Clothestime), which buy seconds, irregulars, canceled orders, overages, or leftover goods from manufacturers or other retailers.[38] A key concept in the off-price retailer's strategy is selling designer labels and branded merchandise; consumers know that the price is an "off-price" if they can make price comparisons on like goods.

The off-price retailer's mode of operation can be described as follows:

- Low buying prices, often lower than for conventional discounters and lower than could be expected on the basis of quantity discounts
- A high proportion of established, often designer brands from manufacturers that seek the highest prices they can get for distressed and leftover merchandise, overruns, and irregulars
- Merchandise often of higher quality than that usually found in "discount stores"
- A changing and unstable assortment in that the customer can't confidently predict exactly what the retailer will have on a given day—a major factor distinguishing off-pricing from simple discounting
- Customer services varying from minimal to extensive, sometimes including wrapping, exchanges, refunds, and credit card acceptance
- Variety ranging from very narrow (men's suits) to very broad (family apparel)[39]

One explanation for the ability of off-price retailers to secure favorable terms is that they tend to pay promptly and do not ask for extras such as advertising allowances, return privileges, and markdown adjustments.

On the selling side, off-price retailers strive to keep their overhead low to maintain lower margins. They reduce operating expenses by operating out of modest facilities located in strip malls, where rent is usually half that charged by large shopping centers.

One variation of the off-price retailer is the **closeout store**—an outlet that specializes in the retailing of a wide variety of merchandise obtained through closeouts, retail liquidations, and bankruptcy proceeds. The merchandise mix depends on buying opportunities; an 80/20 product mix (hard goods to soft goods) is common for closeout operations. The typical closeout store layout lacks organization; searching for bargains is part of the traditional appeal of shopping for closeout merchandise.[40] Like other off-pricers, closeout stores strive to keep operating expenses at a minimum. Consolidated Stores of Columbus, Ohio, operators of Odd Lots and Big Lots stores, Job Lot Trading of New York, and Pic n' Save of Los Angeles are the major players in this form of off-price retailing.

Another variation of the off-price retailer is the **one-price retailer**—a store that offers all merchandise (e.g., overruns, odd lots, cancelled orders, and closeouts) at a single, fixed price. The One Price Clothing Company, One Price Shops, $10 More or Less, and Simply $6/Simply $8 are some of the firms operating this type of off-price enterprise. The one-price clothing chains are (1) working best in smaller communities,

(2) offering "true value" at discount prices to gain return trade, (3) favoring the \$6, \$8, and \$9 price points, and (4) selecting strip center locations.[41]

Supermarket Retailing

No commonly accepted definition of a **supermarket** exists because of the wide range of business formulas used in this industry. Several commonly used definitional classifications of supermarkets follow:

- *Conventional supermarket:* a self-service grocery store that offers a full line of groceries, meat, and produce with at least \$2 million in annual sales
- *Superstore:* a modern, upgraded version of the conventional supermarket with at least 30,000 square feet in total area and more than \$8 million in annual sales; offers an expanded selection of nonfoods and service departments (e.g., deli, bakery, seafood)
- *Food and drug combo:* a combination of superstore and drugstore under a single roof and common checkout; drugstore merchandise represents at least one-third of the selling area and a minimum of 15 percent of store sales
- *Warehouse store:* a low-margin grocery store that combines reduced variety, lower service levels, simpler decor, streamlined merchandising presentation, and aggressive pricing
- *Superwarehouse store:* a high-volume hybrid of the superstore and the warehouse store offering full variety, quality perishables, and low prices
- *Limited-assortment store:* a very "bare-bones," low-price grocery store that eliminates services and carries fewer than 1,000 items with few, if any, perishables[42]

Figure 2–12 shows the market share of each of these formats. The growth of the economy (price-oriented) and extended (selection-oriented) formats come at the expense of the more traditional supermarket operation. Figure 2–13 identifies the top 15 supermarket chains.

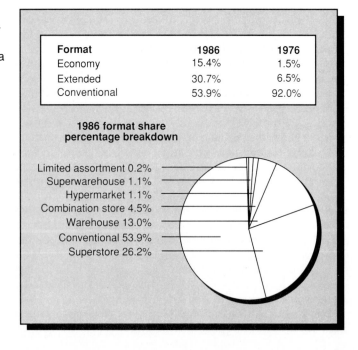

Format	1986	1976
Economy	15.4%	1.5%
Extended	30.7%	6.5%
Conventional	53.9%	92.0%

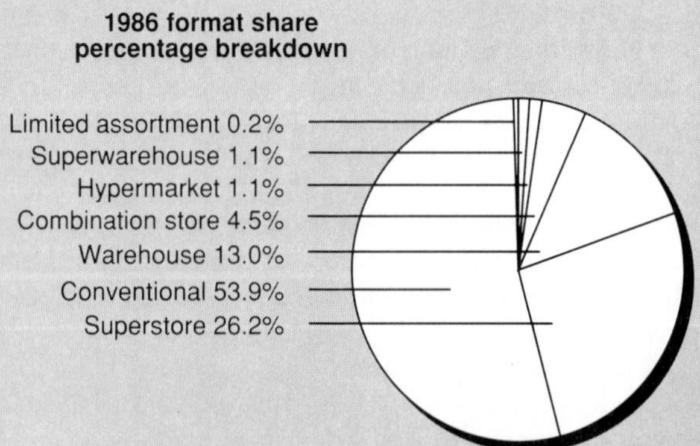

FIGURE 2–12
U.S. supermarkets' format share (source: Cynthia Valentino, "In a fragmented market." Reprinted with permission of *Advertising Age,* May 4, 1987. Copyright © Crain Communications, Inc.)

FIGURE 2–13
The top 15 supermarket chains

Company	1988 Sales (000 Omitted)	Stores
1. Kroger Co., Cincinnati	$19,050,000	2206
2. American Stores, Irvine, Calif.	18,478,000	1285
3. Safeway Stores, Oakland, Calif.	13,612,300	1261
4. A&P, Montvale, N.J.	10,067,800	1241
5. Winn-Dixie Stores, Jacksonville, Fla.	9,007,700	1246
6. Albertson's, Boise, Idaho	6,773,100	497
7. Supermarkets General Holdings Corp., Carteret, N.J.	5,962,200	268
8. Publix Super Markets, Lakeland, Fla.	4,848,000	353
9. Vons Cos., El Monte, Calif.	3,916,600	350
10. Food Lion, Salisbury, N.C.	3,815,400	567
11. Ahold USA, Parsippany, N.J.	3,514,000	329
12. Giant Food, Landover, Md.	2,987,200	145
13. Grand Union Co., Wayne, N.J.	2,872,000	300
14. Stop & Shop Cos., Braintree, Mass.	2,517,363	114
15. Ralphs, Compton, Calif.	2,380,700	134

Source: Reprinted by permission from *Chain Store Age Executive* (August 1989): 34. Copyright © Lebhar-Friedman, Inc., 425 Park Avenue, New York, New York 10022.

The products a supermarket offers include a relatively broad variety and complete assortment of dry groceries, fresh meats, produce, and dairy products. In recent years, the basic food lines have been supplemented by a variety of prepared food lines (deli department) and nonfood lines. By adding prepared foods, the supermarkets hoped to negate the threat posed by the fast-food restaurants. The addition of carryout services and eating-in areas for foods such as deli products, fresh bakery products, and fast-food restaurant lines (e.g., hamburgers, hot dogs, chicken, tacos, and fish) represents a direct effort to obtain a large share of this eating-out business. Currently 33 percent of the typical American's food dollar is consumed away from home.[43] "The supermarket used to be America's pantry, now it's America's Kitchen."[44]

By broadening their merchandise lines to include nonfood products, supermarkets have successfully increased sales and profits. With large numbers of customers moving through their stores each week, this product strategy has resulted in numerous sales of convenience and shopping goods. Today supermarkets' upgraded and upscaled operations include nonfood lines such as prescription drugs, small appliances, linens, auto accessories, books, magazines, clothing, flowers, and housewares. Recently many supermarkets have added numerous services, including dry cleaning, post office, banking, tailoring, medical, dental, insurance, and legal services. Safeway currently is testing Service Village, a kiosk offering shoe repair, key cutting, and fax machines together with additional convenience services.[45] If the "scrambling" process continues, the supermarket of the future could well become the modern version of the "general store."

Supermarkets tend to be low-margin operations that depend on very high stock turnover rates to sustain profits. Operating out of clean, modern facilities (an extremely important patronage motive for most food shoppers), the supermarket is basically a self-service operation supported by services such as parking, check cashing, fast checkout, and bagging. Although some supermarkets accept credit cards[46] and offer tote-to-automobile services, cash-and-carry is the preferred method of doing business. The most distinguishing promotional characteristic of supermarkets is the weekly advertising of loss or low-price leaders (products sold below or at cost). Leader pricing is aimed at attracting consumers into the store in the hope that they will purchase the rest of their weekly shopping list at full markup prices.

Convenience Store Retailing

The modern-day version of the corner "mom-and-pop" grocery store is the **convenience store**. As its name suggests, the convenience store offers customers a convenient place to shop. In particular, it offers time convenience by being open longer and during the inconvenient early morning and late night hours and place convenience by being a small, compact, fast-service operation that is close to consumers' homes and places of business.

The basic premise of the convenience store is capturing fill-in or emergency trade—after the consumer has forgotten to purchase a needed product during the planned weekly trip to the supermarket or has unexpectedly run out of a needed product before the next planned supermarket trip. Because these stores frequently are located between the consumer's home and the nearest supermarket, they serve as effective "interceptors" of fill-in and emergency trade.

Convenience stores carry both food and nonfood merchandise lines. Like supermarkets, convenience stores have broadened their basic product mix to include items such as motor oil, toys, prepared foods (7-Eleven's Hot-To-Go), firewood, cold drinks, and self-service gasoline. Product assortment within each line is very limited. Major national brands dominate the product line, although some of the major chain organizations offer private labels in beverages and some canned goods.

Because they provide time and place utilities, convenience stores charge appreciably higher prices than other stores. From a promotional viewpoint, the store's sign and location are the most important weapons in the war to attract consumers. The convenience store's facilities include buildings that range from 1,000 to 3,200 square feet and parking areas that accommodate 5 to 15 cars. Store layouts are designed to draw customers through the store to increase impulse purchasing. To accomplish this, convenience store managers place high-volume items (e.g., beer and soft drinks) at or near the back of the store.

Contractual Retailing

Independent retailers often attempt to achieve economies of operations and an increased market presence by integrating their operations with those of other retailers and wholesalers. By entering into contractual arrangements, retailers can formalize the rights and obligations of each party in the contract. The terms of the contract can, and often do, cover all aspects of the retailer's product, place, price, and promotional activities. **Contractual retailing** exists in several forms, but the four most common forms are retailer-sponsored cooperative groups, wholesaler-sponsored voluntary chains, franchised retailers, and leased departments.

Retailer-Sponsored Cooperative Group

The **retailer-sponsored cooperative group** is a contractual organization formed by many small independent retailers and usually involves the common ownership of a wholesaler. Originally formed to combat competition from large chain organizations, this type of contractual system allows the small independent to realize economies of scale by making large-quantity group purchases. The contractual agreement usually requires individual members to concentrate their purchases of products from the cooperative wholesaler and in turn receive some form of patronage refund. Associated

Grocers and Certified Grocers are two large food wholesalers that have cooperative contractual arrangements with independent food retailers.

Wholesaler-Sponsored Voluntary Chain

The **wholesaler-sponsored voluntary chain** is a contractual arrangement in which a wholesaler develops a merchandising program that independent retailers join voluntarily. By agreeing to purchase a certain amount of merchandise from the wholesaler, the retailer is assured of lower prices. These lower prices are possible because the wholesaling organization can buy in larger quantities with the knowledge that it has an established market. The Independent Grocers Alliance (IGA) and Super Valu Stores, Inc. are food wholesalers that sponsor voluntary chains.

Franchised Retailer

Today, a large and growing percentage of retail marketing is conducted through a franchise system—a form of retailing in which a parent company (franchisor) obtains distribution of its products, services, or methods through a network of contractually affiliated dealers (franchisees). The International Franchise Association defines **franchising** as "a continuing relationship in which the franchisor provides a licensed privilege to do business, plus assistance in organizing, training, merchandising, and management, in return for a consideration from the franchisee."[47] In other words, the franchisor offers the franchisee a patterned way of doing business that includes product, price, place, and promotional strategies.

In practice, this means that the franchisee is the owner of his or her own business, distributing the goods or services of the franchisor and paying for that privilege through an initial fee and/or a percentage of future sales or profits.[48] Although the franchisee owns the business, the franchisor usually exercises control over some aspects of its operation to ensure conformity to the franchisor's proven methods and standards for products, services, quality, and methods.

In return for the fees and royalties paid by the franchisee, the franchisor may provide some or all of the following services: (1) location analysis and counseling; (2) store development, including lease negotiations; (3) store design and equipment purchasing; (4) initial employee and management training and continuing management counseling; (5) advertising and merchandising counsel and assistance; (6) standardized procedures and operations; (7) centralized purchasing with consequent savings; (8) financial assistance in the establishment of the business; (9) an exclusive territory in which to operate; and (10) the goodwill and recognition of a widely known brand or trade name.

Franchisors expect franchisees to conform to the business pattern and also to provide them with some form of compensation for their right to use the franchise. Franchisor compensation usually involves either one or a combination of the following:

1. *Initial franchise fee*—a fee the franchisor charges up front for the franchisee's right to own the business and to receive initial services
2. *Royalties*—an operating fee imposed on the franchisee's gross sales
3. *Sales of products*—profits the franchisor makes from sales to the franchisee of raw and finished products, operating supplies, furnishings, and equipment
4. *Rental and lease fees*—fees the franchisor charges for the use of its facilities and equipment
5. *Management fee*—a fee the franchisor charges for some of the continuous services it provides the franchisee[49]

Among the primary advantages of owning a franchise unit are that it usually requires less capital to set up a franchise than it would to start up independently; franchisor training programs often make it unnecessary to possess knowledge about the particular type of business; and business risk frequently is reduced because of the recognition and goodwill of the franchisor's name and product and the initial and continued help the franchisor provides in running the business.

However, franchising is not an easy and failure-proof way to financial success. The franchisee faces a number of disadvantages. First, the franchisor usually controls many aspects of the franchisee's business operations, which may inhibit the franchisee's creativity and independence. Second, acquiring a blue-chip franchise such as a McDonald's or Pizza Hut requires considerable financial resources and high royalty payments. Third, the success of each individual franchise unit depends on the workings of the parent company, and even the best managers can find their business—and investment—jeopardized if trouble develops in the franchisor's operations. Finally, experts urge those thinking of purchasing a franchise to remember that it usually is much more a full-time job than an investment, with most new owners putting in well over an average workweek.

Today there are over 2,000 franchise companies involved in almost every type of retail business area from molars to mufflers, as evidenced by the American Dental Centers joining Midas shops on the scene. New franchises follow new trends; the growing desire to work at home is leading to several franchising formats that are home bound—home food delivery, home improvement, home maintenance, and home entertainment businesses are thriving.[50]

Franchise companies can be divided into two main types. The first, *product* or *trade name franchises,* is characterized by franchised dealers that carry one company's product line and identify their business with that company and product. Examples include automobile dealers, gasoline stations, and soft-drink bottlers. These types of operations often are referred to as *manufacturer-sponsored* and *wholesaler-sponsored* retailing (see Figure 2–14).

The second type, *business format franchises* or service firm–sponsored retailers, is a system in which the franchisee not only carries the franchisor's products and trade name but adopts the entire business format itself, from merchandising to store design (see Figure 2–14). Most aspects of the franchisee's operations are coordinated to ensure a specific and consistent image designed to appeal to particular market segments. This category includes restaurants (McDonald's), auto repair shops (MAACO), personal and business services (H&R Block), and many others and is increasing at a much greater rate than product franchises.

The rapid rate of franchise sales growth experienced in the past three decades is expected to continue. This trend will be fueled by the entrance of many new, small companies into the franchise system, attracted by both the ability to expand rapidly despite limited company capital and the competitive advantages that franchising often provides. Growing customer preference for convenience and consistent quality—two of franchising's principal strengths—should also accelerate franchise growth. Another important factor will be increasing activity by U.S. franchisors in foreign markets.

Much of the increase in domestic franchise sales is expected to come from the service sector. With the average age of the U.S. population rising and the increasing number of dual-earner families, forecasters see creation of further franchise opportunities in areas such as housecleaning services, repair and home remodeling, carpet and other cleaning services, and various maintenance functions. Franchises specializing in business services are expected to grow at an even faster rate, a product of the so-called "age of information" and the increasing preference of many firms to contract out functions they once performed internally. Growth is expected to occur in franchises that supply services for businesses such as accounting, advertising, packaging and shipping, consulting, security, personnel, and copying and printing. Other specific types of franchises expecting above-average growth are weight control centers, hair salons, temporary help services, and medical centers.

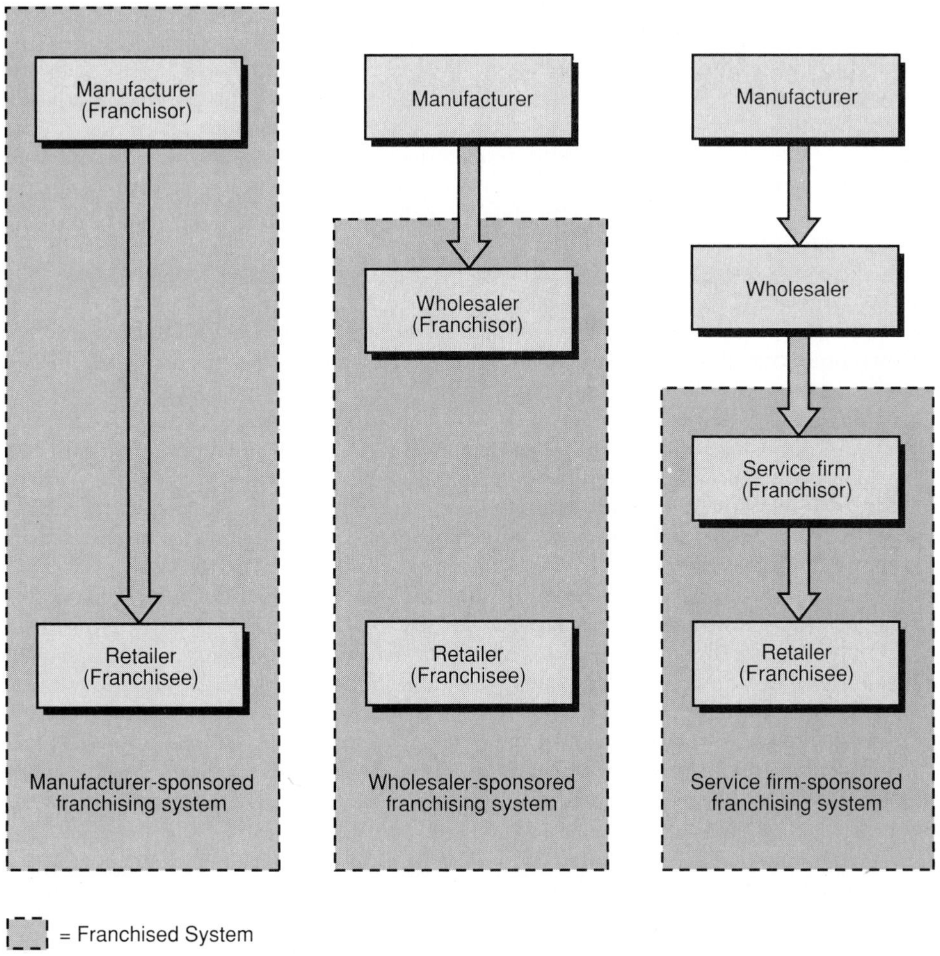

FIGURE 2–14
Types of franchising systems

Leased Department

Leased departments are retailers that operate departments (usually in specialized lines of merchandise) under contractual arrangements with conventional retail stores. Many supermarkets and department stores, for example, lease space to outside organizations to sell magazines (as in supermarkets) and auto supplies and shoes (as in many department and discount stores). The most frequently leased-out departments are beauty salon, books, cameras, candy, costume jewelry, electronics, family shoes, fine jewelry, furs, and photo. The lessor usually furnishes space, utilities, and basic in-store services necessary to the lessee's operation. In turn, the lessee agrees to provide the personnel, management, and capital necessary to stock and operate a department with carefully defined merchandise. Generally the contract calls for the lessee to pay the lessor either a flat monthly fee, a percentage of gross sales, or some combination of the two.

A rapidly growing trend in space subleasing is the *in-store vendor shop:* "Montgomery Ward already has become the landlord to a host of diverse tenants including Toys 'R' Us, Peppers Waterbeds, Gymees, Pro Jersey, Quaker State . . . with virtually no investment, Montgomery Ward expands its offerings through other recognized retailers in a specific category of business that would be very costly to develop internally."[51]

Warehouse Retailing

The typical **warehouse retailing** operation involves some combination of warehouse and showroom facilities. In some cases, these facilities are located in separate but adjacent areas; in others, the warehouse and showroom are combined into one large physical structure. Generally the warehouse retailer uses warehousing principles to reduce operating expenses and thereby offer discount prices as a primary customer appeal. There are four types of warehouse retailers: warehouse showroom, catalog showroom, home center, and warehouse club.

The **warehouse showroom** generally is a single-line, hard-goods retailer that stocks merchandise such as furniture, appliances, or carpeting. To help the consumer make price comparisons with conventional home furnishings retailers, the warehouse showroom typically stocks only well-known, nationally advertised brands. These retailers set up sample merchandise displays in showrooms so potential consumers can get an idea of what the products will look like in their homes. After making their selections, consumers immediately receive the merchandise in shipping cartons from the completely stocked adjacent warehouse. Although they prefer the "cash-and-carry" mode of operation, most warehouse retailers offer credit, delivery, and installation services at an additional fee over the selling price. Because of space and delivery requirements, plus the need to attract consumers from a large market area, warehouse showroom locations usually are free-standing sites near major traffic intersections such as interstate highway systems.

The **catalog showroom** features hard goods such as housewares, small appliances, jewelry, watches, toys, sporting goods, lawn and garden equipment, luggage, stereos, televisions, and other electronic equipment at a discount. The distinguishing feature of the catalog showroom is that a merchandise catalog is combined with the showroom and an adjacent warehouse as part of the retailer's operation. By adding a catalog of products to showroom products, the retailer provides consumers with both an in-store and an at-home method of buying merchandise. Like the warehouse showroom, the catalog showroom features nationally branded merchandise that facilitates consumer price comparisons with conventional hard-goods retailers.

For consumers, the typical shopping trip to a catalog showroom involves (1) filling out an order form using the merchandise/price code found on either the showroom price tag or in the catalog, (2) ordering and paying for the merchandise at a cashier's desk, and (3) picking up the merchandise at a pickup desk. The pickup desk is directly connected to an adjacent warehouse containing a complete stock of merchandise. Best Products and Service Merchandise typify the catalog showroom format.

The modern **home center** combines the traditional hardware store and lumber yard with a self-service home improvement center. The typical merchandise mix includes a wide variety and deep assortment of building materials, hardware, paints, plumbing and heating equipment, electrical supplies, power tools, garden and yard equipment, and other home maintenance supplies. Some home centers have expanded their merchandise offerings to include household appliances and home furnishings. Home centers usually have large showrooms that display sample merchandise (large, bulky items) and complete stock (small, standardized items). Consumers purchase showroom sample merchandise by placing orders at the order desk, and clerks pull the orders from adjacent warehouse stocks. Customers simply serve themselves with showroom stock. While it appeals to all homeowners, the home center has been particularly successful with the "do-it-yourselfer." By providing customers with information on materials and equipment and offering "how-to" services, home centers have developed a strong customer following. Figure 2–15 lists the top 15 home center operators.

Warehouse clubs are huge outlets that cater to customers who have joined the club to secure merchandise at 20 to 40 percent below supermarket and discount store

FIGURE 2–15
The top 15 home center chains

Company	1988 Sales (000 Omitted)	Stores
1. Lowe's Cos., North Wilkesboro, N.C.	$2,516,879	296
2. The Home Depot, Atlanta	1,999,514	96
3. Payless Cashways, Kansas City, Mo.	1,900,000	195
4. Builders Square, San Antonio, Tex.	1,700,000	133
5. Wickes Lumber, Vernon Hills, Ill.	1,200,000	210
6. Grossman's, Braintree, Mass.	1,142,000	246
7. Hechinger, Landover, Md.	1,019,399	92
8. 84 Lumber, Eighty-Four, Pa.	900,000	369
9. HomeClub, Fullerton, Calif.	775,000	46
10. Builders Emporium, Irvine, Calif.	700,000	119
11. Channel Home Centers, Whippany, N.J	675,000	161
12. Sutherland, Kansas City, Mo.	660,000	85
13. Menard's, Eau Claire, Wis.	620,000	40
14. Scotty's, Winter Haven, Fla.	551,000	160
15. Rickel, South Plainfield, N.J.	503,000	51

Source: Reprinted by permission from *Chain Store Age Executive* (August 1989): 39. Copyright © Lebhar-Friedman, Inc., 425 Park Avenue, New York, New York 10022.

prices. As a special type of discount house, the warehouse club is also referred to as a *wholesale club, membership club,* and *wholesale center.*[52] The principal players in the warehouse club market are identified in Figure 2–16. Most warehouse clubs have a two-tiered membership plan: (1) wholesale members, who pay an annual fee and must be operators of small businesses, and (2) group members, who usually pay about 5 percent above the ticket price of the merchandise. The principal retail mix strategies are as follows:

- *Product mix*—a vast array of product categories but a limited selection of the best-selling brands, sizes, and models in each category
- *Service mix*—cash-and-carry business with limited hours and no amenities (e.g., restrooms)
- *Place mix*—large (100,000-square-foot), bare-bones facilities (warehouse) located in out-of-the-way, low-rent locations
- *Price mix*—rock-bottom wholesale prices that produce paper-thin gross margin profits (10 to 11 percent)
- *Promotional mix*—minimal advertising (less than .5 percent of sales) supported by minimal sales support, visual merchandising, and sales incentives

Superstore Retailing

"Ever since the general store was split up into hardware, drug, variety, grocery, automotive, and department stores, retailers have been trying to figure out a way to put them all back together again. Since the advent of the discount store, the urge to get low-priced groceries and discounted general merchandise together has been even greater."[53] While the term *superstore retailing* can refer to any store that is bigger than one would normally expect to find selling a particular product line (e.g., a 50,000-square-foot shoe store),[54] in this discussion **superstore retailing** refers to huge combination supermarkets and discount general-merchandise stores that stock and sell a complete selection of food products together with a wide variety of hard and soft goods at deep-discount prices. For the consumer, it is the "fulfillment of the bigger-is-better, shop-till-you-drop spirit."[55] The superstore concept is in part the

Company	Number of Outlets	Membership Policy: Wholesale	Membership Policy: Retail
B. J.'s Wholesale Club (Zayre)	8	$30 annual fee; up to two additional memberships $10 each	5% markup
Buyers Club	2	[not available]	
Club Mart of America	1	[not available]	
Club Wholesale (Elixir)	2	$25 annual fee	5% markup
Costco Wholesale Club	21	$25 annual fee	5% markup
Metro Cash & Carry of Illinois	3	No fee	5% markup
Money's Worth	1	$25 annual fee	5% markup
Pace Membership Warehouse	15	$25 annual fee	5% markup
Price Club	24	$25 annual fee	Either $15 annual fee and 5% markup or $25 annual fee without 5% markup
Price Savers (Kroger)	5	$25 annual fee	5% markup
Sam's Wholesale Club	23	$25 annual fee	5% markup
Super Saver	9	[not available]	
The Warehouse Club (joint partnership with W. R. Grace)	7	$25 annual fee	5% markup
The Wholesale Club	5	$25 annual fee	5% markup
Wholesale Plus	1	$25 annual fee	5% markup
Value Club	5	$25 annual fee	$5 fee and 5% markup

Source: Jack G. Kaikati, "The Boom in Warehouse Clubs," *Business Horizons* (March–April 1987): 72. Compiled from: Molly Brauer, "Membership Retailing Trend Taking Off," *Chain Store Age Executive,* November 1984: 18; and Joseph H. Ellis, *The Warehouse Club Industry: An Update* (New York: Goldman Sachs & Co., July 25, 1986).

FIGURE 2–16
Top warehouse club merchandisers

competitive counterattack of discount chains (e.g., K mart, Wal-Mart, and Shopko) on the successful large food-drug combo stores operated by supermarket chains. Superstores can be differentiated into two size categories—the large supercenters and the jumbo hypermarkets.

Supercenters are large combination supermarket/discount stores that typically range from 100,000 to 130,000 square feet. Wal-Mart's *Super Center Stores* stock 65,000 SKUs (stock keep units) and operate with gross margins of 18 percent. K mart's *Super K marts* are combination stores that devote 23,000 square feet to grocery merchandise and 87,000 square feet to general merchandise.[56] The downsized supercenters have greater flexibility in market selection than the larger hypermarkets; they can survive in smaller trading areas.[57]

Hypermarkets are huge combination stores that average 220,000 square feet; the largest is the 330,000-square-foot Carrefour Hypermarket in Philadelphia.[58] To succeed, this "mall-without-walls" concept must become a destination-type store capable of attracting customers from a radius of 50 to 60 miles.[59] The primary trading areas (e.g., 20-minute drive time) needs to "contain 500,000 households, with customers in their 20s and 30s, earning $25,000 to $55,000 per household annually, with at least two children."[60] A self-service retailer with central checkouts (typically 50 or more) and a sophisticated system of materials handling, the hypermarket attempts to underprice traditional retailers by as much as 20 to 40 percent. Hypermarket USA (Wal-Mart), Twin Value (Shopko/Super Valu), American Fare (K mart), and Biggs and Carrefour (both French owned) are the principal players in today's hypermarket experiment.

Nonstore Retailing

Nonstore retailing involves retailers that do not use conventional store facilities as part of their standard mode of operation; rather, they use nonstore, direct marketing methods to target a select group of consumers.[61] A major strategy of the nonstore retailer is to take the "store" (i.e., party, catalog, videodisc) to the customer rather than wait for the customer to come to the retailer (i.e., store). Nonstore retailers include a wide variety of retailing formats; Figure 2–17 identifies those formats.

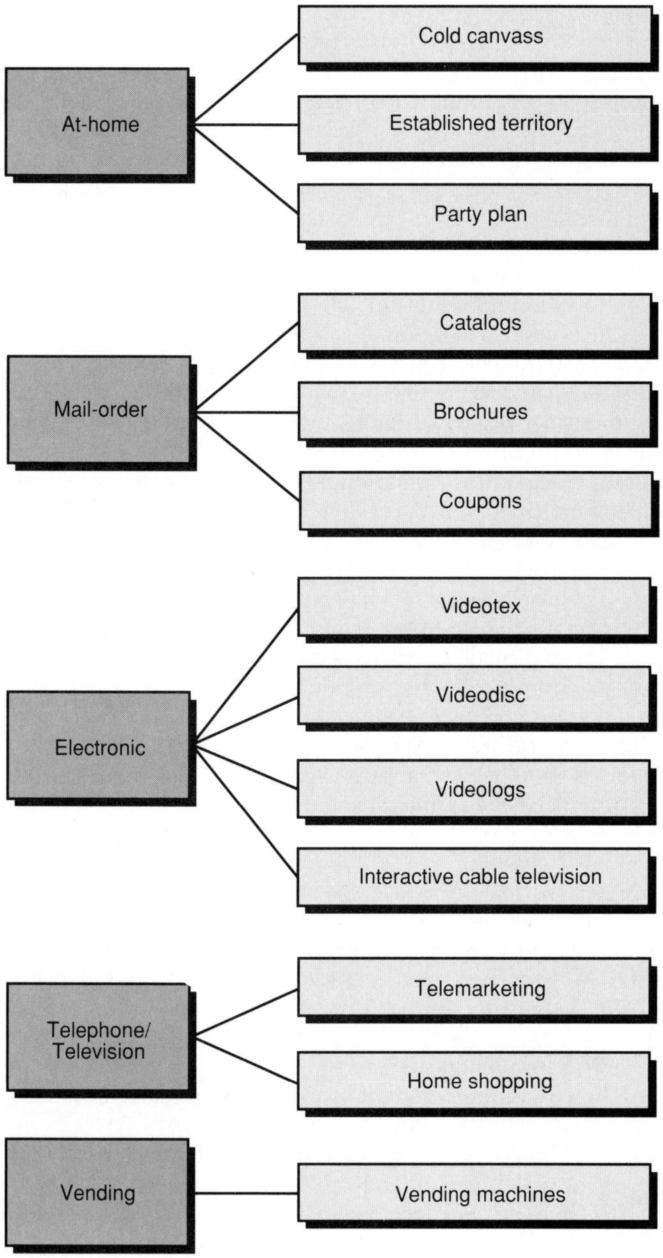

FIGURE 2–17
Nonstore retailing formats

At-Home Retailing

At-home retailing, also called *door-to-door* and *house-to-house selling,* is the market approach of making personal contacts and sales in the consumer's home. This form of retailing offers the consumer the ultimate in *place convenience* and, with some planning on the salesperson's part (such as making an appointment), can provide an equal amount of *time convenience*. At-home retailing provides several other advantages to the consumer. First, it is highly personalized because of the one-on-one relationship between the customer and the salesperson. Second, it helps consumers make a product evaluation before the purchase by letting them try the product in a home setting. Third, it saves the consumer the time and effort of going to the store, searching for needed merchandise, and waiting in checkout lines. Finally, it usually includes home delivery, which appeals to most customers, especially the elderly.

At-home retailing also offers the seller certain advantages, including (1) no direct competition because the seller presents its products in "isolation" in the home, where consumers cannot make direct comparisons with similar products; (2) avoidance of uncontrollable intermediaries; and (3) elimination of investments in stores and other facilities because sales representatives are compensated on a commission basis and pay their own expenses.

The at-home method of retailing exists in several forms. The three principal forms are the cold canvass, the established territory or route, and the party plan.

The *cold-canvass method* involves soliciting sales door-to-door without either advanced selection of homes or prior notice of an intended sales call to potential customers. Vacuum cleaners, magazine subscriptions, and encyclopedias are some of the more common products sold by the cold-canvass method.

The *established-territory method* assigns salespeople to prescribed geographical areas in which they make their door-to-door sales and delivery calls at regular, predetermined time intervals. Some of the best-known users of the established-territory method are Avon (cosmetics), Fuller Brush (household products), Stanley Home Products (household products), and Sarah Coventry (jewelry). Avon currently is testing door-to-door sales of toys and videotapes.[62]

The *party plan method* of at-home retailing requires a salesperson to make sales presentations in the home of a host or hostess who has invited potential customers to a "party." Usually the party plan includes various games and other entertainment activities in which participants receive small, inexpensive gifts. Closing the sale occurs when the salesperson takes orders from the people attending the party. As a reward for holding the party, the host or hostess receives either cash or gifts. Tupperware and Wearever Aluminum Products use the party plan method extensively. Toys, books, home decorating products, household goods, jewelry, health and beauty aids, and apparel are just a few of the products sold in this manner.

Mail-Order Retailing

Mail-order retailing is a business format in which the retailer contacts prospective customers by mail, receives customer orders by mail, and/or makes merchandise deliveries by mail. Mail-order operations vary significantly in terms of merchandise lines and operations (i.e., methods of customer contact, order placement, and delivery arrangements). As we shall see, *mail-order* probably is a misnomer for the modern mail-order retailer.

Mail-order operations differ tremendously in the variety and assortment of merchandise lines they offer. Three important types of mail-order operations have been identified.

The *general-merchandise mail-order house* offers a wide variety of merchandise lines. The depth of the assortment within each merchandise line varies among houses and among lines. Sears, J. C. Penney, and Spiegel operate general-merchandise mail-order operations. To differentiate itself, Spiegel has shifted its marketing focus "to the upper 30% of U.S. households. The company now primarily targets working women. . . . Spiegel considers its main rivals the upscale department store chains."[63]

The *novelty mail-order retailer* carries lines often limited to products not normally carried by conventional retailers. Frequently the novelty operator directs merchandise appeals to a small market segment. Intimate apparel, unusual reading materials, specialized sporting equipment, exotic foods, unusual hobby equipment, and novelty gifts are among the kinds of merchandise that novelty mail-order retailers sell. The Sharper Image is an excellent example of this type of cataloger.

Supplementary mail-order operations of department and specialty stores are the third type of mail-order retailer. Many conventional department and specialty stores offer mail-order service for the convenience of their customers. The Neiman Marcus Christmas catalog (Holiday Planner), The Broadway Home Style, and Saks Fifth Avenue's "The Works" exemplify this type of mail-order retailing.[64]

Because of different operating characteristics, three forms of mail-order retailing have emerged: catalogs, brochures, and coupons. Any given mail-order retailer can use one or any combination of these three forms.

Catalog operations involve the use of specially prepared catalogs that present the retailer's merchandise both visually and verbally. Basic product assortment (sizes, colors, materials, styles, models, etc.) and pricing information are included, along with directions for ordering on the order blanks provided. Modern catalog operations allow the customer to place orders by mail, via telephone, or in person at a catalog desk. In addition, catalog operations offer a variety of delivery arrangements such as mail, parcel post, express service, customer pickup, and store delivery.

Some retailers use a *brochure* form of mail-order retailing by preparing a small booklet or leaflet that they mail to potential consumers. The distinguishing feature of this type of brochure is that it usually displays only a limited number of product items to attract consumer interest. These interesting and attention-getting brochures usually emphasize either the innovative nature or the good value of the product.

The *coupon* form of mail-order retailing involves using magazine and newspaper advertisements. Advertisements featuring special merchandise and mail-order coupons are placed in magazines and newspapers that appeal to specific market segments. To some extent, most magazines and newspapers segment their markets either geographically (regional or local editions) or psychographically (subscribers to specialty publications usually have certain common activities, interests, and opinions).

Electronic Retailing

Electronic retailing via electronic and video systems is in the innovation stage of the retail life cycle. Although a large number of potential electronic retailing options exist and the number of options are expected to expand as new technologies are brought online, retailers currently are focusing their attention on videotex, videodisc, videologs, and interactive cable television.

Videotex is "an interactive electronic system in which data and graphics are transmitted from a computer network over telephone or cable lines and displayed on a subscriber's TV or computer-terminal screen."[65] The basic components and interactions of a videotex system appear in Figure 2–18. Shopping with a videotex system consists of selecting from a series of choices, called *menus*, displayed on the screen. For example, a shopper narrows down the choice by selecting from a menu of product lines and product items (brands, styles, sizes, colors, prices, etc.). In addition to at-home shopping, videotex systems can provide subscribers with a wide selection of services, including news, weather, sports, financial, and consumer information; at-home banking, reservations, and travel information; electronic encyclopedias and magazines, videocoupons and educational/instructional games; directories; real estate and employment listings; home energy management; security, medical, and fire monitoring; and

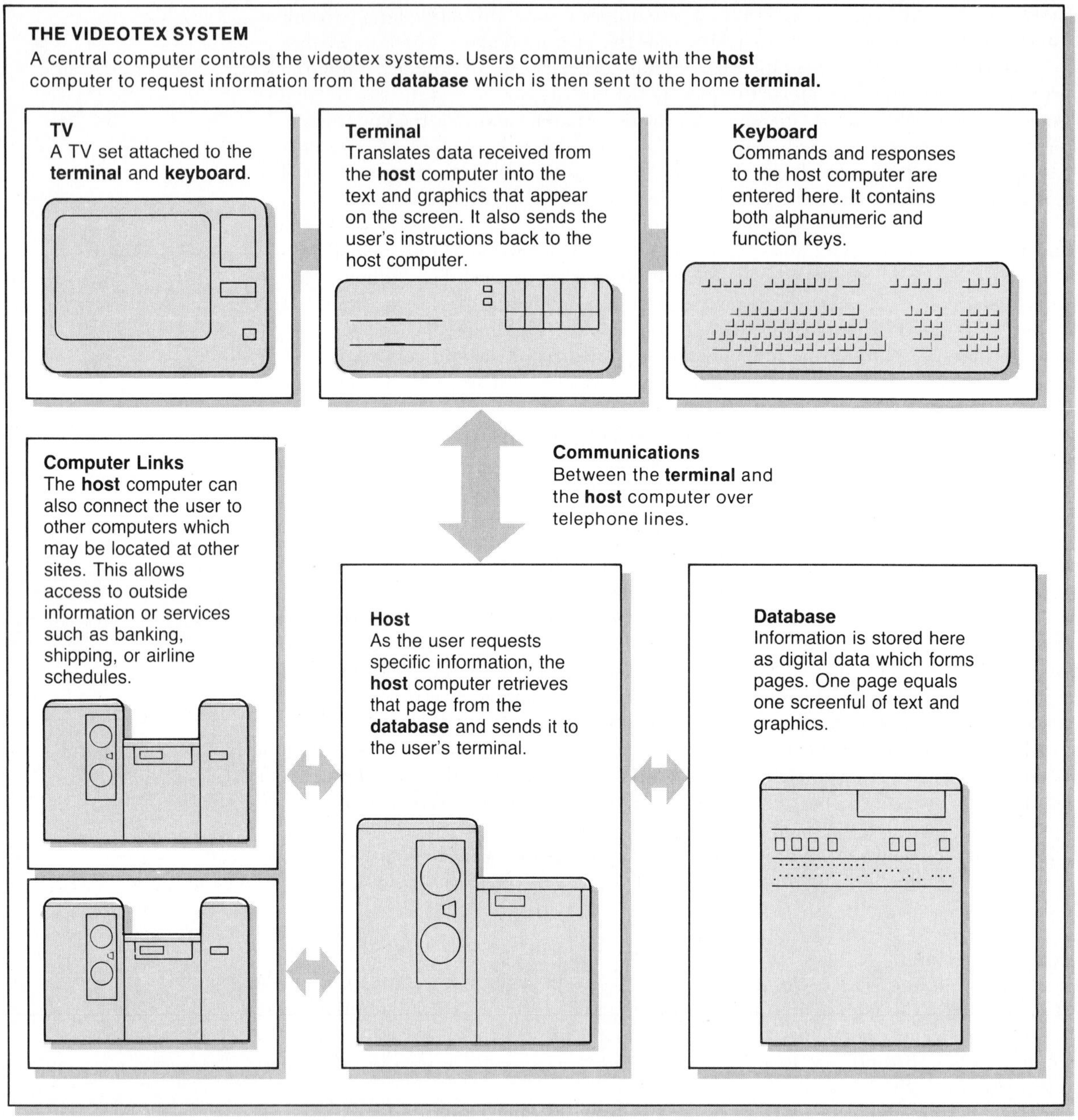
THE VIDEOTEX SYSTEM
A central computer controls the videotex systems. Users communicate with the host computer to request information from the database which is then sent to the home terminal.
TV
A TV set attached to the terminal and keyboard.
Terminal
Translates data received from the host computer into the text and graphics that appear on the screen. It also sends the user's instructions back to the host computer.
Keyboard
Commands and responses to the host computer are entered here. It contains both alphanumeric and function keys.
Computer Links
The host computer can also connect the user to other computers which may be located at other sites. This allows access to outside information or services such as banking, shipping, or airline schedules.
Communications
Between the terminal and the host computer over telephone lines.
Host
As the user requests specific information, the host computer retrieves that page from the database and sends it to the user's terminal.
Database
Information is stored here as digital data which forms pages. One page equals one screenful of text and graphics.

FIGURE 2–18
Basic components and interactions of a videotex system (source: Tom Mach, "High-Tech Opportunities Getting Closer to Home," *Advertising Age,* 16, April 1984. Copyright Crain Communications Inc. Reprinted by permission.)

electronic mail/messaging.[66] The Prodigy network, a joint venture between IBM and Sears, "allows subscribers at home to get information from a number of sources over telephone lines. Subscribers can also shop at home and send messages . . . access to 500 services . . . shop not only at Sears, but at J. C. Penney and some 45 more direct-shipping merchants."[67]

Videodisc is "an interactive electronic system that uses flat optical discs capable of storing vast amounts of information in the form of moving pictures, still pictures, printed pages, and sound—for display on a TV screen."[68] One such system is the "Electronic Bed and Bath Fashion Center" developed by J. P. Stevens Co., an in-store videodisc, text, and printer information system that allows consumers to see and purchase virtually the entire product line. "A printout from the Stevens unit gives a record of the entire order for the customer . . . the customer is helped at the console by a store salesperson specially trained by Stevens. After she punches all her keypad buttons, she is given the order printout, which must be taken to a cashier for completion of the sale."[69]

Videologs are shop-at-home videotapes. In essence, they are the next wave of catalog shopping. Customers either receive the video at no charge by mail or pay a fee that is credited toward any purchase.[70] A third distribution alternative is to make the videologs available free of charge to customers through video stores; however, the video must be returned to the video store. Videologs can be produced to reflect product usage, consumers' lifestyles, or any other merchandising theme that might prove successful. The twofold sight-and-sound appeal provides a competitive edge over the sight-oriented printed catalog.

Interactive cable television provides the ultimate in shopping convenience; it "permits viewers to purchase merchandise displayed on their television screens and charge the cost to a credit card or bank account by punching a keypad."[71] Due to their access to consumer households, cable companies will increasingly play a more active role as a nonstore retailer.

Telemarketing and Home Shopping

Telephone (telemarketing) and the telephone/television (home shopping) business formats are two more methods of nonstore retailing that are experiencing impressive growth rates. In recent years, **telemarketing**—the selling of goods and services through telephone contact—has helped some retailers increase customer service satisfaction by providing greater convenience. For customers who want to avoid traffic congestion and parking problems, telephone shopping is a desirable alternative. This form of retailing also can benefit shut-ins, the elderly, parents with babysitting problems, working people who do not have time to shop, and consumers who dislike shopping. Figure 2–19 profiles the "teleshopping-prone" consumer and the "ideal product" for teleshopping.

Retailers' major reasons for using telephone retailing are that it (1) provides customers with information on new merchandise and upcoming sales events, (2) allows customers to order merchandise that retailers are willing to deliver to customers'

FIGURE 2–19
Teleshopping profiles

Profile of the "teleshopping-prone" consumer
- younger female who:
  - is part of a two-career household
  - has heavy demands on her time
  - is affluent
  - has above-average education
  - takes risks
  - seeks information
  - uses direct mail
  - is technology-fluent

Profile of the "ideal product" for teleshopping
- a product that:
  - has a strong brand with identifiable model number
  - comes in a few standard sizes
  - does not need special customization and prepurchase service
  - does not involve considerable sensual experience in customer evaluation process
  - has a low bulk to value ratio
  - has a medium-to-low level of complexity
  - has a limited number of attributes important to consumer decision making
  - is nonperishable and not subject to price negotiation at point-of-sale
  - is a planned-purchase-type product

Source: "Videotex to Curtail Canada In-Store Retailing: Study Predicts 15% Home Penetration by 1990," *Marketing News* (November 25, 1983): vol. 17, p. 20. Reprinted from *Marketing News,* Published by the American Marketing Association, Chicago, IL 60606.

homes, and (3) gives customers a convenient way to hold merchandise to pick up at a later date.

Home shopping combines two of America's favorite pastimes—watching television and going shopping. A price/value-oriented retailing operation, **home shopping** is a business format in which (1) merchandise items are displayed, described, and demonstrated on television; (2) customers order the merchandise by calling a toll-free number; (3) customers pay for the orders by credit cards, C.O.D., or check; (4) the retailer (home-shopping network) delivers the merchandise by United Parcel Service (UPS) or some other parcel post company; and (5) the retailer typically offers money-back guarantees if merchandise is returned within 30 days.[72] The principal players in the shop-by-television game are Home Shopping Network, Inc., Clearwater, Florida; Television Auction Shopping Program, Inc., of San Jose, California; and Cable Value Network of Minneapolis. An analysis of the largest system, Home Shopping Network (HSN), found that

1. Seventy-five percent of the merchandise offered by HSN consists of manufacturers' overruns and closeouts and the overstock inventory of wholesalers and retailers.
2. Twenty-five percent of the goods sold are special-order merchandise, much of it from foreign sources of supply.
3. The product mix is 25 percent jewelry, 15 to 20 percent electronics and telephones, 15 percent soft goods, and the remainder miscellaneous items.
4. Gross margins are 50 to 75 percent on jewelry and soft goods, with price points of \$30 to \$70.[73]

Vending Machine Retailing

Vending machine retailing is similar to convenience store retailing in that it usually serves to meet the "fill-in," "emergency," and "after-" or "off-hour" needs of consumers. Products that vending machines dispense share several characteristics: Typically they are small, branded, and standardized products of low-unit value. Candies, soft drinks, hot beverages, and cigarettes are the most popular vending machine items. Among other food products commonly sold in vending machines are milk, snack foods, bakery products, and sandwiches. Nonfood products frequently sold by vending machine include life insurance policies for air travel, postage stamps, newspapers, ice, health and beauty aids, and some novelty items. One of the most significant developments in the use of vending machines is in the field of entertainment. Jukeboxes, pinball machines, and electronic games have greatly expanded the sales potential of vending operations.

THE CHANGING CHARACTER OF RETAIL COMPETITION

Retailing and retailing institutions are still undergoing numerous changes in response to several environmental trends. Innovative merchandising strategies and operational methods are constantly being developed to meet the competitive challenges. What the future will bring to the ever-changing retailing world is a matter of speculation. Given that "the past is the key to the future," however, some retailing experts have identified patterns of competitive change that they express as theories of retail institutional change. Five of the most commonly accepted theories are the *wheel of retailing*, the *dialectic process*, the *retail accordion*, *natural selection*, and the *retail life cycle*.

Wheel of Retailing

One of the most widely recognized theories of retail institutional change is the **wheel of retailing**. First hypothesized by Malcolm P. McNair, the wheel of retailing theory states that the dynamics of institutional change are a "more or less definite cycle"; the cycle "begins with the bold new concept, the innovation" and ends with "eventual

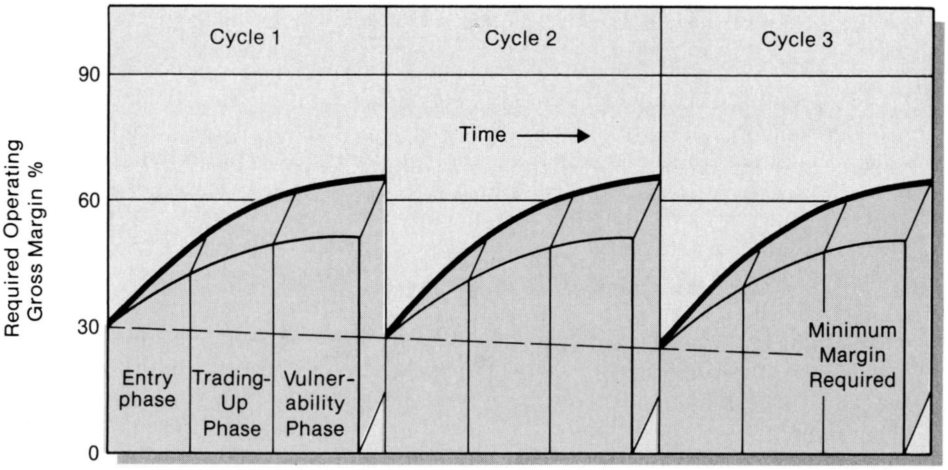

FIGURE 2–20
The wheel of retailing

vulnerability . . . to the next fellow who has a bright idea."[74] A careful examination of the wheel theory reveals three distinct phases to each cycle and that a pattern of cycles will develop over time. Figures 2–20 and 2–21 illustrate the three phases of the wheel of retailing—entry, trading up, and vulnerability—and how each cycle might repeat to form a wavelike pattern.

Entry Phase

In the entry phase of the cycle, an innovative retailing institution enters the market as a low-status, low-price competitor. By reducing operating expenses to a minimum, the new institution can operate at a gross margin substantially below (e.g., 30 versus 50

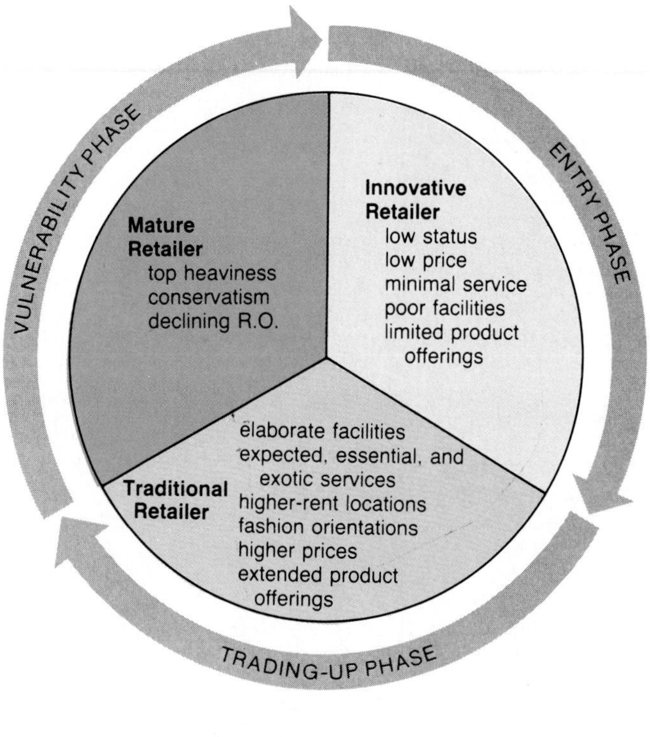

FIGURE 2–21
The retailer and the wheel of retailing

percent) the required gross margins of the more established retailers in the market. Operating expenses usually are maintained at low levels by (1) offering minimal customer service, (2) providing a modest shopping atmosphere in terms of exterior and interior facilities, (3) occupying low-rent locations, and (4) offering limited product mixes. Generally market entry is easier for retailers selling low-margin, high-turnover products. Consumers and competitors consider the innovative institution low-status, and the institution gains market penetration primarily on the basis of price appeals. Once the new form of retailing has become an established competitor, it enters the second phase of the cycle.

Trading-Up Phase

Emulators quickly copy the successful innovation. The competitive actions of these emulators force the original business to differentiate itself by engaging in the process of trading up. The trading-up phase of the cycle involves various changes to upgrade and distinguish the innovative institution.[75] Trading up usually takes the form of acquiring more elaborate facilities, offering expected and exotic as well as essential services, and locating in high-rent neighborhoods. Also, product lines frequently are traded up to include high-markup items, often with a fashion orientation. At the end of the trading-up phase, the original institution has matured into a higher-status, higher-price operation with a required operating gross margin comparable to that of many established competitors. In other words, the innovative institution has matured into a traditional retail institution.

Vulnerability Phase

With maturity, the now established innovative institution enters a phase "characterized by top-heaviness, conservatism, and a decline in the rate of return on investments."[76] Eventually the original innovator becomes vulnerable "to the next fellow who has a bright idea and who starts his business on a low-cost basis, slipping in under the (price)

FIGURE 2–22
The dialectic process

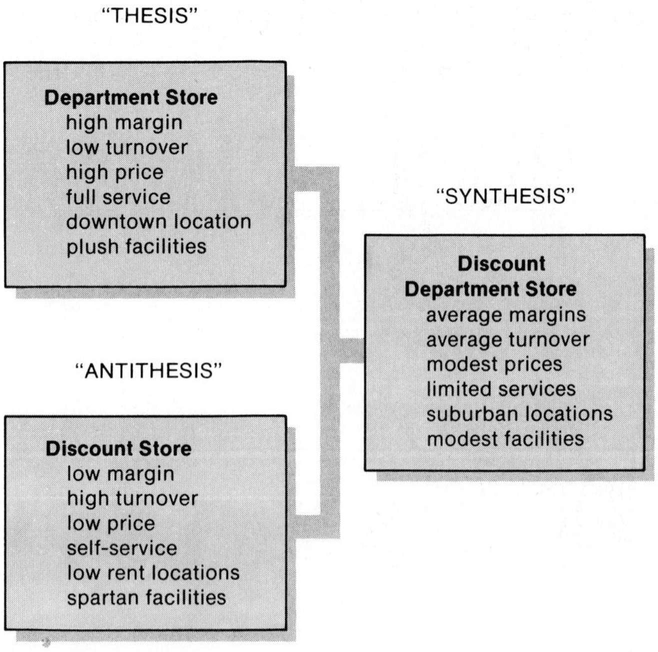

Superstore Building…
is bigger always better?

The superstore retailing concept is the ultimate in the "shop-til-you-drop" spirit. The average shopping time for one of these mammoth shopping experiences is over two hours. It is the current fulfillment of the American belief that "bigger is better."

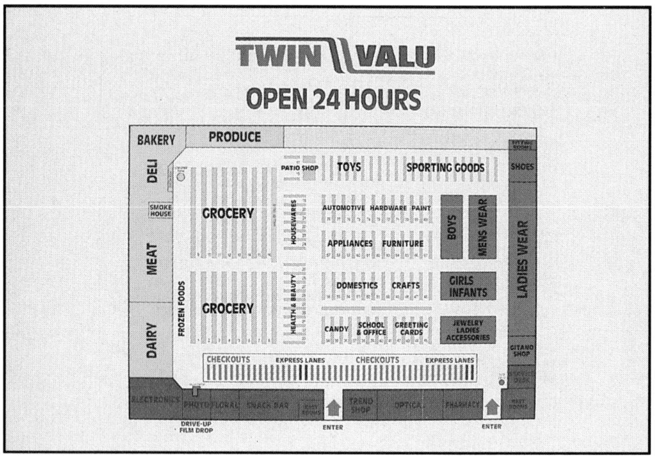

Superstore retailers live up to their namesake by operating out of jumbo-size stores that range from 100,000 to 300,000 square feet. Typically, this retailing format is a combo-store operation that combines a large supermarket with a discount general-merchandise store. K mart's Super K mart and American Fare and Wal-Mart's Super Center Store and Hypermarket USA are excellent examples of this trend toward larger size operations.

Off-Price Retailers—Taking a Turn on the Wheel of Retailing

RETAIL STRATEGIES AND TACTICS

Having reached the mature stage of the retail life cycle, off-price retailers such as T. J. Maxx, Marshall's, and Ross Stores are finding that low prices alone are insufficient to attract and keep customers. As newer and lower-price-oriented retailers (e.g., warehouse clubs, superstores, and hypermarkets) enter the market, off-price retailers are feeling the squeeze. Additional stress is resulting from the promotional sales activities of department stores and the everyday-low-price strategy of many discount and chain stores. To become more competitive, off-price retailers are attempting to increase their customer appeal by expanding and enhancing their merchandising programs. Having been the innovators, they are now trying to differentiate themselves from other, more efficient price-oriented retail formats; in other words, they have entered the trading-up phase of the wheel of retailing.

Taking their turn on the wheel of retailing, off-price retailers are (1) departmentalizing their stores into natural product line groupings; (2) merchandising with brighter and more colorful visual displays, signs, and fixtures; (3) redesigning store layouts to facilitate customer movement and enhance shopping comfort; (4) offering store credit cards; (5) emphasizing customer service; (6) showcasing individual products in their advertisements; (7) becoming more fashion current by eliminating packaways; and (8) establishing more product lines and brands and offering them in complete assortments on a continuing basis. By riding the wheel of retailing, off-price retailers hope to differentiate themselves from emulators such as closeout discounters.

umbrella that the old-line institutions have hoisted."[77] The entry of a new low-price innovator into the retail market signals the end of one cycle and the beginning of a new, competitive cycle.

In practice, the theory of the wheel of retailing has been used to explain numerous changes in the institutional structure of U.S. retailing. In the food industry, the independent corner grocery store was largely replaced by the chain grocery store, which in turn became vulnerable to the competition of the supermarket operation. A second commonly cited example of the "wheel" concept is the emergence of the department store innovation as an alternative to the small specialty retailer and its subsequent vulnerability to discount retailers. Recently some discount retailers have progressed far enough into the trading-up phase that they are becoming vulnerable to discount warehouses, showroom operations, and off-price retailers.

Dialectic Process

The **dialectic process** is a "melting pot" theory of retail institutional change in which two substantially different competitive forms of retailing merge to form a new retailing format. Figure 2–22 illustrates the dialectic process: a thesis (the established institutional form), an antithesis (the innovative institutional form), and a synthesis (the new, combined form). Maronick and Walker describe the dynamics of the dialectic process as follows:

> In terms of retail institutions, the dialectic model implies that retailers mutually adapt in the face of competition from "opposites." Thus, when challenged by a competitor with a differential advantage, an established institution will adopt strategies and tactics in the direction of that advantage, thereby negating some of the innovator's attraction. The

innovator, meanwhile, does not remain unchanged. Rather, as McNair noted, the innovator over time tends to upgrade or otherwise modify products and institutions. In doing so, he moves toward the "negated" institution. As a result of the mutual adoptions, the two retailers gradually move together in terms of offerings, facilities, supplementary services, and prices. They thus become indistinguishable or at least quite similar and constitute a new retail institution, termed the synthesis. This new institution is then vulnerable to "negation" by new competitors as the dialectic process begins anew.[78]

Retail Accordion

The **retail accordion** theory, also known as the *general-specific-general process,* is based on the premise that the changing character of retail competition stems from strategies that alter the width (selection) of the merchandise mix.[79] Historically retail institutions have evolved from the general store (offering a wide variety of merchandise) to the specialty store (offering a limited variety of merchandise) back to the general store and so on. The term *accordion* suggests the alternating expansion and contraction of the retailer's merchandise mix. As Ralph Hower describes it in *The History of Macy's of New York,*

> Throughout the history of retail trade (as, indeed in all business evolution) there appears to be an alternating movement in the dominant method of conducting operations. One swing is toward the specialization of the function performed on the merchandise handled by the individual firm. The other is away from such specialization toward the integration of related activities under one management or the diversification of products handled by a single firm.[80]

Figure 2–23 provides one interpretation of the retail accordion.

Natural Selection

The concept of the "survival of the fittest" is the central theme in Darwin's theory of **natural selection**. Environmental suitability and adaptive behavior are necessary traits

FIGURE 2–23
The retail accordion theory

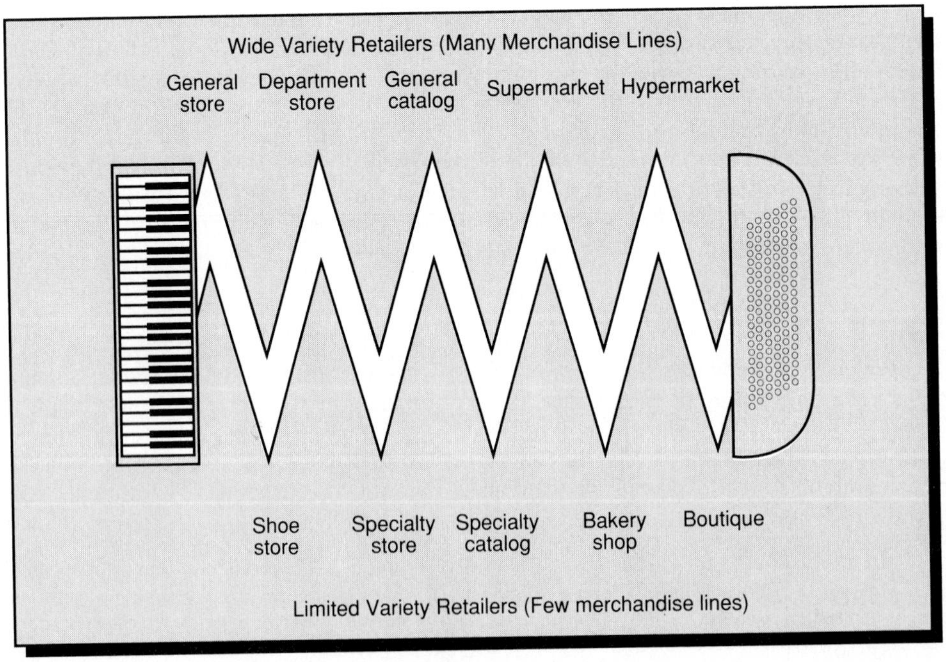

for the long-term survival of a species. The species most willing and able to adapt to changing environmental conditions is the one most likely to prosper and grow. An unwillingness or inability to change could result in stagnation or possible extinction of the species. As an economic species, competitive retailers are both willing and able to change and adapt to the environmental conditions under which they operate. The potential list of environmental conditions that might require adaptive behavior on the retailer's part is almost endless. In general terms, the dynamic environments of retailing include changes in the social, cultural, political, legal, technological, economical, and competitive structure of the marketplace. Required adaptations by retailers might include alterations in the product, price, place, and/or promotional mix offered to targeted consumers. Figure 2–24 identifies the various adaptive behaviors practiced by retailers during the 1980s.

Retail Life Cycle

The **retail life cycle** theory hypothesizes that all retail institutions pass through a series of four life stages: innovation, accelerated development, maturity, and decline. At each stage, retailers must be willing to adapt their merchandising efforts and operating methods to meet the environmental (e.g., consumer expectations, competitive actions, and economic conditions) circumstances of that stage. Both risks and opportunities exist at each stage; it is management's responsibility to reduce the risks and take advantage of the opportunities. Figure 2–25 identifies the basic circumstances found within each life cycle stage.

During the *innovation stage,* a technological, operational, and/or marketing innovation generally is the foundation for the origin of a new retailing institution. The jumbo size of the hypermarket and its food/general merchandise combination is one example of a retail institution in the innovation stage. Video catalogs, videotex, and other electronic retailing formats are also in this origination state of the retail life cycle.

FIGURE 2–24
Adaptive behaviors practiced by retail institutions during the 1980s

Behavior	Form	Example
Experimentation	Trying out the innovation in the retail mix on a small scale	Kroger's testing of self-service check-out scanners
Copycatism	Rapidly duplicating the successful innovation of another institution	The many newly emerging home shopping programs
Joint retailing	Combining two normally separate institutions under a single roof	7-Eleven outlets selling Kentucky Fried Chicken
Vertical integration	Taking over an added function performed either higher or lower in the channel	Benetton building U.S. factories; The Sharper Image opening retail stores
Horizontal integration	Acquiring control over similar retail institutions	Dillards of Little Rock acquiring Cain Sloan of Nashville
Physical premises mutation	Changing the normal locations or combinations of the institution	Off-price store cluster in strips and malls
Focused or Micromerchandising	Identifying a demographic/lifestyle segment, then creating a store for it	Waldenkids books; Gap Kids clothing

Source: Gary R. Brockway and Phillip B. Niffenegger, "Retailing Evolution in the 1980s: Survival Through Adaptive Behavior," *Journal of Midwest Marketing* 3 (Fall 1988): 5.

FIGURE 2–25
The retail life cycle

	Area or Subject of Concern	Stages in the Life Cycle			
		Innovation	Accelerated Development	Maturity	Decline
Market characteristics	Number of competitors	Very few	Moderate	Many direct competitors; moderate indirect competition	Moderate direct competition; many indirect competitors
	Rate of sales growth	Very rapid	Rapid	Moderate to slow	Slow or negative
	Level of profitability	Low to moderate	High	Moderate	Very low
	Duration of new innovations	3–5 years	5–8 years	Indefinite	Indefinite
Appropriate retail actions	Investment/ growth/risk decisions	Investment minimization, high risks accepted	High level of investment to sustain growth	Tightly controlled growth in untapped markets	Marginal capital expenditures and only when essential
	Central management concerns	Concept refinement through adjustment and experi- mentation	Establishing a preemptive market position	Excess capacity and "over- storing," prolonging maturity and revising the retail concept	Engaging in a "run-out" strategy
	Use of manage- ment control techniques	Minimal	Moderate	Extensive	Moderate
	Most successful management style	Entrepreneurial	Centralized	"Professional"	Caretaker

Source: Adapted from an exhibit in William R. Davidson, Albert D. Bates, and Stephen J. Bass, "The Retail Life Cycle," *Harvard Business Review* 54 (November-December 1976): 92. Reprinted with permission of the *Harvard Business Review*.

Customer acceptance, cost controls, profit margins, operational feasibility, and competitors' responses to these innovators will determine which institutions have a business format capable of carrying them into the growth stage of the life cycle.

During the *accelerated development stage,* sales increase rapidly and profits are high; to sustain the growth, however, the retailer must invest heavily in all aspects of the business. In an attempt to retain their status as growth institutions, specialty retailers (e.g., super specialists, niche specialists, and category killers) are opening new stores, refurbishing existing stores, altering merchandise mixes, upgrading service offerings, automating store operations, and developing better management controls. Closeout stores, home shopping networks, warehouse clubs, and catalog retailers are all growth retailers that are refining their merchandising and operating methods in an effort to sustain their growth.

The *maturity stage* involves increased competition, leveling sales, moderate profits, overstored markets, and more complex operational problems. Chain stores, department stores, and off-price retailers have all entered the maturity stage. The adaptive behavior of chain stores has been to develop their "store-within-a-store" concept to better target more profitable customer segments. Department stores are becoming more focused in their merchandising strategies and are enhancing their service offerings to better deal with the competitive challenge of specialty retailers. Off-price retailers are trading up by offering more services and sales assistance and improved store atmospherics. Video stores are coping with early maturity by developing the superstore concept typified by Blockbusters Video.[81] Extending the retail institution's mature life while retaining acceptable profitability levels is the key institutional goal during this stage of the life cycle.

Variety stores and conventional supermarkets entering the *decline stage* of the cycle are experiencing market share losses, marginal profitability, and an inability to compete. By finding small marginal and unserved markets (e.g., older strip centers, small towns, and decaying neighborhoods), declining institutions can survive for a while if they are willing to accept the weak profit performances of their outlets; the small general store still exists in sparsely populated areas.

SUMMARY

The retailer must operate in a very complex competitive environment. Retail competition can take one of several forms: intratype, intertype, vertical, and systems. Retailers also face different levels of competition as defined by the number, size, and quality of competitors.

The various types of retailing institutions are distinguishable on the basis of product line variety, organizational structure, price appeals, customer convenience, and many other criteria. Based on the variety of product lines offered and their organizational structure, retailers are classified as either specialty or department stores. Chain stores are multiunit retailers that use a high degree of centralization in their operations. The full-line discounter and off-price retailer emphasize price by offering nationally branded and designer merchandise at below-market prices. A major development in food retailing has been the supermarket with its emphasis on a complete, self-serve product offering. Time and place convenience distinguish the convenience store in its efforts to provide the "fill-in" and "emergency" needs of consumers. Some retailers try to formalize their relationships with suppliers and other retailers by entering a contractual arrangement. The retailer-sponsored cooperative group, the wholesaler-sponsored voluntary chain, the franchising organization, and the leased department are all examples of contractual retailing. Other retailers tend to stress a certain method of operation. Warehouse showrooms, catalog showrooms, and home centers use warehouse methods of operation. Superstores, such as supercenters and hypermarkets, are jumbo-size stores that offer a combination of food and general merchandise. At-home, mail-order, telephone, electronic, and vending machine retailing are nonstore retailers that attempt to serve potential customers where they live, work, and play.

Theoretically, retail institutions undergo certain competitive changes over time. Five theories that help to explain these competitive changes are the wheel of retailing, the dialectic process, the retail accordion theory, the theory of natural selection, and the retail life cycle theory.

STUDENT STUDY GUIDE

Key Terms and Concepts

at-home retailing (p. 68)
catalog showroom (p. 64)
category killer (p. 45)
chain store (p. 51)
closeout store (p. 57)
contractual retailing (p. 60)
convenience store (p. 60)
department store (p. 45)
dialectic process (p. 75)

electronic retailing (p. 69)
factory outlet (p. 57)
franchising (p. 61)
full-line discount store (p. 55)
home center (p. 64)
home shopping (p. 72)
hypermarket (p. 66)
independent (p. 57)
intertype competition (p. 38)
intratype competition (p. 38)
leased department (p. 63)
mail-order retailing (p. 68)
mini-department specialist (p. 45)
natural selection (p. 76)
niche specialist (p. 42)
nonstore retailing (p. 67)
off-price retailer (p. 57)
one-price retailer (p. 57)
retail accordion (p. 76)
retail life cycle (p. 77)
retailer-sponsored cooperative group (p. 60)
specialty store (p. 39)
supercenter (p. 66)
supermarket (p. 58)
super specialist (p. 42)
superstore retailing (p. 65)
systems competition (p. 39)
telemarketing (p. 71)
vending machine retailing (p. 72)
vertical competition (p. 39)
warehouse club (p. 64)
warehouse retailing (p. 64)
warehouse showroom (p. 64)
wheel of retailing (p. 72)
wholesaler-sponsored voluntary chain (p. 61)

Review Questions

1. Identify the four types of retail competition. Describe and provide two nontext examples of each type.
2. How are retailers classified? Identify the classification criteria and the types of retailers within each. Provide trade examples (e.g., Sears, Ace Hardware) of each type of retailer.
3. What distinguishes the specialty store from other forms of retailing? Describe the key merchandising strategies used by the various specialty retailers.
4. Develop a profile of the operational and merchandising strategies of department stores.
5. What are chain stores doing in response to the competitive threat of specialty retailers? Discuss their new competitive strategies.
6. Compare the merchandising tactics of the full-line discounter and the off-price retailer. How are they alike? How do they differ?
7. How are supermarkets attempting to offset the competitive threat posed by the fast-food industry? What other competitive merchandising trends is the supermarket industry currently using to be more competitive?
8. What is contractual retailing? Describe the four types of contractual retailer.
9. Describe the similarities and differences of the various types of warehouse retailer.
10. Profile the two types of superstore retailer.
11. What are the customer and retailer advantages and disadvantages of at-home shopping? Do the advantages and disadvantages vary with the form of at-home retailing?
12. Why do retailers use telephone retailing?
13. Outline the differences among the videotex, videodisc, and videolog methods of electronic retailing.
14. What is the basic premise of the wheel of retailing theory of institutional change? Characterize the three phases of the wheel.
15. What does the dialectic model of retail institutional change imply?
16. How does the concept of "survival of the fittest" describe the competitive conditions retailers face?
17. Describe the four stages of the retail life cycle.

Review Exam

True or False

_____ 1. Intertype competition exists between two or more retailers using different types of business formats to sell the same type of merchandise.

_____ 2. Specialty store retailers typically stock a limited variety of product lines with a limited assortment or selection within each line.

_____ 3. To appeal to both middle- and upper-income consumers, many department stores use two or three pricing points for most merchandise lines.

_____ 4. A local retail firm operates a hardware store, a drugstore, a sporting goods shop, and a supermarket; it is by definition a retailing chain.

_____ 5. A major reason why conventional discount stores sell name-brand merchandise at below-market prices is to enhance their discount image.

_____ 6. The hypermarket is a general-merchandise warehouse retailer that stocks and sells food products as well as a wide variety of hard and soft goods.

_____ 7. Videotex is an interactive electronic system in which data and graphics are transmitted from a computer network over telephone or cable lines and displayed on a subscriber's TV or computer terminal screen.

_____ 8. The basic premise of the retail accordion theory is that a retail institution facing competition will adopt strategies and tactics of the competition and eventually will become just like the competitors.

Multiple Choice

_____ 1. The best description of the market strategy aims of a specialty retailer is to serve
a. All consumers in one market
b. All consumers in many markets
c. Some consumers in many markets
d. Some consumers in one market
e. All consumers all the time

_____ 2. The advantages of a _____ store organization are that it allows functional (buying, selling) and merchandise (apparel, furniture, jewelry) specialization while gaining the economies of scale associated with larger retailing operations.
a. Franchised
b. Contractual
c. Warehouse
d. Departmentalized
e. Horizontal

_____ 3. A specialty retailer that sells mainly fashion apparel and other soft goods at discount prices significantly (20 to 60 percent) below regular retail prices is referred to as a(n)
a. Off-price retailer
b. Conventional discounter
c. Discount department store
d. Low-ball retailer
e. Fashion mart

_____ 4. In recent years, supermarkets have added nonfood lines such as prescription drugs, small appliances, linens, and housewares to their traditional product mix. This process is referred to as _____.
a. Trading up
b. Opening the door
c. Scrambling
d. Hit-and-miss merchandising
e. Trading out

_____ 5. The franchisor compensation method, which involves imposing an operating fee on the franchisee's gross sales, is called a(n)
a. Royalty
b. Rental fee
c. Management fee
d. Initial franchise fee
e. Service fee

_____ 6. The _____ approach to at-home retailing involves door-to-door sales and delivery calls at regular and predetermined time intervals.
a. Cold-canvass
b. Hot-pavement
c. Party plan
d. Back-door
e. Established-territory

_____ 7. When a retail institution is operating at gross margins substantially below the required gross margins of the more established retailers in the market, the retail institution is in the _____ phase of the wheel of retailing.
a. Trading-up
b. Trading-down
c. Entry
d. Vulnerability
e. Spoke

STUDENT APPLICATIONS MANUAL

Investigative Projects: Practice and Applications

1. Retail competition intensifies each year. Thus, more and more retailers are relying on price reductions to sustain sales volume. Having no unique differential advantage, me-too retailers are competing with one another to become the lowest-cost supplier of goods to the ultimate consumer. Conduct a search of the trade literature, and find the answer to these questions: (1) Why is retail competition increasing? Identify the major reasons or causes for this increase. (2) What methods are retailers using to avoid or lessen the effects of greater competition? (3) How are retailers differentiating themselves from their competitors?
2. Many upscale department stores are turning to private brands and labels to offset the inroads made by off-price retailers. Sears, on the other hand, is pursuing the opposite strategy. As a major private-label merchandiser of hard goods (e.g., Kenmore and Craftsman), Sears is now adding national brands of hard goods to its product mix to expand its market appeal. Evaluate this product strategy. Do you think

it is a good merchandising tactic? Explain and justify your answer.

3. Referring to the hypermarket format, the respected New York retail consultant, Arthur B. Britten, made the following statement: "I question whether people want to do their food shopping on the same trip that they do their clothes shopping." Do you agree with this statement? Why or why not? What merchandising tactics might the hypermarket use to overcome the objection raised by Mr. Britten?

4. To compete in today's dynamic retailing environment, specialty retailers in many product categories are considering upsizing their stores to "superstore" or "category killer" status. What are the advantages and disadvantages of upsizing? What market conditions would increase the likelihood of success? Describe any other conditions that would contribute to a successful upsizing of a specialty store.

Tactical Cases: Problems and Decisions

■ CASE 2–1

McDonald's: From the "Burger Wars" to the "Big Food Fight"*

The "burger wars" of the 1980s has grown into the "big food fight" of the 1990s. McDonald's, the unquestionable winner in terms of market share, battles with Burger King and Wendy's for the hamburger segment of the $70 billion fast-food market and is facing an even greater battle for a larger share of the $155 billion food service market. No longer content with reaping the spoils (increased market share) of the burger wars, McDonald's is in head-to-head competition with the giants of the packaged-food industry (Kraft, General Foods, Oscar Mayer, Campbell, etc.) for a bigger portion of the nation's $400 billion food market. At the same time, the struggle for market share among the various fast-food segments such as pizza (Domino's and Little Caesar's), chicken (Popeye's and Church's), and roast beef (Arby's and Roy Rogers') is intensifying. The strongest force in this intersegment conflict is "Pepsi Power"—PepsiCo's 1-2-3-punch strategy of aggressively expanding its Kentucky Fried Chicken, Pizza Hut, and Taco Bell restaurants. Additional intersegment competition is coming from midpriced, extended-menu eateries such as the Olive Garden, T.G.I. Friday, Chili's, Red Lobster, and Western Sizzler. The final element in this gastronomical battleground is a guerrilla force of supermarkets, convenience stores, delis, and gas stations that offer carryout meals and reheatable packaged foods.

What makes the "big food fight" of the 1990s a particularly grueling time for fast-food restaurateurs is the maze of marketing and operational problems that are an inherent part of the 1990s and the fast-food industry. Some of the most troublesome problems include:

- Competition: A glut of outlets (one restaurant for every 2,700 Americans), resulting in overcapacity and overstored conditions in many of the country's prime trading areas; adding to the problem are the 3,700 new outlets being built each year.
- Sales: Sales growth has slowed in the fast-food market from 7.1 percent in the 1970s to 4.9 percent in the 1980s to 3.0 percent in 1990.
- Profitability: Profit margins are being squeezed by increased costs of commodities (e.g., beef and chicken) and labor on the one hand and lower prices stemming from stiff competition on the other.
- Lifestyles: Frazzled dual-income couples under extreme time constraints prefer the conveniences of eating at home; they are becoming part of the "nuke-it" generation. (Note: microwave ovens are now in 75 percent of American households.)
- Concerns: Nutrition and health studies and reports have heightened public concern over the fat and sodium content of fast foods. Americans of all ages are into the wellness and fitness craze. Menu items high in fat, sodium, and cholesterol are inconsistent with this changing consumer behavior pattern.
- Operations: The shortfall in potential hamburger flippers is crucial in many areas. Labor shortages in low-end jobs are expected to continue throughout the 1990s. To obtain and retain employees will require considerable effort and cost in recruiting, training, motivating, and compensating new and old employees.
- Product: Niche marketing through product (menu) item proliferation by all of the fast-food chains (e.g., McRib by McDonald's, SuperBar by Wendy's, and Chicken International by Burger King) is making it difficult to be a limited-menu restaurant. On the other hand, an increase in product lines and items typically results in rising operations-related expenses.
- Price: The continuous use of consumer sales incentives (coupons, premiums, discounts, and special promotions) adds costs, lowers prices, and increases customer expectations.

Considering the competitive nature and the inherent problems of the fast-food industry, McDonald's is facing a difficult task in its efforts to retain its decade-long record of 15 percent annual compounded-earnings growth. To sustain growth, McDonald's has increasingly relied on overseas expansion in recent years. Today 25 percent of McDonald's restaurants are overseas; one of the more notable overseas outlets is the 900-seat restaurant in Moscow's Pushkin Square. Domestically the average number of customers per restaurant hasn't grown in the last five years; hence, sales growth has had to be achieved by offering new product lines, charging higher prices, and increasing average customer order size. The slowing of the domestic sales growth to 6 percent has some Mickey-D watchers concerned.

Operating on the belief that product line extensions are a necessary part of the overall program needed to meet its sales growth objectives, McDonald's has test-marketed a pizza line of 14-inch pies made with frozen dough and fresh toppings. McDonald's has developed a pizza oven that is capable of baking a pizza in 5½ minutes or in less than one-half the time it takes most ovens to bake a pizza. The eight-slice pizza can be ordered in four varieties (cheese, sausage, pepperoni, and deluxe) with a price range from $5.84 to $9.49. Pizza will be served after 4 P.M., a time when pizza has surpassed the hamburger as Americans' most popular evening meal. As one McDonald's executive says, "We can't be all things to all people, but we can be a few more things to a few more people every year."

ASSIGNMENT

1. What strategies might McDonald's use to effectively compete against the nonrestaurant segment (e.g., large packaged-goods companies) for the American food dollar?
2. How should McDonald's respond to each of the major problems facing the fast-food industry? How might McDonald's (1) reduce the squeeze of profit margins, (2) benefit from the trend to eat at home, (3) alleviate customer concerns regarding nutritional value of fast foods, (4) ensure an adequate labor supply in the future, (5) counter the competitive advantages achieved by competitors who are expanding their menus (especially the 1-2-3-punch strategy of Pepsi Power), and (6) retain its price competitiveness?
3. Evaluate McDonald's product line extension strategy of adding pizza to its menu. What are the strengths and weaknesses of the strategy? Will it be successful? Why or why not?

*This case was prepared by Dale Lewison and John Thanopoulos, The University of Akron.

Sources: Brian Bremner, "Fast-Food Joints Are Getting Fried," *Business Week,* January 8, 1990, 90; Ronald Henkoff, "Big Mac Attacks with Pizza," *Fortune,* February 26, 1990, 87–89; Brian Bremner and Gail DeGeorge, "The Burger Wars Were Just a Warmup for McDonald's," *Business Week,* May 8, 1989, 67–70; Brian Bremner, "Two Big Macs, Large Fries—and a Pepperoni-Pizza, Please," *Business Week,* August 7, 1989, 33; Stuart Elliott, "It's Eating Fast-Food Rivals' Lunch," *USA Today,* March 10, 1989, B-1; Richard Gibson, "McDonald's Makes a Fast Pitch to Pizza Buffs Who Hate to Wait," *The Wall Street Journal,* August 28, 1989, B-3.

■ CASE 2–2
Quinn's Department Store—Utilizing Leased Departments*

In his five years as president of Quinn's department stores, John Spalding had continued the local chain's successful strategy of catering to the upper-end consumer market with high-quality, distinctive merchandise, excellent service, and innovative product and marketing techniques. Sales growth at the flagship store downtown and the six branch stores in area shopping malls had been impressive under Spalding's leadership, attributable in part to his ability to identify and support profitable changes and innovations that maintained the stores' fashionable image and developed better ways to meet customer needs.

In this tradition, Spalding and other company executives recently had decided to add a new food department and accompanying "café" in the downtown store. Though many of the details had yet to be finalized, the plan called for the department to offer a variety of fancy, gourmet, and hard-to-find food and wine items, including many imported goods. Complementing this shop would be a delicatessen serving specialty salads and light meals for take-home or on-premise dining inside an open store "sidewalk café." The atmosphere of both the mini-grocery and café was planned to exude fashionable elegance and feature expensive fixtures, lighting, and displays.

Spalding was convinced the concept would work. A few department stores in other areas of the country had been successful with similar ventures, and Spalding felt that Quinn's customer base would be especially receptive to the new offering, particularly since no grocery retailers in the downtown area offered the type of foods Quinn's planned to carry. "This department will have great appeal to the upscale shoppers whom we serve, provide them with an extra service not currently available in our market area, and make Quinn's a more enjoyable and distinctive place to shop," Spalding had told upper management at a recent meeting.

But while there was general agreement among store executives that the new department was right for Quinn's, there was considerable difference of opinion as to whether the grocery and deli should be run entirely by company personnel or be created and managed by an outside operator on a lease basis. Leased departments have been used by retailers for many years, particularly by department stores in product areas such as shoes, jewelry, millinery, books, and photography. After a period of decline in the early 1980s, these leased departments have enjoyed a recent resurgence in popularity.

Under most lease agreements, customers are unable to distinguish leased departments from store-owned ones. These departments are, however, operated by the lessee, who is responsible for buying and pricing its merchandise, hiring its employees, and managing daily operations. In return for a monthly rental and/or a percentage of department sales, the leasing store typically provides services such as delivery, credit, payroll, accounting, utilities, and space lighting to the lessee. Many of these lessees are national companies that have departments in hundreds of stores, though some operate on a much smaller (regional or local) basis.

Alex Archwell, Quinn's vice-president of marketing, favored leasing the new department and already had conducted some preliminary discussions with a food retailer in a nearby city that operated several specialty food stores very similar in style and merchandise to that Quinn's was considering. Though this company had never before operated a leased department, its owner was enthusiastic about the prospect. "John, these people are just what we need to make a success of this thing," Archwell told his boss. "While I think the idea is great, what do we know about food retailing? For instance, I could see significant problems developing in inventory management. I think that leasing will enable us to provide the service we want as well as make a profit—with considerably less risk."

Jane Roberts, manager of the downtown store, disagreed. "Who knows, and can serve, our customers better than we can?" she asked. "Isn't that one of the reasons we have avoided any lease agreements in the past, such as in shoes or jewelry? Besides, I think the quality of our in-store management is one of the chief factors in Quinn's success, and putting outsiders in control of even one of our departments is asking for trouble."

John Spalding had always had great faith in the judgment of both Archwell and Roberts and recognized that each had raised important points with regard to the decision to lease or not lease the new department. He also realized that the new department's eventual success might well depend on the right decision regarding leasing. Earlier he had been so confident that the fancy-foods and sidewalk café idea would work in the main store that he already had thought about how long it would take before he could introduce similar departments in Quinn's branch stores. Now he realized he would have to take a closer look at the practice of leasing and its desirability for Quinn's fancy-foods department and café.

ASSIGNMENT

1. Assume John Spalding has asked you, a new Quinn's employee with college coursework in retailing, to help him analyze this situation. What do you see as the pros and cons of leased departments?
2. What decision would you recommend to Spalding for Quinn's fancy-foods department and sidewalk café? Justify your decision.
3. If Quinn's decides to lease the new department, what can management do in terms of its relationship with the lessee to help ensure the project's long-term success?

°This case was prepared by Dan Gilmore, The University of Akron.

ENDNOTES

1. See Stanley C. Hollander and Glenn S. Omura, "Retail Census Findings and Strategic Implications," *Retail Issues Letter* (Arthur Andersen & Co. in conjunction with the Center for Retailing Studies, Texas A&M University, February 1988), 1–3.
2. See Stephen Phillips and Michele Galen, "Can Allen Questrom Clean Up Campeau's Mess?", *Business Week,* February 19, 1990, 40; Larry Reibstein, "The Fall of a Retail Empire," *Newsweek,* January 22, 1990, 44; Eva Pomice, *U.S. News & World Report,* October 9, 1989, 39.
3. Penney Gill, "Department Stores: Finding a New Niche," *Stores,* February 1990, 17.
4. Christopher Power, Amy Dunkin and Laura Jereski, "Slugging It Out for Survival," *Business Week,* January 8, 1990, 32–33.
5. Avijit Ghost, "Customer Service: The Key to Successful Retailing," *The Channel of Communication* 3 (Winter 1988): 1.
6. Joseph Barry Mason, "Redefining Excellence in Retailing," *Journal of Retailing* 62 (Summer 1986): 115.
7. Amy Dunkin and Michael Oneal, "Power Retailers," *Business Week,* December 21, 1987, 86–89, 92.
8. Denise Gallagher, "Tabletop Shops," *Stores,* February 1989, 39.
9. See Denise Gallagher, "Hot Socks Shops!" *Stores,* May 1989, 45–50.
10. See Juriel J. Adams, "Kids' Specialty Retailing," *Stores,* March 1990, 18–19, 23–24.
11. See "Do All Category Killers Succeed?", *Chain Store Age Executive,* March 1990, 88.
12. See Gail deGeorge, "The Video King Who Won't Hit 'Pause'," *Business Week,* January 22, 1990, 47–48.
13. See Renee Rouland, "Today's Man: Off-Price Superstores," *Discount Merchandiser,* March 1990, 45–47.
14. See Jennifer Pellet, "At Sports Authority: 40,000 SKUs," *Discount Merchandiser,* August 1989, 88–92.
15. See Susan Caminiti, "Seeking Big Money in Paper and Pens," *Fortune,* July 31, 1989, 173–174.
16. See David Churbuck, "Attention PC Shoppers!", *Forbes,* March 5, 1990, 128–129.
17. Jacquelyn Bivins, "Superstore Retailing, Bigger Formats for Smaller Stores," *Stores,* July 1989, 46.
18. See Jacquelyn Bivins, "One-Price Clothing Stores," *Stores,* October 1989, 39–42.
19. See Mary Krienke, "Men's Wear in London," *Stores,* October 1989, 27–34.
20. Penney Gill, "What's a Department Store?", *Stores,* February 1990, 8.
21. See Amy Dunkin and Chuck Hawkins, "Breathing Easier," *Business Week,* October 2, 1989, 28.
22. Gill, "What's a Department Store?", 8.
23. Joseph B. Siegel, "Retailing: Back to Fundamentals," *Retail Control,* February 1990, 24.
24. Francine Schwadel, "As Retailing's Chic and Indebted Stumble, Bland May Co. Thrives," *The Wall Street Journal,* January 19, 1990, A1, A5.
25. Gill, "What's a Department Store?", 9.

26. Gail Hutchinson Kirby and Rachel Dardis, "Research Note: A Pricing Study of Women's Apparel in Off-Price and Department Stores," *Journal of Retailing* 62 (Fall 1986): 329.
27. See Susan Caminiti, "What Ails Retailing," *Fortune*, January 30, 1989, 61–64; Stanley J. Winkleman, "Why Big-Name Stores Are Losing Out," *Fortune*, January 16, 1989, 131–132.
28. Gill, "Department Stores: Finding a New Niche," 17.
29. Anthony Ramirez, "Department Stores Shape Up," *Fortune*, September 1, 1986, 51–52.
30. See Monica Roman, "Another Swan Dive for Profits," *Business Week*, March 19, 1990, 64.
31. Brian Bremner, "The Big Stores' Big Trauma," *Business Week*, July 10, 1989, 50.
32. James E. Ellis, Brian Bremner, and Michael Oneal, "Will the Big Markdown Get the Big Store Moving Again?", *Business Week*, March 13, 1989, 110.
33. Amy Dunkin and Brian Bremner, "The Newly Minted Penney: Where Fashion Rules," *Business Week*, April 17, 1989, 88.
34. See David P. Schulz, "What the Giants Are Up To," *Stores*, July 1989, 26.
35. Brian Bremner, "Bernie Brennan Has Last Laugh at Ward's," *Business Week*, January 15, 1990, 70.
36. Jacques DeLors, "Attention, K mart Shoppers," *Fortune*, January 2, 1989, 41.
37. David Woodruff, "Will K mart Ever Be a Silk Purse?", *Business Week*, January 22, 1990, 46.
38. "Off-Pricers Grab Growing Retail Market Share," *Marketing News*, March 3, 1987, 9, 14.
39. Ibid.
40. See Michael Selz, "Consolidated Stores Discovers Bigger Isn't Always Better," *The Wall Street Journal*, January 18, 1990, B-2.
41. Jacquelyn Bivins, "One-Price Clothing Stores," 39–42.
42. "There's One for All," *Advertising Age*, October 1983, M11; *Competitive Edge* (Barrington, Ill.: Willard Bishop Consulting Economists, June 1983).
43. See Walter Heller, "Supermarkets 2000, 45 'Insider' Predictions," *Progressive Grocer*, January 1990, 28.
44. John Freeh, "Supermarkets Find New Ways to Lure More Shoppers," *Cleveland Plain Dealer*, April 1, 1990, 1-E.
45. See Ronald Grover, "How Two Big Grocers Are Bringing Home the Bacon," *Business Week*, April 24, 1989, 141–143.
46. See Cynthia Crossen, "Putting Plastic on the Check-out Lanes: More Supermarkets Accept Credit Cards," *The Wall Street Journal*, February 5, 1990, B-1.
47. U.S. Department of Commerce, *Franchise Opportunities Handbook* (Washington, D.C.: U.S. Government Printing Office, November 1986): XXIX.
48. See "Why Franchising Is Taking Off," *Fortune*, February 12, 1990, 124.
49. Louis W. Stern and Adell I. El-Ansary, *Marketing Channels* (Englewood Cliffs, N.J.: Prentice-Hall, 1988), 341.
50. Christine Forbes, "The Franchise Forecast," *Entrepreneur*, April 1990, 124.
51. "Alliances Yield Mutual Gain," *Chain Store Age Executive*, January 1990, 33.
52. This description of warehouse clubs is based on Jack G. Kaikati, "The Boom in Warehouse Clubs," *Business Horizons* (March-April 1987): 68–73.
53. Ken Partch and Leo J. Shapiro, "What Makes Price Clubs Fly?", *Supermarket Business*, May 1989, 24.
54. Bivins, "Superstore Retailing," 40.
55. "'Shop-Til-You-Drop' Theme Killing Most Hypermarkets," *Cleveland Plain Dealer*, April 1, 1990, 4-E.
56. Bivins, "Superstore Retailing," 43.
57. See Steve Weinstein, "The Hypermarket Jury Is Still Out," *Progressive Grocer*, January 1990, 68–74.
58. Diana Fong, "Cherchez la Store," *Forbes*, January 9, 1989, 311–314.
59. Christy Fisher and Patricia Strned, "Wal-Mart Pulls Back on Hypermarket Plans," *Advertising Age*, February 19, 1990, 49.
60. " 'Shop-Til-You-Drop', 4–E."
61. Jean C. Darian. "In-Home Shopping: Are There Consumer Segments?", *Journal of Retailing* 63 (Summer 1987): 163–186.
62. See Kathleen Deveny, "Can Avon Get Wall Street to Answer the Door?", *Business Week*, March 20, 1989, 124.
63. "Spiegel, Inc.," *Barron's*, August 14, 1989, 102.
64. Rayna Skolnik, "Selling via Catalog," *Stores*, October 1989, 52.
65. "Videotex: What It's All About," *Marketing News*, November 1983, 16.
66. See Gary Robins, "On-Line Service Update," *Stores*, February 1990, 24–31.
67. Subrata N. Chakravarty and Evan McGlinn, "This Thing Has to Change People's Habits," *Forbes*, June 26, 1989, 118–119.
68. Stern and El-Ansary, *Marketing Channels*, 81.
69. JoAn Paganetti, "High-Tech Ads Gleam to Service with a Smile," *Advertising Age*, July 25, 1983, M24.
70. Wayne Walley, "Home Shopping Moves onto Tape," *Advertising Age*, November 16, 1987, 76.
71. Stern and El-Ansary, *Marketing Channels*, 81.
72. Betsy Lammerding, "Shopping by TV a Big Turn-On for Many Buyers," *Akron Beacon Journal*, January 25, 1987, A-1, A-15.
73. Jules Abend, "Electronic Selling," *Stores*, November 1986, 23.
74. Malcolm P. McNair, "Significant Trends and Developments in Post War Period," in *Competitive Distribution in a Free, High-Level Economy, and Its Implications for the Universities*, ed. A. B. Smith (Pittsburgh: University of Pittsburgh Press, 1958), 18.
75. Arieh Goldman, "The Role of Trading-Up in the Development of the Retailing System," *Journal of Marketing* 39 (January 1975): 54–62.
76. Arieh Goldman, "Institutional Changes in Retailing: An Updated 'Wheel of Retailing' Theory," in *Foundations of Marketing Channels*, ed. A. G. Woodside,

J. T. Sims, D. M. Lewison, and I. F. Wilkinson (Austin, Tex.: Lone Star, 1978), 193.
77. McNair, "Significant Trends and Developments," 18.
78. Thomas J. Maronick and Bruce J. Walker, "The Dialectic Evolution of Retailing," in *Proceedings: Southern Marketing Association,* ed. Burnett Greenburg (1974), 147.
79. See Stanley C. Hollander, "Notes on the Retail Accordion," *Journal of Retailing* 42 (Summer 1966): 20–40, 54.
80. Ralph Hower, *The History of Macy's of New York, 1858–1919* (Cambridge, Mass.: Harvard University Press, 1943), 73.
81. See Peter Newcomb, "Can Video Stores Survive?", *Forbes,* February 5, 1990, 39–41. See also Pete Engardio and Antonio N. Fins, "Will This Video Chain Stay on Fast-Forward?", *Business Week,* June 12, 1989, 72, 75; Gail DeGeorge, "The Video King Who Won't Hit 'Pause,'" *Business Week,* January 22, 1990, 47–48.

PART I

CHAPTER 3

THE BUYING BEHAVIOR OF CONSUMERS

OUTLINE

THE MARKET
- Structure of Buying Populations
- Nature of Buying Behavior

CONSUMER MARKETS

POPULATION ANALYSIS

DEMOGRAPHIC ANALYSIS
- The Aging Population
- The Shrinking Household
- The Working Woman
- The Diversified Minorities

GEOGRAPHIC ANALYSIS
- Regional Markets
- Metro Geography
- Nonmetro Geography

CONSUMER BUYING BEHAVIOR

BUYING CONSIDERATIONS
- Product Tangibility
- Product Durability
- Product Availability

BUYING SITUATIONS
- Consumer Population
- Consumer Requirements
- Consumer Potential

BUYING CENTERS

BUYING INFLUENCES
- Psychological Factors
- Personal Factors
- Social Factors

THE CONSUMER BUYING PROCESS
- Stage 1: Problem Recognition
- Stage 2: Information Search
- Stage 3: Alternative Evaluation
- Stage 4: Purchase Decision
- Stage 5: Postpurchase Evaluation

BUYING SCENES

OBJECTIVES

- Delineate the structure of buying populations and the nature of buying behavior.
- Identify and explain U.S. population trends.
- Describe the major demographic trends and their impact on retailing practices.
- Discuss the major geographic population patterns and their effect on retailing strategies.
- Understand the concepts of product tangibility, durability, and availability and their impact on consumer buying behavior.
- Explain the concept of market potential and discuss the elements of the market potential equation.
- Describe the psychological, personal, and social factors that influence consumer buying behavior.
- Outline and discuss the five stages of the consumer buying process.

BACK TO THE FUTURE

If there is a secular religion in the U.S., a case can be made that its name is Growth. For as long as any of us can remember, this country has equated growth with progress . . . But now it's over. The single most important finding of the 1990 census [was] a population growth rate of less than 1% a year and a rate of new household formation under 2% a year—the slowest growth rate since the Great Depression.[1]

The shrinking of consumer and household markets is expected to continue through the 1990s. This lack of market growth has effectively ended the mass market concept as retailers scramble for market share. "America is no longer a melting pot. It's a mosaic."[2]

The diffusion of the American mass market has created a more fractionalized marketplace. The market has become a multitude of customer segments; each segment is "an individual entity endowed with its own uniqueness screaming for recognition of its needs. And, unfortunately or fortunately, the needs and wants of these segments are constantly shifting, creating . . . opportunities."[3] For most retailers, success in the future will require that they return to the philosophy that "the customer is king (or queen"). "As the gospel of customer focus spreads, more companies will try to convince employees, investors, and themselves that the customer really does come first."[4]

The consumer marketplace is the battleground for the recognition, acceptance, and adoption of various merchandising programs offered by competing retailers. An understanding of consumers and their behavior is essential to any successful marketing effort. After studying this chapter, you will have a deeper appreciation for the terrain on which the battle for profitable sales rages. More importantly, you will acquire the information vital to developing a viable retailing plan and waging a successful merchandising campaign.

THE MARKET

Fundamental to an understanding of the marketplace and its behavior is a definition of a market. The term *market* can be used in conjunction with a variety of places (a farmers' market or a trade show), products (the bond or housing market), levels (the wholesale or retail market), and activities (marketing a good or a service). In this text, however, the term *market* has a precise meaning and usage. As Figure 3–1 shows, a **market** is a group of actual and potential buyers at a given time and place whose actions lead to an exchange of goods and services or create the potential for an exchange process. In essence, a market is a buying population and its corresponding buying behavior. An appreciation of the concept of a market requires an understanding of both the structure of buying populations and the nature of their buying behavior.

Structure of Buying Populations

Buying populations can be classified into one of two groups—consumer markets and organizational markets. **Consumer markets** are composed of individuals and/or households who are the ultimate consumers of goods and services. **Organizational markets** consist of industrial firms, resellers, and governments that represent intermediate consumers of goods and services. This market accounts for the nonretail sales made by retailers. This chapter deals exclusively with consumer markets and their

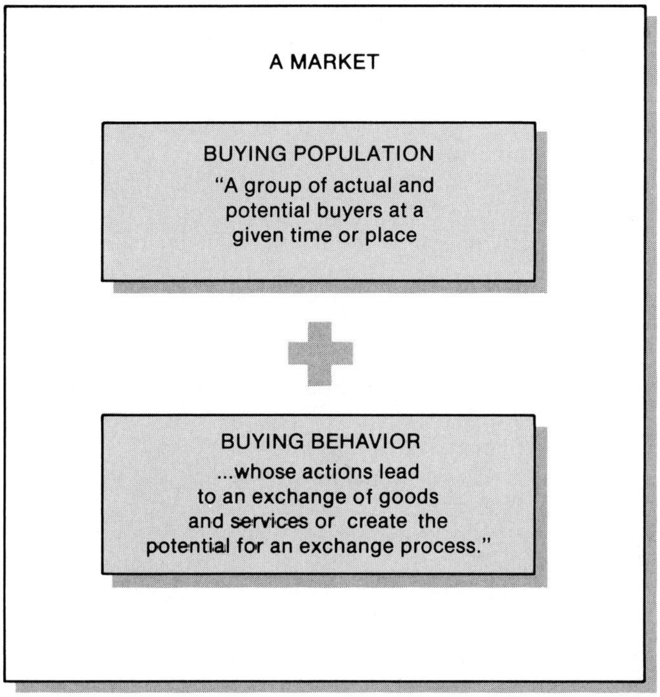
A MARKET
BUYING POPULATION
"A group of actual and potential buyers at a given time or place
BUYING BEHAVIOR
...whose actions lead to an exchange of goods and services or create the potential for an exchange process."

FIGURE 3–1
Definition

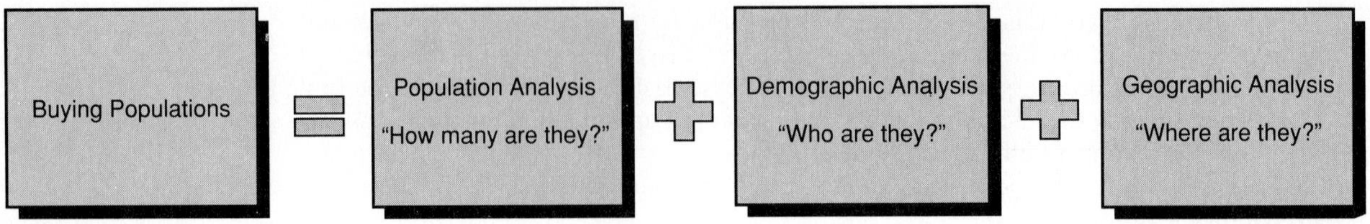

FIGURE 3–2
The structure of buying populations

impact on retail decisions. Regardless of consumer type, the structure of buying populations, as Figure 3–2 shows, needs to be examined in terms of "how many are they" (population analysis), "who are they" (demographic analysis), and "where are they" (geographic analysis).

Nature of Buying Behavior

The second part of the market equation (see Figure 3–1) is buying behavior. Buyers act in a variety of ways when faced with a market situation that requires a purchase decision. The nature of buying behavior involves a number of issues. An analysis of **buying behavior** is directed at answering the questions of "what buyers buy," "how much buyers buy," "who does the buying," "why buyers buy," "how buyers buy," and "where buyers buy" (see Figure 3–3).

The remainder of this chapter is devoted to the structure of consumer markets (population, demographic, and geographic analysis) and the nature of consumer buying behavior (what, how much, who, why, how, and where buyers buy).

CONSUMER MARKETS

The consumer market is made up of ultimate consumers. Who are they? **Ultimate consumers** are individuals who purchase goods and services for their own personal use or for use by members of their households. The purchase intent of an ultimate consumer is to consume the utility of a product. As discussed in Chapter 1, sales to the ultimate consumer represent retail sales transacted by retailers, service firms, and, to a lesser extent, wholesalers and other organizations.

POPULATION ANALYSIS

In this section, we will examine the question "How many ultimate consumers are there?" The actual and potential market for any particular product is determined in part by **total population**—the total number of persons residing within an area at a given time. The total population of the United States grew from 227 million in 1980 to 250 million in 1990; this population increase represents an annual growth rate of less than 1 percent.[5] An area's total population is determined by relationships between birthrates and deathrates and immigration and emigration rates. As Figure 3–4 illustrates, births and immigration are net contributors to an area's population while deaths and emigration reduce total population. "America has a long heritage of welcoming immigrants, and throughout its history, the country has been reshaped and renewed by the talents, energy, and enterprise of those new citizens. They may prove to be a crucial advantage in the global economic competition of the 1990's."[6]

The ebb and flow of U.S. population growth has and will continue to have profound merchandising implications. As each new population wave breaks over the retailing system, new target market opportunities emerge that require continuous and innovative adjustments. Retailers react to these population changes by (1) altering the width and depth of their product lines, (2) adjusting the amount and location of display space devoted to a particular product item, (3) changing the type and amount of promotional support used to enhance sales of certain products, and (4) adapting product line pricing points to current market expectations.

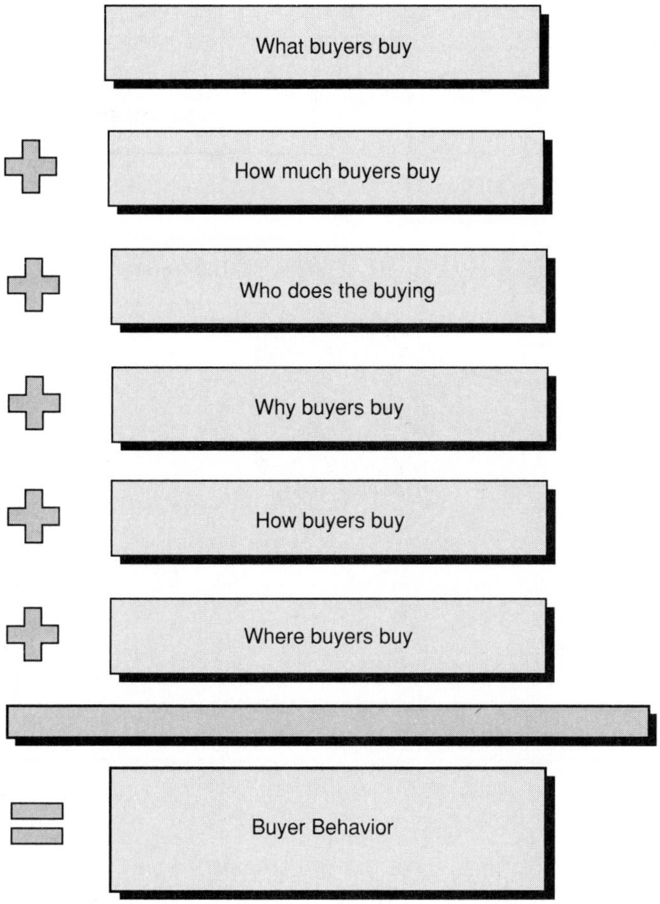

FIGURE 3–3
The nature of buying behavior

DEMOGRAPHIC ANALYSIS

Who is the "average American" or the "typical American family"? In past years, reasonably descriptive profiles were possible. Today, under novel family, marriage, living, and working arrangements, the average or typical profile is considerably less representative of the population as a whole. This section addresses the question of who the ultimate consumers are in terms of their demographic makeup. **Demography** is the study of statistics used to describe a population. Each person can be characterized in terms of age, sex, education, income, occupation, race, nationality, family size, and family structure. These individual characteristics can be aggregated into relatively homogeneous profiles of population groupings that represent consumer market segments and the opportunity to tailor a firm's marketing efforts to one or more of these segments (see Figure 3–5).

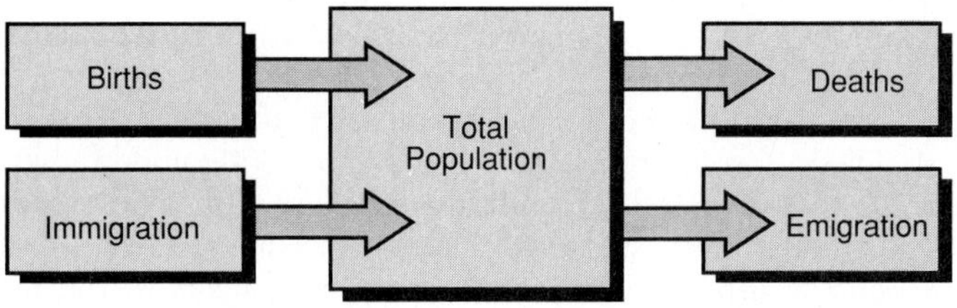

FIGURE 3–4
Determinants of total population

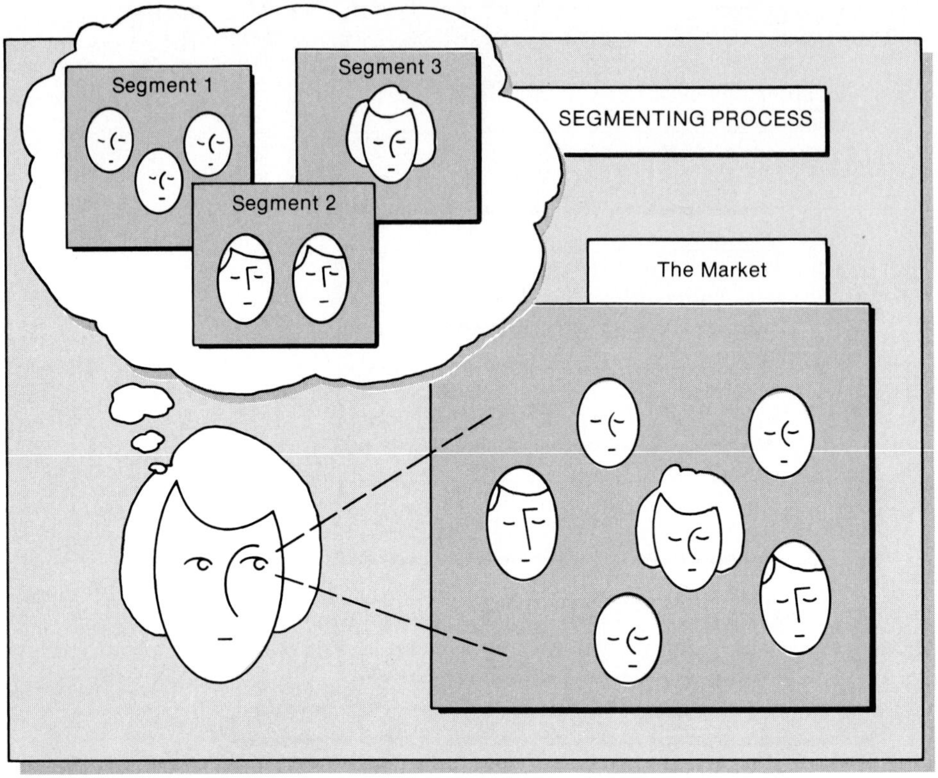

FIGURE 3–5
The market segmentation view of the total market

In the following discussion, we will examine some of the more pronounced historical shifts in the demographic makeup of the U.S. population and the changes in marketing strategies and tactics that were required to accommodate those shifts. Although we will treat demographic shifts individually, you should be aware that all or most of these changes are interrelated. Future demographic trends and their potential impact on retailers in the 1990s are discussed in Chapter 19.

The Aging Population

The American population has aged as a result of a declining fertility rate and an increasing life expectancy. Consumer markets in the 1990s will be reshaped by the same baby boom generation that has had such a profound effect on marketing strategies for the last 30 years. It is the age group that created the 1950s infant market, the 1960s teenage market, the 1970s young adult market, and the 1980s middle-aged market. Figure 3–6 depicts the realignment of the nation's population by age group.

As Figure 3–6 shows, the **youth market** (age 17 and under) is in the process of registering a notable 7.63 percent decrease, from 34.11 to 26.48 percent of the total U.S. population. Although this decline has signaled a deemphasis in the youth-oriented marketing that has held center stage since World War II, the absolute size of this age group (approximately one-fourth of the population) still makes it a formidable retail market.

The importance of the youth market to most retailers is threefold. First, older youths have billions of dollars for discretionary spending on both nondurable and durable goods. Important teen-oriented expenditures include fast foods, sporting equipment, casual clothing, audio and visual entertainment products, soft drinks, and personal accessories. Second, youths of all ages are major influencers of the buying behavior of their parents. They play an important role in deciding what products and brands are purchased, as well as when and where purchases are made. Finally, youths are increasingly becoming the purchasing agent for the family as more and more mothers enter the work force. In this role, they make decisions as to what to buy and from whom to buy.[7]

The coming of age of the baby boom generation is reflected in the significant growth of the **young-adults market** (ages 18 to 34—see Figure 3–6). Within this age group, the older half (ages 25 to 34) accounts for most of the growth. Some demographers have painted a somewhat bleak picture for these tail-ended members of the baby boom. With entry- and lower-level employment positions bulging with earlier baby boomers, these later cohorts are experiencing difficulties in satisfying career aspirations. The demand for housing will continue to increase for both the single-family homes and apartments that cater to the growing number of single-adult, one-child, and childless households. Smaller domiciles and limited incomes suggest that in the future, successful merchandising to this group will require smaller, multipurpose appliances, do-it-yourself products, and durable household furnishings.

As Figure 3–6 shows, a modest increase (from 31.28 to 33.75 percent of the total U.S. population) has characterized the growth pattern for the **middle-aged market** (ages 35 to 64). Early middle-agers (ages 35 to 44) typically are characterized as a higher-income, free-spending group whose purchase motives are directed more at quality, durability, and variety. Today's late middle-agers (ages 45 to 64) comprise a large number of empty-nest families wherein the parents feel free to spend on themselves and seem less intent on leaving an estate for their offspring. This group has the highest household net worth of any age group (almost $75,000).[8] In general, consumers in their middle years will heighten demand for entertainment, travel,

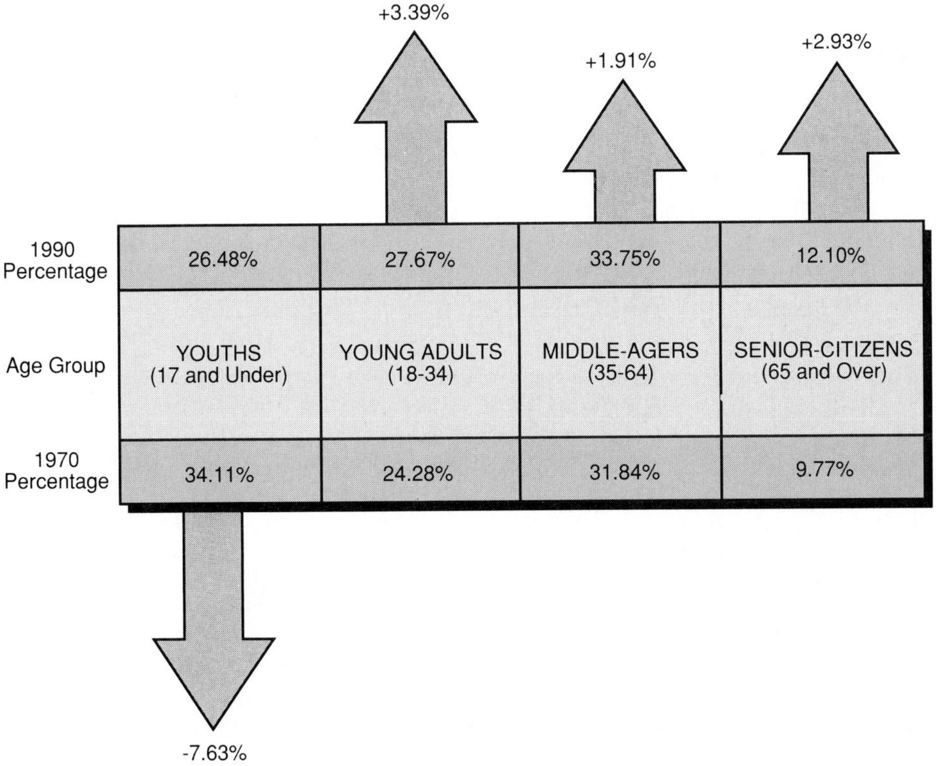

FIGURE 3–6
Percentage change in total population by age group, 1970–1990 (source: U.S. Bureau of the Census. *Projections of the Population of the U.S., 1977 to 2050* [Washington, D.C.: U.S. Government Printing Office])

recreation, adult education, and other convenience- and experience-oriented goods and services.

The **senior-citizens market** has increased notably (see Figure 3–6). Marketers should also note that the market potential of the upper end of the senior-citizens market will be significantly greater in the future. The senior-citizen market has changed drastically in recent years. Because people are living longer—an expected life span of 20 to 25 years following retirement—they face a wide variety of buying concerns. Age-based merchandising strategies often are inappropriate, because it is usually a mistake to sell products to older people by telling them the products are designed for the elderly (e.g., 40-Plus Bran Flakes): "Marketers should avoid age typing products in their messages."[9] Consumer research shows that "older buyers see themselves as ten to fifteen years younger than their chronological years."[10] Mature consumers often are more interested in collecting experiences (e.g., travel) than products.[11] A more effective strategy is to sell product benefits that fit the interests and aspirations of this age group. In product and service lines such as food, housing, clothing, transportation, health care, personal care, and recreation, senior citizens' share of the market is greater than that suggested by their numbers.

The Shrinking Household

While the total number of households increased dramatically over the last two decades, the size of each individual household shrank. The average American today lives with fewer people; average household size has decreased to fewer than three people. Americans have fewer children and are less likely to live with a member of the extended family than in past years.[12] Figure 3–7 reveals the changing structure of the shrinking household. Because a major portion of this changing household makeup is associated with the middle-age groups of 35-to-44- and 45-to-54-year-olds, there is a strong underpinning for booming retail sales in household goods and services. Typically these middle-agers are the most lavish spenders; they spend 27 percent more on goods and services than the average domicile. Some of the more direct merchandising impacts of the shrinking household lie with product design and packaging. The adage "bigger is better" is an inappropriate strategy for accommodating this demographic trend.

The Working Woman

Merchandising strategies that cater to working women will become increasingly important during the next several decades. The participation rate of women in the nation's work force has increased dramatically since the post–World War II period; over 60 percent of women over age 18 now work outside the home.[13] The changing

FIGURE 3–7
Changing mix of household types, 1970–1990

Household Type	Year (%) 1970	1990
Family type	81.2	70.1
Husband and Wife	70.6	55.7
Male, no wife	1.9	2.2
Female, no husband	8.7	12.2
Nonfamily type	18.8	29.9
Male	6.4	13.6
Female	12.4	16.3

Source: U.S. Bureau of the Census, *Projections of the Number of Households and Families, 1979 to 1995*, Series P-25, No. 805 (Washington, D.C.: U.S. Government Printing Office).

needs and roles of working women have had a major impact on women's buying behavior. Let's examine the buying behavior of working women by viewing them in their role as a working partner, a head of household, and a working person.

As an equal working partner within a marriage, the "work wife" has shed the stereotypical role of the chief purchasing agent for most of the family's household needs. Today a teamwork trend is emerging wherein the wife and husband share the responsibilities for the decisions about and procurement of household requirements. "Businesses will increasingly find themselves faced with the converged attitudes, expectations, and buying habits of a more androgenous male/female."[14] For the retailer, this shared purchasing behavior requires targeting the products, prices, promotions, and distribution channels toward the team rather than toward the individual spouse.

As the head of a single, separated, widowed, or divorced household, the working woman has become the decision maker and procurer of both traditional household purchases and nontraditional purchases of goods and services. For example, in her role as head of household, the working woman is becoming an increasingly important consideration in the marketing of homes (apartments, condominiums, and houses); financial services (banking, investment, and retirement programs); and professional services (law, tax, and insurance). With more female heads-of-household in the workplace, the traditional distinction between female-dominated purchases (i.e., food and clothing) and male-dominated purchases (i.e., investment and insurance) is fading rapidly.

Employee responsibilities and employer expectations are an integral part of any job. In an attempt to meet these responsibilities and expectations, the product-service needs and the buying behavior of working women have undergone dynamic changes. As an illustration, the professional woman requires a wardrobe that is sufficient in size for and consistent in character with her profession. In contrast with the homemaker who is a "special-occasion" buyer of "better dresses and suits," the professional woman must make such purchases on a regular and frequent basis. As such, she tends to be a "wardrobe builder" in that she considers each new clothing purchase in terms of how well it can be integrated into her current wardrobe. The professional woman also needs tools of the trade such as a briefcase, an appointment book, a tape recorder, recordkeeping ledgers, or a home personal computer.

The Diversified Minorities

The post–World War II mass market "has shattered into millions of pieces. The mythological homogeneous America is gone. We are a mosaic of minorities."[15] The concept that the United States is one large "melting pot" wherein all ethnic groups are assimilated into the American culture is an inappropriate and inoperative assumption for the retailer. Not only are there nonassimilated geographic concentrations of ethnic minorities (e.g., Hispanics in Miami and Los Angeles) within each of the major minority markets (Hispanic and Black Americans); there are also numerous market segments. As in many other American markets, success in reaching minority markets requires market segmentation and tailoring of the firm's retailing mix. One writer notes, "Penney's Hispanic TV commercials bear little resemblance to their general market counterparts. The English-language spots tend to be fast-paced and contemporary, often show just one individual. The Hispanic spots always focus on the family—usually the extended family."[16] Mass-marketing strategies will find limited application in appealing to most minority markets: "What 'minority' consumers respond to most eagerly is a level of respect—targeted advertising, bilingual salespeople, and special events all help to break down barriers. But their long-term value is to confirm for minorities that they are welcome and valued not just as consumers, but as people—and as Americans."[17]

The major trend characterizing minority markets is their growth in both number and income. Ethnic minority groups have increased faster than the population as a whole, and the annual income for these market segments doubled between 1980 and 1990. In addition to demographic diversity, minority groups show considerable variance in their lifestyles as defined by the activities they engage in, their interests, and their opinions.

GEOGRAPHIC ANALYSIS

Americans have tended to be a very mobile society: Approximately one American in five moves every year. However, the mobility of the American consumer is becoming more restricted; with both spouses working, it is harder to find and time two-career moves than it was to accommodate a single career change.[18] Nevertheless, a necessary part of any successful marketing program is the identification of current geographic population patterns and future shifts in those trends. In this section, we will examine where consumers are today and where they will be tomorrow.

Regional Markets

The dimensions of a market area are defined by several factors. One of the most important is *population density*—the number of persons living within a delineated geographic area. By knowing how many people occupy an area, the retailer has one major element in the equation for determining the area's consumption potential. According to the Bureau of the Census, one-third of the nation's population now lives in the South. The second largest concentration of population—26 percent—is in the North Central region. Following in order of size of population are the Northeast region (21.6 percent) and the West (19 percent). Of the ten largest states, three are in the Northeast (New York, Pennsylvania, and New Jersey), three are in the North Central region (Illinois, Ohio, and Michigan), three are in the South (Texas, Florida, and North Carolina), and one is in the West (California). Conversely, one-half of the least populated states are in the West (Idaho, Nevada, Montana, Wyoming, and Alaska). Judging from these patterns, it appears that the previous population dominance of the Northeast/Great Lakes manufacturing belt has been replaced by a somewhat more even regional distribution of population.

If the adage "retailers follow markets" is true, retailers are shifting their attention toward the West and South. The ten fastest-growing states (percentage change) are in the West (Nevada, Arizona, Wyoming, Utah, Alaska, Idaho, Colorado, and New Mexico) and the South (Florida and Texas). A similar trend is evident when we view population change in terms of absolute numbers of people. California, Texas, and Florida are the most powerful population magnets. Other major absolute population gainers include Arizona, Georgia, North Carolina, Washington, Virginia, Colorado, and Tennessee.

What do these population shifts mean to the retailer? Regional differences stimulate new expenditure patterns. Different climates, lifestyles, and customs necessitate modification of existing merchandising programs and development of new retailing strategies. From the more formal lifestyles of the Northeast to the informality of the West, from the rigorous climates of the North to the moderate environs of the South, from southern fried chicken to New England boiled lobster, the retailer faces different customer expectations requiring different marketing tactics.

Metro Geography

America is an urbanized society; 75 percent of the nation's population lives within one of the 318 metropolitan areas. This is almost a complete reversal from 1880, when three out of four Americans lived in largely rural areas. Metro-area residents are of two types: urbanites who dwell in the central cities and suburbanites who live in the suburbs surrounding the core city. The suburbs have continued to dominate the population growth pattern of the metro areas. While the percentage increase for all metropolitan areas registered approximately 10 percent, suburbanites increased 18 percent and gains in central-city populace were almost stagnant at 0.1 percent.

Nonmetro Geography

Nonmetro markets consist of the many small hamlets, villages, and towns that dot the nation's countryside together with the rural farm areas. Since 1800 the population of nonmetro areas has been declining, largely as a result of migration to the metropolitan areas. During the last two decades, however, the migration process reversed itself as nonmetro markets experienced both a population growth and a net in-migration.[19]

In the migrational interchange of population between metro and nonmetro markets, the nonmetro areas experienced a net gain. A number of reasons for this turnabout have been cited. Nonmetro areas appear to be attracting population because of (1) more casual lifestyles, (2) greater opportunities for outdoor experiences, (3) a more leisurely living pace, (4) a lower cost of living, (5) a less competitive environment, and (6) changing preferences from cultural amenities to physical/environmental amenities.

CONSUMER BUYING BEHAVIOR

Consumer buying behavior is the manner in which consumers act, function, and react to various situations involving the purchase of a good or service or the acceptance of an idea. Effective retailing requires both an understanding and an appreciation of the buying behavior of consumers. Retailers require such buying behavior information as what and how much consumers buy, who does the buying, and how and where consumers buy (see Figure 3–8). This section examines the ultimate consumer's actual act of buying and the situations and influences that affect the consumer's choice of retailers and their products and services.

BUYING CONSIDERATIONS

"What do consumers buy?" is the first question we need to answer to gain an understanding of consumer buying behavior. Consumers buy products. **Products** are bundles of benefits capable of satisfying consumer wants and needs. A product is anything that can be offered to a market as a need and want satisfier. Consumers have "benefit expectations" that need to be realized in buying, using, and possessing products. Successful products are those that provide the tangible and/or intangible features necessary for the realization of the consumer's expectations of benefits. To enhance our conception of what a product is, marketers have developed several classifications based on various product and/or buyer behavior dimensions. Let's look at the dimensions of tangibility, durability, and availability (see Figure 3–9).[20]

Product Tangibility

Tangibility is the degree to which an item has physical and material properties that are capable of being perceived. The sense of touch generally is considered the deciding factor in determining tangibility. Tangible products can be held, hefted, and felt; intangible products cannot be touched.

Product tangibility ranges from goods to services to ideas (see Figure 3–9a). **Goods** are tangible items defined by their size, shape, and weight together with their chemical and/or biological makeup. This book is an example, as is the chair you are sitting in and the desk you are sitting at. **Services** are largely intangible activities that typically involve the application of human skills within a consumer problem-solving context. A service may or may not be associated with the sale of a good. Services range from personal services such as hairstyling and massages to professional services such as medical attention and legal advice, from household services of housekeeping and

FIGURE 3–8
The dimensions of consumer buying behavior

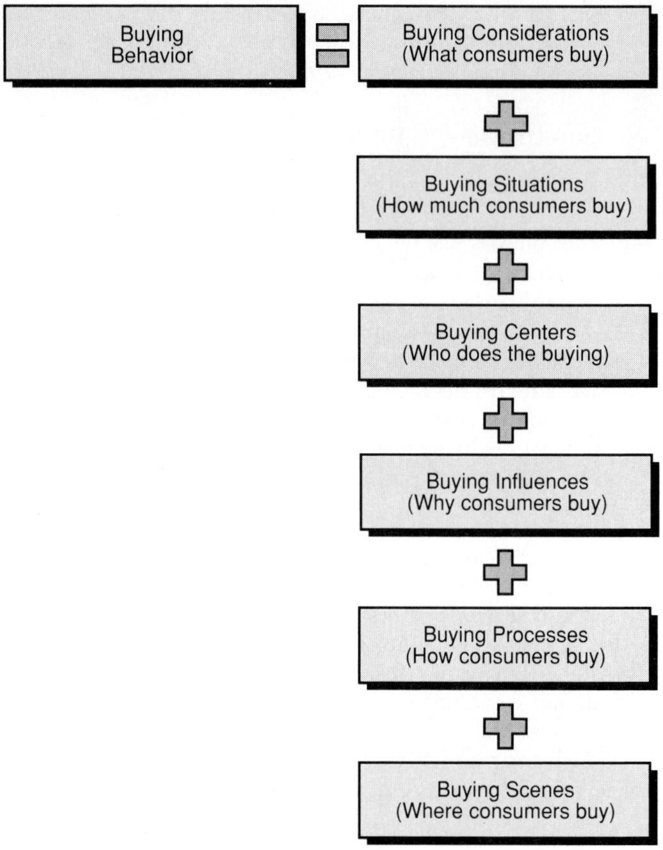

gardening to automotive services of maintenance and repair, from recreational services of amusement parks and campgrounds to cultural services of plays and concerts; the list is almost endless. **Ideas** are concepts and ways of thinking about a particular event or situation. These highly intangible products often are extensions of the opinions, attitudes, and interests of the person marketing the idea. Ideas frequently are categorized as business, religious, political, social, or personal expressions of conceptual thinking.

Product Durability

Durability is the ability of something to endure or to last. **Durables** are products that are capable of surviving many uses. An automobile is a durable good that can provide the transportation function for 100,000 miles or more assuming proper maintenance. Appliances and home furnishings are additional examples of durables. **Nondurables** are perishable products that are used up in one or a few uses. Faddish goods, services, and ideas last for a short period of time and thus have a limited useful life. Figure 3–9b illustrates the continuum of product durability.

Product Availability

Availability is a means of classifying products based on the amount of effort the consumer is willing to exert to secure a particular good, service, or idea (see Figure 3–9c). **Convenience products** are those that the consumer is not willing to spend time,

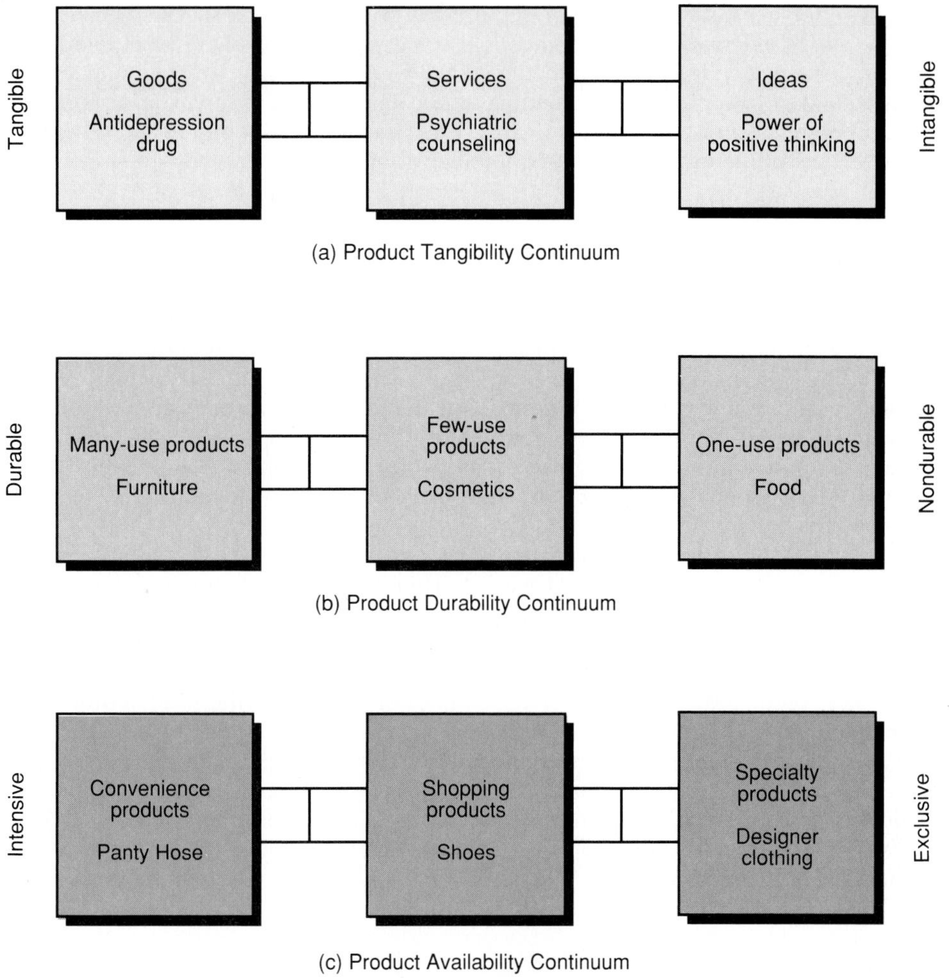

FIGURE 3–9
Product classification continua

money, and effort to locate, evaluate, and procure. For many people, time is a scarcer resource than money.[21] One writer says that time will be "the currency of the Nineties."[22] Hence, more and more goods and services will be treated as convenience goods for which easy and quick availability will be paramount in the consumer's buyer behavior. Consumers expect convenience products to be readily available. If a particular brand of a convenience product is not available, the consumer will select another brand. Bread, cigarettes, and soft drinks are examples of convenience goods, while dry cleaning and automotive maintenance are typical convenience services.

Shopping products are products for which consumers want to make price, quality, suitability, and/or style comparisons. Consumers are willing to spend considerable amounts of time, money, and effort to secure shopping goods; therefore, these goods can be distributed selectively. What constitutes shopping products varies from one consumer to another; however, we usually think of clothing, furniture, and linens as shopping goods. In a similar vein, people shop around for ideas by attending different lectures, churches, and other events and places.

Specialty products are those for which the consumer's buying behavior is directed at securing a particular good, service, or idea without regard for time, effort, or expense. The consumer will not accept a substitute; therefore, he or she will expend whatever effort is required to procure the product. For example, a specialty good may be a specific branded good such as Lagerfeld cologne or a company product line such as Royal Copenhagen figurines. To the individual who insists on a particular hair stylist and is willing to travel to, wait for, and pay the going price, that service is a specialty service. Given the insistent character of the consumer, specialty products tend to be exclusively distributed in a very limited number of outlets.

BUYING SITUATIONS

Consumer Population

This discussion of buying situations focuses on how much consumers buy. Viewed from the perspective of individual consumers, the question of how much they buy is a function of their needs and desires plus the ability, willingness, and authority to buy. Taking a broader, market perspective, how much consumers will buy in total is the problem of determining **market potential**—a market's total capacity to consume a given good, service, or idea. As Figure 3–10 shows, market potential equals the consuming population within a market plus the consumption requirements and potential of that population. Let's examine each of these elements of the market potential equation.

A market's total capacity to consume is, in part, a function of the total number of consumption units that make up that market. Therefore, the first step in determining market potential is to obtain an accurate count of the number of consumption units. However, before consumption units can be counted, they must be defined. The definition of a consumption unit will depend on the type of product that is the focus of the market potential determination. The "number of persons" is the most appropriate population count when market potential is being determined for personal goods and services such as clothing and accessories, health and beauty aids, or medical and legal services. On the other hand, a count of the "number of households" or the "number of residential units" probably is more indicative of a market's consumption capacity for hardware and household goods, furniture, and appliances, lawn and garden equipment, or plumbing and heating services. Although these population figures are important, they

FIGURE 3–10
Market potential as the capacity to consume

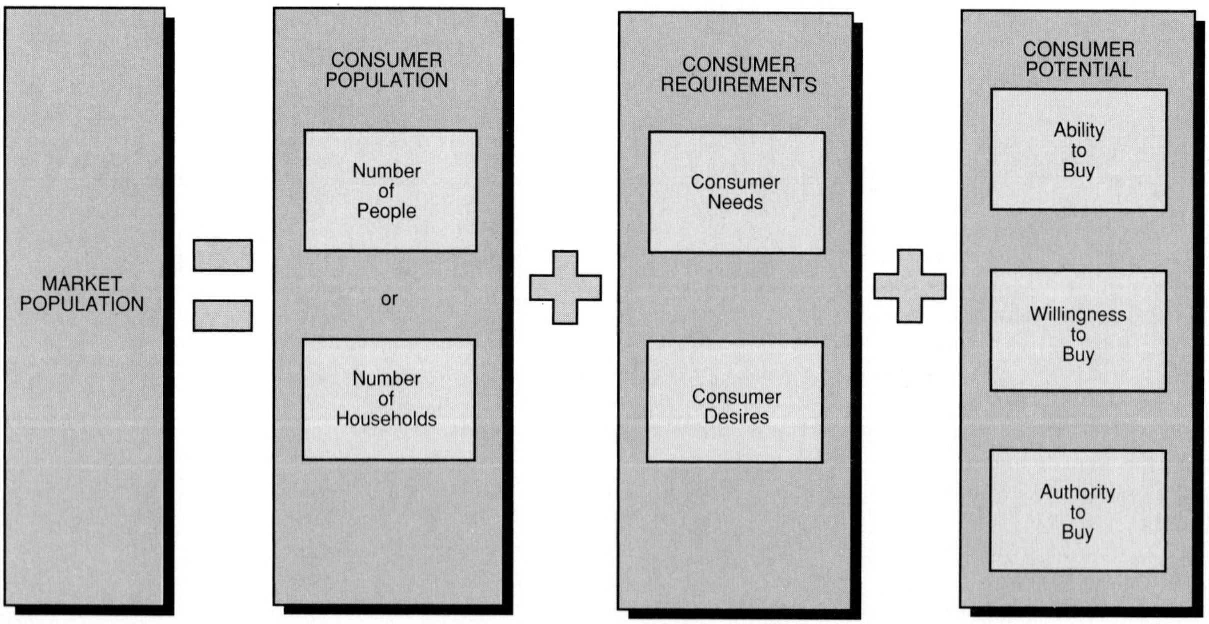

must be qualified in terms of their likelihood of a purchase either now or in the near future.

Consumer Requirements

Prerequisites to the consumer buying process are needs and desires; they motivate and direct consumer's buying activities. Although the distinction between needs and desires is open to debate, the main difference is in their essentiality. **Needs** are essential physiological or psychological requirements necessary for the general physical and mental welfare of the consumer. **Desires** are more akin to wishes in that they are conscious impulses toward objects or experiences that hold promise of enjoyment in their attainment. However, the attainment of desires is less essential to the consumer's well-being than is the satisfaction of needs.

Consumer Potential

Consumers must distinguish between having a need or desire for a product and buying it. Many consumers have product needs (i.e., a new toaster) that go unsatisfied and desires (i.e., a new Porsche) that go unfulfilled. The essential difference between needing or desiring a product and buying it is the consumer's ability, willingness, and authority to purchase the needed or desired good, service, or idea. With respect to product purchases, the list of what each of us would *like* to buy is far more extensive than the list of what we are *willing* and *able* to buy.

Ability to Buy

A consumer's ability to buy is his or her **buying power**—the financial resources available to the consumer for making purchases. The determinants of buying power are the consumer's spendable income, asset position, and available credit.

There are many different expressions of income. **Total income** refers to the total amount of money received from salaries, wages, interest investments, pensions, and profit-making activities. Unfortunately, not all of an individual's or family's total income is available for spending as the individual or family pleases; taxes must be paid, savings increased, and basic living expenses covered. To accommodate these unavoidable expenditures, additional income expressions are in common use. **Disposable income** is the income that remains after taxes and other required payments (e.g., Social Security) have been deducted from total income. It is the total amount of money available for spending and saving. Although disposable income is an appropriate and useful expression of available income for the retailer of essential goods and services, it is not useful for examining the ability of a market to consume nonessential or luxury goods and services. The expression *discretionary income* therefore has evolved. **Discretionary income** is that portion of an individual's or family's disposable income that remains after purchasing the basic necessities of life—food, clothing, and shelter. Consumers are free to purchase whatever they want with their discretionary income. Marketers of many recreation, entertainment, household, automotive, and personal products depend on the amount of discretionary income for satisfactory sales volumes.

The relationships between type of income and consumer expenditure patterns are stated in terms of laws developed from the work of Ernest Engel, a nineteenth-century German statistician. Briefly, these laws state that as a family's income increases, the following result:

1. The percentage of that income spent on food decreases.
2. The percentage of that income spent on clothing is roughly constant.
3. The percentage of that income spent on housing and household operations remains roughly constant.
4. The percentage of that income spent on luxury and other goods increases.

THE WORLD OF RETAILING

■ ■ ■

Ethical Issues

The Income Gap—Wrong Turn on the Path to Prosperity

- In America, hard work and ambition are supposed to bring everyone close to their dreams. And for much of the nation's history, that expectation seemed to come true for more and more people. Year after year, median income and standards of living rose and the gap between the "haves" and "have-nots" shrank. By the 1960s, even unskilled workers in the nation's factories could afford the trappings of the good life. But the path to prosperity took a wrong turn in the early 1970s. For the first time in decades, incomes stopped rising and the gap between rich and poor began to widen again.[1]
- In the 1980s, the pursuit of economic well-being conferred enormous wealth on America and many of its citizens. Yet it left a great many Americans behind. America's real problem is that it has serious deficiencies that one would not expect in so rich a country. . . . That the Great Divide between rich and poor in America has widened is perhaps the most troubling legacy of the 1980s. . . . The family income statistics for the U.S. in the 1980s tell a disturbing tale . . . the richest 5% of American families captured fully 16.9% of aggregate income in the U.S.. . . . By contrast, the poorest fifth of American families—a group four times the size of the richest group just described—earned 4.6% of national income.[2]
- The gap between rich and poor has widened . . . significantly and sometimes dramatically. . . . In the 1980s, the elderly, who previously made up a disproportionate share of the poor, have been replaced by younger adults, who have young children. And children brought up in poverty are more likely to remain poor as adults. The greatest victims are children. The poverty rate of the under-30 crowd has nearly doubled since 1973, to 22%.[3]

Why has the income gap developed? Who is responsible for this inequality? What are the retailer's social responsibilities relative to this issue? What are your recommendations for addressing this problem?

Sources: (1) "A U-Turn in the Road to Riches," *Business Week*, September 25, 1989, 94; (2) Karen Pennar, "The Free Market Has Triumphed, But What about the Losers?", *Business Week*, September 25, 1989, 178; (3) Aaron Bernstein, "America's Income Gap: The Closer You Look, the Worse It Gets," *Business Week*, April 17, 1989, 78–79.

Credit and assets are the second and third buying power determinants. **Credit** is (1) the borrowing power of a consumer, (2) an amount of money placed at a consumer's disposal by a financial or other institution, and (3) a time allowed for payment for goods and services sold on trust. **Assets** are anything of value that an individual owns. The role of assets in determining buying power is twofold: (1) They can be converted to cash, and (2) they are a major factor in determining the amount of credit that creditors are willing to extend.

Willingness to Buy

A consumer may have a need and the ability to satisfy that need, yet for a number of reasons be unwilling to make a purchase decision. As consumers, our willingness to buy or not to buy a product is related to the many influences on us and how we make purchase decisions. Psychologically we may or may not be motivated to make a purchase, or our perception of a product is such that we do not feel it is capable of meeting our needs. The mature consumer, for example, "is much less concerned with the 'hot' fashion than she is with what is stylish, tasteful, comfortable, and flattering."[23] From a personal standpoint, a product may be incongruent with our self-image or our lifestyle. For example, college-educated households are much more likely to buy personal, financial, and entertainment services than are less educated households.[24] On the other hand, our willingness to buy may be based on whether a product meets our "belongingness" need—the need to be accepted by our family, peer groups, or social class. Finally, our willingness or unwillingness to buy may slow our actual buying process. We may postpone a purchase because we need more information about the product or more time to evaluate the information we already have.

Authority to Buy

Even with the ability and willingness to buy, a certain degree of authorization must be present before a consumer will finalize the purchase decision. Authority to buy can be either a formal or an informal type. Formal authorization means that the consumer meets various eligibility requirements such as age, residency, and occupation constraints. For example, minors cannot legally purchase alcoholic beverages. Nonresidents of a state are ineligible for many services provided by that state's government. Many social and professional organizations make their products available only to members of certain professions (e.g., the American Medical Association or the Wisconsin Bar Association).

Informal authorization for making purchases is an expected courtesy when more than one individual is involved and when the purchase can be classified as being of major importance (for a special occasion or very expensive). For example, when one spouse is considering the purchase of a new automobile, the other spouse would expect to be consulted before the purchase is made. The family vacation decision as to what, where, and when is one in which an informal approval and/or other input is expected from all family members.

BUYING CENTERS

A pertinent question in any study of buying behavior is "Who does the buying?" To answer this question, marketers have developed the concept of a buying center. A **buying center** is a basic unit of consumption that engages in the buying process. In consumer products marketing, the basic consumption units tend to be either individuals or households. In certain situations, individuals buy products for their own consumption with no or little regard for the needs or opinions of others. In other situations, purchases are made for a household by one of its members. In a household that is buying, purchase decisions are based on collective needs and therefore are influenced by most or all of the members of the household.

The distinction between individual and household buying centers is important in studying buyer behavior and developing merchandising programs appropriate for that behavior. In the following sections, we will look at the influences on individual and household buying behavior and the processes these two types of buying centers use making purchases.

BUYING INFLUENCES

Why do consumers buy, and what, when, where, and how do they buy? Marketers, like psychologists, do not fully understand the "whys" of human behavior. Although they have a fair understanding of what factors influence behavior, their knowledge of how those factors interact to influence behavior is limited. The human mind is often compared to a "black box"; we know the inputs (stimuli) and the outputs (responses) but not the inner workings of the mind (processes) with respect to the transformation of inputs and outputs. Nevertheless, by detecting patterned buying responses that emerge from planned marketing stimuli, retailers can draw inferences about the processing system of the human mind. One viewpoint on the nature of retailing is that retailing is the art and science of creating and delivering a package of stimuli (products, prices, promotions, and places) that is capable of producing consistent patterns of buying behavior. Fortunately—or unfortunately, depending on your perspective—retailing is still more art than science.

In this section, we will explore the many factors that interact to influence buying behavior and serve as a basis for formulating marketing strategies and tactics. Figure 3–11 overviews the major determinants of the buying behavior of the ultimate consumer.

Psychological Factors

The field of psychology has contributed greatly to the marketer's quest for explanations for the "whys" of consumer behavior. Motivation, perception, learning, and attitude are four major psychological factors that influence consumers' buying choices.

Motivation

Preceding any action are the mental processes of motivation. The act of buying starts with a motive. **Motivation** refers to the process by which consumers are moved or incited to action. Motivation starts with stimulated needs that lead to aroused tensions and results in goal-directed actions. A basic tenet of psychology is "look behind the behavior." What retailers have found upon examining the buying choices of consumers are unsatisfied needs. A **need** is the lack of something that is necessary to the individual's well-being. Needs are the basic source of buyer behavior, but they must be activated before the consumer is driven to action. A need is activated by some internal or external stimulus that arouses tension. A headache is an internal stimulus that creates an uncomfortable feeling (an aroused tension) that activates the goal-directed action of taking aspirin for relief (the need). An external stimulus might be a department store advertisement announcing the arrival of the latest fall fashions; this cue may stimulate one's need to be noticed as a contemporary dresser, thereby promoting the action of purchasing something distinctive to wear.

FIGURE 3–11
Determinants of consumer buying behavior

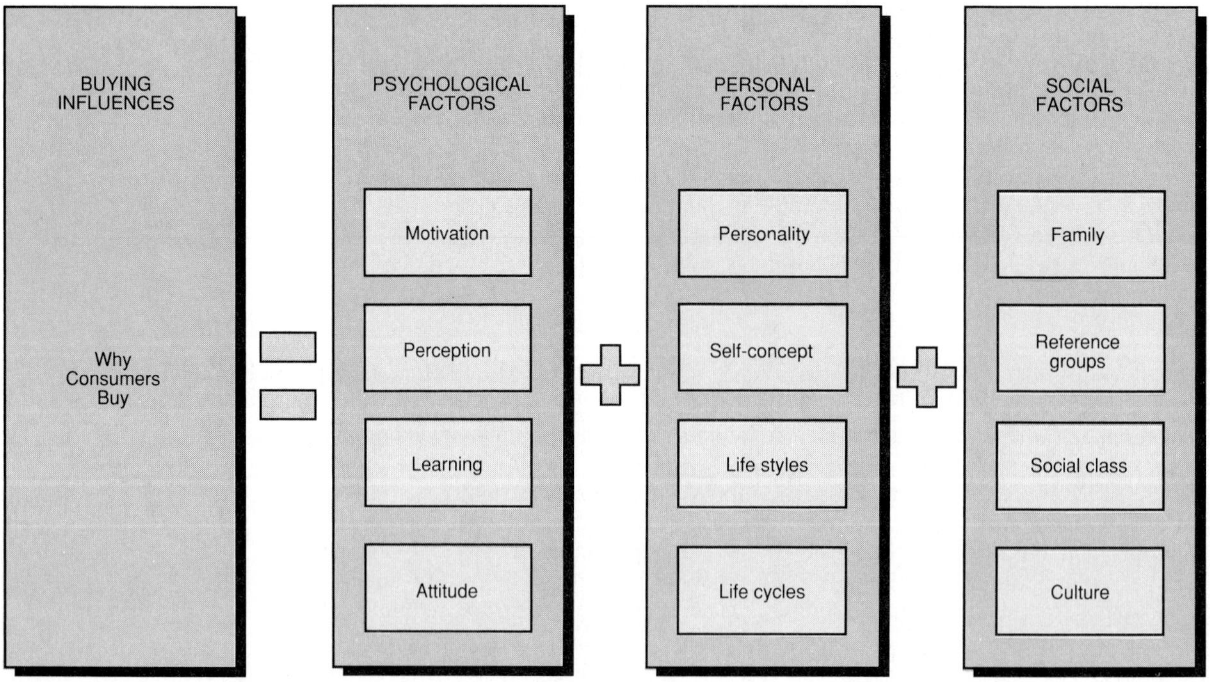

Having portrayed motivation as a needs-based process, we need a further explanation of the nature and intensity of human needs. Needs have been categorized in a variety of ways; one of the more widely accepted need classification schemes is that of psychologist Abraham H. Maslow (see Figure 3–12). According to Maslow, human needs are hierarchical and can be rank ordered on the basis of their motivational power. Lower-order needs—those related to our physiological well-being—are basic, innate needs that must be satisfied before higher-order needs can emerge as strong motivators of our behavior. Higher-order needs are learned needs that are largely psychological in nature. Although higher-order needs are secondary to physiological needs, once these basic needs are satisfied psychological needs will emerge as extremely important motivators of consumer behavior. Let's explore Maslow's hierarchy of needs in more detail.

Physiological needs are life-sustaining and creature comforts that need to be reasonably satisfied before the search for fulfillment of higher-order needs. Food, fluids, shelter, rest, waste elimination, and clothing are all basic to the individual's physiological well-being. In reading this text, for example, your thirst for knowledge and an A on the next exam may be secondary to your need for sleep if you were out partying half the night. On the other hand, if you are well rested, your concern (aroused tension) over improving your grade point average (need) may encourage you to review this chapter several times to earn a grade of B or better on the next exam (goal-directed action). However, you can be sure of one thing—once you have satisfied either or both of these needs, other needs will arise (i.e., getting a date for the weekend).

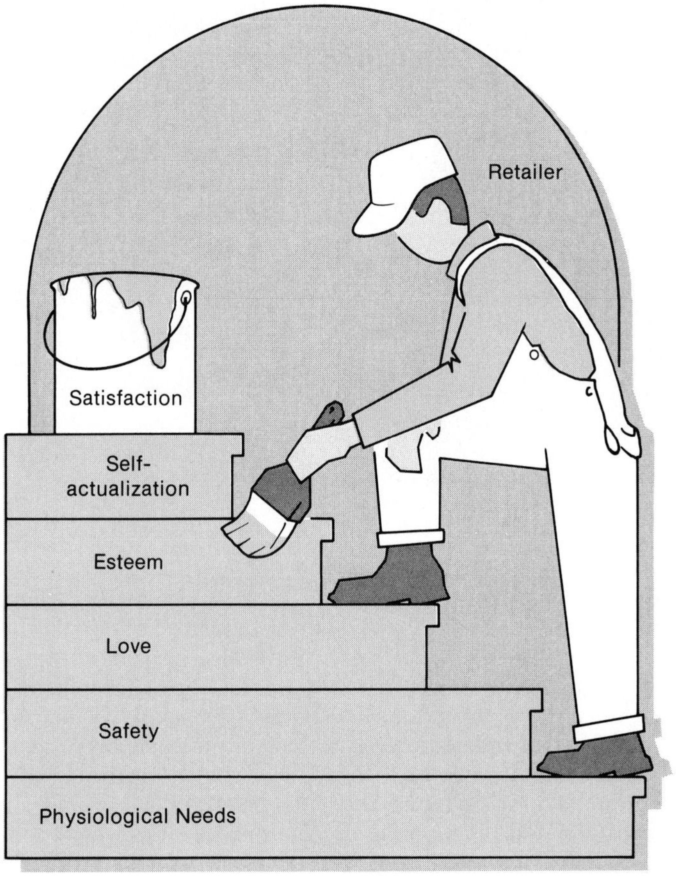

FIGURE 3–12
Maslow's hierarchy of needs

Maslow's hierarchy is concerned with both physiological and psychological needs.

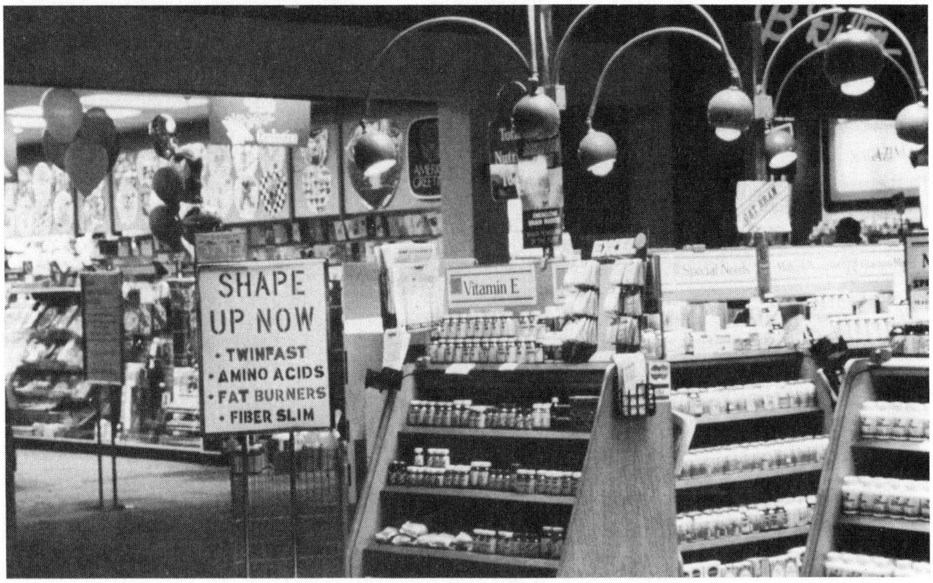

Safety needs are satisfied by feelings of security and stability. To be secure, a person must feel free from physical harm or danger. Product and service retailers that focus on the need for protection include sellers of smoke or burglar alarm systems, insurance and retirement plans, exercise and health programs, warranties and guarantees, and caffeine-free, sugar-free, and salt-free foods and beverages. Stability is an equally important factor in meeting the need for safety. Generally, people feel more secure when there is a reasonable amount of order and structure in their lives. The often heard expressions "I need to simplify my life" and "I need to get organized" are directed at obtaining relief from the tensions aroused by an unstructured, unorganized, and chaotic lifestyle. Simplification and organization are both excellent concepts for retailers to use in developing product lines, designing store and display layouts, creating advertising appeals, and establishing pricing points.

As social creatures, we all have **social needs**—the desire for love, belongingness, affection, and friendship. In our relatively affluent society, social needs have become powerful motivators of our behavior and influential organizers of our perceptions. Capitalizing on this need to "be accepted" or to "fit in," retailers structure many merchandising strategies around the need for satisfying relationships with family, friends, peers, and reference groups. Social need gratification influences where we live, what we wear, what organizations we belong to, what stores we patronize, and what we are willing to pay.

Esteem needs involve aspirations regarding prestige, recognition, admiration, self-respect, success, and achievement. An individual who seeks to fulfill esteem needs wants to "stand out" in contrast to the social need to "fit in." In satisfying esteem needs, a consumer is more likely to (1) purchase "limited-edition" merchandise (i.e., collectible figurines); (2) patronize distinctive outlets (specialty shops); (3) respond to individualist retail promotions (image-building advertisements); and (4) react in a less price-sensitive manner (prestige price preference). The retailer's task in meeting esteem needs is to make the consumer feel special and appreciated. "Nobody buys the Tiffany perfume for its scent. They want the name and blue box."[25]

"Doing what you are capable of doing" is a phrase that summarizes an individual's **self-actualization need**. The desire for self-fulfillment is the highest-order need; it reflects the desire to reach one's full potential as an individual—"what you can be you must be." Many predict that "the real luxury in the 90's will be experiential and not necessarily a possession."[26] This change will result from "possession proliferation"; consumers own more goods but are forced to work harder, longer hours, and under more stress. More and more consumers want fewer goods of better quality to free up time to enjoy life's experiences. The numerous motivational books, tapes, seminars, and programs designed to provide means for self-actualization are good examples of products directed at helping consumers realize their potential. By combining the self-actualization need of self-fulfillment with the social need of recognition, the retailer has target-market opportunities for a wide range of goods and services of a conspicuous nature.

Perception

How motivated consumers act out the buying process is determined, in part, by their perceptions of the buying situation. **Perception** is the process by which consumers attach meaning to incoming stimuli by forming mental pictures of persons, places, and objects. An individual's perception is how he or she views the world. The basic perceptual process consists of receiving, organizing, and interpreting stimuli.

Stimulus reception is accomplished through the five senses of sight, sound, taste, touch, and smell. For most people, the sense of sight is the most used and developed sense mode, a fact that retailers should keep in mind when planning all aspects of their retailing mixes. Exposure is the key to receiving stimuli; perception follows exposure. A major tactic in any retailing program is the inclusion of plans for gaining buyer exposure for the firm's product offering.

Stimulus organization is a mental data processing system whereby incoming stimuli (data) are organized into descriptive categories. The received stimuli must be simplified through organization to be mentally converted into meaningful information that can be useful in problem solving, that is, making purchase decisions. Individuals vary greatly in their ability to mentally receive, store, and organize stimuli; hence, their interpretations of stimuli exhibit equal variance.

Stimulus interpretation is the process of assigning meaning to stimuli. When a consumer attaches meaning to something he or she has sensed, the perceptual process is completed. Interpretation of stimuli is accomplished by the mental comparison of what is sensed to what the individual knows or feels from previous experience.

Selectivity is a natural phenomenon that occurs within the perceptual process of receiving (selective exposure), organizing (selective retention), and interpreting (selective distortion) stimuli: "What you see [hear, feel, taste, and smell] is what you get." What consumers actually perceive is always vastly different from the actual stimuli presented. The selectivity of perception is a key factor in explaining why different people have different perceptions of the same stimuli. **Selective exposure** is the process of limiting the type and amount of stimuli received and admitted to awareness. It is a screening process that allows us to select only the stimuli that interest us. For example, most consumers watch only certain types of television programming or read selected sections of their local newspapers. **Selective retention** is the act of remembering only the information the individual wants to remember. Individuals tend to retain information that is consistent with their feelings, beliefs, and attitudes. Information that is conflicting is likely to be forgotten. Finally, **selective distortion** is the misinterpretation of incoming stimuli to make them consistent with the individual's beliefs and attitudes. By changing incoming information, people can create a harmonious relationship between that information and their mindsets and avoid the tension that results from not having their beliefs supported by new inputs. For example, if we like a particular retail store because of its friendly sales personnel, we might distort the fact that its higher prices are not competitive. The selectivity of perception places a considerable strain on the retailer that must get messages admitted to awareness without being misinterpreted or forgotten.

Learning

The logical extension of the motivational and perceptual process is learning. A considerable amount of human behavior is learned. **Learning** is the process of acquiring knowledge through past experiences. Behavioral psychologists view learning as a stimulus-response mechanism wherein drives, cues, and responses interact to produce a learned pattern of behavior. A **drive** is whatever impels behavior; it arises from a strongly felt inner need that demands action. A fear of failure, for example, may drive an insecure individual to work longer and more efficiently. **Cues** are external stimuli that direct consumers toward specific objects that can satisfy their basic needs and reduce their drives. To illustrate, an advertisement promoting a new book on time management is likely to catch the attention of an insecure individual who is looking for ways to improve his or her work efficiency. **Responses** are the actions taken to reduce a cue-stimulated drive. In a buying situation, these actions typically include identifying, trying, evaluating, and selecting purchase alternatives. To continue the example, our fearful individual may respond by visiting the bookstore and, after previewing the book, may or may not decide to buy it.

The extent to which an individual learns from this stimulus-response mechanism is influenced by three factors: reinforcement, repetition, and participation. **Reinforcement** is the comparing of anticipated results with the actual results experienced from a chosen response. If actual results compare favorably with anticipated results, response reinforcement occurs and learning takes place. **Repetition** is the act of repeating a past experience. Learning is enhanced by performing the same action several times. **Participation** is active involvement in the learning process. An active role in any activity generally results in the acquisition of more knowledge about that activity.

The retailer's efforts regarding the learning process should be directed at enhancing reinforcement, repetition, and participation. Reinforcement may take the form of return and allowance policies that confirm the retailer's intent to correct product deficiencies. Frequent advertisements that expose the consumer to the retailer's products and services are commonly used tactics in supporting the learning process through repetition. Free samples, trial sizes, and demonstrations are participation devices used in marketing to guide the consumer's learning process toward the retailer's products.

Attitudes

An **attitude** is an evaluative mental orientation that creates a predisposition to respond in a certain fashion. People use their attitudes as evaluative mechanisms to pass judgment (i.e., good or bad, right or wrong) and as orientation mechanisms to focus that judgment on particular persons, places, things, or events. Attitudes can simplify the buying process by providing the consumer with a preset way to respond to the object of the attitude. For example, if Bob thinks that department stores are overpriced, he can avoid shopping there.

What forms an attitude? Figure 3–13 portrays the three basic components of an attitude: cognitive, affective, and behavior. The **cognitive component** consists of what the consumer believes about an object based on available information and knowledge. Essentially a cognition is what is known about the object and its attributes. Feelings rather than beliefs are the focal point of the **affective component**—the emotions a consumer feels about an object. The third element of an attitude is the **behavior component**—the predisposition to respond in a certain way to the object based on one's beliefs and feelings.

Attitude formation is the result of past experiences. For example, consumers born during the Depression view spending money very conservatively; they believe in saving for that inevitable rainy day. Consumers in their 50s and 60s experienced both the Depression and the post–World War II boom years; hence, they prefer to save some and spend some. The baby boom generation developed their attitudes during the prosperous postwar period; their attitude is "spend it all, plus some on credit."[27] Attitudes are learned through interactions with family members and a wide range of

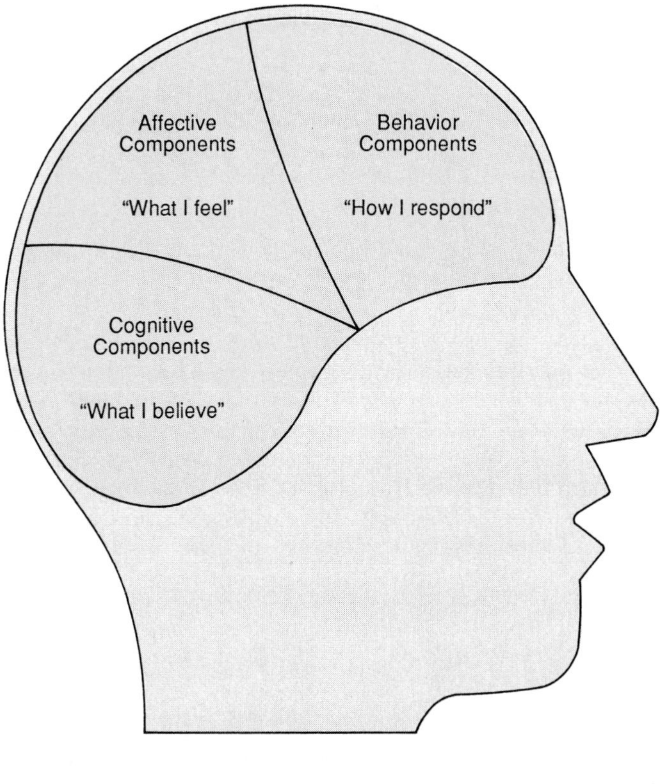

FIGURE 3–13
Components of an attitude (mindset)

peer and reference groups. People often adopt the prevailing attitudes of their associates.

The learning of an attitude takes one of several forms: (1) trial and error (purchasing and using a product), (2) visual observation (watching a product demonstration), and (3) verbal communications (listening to others' opinions about products). Through involvement in trial and error, visual observation, and verbal communication experiences of consumers, retailers can influence attitude formation.

Personal Factors

An individual's personality, self-concept, lifestyle, and position in the life cycle are all personal factors that influence that individual's buying behavior (see Figure 3–13). We will continue our exploration of the "whys" of consumer behavior by discussing the four personal factors.

Personality

Everyone has a personality; unfortunately, there is considerable disagreement as to what personality is and to what extent it influences buying behavior. Because of its complex nature, personality is perhaps best defined in general terms; therefore, **personality** is a general response pattern individuals use in coping with their environment. For example, an individual may be positive or negative, pessimistic or optimistic, aggressive or passive, independent or dependent, sociable or unsociable, and friendly or withdrawn. Logically, the existence of a particular personality trait will affect an individual's buying behavior. For example, a person with a pessimistic personality will approach buying situations with a considerable amount of doubt, while an optimistic individual will be more impulsive and confident about buying choices. Market researchers, however, have been largely unsuccessful in their efforts to find significant statistical relationships between personalities and buying behavior. Take the junior customer—who and what is she? Demographically speaking, she is 18 to 25 years old, a high school girl, a college student, or a young career woman. Her personality is complex, as described by one writer:

> She is sexy and innocent, fickle, fun loving and fashion crazed; she is moody, wild for music, and demands to be entertained; she loves to be courted, but refuses to be loyal; she hasn't much money, never spends her dollars on long term investments, but splurges on instant fads; she's a non-conforming conformist who rebels daily against the establishment, but yearns just as much to be exactly the same as every one of her peers.[28]

Most department stores and specialty shops have been mystified by this consumer group and continue to look for the right definition.

Self-Concept

Who are we? One answer to that question is that we are what we perceive ourselves to be, that is, our **self-concept**—the set of perceptions we have of ourselves within a social context. Each individual has a general awareness of his or her capabilities and attributes and how they are perceived within a social setting. The optimal lifestyle arrangement for most baby boomers is a more even blend of work, home, and recreation; they are just as likely "to define themselves as mothers and fathers, wind-surfers and skiers, as to talk about themselves as accountants and lawyers, carpenters, and secretaries."[29] The self-concept consists of four parts:

1. Real self—the way you actually are
2. Ideal self—how you would like to be
3. Looking-glass self—how you think others see you
4. Self-image—how you see yourself

As Figure 3–14 illustrates, our self-images are, to some extent, a composite of our real, ideal, and looking-glass selves.

The importance of the self-concept to retailers in understanding consumer behavior is twofold. First, consumers often purchase products and/or brands that they feel support and reinforce their self-concepts. Second, consumers never consciously purchase products that are incompatible with their self-concepts. For example, the "contemporary conservative" pictured in Figure 3–14 may purchase a blue blazer with gray slacks because this outfit is consistent with each of his "selfs"; this apparel selection will allow this individual to fantasize about being a swinging bachelor (what he would like to be) while preserving his image as an average (what he really is) and ordinary (what others see him as) guy.

One major use of the self-concept by retailers is in the creation of advertising appeals. By directing an advertising message to self-images such as the "homebody," the "good provider," the "budding scholar," and the "professional," the retailer has an additional tool for targeting selected consumer markets, developing product lines, planning price tactics, and designing store layouts.

Lifestyles

Some people lead an active life; others' lifestyles are more sedentary. Some people's lives are centered around their home and family; others center their lives around jobs, organizations, hobbies, or events. "Couch potatoes and their couch potatoes life-style involves members of the baby boom generation who are simultaneously settling down while becoming bored with nightlife and its related expenses—find it trendy to stay home."[30] Consumers' lifestyles affect what, when, where, how, and why they buy. **Lifestyle** can be defined as the way consumers live. It is a patterned style of living that stems from the individual's needs, perceptions, and attitudes; as such, it represents a behavioral profile of the individual's psychological makeup. How consumers choose to live also reflects the influences exerted by family members, peers, and other groups.

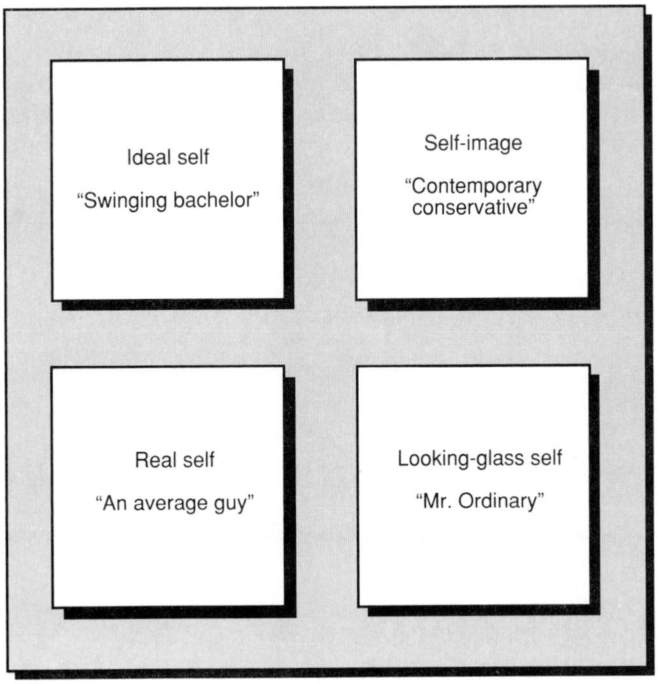

FIGURE 3–14
The four parts of the self-concept

Both conforming and nonconforming lifestyles are behavioral reactions to expected and accepted modes of living.

Marketing researchers use lifestyle analysis (psychographics) to develop consumer profiles based on consumers' ways of living. Lifestyle profiles are composite pictures of consumers' **activities, interests, and opinions (AIO)**, together with their demographic makeup. Figure 3–15 identifies a commonly used enumeration of AIO variables. To develop lifestyle profiles, consumers are asked to respond to a multitude of AIO statements by indicating their degree of agreement or disagreement with those statements (see Figure 3–16). By finding patterned responses to AIO statements (e.g., strong agreement with all statements that reflect favorably on work-oriented activities, job-related interests, and probusiness opinions), the retailer is better able to identify market segments and to target marketing programs.

Lifestyle analysis tends to be special-purpose research; that is, it is directed at determining lifestyle profiles relative to a particular market, product, or retailing program. As an illustration, let's assume that a retailer wants to develop a fashion merchandising program based on lifestyle dimensions. After administering a series of AIO statements to a represented sample, the following lifestyle profiles emerge:

1. The "perfectionist"—a career-oriented, free-spirited, active fashion leader who is concerned with uniqueness and individuality to support her avant-garde image; an individual who can be nonconforming and impractical when in an adventurous mood
2. The "traditionist"—a job-oriented, conforming fashion follower who is extremely label conscious and interested in being accepted as well as presenting a dignified and practical image

Having identified two distinct market segments based on lifestyle dimensions, the retailer can choose to (1) appeal to the perfectionist by offering the most advanced fashion apparel, stocking only one of each type of garment and timing new arrivals every week, or (2) appeal to the traditionist by offering stylish but accepted fashions, stocking well-established labels, and creating displays in practical combinations (outfits) of apparel.

Life Cycle

Are you single, married, widowed, or divorced? Are you with or without children? Are you young, middle-aged, or elderly? These are some of the factors that determine which stage of the life cycle you are in. The **life cycle** is a description of the changes that occur in an individual's demographic, psychographic, and behavioristic profile while progress-

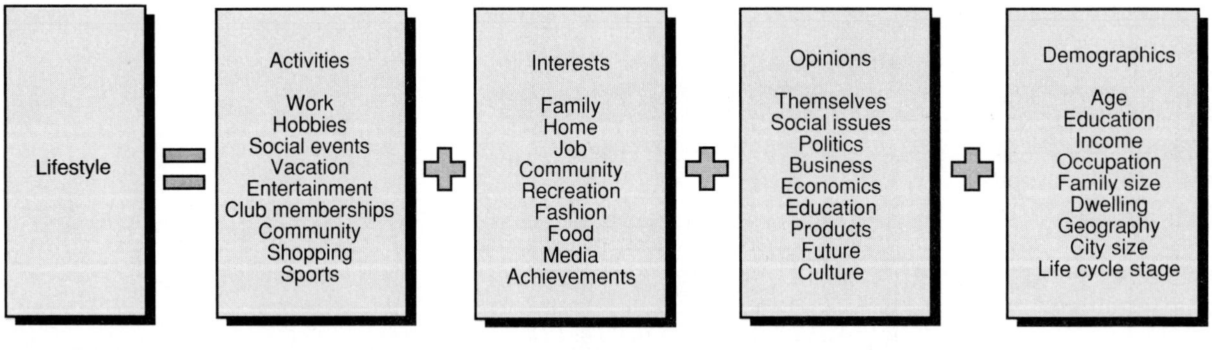

FIGURE 3–15
Dimensions of lifestyle (source: Joseph T. Plummer, "The Concept and Application of Life-Style Segmentation," *Journal of Marketing* 38 [January 1974]: 34. Reprinted from the *Journal of Marketing*, published by the American Marketing Association, Chicago, IL 60606.)

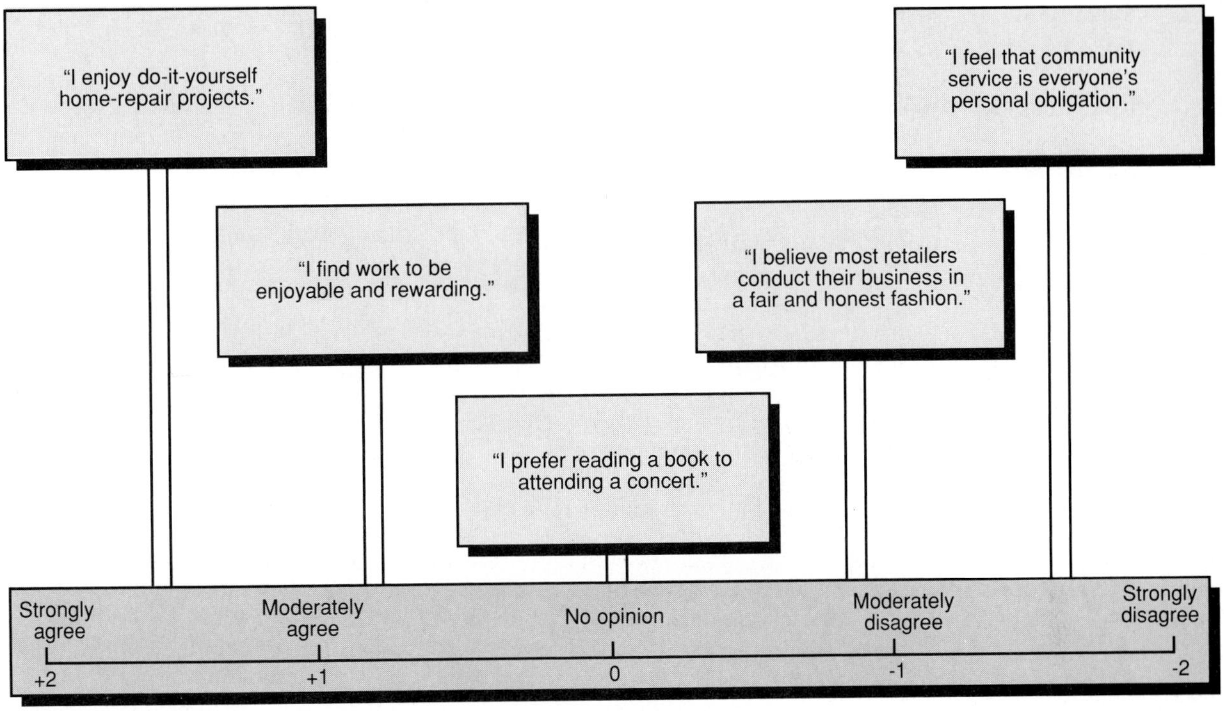

FIGURE 3–16
AIO (activities, interests, and opinions) statements

ing through a series of stages during his or her lifetime. The life cycle starts with the singles stage and ends with the retired solitary survivor of a family. Figure 3–17 portrayes the nine stages of the life cycle and their key demographic, psychographic, and behavioristic elements. The differences in buyer behavior often can be explained by very practical considerations. Families with children buy toys, large families buy economy-size packages, and empty-nest families can more readily afford the purchase of luxury products and services.

Social Factors

Conformity to group expectations is a basic element of human behavior. Much of what we do is directed at gaining acceptance from other people; so it is with our buying behavior. We buy certain products, select particular brands, and patronize specific stores because we want the approval and support of others. The importance of group influences on individual buying behavior is great. The following discussion examines the impact of the family, reference groups, social class, and culture on our individual buying behavior (see Figure 3–11).

The Family

A family can be described in terms of the *nuclear family*, consisting of a father, a mother, and their children, or as the *extended family*, which includes the nuclear family plus grandparents, aunts, uncles, and cousins. Regardless of how the family unit is defined, it represents one of the most important social influences on our buying behavior. *Family influences* on individual buyer behavior stem from childhood. Consciously or unconsciously, we adopt many of our parents' attitudes, values, morals, and ways of doing things. These basic orientations remain with us long after we have left our family of origin. As we establish a new family by getting married and having

RETAIL STRATEGIES AND TACTICS

Lifestyle Segmentation—Using The VALS 2 System

Marketing research has produced a large number of different lifestyle profiles designed for a specific product or company. A more universal lifestyle typology was developed by SRI International, a nonprofit think tank. They developed the original VALS system that grouped individuals on the basis of their values (VA) and lifestyles (LS). VALS 2 is a revision of the earlier system and divides consumers into eight groups as defined by their psychological makeup or self-orientation (i.e., patterns of attitudes and activities that help people reinforce, sustain, or even modify their social self-image) and their available resources (i.e., education, income, self-confidence, health, eagerness to buy, intelligence, and energy level). The eight VALS 2 customer segments are:

- *Actualizers:* Successful, sophisticated, active, "take-charge" people with high self-esteem and abundant resources. They are interested in growth and seek to develop, explore, and express themselves in a variety of ways—guided sometimes by principle and sometimes by a desire to have an effect, to make a change. Their possessions and recreation reflect a cultivated taste for the finer things in life.
- *Fulfilleds:* Mature, satisfied, comfortable, reflective people who value order, knowledge and responsibility. Most are well educated, and in, or recently retired from, professional occupations. Content with their careers, families, and station in life, their leisure activities tend to center around their homes. Although their incomes allow them many choices, they are conservative, practical consumers, concerned about functionality, value, and durability in the products they buy.
- *Believers:* Conservative, conventional people with concrete beliefs and strong attachments to traditional institutions: family, church, community, and the nation. They follow established routines, organized in large part around their homes, families, and social or religious organizations. As consumers, they are conservative and predictable, favoring American products and established brands.
- *Achievers:* Successful career- and work-oriented people who like to, and generally do, feel in control of their lives. They value structure, predictability, and stability over risk, intimacy, and self-discovery. They

children, the influences of our spouse and children assume a primary role in our acquisition of new orientations and development of new behavioral patterns.

Family buying roles are a key issue in understanding consumer behavior. From a merchandising perspective, a consumer often is not an individual but a family represented by an individual. Therefore, retailers must recognize and understand the various roles played by various family members within a given purchase situation. Five specific roles have been identified:

1. *Initiator*—the family member who first recognizes the problem
2. *User*—the family member who will actually use or consume the product or service
3. *Decision maker*—the family member who decides what will be bought and at what time, place, and source
4. *Decision influencer*—the family member who has input that affects the choice of the decision maker
5. *Purchasing agent*—the family member who actually visits the store and makes the purchase

are deeply committed to their work and their families. As consumers, they favor established products that demonstrate their success to their peers.

- *Strivers:* Seek motivation, self-definition, and approval from the world around them. They are striving to find a secure place in life. Unsure of themselves, and low on economic, social, and psychological resources, they are deeply concerned about the opinions and approval of others. They emulate those who own more impressive possessions, but what they wish to obtain is generally beyond their reach.
- *Experiencers:* Young, vital, enthusiastic, impulsive, and rebellious. They seek variety and excitement, savoring the new, the offbeat, and the risky. Still in the process of formulating life values and patterns of behavior, they quickly become enthusiastic about new possibilities but are equally quick to cool. They are avid consumers and spend much of their income on clothing, fast food, music, movies, and videos.
- *Makers:* Practical people who have constructive skills and value self-sufficiency. They live within a traditional context of family, practical work, and physical recreation and have little interest in what lies outside that context. They experience the world by working on it (for example, building a house or canning vegetables) and have sufficient skill, income, and energy to carry out their projects successfully. They are unimpressed by material possessions other than those with a practical or functional purpose.
- *Strugglers:* Strugglers' lives are constricted. Chronically poor, ill educated, low-skilled, without strong social bonds, aging, and concerned about their health, they are often despairing and passive. Their chief concerns are for security and safety. They are cautious consumers; and while they represent a very modest market for most products and services, they are loyal to favorite brands.

By targeting one (e.g., Experiencers) or a limited number of lifestyle segments (e.g., Fulfilleds and Believers), the retailer can create a customer focus through a carefully constructed mix of product lines, pricing points, service offerings, store environments, and promotional appeals.

Source: Adapted from Penney Gill, "New VALS 2 Values and Lifestyles Segmentation," *Stores,* November 1989, 35. Copyright © National Retail Federation, Inc., New York, New York.

To be effective, a merchandising program must take into account each family member and his or her role. For example, the retailer's persuasive and informational advertising might be directed at (1) the initiator to create awareness, (2) the decision influencer and decision maker to develop comprehension and conviction, (3) the user to provide reinforcement, and (4) the purchasing agent to guide shopping behavior. Role specialization in family buying is common in most families. Although some purchase decisions are made jointly or independently, others are dominated by either the husband or the wife. With the increase in working mothers, many teens are taking on adult buying roles of decision maker and purchasing agent. As the purchase decisions become more diffused, people within the household are playing it safe—buying brands they trust—because everyone else in the household will agree it's a better purchase decision than buying a generic or unknown brand.[31] To the retailer, this behavior pattern suggests that nationally advertised brands will continue to be an important part of the product mix.

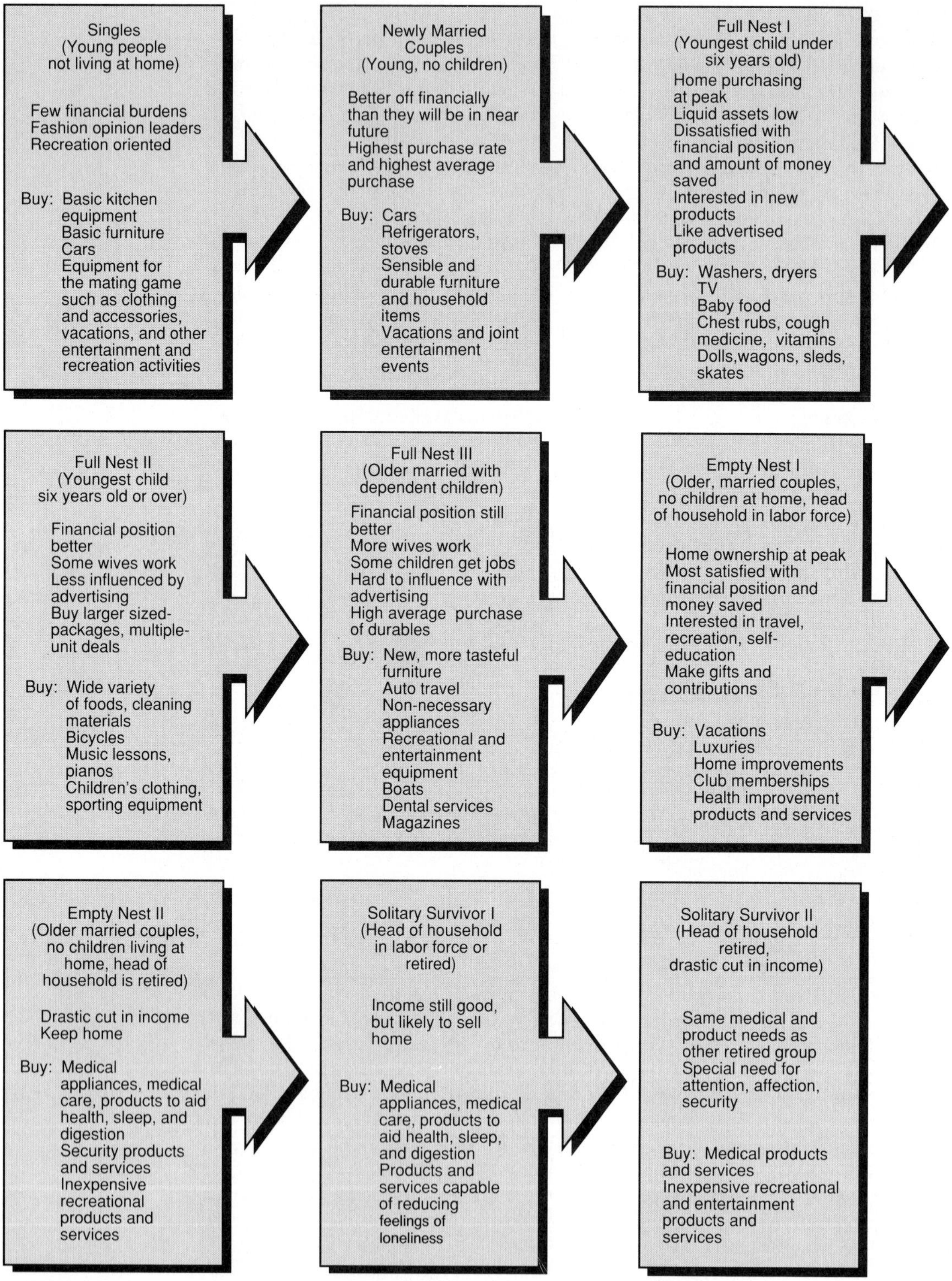

Singles (Young people not living at home)
Few financial burdens
Fashion opinion leaders
Recreation oriented
Buy: Basic kitchen equipment
Basic furniture
Cars
Equipment for the mating game such as clothing and accessories, vacations, and other entertainment and recreation activities
Newly Married Couples (Young, no children)
Better off financially than they will be in near future
Highest purchase rate and highest average purchase
Buy: Cars
Refrigerators, stoves
Sensible and durable furniture and household items
Vacations and joint entertainment events
Full Nest I (Youngest child under six years old)
Home purchasing at peak
Liquid assets low
Dissatisfied with financial position and amount of money saved
Interested in new products
Like advertised products
Buy: Washers, dryers
TV
Baby food
Chest rubs, cough medicine, vitamins
Dolls,wagons, sleds, skates
Full Nest II (Youngest child six years old or over)
Financial position better
Some wives work
Less influenced by advertising
Buy larger sized-packages, multiple-unit deals
Buy: Wide variety of foods, cleaning materials
Bicycles
Music lessons, pianos
Children's clothing, sporting equipment
Full Nest III (Older married with dependent children)
Financial position still better
More wives work
Some children get jobs
Hard to influence with advertising
High average purchase of durables
Buy: New, more tasteful furniture
Auto travel
Non-necessary appliances
Recreational and entertainment equipment
Boats
Dental services
Magazines
Empty Nest I (Older, married couples, no children at home, head of household in labor force)
Home ownership at peak
Most satisfied with financial position and money saved
Interested in travel, recreation, self-education
Make gifts and contributions
Buy: Vacations
Luxuries
Home improvements
Club memberships
Health improvement products and services
Empty Nest II (Older married couples, no children living at home, head of household is retired)
Drastic cut in income
Keep home
Buy: Medical appliances, medical care, products to aid health, sleep, and digestion
Security products and services
Inexpensive recreational products and services
Solitary Survivor I (Head of household in labor force or retired)
Income still good, but likely to sell home
Buy: Medical appliances, medical care, products to aid health, sleep, and digestion
Products and services capable of reducing feelings of loneliness
Solitary Survivor II (Head of household retired, drastic cut in income)
Same medical and product needs as other retired group
Special need for attention, affection, security
Buy: Medical products and services
Inexpensive recreational and entertainment products and services

FIGURE 3–17
The life cycle progression (source: William D. Wells and George Gubar, "Life Cycle Concept In Marketing Research," *Journal of Marketing Research* 3 [November 1966]: 362)

Reference Groups

Reference groups provide individuals with a "frame of reference" in making purchase decisions such as what and where to buy. A **reference group** is a group that serves as a model or standard for an individual's behavior and attitudes. An individual may develop associations with reference groups such as friends, colleagues, coworkers, clubs, and associations.

Reference group influences on purchase behavior vary by product and brand. Purchases of highly conspicuous and visible products such as clothing, furniture, and automobiles are strongly influenced by reference groups.[32] Figure 3–18 illustrates the importance of peer group influence in the purchase of fashion. If the brand name, style, or design is uniquely conspicuous, reference group influences become an important decision factor. The retailer's image as the "right" or "in place" for a particular reference group also can be important in deciding which retailer to patronize. The colorful and distinctive clothing offered by Esprit and the unusual and adventurous apparel sold by Banana Republic are good examples of retailers that have been successful with a specialty business format in which reference group influence is a key focal point for merchandising decisions. The distinctive package of a distinctive retailer may be as important as the product in a group gift-giving situation.

Social Class

Based on occupation, education, place of residence (i.e., prestige of neighborhood), income, and wealth, social scientists have developed societal, rank-ordered groupings of individuals and families known as **social classes**. The higher the class rank, the higher the status (greater prestige) of the class. A widely used classification scheme of American social classes is that developed by W. Lloyd Warner. His scheme, shown in Figure 3–19, consists of six levels ranging from upper-upper class to lower-lower class.

A number of generalizations can be made concerning the marketing implications stemming from our social class groupings:

- *Upper-upper class* consumers typically do not engage in conspicuous consumption; rather, they tend to be governed by conservative tastes and a selective buying process. They represent potential markets for unique and expensive products (e.g., "originals" in fashion apparel). Patronage motives tend toward personalized services and individualistic merchandising at exclusive retailers. The buying patterns of this class often serve as a reference point for the consumption activities of lower classes.
- *Lower-upper class* consumers engage in conspicuous consumption of a wide range of highly visible personal, recreational, and household products and services. This buying behavior often is directed at impressing lower social classes. A primary

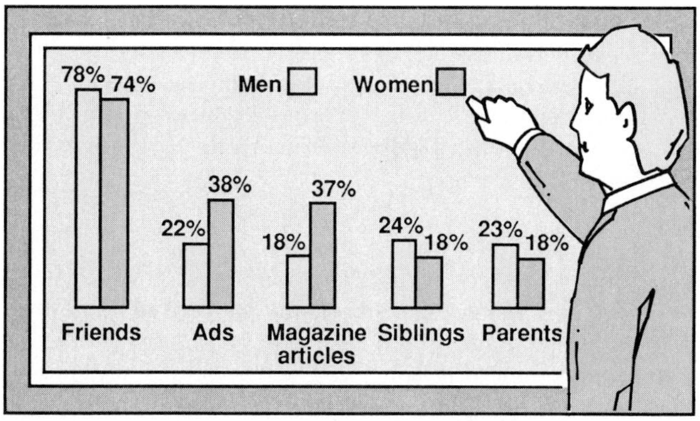

FIGURE 3–18
Setting the style on campus: When it comes to fashion, most college students are influenced by their friends (source: Elys McLean-Ibrahim, "What makes workers succeed," *USA Today* [September 1987], B-1. Copyright © 1987 USA TODAY. Reprinted with permission.)

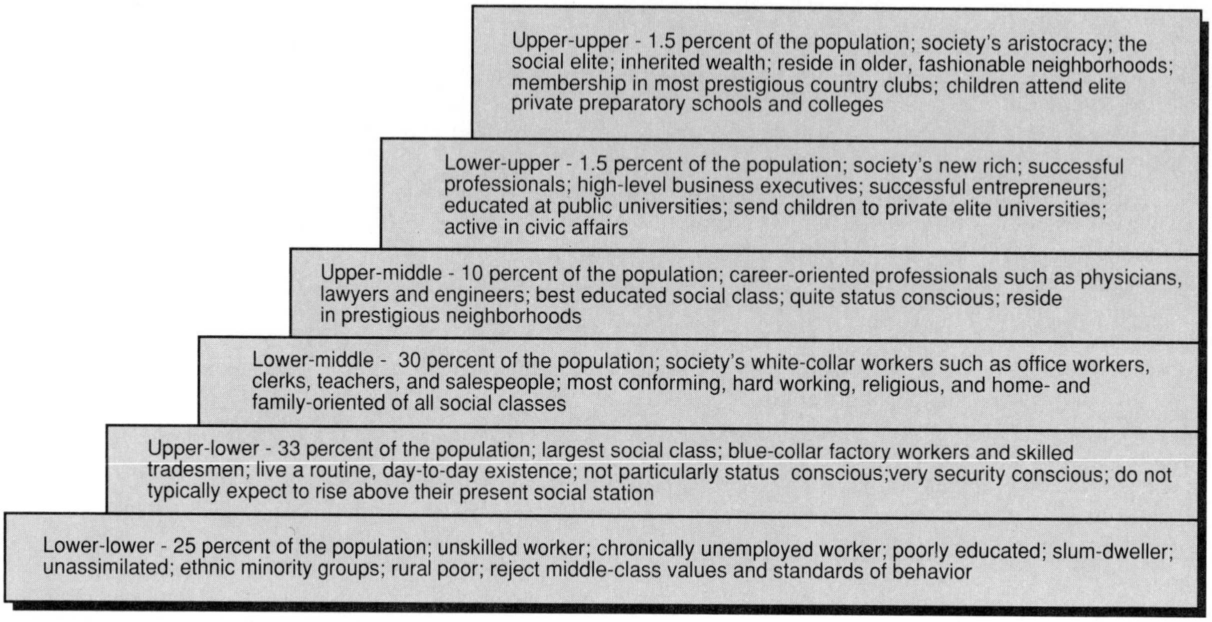
Upper-upper - 1.5 percent of the population; society's aristocracy; the social elite; inherited wealth; reside in older, fashionable neighborhoods; membership in most prestigious country clubs; children attend elite private preparatory schools and colleges
Lower-upper - 1.5 percent of the population; society's new rich; successful professionals; high-level business executives; successful entrepreneurs; educated at public universities; send children to private elite universities; active in civic affairs
Upper-middle - 10 percent of the population; career-oriented professionals such as physicians, lawyers and engineers; best educated social class; quite status conscious; reside in prestigious neighborhoods
Lower-middle - 30 percent of the population; society's white-collar workers such as office workers, clerks, teachers, and salespeople; most conforming, hard working, religious, and home- and family-oriented of all social classes
Upper-lower - 33 percent of the population; largest social class; blue-collar factory workers and skilled tradesmen; live a routine, day-to-day existence; not particularly status conscious;very security conscious; do not typically expect to rise above their present social station
Lower-lower - 25 percent of the population; unskilled worker; chronically unemployed worker; poorly educated; slum-dweller; unassimilated; ethnic minority groups; rural poor; reject middle-class values and standards of behavior

FIGURE 3–19
The staircase of social classes (source: Adapted from W. Lloyd Warner, *American Life, Dream and Reality* [Chicago: University of Chicago Press, 1953])

consideration of lower-upper class purchase behavior is social acceptability of their peer class and the acceptance of the upper-upper class; in other words, much of this class's buying behavior is directed at achieving status. Hence, these higher-class consumers are unlikely to shop at stores with lower-class stereotypes.[33]

- *Upper-middle class* consumers are quality conscious and purchase products that are acceptable to the upper class; hence, they tend to be cautious consumers of prestigious products that communicate "who they are" to others. On the other hand, they tend to be venturesome, trying new products and seeking new places to shop. For the upper-middle class, their homes are the center of their personal and social lives and therefore are a focus for their buyer behavior.
- *Lower-middle class* consumers focus a considerable amount of their buying behavior around maintaining a respectable home within a do-it-yourself context. They tend to be quite value conscious in that they seek an acceptable relationship between lower prices and good quality. Standardization is a key factor in their buying behavior; they therefore purchase products of standard design from traditional retail operations.
- *Upper-lower class* consumers are less concerned with purchasing products that enhance status; they buy goods and services for personal enjoyment. This class spends a lower proportion of their incomes on housing and a higher proportion on household goods than do the higher classes. They tend to be impulsive buyers, yet remain loyal to previously bought brands that they believe reflect good quality. As heavy users of credit, this class is hesitant to try new retail outlets.
- *Lower-lower class* consumers use credit extensively and impulsively to purchase highly visible products of a personal nature. They prefer well-known brands and local stores with easy credit terms.

Culture

The final social influence on our behavior is the cultural environment in which we live. **Culture** is the sum total of knowledge, attitudes, symbols, and patterns of behavior that are shared by a group of people and transmitted from one generation to the next. Cultural traits include (1) profound beliefs (e.g., religious); (2) fundamental values (e.g., achievements); and (3) customs (e.g., ladies first). Because cultural environmental influences are a major determinant of human behavior, it is essential that the retailer adapt and conform merchandising programs to the cultural heritage of its chosen markets.

The American culture is undergoing changes that have profoundly affected consumption patterns and buying behavior. For some products and firms, ongoing cultural trends spell new opportunities and merchandising success; for others, they create new threats and possible market failure. In developing and implementing merchandising programs, the retailer must ascertain the type and extent of influence exerted by the cultural traits of its local market.

THE CONSUMER BUYING PROCESS

Being loved and accepted, overcoming loneliness and insecurity, or gaining status and prestige are all problems that consumers attempt to solve in part by engaging in buying activities. Individuals make purchase decisions by passing through the five stages of the consumer buying process. The **consumer buying process** is the sum of the sequential parts of problem recognition, information search, alternative evaluation, purchase decision, and postpurchase evaluation. The duration and extent to which an individual undergoes any one stage of the buying process varies greatly depending on factors such as urgency of need, frequency of purchase, importance of purchase, and so on. The following discussion outlines each stage; see if you can recognize these stages in your own buying behavior.

Stage 1: Problem Recognition

A perceived discrepancy between an ideal state of affairs and the actual state of affairs starts the consumer's buying process by creating an awareness that a problem exists. Problem recognition, then, is a belief that things are not what they should be. Internally felt physiological and psychological needs are tension-producing stimuli that create an awareness that something is lacking. In addition, external cues attract and direct the consumer's attention toward the recognition that he or she is unsatisfied with the state of affairs. Exposure to the retailer's stores, products, advertisements, merchandising incentives, personal selling efforts, and price structures are all potential reminders to consumers of unfulfilled needs and wants.

Based on importance, cost, knowledge, and/or experience factors, there are three types of problem-solving situations—extensive, limited, and routinized. **Extensive problem solving** involves a buying situation in which the consumer is considering the purchase of an important and costly product under the unfavorable circumstances of having no knowledge or experience with it. First-time purchases, once-in-a-lifetime purchases, and highly infrequent purchases are all buying situations that require extensive consumer effort in achieving a satisfactory solution. Providing useful and readily available information and reducing risk and uncertainty of the purchase are key variables the retailer must consider when developing merchandising tactics to assist the consumer faced with an extensive problem-solving situation.

Limited problem solving occurs when the consumer has some knowledge and experience with purchasing and using the product under consideration. The problem may or may not involve an important purchase and/or costly product. In either case, the buyer is able to limit the range of considerations (e.g., brands, sizes, colors, materials, and so on) because of existing knowledge and previous experience. The retailer's task is to discover which limited decision factors the consumer is using in making product selections; and use these selective factors as focal points in developing appropriate product, price, distribution, and promotion strategies.

Routinized problem solving involves making the same purchase decision time after time. Consumers purchase many products frequently and regularly. Typically these purchases involve products of lower importance and cost that occur as repurchase needs. The typical weekly grocery list represents this type of purchase. Consumers simply repeat a previous purchase decision with little thought or deliberation because they feel there is no reason to change.

Stage 2: Information Search

Gathering information and gaining experience make up the second stage of the consumer buying process. A *low-level information search* involves an increased awareness of readily available information. The consumer pays closer attention to advertisements, store displays, sales pitches, and comments of others in an effort to gather additional information to supplement existing product knowledge. A *high-level information search* is a conscientious effort to seek out and gather new and supplementary information from new and existing sources. It involves actively talking with, reading from, and observing information sources that will be useful in an extensive problem-solving situation involving reevaluation and reinforcement purchases. Retailers that expect to capture the wealthier, healthier, and better-educated 50-plus consumers had better be able and willing to provide plenty of stores and product information; this growth market demands it.[34]

Stage 3: Alternative Evaluation

Product, brand, and store information must be processed before it can be useful in the evaluation of purchase alternatives. Consumers use a variety of criteria in making different purchase decisions. What evaluation criteria would you use in purchasing a tube of toothpaste, a desk lamp, a winter coat, a color television, and a new automobile? A comprehensive list of evaluation criteria consumers use in purchasing these products is far too complex and extensive to fully enumerate here; Figure 3–20 presents a general list of potential evaluation criteria.

Criteria do not carry the same weight in a purchase decision. In some cases, we are interested simply in having the product do what it was designed to do (e.g., clean, polish, cool, or heat); therefore, we place greater weight on the functional features of the product. In other cases, our needs are more social in character; hence, we emphasize the psychological features of the product or brand and the personal considerations of its appropriateness to our lifestyle and circle of friends. In essence, criteria for a given purchase may be weighted along an importance scale as illustrated in Figure 3–21.

Stage 4: Purchase Decision

The purchase decision is actually two decisions: *if* and *when*. The "if" decision concerns whether or not to make a purchase. Based on the previous evaluation stage, the consumer may decide that there are several products, brands, or stores capable of resolving the problem identified in the first stage of the buying process—the *buy decision*. On the other hand, the consumer may conclude that of the known alternatives evaluated, none meet minimum expectations for need satisfaction—the *no-buy decision*. A no-buy decision terminates the current cycle of the buying process; the consumer can either dismiss the problem or start the buying process anew with the hope of gaining a different perspective on the problem.

The "when" decision concerns deciding whether to make a purchase immediately or to wait until some future date. A *decision to proceed* with the purchase may stem from urgently felt needs, currently available opportunities, and other circumstances that mediate against delaying the decision. A *decision to postpone* a purchase frequently is associated with a high level of perceived risk. The consumer becomes anxious because of the importance, cost, and/or uncertainty of the decision.

I. Product Evaluation Criteria
  A. Functional Features
    1. Size
    2. Shape
    3. Weight
    4. Material
    5. Workmanship
  B. Aesthetic Features
    1. Color
    2. Texture
    3. Odor
    4. Taste
    5. Sound
    6. Style
  C. Service Features
    1. Delivery
    2. Alteration
    3. Installation
    4. Warranty
    5. Maintenance
  D. Psychological Features
    1. Prestige
    2. Image
    3. Acceptability
    4. Safety
    5. Security
    6. Uniqueness

II. Merchandising Evaluation Criteria
  A. Price Features
    1. Selling Price
    2. Perceived Value
    3. Credit Terms
  B. Place Features
    1. Convenience
    2. Availability
    3. Prestige
  C. Promotional Features
    1. Labels
    2. Logos
    3. Packages

III. Personal Evaluation Criteria
  A. Compatability Considerations
    1. Substitutive
    2. Complement
    3. Different
  B. Appropriateness Considerations
    1. Life-Style
    2. Life Cycle
  C. Other Considerations
    1. Durability
    2. Suitability
    3. Quality

FIGURE 3–20
Product, brand, and store evaluation criteria

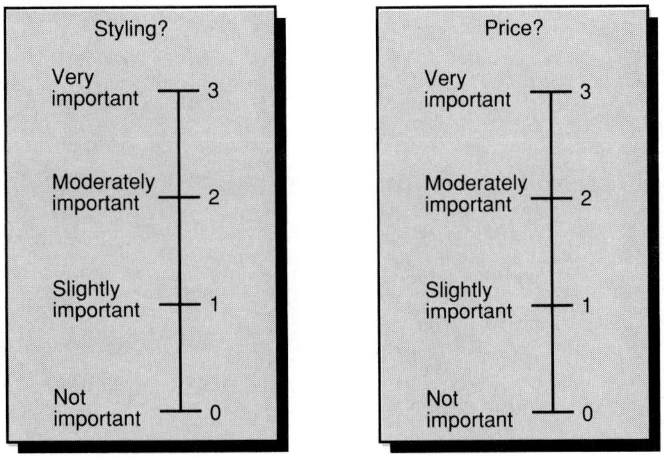

FIGURE 3–21
Criteria-weighting scale

Stage 5: Postpurchase Evaluation

The purchasing of a product does not end the consumer buying process. Once a purchase has been made, the consumer proceeds to reevaluate the decision to judge whether or not he or she made the right (e.g., best or acceptable) decision. Essentially the postpurchase evaluation stage consists of comparing the actual performance of the product/service or the actual experience with the store with the expected or hoped for performance or experience. The basic question to be answered by the consumer in the postpurchase evaluation stage is "Did the product or store relieve aroused tensions stemming from felt needs?" In other words, "Did the product or store solve the problem?" An affirmative answer promotes *postpurchase satisfaction* and encourages the consumer to repeat the purchase behavior at the same outlet when the same or a similar problem arises. A negative answer results in *postpurchase dissonance*—dissatisfaction with the purchase and the process that led to it. To relieve the feelings of uneasiness associated with an unsatisfactory product, the consumer may engage in a variety of actions: (1) discard the product and write it off as a bad experience; (2) obtain some type of allowance from the retailer, thereby increasing the product's perceived value; (3) return the product to the retailer and attempt to improve on his or her purchase decision process; or (4) write off the retailer as a poor place to shop.

Often consumers have mixed feelings concerning their purchases—a mild case of postpurchase dissonance. In such cases, they attempt to confirm a right decision, or at least an acceptable decision, by (1) seeking positive comments from others,

These are examples of the four buying scenes.

(2) distorting information so that it fits the purchase decision, or (3) emphasizing positive and deemphasizing negative information.

BUYING SCENES

The final buyer behavior issues to consider are buying scenes—where consumers buy. A **buying scene** is the actual place where the consumer completes a purchase transaction. There are four possible buying scenes: (1) a retail store, (2) a consumer's home, (3) a consumer's workplace, and (4) a parasite point of consumption.

Americans make most of their purchases by visiting a retail store or responding to in-the-home marketing efforts. While a consumer's place of work is a place of production rather than of consumption, some retailers (e.g., hair stylists and food vendors) have had success by providing the consumer with a high level of time and place convenience. Avon is following women to work; for some sale representatives, 50 percent of their business is generated through offices.[35] Beauti Control targets career-oriented and professional women by holding grooming seminars on their employers' premises.[36] Snap-on Tool Corp. uses step vans to take its products to the customer.[37]

Convenience is also the key for successfully marketing a limited number of products at "parasite" scenes (e.g., a newspaper stand at a restaurant, a hot dog vendor at a football game, and a magazine rack at an airport). A rapidly growing example of this retail format is the pushcart market—temporary (seasonal) tenants in various malls, marketplaces, and airports. Hickory Farms of Ohio operates more than 1,000 such operations in addition to its 500 stores. Jubilee Market at Jackson Brewery in New Orleans offers one-week leases, illustrating the temporary nature of such activities.[38]

SUMMARY

A market is a buying population and its buying behavior. Buying populations can be classified into one of two groups—consumer markets (ultimate consumers of goods and services) and organizational markets (intermediate consumers of goods and services). We examined the structure of buying populations from the perspective of population, demographic, and geographical analyses. Population analysis answers the question "How many are they?" The total population of a consumer market determines in part the actual and potential market for a particular area. Demographic analysis answers the question "Who are they?" Demography is the study of statistics used to describe a population. People can be described in terms of age, sex, education, income, occupation, race, nationality, family size, and structure. Major demographic trends are (1) an aging population, (2) a shrinking household, (3) a changing role for women, and (4) an increasing role of many diversified minorities. Geographic analysis answers the question "Where are they?" People move; therefore markets change. Some important geographic trends and patterns are as follows: (1) Population is shifting from the north and eastern United States to the south and western sectors; (2) America is an urbanized society (e.g., 75 percent reside in urban areas); (3) there are more suburbanites than urbanites; and (4) nonmetro areas are making a comeback.

Buying behavior is the manner in which consumers act, function, and react to various situations involving the purchase of a good or service or the acceptance of an idea. The dimensions of consumer buying behavior include understanding buying considerations, situations, centers, influences, processes, and scenes. Buying consideration concerns the question "What do consumers buy?" Consumers buy products—bundles of benefits capable of satisfying their wants and needs. Products are viewed in terms of their tangibility (goods, services, or ideas); durability (durables and nondurables); and availability (convenience, shopping, and specialty products).

Buying situations concern the question "How much do consumers buy?" The answer is a function of an individual's needs and desires together with the individual's ability to buy (the financial resources—income, credit, assets—available to the consumer); willingness to buy (psychological, personal, and social reasons for buying); and authority to buy (formal and informal authorization).

Buying centers deal with the issue "Who does the buying?" A buying center is a basic unit of consumption that engages in the buying center. Basic consumption units tend to be either individuals or households.

Buying influences concern "Why consumers buy." The major influences of consumer buying behavior include psychological, personal, and social factors. Motivation, perception, learning, and attitudes are the four major psychological factors that influence consumers' buying choices. An individual's personality, self-concept, lifestyle, and position in the life cycle are all personal factors that affect his or her buying behavior. Conformity to group expectations (family, reference groups, social class, and culture) is the basic premise behind the impact of social factors on consumer buying behavior.

The buying process is the sum of the sequential arts of problem recognition, information search, alternative evaluation, purchase decision, and postpurchase evaluation. In other words, the buying process answers the question "How do consumers buy?"

The four buying scenes describe "Where consumers buy." A buying scene is the actual place where consumers complete a purchase transaction; it can be at a retail store, a consumer's home, a consumer's workplace, or a parasite point of consumption.

STUDENT STUDY GUIDE

Key Terms and Concepts

activities, interests, and opinions (AIO) (p. 112)
affective component (p. 109)
attitude (p. 109)
asset (p. 102)
behavior component (p. 109)
buying behavior (p. 90)
buying center (p. 103)
buying power (p. 101)
buying scene (p. 123)
cognitive component (p. 109)
consumer buying behavior (p. 97)
consumer buying process (p. 119)
consumer market (p. 89)
convenience product (p. 98)
credit (p. 102)
cue (p. 108)
culture (p. 118)
demography (p. 91)
desire (p. 101)
discretionary income (p. 101)
disposable income (p. 101)
drive (p. 108)
durable (p. 98)
esteem needs (p. 107)
extensive problem solving (p. 119)
family buying roles (p. 114)
good (p. 97)
idea (p. 98)
learning (p. 108)
life cycle (p. 112)
lifestyle (p. 111)
limited problem solving (p. 119)
market (p. 89)
market potential (p. 100)
middle-aged market (p. 93)
motivation (p. 104)
need (p. 101)
nondurable (p. 98)
organizational market (p. 89)
participation (p. 108)
perception (p. 107)
personality (p. 110)
physiological needs (p. 105)
product (p. 97)
reference group (p. 117)
reinforcement (p. 108)
repetition (p. 108)
response (p. 108)
routinized problem solving (p. 119)
safety needs (p. 106)
selective distortion (p. 108)
selective exposure (p. 108)
selective retention (p. 108)
self-actualization need (p. 107)
self-concept (p. 110)
senior-citizens market (p. 94)
service (p. 97)
shopping product (p. 99)
social class (p. 117)
social needs (p. 107)
specialty product (p. 99)
total income (p. 101)
total population (p. 90)
ultimate consumer (p. 90)
young-adults market (p. 93)
youth market (p. 92)

Review Questions

1. What are the two major components of a market? Provide a brief description.
2. Who are ultimate consumers? What are their purchase intentions?
3. What is demography? On what variables is a demographic description based?
4. Profile the changing age structure of the U.S. population. Discuss the impact of these changes on the retailing of goods.
5. How is the U.S. household mix changing? Is it good or bad news for American retailers? Explain.
6. What are the three working-women roles? Describe the impact of these roles on the merchandising of goods and services.
7. Illustrate the basic geographic shifts in the distribution of the nation's population.
8. Define *product*. Develop a graphic presentation of the various product classifications. Provide a description of each product class.
9. Describe the determinants of consumer buying power.
10. Identify the elements of the motivational process. Distinguish between the various types of needs that direct individual consumer behavior.
11. How is perception accomplished? Delineate between the various forms of selectivity that are portrayed in the perception process.
12. Discuss the stimulus-response mechanism inherent in the learning process.
13. What are attitudes used for? Describe the components of an attitude.
14. Who are we? Identify and define the four parts of the self-concept.
15. Lifestyle profiles are composite pictures of what factors? How do lifestyles affect buying behavior?
16. Portray the roles various family members might play in a given purchase situation.
17. Outline the stages of the consumer buying process.

Review Exam

True or False

_____ 1. A market consists of a buying population and its corresponding buying behavior.

_____ 2. One of the major retailing implications of the increasing number of working women is the need to develop strategies that are not aimed solely at women as the family's major purchasing agent.

_____ 3. Durables are perishable products that are used up in one or a few uses.

_____ 4. Selective retention is the act of remembering only that information the individual wants to remember.

_____ 5. The AIO variables in lifestyle profiles are attitudes, influences, and opportunities.

_____ 6. Upper-upper social class consumers often engage in conspicuous consumption to meet their need for recognition.

_____ 7. Realization of a discrepancy between an ideal state of affairs and the actual state of affairs is the initial stage of the buying process called *problem recognition*.

Multiple Choice

_____ 1. An area's total population is determined by relationships between
   a. Birthrates and deathrates
   b. Immigration and emigration
   c. Birthrates and fertility rates
   d. a and b
   e. a, b, and c

_____ 2. The determining elements of consumer buying power are the consumer's _____.
   a. Spendable income
   b. Asset position
   c. Available credit
   d. a and c
   e. a, b, and c

_____ 3. Andy Lloyd enjoys shopping stores that allow him the freedom to find products that enhance his individuality and his need to be what he wants to be. In this case, Andy is expressing his need for _____.
   a. Safety
   b. Love
   c. Belongingness
   d. Esteem
   e. Self-actualization

_____ 4. A retailer's store sign, newspaper advertisement, and point-of-purchase display serve as a(n) _____ to guide individuals in their buying behavior.
   a. Need
   b. Motive
   c. Cue
   d. Attitude
   e. Roadmap

_____ 5. Mike sees himself as a budding scholar who forgos conspicuously expensive clothing and buys goods and services for mental enhancement. What part of the self-concept is Mike expressing in this case?
   a. Real self
   b. Looking-glass self

c. Ideal self
d. Self-image
e. Hopeful self

_____ 6. A _____ is a group that serves as a model or standard for an individual's behavior and attitudes.
a. Social class
b. Subculture
c. Reference group
d. Culture
e. Society

_____ 7. From past experience, Ted Lewis knows that he wants steel-belted radial tires. However, he is not sure which brand is best, what would constitute a fair price, and which retailer offers the best service. Ted Lewis is faced with a(n) _____ problem-solving situation.
a. Extensive
b. Limited
c. Exclusive
d. Routinized
e. Convenient

STUDENT APPLICATIONS MANUAL

Investigative Projects: Practice and Applications

1. Population and demographic profiles are essential in determining the market potential of a given area. Develop complete population and demographic profiles of your town, city, or county. Consult several sources (e.g., census bureau reports, *Survey of Buying Power*), and prepare a list of the ten most important population or demographic trends in your area. For each trend identified, provide two or more merchandising implications that retailers should consider in the future.
2. Classify each item on the following list of products as to its (1) tangibility, (2) durability, and (3) availability.

1. meat	15. pencil
2. pet food	16. film
3. furniture	17. business suit
4. electricity	18. prescription drug
5. church service	19. haircut
6. auto insurance	20. music concert
7. legal advice	21. college course
8. movie	22. candy bar
9. Datsun 300 ZX	23. wedding ring
10. air conditioner	24. gasoline
11. Big Mac	25. lawn mower
12. bag of apples	26. open-heart surgery
13. telephone service	27. birthday dinner
14. tennis shoes	28. textbook

3. Determine your ability to buy by estimating your buying power.
4. Consult the list of products in project 2. Which products do you purchase to meet (1) physiological needs, (2) safety needs, (3) social needs, (4) esteem needs, and (5) self-actualization needs?
5. Describe specific examples of your selective perception in terms of your selective exposure, retention, and distortion.
6. Lifestyle is the way people live. One interesting lifestyle segmentation scheme for high school students was uncovered by Bickley Townsend, associate editor of *American Demographics*. Review the six high school lifestyles described below. Assume the role of a small specialty clothing store, and develop some merchandising strategies that you believe would be appealing to each of the six lifestyle segments.

Greaseballs: At one end of the high school lifestyle spectrum are the Greaseballs, including Farmers and Farmers' Daughters. The boys wear brown jackets from Agway and tractor caps that say "Brooktondale Volunteer Firemen." The girls sport heavy makeup and tight sweaters. Also in the Greaseball segment are Wrestlers (other jocks have status, but wrestlers do not) and Headbangers. Headbangers wear chains and black concert shirts that say "Twisted Sister"; advanced cases are called Burnouts.
Rah-Rahs: This psychographic segment includes jocks, their girlfriends, and the guys who wish they were jocks. Rah-Rahs are popular conformists, with few intellectual or political interests. They used to include Preppies, but this segment is disappearing, reflecting the temporariness of teenage fashion.
New Wavers: Also popular but more involved in current events, New Wavers are fashion conscious in an attention-getting way. They are distinguished by melon and light-green clothing, including color-coordinated socks, all carrying an Esprit label. New Wavers are emulated by Pseudo-Wavers, who want to be Wavers but don't quite make it.
Apes: These are the smart kids, the ones who take the advanced placement (A.P.) courses. They are arrogantly articulate and fiercely competitive for 4.0 averages. They are the driving force behind the student newspaper. Although they think of themselves as Achievers, they are known to outsiders as Encyclopedias.
Zobos: Mostly female, Zobos are distinguished by their high political consciousness and studied bag-lady fashion look. Zobos shop in used-clothing stores and eschew high heels. A typical Zobo outfit is a long skirt made from an Indian bedspread, accompanied by high, laced-up hiking boots. Zobos spend a lot of time on

worthwhile causes like sponsoring Laotian refugees, and they carry hand-woven purses from Guatemala to demonstrate their solidarity with the Third World.
Resisters: This category represents the pinnacle of psychological development. Resisters defy psychographic classification or fashion identification, evident in their uniform of T-shirts, sweatshirts, and chinos. Their message is that they are totally unaware of image, being above such trivia.

7. A consumer's "values" play an important role in his or her buying behavior. Develop a list of five or six values that you believe are basic to most consumers. Describe each key value and provide an example of how each might affect the consumer's buying behavior.

Tactical Cases: Problems and Decisions

■ CASE 3–1
Doug's Video—Developing Competitive Positioning Strategies Based on Consumer Patronage Behavior*

Doug Deitz's story was not unlike those of many other New Englanders who successfully survived the migration to the Sunbelt of many types of manufacturing. Doug had graduated from high school in the late 1940s, taken a job in a textile mill, enlisted in the Army Reserve, spent two years on active duty during the Korean conflict, and returned to the mill. When the mill headed south in the sixties, Doug took advantage of his G.I. bill and completed an associate degree in business.

He started his retailing career with a family-owned department store. Failure of the store's management to follow the movement into shopping centers led to the sale of the store to a chain. It became apparent to Doug that the new management favored persons with baccalaureate degrees. When Doug realized how long it would take him to complete his degree on a part-time basis, he regretted his decision not to continue his education at the time he completed the associate degree. Like others with less experience receiving promotions to buying responsibility, Doug sought a change of scenery and obtained more managerial responsibility in the employ of a discount store chain. He worked for two discount chains until two years ago when, with the benefit of an inheritance from the passing of his parents, he acquired a video store.

While Doug benefited from the increasing popularity of video rentals and the sale of video equipment, the success of his business seemed to indicate that he had more managerial talent than former employers had perceived. Proof of self-perception is the additional success Doug achieved in providing unique and profitable video services. His first video service was videotaping of houses for sale. The tapes were sold to more progressive area realtors, who used them to screen home buyers' interests. Since it benefited both the realtors and the prospective home buyers, it had been very successful. Recently Doug had expanded the video service to include videotaping of homes and their contents for insurance purposes. While the insurance service didn't generate the volume or the regularity of revenues that the realtor service had, it required no additional investment in equipment and staff. The only added cost was for promotion; hence it represented the addition of a very complementary line of service.

Doug's Video was located in a community shopping center complex that had been built as part of a relatively new housing development. The introduction and expansion of local high-tech industries had created a miniboom for the local economy. New people were attracted by these high-tech firms because salaries in the \$50,000-to-\$100,000 range were common. These high-income families constituted the majority of the buyers of the homes in the housing development that surrounded the shopping center. Additional retailers in the complex were a junior department store, a large food store, a dry cleaner, a bakery, a hardware store, a small pharmacy, three apparel stores, a pizza/sub shop, and a delicatessen.

The video rental business generated a fairly lively traffic volume into the store. Doug's prior expansion of services had taken advantage of existing products and staff capabilities, but only indirectly of the high-volume in-store traffic. Since all systems seemed to be "go" in terms of the local economy, Doug was seriously considering some type of expansion.

One expansion idea was to add a complementary line of merchandise that would fit into the current business format and capitalize on the high in-store traffic generated by the video rental business. The addition of a complete line of cameras and accessories was a product extension strategy that Doug felt that he and his staff could handle within current operating capabilities. The buying and merchandising aspects of adding new camera and accessory lines did not create any major obstacles. What concerned Doug was developing a business format that would be competitive with other retailers and consistent with consumer patronage behavior. Recently Doug had obtained from a vendor an excellent trade survey on what factors influenced consumers' choice of outlet for camera purchases. The survey revealed that the importance of patronage factors varies for different types of retailers (see Exhibit A). The discount store camera customer differs from the department store customer. Through experience, Doug learned that "competitive positioning" often is a key variable in introducing a new product or service. A quick mental survey of local retailers that sell cameras revealed that Doug would face each of the six types of competitors identified in the trade report.

ASSIGNMENT

1. Based on the consumer patronage behavior for camera purchases, develop three competitive positioning strategies Doug might pursue in establishing his camera department. Provide an analysis for each strategy, and make a recommendation.
2. Based on your competitive positioning recommendation, identify key merchandising tactics that Doug should use to successfully introduce this new line of products.

*This case was prepared by Ken Mast and Dale Lewison, the University of Akr

EXHIBIT A
Patronage factors

Retail Setting	Rank	Influencing Factor	Outlet Rating	Overall Average
Discount store	1	Low price	5.77	5.36
	2	Services offered	4.92	5.08
	3	Quality reputation	4.59	5.00
	4	Knowledgeable sales staff	4.40	5.03
	5	Selection of photo goods	4.12	4.44
	6	Close to home or work	4.07	3.90
	7	Selection of other goods	3.60	2.83
	8	Attractive atmosphere	3.25	3.07
Camera store	1	Knowledgeable sales staff	5.84	5.03
	2	Services offered	5.73	5.08
	3	Quality reputation	5.64	5.00
	4	Selection of photo goods	4.91	4.44
	5	Low price	4.80	5.36
	6	Close to home or work	4.00	3.90
	7	Attractive atmosphere	3.15	3.07
	8	Selection of other goods	2.19	2.83
Mail order	1	Low price	5.81	5.36
	2	Quality reputation	5.40	5.00
	3	Selection of photo goods	5.00	4.44
	4	Services offered	4.68	5.08
	5	Knowledgeable sales staff	4.44	5.03
	6	Close to home or work	2.75	3.90
	7	Selection of other goods	2.16	2.83
	8	Attractive atmosphere	2.00	3.07
Department store	1	Low price	5.36	5.36
	2	Services offered	5.18	5.08
	3	Knowledgeable sales staff	4.98	5.03
	4	Quality reputation	4.97	5.00
	5	Selection of photo goods	4.25	4.44
	6	Close to home or work	4.15	3.90

EXHIBIT A
continued

Retail Setting	Rank	Influencing Factor	Outlet Rating	Overall Average
	7	Attractive atmosphere	3.46	3.07
	8	Selection of other goods	3.19	2.83
Catalog showroom	1	Low price	5.73	5.36
	2	Services offered	4.90	5.08
	3	Quality reputation	4.80	5.00
	4	Knowledgeable sales staff	4.63	5.03
	5	Selection of photo goods	4.60	4.44
	6	Close to home or work	3.81	3.90
	7	Attractive atmosphere	3.41	3.07
	8	Selection of other goods	3.34	2.83
Discount camera store	1	Low price	5.56	5.36
	2	Knowledgeable sales staff	5.26	5.03
	3	Quality reputation	4.79	5.00
	4	Services offered	4.69	5.08
	5	Selection of photo goods	4.64	4.44
	6	Close to home or work	3.36	3.90
	7	Attractive atmosphere	2.39	3.07
	8	Selection of other goods	1.87	2.83
Overall factors	1	Low price		5.36
	2	Services offered		5.08
	3	Knowledgeable sales staff		5.03
	4	Quality reputation		5.00
	5	Selection of photo goods		4.44
	6	Close to home or work		3.90
		Attractive Atmosphere		3.07
	8	Selection of other goods		2.83

Source: *1985 Consumer Photographic Survey* (Jackson, Miss.: Photo Marketing Association International), 21.

■ CASE 3–2
Esprit de Corps: A Merchandising-Philosophizing Mix*

Esprit de Corps, a San Francisco–based clothing manufacturer and retailer, has enjoyed considerable success both domestically and abroad. Originally Esprit offered its line of contemporary women's clothing through department and specialty stores. Today these avenues of distribution have been supplemented by company-owned and operated stores. A skilled merchandiser, Esprit offers over ten complete collections each year—about double the number of lines most competitors offer. To protect its image, Esprit has strict merchandising programs that dictate how merchandise is to be displayed and promoted. Esprit requires that to remain an active account, each retailer carry a representative assortment of the Esprit collection.

To further enhance customers' product awareness and shopping convenience, Esprit produces a carefully orchestrated seasonal catalog showing what merchandise will be

EXHIBIT A
Eternal Spring? Maybe not! (source: The 1990 Esprit Spring Catalog, Esprit de Corp, San Francisco, California. Copyright © Esprit de Corp, 1990)

What you see here is a glimpse of Esprit's Spring products. The coming of Spring is also an appropriate time to remind us of the preciousness of the cycle of renewal; when the earth is annually reborn. As the seasons pass and as we are living in more urbanized environments, we are rapidly losing our sense of Nature's cycles. We live in isolated and insulated buildings. We drive in enclosed climate controlled cars, and we pass through a landscape altered, polluted and ravaged by humans. This pollution is by and large the result of an economic system gone out of control, where individuals, businesses, and governments have become slaves to the gods of expansion, "progress," profit and excess copnsumption. We have lost sight of Nature's gifts; her strengths, and most of all, her vulnerabilities. We are living in a world which continues to act as if resources are infinite and as if the cataclysmic problems of global warming, overpopulation, rain forest depletion, air and water pollution, and the annihilation of species can be dealt with by the next technological fix. The trouble is that real solutions lie only within ourselves; within our minds and our behaviors. We must change if we wish to have a decent world for ourselves and our children. This change must come not only in the form of conservation, but also in a renewed consciousness about Nature and our place in the Natural World. We need to return Nature to the center of our universe, to reverse the idea that nature is to be tamed and dominated for humans only. This is a difficult challenge for all of us because it requires that we rethink the most basic assumptions upon which we conduct our lives.

As you read this, you might be asking yourself why Esprit, a clothing company, interested in promoting itself and expanding, is speaking this way? It is simply because, though we need to continue in business, we also need to be responsible citizens of the planet; to implore consumers to temper their appetities, and also to temper our own, changing some of our own business practices. Consumers should evalute carefully what they need, and buy accordingly, whether it is clothing, cars, televisions, or whatever. The resources of the earth are finite. World economics based on exponential growth and expanding consumptive appetites cannot be sustained forever. For our own part, at Esprit, we have already begun. This catalog is printed entirely with recycled paper. We are redesigning all of our packaging to reflect emerging environmental realities. We are instituting anti-waste procedures throughout the company, from reducing waste in our cafeteria to using fewer xerox copies, computer paper, IBM reports, and less "stuff" overall. In addition, we're working hard to raise our own consciousness, and that of all our staff and employees toward population issues, conservation and the environment. We must all change. This is obvious. It starts at home, where we live and work. We make our plea to you, but we know we have a long way to go as well. It will be all of us, each in our own way, that will contribute. Please—be good to our Earth, its air, its water, its natural resources. Thank you.

available through the firm's outlets. The 1990 spring catalog of colorful and casual apparel looks like a typical Esprit book, but with a significant difference—Esprit management decided to make statements regarding various environmental and social issues. Printed on recycled paper, the spring catalog uses an environmental/social responsibility theme to make a dramatic and pointed presentation of both products and ideas. The catalog carries a "social note" explaining management's position and reasoning.

The catalog itself was introduced under the title "Eternal Spring? Maybe Not!" The text of the introduction is covered in Exhibit A. The copy on each page of the catalog identifies an environmental or social theme designed to provoke personal introspection on the part of the reader. The environmental and social themes are listed in Exhibit B.

ASSIGNMENT

From a consumer behavior perspective, evaluate Esprit's strategy of using a merchandising vehicle (catalog) to promote consumer awareness of and concern for various social and environmental issues. What might be the positive and negative outcomes of such a strategy? How will it affect Esprit's image? What will be the impact on product sales? Review all of the catalog copy (Exhibits A and B). Are there any changes you would recommend? Explain and justify those changes with respect to the appropriate consumer behavior principles.

*This case was prepared by Dale Lewison and Amy Morgan, The University of Akron.

Sources: Adrienne Ward, "Esprit Catalogs Catching the Recycling Spirit," *Advertising Age*, February 19, 1990, 49, and the 1990 Esprit Spring Catalog, Esprit de Corps, San Francisco, California.

- Earth First! or Man First?
- Rainforests or Acid Rain?
- Are 6,000,000,000 People Enough?
- Ecology or Deep Ecology?
- Personal Commitments or Group Apathy?
- TV or the Real Thing?
- The End of Nature or a Techno-fix?
- If Small Is Beautiful, How about Slow?
- Conservation or Consumption?
- "Progress" or Is It Regress?
- Star Wars or Eco-raiders?
- Birth Control or Population Drawdown?
- Wildlife Habitats or an Astroturf World?
- Your Children or Your Children's Children?
- Human Solidarity or Personal Gain?
- Green or Greed?
- A Concrete Continent 90 Lanes Wide?
- Paper or Plastic?
- Eco-Immunology or Techno-Medicine?
- The Short-Term or the Future?
- Recycle or Resource Waste?

EXHIBIT B
Environmental and social themes (source: The 1990 Esprit Spring Catalog, Esprit de Corp, San Francisco, California. Copyright © Esprit de Corp, 1990)

ENDNOTES

1. Kathleen Deveny and Peter K. Francese, "Shrinking Markets," *The Wall Street Journal,* March 9, 1990, R29.
2. Ibid.
3. Joe Mandese, "Who Are the Targets?", *Marketing and Media Decisions,* July 1989, 29.
4. Stephen Phillips, Amy Dunkin, James B. Treece, and Keith H. Hammonds, "King Customer," *Business Week,* March 12, 1990, 91.
5. "Snapshots of the Nation," *The Wall Street Journal,* March 9, 1990, R12.
6. John Carey, "The Changing Face of a Restless Nation," *Business Week,* September 25, 1989, 106.
7. See Bernice Kanner, "Kids' Clubs Mean Big Money," *Cleveland Plain Dealer,* April 1, 1990, 1E, 4E.
8. Stephanie Cook, "Riding the Silver Streak," *Retailing Issues Letter* (published by Arthur Andersen & Co. in conjunction with the Center for Retailing Studies, Texas A&M University, September 1989), 2.
9. David B. Wolfe, "The Ageless Market," *American Demographics* (July 1987): 28.
10. Rolph Anderson, "Yo, Marketers, Get Hip!", *Marketing and Media Decisions,* January 1990, 88.
11. "Retailing and the Older Consumer," *The Retail Report,* 2, no. 3 (Newsletter of the Center for Retailing at the University of Florida, 1990), 1.
12. See Blayne Cutler, "Meet Jane Doe," *American Demographics* (June 1984): 25–28.
13. Ken Dychtwald and Greg Gable, "Portrait of a Changing Consumer," *Business Horizons* (January-February 1990): 64.
14. Ibid., 70.
15. Zachary Schiller, "Stalking the New Customer," *Business Week,* August 28, 1989, 55.
16. Lori Keslar, "Efforts by Big Retailers Gaining Notice," *Advertising Age,* February 8, 1988, 5–6.
17. Joel Kotkin, "Selling to the New America," *INC,* July 1987, 47.
18. See Penney Gill, "Know Your Customer," *Stores,* November 1989, 31.
19. See Eugene Carlson, "The Rural Observer," *The Wall Street Journal,* March 9, 1990, R16.
20. Martin L. Bell, "Some Strategy Implications of a Matrix Approach to the Classification of Marketing Goods and Services," *Journal of the Academy of Marketing Sciences* 14 (Spring 1986): 13–20.
21. Laurel Culter, "Consumers Are Tougher Customers," *Fortune,* July 3, 1989, 76.
22. Anne B. Fisher, "What Consumers Want in the 1990s," *Fortune,* January 29, 1990, 108.
23. See Joseph Ellis, "New Opportunities in the Retail Marketplace," *Retail Control* (March 1990): 6.
24. See Judith Waldrop, "Spending by Degree," *American Demographics* (February 1990): 23–26.
25. Jeffrey A. Trachtenberg, "Cocktails at Tiffany," *Forbes,* February 6, 1989, 129.
26. "Luxury of the '90s: Time," *Advertising Age,* January 8, 1990, 31.
27. "Population Counts! And How," *Stores,* November 1989, 41.
28. Janet Wallach, "The Junior Customer: Who Is She, and What Does She Want?", *Stores,* January 1988, 53.
29. Dychtwald and Gable, "Portrait of a Changing Consumer," 67.
30. Joe Agnew, "Targeting the Couch Potato," *Marketing News,* February 15, 1988, 1.
31. Joe Mandese, "Who Are the Targets?", *Marketing and Media Decisions,* July 1989, 30.
32. See Faye Rice, "Yuppie Spending Gets Serious," *Fortune,* March 27, 1989, 147–149.
33. See Douglas L. MacLachlan and John P. Dickson, "Do People Avoid Some Stores Because of 'Social Distance'?", *The Channel of Communication* (Center for Retail and Business Market Strategy, University of Washington, Winter 1990), 5–6.
34. See Walecia Konrad and Gail DeGeorge, "U.S. Companies Go for the Gray," *Business Week,* April 3, 1989, 64–67.
35. See Kathleen Deveny, "Can Avon Get Wall Street to Answer the Door?" *Business Week,* March 20, 1989, 129.
36. See William P. Barrett, "See Dick and Jinger Sell," *Forbes,* August 7, 1989, 48.
37. "Step Vans Serve as Store on Wheels," *Marketing News,* June 1987, 6.
38. Eric C. Peterson, "Temporary Tenants," *Stores,* January 1987, 144; Barbara Bryan, "Airport Retailing," *Stores,* July 1987, 37; "Airport Retailers Expected to Reach New Sales Heights," *Marketing News,* February 15, 1988, 23.

PART I

THE LEGAL AND ETHICAL ASPECTS OF RETAILING

CHAPTER 4

OUTLINE

THE LEGAL ENVIRONMENT

THE LEGAL ASPECTS OF RETAIL COMPETITION

- Present Restraints on Trade
- Probable Restraints on Trade
- Unfair Trade Practices

THE LEGAL ASPECTS OF STORE OPERATIONS

- Store Organization and the Law
- Personnel Management and the Law
- Store Facilities and the Law

THE LEGAL ASPECTS OF RETAIL MERCHANDISING

- Product Legalities
- Price Legalities
- Promotion Legalities
- Distribution Legalities

THE ETHICAL ASPECTS OF RETAILING

OBJECTIVES

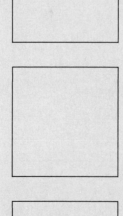

- Respect the legal complexities under which the retailer must operate.
- Understand the legal framework establishing the lawful limits within which retailing activities must be conducted.
- Identify and discuss the legal aspects of retail competition.
- Distinguish the legal aspects of retail store operations.
- Describe the legal aspects of retail merchandising.
- Judge the ethical nature of various behaviors and situations.

THE PENNEY IDEA[1]

The Penney Idea
(Adopted 1913)

1. To serve the public, as nearly as we can, to its complete satisfaction.
2. To expect for the service we render a fair remuneration and not all the profit the traffic will bear.
3. To do all in our power to pack the customer's dollar full of value, quality and satisfaction.
4. To continue to train ourselves and our associates so that the service we give will be more and more intelligently performed.
5. To improve constantly the human factor in our business.
6. To reward men and women in our organization through participation in what the business produces.
7. To test our every policy, method and act in this wise: "Does it square with what is right and just?"

J. C. Penney "understood exactly what he believed and [had] the ability to translate these beliefs about human behavior into practical, everyday behaviors for those who worked in his organization."[2] The company "enjoys the reputation of being a character and man-builder as well as a builder of profits. It is because there always has been and always will be that energetic spirit of efficient honesty directing and developing its affairs, not because honesty is the best policy, but because honesty is right and always has been and always will be until the end of time."[3] Legal and ethical business practices make good business sense. Legal and ethical business conduct is "a pragmatic, no-nonsense, bottom-line way of running your business for the long-term welfare of everyone involved."[4]

Legal and ethical business practices stem from a corporate culture that demands, promotes, and supports behavior that conforms to the laws of the land and the codes of the professional. In this chapter, we examine the retailer's legal and ethical behavior.

THE LEGAL ENVIRONMENT

The legal environment is the framework that establishes the lawful limits within which retailing and other business activities must be conducted. It is the attempt by various government bodies to modify or control the retailer's behavior and activities through various statutory measures and regulatory instruments. The legal environment and the need for a legal framework are the result of our increasingly complex business and social climate.

The legal environment is defined by the actions of the legislative, executive, and judicial branches of federal, state, and local governments. As Figure 4–1 illustrates, the principal legal measures and regulatory instruments used in defining the environment are statutes, ordinances, administrative regulations, contracts, certificates, licenses, taxes, and emergency controls. Governments have other means of influencing the general legal environment; subsidies and government ownership are two examples. In this chapter, we examine the retailer's concerns with the legal aspects of retail competition, store operations, and retail merchandising. Figure 4–2 summarizes the major legal issues we address in this chapter.

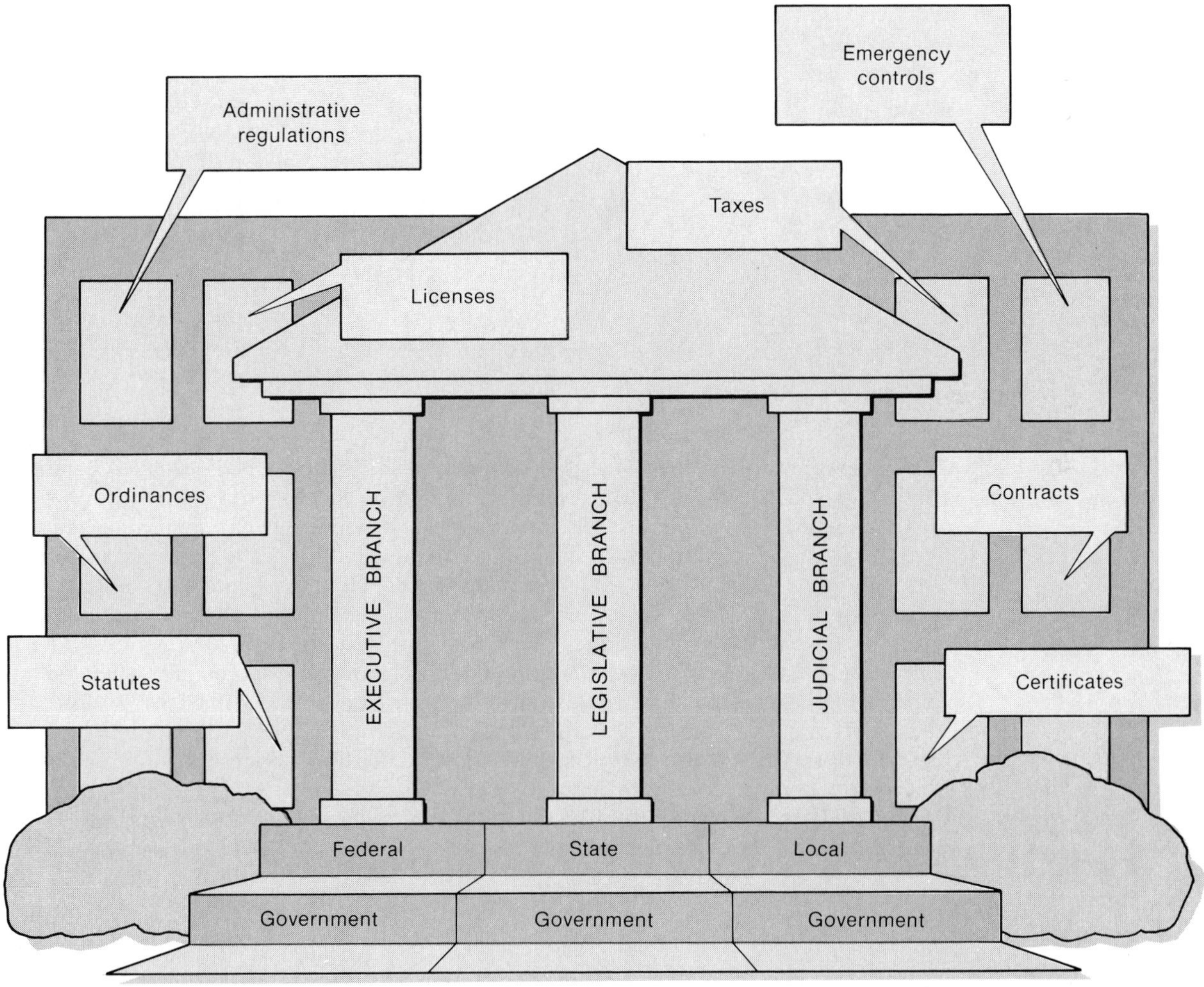

FIGURE 4–1
The legal environment

FIGURE 4–2
The retailer and the law

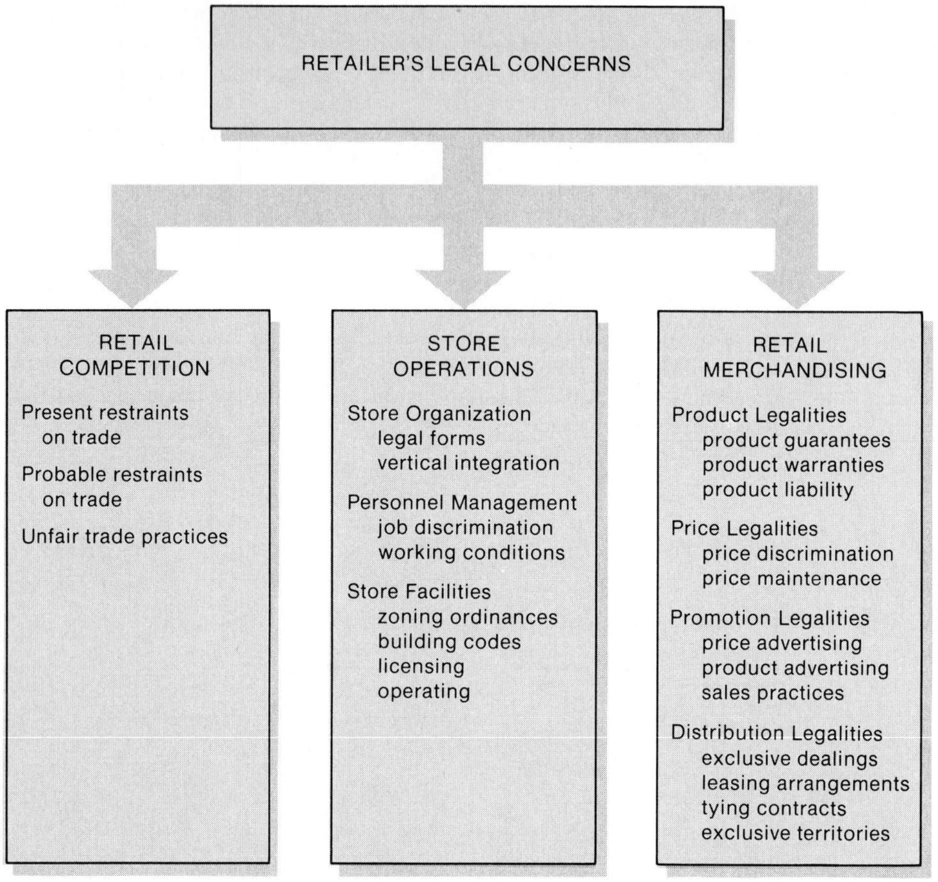

THE LEGAL ASPECTS OF RETAIL COMPETITION

Retail competition involves the actions of one retailer against other retailers in securing resources and patronage of consumers. Competitive actions include both the actual operation of stores and merchandising strategies and tactics. Governments make laws to ensure that these competitive actions are conducted under equitable rules and circumstances. What is fair or equitable naturally is open to interpretation; generally the court system and various government regulatory agencies make such interpretations.

One effort to create and maintain a competitive business environment has taken the form of antitrust legislation. **Antitrust legislation** is a set of laws directed at preventing "unreasonable restraints on trade" and "unfair trade practices" to foster a competitive environment. Concerning "what" exactly it is preventing and "when" it seeks to prevent it, government antitrust legislation aims to protect consumers and businesses from (1) present restraints on trade, (2) probable restraints on trade, and (3) unfair trade practices. Figure 4–3 identifies the principal legislative measures (laws) associated with each classification.

Present Restraints on Trade

In 1890 the federal government, in an attempt to control big business's control or restraint of free trade, passed the **Sherman Antitrust Act**. The existence of cartels, pools, and trade associations during the post–Civil War years led to fear that big business might control prices and supplies of products in the marketplace. In passing

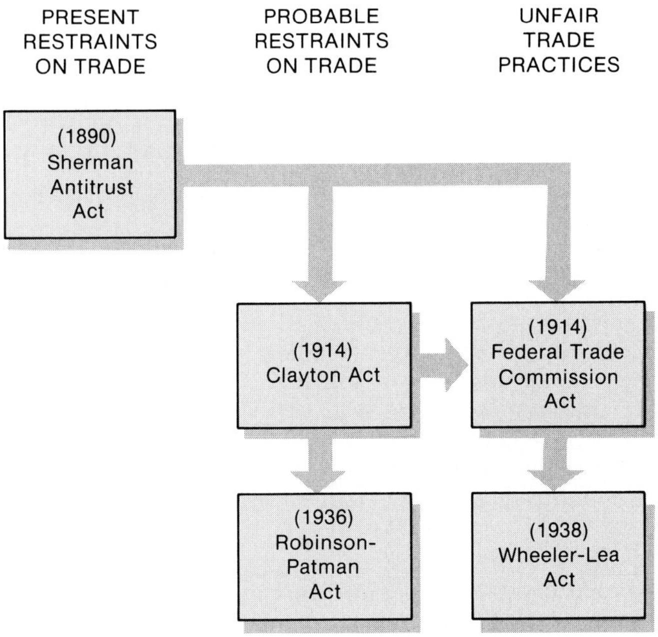

FIGURE 4–3
Principal federal antitrust legislation (source: Adapted from Larry J. Rosenberg, *Marketing*. [Englewood Cliffs, N.J.: Prentice-Hall, 1977], 59)

the Sherman Antitrust Act, the federal government restricted the size and economic power of any given organization with the purpose of correcting existing—and preventing future—unreasonable restraints of trade. Sections 1 and 2, the key provisions of the act, state that every contract, combination, or conspiracy in restraint of trade is illegal and prohibit all monopolies or attempts to monopolize. Because the language of the Sherman Antitrust Act is vague, however, the Supreme Court ruled that the company's act must constitute an *unreasonable* restraint of trade to be unlawful. This ruling became known as the "rule of reason" and made the Sherman Antitrust Act ineffective because each case had to be tried against this rule. Later legislation filled the gaps in the Sherman Act.

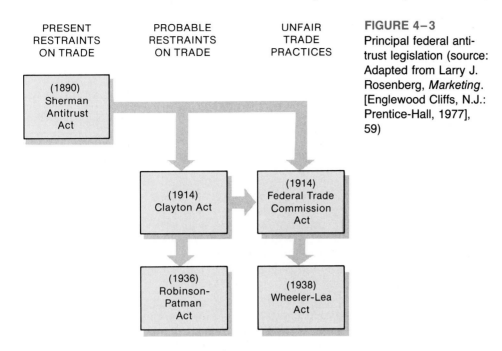

Probable Restraints on Trade

To overcome the shortcomings of the Sherman Antitrust Act, the federal government passed several pieces of legislation to prevent rather than correct restraints of trade. The first of these legislative amendments was the Clayton Act, passed by Congress in 1914. The **Clayton Act** dealt with several specific anticompetitive actions such as price discrimination, tying contracts, exclusive dealings, and interlocking boards of directors (we will discuss each of these actions later in the chapter). It declared such actions illegal where the effect may be to "substantially lessen competition" or "tend to create a monopoly." With passage of the Clayton Act, the government no longer had to prove that either a restraint of trade or a monopoly existed. Instead, it was sufficient to show that a *probable* restraint of trade or monopoly *might* result if certain competitive actions were allowed to continue.

The **Robinson-Patman Act** of 1936 amended the Clayton Act by broadening its scope and clarifying the meaning of "unlawful competition." Under the Robinson-Patman Act, unlawful competition included any competitive action that would tend "to injure, destroy, or prevent competition." Subsequent interpretation extended the intent of the law to include injury to "competitors." The major thrust of the Robinson-Patman Act was at various means of price discrimination.

Unfair Trade Practices

In 1914 Congress passed the **Federal Trade Commission (FTC) Act,** prohibiting unfair trade practices that could injure either competition or competitors. To determine what constitutes fair and unfair trade practices, the FTC was established as a quasi-judicial agency having limited judicial powers. In 1938 Congress amended the 1914 act by passing the **Wheeler-Lea Act,** which banned unfair and deceptive business acts or practices. The significance of this amendment is that it outlaws unfair and deceptive activities regardless of their effects on competition or competitors. Armed with this amendment, the FTC has become the single most important regulatory agency for most retailers. The rules and regulations the FTC administers affect primarily deceptive advertising and sales practices.

The procedures the FTC uses to enforce these rules and regulations include (1) individual-firm or industrywide conferences to secure voluntary compliance, (2) consent orders whereby the firm or industry agrees to abandon an unfair trade practice, and (3) formal court action to force the firm or industry to comply with FTC decisions. The first two procedures have been so successful in preventing and correcting unfair or deceptive trade practices that reliance on formal legal action has been significantly reduced.

THE LEGAL ASPECTS OF STORE OPERATIONS

Government regulations and controls extend to all aspects of the physical operations of the store. In "running" the store, the retailer must follow laws pertaining to its organizational structure, store personnel, physical facilities, and other aspects of the operation.

Store Organization and the Law

The law imposes certain restrictions and controls on establishing, expanding, contracting, and discontinuing a retail business. The influence of the law is especially important in store organization.

Legal Forms of Retail Organization

The law recognizes three basic forms of business organization: the sole proprietorship, the partnership, and the corporation.

The **sole proprietorship** is a business owned and managed by a single individual. Having its origins in common law, the sole proprietorship is the simplest legal form of organization. The principal legal advantages of this form of organization are the following:

1. No formal legal requirement other than a business license, so the retailer need not obtain authorization from state or federal governments to form the business
2. Greater flexibility in operations—the retailer is not expected to meet the maze of state regulations imposed on corporations
3. Single taxation—all profits are taxed at once as personal income

Unlimited liability is the major legal limitation of a sole proprietorship. *Unlimited liability* means that the sole proprietor assumes total responsibility for all debts stemming from the business and that responsibility extends to current and future *personal* as well as *business* assets. In other words, not only is the proprietor's business in jeopardy should the business fail in some way; personal assets also can be seized to cover bad debts.

When two or more persons form a business without incorporating, the business is a **partnership**. Partnerships can consist of any number of partners whose share and control of the business is determined at the time the organization is formed. In a **general partnership**, all partners participate in the control and operation of the partnership; hence, all partners can be held jointly and severally liable for the partnership's debts. The unlimited liability of all general partners represents substantial personal risk, since each partner is legally liable for the actions of all other partners. When one partner makes a business commitment, that commitment is legally binding on all of the other partners. Not only are commonly owned business assets therefore subject to legal judgments; each of the other partners' personal assets can be used to pay off the business liabilities of another partner.

An alternative partnership arrangement is the **limited partnership**, a legal form of organization in which one or more members contribute capital to the formation and running of the partnership, but these limited partners do not take part in managing the firm's retail operations. The main advantage of the limited partnership is that creditors cannot seize the personal assets of limited partners. In exchange for this limited liability, the limited partner forgoes control over the partnership's management.

A **corporation** is a business entity authorized by state law to operate as a single person even though it may consist of many persons. Limited liability is the principal legal advantage of this type of organization. The liability of any given owner (shareholder) is limited to equity money, or the amount of stock owned. The nonlegal advantages of being able to raise investment capital and engage in a greater degree of operational and managerial specialization are equally appealing to many retailers. However, corporations are subject to a greater number of legal controls (e.g., public financial accountability, public stockholders' meetings, certificates of incorporation) and possibly double taxation (the corporation pays a corporate income tax, and stockholders pay personal income tax on any dividends they receive).

Limitations on Vertical Integration

The law places certain limitations on retailers' attempts to integrate vertically. **Vertical integration** is the merger of two organizations from different levels within a channel of distribution. Examples of vertical integration are the merger of a retailer and a wholesaler or a retailer and a producer. A **merger** occurs when one firm acquires the stocks or assets of another firm. Mergers are regulated by Section 7 of the Clayton Act of 1914 as amended by the Celler-Kefauver Act of 1950. These acts prohibit a company from acquiring the stocks or assets of other firms in any line of commerce in any part of the country if this action will substantially reduce competition or tend to create a monopoly. The federal government views mergers as monopolistic when they tend to either cut off other retailers from a source of supply or close out other suppliers from a market area.

Personnel Management and the Law

The law protects the retail employee in a variety of ways. Therefore, a store's personnel manager must be acquainted with the legal environment surrounding job discrimination, working conditions, and various compensation requirements.

Job Discrimination

Equal employment opportunity is a civil right. The **Civil Rights Act of 1964** makes job discrimination illegal if it is based on the applicant's or employee's sex, race, color, creed, age, or national origin. Essentially the purpose of the Civil Rights Act is to eliminate both intentional and inadvertent discriminatory employment practices. It charges the Equal Employment Opportunity Commission (EEOC) with administering the act, and it charges each employer with the implicit obligation to uncover and eliminate discriminatory practices.

The two most prevalent forms of employment discrimination are personal and systematic. *Personal discrimination* occurs when the personal biases of an individual in authority enter the decision-making process in employment matters to the detriment of applicants or employees. *Systematic discrimination* is inadvertent discrimination resulting from policies, practices, and decision-making criteria that negatively affect protected classes. In all areas of staffing (job description and specification, recruitment and selection, training and supervision, evaluation and compensation), the retailer must take every precaution to ensure compliance with the intent of the law.

To eliminate discriminatory employment criteria and measurements (age, sex, race, etc.), the retailer should follow two basic guidelines to help ensure compliance with the law: consistency and supportability. *Consistency* means treating all employees and job applicants in a uniformly fair and equitable manner. Also, all actions the retailer takes for or against an employee should be carefully *documented and supported* on the basis of legally defensible economic and/or social terms. If an employer can show due cause through documentation for firing, promoting, or creating a new position for an employee, the employer probably has reasonably safe grounds for actions and employees are likely to be protected from bias and job discrimination.

Working Conditions and Compensation

Numerous legal requirements govern the conditions under which retail employees work. Important to the retailer are wage and hour requirements, restrictions on the use of child labor, and provisions regarding equal pay, workers' compensation, and unemployment benefits.

The **Fair Labor Standards Act (FLSA)** of 1938 sets the legal requirements for both minimum wages and maximum working hours. The FLSA established a 40-hour workweek. Employees working in excess of this maximum are entitled to overtime benefits (extra compensation).

The FLSA also restricts the use of child labor. It determines the age at which minors can work, the types of jobs (hazardous versus nonhazardous occupations), and when they can work (hours, days, etc.). The FLSA also contains an equal-pay provision prohibiting wage differentials for doing work requiring equal skill, effort, and responsibility. Legal wage differentials are justified on the basis of training, education, and experience.

The **Williams-Steiger Occupational Safety and Health Act** of 1970 established the Occupational Safety and Health Administration (OSHA). This agency is charged with enforcing the provisions of the act—to have each employer "furnish . . . a place of employment which is free from recognized hazards that cause or are likely to cause death or serious physical harm to employees." Compliance officers from OSHA make unannounced workplace inspections to ensure conformity.

Workers' compensation is an employee accident and disability insurance program required under various state laws. It covers employees who are accidentally injured while working or are unable to work as a result of a disease associated with a particular occupation. While these programs vary among states, they generally provide coverage for medical expenses and basic subsistence during the disability period. Both public (state-operated) and private (insurance company) programs are available to companies and employees in most states.

Unemployment compensation is a tax levied by the state on each retailer's payroll. The state uses the revenue to create an unemployment fund for the retailer. Qualified former employees of the retailer can draw unemployment benefits from the fund, whose amount and duration are prescribed by state law. Employees who are either laid off or fired usually qualify for benefits; employees who simply quit typically do not qualify.

Store Facilities and the Law

A number of local regulations bear directly on the retailer's facilities. Zoning ordinances, building codes, licensing requirements, and operating requirements are the most common forms of local controls on the retailer's facilities and operations.

Zoning Ordinances

Zoning ordinances are controls that local governments place on land use by regulating the types of activities and buildings located in certain areas. Land is zoned according to residential, commercial, and industrial uses. By controlling the use of land, local governments offer the retailer (1) protection against undesirable neighbors by ensuring that land users are properly situated in relation to one another, (2) assurance that an orderly growth of business will occur only in those areas zoned for business activities, and (3) certainty that adequate government services, such as trash removal, street maintenance, and police protection, will be available to businesses.

Building Codes

Local governments enact numerous regulations affecting the design and construction of retail facilities. Design regulations include local authority over the (1) size of the building relative to the size of the site; (2) height of the building; (3) number of entrances and exits; (4) architectural style (some communities, such as Sante Fe, New Mexico, require businesses to conform to a particular style); and (5) safety features such as plumbing, electricity, and fire protection.

Construction regulations control both the methods and the materials used in construction. Public safety and convenience, such as access for the handicapped, are two major guidelines local governments use in developing construction regulations. Associated with building codes are inspection requirements the retailer must meet before it can open the facility to the public.

Licensing Requirements

Retailers usually must meet two types of local licensing requirements before they can begin operations. Many local communities require retailers to obtain a **general business license** before they can operate a business. In most cases, the license is nothing more than a registration fee to operate a business. A major purpose of the general business license is to generate a source of revenue for a community. A **special business license** applies to either the sale of certain types of products (e.g., guns, prepared foods, drugs, gasoline) or the operation of a particular type of retail organization (e.g., vending machines, door-to-door selling, telephone selling, various types of personal services). A recent U.S. Supreme Court case ruled that local ordinances or licenses cannot be too restrictive; for example, unreasonable door-to-door time restrictions were found unconstitutional because they violated free-speech rights.[5]

Operating Requirements

Many of the retailer's day-to-day operations also are controlled by state and local regulations. In some states and communities, a host of **blue laws** regulate everything from operating hours (such as "sundown laws" that prohibit the sale of liquor after sundown) and days (Sunday closing laws that limit the types of goods consumers can purchase on Sunday) to operating locations (prohibiting the sale of certain products such as liquor and beer within a prescribed distance of a church, school, or some other community facility).[6] Retailers should learn which blue laws affect their businesses, the legal and social implications of such laws on the businesses, and where and when they can operate successfully and legally. In addition, local ordinances regulate trash pickup, snow removal, sign placement, the number and width of entrances and exits (curb cuts), customers' minimum age (e.g., for liquor), and many other factors.

THE LEGAL ASPECTS OF RETAIL MERCHANDISING

Legal requirements govern all aspects of the retailer's merchandising efforts. Strategies for pricing, promoting, and distributing products must fall within certain legal limits.

Product Legalities

As a reseller of products, the retailer assumes three major responsibilities in the areas of product guarantees, product warranties, and product liability. Because of these responsibilities, retailers incur additional operating expenses; however, sales volume can offset these expenses and help a retailer establish a reliable and dependable reputation.

Product Guarantees

Product guarantees are policy statements expressing retailers' general responsibility for the products they sell. Some retailers offer very broad guarantees, such as "complete satisfaction or your money back." Other retailers limit their guarantee statements to certain aspects of the product (e.g., six months from date of purchase). Often consumers and retailers disagree about what is guaranteed; "consumers interpret satisfaction to apply not only to the products they acquire but also to the shopping experience that results in these acquisitions."[7] Given these customer expectations and the legal requirement to fulfill the general intent of any guarantee made, the retailer needs to carefully monitor all guarantee statements.

Product Warranties

A **warranty** is a specific statement by the seller of the quality or performance capabilities of the product and the exact terms under which the seller will take action to correct product deficiencies. There are two basic types of warranties—expressed and implied.

Expressed warranties are written and oral statements that the seller makes to consumers about a product and performance and that the retailer is legally obligated to honor. While written statements of fact are expressed in fairly specific terms and subject to precise interpretation, oral statements of fact and promises are more difficult to interpret. A fine line distinguishes oral promises from mere sales talk. Often the distinction is made on the basis of whether the statements made during a sale are expressions of opinion or of fact. Courts have recognized the difference between "puffing" and promise. To avoid being charged with engaging in unfair competitive acts, the retailer must be careful that its sales "puffery" is not construed as a legally binding promise of product performance.

Implied warranties are the seller's implied or "intended" promises of product performance even though they are not expressed in either written or oral form. Under the Uniform Commercial Code, every sale is subject to a warranty of merchantability and a warranty of title. The *warranty of merchantability* implies that all merchandise retailers offer for sale is fit for the purpose for which it was sold. For example, a clothes dryer that scorches clothes is not fit for its intended purpose. The *warranty of title* implies that the seller has offered the buyer a free and clear title to the product. Consumers have the right to assume they own the product and have full use of it without fear of repossession. That assumption is not valid, however, when the consumer elects to purchase an item from a questionable source (e.g., a car from "Midnight Auto Sales").

The most significant piece of federal legislation concerning warranties in recent years is the Magnuson-Moss Warranty Act of 1975. This act has greatly strengthened consumers' rights by substantially increasing the responsibilities of retailers and other sellers of products under warranty. Important to retailers are the first three regulations the FTC issued under this act. These require the retailer to (1) provide consumers with warranty information before they buy the product, (2) disclose the terms of the product warranty in "simple and readily understood language," and (3) establish and maintain procedures for handling customer complaints.

Product Liability

The retailer, as well as the manufacturer, can be held liable for an unsafe product. The retailer's **product liability** can result from failing to inform the customer of the dangers associated with using the product; misrepresenting the product as to how, when, and where it should be used; or selling a product that causes injury as a result of its failure to meet warranty standards. Much confusion exists over the exact nature of the retailer's product liability. The retailer's best protection is to provide the consumer with adequate product safety information, to correctly represent the product, and to obtain adequate liability insurance.

Price Legalities

The most regulated aspect of a retailer's merchandising program is pricing. Government regulations influence the prices the retailer pays the supplier, the prices the retailer charges customers, the conditions under which prices are set or adjusted, and the impact of the retailer's prices on the competitive structure of the marketplace.

Price Discrimination

In a very broad sense, **price discrimination** covers a number of situations involving pricing arrangements under various buying and selling circumstances. The law recognizes both illegal and legal price discrimination. *Illegal pricing* potentially exists when different prices are offered or received under similar circumstances or when similar prices are offered or received under different circumstances. *Price discrimination* can be legally justified when different prices are offered or received under different circumstances. Obviously the size of the price differential, the exact nature of the circumstances, and the differential's effects on all parties involved determine the precise legalities of the situation.

Retailers become involved with price discrimination in a number of ways. As Figure 4–4 illustrates, the retailer can be both a victim and a perpetrator of price discrimination as a result of buying activities with suppliers and selling activities with consumers. We will examine each of these circumstances individually.

PRICE DISCRIMINATION AGAINST	THE RETAILER'S ROLE IN PRICE DISCRIMINATION	
	Victim	Perpetrator
Buying Activities Supplier Interactions	product discrimination quantity discrimination allowance discrimination service discrimination	coercive buying dummy brokerage
Selling Activities Customer Interactions		predatory pricing price fixing

FIGURE 4–4 The retailer's involvement with price discrimination

When a supplier treats one retailer unequally or differently from the way it treats other retailers, the single retailer becomes a potential victim of price discrimination. As defined by Section 2 of the Robinson-Patman Act, unequal treatment or price discrimination is illegal when its effect "may be to substantially lessen competition or tend to create a monopoly . . . or to injure, destroy, or prevent competition." Price discrimination against retailers can result when a supplier treats one retailer differently from others with respect to product characteristics, quantity discounts, special allowances, and special services.

Product Characteristics. It is unlawful for any business to discriminate either directly or indirectly in price among different purchasers of commodities of like grade and quality. *Competing retailers are entitled to pay the same price for the same type of merchandise.* While the meaning of "like grade and quality" is ambiguous, the courts generally have interpreted the phrase to mean that there must be clearly distinguishable differences in either materials or workmanship. Courts typically have found products with minor differences in materials and workmanship to be of "like grade and quality." Thus, where minor differences exist, sellers run the risk of price discrimination if they sell to different buyers at different prices under similar circumstances.

Quantity Discounts. The general principle regarding quantity discounts is that *all competing retailers are entitled to pay the same price for the same quantity of "like" merchandise.* Suppliers often try to encourage volume buying by offering their customers (retailers) discount prices for large-quantity orders. However, even this form of seller inducement is illegal unless the seller can show that the lower prices for volume buyers result from cost savings from producing and selling the larger quantity.

Sellers offer quantity discounts in two ways—cumulative and noncumulative. *Cumulative* quantity discounts apply to customers' purchases over an extended period. For example, if a buyer purchases a certain quantity of merchandise over a 12-month period, the seller will give the buyer a discount on any additional purchases. *Noncumulative* quantity discounts apply only to a single large-volume purchase. Because cumulative discounts do not represent cost savings equal to those for noncumulative discounts, the courts have ruled that cumulative discounts cannot be as large.

Special Allowances. The Robinson-Patman Act makes it unlawful for a seller to grant payment of any special allowances for any services that a retailer might provide to attempt to sell, advertise, or distribute a product unless those allowance payments are also made available to all competing retailers on proportionately equal terms. Therefore, *all competing retailers are entitled to the same opportunities to receive the same allowance payments for providing the same special services.* Of special interest to the retailer is the "push money" that various suppliers provide. Push money is money that suppliers pay the retailer's sales personnel for making a special selling effort on their brands. Push money is legal if the same incentives are available to all competing retailers, if the retailer gives its consent, and if it does not reduce competition or severely affect competitive products.

Special Services. It is unlawful for a supplier to provide retailers with services and facilities that aid them in selling merchandise unless it makes the same favors available to all competing retailers on proportionately equal terms. Thus, *all competing retailers are entitled to receive the same support in services and facilities to sell the same goods.* When the original service or facility offer is impractical for competing retailers, regulatory agencies have allowed sellers to substitute different but equal services or facilities more suitable to their operations.

THE WORLD OF RETAILING

■■■

Ethical Issues

Street Money—Is It Legal, Is It Ethical?

In the past year, the trend has been toward lower, more uniform case rate deals, with the balance going into market development funds—sometimes referred to as street money. These generally are lump sum payments, purportedly associated with participating in a particular event. . . . Street money is very selective. . . . Therefore its unfair and patently illegal . . . manufacturer programs are geared toward chains. . . . Many in the industry avoid using the term "street money" because they feel that it has a nasty connotation, no matter how equitably it is administered. One supplier executive differentiates between market development funds and street money. The former goes to corporate headquarters . . . while the latter goes to stores. Street money is a retail certificate stating that the manufacturer will pay a certain amount of money if the store puts up a display or some type of point-of-sale material. Street money can be dirty if it is paid to some and not to others, and nobody knows what was paid or even what is available.

Source: Steve Weinstein, "New Deal: Out of the Case and into the Street," *Progressive Grocer,* February 1990, 40–41.

Price Discrimination Defenses. Although each of the seller activities just discussed could lead to price discrimination suits, the Robinson-Patman Act contains provisions for a legal defense for price differentials. Cost justification and good faith are two of the most common defenses.

The *cost justification defense* makes it lawful for a supplier to charge retailers different prices if it can justify the price differentials on the basis of its cost of doing business with each competing retailer. If it costs a supplier more to do business with one retailer than with another, the supplier can legally charge that retailer a higher price. The courts have placed the burden of proof on the seller, however, and have been quite particular about which costs (e.g., overhead) the seller can include in estimates and how cost calculations can be made.

The *good-faith defense* makes it lawful for a seller to discriminate in price if such action is done in good faith to meet an equally low price of a competitor. The essential factor in using the good-faith defense is whether the discriminatory price was necessary to *meet* competition rather than an offensive move to *beat* competition. Defensive price discrimination is legal; offensive price discrimination is illegal.

The retailer assumes the role of a perpetrator of illegal price discrimination when it uses coercive buying techniques or deceptive brokerage practices to obtain a lower price than that available to competing retailers. **Coercive buying** is the retailer's use of financial, distribution, marketing, and other powers to gain lower prices from sellers. Since some retailing organizations are larger than their suppliers, they are in a position to force favorable but unfair price treatment. However, Section 2(f) of the Robinson-Patman Act makes it unlawful for a retailer to knowingly receive or induce a discriminatory price or special allowance and service.

Deceptive brokerage activities involve the establishment and use of "dummy" brokerage firms to secure a brokerage allowance from suppliers that give retailers an unfair purchase-price advantage. A *dummy brokerage firm* is a brokerage company that is owned and operated by a retailer but represents itself as an independent operation. As such, the brokerage firm does not charge its parent retailing firm a brokerage fee for bringing the buyer and seller together, and such "savings" in brokerage fees are passed on to the retailer. In this situation, the retailer with a dummy brokerage firm pays less for merchandise and therefore can sell products at a lower price, thus creating an unfair competitive advantage. Section 2(c) of the Robinson-Patman Act makes it unlawful for a company to receive brokerage allowances (fees and/or discounts) unless the broker is completely independent of both the supplier and the retailer.

Retailers can also run the risk of price discrimination in selling activities by engaging in predatory pricing and price fixing. **Predatory pricing** is a pricing tactic whereby the retailer charges customers different prices for the same merchandise in different markets to eliminate competition in one or more of those markets. Such pricing practices are illegal except when the firm can show a cost justification. **Price fixing** is an illegal pricing activity in which several retailers establish a fixed retail selling price for a particular product line within a given market area.

Resale Price Maintenance

Resale price maintenance legislation, commonly referred to as "fair-trade laws," was designed to permit manufacturers and wholesalers to set retail prices by requiring retailers to sign contracts agreeing to sell their products at the "suggested" prices.[8] The primary purpose of these laws was to protect the small, independent retailer that could not compete effectively on a price basis with large chains and discount operations. Although **resale price maintenance** is no longer legal, a limited type of resale price maintenance exists in some states in the form of **unfair trade practice acts**. These state laws regulate retailers' right to sell either below cost or at cost plus some minimum markup (e.g., cost plus 5 percent). The intent of these laws is to preserve competition by eliminating predatory price cutting and loss-leader selling (the use of a below-cost price on a popular item to attract customers into the store).[9] These laws have been ineffective due to enforcement problems and the large number of exceptions. Typical exemptions permitting sales below cost include clearance sales, closeout sales, business liquidation sales, sales to relief agencies or for charitable purposes, and sales of products with deteriorating marketability (such as seasonal, damaged, and perishable goods).

Promotion Legalities

Freedom of speech for the retailer is not without its limitations. Numerous laws govern what retailers may communicate to their customers and how they may communicate it. The principal legal vehicles through which the federal government regulates promotional activities are the Federal Trade Commission Act of 1914 and the Wheeler-Lea Amendment to that act. Together these laws make it illegal for a retailer to engage in any unfair method of competition or unfair or deceptive act or practice in commerce. If retailers are caught using either deceptive price advertising, deceptive product advertising, or misleading personal sales information, the FTC can take legal action against them.

Deceptive Price Advertising

Retailers can express price information in a number of confusing and misleading ways. For example, prices expressed as the "suggested retail price," the "original price," the "regular price," "our price and our competitor's price," "two for the price of one," "buy one and get one free," "50 percent off," and "reduced one-half" can mislead consumers into believing that they are receiving a better price or a larger discount than is actually being offered. To prevent **deceptive price advertising**, the FTC has established several guidelines for the use of such pricing terms.

Former-Price Comparisons. The retailer that uses pricing terms such as "originally," "usually," or "regularly" is using a former-price comparison that suggests an item is selling at a price lower than its former price. To avoid charges of deceptive price advertising, the retailer should determine whether the former price was as established as the original, usual, or regular selling price. When the former price was established, the retailer's advertisements can inform consumers that the "new" price is a discount price. If the former price was not established, the retailer cannot make a former-price comparison.[10] Also, for a sale price to be legal, the price reduction must be for a specific and reasonable period of time and be accompanied by a price increase at the end of the sales period. A new law passed in Massachusetts requires that "sales advertised in retail catalogs, which are printed months in advance, must disclose that the so-called original price is really only a reference price and not necessarily the actual former selling price."[11]

Competitive-Price Comparisons. When making an advertising claim that its prices are lower than its competitors', the retailer must establish that the competitors' prices are in fact prices that they regularly charge. In addition, under FTC guidelines, the competitive-price comparison must be made on identical products. If the retailer wishes to make competitive-price comparisons on similar but not identical products, the advertisement must make it clear that the price comparison is being made on "comparable" and not "identical" products. The FTC guidelines allow the retailer to make price comparisons on comparable products of "like grade and quality" as long as it clearly states that different products of essentially the same quality and quantity are being compared. Hence, a retailer can make price comparisons between a private-label brand and a nationally advertised brand if the brands are of the same quality and quantity.

Free Merchandise. Advertisements offering free merchandise represent a price reduction, since the offer usually depends on the consumer meeting certain conditions (e.g., "buy one, get one free"). These promotional pricing practices are not considered deceptive if the advertisement clearly states the conditions under which the merchandise is "free."

Cents-off Pricing. When a retailer's advertisement contains a cents-off coupon, the coupon should be based on the regular price. If the retailer raises the product's price to inflate the coupon value, the FTC will consider this promotional effort deceptive.

Another deceptive act is the retailer's failure to stock sufficient quantities of the coupon product to meet the normal demand associated with such a sale. The FTC does consider "rain checks" (for the same or comparable product at a later date at the same price) an adequate substitute when an unusual demand or out-of-stock problem unexpectedly arises. However, if the retailer uses rain checks in conjunction with planned shortages of advertised products hoping that only a small percentage of the rain checks will be redeemed, it is engaging in a deceptive practice. As with free merchandise offerings, any conditional aspects of the cents-off offering (e.g., quantity limitations) must be clearly stated in the advertisement.

Deceptive Product Advertising

Deceptive product advertising involves making a false or misleading claim about the physical makeup of the product, the appropriate uses for the product, or the benefits from using the product, as well as using packages and labels that tend to mislead the customer about the exact contents, quality, or quantity of the package. In April 1987, several state attorneys general asked McDonald's to "cease and desist" further "use of print ads extolling the quality and nutritional makeup of its foods or face legal action for violating state false-advertising statutes. . . . [I]t charges that one ad's claim that 'our sodium is down across the menu' is false because the ad mentions four products for which the sodium content has not been lowered."[12] Several laws have been enacted to control the various claims about the physical makeup of the product.[13]

Other legislation has been directed at identifying appropriate product usage. For example, the Child Protection and Toy Safety Act of 1965 instructs manufacturers to identify the appropriate age group for a particular toy. The FTC has taken an active role in correcting false claims concerning product benefits by requiring companies to use promotional messages correcting these previous false claims.

Finally, the Fair Package and Labeling Act of 1966 prohibits companies from using deceptive packaging and labeling methods. Companies must properly label the contents, ingredients, net quantity, and name and address of the manufacturer on the package. Also, the act contains guidelines regarding deceptive package sizes and shapes as well as the misleading use of printed material on packages.

Deceptive Sales Practices

The law also places restrictions on several kinds of personal selling that constitute **deceptive sales practices**. One is called **bait and switch**. The "bait" is an advertised low price on a product that the retailer does not intend to sell.[14] The "switch" involves personal selling techniques that induce the customer to buy a higher-priced product that will provide the retailer with greater profits. These selling techniques involve (1) making disparaging remarks about the product, (2) either failing to stock the product or planning a stockout, (3) refusing to show or demonstrate the product to the consumer on some false pretense, or (4) denying credit arrangements in conjunction with the sale of the product.[15] To protect the consumer, the FTC can require any retailer to make good any "bait" offer extended to consumers.

A legal issue related to sales transactions involves **deceptive credit contracts**. In 1960 Congress passed the **Truth-in-Lending Act**, which requires full disclosure of credit terms. Retailers must give borrowers a disclosure statement detailing the exact terms of their contracts. Terms such as the loan amount, finance charges, annual percentage rate, miscellaneous charges, number of payments, and the amount of each payment, as well as a description of any property held by the lender as security, must be clearly stated in the disclosure statement. Additional legal requirements of retail lenders have been enacted through amendments to further protect the consumer. These amendments state the following:

1. Monthly statements (bills) must include information (address and telephone number) about where inquiries about them can be made.
2. Consumers have 60 days to lodge complaints concerning billing errors; retailers have 30 days to reply to complaints and must make a reasonable effort to resolve each complaint.
3. All credit arrangements containing a "free period" provision require retailers to mail monthly statements 14 days before assessment of finance charges.
4. Credit payments must be credited to the customer's account on the day they are received.
5. Credit card issuers cannot restrict the retailer from offering the final consumer a cash discount.

Distribution Legalities

Retailers often enter into agreements with suppliers that might give them a competitive edge in the marketplace. These agreements are legal in some circumstances but illegal in others. Some of these competitively advantageous but potentially illegal arrangements are exclusive dealings, anticompetitive leasing arrangements, tying contracts, and exclusive territories.

Exclusive Dealings

Exclusive dealings are arrangements between retailers and suppliers in which the retailer agrees to handle only the supplier's products and no other products that pose direct competition. Benetton, the upscale apparel retailer, requires no fees or royalties from its independent licensees; however, each shopkeeper "agrees to sell only

Benetton-made goods through one of several standard store formats."[16] Such agreements are not illegal per se; however, Section 3 of the Clayton Act declares exclusive dealings illegal where the effect may be to substantially lessen competition or to create a monopoly. The courts generally have viewed exclusive dealings as illegal when they exclude competitive products from a large share of the market and when they represent a large share of the total sales volume for a particular product type.

Anticompetitive Leasing Arrangements

A variation of exclusive dealings involves several forms of **anticompetitive leasing arrangements.**[17] The purpose of these contracts is to limit the type and amount of competition a particular retailer faces within a given area. Generally associated with shopping centers, anticompetitive leasing arrangements grant some retailers certain rights such as "(1) the right to be the only retailer of its kind, (2) the right to reject or accept the opportunity to operate an additional outlet in a shopping center where it already has one, (3) the right to prohibit or control the entrance of tenants into shopping centers, and (4) the right to restrict the business operations of other tenants in shopping centers."[18] Under Section 5 of the Federal Trade Commission Act, the FTC has the power to enforce rules prohibiting one retailer in a shopping center from limiting the competitive activities of another retailer.

Tying Contracts

Tying contracts are conditional selling arrangements between retailers and suppliers in which a supplier agrees to sell a retailer a highly sought-after line of products if the retailer agrees to buy additional product lines in return (usually those not frequently sought) from the same supplier. An extended version of the tying contract concept is **full-line forcing,** in which the supplier requires the retailer to carry the supplier's full line of products if the retailer wishes to carry any part of that line. The FTC views both tying contracts and full-line forcing as illegal when the supplier has sufficient coercive powers to force competition.

The most serious problems involving tying arrangements are those associated with franchise retailing. Often franchise agreements contain provisions requiring the franchisee to purchase all raw materials and supplies from the franchisor. The courts generally consider tying provisions of a franchise agreement legal as long as there is sufficient proof that these arrangements are necessary to maintain quality control; otherwise, they are viewed as unwarranted restraints of competition.

Exclusive Territories

Exclusive territories are agreements under which a supplier grants a retailer the exclusive right to sell its products within a defined geographic area; in return, the retailer agrees not to sell the product anywhere except within the agreed-upon area. In essence, this creates a geographic monopoly for a particular product line. For obvious reasons, these territorial arrangements generally are viewed as unlawful systems of distribution. The law does not, however, prevent suppliers and retailers from establishing territorial responsibilities as long as these arrangements are not exclusive and do not restrict the resale of products.

THE ETHICAL ASPECTS OF RETAILING

Is the marketing concept of "customer satisfaction at a profit" a sufficient guideline for conducting an honest, fair, and equitable retail business? For most retail organizations, the answer clearly is no. The reason for this negative response lies in the reality that retailers are part of a much larger environment that incorporates the competing interests of shareholders, managers, employees, vendors, and the community as well as the needs and wants of the firm's customers. While being "customer focused" is an

FIGURE 4–5
American Marketing Association code of ethics

Responsibilities of the Marketer

Marketers must accept responsibility for the consequences of their activities and make every effort to ensure that their decisions, recommendations, and actions function to identify, serve, and satisfy all relevant publics, customers, organizations, and society.

Marketers' professional conduct must be guided by:

1. The basic rule of professional ethics; not knowingly to do harm;
2. The adherence to all applicable laws and regulations;
3. The accurate representation of their education, training, and experience; and
4. The active support, practice, and promotion of this Code of Ethics.

Honesty and Fairness

Marketers shall uphold and advance the integrity, honor, and dignity of the marketing profession by:

1. Being honest in serving consumers, clients, employees, suppliers, distributors, and the public;
2. Not knowingly participating in conflict of interest without prior notice to all parties involved; and
3. Establishing equitable fee schedules including the payment or receipt of usual, customary, and/or legal compensation for marketing exchanges.

Rights and Duties of Parties in the Marketing Exchange Process

Participants in the marketing exchange process should be able to expect that:

1. Participants and services offered are safe and fit for their intended uses;
2. Communications about offered products and services are not deceptive;
3. All parties intend to discharge their obligations, financial and otherwise, in good faith; and
4. Appropriate internal methods exist for equitable adjustment and/or redress of grievances concerning purchases.

It is understood that the above would include, but is not limited to, the following responsibilities of the marketers:
In the area of product development and management,

- Disclosure of all substantial risks associated with product or service usage;
- Identification of any product component substitution that might materially change the product or impact on the buyer's purchase decision;
- Identification of extra-cost added features.

absolute credo for most retailers, customers' wants and needs can and often do conflict with society's long-run interest. "History teaches that the marketer who has his eyes *only* on the bottom line will not last in the long run, although he might make a profit in the short run."[19] Successful retailers keep their eyes on all of the firm's stakeholders—all individuals who have a stake in any aspect of the firm's business.

It is the retail firm's organizational culture that guides its employees and managers in determining right from wrong, fair from unfair, loyal from disloyal, trustworthy from untrustworthy, and a host of other ethical value distinctions. **Ethics** can be defined as "a system or code of conduct based on universal moral duties and obligations which

FIGURE 4–5
continued

In the area of promotions,

- Avoidance of false and misleading advertising;
- Rejection of high-pressure manipulations or misleading sales tactics;
- Avoidance of sales promotions that use deception or manipulation.

In the area of distribution,

- Not manipulating the availability of a product for purpose of exploitation;
- Not using coercion in the marketing channel;
- Not exerting undue influence over the reseller's choice to handle a product.

In the area of pricing,

- Not engaging in price fixing;
- Not practicing predatory pricing;
- Disclosing the full price associated with any purchase.

In the area of marketing research,

- Prohibiting selling or fundraising under the guise of conducting research;
- Maintaining research integrity by avoiding misrepresentation and omission of pertinent research data;
- Treating outside clients and suppliers fairly.

Organizational Relationships

Marketers should be aware of how their behavior may influence or impact on the behavior of others in organizational relationships. They should not demand, encourage, or apply coercion to obtain unethical behavior in their relationships with others, such as employees, suppliers, or customers. Marketers should:

1. Apply confidentiality and anonymity in professional relationships with regard to privileged information;
2. Meet their obligations and responsibilities in contracts and mutual agreements in a timely manner;
3. Avoid taking the work of others, in whole, or in part, and represent this work as their own or directly benefit from it without compensation or consent of the originator or owner; and
4. Avoid manipulation to take advantage of situations to maximize personal welfare in a way that unfairly deprives or damages their organization or others.

Source: "AMA Adopts New Code of Ethics," *Marketing News,* September 11, 1987, 1, 10.

indicate how one should behave."[20] **Values** are "core beliefs or desires which guide or motivate attitudes and actions."[21] Not all values are concerned with ethics. Ethical values such as honesty, fairness, and loyalty involve the notion of moral duty and "reflect attitudes about what is right, good, and proper rather than what is pleasurable, useful, or desirable."[22] Values such as happiness, fulfillment, pleasure, personal freedom, and being liked and respected are all ethically neutral because they deal with matters other than moral duty and obligation.[23]

The morality of a particular action can be judged using either relative or absolute standards. In using relative standards, the retailer judges the morality of an action based on the particular circumstances surrounding it. Because there are no absolutes when using relative standards, ethical behavior involves making judgments using subjective,

FIGURE 4–6
Ethical principles for business executives

Ethical values, translated into active language establishing standards or rules describing the kinds of behavior an ethical person should and should not engage in, are ethical principles. The following list of principles incorporates the characteristics and values that most people associate with ethical behavior. Ethical decision making systematically considers these principles.

I. *Honesty*. Ethical executives are honest and truthful in all their dealings and they do not deliberately mislead or deceive others by misrepresentations, overstatements, partial truths, selective omissions, or any other means.

II. *Integrity*. Ethical executives demonstrate personal integrity and the courage of their convictions by doing what they think is right even when there is great pressure to do otherwise; they are principled, honorable and upright; they will fight for their beliefs. They will not sacrifice principle for expediency, be hypocritical, or unscrupulous.

III. *Promise-Keeping and Trustworthiness*. Ethical executives are worthy of trust, they are candid and forthcoming in supplying relevant information and correcting misapprehensions of fact, and they make every reasonable effort to fulfill the letter and spirit of their promises and commitments. They do not interpret agreements in an unreasonably technical or legalistic manner in order to rationalize non-compliance or create justifications for escaping their commitments.

IV. *Loyalty*. Ethical executives who are worthy of trust demonstrate fidelity and loyalty to persons and institutions by friendship in adversity, support and devotion to duty; they do not use or disclose information learned in confidence for personal advantage. They safeguard the ability to make independent professional judgments by scrupulously avoiding undue influences and conflicts of interest. They are loyal to their companies and colleagues and if they decide to accept other employment, they provide reasonable notice, respect the proprietary information of their former employer, and refuse to engage in any activities that take undue advantage of their previous position.

V. *Fairness*. Ethical executives are fair and just in all dealings; they do not exercise power arbitrarily, and do not use overreaching nor indecent means to

situational, and culturally determined criteria. The relative type of situation ethic comes in two basic forms:

Utilitarianism—"judges not the act itself but the consequences of the act. If the results mean a net increase in society's happiness or welfare, then the act is believed to be morally right . . . akin to saying that the end justifies the means."[24]

Intuitionism—"decision is right if the individual's intuition or conscience tells him that it is right. If the person's sixth sense or gut feeling says that it is okay, that his motives are good, and that he doesn't intend to hurt anyone, then he can go ahead with it."[25]

Absolute standards are rigid rules that clearly state whether an act is right or wrong; using these standards constitutes ethical behavior regardless of the circumstances surrounding the situation. These timeless truths typically are based on religious teachings; for example, the Bible has provided permanent guidelines that have evolved into the Judeo-Christian value system. Rules such as "Do unto others as you would have them do unto you" (the Golden Rule or Rule of Reciprocity), "Thou shall not lie," and "Thou shall not steal" provide direct answers that appeal to some decision makers.[26]

FIGURE 4–6
continued

gain or maintain any advantage nor take undue advantage of another's mistakes or difficulties. Fair persons manifest a commitment to justice, the equal treatment of individuals, tolerance for and acceptance of diversity, and they are open-minded; they are willing to admit they are wrong and, where appropriate, change their positions and beliefs.

VI. *Concern for Others*. Ethical executives are caring, compassionate, benevolent and kind; they live the Golden Rule, help those in need, and seek to accomplish their business objectives in a manner that causes the least harm and the greatest positive good.

VII. *Respect for Others*. Ethical executives demonstrate respect for the human dignity, autonomy, privacy, rights, and interests of all those who have a stake in their decisions; they are courteous and treat all people with equal respect and dignity regardless of sex, race or national origin.

VIII. *Law Abiding*. Ethical executives abide by laws, rules and regulations relating to their business activities.

IX. *Commitment to Excellence*. Ethical executives pursue excellence in performing their duties, are well informed and prepared, and constantly endeavor to increase their proficiency in all areas of responsibility.

X. *Leadership*. Ethical executives are conscious of the responsibilities and opportunities of their position of leadership and seek to be positive ethical role models by their own conduct and by helping to create an environment in which principled reasoning and ethical decision making are highly prized.

XI. *Reputation and Morale*. Ethical executives seek to protect and build the company's good reputation and the morale of its employees by engaging in no conduct that might undermine respect and by taking whatever actions are necessary to correct or prevent inappropriate conduct of others.

XII. *Accountability*. Ethical executives acknowledge and accept personal accountability for the ethical quality of their decisions and omissions to themselves, their colleagues, their companies, and their communities.

Source: Michael Josephson, "Ethical Principles for Business Executives," *Ethical Decision Making in the Trenches*, 1989, 3. Copyright © The Joseph and Edna Josephson Institute for the Advancement of Ethics, Marina del Rey, California.

As we can infer from the above discussion, developing a practical and operational code of ethics or establishing a set of principles for ethical decision making is a difficult and complex task.[27] Studies have drawn similar conclusions regarding the implementation of an ethics program for business organizations:

1. Codes of ethics must be more than legal or public relations ploys; they must be useful, understandable and practical.
2. Visible signs of support for ethical behavior must be forthcoming from management.
3. There is no single approach to business ethics that is ideally suited to a particular organization.
4. Top management must champion their demand for the highest ethical posture for their companies.[28]

Retailers can implement ethics programs by adopting already established ethics codes. Figure 4–5 presents the Code of Ethics governing all members of the American Marketing Association; it represents a code of behavior for a particular profession or trade. Figure 4–6 lists 12 ethics principles that business executives need to follow in making decisions. You will get a chance to apply these ethical standards and principles

THE WORLD OF RETAILING

■ ■ ■

Ethical Issues

Ethics—Just the Way It Ought to Be

How does a local supermarket chain that closes on Sundays and doesn't sell beer beat out a national chain and make it to the top of the grocery store heap? The personal touch . . . Ukrop's Super Markets, Inc. . . . Getting a personal reply from the president of Ukrop's wouldn't surprise most regular customers of the Richmond stores, where clerks are unflaggingly friendly; baggers insist on carrying shoppers' groceries; and a framed statement declares that the store's mission is "to serve our customers and community more effectively than anyone else by treating our customers, associates, and suppliers as we personally would like to be treated." . . . There's never been a conflict between family values and running the company . . . we knew what the golden rule was. . . . We've never had to make a decision that wasn't consistent with our values. . . . If you want to be the best place to shop, you have to be the best place to work. . . . Ukrop's also gives 10% of its pre-tax profits to charity, and for the last two years has donated more than $1 million to nonprofit groups that get 2% of the sales receipts they collect. Giving to charity is "just the way we think it ought to be."

Source: "Personal Touch, Traditional Values Help Family Grocery Beat 'Giants,'" *Marketing News,* June 5, 1989, 6.

in the investigative projects and cases at the end of this chapter and throughout the remainder of the text (see "The World of Retailing—Ethical Issues").

SUMMARY

Legal considerations are an integral part of the retailer's daily operations. The retailer must consider the legal aspects of retail competition, store operations, and retail merchandising within the legal environment created by the federal, state, and local legislative, executive, and judicial branches of government.

The legal aspects of competition deal with attempts by various government bodies to correct present restraints on trade and to prevent probable trade restraints and unfair trade practices. The major laws dealing with maintaining a competitive environment are the Sherman Antitrust Act, the Clayton Act, the Robinson-Patman Act, the Federal Trade Commission Act, and the Wheeler-Lea Act.

The legal forms of store organization (sole proprietorship, partnership, and corporation), the limitations of vertical integration, the laws governing personnel management (job discrimination, working conditions, and compensation requirements), and the restrictions on store facilities (zoning ordinances, building codes, licensing requirements, and operating requirements) are central legal issues in store operations.

The legal aspects of merchandising require the retailer to carefully consider the legalities of its product, price, promotion, and distribution mix. Guarantees, warranties, and liability are three of the more important legalities associated with the product. Price discrimination in terms of product characteristics, quantity discounts, and special allowances or services, together with resale price maintenance activities, are the retailer's chief legal concerns regarding price. Deceptive price and product advertising and deceptive sales practices are illegalities of promotion that retailers must avoid. Finally, the laws pertaining to distribution call for careful consideration of exclusive dealings, anticompetitive leasing arrangements, tying contracts, and the use of exclusive territories.

Ethical behavior is based on a system or code of conduct derived from a universal moral duty or obligation. Honesty, fairness, and loyalty are ethical values that help an individual determine what is right, good, and proper. Retail businesses use both relative and absolute approaches in judging the morality of a particular action.

STUDENT STUDY GUIDE

Key Terms and Concepts

anticompetitive leasing arrangement (p. 149)
antitrust legislation (p. 136)
bait and switch (p. 148)
blue laws (p. 141)
Civil Rights Act of 1964 (p. 139)
Clayton Act (p. 137)
coercive buying (p. 145)
corporation (p. 139)
deceptive brokerage activities (p. 145)
deceptive credit contracts (p. 148)
deceptive price advertising (p. 146)
deceptive product advertising (p. 147)
deceptive sales practices (p. 148)
ethics (p. 150)
exclusive dealings (p. 148)
exclusive territories (p. 149)
expressed warranty (p. 142)
Fair Labor Standards Act (FLSA) (p. 140)
Federal Trade Commission (FTC) Act (p. 138)
full-line forcing (p. 149)
general business license (p. 141)
general partnership (p. 139)
implied warranty (p. 142)
intuitionism (p. 152)
limited partnership (p. 139)
merger (p. 139)
partnership (p. 138)
predatory pricing (p. 146)
price discrimination (p. 143)
price fixing (p. 146)
product guarantee (p. 142)
product liability (p. 143)
resale price maintenance (p. 146)
retail competition (p. 136)
Robinson-Patman Act (p. 137)
Sherman Antitrust Act (p. 136)
sole proprietorship (p. 138)
special business license (p. 141)
Truth-in-Lending Act (p. 148)
tying contracts (p. 149)
unemployment compensation (p. 140)
unfair trade practice acts (p. 146)
utilitarianism (p. 152)
values (p. 151)
vertical integration (p. 139)
warranty (p. 142)
Wheeler-Lea Act (p. 138)
Williams-Steiger Occupational Safety and Health Act (p. 140)
workers' compensation (p. 140)

Review Questions

1. Whose actions define the retailer's legal environment?
2. What is antitrust legislation? What action did Congress take to overcome the shortcomings of the Sherman Antitrust Act? Be specific.
3. Compare and contrast the legal and operational advantages and disadvantages of the sole proprietorship, partnership, and corporate forms of retail organization.
4. What are the two most prevalent forms of employment discrimination? Describe each.
5. Which two basic guidelines should a retailer follow to ensure compliance with the provisions of the Civil Rights Act?
6. Who qualifies for unemployment compensation?
7. Why do local governments enact zoning ordinances? What are the benefits and limitations for the retailer?
8. What two types of local licensing requirements do retailers usually have to meet before they can begin operations? Define each.
9. Compare and contrast product guarantees and product warranties.
10. What are the two basic types of warranties? Describe each type.
11. Under what conditions can the retailer be held liable for an unsafe product?
12. What is price discrimination? When is price discrimination illegal? Describe the two legal defenses for price discrimination.
13. To avoid charges of deceptive price advertising when using former- and competitive-price comparisons, the retailer should follow which practices?
14. What is deceptive product advertising? What is the major weapon the FTC uses in correcting false claims concerning product benefits? Explain.
15. Describe the sales practice of bait and switch. When is it illegal?
16. Compare and contrast the distribution arrangements of exclusive dealings, tying contracts, and exclusive territories. When are they illegal?
17. Is the marketing concept of "customer satisfaction at a profit" an adequate guideline for judging the ethics of business practices? Why or why not?
18. Describe the two approaches for judging the morality of a particular business action.

Review Exam

True or False

_____ 1. A major advantage of a general partnership over a sole proprietorship form of organization is that the partnership represents a substantially reduced financial liability for each partner in the organization.

_____ 2. Before using training, education, and experience to justify wage differentials among employees, the retailer should be able to prove that these factors have a direct bearing on job performance.

_____ 3. Retailers can be held liable for unsafe products if they fail to inform consumers of the dangers associated with using the product.

_____ 4. If the retailer wishes to make competitive-price comparisons on products that are similar but not identical, the advertisement must make it clear to the consumer that the price comparison is being made on comparable and not identical products.

_____ 5. Exclusive dealing arrangements between retailers and suppliers generally are viewed as a per se violation of the law.

_____ 6. Ethics can be defined as an individual's core beliefs or desires that guide or motivate attitudes and actions.

_____ 7. Applying the Golden Rule or the Rule of Reciprocity is an example of using situational ethics to judge behavior.

Multiple Choice

_____ 1. Antitrust legislation was initiated to protect consumers and businesses from
a. Present restraints on trade
b. Probable restraints on trade
c. Unfair trade practices
d. a and c
e. All of the above

_____ 2. The inadvertent discrimination resulting from policies, practices, and decision-making criteria that negatively affect protected classes is termed _____ discrimination.
a. Personal
b. Organizational
c. Social
d. Systematic
e. Pragmatic

_____ 3. The warranty of _____ is the implied warranty that all merchandise offered for sale by the retailer is fit for the purpose for which it was sold.
a. Liability
b. Title
c. Merchantability
d. Performance
e. Price

_____ 4. Price discrimination is legal when
a. Different prices are offered under similar circumstances
b. Different prices are received under similar circumstances
c. Similar prices are received under different circumstances
d. Different prices are offered under different circumstances
e. None of the above

_____ 5. A retailer may be charged with predatory pricing if
a. It charges customers different prices for the same product in different markets to eliminate competition in one or more of those markets.
b. It establishes a fixed retail selling price for a particular product line within a market area.
c. It secures a brokerage allowance from suppliers, giving it an unfair purchase-price advantage.
d. It uses financial, distribution, and marketing powers to gain lower prices from sellers.
e. It uses bait-and-switch tactics to attract customers and capture markets.

_____ 6. Which of the following criteria would best represent the utilitarianism view of ethical behavior?
a. My conscience tells me it is right.
b. Thou shall not lie.
c. The end justifies the means.
d. Do unto others as you would have them do unto you.
e. If it is legal, it is ethical.

STUDENT APPLICATIONS MANUAL

Investigative Projects: Practice and Applications

1. Obtain product guarantee statements from three different retailers. Analyze each statement to determine your view of the legal obligations of the retailer regarding its responsibility for the products it sells. Then interview the store manager to ascertain his or her view of the store's product guarantee obligations. Does the store manager's view match your view? Explain. How might any differences be reconciled?
2. Conduct personal interviews with three or more retail buyers to determine whether they have been victims of vendor price discrimination. Determine how they were discriminated against (e.g., product, quantity discount, special allowances, special services). What was their

response? What other alternatives did they have? Would any of the other alternatives have been a better reaction? Explain.

3. Survey your local newspaper to identify three or four potential examples of deceptive retail price advertisements. Describe how the advertisement might be deceptive. Visit the local store, and investigate how the retailer supports the advertising claim. Was the advertisement deceptive? Was it legal or illegal? Explain. If it was legal, was it ethical? Explain.
4. Are retail price-matching policies (promising to match the lowest advertised prices a shopper can find) legal? Critics question the fairness of a policy that allows retailers to make deals with certain vocal customers while charging loyal customers higher prices. Do you agree? Describe the ethics of this practice.
5. One of the nation's fastest-growing supermarket chains has been criticized for some of its expansion tactics. The firm employs part-time labor, which it pays at the lowest possible rates. Because of high turnover, most of its labor force never qualifies for the firm's employee benefit plan. Extremely low labor costs allow the chain to be very competitive; hence, it has been able to squeeze out many of its competitors. Customers benefit because in all of its market areas, the chain has been able to substantially lower the total price of a market basket of food. Evaluate the ethics of this behavior using both the relative and absolute approaches to judging retailing behavior.

Tactical Cases: Problems and Decisions

■ CASE 4–1
Is It Bait and Switch, or Is It Trading Up?*

BACKGROUND

The morning edition of the *Cleveland Gazette* carried two sales advertisements featuring special promotions on color television sets. Prough Home Centers, a chain of home appliance stores with 84 outlets in 14 states, ran an advertisement featuring repossessed color televisions:

> PROUGH HOME CENTERS
> "The Professionals in Home Appliances"
> Saturday Only
> Repossessed, Repaired, Resold
> COLOR TELEVISIONS
> At Rock-Bottom Prices
> Starting at $99.95
> LIKE NEW

The second advertisement was placed by The World of Entertainment, a specialty electronics store chain with outlets in eight states; it featured deep discounting of new, brand-name color televisions:

> THE WORLD OF ENTERTAINMENT
> Proudly Presents
> NEW, NAME-BRAND, FAMILY-SIZE
> COLOR TELEVISIONS
> $279.95
> "We Buy Straight from the Factory"
> DON'T MISS THIS DEAL
> SALE ENDS SOON

CURRENT SITUATION

The Johnsons' Experience

Dave and Carol Johnson, a newlywed couple, had been holding off purchasing a new color television until the right sale came along. The Prough Home Center ad caught Dave's attention. The price of $99.95 seemed almost too good to be true. Since the Johnsons lived only six blocks from the nearest outlet, they decided to check out what specific items were available. While Carol reminded Dave that the advertisement did specify "repossessed" color televisions, Dave dismissed Carol's comment, saying, "At $99.95, who cares! So long as we can get a couple of good years of trouble-free service out of it, I'll be happy."

Entering the store, the Johnsons were met by Kathy O'Brian, a top performer in the store's sales department. Dave told O'Brian they had seen Prough's newspaper advertisement, and he expressed an interest in seeing which sets were available. O'Brian informed the Johnsons that although the used sets were in good working order, many of the models had nicks and scratches and the lower-priced sets generally were smaller portable models with even more wear and tear. To support her statement, O'Brian explained that the set advertised for $99.95 was a 12-inch, two-year-old model. Dave replied that he expected as much but still wanted to see the selection of used sets.

As they started to the back of the store where the used sets were on display, O'Brian stopped them at a 14-inch Sony with remote control. "You know," she said, "this is the best set in the store. It's also the best value. This color portable comes complete with remote control and automatic tuning. The regular price on this Sony is $499, but it is currently on sale for $399, and terms are 90 days, same as cash. Also, Sony has a great limited warranty, so you would not have to worry about any major repair bills. I think this set offers excellent value. You really should consider taking advantage of this offer." As a commissioned salesperson, O'Brian stood to benefit financially from the sale of a more expensive set.

"We really would like to look at the used sets if we could," Dave said.

"Sure," O'Brian replied. "I just wanted to show you an opportunity to make a real value purchase. Personally, I feel the smart buy is a new set, because there is very little risk with such a purchase."

"What risk?" Carol asked.

"Well, as you would expect, the manufacturer's warranties are no longer in force on the used sets," O'Brian replied. "And the store's guarantee is limited to 30 days." Seeing that this final clincher had sold the Johnsons, O'Brian hurriedly started writing up the sales contract on the new Sony.

The Criss's Experience

The same day across town, Betty Criss was skimming the *Cleveland Gazette*. The sales promotion advertisement by The World of Entertainment caught Betty's eye. Betty and her husband, Dick, had been watching television on a portable set for a long time, and she thought it was time to get a big, 24-inch console television. When Betty saw The World's offer of "family-size" color televisions for $279.95, she knew the time to buy a new color television had come. Dick expressed some concern about this "almost too good to be true deal" but agreed to accompany Betty to the local outlet in Leipply Square.

Betty walked confidently into The World of Entertainment that night and expressed her interest in the color television console she had seen advertised. Bob Sproat, department manager, led Betty and Dick to a 19-inch color portable. "This is it! This is as family size as you can get," Sproat said. "We've been having trouble with the picture on this one all day, so let's see if I can get one in for you now."

Much to Sproat's delight, Betty's face shriveled at the sight of this family-size portable. The truth was that The World of Entertainment had none of these sets in stock at the moment and the earliest Sproat could get one with an immediate order was 60 days—if he was lucky. He sensed an excellent opportunity to unload one of the many big console sets in stock. "This portable set has a very limited manufacturer's warranty, and the store's guarantee is limited to 30 days. You've already seen the tough time I've had getting a clear picture. This particular model has already given us nothing but trouble. I doubt that it would last more than a couple of years, if that long."

Sproat stepped around the set on sale to a big color console on display in an adjacent setting. Betty's face lit up. Sproat kicked his sales pitch into high gear: "Look at this beautiful console. It's got a great finish and would complement the decor of any home. The manufacturer's warranty is excellent, and we have a full service department to support the warranty. It's a bit more in price than the one on sale, but look at how much more you're getting. At this price, I think we can even throw in a remote control. Personally, I would hate to see you get stuck with that other troublemaker when I can let you walk out of here today with this set."

After extolling all the virtues of the big console, Sproat tried once again to get a clear picture on the portable, but without success.

As Betty and Dick stared at the fuzzy picture, Bob whipped out a sales contract and started filling in the necessary information. Within 20 minutes, Betty and Dick were driving home with a new 24-inch console in the back of the station wagon. "I thought he said he would deliver this thing," Dick said. "For $625.95, you would think he would at least have it delivered."

"He would have," Betty replied, "but they wouldn't be able to deliver it until the end of next week."

ASSIGNMENT

1. Discuss the legal implications concerning the two sales experiences. What remedies, if any, might each family attempt?
2. Discuss the moral and ethical implications of the advertising and selling techniques employed by each retailer. Look at the transaction from both sides. Do retailers and consumers really deal at arm's length (with equal knowledge of the product and its value)?

*This case was prepared by Joseph McCafferty, The University of Akron.

■ CASE 4–2
"Risk": Good Business or Questionable Ethics?*

Athena Demou and her sister Areti, former national sales manager for a major U.S. manufacturer and marketer of teenage clothing in Greece, decided to start a small boutique of high-fashion apparel for young, well-to-do Athenians. For both sisters, the undertaking, "Risk," was the culmination of years of preparation. They located an 800-square-foot store in a posh suburb of southern Athens surrounded by four dozen other retailers. They created the most desirable atmospherics and ambiance to lure their under-25 target segment. Finally, through Areti's contacts, they managed to secure exclusive, international, branded merchandise not otherwise available in their immediate market. Risk, despite high overhead, started producing a reasonable profit within a year and soon became the envy of many other established retailers in the area.

But soon the exclusive boutique was to face the realities of Greek production and merchandising practices. Customer knowledge and the influence of high-fashion trends from a variety of European sources (French, Italian, etc.) require a great degree of flexibility on the retailer's part in choosing merchandise and changing the store product mix on short notice. Often the retailer is expected to coordinate outfits or match styles from different international designers. For small, independent, specialty boutiques, it could be impossible to secure and stock representative merchandise from all or most of these international designer houses. Therefore, a large number of local small manufacturers offer short runs of complementary private-label products, often covering only part of the total width or depth of the needs of a single retailer. These manufacturers usually copy a success story (e.g., Levi's 501) and adapt it to the merchandise mix requirements of a specific retailer. Actually, patent infringement is avoided by altering the name of the product somewhat (e.g., Lefi 502). In most cases, the new product is of better or as good quality as the original and significantly cheaper. For many retailers, it makes good business sense to carry this type of infringement or immolation merchandise.

Athena and Areti quickly learned that they had to adapt to this practice to survive. However, the distributors that gave them exclusive rights for their prestigious international labels were now quite upset. Their products effectively were used as leaders to attract customers (who in the end often purchased the locally produced private labels). Given the realities of this industry, the international producers needed the smaller boutique to achieve full coverage in the Athens market.

The two sisters opened a second store ("Challenge"), which copied the character of Risk. However, since the second store was in a neighboring market with less affluent customers, much of its private-label merchandise was supplied by channels that were directly importing goods that were from less recognized sources (Korea, Macao, etc.), but conformed to the standards of name brands.

To improve the new store's image, Athena and Areti routinely sold through Challenge exclusive merchandise that was moving very slowly in Risk. This practice was allowing them to keep both stores at the cutting edge of new fashion entries by coordinating styles and lines from different origins using the expertise and quick responses of small local manufacturers to provide the missing links to a relatively complete line of comfortable, sporty, and stylish clothing for their young, upscale customers.

With the opening of the new store came new policies. All represented products were chosen only if the very best quality was assured, and service support was paramount. Some of the better-known international labels in apparel were not even carried in the stores on the belief that these brands had a lesser quality than desired. The two sisters started becoming very selective about their channels and often supplemented lesser-quality items of major international labels with what in their opinion were better private-label lines. Soon the stores' ambiance, vibrant character, fashion-forward merchandise, and quality of product lines carried resulted in a high level of customer loyalty and patronage.

Nevertheless, eight major international brands continued to wield the primary customer drawing power due to their strong name recognition. However, in terms of total sales volume, the international labels accounted for less than half the total revenues. The rest were produced by private-label manufacturers and were of the highest possible quality, with names that often resembled those of the major brands. That was another frustrating reality to the established international channels, which could hardly even detect this type of infringement. The goods were moving very quickly and in small quantities. To identify and monitor this type of activity would be a very expensive and time-consuming exercise for the international producers. In addition, nothing technically "illegal" was going on. None of the complementary products pretended to be from well-known manufacturers. And they usually had better prices, higher quality, and better fit. Athena and Areti believed they had helped the private-label manufacturers challenge the international labels in both quality and design.

Despite their lower volume, the quality and customer base of Risk and Challenge made the stores highly desirable outlets for the channels of major international brands. Customers were sporting their fashions in the better gatherings of young Athenians and presumably were responsible for significant brand-name exposure and word-of-mouth publicity. At the same time, the pro-quality emphasis of the two stores had generated strong store loyalties, perhaps greater than the advertised loyalties of their international-label merchandise.

ASSIGNMENT

1. Are Athena and Areti's merchandising practices good business practices? Why or why not? Explain.
2. Are Athena and Areti's merchandising practices ethical? Why or why not? Explain.
3. Could there be any cross-cultural differences in determining what might be good or ethical business practices? Do different cultures use different criteria or approaches in judging good versus ethical business actions?

*This case was prepared by John Thanopoulos and Jon Hawes, The University of Akron.

ENDNOTES

1. J. C. Penney archives.
2. Mary Ellen Oliverio, "The Implementation of a Code of Ethics: The Early Efforts of One Entrepreneur," *Journal of Business Ethics* 8 (May 1989): 369.
3. J. C. Beatly, "Faith in the J. C. Penney Company," *The Dynamo,* September 1917, 10.
4. Hershey H. Friedman and Linda Weiser Friedman, "Framework for Organizational Success," *Journal of Business Ethics* 7 (March 1988): 220.
5. Diane Schneidman, "Door-to-Door Time Restrictions Found Unconstitutional," *Marketing News,* March 13, 1987, 4.

6. Joe Agnew, "Small Retailers Help Retain North Dakota Sunday Blue Law," *Marketing News,* March 13, 1987, 8.
7. Sandra L. Schmidt and Jerome B. Kernam, "The Many Meanings (and Implications) of 'Satisfaction Guaranteed,'" *Journal of Retailing* 61 (Winter 1985): 89.
8. See Robert J. Aalberts and Ellen Day, "Is Discounting Destined for Difficult Times?", *Business,* January-March 1989, 27–31.
9. See Willard F. Mueller and Thomas W. Paterson, "Effectiveness of State Sales-Below-Cost Laws: Evidence from the Grocery Trade," *Journal of Retailing* 62 (Summer 1986): 166–169.
10. See Francine Schwadel, "Sears Cails It 'Low Prices, New York Calls It Misleading," *The Wall Street Journal,* January 22, 1989, B-1, B-4.
11. Teri Agins, "As Retailers' Sales Crop Up Everywhere, Regulators Wonder If the Price Is Right," *The Wall Street Journal,* February 13, 1990, B-1.
12. Scott Hume, "Big Mac Attacked," *Advertising Age,* May 4, 1987, 110.
13. See Lynn Scarlett, "Forced Food Labeling Will Hurt Consumers," *USA Today,* March 12, 1990, 6A.
14. See Susan M. Thomas, Doris C. Van Doren, and Louise W. Smith, "Bait and Switch May Be Getting Passé; Consumers Want Information Respect," *Marketing News,* February 15, 1988, 3.
15. Asra Q. Nomani, "Best Buy, Sued on Sales Tactics, Dispute Rules," *The Wall Street Journal,* October 18, 1989, B-6.
16. Amy Dunkin, "Why Some Benetton Shopkeepers Are Losing Their Shirts," *Business Week,* March 14, 1988, 78.
17. See Udayan Gupta, "At the Mall, Tenants Press Grievances as Never Before," *The Wall Street Journal,* June 15, 1989, B-2.
18. Louis W. Stern and Adel I. El-Ansary, *Marketing Channels,* 2d ed. (Englewood Cliffs, N.J.: Prentice-Hall, 1982), 368.
19. Geoffrey P. Lantos, "An Ethical Base for Marketing Decision Making," *Journal of Business and Industrial Marketing* 2 (Spring 1987): 13.
20. Michael Josephson, *Ethical Decision Making in the Trenches* (Marina del Rey, Cal.: The Joseph and Edna Josephson Institute for the Advancement of Ethics, 1989), 1.
21. Ibid.
22. Ibid.
23. Ibid.
24. Lantos, "An Ethical Base," 14.
25. Ibid., 15–16.
26. Ibid.
27. See Gael M. McDonald and Raymond A. Zepp, "What Should Be Done? A Practical Approach to Business Ethics," *Management Decision* 28 (1990): 9–14.
28. See Patrick E. Murphy, "Creating Ethical Corporate Structures," *Sloan Management Review* (Winter 1989): 1–7; Patrick E. Murphy, "Implementing Business Ethics," *Journal of Business Ethics* 7 (December 1988): 907–915.

PART I

RETAIL INFORMATION SYSTEMS AND TECHNOLOGIES

CHAPTER 5

OUTLINE

OBJECTIVES

- Describe how to reduce the risks of doing business through an adequate retailing information system.
- Determine what information is available, what information is needed, how information is gathered and processed, and where information is obtained.
- Productively use information in retail problem-solving and decision-making situations.
- Recognize the key considerations in effective management of the retailing information system.
- Design, implement, and manage a retail research project.
- Understand and appreciate the role of the electronic data processing system within the retailing information system.
- Discuss the role of automatic identification systems in the management of effective and efficient retail organizations.
- Profile the various types of integrated information systems used in sharing information and developing company teamwork.

THE RETAILER'S NEED TO KNOW

To succeed in today's complex dynamic retailing environment, the retailer must learn how to reduce the risks of doing business. Basing decisions on reliable information is perhaps the single most effective way to reduce business risks.

Retailers need to know what information is available, what information they need, how and where to obtain information, how to effectively communicate information within and beyond the organization, and how to use the information obtained productively. The kinds of information that interest the retailer are those that can make problem solving and decision making as effective as possible. Successful information systems and technologies, by necessity, are future oriented. A major function of any information and technology system is to predict today what is going to happen tomorrow. Equally important is the ability of the information and technology system to reduce the time span required to make a decision. Because good information is the precursor to effective decision making and problem solving, we turn to this subject early in the text.

THE RETAILING INFORMATION SYSTEM

Because successful retailing starts with the possession and proper use of business information, many retailers have developed and implemented some form of retailing information system. A **retailing information system (RIS)** is an interacting organization of people, machines, and methods designed to produce a regular, continuous, and orderly flow of information necessary for the retailer's problem-solving and decision-making activities. The RIS is a planned, sequential flow of information tailored to the needs of a particular retail operation. As Figure 5–1 shows, the four basic activities of the RIS are locating, gathering, processing, and utilizing pertinent retailing information.

Locating Information

The fundamental purpose of the RIS is to provide a framework for gathering input (information) from the retailer's external and internal environments to enable the retailer to develop the best possible output ("correct" decisions). In the first stage, the decision maker must locate information relevant to its business. Before this, however, the retailer must understand the two basic *types* of information—secondary and primary—and the two *sources* from which it can obtain this information—external and internal.

Types of Information

Secondary information is existing, often published information that has been collected for another purpose. Although the information was intended for some other purpose, a retailer often can adapt it to its own needs. Given the tremendous wealth of secondary information collected and published by government agencies, trade associations, and other research groups, the chance of finding useful information collected for other purposes is very high. Even though secondary information might not fit the retailer's *precise needs,* a major function of the RIS is to convert this information into a reservoir of useful knowledge. Like any type of information, secondary information has advantages and disadvantages (see Figure 5–2).

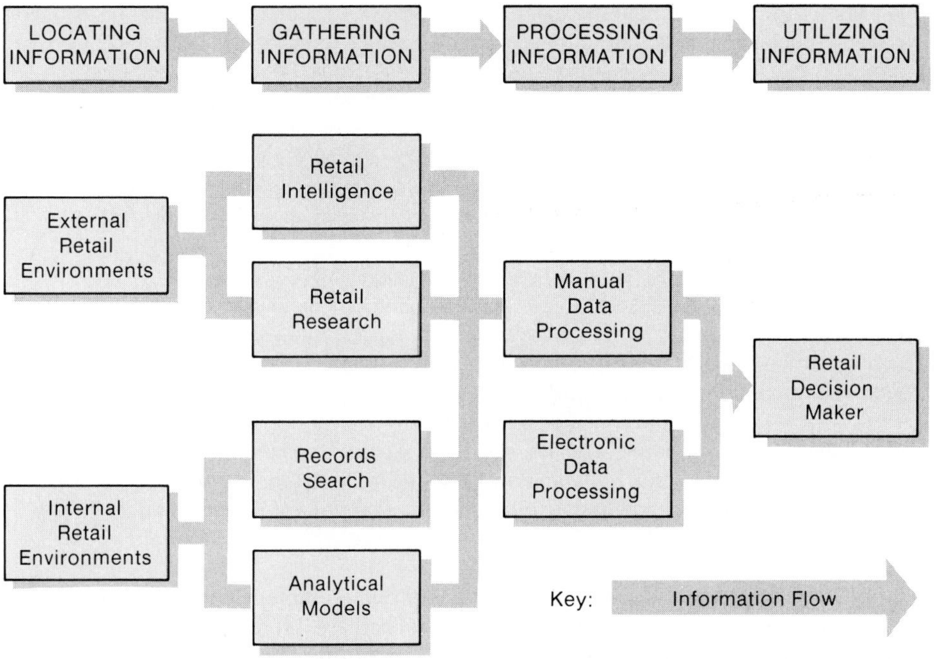

FIGURE 5–1
The retailing information system

FIGURE 5–2
Advantages and disadvantages of secondary information

DISADVANTAGES

Lack of Suitability

Suitability is the "match" between pertinent secondary information and the information needs of the retailer. Where there is a lack of suitability, there is a poor match between the secondary information and the retailer's information needs. Lack of suitability can be the result of either geographic or class conformity. Geographic conformity is concerned with whether the information is broken down by geographic units (census areas, cities, counties, states, etc.) which are consistent with the retailer's needs. Class conformity is concerned with how information is classified and defined, as well as what units of measurements are used in measuring each class. Sales, for example, can be defined as gross *or* net sales per square *or* linear foot.

Lack of Accuracy

Secondary data can be inaccurate for a number of reasons: (1) a considerable amount of secondary information is reported without sufficient comment on how, when, and under what circumstances the information was collected and tabulated; (2) some secondary sources get their information from other sources, with the result being third-hand information for the retailer, for whom the problems of accuracy are substantially increased; and (3) secondary information was collected for a specific purpose and frequently that purpose was to promote a particular idea, position, or organization. By definition and design, such information is biased and often inaccurate.

Obsolescence

The usefulness of secondary information is sometimes limited by its obsolescence. In the time it takes to collect, tabulate, and publish secondary information, it can become quite dated. Census information, for example, is collected at 5-, 7-, and 10-year intervals, depending on the particular type of census.

ADVANTAGES

Less Costly

Secondary information generally costs less to obtain than primary information. By using published sources of information, the very expensive collecting, editing, and tabulating phases can be avoided. The use of unpublished secondary information requires a more extensive search process; however, such information usually can be obtained at costs below primary information. Many governmental agencies and trade associations provide vast amounts of information either free of charge or at some minimal charge. Private commercial sources normally charge substantial fees; nevertheless, due to their operating economies and efficiencies, they frequently can provide secondary information at rates lower than the costs of the retailer doing it.

Greater Speed and Availability

Secondary information often can be obtained immediately or in a matter of days, whereas the collection of primary information can take several weeks or months. When the firms's decision makers require at least some information, secondary information may be the only feasible alternative.

Greater Familiarity

Since the firm's managers have been exposed at one time or another to many of the standard types of secondary information, they tend to be more comfortable with that information because they are more aware of its uses and its limitations.

Possible Greater Credibility

Secondary information has greater credibility when the original source is highly credible. Sources with questionable reputations are usually perceived as having less credible information.

Primary information is new information tailored to the purpose at hand. Original data are collected using survey, panel, laboratory, and statistical techniques. Sometimes the retailer collects primary information because it can find no secondary sources to help make an important decision. At other times, the retailer obtains primary information to corroborate the secondary information gathered.

By using primary information, the retailer overcomes most of the disadvantages associated with secondary information. Primary information generally is more accurate, more current, and more suitable to the problem at hand. Unfortunately, primary information usually is more costly and time consuming to obtain. Further, gathering primary information normally requires investment in specialized equipment and personnel.

Sources of Information

The retailer has two sources of information—external and internal. **External information** is information obtained from outside the firm. It originates from formal (library, government, trade, and commercial) organizations and from informal (supplier, competitor, and consumer) sources. Given the great variety of outside sources, the task of locating and collecting external information often is very tedious and time consuming.

Internal information is information found within the firm. For example, various departments and divisions generate a wide range of information in the normal course of their operations. Sources include operating statements, sales records, expense records, purchasing and inventory records, accounts receivable and payable records, and prior written reports. Other information comes from employee surveys and employment records. By applying certain statistical and analytical procedures, the retailer can generate additional information.

Gathering Information

Once the information has been located, the second stage is to gather it. Figure 5–3 represents a taxonomy of information-gathering methods, including retail intelligence, retail research, records search, and analytical models. In this section, we briefly define and describe each of these methods. Later in the chapter, we discuss retail intelligence and retail research in more depth.

Retail intelligence is any method or combination of methods used to obtain external secondary information. To keep the firm's decision makers current, the retailing information system must be able to monitor the daily developments of the

DIMENSIONS OF INFORMATION		Types of Information	
		Secondary	Primary
Sources of Information	External	retail intelligence	retail research
	Internal	records search	analytical models

FIGURE 5–3
A taxonomy of information-gathering methods

marketplace. Retail intelligence involves search procedures to comb libraries and government and trade sources for pertinent information regularly and systematically. For a fee, additional retail intelligence can be secured from various commercial organizations that specialize in monitoring certain aspects of the marketplace.

Retail research involves using a set of scientific procedures to gather external primary information from consumers, suppliers, and competitors. Typically retail research is project oriented, that is, directed at a particular decision-making or problem-solving situation. Two major characteristics of retail research are that (1) it is conducted in a fragmented, intermittent fashion and (2) a computer usually processes the data. Surveys, panels, and laboratory experiments are the most common information-gathering techniques used in retail research.

Records search includes all methods used in gathering internal secondary information. The firm's internal accounting system and various operational control subsystems can provide a wealth of information on all aspects of the retailer's operations. A records search can generate information on both past and current performances and activities. Such internal records contain information on sales, expenses, inventories, purchases, potential vendors, and a host of other factors. They also indicate a great deal about the relationship between these factors and the retailer's products, prices, promotions, facilities, and personnel.

Analytical models are various statistical and quantitative methods that researchers use internally to generate primary information. Used mostly by large retailers, analytical models employ mathematical techniques to find the best solution to a particular problem. Retailers use analytical models to estimate a trading area's sales potential, evaluate an advertising campaign, predict operating expenses under various circumstances, and analyze stocking and handling procedures. Essentially analytical models generate primary information from secondary information using a complex set of quantitative procedures.

Processing Information

After locating and gathering information, the RIS must be able to process the information effectively. The information-processing system consists of (1) selecting and preparing input; (2) evaluating, storing, and retrieving processed information; and (3) preparing and disseminating output. As Figure 5–1 shows, the information-processing system can be either manual or electronic.

Manual data processing uses human labor to process information. The hardware in such a system usually consists of typewriters, calculators, filing cabinets, and hand-carried files. The software typically consists of written instructions on how to conduct each processing function. For small retailers, manual data processing is practical and can be highly effective if the system is carefully developed and maintained.

Electronic data processing is a computer-based system of processing information. The computer is the principal piece of hardware used in preparing, evaluating, storing, retrieving, and disseminating information. It has three major components: an input system, a central processing unit, and an output system. The software consists of the instructional procedures for programming the computer. Traditionally only large retailing organizations could afford a computer-based electronic data processing system. The development of the personal computer, however, has made electronic data processing a much more accessible option for all retailers.

Utilizing Information

No matter how well the RIS accomplishes the tasks of locating, gathering, and processing information, the total system will fail if the decision maker does not fully utilize the information. Information, the principal input into every decision-making and problem-solving situation, is crucial for establishing goals and objectives, identifying and analyzing alternatives, developing plans, and making recommendations and decisions. To avoid "muddling through" problems and making decisions with crude rules of thumb and rough approximations, reliable and pertinent information must be available—and used.

RETAIL INTELLIGENCE

Gathering retail intelligence from library, government, association, and commercial sources provides the retailer with information about the legal, political, social, economic, and technological environments. For any one of these sources, the information can be published or reported in the form of books, monographs, reports, periodicals, bulletins, tapes, films, or several types of special publications.

Library Sources

The library not only is a source of information on a wide variety of subjects but also frequently serves as a means for locating other sources of retail intelligence. For the retailer seeking external secondary information, the library is a good starting point. Library research skills are developed by using the library and becoming familiar with its information retrieval systems (e.g., card catalogs, visual display terminals, and computer search technologies). Also, many libraries have specialized personnel (e.g., a government documents librarian), trained in finding specific information.

Government Sources

The most prolific compilers of external secondary information are federal, state, and local governments. While government sources collect and disseminate an enormous amount of information on a wide variety of subjects, the types of information retailers use most often are census and registration data.

Census Information

The U.S. Bureau of the Census of the Department of Commerce regularly conducts nine different censuses. These constitute the most important sources of external secondary information for most businesses.[1] The nine censuses are as follows:

- Census of Population
- Census of Housing
- Census of Governments
- Census of Agriculture
- Census of Construction
- Census of Business
- Census of Manufacturing
- Census of Mineral Industries
- Census of Transportation

The *Census of Population* and the *Census of Housing* contain a vast amount of detailed information broken down according to predefined geographical reporting units. Information for both censuses is reported by states, counties, cities, and various urban area classifications. Within urban areas, population and housing characteristics are available on a very localized level. Urban areas are subdivided into census tracts, enumeration districts, and census blocks for reporting purposes. In addition to population, housing counts and density measurements (persons or units per area), each census contains an extensive amount of information concerning each person or unit. For example, the *Census of Population* provides statistics on the demographic makeup of a given reporting area, including age, sex, race, education, occupation, income, marital

RETAIL STRATEGIES AND TACTICS

"TIGER": Targeting the Target Market

Not many people wait in line to greet a tiger face-to-face. But the Census Bureau's TIGER is on the loose, and marketers, researchers, and demographers are ready to gobble it up.

For businesspeople and researchers, it means the ability to chart every block in every county in the U.S. topologically and demographically. It means pizza delivery drivers can more easily locate their targeted destinations while the pizzerias more accurately keep track of who their customers are and where they come from.

It means direct marketers can physically see their customers' locations, with the subsequent ability to cluster them for targeted marketing.

It means businesses can more accurately define the geographic boundaries of their customers, enabling them to allocate resources better. . . . TIGER, in its purest form, links addresses to specific blocks. TIGER stands for Topologically Integrated Geographic Encoding and Referencing . . . it will cover all 3,200 counties in the U.S., including addresses from the most intense urban areas to the most remote rural areas. Direct marketing and delivery-intensive businesses will benefit greatly from it . . . because of its ability to pinpoint addresses on every city block.

Source: Howard Schlossberg, "Census Bureau's TIGER Seen as a Roaring Success," *Marketing News* (April 30, 1990): vol. 24, p. 2. Reprinted from *Marketing News*, published by the American Marketing Association, Chicago, IL 60606.

status, living arrangements, and family structure. The *Census of Housing* gives additional information on the occupancy status and the financial and structural characteristics of the housing stock.

The *Census of Governments* describes the operating characteristics of all levels of government—federal, state, and local. The economic censuses of agriculture, construction, business, manufacturers, mineral industries, and transportation are presented by geographical areas and by Standard Industrial Classification (SIC) system codes. In some cases, states, counties, and cities are the most common reporting units for the economic censuses. The SIC is a standardized code that categorizes industries into major groups and subclassifies them into highly descriptive groups. Each of the economic censuses provides information on the number of establishments and their sales, expenditures, number of employees, size of operation, and types of facilities and equipment used in their operations. The most important economic census for the retailer is the *Census of Business*, which consists of three parts: "Retail Trade," "Wholesaler Trade," and "Selected Services."

Registration Information

All levels of government at various times require individuals and organizations to register and report activities in which they are engaged. This routinely collected data can provide the retailer with a tremendous amount of useful information if the retailer knows how and where to secure it. Some of the more common forms of registration include public records on (1) births, (2) deaths, (3) marriages, (4) school enrollments, (5) income, (6) sales tax payments, (7) automobile and recreational vehicle registration, and (8) general and special business licenses and crime statistics.

Association Sources

A third major source of external secondary information is the large group of trade and professional associations that collect and publish highly specialized information. It would be difficult to find a subject on which one or more of these groups or associations could not provide information. Their charges for information range from none to various organization membership fees and publication subscription rates. To contact these organizations, the retailer can consult the *World Almanac*, the *Encyclopedia of Associations*, or the *Writer's Guide*. Most associations publish either a magazine, a journal, or a newsletter; they usually issue special reports, maintain files of information, and send out promotional literature as well. Figure 5–4 lists some of the more important trade and professional associations and publications of particular interest to retailers.

Trade and Professional Associations

American Booksellers Association
American Management Association
American Marketing Association
American Retail Federation
Automotive Parts and Accessories Association
Better Business Bureau
Chamber of Commerce
International Franchise Association
Mass Retailing Institute
Menswear Retailers of America
National Appliance and Radio-TV Dealers Association
National Association of Retail Druggists
National Association of Retail Grocers
National Association of Variety Stores
National Home Furnishing Association
National Industrial Conference Board
National Jewelers of America
National Lumber and Building Materials Association
National Retail Federation, Inc.
National Retail Furniture Association
National Retail Hardware Association
National Shoe Retailers Association
National Sporting Goods Association
Sales and Marketing Executives
Urban Land Institute

Trade and Professional Publications

Advertising Age
American Fabrics and Fashions
Auto Merchandising News
Business Week
California Apparel News
Chain Store Age Executive
Clothes
Curtain, Drapery and Bedspread Magazine
Dealerscope (Appliances)
Discount Merchandiser
Drug Topics
Earnshaw's Infants, Girls, and Boyswear Review
Floor Covering Weekly
Florist
Fortune
Furniture News
Hardware Age
Hardware Merchandiser
Harvard Business Review
Home and Auto
Journal of Advertising Research
Journal of Marketing
Journal of Marketing Research
Journal of Retailing
Juvenile Merchandising
Luggage and Leather Goods
Mart Magazine
Merchandising Week
Modern Jeweler
Office Products News
Progressive Grocer
Publishers Weekly
Retail Advertising Week
Sales and Marketing Management
Sports Merchandiser
Sporting Goods Business
Stores
Visual Merchandising
Volume Retail Merchandising
Women's Wear Daily

FIGURE 5–4
Association sources of retail intelligence

FIGURE 5–5
Selected examples of standardized information sources

Survey of Buying Power .... Sales and Marketing Executives	Information on population, retail sales by store group, and effective buying income.
Market Survey .... The Editor and Publisher Market Guide	Information on the number of retail stores and their sales, population, disposable personal income, number of households, and household income.
Retail Index .... A. C. Nielsen Co.	Information on retail sales by product class and brand, purchases by retailers, retail inventories and stock turn, and retail and wholesale prices.
Consumer Panel .... Market Research Corporation of America	Information on product and brand sales by type of consumer, type of household, and type of retailer.
Supermarket Audit .... Market Research Corporation of America	Information on in-store type and amount of stock, prices of products, and shelf space assignments.
Channel Survey .... Selling Areas-Marketing, Inc.	Information on movements of products from suppliers to retailers.
Television Index .... A. C. Nielsen Co.	Information on size of television audience, viewing habits, flow of audience, and cost per 1,000 homes reached.
Media Survey .... Audit Bureau of Circulation	Information on readership of newspaper and magazine ads.
Media Survey .... Standard Rate and Data Service	Information on advertising rates for various media.

Commercial Sources

The need for marketing information has led many firms into the business of providing it commercially. Commercial sources collect, tabulate, analyze, and report information. *Bradford's Directory* lists more than 350 firms engaged in the commercial gathering and selling of information. Typically commercial information sources provide either a standardized information service or a service tailored to the informational needs of a particular customer.

Standardized information services provide a prescribed type of information continuously and regularly. Figure 5–5 illustrates several examples of standardized information sources and the types of information they provide.[2] *Tailored information services* provide customized information for the specific needs of the retailer. These services typically are performed on either a single occasion or an irregular, contractual basis.

RETAIL RESEARCH

Retail research is the systematic process of gathering and analyzing primary, external information about consumers, suppliers, and competitors. It is conducted on a project-by-project basis and directed at a particular problem-solving or decision-making situation. The main purpose of the research is to obtain specific information to help

RETAILING IN THE 90's

Retail Technologies...

ensuring merchandising effectiveness and operational efficiency.

Bar coding symbologies are a series of light and dark bars attached to products, product packages, and shipping cartons. Bar codes are part of the interacting technologies that enable machines to recognize and enter data into a computer system. For the retailer, fast and accurate data collection and processing are vital to effective merchandising strategies and efficient daily operations.

Bar code technologies permit the retailer to offer faster checkout, itemized receipts, price verification, coupon redemption, credit and check authorization, and a host of other customer conveniences. Bar code technologies are an integral part of the retailer's daily operations — electronic purchase order systems, in-store sales, audits, merchandise ticketing, inter-store merchandise transfer processes, direct store delivery systems, and staff productivity reports.

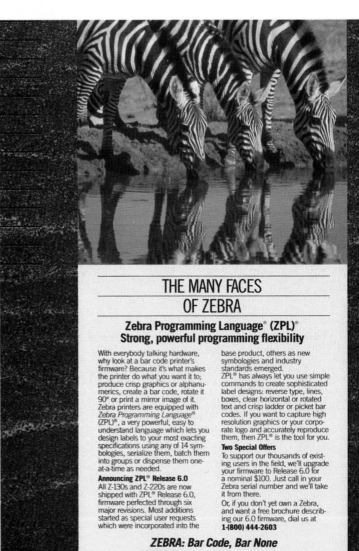

reduce the risks in making a decision. Conducting research can be an expensive and time-consuming venture, so each research project must be selected carefully on the basis of its potential for providing meaningful, useful information.

Research projects that have proven to be productive ventures for the retailer include studies on (1) consumer attitudes toward the retailer and its merchandising efforts, (2) consumer purchase motives and preferences, (3) demographic and psychographic profiles of both customers and noncustomers, (4) buyer behavior patterns and their relationships to the retailer's mode of operations, (5) service and performance records of suppliers, (6) price and cost comparisons among suppliers, (7) merchandising and operational strengths and weaknesses of competitors, and (8) employees' perceptions of the company and its dealings with them. Retail research also provides information on the sales potential and customer acceptance of product lines, advertising and personal selling effectiveness, locational attributes of the retailer's outlets, and consumer service and price perceptions. To conduct retail research, a basic understanding of the scientific method is useful.

The Scientific Method

The **scientific method** is a set of procedures that allows the retailer to gather and analyze data in a systematic, controlled fashion. It is perhaps the most commonly used method of producing defensible results and drawing reliable conclusions. The accepted stages of the scientific method are:

- Identifying the problem
- Developing a hypothesis
- Collecting information
- Analyzing information
- Drawing conclusions

Its objectivity in the midst of creative and mechanical processes gives the scientific method its unusually high level of acceptance.

The Creative Process

The creative aspect of the scientific method consists of identifying problems and developing hypotheses, the most critical part of any research project. The *problem identification process* requires the retailer to clearly identify the problem and then state it in precise terms. Problem statements take the form of a declarative sentence ("The problem is to determine the relationship. . . . ") or a question ("What is the relationship between . . . ?"). The importance of the problem identification process perhaps is best expressed by the adage "A problem well defined is a problem half solved." Problem identification demands more than basic knowledge and skills; it requires creative perception and insight and the ability to look beyond the "symptoms" of a problem to find its causes.

The *hypothesis development* process is the most important stage in the scientific method. This stage characterizes the whole process of scientific investigation by focusing that investigation. In developing a hypothesis, the researcher formulates a definite position that will be either accepted or rejected in the analysis stage. In essence, the hypothesis is simply a statement of the researcher's tentative solution to the identified problem. A hypothesis takes a known fact and proposes a relationship one step beyond existing knowledge. Once the hypothesis has been developed, it is considered "cast in concrete." Based on the outcome of the analysis, the researcher's decision is automatic: either accept or reject the hypothesis. The hypothesis can be expressed in statistical or verbal terms.

The Mechanical Process

Compared to the creative stages of the scientific method, the last three stages (collection, analysis, and conclusion) are largely mechanical. In the *information collection process*, the researcher selects and uses one or more research methods, such as surveys, observation, focus groups, interviews, or experimental, in association with a research instrument such as a questionnaire. This process also involves the use of some form of scientific sampling.

The *information analysis process* consists of several mechanical activities. The first is to prepare the information for analysis; examples are editing and tabulating raw data. The second step is to calculate statistical expressions such as percentages, averages, and measures of central tendency. The third activity is to observe the relationships among these statistical expressions; for example, the researcher might want to observe similarities and differences among the statistics. The fourth step is to test the degrees of relationship among the statistical expressions. The degrees of relationship can be determined through a variety of statistical tests that measure how significant the differences are and how strongly the data are associated.

Drawing conclusions is the final stage of the scientific method and should evolve naturally from the problem-identification, hypothesis development, information collection, and analysis stages. Conclusions usually state whether the hypothesis was accepted or rejected, together with an operational interpretation of the results. Because the retailer's decisions are based on the final conclusions of the research, the research analyst should take considerable care to present the results clearly, concisely, and professionally.

Collecting Primary Information

The following discussion identifies and examines the most common of the various methods and instruments used to collect information in retail research.

Research Methods

Retail analysts use four basic methods to collect external primary information: surveys, observation, the purchase intercept technique, and experimentation. The method used depends on the nature of the research problem.

The Survey Method. With the **survey** method, the researcher systematically gathers information directly from the appropriate respondents. Generally the researcher uses a questionnaire administered either in person, over the telephone, or by mail. The *personal interview* is a face-to-face question-and-answer session between the interviewer and the respondent.[3] Interviewers can contact respondents either at their homes or places of employment or at public places (street corners, shopping centers, retail stores).[4] Typically the personal interview consists of these steps:

1. Identification—a statement of who is conducting the interview, what the survey is about, for whom it is being conducted, and why it is being conducted
2. Permission—a request of the respondent for an interview
3. Administration—asking a predetermined list of questions and recording the respondent's answers
4. Closure—the terminating step in which the interviewer thanks the respondent for his or her cooperation

Two other survey methods retailers use are the telephone survey and the mail survey. In a *telephone survey*, the interviewer phones potential respondents at their homes. Successful telephone interviews take no more than three or four minutes of the respondent's time. The basic survey steps of identification, permission, administration,

Selection Criteria	Survey Method		
	Personal Interview	Telephone Survey	Mail Survey
Cost:[1] What is the most expensive method of collecting information?	Most expensive	Intermediate	Least expensive
Speed: What is the fastest method of collecting information?	Slowest method	Fastest method	Intermediate
Accuracy: What is the most accurate method of collecting information?	Most accurate	Intermediate	Least accurate
Volume: Which method is capable of collecting the most information?	Most information	Least information	Intermediate
Response rate: Which method results in the highest number of completed interviews?	Highest response	Intermediate	Lowest response
Flexibility: What method is most capable of adjusting to changing interviewing conditions?	Most flexible	Intermediate	Least flexible
Sample control:[2] Which method is capable of securing the best representative sample of the total population?	Intermediate	Worst representation	Best representation
Interview control: What method provides the interviewer the greatest amount of control over the interview situation?	Greatest control	Intermediate	Least control
Administrative control: Which method provides the retailer the greatest amount of control over the actions of the interviewer?	Least control	Intermediate	Greatest control

[1]Where the sample is scattered over a wide geographic area.
[2]Assumes an accurate mailing list.

Source: Adapted from K. L. McGown, *Marketing Research: Text and Cases* (Cambridge, MA: Winthrop Publishers, 1979), 135.

FIGURE 5–6
Determining which survey method to use

and closure are essentially the same for telephone surveys as they are for personal surveys.

Mail surveys differ from personal interviews and telephone surveys in that the questionnaire is administered in writing. The potential respondent receives and returns the questionnaire by mail. The survey director also can administer the survey by attaching questionnaires to products or packages, passing them out in a store or on the street, or placing them in newspapers. In these cases, respondents are asked to return the questionnaire in a self-addressed, postage-paid envelope. Because the questionnaire is in written form and the interviewer is not available to ask or answer questions, the questionnaire should be short and simple and have complete instructions.

Figure 5–6 summarizes the relative strengths and weaknesses of each survey method.

The Observation Method. Researchers can obtain significant amounts of primary information simply by observing consumers' behavior. **Observation** is a method of recording some aspect of consumers' overt behavior by either personal or mechanical means. What the consumer does rather than says is the principal focus of the observation method. The advantages of this method are that it (1) eliminates any interviewer bias associated with the survey method and (2) does not require the respondent's cooperation. The major disadvantage of the observation method is that the retailer cannot investigate the consumer's motives, attitudes, beliefs, and feelings. If the retailer uses this method, it must decide which observation and recording techniques to use, the setting in which to make the observation, and whether to inform consumers that they are being observed. Figure 5–7 outlines each of these decisions.

The Purchase Intercept Technique. By combining the observation method with the survey (self-report) method, the **purchase intercept technique (PIT)** capitalizes on "the advantages of observation (e.g., accuracy and objectivity) and the significant information gained through self-report (e.g., information about why the specific behavior takes place)."[5] The PIT is an in-store information-gathering technique consisting of the following steps:

1. Observe customer's in-store shopping behavior.
2. Record pertinent shopping behavior information.
3. Interview the customer immediately (at the time of observable product selection or other significant behavior trait under study—reaction to displays and signs) about his or her purchase or shopping behavior.[6]

The Experimentation Method. Researchers use **experimentation** to determine a cause-and-effect relationship between two or more factors. An experiment usually is conducted under controlled conditions; that is, the factors under study are manipulated while all other factors are held constant. For example, a retailer might increase the price of a product by $5.00 to see what effect the price change has on sales and profits, while holding constant all other factors, such as location, amount of shelf space, advertisements, and in-store displays. Figure 5–8 illustrates a number of experimental designs.

The before-after design *without* control group measures the dependent factor (sales volume) before and after the factor has been manipulated (e.g., change from a middle- to end-of-aisle display). The researcher assumes that the difference in sales volume is caused by the change in location, since all other factors affecting the sale of the product were held constant (see Figure 5–8a).

The before-after design *with* control group is essentially the same as the design just described except that a control group is used to determine if any changes in sales volume would have occurred regardless of any manipulation. For example, in Figure 5–8b, Store A's sales volume is measured before and after an advertising campaign to determine the effects of advertising. To prove that all changes in sales volume resulted from advertising, any changes in the sales volume of control Store B, which is unaffected by the advertising campaign, are also measured over the same period. If control Store B experienced no change in sales volume, the researcher can reasonably state that changes in sales volume for Store A resulted from the advertising campaign, everything else being equal.

The after-only *with* control group design is the most widely used design because of its simplicity and ease of implementation. As Figure 5–8c shows, it involves measuring the dependent factor (sales volume of Department A in Store A) for one group that has been manipulated (increased size of display area) and comparing it with the same dependent factor (sales volume of Department A in Store B) for the control group that was not manipulated.

Decision	Description	Example
Observation methods:		
1. Direct	Observing current behavior	Watching the number of consumers who stop to inspect a store display
2. Indirect	Observing past behavior	Counting the number of store-branded products (e.g. Sears) found in the consumer's home
Recording methods:		
1. Personal	Recording observations by hand	Logging customer reactions to a sales presentation by visually observing and manually recording the process
2. Nonpersonal	Recording observations mechanically or electronically (counters, cameras, sensors)	Measuring television viewing habits using an "audiometer," measuring pupil dilation while an advertisement is viewed as an indication of interest using a "perceptoscope," and using an "eye camera" to measure eye movement of a consumer as he or she views a display
Observation setting:		
1. Natural	Observing behavior in an unplanned and real setting	Observing the customer's natural and unobstructive trip behavior through the store
2. Artificial	Observing behavior in a planned and contrived setting	Observing sales personnel reaction to various customer "plants" who dress in a different fashion (e.g. well-dressed or shabbily dressed)
Observation organization:		
1. Structured	Observing specific behavior patterns	Observing the actions of only female customers who purchase a particular product
2. Unstructured	Observing general behavior patterns	Observing all of the actions of all customers regardless of who they are or what they buy
Observation situation:		
1. Disguised	Observing behavior without the person being aware that he or she is being observed	Using a two-way mirror to observe how customers inspect a display
2. Nondisguised	Observing behavior in an open fashion, thereby allowing the person to be aware that he or she is being observed	Following the customer around the store to observe shopping patterns

FIGURE 5–7
Using the observation method

FIGURE 5–8
Experimental research designs

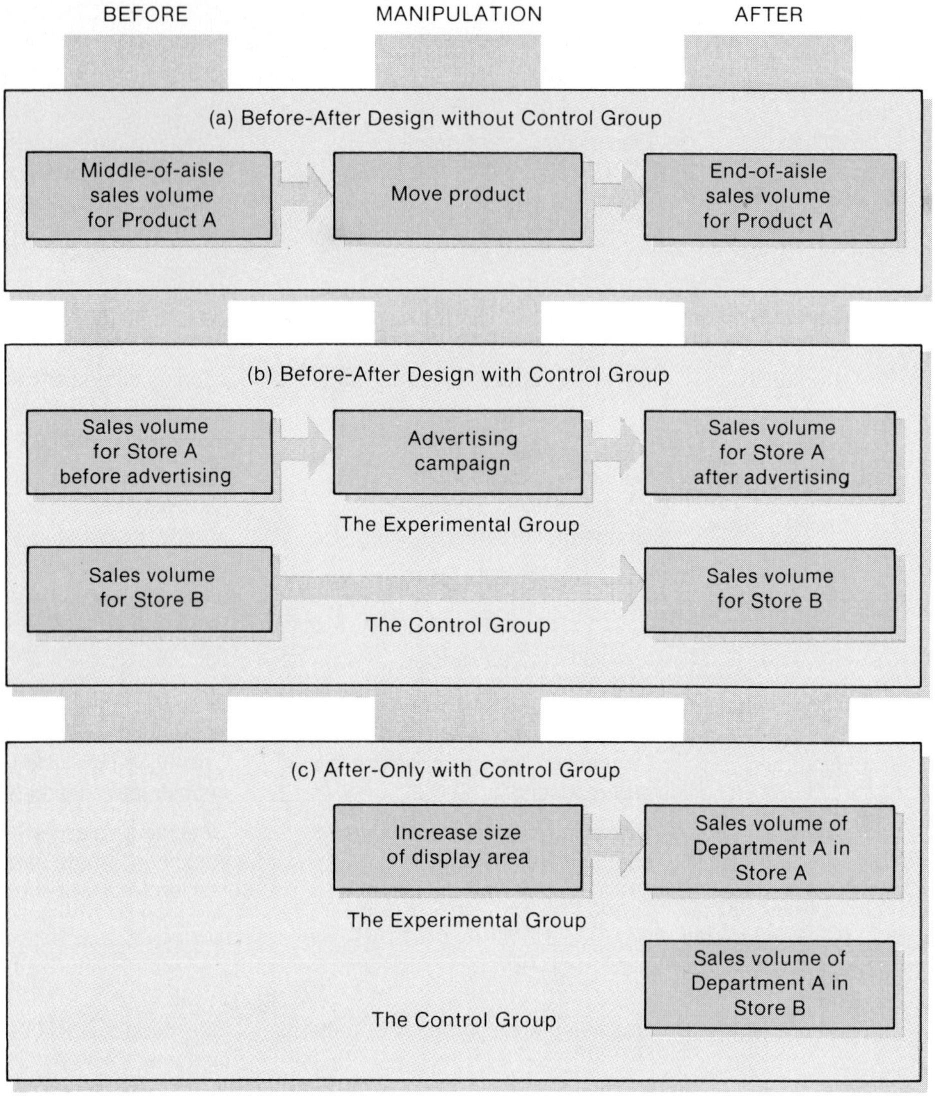

In general, the major advantage of using the experimentation method is that it systematically demonstrates cause-and-effect relationships. Its principal limitations are high costs, artificial settings, and the difficulties of controlling all the factors that might influence the results of the experiment.

Research Instruments

By far the most widely used research instrument in retail research is the questionnaire. This discussion therefore is limited to this particular instrument. The four major factors a researcher must carefully consider are structuring, wording, and sequencing questions and scaling answers in the questionnaire.

Structuring Questions. Questions can be either open-ended (unstructured) or closed-ended (structured). *Open-ended* questions allow respondents to answer questions in their own words, thereby giving them greater freedom in communicating their responses. Used extensively in motivation research, the open-ended question allows respondents to project their feelings about the retailer's merchandising and operational activities.

Retailers can use a number of open-ended or projective techniques. One is the **word association test**, a set of words or phrases to which respondents give their immediate reactions:

Retailer (Interviewer)	Consumer (Respondent)
Store	Clean
Products	Good selection
Services	Courteous salespeople
Prices	Low

A second projective technique is the **sentence completion test**, which simply asks respondents to finish a set of sentences. Examples follow:

Store personnel should be ______.
Store advertising should stress ______.
Store convenience is a matter of ______.

A third technique is the **narrative projection test**, in which the researcher provides respondents with a descriptive situation and asks them to write a paragraph in response.[7] An example of a descriptive situation the researcher might give respondents is the following:

A neighbor asks you what is the best store in town for buying draperies and why you think it is best. What would you tell her?

Respondents then write their reactions to this description.

A fourth projection technique is the **thematic apperception test**. In this test, respondents are shown a cartoon, drawing, or picture and then asked to project themselves into the situation and tell a story about what is happening or what they would do:

A picture showing one customer observing a poorly dressed elderly woman placing merchandise into a pocket.

A typical response to this picture might be "She lives on welfare, has very little money, and must resort to shoplifting."

The major purpose of most **open-ended questionnaires** is to explore and identify potential problems and to obtain information for inclusion in a structured research study. Because of the numerous difficulties in classifying and interpreting the results of open-ended questionnaires, many retailers prefer to use structured questioning. The closed-ended questionnaire meets this need. The **closed-ended questionnaire** is a highly structured format giving respondents a set of answers from which to choose. The three most common closed-ended questionnaires are in the form of dichotomous, multiple-choice, or rank-ordered questions.

Dichotomous questions limit the respondent's answer to only one of two choices. Examples of dichotomous questions follow:

Is our store the closest food store to your home?
_____ Yes _____ No

Is price the most important factor in comparing products?
_____ True _____ False

Multiple-choice questions provide several possible answers from which the respondent selects the best answer, for example:

What is your favorite type of television program?
_____ Sports
_____ News
_____ Comedy
_____ Mystery
_____ Drama
_____ Variety
_____ Other

What is your approximate income?
_____ Under $15,000
_____ $15,000–$24,999
_____ $25,000– $34,999
_____ Over $35,000

Rank-ordered questions ask the respondent to rank a list of factors in order of their importance. An example of a rank-ordered question is the following:

Please rank the following store services in terms of their importance in attracting you as a customer. Let 1 be the most important service, 2 the second most important service, and so on until each service has been ranked.

_____ Easy credit terms
_____ Liberal return policy
_____ Free home delivery
_____ Free layaway service
_____ Good repair service
_____ Long store hours

Many researchers prefer structured questions because they are easier to tabulate and analyze and eliminate the ambiguity of answers and interpretation problems associated with unstructured questions. The major disadvantage of structured questions is that they limit the amount and types of answers the respondent can make.

Scaling Answers. To overcome the high cost and interpretation problems associated with unstructured questions and to gain more information than structured questions provide, many researchers prefer to use questions whose answers reflect the relative degree of the respondent's attitudes and opinions on a subject. The two most commonly used scales in retail research are Likert's summated ratings scale and Osgood's semantic differential.

Likert's summated rating scale measures attitudes and opinions by asking respondents to indicate the extent of their agreement or disagreement with a list of statements concerning the issue being studied. The answers to several statements concerning a clothing store's merchandise offering could be scaled as follows:

	Strongly Agree	Agree	Undecided	Disagree	Strongly Disagree
The Castle Shop Stocks a wide assortment of products	(+2)	(+1)	(0)	(−1)	(−2)
Stocks only high-quality products	(+2)	(+1)	(0)	(−1)	(−2)

The responses for each statement are given a numerical weight of either +2, +1, 0, −1, and −2, or 5, 4, 3, 2, and 1. An overall measure of opinion and attitudes is determined either by summing all subjects' responses to a particular statement or by summing one subject's responses to all statements.

One of the most popular scaling instruments in recent years is the semantic differential. The **semantic differential rating scale** is a set of seven-point, bipolar scales that measure people's meanings and attitudes regarding some object. The respondent is asked to mark one of seven positions on a scale, with ends identified by opposite descriptive terms. For example, a retailer that wants to obtain information concerning the appearance of its store might use the following scale:

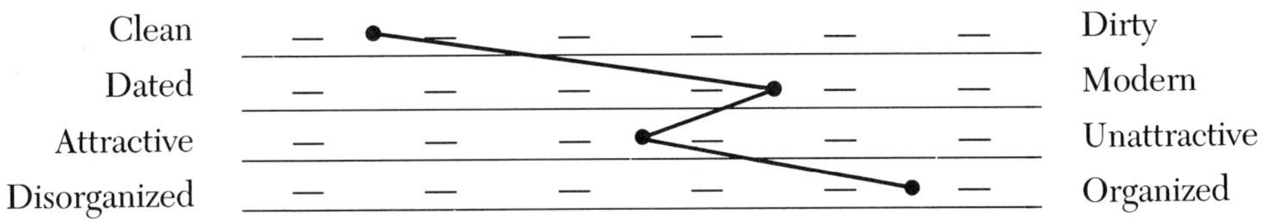

Each position on the semantic scale is assigned a numerical value that can be used to calculate arithmetic means for all respondents' answers to each scale. These figures can be used to profile a store's image, as illustrated by the connected lines.

Wording of Questions. If questions are leading, ambiguous, poorly worded, or use a vocabulary with which respondents are unfamiliar, the resulting answers will not be helpful—in fact, they might be meaningless. To avoid wording problems, the researcher should use the following guidelines:

1. Keep each question as short as possible.
2. Limit each question to one idea.
3. Use simple, concise language.
4. Avoid technical or "buzz" words.
5. Ask questions whose answers the respondent can be expected to know and remember.
6. Ask personal questions in a generalized way.

These guidelines, along with common sense, will help the researcher avoid many of the pitfalls in wording questions.

Sequencing of Questions. Once the researcher has carefully worded the questionnaire, the next step is to order the questions. Order is an important aspect of developing any questionnaire, because the sequence can affect the final results. To sequence questions, the researcher should use the following three guidelines:

1. Use an "attention getter" for the opening question.
2. Ask general questions first, specific questions last.
3. Place personal questions at the end of the questionnaire.

Sampling Procedures

After selecting the type of research method and the instrument, the retailer must decide on the sampling procedure to use in collecting information; that is, once the retailer has decided "what" information it needs and "how" to obtain it, it must determine "whom" to ask to obtain the desired information. The "whom" in this case is a **sample**, or some portion of a predefined population. A **population** is the total membership of a defined group of individuals or items. For example, a population could be defined as either all potential consumers or all actual consumers of a particular product. Researchers use samples instead of an entire population because it is too costly and time consuming to observe or survey an entire population. With proper sampling procedures, the researcher can draw valid conclusions about the attitudes, opinions, makeup, or behavior of the total population without contacting its entire membership. The retailer's sampling procedures follow three essential steps: (1) identifying the sampling frame, (2) determining the size of the sample, and (3) selecting the sample items.

Identifying the Sample Frame. The first step in sampling is to either create or find a list of individuals included in the defined population being investigated from which to draw the sample. For example, the list could be the names of retail businesses listed in the phone book, names and addresses of all adults age 18 and over living within a defined trading area, or a list of a store's credit card holders. The sample frame must be carefully identified to obtain meaningful and appropriate information.

Determining the Sample Size. The sample size is the number of people the researcher wants to survey. A large sample normally results in greater accuracy and more reliable information; however, as the size of the sample increases, so do the costs of obtaining the sample. If scientific sampling procedures are followed carefully, small samples such as 400 or 500 people can provide satisfactory results and reliable information. (Almost any marketing research text explains the necessary procedures for calculating the required sample size for a predetermined level of reliability.)

FIGURE 5–9
Types of probability and nonprobability samples

Probability Samples	Nonprobability Samples
1. *Simple random:* A sampling procedure in which one sample is drawn from the entire population, with each individual or item having an equal probability of being selected. 2. *Stratified random:* A sampling procedure in which the population is first subdivided into groups based on some known and meaningful criteria (e.g., sex, age). Then a simple random sample is drawn for each subgroup. 3. *Cluster or area:* A sampling procedure in which geographical areas (e.g., census tracts or blocks) are randomly selected. Then a simple random sample is used to select a certain number of individuals or items (e.g., houses) from each of the selected geographical areas. 4. *Systematic:* A sampling procedure in which the first individual or item of a sampling frame is selected randomly. Then each subsequent individual or item is selected at every *n*th interval (e.g., every fifth item on the list).	1. *Convenience:* A sampling procedure in which each sample individual or item is selected at the convenience of the researcher (e.g., whoever walks in the store). 2. *Judgment:* A sampling procedure in which each sample individual or item is selected by the researcher based on an idea of what constitutes a representative sample (e.g., every seventh person who walks past the display counter). 3. *Quota:* A sampling procedure in which the researcher divides the total population into several segments based on some factor believed to be important (e.g., sex and age). Then the researcher arbitrarily selects a certain number (quota) from each segment (e.g., selects five females over age 40, five females under age 40, five males over age 40, and five males under age 40).

Selecting the Sample Item. The last sampling procedure is selecting the sample—determining how the sample items or individuals are to be chosen. There are two general types of samples: probability and nonprobability. In a **probability sample**, each individual in the total population has a known and equal chance of being selected. In a **nonprobability sample**, each individual in the total population does not have a known and equal chance of being selected, but the researcher controls selection. Whenever possible, the researcher should use a probability sample because it provides more reliable results and permits the use of more sophisticated analytical techniques. Figure 5–9 identifies and briefly defines the various types of probability and nonprobability samples.

Analyzing Primary Information

The retailer's second major concern in conducting retail research is to analyze the collected information. We cannot describe here all the possible techniques for analyzing information, but Figure 5–10 identifies the basic approaches researchers use.

Researchers use summarization procedures to simplify and organize information into meaningful descriptive measurements. **Statistical inferences** are used to make interpretations from a sample about the total population under study. **Bayesian analysis** attempts to combine managerial judgment and objective information to assess dollars-and-cents consequences of alternative decisions. **Mathematical programming** involves the use of mathematics to find optimal solutions to problems. **Simulation** uses mathematics to develop models of retailing situations and to provide solutions by using various parameter values and observing the results. A more complete description of each of these approaches, together with their respective techniques, can be found in most marketing research textbooks.

ELECTRONIC DATA PROCESSING SYSTEMS

Processing information is the third basic activity of the retailing information system. An integral part of this processing activity is the **electronic data processing system (EDPS)**. Electronic data processing is that part of the information processing system built around a computer. As Figure 5–11 illustrates, the EDPS consists of three basic

FIGURE 5–10
Processing techniques for information analysis

1. Summarization procedures
   - Percentages
   - Measures of central tendency
   - Trend analysis (time series)
2. Statistical inference
   - Estimation
   - Hypothesis testing
   - Analysis of associative data
3. Bayesian analysis
   - Prior
   - Preposterior
   - Posterior
4. Mathematical programming
   - Linear programming
   - Nonlinear programming
   - Critical path scheduling
5. Simulation
   - Micro models
   - Organization models
   - System models

Source: Keith K. Cox and Ben M. Enis, *The Marketing Research Process* (Pacific Palisades, CA: Goodyear Publishing, 1972), 351.

FIGURE 5–11
The electronic data processing system (EDPS)

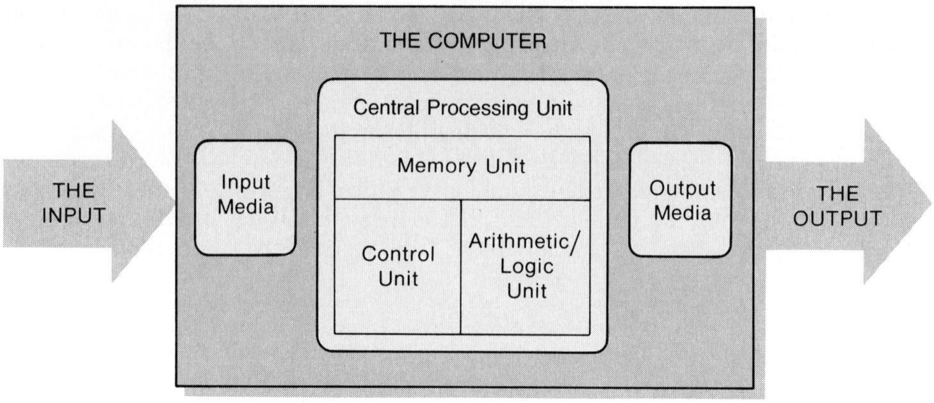

elements: the input, the computer, and the output. The computer's ability to process large volumes of data with incredible speed and accuracy makes it a valuable tool.

The Input

Any system must have the right input in the right form with the right directions to produce the desired results. This is especially true when putting data into a computer. The input element of an EDPS requires the retailer to carefully select and prepare the data and provide the computer with instructions on exactly what to do with them.

The data selected as input will depend on the retailer's needs. Before feeding any data into the computer, the retailer must clearly identify what information is needed, for what purpose, when, and in what form. If the retailer has clearly identified the problem, the data selection method already has been determined. The actual data to be put into the EDPS can come from any of the previously discussed sources—retail intelligence, retail research, internal records, or analytical models. After the right data have been selected, they must be prepared to meet the input requirements of the computer.

The computer is fussy. It will accept only data in its own machine language. The basic machine languages of the computer consist of binary numbers—various combinations of ones and zeros. After the data are transformed into machine language, they are fed into the computer. The data can be fed in batches or in a continuous fashion (real time). In **batch processing,** the retailer waits until considerable amounts of data have been collected and then processes the entire batch at one time (e.g., at the end of the day or week). **Real-time processing** involves continuous feeding of data from input devices connected directly to the computer; it allows immediate processing of all data.

Regardless of which processing method is used, all input must be accompanied by instructions to the computer about what to do with the data. In many cases, the instructions simply have the computer recall earlier, more detailed instructions. Instructions to the computer are in the form of computer programs that the retailer can write or obtain as part of a "software package" from either the computer manufacturer or various software firms.

The Computer

The heart of the electronic data-processing system is the computer—an information-processing machine. To be functional, a computer must consist of three hardware components: an *input medium* for feeding information into a *central processing unit (CPU),* which stores and manipulates information, and an *output medium* for delivering the results (see Figure 5–11).

Based on the number of input and output devices that can be handled simultaneously, the amount of storage or memory, and the speed of processing, computers fall into one of three categories:

1. **Mainframe computers** are large machines with large CPUs and vast amounts of memory. They can handle a large number of terminals simultaneously and have incredibly fast processing speeds.
2. **Microcomputers** are small personal computers that have self-contained CPUs and a single, attached input terminal but still have many of the processing capabilities associated with mainframes. Use ranges from sophisticated desktop computers to portable, typewriter-size models.
3. **Minicomputers** are medium-size computers designed for business use. They are capable of handling several terminals. Minis have memory and processing speeds sufficient for most small-business systems.

Computers can accept data via punched cards, punched paper tapes, magnetic tapes and disks, keyboards, teletypes, and optical scanners. Thus, the input medium can be any one or a combination of the following: card readers, tape readers, teletypewriters, and wand readers.

The CPU consists of three basic units: a memory unit for internal storage of data and instructions, an arithmetic/logic unit for making the necessary mathematical computations, and a control unit for guiding the operations of the other two units. The principal output media available to the retailer are those that produce printouts and visual displays. Output in the form of punched cards, floppy disks, and magnetic tapes also is available for storing data for future use.

The output from the EDPS should be meaningful information. The whole purpose of an EDPS is to process raw data into useful information. The application of electronic data processing to the retailer's merchandising and operating activities can be quite extensive depending on the retailer's willingness to invest in the equipment, facilities, and personnel necessary for its operation.

THE TECHNOLOGICAL ENVIRONMENT

The retailer's **technological environment** incorporates the various improvements in the technical processes that increase the productivity and efficiency of machines and eliminate or reduce manual operations. Improved technologies are most often achieved through mechanical, electrical, and computerized automation of the retailer's merchandising and operational tasks. At the turn of this decade, retail organizations that had invested in modern technologies had a decidedly competitive advantage over the technological laggards. By the year 2000, modern retail technologies will be essential for survival in the high-tech marketplace: "One of the characteristics of retailing in the year 2000 is that technology will increasingly drive strategy and substantially change the way the retail business is operated."[8]

The development of modern electronic and computer-based retail technologies began around 1960 and is still going on. As Figure 5–12 illustrates, the development of modern retail technologies was an evolutionary process consisting of three phases or waves.[9] In each wave, development of both electronic or computer technologies and agreed-upon industry standards were necessary for overall technological progress.[10] The first wave (1960–1974) saw the conceptualization of and experimentation with new technologies and the struggle among various parties (retailers, equipment vendors, manufacturers) over what standards would prevail. The next 15 years (1975–1989) involved the adaptation and refinement of standards and technologies. Now, in the third wave (1990 and beyond), retailers are scrambling to apply and implement the tremendous number of sophisticated and costly technologies. The winners in the application and implementation battle will have strategic and tactical advantages in the competitive warfare of the marketplace.

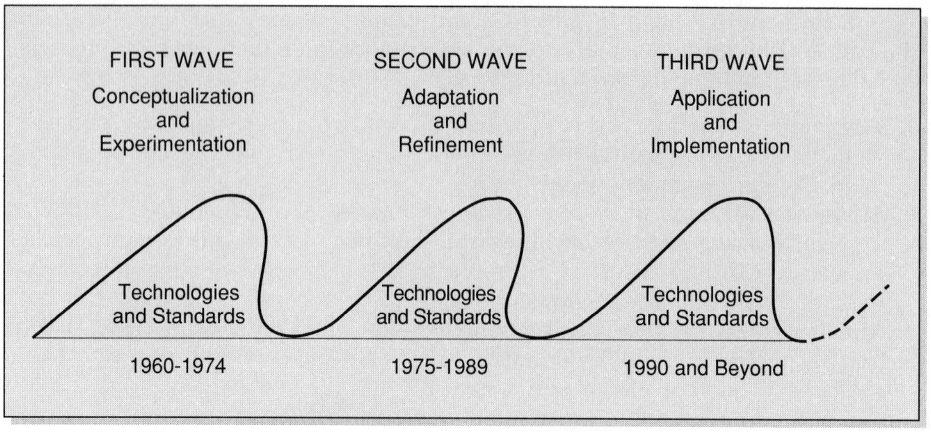

FIGURE 5–12
The waves of technological development in retailing

Automatic Identification Systems

Fast and accurate data collection and processing are vital to effective merchandising and efficient operations. The Automatic Identification System (AIS) is a group of several interacting technologies that enables machines to recognize and enter data into a computer system.[11] In the merchandising program, the AIS permits the retailer to offer faster checkout, itemized receipts, price verification, coupon redemption, credit and check authorization, and a host of other customer conveniences. Operationally, automatic identification systems are an integral part of the retailer's electronic purchase order systems, in-store sales audits, merchandise ticketing, interstore merchandise transfer processes, direct store delivery/receiving, staff productivity reports, and a variety of other operational functions. Some of the more promising automated identification technologies include (1) bar coding, (2) radio frequency data communication, (3) radio frequency identification, (4) magnetic strips, (5) voice recognition, (6) machine vision, and (7) smart cards.

Bar Coding

A **bar code** is a series of light and dark bars that constitute a symbol that typically is attached to a product package or shipping carton. While a number of different bar code symbologies (e.g., code 128 or code 39) exist, the Universal Product Code (UPC) that appears on almost every consumer packaged good is the most widely used bar coding system. Bar coding is also being used on shipping cartons to facilitate the distribution function.

Figure 5–13 illustrates the numeric UPC bar coding system. The UPC identifies the manufacturer and the product item down to the size and color level. It is designed for scanning in both directions and has a built-in system (module check character) to confirm an accurate scan.[12] Information obtained from scanning a bar code is fed directly into a central computer for additional processing.

The information gathered from bar codes can assist the retailer in a variety of ways. "Although retailers originally got into scanning for the 'hard benefits' of inventory and labor savings, they are now beginning to focus on 'soft benefits' of the data . . . can expect retailers to apply their scanner data to promotion and merchandising decisions . . . shelf management, item forecasting, automated ordering, local marketing, shopping-trip analysis,"[13] and other means to control their business and relationships with vendors. Better and more timely information also equals better customer service through more complete product assortments, fewer stockouts, and faster, more

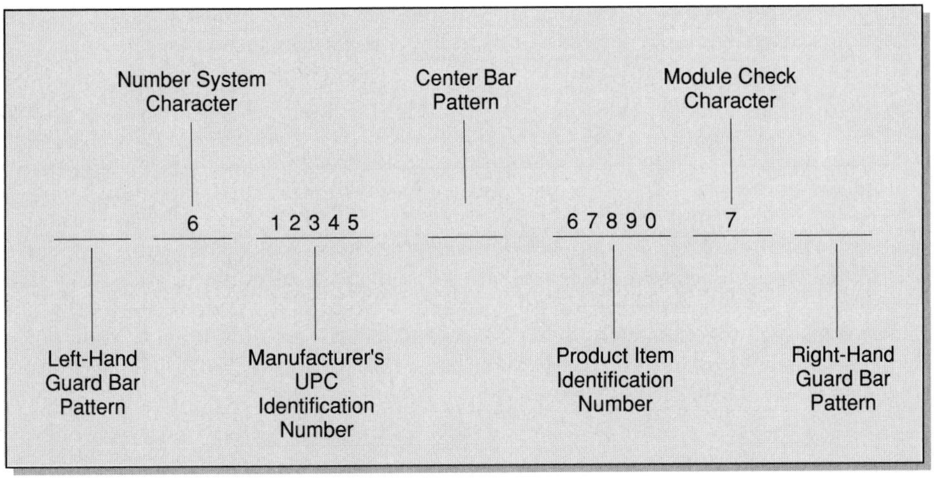

FIGURE 5–13
Universal product code (UPC)

accurate customer checkout. By bar coding shipping cartons, retailers can streamline their receiving and handling of incoming merchandise shipments.[14]

Radio Frequency Data Communication

An emerging technology is the transmitting of data through the air waves between a hand-held data collection device and a host computer; this technology is referred to as **radio frequency data communication (RFDC)**. Retailers are experimenting with RFDC for a wide range of applications; the most common application is to attach portable scanners to a hand-held device and use it as a data entry instrument to identify items via their bar-coded labels.[15] Essentially this direct, two-way communication system allows the retailer to take the equivalent of a portable computer to the store shelf, the receiving dock, the warehouse bin, the supply room, or any place where valuable data are located. Once there, the data can be electronically collected and transmitted back for analysis and conversion into useful information. When the data transformation is completed, the data can then be transmitted back to management and staff for real-time decision making. RFDC is used (1) to check the accuracy of the price match between the Price Lookup (PLU) file and the shelf label price or product price tag; (2) to take a physical inventory count on a more frequent and regular basis; (3) to verify prices on returned merchandise; (4) to identify low-stock conditions and automatically reorder merchandise; (5) to request out-of-stock merchandise from the distribution center or another store; and (6) to verify electronic invoices for incoming shipments.[16]

Radio Frequency Identification

Radio frequency identification is a technology that has found extensive use in the retailer's electronic article surveillance system. It involves the attachment to a product of a tag that contains a small circuit or target that is capable of emitting a radio signal; the signal is picked up as it passes by a security detection device typically located at store exits. Security tags "can be either disposable or reusable. The disposable tags leave the store with the merchandise and are deactivated at the point of sale by passing the item across a deactivation panel. The reusable tags must physically be removed from the item."[17] These electronic security tags are recognized as one of the most effective devices for combating customer and employee theft.

Magnetic Stripes, Voice Recognition, Machine Vision, and Smart Cards
Magnetic stripe technology is used in conjunction with financial cards, store-service cards, and employee security cards.[18] Financial cards such as credit cards (e.g., VISA) and automated teller machines (ATM) cards use magnetic stripes to identify the card user. Check-cashing and frequent-buyer cards are the two most common types of store-service identification cards. Employee security cards simply identify employees to permit their access to secured areas, whether rooms or computer terminals. This type of automatic identification allows the retailer to expand its service offering through convenient and secure transactions. **Voice recognition** (in which computers respond to the human voice for data input or operating commands), **machine vision** (using video cameras to read bar codes or identify a product through its signature—size, shape, color of package together with its bar code), and **smart cards** (an identification device with an embedded microprocessor) are emerging technologies. For retail applications, they are in the developmental stages.[19]

Integrated Information Systems

Successful retail operations are team operations. For operation as a team, each member must have access to all of the information needed to successfully complete the assigned task and make the right decision. Wal-Mart's highly publicized success with its employees involves creating entrepreneurial partnerships with department heads and associates by providing employees with extensive information about their areas of responsibility that many companies never show their general managers. Operating information concerning costs, freight charges, and profit margins assists the local entrepreneur in managing an effective and profitable department. Wal-Mart also shares information with its vendors. By trying a nonadversarial approach in which the company shares sales projection data through computer links, it is hoped that the vendor can anticipate Wal-Mart's needs.[20] The sharing of information through integrated information systems is and will continue to be a key to developing mutually supportive partnerships within the company and between the company and its various publics (consumers, vendors, and support organizations).

The following discussion profiles technology-based means for integrating the retailer's information system.

Point-of-Sale (POS) Systems
Computer-based **point-of-sale (POS) systems** essentially are computerized checkout counters that are in wide use within the retail industry. POS systems involve a computerized cash register or terminal connected to a central computer. While some retailers still capture data by keying them into the terminal, most retailers have converted, or are in the process of converting, to scanner technologies capable of reading bar codes. This automated system offers the benefits of transactional efficiency (fast, accurate checkout) and inventory control (automatic adjustments on book inventory). Customers receive an itemized receipt, and the retailer obtains detailed information on sales and inventories.

A technological extension of the computerized POS system is the **electronic point-of-sale system.**[21] Using one of the many available computer software packages, the retailer can capture and use sales and inventory data to (1) ascertain sales levels and issue sales reports; (2) determine inventory levels and activate an automatic merchandise replenishment system; (3) verify prices (via price lookup files) and monitor price changes;[22] (4) check electronic invoices and authorize receiving activities; and (5) interact with the rest of the retailer's information systems to generate financial statements (e.g., income statements) and operational reports (e.g., labor productivity reports).

Electronic Date Interchange (EDI)

Electronic data interchange (EDI) is "a communication protocol that allows stores and their suppliers to conduct business transactions electronically instead of manually. With EDI, money is saved by eliminating the amount of time, human intervention, and paperwork that would otherwise be needed to process a single purchase order."[23] Using the EDI system, Dayton Hudson has achieved a 50 percent increase in its inventory turnover rate and drastically reduced inventory levels.[24]

Electronic Banking

Electronic banking activities in the form of **automated teller machines (ATMs)** are being intensively distributed in a wide variety of locations. Supermarkets are now becoming popular sites for ATMs. A 24-hour-a-day, everyday service, these machines allow patrons continuous access to basic banking transactions (account deposits, withdrawals, and transfers). ATMs also allow users to pay utility bills, make loan payments, and check account balances. In-store use of ATMs offers the retailer the advantage of instant funds availability at the time of the transaction: Funds are automatically transferred from the customer's account to the retailer's account.

An extension of the electronic banking concept is the **debit card**, which essentially is an electronic checkbook that allows the retailer to automatically subtract payments from a customer's checking account at the time of sale. For the retailer, the advantages include immediate access to cash, lower transaction costs, faster transaction time, and greater transaction accuracy. However, "debit cards and electronic funds transfer (EFT) are technologies still in search of a market. . . . [C]ustomers . . . prefer to pay for goods and services with checks, cash, and credit cards."[25] For the consumer, there is no advantage to using debit cards: "You still have to record the purchase in your ledger and you lose the float you get with checks."[26]

Automated Checkout Machines (ACMs)

Supermarket chains currently are experimenting with new technologies that allow customers to (1) scan their own purchases at point-of-sale terminals, (2) identify themselves by using a magnetic-stripe type of identification card, (3) pay for purchases using a debit card, and (4) clear themselves from the checkout station. While still experimental in nature, these **automated checkout machines (ACMs)** are expected to receive considerable attention as the entry-level labor pool declines.

Digital Imaging (DI)

Digital imaging (DI) is "the process whereby images are digitized directly from a video camera, stored in a computer, modified, combined with other images and text, and then sent (possibly all over the world) through networks and satellites, while maintaining photographic quality throughout the process."[27] J.C. Penney currently is using DI technology to convert customers' checks and payment stubs into electronic images for fast, accurate, and efficient processing.[28]

Expert Systems (ES)

Many retailing decisions and actions do not lend themselves to traditional programming techniques; subjective evaluations, "guesstimates," and gut feelings are all part of the reality of retail decision making. **Expert systems (ESs)** are computer software packages that "differ from traditional computer programs . . . in that they make inferences, have no set path, and can recommend various possible solutions. Their approach to logic seeks to emulate the human mind."[29] Publix Super Markets of Florida uses its expert system to help train the staff of its "help desk" so that they in turn can help find solutions to a wide variety of problems phoned in by individual store managers (e.g., problems resulting from the newly installed POS system).[30]

RETAIL STRATEGIES AND TACTICS

■■■

Expert Systems—Finetuning Operations Technologically

To access The Broadway's (a division of Carter Hawley Hale Stores of Los Angeles) expert systems, the user logs on to the terminal and is presented with a menu, which allows a choice of any of six defined areas where help may be needed: sales technique, procurement, staffing, motivation, floor layout, and product knowledge.

These areas were determined by the eight expert area sales managers. They were not structured from the training department or any company procedure manual.

In some instances, users may choose to submit to questions and let the system determine which area they are having trouble in.

Once the area is determined, the system will ask the user further questions: How is the user now doing things? What changes have been instituted? What sales figures have resulted? What are sales per hour?

Users who wonder why a particular question is being asked can go into a help mode that explains the significance of the question and why the answer can assist in the overall judgment process.

Based on the answers provided by the user to the questions, the system assesses weaknesses and makes recommendations on how to improve performance. It acts as a consultant, offering some of the "tricks of the trade" employed by the best area sales managers.

It also provides reasons for the recommendations, explaining in each case how the judgment was reached.

Source: Reprinted by permission from "Retail Technology," *Chain Store Age Executive* (August 1989):113. Copyright © Lebhar-Friedman, Inc., 425 Park Avenue, New York, NY 10022.

SUMMARY

Information is the key to reducing the risks associated with retail decision making and problem solving. Retailers need to know what information they need, what information is available, how to gather information, where to obtain information, and how to use information once it has been obtained.

The retailing information system consists of four basic activities: locating, gathering, processing, and utilizing information. Locating information requires the retailer to be acquainted with the various types (primary and secondary) and sources (external and internal) of information. In gathering information, the retailer engages in the four basic activities of retail intelligence, retail research, records search, and constructing analytical models. Having located and gathered the necessary information, the retailer then processes it, using either manual or electronic data-processing techniques. Each of the three preceding steps is useless unless the retailer uses the information in daily operations.

Retail intelligence is any method or combination of methods used to obtain external secondary information. The principal sources of retail intelligence are libraries, government publications (e.g., census and registration information), association information (trade and professional organizations), and commercial providers (organizations that make a business out of collecting, analyzing, and reporting information).

Retail research uses a set of scientific procedures to gather external primary information from consumers, suppliers, and competitors. These scientific procedures are best described in the five stages of the scientific method: (1) identifying problems, (2) developing hypotheses, (3) collecting information, (4) analyzing information, and (5) drawing conclusions. Collection of primary information is accomplished using research methods such as surveys, observations, the purchase intercept technique, and experiments. Sampling procedures are crucial in conducting primary retail research. The retailer must develop the skills for identifying the sample frame, determining the sample size, and selecting the sample item. The last issue in retail research is analyzing primary information. Summarization procedures, statistical inferences, Bayesian analysis, mathematical programming, and simulation are the methods used in the analysis process.

Electronic data-processing systems are computer-based procedures for analyzing information. The retailer requires sound input, computer, and output systems to process information effectively.

Information technologies are vital to any successful retail organization. Fast and accurate data collection is achieved via the automatic identification system. Bar coding, radio frequency data communication, radio frequency identification, magnetic stripes, voice recognition, machine vision, and smart cards are some of the identification technologies being used or tested by retailers. Teamwork is a common trait of all successful retailers; sharing of information is a necessary ingredient for teamwork. Integrating the retailer's information system involves technologies such as point-of-sale terminals, electronic data interchange protocols, electronic banking hardware, automatic checkout machines, digital imaging, and expert systems software.

STUDENT STUDY GUIDE

Key Terms and Concepts

analytical models (p. 166)
automated checkout machine (ACM) (p. 187)
automated teller machine (ATM) (p. 187)
automatic identification systems (p. 184)
bar code (p. 184)
batch processing (p. 182)
Bayesian analysis (p. 181)
closed-ended questionnaire (p. 177)
debit card (p. 187)
dichotomous question (p. 177)
digital imaging (p. 187)
electronic banking (p. 187)
electronic data processing (p. 166)
electronic data processing system (EDPS) (p. 181)
electronic data interchange (p. 187)
electronic funds transfer system (p. 187)
electronic point-of-sale system (p. 186)
experimentation (p. 174)
expert system (p. 187)
external information (p. 165)
integrated information system (p. 186)
internal information (p. 165)
Likert's summated rating scale (p. 178)
machine vision (p. 186)
magnetic stripes (p. 186)
mainframe computer (p. 183)
manual data processing (p. 166)
mathematical programming (p. 181)
microcomputer (p. 183)
minicomputer (p. 183)
multiple-choice question (p. 178)
narrative projection test (p. 177)
nonprobability sample (p. 181)
observation (p. 173)
open-ended questionnaire (p. 177)
point-of-sale systems (p. 186)
population (p. 179)
primary information (p. 165)
probability sample (p. 181)
purchase intercept technique (PIT) (p. 174)
radio frequency data communication (RFDC) (p. 185)
radio frequency identification (p. 185)
rank-ordered question (p. 178)
real-time processing (p. 182)
records search (p. 166)
retail intelligence (p. 165)
retail research (p. 166)
retailing information system (RIS) (p. 163)
sample (p. 179)
scientific method (p. 171)
secondary information (p. 163)
semantic differential rating scale (p. 179)
sentence completion test (p. 177)
simulation (p. 181)
smart cards (p. 186)
statistical inference (p. 181)
survey (p. 172)
technological environment (p. 183)
thematic apperception test (p. 177)
voice recognition (p. 186)
word association test (p. 177)

Review Questions

1. Define *RIS*. What are the four basic activities of an RIS?
2. Compare and contrast secondary and primary information. What are their relative advantages and disadvantages?

3. Compare and contrast external and internal sources of information.
4. Identify and define the four information-gathering methods.
5. What are the two types of systems used in processing information? Briefly describe each.
6. How do the two general forms of commercial sources of retail intelligence differ?
7. What are the five stages of the scientific method? Describe the major task to be accomplished in each stage.
8. What are the three basic methods of collecting external primary information? Describe each method.
9. Explain the personal interview process. How should a personal interview be conducted?
10. How do mail surveys differ from personal and telephone surveys?
11. How are mail surveys administered?
12. Develop a graphic presentation of the three experimental designs used by researchers.
13. Describe the four open-ended or projective techniques for collecting primary information.
14. Develop a questionnaire that explores why a consumer has selected a particular product brand. Use each of the three types of closed-ended questions in developing your questionnaire.
15. What guidelines should be followed to avoid the many pitfalls in wording questionnaire items?
16. How should questions be sequenced?
17. What is a sample frame?
18. Briefly describe the various types of probability and nonprobability samples.
19. In an EDPS, what is the difference between batch and real-time processing?
20. Profile each of the seven automated identification technologies.
21. What is EDI?
22. Why should a retailer develop an expert system?

Review Exam

True or False

_____ 1. Primary information generally costs less to obtain than secondary information.

_____ 2. Standardized information services are commercial sources of retail intelligence that provide prescribed types of information on a continuous, regular basis.

_____ 3. Mail surveys provide the interviewer with the greatest amount of control over an interview situation.

_____ 4. The major disadvantage of the observation method is that the retailer cannot investigate the consumer's motives, attitudes, beliefs, and feelings.

_____ 5. The after-only with control group design is the most widely used experimental design because of its simplicity and ease of implementation.

_____ 6. Nonprobability samples should be used whenever possible because they permit the use of more sophisticated analytical techniques.

_____ 7. Debit cards are electronic checkbooks that allow retailers to automatically subtract payments from a customer's checking account at the time of sale.

Multiple Choice

_____ 1. The retailing information system (RIS) consists of four basic activities. Which of the following activities is *not* one of those four?
a. Locating information
b. Fabricating information
c. Gathering information
d. Processing information
e. Utilizing information

_____ 2. Any method or combination of methods used to obtain external secondary information is termed
a. Retail search
b. Retail intelligence
c. Records search
d. Survey research
e. Analytical models

_____ 3. What survey method is the most expensive, the most accurate, and the most flexible?
a. Observation
b. Mail
c. Personal
d. Telephone
e. Experiential

_____ 4. A retailer wanted to know the effects of a price increase on the sale of oxford dress shirts. Unit sales were carefully recorded for a month prior to the price increase. Following the price increase, the unit sales of oxford shirts again were carefully recorded to ascertain the changes in unit sales volume. What type of experimental design did the retailer use?
a. Before-after design without control group
b. Before-after design with control group
c. After-only design without control group
d. After-only design with control group

_____ 5. All of the following instruments are open-ended projective techniques *except*
a. Word association tests
b. Sentence completion tests
c. Thematic apperception tests
d. Rank-ordering tests

_____ 6. When designing a questionnaire, the wording of each question is extremely important. To

avoid wording problems, all of the following guidelines should be observed *except:*
a. Limit each question to one idea.
b. Use concise and simple words.
c. Avoid technical or "buzz" words.
d. Ask personal questions in a specific manner.
e. Keep each question as short as possible.

_____ 7. Electronic article surveillance systems use a technology known as
a. Radio frequency identification
b. Voice recognition
c. Machine vision
d. Electronic data interchange
e. Radio frequency data communication

STUDENT APPLICATIONS MANUAL

Investigative Projects: Practice and Applications

1. Do you agree with the statement "Some information is better than no information"? Why or why not?
2. Consult the following government sources of information and compile a list of specific types of information available to the retailer: (1) *Census of Population,* (2) *Census of Housing,* and (3) *Census of Business.* Explain how each information type cited might be useful to the retailer.
3. What factors should the retailer consider when evaluating the services of a commercial source of retail intelligence?
4. The manager of a specialty furniture accessories shop is considering adding a line of ceiling fans. Before making this product line addition, the manager wants more information concerning (1) consumers' attitudes regarding product features, preferred brands, and desired price ranges and (2) consumers' past purchases of ceiling fans and their future buying intentions. Design an effective, efficient consumer survey research instrument that will obtain the desired information.
5. Consider the problem outlined in question 4. Design a sampling procedure that will allow the retailer to draw valid conclusions about the attitudes, behavior, and intentions of the total population without contacting its entire membership. Be sure to include in your design a discussion of the sample frame, the sample size, and the procedures for selecting each sample item.
6. Contact a local supermarket chain, department store chain, and specialty store chain. Evaluate their technological environments in terms of their current and planned automatic identification systems and integrated information systems. Which of the three types of chains are the most advanced technologically? What competitive advantages do they enjoy from this advanced technology?

Tactical Cases: Problems and Decisions

■ CASE 5–1
Classic Tailoring*

Over the last five years, Bonnie Griffith developed quite a business for herself making and repairing clothing. After starting out doing a few things for a couple of friends, Bonnie now had enough tailoring to keep her busy for several hours each day.

Currently Bonnie was going to customers' homes for measurements and fittings. This took a couple of hours each week but was greatly appreciated by the young professionals for whom she sews. With dual-income families, neither women nor men had the time to add one more errand to their schedule.

Most of Bonnie's clients worked in the downtown area. They seemed to find out about her through word of mouth from satisfied customers showing off their new clothing. Bonnie contacted her customers at the office but seldom did fittings there. After one or two sets of garments, Bonnie generally could do alterations or completely new garments based on the measurements she had on record.

Most of the fitting sessions occurred in the western suburbs and condominium areas where Bonnie lived. Bonnie wanted to reduce the number of trips into town and was considering opening a shop. She began investigating the feasibility of starting "Classic Tailoring."

In a book from the public library, *How to Plan a Small Business,* Bonnie found that it is very important to be able to estimate demand to justify the risk of a small business. However, the book was vague about how to do this and made several references to the need for "market research." She couldn't find anything else helpful in the public library, so Bonnie tried the local college. She was able to borrow a textbook on marketing research and settled in to see what it had to offer.

A chapter on product testing suggested conducting consumer interviews to generate concepts for new products. When Bonnie talked this over with her customers, friends, and sister-in-law, several ideas came up. While some liked the concept of opening a tailor shop as a storefront location on the west side of Summit City, the choice was not unanimous. Some customers were fond of the in-home service. Some friends indicated that they never shopped anywhere but a mall. Her sister-in-law suggested, "My neighbor, Barney, runs an automobile fix-it shop from a van. He carries all the tools and equipment he needs to the car and does the job right there. Couldn't you do that with a van or RV?" Bonnie agreed that it was a novel suggestion and should be considered.

By the end of that week, Bonnie wasn't sure whether she had made any progress. She had thought that her question was "Do I open a shop?" Now it seemed to be "Do I open a shop, or go into full-scale in-home service, or become a mobile service, or not expand at all?" Each of these options would have different costs associated with it. When she first went into the business, Bonnie thought "a hem is a hem" and price was pretty well fixed. But *How to Plan a Small Business* seemed to suggest that the price a consumer is willing to pay might vary with the convenience of the service. How could Bonnie tell for sure?

ASSIGNMENT

1. Define the research questions Bonnie faces.
2. What kind of research design would you recommend to Bonnie?
3. What population can give Bonnie the best answers to her questions?
4. How would you draw a sample from this population? By what method (telephone, mail, etc.) would you contact them?
5. Design a questionnaire that can get answers to the research questions using the methodology you have described.

*This case was written by Douglas Hausknecht, The University of Akron.

■ CASE 5–2
College Stores, Inc.*

College Stores, Inc. (CSI) was a chain of varsity specialty shops that operated near college and university campuses. They targeted students, staff, and faculty with lines of college-related items and licensed products. The stores also carried basic toiletries, household goods, stationery, and some food items. They were open late and carried the goods that "will get you through the night." The firm had been very successful at large (50,000 plus) state and private universities and was now expanding into other schools.

The basic business goals and operations were controlled by a centralized management team. Each store was adapted to the school at which it was located. This required an assessment of the needs of each market and tailoring the store to the competitive environment. This was particularly evident in the management of licensed products. Some schools licensed long lines of products bearing their logo or mascot; others had very few. Some schools jealously guarded exclusive rights to such items; others welcomed the wider distribution that CSI and similar firms could offer.

While examining a list of NCAA Division I schools, Becky Bush, vice-president of real estate at CSI, noticed City University. She had heard of the school but was not certain about its size or the characteristics of its students. She checked the *Atlas of Colleges and Universities* and found that CU was an urban school serving 32,000 students. Most of the students lived off campus or commuted from nearby communities. Only about 3,200 lived in on-campus residence halls or fraternity or sorority housing. There was an active intercollegiate athletic program, but it was not well supported by the community. Professional sports dominated the area and generated the greatest loyalty.

Other secondary sources confirmed the size of the school. The basic data fit the profile of the type of institution to which CSI wanted to expand. The decision was made to visit the campus and conduct a more in-depth assessment. This usually entailed an examination of competition in the area, including the school's own store. It was also necessary to evaluate the needs and desires of the expected clientele. Becky chose to conduct a telephone survey to accomplish this.

Using the telephone directory supplied by the registrar's office, Becky called 200 of the university's students. Based on her experience with other schools, she felt that needs and perceptions would differ between on- and off-campus students. Therefore, the sampling was conducted separately and the responses for each group were recorded separately.

The major goals of the study were to determine students' attitudes toward the school and its store and preferences for products and price levels among the target market. With a limited budget for research, there was little chance for follow-up or an elaborate design.

Exhibit A displays the responses obtained.

ASSIGNMENT

1. What can you conclude from the results given in Exhibit A?
2. Did Becky ask the right questions?
3. Did Becky ask the right people (i.e., was the sample correct)?
4. Did the on-campus versus off-campus distinction prove useful? Would other breakdowns have been equally useful?
5. Should Becky have performed this survey at all? That is, could other information-gathering methods have been as useful? Is primary data collection always the best alternative?
6. What changes would you recommend if a new study were undertaken? Consider sampling and questionnaire design issues.

*This case was written by Douglas Hausknecht, The University of Akron.

EXHIBIT A
City University survey responses

	On-campus students (n = 80)	Off-campus students (n = 120)
What is your year in school?		
Freshman	35	12
Sophomore	29	20
Junior	8	35
Senior	6	31
Graduate student	2	22
My overall opinion of the university is		
Very favorable	30	48
Favorable	29	45
Neutral	14	20
Unfavorable	5	4
Very unfavorable	2	3
In business dealings with students, the campus bookstore is		
Very fair	10	25
Fair	40	65
Unfair	23	15
Very unfair	7	5
I would be interested in purchasing the following university items at some place other than the campus bookstore. (check all that apply)		
T-shirts/sweatshirts	61	75
Other clothing articles	47	90
Decals/pennants	32	12
Steins/mugs	12	13
Bumper stickers	49	52
Caps	23	19
Textbooks	20	80
Toiletries	15	80
Stationery/school supplies	45	100
Convenience food items	30	93
How much would you be willing to pay for these items?		
20% less than the campus bookstore	62	20
10% less than the campus bookstore	10	63
5% less than the campus bookstore	7	15
Same as the campus bookstore	1	12
5% more than the campus bookstore	—	10
10% more than the campus bookstore	—	—
20% more than the campus bookstore	—	—

ENDNOTES

1. See Stanley C. Hollander and Glenn S. Omura, "Retail Census Findings and Strategic Implications," *Retailing Issues Letter* (Published by Arthur Andersen & Co. in conjunction with the Center for Retailing Studies, Texas A&M University, February 1988), 1–3.
2. See David J. Curry, "Single-Source Systems: Retail Management Present and Future," *Journal of Retailing*, 65 (Spring 1989): 1–20.
3. See Judith Langer, "Getting to Know the Customer through Qualitative Research," *Management Review* (April 1987): 42–46.

4. See David Rodgers, "Market Research: The Ins and Outs," *Discount Merchandiser,* August 1989, 64–65.
5. Shelby H. McIntyre and Sherry D. F. G. Bender, "The Purchase Intercept Technique (PIT) in Comparison to Telephone and Mail Surveys," *Journal of Retailing* 62 (Winter 1986): 364.
6. Ibid.
7. See Sharon L. Hollander, "Projective Techniques Uncover Real Consumer Attitudes," *Marketing News,* January 4, 1988, 34.
8. "Strategies for the New Strategy," *Chain Store Age Executive,* January 1990, 27.
9. See "J.C. Penney: Ready to Ride the Third Wave," *Chain Store Age Executive,* January 1990, 72–74.
10. See Al D. McCready, "Paperless Retailing," *Retail Control,* December 1989, 17–21.
11. Gary Robins, "Auto Id," *Stores,* September 1989, Section 2.
12. See Richard Weizel, "The Price Is Right?", *Akron Beacon Journal,* February 22, 1990, D1–D3.
13. Lynn G. Coleman, "Retailers Set to Arm Themselves with Scanner Data as They Battle Suppliers," *Marketing News,* July 3, 1989, 6.
14. Robins, "Auto Id."
15. Ibid., 6–7, 10.
16. See "Price Chopper Quiets Backroom Chaos," *Chain Store Age Executive,* January 1990, 76–80.
17. Robins, "Auto Id," 15–16.
18. Ibid.
19. Ibid.
20. See Jon Huey, "Wal-Mart—Will It Take Over the World?", *Fortune,* January 30, 1989, 52–58.
21. See "Barney's Updates POS as Chain Expands," *Chain Store Age Executive,* October 1989, 52–54.
22. See Gary Robins, "Price Lookup: How It Works," *Stores,* August 1989, 45–48; "At McKids, The Price Is Right," *Chain Store Age Executive,* March 1990, 57, 60.
23. Kathy Chin Leong, "Store Systems Help Retailers Give Shoppers What They Want," *Computerworld,* November 28, 1988, 68.
24. "Quick Response: The Right Thing," *Chain Store Age Executive,* March 1990, 49–51.
25. "Debit Cards, EFT Still Grasping for Toehold," *Chain Store Age Executive,* February 1989, 67.
26. Ibid.
27. Renee Rouland, "Image Technology: A New Retail Vision," *Discount Merchandiser,* March 1990, 54.
28. See "Digital Imaging Keeps Checks Moving," *Chain Store Age Executive,* March 1990, 84, 86.
29. "Retail Technology," *Chain Store Age Executive,* August 1989, 133.
30. See "Expert Systems Gain Expertise," *Chain Store Age Executive,* March 1989, 51–53.

PART II

FINANCIAL MANAGEMENT

Managing and Controlling the Retailer's Finances

CHAPTER 6

OUTLINE

OBJECTIVES

- Defend the need for fiscal control as an essential ingredient in any successful retail operation.
- Identify and define the basic financial records required to accomplish fiscal control.
- Prepare a basic income statement for a retailing enterprise.
- Prepare a basic balance sheet for a retailing enterprise.
- Analyze and evaluate the operational and financial performance of a retail firm.
- Explain how to generate and maintain sufficient capital to conduct a retail business.
- Describe the procedures for managing the retailer's operating expenses.

A KEY TO CORPORATE EXCELLENCE[1]

What organizational and managerial traits, practices, and strategies explain why some retailers excel while others falter? The keys to corporate excellence are as numerous as the number of individuals who have studied and written about the topic. However, there are some keys that appear on everyone's list—financial planning and control is one of those keys. The financial management component of retail corporate excellence has been described in various studies in the following manner.

- *Fortune's* Corporate Stars—excellent retailers have tight controls, time information systems, and a high level of cost consciousness.
- *Business Week's* Power Retailers—excellent retailers possess the ability to combine state-of-the-art information systems and excellent management to gain superior knowledge of the markets they serve.
- Donaldson, Lufkin & Jenrette's Great Retailing Companies—excellent retailers invest in systems capability as a key to effective inventory control and management, identify and capitalize on trends, and improve gross margins and operating margins through better buying, planning, and control decisions.
- Varadarajan and the Center for Retailing Studies—excellent retailers closely monitor performance through a system of constant communication, planning and budgeting, time reporting, and strict financial controls. Emphasis on cost controls is widely prevalent.

Fiscal control is an essential ingredient in the success of any retail operation. To develop and maintain a viable retail enterprise, the retailer must control the firm's financial health. Many retailers encounter financial trouble despite respectable sales volumes. A common cause of such trouble is insufficient planning and control of the firm's financial affairs. Before the retailer can improve operations, it must be fully aware of the present state of operations. In this chapter, we examine the retailer's financial system. As Figure 6–1 illustrates, the retailer's financial system consists of (1) developing and maintaining good financial records, (2) preparing and analyzing financial statements, (3) constructing and evaluating financial performance ratios, (4) obtaining and managing capital funds, and (5) planning and controlling operating expenses. We will examine each of these tasks.

THE RETAILER'S FINANCIAL RECORDS

The size and operational complexities of the retail firm determine the type and level of sophistication of the financial recordkeeping system the retailer uses. Most retailers maintain a number of ledger accounts. An **account** is a record of the increases and decreases in one type of asset, liability, capital, income, or expense. A **ledger** is a book or file that stores a number of accounts together. The following basic ledger accounts or records are fairly standard:

- *Cash receipts*— record the cash received
- *Cash disbursements*— record the firm's expenditures
- *Sales*— record and summarize monthly income
- *Purchases*— record the purchases of merchandise bought for processing or resale
- *Payroll*— records the wages of employees and their deductions, such as income tax and social security
- *Equipment*— records the firm's capital assets, such as equipment, office furniture, and motor vehicles
- *Inventory*— records the firm's investments in stock; needed to arrive at a true profit on financial statements and for income tax purposes
- *Accounts receivable*— record the balances customers owe to the firm
- *Accounts payable*— record what the firm owes its creditors and suppliers

THE RETAILER'S FINANCIAL STATEMENTS

To gain a clear picture of the firm's financial position, the retailer must prepare two standard financial statements: the income statement and the balance sheet. The **income statement,** also referred to as the *profit and loss statement, operating statement,* or *earnings statement,* depicts the retailer's profits or losses over a given period of time; it summarizes the firm's income and expenses. The **balance sheet** lists the firm's assets,

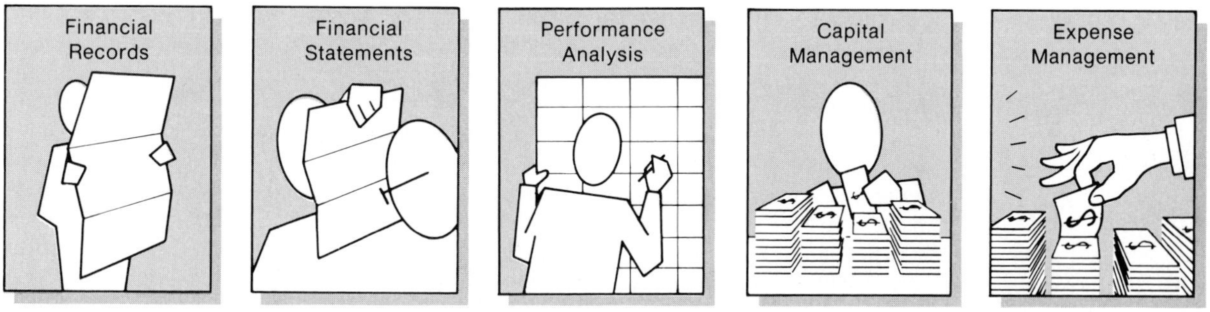

FIGURE 6–1
The retailer's financial system

liabilities, and net worth on a given date; it summarizes the basic accounting equation of assets equal liabilities plus net worth.

The Income Statement

To fully understand the many dimensions of profit, the retailer must have some procedure for organizing these dimensions. The income statement is an excellent means for organizing and understanding the many facets of profit. The income statement summarizes the retailer's financial activity for a given period. The principal objective of the income statement is to show whether the retailer had a profit or a loss during the stated period.

The Profit Concept

The term *profit* is a relative word that can be determined and expressed in a variety of ways depending on the context in which it is used. For example, profit can be expressed as either operating or net profit, dollar or percentage profit, or before- or after-tax profit. Also, profit can be expressed in relation to sales, selling space, number of transactions, net worth, and average inventory investment.

Preparation of the Income Statement

Time, unit, and usage are three important variables retailers must consider in preparing the income statement. *Time* considerations concern when income statements are prepared. Federal and state income tax regulations require retailers to prepare at least an annual income statement. By preparing an income statement more frequently, however, the retailer can maintain closer control over operations.

Unit considerations influence how many income statements are prepared and at what organizational level. For the small, independent retailer, a single income statement should suffice for the entire store. For a departmentalized chain store operation, income statements are prepared for the department and store units as well as for the entire chain organization. Like more frequent preparation, greater control of operations is the primary advantage of preparing income statements for each of the retailer's operating units.

Usage considerations involve the type of format to use in preparing income statements. A retailer should select an appropriate standardized format, because standardization will allow the retailer to (1) compare current income statements to previous statements and (2) analyze trends in sales, expenses, profits, and losses.

Elements of the Income Statement

Every income statement has at least nine basic elements, regardless of the size, type, or organizational structure of the retail enterprise. Figure 6–2 illustrates the nine elements and the relationships among them. It shows that the elements of an income statement are divided into two major groups: income measurements and income modifications.

Income measurements are various expressions of the monetary gain the retailer realizes from retailing activities. The exact nature of each income measurement depends on where it appears in the income statement and the income modifications that have been applied in calculating it. Figure 6–2 shows five income measurements—gross sales, net sales, gross margin, operating profit, and net profit.

Income modifications are monetary additions or reductions applied to one income measurement to calculate another income measurement. These income modifications simply reflect normal adjustments required by the retailer's operating characteristics. Most income modifications are reductions; they represent the various costs the retailer incurs in conducting the business, and they are necessary for arriving

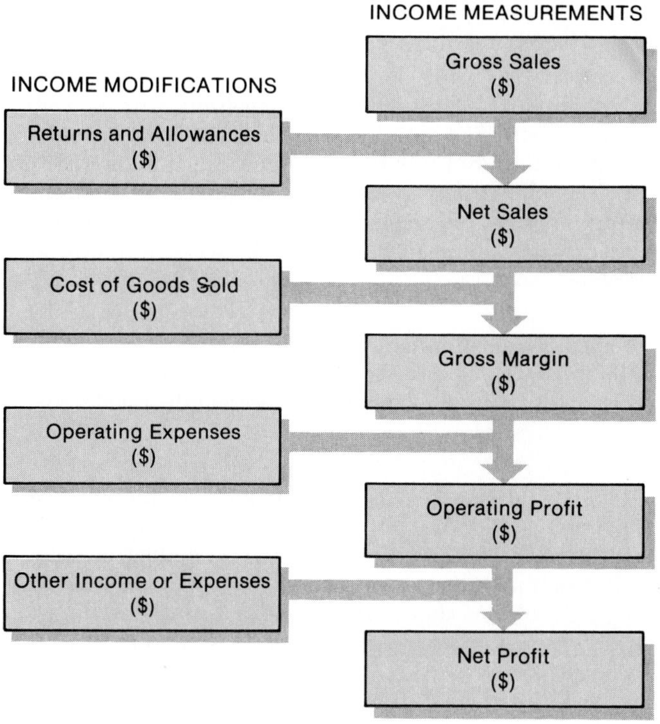

FIGURE 6–2
Elements of the income statement

at the retailer's true income—the bottom line of the income statement or net profit before taxes. In one case, an income modification represents an addition to an income measurement. This "other income" usually represents income the retailer generates outside of normal retailing activities. As Figure 6–2 illustrates, there are four general income modifications—returns and allowances, cost of goods sold, operating expenses, and other income or expenses. Figure 6–3 shows the basic format for the income statement.

Gross Sales. **Gross sales** are the total dollar revenues the retailer receives from the sale of merchandise and services. The gross sales figure, which includes both cash and credit sales, is obtained by first posting in a sales ledger all cash and credit sales at the price actually charged customers and then totaling those sales for the appropriate accounting period. The gross sales figure is important because it reflects the total dollar

Gross sales		$_____
— Returns and allowances	$_____	
Net sales		$_____
— Cost of goods sold	$_____	
Gross margin		$_____
— Operating expenses	$_____	
Operating profit		$_____
± Other income or expenses	$_____	
Net profit before taxes		$_____

FIGURE 6–3
Format of the income statement

amount that not only must cover all of the retailer's costs of doing business but must provide a reward (profit) for conducting that business.

Returns and Allowances. Not all customer purchases are finalized with the initial sale. Some customers will become dissatisfied with their purchases and will expect the retailer to make some sort of adjustment. **Returns from customers** and **allowances to customers,** two means by which retailers adjust for customer dissatisfaction, represent cancellation of sales; therefore, the gross sales figure must be adjusted to reflect the cancellations. While some returns and allowances are expected, excessive returns and allowances can be a major problem.

Net Sales. Net sales, the income measurement that results when returns and allowances are subtracted from gross sales, represent the amount of merchandise the retailer actually sold during the accounting period. Net sales represent the retailer's true sales revenue picture.

Cost of Goods Sold. The value of the merchandise the retailer sells during a given accounting period is the **cost of goods sold**. The cost of goods sold is a function of six factors: opening inventory, net purchases, transportation charges, ending inventory, cash discounts earned, and alteration and workroom costs. Figure 6–4 illustrates the format for calculating cost of goods sold. As shown, the calculating procedures consist of determining total goods handled, gross cost of goods sold, net cost of goods sold, and total cost of goods sold.

Gross Margin. Gross margin is the dollar difference between the retailer's net sales and the total cost of goods sold (see Figure 6–3). It represents the funds available for covering operating expenses and generating a profit. Gross margins for department stores average about 40 percent of net sales, while specialty stores' gross margins average about 2 percent higher.[2]

Operating Expenses. Every retailer incurs certain expenses (payroll, rent, utilities, supplies, etc.) in operating a business. To realize a profit, the retailer's **operating expenses** must be less than the gross margin figure. Therefore, every retailer must fully understand the management of operating expenses.

FIGURE 6–4
Calculating cost of goods sold

Opening inventory	($)
+ Net purchases	($)
+ Transportation charges	($)
Total goods handled	($)
− Ending inventory	($)
Gross cost of goods sold	($)
− Cash discounts earned	($)
Net cost of goods sold	($)
+ Alteration and workroom costs	($)
Total cost of goods sold	($)

Operating Profit. The difference between gross margin and operating expenses is the retailer's **operating profit** (see Figure 6–3); it is what remains after the retailer has covered the cost of goods sold and cost of doing business. Operating profit defines productivity of the capital and labor invested in the retail store; it is derived from retail management's skill in maintaining a reasonable spread between operating expenses and gross margin. For any given operating unit within the retailer's organization (e.g., a department within a store), operating profit represents the final expression of profit. Operating profit, however, is not the figure that determines the retailer's tax liability; net profit must be determined by considering other income and expenses associated with the operation.

Other Income and/or Expenses. The final modification to the income statement is other income the retailer receives and other expenses incurred in conducting the business. **Other income** consists of additional revenues resulting from retailing activities other than the buying and selling of goods and services. Rent from a leased department, interest on installment credit, and interest on deposited bank funds are all examples of other income. Before the retailer can compute the final net sales figure, however, some additional expenses must be deducted from the operating profit figure. Interest paid by the retailer on borrowed funds is an example of **other expenses**.

Net Profit. Net profit is operating profit plus other income and minus other expenses (see Figure 6–3). Net profit is the figure on which the retailer pays income tax, and it is usually referred to in terms of either *net profit before taxes* or *net profit after taxes*.

The Balance Sheet

The second accounting statement used in reporting financial information is the balance sheet—a statement of the retailer's financial condition as of a given date. In its most basic form, the balance sheet summarizes the relationships among the retailer's assets, liabilities, and net worth. The following equation shows this basic balance sheet relationship:

$$\text{assets} = \text{liabilities} + \text{net worth}$$

The balance sheet is prepared to show what the retailer owns (the amount and distribution of assets), what the retailer owes (the amount and distribution of liabilities), and what the retailer is worth (the difference between assets and liabilities). By comparing the current year's balance sheet to those of previous years, the retailer can identify any changes in the firm's financial position and determine whether any operational improvements are possible.

A typical balance sheet format, illustrated in Figure 6–5, consists of two major parts. The first part lists assets; the second part lists the retailer's liabilities and states the equity position (the net worth of the owners). As Figure 6–5 shows, the total-assets figure always equals the sum of total liabilities plus net worth.

The Retailer's Assets

The first part of the balance sheet reports the retailer's asset position. An **asset** is anything of value owned by the retail firm. Assets are categorized into two groups: current assets and fixed assets.

Current assets include all items of value that the retailer can easily convert into cash within a relatively short time, *usually within one year or less*. In addition to cash on hand, current assets include accounts receivable, merchandise inventory, and supply inventory. Accounts receivable are amounts that customers *owe* the retailer for goods

FIGURE 6–5
Balance sheet format

Assets		
Current assets		
Cash	$10,000	
Accounts	15,000	
Merchandise inventory	90,000	
Supply inventory	5,000	
Total current assets		$120,000
Fixed assets		
Building (less depreciation)	75,000	
Fixtures and equipment (less depreciation)	25,000	
Total fixed assets		100,000
Total assets		220,000
Liabilities and net worth		
Current liabilities		
Accounts payable	$25,000	
Payroll payable	10,000	
Taxes payable	5,000	
Notes payable	15,000	
Total current liabilities		$55,000
Fixed liabilities		
Mortgage payable	50,000	
Notes payable	20,000	
Total fixed liabilities		70,000
Net worth		
Capital surplus	85,000	
Retained earnings	10,000	
Total net worth		95,000
Total liabilities and net worth		$220,000

and services. Frequently the retailer reduces the accounts receivable figure by some fixed percentage (based on past experience) to take into account customers that eventually will default on their payments. The retailer makes this adjustment to avoid overstating assets.

The value of the merchandise on hand at the time of preparing the balance sheet is part of the retailer's current assets. Stating the merchandise inventory in terms of "cost or current market value, whichever is lower" is a conservative approach that helps the retailer avoid overstating its assets. Supply inventory reflects operating supplies on hand that have been paid for but not used; in effect, they represent prepaid expenses. The retailer arrives at the total current-asset figure by totaling cash on hand, accounts receivable, merchandise inventory, and supply inventory (see Figure 6–5).

Fixed assets are assets that require a significant length of time to convert into cash (more than one year). These long-term assets include buildings, fixtures (e.g., display racks), and equipment (e.g., delivery trucks). The value of fixed assets is expressed in terms of their cost to the retailer minus an assigned depreciation. This depreciation is necessary because fixed assets have a limited useful life; therefore, depreciation better reflects their true value. The depreciation also helps the retailer avoid overstating total

Merchandise inventory and supply inventory are two of the retailer's current assets that can be converted to cash within a relatively short time.

assets. Some retailers include a fixed-asset value (not illustrated) for intangibles such as goodwill or store loyalty. The value assigned to intangible assets usually is minimal.

Total assets equal current assets plus fixed assets (see Figure 6–5).

The Retailer's Liabilities

The second part of the balance sheet reflects the retailer's liabilities and net worth. A **liability** is a debt owed to someone. On the balance sheet, liabilities represent a legitimate claim against the retailer's assets. Liabilities are classified as either current or long-term.

Current liabilities are short-term debts that must be paid during the current fiscal year. Included in the current-liabilities column are accounts payable, payroll payable, and notes payable that are due within one year. Accounts payable represent money owed to suppliers for goods and services provided. Payroll payable is money owed to store employees for labor performed. Principal and interest the retailer owes on a bank loan (notes payable) and taxes the retailer owes local, state, and federal governments (taxes payable) also are classified as current liabilities.

Long-term liabilities are long-term indebtedness. Mortgages and long-term notes and bonds not due during the current fiscal year are the most common long-term liabilities. Another category sometimes treated as a long-term liability is a reserve account to provide the retailer with funds for emergencies. The total-liability figure is computed by combining the current and long-term liabilities.

The Retailer's Net Worth

Net worth represents the owner's equity in the retail business and is defined by the following equation:

$$\text{net worth} = \text{total assets} - \text{total liabilities}$$

Another way to look at net worth is as the owner's share of the firm's total assets.

The Financial Status Checklist

To achieve sound fiscal control over the retail operation, the retailer must maintain accurate and timely records and statements. Figure 6–6 illustrates a **financial status checklist** of the kinds of financial information retailers need and how frequently (daily, weekly, or monthly) they should compile this information. By carefully checking the status of each financial record on a frequent, regular basis, retailers can identify problem situations and take the necessary action to correct or eliminate them.

FIGURE 6–6
Financial status checklist for retailers

Daily

1. cash on hand
2. bank balance (business and personal funds kept separate)
3. daily summary of sales and cash receipts
4. all errors in recording collections on accounts corrected
5. a record maintained of all monies paid out, by cash or check

Weekly

1. accounts receivable (action taken on slow payers)
2. accounts payable (advantage taken of discounts)
3. payroll (records include name and address of employee, social security number, number of exemptions, date ending the pay period, hours worked, rate of pay, total wages, deductions, net pay, check number)
4. taxes (sales, withholding, social security, etc.) paid and reports to state and federal government completed on time

Monthly

1. all journal entries classified according to like elements (these should be generally accepted and standard for both income and expense) and posted to general ledger
2. income statement for the month available within a reasonable time—usually 10 to 15 days following the close of the month
3. balance sheet accompanying the income statement, showing assets (what the business has), liabilities (what the business owes), and the investment of the owner
4. bank statement reconciled (that is, the owner's books are in agreement with the bank's record of the cash balance)
5. petty cash account in balance (that is, the actual cash in the petty cash box, plus the total of the paid-out slips that have not been charged to expense, total the amount set aside as petty cash)
6. all federal tax deposits, withheld income and FICA taxes, and state taxes paid
7. accounts receivable aged—i.e., 30, 60, 90 days, etc., past due (all bad and slow accounts pursued)
8. inventory control worked to remove dead stock and order new stock (What moves slowly? Reduce. What moves fast? Increase.)

Source: Adapted from John Cotlon, *Keeping Records in Small Business*, Small Marketers Aids No. 155 (Washington, D.C.: Small Business Administration, May, 1974), 8.

PERFORMANCE ANALYSIS

The income statement and the balance sheet provide the retailer with a wealth of data. To convert these data into meaningful information, retailers rely on **ratio analysis**—an examination of the relationships among elements in the income statement and/or balance sheet. A number of different ratios and relationships can assist the retailer in appraising its past and present performances and provide some insight into its future performances. By making comparisons among the firm's past ratios and the ratios of similar national and local firms, the retailer can constructively evaluate its performance. Ratios can be grouped into two general categories: operating ratios and financial ratios.

Operating Ratios

Operating ratios express relationships among elements of the income statement. They are used to judge how efficiently the retailer is generating sales and managing expenses. To obtain operating ratios, one element of the retailer's income statement is divided by another element and multiplied by 100.

FIGURE 6–7
The use of operating ratios

(a) 1990 Income Statement: The Smart Shop

Gross sales		$220,000
− Returns and allowances	$ 4,000	
Net sales		$216,000
− Cost of goods sold	$104,000	
Gross margin		$112,000
− Operating expenses	$ 80,000	
Operating profit		$ 32,000
+ Other income	$ 1,000	
− Other expenses	$ 3,000	
Net profit		$ 30,000

(b) 1990 Operating Ratios The Smart Shop

Ratio	Calculation	Interpretation
$\frac{\text{Gross sales}}{\text{Net sales}}$	$\frac{\$220,000}{\$216,000} \times 100$	Gross sales equal 102 percent of net sales.
$\frac{\text{Cost of goods sold}}{\text{Net sales}}$	$\frac{\$104,000}{\$216,000} \times 100$	Cost of goods sold equals 48.1 percent of net sales.
$\frac{\text{Gross margin}}{\text{Net sales}}$	$\frac{\$112,000}{\$216,000} \times 100$	Gross margin equals 51.9 percent of net sales.
$\frac{\text{Operating expenses}}{\text{Net sales}}$	$\frac{\$\ 80,000}{\$216,000} \times 100$	Operating expenses equal 37 percent of net sales.
$\frac{\text{Operating profit}}{\text{Net sales}}$	$\frac{\$\ 32,000}{\$216,000} \times 100$	Operating profit equals 14.8 percent of net sales.
$\frac{\text{Net profit}}{\text{Net sales}}$	$\frac{\$\ 30,000}{\$216,000} \times 100$	Net profit equals 13.9 percent of net sales.

Figure 6–7 illustrates the use of operating ratios. It uses information from an income statement (Figure 6–7a) to calculate several operating ratios (Figure 6–7b) that show the basic relationship between net sales and (1) gross sales, (2) cost of goods sold, (3) gross margin, (4) operating expenses, (5) operating profit, and (6) net profit. By making historical comparisons with past years, the retailer can detect any positive or negative changes that might be significant in judging operating efficiency. Comparisons with trade data allow the retailer to determine whether significant differences between its operation and national operating norms exist.

Financial Ratios

Financial ratios express relationships among the elements of a balance sheet or between a balance sheet element and an element in the income statement. They are

RETAIL STRATEGIES AND TACTICS

Catalog Warehouse: Applying the Strategic Profit Model

I. Information

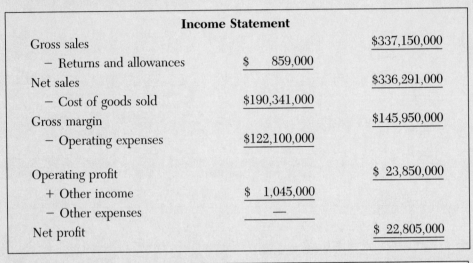

Income Statement

Gross sales		$337,150,000
− Returns and allowances	$ 859,000	
Net sales		$336,291,000
− Cost of goods sold	$190,341,000	
Gross margin		$145,950,000
− Operating expenses	$122,100,000	
Operating profit		$ 23,850,000
+ Other income	$ 1,045,000	
− Other expenses	—	
Net profit		$ 22,805,000

Balance Sheet

Assets		Liabilities and Net Worth	
Current	$ 78,948,000	Current	$ 39,204,000
Fixed	$ 29,052,000	Fixed	$ 11,556,000
		Net worth	$ 57,240,000
Total assets	$108,000,000	Total liabilities and net worth	$108,000,000

used to identify relative strengths and weaknesses in the retailer's financial status and to uncover trends that will affect future performance capabilities. Liquidity, leverage, and profitability ratios are the three key financial areas of concern.

Liquidity Ratios

Liquidity determines whether the retailer can meet payment obligations as they mature. It means possessing sufficient liquid assets that can be quickly and easily converted to cash to meet scheduled payments or to take advantage of special merchandising opportunities. **Liquidity ratios** answer the question "How solvent is the retailer?" The current ratio and the quick ratio are the two most common measures of a retailing enterprise's solvency or insolvency.

The **current ratio** represents the retailer's ability to meet current debts with current assets; it is computed by dividing current assets by current liabilities (see previous definitions of current assets and liabilities). While the desired current ratio will depend on the nature of the retailer's operation (i.e., high-volume, high-turnover operations do not require as high a ratio as low-volume, low-turnover retailers), a current ratio of 2:1—$2 of current assets to $1 of current liabilities—is the most common benchmark used in retailing.[3] Low current ratios suggest liquidity problems;

II. Calculation

$$\frac{\text{net profit}}{\text{net sales}} \times \frac{\text{net sales}}{\text{total assets}} = \frac{\text{net profit}}{\text{total assets}} \times \frac{\text{total assets}}{\text{net worth}} = \frac{\text{net profit}}{\text{net worth}}$$

$$\text{profit margin} \times \text{asset turnover} = \text{return on assets} \times \text{financial leverage} = \text{return on net worth}$$

$$\frac{22{,}805}{336{,}291} \times \frac{336{,}291}{108{,}000} = \frac{22{,}805}{108{,}000} \times \frac{108{,}000}{57{,}240} = \frac{22{,}805}{57{,}240}$$

$$.0678 \times 3.113 = .2111 \times 1.886 = .3984$$

$$6.8\% \times 3.1x = 21.1\% \times 1.9x = 40\%$$

III. Interpretation

- *Profit margin*—Catalog Warehouse is realizing an after-tax profit of 6.8 percent, an excellent performance by industry standards. To increase the profit margin, the firm needs to increase sales without a corresponding increase in operating expenses or lower operating expenses while maintaining sales levels.
- *Asset turnover*—Catalog Warehouse's asset turnover is 3.1, or an average of $3.10 in sales per dollar of total assets. This value suggests that the firm is quite productive in terms of asset utilization.
- *Return on assets*—Catalog Warehouse is achieving an excellent return on its entire investment in the firm; 21.1 percent is well above the industry norms.
- *Financial leverage*—Catalog Warehouse's financial leverage of 1.9 suggests that owner equity is quite high. There is money available in the owners' equity if shareholders wish to take money out of the firm.
- *Return on net worth*—Catalog Warehouse's return on net worth is exceptional. At 40 percent, the firm's owners are getting an excellent return on their investment funds.
- *Conclusion*—Catalog Warehouse's overall financial performance is excellent. It would be an upper-quartile performer in all categories.

high ratios indicate good long-term solvency. If a retailer's current ratio is too high, however, management may not be using the firm's assets to their full potential.

The **quick ratio,** or *acid test,* is a more severe measure of the retailer's liquidity position. It measures the retailer's ability to meet current payments with assets that can be immediately converted to cash. To calculate the quick ratio, the retailer simply divides its quick assets by its current liabilities. Quick assets include cash, readily marketable securities, notes receivable, and accounts receivable.[4] Typically a quick ratio of 1:1 is deemed satisfactory for most retailing organizations.

Leverage Ratios

Owner financing versus creditor financing is addressed by leverage ratios. A **leverage ratio** measures the relative contributions of owners and creditors in the financing of the firm's operations. One type of leverage ratio is the **debt ratio**—total debt (current plus long-term liabilities) divided by total assets (current plus fixed assets). The higher the debt ratio, the greater the role of creditors in the firm's total financing.[5] Within reason, owners like to limit their own financial investment; hence, they prefer high debt ratios, while creditors prefer the lower risks associated with more moderate debt ratios.

Profitability Ratios

An overall assessment of a retailer's performance in terms of profit can be obtained from the **strategic profit model (SPM)**. The formula for the SPM is

$$\text{profit margin} \times \text{asset turnover} = \text{return on assets} \times \text{financial leverage} = \text{return on net worth}$$

where **profit margin** is net profit (after taxes) divided by net sales. This ratio measures the after-tax profit per dollar of sales.

Asset turnover is net sales divided by total assets; it measures the productivity of the firm with respect to asset utilization. **Return on assets** is net profit (after taxes) divided by total assets; it measures the return on all funds invested in the firm by both owners and creditors. **Financial leverage** is total assets divided by net worth; it indicates the relative owner/creditor contributions in the firm's capital structure. **Return on net worth** is net profit (after taxes) divided by net worth; it measures the return on funds invested in the firm by its owners.

Profitability goals can be established by setting a target rate of return on net worth. Profit performance can be judged by how well the firm is achieving its targeted return. What constitutes a high performer in the retail industry has varied considerably over the last few decades; the definition of "high performance" increased from 4.4 percent return on net worth in 1960 to 10.0 percent in 1980.[6] To improve its return-on-net-worth ratio, a retailer can strive to improve profit margins, increase its asset turnover rate, or seek higher leverage ratios.

A widely used source of financial ratios is Dun & Bradstreet's *Industry Norms and Key Business Ratios*. An example of these ratios is shown in Figure 6–8. These key performance measurements help the retailer make meaningful comparisons between its financial performance and the national median performance of similar retailers. These ratios are also useful in establishing realistic financial objectives.

CAPITAL MANAGEMENT

A major concern of every retailer is how to create and maintain sufficient capital to conduct business. Careful financial planning and control are ways to alleviate this concern. Few retailers, if any, have enough money available at all times to finance daily business operations and meet long-term investment requirements. Hence, the retailer's ability to *obtain* money and secure *credit* is essential to sustaining a healthy financial situation.

Capital management involves planning and controlling the retailer's **equity capital** (what the retailer owns) and **borrowed capital** (money the retailer has obtained from outside sources). The following discussion examines the retailer's capital requirements, types of retail financing, and various sources of funds.

Capital Requirements

A retailer needs money for a variety of purposes. **Fixed capital** is money needed to purchase physical facilities such as buildings, fixtures, and equipment. This type of capital requirement represents long-term investments that tie up capital for extended periods. **Working capital** is money needed to meet day-to-day operating costs. It is used to pay rent and utility bills, purchase inventories, and cover payroll expenses. **Liquid capital** is money held in reserve for emergency situations, usually in the form of cash or disposable securities (e.g., stocks, bonds, certificates of deposit).

The amount of fixed, working, and liquid capital required by a particular retail operation is a function of the enterprise's size and nature. Capital requirements for larger retailers are greater than for smaller retailers, other things being equal. Upscale retail operations featuring complete product assortments, plush facilities, personal

	SIC 5271 Mobile Home Dealers (no breakdown)		SIC 5311 Department Stores (no breakdown)		SIC 5331 Variety Stores (no breakdown)		SIC 5399 Misc Genl Mdse Stores (no breakdown)	
	1989 (2192 Estab)		1989 (1892 Estab)		1989 (1496 Estab)		1989 (1740 Estab)	
	$	%	$	%	$	%	$	%
Cash	55,638	10.4	120,590	10.2	32,305	13.0	37,844	14.0
Accounts receivable	40,124	7.5	183,249	15.5	11,680	4.7	20,003	7.4
Notes receivable	7,490	1.4	4,729	0.4	1,491	0.6	1,892	0.7
Inventory	282,472	52.8	533,195	45.1	139,657	56.2	132,455	49.0
Other current	19,794	3.7	44,926	3.8	7,455	3.0	8,920	3.3
Total current	405,518	75.8	886,688	75.0	192,588	77.5	201,116	74.4
Fixed assets	62,593	11.7	144,235	12.2	30,069	12.1	41,629	15.4
Other noncurrent	66,873	12.5	151,328	12.8	25,844	10.4	27,572	10.2
Total assets	534,984	100.0	1,182,250	100.0	248,500	100.0	270,317	100.0
Accounts payable	34,239	6.4	130,048	11.0	30,566	12.3	25,139	9.3
Bank loans	3,745	0.7	10,640	0.9	1,988	0.8	1,352	0.5
Notes payable	66,338	12.4	41,379	3.5	7,704	3.1	10,813	4.0
Other current	169,055	31.6	109,949	9.3	25,099	10.1	23,788	8.8
Total current	273,377	5.1	292,016	24.7	65,356	26.3	61,092	22.6
Other long term	70,618	13.2	184,431	15.6	28,826	11.6	31,897	11.8
Deferred credits	1,605	0.3	3,547	0.3	249	0.1	270	0.1
Net worth	189,384	35.4	702,257	59.4	154,070	62.0	177,058	65.5
Total liab. & net worth	534,984	100.0	1,182,250	100.0	248,500	100.0	270,317	100.0
Net sales	1,286,021	100.0	1,673,899	100.0	482,319	100.0	521,972	100.0
Gross profit	302,215	23.5	580,843	34.7	161,095	33.4	159,201	30.5
Net profit after tax	38,581	3.0	33,478	2.0	20,257	4.2	22,967	4.4
Working capital	132,141	—	594,672	—	127,232	—	140,024	—

Ratios	UQ	MED	LQ	UQ	MED	LQ	UQ	MED	LQ	UQ	MED	LQ
Solvency												
Quick ratio (times)	0.7	0.3	0.1	2.5	1.3	0.4	1.7	0.6	0.2	2.8	0.9	0.3
Current ratio (times)	2.1	1.3	1.1	6.3	3.7	2.1	8.2	3.7	2.0	9.4	4.3	2.2
Curr liab to nw (%)	49.0	156.9	338.8	14.3	32.3	76.8	10.5	30.8	82.2	8.8	23.2	57.8
Curr liab to inv (%)	71.8	100.2	118.0	28.1	50.1	77.9	15.5	36.0	68.7	17.0	35.5	66.6
Total liab to nw (%)	85.1	201.0	388.6	17.2	55.1	146.3	14.8	44.0	115.1	12.6	36.5	94.0
Fixed assets to nw (%)	14.1	35.3	79.2	6.0	18.2	52.1	6.3	18.1	46.1	7.1	22.1	54.6
Efficiency												
Coll period (days)	2.9	8.0	18.6	6.2	24.1	52.6	2.6	7.7	24.1	2.9	9.1	23.0
Sales to inv (times)	6.4	4.4	3.1	6.2	4.5	3.2	6.1	3.9	2.7	7.7	4.5	2.8
Assets to sales (%)	27.5	39.8	62.1	37.4	49.2	69.0	30.3	43.7	68.4	30.0	45.8	75.3
Sales to nwc (times)	26.0	12.1	5.4	6.7	3.8	2.5	7.5	4.4	2.5	7.6	4.4	2.5
Acct pay to sales (%)	0.5	1.2	3.0	2.8	4.8	7.7	2.5	4.6	8.1	1.6	3.7	7.1
Profitability												
Return on sales (%)	5.8	2.5	0.7	3.9	1.7	0.3	7.6	3.2	0.9	7.8	3.1	0.6
Return on assets (%)	10.5	4.8	1.2	7.6	3.3	0.6	14.4	7.1	2.0	14.8	5.9	1.3
Return on nw (%)	41.2	17.5	4.0	15.7	6.6	1.2	24.9	12.0	3.8	26.0	9.4	2.2

Source: *Industry Norms and Key Business Ratios* (1989 Edition) © Dun & Bradstreet Credit Services, 1990.

FIGURE 6–8
The ratios of retailing

selling, and many services have a greater need for capital than retailers offering limited product assortments, spartan facilities, and limited services.

Types of Financing

The first step a retailer takes in securing capital funds is determining what kind of money it needs. The retailer's purpose for the money (e.g., for use as fixed, working, or liquid capital) determines the type of financing. There are three types of financing: short-, intermediate-, and long-term credit.

Short-term credit is money the retailer can borrow for less than one year. Lending institutions provide retailers with short-term loans primarily for working capital. For example, banks extend short-term credit to retailers to purchase next season's inventory. In such cases, the loans are self-liquidating because they generate sales dollars.

Intermediate-term credit usually is offered for periods longer than one year but less than five years. Retailers secure such loans to finance smaller, fixed-capital expenditures (e.g., fixtures and equipment).

Long-term credit takes the form of loans that retailers secure for periods longer than five years. Typically retailers use long-term financing to purchase major fixed-capital investments such as buildings and land. For both intermediate- and long-term credit, the retailer must make periodic installment payments (monthly, quarterly, or annually) from earnings.

Sources of Funding

To obtain funds retailers can turn to a number of sources, including equity, vendors, lending institutions, and the government. Most retailers find it necessary to tap several sources of funds.

Equity sources of funds are obtained by selling part ownership in the business. Equity sales allow the retailer to raise funds without having to borrow money or pay interest and repay a loan. Investors in a retail business are individuals willing to accept a certain amount of risk (i.e., the amount of their investment) for potential long-term gains. Before selling equity shares, however, the retailer should determine how much control over the business it would relinquish by making the sale.

Vendors supply retailers with merchandise and are frequently used as sources for short-term credit. Vendors make this form of "trade credit" available when they extend dating terms—the amount of time the retailer has to pay the net invoice price for a shipment of merchandise. By extending dating terms to 60, 90, or even 120 days, the vendor is effectively financing the retailer's inventory for that period. Favorable dating terms often give the retailer time to sell the merchandise before it has to pay for it.

Lending institutions are sources of short- and long-term retail financing. Commercial banks, credit associations, and insurance companies are the lending institutions most often willing to make loans to creditworthy retailers. When lending institutions make short-term, working-capital loans, they expect repayment immediately after the loans have served the purpose for which they were made. For example, a seasonal inventory loan must be repaid at the end of the season. The lender carefully specifies repayment and other terms associated with fixed-capital loans in written contractual agreements.

Commercial lending institutions make both secured and unsecured loans. Retailers with good credit ratings often can get unsecured loans on their signatures alone. Figure 6–9 identifies the various methods by which a loan can be secured.

Government sources of funds usually are the only viable alternative for the small retailer whose credit rating is either uncertain or unestablished. The Small Business Administration (SBA) also makes financial resources available for small businesses,

Endorser	A third party signs a note to bolster the retailer's credit. If the retailer fails to pay the note, the bank expects the endorser to make the payments.
Comaker	A third party creates an obligation jointly with the retailer. The bank can collect directly from either the retailer or the comaker.
Guarantor	A third party guarantees the payment of a note by signing a guaranty commitment.
Assignment of leases	An arrangement in which the bank automatically receives the rent payments from a leasing agreement made between a retailer and a third party. Used in franchising to finance buildings.
Warehouse receipts	An arrangement in which the bank accepts commodities as security by lending money on a warehouse receipt. Such loans are generally made on staple merchandise that can be readily marketed.
Floor-planning	An arrangement in which banks accept a trust receipt for display merchandise as collateral. Used for securing loans on serial-numbered merchandise (automobiles, appliances, boats). When the retailer signs a trust receipt, it (1) acknowledges receipt of the merchandise, (2) agrees to keep the merchandise in trust for the bank, and (3) promises to pay the bank as soon as the merchandise is sold.
Chattel mortgage	An arrangement in which the bank accepts a lien on a piece of new equipment as security for the loan needed to buy the equipment.
Real estate	An arrangement in which the bank accepts a mortgage on real estate as collateral for a loan.
Accounts receivable	An arrangement in which the bank accepts accounts receivable (money owed the retailer) as collateral for a loan. Under the *notification plan* the retailer's customers are informed by the bank that their accounts have been assigned to the bank and all payments are made to the bank. Under the *nonnotification plan,* the retailer's customers are not informed of the assignment to the bank. The customer continues to pay the retailer who, in turn, pays the bank.
Savings accounts or life insurance	An arrangement in which the bank extends a loan to a retailer that assigns to the bank a savings account or the cash value of a life insurance policy as collateral.
Stocks and bonds	An arrangement in which the bank accepts as collateral marketable stocks and bonds. Usually the bank will accept as collateral only a certain percentage of the current market value of the stock or bond.

Source: Adapted from *ABCs of Borrowing*, Management Aids No. 170 (Washington, D.C.: Small Business Adminstration, April, 1977) 2–3.

FIGURE 6–9
Methods for securing a retail loan

including retailers, that have exhausted all other avenues (e.g., traditional sources such as banks) for financing. The SBA provides financing by acting as a (1) "guarantor," guaranteeing a loan made by a bank to a retailer, or (2) "lender," directly lending money to a retailer when local banks will not.

EXPENSE MANAGEMENT

Expense management is the planning and control of operating expenses. To ensure an operating profit, operating expenses must be less than the retailer's gross margin. The retailer that fails to plan and control operating expenses risks losing financial control over an important segment of the business. Expense management entails three basic planning and control activities: classifying expenses, allocating expenses, and budgeting expenses.[7]

Expense Classification

All planning and control activities require careful identification and classification of every relevant factor. Hence, the first step in expense management is to recognize the various costs of doing business and classify these costs into logical groupings based on some common feature. In retailing, four fundamental perspectives on operating expenses will lead to different classifications: sales, control, allocation, and accounting perspectives.

Sales Perspective

One way to look at operating expenses is to see how such expenses are affected by sales. From a sales perspective, operating expenses are classified as fixed and variable. **Fixed expenses** usually are fixed for a given period (e.g., the life of a contract or a planning or operating period). Expenses are classified as fixed when they remain the same regardless of the sales volume; as sales increase or decrease, fixed expenses remain constant.

Expenses that vary with the volume of sales are called **variable expenses**; as sales increase or decrease, variable expenses also increase or decrease. Although the relationship between sales and expenses is not always directly proportional, they are sufficiently related that the retailer can reasonably predict changes in operating expenses. By being attentive to specific relationships between a variable expense and sales, the retailer can identify opportunities for increasing profits. For example, initial increases in advertising expenditures could increase sales to such a degree that profit increases are greater than the advertising expense.

Control Perspective

The second way to look at operating expenses is to see whether a particular expense is controllable. As the term implies, **controllable expenses** are those over which the retailer has direct control. Retailers can adjust these expenses as operating conditions warrant. For example, part-time help can be reduced during slack sales periods. **Uncontrollable expenses** are outlays over which retailers have no control and that they cannot adjust to current operating needs in the short run. Expenses incurred as a result of long-term contractual arrangements are uncontrollable over the short run. Given their adaptability, controllable expenses should be the focus of the retailer's attention. Daily or weekly monitoring of these expenses helps maintain operating expenses at acceptable levels.

Allocation Perspective

In using the allocation perspective, the retailer looks at operating expenses to see if they can be directly attributed to some operating unit. Many retailers find it useful for purposes of analysis and control to allocate operating expenses to various operating units, such as store units or departmental units. With this approach, retailers classify operating expenses as either direct or indirect. **Direct expenses** are those directly attributable to the operations of a department or some other defined operating unit. If the retailer eliminated a department or unit, the direct expenses associated with that department also would be eliminated. Salaries and commissions of departmental sales personnel are examples of direct expenses. Expenses not directly attributable to the operations of a department are classified as **indirect expenses**. These costs cannot be eliminated if a particular department is dropped. Indirect expenses are general business expenses that a retailer incurs in running the entire operation.

Accounting Perspective

A final way to look at operating expenses is to classify them into well-defined groups that the retailer can use to identify year-to-year trends for each expense class and to make comparisons with trade averages of similar retailers. This expense classification system helps the retailer identify, analyze, and initiate controls for expenses that are out of line with either last year's figures or those of similar retailers. Using the accounting approach, the retailer can classify operating expenses using either a natural division of expenses or expense-center accounting.

With the **natural division of expenses** (see Figure 6–10), the retailer classifies expenses on the basis of the kind of expense each is without regard for (1) which store functions (e.g., selling, buying, or receiving) incurred the expense or (2) where (e.g., which store or department) the expense was incurred. The natural division method of expense classification is used primarily by small and medium-size retailers looking for simple but acceptable means of classifying expenses.

The second accounting method for classifying operating expenses is **expense-center accounting**. An *expense center* is a functional center within the store's operation or a center of a certain store activity. The center incurs expenses in the process of providing its assigned functions or performing its required activities. Expense-center accounting is a system of classifying operating expenses into functional or activity classes such as management, direct selling, customer services, and so on. The National Retail Merchants Association has identified 54 major expense centers, shown in Figure 6–11. Expense-center accounting is used most frequently by large, departmentalized retailers.

FIGURE 6–10 Natural division of expenses

01 Payroll	13 Depreciation
02 Allocated fringe benefits	14 Professional services
03 Media costs	16 Bad debts
04 Taxes	17 Equipment rentals
06 Supplies	18 Outside maintenance and equipment service contracts
07 Services purchased	20 Real property rentals
08 Unclassified	90 Expense transfers in
09 Travel	91 Expense transfers out
10 Communications	92 Credits and outside revenues
11 Pensions	
12 Insurance	

Source: Adapted from *Retail Accounting Manual*, rev. ed. (New York: Financial Executives Division, National Retail Federation, Inc., 1978), III-3.

FIGURE 6–11
Major expense centers

010 Property and equipment
- 020 Real estate, buildings, and building equipment
- 030 Furniture, fixtures, and nonbuilding equipment

100 Company management
- 110 Executive office
- 130 Branch management
- 140 Internal audit
- 150 Legal and consumer activities

200 Accounting and management information
- 210 Control management, general accounting, and statistical
- 220 Sales audit
- 230 Accounts payable
- 240 Payroll and time-keeping department
- 280 Data processing

300 Credit and accounts receivable
- 310 Credit management
- 330 Collection
- 340 Accounts receivable and bill adjustment
- 350 Cash office
- 360 Branch/store selling location offices

400 Sales promotion
- 410 Sales promotion management
- 420 Advertising
- 430 Shows, special events, and exhibits
- 440 Display

500 Service and operations
- 510 Service and operations management
- 530 Security
- 550 Telephones and communications
- 560 Utilities
- 570 Housekeeping
- 580 Maintenance and repairs

600 Personnel
- 610 Personnel management
- 620 Employment
- 640 Training
- 660 Medical and other employee services
- 670 Supplementary benefits

700 Merchandise receiving, storage, and distribution
- 710 Management of merchandise receiving, storage, and distribution
- 720 Receiving and marking
- 730 Reserve stock storage
- 750 Shuttle services

800 Selling and supporting services
- 810 Selling supervision
- 820 Direct selling
- 830 Customer services
- 840 Selling support services
- 860 Central wrapping and packing
- 880 Delivery

900 Merchandising
- 910 Merchandising management
- 920 Buying
- 930 Merchandise control

Source: *Retail Accounting Manual,* rev. ed. (New York: Financial Executives Divison, National Retail Federation, Inc., 1978), III-3.

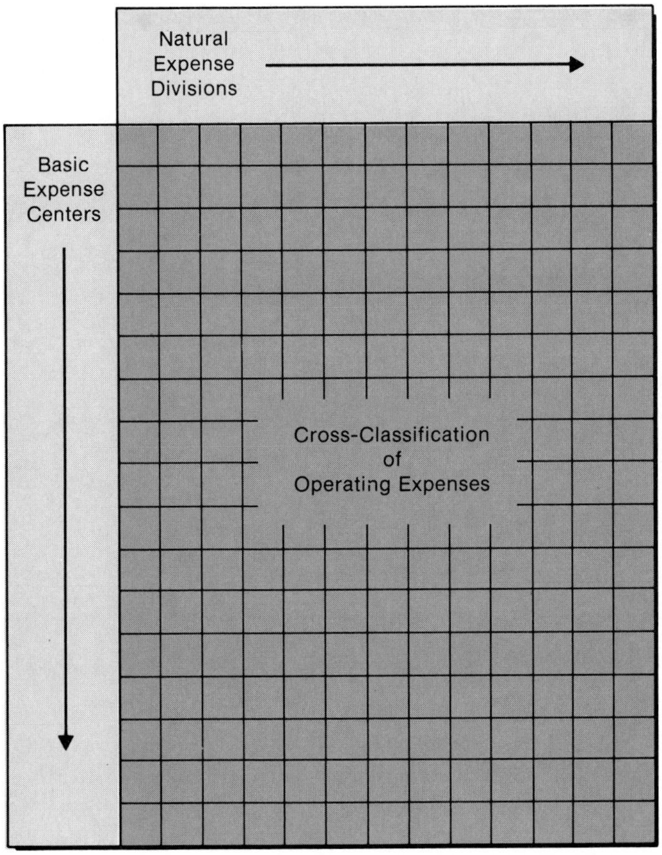

FIGURE 6–12
Expense-center accounting system

In using the expense-center accounting system, the retailer follows a two-step procedure. The first step is to classify operating expenses according to natural divisions. The second step is to cross-classify each natural expense with each of the 54 expense centers. As Figure 6–12 illustrates, the retailer can use expense-center accounting to identify, analyze, and control operating expenses either by the kind or type of expense (i.e., natural divisions) or by the function or activity that incurred the expense (i.e., the expense center). Typically the expense-center accounting system provides greater detail in classifying operating expenses than do other methods. After operating expenses have been classified, the retailer's second task is to allocate expenses to each of the operating units, such as departments within a store or stores within a chain organization.

Expense Allocation

Large retailers typically are either departmentalized or multiunit (chain) operations that have a great need for examining the operating expenses of individual operating units. Three methods by which retailers allocate operating expenses to operating units are (1) the net profit plan, (2) the contribution plan, and (3) the net profit contribution plan. Figure 6–13 illustrates each of these expense allocation plans. Two points are notable. First, the bottom line for a departmental income statement is its operating profit. However, this profit expression often is referred to as the department *net profit*. Second, the allocation methods are quite similar; the principal differences are in treatment of direct expenses and calculation criteria for the operating unit.

FIGURE 6–13
Allocating operating expenses

Net profit plan	
Department gross margin	($)
− Direct expenses of the department	($)
− Indirect expenses charged to department	($)
Department net profit	($)*
Contribution plan	
Department gross margin	($)
− Direct expenses of the department	($)
Contribution of the department	($)*
Net profit contribution plan	
Department gross margin	($)
− Direct expenses of the department	($)
Contribution of the department	($)*
− Indirect expenses charged to department	($)
Department net profit	($)*

*Measurement used to evaluate departmental performance.

Net Profit Plan

When using the **net profit plan**, the retailer allocates all direct and indirect expenses. Direct expenses are directly attributed to the particular department that incurred them. Indirect expenses are not directly attributed to a particular department but instead are allocated to departments based on a prejudged set of criteria. Figure 6–14 lists common criteria for retailers. To illustrate, the salary of a department manager would be considered a direct expense that could be allocated to the department. The salary of the store manager, however, would be an indirect expense to any given department, and the store manager's salary could be allocated to various departments based on each department's percentage of total net sales.

As Figure 6–13 shows, the department's gross margin minus the department's direct and indirect expenses equals the department's net profit. The treatment of each department as a profit-producing center has the advantage of providing a "hard-figure" (net profit) evaluation of departmental operations and encourages each department to be expense-control conscious. On the other hand, unfair or questionable allocations of indirect expenses to the department can distort the department's profit picture and

FIGURE 6–14
Selected expense-center allocation criteria

Type of Expense	Allocation Criteria
Property and equipment	Weighted floor space
Company management	Net sales
Accounting and management information	Gross sales
Credit and accounts receivable	Number of transactions
Sales promotion	Number of displays
Personnel	Number of employees
Merchandise receiving storage and distribution	Number of invoices
Selling and supporting services	Number of units
Merchandising	Net sales

create considerable dissatisfaction among departmental managers whose careers are on the line.

Contribution Plan

The **contribution plan** can be characterized as follows: (1) Direct expenses are allocated to the departments that incurred them, and (2) indirect expenses are allocated not to departments but to a general expense account. The department's *contribution* is defined as the department's gross margin minus its direct expenses. Again referring to Figure 6–13, we see that each department is judged on the basis of its contribution to the store. The sum of the contributions from each department is treated as a "reservoir" to cover the indirect expenses in the general expense account and to provide an operating profit for the store.

Net Profit Contribution Plan

Using the **net profit contribution plan**, the retailer calculates both the department's net profit and its contribution (see Figure 6–13). This plan involves a two-step procedure. First, the department's contribution is calculated by subtracting the department's direct expenses from its gross margin. Second, the department's net profit is calculated by subtracting the department's indirect expenses from its contribution. The combination net profit contribution plan allows examination of departmental performance from both the contribution and net profit perspectives.

Expense Budgeting

An **expense budget** is a plan or set of guidelines that a retailer uses to control operating expenses. It is an estimate or forecast of the amount of money needed during a given accounting period to operate the business. An annual expense budget for the entire store is the normal starting point in expense control. Then the annual budget is broken down into monthly and weekly expense plans. While small retailers typically operate on a storewide expense budget, larger, departmentalized retailers usually find it necessary to prepare departmental expense budgets separately from the store budget.

In practice, expense budgets should act as a general game plan, not as a straitjacket of unbreakable rules. As a plan of action, budgets must be flexible enough for management to adjust them as conditions warrant but rigid enough to provide meaningful guidance.

The first step in preparing an expense budget is to determine an overall expense figure for the prescribed operating period. This figure is a general estimate of the amount of money the retailer will have available to cover operating expenses. The second step is to select a budgeting method. The retailer can elect to use any one of three approaches to expense budgeting: zero-based budgeting, fixed-based budgeting, and productivity-based budgeting.

Zero-Based Budgeting

As the term implies, under **zero-based budgeting**, each operating department or unit starts with no allocated operating expenses. To secure operating funds, each operating department must justify its need for each expense item on the budget. While past expenditures may be considered supporting evidence, management does not accept past expenditures as total justification for future expense allocations. To obtain operating funds, department personnel must use justifications based on current merchandising plans, market conditions, competitive atmospheres, and operating requirements. Although zero-based budgeting generally is time consuming and costly, it forces each operating department to reevaluate its expenses and define the needs and benefits each expenditure should generate. Zero-based budgeting is the most appropriate way to establish an expense budget for a new retailer or a new department.

Period: Third Quarter				Store: 12		Expense Center:	721-Receiving		
Natural Division		Current Period				Year-to-Date			
		Amount		Variance		Amount		Variance	
No.	Expense	Actual	Budget	Dollar	Percent	Actual	Budget	Dollar	Percent
01	Payroll	4,000	4,000	00	00	12,000	12,000	00	0.0
06	Supplies	1,000	800	(200)	(25)	2,600	2,400	(200)	(8.3)
07	Services Purchased	500	600	100	16.7	1,400	1,800	400	22.2
10	Communications	100	100	00	00	270	300	30	10.0
	Total	5,600	5,500	(100)	1.8	16,270	16,500	230	1.4

FIGURE 6–15
Fixed-based budgeting form

Fixed-Based Budgeting

In the **fixed-based budgeting** process, each expense (e.g., payroll, supplies) is budgeted at a specific dollar amount. The predetermined amount is based on past experience as well as on the need for incurring the expense in the forthcoming budgeting period. Figure 6–15 illustrates a fixed-based budgeting form. To facilitate control, the retailer should fill in the form for both the budgeted and the actual expenditure in the current budget period as well as complete a year-to-date summary.

The form also provides space for the retailer to report variances between actual and budgeted amounts in both dollars and percentages. Management carefully scrutinizes these variances; when they exceed either a predetermined dollar or

Natural Division		Period: April		Store: 12		Expense Center: 410—		Sales Promotion	
		Unit Sales							
No.	Expense	500	1000	1500	2000	2500	3000	3500	4000
01	Payroll	$2,000	$2,000	$2,500	$2,500	$3,000	$3,500	$4,000	$4,500
03	Advertising	500	1,000	1,500	2,000	2,500	3,000	3,500	4,000
06	Supplies	500	550	600	700	800	1,000	1,200	1,400
	Total	$3,000	$3,550	$4,600	$5,200	$6,300	$7,500	$8,700	$9,900

FIGURE 6–16
Productivity-based budgeting form

percentage amount, the manager of the operating department should examine and correct the situation and submit either a written or oral report to the supervisor. The example in Figure 6–15 shows that the manager of the receiving department appears to be controlling the department's expenses quite adequately. Although the current period shows the department is slightly over budget, the year-to-date expenses are slightly below the amount budgeted for the department.

Productivity-Based Budgeting

Expense budgets based on levels of productivity provide a high degree of flexibility in the budgetary process. Under a **productivity-based budget,** the retailer prepares a series of expense budgets to correspond to various sales levels (or to some other productivity measure). As Figure 6–16 illustrates, an increase in unit sales automatically increases the amount budgeted for each item in the department's expense budget. Given that numerous operating expenses are either directly or indirectly related to sales, a budget based on sales productivity should help the retailer make operational adjustments to meet changing market conditions. Some retailers think that a productivity-based budget is the most appropriate approach to expense budgeting, especially when reliable sales estimates are difficult to make or when there is a high likelihood for extreme sales variations. Essentially this budget approach allows the retailer to allocate limited financial resources based on actual need as opposed to anticipated requirements.

SUMMARY

A key means of gaining retailing success is fiscal control. To ensure an adequate degree of control over financial affairs, the retailer must develop and maintain a set of financial records that provide a broad picture of its financial condition. A typical set of records includes a separate record for sales, cash receipts, cash disbursements, purchases, payroll, equipment, inventory, accounts receivable, and accounts payable. The retailer then uses these records to prepare two essential financial statements: the income statement and the balance sheet.

The income statement summarizes the retailer's financial activity for a stated accounting period. It is prepared to show the profit (or loss) the retailer has experienced during the accounting period. The income statement is a systematic set of procedures that helps the retailer identify five income measurements: gross sales, net sales, gross margin, operating profit, and net profit.

The balance sheet is a statement of the retailer's financial condition on a given date. It summarizes the basic relationships among the retailer's assets, liabilities, and net worth. The balance sheet shows how the sides of the accounting equation (assets = liabilities + net worth) are balanced.

The financial status checklist allows the retailer to check the status of each financial record or statement and identify financial problems requiring corrective action.

In performance analysis, the retailer must make judgments on operating and financial performance. By using several standardized operating and financial ratios, the retailer can compare performance, on a historical or trade basis, to national norms.

Capital management involves planning and controlling the retailer's equity capital (what the retailer owns) and borrowed capital (what the retailer owes). A retailer needs money for a variety of reasons, including funds for fixed, working, and liquid capital requirements. The type of financing a retailer needs depends on its capital requirements. The retailer uses short-term credit when it needs working capital and intermediate- and long-term credit to meet fixed capital requirements. Equity sales, vendor credit, and loans from lending institutions and government agencies are the major sources of funds for the retailer.

In departmentalized or chain store organizations, operating expenses must be allocated to various operating units. Expense allocation is accomplished by using the net profit plan, the contribution plan, and the net profit contribution plan. An expense budget is used to plan and control operating expenditures. The retailer can elect to use one of three budgeting procedures: zero-based, fixed-based, or productivity-based.

STUDENT STUDY GUIDE

Key Terms and Concepts

account (p. 197)
allowances to customers (p. 200)
asset (p. 201)
asset turnover (p. 208)
balance sheet (p. 201)
borrowed capital (p. 208)
contribution plan (p. 217)
controllable expenses (p. 212)
cost of goods sold (p. 200)
current assets (p. 201)
current liability (p. 203)
current ratio (p. 206)
debt ratio (p. 207)
direct expenses (p. 213)
equity capital (p. 208)
expense budget (p. 217)
expense-center accounting (p. 213)
financial leverage (p. 208)
financial ratios (p. 205)
financial status checklist (p. 203)
fixed assets (p. 202)
fixed-based budgeting (p. 218)
fixed capital (p. 208)
fixed expenses (p. 212)
gross margin (p. 200)
gross sales (p. 199)
income measurements (p. 198)
income modifications (p. 198)
income statement (p. 197)
indirect expenses (p. 213)
intermediate-term credit (p. 210)
ledger (p. 197)
leverage ratios (p. 207)
liability (p. 203)
liquid capital (p. 208)
liquidity ratios (p. 206)
long-term credit (p. 210)
long-term liability (p. 203)
natural division of expenses (p. 213)
net profit (p. 201)
net profit contribution plan (p. 217)
net profit plan (p. 216)
net sales (p. 200)
net worth (p. 203)
operating expenses (p. 200)
operating profit (p. 201)
operating ratios (p. 204)
other expenses (p. 201)
other income (p. 201)
productivity-based budgeting (p. 219)
profit margin (p. 208)
profitability ratios (p. 208)
quick ratio (p. 207)
ratio analysis (p. 204)
return on assets (p. 208)
return on net worth (p. 208)
returns from customers (p. 200)
short-term credit (p. 210)
strategic profit model (SPM) (p. 208)
total assets (p. 203)
uncontrollable expenses (p. 212)
variable expenses (p. 212)
working capital (p. 208)
zero-based budgeting (p. 217)

Review Questions

1. What is the purpose of an income statement? Identify and define the role of the nine elements of an income statement.
2. Why is a balance sheet prepared? Describe the basic balance sheet equation.
3. Distinguish between current and fixed assets and current and long-term liabilities. Provide specific examples of each.
4. How should the retailer view the concept of net worth?
5. What is ratio analysis?
6. Describe the relationships expressed by operating ratios. Cite examples of these relationships.
7. Compare and contrast current ratios and leverage ratios. What does each ratio measure?
8. What are fixed, working, and liquid capital needed for?
9. What types of financing are available to the retailer? Where would the retailer find this financing?
10. How can expenses be classified? Describe the various expense classification systems.
11. Describe the three methods of expense allocation.
12. Describe the three approaches to expense budgeting.

Review Exam

True or False

_____ 1. The income statement is a picture of the retailer's assets, liabilities, and net worth on a given date; the balance sheet is a picture of the retailer's profits or losses over a stated period of time.

_____ 2. Operating profit is the difference between gross margin and other income and expenses; it is the figure that determines the retailer's tax liability.

_____ 3. Fixed assets are assets that require a significant length of time to convert to cash.

_____ 4. A high current ratio suggests liquidity problems; a low current ratio indicates good long-term solvency.

_____ 5. If a retailer eliminated a department, the indirect expenses allocated to that department would not be eliminated and would need to be allocated elsewhere.

_____ 6. The contribution plan of expense allocation will almost always show a positive contribution. This means the department is contributing its fair share to the store's profit.

_____ 7. Productivity-based budgeting is characterized by a high degree of flexibility.

Multiple Choice

_____ 1. For a departmentalized chain store operation, income statements are prepared for
- a. Each department
- b. Each store
- c. The whole chain
- d. All of the above
- e. None of the above

_____ 2. Gross margin
- a. Is the dollar difference between net sales and the total cost of goods sold
- b. Is the dollar difference between gross sales and net returns and allowances
- c. Represents the funds available for covering operating expenses and generating a profit
- d. a and c
- e. b and c

_____ 3. A _____ ratio measures the relative contributions of owners and creditors in the financing of the firm's operation.
- a. Leverage
- b. Current
- c. Debt
- d. Liquidity
- e. Operating

_____ 4. The Small Business Administration (SBA) may provide the following services to the small retailer whose credit rating is uncertain or unestablished
- a. Guaranteeing loans made by a bank to the retailer
- b. Direct loans to the retailer
- c. Information and advice
- d. All of the above

_____ 5. A loan is self-liquidating when
- a. The terms include a provision indicating it can be renewed when it comes due.
- b. The goods purchased with the proceeds from the loan generate sales, and therefore funds, with which to repay the loan.
- c. The interest rate declines as the balance of the loan declines.
- d. It is due within 30 days.

_____ 6. Floorplanning is an arrangement in which the bank holds a trust receipt for display merchandise as collateral for a loan. When the retailer signs the trust receipt, it
- a. Agrees not to sell the merchandise until the loan is repaid
- b. Agrees to keep the merchandise in trust for the bank until it is sold
- c. Agrees to pay the bank as soon as the merchandise is sold
- d. a and b

_____ 7. Using the natural division of expenses, the retailer classifies expenses on the basis of
- a. Which store function incurred the expense
- b. Where (e.g., which store or department) the expense was incurred
- c. Fixed or variable
- d. Kind of expense

STUDENT APPLICATIONS MANUAL

Investigative Projects: Practice and Applications

1. Excessive customer returns and allowances can be a major problem for the retailer. Control procedures should be initiated to identify and analyze the causes of returns and allowances. Review the causes of returns and allowances in Chapter 12. Then develop a customer survey instrument that a department store retailer could use to identify and analyze customer returns and allowances.
2. The value of fixed assets equals their cost to the retailer minus an assigned depreciation. Identify and describe some of the methods retailers might use to depreciate their fixed assets.

3. Interview several vendors (e.g., wholesalers) and determine the terms and conditions under which they are willing to extend short-term (less than one year) and intermediate-term (one to five years) credit to retailers. Evaluate these terms and conditions from the viewpoint of the retailer. Are they acceptable? Why or why not?
4. Contact your local Small Business Administration (SBA) office, and determine the procedures and requirements for obtaining a small-business loan.
5. Classify the following list of expenses as either fixed or variable and controllable or uncontrollable: (1) sales commissions, (2) store manager's salary, (3) a weekly newspaper advertisement, (4) a business license, (5) employees' health insurance payments, (6) the services of an accounting firm, (7) a donation to the United Way, (8) cost of new fixtures, (9) store rent, and (10) monthly telephone bill. Explain your classification.
6. The Family Shoe Shop is an independently owned and operated shoe store located in a large regional shopping center. R. P. Evans, the proprietor, has organized the store around three departments: 1,800 square feet of selling space is devoted to men's shoes, 1,600 square feet to women's shoes, and 1,200 square feet to the children's department.

   Each year Evans must complete the store's annual income statement. With this year's gross sales totaling $250,000, Evans hopes he will end the year with a greater operating profit than last year's $39,800. An examination of the current year's sales records shows that it took 8,450 sales transactions and an average investment in inventory of $88,000 to generate the $250,000 figure. Further examination of various records has provided Evans with the following information: (1) The store opened the year with $48,000 of inventory; (2) the beginning inventory was supplemented throughout the year by net purchases of $112,000; (3) the year ended with an inventory on hand conservatively valued at $36,000; (4) workroom costs of $1,000 were incurred in getting the products ready for sale, and $4,000 was spent on transportation charges in getting the products to the store; and (5) the store earned a $2,000 cash discount by paying for the goods as soon as it received the invoice.

   One figure that greatly disturbed Evans was the $1,100 in goods returned by customers. In addition, he had to make allowances totaling $250 for damaged merchandise. Another major concern is operating expenses. After a concerted effort to control this year's operating expenses, he hopes that a lower expense figure will substantially improve his profit picture. Records kept by natural divisions reveal the following expenses:

Payroll	$26,000
Advertising	3,000
Taxes	1,700
Supplies	900
Services purchased	500
Unclassified	100
Travel	350
Communications	550
Insurance	2,600
Pensions	1,100
Depreciation	1,450
Professional services	3,500
Donations	250
Bad debts	400
Equipment	600
Real-property rentals	36,000

   In addition to these operating expenses, Evans is very concerned about the $2,500 interest payments to the First Republic Bank. Something will have to be done to reduce the principal on that business loan. If nothing else works out, at least the income from the candy machine increased 100 percent, from $75 last year to $150 this year.

   Given the information in the case, lend Evans a hand by developing a complete income statement.

Tactical Cases: Problems and Decisions

■ CASE 6–1
The Lost Weekend: Making a Performance Analysis*

It was late Friday afternoon. Mike Showater had been trying to finish up some work before heading off to the lake for a weekend of rest and relaxation when Art Weiss, V.P. of finance, stopped by Mike's office. With his usual lack of consideration, Art threw down a set of financials and told Mike he expected a complete financial analysis by Monday morning. When Mike inquired about the purpose of the analysis, Art informed him that he had to catch a plane and didn't have time to explain any further. So much for a weekend of fun in the sun!

The financial statements consisted of the basic income statement and balance sheet for two respected apparel retail chains—The Apparel Mart and Status Clothiers. Speculating on the reason for the analysis, Mike wondered if Retail International was on the hunt for a new acquisition; surely it would have more information than one year's financials. Nevertheless, having recently joined Retail International, takeover speculation was not in Mike's job description, but financial analysis was. Who knows—maybe this was just the job to keep from getting bored at the lake. Grabbing the financial statements and his laptop, Mike headed for the door.

ASSIGNMENT

Using the information in Exhibits A and B, assume Mike Showater's responsibilities and conduct a complete finan-

EXHIBIT A
The Apparel Mart financial statement for the year ending January 1, 1992

Income Statement

Gross sales		$123,425,000
− Returns and allowances	$ 700,000	
Net sales		$122,725,000
− Cost of goods sold	$60,872,000	
Gross margin		$ 61,853,000
− Operating expenses	$53,753,000	
Operating profit		$ 8,100,000
+ Other income	$ —	
− Other expenses	117,000	
Net profit		$ 7,983,000

Balance Sheet

Assets		Liabilities and Net Worth	
Current	$52,326,000	Current	$22,873,000
Fixed	$24,174,000	Fixed	$17,748,000
		Net worth	$35,879,000
Total assets	$76,500,000	Total liabilities and net worth	$76,500,000

EXHIBIT B
Status Clothiers financial statement for the year ending January 1, 1992

Income Statement

Gross sales		$33,811,000
− Returns and allowances	$ 820,000	
Net sales		$32,991,000
− Cost of goods sold	$16,463,000	
Gross margin		$16,528,000
− Operating expenses	$14,913,000	
Operating profit		$ 1,615,000
+ Other income	$ 74,000	
− Other expenses	10,000	
Net profit		$ 1,679,000

Balance Sheet

Assets		Liabilities and Net Worth	
Current	$5,527,000	Current	$3,093,000
Fixed	$3,873,000	Fixed	$ 263,000
		Net worth	$6,044,000
Total assets	$9,400,000	Total liabilities and net worth	$9,400,000

cial analysis for The Apparel Mart and Status Clothiers. Compare the performance of the two firms. Given that the purpose of the analysis is not entirely known, be sure to provide a clear interpretation of your findings.

■ CASE 6–2 The Island Shops Franchise: Making a Financial Investment Decision*

*This case was prepared by Dale Lewison and John Thanopoulos, The University of Akron.

CURRENT SITUATION

Penny and Dan Shaheen were listening intently to the presentation being given in their home by a representative of The Island Shops, a chain of franchised clothing outfits in the Midwest that featured casual Hawaiian and safari-style clothing and accessories. The franchise was of the business format type, which meant that it provided not only the right to do business under The Island Shops name but a standardization of store design and operations as well as assistance at some specified level in areas such as management training, accounting, merchandising, site location, and many others. The representative, Debra Long, was here because Penny had called the company after seeing a franchise opportunity ad in a well-known national business publication. The company had set up this initial meeting. Though she had called the firm on little more than a whim, Penny had been considering the idea of leaving her present job and starting her own business for some time. She had read that franchising might be a good choice for achieving this goal, and The Island Shops advertisement had made the opportunity it offered sound quite appealing.

"The fact that you have no retail management experience, Mrs. Shaheen, should not be of concern," said Debra shortly after she began her presentation. "Believe me, our complete training and assistance program will enable you to learn successful operating procedures with little difficulty. That's one of the great advantages of franchising."

Debra went on to explain that becoming an Island Shops store owner, or franchisee, required payment of an initial franchise fee of $60,000 plus the ability to secure an additional $40,000 of capital. On top of that, continuing royalty fees of 3 percent of gross sales were required.

"Our franchise fee is somewhat high for this type of store," Debra conceded, "but that is more than balanced by the low royalty fees we collect." She noted that McDonald's, for instance, charges franchisees an 11.5 percent royalty fee plus another 4 percent for advertising.

As required by Federal Trade Commission law, Debra gave Penny a franchise disclosure statement, or prospectus. This document must give detailed information concerning 20 subjects of interest to potential franchise investors, such as terms of sale, any continuing fees, operating restrictions, and a variety of financial and business figures, including a company balance sheet, income statement, and a statement of changes in financial position. A copy of a sample franchise contract must also be attached. (A selected sample of the information in the

Name of Company: The Island Shops, Inc.
310 Riverside Drive
Rock Island, IL 50432
(242) 555-6812

The Island Shops is a wholly owned subsidiary of Omega, Inc., San Jose, California.

Description of Operations: Franchised and company-owned retail clothing stores. The Island Shops, typically located in shopping malls and plazas, carry an exciting line of Hawaiian and safari-style clothing and accessories for men and women.

Number of Stores: 20 franchise stores and 5 company-owned stores in five states.

Number of Franchises Sold in 1987: 14

In Business Since: 1985

Managerial Assistance Provided: Initial and continuing management assistance in the areas of general retail management, accounting merchandising, site selection, lease negotiations, and advertising is provided for franchisees at company expense.

EXHIBIT A
Disclosure statement as of February 1, 1988

Total revenue (stores, royalties, franchise sales)	$2,912,000
Cost of goods sold	$1,450,000
Income from operations	$1,462,000
Administrative and other expenses	$ 720,000
Net income before taxes	$ 742,000

List of Franchises: 1543 Boucher Blvd.
Indianapolis, IN 49202
(315) 555-9123
Owner: Jim Plezak
(The remaining franchisees were listed)

EXHIBIT B
The Island Shops income statement for year ending 12/31/87

disclosure statement for The Island Shops is provided in Exhibits A and B).

"I know it's a lot to think over," said Debra, "but you'll need to make a decision rather quickly. You are just one of many people we're interviewing, and only one franchise is available in this area. I can give you a week, but after that I'm afraid someone else will snap up this opportunity." She continued, "I've been impressed by our meeting here, however. If you can meet our capital requirements, I can say with near certainty you will be selected as this area's Island Shops franchisee."

Penny had never been to an Island Shops store, but the concept did sound appealing. She had purchased a Hawaiian outfit herself recently and knew that this type of clothing currently was quite popular.

"Let me tell you, these stores are hot," said Debra. "The merchandise really moves. Everybody is interested in this type of clothing now, as some of our other franchisees could tell you. I would suggest if you want to find out more about the stores that you call Jim Huscroft in Toledo or Alice Schaub in Ft. Wayne. They're both fairly typical of our owners and very easy to talk to."

The presentation lasted nearly two hours in total, after which Penny and Dan felt they knew a great deal about both the chain and the opportunity. Debra had been very informative and thorough. Having read a little bit about franchise deals, the Shaheens were pleased about several aspects of the opportunity, including the low royalty payments and Debra's promise that the outlet would have an exclusive territory; that is, no other company stores would be opened in their defined territory during the first five-year contract.

As she was leaving, Debra said, "You know, not many franchisors can advertise in the type of prestigious publication like the one in which you saw our ad. I think that tells you something about our company's commitment to quality." Then she added, "And one more thing—please review our standard contract. I think you'll find it is written quite favorably for franchisees."

After Debra left, Penny and Dan talked things over. The opportunity sounded great, but it was an awfully big decision to make in a short time. Penny was unhappy with her insurance job, though as a district manager for claims adjustment she was earning nearly $40,000 per year. But her job dissatisfaction, combined with her long-standing desire to own her own retail clothing business, made the offer attractive. The Shaheens decided they could raise the capital required without too much strain and that if the store were successful their return on the investment would be substantial. Nevertheless, both agreed that they had a lot to think over and do in the next week before making a decision.

ASSIGNMENT

1. If you were Penny Shaheen, what steps would you take to help you make your decision? Outline a plan, including what you would do and why, for making a franchise investigation and investment decision.
2. Critique the proposal and presentation given by Debra Long and The Island Shops from an investor's perspective. Are there any actions, evidence, or statements that you feel are misleading or otherwise a cause for concern?

*This case was prepared by Dan Gilmore, The University of Akron.

ENDNOTES

1. Based on P. "Rajan" Varadarajan, "Pathways to Corporate Excellence in Retailing," *Retailing Issues Letter* (Published by Arthur Andersen & Co. in conjunction with the Center for Retailing Studies, Texas A&M University, February 1989), 1–3.

2. See David P. Schulz, "NRMA's New 1988 MOR," *Stores,* December 1989, 31.
3. See "Mercantile Most Profitable," *Stores,* July 1989, 17.
4. See Norman M. Scarborough and Thomas W. Zimmerer, *Effective Small Business Management* (Columbus, Ohio: Merrill, 1988), 170.
5. Ibid., 171.
6. Robert F. Lusch, *Management of Retail Enterprises* (Boston: Kent, 1982), 25.
7. Nathan Katz, "12 Keys to Effective Expense Control," *Retail Control,* February 1987, 11–21.

PART II

ORGANIZATION MANAGEMENT

Organizing and Staffing the Retail Firm

CHAPTER 7

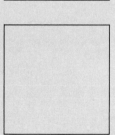

OUTLINE

OBJECTIVES

- Develop organizational objectives that will provide a focus for the structure and activities of the retail firm.
- Identify the organizational tasks necessary to realize the firm's organizational objectives.
- Explain the basic principles of organization that are an inherent part of any effective retail structure.
- Distinguish among the organizational patterns of various types of retailers.
- Write a job description and develop specifications for each position.
- Identify potential sources of store employees and describe the criteria and methods for screening job applicants.
- Understand and use the basic techniques for matching job requirements with employee attributes.
- Specify the procedures used in training and supervising store personnel.
- Discuss when to evaluate, what to evaluate, and how to evaluate employees and their performances.
- Evaluate the various methods used in compensating store personnel.

CORPORATE CULTURE: WHAT IS IT?

A company's culture is almost as obvious to its customers—and to its competitors—as the merchandise on its selling floors. It is most obviously displayed by the behavior of salespeople in their face-to-face contacts with customers. Often it's the little things that matter in the treatment of customers—an employee's smile, for example—and the treatment of employees—a manager's smile—that make a big difference in a company's culture and its effectiveness.

One company that most consistently communicated its culture is the Dayton Hudson Corp. Management has even collected all its thoughts on the subject into a book, *Management Prospectives,* and makes a copy of the executive summary available to all employees.

This summary includes the company's mission statement, which begins, "We are in business to please our customers." It goes on to explain that the company does this by emphasizing value, by having the most wanted merchandise in stock, in depth, and "by giving them a total shopping experience that meets their expectations for service, convenience, environment, and ethical standards."

Other key sections in the summary include an introduction to the business itself; an explanation of the corporation's commitment to serving society; the corporation's belief in "making the difference with people"; descriptions of the positioning, managing, and governing of the business; how the business is operated and merchandised (including use of "trend merchandising" to identify where the customer's emphasis is and how it is changing); how business performance is measured; how the balance sheet is managed; and how the company communicates with the public—its customers.[1]

It is people who make a successful business! However, organization is essential to any group with a common purpose or goal; organization is the binding force that coordinates, channels, and propels the group toward its stated mission. Retailers use a vast number of organizational structures to organize their people. All retailing organizations, however, incorporate certain organizational elements and principles structured around one of several basic organizational forms. In this chapter, we examine these organizational elements, principles, and forms and the general organizational patterns that small, independent retailers, department store retailers, and chain store retailers use in organizing groups of people. In addition, we look at the retailer's staffing process. Figure 7–1 illustrates the issues of retail organization and the eight steps of the retail staffing process.

ELEMENTS OF RETAIL ORGANIZATION

The particular organizational foundation a retail firm adopts depends on several factors, including (1) the type of merchandise to be offered, (2) the variety and assortment of merchandise stocked, (3) the type and number of customer services performed, (4) the type and number of locations used, (5) the availability and quality of personnel employed, and (6) the legal requirements and/or restrictions. Given this vast array of influential factors, the firm's organization must center around specific organizational objectives and tasks.

Organizational Objectives

In retailing, the firm's organizational foundation focuses on achieving the firm's objectives. Establishing well-defined organizational objectives is an important step,

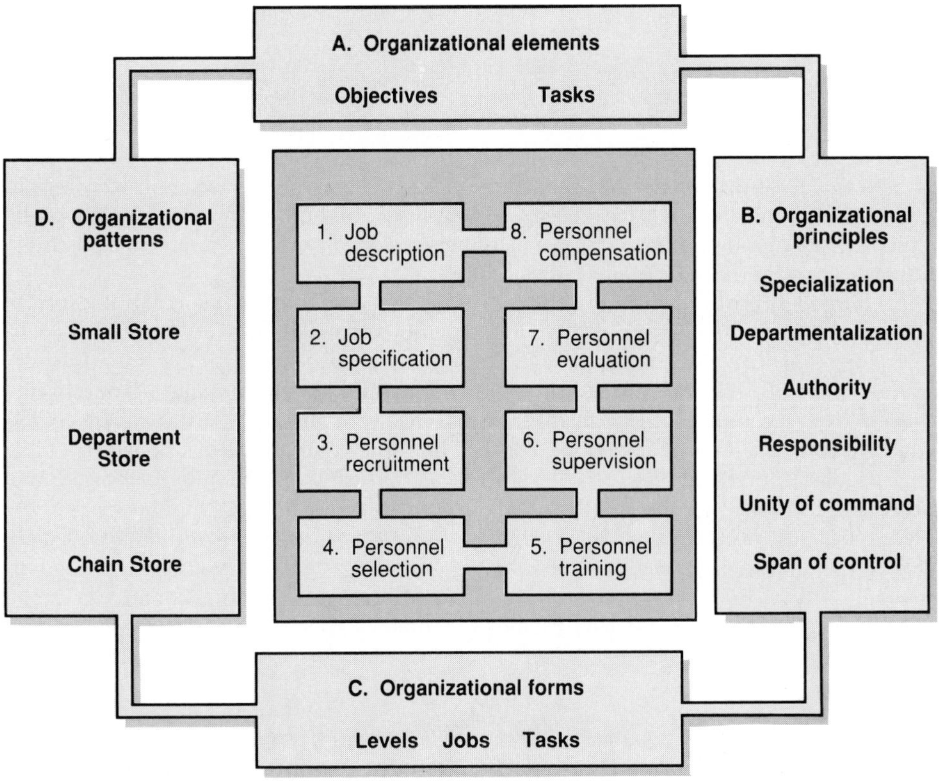

FIGURE 7–1
The organizational and human resource components of the retailing plan

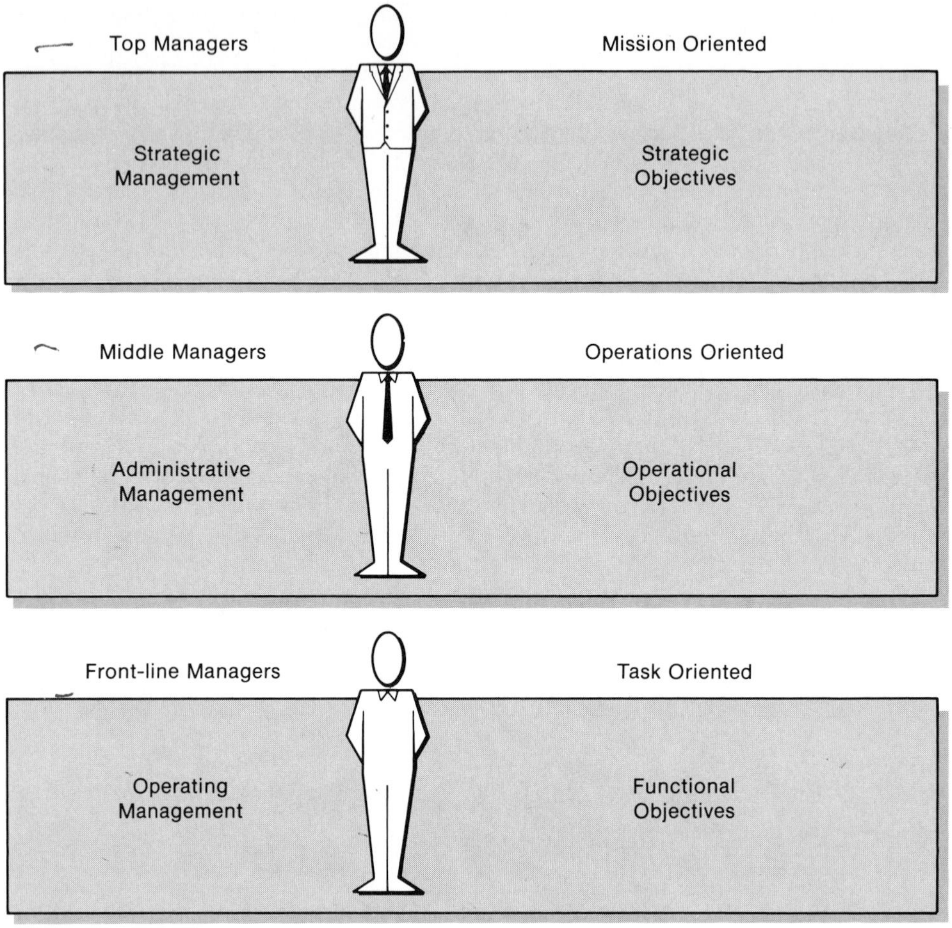

FIGURE 7–2
Managerial levels and organizational objectives

because it forces the retailer to think through what it is trying to accomplish, where it is going, and how it intends to get there. In addition, organizational objectives provide a realistic orientation for the retailer's planning process as well as a means of evaluating the firm's past performance and current status.

Three levels of organizational objectives correspond to the three general levels of retail management (see Figure 7–2). **Strategic objectives** are general, long-term goals that the retail firm intends to pursue. Essentially a strategic objective identifies an overall mission that the firm's management wishes to accomplish. **Operational objectives** are general, long-term operational requirements necessary for achieving a strategic objective. Operational objectives establish the general framework within which a particular merchandising or operating function can be identified. **Functional objectives** are specific task objectives that identify a specific function and how it is to be accomplished. The unique value of functional objectives is their quantifiability, which makes them especially useful in planning, executing, and controlling a particular retailing activity. Figure 7–3 provides examples of strategic, operational, and functional objectives for an upscale specialty retailer of women's apparel.

Organizational Tasks

In developing the retail organization, the retailer must identify and assign the various tasks necessary for realizing its stated organizational objectives. Figure 7–4 lists the

Strategic Objectives	Operational Objectives	Functional Objectives
To appeal to the "perfectionist," the "updated," the "traditionalist," and the "establishment" consumer	To offer the "perfectionist" consumer the most advanced fashion apparel	To ensure the "perfectionist" consumer a new and fresh selection of fashionables by stocking only one garment in each size category (e.g., Misses 4–14) and by timing new arrivals every week
	To offer the "updated" consumer new styles that have gained wide acceptance	To ensure the "updated" consumer stylish yet not extreme fashion apparel by stocking a limited selection of last season's perfectionist styles in Misses sizes 4–16
	To offer the "traditionalist" and the "establishment" consumer well-established yet fashionable apparel	To ensure the "traditionalist" and "establishment" consumer a complete selection of stylish yet dignified fashion apparel by stocking a representative offering of well-established designer labels in Misses sizes 8–20

FIGURE 7–3
Examples of organizational objectives

basic organizational tasks inherent in any retail organization. Although this list can help a retailer develop a general organizational structure, a more detailed description of tasks is necessary for assigning responsibilities and authority to each position in the organization.

PRINCIPLES OF RETAIL ORGANIZATION

There are several basic principles of organization that every retailer should consider in establishing a retail organization. Organizational principles that are particularly appropriate to the retail firm are specialization and departmentalization, lines of authority and responsibility, unity of command, and span of control.

Specialization and Departmentalization

Specialization and departmentalization are inherent parts of any efficient retail organizational structure. With job **specialization,** employees concentrate their efforts on a limited number of tasks. Retailers have learned that specialization improves the speed and quality of employee performance.

Departmentalization, an extension of the specialization principle, occurs when tasks and employees are grouped into departments to achieve the operating efficiencies of specialization for a group performing similar tasks. Specialization and departmentalization can be based on *product type* (e.g., apparel, home furnishings, and appliances), *activity* (buying, selling, and stocking), *activity location* (main store, branch store, and warehouse), and *consumer type* (household consumer and business customers). In choosing which of these bases to use in departmentalizing the store, the retailer should select the one that will give management the highest level of control and produce the highest employee efficiency.

FIGURE 7–4
Basic organizational tasks

1. **Operating the store**
   a. Recruiting store personnel
   b. Training store personnel
   c. Supervising store personnel
   d. Planning information systems
   e. Meeting legal obligations
   f. Designing store facilities
   g. Maintaining store facilities
   h. Ensuring store security

2. **Finding the best location**
   a. Analyzing regional markets
   b. Assessing trading areas
   c. Appraising site locations

3. **Developing the merchandise mix**
   a. Determining consumer product needs
   b. Evaluating product alternatives
   c. Planning product-mix strategies
   d. Determining consumer-service requirements
   e. Evaluating service alternatives
   f. Planning service-mix levels

4. **Buying the merchandise**
   a. Identifying sources of supply
   b. Contacting sources of supply
   c. Evaluating sources of supply
   d. Negotiating with sources of supply

5. **Procuring the merchandise**
   a. Ordering merchandise
   b. Receiving merchandise
   c. Checking merchandise
   d. Marking merchandise
   e. Stocking merchandise

6. **Controlling the merchandise**
   a. Planning sales
   b. Planning stocks
   c. Planning reductions
   d. Planning purchases
   e. Planning markups
   f. Planning margins
   g. Controlling inventories
   h. Taking inventory
   i. Valuating inventory
   j. Evaluating inventory

7. **Pricing the merchandise**
   a. Setting prices
   b. Adjusting prices

8. **Promoting the merchandise**
   a. Planning advertising strategies
   b. Selecting advertising media
   c. Preparing advertisements
   d. Designing promotional displays
   e. Planning promotional events
   f. Gaining favorable publicity
   g. Managing the personal-selling effort

Authority and Responsibility

Lines of authority and **lines of responsibility** are the organizational principle that each store employee (managerial and nonmanagerial) should receive the authority to accomplish whatever responsibilities have been assigned to that individual. Figure 7–5 demonstrates the relationship between the responsibilities and the authority of a sales manager whose general charge is to direct the customer service, personnel, sales, merchandising, and operations activities of a department to achieve sales goals and maximize profit. To assume certain responsibilities and accomplish them most efficiently, an employee must receive sufficient authority to call on whatever resources are necessary to complete the task.

An equally important aspect of this principle is that all members of the organization must know and respect the established lines of authority and responsibility. A retailer's "chain of command" comprises lines of authority that link the various managerial levels of the organization. Line and staff relationships are the linkages that join management levels and create organizational hierarchies.

Line relationships are affiliations among managers at different organizational levels or between a manager and a subordinate within the same level who are directly

Department Sales Manager's Responsibilities	*Equals*	Department Sales Manager's Authority
1. to ensure that the store's customer service standards and policies are maintained		1. to direct customer service standards and procedures; make customer adjustments
2. to provide (ensure) adequate floor coverage while controlling personnel budgets		2. to assign personnel within area; prepare weekly personnel schedule; request additional personnel
3. to ensure that the physical appearance of the area is visually appealing and orderly		3. to determine the merchandising set-up of area; request the removal or addition of fixtures; request and followup maintenance services
4. to communicate selling trends and other merchandise information to merchants and associates		4. to request sales and merchandising information; analyze current reports and information
5. to supervise the receipt, movement, maintenace, and display of merchandise on the selling floor and in the stockroom area		5. to determine merchandising set-up of selling-floor area; coordinate merchandising set-up of stockroom area; maintain a merchandise-movement information file
6. to ensure that advertised merchandise is available and properly priced, ticketed, and displayed		6. to communicate information about advertised merchandise to Central Stock, Receiving, and/or the merchandising staff; make necessary price and/or ticket changes
7. to shop the competition		7. to visit the competition to determine competitive pricing; communicate and/or adjust price changes for competition
8. to lead, delegate, control, discipline, and train associate employees		8. to establish, monitor, and appraise selling personnel on standards of performance; enforce store policies and procedures; communicate all information pertinent to the department operation
9. to maintain inventory control		9. to inspect and approve all paperwork within area; ensure that adjustments are properly recorded

FIGURE 7–5
Authority should equal responsibility

responsible for achieving the firm's strategic, operational, and/or functional objectives. In a line relationship, the manager has direct authority over the subordinate. On an organizational chart, line relationships typically are shown as solid lines.

Staff relationships are advisory or supportive and appear on organizational charts as broken lines. Staff employees typically are specialists with expertise in a particular area (e.g., legal affairs, taxation, or market analysis), and their primary function is to assist line managers in realizing their objectives. To avoid confusion, duplication of effort, and territorial disputes, an organization needs to clearly distinguish the responsibilities and authority of each line manager and supportive staff. To gain more control and efficiency, Sears is in the process of shortening lines of authority; its massive field organization will be under the control of headquarters for the first time in decades.[2]

Unity of Command

The principle of **unity of command** states that the organizational structure of the retail firm should ensure that each store employee is directly accountable to only one immediate supervisor at any one time for any given task. Most employees find it difficult, if not impossible, to satisfy several superiors at the same time. It is not unusual for different supervisors to want subordinates to accomplish a particular task in a different way at a different time. The store employee who must serve several "masters" at one time often is confused, inefficient, and frustrated.

Span of Control

Every organization must determine how many subordinates one person can manage. One rule of thumb suggested by authorities on management is that the ideal number of subordinates ranges from four at the highest levels to twelve at the lowest levels of the organization. The principle of **span of control** sets guidelines for the number of subordinates a superior should control, depending on the level within the organization and the nature of the tasks being performed. Three of the guidelines follow:

1. As employees' tasks become more complex and unstandardized, their supervisor's span of control should narrow.
2. Where supervisors and employees are highly competent and well trained, the supervisor's span of control can be broader.
3. Where tasks are highly centralized in one location, a person can supervise more subordinates than if the tasks are scattered throughout a location.

These guidelines suggest the latitudes within which organizers vary the "4–12" rule for supervisors. In retailing, these guidelines can help determine the size of the various merchandising and operating departments and divisions.

FORMS OF RETAIL ORGANIZATION

The organizational structure of the retail firm can assume many forms. To help employees understand the organizational structure, the retailer prepares organizational charts that show the formal relationships among various parts of the organization. Organizational charts also describe the hierarchy of authority, the areas of responsibility, the span of control, the type and degree of specialization and departmentalization, and the reporting relationships among employees at different levels.

In planning an organizational structure, the retailer must ask two critical questions: (1) how many organizational *levels* are needed for effective and efficient operation of the firm and (2) how the various tasks should be organized into *areas of responsibility* (jobs) and how many of these areas should be designated.

Number of Organizational Levels

The number of levels separating the firm's top manager from its lowest-level employee can be viewed as a hierarchy of organizational levels. Firms that limit the number of organizational levels to one or two are using a **flat organizational structure**, as Figure 7–6a illustrates. Small, independent retailers and low-margin retailers attempting to keep their operating expenses at the lowest possible level typically use a flat organizational structure. In addition to lower operating expenses, the flat organizational structure fosters direct communication with employees, higher employee morale, and quicker reaction time to problems that arise. However, this structure often is wide, meaning that the supervisor may have too many people to manage at one time.

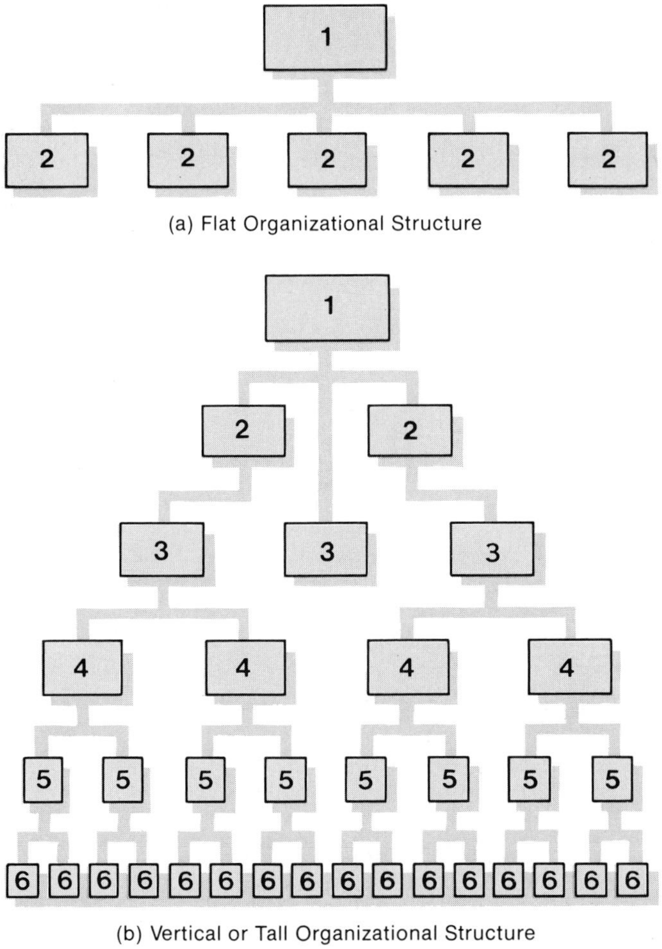

FIGURE 7–6
Number of organizational levels

Vertical, or **tall**, **organizational structures** have many layers of supervisor-subordinate relationships. As Figure 7–6b shows, a large number of levels separate top management from employees at the bottom of the organization. Large retailers (e.g., department stores) and multiunit retailers (e.g., chain stores) typically use a taller organizational structure. The impersonal nature, lack of direct communications, and rigidity associated with a large number of organizational levels are the primary limitations of this type of structure. These limitations may be offset by the benefits of having well-defined areas of responsibility and gaining increased supervision over employees and their assigned tasks.

Job and Task Organization

The exact form of organizational structure for any retailer depends on how the retailer classifies jobs that employees must perform. A retailer can classify jobs on the basis of their functional nature, geographic location, product involvement, or some combination of the three.

With the **functional approach** to retail organizational structure, the retailer groups tasks and classifies jobs according to functional areas such as store operations,

RETAIL STRATEGIES AND TACTICS

The Inverted Organization: Creating a Customer Service Perspective

By all accounts, customer service will be a cornerstone of any successful merchandising strategy in the 1990s. To fully support their customer service philosophy, retailers that have a reputation for superior service are viewing their organizations as an inverted pyramid.

At the top of the organizational pyramid are the stores' sales associates and their support staff. If customer needs and expectations are to be met, the entire organization must be dedicated to supporting the customer-satisfying activities of the sales associates. By developing an organizational structure in which each management level supports the next level and everyone supports front-line salespeople, the retail organization truly becomes "customer focused" and a practitioner of the marketing concept. The superior customer service reputation of Nordstrom, Inc., the Seattle-based retailer, is based in part on the firm's inverted organizational chart.

buying and selling merchandise, promotional activities, or recruiting and training store personnel. Small, independent retailers usually have a two-function organizational structure, which limits specialization. As Figure 7–7a illustrates, merchandising and store operations are the first two functional divisions that retailers usually create. As their firms become larger and more complex, retailers create additional functional divisions. In the three-function organizational structure, shown in Figure 7–7b, retailers add a third division to the basic merchandising and operating divisions, typically one of the following: a financial controls division, a sales promotion division, or a personnel division. Figure 7–7 illustrates only the two- and three-function organization, but many retailers create four, five, or more functional divisions. (Four- and five-function organizations are illustrated and discussed in a later section).

With the **geographic approach** to organizational structure, the retailer organizes tasks and assigns jobs on the basis of where those tasks and jobs are performed. Multiunit retailers, such as chain stores, frequently use the geographic approach. The geographic size of the retailer's market influences both the number of organizational levels and the degree of market specialization at each level. A multiunit retailer with a

FIGURE 7–7
Functional organizational structures

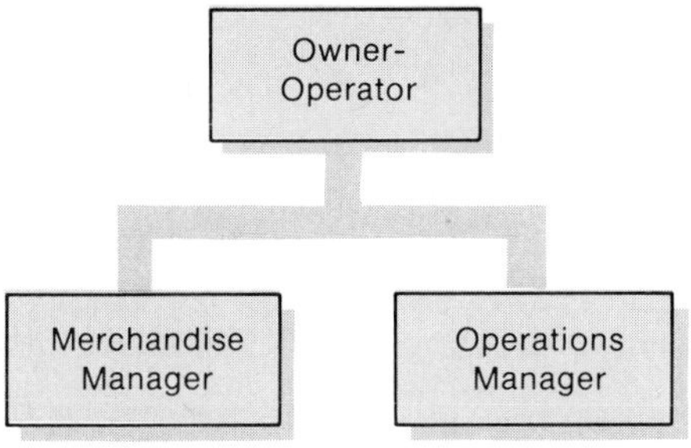

(a) The Two-Functional Organization

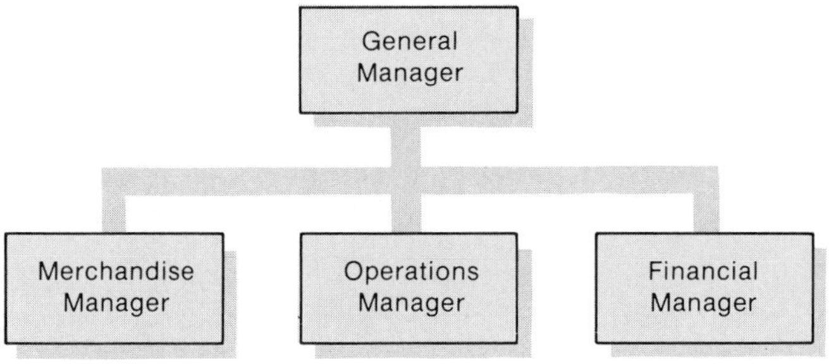

(b) The Three-Functional Organization

limited number of stores within a concentrated geographic market usually has only two levels (the main store and several branch stores) and a local market specialization (neighborhood or community). On the other hand, large chain organizations with many stores operating nationwide typically form organizational structures with several levels and degrees of market specialization. Figure 7–8 illustrates a national retail firm that uses the geographic approach to organization.

With the **product approach** to retail organizational structure, the retailer organizes the store by product line. This organizational form centers around task and job specialization to meet consumers' buying needs for certain products. For many shopping and specialty goods, for example, consumers think, shop, and buy in terms of product groupings. Figure 7–9 illustrates a family apparel store organized around the general product lines of women's, men's, and children's apparel and accessories.

PATTERNS OF RETAIL ORGANIZATION

Over the years, various retail organizational patterns have emerged as the result of the diverse sizes and natures of firms. To characterize these patterns, we will look at the organizational structures of small, independent retailers, department store retailers, and chain store retailers.

Small Store Organization

Many retailers began business as one-person, owner-operator shops. In these cases, the owner-operator *was* the organization. As such, the individual had the responsibility and authority for all organizational tasks. As the firm grew, the owner-operator hired additional store personnel to handle the increasing number of complex tasks that accompany a larger, more formal organizational structure.

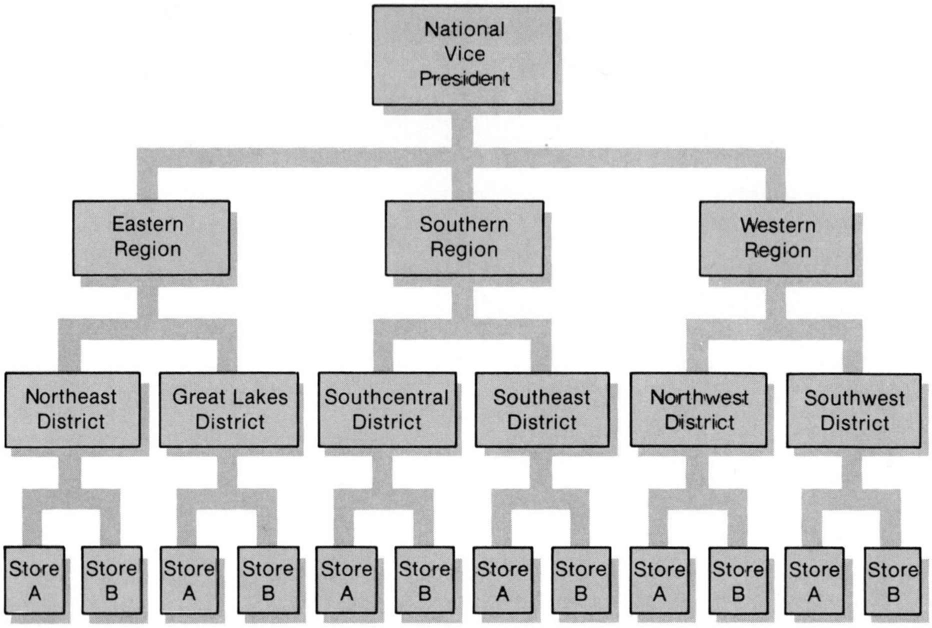

FIGURE 7–8
Geographic organization structure

The typical organizational structure of the small, independent retailer previously was characterized as flat, typically with two levels and a general organization and a limited amount of specialization. As Figure 7–10 illustrates, the owner-manager develops store and personnel policies; administers expense, sales, and merchandising budgets; and oversees accounting and other control procedures. Also illustrated in Figure 7–10 are the two most common functional divisions that small retailers use: the merchandising and operations divisions.

Department Store Organization

Department store organizations are more formal and complex than small retailers'. As mentioned earlier, the organizational structure of department stores is taller and more specialized than that of small retail stores. To understand department store organization, we will examine the Mazur plan of retail organization and its functional and geographic modifications.

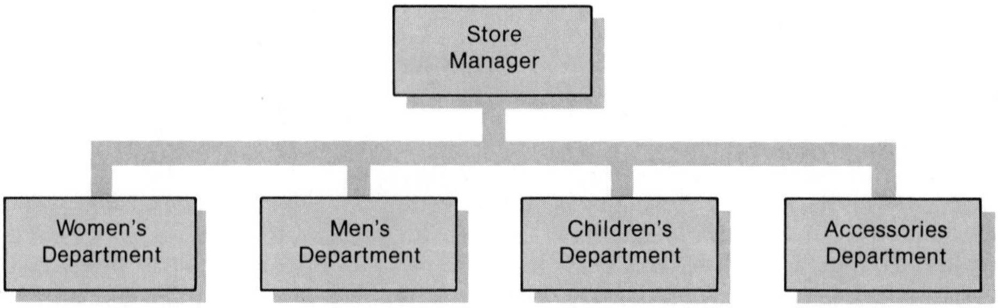

FIGURE 7–9
Product organization structure

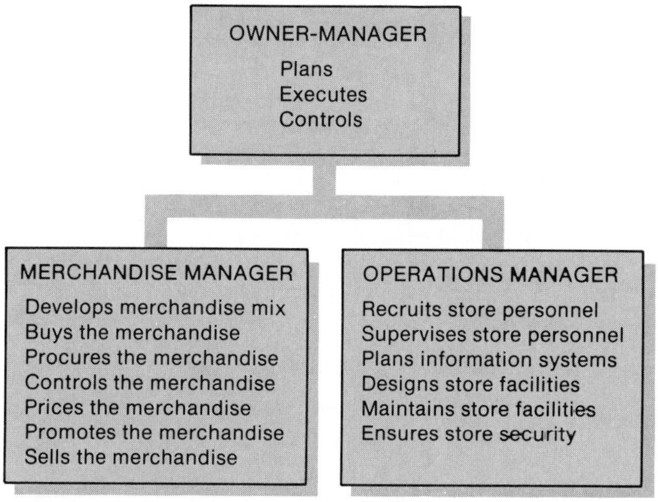

FIGURE 7–10
Small, independent retail organization

The Mazur Plan

Most retailing experts date modern retail organizational structures from 1927, when an investment banker named Paul Mazur introduced his ideas on how to structure a retail store.[3] The **Mazur plan** divides the retail organization into four functional divisions: finance, merchandising, promotion, and operations. Each division manager has specific responsibilities (see Figure 7–11). The *finance manager's* chief responsibilities are to control the firm's assets and to ensure that sufficient working capital is available for each of the firm's functional divisions. The *general merchandising manager* is responsible primarily for supervising the firm's buying and selling activities. The *promotions manager* is responsible for directing the firm's persuasive communications to consumers. Specifically, the promotions manager oversees all advertising, sales promotion activities (e.g., fashion shows, demonstrations), interior and window displays,

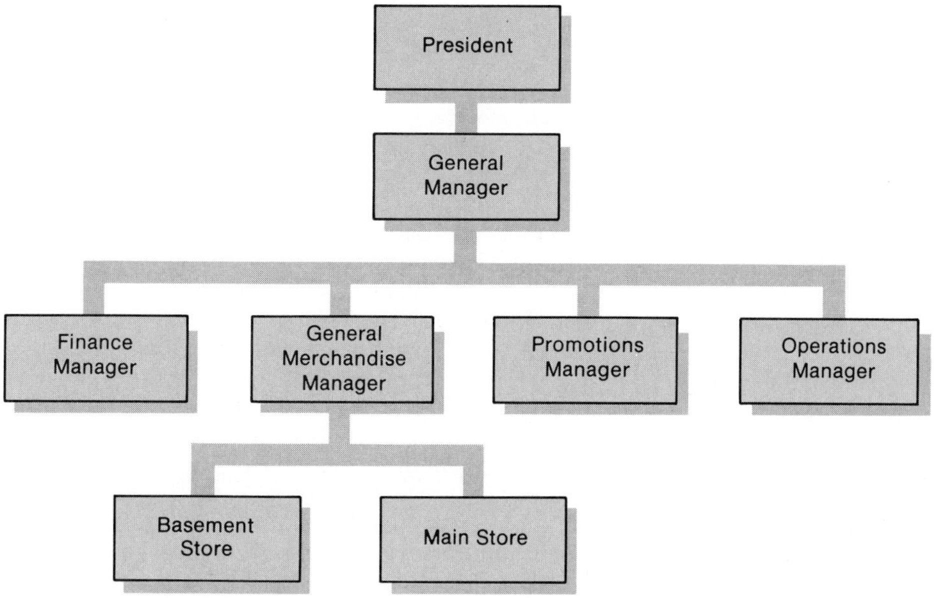

FIGURE 7–11
The Mazur plan for department store organization

public relations, and publicity. The *operations manager* generally is responsible for all the physical operations of the store that are not directly assigned to one of the other divisions. Major tasks include facilities development and maintenance; customer services and assistance; receiving, checking, marking, and stocking of incoming merchandise; store security; and general store housekeeping.

Functional Modifications. The two most common functional modifications in the Mazur plan are (1) changing the number of functional divisions and (2) separating the buying and selling functions. In changing the Mazur plan, department stores most often create a five-function organization by establishing a personnel division equal in status to the other four divisions. Other functional activities that retailers might consider for separate divisional status are distribution, real estate and construction, and catalog operations.

According to the Mazur plan, both the buying and selling functions fall under the direct supervision of the general merchandise manager. Some retailing experts argue, however, that these functions should be separated. Proponents of separation believe that (1) buying and selling require different skills, talents, and training; (2) selling activities suffer because buying takes up a considerable amount of the buyer's time spent away from the store; (3) feedback on consumer needs can be handled better by a well-developed and maintained merchandise control system; (4) greater flexibility in the use of sales and buying personnel is possible when these individuals specialize in either selling or buying activities; and (5) in-store grouping of merchandise should be based on selling, not buying, activities. Those who argue against separation of buying and selling activities, however, hold that (1) the buyer must have direct contact with customers to determine their needs; (2) if the individuals who buy the merchandise are responsible for selling it, they will exercise greater care in buying activities; and (3) it is easier to assign responsibility for the department's profit performance if buying and selling are conducted by the same person, because the buyer cannot blame the seller for not putting out the necessary selling effort and the seller cannot blame the lack of a good profit performance on buying mistakes. Both sides of the issue offer valid arguments.

Geographic Modifications. When department stores began to branch out into other geographic areas, they necessitated several additional changes in the basic Mazur plan.[4] These new geographically based organizational arrangements were the main-store approach, the separate-store approach, and the equal-store approach.

With the **main-store approach** to branch organization, the parent organization (the main store) exercises control over branch stores. As Figure 7–12 illustrates, main-store managers of finance, general merchandise, promotion, and operations are responsible for supervising the same functions in the branch stores as at the main store. Under this organizational plan, main-store buyers and their assistants are responsible for securing merchandise for the main store and all branches. Sales activities in the main store are under the direct supervision of buyers, while those in all branch stores are the responsibility of branch sales managers. Used by department stores in the initial stages of expansion, the main-store approach is most appropriate when (1) there are only a few branches; (2) customer preferences and the merchandise mix are fairly similar for the main and branch stores; (3) branch stores are located near the main store; and (4) main-store management and supporting staff can comfortably supervise branches without overextending themselves.

The **separate-store approach** to branch department store organization treats each branch as an independent operation with its own organizational structure of managers, buyers, and sales personnel. Under this plan, branch-store management assumes both the merchandising responsibilities of buying and selling and the routine responsibilities

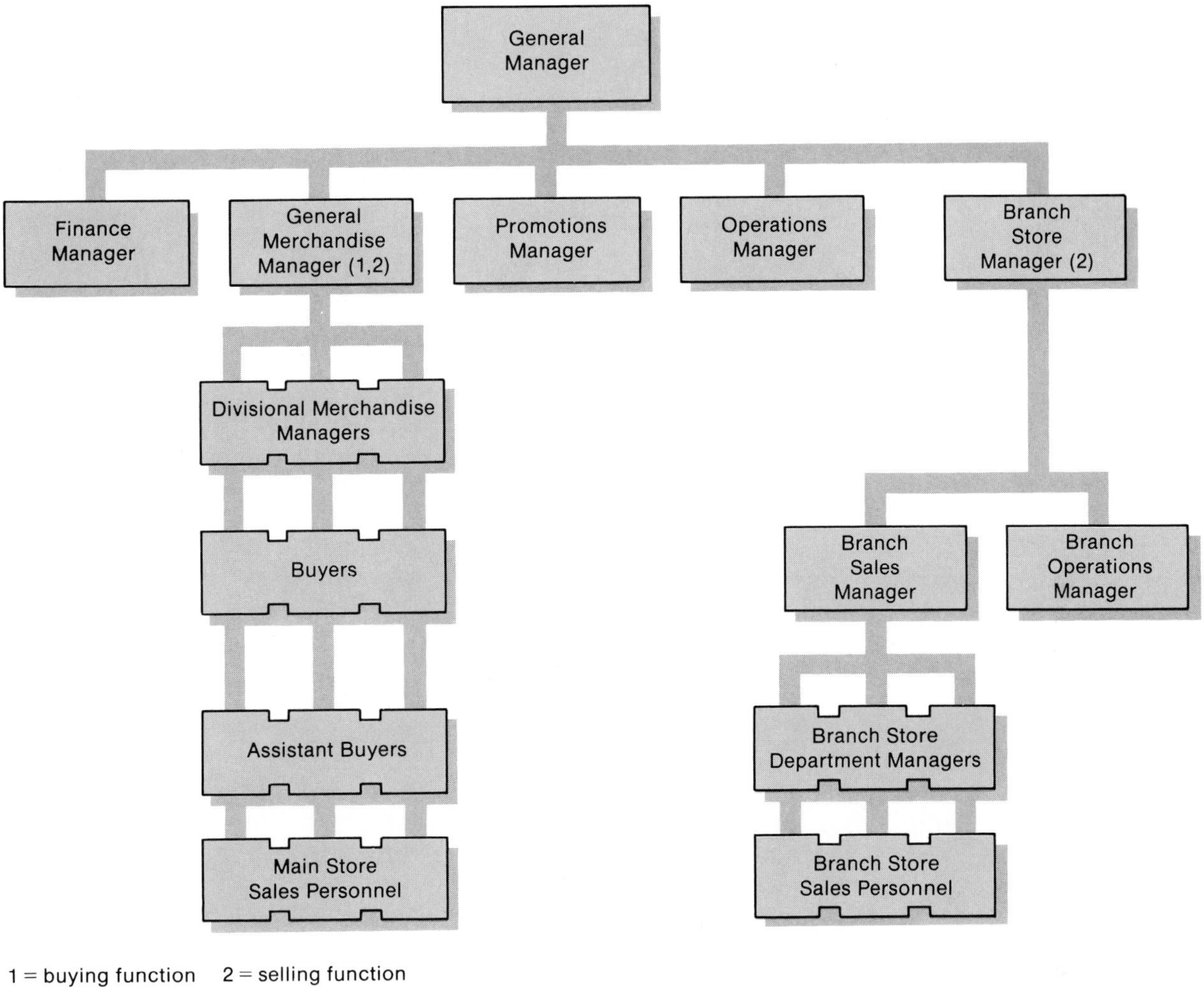

FIGURE 7–12
The main-store approach to branch department store organization

of operating the branch store. As Figure 7–13 shows, each branch has its own store manager as well as personnel, merchandise, and operations managers, who operate separately from the parent organization. Although the parent organization has little direct involvement in the day-to-day operations of the branch store, it does have the general responsibilities of serving in an advisory and policy making capacity.

The separate-store approach generally is used by department stores that have four to seven branches approximately the size of the main store. The major advantage of this approach is that each branch has great flexibility in tailoring its merchandise and operations to meet the needs of its local clientele. The principal disadvantages are (1) a loss in economies of scale in buying; (2) an increase in operating costs because of additional management and staff needs; (3) increased difficulties in maintaining a consistent image from store to store; and (4) increased problems of coordination (e.g., stock transfers, promotion activities).

The **equal-store approach** (see Figure 7–14) emphasizes centralization of authority and responsibility. Under the equal-store plan, all major managerial functions are controlled from a central headquarters. The finance, merchandise, promotions, and operations functions are under the direct supervision of headquarters managers. This approach has two unique features. First, the buying and selling functions are separated;

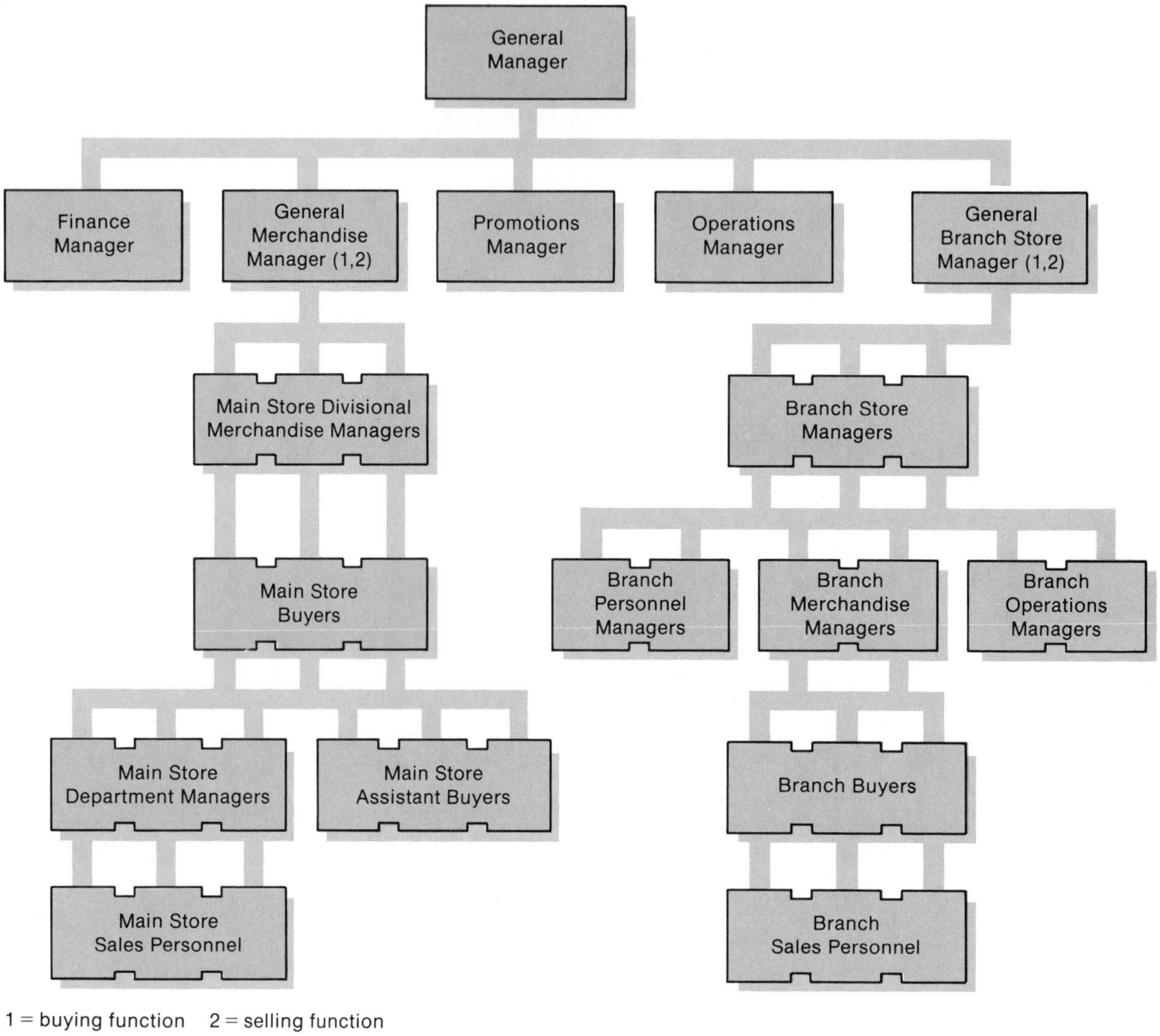

FIGURE 7–13
Separate-store approach to branch department store organization

the buying function remains a centralized activity under the general merchandise manager, and the selling function becomes a decentralized activity under the store manager. Second, all stores (main and branches) are treated equally as basic sales units. The equal-store plan attempts to combine the advantages of centralized buying (economies of scale) with the advantages of localized selling (target-market selling).

Chain Store Organization

Chain store organizations vary considerably in size, geographic spread, local markets, product mix, and number of operating units. Although all of these factors influence how a chain store will organize, three distinctive elements characterize all chain store organizations: centralization, specialization, and standardization.

Centralization is the concentration of policy and decision making in one location, called either *central headquarters* or the *home office*. Within the chain store organizational structure, the authority and responsibility for most operating and

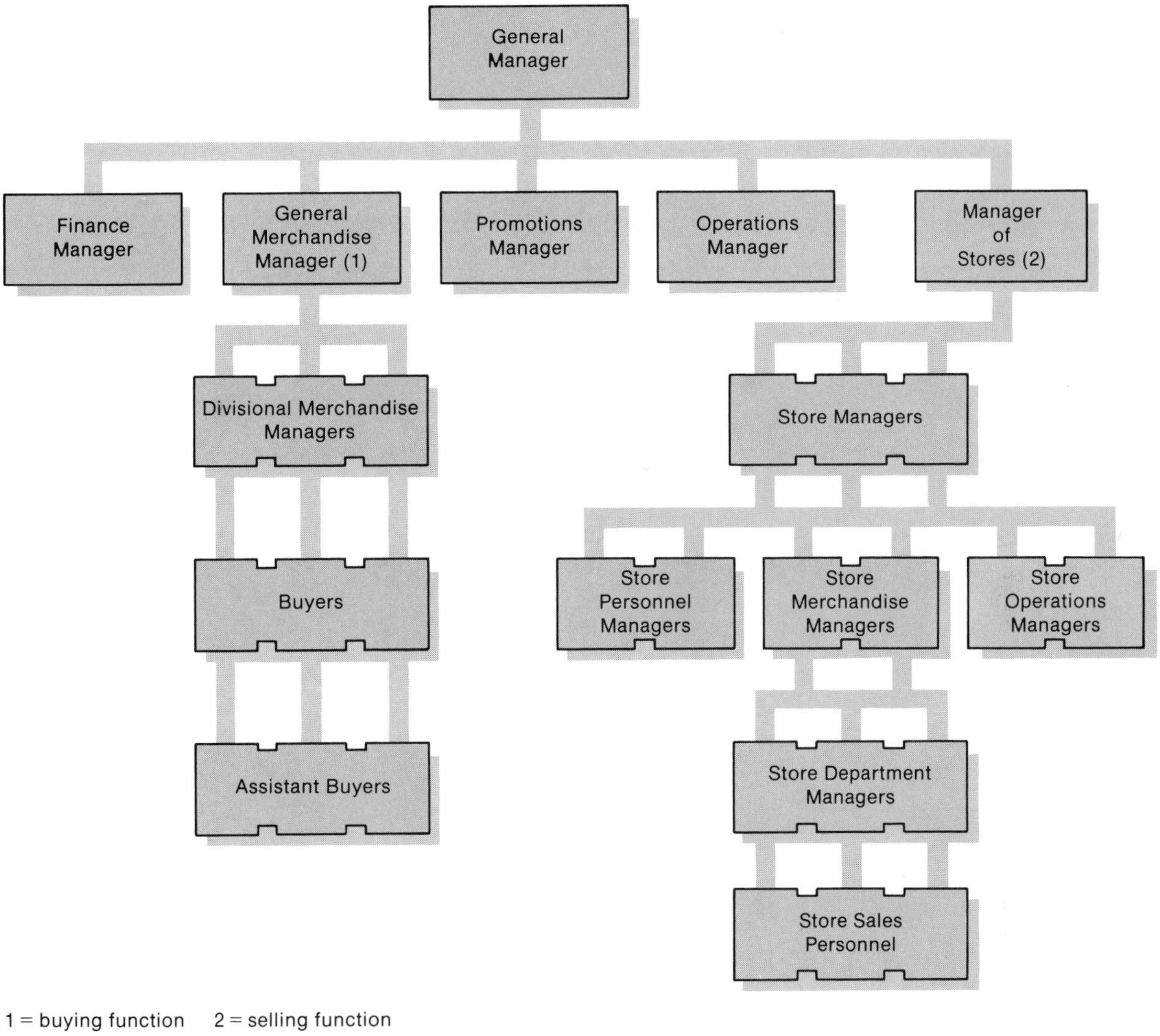

FIGURE 7–14
Equal-store approach to branch department store organization

merchandising functions are assigned to home office management personnel. The primary exception is sales, which are under the decentralized control of local management. In recent years chain store organizations have tended to adopt limited decentralization. Thus, more and more functional authority and responsibility are being given to regional and divisional levels of the organization. The main reason behind this change is the gigantic size of many chain store retailers (see Figure 7–15).

A high degree of **specialization** is another distinguishing feature of chain store organizations. Typically the chain store incorporates a greater number of functional divisions in its organizational structure. In addition to the four basic functional divisions of finance, merchandising, operations, and promotions, many chain stores include one or more of the following functional divisions: distribution (traffic and warehousing), marketing, real estate and construction, personnel, and industrial relations. Some large chains also specialize geographically.

The third distinguishing feature of chain organizations is a high degree of **standardization**, or similarities between the operating and merchandising operations of

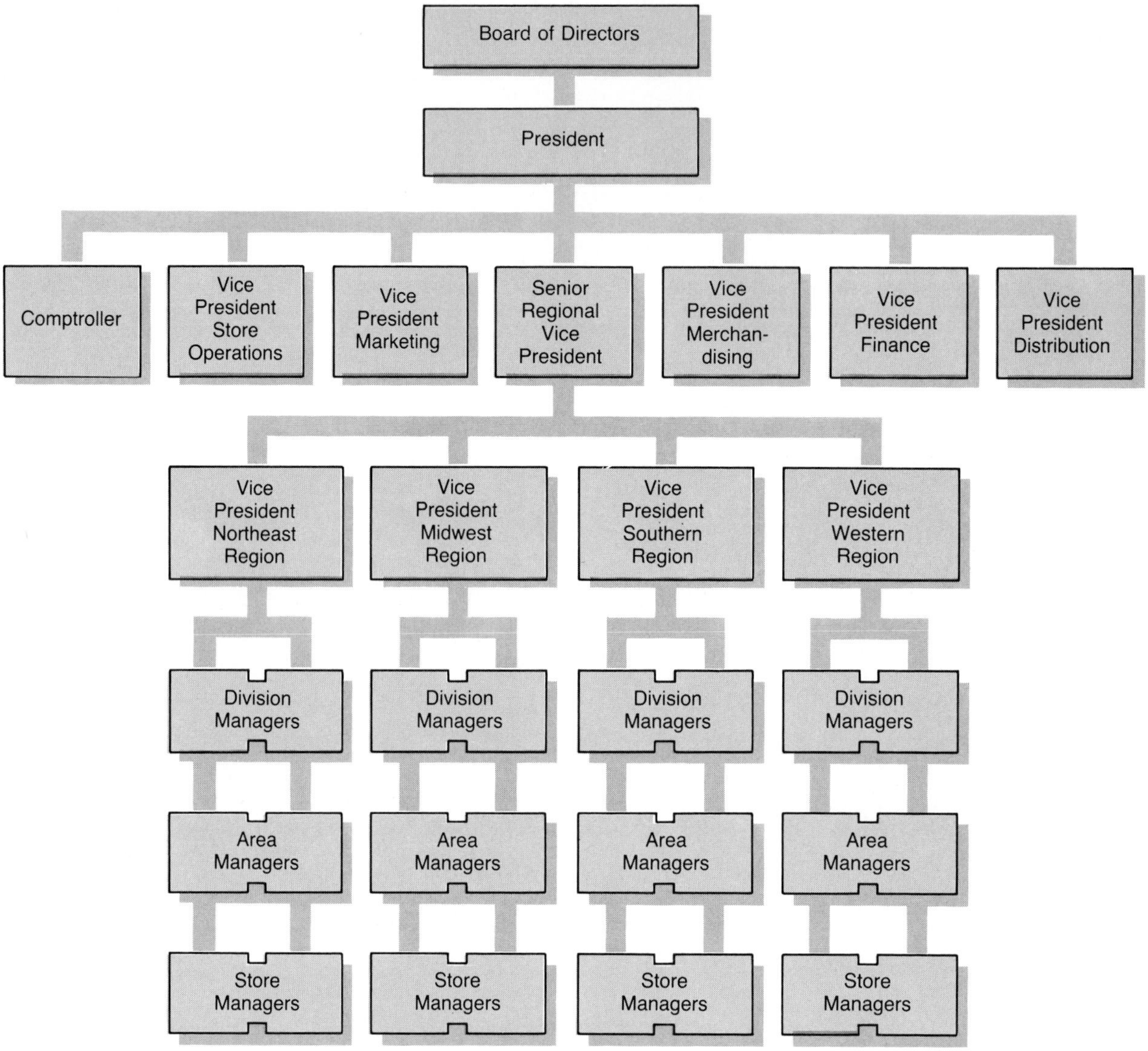

FIGURE 7–15
Chain store organization

the business. To support standardization, chain store management establishes an elaborate system of supervision and control mechanisms to keep themselves fully informed. Through standardization, the chain projects a consistent company image and minimizes the total costs of doing business.

Having examined the issues surrounding the organization of the retailer's human resources, let's turn to the process of staffing the retail firm. Figure 7–16 illustrates the eight steps of the staffing process. A shortage of qualified people will be one of the biggest problems that retailers will have to overcome during the 1990s.[5] One writer notes, "Recent waves of immigration, coupled with faster population growth in certain minority components of our society, have resulted in a pool of potential retail employees who are culturally different from their predecessors and a majority of retail customers. . . . These are the people who now form a large population or available workers at prices retailer can pay."[6]

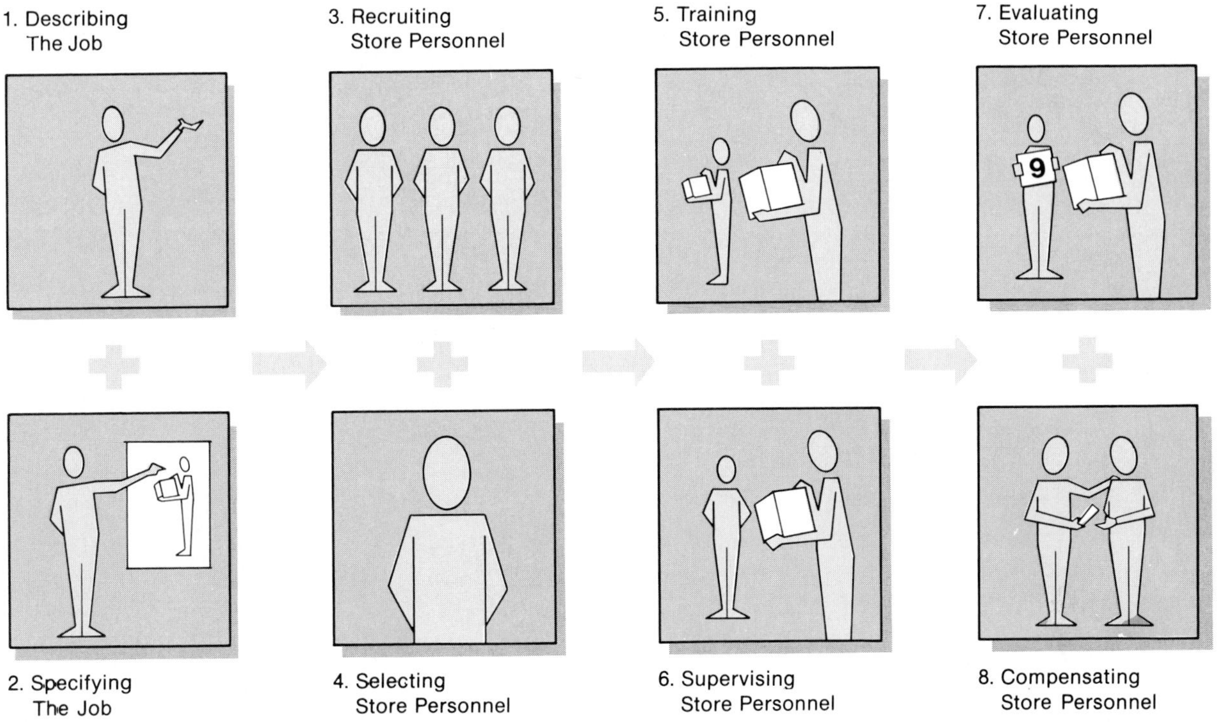

FIGURE 7–16
The retail staffing process

DESCRIBING THE JOB

The first step in the staffing process is to develop a well-defined and clearly expressed **job description**. This step not only forces the retailer to carefully determine its personnel needs; it also provides the potential employee with a means of evaluating the job. Before writing a job description, the retailer should conduct a job analysis to determine (1) specific job performance objectives and standards; (2) the tasks, duties, and responsibilities of the job; and (3) the skills, aptitudes, experience, education, and physical abilities that potential employees must possess to meet the minimum job requirements.[7] Figure 7–17 illustrates a job analysis questionnaire for a retail salesperson.

After completing the job analysis, the retailer can write a job description containing the following items: (1) the job title (e.g., sales representative, assistant store manager); (2) the job location (e.g., store, department); (3) the job position and relationships with the firm's organizational structure (e.g., identify superiors and subordinates, if any); and (4) the job description (i.e., duties and responsibilities). Figure 7–18 presents a typical job description for a sales manager position.

SPECIFYING THE JOB

To meet federal, state, and local regulations on hiring practices, many retailers provide potential employees with a written job specification. A **job specification** clearly states the minimum qualifications a person must have to obtain the job applied for. Qualification criteria include education and training requirements and/or basic knowledge and skill requirements. Because of recent legislation, retailers need to recognize that they might be asked to prove that their qualifying criteria are directly related to successful performance in the positions outlined in their job descriptions. To avoid costly lawsuits, they must establish the validity of the relationship between job

Salesperson

Job Title: ____________________ Store Name ____________________

Supervisor's Position: ____________ Location: ____________________

Store Department: ______________ Approvals: ______________ (Incumbent)

______________ (Supervisor)

1. *Major Function:* (Write a brief statement on the reason for the job's existence).
2. *Dimensions:* (This section should give pertinent statistics about the job. What is the individual sales volume? What are the department and store sales volumes? What are the numbers of sales people on the [illegible] average, during store-opening time?)
3. *Merchandise:* (List here the lines sold—number and/or types of merchandise.)
4. How is the department merchandised?
5. Does merchandise need fitting or alterations?
6. Are deliveries involved?
7. List specific duties:
   a.
   b.
   c.
   etc.
8. Who assigns, reviews, and/or approves work?
9. What responsibility or decision-making authority have you?
10. Do you prepare reports and, if so, what are they and what are they used for?
11. Do you operate or service any equipment, fixtures or machinery?
12. What is the hardest part of the job?
13. What experience is necessary to perform the job adequately?
14. How long does it take to learn the job adequately?
15. How would you describe the working conditions in which you perform?
16. Additional useful information.

FIGURE 7–17
Job analysis questionnaire

success and the stated job qualifications. Before filling any position, the retailer should protect itself by gathering evidence that the job qualifications actually enable an employee to meet job expectations. The retailer must avoid certain illegal conditions for employment in writing job qualifications, such as any requirement related either directly or indirectly to the applicant's race, age, creed, color, sex, religion, or national origin. With today's labor shortage, many retailers are now writing job specifications designed to attract a class of workers that previously might have been overlooked or undervalued. One such group is older workers, who are proving to be an excellent source of reliable and productive associates.[8]

RECRUITING STORE PERSONNEL

Recruiting is the active search for qualified employees. The astute manager recruits personnel by aggressively *seeking* lists of qualified prospects, *screening* large numbers of applicants, and *maintaining* a pool of prospective employees. Successful recruiting is the process of knowing where to look, what to look for, and how to find qualified people.

Job title:	Sales manager
Job location:	Men's shoe department Walnut Valley Branch Selmer's Department Stores
Job position:	Reports to assistant store manager
Job description:	To achieve sales goals by setting and maintaining customer service standards, training and motivating a professional sales staff, and maintaining merchandise presentation standards.
Job objectives:	1. To work as a partner with the merchandise analyst to develop sales plans and to reach sales goals within the area of responsibility. 2. To ensure that the store's customer service standards and policies are maintained. 3. To train, develop, motivate, and appraise the sales associates working within the area of responsibility. 4. To work as a partner with the merchandise analyst and assistant store manager in developing stock assortments and quantities. 5. To verify that the appearance and presentation of merchandise on the selling floor adhere to the visual merchandising guidelines. 6. To ensure that selling services provide appropriate floor coverage to meet or exceed productivity goals. 7. To communicate with the branch store coordinator, assistant store manager, and merchandise analyst concerning floor presentation. 8. To ensure that advertised merchandise is properly priced, ticketed, and displayed and to ensure that sales associates are aware of this merchandise. 9. To control merchandise inventories, including but not limited to receiving, pricing, transfers, price changes, security, and damages. 10. To conduct all stock counts. 11. To supervise the control of sales register media and cash register shortage. 12. To shop the competition. 13. To input information into major sale resumes. 14. To disseminate all pertinent information to all sales associates including night contingents. 15. To ensure the correct documentation of time sheets within the area. 16. To implement credit promotions and other programs in the area.

FIGURE 7–18
A typical job description

Finding Employees

Several internal and external sources can provide the names and general backgrounds of prospective employees. Internal sources include lists of current and past employees as well as employee recommendations. *Current employees* should be considered if they possess the necessary qualifications for the job. Promotions and transfers not only are a means of finding qualified persons; they also improve employee morale by demonstrating that advancement within the firm is possible. *Past employees* with satisfactory service records are an internal source of employees that retailers often overlook. By maintaining files on past employees (full- and part-time), the personnel manager has access to individuals who could be productive immediately with minimal training. The third internal source comprises *employee recommendations*. Frequently the firm's employees know of friends, relatives, and acquaintances who are in the job market and have the necessary skills and training to fill a position. Neiman Marcus has a hiring bonus program for employees who recommend qualified persons who are hired and stay for a prescribed period of time.[9]

External sources of prospective employees include advertisements, employment agencies, educational institutions, and unsolicited applications. *Advertisements* in newspapers, trade publications, and professional papers and journals are common vehicles for attracting applicants. Printed media frequently devote sections to employment opportunities at certain times or in particular issues. Private and public *employment agencies* offer the advantages of providing initial screening for a large number of prospects and maintaining the retailer's anonymity during the initial stages of the recruiting process. Before using the services of a private or government employment agency, the retailer should determine the agency's fee structure and whether the employer or the employee is responsible for paying the fee. *Educational Institutions* offer many sources of perspective employees. Career counselors at most high schools often can provide a list of suitable prospects for part-time and entry-level positions. Placement offices at junior and four-year colleges and universities are always eager to supply retailers and other businesses with the names and qualifications of prospective employees for low- and middle-management positions. Walk-ins and mail-ins represent *unsolicited applications* that retailers should keep on file and periodically review when a job becomes available.

One additional external source of employees is *pirating*—hiring an employee who works for a noncompeting retailer. The major advantage of pirating is the retailing experience the prospective employee undoubtedly has. However, the retailer should proceed cautiously when hiring another retailer's employee. Neiman Marcus filed suit against Federated Department Stores and Allied Stores for enticing its chief executive while he was under contract to head Neiman's retail divisions.[10]

Screening Applicants

In the screening process, personnel managers examine the applicant's qualifications to determine whether the person has the requisite background and capabilities to perform the job. The most common criteria retailers use in the initial screening process are educational background, ability to communicate in oral and written form, experience in working with people, and knowledge, experience, or skills in performing specific activities (e.g., typing). Other screening criteria retailers use indirectly and subjectively are personal appearance, general attitude, motivation, and personality.

SELECTING STORE PERSONNEL

From the list of qualified applicants, the retailer must select the individual best suited to the job. Matching job requirements to employee attributes is the purpose of the selection step of the staffing process. In finding the best match, the retailer has available several methods of generating additional information on the prospective employee before deciding to make an offer. These methods include application forms, reference checks, personal interviews, testing instruments, and physical examinations.

Application Forms

All retailers should require each prospective employee to complete an application form as a prerequisite for further processing. Application forms provide the retailer with preliminary information on each applicant and (1) serve as a means of checking minimum qualifications during initial screening; (2) provide basic information to guide the interviewer during the personal interview process; (3) allow a preliminary check on the applicant's ability to follow instructions; and (4) provide background information for a permanent record if the applicant is hired.[11] The typical application form provides space for the applicant's name, address, telephone number, employment history (when and where the applicant has previously worked, levels of compensation, and reasons for leaving previous jobs), formal education and training, personal health history, and demographic information allowed by state and federal regulations. The application form also usually includes space for a list of personal references. Although the retailer should carefully review all the information on the application form, it should give special attention to *omissions* and *job changes*. What is *not* on the application form could be as important as what *is*. The retailer should seek clarification of all omissions on application forms. Frequent job changes without good cause also can reveal something about the applicant's character.

Reference Checks

After the retailer has initially screened prospective employees' application forms and eliminated those who are unqualified, it should contact the references of the remaining prospects. Although most references applicants list are favorably biased, they give the retailer a way to verify the accuracy and completeness of the applicant's form. Telephone calls to references normally provide more complete and honest evaluations than do letters, mainly because of the immediate and personal two-way communication telephone conversations allow. Telephone contact gives the retailer a chance to ask questions about issues of particular concern. To reinforce reference checks, many retailers contact former employers, teachers, and other individuals who might have specific knowledge about the applicant's character and abilities. Some retailers even check applicants' credit by contacting local credit bureaus.

Personal Interviews

Retailers use personal interviews to question and observe applicants in a face-to-face situation. Formal, highly structured interviews establish the relative roles of each party in the interview, permitting a controlled interviewing environment, and facilitate complete, effective information gathering. Informal and unstructured interviews help the applicant to relax, talk freely, and act naturally, thereby allowing the interviewer to observe the applicant in an unguarded state. Most retailers prefer to compromise by injecting enough formality and structure into the interview to promote efficiency but not so much as to create undue tension in the applicant.

The number of interviews usually depends on the level of the position to be filled. When retailers are trying to fill upper-level managerial positions, they normally interview each applicant several times; for entry-level positions, one interview generally suffices. Many retailers find it advantageous to have the applicant interview with several of the firm's managers so they can elicit several opinions of the applicant's qualifications.

The personal interviewing process should fully comply with state and federal equal employment opportunity regulations. Questions asked must be job related and necessary for judging the applicant's qualifications and abilities. To avoid charges of discrimination, the retailer should construct a list of questions to use in the interviewing process and have the store's legal department review it for any possible discriminatory inquiries.

Testing Instruments

In the hiring process, some retailers use testing instruments to evaluate prospective employees. These include pencil-and-paper tests to demonstrate applicants' ability to handle a job. Although the validity and usefulness of these instruments have been debated, many retailers believe they provide valuable insights into a person's qualifications for employment. Retailers use two general types of instruments to evaluate applicants: psychological tests and achievement tests.

Psychological tests are designed to measure an applicant's personality, intelligence, aptitudes, interests, and supervisory skills. Regardless of which tests are used, the retailer needs trained personnel to administer and interpret the results.

Achievement tests are questionnaires designed to measure a person's basic knowledge and skills. Tests that measure an applicant's ability to do basic arithmetic computations or to operate mechanical devices such as cash registers, typewriters, and calculators are examples. Generally retailers prefer achievement tests to psychological tests because they are easier to administer and interpret. Also, most retailers believe that achievement tests are more valid than psychological tests because the statistical relationship between the skills they measure and job success is stronger—a particularly important consideration in light of recent court rulings regarding equal employment opportunities.

Physical Examinations

Some retailers require applicants to undergo a physical examination. Usually this examination is requested only after the applicant has been judged the most qualified person for the job. Some states have laws requiring a physical examination for prospective employees who will handle food and drug products. In addition, some firms' health, life, and disability insurance programs require exams. Testing for drug use and acquired immune deficiency syndrome (AIDS) is another issue some retailers are addressing. Because an estimated 50 percent of internal theft cases are drug related, Marshall Field's of Chicago has joined the growing ranks of retailers that are testing applicants for drug use.[12]

Final Selection

Ultimately the retailer must make a final selection among the qualified applicants. No absolute, totally objective method can determine the most qualified person; rather, the final selection is largely a subjective choice based on all available information. An experienced personnel manager with good intuition is perhaps one of the most valuable assets a firm can have for selecting employees who will make a significant contribution over an extended period. Objective tests, experience, and good personal judgment are the tools a personnel manager needs to make the final selection.

TRAINING STORE PERSONNEL

The fifth step in the staffing process is employee training. Training programs are needed not only for new employees but for existing employees to update their knowledge and skills. Training programs are designed to help both employer and employee reach mutually beneficial goals.

Regardless of the retailer's individual situation, however, every sound retail training program should address three basic questions: *what type* of training the employee should have, *where* the training should take place, and *how* the training should be done. Figure 7–19 identifies these basic elements.

What Training to Give

Two basic kinds of training that both new and old employees need are organization orientation and functional training.[13] **Organization orientation** either initiates new employees or updates old employees on the general organizational structure of the firm and its policies, rules, and regulations. It also acquaints employees with the company's

WHAT	Organizational orientation
	Functional training
WHERE	On the job—decentralized training
	Off the job—centralized training
HOW	Individual methods
	"on your own"
	programmed learning
	Sponsor method
	Group methods
	lectures
	demonstrations
	case studies
	role playing
	Executive training programs

FIGURE 7–19
Elements of a retail training program

history, objectives, and future expectations. Essentially an organization orientation program makes employees aware of what the firm is trying to accomplish and how it plans to do so. One aim of this program is to improve employees' morale and make them feel they are members of the "team."

Functional training develops and expands the basic skills and knowledge employees need to perform their jobs successfully.[14] Training sessions on selling techniques, customer service procedures, and inventory control are three examples of functional training directed at improving basic employee skills. Increasing employees' knowledge of the company's product lines and helping them understand customer purchase motives are examples of knowledge-oriented, functional training.

Where to Train

The second element of the training program concerns where training is to take place and under whose supervision. Normally training occurs either on the job during regular working hours, off the job during scheduled training periods, or some combination of both. **On-the-job training** is a decentralized approach that occurs on the sales floor, in the stockroom, or in some other work environment where employees are performing their jobs. The trainee usually is under the direct supervision of the department manager or some other designated person responsible for handling the training program. **Off-the-job training** is conducted in centralized training classrooms away from the employees' work environment. In centralized classrooms, the trainer can use various learning aids (e.g., films, demonstrations, and role playing) under controlled conditions, allowing the employee to focus on the learning experience without interruption.

How to Train

The third element in the retailer's training program is how each employee should be instructed; that is, which methods to use in the training process. As Figure 7–19 outlines, there are four general training methods: individual, sponsor, group, and executive. With the **individual training method**, employees "train" themselves. One individual training method is the "on-your-own" approach. In this training situation, the employee is put on the job and expected to learn by trial and error, observation, and asking questions. In essence, this sink-or-swim approach includes no formal training. Although the retailer incurs no training costs in the short run, the total long-run costs could be substantial because of potential low employee productivity, high employee turnover, employee errors, and dissatisfied customers due to improper service.

An alternative method retailers use is **programmed learning,** which uses a highly structured format. First, employees study a unit of material. Second, they respond to a series of questions (true/false, multiple-choice, fill-in-the-blank, etc.) on the material they have read. Third, they receive immediate feedback on their performance in answering the questions. Fourth, they continue to repeat the first three steps until they master the material. Once the employees achieve an acceptable competence level on a unit of material, they move on to the next level of instruction. Repetition is the key to programmed learning. These training devices are available in both written (pencil-and-paper) and machine (mechanical and computer) form.

The **sponsor training method** uses an experienced employee to assume part or all of the responsibility for training a new employee. Most retailers believe that this one-on-one approach is the best method for teaching new employees the basic skills of selling, buying, promotion, and so forth. The sponsor's responsibilities also extend to introducing the employee to fellow workers, evaluating the employee's progress, and providing advice on the employee's problems and concerns. Successful sponsor training programs involve individuals who volunteer for the assignment and are compensated for their efforts (e.g., with money or time off).

Group training methods involve the simultaneous training of several employees through lectures (or discussion, films, or slides), demonstrations (on sales or marketing and stock presentations), case studies (e.g., oral and written problem-solving situations), role-playing activities (e.g., a sales or customer complaint situation), computer simulations, and interactive videos.[15] Large retailers use group training in centralized training facilities with specialized personnel. Lexus, Toyota Motor Corp.'s new

On-the-job training takes place in the environment in which the employee will work.

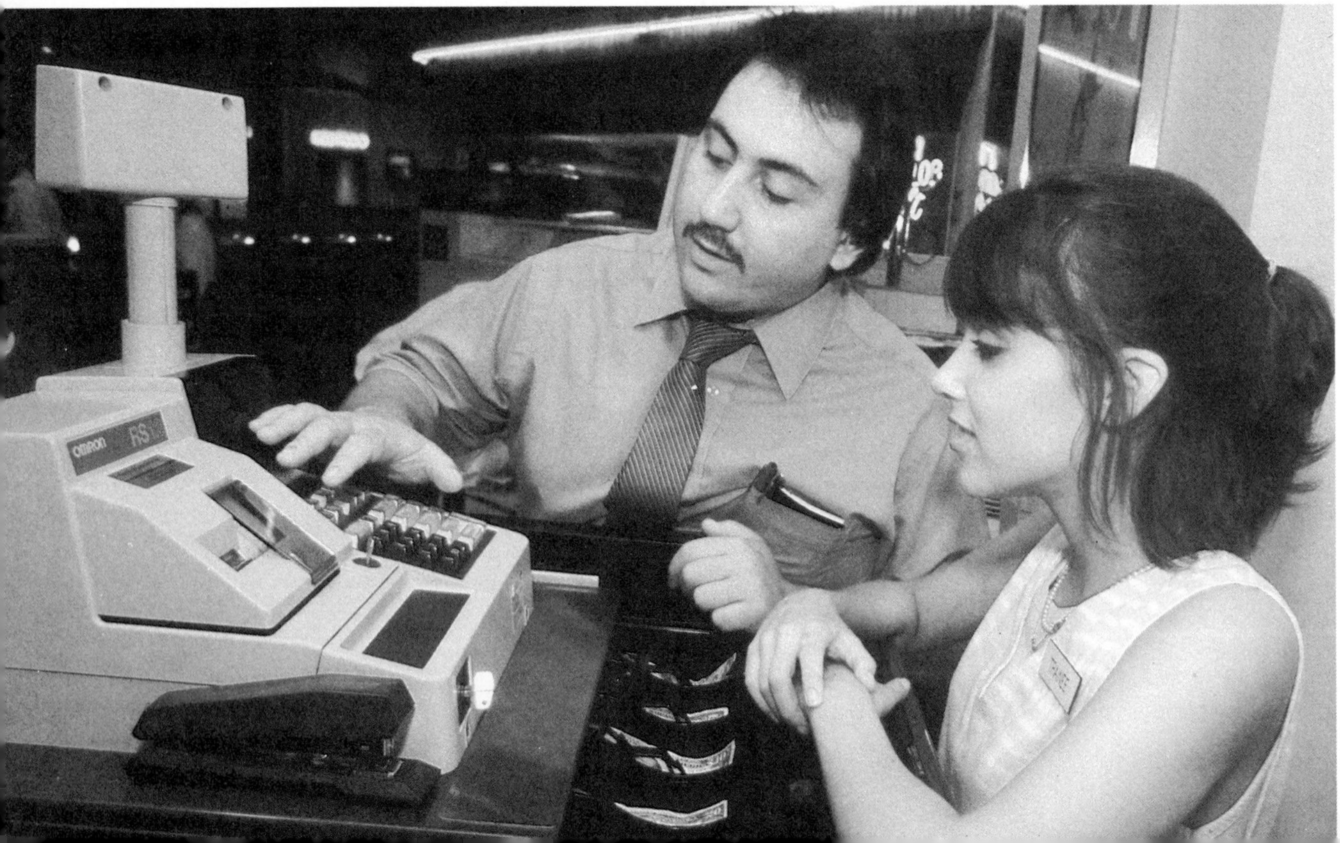

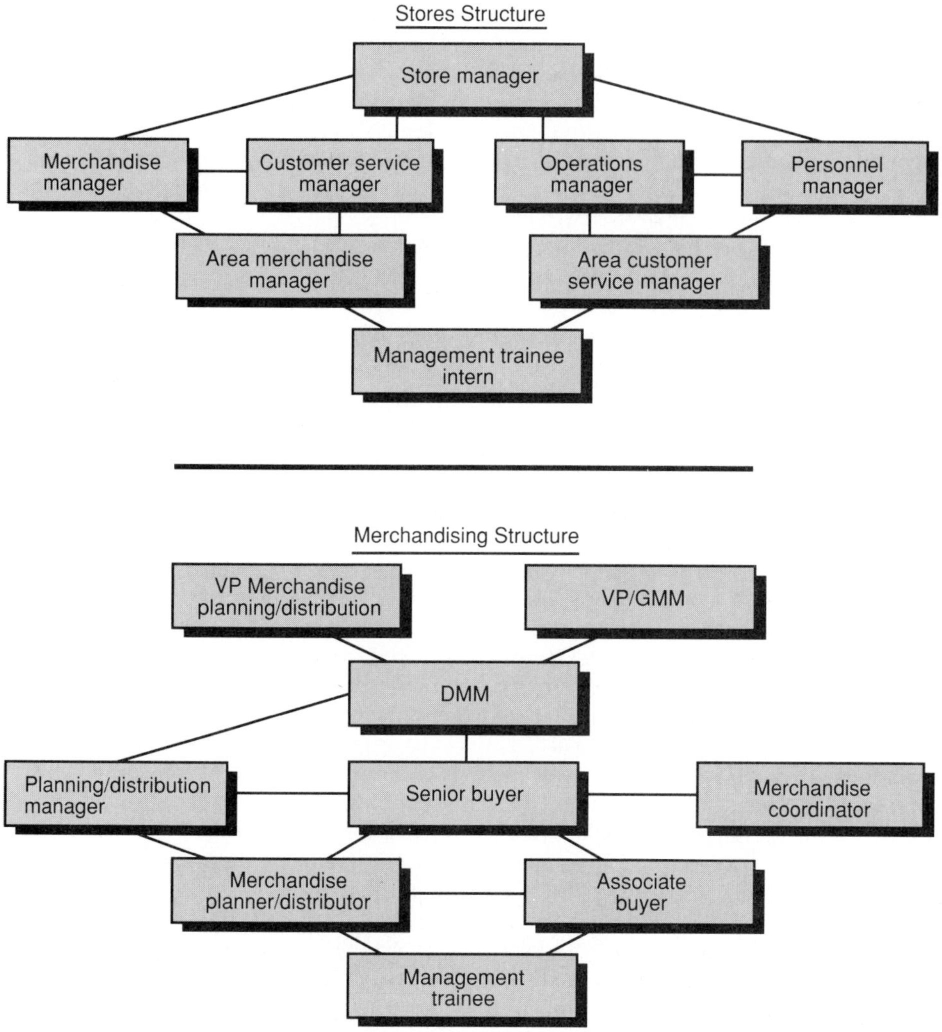

FIGURE 7–20
An executive training program—Dayton Hudson department stores (source: James Abend, "The Fast Track," *Stores,* September 1985, 63. Reprinted by permission of *Stores*. Copyright by National Retail Federation, Inc.)

luxury-car division, conducts group training courses in which "sales and service people are learning how to build the classy image the Lexus division thinks it needs. . . . The two-day seminar in Chicago is a marathon of lectures, quizzes, and role playing. Constant reiteration of the division's highbrow philosophy sometimes gives it the feeling of a revival meeting."[16] The advantage of group training is the low cost of training several employees at one time; the principal drawback is the lack of individual attention.

Executive training programs (ETPs) are educational sessions directed at supervisors, managers, and executives. Common among large department store and chain organizations, ETPs are designed to recruit personnel who have executive potential and to provide them with the opportunity to gain management experience. The typical ETP is a step-by-step training procedure whereby the executive trainee gains practical management experience by progressing from low- to higher-level management positions. Figure 7–20 illustrates the ETP for Dayton Hudson department stores. Dayton Hudson creates two separate but parallel routes to senior management. This example shows several alternative routes that a trainee might follow. An executive trainee is first promoted to either an associate buyer or area sales manager position. The progression from that point varies according to the individual and the company's needs. The amount of time one spends at any position depends on one's ability, the type and complexity of the position, and the number of positions open at any given time. Lower-level positions usually involve several months of training, while middle- and upper-level positions frequently necessitate several years' experience. By moving potential executives from one position to another, the retailer gives them complete exposure to all or most of its operations, policies, and procedures.

Many large retail organizations also have special executive development programs for new and veteran employees with extensive educational backgrounds and experience. These programs normally include orientation programs, project assignments, executive seminars, and sponsorship programs with one of the firm's top executives. May Department Stores' divisional merchandise managers are given actual merchandising problems as case studies and must present their solutions to the chairperson and president of the firm during week-long retreats.[17] Many companies also encourage a wide range of self-development activities.

SUPERVISING STORE PERSONNEL

Supervision is the process of directing, coordinating, and inspecting the efforts of store employees to attain both company and individual goals. Effective supervisors can successfully satisfy the needs of the retailer (e.g., quality job performance, company loyalty, satisfactory profits) and the needs of the employee (e.g., fair treatment, a decent standard of living, a chance for advancement). The West Point Market in Akron, Ohio, one of the country's most successful specialty food markets, has created an innovative work environment; its owner describes it as a "'tight-loose environment', tight enough to make a profit, yet loose enough to have fun by making work something enjoyable."[18]

The key to good supervision is knowing how to motivate employees. **Motivation** is the drive that moves people to act. Employees are driven to excel in a variety of ways. Some employees are motivated by money, others by praise, and still others by the promise of free time to spend with their families. Stew Leonard's, the Norwalk, Connecticut, supermarket chain, uses a motivation device called the "ladders of success": "Promotion is strictly from within, and as an employee climbs the 'ladders,' he or she has a chance at becoming the 'superstar of the month.' That employee is honored with a parade and in-store party. Recognition and appreciation are essential to a motivated work force."[19] Undoubtedly, "money can be a strong incentive for employee productivity, but it may not be a sufficient condition for it. The link between pay and performance is a bit more complex than the simple formulation that incentive pay increases motivation and performance."[20] The supervisor must discover the key that motivates each employee.

How to Motivate

Frederick Herzberg offers one method of motivation in his theory of satisfiers and dissatisfiers.[21] **Satisfiers** are employment factors that produce pleasurable reactions within people's work lives. Herzberg found that the primary employment satisfiers were a challenging job, recognition of achievement, a responsible position, a chance for advancement, and professional and personal growth. In essence, motivation factors are conditions that enhance the employee's personal needs for self-esteem and self-actualization.

Dissatisfiers are employment factors that make workers unhappy with their job, leading to high turnover and weak performance. Oversupervision, poorly developed work rules, undesirable working conditions, restrictive company policies, and inadequate wages and fringe benefits are common dissatisfiers. In general, dissatisfiers are closely associated with an individual's physiological and security needs. Given Herzberg's findings, the answer to the question "How to motivate?" is to eliminate conditions that generate dissatisfiers and initiate programs and policies that promote satisfiers.

How to Supervise

The optimal level of employee supervision depends largely on how motivated employees are. Two opposing schools of thought on the amount of supervision that employers should exercise are the heavyhanded approach and the lighthanded approach.

Those who support **heavyhanded supervision** assume that employees are lazy, passive, self-centered, and irresponsible. They maintain that employers must closely supervise and control their employees to motivate them to work toward company goals and to assume responsibilities. Retailers that subscribe to this school of thought view economic inducements as the primary means of motivation (McGregor's Theory X).[22] In particular, some retailers consider the heavyhanded approach the only way to motivate people in the lower-level positions of their stores. In modern society, however, the heavyhanded approach may not apply: "If a top executive is heavy-handed, taking all decisions unto himself, those working for him will be reluctant to act on their own . . . and then you get reverse delegation. Everything gets delegated upstream."[23]

A more contemporary view of motivation and supervision is the lighthanded approach. Retailers that support **lighthanded supervision** believe that providing

Theory X states that efficiency will be high when:

- Authority flows down a hierarchical chain in which each subordinate has but one supervisor or manager.
- Work is divided into the smallest number of sets of similar functions.
- Span of management is kept small, but balanced against the number of levels of management.
- Jobs are carefully defined and the worker is hired to fit the job.

Theory X assumes that:

- Most people prefer to be directed and have little desire for responsibility and creativity.
- Motivation occurs only at an economic level. The worker is resistant to change.
- People must be closely supervised. They have a short time span of responsibility. People are by nature indolent.
- People can be considered alike as units of production. No differentiation of jobs to utilize different interests and capacities is desirable. The worker is self-centered and indifferent to organizational needs.

Theory Y states that efficiency will be high when:

- Authority and communication flow in all directions in both formal and informal systems.
- Work is varied and enriched.
- Span of management is as broad as possible as long as major objectives can be achieved.
- Tasks are grouped into different meaningful jobs to accommodate individual talents and capacities.

Theory Y assumes that:

- Workers are social beings who can work together for organizational and personal goals.
- Capacity for creativity is present to some degree in everybody. Needs at the level above the economic level are powerful motivators.
- People desire self-fulfillment through directing their own activities and participating in setting their own objectives.
- Workers achieve their fullest potential when their aspirations and job challenges are matched to their capabilities.

Source: Norman M. Scarborough and Thomas W. Zimmerer, *Effective Small Business Management* (Columbus: Merrill Publishing Co., 1984), 503

FIGURE 7–21
McGregor's Theory X and Theory Y models of motivation

employees with a favorable work environment can create a situation in which employees will obtain job satisfaction and achieve their personal goals by directing their efforts toward the firm's needs (McGregor's Theory Y).[24] Retailers that use the lighthanded approach believe that close supervision and control are unnecessary, employees will assume their responsibilities and, in part, supervise themselves if a desirable social and psychological environment is present. To heighten associates' sense of mission, Wal-Mart "expects managers for each of the 34 departments within a typical Wal-Mart to run their operations as if they were running their own businesses."[25] Wal-Mart has 250,000 entrepreneurs in all of their stores running their part of the business. The previously discussed satisfiers are the keys to creating this desirable social and psychological condition. Within this kind of working environment, less supervision produces better job performance.

A summary of Douglas McGregor's two contrasting models of motivation, Theory X and Theory Y, appears in Figure 7–21.

EVALUATING STORE PERSONNEL

The seventh step in the store staffing process is the development of personnel evaluation procedures.[26] Each store employee, regardless of position or level, should be evaluated periodically. The purpose of personnel evaluations are to (1) determine compensation, (2) recommend or deny promotions and transfers, and (3) justify demotions and terminations. Conducted constructively, personnel evaluations can be used to motivate employees, improve store morale, generate information for planning purposes, encourage employee self-development, and improve communications between employee and employer. In developing the store's personnel evaluation methods and procedures, the retailer should decide when to evaluate, what to evaluate, and how to evaluate.

When to Evaluate

A smart retailer evaluates personnel continuously. It would be unfair to judge an employee's contribution and performance at the end of an arbitrary time period, such as the end of the fiscal year. Instead, the retailer should provide its employees with immediate feedback on their progress. This informal feedback, however, should be accompanied by an established, formal evaluation in which employees receive a detailed account of their job performance. Formal evaluations tell employees exactly what their status is. Often new employees are evaluated weekly or monthly. Established lower-level employees, however, typically are evaluated on a formal basis every six months, while annual evaluations for upper-level management and executive personnel are the norm.

What to Evaluate

Retailers have learned that the most important employee factors to evaluate are performance-demonstrated skills and personal attributes; these factors relate most closely to employee success. Examples of such characteristics appear in Figure 7–22. Figure 7–23 identifies those traits that executives believe are most important to employee success.

In selecting evaluation criteria and their respective measuring instruments, the retailer must consider the legal ramifications of each decision and the influence of any labor union that might be involved. It often is a good policy to seek advice regarding the legality of the employee evaluation system. In areas where unionization of labor is present, management consults with appropriate union representatives before formulating evaluation methods and procedures.

Performance characteristics	Personal attributes
Job knowledge	Enthusiasm
Quality of work	Loyalty
Quantity of work	Dependability
Organizing capabilities	Leadership
Supervision requirements	Maturity
Promptness	Stability
Peer relationships	Creativity
Customer relations	Honesty
Analytic abilities	Initiative

FIGURE 7–22
Employee evaluation factors

How to Evaluate

Retailers use a variety of methods for evaluating store personnel; the method used depends on the degree of objectivity and formality the retailer wants. Figure 7–24 identifies several objective employee evaluation methods, which are based largely on factual and measurable criteria, and subjective methods, which are based on the evaluator's perceptions, feelings, and prejudices. Formal methods are regularly scheduled evaluations; informal methods follow no set schedule, and the criteria and procedures may or may not be known to the employee.

Formal Objective Evaluation Methods

Formal objective evaluation methods include performance records and management by objectives (MBO) procedures. Performance records are quantitative measures of the employee's performance and include varied statistics such as (1) total sales dollars, (2) total number of sales transactions, (3) number of customer complaints, (4) number of merchandise returns and their dollar value, (5) number of times an employee is absent or late for work, and (6) net sales per working hour or per hourly wage. By comparing the employee's performance against the store average for any one of these criteria, the retailer can identify above-, at-, and below-average performers. These MBO procedures set measurable performance objectives for employees that should match their job descriptions. Employees are then evaluated on how well they achieved their objectives. Using MBO procedures offers the advantage of drawing the employee into the evaluation process and thereby encouraging self-development and self-evaluation. The employee is asked to (1) set objectives in specific terms, (2) determine the method of

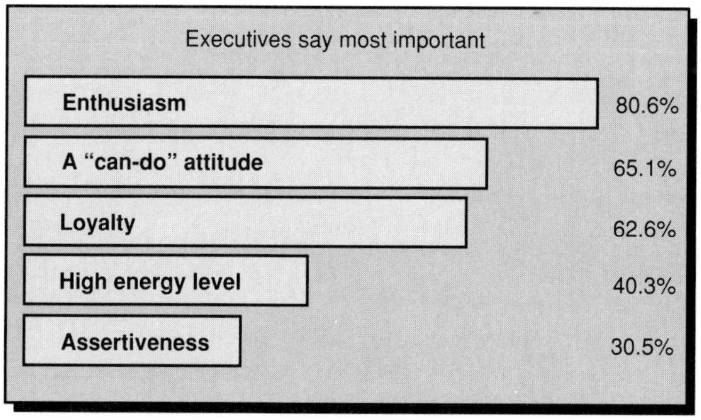

FIGURE 7–23
Employee traits that executives believe are most important to employee success (source: Elys McLean-Ibrahim, "What Makes Workers Succeed?" *USA Today*, September 25, 1987, p. B–1. Copyright © 1987 *USA Today*. Reprinted with permission.)

FIGURE 7–24
Store personnel evaluation methods

Degree of Formality \ Degree of Objectivity	Objective	Subjective
Formal	performance records MBO (management by objectives)	rating scales checklists
Informal	professional shoppers	intuition

accomplishment, (3) set an accomplishment time frame, and (4) determine the measure of accomplishment.

Formal Subjective Evaluation Methods

Rating scales and checklists constitute two of the more common **formal subjective evaluation methods**. The typical procedure is to identify and list several criteria in checklist form. The evaluator may weight the individual criteria according to their importance (see Figure 7–25). Typical scales are (1) satisfactory or unsatisfactory; (2) below average, average, or above average; and (3) poor, fair, average, good, and excellent. Given the subjective character of these ratings, many retailers prefer to have several supervisors rate each employee. The average of these ratings forms the basis for the employee's evaluation. When using rating scales, retailers should recognize the central tendency effect: the tendency of evaluators to rate everyone at or near the midpoint of the scale.

Informal Objective Evaluation Methods

The most common **informal objective evaluation method** in retailing is to use professional or mystery shoppers. Professional shoppers are people who wander into a store to "shop" for merchandise in a "typical" way but in fact are professional investigators who attempt to learn how a retailer's employees behave toward them. Domino's Pizza tries to evaluate and compensate its employees "by paying 10,000 'mystery customers' $60 each to buy 12 pizzas throughout the year at its 5,000 units and evaluate quality and service."[27] This evaluation method should not be the *basis* of employee evaluation but a *supplement* to the retailer's assessment of employees' job performance.

Informal Subjective Evaluation Methods

Informal subjective evaluation methods have no structure and rely heavily on the supervisor's intuition. Although a supervisor's feelings and perceptions might represent a correct evaluation of an employee, the lack of objectivity and formality leaves such a method open to criticism by both employees and outside concerns (e.g., the Fair Labor Standards Act). A constant danger in using intuition as an evaluative method is the "halo effect" or the "good old boy syndrome." An employee who is a good person is not necessarily contributing effectively to the firm's efforts; in fact, such considerations often lead to other employees' accusations of favoritism.

Regardless of the method used to evaluate store personnel, employees should be made aware of the method (its criteria, measurements, and procedures), receive feedback after each evaluation, and be permitted to appeal the evaluation.

COMPENSATING STORE PERSONNEL

Equitable compensation is an integral part of the retailer's staffing process.[28] A well-designed compensation package is not only an important factor in rewarding past performance but a significant incentive for future performance.[29] Compensation methods include the straight-salary plan, the straight-commission plan, the salary-plus-

Employee's name ____________________ Date ____________________

Employee's title ____________________ Supervisor ____________________

Instructions: Please review the performance of the employee whose name is listed above on each of the following items. In order to guide you in your rating, the five determinants of performance have been defined

Rating Points

5 OUTSTANDING
A truly outstanding employee whose achievements are far above acceptable. Has consistently performed far beyond established objectives and has made significant contributions beyond current position. Requires minimal direction and supervision. (Relatively few employees would be expected to achieve at this level.)

4 SUPERIOR
An above-average employee whose performance is clearly above acceptable. Has usually performed beyond established objectives and, at times, has made contributions beyond responsibilities of present position. Requires less than normally expected degree of direction and supervision.

3 AVERAGE
A fully acceptable employee who consistently meets all requirements of position. Has consistently met established objectives in a satisfactory and adequate manner. Performance requires normal degree of supervision and direction. (The majority of employees should be at this level.)

2 BELOW AVERAGE
A somewhat below-average employee whose performance, while not unsatisfactory, cannot be considered fully acceptable. Generally meets established objectives and expectations, but definite areas exist where achievement is substandard. Performance requires somewhat more than normal degree of direction and supervision.

1 UNACCEPTABLE
A far-below-average employee whose performance is barely adequate to meet the requirements of the position. Generally performs at a level below established objectives with the result that overall contribution is marginal. Performance requires an unusually high degree of supervision. (This level is considered acceptable only for employees new to the job.)

JOB CRITERIA POINTS

1. Amount of work. Consider here only the **quantity** of the employee's output. ____________
   Supervisor's comments:

2. Quality of work. Consider how well the employee does each job assigned. Include your appraisal of such items as accuracy, thoroughness, and orderliness. ____________
   Supervisor's comments:

3. Cooperation. How well does this employee work and interact with you and coworkers for the accomplishment of organization goals? ____________
   Supervisor's comments:

4. Judgment. Consider this employee's ability to reach sound and logical conclusions. ____________
   Supervisor's comments:

FIGURE 7–25
A formal subjective employee evaluation form

5. Initiative. The energy or aptitude to originate action toward organization goals. __________
   Supervisor's comments:

6. Job knowledge. How well does the employee demonstrate an understanding of the basic fundamentals, techniques, and procedures on the job? __________
   Supervisor's comments:

7. Interest in job. Does the employee demonstrate a real interest in the job and the organization? __________
   Supervisor's comments:

8. Ability to communicate. How well does this employee exchange needed information with others in the work group and with supervisors? __________
   Supervisor's comments:

9. Dependability. Consider the employee's absences, tardiness, punctuality, timeliness in completing job assignments, and the amount of supervision required. __________
   Supervisor's comments:

10. Adaptability. Consider the degree to which this employee demonstrates adjustment to the varying requirements of the job. __________
    Supervisor's comments:

TOTAL POINTS __________

Supervisor's general comments:

Instructions: After you have rated the employee and made whatever comments you feel are pertinent to each criterion and the overall evaluation, schedule a meeting to review each item with the employee. An employee wishing to make comments about the evaluation should be asked to do so in the following space.

Employee's comment:

Date: ____________________

Supervisor present (Name): ____

Employee's signature: ______________________________ Date: ____________________

Notice to employee: Signing the form does not imply that you either agree or disagree with the evaluation.

Source: Norman M. Scarborough and Thomas W. Zimmerer, *Effective Small Business Management* (Columbus: Merrill Publishing Co., 1984), 521–23.

FIGURE 7–25
continued

commission plan, and the salary-plus-bonus plan. Long-term incentives (top-level management), annual bonuses (mid-level management) and short-term incentives (sales personnel) are becoming increasingly important in all retail compensation practices.

Straight-Salary Plan

The **straight-salary plan** is a fixed amount of compensation for a specified work period such as a day, week, month, or year. For example, an employee's salary might be set at $200 per week or $4 per hour. Younkers Department Store's Satisfactory Plus program pays sales associates one of four different per-hour wage rates depending on their productivity. The program involves a 12-month review period during which an employee's productivity is evaluated and wage level assigned.[30]

For the retailer, the straight-salary plan offers the advantages of easy administration and a high level of employer control. Under the straight-salary plan, the retailer can expect employees to engage in nonselling activities such as stocking and housekeeping. For the employee, the straight-salary plan offers a known level of financial security and stability. The disadvantages of this plan for the retailer are (1) limited incentives to increase employee performance, (2) fixed costs that result in a high wage cost/sales ratio, and (3) lack of downward salary adjustments during periods of sales decline.

Retailers typically use straight-salary plans when a job involves a considerable amount of customer service and nonselling time, such as stocking, receiving, clerking, and checking out. Home Depot, the nation's largest home center chain, prefers the straight-salary plan because management wants employees to take the time to provide the do-it-yourself home repair customer with the information and products necessary to ensure success in his or her home repair projects.[31]

Straight-Commission Plan

A quiet revolution is sweeping department store retailing: "To boost sales and upgrade service, major retail chains are converting thousands of hourly sales employees to commission pay."[32]

Under a **straight-commission plan,** a store employee receives a percentage of what he or she sells. The commission percentage is either fixed (e.g., 5 percent on all sales) or variable (e.g., 6 percent on high-margin lines and 3 percent on low-margin lines). Retailers usually calculate an employee's commission on the basis of *net sales* (gross sales dollars minus dollar value of returned merchandise).

The major advantage of a straight-commission plan is the monetary incentive it creates for employees. However, this incentive often causes several problems. Salespeople on commission often become overly aggressive in trying to make a sale. High-pressure selling is also a temptation when commission sales are involved. By exerting undue pressure on the customer to buy now (as opposed to later, when a different salesperson might be serving the customer), the retailer could lose the sale altogether. Also, commission sales tempt many salespeople to attempt to trade up customers to more expensive merchandise. This practice can backfire, however, when trading up leads to a large number of returns: Not only does the salesperson lose the commission; the retailer loses a sale and very likely the goodwill of the store's clientele.

For the commissioned salesperson, the straight-commission plan has the weaknesses of financial insecurity and instability. To overcome these limitations, many retailers have established "drawing accounts" that allow employees to draw a fixed sum of money at regular intervals against future commissions.

Salary-Plus-Commission Plan

As the term implies, the **salary-plus-commission plan** provides employees with a salary and a commission. There are a number of variations to this plan. The *straight-salary/*

RETAIL STRATEGIES AND TACTICS

Dayton Hudson Department Stores: Performance Plus Program

Dayton Hudson's Performance Plus program involves a fundamental change in the way sales associates are compensated and it represents a fundamental cultural shift at each of its stores. The goals of the program are (1) to reward salespeople for customer service, (2) to provide superior customer service, and (3) to retain sales associates.

Under the Performance Plus program, each salesperson "is expected to sell x dollars per hour depending on the area where he or she is working." Each person receives his own financial rewards based on how much his individual sales go above that rate.

The exact calculations include an hourly multiplier that has been predetermined for each department. For example, "If a salesperson is being paid $5.65 per hour and the multiplier for her department is 17, then the hourly rate of sales comes out to $96.05. Therefore, if she is employed 300 hours, she should sell $28,815 worth of merchandise. But if the employee actually sells $50,000 net sales (which excludes returns) her sales over the average for that area are $21,185. Using a bonus percentage that has also been predetermined for each department, say six percent times the incremental pay, then the bonus would be equal to $1,271.10."

As an employee's track record becomes established, the salesperson is able to increase his or her base rate up to $8 an hour, provided this doesn't go into a deficit situation and there is a track record that can show the sales the person has been generating.

Another ramification: When it comes to compensation, we can show each sales associate an earnings matrix. "If someone is making $14,000 a year and wants to make $18,000 we can show her exactly what she has to sell to get there. For example, it may be another blouse a day. But we are able to track precisely what the salesperson is selling."

Source: Jacquelyn Bivins, "Commissions and More," *Stores,* (September 1989): 26.

single-commission variation uses a base salary (e.g., $200 per week) plus (1) a single commission (e.g., 1/2 percent) on all net sales up to the sales quota and a larger commission (e.g., 2 percent) on all sales in excess of sales quota or (2) a commission only on net sales that exceed the quota. As a general rule, the base salary constitutes the greatest share of the employee's total compensation. To offer greater sales incentive, however, a retailer can increase the commission rate to make commission income a significantly higher proportion of the employee's total income. For example, "Sears sharply reduced the salespeoples' base pay when it installed Brand Central departments in their stores . . . instead of continuing its past practice of paying an additional commission of 3% of sales and then bumping up the rate of 6% once salespeople met annual sales quotas. Sears now pays them commissions that range from 2% to 8%, depending on the item sold."[33]

The strengths of this plan are that it provides employees with financial security and stability while helping the retailer control and motivate personnel. Although the combination plan is more difficult to administer, its benefits generally outweigh its costs.

Salary-Plus-Bonus Plan

A popular method for compensating middle-management personnel such as department managers, store managers, and buyers is the **salary-plus-bonus plan,** which

Retail firms recently have begun to offer employees the use of physical fitness centers as a fringe benefit.

involves a straight monthly salary supplemented by either semiannual or annual bonuses for exceeding performance goals. Performance goals and related bonuses usually are set by upper management for each operating unit and typically are expressed in the form of increased sales or profits, decreased operating costs, or some other measure of the operating unit's productivity. The most common problems associated with the salary-plus-bonus plan are employees' difficulty in understanding such plans and administrators' problems in setting up the performance criteria and measurement instruments to make the system work.

Fringe Benefits

The employee's total compensation package also includes fringe benefits, which vary greatly from one retail firm to another. In recent years, fringe benefits have become more important in the retailer's efforts to attract and keep qualified personnel. Fringe benefits are much more important for middle- and upper-level positions than for entry-level positions. As unionization of lower-level personnel becomes more common, however, benefit packages at that level will increase in significance.

Among the most popular fringe benefits are (1) insurance programs covering life, health, accident, and disability;[34] (2) sick leave; (3) personal leave time; (4) holiday leave and paid vacations; (5) pension plans; (6) profit sharing; (7) employee discounts; (8) recreational facilities; (9) coffee breaks; (10) employee parties; and (11) team sponsorships. As more women enter the labor force, day care is becoming an important benefit in attracting and retaining productive employees. On-site day-care centers, child-care allowances, and cooperative day-care centers are all new additions to the benefit packages that retailers currently are reviewing.[35] Fringe benefits are becoming a more important form of compensation in today's leisure-oriented society, with the goal of making employees happy, content, and loyal to the store. J. C. Penney's comprehensive benefit package includes "a savings and profit-sharing program, a pension plan for all associates, no-cost life insurance, medical and dental insurance, three weeks of vacation after five years, and 15% off all Penney merchandise. Anyone who works more than 20 hours a week is eligible for the benefits."[36] Additional perks for company executives include club memberships, company cars, financial counseling, and spouse travel.

SUMMARY

Retailers use numerous structures to organize their people, tasks, and operations. The retailing firm's organization is directed at accomplishing certain strategic, operational, and functional objectives. Also, retailers must organize so as to facilitate the basic operational tasks of planning and controlling the product, price, promotion, and distribution.

The retailer should consider several basic principles of organization in developing its organizational structure. Of particular interest are the organizational principles of specialization and departmentalization, lines of authority and areas of responsibility, unity of command, and span of control.

Many retailers prepare charts to illustrate their form of retail organization. Some retail organizational structures are characterized by a limited number of levels (flat organizations), while others incorporate several levels (vertical structures). Organizational forms are strongly influenced by how retailers classify jobs and tasks. Depending on the firm, jobs and tasks can be classified on the basis of their functional, geographic, or product relationships or a combination of these three factors.

Patterns of retail organization vary considerably between the simple structures of the small, independent retailer and the often complex organization of the department and chain store retailer. Centralization, specialization, and standardization are the key characteristics of chain store organizational structures. The Mazur plan and its variations characterize department store structures.

The staffing process consists of eight steps. The first is describing the job, including developing job descriptions and conducting job analyses. The second is specifying the job— writing job classifications that both outline the responsibilities of the position and avoid charges of unfair employment practices. The third is recruiting store personnel, including both finding and screening potential employee candidates. The fourth is selecting from the list of qualified applicants the individuals best suited to the job by carefully reviewing application forms, personal interviews, reference checks, testing instruments, and physical examinations. Fifth is training store personnel. It requires the retailer to know what to train (organization orientation and functional or task training), where to train (on-the-job or off-the-job), and how to train (individual training method, programmed learning, sponsor or group training methods). Executive training programs are sessions directed at store supervisors, managers, and executives. Sixth is supervision, including motivation of employees. One method of motivation is to eliminate conditions that generate job dissatisfaction and to initiate programs that promote satisfaction. Supervising can be approached in a heavyhanded manner (close supervision) or in a lighthanded fashion (limited supervision). The seventh step is evaluating store employees. The retailer must address issues such as when to evaluate, what to evaluate, and how to evaluate personnel. In the final step, the retailer determines the type of compensation system to use. Alternatives are the straight-salary plan, straight-commission plan, salary-plus-commission plan, and salary-plus-bonus plan, all of which might involve various fringe benefits.

STUDENT STUDY GUIDE

Key Terms and Concepts

achievement tests (p. 250)
centralization (p. 242)
departmentalization (p. 231)
dissatisfier (p. 254)
equal-store organization (p. 241)
executive training programs (ETPs) (p. 253)
flat organizational structure (p. 234)
formal objective evaluation methods (p. 257)
formal subjective evaluation methods (p. 258)
functional approach to organizational structure (p. 235)
functional objectives (p. 230)
functional training (p. 251)
geographic approach to organizational structure (p. 236)
group training method (p. 252)
heavyhanded supervision (p. 255)
individual training method (p. 251)
informal objective evaluation methods (p. 258)
informal subjective evaluation methods (p. 258)
job description (p. 245)
job specification (p. 245)
lighthanded supervision (p. 255)
line relationships (p. 232)
lines of authority (p. 232)
lines of responsibility (p. 232)
main-store organization (p. 240)
Mazur plan (p. 239)
motivation (p. 254)
off-the-job training (p. 251)
on-the-job training (p. 251)
operational objectives (p. 230)
organization orientation (p. 250)
product approach to organizational structure (p. 237)
programmed learning (p. 252)
psychological tests (p. 250)
salary-plus-bonus plan (p. 262)
salary-plus-commission plan (p. 261)
satisfier (p. 254)
separate-store organization (p. 240)
span of control (p. 234)
specialization (p. 231)
sponsor training method (p. 252)
staff relationships (p. 233)
standardization (p. 243)
straight-commission plan (p. 261)
straight-salary plan (p. 261)
strategic objectives (p. 230)
supervision (p. 254)
unity of command (p. 234)
vertical (tall) organizational structure (p. 235)

Review Questions

1. What are the three levels of organizational objectives? Define each and describe its relationship to the general levels of retail management.
2. Describe the organizational principles of specialization and departmentalization. How can specialization and departmentalization be accomplished?
3. Distinguish between line and staff relationships. How do these relationships affect the organizational chart?
4. What is unity of command? Why is this principle important?
5. What is span of control? Is there an ideal span of control? Describe the guidelines for determining span of control.
6. Compare and contrast the pros and cons of vertical and flat organizational structures.
7. Describe the three criteria used in job classification.
8. What are the four functional divisions in the Mazur plan of retail organization? How is this plan usually modified?
9. Outline the advantages and disadvantages of separation of buying and selling activities.
10. Compare and contrast the main-store, separate-store, and equal-store approaches to branch department store organization.
11. What elements distinguish chain store organizations? Discuss each.
12. What specific information should be obtained in a job analysis? Why should a written job specification be given to a potential employee?
13. Identify the internal and external sources of prospective employees.
14. What is the most effective way to check an applicant's references?
15. List the relative advantages of a formal, highly structured interviewing process and the informal, unstructured method of interviewing.
16. What two general types of testing instruments are used to evaluate applicants? Describe each type. Which instrument is generally preferred? Why?
17. Describe the two types of training needed by both veteran and new employees.
18. How do on-the-job and off-the-job training differ?
19. What methods are available to the retailer for training employees? Briefly describe each method.
20. What are satisfiers and dissatisfiers? How do they affect employee motivation?
21. Compare and contrast McGregor's Theory X and Theory Y.
22. What are the advantages of the straight-salary compensation plan? What problems result from the monetary incentive created by the straight-commission plan?

Review Exam

True or False

_____ 1. Operational objectives are general statements of long-term operational requirements that are necessary to achieve a strategy objective.

_____ 2. Line managers typically are specialists whose primary function is to assist staff managers in realizing their objectives.

_____ 3. Where tasks are highly centralized in one location, the supervisor's span of control can be broadened.

_____ 4. The organizational structure of department stores is flatter and more generalized than that of small, independent retail organizations.

_____ 5. Small, independent retailers usually have a two-function organizational structure, thereby limiting specialization.

_____ 6. A major argument for combining the buying and selling functions is that it makes it easier to assign responsibility for the department's profile performance.

_____ 7. Under the equal-store approach to branch department store organization, each branch has its own store manager as well as personnel, merchandise, and operations managers, who operate separately from the parent store.

Multiple Choice

_____ 1. A _____ clearly states the minimum qualifications a person must have to obtain the job.
- a. Job description
- b. Job analysis
- c. Job specification
- d. Job objective
- e. Rack jobber

_____ 2. Initial prospect screening and retailer anonymity during the initial recruiting stages are two advantages associated with which source of prospective employees?
- a. Newspaper advertisements
- b. Public employment agencies
- c. Private employment agencies
- d. Journal advertisements
- e. b and c

_____ 3. Applicants' _____ should *not* be requested on the retailer's application form.
- a. Name, address, and telephone number
- b. Employment history
- c. Formal education and training
- d. Complete demographic makeup
- e. List of references

_____ 4. Which of the following is *not* an advantage of a formal, highly structured personal interview situation?
- a. It establishes the relative roles of each party in the interview.
- b. It permits a controlled interviewing environment.
- c. It allows the applicant to be viewed in an unguarded state.
- d. It facilitates complete, effective gathering of information about the applicant.

_____ 5. Group training methods involve the simultaneous training of several employees through the use of _____.
- a. Lectures
- b. Demonstrations
- c. Case studies
- d. Role-playing activities
- e. All of the above

_____ 6. Theory Y assumes that
- a. Motivation occurs only at an economic level.
- b. People must be closely supervised.
- c. Workers are social beings who can work together for organizational and personal goals.
- d. People can be considered alike as units of production.
- e. People are indolent by nature.

_____ 7. The "halo effect" or "good-old-boy syndrome" is a constant danger associated with the _____ employee evaluation method.
- a. Informal subjective
- b. Formal subjective
- c. Informal objective
- d. Formal objective

STUDENT APPLICATIONS MANUAL

Investigative Projects: Practice and Applications

1. Obtain an organizational chart from a department store chain and a specialty store chain. Compare and contrast the two organizational charts. What are the strengths and weaknesses of each organizational form? On the basis of organizational structure, which organization would you prefer as a career path? Why?
2. Outline two specific examples of strategy, operational, and functional objectives for a stereo system department.
3. Explain how specialization, departmentalization, lines of authority and responsibility, unit of command, and span of control help the retailer avoid managerial confusion and employee discontent.

4. What are the advantages and disadvantages of working for a retail organization characterized by a flat organizational structure? For one having a vertical organizational structure?
5. Describe the conditions under which the retailer should consider a functional approach to retail organizational structure and the classification of jobs and tasks. Explain why he or she might consider adopting a geographic approach.
6. Obtain and analyze three retail job descriptions from your local newspaper or from the personnel director for a local retailer. Judging from the advertised job description, has the retailer made a careful determination of its personnel needs? Does the retailer provide the applicant with the means to evaluate the job as a potential source of employment?
7. Assume you are the manager of the sporting goods department of a large department store and are responsible for conducting the initial personal interviews with the applicants for the assistant department manager position. Develop a list of potential questions to ask each applicant. Explain your reason for asking each question, as well as what answers you would view favorably for each.
8. What are the advantages and disadvantages of on-the-job and off-the-job training? Contact a major retail organization in your community, and obtain the specifics of its executive training program. After reviewing the program, explain whether or not you would seriously consider the firm as a potential employer when you graduate.
9. Under what circumstances should the retailer consider using the heavy-handed approach to employee supervision?
10. Obtain employee evaluation forms and procedures from a local retailer. Classify these forms and procedures as to their objectivity and formality. Assess the forms and procedures as to their effectiveness as employee evaluation instruments and their fairness to employees.

Tactical Cases: Problems and Decisions

■ CASE 7–1
The Case of the Organic Gardener: Investigating Various Forms of Business Ownership*

Gareth Reed was known for his melons, particularly among organic gardening enthusiasts. Organic gardeners use only natural fertilizers and forms of insect control. Compost, natural or dehydrated manures, and dehydrated seaweed are some of the fertilizers used; bug traps using feromes, powders, or sprays with rotenone or pyrethrins and side-by-side planting or combinations of vegetables or of flowers and vegetables are means of insect control.

Reed had graduated with a bachelor's degree in biology and, after a couple of false starts, had become a medical laboratory technician. He had enjoyed doing the individual tests in serology, hematology, and blood chemistry. Now, however, one blood specimen could be run through an automatic "hemoanalyzer," which performed several diagnostic tests. The loss of opportunity for individual investigation had diminished his enthusiasm for that line of work.

Reed had learned that a lawn and garden store he occasionally patronized was for sale because the owner was ill. He knew of no lawn and garden store within a 30-mile radius of this store that carried a full line of organic gardening products and seeds that were not treated with chemicals or poisons to repel birds and other scavengers. Presently he had to drive 40 miles to patronize his preferred source of organic garden supplies but figured that not all organic gardeners were as persnickety as himself. Thus, he figured he could enhance the business of the store that was for sale by carrying a full line of organic gardening supplies due to his popularity with organic gardeners throughout the county.

Reed felt quite comfortable with the prospect of the operations aspect of a lawn and garden store, because he had worked in a hardware store part time for many years. However, he had taken no business courses in college and never been involved in the financial aspects of running a business. There was also the issue of raising the necessary capital in buying the business from the present owner.

Reed stopped in the store one day on his way home from work. He talked with the owner and his wife, the Mofits, who had living quarters in the back of the store. It was around closing time, and when the Mofits became convinced that Reed's interest was more than a casual inquiry, they closed for the day and invited him to ask any questions he wished. While Mrs. Mofit prepared supper, Mr. Mofit showed Reed the financial records and even quoted his asking price. When Reed expressed concern, Mr. Mofit even indicated that he and Mrs. Mofit would consider staying on as partners with the "right" person.

Following his visit with the Mofits, Reed decided to do some further investigation. A high school classmate, Kim Falanga, was a managing partner in a highly successful certified public accounting firm. Reed arranged an appointment and was pleased to find Falanga cordial, professional, and well prepared to discuss all financial aspects of retail ventures similar to and including lawn and garden stores. She asked some questions that he hadn't thought about and was embarrassed by some of his answers. He was surprised that she encouraged him to develop a formal proposal for funding along guidelines that she provided. His surprise turned to amazement when she hinted that she might personally be interested in investing in this venture.

He got another surprise when he contacted a number of fellow organic gardeners. His purpose was merely to ascertain their interest in a more accessible source of full-line organic gardening supplies. But he discovered not only interest but inquiries about investing and, in one instance, about part-time employment. One thing led to another and eventually to a meeting at his house of the organic gardeners who had expressed unexpected interest beyond just a closer source of supplies. In this group was a lawyer, who was knowledgeable and helpful in explaining the advantages and disadvantages of general and limited partnerships as well as corporations. Although no consensus as to the form of ownership was established, only a couple of those present appeared to have any reservations about some type of financial interest in the venture. No one indicated dollar amounts, but there were indications that all were reasonably well established financially.

After everyone left, Reed pondered his situation. He wasn't sure he could raise enough money to buy the lawn and garden store by liquidating his own resources. Even if he could, the risk would be high since everything he had would be invested in the store. Further, selling his house would leave him without a place to garden. He could rent a plot of ground, but he hated the thought of parting with all that compost-rich soil he had so carefully nurtured over the years.

His discussion with the Mofits had revealed little interest on their part in carrying a full line of organic supplies. Mr. Mofit claimed that even the limited organic supplies he carried didn't "move very fast." As for Kim Falanga, he wistfully wondered if the heart of an organic gardener beat beneath her tailored business suits. Her polished nails probably had never turned the handle of a compost maker. The "organic group" was long on enthusiasm but other than the lawyer, appeared to have relatively little business background that would compensate for Reed's inexperience with the financial management.

ASSIGNMENT

1. Outline the advantages and disadvantages of the alternative forms of business ownership available to Gareth Reed.
2. Rank the form of business that you think would be best for Reed based on the information provided. Justify your ranking.
3. What additional information, if any, do you believe would be particularly helpful if you were in Reed's garden shoes?

*This case was prepared by Ken Mast and Jon Hawes, The University of Akron.

■ CASE 7–2
Braddock's Department Stores: Facing Up to the Growing Retail Labor Crunch*

As president of Braddock's Department Stores, a chain of nine stores located in central and southern California, Amy Whitmeyer usually spent her time dealing with sales volume promotions, marketing and merchandising strategies, and long-term planning. Lately another problem was developing that required increasing attention—the growing shortage of sales, clerical, and management personnel. In many areas of the country, particularly on the East and West Coasts, the personnel shortage problem was acute; it was hampering store operations and impeding growth. Reasons for this shortage were many, but among the most prominent were (1) a shrinking number of people in the 16-to-24 age group, which traditionally staffed most lower-level retail positions; (2) the rapid growth of the retail sector in terms of job creation; and (3) the low wages, poor working conditions, and meager benefits associated with lower-echelon positions.

Whitmeyer feared the labor crunch would soon affect Braddock's. She was especially concerned because the turnover rate among both sales and management personnel at the company was already high. Nearly 40 percent of the individuals hired for Braddock's management trainee program had left the company after one year, a figure similar to that in much of the industry. The company had not fully investigated the reason for this high rate, but someone from human resources told Whitmeyer that many management trainees quit because they were unable to adjust to the hard first year of job training (e.g., long hours, weekend hours, physical work, dealing with customers). After a year or two, things became easier. Many trainees left before then, however, although company data showed that within a few years Braddock's managers had greater opportunities and better compensation than many other firms or industries (i.e., jobs in banking and insurance) offered.

Whitmeyer was studying a report supplied by the human resources department that outlined most of Braddock's personnel policies. As expected, the report showed that for lower-level sales and clerical employees, Braddock's hired primarily high school and college students to work part time; however, a few worked full time. The firm usually relied on walk-in applicants to fill lower-level positions or used newspaper want ads if the need was great enough. For store and corporate management positions, Braddock's hired only college graduates who entered the firm's management training program. These trainees were chosen from unsolicited applications and from the twice-yearly recruiting trips to the two local universities.

The report also contained some of the gloomy projections about personnel shortages the company would experience in coming years. It warned that the pool of candidates from which the company now drew its applicants was contracting and there would be increasing competition with other retailers for available candidates. The report also discussed the turnover problem within the company. Though Braddock's had not conducted any studies on the problems particular to its own employee turnover, the human resources department had been looking at some research showing that although pay and benefits were important components of an employee's decision to stay with a retail firm, other factors were influential. Specifically the report identified five factors especially important to lower level employees:

1. Skill variety—the number of skills and talents the job required
2. Task identity—the degree to which an employee did a job from beginning to end with a visible outcome
3. Task significance—the impact of that job on other people
4. Autonomy—the freedom and independence an employee had to determine his or her own work procedures
5. Feedback—the direct information an employee received about the effectiveness of his or her performance.

In short, the report said these psychological aspects of the job could be as important as the monetary ones for retaining and motivating sales and clerical employees who felt jobs were not valued by the company and they were treated poorly by their supervisors.

The report concluded that wages and benefits probably would have to be raised for both management and lower-level employees to attract and retain the people the company would need in the coming years. However, Whitmeyer felt this would not be sufficient. She realized that although Braddock's would have to increase the monetary aspects of the job, everyone in the business, including many of Braddock's competitors, would be forced to do the same to compete with other industries for employees. The net result would be that while wages, and therefore costs, would be higher than at present, the personnel shortage likely would remain.

Whitmeyer was convinced that it would be necessary to come up with some creative techniques for attracting employees and keeping them with the company. She realized the company couldn't overhaul its personnel policies overnight, but she thought it had better start preparing now before Braddock's found it had stores full of customers and too few employees to service them.

ASSIGNMENT

Assume you are Braddock's SPO (senior personnel officer). Whitmeyer has asked you to prepare a report dealing with the following issues:

1. Evaluate Braddock's recruitment process for both management and sales employees. In light of the predicted retail labor shortage, what actions can you suggest to improve the process?
2. The employee turnover rate is high for Braddock's. Identify possible causes. What policies or practices can you recommend that might help Braddock's retain both sales and management employees? Be creative.
3. Now you have come up with some solid suggestions for improving the recruiting, retaining, and motivation of employees for Braddock's. Whitmeyer will also want to know what disadvantages the company might run into if the firm adopts your suggestions. Help her out.

*This case was prepared by Daniel Gilmore, The University of Akron.

ENDNOTES

1. Jackie Bivins, "Corporate Cultures," *Stores* (February 1989): 9. Copyright © National Retail Federation, Inc. New York, New York.
2. See Brian Bremner and Michael Oneal, "The Big Store's Big Trauma," *Business Week*, July 10, 1989, 50–55.
3. Paul M. Mazur, *Principles of Organization Applied to Modern Retailing* (New York: Harper & Row, 1927).
4. See, for example, Carole Sloan, "Merchandising the Branches," *Stores*, January 1988, 71–74.
5. See Anthony Redwood, "Human Resources Management in the 1990s," *Business Horizons* (January-February 1990): 74–80; Bill Richards, "Wanting Workers," *The Wall Street Journal*, February 9, 1990, R10–R11.
6. Arthur J. Rawl, "Training Programs Must Reflect Today's Environment," *Chain Store Age Executive*, June 1989, 61.
7. Neil M. Ford, "Recruitment and Selection—Are There Easy Answers?", *Sales Management Bulletin* 2 (Summer 1987): 3–4.
8. See Paul Spiers, "Older Workers Are Ready, Willing, and Able," *Business and Society Review* (Winter 1990): 68–69.
9. Jules Abend, "Taking Care of Your Own," *Stores*, November 1987, 98.
10. "Neiman Marcus Tries on a New Suit," *Business Week*, February 26, 1990, 49.
11. Robert F. Hartley, "The Weighted Application Blank," *Journal of Retailing* 46 (Spring 1970): 32–40.
12. "Marshall Field Implements Drug Testing," *Chain Store Age Executive*, March 1990, 83.
13. See "New Study: How Stores Are Paying," *Stores*, September 1989, 27–28.
14. See Marji Charlier, "Back to Basics," *The Wall Street Journal*, February 9, 1990, 14–15.
15. See J. B. Robinson, "Role Playing as a Sales Training Tool," *Harvard Business Review* (May-June 1987): 34–35; "Trainees Build Skills in Risk-Free Contest," *Chain Store Age Executive*, June 1987, 56,58; Robert Neff, "Videos Are Starring in More and More Training Programs," *Business Week*, September 7, 1987, 108–109.

16. Wendy Zellner, "Two Days in Boot Camp—Learning to Love Lexus," *Business Week,* September 4, 1989, 87.
17. Franchine Schwadel, "As Retailing's Chic and Indebted Stumble, Bland May Co. Thrives," *The Wall Street Journal,* January 19, 1990, A5.
18. Richard M. Petreycik, "Teamwork," *Progressive Grocer,* March 1990, 30.
19. Richard M. Petreycik, "Creative Recruiting That Works," *Progressive Grocer,* January 1990, 45.
20. Richard A. Femberg, Richard Widdows, and Amy Rummel, "Paying for Performance: What You Need to Know," *Retail Control* (April-May 1987): 40–41.
21. Frederick Herzberg, "One More Time: How Do You Motivate Employees?", *Harvard Business Review* 46 (January-February 1968): 53–62.
22. See Douglas McGregor, "The Human Side of Enterprise," in *Leadership and Motivation: Essays of Douglas McGregor,* ed. W. G. Bennis and E. Schein (Cambridge, Mass.: MIT Press, 1966).
23. Stephen Bennett, "Life on the Leading Edge," *Progressive Grocer,* February 1990, 71.
24. McGregor, "The Human Side of Enterprise."
25. Sarah Smith, "Leaders of the Most Admired," *Fortune,* January 29, 1990, 46.
26. See Alan J. Dubinsky and Michael Levy, "Influence of Organizational Fairness on Work Outcomes of Retail Salespeople," *Journal of Retailing,* 65 (Summer 1989): 221–243.
27. Patricia Sellers, "Getting Customers to Love You," *Fortune,* March 13, 1989, 40.
28. See William Weitzel, Albert B. Schwarzkopf, and E. Brian Peach, "The Influence of Employee Perceptions of Customer Service on Retail Store Sales," *Journal of Retailing* 65 (Spring 1989): 27–39.
29. James R. Terborg and Gerardo R. Ungson, "Group-Administered Bonus Pay and Retail Store Performance: A Two-Year Study of Management Compensation," *Journal of Retailing* 61 (Spring 1985): 63.
30. "How Younkers' 'Satisfaction Plus' Program Works," *Stores,* September 1989, 29.
31. Chuck Hawkins, "Will Home Depot Be 'The Wal-Mart of the 90's?' ", *Business Week,* March 19, 1990, 124.
32. Amy Dunkin and Kathleen Kerwin, "Now Salespeople Really Must Sell for Their Supper," *Business Week,* July 31, 1989, 50.
33. Francine Schwadel, "At Sears, Unpopular Pay Policy Reflects Fuss in Retail Industry," *The Wall Street Journal,* January 31, 1990, B-2.
34. Jacqueline Bivins, "The Cost of Benefits," *Stores,* June 1989, 29–32.
35. See Dyan Machan, "The Mommy and Daddy Tract," *Forbes,* April 16, 1990, 162–164. See also "Child Care and Retailing," *Stores,* June 1989, 32–33.
36. "How Other Industries Are Handling the Crunch," *Progressive Grocer,* January 1990, 48.

PART II

FACILITIES MANAGEMENT

Designing and Securing the Retail Store

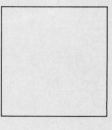

CHAPTER 8

OUTLINE

OBJECTIVES

- Appreciate the physical and psychological impacts that store facilities have on customer attraction, employee morale, and store operations.
- Distinguish design features vital in creating a desirable store image, in targeting the appropriate consumer group, and in communicating the right impression.
- Understand the design features necessary to create a store atmosphere conducive to buying.
- Identify and explain the major considerations in planning store exteriors capable of stopping and attracting customers.
- Specify and discuss the key features of the store's interior and their role in creating an inviting, comfortable, and convenient facility.
- Discuss the unique contribution of visual merchandising in the retailer's customer communication program.
- Plan and construct an effective in-store display.
- Identify the various types of security problems and their causes.
- Distinguish among the various devices and techniques used by thieves.
- Outline the methods retailers use to detect and prevent criminal activities.

With nine distinct divisions, each appealing to different consumer segments, The Limited, Inc. is the nation's largest specialty retailer. To meet the shopping needs of such a diverse consumer base, James D. Mansour, director of design and research, has created for each Limited store "a unique specialty store environment that reflects the aspirations of the customer. We don't underestimate the customers' taste levels. We don't look at the moderate business and schlock it up, we bring in what captures the integrity of the business."[1] Some of the store atmospherics created by Mansour include:

- Abercrombie & Fitch—very traditional, not trendy, reflects the heritage of two real people who happen to be real sportsmen, rugged individualists. Based on the original coat of arms and the Abercrombie family tartan, stuffed leather figures were incorporated into the store as footstools and accoutrements. Most of the store's fixturings are London antiques and furnishings. Nonantique fixtures were made by traditional craftsmen who beat them until they took on a worn, comfortable feeling.[2]
- Victoria's Secret—distinctive personality, an English lady, a traditional English-looking store, yet sensuous and feminine; not a Victorian store, but an inner sanctum, a secret. Everything in the store speaks of that culture.[3]
- Compagnie Internationale Express—formerly Limited Express, a mixture of some very contemporary pieces with antiques that reflect the company internationale. Antiques are of the French persuasion, mostly 18th century. The old and new live simultaneously.[4] "From the grainy wood floors to the black-lacquered display cases, the store serves as a stage for up-to-the-moment sportswear for women and now men."[5]
- The Limited—the new-generation store was designed to be comfortable and appropriate on any of the greatest shopping streets in the world—an international fashion destination. Poshness is a big lure; the white-and-black marble floors and antique furniture titillate customers.[6] The idea behind the upscaled store design is to overshoot the customer in every way possible except price.[7]

A store and its immediate area create the environment within which the retailer operates. This environment either attracts or repels potential customers. Accordingly, the retailer must make a concentrated effort to ensure that the store's environment is conducive to both retail operations and consumers' shopping needs. In this chapter, we explore the elements of store design, visual merchandising, and store security.

THE STORE'S ENVIRONMENT

In selecting and developing a store's environment, the retailer must consider its *physical* and *psychological* impacts on customer attraction, employee morale, and store operations. Both store operations and customer shopping are enhanced by a well-planned and well-designed setting. A store's physical environment is a composite of the tangible elements of form reflected in the way land, building, equipment, and fixtures are assembled for the convenience and comfort of both customers and retailer. Equally important is the store's psychological environment—the perceived atmosphere the retailer creates. In essence, a store's psychological environment is the mental image of the store produced in customers' minds. A store's effectiveness and uniqueness lie in the retailer's ability to plan, create, and control both the store's physical and psychological setting. A Laura Ashley store, for example, "with its dark green front and blackberry sprig motif, woodsy interior and heathery scents, conjures up images of the cozy, privileged gentry of England."[8] The psychological impressions a store makes on consumers depend on the store's image and buying atmosphere: "For a consumer to want to go to a store . . . he or she is going to need a reason. . . . Retailers will have to offer a theatrical approach."[9] Further, "one important aspect of all theater is escapism, and for many shoppers, the retail store can offer that quick escape. Ralph Lauren is an escapist design, pseudo British."[10]

Creating a Store Image

Creating a **store image** is one of the retailer's principal concerns. Because it represents to the consumer a composite picture of the retailer, image is one of the most powerful tools in attracting and satisfying consumers. Creating an image, however, is a very difficult task. An *image* is a mental picture that forms in the human mind as a result of many different stimuli. These stimuli include the retailer's physical facilities, the store's location, product lines, service offering, pricing policies, and promotional activities. A store's image is the store's personality. It is how the consumer *sees* the store as well as what the consumer *feels* about the store. Therefore, it is important that retailers know and plan what they want the consumer to see and feel.

The store's exterior and interior are key factors in the retailer's image-creating efforts. *Externally*, the position of the store on the site, its architectural design, its storefront, and the placement of signs, entrances, and display windows all contribute to the store's image. *Internally*, a store's image can be created in part by the layout of departments and traffic aisles, the use of store displays, and the selection of store fixtures and equipment.[11] No standard combinations of external and internal store factors can produce a given image.

In designing the image-creating features of the store's physical facilities, the retailer must work with a particular target consumer in mind. Neither the retailer nor the store can be all things to all people. Likewise, a single image that will appeal to *all* consumers cannot be created. Therefore, a store's facilities should be tailored to the psychological and physical needs of a selected customer group.

The physical facilities of a retail store can be an important vehicle for nonverbal communication. Communicating the right impression means that the store's personality helps "position" one retailer against other retailers, thereby facilitating the store selection process for consumers. Communicating the desired impression, then, is a problem of how to best use physical facilities to convey to consumers what the retailer wants them to see and feel.

Creating a Buying Atmosphere

To create an atmosphere conducive to buying, a retailer should establish in the consumer a frame of mind that will promote a buying spirit. Even the economy-minded consumer wants something more than a shopping atmosphere with only the bare essentials. Today's shoppers, regardless of their principal shopping motives, are drawn to safe, attractive, and comfortable shopping environments. The store's atmosphere should be an agreeable environment for both the consumer and the retailer. The tropical decor of Burdine's department store in TownCenter Mall in Boca Raton, Florida, helps to distinguish it from the more somber, mahogany-and-brass decor of Saks Fifth Avenue and Lord & Taylor stores. Burdine's light and breezy decor fits the Florida environment: "Complementing the pink-hued floors and walls, some ceilings have been painted to resemble skies dotted with puffy clouds. Most of the wood is bleached and many of the building's support columns are housed in white fiberglass palm trees. A center atrium brings in natural light."[12]

The retailer wants to influence the consumer's mood by creating an atmosphere that will positively influence buying behavior. An appealing buying atmosphere uses cues that appeal to the consumer's five senses of sight, hearing, smell, touch, and taste. Waldenbooks, Inc. introduced its WaldenKids stores, which sell books and educational toys and games. The WaldenKids stores mimic a playground: "Kids can even crawl into the store through a carpeted tunnel. Inside, children are greeted by a video monitor playing cartoon fairy tales—painted primary red, yellow, and blue—toys from computer games to wooden railroads are just waiting for eager little hands."[13]

Sensory cues can be strongly reinforced if they are structured around shopping themes that unify and organize the store's atmosphere. The following sections discuss how a retailer can use sensory appeals to effect a favorable store image and pleasant shopping environment.

Sight Appeal

The sense of sight provides people with more information than any other sense mode and therefore must be considered the most important means by which retailers can appeal to consumers. For our purposes, and for the sake of simplicity, we can view **sight appeal** as the process of imparting stimuli, resulting in perceived visual relationships. Size, shape, and color are three primary visual stimuli a retailer can use to arouse the consumer's attention. Visual relationships are interpretations made by the "mind's eye" from visual stimuli consisting of harmony, contrast, and clash. *Harmony* is "visual agreement"; *contrast* is "visual diversity"; and *clash* is "visual conflict" that can occur among the many parts of any display, layout, or physical arrangement. In any given situation either harmony, contrast, or clash may be the best way to create an appealing shopping atmosphere. Harmonious visual relationships generally are associated with a quieter, plusher, and more formal shopping setting, while contrasting and clashing visual relationships can promote an exciting, cheerful, or informal atmosphere. To control these environmental impressions, the retailer must understand the basics of visual stimuli.

Size Perceptions. The sheer physical size of a store, display, sign, or department can communicate many things to many people. Size can communicate relative importance, success, strength, power, and security. Some consumers feel more secure when they buy from large stores because they believe large stores are more capable and more

Display harmony (visual agreement) and clash (visual conflict) affect consumer buying moods.

willing to fix, adjust, or replace faulty merchandise. Other consumers prefer large stores because of the prestige they associate with such operations. A smaller store, display, or department may be perceived as less important, successful, or powerful than its larger counterparts, but it could be viewed as more personal, intimate, or friendly.

Size is a key element in creating harmony, contrast, and clash. To achieve a harmonious atmosphere in a store department or display, the retailer should maintain a consistent size relationship among its various elements. Using *moderately* different size elements can create contrast among various departments within the store or different displays within the department. Clashing relationships can be created by using substantially diverse size elements.

Shape Perceptions. Shapes arouse certain emotions within buyers. In planning store layouts and designing store displays, the retailer should recognize that a vertical line gives "a rigid, severe, and masculine quality to an area. It expresses strength and stability . . . gives the viewer an up-and-down eye movement . . . tends to heighten an area, gives the illusion of increased space in this direction."[14] Similarly, horizontal lines promote a feeling of rest, relaxation, and repose; diagonal lines connote action and movement and sometimes give the illusion of instability;[15] and curved lines suggest a feminine atmosphere and add a flowing movement that directs the eye to a display or department. Equally important in facilities planning is the similarity or dissimilarity among shapes: "For the creation of perfect harmony in a display, shapes that correspond exactly to one another are used exclusively. Inharmonious or dissimilar shapes may be used in a display to create contrast and, in some instances, a point of emphasis."[16]

Different lines and shapes give various impressions to store displays and contribute to the overall atmosphere of the store layout.

Color Perceptions. Color makes the first impression on someone looking at an object. Color often is what catches customers' eyes, keeps their attention, and stimulates them to buy. The U.S. consumer is becoming increasingly color conscious. For most customers, if the color is wrong, everything is wrong.

The psychological impact of color results from the three color properties of hue, value, and intensity. *Hue* is the name of the color. *Value* is the lightness or darkness of a hue. Darker values are referred to as *shades,* while lighter values are called *tints*. The brightness or dullness of a hue is its *intensity*. For the retailer, color psychology is important not only in selling merchandise, but in creating the proper atmosphere for selling that merchandise.

The impact of color psychology becomes apparent as soon as we classify hues into *warm* and *cool* tones. The warm colors (red, yellow, and orange) and the cool colors (blue, green, and violet) symbolize different things to different consumer groups. Figure 8–1 identifies some of the associations and symbols consumers attach to colors. Warm colors connote a comfortable, informal atmosphere. Cool colors, on the other hand, project a formal, aloof, icy impression. When used properly, however, both warm and cool colors can create a relaxing yet stimulating atmosphere in which to shop.

Red is one of the most stimulating colors and should be used with considerable care. Too much red can be overpowering; thus, it should be used as an accent color rather than as a basic background color. To attract attention and stimulate buyer action, red frequently appears on building signs, fixtures, and displays. Two exceptions to using red only as an accent color are restaurants and cocktail lounges, in which red is thought to stimulate people's appetites. Christmas and Valentine's Day are two holiday seasons when red is an appropriate display color. Shades of red are also appropriate for certain decorative themes, such as carnivals and sports.

Yellow, like red, is a stimulating color that must be used with caution. Yellow's principal asset is its visibility at long distances, which makes shades of yellow a logical color selection for signs, walls, and poorly lit areas. The time to use yellow is in the spring, particularly around Easter. Yellow is also considered a color for children, so it is appropriate for decorating infants', children's, and toy departments.

Packaging relies heavily on the psychological effects of color.

Orange is used sparingly because of its high intensity and its tendency to clash with other colors. Most often thought of as a fall color (fall foliage, harvest, and Halloween), orange is used primarily for accent and not as a basic decorative color. Orange, like yellow, is a children's color and livens up a children's department by evoking warm, cheerful surroundings.

Blue is associated with the cool, blue sky and the calm, blue sea. As a result, retailers use blues to create a serene, relaxing shopping atmosphere. Because blue also connotes masculinity, shades of blue often appear in men's departments. In addition, blue works well as a trim and as a basic background.

Like blue, *green* has many pleasant associations—the newness and freshness of spring and the peacefulness of the great outdoors. Many experts believe that green is probably the single most popular and accepted color. Its soft and relaxing qualities make green an ideal choice for many uses. Green is perceived as a spacious color and

FIGURE 8–1
Perceptions of colors

Warm Colors			Cool Colors		
Red	Yellow	Orange	Blue	Green	Violet
Love	Sunlight	Sunlight	Coolness	Coolness	Coolness
Romance	Warmth	Warmth	Aloofness	Restful	Retiring
Sex	Cowardice	Openness	Fidelity	Peace	Dignity
Courage	Openness	Friendliness	Calmness	Freshness	Rich
Danger	Friendliness	Gaiety	Piety	Growth	
Fire	Gaiety	Glory	Masculine	Softness	
Sinful	Glory		Assurance	Richness	
Warmth	Brightness		Sadness	Go	
Excitement	Caution				
Vigor					
Cheerfulness					
Enthusiasm					
Stop					

therefore is useful for making small areas appear larger. Its softness also helps accentuate displayed merchandise.

Violet is little used in retail displays except to achieve special effects. Overuse of this hue is thought to dampen shoppers' spirits.

The lightness and darkness of colors create optical illusions that retailers can use to modify stores' physical characteristics. Generally lighter colors make a room or an object appear larger, while darker colors create an illusion of smallness. Light neutral tones (e.g., beige) are popular as fixture colors, because they are perceived as warm and soft and do not detract from the displayed merchandise. Darker colors, on the other hand, have attention-grabbing ability; for example, by using darker colors at the back of a store, a retailer can draw consumers' attention to that area and increase the flow of customer traffic throughout the store.

The brightness and dullness of different physical facilities also affect the buying atmosphere. Like color value, color intensity can create illusions. Bright graphics and multicolor, flashing, sequenced neon signs are used by one chain of appliance superstores for both functional and aesthetic purposes: They identify the different departments while adding color and excitement to the warehouse atmosphere.[17] Bright colors make the facilities appear larger than do duller colors. However, a bright color tends to create an illusion of hardness, while a dull color appears softer. As a rule, children react more favorably to brighter colors; hence, these colors are widely used in children's departments. Adults, on the other hand, prefer softer tones, which may explain why many retailers use pastels.

Sound Appeal

Sound appeal is another important dimension of a store's buying atmosphere. In planning store facilities, it is as important to avoid undesirable sounds as it is to create desirable ones. Disturbing noises detract from a store's appeal, while pleasant sounds can attract customers.

Sound Avoidance. Obtrusive sounds distract consumers, interrupting the buying process. Whether these sounds originate inside or outside of the store, they must be either controlled or eliminated. Noise avoidance is a problem tailor-made for physical facilities planning. Careful use of architectural design, construction materials, equipment, and interior decors can eliminate or at least substantially reduce most obtrusive sounds. For example, the sound of clicking heels can be eliminated by heavy, durable carpeting, humming air conditioners can be strategically positioned away from selling areas, and rattling jackhammers and undesirable external music can be neutralized by proper insulation. Lower ceilings and sound-absorbing partitions and fixtures reduce unwanted sounds even further.

Sound Creation. To create an atmosphere that encourages buying, the retailer can use sound appeal in a variety of ways. Sound can be a mood setter, an attention getter, and an informer. Music can relax the customer, promote a buying spirit, set the stage for a particular shopping theme (e.g., a Mexican fiesta), or remind the customer of a special season or holiday (particularly Christmas), as well as provide a generally pleasant background of familiar sounds. Jungle Jim's, a supermarket in Fairfield, Ohio, has "life-size replicas of elephants squirting water inside the store and a pond filled with birds greeting visitors upon their arrival. A singing hippopotamus serenades shoppers at the checkout."[18] Music must complement the selling scene, however, not detract from it. The type (rock, classical, soul, etc.) and volume of music must be suitable to the retailer's consuming public: "If a store chooses to play music, the selection should match its image and audience—music should enhance the environment, not overwhelm it. In Ralph Lauren's Madison Avenue store the stereo plays Vivaldi and jazz in the morning and Frank Sinatra at 5 P.M."[19]

Sound has been used as an attention getter in a variety of circumstances. Attention-getting sounds can draw customers to a particular display or department. Noise-making toys attract both children and adults to the toy department. K mart stores draw attention to their "specials" with loud announcements: "Attention, K mart shoppers." Finally, fast, convenient, and pleasurable shopping requires that the customer have sufficient information about the store, its merchandise, and its operations. Frequently the retailer must inform the consumer about where to go, when to go, how to get there, and what is available. Because this basic information is a prerequisite to the buying process, the *informer* role of sound is a key element in creating a buying atmosphere. The Music Sampler is an interactive kiosk that "lets customers listen to musical excerpts from new releases while watching a video slide show for each album."[20]

Scent Appeal

The creation of **scent appeal** is a problem similar in scope to that of the sound appeal problem: how to avoid unpleasant odors and create pleasant scents. Stale, musty, and foul odors offend everyone and are sure to create negative impressions. Inadequate ventilation, insufficient humidity control, and poorly placed and maintained sanitation facilities are frequent causes of undesirable odors. Store facilities should be designed to minimize these problems or eliminate them entirely. Pleasurable scents, on the other hand, are key ingredients in creating atmospheric conditions that induce the customer to buy. A strategically placed fan in a bakery shop, candy store, or delicatessen attracts the passerby to these almost unavoidable pleasurable scents of products frequently bought on impulse. Retailers of foods, tobacco, flowers, perfumes, and other scented products know the value of exposing their customers' noses to the scents. A store should smell like it is supposed to smell. Some stores, such as a drugstore, should smell clean and antiseptic. For others, such as an antique store, a dusty, musty smell could enhance the buying atmosphere.

Touch Appeal

At one point in the history of retailing, the vending machine was considered the retailing store of the future. Today, although the vending machine admittedly is an important retailer of some standardized products, it is still an unacceptable way to sell most goods. The vending machine's lack of acceptance is largely the direct result of the machine's inability to provide **touch appeal**. For most products, personal inspection—handling, squeezing, and cuddling—is a prerequisite to buying. Before buying a product, the average consumer must at least hold it, even if it cannot be removed from its package. Store layouts, fixtures, equipment, and displays encourage and facilitate the consumer's sense of touch. The chances for a sale increase substantially when the consumer handles the product. The expression "I just couldn't put it down" underscores the importance of getting the consumer to pick up a product.

Good facilities planning not only encourages the consumer to pick up the product; it helps protect the product. Displays and fixtures should be designed to (1) provide consumers with samples to handle, thereby protecting products for sale from unnecessary handling, and (2) provide product protection from normal store dust and dirt.

Taste Appeal

For some food retailers, offering the consumer a taste might be a necessary condition for buying. This often is the case with specialty foods such as meats, cheeses, and bakery and dairy products. Hickory Farms and Baskin Robbins are two specialty food retailers that use **taste appeal** as part of their selling operations. In designing in-store displays, such retailers provide potential customers with a sample of the product under clean and sanitary conditions.

This display appeals directly to several of the physical senses.

Theme Appeal
Many retailers find that a *shopping theme* helps provide a focus in planning physical facilities. **Theme appeal** is a useful vehicle around which to organize the five sensory appeals. Any number of themes can be used. Common themes center around natural and holiday seasons, historical periods, current issues (energy, environment), and special events (anniversaries). Shopping themes can be organized on either a storewide, department, or product line basis.

THE STORE'S EXTERIOR

First impressions are so important that they often are the swing factor in a consumer's decision to stop at one store or another. Frequently a consumer's first impression about a store is created by the store's exterior. The exterior is a key factor in stopping and attracting new customers and retaining existing ones. The major considerations in planning store exteriors are the store's position, architecture, sign, and front.

The Store's Position

How and where the store is positioned on the site affects the retailer's ability to attract customers. In evaluating existing store facilities or planning future site layouts, the retailer should consider at least these three questions: (1) How visible is the store?; (2) is the store compatible with its surroundings?; and (3) are store facilities placed for consumer convenience?

Ensuring Store Visibility
For the physical exterior to accomplish its goals of stopping, attracting, and inviting customers to shop, customers must see it. A visible store becomes part of the consumer's mental map of where to shop for a certain product or service. Visual

awareness of a store's existence has the short-run benefit of alluring impulse shoppers and the long-run benefit of attracting customers who develop a particular need for the retailer's products. Simply put, people shop more frequently at stores they are aware of, and **store visibility** is an important factor in developing that awareness. Ideally a store should be positioned so that it is clearly visible from the major traffic arteries (foot and/or vehicle) adjacent to the site. The retailer improves the store's visibility by using the three interacting factors of setback, angle, and elevation to advantage.

Reduced visibility can result either from setting the store too far back from a traffic artery or from positioning it too close to the street. Ideally a store should be set back far enough to give passersby a broad perspective of the entire store but close enough to let them read major signs and see window displays. Visual impressions also can be enhanced or hindered by the angle of the store relative to a traffic artery. In positioning the store, the retailer should place the building at an angle to the traffic artery that will maximize exposure. The elevation of a site can place the retailer's store above or below the main traffic artery level. Most consumers do not see stores that are too high or too low. These stores are also perceived as having accessibility problems.

Designing Site Compatibility

Fitting the store to the natural lay of the land and the natural habitat can reap substantial benefits for the retailer in terms of visual impressions. In designing for **site compatibility**, the retailer should ensure that the size of the facility is appropriate for the size of the site. Placing an oversize building on a small site distorts proportion. Also, architectural design and construction materials should demonstrate a harmonious relationship with the immediate environment.

Planning Consumer Convenience

In planning the store's on-site position, the retailer should consider how the position affects consumer convenience. The retailer might ask a number of questions. Does the store's position allow enough parking spaces and permit easy access to them? Can cars and trucks turn around in the parking lot? Does the position permit safe, convenient pedestrian traffic? Does the position enhance or hinder pedestrian access to the store?

The Store's Architecture

Architecture is a major factor in both making the right impression on the consumer and developing an efficient retail operation. In most cases, the store's architecture is a compromise between these two objectives.

Making an Impression

The store's architectural motif can convey any number of impressions as well as communicate a considerable amount of information. A certain architectural style can indicate the size and prestige of the retailer's operation, the nature of the retailer's principal product line (e.g., Taco Bell), and the retailer's affiliation (e.g., store designs). In addition, architectural design can support a central theme or focal point for the retailer's merchandising activities. For example, the use of open space can suggest a *marketplace* theme—open storefronts, central squares, and outdoor shopping stalls.

Designing a Functional Facility

The impression-creating elements of the architecture must be balanced against the functional needs of retailer and consumer. Functional considerations that are paramount in the store's design are costs, energy efficiency, security, operational efficiency, and customer convenience.

Rapidly rising land, construction, and materials *costs* have made differentiating a store from the competition increasingly difficult. In addition, the costs associated with

Note the different impressions projected by each of these store facilities.

maintenance limit architectural freedom. Conversely, architectural designs that reduce maintenance costs often hinder customer convenience and store attractiveness.

With increased *energy* prices, the retailer has an overriding obligation to minimize energy costs. Energy-saving construction methods include lower ceilings, less window space, proper air circulation, controlled entrances and exits, proper insulation, and energy-efficient lighting.[21]

Because of the rising crime rate, modern retailers have had to design facilities that increase store *security*. In their architectural plans, retailers include security features such as reduced window space, elimination of unexposed areas, controlled entrances and exits, proper lighting, limited exposure of high-value products, and security devices such as television monitors, two-way mirrors, and observation areas.

Another architectural design consideration is *operational efficiency*. The best allocation of store space for operational activities is one that facilitates movement of customers, sales personnel, and merchandise and gives the retailer maximum product exposure. Maximizing selling areas and creating the highest possible level of product exposure are the chief architectural concerns.

The final architectural design consideration is *customer convenience*. For example, new government regulations and public pressure require the retailer to remove all possible physical barriers to handicapped consumers.

The Store's Sign

A store's sign (marquee) often is the first "mark" of the retailer that a potential customer sees. It serves the two key purposes of identifying the store and attracting the consumer's attention.

Signs identify the who, what, where, and when of the retailer's offering. Signs indicate *who* the retailer is with a name, logo, or some other symbol. Sears, Safeway, and Holiday Inn are immediately recognized by most consumers. Signs also inform consumers about *what* the retailer's operation is. They transmit information concerning the type of retail operation (department store, supermarket, catalog showroom), the nature of the product line (food, hardware, clothing, gifts), the extent of the service offering (full-service bank, self-service gasoline station), and the character of the pricing strategy (discount prices, family prices). Signs inform the consumer *where* the retailer is located and, in some cases, how to get there (e.g., "Located at 5th and Main"). Finally, some retailers use signs to inform the consumer *when* they are willing to provide service or when they are open (e.g., 24 hours).

The store's sign should create awareness, generate interest, and invite the consumer to try the store. The size, shape, color, lighting, and materials all contribute to the sign's distinctiveness and ability to create awareness and interest. McDonald's golden arches have become one of the most highly recognized signs in the United States.

The Store's Front

A store's front is the first major impression consumers get of a store. The three primary design elements in a facade are storefront configuration, window displays, and store entrances.

Storefront Configurations

The three basic storefront configurations are the straight, angled, and arcade fronts.

As Figure 8–2 illustrates, the **straight front** runs parallel to the sidewalk, street, mall, or parking lot. Usually the only break in the front is a small recess for an entrance. This storefront design is operationally efficient because it does not reduce interior selling space. It lacks consumer appeal, however, because it is monotonous and less attractive than the other two configurations. Reflective glare from windows can inhibit window shopping. When retailers use the straight-front configuration, window shoppers can inspect only a small part of any display from one position.

The **angled front** overcomes the monotony of the straight front by positioning the front at a slight angle to the traffic arteries. To create a more attractive and interesting front, retailers that use the angled-front approach place windows and entrances off center or at one end of the store's front. Angled fronts also give the window shopper a better viewing angle of the merchandise in the window and reduce window glare. The entrance in an angled front usually is located at the most recessed part to funnel and direct consumers into the store; thus, it provides more protection for the window

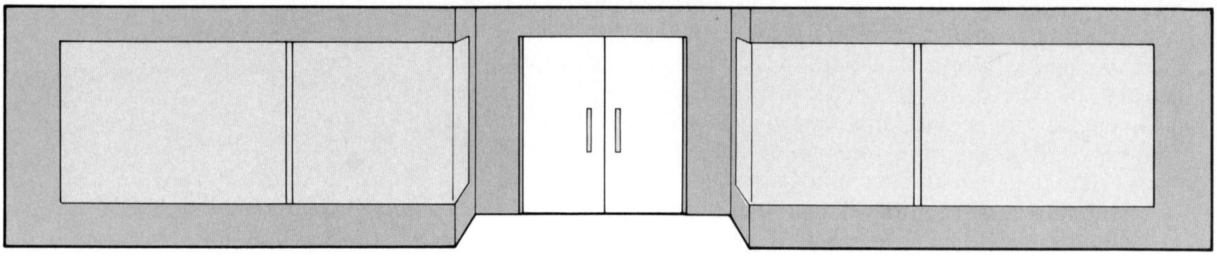

The Straight Front

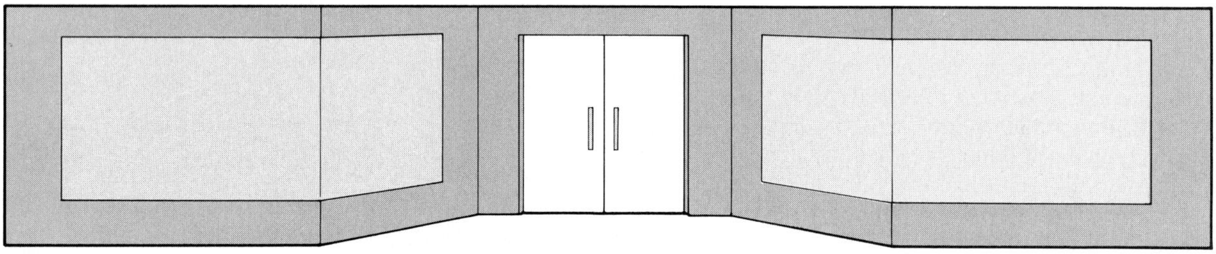

The Angled Front

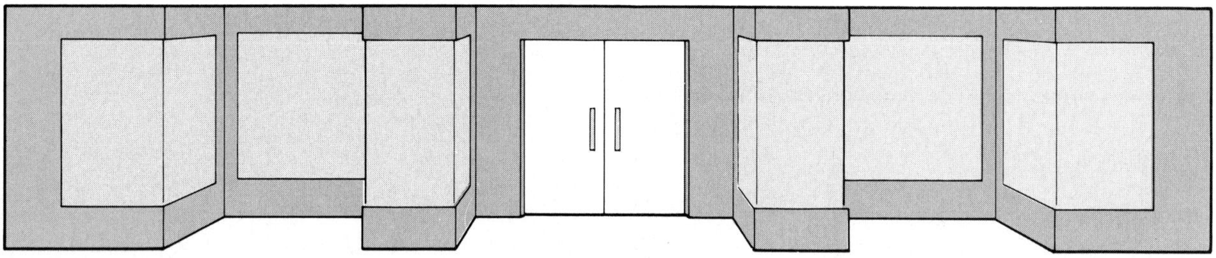

The Arcade Front

FIGURE 8–2
Storefront configurations

shopper than the straight front. The main limitation of the angled front is that it reduces the interior space available for selling.

The **arcade front** is characterized by several recessed windows and/or entrances. Its advantages are that it (1) increases the store's frontage exposure and display areas; (2) provides shoppers with several protected areas for window shopping; (3) increases privacy for window shoppers; (4) creates an attractive, relaxing atmosphere for shoppers; and (5) reduces glare for a substantial part of the storefront. Its disadvantages are that it considerably reduces interior selling and display space; requires a substantial investment in construction and materials; and requires a professional display staff to make full use of the arcade concept of window settings.

Window Displays

The number, size, depth, and type of windows a store has can substantially alter the store's exterior appearance and the general impression it produces on consumers. To create the desired impression, the retailer can use one or a combination of the elevated, ramped, shadow box, or island displays.

Elevated windows are display windows with floors of varying heights. The floor elevations range from 12 to 36 inches above sidewalk level. The choice of floor height depends on the kind of merchandise and the elevation necessary to place the display at the typical shopper's eye level. Small merchandise such as shoes, jewelry, books, and cosmetics normally is displayed in windows with a floor elevation of 36 inches, while large merchandise such as clothing displayed on mannequins usually appears in windows with a floor elevation of 12, 18, or 24 inches. Elevated windows give consumers an excellent visual perspective of the retailer's merchandise.

Ramped windows are standard display windows with a display floor higher in back than in front. The floor ramp either is a wedge or is tiered, while the backing may be open, partially opened, or closed. The principal advantage of the ramped display window is the greater visual impact of merchandise displayed in the rear.

Shadow box windows are small, boxlike display windows set at eye level. They usually are completely enclosed and focus the shopper's attention on a selected line of merchandise. Jewelry stores use this type of window display extensively.

Island windows are four-sided display windows isolated from the rest of the store. Used in conjunction with the arcade-storefront configuration, the island window can

(Left) Shadow box windows focus the customer's attention on a particular merchandise item on display. (Right) Island windows effectively highlight merchandise from all angles.

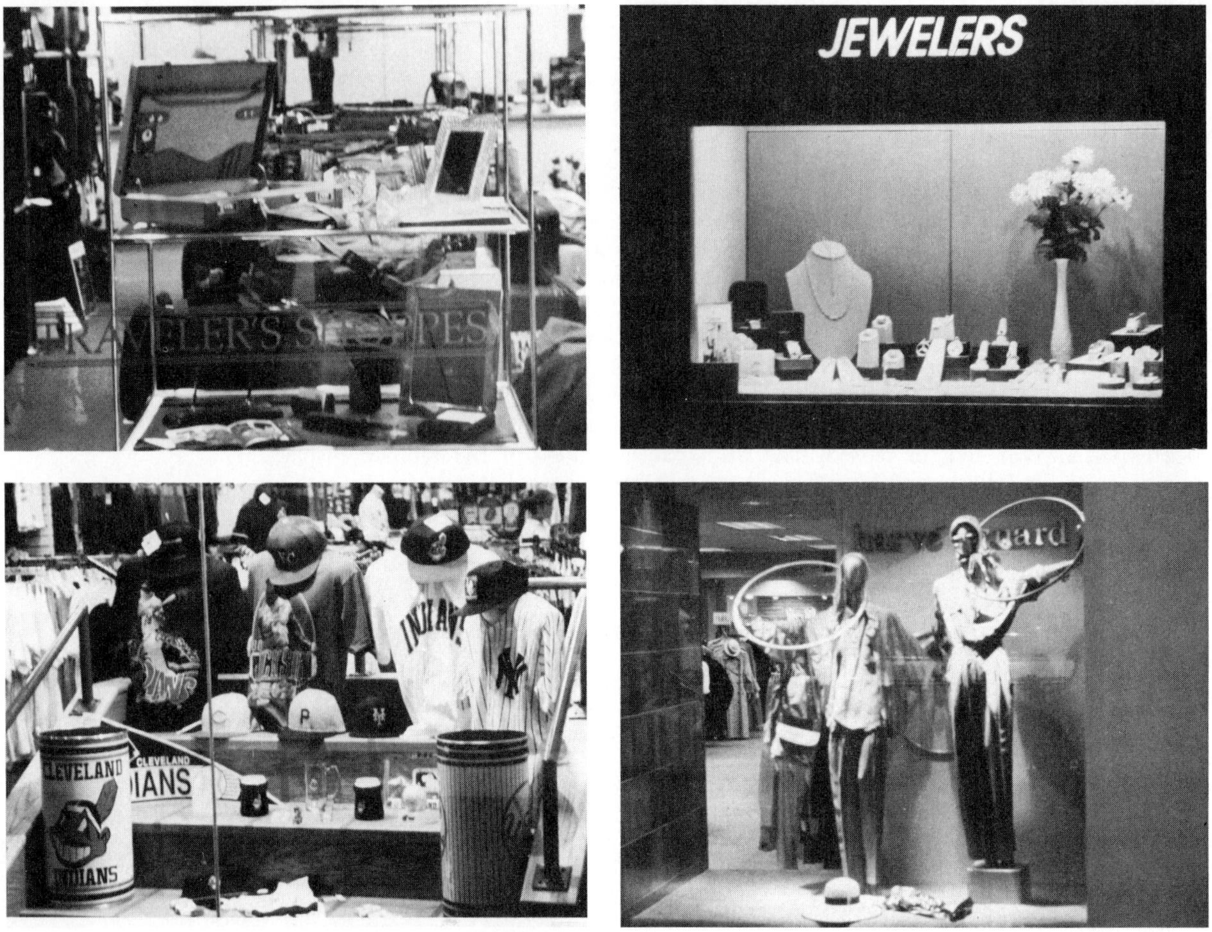

Explain why these window displays are effective or ineffective.

effectively highlight merchandise lines from all angles. This display advantage can become a disadvantage, however, if the retailer does not carefully select and position merchandise.

Store Entrance

Retailers should design store entrances for customers' *safety, comfort, and convenience,* as well as for guiding customers into the store. Design considerations for store entrances include (1) good lighting, (2) flat entry surfaces (no steps), (3) nonskid materials, (4) easy-to-open doors (slide-away or air curtains), (5) little or no entrance clutter, such as merchandise tables, and (6) doors wide enough for people carrying large parcels. In addition, store entrances must meet all access regulations for handicapped persons.

THE STORE'S INTERIOR

The store's interior must contribute to the retailer's basic objectives of minimizing operating expenses while maximizing sales and customer satisfaction. To accomplish these goals, the store's interior not only must be inviting, comfortable, and convenient for the customer; it must permit the retailer to use interior space efficiently and effectively.

The Store's Space

Not all of the interior space is of equal value when judged against its revenue-producing capabilities. The consumer's in-store shopping responses to different interior arrangements vary substantially. Specifically the value of any unit of store space will vary with the floor location, the area position within each floor, and its location relative to various types of traffic aisles. Many retailers recognize these variations in the value of store space and allocate total store rent to sales departments according to where they are located and how valuable each space is.

Floor Values

The value of space in multilevel stores decreases the further it is from the main or entry-level floor. Although experts have different opinions on exactly how to allocate rental costs to each floor, they all agree that sales areas on the main floor should be charged a higher rent than those in the basement or on higher floors (see Figure 8–3). The additional customer exposure associated with entry-level floors justifies both the greater sales expectations (value of space) and the higher rent allocation of total store rent by floors. Casual Corner's remodeled flagship store in Union Square (San Francisco) features as its interior focal point a grand circular staircase that moves customers easily through the lower and mezzanine levels; the staircase has proven a successful solution to the challenge of getting customers to go to the lower level.[22]

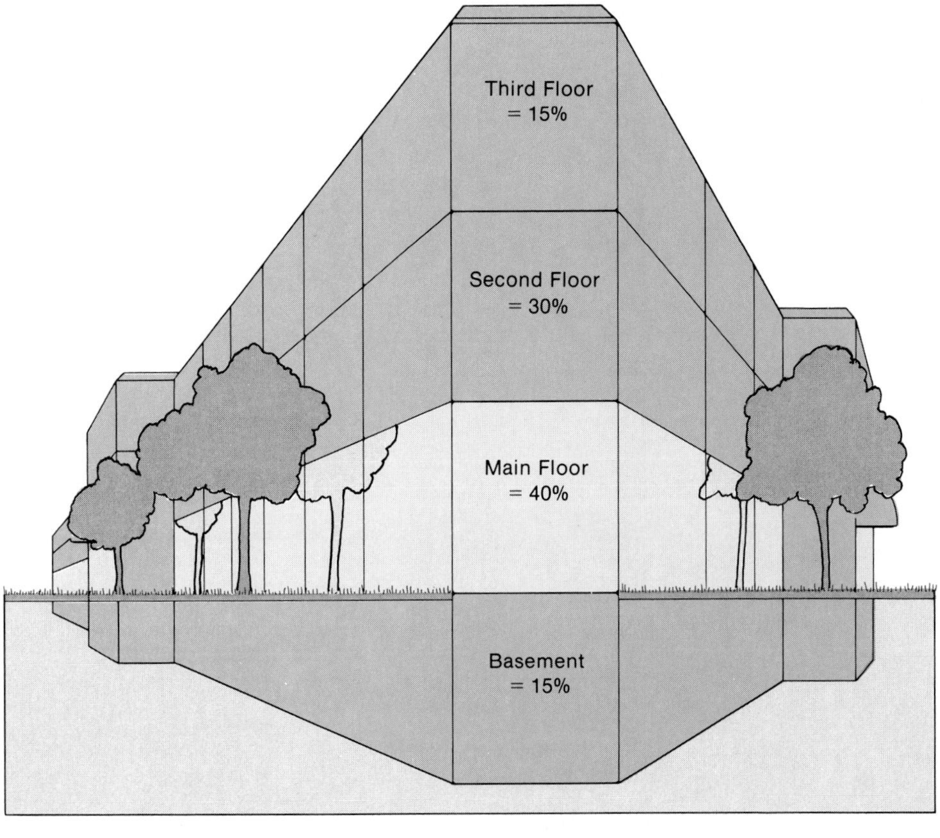

FIGURE 8–3
Rent allocation by floors

Area Values

The value of space also varies depending on where customers enter and how they traverse the store. In assigning value to interior store areas (and in making rent allocations), the retailer should consider three factors. First, the most exposed area of any floor is the immediate area surrounding the entrance. Second, most consumers tend to turn right when entering a store or floor. Third, a general rule of thumb is that only one-quarter of the store's customers will go more than halfway into the store. Based on these three considerations, Figure 8–4 provides one of several variations for allocating store rents to a floor area. Another rule of thumb in assigning rent allocations is the **4-3-2-1 rule** (see Figure 8–5).

Aisle Values

Because merchandise located in primary traffic aisles greatly benefits from increased customer exposure, the retailer should assign a higher value and a higher rent to space along these aisles than to that along secondary aisles. To illustrate, Figure 8–6 classifies interior store space into high-, medium-, and low-rent areas based on their position relative to primary and secondary traffic aisles. A high-rent area is exposed to two primary traffic aisles; a low-rent area is exposed only to secondary aisles; and medium-rent areas are exposed to one primary and one secondary aisle.

The Store's Layout

A store's interior can be divided into two general areas according to usage: sales support areas and selling areas. Store size averages for various types of retailers and the typical amount of space devoted to selling activities are shown in Figure 8–7. Selling space usually accounts for 75 to 80 percent of the total space available.

FIGURE 8–4
Rent allocations by areas

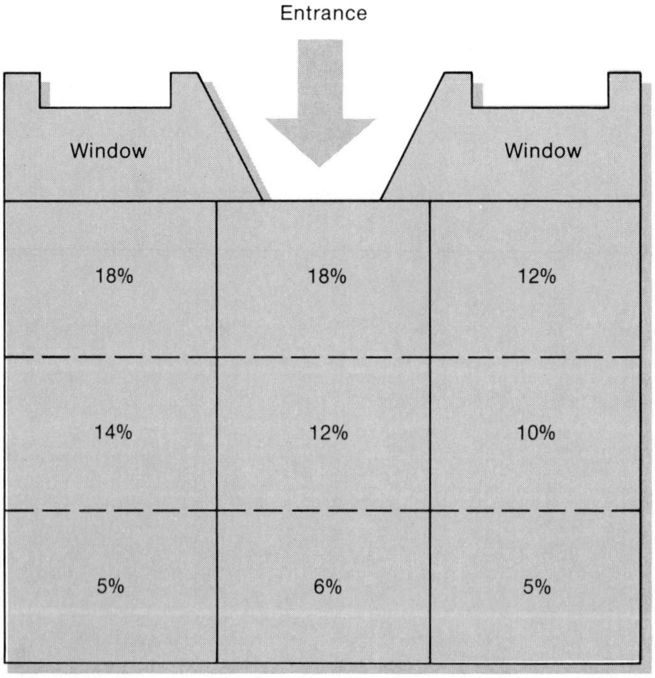

FIGURE 8–5
The 4-3-2-1 rule

The decline in value of store space from front to back of the shop is expressed in the 4-3-2-1 rule. This rule assigns 40 percent of a store's rental cost to the front quarter of the shop, 30 percent to the second quarter, 20 percent to the third quarter, and 10 percent to the final quarter. Similarly, each quarter of the store should contribute the same percentage of sales revenue.

For example, suppose that a small department store anticipates $120,000 in sales this year. Each quarter of the store should generate the following sales volume:

Front quarter	$120,000 · .40 =	$ 48,000
Second quarter	120,000 · .30 =	36,000
Third quarter	120,000 · .20 =	24,000
Fourth quarter	120,000 · .10 =	12,000
Total		$120,000

Source: Norman M. Scarborough and Thomas W. Zimmerer, *Effective Small Business Management* (Columbus: Merrill Publishing Co., 1984), 339.

Sales Support Areas

A *sales support area* is space devoted to customer services, merchandise processing, and management and staff activities. Figure 8–8 identifies some common sales support areas.

The four general approaches to locating sales support areas capable of satisfying both customer convenience and employee productivity needs are the sandwich, core,

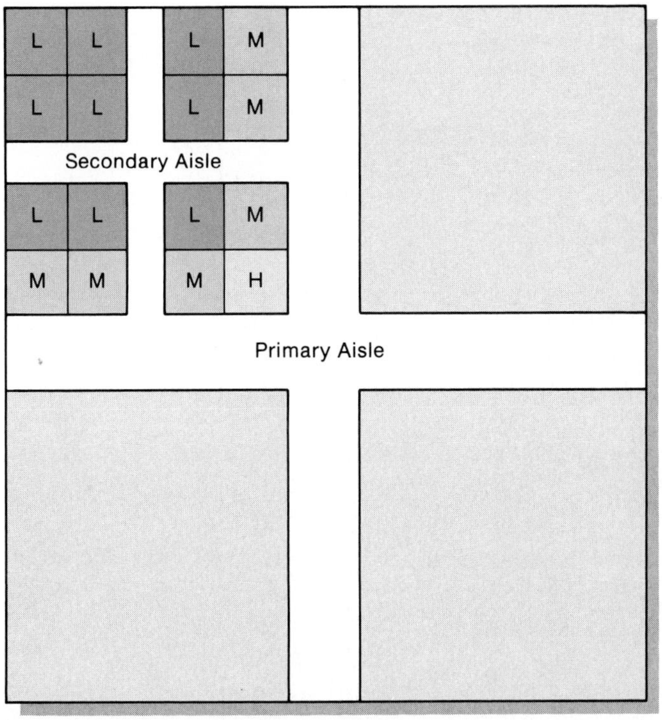

H = High-Rent Area M = Medium-Rent Area L = Low-Rent Area

FIGURE 8–6
Rent allocations based on traffic aisles

FIGURE 8–7
Store size and selling space for selected retailing formats

Type of Retailer	Average Total Store Size: Square Feet (%)	Average Selling Space Available: Square Feet (%)
Supermarkets	48,800 (100)	36,209 (74.2)
Department stores	148,300 (100)	119,975 (80.9)
Discount stores	88,700 (100)	69,097 (77.9)
Apparel specialty stores	21,200 (100)	16,536 (78.0)
Drug stores	14,300 (100)	11,440 (80.0)
Home centers	28,300 (100)	22,753 (80.4)

Source: Reprinted by permission from "Annual Decision-Makers' Digest," *Chain Store Age Executive* (July 1987), pp. 36–37. Copyright © Lebhar-Friedman, Inc. 425 Park Avenue, New York, NY 10022.

FIGURE 8–8
Selected examples of sales support areas

CUSTOMER SERVICE AREAS

- Checkout areas
- Dressing rooms
- Wrapping desk
- Complaint desk
- Credit desk
- Catalog desk
- Repair counter
- Return desk
- Rest rooms
- Restaurants

MERCHANDISE SERVICE AREAS

- Receiving areas
- Checking areas
- Marking areas
- Stocking areas
- Merchandise control areas
- Alteration and work rooms

MANAGEMENT/STAFF AREAS

- Offices
- Lounges
- Locker rooms
- Conference rooms
- Classrooms
- Training areas

peripheral, and annex approaches. The **sandwich approach** involves using one floor of a multilevel store for sales support activities (Figure 8–9a). The **core approach** is the location of all nonselling areas within a central core area surrounded by selling areas (Figure 8–9b). The **peripheral approach** locates sales support areas around the exterior of the store or floor (Figure 8–9c). The **annex approach** locates all nonselling activities away from the sales floor in a sales support annex. Usually the annex is an appendage to the back of the store (Figure 8–9d).

Selling Areas

Selling space is the area of the store devoted to the display of merchandise and the interaction between customers and store personnel. In planning the store's interior

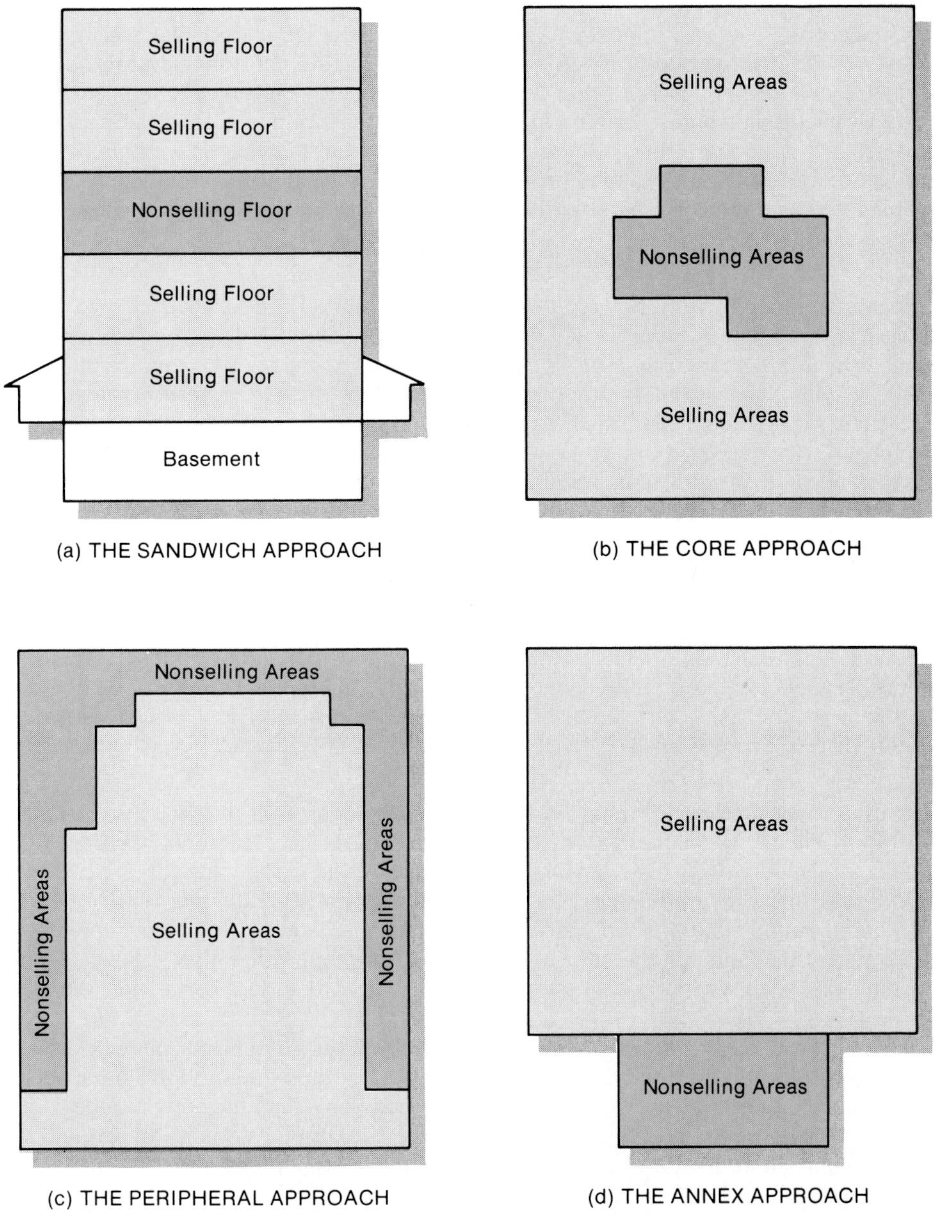

FIGURE 8–9
General approaches to locating nonselling areas

selling areas, the designer must organize merchandise into logical selling groups and allocate space, locate merchandise, and design layouts that are conducive to both the selling function and efficient overall operations.

Grouping Merchandise. Better merchandise *planning*, greater merchandise *control*, and a more *personalized shopping atmosphere* are three important reasons for assembling merchandise into some type of natural grouping. A logical grouping of merchandise also helps customers find, compare, and select merchandise suited to their needs. Some off-price retailers, such as T. J. Maxx and Ross Stores, sensitive "to shoppers' criticism that their stores are hard to shop in because they are too crammed with merchandise on racks and piles, are trying to do a better job at presenting their wares . . . a remodeling program to group apparel for men and women by segment . . . by life-style and attitude."[23] The most common criteria the retailer uses are (1) functional (footwear, underwear, outerwear), (2) storage and display (racks, bins, shelves or dry, refrigerated, frozen), and (3) target-market consumer criteria (men's, women's, children's or economy minded, prestige oriented, convenience directed). The key factors retailers must ensure in grouping merchandise are that the customer understands and appreciates the organization and that merchandise groupings are consistent with efficient operating principles. Figure 8–10 illustrates the floor plan and merchandise grouping of Hypermarket USA, Wal-Mart's entry into the hypermarket business in Garland, Texas.

Allocating Space. After the retailer has grouped merchandise according to some logical criteria, it must allocate selling space to each merchandise group. Given that each store has a limited amount of space, the retailer must select some method to allocate selling space. One method is the *model stock method*, whereby the retailer determines the amount of floor space needed to stock a desired assortment of merchandise for each grouping. For the more important merchandise groupings, the retailer allocates a sufficient amount of space to achieve the desired assortment. Merchandise groupings of lesser importance are allocated space based on their assortment needs and the remaining available space.

A second method by which retailers allocate selling space is the *sales/productivity ratio*. This method allocates selling space on the basis of sales per square foot for each merchandise group. Figure 8–11 identifies some of the best and the worst merchandise lines for department and specialty stores in terms of sales-per-square-foot performance. Some retailers use profit per square foot or gross margin return per square foot as the basis for space allocation.[24] Merchandise groups with lower sales or profit productivity are assigned space on an availability and needs basis.

Locating Merchandise. Where on the sales floor to put each merchandise group is the third factor in planning the sales floor. Criteria that retailers consider are rent-paying ability, consumer buying behavior, merchandise compatibility, seasonality of demand, space requirements, and display requirements.[25]

Rent-paying ability is the contribution that a merchandise group can generate in sales to pay the rent for the area to which it is assigned. Other things being equal, merchandise groups with the highest rent-paying ability are located in the most valuable space.

Consumer buying behavior criteria are based on the recognition that consumers are willing to spend different amounts of time and effort in searching for merchandise. For example, the retailer should place impulse and convenience goods in areas with high exposure (major aisles, checkout stands, etc.), because customers will exert little effort to find them. In contrast, the retailer should locate shopping and specialty goods

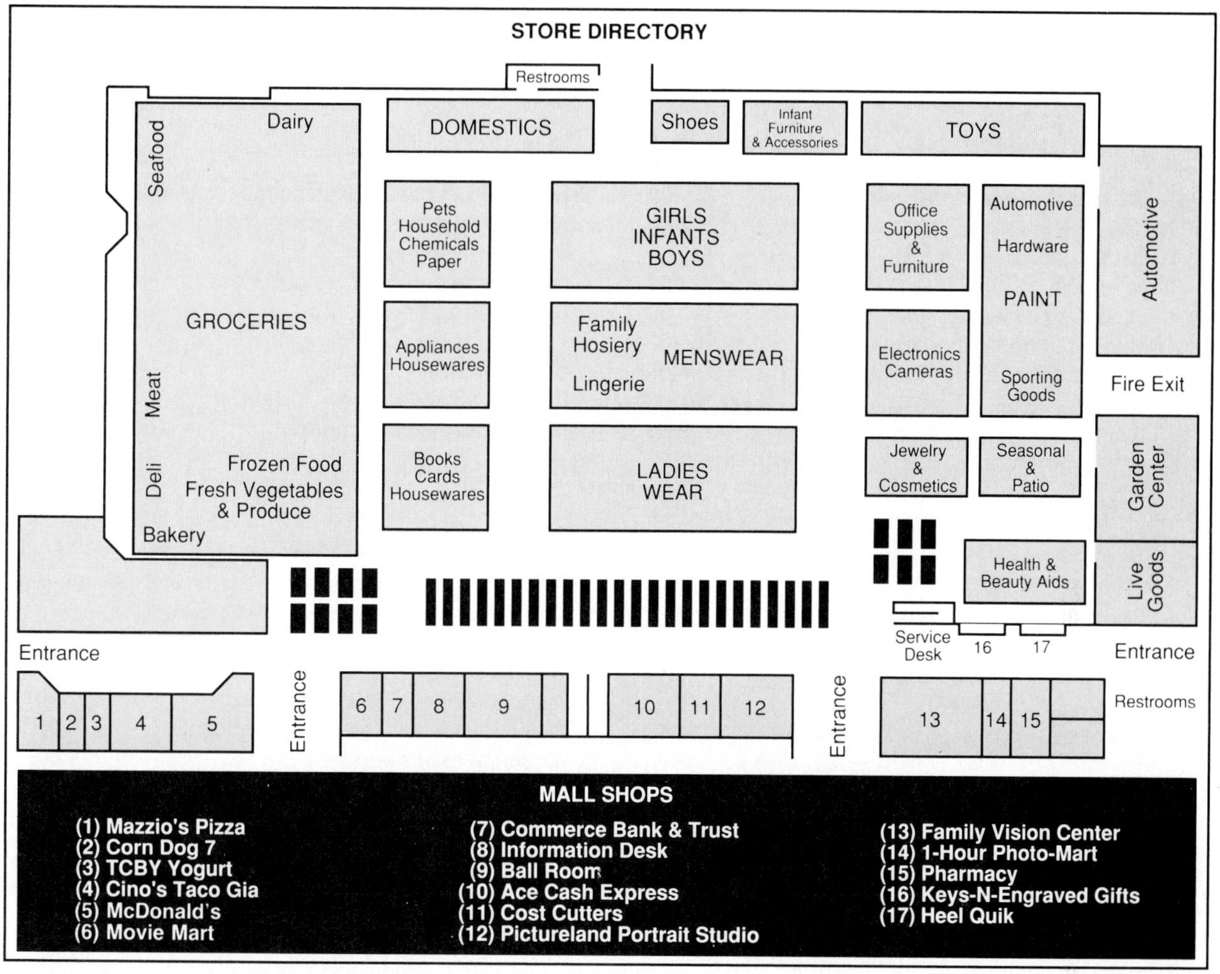

FIGURE 8–10
Merchandise groupings and floor plan, Hypermarket USA (source: *Stores,* March 1988, 56. Reprinted by permission of *Stores*. Copyright by National Retail Federation, Inc.)

in less accessible areas, because consumers' purchase intents are well established and they will exert the effort necessary to find them.

The degree of relationship among various merchandise groups is termed *merchandise compatibility*. This concept states that closely related merchandise should be located together to promote complementary purchases. For example, the sale of a man's suit will increase the chances of selling men's ties and shirts if those products are located close to and are visible from the men's suit department.

Merchandise characterized by *seasonality of demand* often is accorded valuable, visible space during the appropriate season. In addition, merchandise groups with different seasonal selling peaks typically are placed together to allow the retailer to expand or contract these lines without making major changes in the store's layout. Examples are Christmas toys, lawn and garden equipment, women's coats, and women's dresses.

Space requirements for each merchandise group also must be considered in making in-store location decisions. For example, merchandise groups that require large amounts of floor space (e.g., a department store's furniture department) use less valuable space at the rear of the store, on an upper floor or in the basement, or in an

Department Stores					
Sales per Square Foot					
Rank	Best	Sales ($)	Rank	Worst	Sales ($)
1.	Fine jewelry and watches	332.00	1.	Millinery	36.00
2.	Cosmetics, fragrances, toiletries	221.00	2.	Gifts, Christmas decorations	51.50
3.	Costume jewelry	204.00	3.	Notions and closet accessories	53.00
4.	Ladies' gloves	187.50	4.	Floor coverings	55.00
5.	All shoes	178.50	5.	Window and furniture coverings	56.00
6.	Ladies' small leather goods	158.50	6.	Linens and domestics	70.00
7.	Men's and boys' sportswear	158.00	7.	Toys, hobby goods, games	71.50
8.	Men's and boys' furnishings	154.00	8.	Furniture and bedding	74.50
9.	Hosiery	151.00	9.	Little boys' (ages 4–7) wear	81.00
10.	Women's and misses' sportswear	148.00	10.	Lamps, pictures, mirrors	82.00
Specialty Stores					
Sales per Square Foot					
Rank	Best	Sales ($)	Rank	Worst	Sales ($)
1.	Cosmetics, toiletries and fragrances	340.00	1.	Infants' and children's clothing and accessories	108.00
2.	Women's and misses' dresses	271.00	2.	Men's and boys' apparel and accessories	142.00
3.	Women's and misses' sportswear	252.00	3.	Women's, misses' and junior coats	173.00
			4.	Junior sportswear	179.00
			5.	Hosiery	184.00

Source: David P. Schulz, "New MOR: New Data," *Stores* (January 1988): 124, 126. Reprinted by permission of *Stores*. Copyright by National Retail Federation, Inc.

FIGURE 8–11
The best and worst merchandise performers based on sales per square foot

annex. Normally the bulky nature of such products cannot justify their placement in higher-rent locations.

Display requirements also influence where the retailer places a particular group of merchandise. For example, merchandise such as clothing, which must be hung for display, usually is located along the sides of walls or at the rear of the store, where it will not interfere with the customer's needs for convenience and comparison shopping and the retailer's selling and operating needs.

Designing Layouts. When designing sales floor layouts, the retailer must consider the arrangement of merchandise, fixtures, displays, and traffic aisles so that they accommodate the spatial and locational requirements of different merchandise groups. Selling floor layouts are extremely important, because they strongly influence in-store traffic patterns, shopping atmosphere, shopping behavior, and operational efficiency. American Fare, the 244,000-square-foot hypermarket near Atlanta, makes a bold high-tech statement using "black fixtures on locking wheels that permit great mobility of space use . . . store people can reconfigure a department overnight."[26] Some of the factors the retailer must consider in designing the sales floor layout include the following:

- *Type of displays* (shelves, tables, counters) and *fixtures* (stands, easels, forms, platforms)
- *Size* and *shape* of fixtures

Planograms: Planning Efficient Space Utilization

RETAIL STRATEGIES AND TACTICS

A *planogram* is a visual diagram or plan detailing how much space is to be allocated to each product item (or SKU—stock-keeping unit) and the location of each item relative to other SKUs. As a planning and control device, planograms assist the retailer in making decisions regarding the effective merchandising and efficient operational use of both vertical space (e.g., shelf facings—linear feet) and horizontal space (e.g., sales floor area—square feet). In creating standardized presentations of product items, the retailer uses a computer-generated plan for (1) grouping products into sales compatibility units, (2) allocating space to each product grouping, and (3) locating product groupings within well-conceived store and display designs. Planograms use a host of criteria in developing plans, including sales levels, gross margins, product compatibility, package size and shape, storage requirements, display needs, and inventory turnover rates. Planograms typically are generated by corporate merchandising and facility planners and distributed to individual stores.

Target, the Minnesota-based discount retailer, maintains a computer database of over 3,400 planograms in any running length from 16 to 24 feet for its standardized gondola sections and display platforms. It uses a computer-assisted design (CAD) system to customize the merchandise presentation of each outlet. When Target needs a plan for a store, it performs space analysis to determine what and how much area is needed and what product adjacencies are appropriate. The CAD system then indicates which planogram(s) are appropriate for that store. Merchandise flexibility is the major benefit Target receives from its store-planning infrastructure.

Source: R. Lee Sullivan, "Target's Customized Store Design," *Discount Merchandiser* (February 1990): 32. Copyright © Schwartz Publications, New York, New York.

- *Permanence* of displays and fixtures
- *Arrangement* (formal or informal balance) of displays and fixtures
- *Width* and *length* of traffic aisles
- *Positioning* of merchandise groups, customer services, and other customer attractions

Three basic layout patterns are the grid, free-form, and boutique layouts. The **grid layout** is a rectangular arrangement of displays and aisles that generally run parallel to one another. As Figure 8–12 illustrates, the grid layout represents a formal arrangement in which the size and shape of display areas and the length and width of the traffic aisles are homogeneous throughout the store. Although the retailer can develop various modifications in this layout to create variety and to respond to operational needs, this grid pattern essentially retains its formal arrangement.

Figure 8–13 illustrates this twist in the old supermarket layout. Used most frequently by supermarkets and convenience, variety, and discount stores, the grid layout offers several advantages. First, it allows the most efficient use of selling space of any of the layout patterns. Second, it simplifies shopping by creating clear, distinct traffic aisles. Third, it promotes the image of a clean, efficient shopping atmosphere. Fourth, it facilitates routine and planned shopping behavior as well as self-service and self-selection by creating a well-organized environment. Finally, it allows more efficient operations by simplifying the stocking, marking, and housekeeping tasks and reduces some of the problems associated with inventory and security control.

The major disadvantage of the grid layout is the sterile shopping atmosphere it creates. For this reason, the grid pattern is simply inappropriate for most shopping- and specialty-goods retailers.

FIGURE 8–12
The grid layout

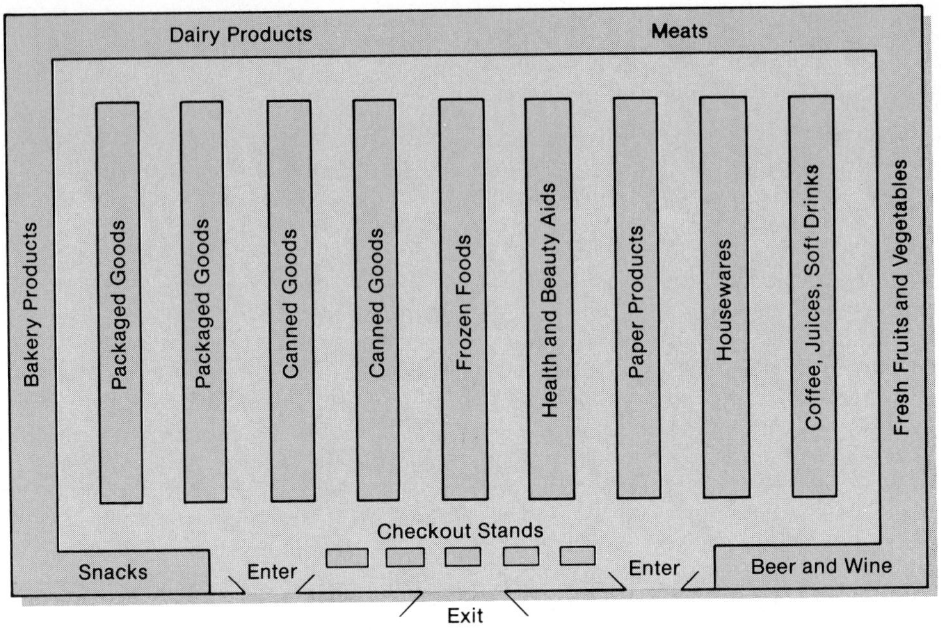

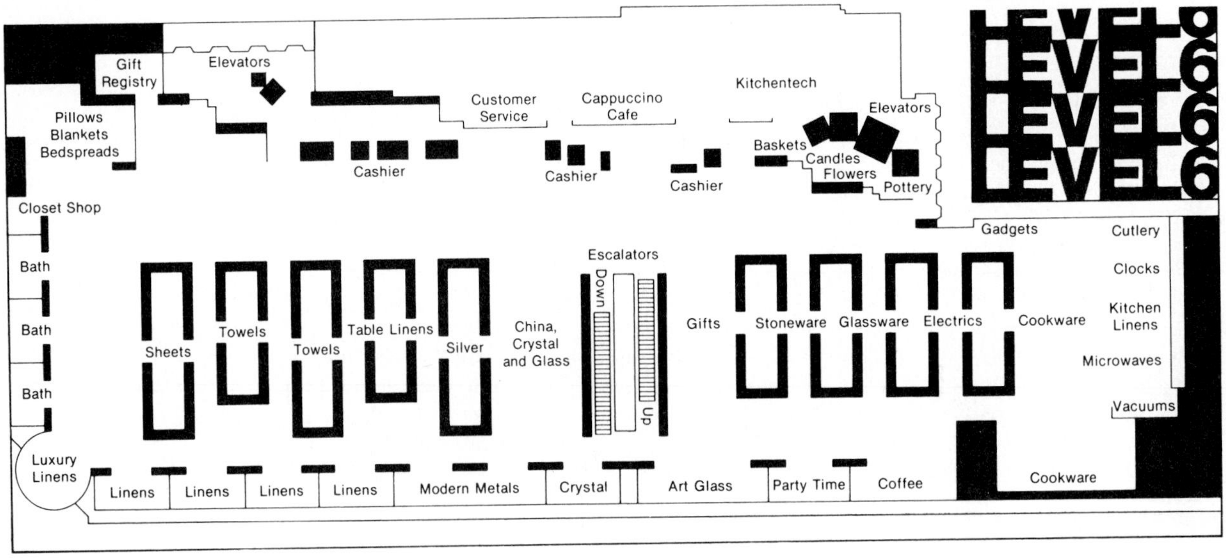

FIGURE 8–13
Retail floor plan (source: "Carson's Level 6: Supermarket Style," *Stores,* August 1985, 62–63. Reprinted by permission of *Stores*. Copyright by National Retail Federation, Inc.)

The **free-form layout,** on the other hand, arranges displays and aisles in a free-flowing pattern (see Figure 8–14). This layout uses a variety of sizes, shapes, and styles of displays, together with fixtures positioned in an informal, unbalanced arrangement. The main benefit retailers derive from the free-form layout is the pleasant atmosphere it produces—an easygoing environment that promotes window shopping and browsing. This comfortable environment increases the time the customer is willing to spend in the store and results in an increase in both planned and unplanned purchases. These benefits of a superior shopping atmosphere, however, are partially offset by the increased cost of displays and fixtures, high labor requirements, additional inventory and security control problems, and the wasted selling space that normally accompany a free-form layout.

The **boutique layout** arranges the sales floor into individual, semiseparate areas, each built around a particular shopping theme. The boutique layout illustrated in Figure 8–15 divides the sales floor into several small specialty shops. By using displays and fixtures appropriate to a particular shopping theme and stocking the boutique accordingly, the retailer can create an unusual and interesting shopping experience.

For example, a "Leisure World" boutique might include an unconventional merchandise assortment such as sporting goods, exercise equipment, home electronics (computer games, stereos, televisions), and art and music supplies. The "Naturals Shop" could feature apparel and food products along with home furnishings, all made from natural materials. To reinforce the theme, the fixtures could be constructed out of natural, unfinished woods. The new generation of Fred Meyer megastores (187,000 square feet) in the Pacific Northwest features "a 'race track' layout that leads customers past 29 specialty shops that together create 11 main store departments. The main aisle contains park benches surrounded by tall ficus trees, vendor carts, and product demonstrations—adding to the sense of theater."[27] Boutique layouts have essentially the same advantages and disadvantages as free-form layouts.

VISUAL MERCHANDISING

Advertising may attract consumers to the store, but it is either the retailer's visual displays or sales personnel that make the sale once the consumer is there. **Retail displays** are nonpersonal, in-store presentations and exhibitions of merchandise together with related information. In practice, retail displays are used to (1) maximize

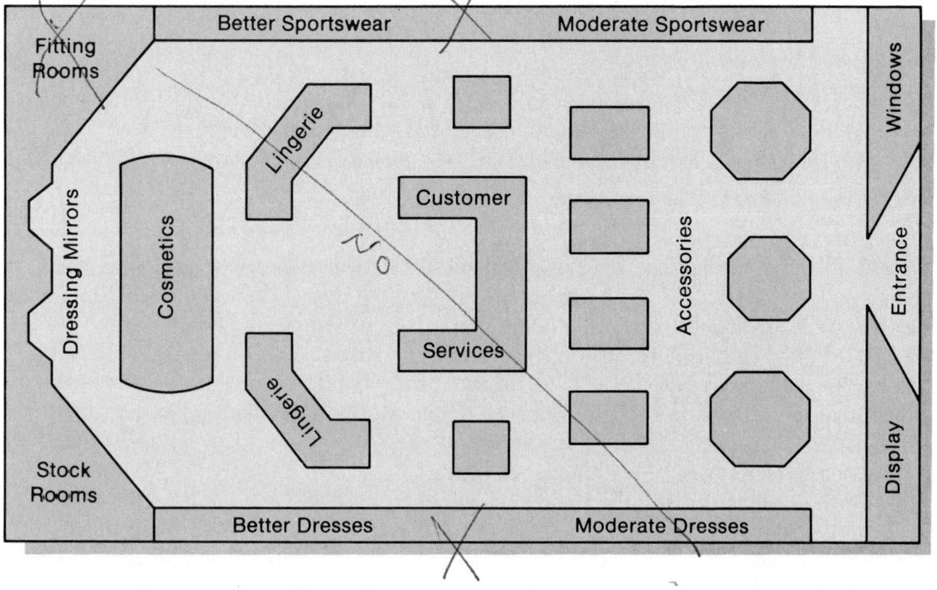

FIGURE 8–14
The free-form layout

FIGURE 8–15
The boutique layout

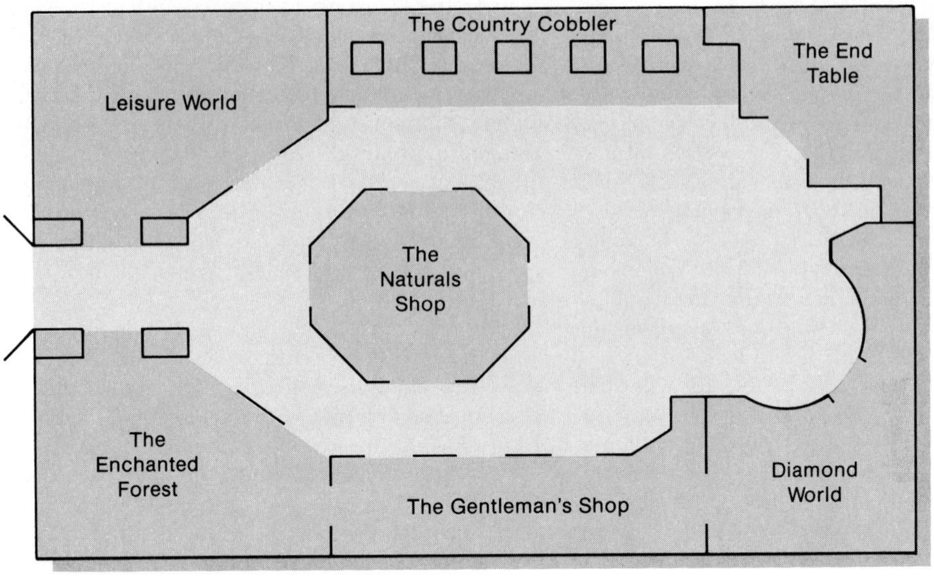

product exposure, (2) enhance product appearance, (3) stimulate product interest, (4) exhibit product information, (5) facilitate sales transactions, (6) ensure product security, (7) provide product storage, (8) remind customers of planned purchases, and (9) generate additional sales of impulse items. Retail displays are essential ingredients in creating the store's shopping atmospherics, because the sight, sound, touch, taste, and scent appeals are largely the result of in-store displays. In apparel retailing, a new philosophy of presentation has taken over. To compete with the fashion-forward presentation of The Limited stores, even price-oriented retailers are stressing the need for superiority of presentation: "While volume and space considerations are still vital, they've been joined by the necessity for a store to have an updated, upscale look and a fashion identity, and most of all, to present merchandise in a simplified layout for easier shopping."[28]

Types of Displays

Store interiors are the sums of all the displays designed to sell the retailer's merchandise. While retail displays can be classified in various ways, we will focus on four general types: selection, special, point-of-purchase, and audiovisual.

Selection Displays

Nearly all the merchandise for which retailers rely on self-service and self-selection selling is presented to the consumer in the form of **selection displays**. These mass displays typically occupy rows of stationary aisle and wall units (shelves, counters, tables, racks, and bins) designed to expose the complete assortment of merchandise. Selection display units generally are "open" to promote merchandise inspection. Their primary functions are to provide customer access to the store's merchandise and to facilitate self-service sales transactions. As a rule, retailers use selection displays to exhibit their everyday assortments of convenience and shopping goods. Effective selection displays present the merchandise in (1) logical selling or usage groupings; (2) a simple, well-organized arrangement; (3) a clean, neat condition; (4) an attractive, informative

Storefronts…
inviting the customer in.

Storefronts can play a crucial role in attracting initial visits by new customers and return visits by existing customers. Retailers need to extend an invitation for the customer to come in, look around, and stay a while. Storefronts create different images and invite different customers, depending on the character of the store's exterior as defined by marquees, store entrances, display windows, lighting schemes, and construction materials.

Just as people judge books by their covers, customers judge stores by their fronts. Storefronts should effectively communicate who and what the retailer is. Are these storefronts effective communicators?

RETAILING IN THE 90's

Store Atmospherics...

inviting the
customer to stay.

This photograph was originally published in Self.

A store interior has both a physical and psychological atmosphere that can either promote or discourage customer interaction with retailers' products and personnel. Store atmospherics should encourage customers to make full use of all their senses and to become involved with the retailer's total offering of shopping and nonshopping experiences.

setting; and (5) a safe, secure state. Customer convenience and operational efficiency are the watchwords for good selection displays.

Special Displays

A **special display** is a notable presentation of merchandise designed to attract special attention and make a lasting impression on the consumer. A huge $549 bottle of champagne helped attract plenty of attention to the wine department of Spokane, Washington's Rosauers Supermarket.[29] Special displays use highly desirable in-store locations, unique display equipment or fixtures, and distinctive merchandise.

Placing special displays in highly desirable locations ensures maximum exposure for the display and its merchandise, thereby significantly affecting the number of units sold.[30] Ends of aisles, countertops, checkout stands, store entrances and exits, and free-standing units in high-traffic areas are all preferred locations for attracting special attention from shoppers. Unique combinations of display equipment (counters, tables, racks, shelves, bins, mobiles) and display fixtures (stands, easels, millinery heads, forms, set pieces) help create a dramatic setting that will attract consumers' attention and build their interest. The choice of display equipment and fixtures depends on the merchandise, the amount of space available, and the effect sought.

Special displays highlight merchandise that can attract customers into the store, build the store's image, improve sales volume, or increase net profits. Special displays therefore are reserved for advertised, best-selling, high-margin, and high-fashion merchandise, together with product items suitable for impulse and complementary buying behavior. Merchandise selected for special displays should also lend itself to good display techniques, which create a favorable sight, sound, taste, touch, or scent appeal.

A selection display.

A special display.

Point-of-Purchase Displays

A **point-of-purchase (POP) display** is a particular type of special display. Retailers make heavy use of POP materials to stimulate immediate purchase behavior. The POPs often are the first and last chance retailers and manufacturers have to tell customers about merchandise. Point-of-purchase displays include items such as counter displays, window displays, shelf extenders, grocery-cart ads, floor-stand displays, dump bins, end-aisle stands, banners, shelf talkers, clocks, counter cards, sniff teasers, and video screen displays. They are designed to attract customers' attention and interest, reinforce the store's creative theme, and fit in with the store's interior decoration.

A point-of-purchase display.

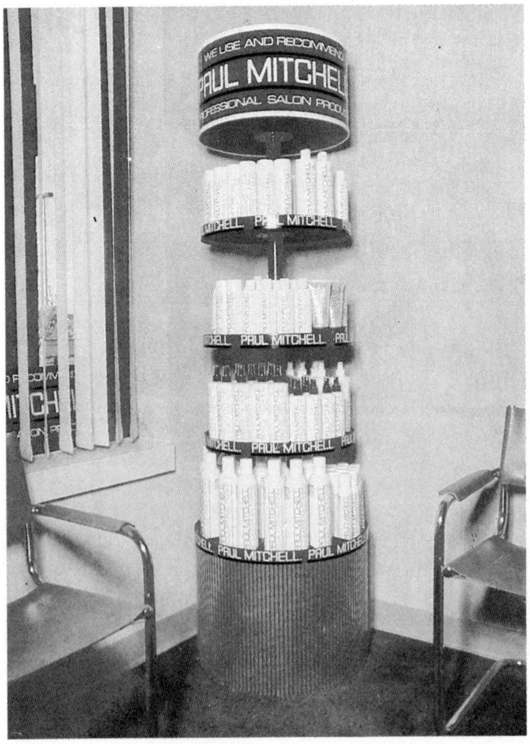

The Concept Shop: A Lifestyle POP Display

RETAIL STRATEGIES AND TACTICS

Matching consumer lifestyles to branded products is reaching unprecedented sophistication as manufacturers invest in innovative brand image-building tactics at the retail level.

This point-of-purchase trend toward lifestyle marketing manifests itself with an emerging class of displays called concept shops, which create a store-within-a-store and establish an image for the brand that matches the lifestyle of the consumer.

Some leading retailers are dramatically restaging their stores to better address the interests of various consumer segments, adjusting and redesigning displays by size, location, and style based on research into how shoppers respond.

Wal-Mart has even established an experimental "vendor store," where manufacturers can test the effectiveness of their displays before deploying them in the field.

Translating lifestyles into displays, however, is not a simple process. While point-of-purchase displays are well-suited to lifestyle marketing because they reach the consumer at the moment a decision is being made, POP has not traditionally been designed to build a brand's image. The primary purposes were to prompt an impulse purchase and reinforce an established image.

Concept shops are becoming the method of choice to achieve lifestyle marketing objectives at the retail level among a variety of trade categories. . . . Currently, concept shops are mostly found within the domain of fashion retailing businesses. This should come as no surprise, because fashion is so integrally entwined with consumer lifestyles.

A concept shop . . . for Sperry Top Sider's line of footwear creates the ambiance of a classic yacht club representing the image and lifestyles of the line.

The shopper is coaxed into a comfortable setting amid the general marketplace of a department store. The shopping experience becomes more directly related to the product, helps build the brand's image, and creates a relaxed atmosphere that is conducive to a favorable purchasing decision.

Concept shops are not rigid, permanent displays. Quite the opposite, in fact. The Top Sider display can work in areas as small as 8-by-8 feet. The system is modular and flexible within a variety of floor plans. Based on square footage available on the selling floor and the amount of stock numbers carried, a combination of fixtures can be selected to maximize use of the space.

The display is essentially nonstructural, making installation simple and involving relatively little assembly for the retailer.

Source: Douglas B. Leeds, "Concept Shops Meld Consumer Lifestyles with Brand Image," *Marketing News* (November 6, 1989): vol. 23, pp. 25, 29. Reprinted from *Marketing News*, published by the American Marketing Association, Chicago, IL 60606.

Audiovisual Displays

The current trend in fashion retailing is to make a video statement by applying current technology to stimulate consumer purchases. Retailers now use **visual merchandising, audio merchandising,** and/or **audiovisual merchandising** to sell their products. Three key applications of audiovisual merchandising are (1) to display the depth and breadth of product lines (e.g., Florsheim Express Shops can show all shoe sizes and styles); (2) to use kiosks to explain the benefits of different products (e.g., Best Products, a catalog showroom, uses kiosks to help merchandise electronic products); and (3) to provide customers with basic price information (e.g., customers at Zale jewelers can view video

Audiovisual displays are effective because they have multisensory impact.

displays to determine price and quality ranges before seeing a salesperson).[31] These display approaches use technology to "speak" to and "show" the consumer available merchandise. Devices include *shelf talkers* (tape recordings describing the merchandise audibly); *rear-screen projections* (slide projectors that present wide-screen, color pictures of the merchandise and its use); and *audiovisual displays* (a combination of sound and videotape or slides to present the product's story).

Display Elements

To communicate the desired message effectively, the retailer must carefully consider and plan each element of a display. Display elements include the merchandise, shelf display areas or window displays, props, colors, background materials, lighting, and signs. The retailer must consider the contrast, repetition, motion, harmony, balance, rhythm, and proportion of each display to draw attention to it (see Figure 8–16).

Display Content

Display content is the type and amount of merchandise to be set off. Cluttered displays of unrelated merchandise attract little attention and are ineffective in stimulating customer interest. To ensure good display content, many retailers confine their efforts to one of three groupings.

Unit groupings of merchandise highlight a separate category of product items (e.g., shoes, shirts, cocktail dresses, or handbags). Unit groupings contain merchandise that is almost identical (five black leather handbags of different sizes) or closely related (three red leather handbags and five brown suede bags). If a single vendor is featured in a unit grouping display, the display often is referred to as a "vendor statement."

Related groupings of merchandise are ensemble displays that present accessory items along with the featured merchandise; for example, a mannequin may be dressed in a coordinating sportswear outfit with sporting accessories (e.g., tennis racket and bag). The principal idea behind the inclusion of accessory items is to remind the customer of a need for more than the featured item; in other words, the retailer is using suggestive selling. A display of either unit or related groupings should contain an odd number of product items. Consumers perceive an odd number of items as more

Display elements must be evaluated to determine how well and if they attract and hold the attention of passersby.

Contrast is one way to attract attention. Contrast is achieved by using different colors, lighting, form (size and shape), lettering, or textures.

Repetition attracts consumer attention by duplicating an object to reinforce and strengthen the impression. By displaying 20 tennis rackets, the image is created of a store with a wide assortment of merchandise in that category.

Physical motion is a powerful attention getter, as is dominance. If an item is much larger than other items in a display, it will be the dominant item and will draw attention to the entire display.

Once attention has been harnessed, the next step is to direct that attention to the intended message. Harmony and graduation frequently are used to accomplish this.

Harmony refers to the unification of merchandise, lighting, props, shelf space, and showcards to create a pleasing effect. Balance, emphasis, rhythm, and proportion work to focus attention on the central point.

Formal balanced displays in which one side is duplicated by the other tend to produce feelings of dignity, neatness, and order. Informally balanced displays in which one side does not exactly match the other tend to generate excitement and are less stuffy.

Rhythm refers to the eye's path after initial contact with the display. The objective is to hold the eye until the entire display is seen.

Design specialists use vertical lines to create the image of height, strength, and dignity. Horizontal lines connote calmness, width, and sophistication; diagonal lines create action, and curved lines suggest continuity and femininity.

Proportion concerns the relative sizes of the display's various objects. Attention can be directed to the desired focal point by arranging items in a graduated pattern from the small to the large.

The proportion concept also involves the positioning of objects in patterns. Popular display patterns include pyramids, steps, zigzags, repetition, and mass.

The image of height and formality is created with pyramids, while the zigzag is a popular method of displaying clothing to create an aura of excitement.

Repetition arrangements are used primarily in shelf merchandising situations. Merchandise items are placed equidistant from one another in a straight, horizontal line.

The mass arrangement is the placement of a large quantity of merchandise in either neatly stacked lines or in jumbled dump bins to convey the image of a sale item.

Source: Ray Marquardt, "Merchandise Displays Are Most Effective When Marketing, Artistic Factors Combine," *Marketing News* (August 16, 1983): vol. 17, p. 3. Reprinted from *Marketing News,* published by the American Marketing Association, Chicago, IL 60606.

FIGURE 8–16
Developing an attractive display

intriguing; hence, the items attract more attention and create a more dramatic setting. When displaying an even number of merchandise items (e.g., a set of eight stemmed glasses), it is recommended that one item be set apart from the rest or differentiated in some other way (e.g., elevated).

Theme groupings display merchandise according to a central theme or setting. Sometimes referred to as presentational theater, themes provide a focus in planning displays and are useful vehicles around which the five sensory appeals can be employed. The number of possible display themes is unlimited. For example, there are product themes ("Shoes complete the appearance"), seasonal themes ("Swing into spring"), patronage themes ("Cheaper by the dozen"), usage themes ("Mealtime magic"), occasion themes ("Along the bridal path"), color themes ("Pastel softness"), life-style themes ("The swinging singles set"), holiday themes ("Santa approved") as well as themes based on historical, current, and special events.

Display Arrangement

Display arrangement is organizing display merchandise into interesting, pleasing, and stimulating patterns. Haphazard arrangement of merchandise items can substantially

A unit grouping display.

reduce a display's effectiveness. Selection displays are simply arranged in some well-organized fashion, but special-display merchandise frequently is presented in one of four definitive arrangement patterns: the pyramid, zig-zag, step, or fan arrangement. Figure 8–17 illustrates these patterns.

Pyramid arrangements are triangular displays of merchandise in vertical (stacked) or horizontal (unstacked) form. "The pyramid begins at a large or broad base and progresses up to an apex, or point, at the highest level."[32] The vertical pyramid can be two or three dimensional and is well suited to displaying boxed and canned merchandise; it also represents efficient use of space. The base of a horizontal pyramid is placed in the rear of the display to achieve the proper visual perspective. When displaying different-size merchandise items, larger items are positioned at the base and the smallest item occupies the apex. Figure 8–17a illustrates the use of pedestal displayers arranged in a pyramid fashion—an effective arrangement pattern for window, counter, and table displays.

Zig-zag arrangements are modified pyramids that zig and zag their way to the apex of the display. No two display levels are at the same height. This arrangement is less monotonous than the pyramid; it is perceived to be more fluid and graceful and,

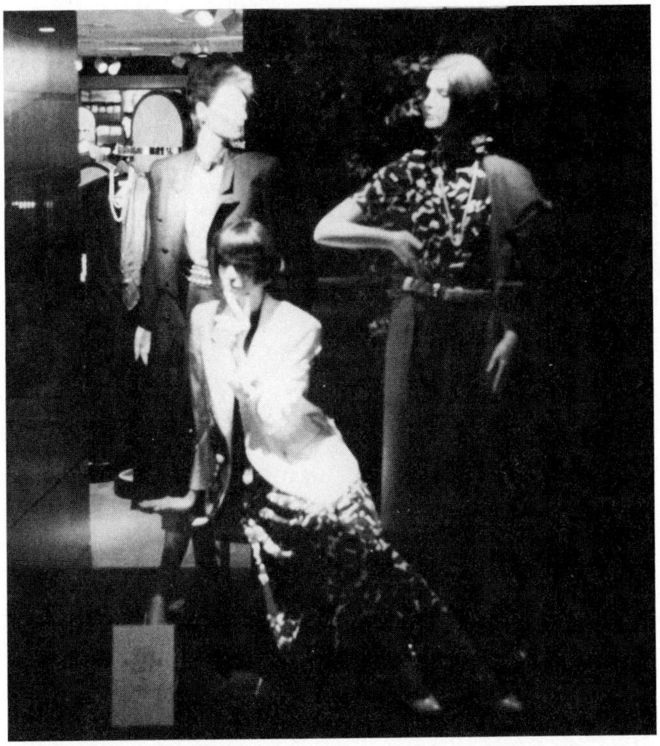

A related grouping (ensemble) display.

perhaps, more feminine. A zig-zag pattern of pedestal displayers (such as the one shown in Figure 8–17b) is especially appropriate for displaying women's jewelry, cosmetics, small apparel items, and shoes.

Step arrangements are essentially that: a series of steps. "Step arrangements lead the eye in a direct line; they begin at a low point on one side of a display area and progress directly to a higher point on the opposite side of that area."[33] Typically step displays are constructed so that the base of each step increases in area (see Figure 8–17c); the larger base area is used for displaying accessory items, while the steps display the featured merchandise. The step arrangement is well suited to displaying a wide variety of merchandise.

Fan arrangements spread up and out from a small base, thereby directing the viewer's eyes upward and outward.[34] Figure 8–17d illustrates this inverted-pyramid arrangement. The fan pattern is appropriate for displaying merchandise ranging from clothing to sporting goods.

STORE SECURITY

Customer theft, employee pilferage, supplier pilferage, bad checks and credit cards, burglary, and robbery are everyday facts of life that every retailer must face and protect itself against. Collectively these protective measures are called *store security,* which must include not only the store and its merchandise but its customers and employees. This section describes how a retailer can detect and prevent many of the losses that might result from criminal activities such as shoplifting by customers, pilferage by employees and suppliers, passing of bad checks and credit cards, and thefts by burglary and robbery. While estimates vary greatly, about five cents out of every dollar spent in a retail store goes to cover the losses resulting from these criminal activities and the security measures used to prevent them.

A display is more interesting and intriguing when it exhibits an odd number of items.

CUSTOMER THEFT

Shoplifting is the act of pilfering merchandise from a store display by customers and individuals posing as customers. To **pilfer** is to commit or practice petty theft. This form of petty thievery can account for 30 to 40 percent of all stock losses the retailer suffers. Unfortunately for the store's customers, retail prices must be set high enough to cover these losses. Shoplifting occurs in three basic ways: (1) outright theft of merchandise, (2) alteration of the retailer's price tag to reflect a lower price, and (3) switching or substituting a lower price tag for the original tag. Shoplifters fall into two general categories: the amateur who steals to satisfy physical or psychological needs and the professional who steals for a living.

Devices and Techniques

Both the amateur and the professional use a variety of devices in shoplifting. The main purpose of shoplifting devices is to conceal both the actual act of stealing and the stolen merchandise. Shoplifting devices include various types of clothing (e.g., coats, "booster" panties, wide-top boots, and other loose-fitting garments) and parcels (e.g., booster boxes, purses, umbrellas, newspapers, magazines, and shopping, school, and knitting bags).

Shoplifters use a number of techniques in their pilfering activities. The **booster** shoves merchandise into concealed areas of parcels and/or clothing. Booster boxes are carefully constructed boxes that appear to be authentic, tightly wrapped packages but contain trap doors that allow the shoplifter to slip merchandise into the box quickly and easily. Other booster devices are *booster hooks* and *bags* securely fastened to the inside

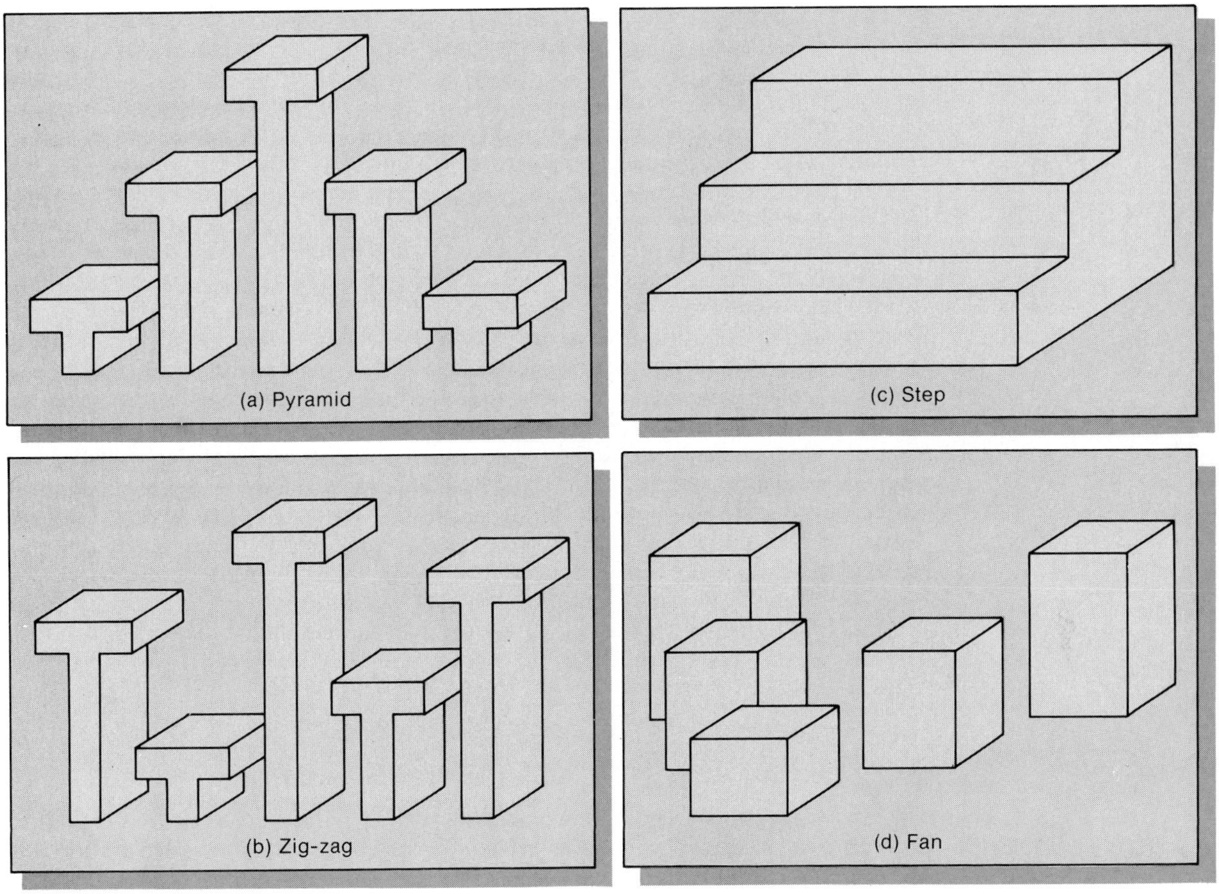

FIGURE 8–17
A gallery of display arrangements

of a large, bulky coat; the shoplifter simply slips merchandise onto the hooks or into the bags and walks away. Some shoplifters use *booster coats* constructed to conceal merchandise. Still others wear *booster panties*, loose-fitting bloomers that are fastened tightly around the knees and worn under bulky clothing; the shoplifter drops merchandise into them at the waist.

The **diverter** is one member of a team of shoplifters who attempts to divert the attention of the store's personnel while a partner shoplifts. Diverters use several techniques to attract store personnel's attention, including (1) engaging the salesperson in conversation, (2) creating an attention-grabbing disturbance, and (3) requesting merchandise that requires the salesperson to go to the stockroom. If the diverter manages to draw attention, the shoplifter partner can secure the merchandise and be out of the store before anyone realizes what has happened.

Obstructing the vision of store personnel while they or a partner shoplift is the principal technique of **blockers**. In a team effort, the blocker simply stands between the salesperson and a shoplifting partner. Working singly, the blocker might use a topcoat draped over the arm to shield the shoplifting activities of the other hand.

The **sweeper** simply brushes merchandise off the counter into a shopping bag or some other type of container. Typically the sweeper reaches over a counter, pretending to examine a piece of merchandise, but in the process of bringing the arm back sweeps merchandise off the counter and into the container.

Walkers have perfected the technique of walking naturally while carrying concealed merchandise between their legs. The walker is usually a woman. Shoplifters who have developed this skill are capable of carrying both small items such as jewelry and large items such as small appliances in a completely natural way.

The **wearer** tries on merchandise, then wears it out of the store. The *open-wearer* is a bold shoplifter who tries on a hat, coat, or some other piece of clothing, removes the tags, and then openly wears it while shopping and exiting the store. It is the boldness of this technique that makes it successful. *Under-wearers* steal clothing items by wearing them under their own loose outerwear. The most common technique is to take several items into the fitting room and return fewer items to the racks.

Several other shoplifting techniques are used by both amateur and professional shoplifters. The **carrier** walks in, picks up a large piece of merchandise, removes the tags, affixes a fake sales slip, and walks out. **Self-wrappers** use their own wrapping paper to wrap store merchandise before removing it from the store. The **price changer** pays for the merchandise after taking a reduction by altering or switching the store's price tag or removing the store tag and substituting a realistic-looking fake. The **spoiler** purposely damages merchandise, then takes it up to the store manager to obtain a markdown; in essence, the customer is attempting to steal the difference between the full price and the customer-induced markdown price.[35] Finally, the **returner** uses the store he or she shoplifts from as a fence, that is, steals the merchandise and then returns it for a refund. The returner's activities are why a "no receipt, no refund" policy makes good security sense for most retailers.[36]

Detection and Prevention

The retailer's security program should include both shoplifting detection and shoplifting prevention measures. Detecting shoplifters is largely a matter of good observation. Training store employees to be better observers not only increases the chances of detecting actual shoplifting activities but raises the likelihood of discouraging potential shoplifters. Following are basic observation rules for spotting shoplifting activities:

- *Watch the eyes*. Some shoplifters often focus undue attention on the merchandise they are about to steal.
- *Watch the hands*. It is important to watch *both* hands. While one hand may be visibly handling merchandise on top of the counter, the other may be busily engaged in shoplifting activities.
- *Watch the body*. Unnatural body movements are more common with amateur shoplifters than with professionals, who have been trained to use smooth, fluid body movements.
- *Watch the clothing*. When clothing is out of season (e.g., winter clothing in the summer), appears to be inconsistent with the individual wearing it (e.g., large, bulky clothing on a small person), and is inconsistent with the weather (e.g., a raincoat on a bright sunny day), the likelihood that the customer is a potential shoplifter is substantially increased.
- *Watch for devices*. Anything the customer carries is a potential concealment device. If the object appears out of place, such as an umbrella on a sunny day or gloves on a warm day, store personnel should pay special attention to the individual.
- *Watch for groups*. Amateur teenage shoplifters often travel in groups or gangs; while two or three members divert attention, the other members shoplift.
- *Watch for loiterers*. Many shoplifters must work up the nerve to steal. In doing so, they frequently loiter around the area containing the merchandise they have targeted.

Excessive time spent inspecting exposed merchandise is a telltale sign of potential shoplifting activities.

- *Watch for switches*. Shoplifters often work in pairs: One shoplifts the merchandise and then passes it on to a partner. Telephone booths, restrooms, and restaurants are favorite switching places for this team effort, so they should be scrutinized.

To facilitate observation and detection, many retailers use devices such as mirrors, observation towers, closed-circuit television, and electronic bugs (see Figure 8–18).[37]

Prevention is the best way to control losses from shoplifting. While some retailers use door guards, floor walkers, and mechanical detection devices, the best prevention measures are well-trained, observant employees.[38] Store employees should (1) be aware of all individuals in their areas of responsibility, (2) maintain a high profile in terms of visibility, (3) be alert to the actions of others in the department, (4) be available to assist customers, and (5) keep displays neatly organized to facilitate theft detection.

Decide how effective these security devices might be in preventing and detecting shoplifting.

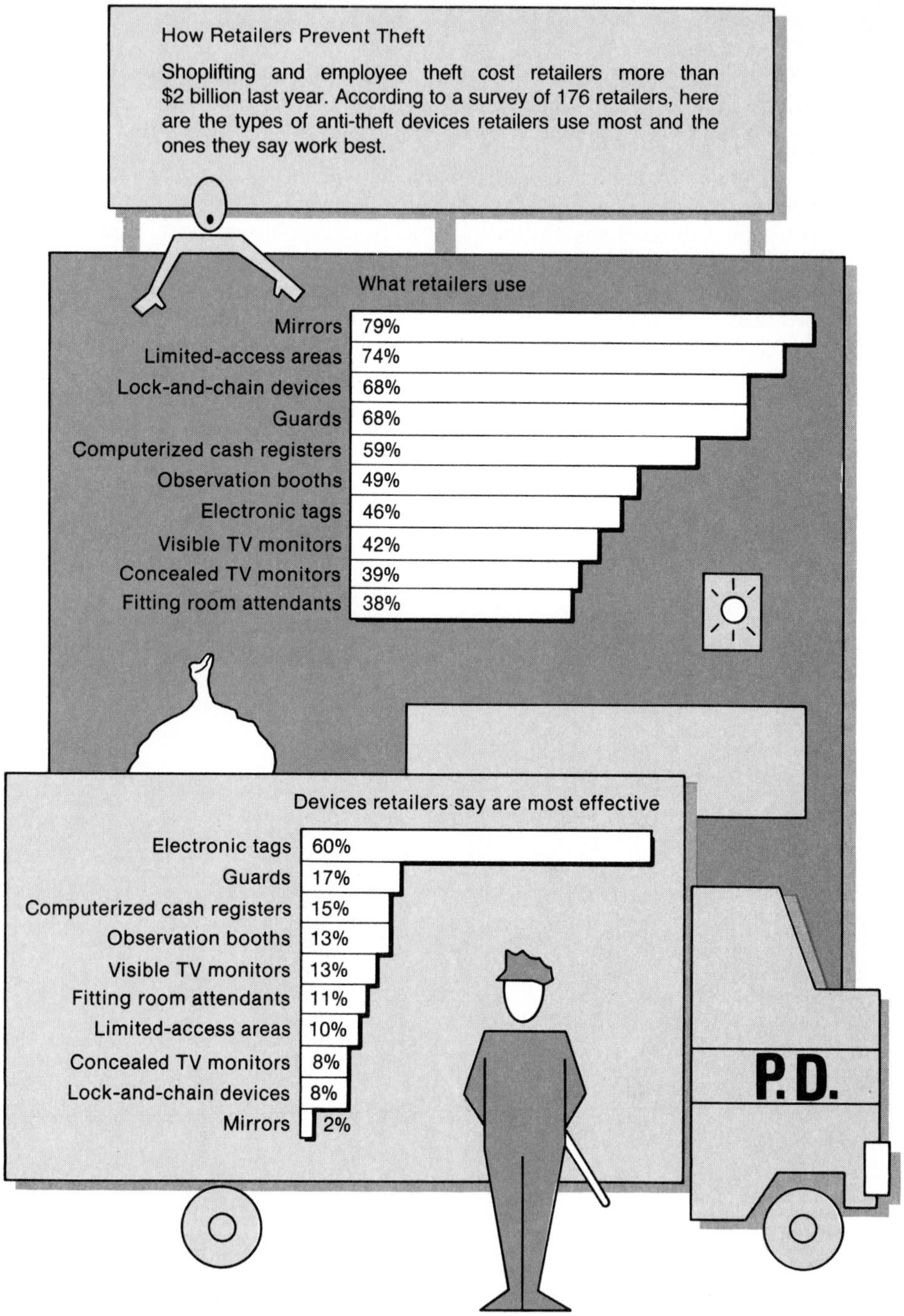

Source: Arthur Young-NMRI 6th annual study of security and shrinkage.

FIGURE 8–18
Observation methods (source: adapted from M. E. Williams, "Theft: Stores Fight Back: For Retailers, 'Tis the Season to be Wary," copyright 1984, *USA Today*. Reprinted with permission.)

Apprehension and Prosecution

Approaching, apprehending, and prosecuting an individual for shoplifting is a tricky business. State and local laws differ concerning the apprehension and prosecution of shoplifters. However, a number of general rules are appropriate in dealing with any shoplifting situation:

1. *Be absolutely certain.* Before approaching or accusing an individual of shoplifting, the retailer should be as certain as possible that the individual has pilfered merchandise.
2. *Use trained personnel.* Only trained personnel (e.g., security personnel or store manager) who are familiar with the legalities and techniques of apprehension should attempt to apprehend shoplifters.
3. *Pick the right place.* In some cases it is best to wait until the shoplifter has left the store, because it can improve the store's legal case in prosecuting the shoplifter and may avoid a scene in front of the store's legitimate customers. In other cases, in-store apprehension is preferable when high-value merchandise is involved or when the shoplifter might successfully leave the store.
4. *Make a positive approach.* Suspected shoplifters should be approached positively and firmly.
5. *Observe individual's legal rights.* Undue harassment of or use of force on shoplifters will eliminate any chance of successful prosecution.
6. *Call the police.* If the retailer decides to detain the suspect for any reason, the police should be called immediately.
7. *Prosecute when warranted.* Most retailers agree that professional shoplifters should be fully prosecuted at every opportunity but prefer to examine the individual circumstances surrounding each case of amateur shoplifting.

EMPLOYEE PILFERAGE

Employee pilferage represents serious losses for many retailers. Employee theft accounts for approximately 42 to 44 percent of retail shrinkage. It is typical for losses from employee theft to exceed those from all other forms of pilferage. Perhaps the single most important factor contributing to these losses is the retailer's belief that trusted employees do not and will not steal. Employee pilferage takes one of two forms: theft of merchandise and theft of money. Opportunity and need are the two most commonly cited factors responsible for the honesty or dishonesty of employees.

Devices and Techniques

Like most thieves, the employee who pilfers money and/or merchandise develops definite patterns or modes of operation. Based on these operational modes, profiles of the typical employee pilferer have been developed.

The **eater** samples the retailer's food and beverage lines or supplements lunch with a soft drink or dessert. Unfortunately, what starts out as a free snack often leads to a six-course feast. For the food store, restaurant, and cocktail lounge, the eater (or drinker) can literally eat up the profits.

The **smuggler** takes merchandise out of the store by whatever means available. Many retailers might be surprised to learn how much merchandise is carried out the back door in trash cans and bags. The smuggler also uses coats, lunchboxes, purses, and various other types of bags and packages to conceal and transport merchandise from the store's premises.

The **discounter** feels entitled to give unauthorized discounts to friends and relatives. By charging $10 for a $16 pair of slacks, the employee may satisfy a "special" customer but certainly not at a profit for the retailer. Other employees give their friends and relatives unauthorized discounts with free merchandise or "two-for-one" sales. The friend or relative who receives two for the price of one is sure to spread the word among other friends and relatives. Before long, the employee is in a compromising position with few alternatives other than to quit the job.

The **dipper** steals money by dipping into the cash register or mishandles cash in some other way, such as making short rings, fraudulent refunds, or false employee discounts. A *short ring* occurs when the employee fails to ring up a sale on the cash register or rings up less than the purchase amount. In either case, the employee pockets whatever money is left over from the transaction. The *fraudulent refund* involves writing up refund tickets for merchandise that has not been returned and pocketing the entire amount of the refund. To use this method, the dipper must have access to refund slips and the authority to issue refunds. *False employee discounts* also allow the dipper to pilfer cash: The employee simply rings up a regular customer sale as an employee-discount sale and pockets the difference.

The **embezzler** is most often a highly trusted employee who takes advantage of that trust to divert the retailer's funds for either permanent or temporary use. Some of the simpler embezzlement schemes are (1) adding the names of relatives and fictitious employees to the payroll and collecting "their" multiple paychecks; (2) creating dummy suppliers and falsifying purchase orders, then collecting for fictitious shipments; (3) accepting kickbacks from suppliers for inflated purchases; (4) padding expense accounts; (5) falsifying overtime records; and (6) using company supplies and facilities for personal use.

The **partner** does not actually pilfer the merchandise or money; instead, he or she supplies outside individuals with information (e.g., security procedures) or devices (e.g., keys) that increase the likelihood of successful theft. In return, the employee receives a cut of the pilfered merchandise.

The **stasher** hides merchandise in a secure place inside the store. Later in the selling season, when the merchandise is marked down for clearance, the employee removes the stashed merchandise from its hiding place and purchases it at the discount price. Essentially the store employee has pilfered the difference between the original price of the merchandise and the discounted price.

Detection and Prevention

To combat employee pilferage, the retailer's security program should include (1) creating a security atmosphere, (2) using security personnel, and (3) establishing security policies.

Creating a Security Atmosphere

One of the most effective methods of controlling employee theft is to create a general store atmosphere in which not even the slightest degree of dishonesty is tolerated and honesty and integrity are rewarded. The first step in creating a security atmosphere is to stop employee theft before it starts by carefully screening employees before hiring them and properly training them after they are employed. The second step is for management to set the example. By engaging in dishonest or questionable behavior, the manager sets the tone for an atmosphere that can lead to employee pilferage. One simple philosophy about controlling shrinkage is that "it starts and ends with the store manager."[39] The third step is to create a work environment that is free from unnecessary temptation. Establishing and enforcing good security policies can substantially reduce opportunities for employee theft. The fourth step is to establish an environment that makes employees feel like trusted and respected members of a team.

Using Security Personnel

To detect, discourage, and prevent employees from pilfering, some retailers use several types of security personnel. Stationing **uniformed guards** at employee entrances/exits and requiring employees to check in and out of the store reduce opportunities for stealing merchandise. The threat of search on a random basis can serve as a major deterrent to employee theft.

Retailers also use **undercover shoppers** to check on the honesty of employees. Posing as a legitimate customer, an undercover shopper often can detect the activities of the eater, the discounter, and the dipper. By informing store employees that such undercover security personnel are present in the store, the retailer has activated an effective preventive measure.

Additional security measures include **silent witness programs** that reward employees with cash for anonymous tips on theft activities of other employees. Tips are transmitted to a third party, who relays the information to the employer.

Establishing Security Policies

Retailers have established a number of store security policies to control employee theft. Some examples of policies aimed at controlling employee pilferage might include the following:

1. All packages, bags, trash cans, and other devices for concealing merchandise are subject to unannounced random inspection.
2. All store employees (including management personnel) will enter and leave the store by designated entrances and exits.
3. All customers' discounts must be specifically approved by the store manager.
4. All sales must be registered and each customer given a sales receipt.
5. All customer returns and refunds must be approved by the department or store manager.
6. All sales involving employee discounts must be approved by the store manager.
7. All cash registers and cash boxes are subject to regularly scheduled checks as well as random checks.
8. All records (sales, purchase, expense, etc.) are audited both regularly and randomly.

Apprehension and Prosecution

The same rules that apply for shoplifters apply in approaching, apprehending, and prosecuting employee pilferers: (1) Be absolutely certain, (2) use trained personnel, (3) pick the right place, (4) make a positive approach, (5) observe legal rights, (6) call the police, and (7) prosecute when warranted.

SUPPLIER PILFERAGE

When developing a store security program, the retailer must remember that suppliers have some of the same security problems with dishonest employees as the retailer. The retailer is very vulnerable to pilfering activities of delivery personnel. These activities include (1) **short counts**—delivering fewer items than were listed on the purchase order and signed for on the invoice—and (2) **merchandise removal**—stealing merchandise from receiving, checking, stocking, and selling areas. In the latter case, dishonest delivery personnel have readily accessible concealment devices, such as empty boxes, delivery carts, and bulky work clothes. There are numerous security requirements and procedures to reduce and eliminate pilferage by supplier personnel, including the following:

1. Establish a receiving area for accepting all incoming merchandise.
2. Supervise all deliveries.
3. Control entry and exit to the receiving area.
4. Use random inspection of all delivery personnel while they are on the store's premises.

5. Check all incoming shipments.
6. Document all incoming shipments as to contents, weight, size, condition of shipment, and any other pertinent information.

BAD CHECKS

Accepting checks in exchange for merchandise has become an essential part of most retailers' service offering. Accepting bad checks, however, is not part of that service. A bad check is, of course, not honored for payment when the retailer presents it to the designated bank. The retailer's security program must include safeguards against accepting worthless checks and appropriate procedures for recovering losses resulting from such exchanges. Bad checks can be stolen and falsely endorsed, written on bank accounts with insufficient funds, and written on nonexistent or closed bank accounts.

It is virtually impossible to avoid some bad checks. Through proper detection and prevention measures, however, the retailer can keep bad-check losses at a minimum. By carefully examining each check not only for fraudulent information but for simple, honest mistakes in writing, the retailer can avoid accepting checks that are intentionally or unintentionally bad. After determining that the check is valid, the retailer must determine whether the customer offering the check is the right person (see Figure 8–19).

No check should be accepted without proper identification. Many retailers require at least two pieces of acceptable identification, most commonly driver's licenses, automobile registration cards, credit cards, and employment identification cards.

The retailer should establish a system that clearly states check-cashing policies. Employees and customers alike should be informed of the types of checks that are acceptable and the conditions under which the retailer will accept them. With a *registration system,* retailers request that their customers register identification information at some prior time with the store's credit or customer service office. Once registered, the customer receives a check-cashing ID card. All pertinent information concerning the customer is gathered at the time of registration and verified by the

FIGURE 8–19
Spotting the bad-check artist

Does the age of the customer match with the identification? Birthdate on ID seem correct for the customer? Is customer with a driver's license old enough to drive?

Does the sex shown on the ID match the customer? Does the name on check and identification match the sex of the presenter?

If photo identification is shown, does the picture look reasonably like the customer, allowing for aging and cosmetic changes, such as hair coloring?

Is the customer nervous? Or appear to be in a rush? Does the customer hesitate when signing the check or when asked to verbally repeat the address or phone number?

Is the customer shopping in a "high risk" merchandise department? These might include: jewelry; consumer electronics; appliances; and other merchandise categories where goods can be sold quickly for cash. Your own store's experiences will help you determine where you are most at risk.

Is the transaction too rapid for the type of merchandise selected? For example, does the customer fail to ask about warranty, delivery, layaway, or other questions which frequently arise in connection with the merchandise being purchased?

Source: *Check Acceptance Policies and Procedures,* Credit Management Division, National Retail Federation, Inc. New York, 1984, 9.

central office. When paying by check, the customer simply shows the ID to the salesclerk, who records the ID number on the check and compares the check signature with the ID signature.

BAD CREDIT CARDS

Sales charged to stolen, fictitious, canceled, and expired credit cards cause substantial losses for retailers each year. To reduce these costs, a good policy for retailers is to exercise as much care in accepting credit cards as in cashing checks. In accepting both third-party credit cards (bank cards, entertainment cards, etc.) and the store's own credit cards, retailers are now using various commercial electronic credit card verification systems.[40]

BURGLARY AND ROBBERY

Retail stores are prime targets for burglary and robbery because they are less secure than most other businesses (e.g., isolated locations, evening hours, exposed cash in registers, etc.). This lack of security results from carelessness as well as from the general nature of the retailing business. While retailers can do little to alter the nature of their business, they can initiate security measures to make their stores a less desirable target for burglary and robbery and reduce their harmful impact. **Burglary** is any unlawful entry to commit a felony or a theft even if no force is used to gain entrance. **Robbery** is stealing or taking anything of value by force, violence, or intimidation. Given the steady increase in the number of burglaries and robberies in recent years, the retailer's security program must incorporate careful measures to prevent such crimes.

Burglars usually operate under cover of darkness, after the store is closed. They gain entry by picking locks, forcing open doors or windows, using duplicate keys, or hiding in the store until it closes. Most security measures are directed at (1) preventing the burglar from gaining entry to the store, (2) securing all high-value merchandise, and (3) informing police and other security personnel of all successful and unsuccessful attempts at entry. Most retailers use locks and lights to discourage attempts at entry, safes to secure valuables, and alarms to alert police.

Good security locks discourage less skilled burglars from attempting entry and require them to make a risky forced entry. A burglar-resistant safe can create another major obstacle to attempted theft. The safe should be well lighted and usually located near the front of the store, where it is visible from the outside. To further boost security, the retailer can bolt the safe to the floor or set it in concrete. Security alarms (1) discourage some burglars from attempting entry; (2) detect entry by burglars who are unaware of the alarms or do not know how to circumvent them; and (3) notify the police or a private security agency that an illegal entry has occurred. The silent, central-station burglary alarm system gives the best protection. Retailers can choose from among several alarm-sensing devices, including radar motion detectors, invisible photo beams, ultrasonic sound detectors, and vibration detectors.

Robbery is far more serious than burglary, because it always holds the potential for loss of life as well as of property. By definition, robbery is a violent crime in which one person uses force, or the threat of it, against another individual. Perhaps the most disturbing aspect of robbery is that many robberies are committed for very small sums of cash or merchandise, often by individuals who are extremely unstable (e.g., drug addicts). Training employees to cope with robbers and limiting the opportunities for robbery help ensure the well-being of store personnel and reduce property losses.

The retailer's first concern in developing any robbery security program is to train store employees to handle an actual robbery situation. The following procedures and instructions can help:

1. Remain as calm as possible.
2. Make no sudden moves.
3. Reassure robbers that they can expect full cooperation in every way.

4. Make no attempt to be a hero by trying to apprehend the robber.
5. Give robbers whatever they want when they want it.
6. Attempt to make mental notes on the robber's description (height, weight, hair and eye color, complexion, voice, clothing, and any other distinguishing characteristics).
7. Remain still until the robber has completely exited the premises. Then call the police and the store's management.
8. Talk only to the police and store manager regarding the robbery situation and the robber.

Several preventive measures might well reduce the number of robbery attempts as well as losses suffered from robberies. To reduce the risk of robbery, the retailer should heed the following guidelines:

1. Keep as little cash in each cash register as possible, and remove excess cash frequently.
2. Maintain a minimal level of operating cash in the store. Bank all excess cash.
3. Use an armored-car service for making bank deposits. If this is impractical, vary bank trip routes and times.
4. Keep store safes locked at all times. Do not leave a safe open during operating hours.
5. Use two people to open and close the store—one for the actual opening and closing of the store and the other as an outside security lookout.
6. Exercise extreme caution when someone asks you to make an emergency opening after store hours. Before going to the store, call the police and make sure they will be there for the unscheduled opening.

Antirobbery defense systems are directed at discouraging and apprehending robbers. Some of the more common robbery protection systems include panic buttons, till traps, video systems, and cash control devices. Panic buttons are hidden alarm devices that silently alert the police or security company that a robbery is in progress. Till traps are devices installed in cash register drawers that trigger a silent alarm when the last dollar bill is removed from the till. In-house video systems are highly visible closed-circuit TV monitors trained on the cash register. They serve the dual purpose of discouraging potential robbers and providing police with pictures of an actual robbery.

SUMMARY

One of the most valuable ways the retailer can attract customers is by the appearance of the store and its immediate surroundings. The store's environment has both physical and psychological repercussions in the battle for the customer's attention and for efficient operations. By identifying the desired image, targeting the right consumer, and communicating the right impression, the retailer creates a store image that is right for shopping and working. Appeals to the five senses promote a favorable buying atmosphere: Sight, sound, smell, touch, and taste appeals have an obvious influence on the consumer's buying behavior.

Communication with the consumer is facilitated by the store's exterior. How and where the store is positioned on the site affect the retailer's ability to attract customers. The store should be positioned so that it is visible to the consumer, compatible with the natural environment, and convenient for on-site movement of people and vehicles. The store's architecture should incorporate features that make a favorable impression while remaining functionally efficient. The store's sign serves two purposes: identifying the store and attracting consumer attention. Because the store's facade often creates the consumer's first impression, an appropriate configuration, attractive window displays, and accessible store entrances are essential.

The store's interior should minimize operating expenses while maximizing sales activities and customer satisfaction. In planning store layouts, the retailer must consider that all space is not equal in terms of sales-producing potential. Also, wise use of nonselling space helps the retailer meet consumers' service needs.

As in-store visual presentations of the merchandise, retail displays assume a key role in creating a shopping atmosphere and enhancing the consumer's buying mood. Depending on their objectives, retailers use a variety of methods to present merchandise, including selection, special, point-of-purchase, and audiovisual displays. To ensure effective displays, retailers plan merchandise exhibits by controlling content (unit, related, and theme groupings) and arrangements (pyramid, zig-zag, step, and fan patterns).

Store security calls for developing the necessary safeguards for the store and its merchandise by initiating programs for detecting and preventing losses resulting from shoplifting by customers, pilfering by employees and suppliers, passing of bad checks and credit cards, and burglary and robbery.

Shoplifting is the theft of merchandise by customers or individuals posing as customers. There are basically two types of shoplifters: those who steal from need and for psychological reasons (amateurs) and those who steal for a living (professionals). Several shoplifting devices and techniques exist, including the booster, the diverter, the blocker, the sweeper, the walker, and the wearer. The best means of detecting shoplifters is good observation—knowing what to look for and where to look. In addition to well-trained personnel, retailers use convex mirrors, one-way mirrors, observation towers, closed-circuit television, and electronic "bugs" to aid in the detection process. Retailers should apprehend shoplifters in full compliance with the law and prosecute shoplifters when conditions warrant.

Store employees also steal; in fact, losses from employee pilferage exceed those from shoplifting. Opportunity and need are the two most critical causes of this type of theft. The eater, the smuggler, the discounter, the dipper, the embezzler, the partner, and the stasher are types of dishonest employees who pilfer merchandise and money. The retailer can reduce this form of theft by creating an atmosphere of honesty, using security personnel, and establishing strict security policies.

STUDENT STUDY GUIDE

Key Terms and Concepts

angled-front configuration (p. 283)
annex approach (p. 291)
arcade-front configuration (p. 284)
audio merchandising (p. 301)
audiovisual merchandising (p. 301)
blocker (p. 307)
booster (p. 306)
boutique layout (p. 297)
burglary (p. 315)
carrier (p. 308)
core approach (p. 291)
dipper (p. 312)
discounter (p. 311)
diverter (p. 307)
eater (p. 311)
elevated windows (p. 285)
embezzler (p. 312)
fan arrangement (p. 305)
4-3-2-1 rule (p. 288)
free-form layout (p. 297)
grid layout (p. 295)
island windows (p. 285)
merchandise removal (p. 313)
partner (p. 312)
peripheral approach (p. 291)
pilfer (p. 306)
point-of-purchase (POP) display (p. 300)
price changer (p. 308)
pyramid arrangement (p. 304)
ramped windows (p. 285)
related groupings (p. 302)
retail display (p. 297)
returner (p. 308)
robbery (p. 315)
sandwich approach (p. 291)
scent appeal (p. 279)
selection display (p. 298)
self-wrapper (p. 308)
shadow box windows (p. 285)
shoplifting (p. 306)
short counts (p. 313)
sight appeal (p. 274)
silent witness program (p. 313)
site compatibility (p. 281)
smuggler (p. 311)
sound appeal (p. 278)
special display (p. 299)
spoiler (p. 308)
stasher (p. 312)
step arrangement (p. 305)

store image (p. 273)
store visibility (p. 281)
straight-front configuration (p. 283)
sweeper (p. 307)
taste appeal (p. 279)
theme appeal (p. 280)
theme groupings (p. 303)
touch appeal (p. 279)
undercover shopper (p. 313)
uniformed guard (p. 312)
unit groupings (p. 302)
visual merchandising (p. 301)
walker (p. 308)
wearer (p. 308)
zig-zag arrangement (p. 304)

Review Questions

1. What is store image? How is it created?
2. Describe the three types of visual relationships.
3. Describe the emotions or feelings consumers associate with horizontal lines, vertical lines, and slanted lines.
4. What determines the psychological impact of color? Explain.
5. What illusions do bright colors create? Which consumers tend to prefer softer tones?
6. Discuss the three uses for sound in creating a buying atmosphere.
7. What three factors determine a store's visibility? Explain.
8. Identify and explain the factors the retailer considers in designing a functional facility.
9. Describe the who, what, where, and when functions of a retail store sign.
10. Compare and contrast the three basic storefront configurations.
11. What is the 4-3-2-1 rule?
12. Compare and contrast the model stock and sales productivity methods of allocating selling space.
13. How can seasonality of demand affect the in-store location of merchandise?
14. Describe the three basic layout patterns. What are the strengths and weaknesses of each pattern?
15. Identify the three basic ways in which shoplifting is accomplished.
16. Identify and describe the various types of shoplifters on the basis of their techniques.
17. Describe the major devices retailers use in observing and detecting shoplifters.
18. What are the two most commonly cited factors contributing to dishonesty of employees?
19. Profile the seven types of employee pilferer.
20. What are the two most common methods of supplier pilferage?

Review Exam

True or False

_____ 1. The sense of sight provides people with more information than any other sense mode.
_____ 2. To create perfect harmony in display, dissimilar shapes should be used.
_____ 3. A retailer using the 4-3-2-1 rule of store rent allocation would assign 1 percent of the store's rental cost to the back quarter of the store.
_____ 4. Using the sales-productivity ratio, the retailer allocates selling space on the basis of sales per square foot generated by a given merchandise group.
_____ 5. The walker is usually a female shoplifter who tries on merchandise, then wears it out of the store.
_____ 6. The most effective method of controlling employee theft is to create a general store atmosphere in which not even the slightest degree of dishonesty is tolerated and honesty and integrity are rewarded.
_____ 7. Short counts involve delivering fewer items than were listed on the purchase order and signed for on the invoice.

Multiple Choice

_____ 1. Visual relationships are those interpretations made by the "mind's eye" from visual stimuli that consist of
a. Harmony, melody, contrast
b. Melody, contrast, clash
c. Clash, melody, harmony
d. Harmony, clash, contrast
e. All of the above

_____ 2. Restful, peace, freshness, and growth are all perceptions normally associated with which color?
a. Red
b. Yellow
c. Blue
d. Green
e. Violet

_____ 3. Which of the following is *not* one of the three interacting factors a retailer uses to improve a store's visibility?
a. Setback
b. Angle
c. Color
d. Elevation
e. Smell

_____ 4. The _____ storefront configuration is characterized by several recessed windows and/or entrances.
a. Straight
b. Arcade
c. Angled
d. Closed
e. Open

_____ 5. If the retailer wishes to achieve the most efficient use of selling space, it should use the _____ layout.
a. Free-form
b. Grid
c. Square
d. Boutique
e. Shoppe

_____ 6. The likelihood that a customer is a potential shoplifter is substantially increased when his or her clothing is _____.
a. Out of season
b. Inconsistent with his or her size
c. Inconsistent with the weather
d. Old and worn
e. a, b, and c

_____ 7. The _____ is a store employee who feels entitled to give unauthorized price reductions to friends and relatives.
a. Dipper
b. Smuggler
c. Discounter
d. Embezzler
e. Stasher

STUDENT APPLICATIONS MANUAL

Investigative Projects: Practice and Applications

1. Compare and contrast the image created by the physical facilities of a local Sears store with that of a local J. C. Penney store. How does each store communicate the right impression and the wrong impression? Provide specific examples.
2. Evaluate the sight, sound, scent, touch, taste, and theme appeals for a major franchised food retailer (e.g., McDonald's, Wendy's, Pizza Hut) in your community. Identify specific examples of both positive and negative appeals. What changes would you recommend to create a more desirable atmosphere?
3. For the retailer selected in project 2, analyze the store's position in terms of visibility, site compatibility, and consumer convenience. Identify and explain positive and negative aspects of the store's position.
4. Draw a comprehensive diagram of the store layout of a local discount store. Redesign the store's layout using the boutique approach. Should a discount store consider using a boutique layout? Explain your reasoning.
5. Survey your local police department to develop a statistical profile of the various types of criminal activities besetting retailers. Identify retail crime patterns (high-crime areas, types of retailers and/or products that appear to be targeted by criminals, etc.). Discuss with the police the preventive measures they recommend for reducing retail security problems.
6. Should the retailer prosecute amateur shoplifters? Discuss the positive and negative sides of this question. Develop a specific set of policies regarding when, who, and how often to prosecute. Justify your policies.
7. Identify and discuss the issues surrounding the use of drug tests as a prerequisite for initial and continued employment. Should retailers be allowed to use such tests? Why or why not?
8. Interview a small, independent retailer regarding its check-cashing policies. Determine what problems the retailer experiences in regard to cashing checks. Are the retailer's check-cashing policies adequate? Why or why not? What changes would you recommend? Justify your recommendations.

Tactical Cases: Problems and Decisions

■ CASE 8–1

Montgomery Ward: From General Merchant to Specialty Mall Operator*

Chicago-based Montgomery Ward & Co. is pursuing a strategy of recasting itself from a dusty, broad-line general merchant into an operator of narrowly focused specialty stores. The strategy consists of remodeling many of Ward's older free-standing stores into a self-contained mall of specialty boutiques. This "store-within-a-store" concept embraces all of the merchandising tactics commonly associated with successful specialists such as The Limited and The Gap. Ward's strategy involves offering both branded and private-label merchandise, complete and compelling assortments, value pricing, and excellent customer service. Ward's current collection of six specialty power formats is shown in Exhibit A. Seventy percent of Ward's product mix consists of hard lines such as automotive supplies, appliances, and home furnishings; soft goods and apparel account for the remaining 30 percent. To expand the drawing power of its new store format and fully utilize the extra space in some stores, Ward is bring-

EXHIBIT A
Ward's six power formats

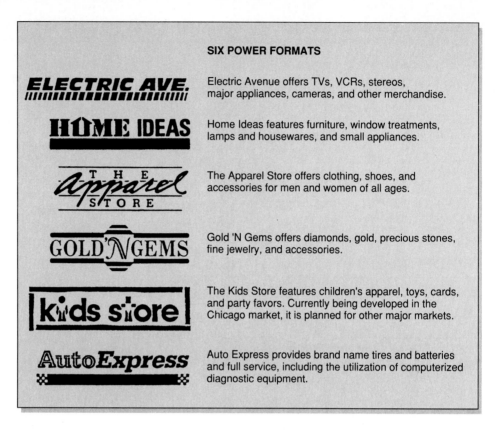

SIX POWER FORMATS

ELECTRIC AVE.	Electric Avenue offers TVs, VCRs, stereos, major appliances, cameras, and other merchandise.
HOME IDEAS	Home Ideas features furniture, window treatments, lamps and housewares, and small appliances.
THE Apparel STORE	The Apparel Store offers clothing, shoes, and accessories for men and women of all ages.
GOLD 'N GEMS	Gold 'N Gems offers diamonds, gold, precious stones, fine jewelry, and accessories.
kids store	The Kids Store features children's apparel, toys, cards, and party favors. Currently being developed in the Chicago market, it is planned for other major markets.
AutoExpress	Auto Express provides brand name tires and batteries and full service, including the utilization of computerized diagnostic equipment.

ing in other, noncompeting retailers that are compatible with its merchandising mix. Synergistic retailers such as Toys 'R' Us, Silk Plants, Waxy Maxy record shops, and Pro Jersey athletic apparel are current tenants in Ward's "mall without walls" format. Ward is also testing several more specialty concepts, including (1) the Party Store (party supplies), (2) Office World (discount office supplies), (3) Doctronics (consumer electronics repair shop), and (4) Four Seasons Shop (a self-contained store area featuring hard and soft seasonal goods).

Bernie Brennan, Ward's CEO, explains his concept this way: "Why can't we have the image of a full line store on the outside and give customers both a choice of a destination store and the overall convenience of being able to go between specialty stores?" The idea is for Ward to externally resemble a power-strip shopping center while internally offering the customer the atmosphere of a specialty shopping mall. On the outside, some or all of the six power formats have their own exterior entrances and signage. On the inside, the illusion of a separate store continues where selective interior walls and display units create a boutique-like layout. All specialty areas are connected by large internal aisles called the Midway. The "nerve center" of the store is a 2,000-square-foot customer service area located at the front of the store. Exhibit B representates one store prototype currently being tested and evaluated.

ASSIGNMENT

1. Evaluate Ward's "store-within-a-store" concept of a self-contained mall of specialty boutiques. What are the strengths and weaknesses of the concept? Describe Ward's competitive position with respect to this concept.
2. From a merchandising and operational standpoint, are the six power formats compatible? Do they go together? Why or why not? How will the additional noncompeting outside retailers fit in? What contribution will Toys 'R' Us, Silk Plants, Waxy Maxy, and Pro Jersey make to Ward's new concept? Will the new specialty concepts have successful test market results? Why or why not?
3. Evaluate the store layout in Exhibit B. Identify its advantages and disadvantages. What improvements would you recommend?

*This case was prepared by Dale Lewison and Jon Hawes, The University of Akron.

Sources: Brian Bremner, "Bernie Brennan Has the Last Laugh at Wards," *Business Week,* January 15, 1990, 70; "Tucson Montgomery Wards: Store or Mall?", *Chain Store Age Executive,* August 1989, 128–129; and Jay L. Johnson, "The Remaking of Montgomery Wards," *Discount Merchandiser,* September 1989, 17–25.

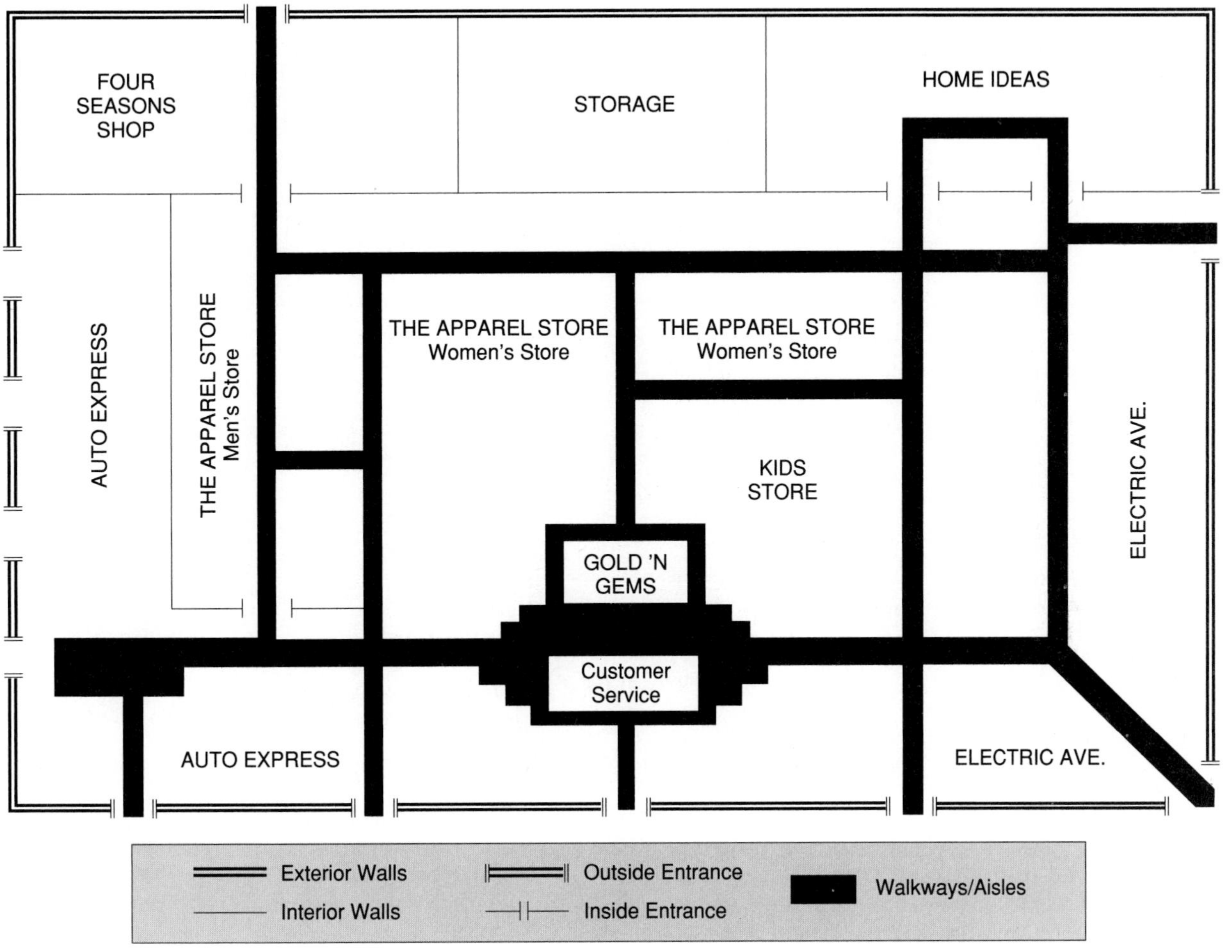

EXHIBIT B
A Montgomery Ward prototype store

■ CASE 8–2
Hoffman–La Roche, Inc.*

Drug abuse is one of our most serious social problems and an important factor to corporations seeking to increase employees' productivity. Experts estimate that 10 to 23 percent of American workers use dangerous drugs while on the job. Employee drug abuse has been estimated to cost American industry $33 billion per year. Obviously, from social and competitive perspectives, U.S. firms are interested in reducing drug abuse among the work force.

Drug abuse testing is seen as a legitimate means for screening prospective employees (nearly one-third of the Fortune 500 companies do this) and discouraging drug use by current employees. Several pharmaceutical companies now manufacture drug abuse tests, and others are considering entry into this potentially lucrative market. In fact, a recent study indicated that the market potential for drug abuse testing has been increasing by 10 to 15 percent annually and could grow to $220 million by 1991.

Hoffman–La Roche, Inc., located in Nutley, New Jersey, already has entered the market for drug abuse testing. The company currently sells about $20 million per year in various drug-testing products. Recently it introduced a service known as Abuscreen and has begun promoting it as 99 percent accurate in testing for the presence of marijuana, LSD, amphetamines, cocaine, morphine, barbiturates, and methaqualone.

The high reliability of Hoffman–La Roche's drug abuse testing is extremely important in marketing these services. The company's reputation, experience, and comprehensive services to potential customers are also important factors and enabled Hoffman–La Roche to sell its services to the 1984 Olympics, the U.S. Department of

Defense, and many other organizations. Although price is a concern, most of the prospective corporate clients place greater emphasis on the quality of the drug abuse tests.

Hoffman–La Roche recently launched a new subsidiary called Diagnostic Dimensions, which markets comprehensive services to fight drug abuse in the work force. It offers training programs, employee education and counseling, and other services to help companies help their employees.

ASSIGNMENT

Assume the role of director of human resources for an 80-unit chain of specialty apparel shops. The president of the firm believes that many of the personnel problems (e.g., employee pilferage, poor employee morale, customer complaints, and store security) are drug related. Although there is no precise information on what percentage of the firm's employees might be using drugs, national averages provide some guidance. Because you are responsible for managing personnel problems, the president has asked you to prepare a report on the following:

1. Is drug usage a security problem?
2. Should the firm initiate a drug-testing program?
3. How might a drug-testing program be administered?
4. What actions should the firm take if an employee is found to be using drugs?

*This case was prepared by Jon Hawes, The University of Akron.

ENDNOTES

1. Marita Thomas, "Visual Merchandiser of the Year—Mansour of the Limited," *Stores,* January 1990, 162.
2. Ibid., 159.
3. Ibid.
4. Ibid.
5. Carol Hymowitz, "Upscale Look for Limited Puts Retailer Back on Track," *The Wall Street Journal,* February 24, 1989, B-1.
6. Ibid., B-4.
7. "Cool Elegance Highlights Lerner New York," *Chain Store Age Executive,* August 1989, 126.
8. Colten Timberlake, "Laura Ashley Chain Enduring Tough Times," *Akron Beacon Journal,* December 18, 1989, C-6.
9. Muriel J. Adams, "Robots in the Future," *Stores,* April 1988, 41.
10. Ibid.
11. See "Grand Tradition Continues in Columbus," *Chain Store Age Executive,* October 1989, 100–101.
12. Jeffrey A. Trachtenberg, "Burdine's Bets It Knows Florida Best," *The Wall Street Journal,* December 18, 1989, B-1.
13. Russell Mitchell, "Waldenbooks Tries Hooking Young Bookworms," *Business Week,* May 11, 1987, 48.
14. Kenneth H. Mills and Judith E. Paul, *Applied Visual Merchandising* (Englewood Cliffs, N.J.: Prentice-Hall, 1982), 47.
15. Ibid., 47–48.
16. Kenneth H. Mills and Judith E. Paul, *Create Distinctive Displays* (Englewood Cliffs, N.J.: Prentice-Hall, 1974), 61.
17. See "Tops' Props, Neon Signage Add Pizzazz," *Chain Store Age Executive,* January 1990, 140.
18. Marjorie Wold, "Creative Merchandising," *Progressive Grocer,* March 1990, 42.
19. Sallie Hook, "All the Retail World's a Stage," *Marketing News,* July 31, 1987, 16.
20. Cyndee Miller, "Interact Updates Old 'Listening Booth' Concept in Record Stores," *Marketing News,* January 1988, 4.
21. See Jennifer Pellet, "The Power of Lighting," *Discount Merchandiser,* February 1990, 71–74. See also "Lighting Dramatizes Filene's Flagship," *Chain Store Age Executive,* September 1989, 84.
22. See "Casual Corner Flagship Gets a Facelift," *Chain Store Age Executive,* August 1989, 132.
23. Teri Agins, "Discount Clothing Stores Facing Squeeze, Aim to Fashion a More Rounded Image," *The Wall Street Journal,* March 15, 1990, B-6.
24. See "The Real Estate Connection," *Chain Store Age Executive,* January 1990, 39.
25. See William R. Davison, Daniel J. Sweeney, and Ronald W. Stampfl, *Retailing Management* (New York: Wiley, 1985), 205–206.
26. Joan Bergmann, "American Fare," *Stores,* May 1989, 42.
27. "Fred Meyer Megastore Goes Hollywood," *Chain Store Age Executive,* March 1990, 77.
28. Pat Corwin, "Fashion-Forward Presentation," *Discount Merchandiser,* March 1990, 58.
29. See Marjorie Wold, "Retailing Roundup," *Progressive Grocer,* February 1990, 15.
30. Jean-Paul Gagnon and Jane T. Osterhaus, "Research Note: Effectiveness of Floor Displays on the Sales of Retail Products," *Journal of Retailing* 61 (Spring 1985): 115.
31. Cyndee Miller, "Trend in Fashion Retailing Is to Make a Video Statement," *Marketing News,* December 4, 1987, 14.
32. See Kenneth Mills and Judith Paul, *Visual Merchandising* (Englewood Cliffs, N.J.: Prentice-Hall, 1983), 37.
33. Ibid.
34. Ibid.

35. See Jennifer Pellet, "Keeping the Peace," *Discount Merchandiser,* September 1989, 55–56.
36. James K. Parmley, "The Risky R's of Retailing," *Security Management,* October 1988, 31–33.
37. See Jules Abend, "More Deterrents to Theft," *Stores,* June 1989, 61–63.
38. See Richard Weizel, "No Petty Theft Here," *Akron Beacon Journal,* August 23, 1989, B-1.
39. Ela Schwartz, "Hecks' Life after Chapter XI," *Discount Merchandiser,* February 1990, 27.
40. See "Talbots Links Banking, Credit Authorization," *Chain Store Age Executive,* January 1990, 81, 84–85.

OUTLINE

OBJECTIVES

- Appreciate the considerable impact that the retail location decision has on all other aspects of the retailer's business.
- Characterize a market and describe its components.
- Delineate and describe regional and local market areas.
- Evaluate regional and local market areas using sales potential and operational suitability.
- Select regional and local market areas capable of meeting the sales and operational needs of the retailing firm.
- Define a retail trading area in terms of its operational dimensions.
- Understand and use various techniques for trading-area identification.
- Ascertain the gross and net adequacy of retail trading areas.
- Evaluate and select retail trading areas in accordance with established minimum criteria.

PART III

RETAIL MARKETS AND TRADING AREAS

Identifying, Evaluating, and Selecting Markets

CHAPTER 9

THE RETAIL MARKET: FINDING THE RIGHT LOCATION

Retail location problems and opportunities are both varied and complex. Consider the following examples:

- Mervyn's, the soft goods department store division of Dayton Hudson Corp., "launched a big push into Texas and the southwest just before the energy crunch. Mervyn's wasn't alone in misreading the oil boom, but it had gotten bigger than most, forcing it into a costly and disconcerting retrenchment."[1]
- "Next to New York, its flashier cousin to the north, the nation's capital used to be something of a fashion backwater. In dress, Washingtonians preferred the preppy over Fifth Avenue chic, the traditional over the sometimes preposterously hip. But today that view of D.C. style is as outdated as bell-bottoms."[2] Washington's coming of age as a fashion center is well documented with strong retailers such as Saks Fifth Avenue, Lord & Taylor, R. H. Macy & Co., Nordstrom, Bloomingdale's, and Neiman Marcus, together with Washington stalwarts such as Woodward & Lothrop, Hecht's, and Garfinckel's.
- The Mall of America in Bloomington, Minnesota, will be the nation's largest mixed-use retail and entertainment project. Complete with a full-fledged theme park, the mall will have an extended drawing power. While mall trading areas usually are in the 10- to 15-mile range, a trading area radius of 200 to 300 miles is expected because of the amusement park's pull.[3]
- "When the Tyler Mall in Riverside, California, had a 'leak,' Nordstrom was called to plug it. The seepage was not a problem suitable for a plumber. It was a loss of customers who were traveling out of the area to shop the more upscale centers in nearby counties."[4] The addition of the upscale Nordstrom store was intended to stop the sales leakage and please the upwardly mobile residents who had become outshoppers.
- Chains now offer various "brands" of supermarkets—A&P operates Sav-a-Centers and Futurestores as well as A&Ps.[5] Using this variety of supermarket format, "the company plugs in the right one to fit market characteristics."[6]
- Sterling, Inc., operator of jewelry store chains such as Hudson Goodman, LeRoy's, Osterman, Rogers, Shaw's, and Belden, uses the strat-

egy of clustering its stores regionally to take advantage of its name recognition and maximize the effectiveness of its ad programs.[7]

- Burdine's, the Miami-based department store chain, must adapt its operations to the many local Florida markets: "Burdine's knows the Gulf Coast has attracted thousands of price-sensitive retirees who lead quiet lives. It knows folks in the Panhandle are more like those in rural Alabama than Miami. It knows that Central Florida has a Midwestern atmosphere, and that flashy South-Seas Florida prides itself on having the latest fashions."[8]

RETAIL LOCATION DECISIONS

The importance of location decisions cannot be overstated. A retailer that selects a poor location will always suffer a competitive disadvantage. To overcome a poor location (a struggle that is not always successful), the retailer must make substantial adjustments in the product, price, and promotional mixes.[9] Because adjustments usually are expensive to implement, they adversely affect the firm's profits.[10] On the other hand, selecting a good location enhances the chance of success, because it allows greater flexibility in developing the product, price, and promotional mixes. Given the long-term commitment, the substantial financial investments, and the effects on all retailing operations, the retailer must consider the location problem extremely carefully.

The retail location problem consists of identifying, evaluating, and selecting (1) regional market areas, (2) local market areas, (3) trading areas, and (4) site locations (see Figure 9–1). In this chapter, we examine regional markets, local markets, and trading areas. In Chapter 10, we will discuss selecting the retail site.

MARKET AREA DIMENSIONS

Market areas come in all sizes, shapes, and descriptions. The dimensions of a market area depend on several factors, including population density and media coverage. The two general problems facing the location specialist are (1) how to identify regional markets and (2) how to identify local markets. These two problems and their particular components are illustrated in Figure 9–2.

Identifying regional markets consists of determining the "right region" of the country and the "right part of the region." The geographic extent of a regional market is not fixed and can include either one state or a multistate area. For many small, independent retailers, the regional market problem is not a concern. They often have narrowed their choice of regions to the ones in which they currently live or work. For the chain organization or the retailer that intends to expand, however, the starting point in the location decision process is to identify regional and subregional markets.

As Figure 9–2 shows, the local market problem is how to find the "right town" and the "right part of town." For our purposes, "town" refers to an urban center of any size that can be associated with a particular regional or subregional market.

IDENTIFYING MARKET AREAS

Retailers use two criteria to identify retail market areas. With the **market potential approach**, retailers select criteria that reflect the support (in sales, number of customers, etc.) that a geographic area will provide a given retail operation. With the **retail operations approach**, the retailer examines factors that might enhance or limit operations.

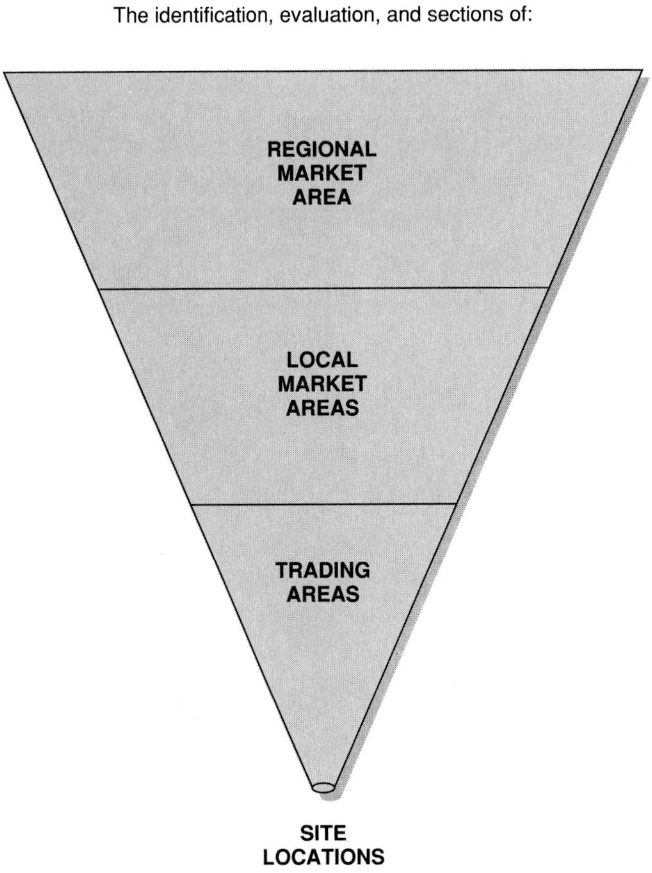

FIGURE 9–1
The retail location problem

Market Potential Approach

With the market potential approach, the retailer uses criteria specific to its class of goods (i.e., retailer-specific criteria) to identify market areas. While certain criteria are useful to one retailer, the same criteria may be of no use to another. Commonly used market identification criteria include those based on population, housing, buyer behavior, and physical environment characteristics.

Population characteristics are the most common segmenting criteria. As Figure 9–3 illustrates, a retailer can describe any geographic area (state, county, city, etc.) with any combination of population characteristics. Although total population figures and population densities are of primary importance, the retailer can get a more detailed profile of a market by examining the demographic characteristics of education, age, income, sex, occupation, religion, race, nationality, and family characteristics data. The retailer's purpose is to match a market's population characteristics to the population characteristics of people who desire its goods and services. Retailers can get population and demographic data from the *Census of Population*.

Housing characteristics are an important criterion for some retailers in determining profitable markets. Hardware retailers, home improvement centers, and home furnishings stores are examples of retailers that rely on data on the housing market. Home Depot, the Atlanta-based operator of the nation's largest home center chain, is preparing to invade the northeast United States because the area has millions of aging suburban houses and apartments that need repair.[11] An aging housing stock is the prime

FIGURE 9–2
Identification of regional and local market areas

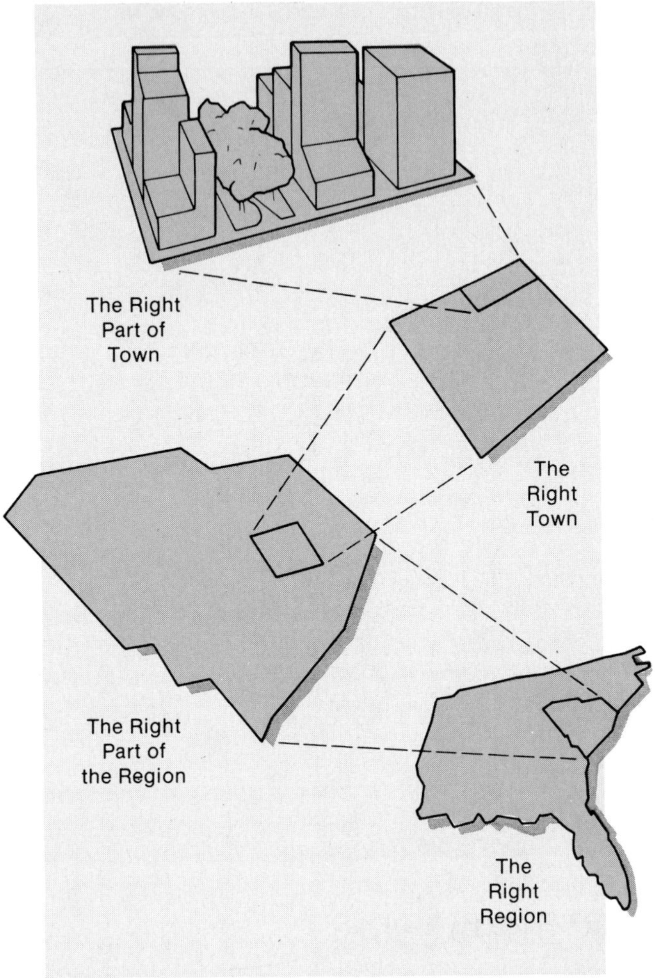

target for this "do-it-yourself" retailer. Figure 9–4 illustrates some of the more important housing characteristics that retailers use to identify lucrative market areas. To locate these data, retailers turn to the *Census of Housing* and the *Annual Housing Survey*.

Buyer behavior characteristics also are extremely useful in identifying and segmenting retail markets, as Figure 9–5 illustrates. Among such characteristics are store loyalty, consumer psychographics, reasons for store patronage, usage rates, lifestyles, benefits sought, and purchase situations. Although buyer behavior characteristics provide retailers with the most useful information for making location decisions, the data are difficult both to measure and obtain.

Another way retailers measure market potential is to examine an area's physical environment. Differing characteristics of their physical environments influence people's choices of clothing, housing, foods, and forms of recreation, as well as their preferences among many other products, services, and activities.

Retail Operations Approach

With the retail operations approach, the location specialist must take into account the nature of the retailer's operations. A profitable retail store not only serves a consumer market of high potential but operates in a market that allows for efficiency and

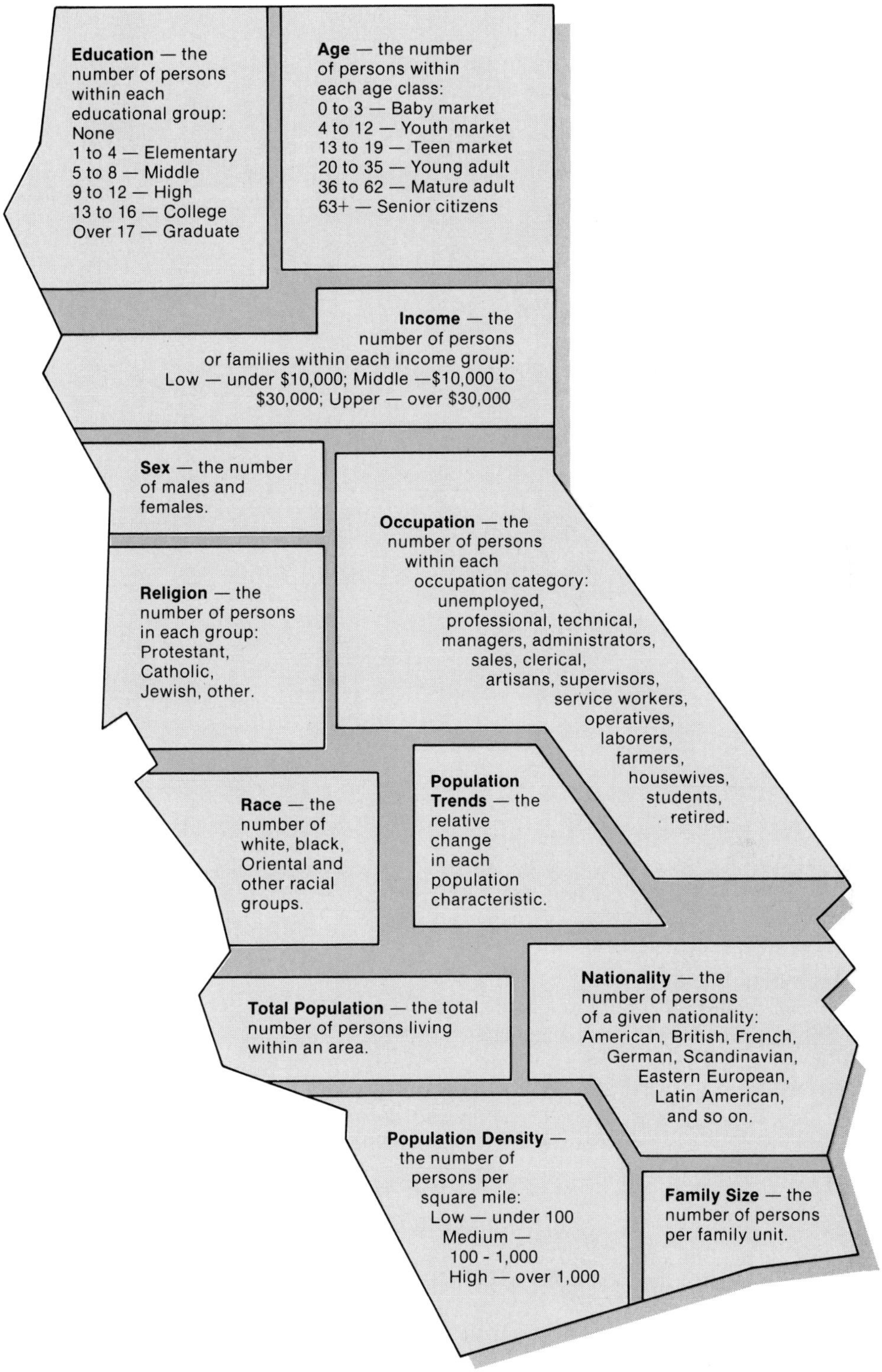
Education — the number of persons within each educational group: None 1 to 4 — Elementary 5 to 8 — Middle 9 to 12 — High 13 to 16 — College Over 17 — Graduate
Age — the number of persons within each age class: 0 to 3 — Baby market 4 to 12 — Youth market 13 to 19 — Teen market 20 to 35 — Young adult 36 to 62 — Mature adult 63+ — Senior citizens
Income — the number of persons or families within each income group: Low — under $10,000; Middle —$10,000 to $30,000; Upper — over $30,000
Sex — the number of males and females.
Occupation — the number of persons within each occupation category: unemployed, professional, technical, managers, administrators, sales, clerical, artisans, supervisors, service workers, operatives, laborers, farmers, housewives, students, retired.
Religion — the number of persons in each group: Protestant, Catholic, Jewish, other.
Race — the number of white, black, Oriental and other racial groups.
Population Trends — the relative change in each population characteristic.
Total Population — the total number of persons living within an area.
Nationality — the number of persons of a given nationality: American, British, French, German, Scandinavian, Eastern European, Latin American, and so on.
Population Density — the number of persons per square mile: Low — under 100 Medium — 100 - 1,000 High — over 1,000
Family Size — the number of persons per family unit.

FIGURE 9–3
Using population characteristics as criteria in identifying market areas

FIGURE 9–4
Using housing characteristics as criteria in identifying market areas

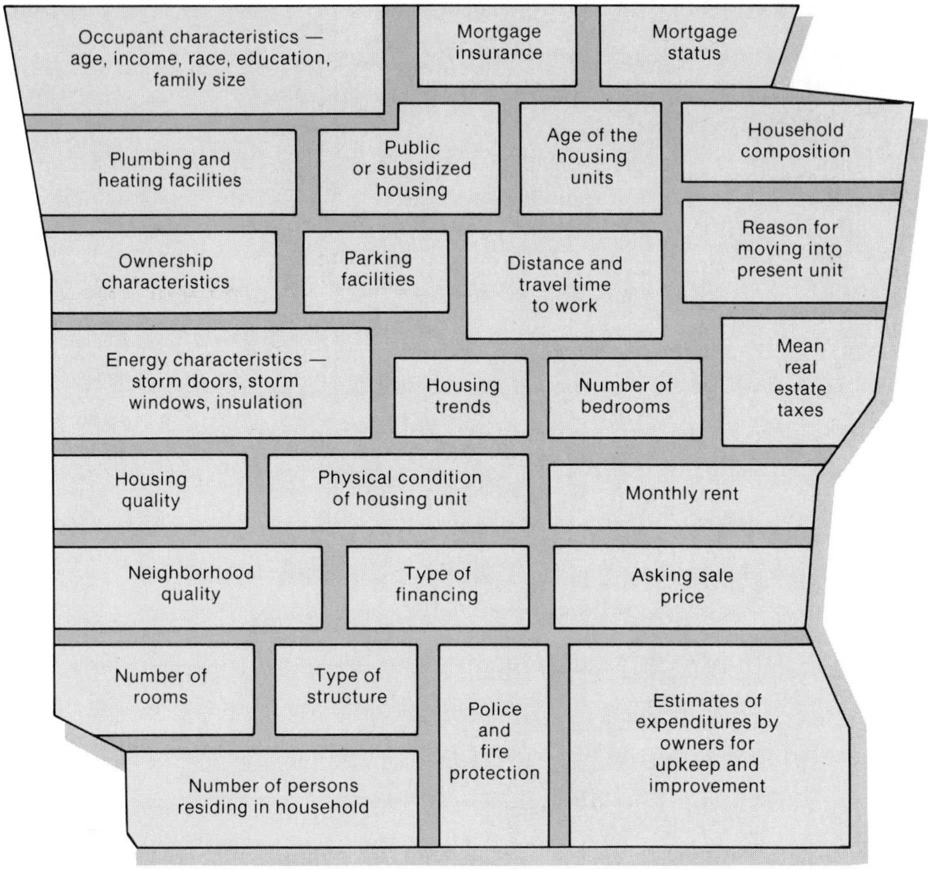

competitiveness. Several factors that directly influence the retailer's chances to operate successfully are (1) distribution, (2) competition, (3) promotion, and (4) legal considerations.

Distribution Factors

A crucial problem for all retailers is to get the product into the store. This involves inventory control—overstocks increase carrying costs, while stockouts cause lost sales and customer illwill. The retailer must consider transportation and handling costs, delivery time, and reliability of delivery services. To identify potential market areas, the retailer also must consider the location and delivery practices of suppliers and the market area's ability to support distribution facilities.

Competitive Factors

It is imperative that the retailer consider the competition when identifying market areas. Competition varies from one area to another and according to the type, number, and size of competitors. Types, levels, and competitive strategies of various retailing formats were discussed in Chapter 2. As a quick review of that chapter would indicate, retail competition is very complex; hence, the market area specialist must carefully audit all competitors, regardless of their form.

Promotional Factors

A retailer that depends heavily on promotional activities can identify market areas by analyzing the advertising media within each market area and the behavior of

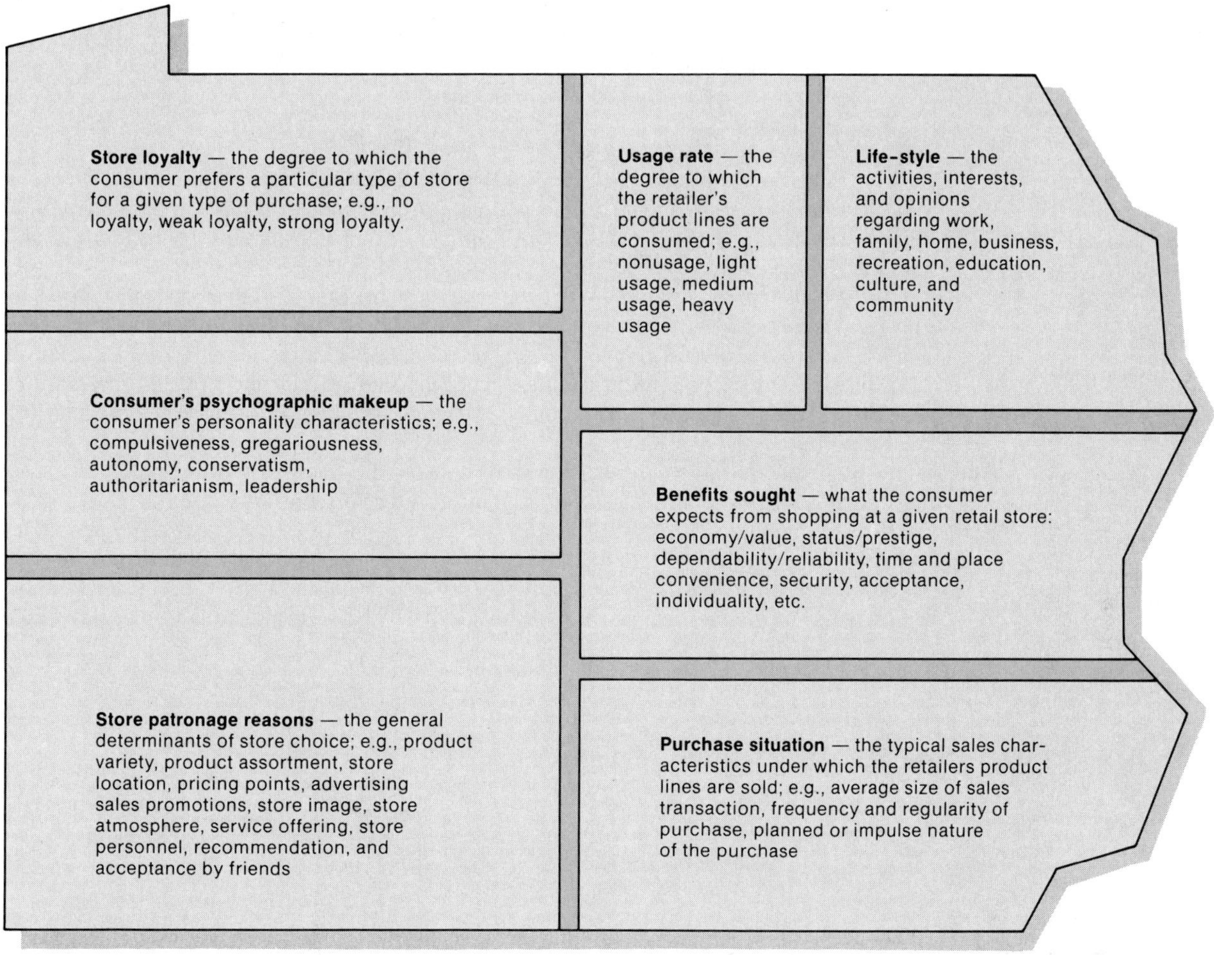
Store loyalty — the degree to which the consumer prefers a particular type of store for a given type of purchase; e.g., no loyalty, weak loyalty, strong loyalty.
Usage rate — the degree to which the retailer's product lines are consumed; e.g., nonusage, light usage, medium usage, heavy usage
Life-style — the activities, interests, and opinions regarding work, family, home, business, recreation, education, culture, and community
Consumer's psychographic makeup — the consumer's personality characteristics; e.g., compulsiveness, gregariousness, autonomy, conservatism, authoritarianism, leadership
Benefits sought — what the consumer expects from shopping at a given retail store: economy/value, status/prestige, dependability/reliability, time and place convenience, security, acceptance, individuality, etc.
Store patronage reasons — the general determinants of store choice; e.g., product variety, product assortment, store location, pricing points, advertising sales promotions, store image, store atmosphere, service offering, store personnel, recommendation, and acceptance by friends
Purchase situation — the typical sales characteristics under which the retailers product lines are sold; e.g., average size of sales transaction, frequency and regularity of purchase, planned or impulse nature of the purchase

FIGURE 9–5
Using buyer behavior characteristics as criteria in identifying market areas

competitive retailers. Media selectivity and coverage are both important. With respect to **media selectivity**, the retailer should look at **geographic selectivity**, the ability of a medium to target a specific geographic market area such as a city or a part of a city, and **class selectivity**, the ability of a medium to target specific kinds of people who have certain common characteristics. In other words, most advertising media are "targeted" to serve certain geographical areas and to appeal to specific groups of consumers. For example, a radio station serves only the geographic area defined by its transmitting power, antenna system, frequency on the dial, and other local conditions. If the station follows a "pop" format, it will attract specific listeners. **Media coverage** is the number of people an advertising medium reaches in a given market area. For example, a newspaper might provide excellent coverage in one county by reaching 90 percent of the homes but cover only 30 percent of the homes in a distant county.

Legal Factors

The final group of criteria that retailers use to identify market areas are state and local legal requirements. Land use regulation in the form of *zoning restrictions, building codes,* and *signing requirements* has a direct bearing on the success of a retailer's operation. State and local taxes on the firm's *real estate, personal property,* and *inventory* can have an equally important impact on the cost of operation. Retailers must also meet certain *licensing requirements* to conduct a business. License availability and cost thus are considerations.

Regional Markets

Most business organizations have regionalized the United States in some way. Regional classification schemes suggest that people perceive social, cultural, and economic differences among various parts of the country. The retailer should try to identify and analyze these perceived differences.

Perhaps the most widely used regional classification system is one developed by the U.S. Bureau of the Census. As Figure 9–6 shows, the bureau divides the United States into nine census regions. The relative importance of this **census market** classification scheme is evident from the fact that many public and private organizations use this system as the organizational framework for their information reporting and analyzing processes.

Regional markets can also be identified on the basis of various types of media coverage; such areas are classified as **communication markets**. In the case of the broadcast media, a 50,000-watt radio station like WGN in Chicago is capable of providing the retailer with multistate regional coverage. On the other hand, a 5,000-watt station like KVI in Seattle/Tacoma covers only a subregional market, because its output is restricted to the western portion of the state of Washington. The large-area coverage

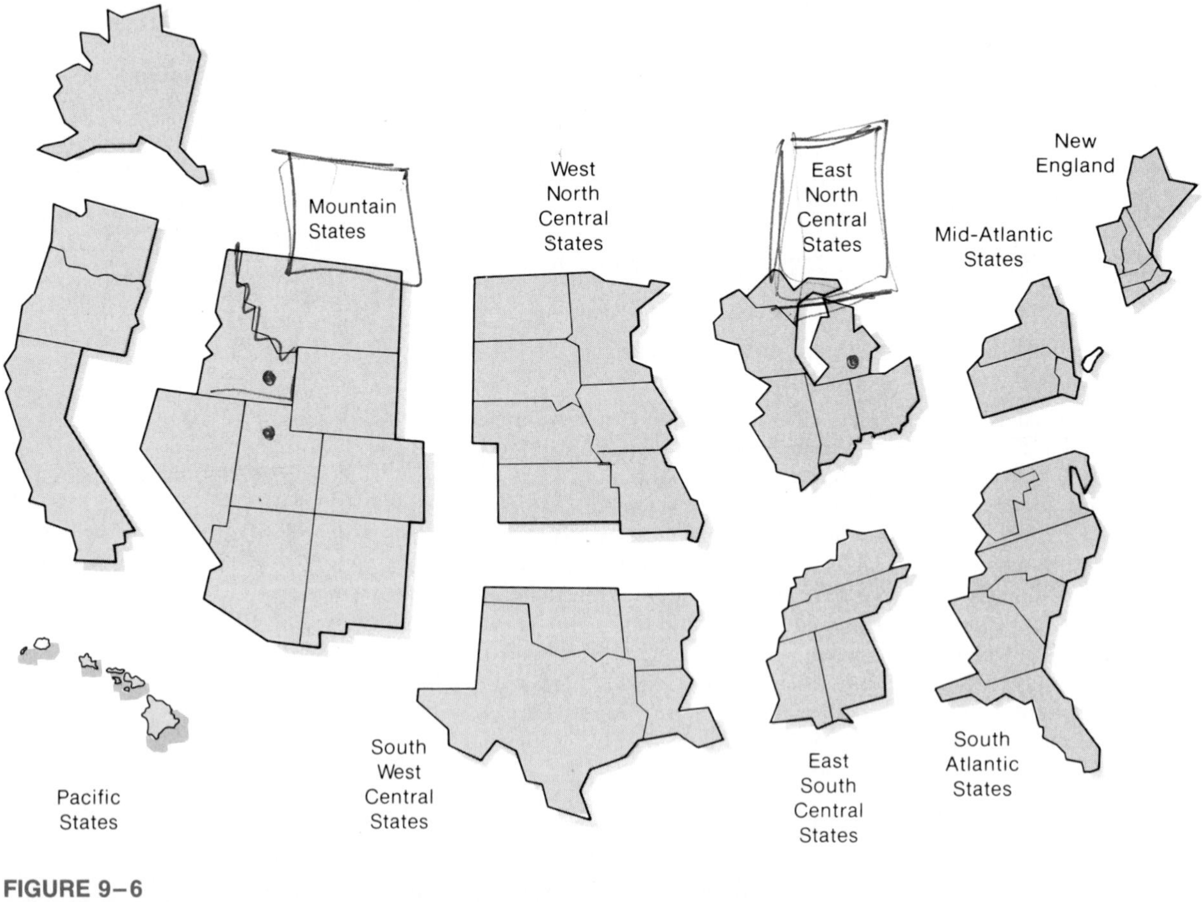

FIGURE 9–6
Census regions as defined by the Bureau of the Census

by WGN is appropriate for the multiunit retailer, such as K mart, that has operations in each state WGN covers. Montgomery Ward has embarked on a program of filling market areas around existing stores. In operationalizing this strategy, Ward tries to keep new stores "within the existing ADI (Areas of Dominant Influence—an area identified by the Arbitron Co. that consists of all counties in which the home market stations receive a preponderance of viewing) for purposes of television advertising. We're going into Appleton, Wisconsin, which has the same ADI as nearby Green Bay where we now have a store."[12]

Print media also provide good operational definitions of regional and subregional markets. For example, the *New York News* has multistate regional coverage. By dividing the total New York regional market into 27 zones (a process referred to as *zoned insert marketing*), the regional market is effectively segmented into subregional markets. Magazines also recognize the value of regional and subregional classifications. *Newsweek*, for example, has segmented the U.S. market into five regions—Western, West Central, East Central, Eastern, and Southern—and three of these regional markets are further segmented into subregional markets. *USA Weekend* uses what it calls "geodemographic marketing"[13] to divide the country into nine "nations" or intranational markets based on demographic and lifestyle characteristics (see Figure 9–7). Regional and subregional issues of magazines such as *Newsweek* and *USA*

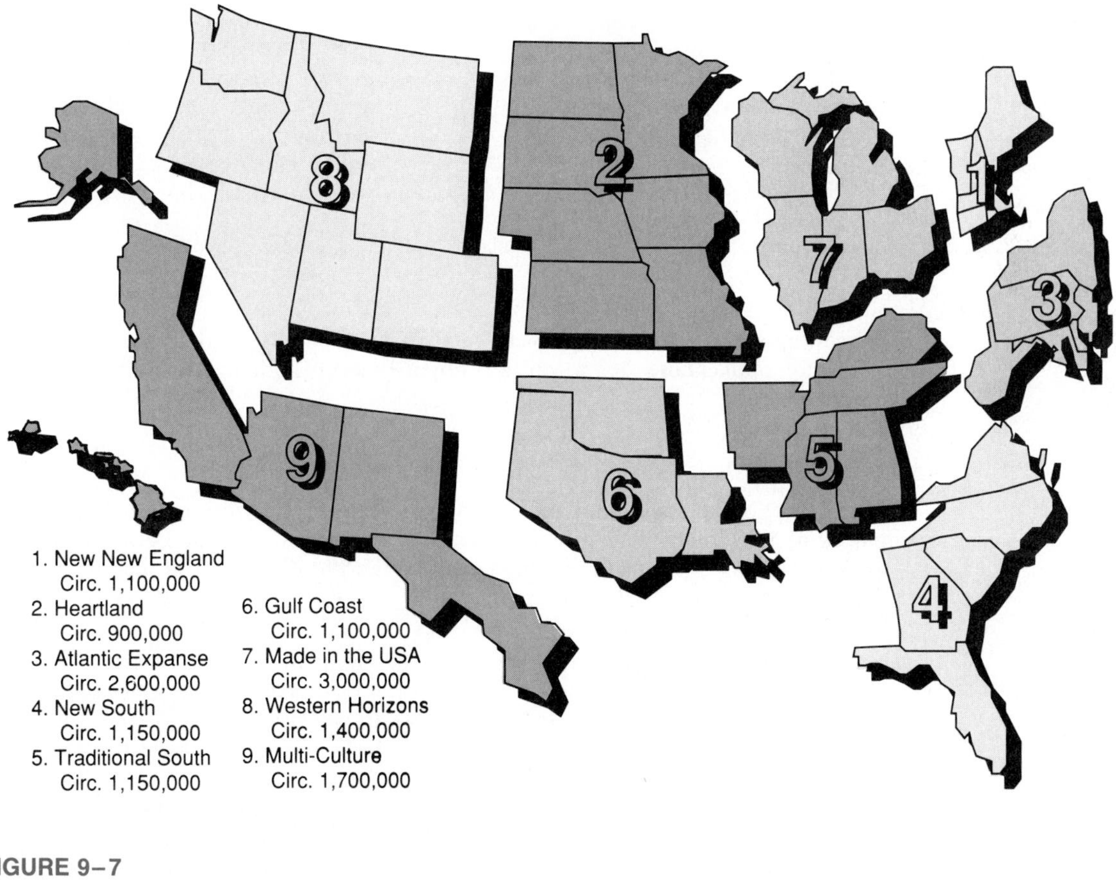

FIGURE 9–7
Market segmentation using geodemographic data

RETAIL STRATEGIES AND TACTICS

Geodemographic Marketing: Finding the Right Part of the Country

Where consumers live may be more important in determining what they'll buy than age, lifestyle, or other demographic and psychographic factors.

At least, that is the contention of proponents of "geodemography," a marketing tool that links households within geographic locations to identify regional lifestyles that impact directly on consumer attitudes, behavior, and buying patterns.

One of the more recent studies in geodemography comes from *USA Weekend,* the Sunday newspaper magazine supplement published by Gannett Co. In 1988, the magazine asked a group of cultural demographers to categorize the nation in terms of regional lifestyles. The result is nine lifestyle "nations," which *USA Weekend* president Ramon G. Gaulke, also vice president of marketing for Gannett, described at a mid-year meeting of the National Retail Merchants Association.

Here are the highlights:

1. *The New England,* containing Maine, Vermont, New Hampshire, Massachusetts, Connecticut, and Rhode Island. Residents are typically older than in other regions and boast the highest proportion of executives and professionals; they reflect a high incidence of two-earner couples, and they are open to alternative shopping methods, such as shopping by mail.
2. *The Atlantic Expanse,* comprising New York, New Jersey, Pennsylvania, West Virginia, Maryland, and Delaware. The most populous and the region with the highest proportion of white-collar workers, it has one of the highest proportions of single, young adults, but is last in terms of households with children. As consumers, they are individualistic in their buying styles; and with a fast-paced lifestyle, prefer the centralized convenience and variety of stores found in malls.
3. *The New South,* lining the southernmost point of the U.S. coastline from Virginia to Key West, Florida. New Southerners are characterized as "belongers," and tend to be conservative in outlook. They are also cosmopolitan and like to keep pace with the trends, bestowing them

Weekend provide regional and local retailers with an opportunity to advertise in prestigious publications to reach an upper-bracket audience within a selective geographic area.

Local Markets

Finding the "right town" and the "right part of town" constitutes the local market identification problem. Faced with an array of thousands of urban centers, the retail location specialist must use some organized method to identify local markets.[14]

ABC Markets: The Right Town

One method of classifying urban centers is to group or rank them on the basis of population, retail sales, employment levels, disposable income, number of households, and a host of other factors. Figure 9–8 identifies the 50 largest metro markets based on 1991 projected population. Figure 9–9 projects the largest markets based on household income.

Many retailing operations use population and demographic analyses to determine each market's sales potential for a particular line of merchandise or a given type of retail operation. Based on their sales volume potential, urban centers can be classified, in with the honor of having among the highest ownerships of compact disk players.

4. *The Traditional South,* with states located in the center of the Cotton Belt. Residents are still struggling with economic and social problems, and retail sales per household are lower by far than any other region of the country. However, these customers are very brand loyal.
5. *The Gulf Coast,* described as a bridge between the South and the West. Populated by more "self-made" men and women, the region's consumers tend to be value-oriented and conformists in their shopping—and shopping is a popular sport for them.
6. *The Heartland,* made up of seven "breadbasket" states and including such urban centers as Kansas City, Des Moines, and Minneapolis. Consumer buying styles reflect conservative values; and shoppers lead the nation in purchases of kitchen conveniences like dishwashers and microwaves. These consumers are also "world-class browsers."
7. *The Made in the USA Nation,* located east of the Heartland and encompassing the U.S. motor capital, Detroit. Living here are the greatest number of economic nationalists; and Sears catalogs are probably the most-thumbed reading in their homes.
8. *Western Horizons,* the largest of the regions and including Wyoming, Montana, Oregon, and the Pacific Northwest. The region boasts a highly-educated populace and more children under 18 than any other. Its consumers tend to be impulsive shoppers, doing more than average buying by mail or telephone.
9. *The Multi-Cultures Region,* dominated by California, plus the states of New Mexico, Arizona, and southern Texas. Residents are young, affluent, highly educated, dynamic and informed, with active lifestyles. As consumers, they reflect their upscale situations in buying patterns and boast above-average per household retail sales.

Source: "Geodemography: Tracking Where Customers Live," *Stores* (November 1989): 42–43. Copyright © National Retail Federation, Inc., New York, New York.

descending order, as either *A, B,* or *C markets*. The exact definition of what constitutes an A, B, or C market varies from one retailing organization to another, because each organization uses different decision variables. Nevertheless, the purpose of identifying various-size markets is to help the retailer adjust the business format to meet the consumption needs of a particular market. Wal-Mart uses different sizes of its Supercenter format depending on the market's sales potential. For example, Wal-Mart has Supercenters in Washington, Missouri; Wagoner, Oklahoma; and Farmington, Missouri covering 126,000, 96,000, and 186,000 square feet, respectively.[15]

Markets designated as **A markets** can provide the highest levels of support for retailers. Typically, A markets have the sales potential to support multiple specialty store units. In addition, A markets provide retailing environments that can support pricing, advertising, and personal-selling strategies ranging from discount to prestige pricing, mass to direct advertising, and store to in-home selling.

Many medium-size cities offer adequate sales potential for a wide variety of retailing activities; the **B market** is still strong for most types and sizes of store operations. Traditionally a B market did not warrant a full-line department store operation unless special circumstances prevailed in the market. However, as A markets have become more saturated, the development of these second-tier markets is receiving considerable attention by the nation's largest retailers and mall developers.[16]

1991 Rank	Metro Market	Projected 1991 Pop. (Thous.)	Projected % Change 1986–91	1991 Rank	Metro Market	Projected 1991 Pop. (Thous.)	Projected % Change 1986–91
1.	Los Angeles-Long Beach	**8,869.6**	+ 6.7%	**27.**	San Francisco	**1,649.6**	+ 4.2
2.	New York	**8,713.0**	+ 2.2	**28.**	Kansas City	**1,582.3**	+ 3.7
3.	Chicago	**6,187.9**	+ 0.4	**29.**	San Jose, CA	**1,484.5**	+ 5.4
4.	Philadelphia	**4,884.2**	+ 1.2	**30.**	Sacramento	**1,450.9**	+11.2
5.	Detroit	**4,412.7**	+ 1.2	**31.**	Cincinnati	**1,421.0**	+ 0.1
6.	Boston-Lawrence-Salem-Lowell-Brockton	**3,752.9**	+ 0.8	**32.**	Fort Worth-Arlington	**1,420.3**	+15.9
7.	Washington, DC	**3,744.8**	+ 5.7	**33.**	New Orleans	**1,402.8**	+ 4.1
8.	Houston	**3,567.9**	+10.4	**34.**	Milwaukee	**1,400.5**	+ 0.4
9.	Atlanta	**2,800.3**	+10.1	**35.**	Norfolk-Virginia Beach-Newport News, VA	**1,394.9**	+ 6.7
10.	Nassau-Suffolk, NY	**2,738.7**	+ 2.8	**36.**	San Antonio	**1,378.6**	+10.2
11.	Dallas	**2,666.3**	+12.1	**37.**	Columbus, OH	**1,334.4**	+ 2.5
12.	St. Louis	**2,498.7**	+ 1.9	**38.**	Bergen-Passaic, NJ	**1,311.1**	+ 0.6
13.	San Diego	**2,466.0**	+11.2	**39.**	Fort Lauderdale-Hollywood-Pompano Beach	**1,280.0**	+ 9.6
14.	Minneapolis-St. Paul	**2,445.9**	+ 5.3	**40.**	Indianapolis	**1,247.2**	+ 2.3
15.	Baltimore	**2,374.7**	+ 3.0	**41.**	Portland, OR	**1,188.3**	+ 2.5
16.	Anaheim-Santa Ana	**2,341.3**	+ 7.5	**42.**	Charlotte-Gastonia-Rock Hill	**1,140.3**	+ 6.4
17.	Riverside-San Bernadino, CA	**2,325.2**	+15.9	**43.**	Salt Lake City-Ogden	**1,139.5**	+ 8.3
18.	Phoenix	**2,221.4**	+15.9	**44.**	Hartford-New Britain-Middletown-Bristol, CT	**1,126.5**	+ 2.6
19.	Tampa-St. Petersburg-Clearwater, FL	**2,133.9**	+11.4	**45.**	Oklahoma City	**1,081.0**	+ 8.9
20.	Pittsburgh	**2,103.4**	− 1.7	**46.**	Monmouth-Ocean, NJ	**1,033.1**	+ 7.9
21.	Oakland	**2,070.6**	+ 6.2	**47.**	Orlando, FL	**1,031.4**	+14.7
22.	Newark	**1,905.4**	+ 0.3	**48.**	Rochester, NY	**1,005.4**	+ 1.3
23.	Miami-Hialeah	**1,901.7**	+ 6.5	**49.**	Nashville, TN	**995.8**	+ 6.3
24.	Seattle	**1,860.5**	+ 5.8	**50.**	Middlesex-Somerset-Hunterdon, NJ	**983.6**	+ 4.0
25.	Cleveland	**1,823.2**	− 1.6				
26.	Denver	**1,796.3**	+ 8.9				

Source: Reprinted from "The 50 Largest Metro Markets Based on 1991 Population and Household Income" from *1987 Survey of Buying Power—Part II* © 1987, Sales and Marketing Management, a Bill Publication.

FIGURE 9–8
The 50 largest metro markets based on 1991 projected population

The **C market** is basically the small-town market. In recent years, many of the country's retailing giants have targeted these markets as major areas for expansion. This once secure market domain of the small, independent retailer has felt the impact of entry by large, multiline chain retailers such as K mart, Wal-Mart, and TG&Y.

Intraurban Markets: The Right Part of Town

For most retailers, there are literally "right" and "wrong" parts of town. An urban center is not simply a homogeneous mass; rather, it is a heterogeneous grouping of people and activities making up **intraurban markets** that can have a profound effect on a retailer's operations. The internal structure of urban centers is composed of many recognizable areas, including the downtown and the suburbs; shopping centers and strip shopping developments; ethnic and racial areas; residential, commercial, and industrial areas; and low-, middle-, and high-income areas. To facilitate understanding of the internal structure of cities, we will examine several theories of urban structure based on *land-use*

1991 Rank	Metro Market	1991 Average Household EBI	1991 Rank	Metro Market	1991 Average Household EBI
1.	Bridgeport-Stamford-Norwalk-Danbury, CT	$73,851	**26.**	Minneapolis-St. Paul	$54,770
2.	Nassau-Suffolk, NY	71,637	**27.**	Kenosha, WI	53,862
3.	Lake County, IL	68,624	**28.**	Chicago	53,679
4.	Washington, DC	64,031	**29.**	Santa Barbara-Santa Maria-Lompoc	53,676
5.	Middlesex-Somerset-Hunterdon, NJ	63,163	**30.**	Aurora-Elgin, IL	53,529
6.	San Jose	62,556	**31.**	Wichita, KS	53,426
7.	Bergen-Passaic, NJ	62,337	**32.**	Seattle	53,416
8.	Grand Forks, ND	61,138	**33.**	Lincoln, NE	53,370
9.	Oxnard-Ventura, CA	60,662	**34.**	Portsmouth-Dover-Rochester, NH	53,264
10.	Trenton, NJ	60,216	**35.**	Omaha	53,216
11.	Anaheim-Santa Ana, CA	59,777	**36.**	Richland-Kennewick-Pasco, WA	53,086
12.	San Francisco	58,959	**37.**	San Diego	52,969
13.	Newark	58,615	**38.**	Santa Cruz, CA	52,437
14.	Midland, TX	58,599	**39.**	Topeka	52,392
15.	Honolulu	58,043	**40.**	Wilmington, DE	52,281
16.	Anchorage	56,403	**41.**	Kalamazoo, MI	52,108
17.	Boston-Lawrence-Salem-Lowell-Brockton	56,325	**42.**	Rochester, MN	52,013
18.	Hartford-New Britain-Middletown-Bristol, CT	56,282	**43.**	Dallas	51,877
19.	Oakland	56,269	**44.**	Ann Arbor, MI	51,375
20.	Monmouth-Ocean, NJ	56,094	**45.**	Grand Rapids, MI	51,152
21.	Poughkeepsie, NY	55,918	**46.**	Salinas-Seaside-Monterey, CA	51,111
22.	Brazoria, TX	55,655	**47.**	Denver	51,096
23.	Manchester-Nashua, NH	55,493	**48.**	Iowa City	51,007
24.	New London-Norwich, CT	55,004	**49.**	Peoria, IL	50,659
25.	New Haven-Waterbury-Meriden, CT	54,999	**50.**	West Palm Beach-Boca Raton-Delray Beach, FL	50,615
				U.S. Average	**$45,362**

Source: Reprinted from "The 50 Largest Metro Markets Based on 1991 Projected Population and Household Income" from *1987 Survey of Buying Power—Part II* © 1987, Sales and Marketing Management, a Bill Publication.

FIGURE 9–9
The 50 largest metro markets based on 1991 projected household income

patterns. Over time, these patterns emerge when certain activities (e.g., commercial, industrial, and residential) tend to dominate the land use of particular areas in and around the urban center.

EVALUATING MARKET AREAS

After identifying potential regional and local market areas, the retail location specialist must evaluate each one. The identification process itself should have provided considerable insight into the various capabilities of each area to support a given type of retail organization. The evaluation process involves collecting and analyzing data pertinent to a particular retailer's operation. Three indices commonly used in measuring the potential of a market area are the market's buying power, sales activity, and retail saturation.

RETAIL STRATEGIES AND TACTICS

Using ZIP Codes to Find the Right Part of Town!

If you thought that your postal ZIP code was only good for getting mail to you more efficiently, think again.

An increasing number of marketers are using "clusters"—computer-generated research that categorizes consumers by ZIP code to determine what they eat, drink, purchase and watch on television.

There's even a book on the subject, called *The Clustering of America*, by Michael Weiss, and it segments the country into some 40 clusters for marketers to target.

Here are just a few:

- *"Furs & Station Wagons"* (3.2% of U.S. households)—Median household income, $50,086. Age group 35–54. New money in metro suburbs; white, college-educated families. Belong to country clubs; have second mortgages; drive BMW 5 series; read *Gourmet, Forbes;* eat cold cereals. Sample ZIPs: Plano, Tex. 75075; Reston, Va. 22091; Glastonbury, Conn. 06033; Needham, Mass. 02192; Pomona, Calif. 91765; Dunwoody, Ga. 30338.
- *"Young Suburbia"* (5.3% of U.S. households)—Median household income, $38,582. Age group 25–44. White, college-educated; upper middle class; child-rearing families. Buy swimming pools, mutual funds; drive Mitsubishi Galants, Toyota vans; read *World Tennis;* eat frozen waffles. Sample ZIPs: Eagan, Minn. 55124; Dale City, Va. 22193; Pleasanton, Calif. 94566; Smithtown, NY 11787; Ypsilanti, Mich. 48197.
- *"Blue-Chip Blues"* (6.0% of U.S. households)—Median household income, $32,218. Age group 25–44. White families, high-school educated; wealthiest blue-collar suburbs. Use CB radios, belong to unions; drive Chevy Sprints, Buick Rivieras; read *Golf, 4 Wheel & Off Road;* eat natural cold cereal, frozen pizzas.

Market Area Buying Power

The ***Survey of Buying Power*** is an annual publication compiled by the editors of *Sales and Marketing Management* magazine. While the survey contains a great deal of information that is useful to the retailer, three basic categories of information are of particular interest to the retail location specialist attempting to evaluate potential market areas: population, retail sales, and effective buying income.

The survey contains information for all census regions, states, metro areas, counties, and cities. Although the population and retail sales figures reported in the survey are self-explanatory, the expression *effective buying income* requires additional explanation. As used in the survey, effective buying income is all personal income (wages, salaries, rental income, dividends, interest, pension, welfare) less federal, state, and local personal taxes, contributions for social security insurance, and nontax payments (fines, fees, penalties). In essence, effective buying income is the rough equivalent of disposable personal income, that is, the spendable income available to the consumer.

The **buying power index (BPI)**, published annually in the *Survey of Buying Power,* is "a measurement of a market's ability to buy."[17] The index is constructed using three criteria:

1. The market area's population expressed as a percentage of the total U.S. population
2. The market area's retail sales expressed as a percentage of total U.S. retail sales
3. The market area's effective buying income expressed as a percentage of the total U.S. effective buying income

Sample ZIPs: Coon Rapids, Minn. 55433; S. Whittier, Calif. 90605; Mesquite, Tex. 75149; Ronkonkoma, N.Y. 11779; St. Charles, St. Louis, Mo. 63301; Taylor, Detroit, Mich. 38180.

- *"Levittown, USA"* (3.1% of U.S. households)—Median household income, $28,742. Age group 55-plus. High school–educated white couples, postwar tract subdivisions. Watch ice hockey, go bowling; read *Stereo Review, Barron's;* drink instant iced tea, eat English muffins. Sample ZIPs: Norwood, Mass. 02062; Cuyahoga Falls, Ohio 44221; Donelson, Nashville, Tenn. 37214; Stratford, Conn. 06497.
- *"New Beginnings"* (4.3% of U.S. households)—Median household income, $24,847. Age group 18–34. Middle-class, urban apartment dwellers; some college education. Use slide projectors, jazz records; drive Mitsubishi Mirages, Hyundais; read *Scientific American, Rolling Stone;* drink bottled water, eat whole-wheat bread. Sample ZIPs: Bloomington, Minn. 55420; Northeast Phoenix 85016; Reseda, Los Angeles 91335; Englewood, Denver 80110; Parkmoor, San Francisco 95126; Park Place, Houston 77061.
- *"Middle America"* (3.2% of U.S. households)—Median household income, $24,431. Age group 45–64. High school educated, white families; middle-class suburbs. Use domestic air charters, Christmas clubs; drive Plymouth Sundances, Chevy Chevettes; read *Saturday Evening Post;* eat pizza mixes, TV dinners. Sample ZIPs: Marshall, Mich. 49068; Sandusky, Ohio 44870; Hagerstown, Md. 21740; Oshkosh, Wisc. 54901; Stroudsburg, Pa. 18360; Elkhart, Ind. 46514.

Source: "Using Zip Codes to Segment Customers," *Stores* (November 1989): 42–43.

The index does not equally weight each criterion as an indicator of a market area's ability to buy. Instead, it weighs each according to the criterion's perceived importance—population by 2, retail sales by 3, and effective buying income by 5. The buying power index is calculated as follows:

$$\text{BPI} = \frac{(\text{population} \times 2) + (\text{retail sales} \times 3) + (\text{effective buying income} \times 5)}{10 \text{ (the sum of the weights)}}$$

The higher the index value, the greater the market area's ability to buy and therefore to support retailing activities.

Although the BPI provides a good estimate of the spendable income within a market area, it does not indicate the area's "distribution of income," "stability of income," or "income trends." As described by the editors of *Survey of Buying Power,* the index "is most useful in estimating the potential for mass products sold at popular prices. The further a product is removed from the mass market, the greater is the need for a BPI to be modified by more discriminating factors—income, class, age, sex, etc."[18]

Market Area Sales Activity

The *Survey of Buying Power* also reports the standardized **sales activity index (SAI)**: "a measure of the per capita retail sales of an area compared with those of the nation."[19] Although the SAI is reported for the nine census regions and for each state within those regions, it can be calculated for any geographic subdivision contained in the survey. The SAI is calculated as follows:

$$\text{SAI} = \frac{\text{market area's percentage of U.S. retail sales}}{\text{market area's percentage of U.S. population}}$$

Because the numerator (retail sales) reflects all sales made in an area regardless of where the consumer is from and the denominator (population) includes only those people who live in the area, the sales activity index does not specify whether a market area's sales activity is the result of the shopping activities of area residents, nonresidents, business concerns, or some combination. Thus, a high index may indicate "a strong influx of nonresident shoppers, heavy buying by business concerns, heavy buying by residents, or all three."[20]

Market Area Saturation

The **index of retail saturation (IRS)** measures the potential sales per square foot of store space for a given product line within a particular market area.[21] As a market area evaluation tool, it incorporates both consumer demand and competitive supply. Essentially the index is the ratio between a market area's capacity to consume and its capacity to retail. The formula of the index of retail saturation is

$$\text{IRS} = \frac{(\text{C})(\text{RE})}{\text{RF}}$$

where

IRS = index of retail saturation for a given product line(s) within a particular market area

C = number of customers in a particular market for a given product line

RE = retail expenditures—the average dollar expenditure for a given product line(s) within a particular market area

RF = retail facilities—the total square feet of selling space allocated to a given product line(s) within a particular market area

To illustrate, assume that a retail operation needs sales of $45 per square foot of selling space for a given product line to operate profitably. Also assume that the retailer currently is examining three potential market areas (see Figure 9–10). Market area A can be eliminated from further consideration because it does not meet the $45 minimum sales-per-square-foot criterion. Both markets B and C meet the minimum sales criterion. If all other location considerations are equal, however, market B will be preferable to C because it offers the retailer more ($3.33 higher) sales potential per square foot of selling space.

The index of retail saturation allows the retailer to classify market areas on the basis of their competitive situation—understored, overstored, or saturated.[22] **Understored market areas** are those in which the capacity to consume exceeds the capacity

FIGURE 9–10
Market area evaluation using index of retail saturation

	Market Area		
	A	B	C
Number of customers (C)	40,000	50,000	70,000
Retail expenditures (RE)	$10	$12	$10
Retail facilities (RF)	10,000	12,000	15,000
Index of retail saturation (IRS)	$40.00	$50.00	$46.67

to retail. In other words, there are too few stores and/or too little selling space devoted to a product line to satisfy consumer needs. **Overstored market areas** occur when the capacity to retail exceeds the capacity to consume. In this situation, retailers have devoted too much space to a particular product line. Finally, a **saturated market area** is one in which the capacity to retail equals the ability of buyers to consume a product line. In this case, the demand for and supply of a given product line are in equilibrium.

The understored market area obviously offers the best opportunity for the retailer seeking a new location. During the last several years, retailers such as IKEA (Scandinavian home furnishings) and Carrefour (European hypermarket) have located in Philadelphia because they considered it understored.[23] AuBon Pain, a Boston-based café chain known for its gourmet sandwiches and fresh juices, pursues a strategy of market saturation in the central business districts of large eastern cities. By grouping cafés close together in high-traffic areas, the firm achieves advantages of high visibility and customer awareness, operational conveniences, and closer employee supervision.[24]

SELECTING MARKET AREAS

On completing the market area identification and evaluation processes, the retailer must select a regional and local market. There are no simple decision rules to aid the retailer in selection. The basis of the location decision varies with the types of retailers, operational characteristics, and stated objectives. At this point, the retailer's *judgment* is the critical factor. Ultimately the retailer should select the regional and local markets that will provide sufficient levels of support (sales potential) conducive to the firm's operational needs. Generally the market area a retailer selects represents a compromise among several promising but diverse market situations.

TRADING-AREA DIMENSIONS

A **retail trading area** is broadly defined as the area from which a store attracts its customers or obtains its business. Depending on the *kind* of retail operation, a retail trading area can be described more specifically in the following terms:

- *Drawing power*—the area from which a *shopping center* could expect to derive as much as 85 percent of its total volume
- *Per capita sales*—the area from which a *general-merchandise store* can derive a minimum annual per capita sale of $1
- *Patronage probability*—the area that includes potential customers who have a probability of greater than zero of purchasing a given class of products or services that either a retailer or a group of retailers offers for sale
- *Retail operations*—the area from which either a marketing unit or group can operate economically depending on volume, cost of operation, and cost of selling and/or delivering a good or service

Two characteristics common to these four definitions are that (1) they identify an area from which retailers *draw customers* over a specific period of time and (2) they identify a *single focal point* (e.g., a town, a shopping center, or a single retail outlet) around which the trading area develops. Essentially, then, retail trading areas are "gravity areas"—retail sites to which consumers will gravitate or be pulled from an identifiable area.

Trading-Area Size

Trading areas range from a few square blocks to a radius of many miles. The size of a trading area is a function of the cumulative effects of several *operational* and *environmental* factors. The two major operational factors are *type* and *size*. *Type of retail operation* means the kind of goods and services offered. Retailers that offer specialty and shopping goods will draw consumers from a wider geographic area than will retailers that offer convenience goods, because consumers are willing to exert greater effort and to travel greater distances to buy specialty and shopping goods than they are to buy convenience goods. *Store size* is directly related to the retailer's trading-area size; that is, the larger the retail store and the greater its selection of merchandise, the larger its trading area will be. Because of their physical size and wide range of merchandise, Bloomingdale's of New York and Rich's of Atlanta are department stores with very large trading areas.

The second set of factors that determine the size of a retailer's trading area are environmental, including (1) the number, size, and type of neighboring stores; (2) the nature and activity of competing stores; and (3) the character of the transportation network. A retailer that locates near other retailers often finds that the combined trading area of all the *neighboring retailers* in the cluster is larger than what the store would enjoy if it were in an isolated location. The size of a retailer's trading area also depends on the location, size, and activity of *competing stores*. One large department store, for example, might locate next to another large department store to facilitate consumers' comparative shopping and thus draw from a larger geographic area. The *transportation network* strongly influences a retailer's ability to attract consumers from an area. The effect of traffic networks on the size of a retailer's trading area becomes apparent when we consider that stores located on major thoroughfares usually have larger trading areas than those located on secondary streets and roads. Thus, the number of traffic lanes, the number and nature of intersections (controlled or uncontrolled), the speed limit, and the presence or absence of barriers to uncongested movement all affect the size of the area from which a retailer can attract consumers.

Trading-Area Structure

A **composite trading area** is a set of trading areas, each of which is structured according to the type of goods the retailer sells. Figure 9–11a illustrates the composite trading area for a store (or shopping center) selling convenience, shopping, and specialty goods. In this case, the retailer draws from a larger trading area for specialty goods than for shopping and convenience goods. The consumer's willingness to exert shopping effort, as described earlier, accounts for the composite-area boundary lines.

FIGURE 9–11
Trading-area structure

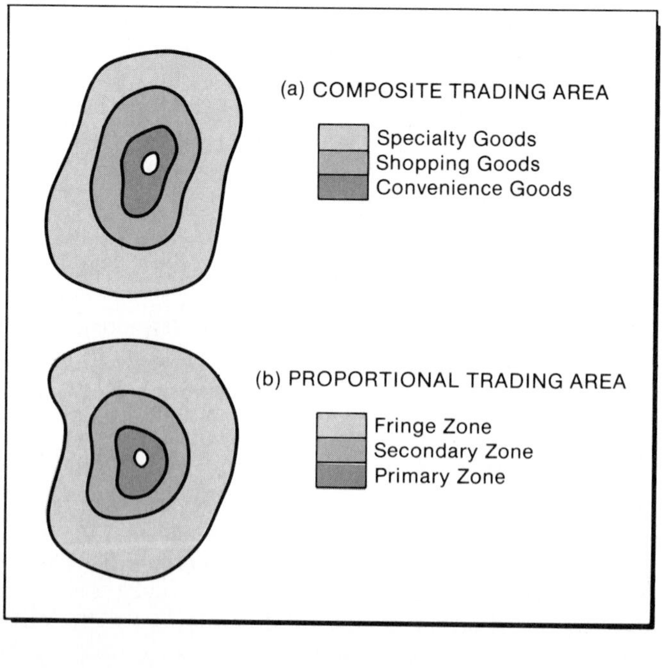

A **proportional trading area** (Figure 9–11b) is based on customers' distance from the store. The further customers are from the retail store, the less likely they are to patronize it, and vice versa. These relationships define what retailers call the "distance decay function"; that is, the number of customers attracted to a given store decreases as their distance from the store increases. As Figure 9–11b illustrates, three distance zones—primary, secondary, and fringe—constitute the proportional trading area.

The **primary trading zone** is the area around which a retailer can expect to attract 50 to 70 percent of its business. The primary trading area might be defined in one of three ways: (1) the area closest to the store; (2) the area in which the retailer has a competitive advantage, such as customer convenience and accessibility; and (3) the area from which the retailer produces the highest per capita sales. The **secondary trading zone** surrounds the primary zone and generally represents 20 to 30 percent of the retailer's total sales volume. From the secondary zone, consumers usually select the store as their second or third shopping choice. The **fringe trading zone** is the area from which the retailer occasionally draws customers (5 to 10 percent of the business). Retailers generally attract customers from this zone either because they "just happened" to be in the vicinity or because they are extremely loyal to the store or its personnel.

IDENTIFYING TRADING AREAS

Two general approaches for identifying trading areas are spotting techniques and quantitative procedures. The latter approach is more appropriate for new or expanding retail operations, while the former technique typically is used by an existing retailer that is seeking to determine the extent of its present trading area.

Spotting Techniques

Spotting techniques include several methods by which the retailer attempts to "spot" customer origins on a map. By carefully observing the magnitude and arrangement of these origins, the retailer can identify the dimensions of the trading area. Retailers normally define customer origins by home addresses, although customers' places of employment also are important. Some of the more common spotting techniques include surveys of customers' license plates, customer surveys, analyses of customer records, and studies of customer activities.

License Plate Surveys

By recording the license plate numbers of automobiles in the store's parking lot, retailers can obtain customers' home addresses. Sampling should include checking license plates at different times of the day, different days of the week, and different weeks of the month to ensure a representative sample. The primary advantage of this technique is that it is relatively inexpensive to administer.[25] License plate surveys also have several limitations, including the following: (1) There is no way to determine who actually drove the car to the store or whether that car represents a regular customer or someone who just happened to be in the neighborhood; (2) a survey of license plates reveals no information on the shopping behavior of customers, such as what they bought, how much they bought, where they bought, why they bought, or if they bought at all; and (3) the number of purchasers in each car cannot be determined.

Customer Surveys

Either a personal interview, mail questionnaire, or telephone survey can provide information on who lives or works in a given area and who current or potential customers are. Actual customers can be surveyed on the premises (within a particular store or shopping mall) through either personal interviews or take-home/mail-back questionnaires. Good surveying techniques must be used to ensure an unbiased, representative sample. Customer surveys can provide a significant amount of information regarding demographics and shopping behavior. Their limitations are the cost, time, and skill required to conduct them efficiently and effectively.

Customer Records Analyses

Retailers have several ways to obtain addresses of current customers as well as additional valuable information. Customer credit, service, and delivery records contain a great deal of information if properly developed and maintained. From their records, retailers can find customer addresses and places of employment, ages, sex, family status, telephone numbers, and types and amounts of purchases. Although customer credit, service, and delivery records are a fast and inexpensive means of obtaining information, they are biased because cash customers, who require no services or delivery, are omitted from the analysis.

Customer Activities Studies

Any method that asks or requires customers to provide their names and addresses can help identify an existing or proposed trading area. Promotional activities such as contests and sweepstakes can be effective ways to obtain names and addresses. Unfortunately, they tend to be biased toward the consumer who is willing to participate (sometimes, for example, the high-income consumer would not think it worth the time). Cents-off coupons that require the consumer to provide minimal information also have been used in identifying trading areas. In identifying the trading area of a supermarket, one research firm dropped coupon packages at households within a general target area. Each package contained eight PIN-coded coupons, thereby allowing identification of coupon redeemers and their addresses; subsequent mapping permitted trade area delineation.[26]

Quantitative Procedures

Retailers have used several quantitative procedures to delineate retail trading areas. The one most retailers use is the **retail gravitation** concept, which provides a measure of the potential interactions among various locations by determining the relative drawing power of each location.[27] Based on the relative drawing power of a location within an area, each area can be identified as being part of a trading area (in some cases, areas can be shared by more than one location). Two of the more widely recognized gravity formulations are Converse's break-even point and Huff's probability model.

Converse's Break-Even Point Model

Paul Converse developed a formula that allows the retailer to calculate the **break-even point** in miles between competing retail centers (stores, shopping centers, or cities).[28] In essence, Converse computes the break-even point as the point between the competing retailing centers at which the probability of a consumer patronizing each retailing center is equal. This break-even point identifies the trading-area boundary line between competing retail trade centers. By identifying the break-even point between one retail center and all competing centers, the retailer can determine the trading area. The break-even point formula is expressed as

$$BP = \frac{d}{1 + \sqrt{\frac{P_1}{P_2}}}$$

where

BP = break-even point between the competing retail center in miles from the smaller center

d = distance between the two competing retail centers

P_1 = population of the larger retail center

P_2 = population of the smaller retail center

Both the distance and population expressions require further explanation. Although distance normally is measured in miles, studies show that many people think of distance in terms of travel time. Retail analysts can use travel time to replace miles for the distance between competing retail centers.

Populations (P_1 and P_2) can be expressed in several ways. The total population in each center is the most common measurement. Another approach is to use the center's total number of retailers or the total retail square footage in the center as the population measurement. Any measurement that reflects a retail center's ability to attract customers can be used as an expression of population. Figure 9–12 illustrates the identification of shopping center trading areas using Converse's breakeven point method.

Huff's Probability Model

The consumer choice of retail store or shopping cluster results from a complex decision-making process. The number and importance of store and cluster attributes used in the selection process vary with each shopper. D. C. Huff's model "was the first to suggest that market areas were complex, continuous, and probabilistic rather than the nonoverlapping geometrical areas of central place theory."[29] The basic premise of Huff's "shopper attraction" model is based on the following empirical regularities:

1. The proportion of consumers patronizing a given shopping area [cluster] varies with distance from the shopping area.
2. The proportion of consumers patronizing various shopping areas [clusters] varies with the breadth and depth of merchandise offered by each shopping area.
3. The distance that consumers travel to various shopping areas [clusters] varies for different types of products purchased.
4. The "pull" of any given shopping area [cluster] is influenced by the proximity of competing shopping areas.[30]

The Huff model computation is shown in Figure 9–13.

EVALUATING TRADING AREAS

The basic problem of any trading-area evaluation is to answer two questions: (1) What is the total amount of business that a trading area can generate now and in the future? and (2) what share of the total business can a retailer in a given location expect to attract? Although there is no standard trading-area evaluation process, most evaluation procedures use the concepts of trading-area adequacy and trading-area potential to predict total trading-area business and the share of business a particular retailer can expect.

Trading-area adequacy is the ability of a trading area to support proposed and existing retail operations.[31] This support capability may be viewed in a gross as well as net form (see Figure 9–14). **Gross adequacy** is the ability of a trading area to support a retail operation with no consideration of retail competition; that is, gross adequacy measures the total amount of business available to all competing retailers within a defined trading area. On the other hand, **net adequacy** is the ability of a trading area to provide support for a retailer after competition has been taken into account. Finally,

FIGURE 9–12
A problem using Converse's break-even point formula

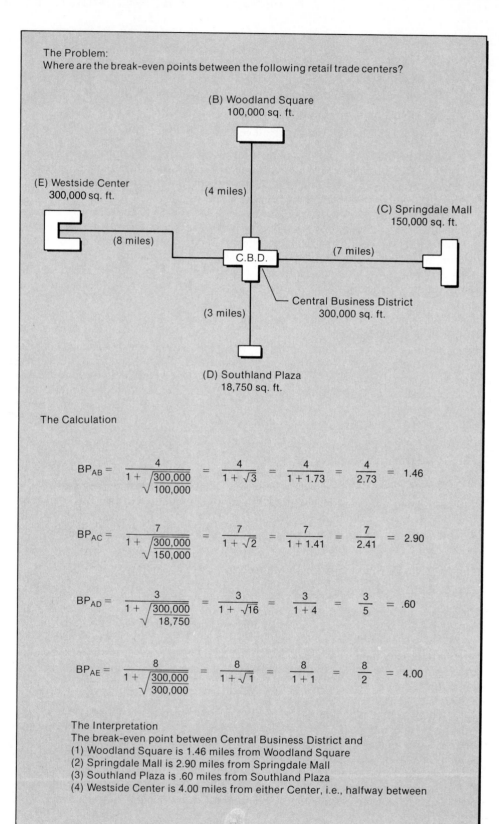

The Problem:
Where are the break-even points between the following retail trade centers?

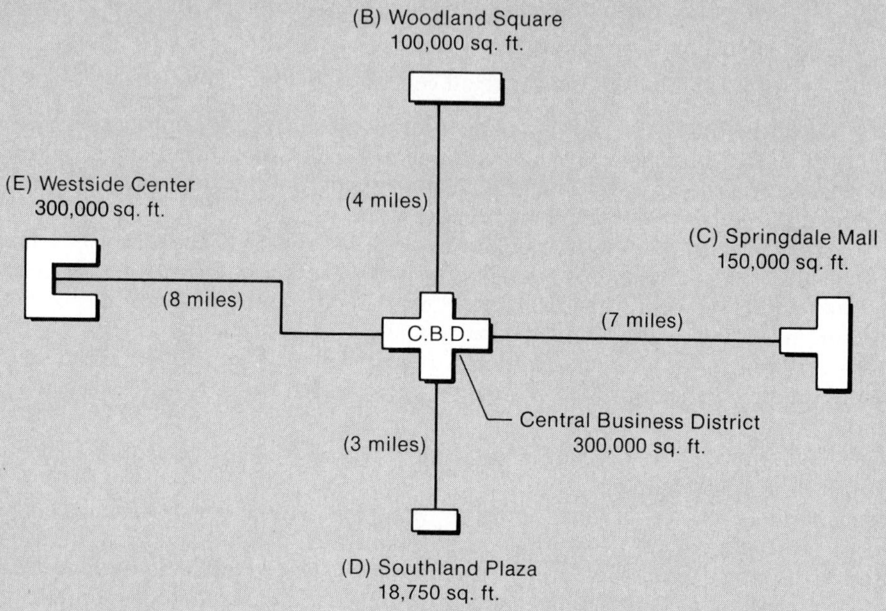

The Calculation

$$BP_{AB} = \frac{4}{1 + \sqrt{\frac{300{,}000}{100{,}000}}} = \frac{4}{1 + \sqrt{3}} = \frac{4}{1 + 1.73} = \frac{4}{2.73} = 1.46$$

$$BP_{AC} = \frac{7}{1 + \sqrt{\frac{300{,}000}{150{,}000}}} = \frac{7}{1 + \sqrt{2}} = \frac{7}{1 + 1.41} = \frac{7}{2.41} = 2.90$$

$$BP_{AD} = \frac{3}{1 + \sqrt{\frac{300{,}000}{18{,}750}}} = \frac{3}{1 + \sqrt{16}} = \frac{3}{1 + 4} = \frac{3}{5} = .60$$

$$BP_{AE} = \frac{8}{1 + \sqrt{\frac{300{,}000}{300{,}000}}} = \frac{8}{1 + \sqrt{1}} = \frac{8}{1 + 1} = \frac{8}{2} = 4.00$$

The Interpretation
The break-even point between Central Business District and
(1) Woodland Square is 1.46 miles from Woodland Square
(2) Springdale Mall is 2.90 miles from Springdale Mall
(3) Southland Plaza is .60 miles from Southland Plaza
(4) Westside Center is 4.00 miles from either Center, i.e., halfway between

The model developed by D. L. Huff to measure the probability of consumers expected to be attracted to a particular shopping cluster can be formally expressed as follows:

$$P_{ij}^{k} = \frac{\dfrac{S_j^k}{(T_{ij})^{\lambda}}}{\displaystyle\sum_{j=1}^{n} \dfrac{S_j^k}{(t_{ij})^{\lambda}}} \qquad \begin{array}{l} i = 1, 2, \ldots, m \\ j = 1, 2, \ldots, n \\ k = 1, 2, \ldots, p \end{array} \qquad (1)$$

where

P_{ij}^{k} = the probability of a consumer at a given origin i traveling to a particular shopping cluster j for a type k shopping trip

S_j^k = the size of the shopping cluster j devoted to shopping trip k (measured in square footage of retail selling area devoted to shopping trip k items)

T_{ij} = the travel time involved in getting from a consumer's point of origin i to a given shopping cluster j

λ = a parameter which is to be estimated empirically to reflect the effect of travel time on various kinds of shopping trips

m = the number of origins in the marketing area

n = the number of shopping clusters in the marketing area

p = the number of different types of shopping trips defined.

FIGURE 9–13
Huff's probability model for defining and estimating a trading area

trading-area potential is the predicted ability of a trading area to provide acceptable support levels for a retailer in the future.

Trading-Area Gross Adequacy

Measuring gross adequacy determines a trading area's total *capacity to consume*. The capacity of a retail market to consume is a function of the total *number of consumers* within a trading area at any given time and their need, willingness, and ability to purchase a particular class of goods (see Figure 9–15). Unfortunately, it is not easy to determine consumers' need, willingness, and ability to buy a certain class of goods. To determine gross adequacy, the retailer must first consider appropriate consumption units (e.g., people, homes, businesses) to count for a general class of goods. Second, the retailer must find an appropriate measure of a consumption unit's need, willingness, and ability to buy. To feel confident in their analyses, retailers must use one or more indicators of their potential buyers' behavior. Finally, the support capabilities of a trading area depend to some extent on sources outside the gross trading area.

Residential Support Levels

After sufficiently identifying the gross trading area, the retailer must concentrate on the most important source of business: the area's residents. To measure a trading area's

FIGURE 9–14
Elements of trading-area adequacy

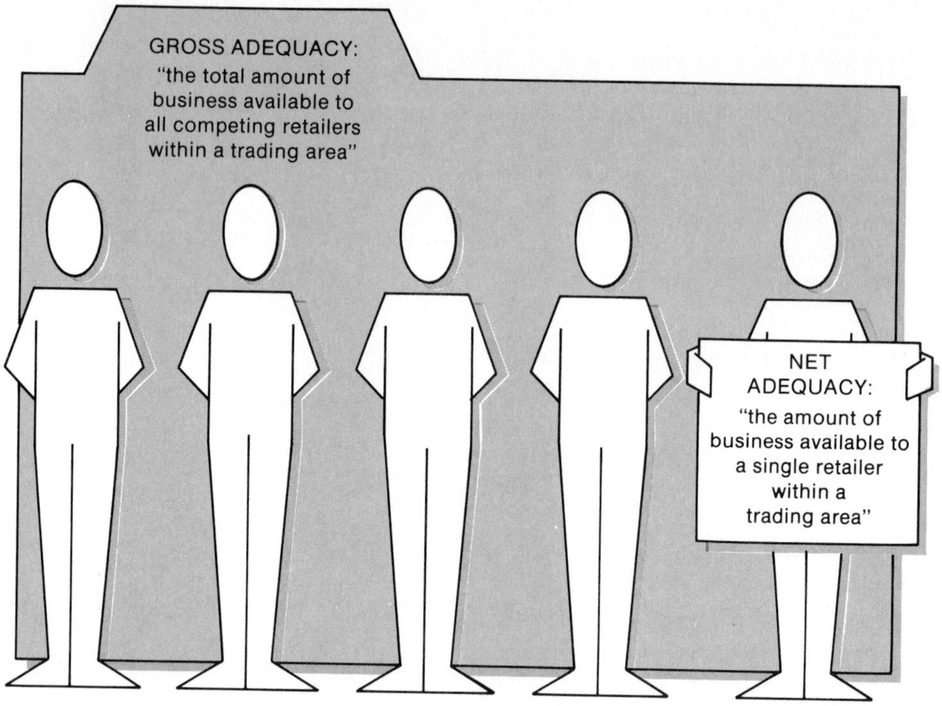
GROSS ADEQUACY:
"the total amount of business available to all competing retailers within a trading area"
NET ADEQUACY:
"the amount of business available to a single retailer within a trading area"

potential consumers, the retailer must analyze population/demographic and household/residential variables.

Population/Demographic Analysis. A trading area's total capacity to consume is partly a function of the total number of people who reside in that trading area. It is important to obtain an accurate population count, because the total population figure plays a part in several quantitative estimates of gross and net adequacy; the population figure must be accurate to produce reliable estimates. Although total population figures are informative, a trading area's capacity to consume may not be directly related to its total population; instead, it may be a function of the number of people who have a certain demographic makeup, such as age, sex, income, occupation, and family status. For example, measurements such as the number of children (bike store), the number of women (women's clothing store), or the number of high-income homeowners (expensive home furnishings) indicate a population count that should produce more reliable gross adequacy estimates. Evaluating gross adequacy is a matter of identifying demographic characteristics that best indicate the consumer's need, willingness, and ability to buy and of obtaining a reliable count of the number of people who have the desired demographic makeup. At the local trading-area level, a good source of population and demographic information is the *Census of Population*.

Household/Residential Analysis. For some retailing operations, a trading area's capacity to consume is more directly related to the *number of households* or *residential units* than to the number of people in the area. For example, a count of household or residential units probably is more indicative than a population count of a trading area for hardware, furniture, and appliances. This relationship simply reflects the fact that the household unit purchases many goods and the consumer's home is the prime determinant of the need for certain product lines. A household unit count by tracts and blocks can be obtained from the *Census of Population*. A residential unit count for

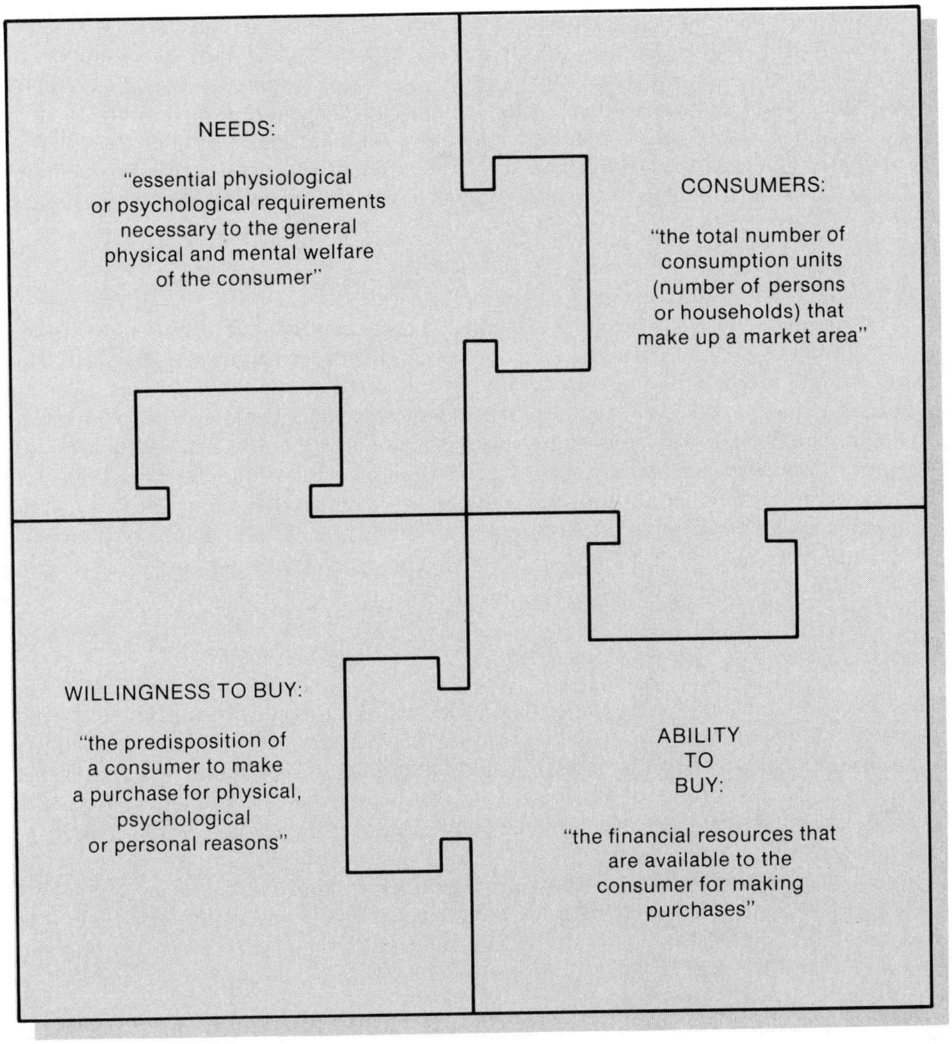
NEEDS:
"essential physiological or psychological requirements necessary to the general physical and mental welfare of the consumer"
CONSUMERS:
"the total number of consumption units (number of persons or households) that make up a market area"
WILLINGNESS TO BUY:
"the predisposition of a consumer to make a purchase for physical, psychological or personal reasons"
ABILITY TO BUY:
"the financial resources that are available to the consumer for making purchases"

FIGURE 9–15 The market potential puzzle: determinants of a market's capacity to consume

either census tracts or blocks is available from the *Census of Housing* and can be checked through field observation and aerial photographs. To reflect their consumption capacity more accurately, each residential unit can be weighted by average value, size, type of construction, and characteristics noted in housing census reports and local building permits.

Nonresidential Support Levels

Although the vast majority of a trading area's consumption capacity comes from people who live in that area, some of the consumption support does not. Consumers who reside outside a trading area contribute significantly to that area's capacity to consume. Most trading areas are characterized by daily inward, outward, and through migration of consumers who are attracted into the trading area for work, recreation, and other reasons, such as the need for professional services. Although these consumers might live many miles away, they represent a significant number of trade customers who visit the area. Some of these customers visit frequently and regularly (work trip); others visit infrequently and irregularly (recreation trip). Nevertheless, this external consumption capacity should be included in assessing a trading area's gross adequacy.

Although it is impossible to accurately count the number of consumers that make up the external consumption capacity, it is possible to count the number of nonresidential units likely to attract consumers to the trading area (e.g., retailers, wholesalers, manufacturers, offices, schools, churches). Because not all nonresidential units have equal consumption-generating abilities, each must be weighted according to its ability to generate traffic. Because some nonresidential units are more compatible with a retail enterprise than others, the weights a retailer assigns to each nonresidential unit should reflect the degree of consumer-retailer compatibility.

Estimating Trading-Area Sales

Several methods are available for estimating trading-area sales. The two most widely used techniques are the corollary data method and the per capita sales method. The **corollary data method** assumes that an identifiable relationship exists between sales for a particular class of goods and one or more trading-area characteristics (e.g., population, residential units). Knowledge of these relationships helps retailers estimate total sales. The **per capita sales method** estimates trading-area sales for a general product line and is a function of the per capita expenditures for that product line times the total population of that trading area. Retailers can obtain reliable population counts from census materials and per capita expenditure figures from consumer surveys and trade source estimates.

Trading-Area Net Adequacy

To answer the question "What is my slice of the pie?" a retailer must estimate the net adequacy of the trading area. As defined earlier, *net adequacy* is the proportion of sales volume a retailer can expect to receive from the total sales in a trading area; that is, net adequacy is the percentage of gross adequacy (or market share) a retailer can expect to get. To determine net adequacy, a retailer must consider the trading area's *capacity to consume* and its *capacity to sell*.

The capacity to consume is the gross adequacy measurement. Having obtained a gross estimate of the trading area's sales volume capabilities, the retailer's problem is to find a method of allocating total sales volume to each of the trading area's existing and proposed competitors. This allocation process consists of (1) analyzing the competitive environment and (2) estimating each retailer's sales and market share.

To determine net adequacy, the retailer must first identify the competitive environment. To analyze the competitive environment, the retailer must examine the types of competition, the number and size of competitors, and the marketing mix of competitors. We discuss these characteristics in Chapter 10 in the analysis of regional and local markets. However, assessing a trading area's net adequacy requires certain refinements. To gain a clearer picture of the competitive environment, a retailer can use two methods: (1) a competitive audit and (2) an outshopper analysis.

Competitive Audit

A **competitive audit** is an arbitrary, composite rating of each competitor's product, service, price, place, and promotion mixes. An audit covers a wide range of activities, including eyeballing competitors' floor space, checking ad results, getting information from media people and vendors, checking competitors' prices, and evaluating competitors' merchandise mixes. The purpose of a competitive audit is to assess the ability of competitors to provide a marketing mix that consumers within the trading area desire. The sum of all audits is a measurement of total competition.

Retailers use a competitive audit in several ways. First, they use it to measure the total competition within the trading area (the sum of all competitors times their competitiveness rating). Second, they derive a measure of each competitor's expected share of total trading-area sales. Third, they gain a picture of an unfulfilled product position or "niche" in the trading area. The last item of information can help the retailer develop a marketing strategy.

Outshopper Analysis

Not all consumers who live within a trading area shop exclusively in that area. A group of consumers known as "outshoppers" frequently and regularly shop outside their local trading area. These consumers spend a considerable amount of time, money, and effort in making inter-trading-area shopping trips. One analyst characterizes outshoppers and their shopping behavior this way:

> Some outshoppers are looking for economic gains resulting from lower prices in larger trading centers where assortments are better and the level of competition more intense. Some outshoppers simply *seek* the diversity of unfamiliar or more stimulating surroundings . . . demographically, outshoppers are younger (25–54 year age group), are relatively well educated (had some college), and the relative income is high . . . psychographically outshoppers are active, on the "go," urban-oriented housewives who are neither time-conscious nor store-loyal shoppers. They tend to manifest a distaste for local shopping and hence a strong preference for out-of-town shopping areas.[32]

To obtain an accurate estimate of total expected sales, the retailer must perform **outshopper analysis**, subtracting outshopping sales, referred to as "sales leakage," from the trading area's gross sales to arrive at a more realistic total sales volume for the trading area. To estimate sales leakage that results from outshopping behavior, a retailer can either conduct consumer surveys or use standard adjustments. In using consumer surveys, the retailer asks trading-area consumers to estimate how much they spend locally on a particular class of goods as a percentage of their total expenditures for those goods. The retailer then can use this percentage to adjust the gross sales figure for the trading area.

A simple and less expensive method is the standard adjustment. A standard adjustment figure depends on prevailing trading-area conditions. For example, if the trading area contains a large number of consumers who are similar to the demographic and psychographic profile of outshoppers, the retailer should make a standard downward adjustment (e.g., 5 percent) in gross sales. Other factors to consider in making standard adjustments are (1) the existence of major shopping centers outside the trading area that are within easy driving distance, (2) the presence of major traffic arteries that facilitate outshopping, and (3) the lack of a sufficient number of competing retailers to facilitate consumers' comparison shopping.

Estimating the Retailer's Sales

After evaluating the competitive environment, a retailer can estimate each competitor's sales. To calculate net adequacy (i.e., the trading-area market share) figure, the retailer can use either the total sales method or the sales-per-square-foot method. Both methods use a ratio of trading-area capacity to consume (gross adequacy) to trading area capacity to sell.

With the **total sales method**, the retailer allocates an equal share of the trading area's total sales for a specific product category to each competing retailer. This calculation is shown in Figure 9–16. The advantage of this method is that it is simple and quick to calculate. However, it assumes that all competing retailers are equal and can generate an equal share of the trading-area sales. Because competing retailers devote different amounts of time, money, space, and effort to sales, the analyst must make adjustments to the "all are equal" assumption. The competitive audit, discussed earlier, can be used to make this adjustment.

Another method for allocating trading-area sales to competitors is the **sales-per-square-foot-method**, whereby the retailer computes a ratio of each retailer's floor space

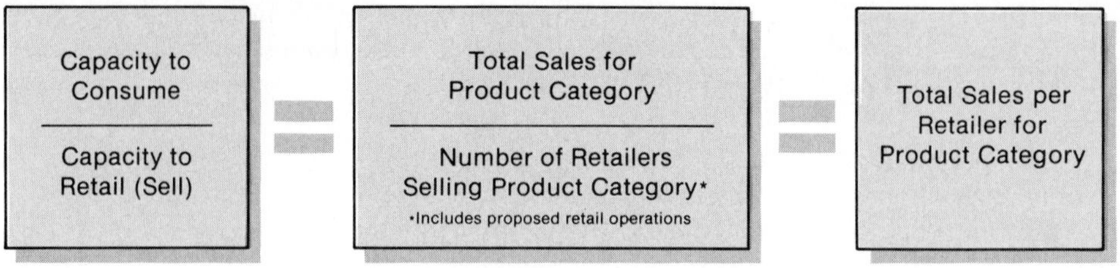

FIGURE 9–16
Total sales method for estimating a retailer's sales

devoted to a specific product category to the total of all retail floor space for the product category in the trading area. Figure 9–17 illustrates the calculation procedure. This method assumes that selling space is a good predictor of a retailer's competitiveness. Variations of this method substitute amounts of shelf space (linear, square, or cubic feet), sales per employee, or sales per checkout counter for sales per square foot.

Trading-Area Growth Potential

Before completing the trading-area evaluation process, the retailer must answer an additional question: What does the future hold for the trading area? Because marketing opportunities can change quickly, dynamic and growing trading areas often become either static or declining markets. Visual observation of an area is a simple method of looking into the future. Although lacking scientific methodology, visual inspection of current activities can produce a useful picture of the future. A retailer should consider several factors:

1. New and expanding residential areas combined with older, stable neighborhoods provide a solid base for future growth.
2. An expanding commercial or industrial base signals growth opportunities.
3. A good balance between items 1 and 2 reflects a stable growth rate that avoids overdependence on limited economic activity.
4. A well-developed transportation network and proposed future transportation networks in the trading area contribute to a trading area's growth.
5. An involved local government that takes an interest in residential and business development is a great asset.
6. A progressive social and cultural environment (theaters, museums, zoos, etc.) is a healthy climate for business.

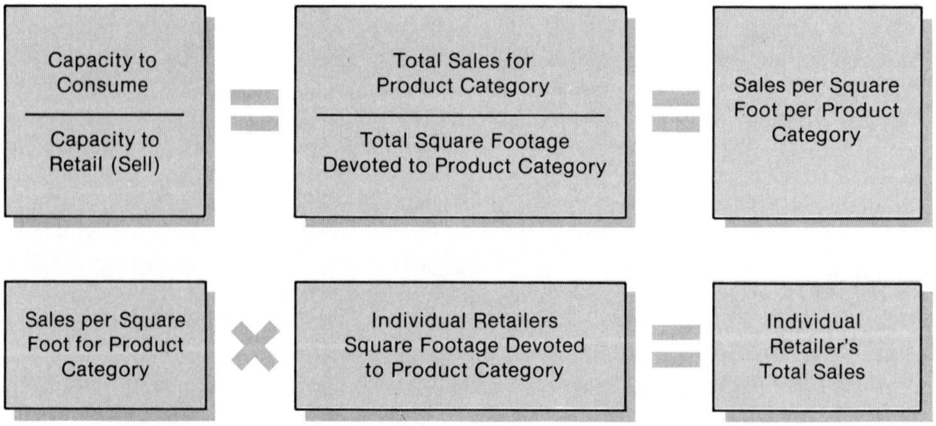

FIGURE 9–17
Sales-per-square-foot method for estimating a retailer's sales

SELECTING TRADING AREAS

To make the final selection of a trading area, the retailer must evaluate the alternatives according to each of the following criteria, referred to as a *minimum threshold:*

1. A stated minimum population having the desired demographic characteristics (e.g., 10,000 persons)
2. A stated minimum sales volume (e.g., $300,000/year)
3. A stated minimum daily traffic count (e.g., 5,000 vehicles per day)

If a trading area does not meet at least one or a certain combination of these minimums, the retailer excludes it from further consideration.

SUMMARY

The retail location decision is multidimensional. To find the "right place," the retailer must identify, evaluate, and select market areas, trading areas, and site locations.

Market areas can be delineated as regional markets (the "right region" and the "right part of the region") and local markets (the "right town" and the "right part of town"). Markets are delineated on the bases of the level of support (e.g., sales) available to the retailer and the ease of operating an outlet within identified areas. Level of support (i.e., market potential) is indicated by the area's population, housing, buyer behavior, and physical environment characteristics. Distribution, competition, promotional, and legal factors are all considered by retailers in assessing a market area.

Regional and local markets commonly are evaluated on the bases of their buying power, sales activity, and level of saturation. Retailers measure a market's ability to buy using the buying power index published in the *Survey of Buying Power*. To obtain the per capita retail sales of an area, retailers consult the sales activity index. A market area's capacity to consume as compared to its capacity to retail is determined by calculating the index of retail saturation. Finally, regional and local markets are selected on the basis of the best compromise among several different market situations.

A trading area is the area from which a store attracts its customers or obtains its business. To delineate trading areas, retailers use spotting techniques (e.g., license plate surveys, customer surveys, analyses of customer records, and studies of customer activities) and quantitative procedures (e.g., Converse's break-even point and Huff's probability models). Trading areas can be viewed from two perspectives. Composite trading areas are based on the type of goods (e.g., convenience, shopping, specialty) the retailer sells. Proportional trading areas are based on the distance customers are willing to travel to get to the store. All trading areas are evaluated with respect to their gross adequacy (their total capacity to consume) and net adequacy (their total capacity to consume divided by their total capacity to retail). A trading area's net adequacy is the relative market shares of each competing retailer in the area. Finally, a trading area's growth potential is assessed by studying the area's infrastructure.

STUDENT STUDY GUIDE

Key Terms and Concepts

ABC markets (p. 334)
break-even point (p. 344)
buying power index (BPI) (p. 338)
census market (p. 332)
communication market (p. 332)
competitive audit (p. 350)
composite trading area (p. 342)
corollary data method (p. 350)
fringe trading zone (p. 343)
geographic selectivity (p. 331)
gross adequacy (p. 345)
index of retail saturation (IRS) (p. 340)
intraurban markets (p. 336)
market potential approach (p. 326)
media coverage (p. 331)
media selectivity (p. 331)
net adequacy (p. 345)

outshopper analysis (p. 351)
overstored market area (p. 341)
per capita sales method (p. 350)
primary trading zone (p. 343)
proportional trading area (p. 343)
retail gravitation (p. 344)
retail operations approach (p. 328)
retail trading area (p. 341)
sales activity index (SAI) (p. 339)
sales-per-square-foot method (p. 351)
saturated market area (p. 341)
secondary trading zone (p. 343)
spotting technique (p. 343)
Survey of Buying Power (p. 338)
total sales method (p. 351)
trading-area adequacy (p. 345)
trading-area potential (p. 347)
understored market area (p. 340)

Review Questions

1. Retail markets can be identified using the market potential approach. Describe the four criteria used in this approach.
2. How might geographic selectivity and class selectivity be used to identify promotional market areas?
3. Describe how area coverage by various types of broadcast and print media are used in identifying market areas. Provide specific examples.
4. How are ABC markets defined?
5. Identify and describe two standard evaluation sources retail analysts commonly use to evaluate retail market areas.
6. What do the buying power index and sales activity index measure?
7. How is the formulation of the index of retail saturation expressed? What relationship does it measure? Describe the three market area classifications resulting from an application of the index.
8. What determines the size and structure of a retail trading area?
9. Describe the various types of composite and proportional trading-area zones.
10. Compare and contrast the various types of spotting techniques.
11. How is Converse's break-even point formula expressed? Define each part of the expression.
12. What determines a trading area's capacity to consume? Describe each factor.
13. Describe the two methods for estimating trading-area sales.
14. Who are outshoppers? Why are they important? Profile this consumer group.
15. How does the total sales method differ from the sales-per-square-foot method of calculating net adequacy?

Review Exam

True or False

_____ 1. The exact definition of what constitutes an A, B, or C market varies from one retailing organization to another.

_____ 2. The *Survey of Buying Power*'s effective buying income measurement is the rough equivalent of disposable personal income.

_____ 3. Overstored market areas are those in which the capacity to consume exceeds the capacity to retail.

_____ 4. The outermost ring of a store's composite trading area is delineated by the demand for the store's convenience goods offering.

_____ 5. The primary advantage of the license plate spotting technique is that it is relatively inexpensive to administer.

_____ 6. When retailers measure gross adequacy, they measure a trading area's total capacity to consume.

_____ 7. An outshopper is a consumer who shops outside his or her local trading area on a frequent and regular basis.

Multiple Choice

_____ 1. Usage rate is a buyer behavior characteristic used in the market potential approach to identifying market areas. Usage rate can be defined as
a. The activities, interests, and opinions regarding work, family, home, and business
b. The typical sales characteristics with which the retailer's products are sold
c. The degree to which the retailer's products are consumed
d. The general determinants of store choice
e. The consumer's personality characteristics

_____ 2. Which of the following factors is *not* associated with the retail operation's approach to identifying retail market area?
a. Distribution
b. Population
c. Competition
d. Promotion
e. Legal factors

_____ 3. The _____ index is a measure of the per capita retail sales of an area compared with those of the nation.
a. Retail saturation
b. Buying power
c. Sales activity
d. Quality
e. Wholesale

_____ 4. Which of the following statements is *not* one of the basic premises of Huff's shopper attraction model?
a. The proportion of consumers patronizing a given shopping cluster varies with distance from the shopping area.
b. The proportion of consumers patronizing various shopping areas varies with the breadth and depth of merchandise offered by each shopping area.
c. The distance that consumers travel to various shopping areas is the same for all product types.
d. The "pull" of any given shopping area is influenced by the proximity of competing shopping areas.

_____ 5. The capacity of a trading area to consume (gross adequacy) is a function of
a. The total number of consumers within the area at any given time
b. The consumer's need to purchase a particular class of goods
c. The consumer's willingness to purchase a particular class of goods
d. The consumer's ability to purchase a particular class of goods
e. All of the above

_____ 6. The _____ method for estimating trading-area sales assumes that an identifiable relationship exists between sales for a particular class of goods and some trading-area characteristic such as the number of residential units.
a. Per capita sales
b. Total sales
c. Sales-per-square-foot
d. Corollary data
e. Random-guess

_____ 7. Bob Smith, manager of the Furniture Mart, is considering the addition of a waterbed department. Bob estimates the total annual waterbed sales for his trading area to be approximately \$100,000. Bob estimates that with the addition of his new, 2,000-square-foot waterbed department, the trading area has a total of 10,000 square feet of selling space devoted to this product line. Using the sales-per-square-foot method, Bob estimates his total sales to be
a. \$ 5,000
b. \$10,000
c. \$20,000
d. \$25,000
e. None of the above.

STUDENT APPLICATIONS MANUAL

Investigative Projects: Practice and Applications

1. Select three radio stations your community receives. Interview the station manager or a sales representative for each station, and determine the geographic and class selectivity of each. Identify the types of retailers that would be best served by each station. Explain your selections.
2. Calculate the sales activity index for your county.
3. Select a neighborhood within your community that has three or four convenience food stores. Using a map of the area, delineate the primary, secondary, and fringe zones for each store's composite trading areas. Illustrate and discuss the impact of any supermarkets within the area.
4. Gain the cooperation of a local retailer and attempt to identify its trading area using one of the spotting techniques—a survey of license plates, customers, customer records, or customer activities. Construct a map illustrating the retailer's trading area. Discuss the strengths and weaknesses of the technique used.
5. Develop the forms (e.g., questions, rating scales, etc.) and procedures necessary for conducting a competitive audit for a general-merchandise retailer.
6. Analyze the retail growth potential of the trading area surrounding (e.g., within five blocks of) your college or university. Identify potentially positive and negative growth factors for existing and potential retailers. Provide some specific examples of retailing opportunities that might develop in the next ten years, and explain why you think these opportunities exist.

Tactical Cases: Problems and Decisions

■ CASE 9–1
To Mall or Not to Mall: Is the Question*

Joe Baldwin, owner and operator of Baldwin's, has had a successful women's apparel store on Main Street for 14 years. Appealing to the more mature consumer (age 30 to 65), Baldwin's offers a complete assortment of moderate and better apparel and accessories for both the professional woman and the home manager (Joe detests the term *housewife*). From Joe's viewpoint, Baldwin's had a secure future within the downtown retailing establishment. Baldwin's success is based on a number of factors, including (1) a loyal customer base due to an excellent reputation for high-quality merchandise, fair value prices, and superior personal service; (2) a desirable, high-traffic location in the middle of the downtown shopping area; and (3) a favorable long-term lease that is largely responsible for the store's relatively low operating costs. However, the store has its problems, the most troublesome being (1) the overcrowded condition of the downtown parking garages and lots, together with a limited number of metered spaces; (2) the lack of additional available selling space to alleviate the store's current overcrowded condition—another 1,000 square feet of selling space is needed to handle present customer traffic; and (3) the numerous problems associated with receiving merchandise—delivery trucks have to either doublepark on the main street or block the alley at the rear of the store. But viewed from a positive standpoint, all this overcrowding is a sign of a thriving downtown.

Mike Strong, proprietor of The Current Affair, is also a long-time member of the downtown retailing establishments. Targeting younger women age 16 to 35, The Current Affair is affiliated with a prominent and trendy Los Angeles clothing manufacturer that furnishes the store with new, exciting, and updated apparel that other local merchants have a hard time obtaining. This vendor relationship is providing The Current Affair with an important competitive advantage: fashion currency. In this medium-size, rather conservative Snowbelt city, younger women, swinging singles, and contemporary, updated, fashion-conscious consumers all depend on The Current Affair for the latest fashion trends. As with all of the merchants in the downtown area, overcrowding is the only dark cloud on the horizon. In short, the store is too crowded for its current sales level and expansion is impossible, yet the store's cost of business is surprisingly low due to a favorable lease and fixturing and decorating expenses that have long since been written off.

Joe Baldwin and Mike Strong are long-time friends and manage to have coffee together almost every morning. Other members of the Downtown Retail Merchants Association often join them at these informal get-togethers to discuss everything from current events to common problems. One of their favorite ongoing discussions centers on whether or not Woodlands Shopping Mall will ever become a reality. The sign on the rock site at the edge of town declaring the "Future Site of the Woodlands Shopping Mall" has been there for two years, and during that time the discussion has always come around to what effect the new mall will have on the downtown if it is ever built. Now that that concern has become a reality; at one of their many coffee klatches, Joe and Mike learned that a large developer had agreed to develop the property.

Shortly after that, every merchant in the downtown area was approached by an experienced mall solicitor who showed beautiful brochures of how the new mall would look, samples of other malls built by the developer, and a mall layout plan showing which locations were still available to local merchants. Already there was pressure to sign up now, before all of the best mall locations were secured by national chain retailers. While both Joe and Mike were satisfied with the status quo, each had to examine what a proposed move to the new mall might do to their business operations, customer relations, and financial statements.

In reviewing the mall developer's proposals, Mike and Joe are shocked at potential increases in the costs of doing business. Minimum base rents in the new mall are three to four times the dollar-per-square-foot costs presently being incurred by Baldwin's and The Current Affair in their downtown locations. If that were not enough, the mall's leasing contract has several clauses, including:

- *Average rent clause*—a charge based on a percentage of sales above a predetermined sales volume that is in addition to the minimum base rent
- *Continuous occupancy clause*—requires tenants to be open for business during certain hours
- *Sales submission report clause*—requires that tenants submit monthly sales reports (thus opening Mike and Joe's financial records to strangers)
- *Radius clause*—prevents tenants from opening a similar business within a five-mile radius (the downtown is 4.9 or 5.1 miles from the mall, depending which route is used)
- *Advertising clause*—requires each tenant to spend 2 percent of gross sales on advertising and 1 percent on advertisements in the mall's tabloid or other cooperative advertising activities such as mall recreation and entertainment events
- *Use clause*—requires tenants to limit their product assortment and service offering to the agreed-upon merchandise mix
- *Maintenance clause*—requires all tenants to pay a maintenance fee to cover the upkeep on central facilities (mall, parking lots, etc.).

After recovering from the initial "sticker price" shock, Mike and Joe have concluded that they are about to make the most important business decision each has made in over ten years.

ASSIGNMENT

1. Assume the role of either Joe Baldwin or Mike Strong, and outline the reasons why you would (select those answers you feel are the best solution and provide a merchandising, operational, and financial justification—advantages and disadvantages—for your decision):
   a. Sign a new lease with the new mall immediately to secure a prime location
   b. Sign a new lease for 50 percent more space to overcome the store space problems currently being experienced in the downtown location
   c. Sign a new lease for double the space of the current downtown store to provide for future sales growth
   d. Close the existing downtown store and move as soon as the new mall location is available
   e. Keep the downtown location and open a second store in the mall

f. Pass up the mall invitation for the time being; keep the downtown store, and defer the decision for another year
g. Decide your business was built on the downtown location, and that is where you are going to stay
h. Develop merchandise plans for your store and action plans for the downtown that would effectively counter the new competition for the mall.

2. Assume that the facts of this case are based on reality. What do you think actually happened?

*This case was prepared by Charles R. Patton, Pan American University.

■ CASE 9–2
The Electronic Mall: Identifying and Evaluating Market Areas*

I think your mall is excellent!

I think your mall is a wonderful place, and I will be shopping here often.

I've used The Mall frequently and have found the service to be excellent—keep up the good work.

What a great idea. Now I won't have to go throughout our fair city looking for gifts for those I know little about. This is my first time on board, and I am looking forward to browsing again.

I would first like to say I'm very impressed with The Mall.

The above are but a few of the encouraging customer comments received by the Mall Manager. In this case, the mall is The Electronic Mall, a shop-at-home service that enables personal computer owners to purchase goods and services via computer. This videotex shopping mall is owned and operated by CompuServe Incorporated of Columbus, Ohio. The Mall is open 24 hours a day, 365 days a year, and offers thousands of brand-name products at the touch of a keystroke.

Shoppers enter The Electronic Mall using a personal computer and a telephone modem. Shoppers can browse The Mall by keying in "This Week's Mall News," a comprehensive product index or a directory of all Mall merchants. Questions are promptly answered by the Mall Manager, an online representative. To make a purchase, the customer keys in the selected product together with his or her credit card number. The system reviews the selection and captures the order. Then the order is sent to a designated address via express mail or some other delivery service. The Buyer receives an electronic receipt, which is sent to his or her online mailbox. If the customer has a question about the product or bill, he or she can send a message directly to the merchant, who will respond via electronic mail.

The Mall layout and design may not look like a "bricks and mortar" facility, but it is organized into departments. A retailer can focus on one department or display merchandise in several departments. The Mall is laid out into 16 departments: (1) apparel and accessories, (2) automotive, (3) books and periodicals, (4) gifts and novelties, (5) computing, (6) gourmet and flowers, (7) hobbies and toys, (8) merchandise and electronics, (9) online services, (10) premium merchants, (11) music and movies, (12) health and beauty, (13) financial, (14) travel and entertainment, (15) office supplies, (16) sports and leisure.

Electronic shopping, a phenomenon of the Information Age, is one of the ways retailers are reaching a lucrative market of busy consumers who want to shop at home. It is a direct-marketing technique that takes the store to the market rather than attracting the market to the store.

ASSIGNMENT

1. Identify and delineate the market area for The Electronic Mall.
2. Profile and characterize the typical consumer (i.e., target market) who patronizes The Mall.
3. List and describe the advantages and disadvantages of this mall location for the consumer and for the retailer.
4. Describe the type of retailing format (products, prices, promotions) that is most compatible with this type of mall. Explain.

*This case was prepared by Dale Lewison and John Thanopoulos, The University of Akron, and Charles R. Patton, Pan American University.

Source: Materials for this case were obtained from promotional brochures, press releases, and advertisements supplied by CompuServe Incorporated of Columbus, Ohio.

ENDNOTES

1. Russell Mitchell, "From Punching Bag to Retailing Black Belt," *Business Week*, November 20, 1989, 62.
2. Ron Stodghill, II, and Paul Magnusson, "Store Wars Break Out All Around the Beltway," *Business Week*, November 10, 1988, 140.
3. "Entertainment Anchors: New Mall Headliners," *Chain Store Age Executive*, August 1989, 63.
4. "Nordstrom Plugs Tyler Leak," *Chain Store Age Executive*, September 1989, 40.
5. "How Supermarkets Reflect Consumer Trends," *The Repository*, February 23, 1989, D-2.
6. Bill Saporito, "A&P: Grandma Turns a Killer," *Fortune*, April 23, 1990, 211.

7. Denise Callagher, "Sterling Jewelry," *Stores,* January 1989, 107.
8. Jeffrey A. Trachtenberg, "Burdine's Bets It Knows Florida Best," *The Wall Street Journal,* January 18, 1989, B-4.
9. See Ronald D. Taylor and Blaise J. Bergiel, "Chain Store Executives' Ratings of Critical Site Selection Factors," *The Journal of Midwest Marketing* (Fall 1988): 37–47.
10. Louis W. Stern and Frederick D. Sturdivant, "Customer-Driven Distribution Systems," *Harvard Business Review* (July–August 1987): 34.
11. Chuck Hawkins, "Will Home Depot Be 'The Wal-Mart of the '90s'?", *Business Week,* March 19, 1990, 124.
12. Jay L. Johnson, "The Remaking of Montgomery Ward," *Discount Merchandiser,* September 1989, 25.
13. See Dwight J. Shelton, "Birds of a Geodemographic Feather Flock Together," *Marketing News,* August 28, 1987, 13.
14. See Peter S. Carusone and Brenda J. Moscove, "Special Marketing Problems of Smaller City Retailing," *Journal of the Academy of Marketing Science* 13 (Summer 1985): 198–211.
15. Jay L. Johnson, "The Supercenter Challenge," *Discount Merchandiser,* August 1989, 72.
16. See "Wal-Mart Puts Indiana in High Gear," *Chain Store Age Executive,* March 1990, 27–28, 31.
17. *1987 Survey of Buying Power, Sales, and Marketing Management,* July 27, 1987, C-3.
18. Ibid.
19. Ibid., C-5.
20. Ibid.
21. The following discussion is based on Bernard J. LaLonde, "New Frontiers in Store Location," *Supermarket Merchandising,* February 1963, 110.
22. Ibid.
23. "Retailers Buy into Philadelphia," *Advertising Age,* March 28, 1988, 48MW.
24. Suzanne Alexander, "Saturating Cities with Stores Can Pay," *The Wall Street Journal,* September 11, 1989, B-1.
25. Larry D. Crabtree, "Survey Car License Plates to Define Retail Trade Area," *Marketing News,* January 4, 1985, 12.
26. Gerald McMahon, "Grocers Need Shopping Data Base to Build Strong Relationships," *Marketing News,* March 19, 1990, 26.
27. See Howard L. Green, "Retail Sales Forecasting Systems," *Journal of Retailing* 62 (Fall 1986): 227–230.
28. Paul D. Converse, *Retail Trade Areas in Illinois,* Business Study No. 4 (Urbana, Ill.: University of Illinois Press, 1946), 30–31.
29. C. Samuel Craig, Avijit Ghosh, and Sara McLafferty, "Models of the Retail Location Process: A Review," *Journal of Retailing* 60 (Spring 1984): 15.
30. D. C. Huff, "Defining and Estimating a Trading Area," *Journal of Marketing* 28 (1964): 34.
31. Dale M. Lewison and Ray Robins, "A Model for Evaluating the Adequacy of a Retail Trading Area," in *Proceedings: Small Business Administration Directors Institute,* ed. David H. Hovey and Ronald S. Rubin (Small Business Administration Directors Institute, 1980).
32. Fred D. Reynolds and William R. Darden, "Internal Patronage: A Psychographic Study of Consumer Outshoppers," *Journal of Marketing* 36 (October 1972): 50–54.

PART III

RETAIL SITE LOCATIONS
Identifying, Evaluating, and Selecting Sites

CHAPTER 10

OUTLINE

OBJECTIVES

- Classify and characterize the various types of site alternatives.
- Identify and use the five principles of site evaluation to assess the value of alternative sites.
- Describe and apply the basic method of retail site evaluation.
- Make a final site selection decision through the process of elimination.

SHOPPING MALLS OR ENTERTAINMENT CENTERS?

The typical shopping center, which consists of a well-balanced tenant mix of specialty stores with major department stores anchoring each end, may no longer be adequate to meet the customer's total need package for socialization, recreation, entertainment, and shopping. Consider these developments:

- "Scala is the lively new anchor at the 'fun' end of Copenhagen's (Denmark) famous Stroget pedestrian shopping street; Sture Gallerian is a stylish shopping arcade built within and around Stockholm's (Sweden) elegant old baths . . . both are based on the shopping-as-entertainment principle . . . their strongest drawing cards are restaurants and fitness and/or entertainment facilities rather than the stores and boutiques that compose the largest percentage of tenants."[1]
- "Visitors to Underground Atlanta will find a lot more than stores, restaurants, and night clubs. . . . Highlights include a 45,000 square foot Coca Cola pavilion, an old-fashioned train ride, and a multimedia historical exhibit. . . . Underground Atlanta, with its mix of retail and entertainment attractions, will offer something for everyone. . . . Entertainment fast is becoming a mall anchor and destination point."[2]
- In the Philadelphia area, Franklin Mills combines entertainment with a power-center-type retail mix to create a "state fair" environment. As part of the project, the "49th Street Galleria" is a large-scale entertainment complex offering a variety of games (laser tag, videos, video games) and sporting activities (bowling alleys and batting cages). The "entertainment aspect is so important that management has begun marketing it as a tourist attraction."[3]
- Carousels, carnival games, games of chance (Bingo), coin-operated amusements, electronic shooting galleries, movie theaters, live theaters, party rooms, comedy clubs, live reviews, roller coasters and other rides, water slides, swimming pools, skating rinks, miniature golf, bowling, tennis courts, and health clubs are but some of the entertainment and recreational activities that are becoming part of the regional mall concept.[4]

SITE LOCATION DIMENSIONS

A **retail site** is the actual physical location from which a retail business operates. Specialists in the retailing field believe that a retailer's site is one of the principal tools for obtaining and maintaining a competitive advantage through spatial monopoly. A given site is unique when its "positional qualities" serve a particular trading-area consumer in a way that no other site can match. Obviously competing sites also are uniquely situated. The *retailer's site problem*, therefore, is how to identify, evaluate, and select the best available site alternative to profitably serve the needs of an identified trading-area consumer (see Figure 10–1).

IDENTIFYING SITE LOCATIONS

The first step in appraising retail site locations is to identify all potential site alternatives. The number of site alternatives in a given trading area can range from an extremely limited choice to a very large selection. Before attempting any formal evaluation, the retailer should screen the alternatives by asking three questions:

1. **Availability:** Is the site available for rent or purchase?
2. **Suitability:** Are the site and facilities of a suitable size and structure?
3. **Acceptability:** Is the asking rental rate within the retailer's operating budget?

To be considered for further evaluation, a site alternative must meet all three screening criteria: It must be available, suitable, and acceptable.

Retail sites can be classified as either isolated or clustered. **Isolated sites** are geographically separated from other retailing sites. They can, however, be located next to other forms of economic and social activity. **Clustered sites** are either next to or in

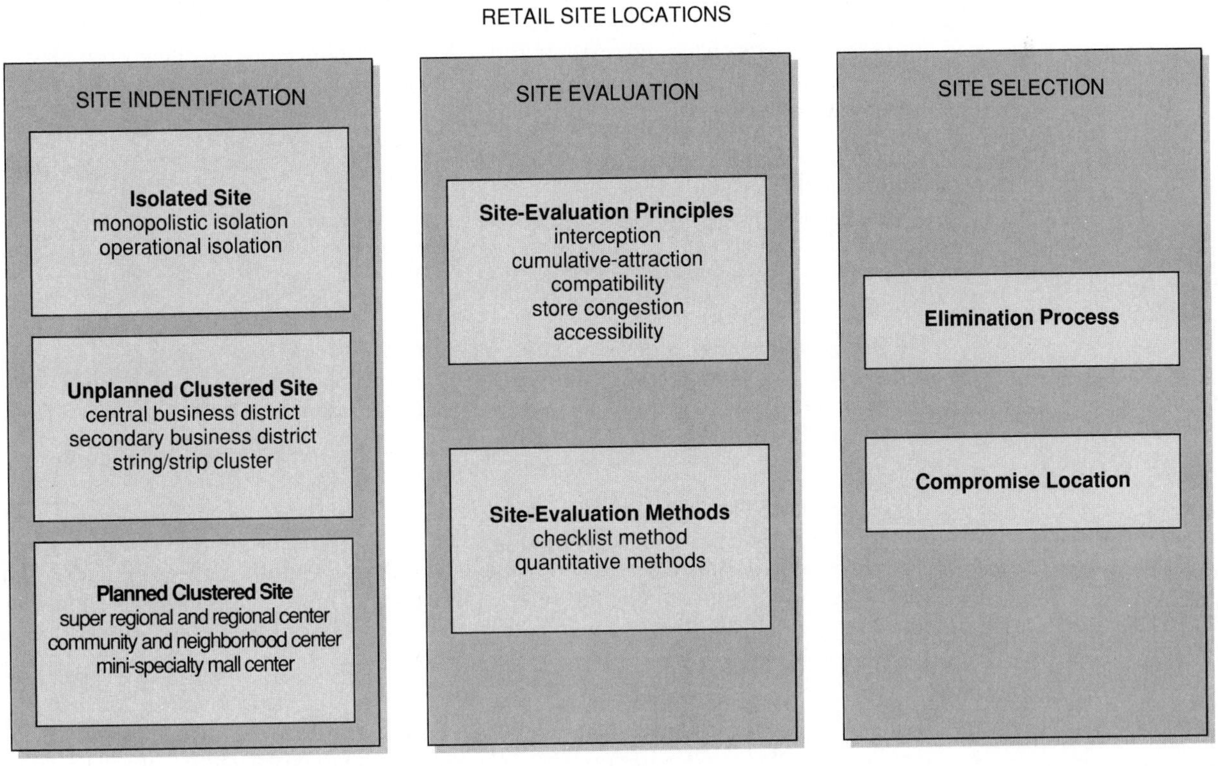

FIGURE 10–1
Appraising retail site locations

close proximity to one another. From a shopping perspective, a cluster is two or more closely located retailers capable of sharing customers with minimal effort. Retail clusters are either unplanned or planned. An *unplanned retail cluster* is the result of a natural evolutionary process; a *planned retail cluster* is the result of planning.

The Isolated Site

One site alternative is to "go it alone" by selecting an absolute location isolated from other retailers. The degree of physical isolation can range from "around the corner and down the block" to "far out on the outskirts of town." In relative location terms, an isolated site is situated so that it will not normally share consumer traffic with other retailers. However, its relative location offers certain advantages in attracting customers from other sources of business. Generally the retailer that selects an isolated site is seeking to gain either a monopolistic or an operational advantage: "Upgraded shopping areas are becoming an important airport marketing tool. . . . Flight delays of more than an hour create a captive, affluent audience . . . mainstream retailers are moving out to the airports."[5] Bloomingdale's led the way in this trend by opening two Bloomie's Express clothing and gift boutiques at Kennedy Airport in New York.

Monopolistic Isolation

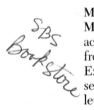

Monopolistic isolation is a site that affords the retailer a uniquely convenient and accessible location to serve consumers. A monopolistically isolated site is segregated from competing retail sites but is uniquely situated for traffic-generating activities. Examples are a convenience food store in a residential area, a neighborhood bar, a local service station, and a cafeteria located in an office complex. Exclusive airport locations, let under concessionaire agreements to the highest bidders, are excellent examples of monopolistic locations. An example of monopolistic isolation familiar to students is the local campus bookstore.

Operational Isolation

Some retailers prefer to locate in isolated areas because they believe it gives them greater flexibility in operating a retail business. A retailer that uses an **operational isolation** strategy can achieve flexibility in a number of areas.

Site Geography. Site alternatives that meet the size, shape, and terrain requirements of the retailer's operation constitute site geography. A home improvement center, for example, normally requires a large, flat site to accommodate large showrooms and storage facilities.

Transportation Network. Some site alternatives have transportation networks that generate good consumer traffic and also have good supply connections. A large warehouse-showroom retailer might consider locating the store at the junction of two major highway systems where customer traffic is high. However, it should also consider whether there is an adjacent railroad spur to handle large numbers of heavy, bulky products efficiently.

Type of Facilities. Certain site alternatives permit installation of facilities that are conducive to the retailer's operations. The store's architectural motif, internal layout, fixturing, and atmosphere, as well as supporting facilities such as parking and signing, are all important considerations for any retailer. Most clustered locations have numerous facility restrictions, while isolation permits great freedom in design.

RETAILING IN THE 90's

Recreation and Entertainment...

providing a total shopping experience.

Greater store and mall loyalty together with longer and more frequent store and mall visits are the advantages that accrue to retailers that support their shopping opportunities with customer recreation and entertainment activities.

Fun, relaxation, and diversion are but some of the additional benefits that many customers hope to find when visiting a store or mall. "To escape from their daily routines" can be a strong motivating factor in attracting shoppers to shopping malls and retail stores.

Central Courts and Facility Restorations...

creating nostalgic images and memories.

The central court is center stage for most large shopping malls; it is the hub of shopping activities. A well-designed and attractive center court is a key element in creating a shopping center's image because it is the feature that customers remember most often and most vividly.

An important trend in shopping center development is the restoration, preservation, and conversion of manufacturing plants, railroad stations, shipping docks, warehouses, and other interesting structures into specialty shopping malls. The uniqueness of such properties creates an interesting and exciting shopping atmosphere with a sense of nostalgia.

Operating Methods. Some sites offer the retailer freedom of operation and avoidance of group rules common to shopping centers. Such restrictions include store operating hours, external displays, and cooperative advertising programs.

Operating Costs. A site must permit the retailer to operate within the business's cost constraints. A low-margin, high-turnover retailer (e.g., discount house) needs to keep operating expenses low to offer discount prices. An isolated site can have low rental costs that help hold prices down.

An isolationist strategy also has several disadvantages. First, the retailer must attract and hold its own customers. An isolationist strategy may cause the shopping-goods retailer to encounter serious problems, since these consumers either prefer to compare brands or are one-stop shoppers. Second, the retailer usually must design and build its own facilities. Only the largest retail organizations have the human and financial resources to engage in such activities. Third, the isolated retailer cannot share operating costs with neighboring establishments. Clustered locations, in contrast, allow retailers to share certain common ground costs such as maintenance, security, lighting, and snow and garbage removal.

The Unplanned Clustered Site

Before widespread urban planning and zoning laws, "unplanned" retailing clusters sprang up, many of which still exist. In cities where local zoning ordinances are not strictly enforced, they continue to form. Unplanned retailing clusters often are part of larger unplanned business districts in which retailers can be either clustered together or scattered with no discernable pattern. The four general types of unplanned clusters are the central business district, the secondary business district, the neighborhood business district, and the string/strip cluster.

Central Business Districts

The **central business district (CBD)** was, and in many cities still is, the single most important retailing cluster. A strong downtown retailing cluster is North Michigan Avenue in Chicago. In recent years, this downtown area has attracted many of the nation's leading merchandisers: Bloomingdale's, Saks Fifth Avenue, Lord & Taylor, and Bonwit Teller from New York; I. Magnin from San Francisco; Neiman Marcus from Dallas; and a host of other well-known specialty stores.[6] Since World War II, however, the CBD's role as the city's principal place to shop has declined. Among the commonly cited reasons for the CBD's decline are the following:

- Migration of middle- and upper-income consumers to the suburbs
- Development of fast, accessible intracity transportation networks, which allow people to live anywhere in the city and still work in the CBD
- General congestion in the CBD and its effects on free movement and accessibility
- Environmental pollution (air, noise, etc.) and its physiological effects
- General decay of the physical facilities in many downtown areas and its psychological effect
- High crime rates in and around the CBD
- Problems associated with the influx of low-income and ethnic groups into the areas immediately surrounding the CBD

Despite its problems and predictions of its extinction, the CBD and the retailing clusters within it have survived. In fact, some CBDs are experiencing a renaissance. Revitalized CBDs have resulted from the following efforts:

- Converting streets to pedestrian malls
- Modernizing physical facilities

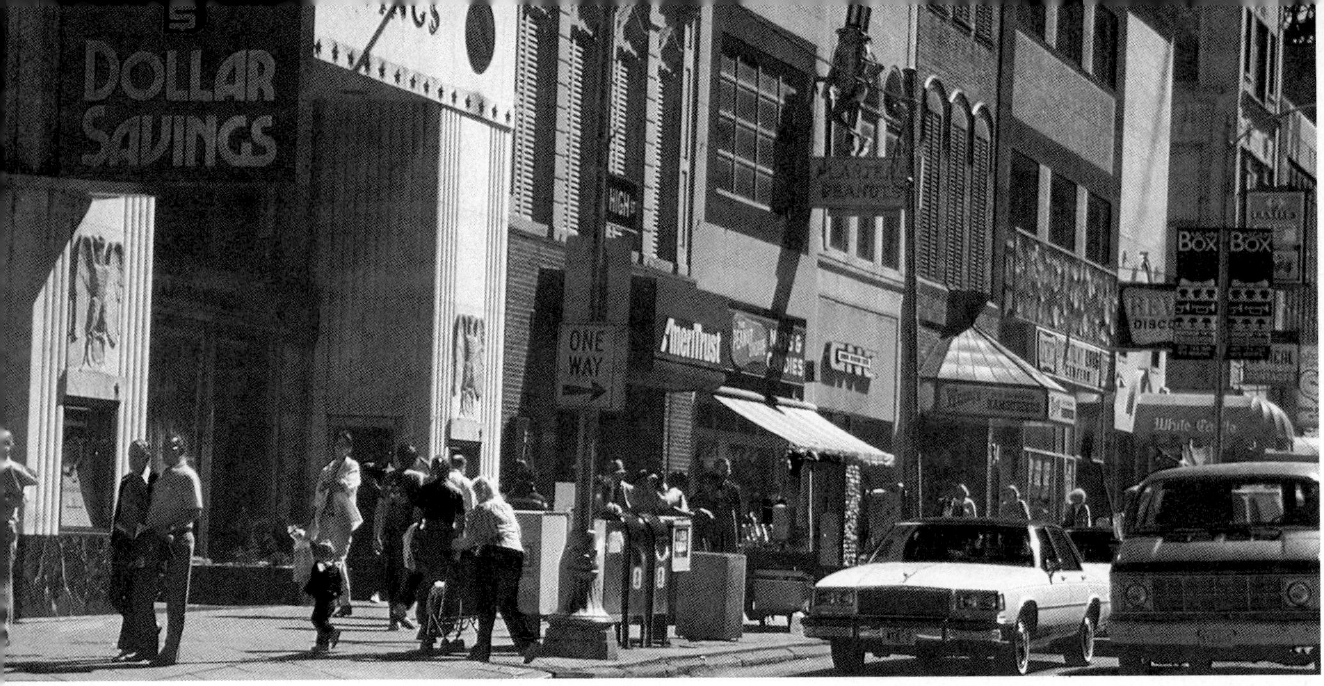

Shopping in the central business district (CBD) offers both advantages and disadvantages.

- Reducing traffic congestion with one-way streets and modern traffic control devices
- Constructing new middle- and upper-income residential complexes
- Renovating low-income residential areas
- Organizing commercial businesses to develop and promote the downtown area

Some CBD revitalization projects have been extremely successful, and others have failed. Successful revitalization projects include the Nicollet Mall in Minneapolis, Ghirardelli Square in San Francisco, Faneuil Hall Marketplace in Boston, and The Gallery at Market Street East in Philadelphia. The key to successful revitalization projects is not so much the development of new and existing facilities as the creation of a safe and pleasant shopping atmosphere. "Festival marketplaces" have long been a key to reversing the flight from center cities and in developing the environment for a successful retail cluster.[7] The new generation of CBD retailing projects are being tailored to the downtown environment; they tend to be vertical, multilevel malls that are reusing existing facilities. Two good examples include the four-level Terminal Tower project in downtown Cleveland[8] and the eight-level conversion of the old Gimbel's flagship store in New York City into the A&S (Abraham & Straus) Plaza.[9]

Secondary Business Districts

Most medium-size and large cities have one or more **secondary business districts (SBDs)** located at the intersections of major traffic arteries. Some SBDs originally were the downtown areas of cities that later were incorporated into larger cities. Others represent the natural evolution of a retailing cluster to meet the convenience shopping needs of adjacent neighborhoods. As their name implies, these clusters are secondary to central business districts. They are similar to CBDs but smaller. A typical SBD generally varies from 10 to 30 stores, radiating from one or more major intersections along primary traffic arteries.

The typical store mix of an SBD includes one or two branch department stores (or some other mass merchandiser) that serve as the principal consumer attraction; several specialty, shopping, and convenience goods retailers; and various service establishments. Often one or more large, nonretailing generators (e.g., hospital, office complex, university, manufacturing plant) are in the immediate vicinity of an SBD. These nonretailing establishments usually are important nonresidential sources of business.

57th Street: The Right Side of the Street

RETAIL STRATEGIES AND TACTICS

The three-and-a-half blocks along New York's 57th Street stretching from Lexington Avenue to halfway between Fifth and Sixth avenues is one of the world's greatest shopping streets. The $500-per-square-foot rental rates are supported by the foot traffic that passes along this street; the corner of 57th Street and Madison Avenue has an estimated 240,000 passersby a day. The uniqueness of 57th Street as a shopping district is that it has the world's highest concentration of high-end retailers offering designer labels. Chanel, Burberry's, Hermes, Ann Taylor, David Webb, Tiffany, Henri Bendel, Bergdorf Goodman, and Bůlgari Jewelers are but a few of the upscale retail establishments found along this street of posh retailers. Strategically, however, both sides of 57th Street are not equal. The north side of the street has always been stronger. Why? During the prime shopping hours of 10 A.M. to 4 P.M., the north side is the sunny side of the street.

Source: Based on Janet White, "57th Street—One of the World's Great Shopping Streets," *Stores*, April 1989, 53–56.

Neighborhood Business Districts

The **neighborhood business district (NBD)** is a small retailing cluster that serves primarily one or two residential areas. The NBD generally contains four to five stores, usually including some combination of food stores and drugstores, gasoline service stations, neighborhood bars, self-service laundries, barber shops, beauty shops, and small, general-merchandise stores. The most common structural arrangement for the NBD is the "four-corners" layout, with a retailer situated on each corner. Although the four-corners layout generally is associated with secondary and residential streets, these streets represent the major "feeder" into the adjacent residential neighborhoods. The NBD is a logical alternative for a convenience retailer that wants to serve a particular neighborhood.

String/Strip Cluster

The **string/strip cluster** develops along a major thoroughfare and depends on the consumption activities of people who travel these busy streets. The size of the string or strip is directly related to the average volume of traffic along the thoroughfare. Some strings stretch for miles along the heavily traveled arteries leading in and out of a CBD, while others are limited to one or two blocks along streets carrying a lower density of traffic. Examples of long strips are those with new and used car lots, rows of mobile home dealerships, strings of home furnishings outlets, and a strand of side-by-side fast-food restaurants or collection of specialty shops.

The positional strengths of the string/strip cluster are their ability to achieve the following:

- Intercept consumers as they travel from one place to another
- Expose consumers to the retailer's operations, thereby creating store awareness
- Attract consumers on impulse due to place convenience
- Offer lower rents than central and secondary business districts

The Planned Clustered Site

Over the last several decades, the growth of suburban populations has given retailers the opportunity to meet the needs of the suburban shopper. Today, "there are 34,683 shopping centers in the U.S., including small community centers, strip centers, and

THE WORLD OF RETAILING

International Retailing

Paris's Avenue Montaigne: The Chicest Shopping Street in the World

From its beginning, a mere Seine-span from the base of the Tour Eiffel to the Rond-Point des Champs-Elysées, Avenue Montaigne is unarguably the most densely packed concentration of chic in Paris, if not the world. This short street has everything going for it: elegant buildings festooned with wrought-iron balconies; glorious chestnut trees down the center; one of the world's most widely acclaimed hotels, the Plaza Athenée; great couture houses and jewelers.

The fashion reign of Avenue Montaigne dates back to 1947, when Christian Dior stepped out onto the balcony of his couture house at 30 Avenue Montaigne to receive accolades for his first collection.

Retailing along the Avenue has evolved gradually and gracefully over 40 years. Early retail activities were limited to discreet couture houses, small, typically Parisian shops, and neighborhood *boulangeries* and *confiseries* until the transformation began in the 1960s.

Today Avenue Montaigne houses many of Paris's chicest couture houses and boutiques: Jean-Louis Scherrer, Nina Ricci, Chanel, Valentino, Ungaro, Guy Laroche, Givenchy, Theirry Mugler, and Torrente. Adding to the glitter of the Avenue are such renowned jewelers as Harry Winston, Bulgari, O. J. Perrin, Patek-Philippe, and Cartier. As the most expensive location and desired address in Paris, firms will pay almost any amount for "Avenue Montaigne" on their letterheads.

Source: Mary Krienke, "Paris' Avenue Montaigne," *Stores* (June 1989): 38, 40–41.

larger regional malls, up 57.3% from 1980."[10] Originally the basic problem was to develop an institution that could satisfy the shopping needs of a geographically dispersed market. The most common solution was (and still is) a one-stop shopping institution such as a planned shopping center. Through careful planning, a developer could offer a merchandise mix—products, services, prices—with which to meet most customer needs for convenience, shopping, and specialty goods.

A planned shopping center is a purposeful cluster of retail and service establishments at a location designed to serve a specific geographic, demographic, and psychographic market segment. Shopping centers vary in nature according to their tenants and the size of the markets they serve.[11] On the basis of type and size, shopping centers are classified as regional, community, neighborhood, and specialty centers. Figure 10–2 shows sales performance (sales per square foot) for various types of retailers at different types of malls. Figure 10–3 shows occupancy costs (total charges equal rent plus common area maintenance [CAM] charges) as a percentage of sales.

Super Regional and Regional Centers

Regional shopping centers serve regional markets varying in size according to the type of transportation network serving the center, the location of competing centers and unplanned business districts, the willingness of consumers to travel various distances to shop, and the tenant mix. The Urban Land Institute identifies two types of regional shopping centers: A **super regional shopping center** is built around at least three and often four major department stores; a **regional shopping center** is built around one or two full-line department stores. Typical sizes range from 400,000 to 600,000 square feet of gross leasable area (GLA) for the regional center to 750,000 to 1,000,000 square feet of GLA for the super regional center.

Regional and super regional centers provide consumers with an extensive assortment of convenience, shopping, and specialty goods as well as numerous personal

Types of Retailers	Super Regional	Regional	Community	Neighborhood
Cameras	553	425	—	—
Jewelry	447	380	207	161
Key shop	362	—	—	—
Computers/calculators	359	—	130	—
Cookie shop	320	188	—	—
Leather shop	313	243	—	—
Film-processing store	295	217	165	141
Costume jewelry	294	274	—	—
Optometrist	287	175	150	—
Photocopy/fast printing	285	163	132	92
Tobacco	281	258	114	—
Candy and nuts	282	239	176	7
Radio/video/stereo	280	230	150	143
Records and tapes	245	229	148	—
Eyeglasses/optician	246	220	150	119
Athletic footwear	252	219	130	—
Superstore (over 30,000 sq. ft.)	—	—	318	307
Supermarket (over 6,000 sq. ft.)	—	—	291	279
Liquor and wine	159	—	186	170
Ladies' shoes	194	166	163	72
Drugstore	182	184	156	144
Fast food/carryout	262	215	155	148
Super drugstore	153	173	140	152
Ladies' specialty	189	169	118	138

Source: *Dollars & Cents of Shopping Centers: 1987* (ULI—the Urban Land Institute, 1987, 1200 18th St. NW, Washington, DC 20036).

FIGURE 10–2
Sales performance for various types of retailers at different types of malls ($ sales per square foot)

and professional service facilities. The trend in tenant mix for shopping centers is "mixed-use developments" (MXDs).[12] In addition to retailing establishments, these MXDs might include office buildings, recreational and entertainment facilities, residential units, hotels, government buildings, wholesaling, and light manufacturing.[13] This extensive assortment is achieved through a balanced tenancy of some 50 to 150 individual stores.

The tenant mix is very important. In the past, shopping malls were built around one or more major department stores whose size and advertising attracted customers to the center. The basic premise of the shopping center was that people would "walk up and down the malls to get to the different department stores, and as they walk, they look at the small stores to see what they like and what they want to buy."[14] Today shopping centers and areas within shopping centers (wings) are being planned as "a collection of stores with a purpose rather than those [stores] offering undefined impulse shopping."[15] The modern mall has become a festival, tourist, theme, recreational, entertainment, and/or specialty center. It caters to multiple market segments, including tourists, conventioneers, sports enthusiasts, shoppers, and locals who are looking to "escape" for a few hours.[16]

While traditional department store anchors will continue as a major element in the shopping center's tenant mix, new and different anchors are becoming more important. Specialty store chains like Mervyn's (apparel), IKEA (home furnishings), and Lechmere (hard goods) are achieving anchor status. In some areas, "category killers" (aggressive, high-volume specialty superstores such as Toys 'R' Us, Circuit City, Cohoes, and The Wiz) and catalog showrooms (e.g., Service Merchandise and Best) are

Types of Retailers	Super Regional	Regional	Community	Neighborhood
Ladies' ready-to-wear	9.91	9.12	8.04	7.92
Jewelry	8.08	7.56	7.06	—
Fast food/carryout	14.69	13.22	9.71	7.14
Men's wear	9.68	9.29	—	—
Ladies' shoes	11.34	10.77	—	—
Family shoes	10.41	12.03	8.69	—
Cards and gifts	13.09	12.12	11.36	—
Ladies' specialty	9.74	9.61	9.07	—
Men's and boys' shoes	11.12	—	—	—
Unisex/jeans shop	10.34	8.95	—	—
Books and stationery	9.49	9.06	—	—
Restaurant with liquor	—	—	7.59	8.50
Beauty	—	—	10.27	10.62
Medical/dental	—	—	9.32	10.39
Restaurant without liquor	—	—	7.59	9.23
Cleaners and dyers	—	—	—	12.57
Supermarket (over 6,000 sq. ft.)	—	—	—	1.51
Drugstore	—	—	—	3.88
Videotape rentals	—	—	—	12.61

Source: *Dollars & Cents of Shopping Centers: 1987* (ULI—the Urban Land Institute, 1987, 1200 18th St. NW, Washington, DC 20036).

FIGURE 10–3
Facilities' cost (total charges as a percentage of sales) for various types of retailers at different types of malls

assuming the role of anchors as a result of their ability to generate high traffic volumes and attract consumers from considerable distances. Equally important is the collection of specialty stores that complete the tenant mix. Each developer must find the right blend of (1) general-merchandise lines (e.g., apparel, shoes, gifts, food); (2) pricing points (e.g., exclusive, upper, middle, value); (3) lifestyles and demographic specialties (e.g., Limited Express For Men, GapKids, Just Sweats, Banana Republic); and (4) national chains and local establishments. A recent trend in planning a center's tenant mix is to lease to temporary retail tenants. These retail alternatives include kiosks, pushcarts, showcase modules, and electronic catalog machines. For a limited time they add merchandise variety, marketplace atmospherics, and a sense of the unusual to the center's normal operational mode. Seasonal rental of vacant stores (e.g., Wisconsin Toy Company during the Christmas season) is also increasing in popularity.[17]

Shopping centers are designed in a variety of shapes and arrangements. A given configuration must conform to the site's terrain and the tenants' space requirements and cost restrictions, as well as provide ease of customer movement.[18] Any number of configurations is possible. Figure 10–4 illustrates four basic shopping center configurations. The "I" plan is the simplest and most common regional shopping center configuration (see Figure 10–4a). Although the "I" plan is efficient for retailer space requirements and customer movement, it does not create an interesting and exciting shopping environment.

For regional and super regional centers containing three or more major anchors, retailers can use either the "Y" plan (Figure 10–4b) or the "L" plan (Figure 10–4c). Examples of a modified "Y" plan include TownEast Shopping Center in Mesquite, Texas, near Dallas; Pompano Fashion Square in Pompano Beach, Florida; and Santa Anita Fashion Park in Arcadia, California. The latest Y-shaped mall is the 1.8-million-square-foot Forest Fair megamall in Cincinnati.[19] Tysons Corner Center in Fairfax

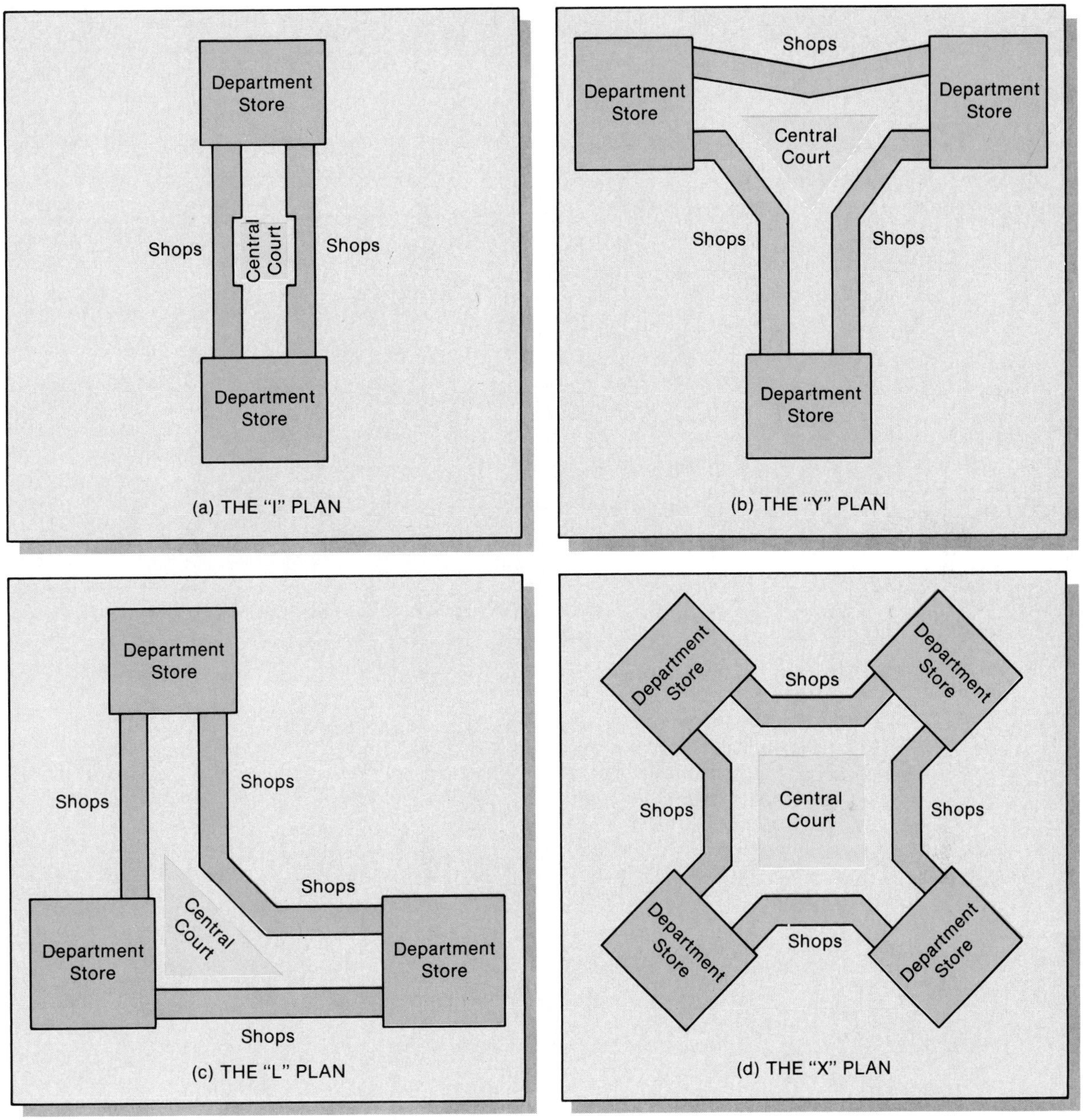

FIGURE 10–4
Basic shopping center configurations

County, Virginia, and the North Park Mall in Dallas represent modifications of the basic "L" plan.

The "X" (Figure 10–4d) plan serves as the basic configuration for the four-anchor, super regional center. The best example of this configuration is Crossroads Center in Oklahoma City.

Regardless of the configuration, a key feature of most super regional and regional shopping centers is the central court. Some super regional centers also have several smaller secondary courts, each with its own character and decor. The importance of

Large, central courts have become the focal point of activity for regional shopping centers.

Because of their socialization and entertainment value, food courts are becoming an essential part of every regional shopping center.

courts lies in their image-creating role. The central court is what consumers remember most often and most vividly. Hence, in recent years more and more emphasis has been placed on court design.

The third design consideration is the planning of mall areas. Mall areas are the center's traffic arteries; as such, they must facilitate movement and exchange of customers throughout the entire complex. The length and width of mall areas are prime considerations in planning for movement and exchange. To overcome the "tunnel effect" commonly associated with long mall areas, retailers have used several design features to create a more comfortable psychological environment.[20] The most common is a "break" in the mall approximately midway between major attractions, such as the central court; however, if the distance between the central court and each department store is too long, additional breaks may be required. Secondary court areas and slight angles in the mall that require shoppers to make short turns before they can see the remainder of the mall can be extremely effective in reducing the tunnel effect.

Besides customer movement and exchange, mall areas should facilitate shopping. Storefronts should give the consumer some privacy for window shopping without jostling from passing pedestrian traffic. On the other hand, some mall designs incorporate kiosks to create the festive, busy atmosphere of an open marketplace. These free-standing booths with highly specialized product lines (greeting cards, cutlery items, T-shirts, candy) and services (minibanks, snack bars, utility cashiers) add a new dimension to the mall's shopping atmosphere and contribute substantially to profitability.

Community and Neighborhood Shopping Centers

Community and neighborhood shopping centers serve the respective market areas that their names suggest. The **neighborhood shopping center** obtains its customers from one or a few neighborhoods within the immediate vicinity. Its trading area can be roughly defined as the area within a five-minute drive of the center, containing anywhere from 7,000 to 50,000 potential customers. The **community shopping center** serves a composite of many neighborhoods within a 10- to 15-minute drive from the center. The number of potential customers within its trading area ranges from 20,000

Kiosks add to a mall's atmosphere and can be highly profitable retail operations.

RETAIL STRATEGIES AND TACTICS

Megamalls: Retailing Juggernauts or Modern Dinosaurs?

Megamalls, supermalls, or the eighth and ninth wonders of the world, whatever they are called, are huge: two to five times the size of a regional mall. The largest of these mammoth structures is the West Edmonton Mall in Edmonton, Alberta. With 5.2 million square feet of retail space, this Canadian mall stretches for eight city blocks. Attracting visitors from all over Canada, the United States, and the world, this retailing juggernaut is composed of a wide variety of traditional and not-so-traditional stores and activities, including:

- 825 convenience, shopping, and specialty store retailers
- 11 department stores
- 2 auto dealerships
- 132 restaurants
- 32 movie theaters
- A 5-acre waterpark with 22 water slides
- The world's largest indoor amusement park with roller coaster
- An 18-hole miniature golf course patterned after Pebble Beach
- An ice-skating rink
- An underground lake
- A bingo parlor
- A medieval torture chamber
- Fantasyland Hotel, with 120 theme rooms
- Marketplace Chapel
- An 80-foot replica of the Santa Maria
- A miniature Bourbon Street
- 4 submarines
- 16 doctors
- Sharks, dolphins, flamingos, jaguars, and alligators
- Golf cart and rickshaw transportation
- Free parking

The Mall of America, currently under construction in Bloomington, Minnesota, will be the largest mall in the United States, with 4.2 million square feet, 2.6 million square feet of which will be devoted to retailing. Bloomingdale's, Nordstrom, Macy's, and Carson Pirie Scott are four of the eight department stores that will anchor the mall. The mixed-use tenant mix will include 600 to 800 specialty stores, 18 theaters, a health club, restaurants, nightclubs, 3 hotels, and a 300,000-square-foot indoor theme family entertainment park. Knott's Camp Snoopy will be built in the center of the mall, with retail shops surrounding it on all sides; the park will have 16 rides and attractions, including a roller coaster, carousel, water flume and chair swing rides, a children's train, and a ferris wheel. Live entertainment, a craft center, and a wilderness theater are also part of the theme park. The trading area of the Mall of America is expected to reach a 200-to-300-mile radius because of the total attraction package offered by the mixed-use tenant mix.

Sources: Based on Joe Queenan, "Will Wonders Never Cease?", *Forbes,* September 4, 1989, 72–73, 76; Eric C. Peterson, "Regional Growth Prospects," *Stores,* November 1989, 63–72; Joseph Queenam, "The Bizarre Bazaar," *GQ,* November 1988, 309–316, 361–363; "Mall of America," *Stores,* August 1989, 43–44.

to 100,000. The community shopping center in a smaller city serves the entire city and often competes with the downtown area.

The size of the market areas for each type of center is a function primarily of the center's number of stores and tenant mix. The neighborhood center usually has five to fifteen stores, with a supermarket as the principal tenant. Composed largely of convenience-goods retailers, the neighborhood center sells products that meet the daily living needs of its local area. With a GLA ranging from 25,000 to 100,000 square feet, the neighborhood center frequently includes a hardware store, drugstore, and various personal service retailers, such as beauty and barber shops.

The community center is considerably larger and more diverse in its tenant mix than the neighborhood center. Containing from 10 to 30 retail establishments with a total GLA of 75,000 to 300,000 square feet, the community center offers a wide range of shopping goods and convenience goods. In recent years, community strip centers have taken on a growing specialty look as more popular-price specialty retailers have moved to strips to avoid the increased costs resulting from upscaling of regional malls.[21] They are likely to be anchored by one or more mass-merchandising stores, most commonly junior department stores, discount stores, and discount department stores. Large food/drug combo supermarkets also are popular anchors for the community center.

A recent development in the evolution of the community shopping center has been the **power strip**, a clustering (planned or unplanned) of retailers next to or near major shopping malls:

> [These power strips] contain strong retail merchants, each being a destination-oriented shopping trip in its own right. Potential anchor tenants include off-price apparel merchants such as T. J. Maxx, promotional department stores such as Mervyn's, children's stores such as Toys 'R' Us, Kids 'R' Us, or Child World, major consumer electronics chains such as Highland Superstores or Fretters, home centers such as Home Depot, and occasionally deep-discount drug stores such as F&M.[22]

Category killers such as Toys 'R' Us, off-price retailers such as T. J. Maxx, and super-store supermarkets such as Finast often serve as anchors for power strips.

Depending on the number and type(s) of anchor(s) used, a power strip can be food based (e.g., large supermarkets), fashion based (e.g., apparel stores), hard goods based (e.g., toys and appliances), or some combination of these three orientations.

Power strips can range in size from 200,000 to 900,000 square feet.[23] Sixty to 70 percent of the space in the typical power strip is occupied by the large destination anchors. Most of the remaining space is leased by national specialty chains; small, local mom-and-pop merchants are excluded from the center due to the high rents. While power strips have destination-type retailers, locations near regional shopping malls are preferred to take advantage of the mall's drawing power. To some extent, power centers are parasites, feeding off the traffic generated by regional malls.[24] It is not unusual to find more than one power strip in and around a regional mall. The drawing power of this "retail mega-cluster" is tremendous and can dominate a local retail market provided the area infrastructure (e.g., adequate transportation network, easy ingress and egress, and sufficient parking) can efficiently handle the increased customer traffic.[25]

Specialty Shopping Centers

The **specialty shopping center** essentially is a cluster of specialty retailers that tends to be more focused in its target market. Offering many of the same features as regional malls, these centers range from 100,000 to 300,000 square feet with 15 to 30 specialty stores, boutiques, and service retailers. The largest store usually does not exceed 25,000 square feet. Specialty malls range from enclosed malls with a common architectural motif and decor to restored manufacturing plants, railroad stations, shipping docks, and warehouses. Quaker Square in Akron, Ohio, is a conversion of the original manufacturing plant and grain elevators of the Quaker Oats Company. Union Station in Indianapolis is the restoration of that city's old Union railroad station.[26]

Additional preservation and restoration examples include Cincinnati's West 4th Street, Denver's Tivoli Union brewery, Bullocks old downtown department store in Los Angeles, the Alabama theater in Houston, and Pioneer Square in Seattle.[27] "There's a uniqueness in converting properties that you can't get in building new properties. . . . Old buildings are especially interesting to young, upwardly mobile people because of their sense of nostalgia."[28]

This "power strip" is located near a major shopping mall and can readily intercept mall shoppers.

These are two views of specialty malls.

Another variation of the specialty mall is the *manufacturers' outlet mall.* These malls specialize in off-price merchandising by the manufacturers themselves (e.g., seconds, irregulars, packaways) and in other forms of discounting. This type of mall tends to be located "along an interstate highway between a metropolitan area and a resort community or tourist attraction."[29]

Specialty malls based on product category are still another variation of the specialty theme. HomeWorld, a home furnishings mall, currently is under construction in Scarborough, a Toronto suburb. The project combines retail, showcases, and home services.[30] These "one-type mission merchant" centers are in the growth cycle.[31]

EVALUATING SITE LOCATIONS

In this section, we discuss the site evaluation process in two phases. First, we examine several principles of site evaluation and how retailers use them to assess the value of alternative sites. Then we look at several methods by which retailers evaluate alternative site locations.

Principles of Site Evaluation

Several consumer-oriented location principles help retailers evaluate site alternatives.[32] Although there are no standard criteria by which all sites can be judged, the following location principles provide the necessary framework for developing practical solutions to the problem of retail site evaluation. These location principles are (1) interception, (2) cumulative attraction, (3) compatibility, (4) store congestion, and (5) accessibility.

Principle of Interception

The principle of **interception** concerns a positional site's qualities that determine its ability to "intercept" consumers as they travel from one place to another. Interception has two distinct elements: (1) a "source region" from which consumers are drawn and (2) a "terminal region" or consumer destination, a region to which consumers are drawn. Examples of source and terminal regions are residential areas, office complexes, industrial plants, business districts, and shopping centers. Any point between the source and terminal regions can be considered a point of interception.

RETAIL STRATEGIES AND TACTICS

Bal Harbour Shops: The Strategy Is Ultra-Upscale Specialty Retail

Bal Harbour Shops, the ultra-upscale specialty shopping mall, has been called a "self-contained Rodeo Drive." This bastion of chic is a unique collection of some of the finest fashion boutiques in the country. The garden setting is a green oasis of sour orange citrus, red bougainvillea, yellow trumpet trees, and silver buttonwoods, accentuated by flowing waterfalls and effervescent fountains. The natural atmosphere is designed to complement the leisurely shopping behavior of its wealthy clientele of tourists and local residents of the stylish village of Bal Harbour, Florida (with an average income in excess of $250,000). The exclusive nature of the three-level mall was part of the original design that called for a foliage screen between the mall and the surrounding streets. Its exclusiveness is further enhanced by its aesthetic sign control policies; illuminated signs are prohibited. Doormen dressed in Bahamianlike police uniforms ensure the security of the mall and its parking lots.

The mall's tenant mix includes many local chic fashion shops together with an invitation-only list of national and international labels. Neiman Marcus and Saks Fifth Avenue anchor the mall and are supported by specialty store complements such as Cartier, Charles Jourdan, Fendi, F.A.O. Schwartz, Gianni Versace, Gucci, H. Stern, Krizia, Louis Vuitton, Mark Cross, Ann Taylor, Banana Republic, Brooks Brothers, Polo/Ralph Lauren Shop, and Waterford/Wedgewood. An interesting shopping list might include:

- $450 DKNY jacket
- $1,000 F. G. Bodner tailored suit
- $1,800 20-inch, rhinestone-studded leather skirt
- $800 leather bag
- $4,500 solid gold eyeglass frames
- $46,000 automatic time piece
- $8,000 his and her matching mummy cases
- $165 vintage Batard-Montrachet, Louis Jadot
- $9.95 Sophia Loren salad
- Under $2—unlimited cups of coffee

Sources: Based on Georgia Lee, "Bal Harbour's New Breed," *Women's Wear Daily,* January 24, 1990, 8–9; "Bal Harbour Shops," *Supershuttle Focus,* Winter 1990, 6; press releases supplied by Bal Harbour Shops, Bal Harbour, Florida.

In assessing a site's interceptor qualities, the evaluator has both an identification problem and an evaluation problem. The identification problem consists of determining (1) the location of source and terminal regions, (2) the lines connecting those regions, and (3) appropriate points (sites) along the connecting line. The evaluation problem is one of measuring the magnitude and quality of these regions, lines, and points. Thus, the evaluator's problem is how to determine whether a site is an efficient "intervening opportunity" between known source and terminal regions. Another perspective of the vulnerability principle is practiced by Vidtron, Inc., which operates "drive-in video rental stores in shopping-mall parking lot kiosks. Vidtron feeds off the frustrations of customers who can't find the current top hits at larger video stores."[33] By carrying a large number of each of the top 40 movies, Vidtron avoids stockouts. By locating next to other video stores with greater variety but less depth of assortment, Vidtron intercepts and captures competitor business.

A different perspective of the interception principle often is expressed as the concept of *location vulnerability*. In this case, the evaluator's job is to determine the source of a competitor's business and then locate a site that will intercept the competitor's customer flow. If such a location exists, the firm's competitor is vulnerable in terms of location, at least regarding one or more source regions.

It is difficult to measure interceptor qualities because of the numerous potential source and terminal regions, connecting lines, and interceptor points (sites) along these lines of movement. Location specialists often use traffic volume as a surrogate measurement of interception.

Principle of Cumulative Attraction

According to the principle of **cumulative attraction**, a cluster of similar and complementary retailing activities generally will have greater drawing power than dispersed and isolated stores engaging in the same retailing activities. Retail location literature often refers to the cumulative attraction effects of the familiar "rows," "cities," and "alleys." In many large cities, certain types of retailing establishments tend to cluster in specific areas. Examples are the familiar automobile rows, mobile home cities, and restaurant alleys.

The evaluator's problem in this case is how to determine whether the retail operation can benefit from the cumulative drawing power of a site's immediate environment.

Principle of Compatibility

Retail **compatibility** refers to the extent to which two retailers interchange customers.[34] As a rule, the greater the compatibility among businesses located in close proximity, the greater the interchange of customers and the greater the sales volume of each compatible business.[35] Compatibility among retailers occurs when their merchandising mixes are complementary, as in the case of an apparel shop, shoe store, and jewelry store that are located very close to one another. If there are several apparel, shoe, and jewelry stores located in the same cluster, all the better! Not only are they complementary, but they also provide a healthy competitive situation that satisfies customers' need for comparison shopping and thus offer greater customer interchange for the retailer. Sometimes shopping center managers reduce cross-shopping (i.e., customer exchange) because they spread "like establishments" (e.g., intratype competitors such as shoe stores) throughout the mall rather than concentrating them in one area. As a rule, good comparative-shopping opportunities benefit all concerned.

A high degree of compatibility is more likely to occur when the pricing structures of neighboring businesses are complementary. Other things being equal, there will be a greater interchange of customers between two high-margin retailers than between a high-margin and a low-margin retailer. Equally important in site evaluation is determining whether neighboring businesses are compatible. For example, an exclusive dress shop would be incompatible with a pet shop because of the odor and noise produced by the animals.

Principle of Store Congestion

At some point, the advantages of cumulative attraction and compatibility end and the problems of site congestion begin. The principle of **store congestion** states that as locations become more saturated with stores, other business activities, and people, they become less attractive to additional shopping traffic. This phenomenon results from the limited mobility of people and cars in the area. Retailers should have learned this lesson from the original congested CBDs. Although the excitement of the crowd can be a positive factor, the aggravation of a mob can be a limitation, discouraging customers from visiting the site. Thus, in the site evaluation process the retailer should estimate at what point the volume of vehicle and foot traffic would limit business, both in the present and in the near future. In measuring store congestion, the retailer should recognize that "the shopper's tolerance for retail crowding may differ across types of

Generally, the greater the compatibility among businesses located in close proximity, the greater the interchange of customers.

retail establishments (for example, discount stores versus department stores) and shopping times (for example, Christmas season, weekends, lunch hour)."[36]

Principle of Accessibility

Perhaps the most basic of site evaluation principles, the principle of **accessibility** states that the more easily potential consumers can approach, enter, traverse, and exit a site, the more likely they will be to visit the site to shop. Accessibility is a function of both physical and psychological dimensions. The physical dimensions of accessibility are tangible site attributes that either facilitate or hinder the actual physical movement of potential consumers in, through, or out of the site. Psychological dimensions of accessibility include how potential customers *perceive* the ease of movement toward and away from a site. If consumers believe that it is difficult, dangerous, or inconvenient to enter a site, a psychological barrier equal to any physical barrier has been created. Retailers should consider both real and apparent barriers to accessibility.

Number of Traffic Arteries. The number of traffic arteries adjacent to a site has a profound effect on the consumer's ability to approach and enter the site. Other things being equal, a corner site that is approachable from two traffic arteries is more accessible than a site served by a single traffic artery. Not all traffic arteries are equal, though. Major thoroughfares provide greater accessibility to trading areas than secondary, feeder, or side streets. Because their function is to provide access for local traffic, side streets are of less value to retailers.

Number of Traffic Lanes. The more lanes in a traffic artery, the more accessible the site located on this artery. Multilane arteries are the consumer's first choice in selecting routes for most planned shopping trips. Multilanes often reduce the consumer's access to a site, however, especially in the case of left turns. Given some drivers' reluctance to turn left across traffic, wide roads create a psychological barrier, especially when consumers must cross two or more lanes of oncoming traffic. In essence, multilanes increase consumers' perceived risks.

Directional Flow of Traffic Arteries. The accessibility of any site is enhanced if the site is directly accessible from all possible directions. Any reduction in the number of directions from which the site can be approached has an adverse effect on accessibility.

Usually several traffic arteries adjacent to the site enhance accessibility. The location analyst should examine local maps to determine directional biases.

Number of Intersections. The number of intersections in the site's general vicinity has both positive and negative effects on accessibility. A large number of intersections offers consumers more ways to approach a site but may also reduce accessibility because of slower speeds and increased risk of accidents. Where intersections are plentiful, the role of traffic control devices (such as traffic lights and stop signs) becomes critical.

Configuration of Intersections. Consumers generally perceive a site located on a three-corner or four-corner intersection as very accessible because these kinds of intersections are fairly standard; consumers are familiar with them and with negotiating them. When there are more than four corners at an intersection, consumers often are confused by the "unstandardized" configuration. This "zone of confusion" exists across the entire intersection and presents the potential consumer with numerous conflict situations.

Type of Median. The type of median associated with each site's adjacent traffic arteries strongly influences accessibility. Some medians are crossable, while others are not. Generally crossable medians increase accessibility, although in varying degrees. Medians that provide a "crossover lane" are more encouraging to potential consumers attempting site entry than those without it. Crossable medians that force consumers to wait in a traffic lane until crossover is possible create a perceived danger. The driver often has to put up with horn honkers and fears being "stuck out there." This situation results in a psychological deterrent to the site's accessibility.

Uncrossable medians are both a physical and a psychological barrier to site entry. Elevated and depressed medians physically separate traffic, but they also separate traffic psychologically. Potential consumers traveling on the right side of an uncrossable median tend to feel isolated from left-side locations and become more aware of right-side locations, where access is substantially easier.

Speed Limits on Traffic Arteries. The speed limit on a traffic artery influences a site's accessibility, because it determines the amount of time customers have to make a decision about entering a site. Experts' opinions vary over what constitutes an ideal speed limit. The limit must be high enough to encourage consumers to use the route but low enough to allow them a safe and easy approach to the site. Most experts believe a speed limit between 25 and 40 mph is best.

Number and Type of Traffic-Control Devices. Of the numerous devices for controlling traffic, the most common are traffic lights, stop signs, rule signs, and guidance lines. In terms of accessibility, *traffic lights* are extremely effective at crossovers because of the protection left-turn arrows allow. Traffic lights may be more important for their psychological value than for their physical value. Consumers perceive retail sites with controlled crossovers as more accessible. "Free left turn" arrows are extremely important to site accessibility.

Stop signs are another major accessibility improvement, in two respects. First, the chances of creating consumer awareness of the retailer's location and product offering are higher if traffic "stoppers" force consumers to halt and look around. Second, stop signs help space the flow of traffic. Psychologically, these breaks in traffic are extremely important to the potential customer attempting to cross over from a left-hand lane.

Traffic rule signs, like speed limit signs, also influence site accessibility. Traffic signs prohibiting U turns and left turns can reduce site accessibility.

Uncrossable medians create both a physical and a psychological barrier.

Finally, one effective way to reduce traffic confusion and increase the actual and perceived safety and ease of entering a site is to use *guidance lines* (turn- and through-arrows and traffic lines) to direct traffic. Guidance lines are especially important at intersection locations. Any means of traffic guidance that tells the consumer how and where to go enhances accessibility.

Size and Shape of Site. The proposed site should be large enough to facilitate all four components of accessibility. Sufficient space should be available to allow ease of parking as well as turning and backing in and out without interfering with consumers who are entering and exiting the site. The shape of the site also can affect accessibility. The wider the site, the greater the exposure to passing traffic, thereby increasing consumer awareness of the retailer's location and activities. Finally, a site should be deep enough to allow ease of entry without interference from exiting traffic or other on-site traffic activities.

Methods of Site Evaluation

Analysts use several methods to evaluate retail site alternatives. Some of these methods are subjective, verbal descriptions of a site's worth; others provide objective, quantitative measurements. The subjective methods lack the qualities for good scientific decision making, while the latter methods require specialized skills and equipment. Certain methods, however, incorporate both simplicity and objectivity without the need for specialized training or equipment. One such method of site evaluation is the checklist.

The Checklist Method

The **checklist method** provides the evaluator with a set of procedural steps for arriving at a subjective but quantitative expression of a site's value.

First, the evaluator enumerates the general factors usually considered in any site evaluation. A typical list of factors includes all or most of the site evaluation principles: interception, cumulative attraction, compatibility, and accessibility.

Second, for each general factor the evaluator identifies several attribute measurements that reflect the location needs of the proposed retail operation. For example, interception, which is a key location attribute for most convenience retailers, can be divided into the volume and quality of vehicular and pedestrian traffic.

Third, each location attribute receives a subjective weight based on its relative importance to a particular type of retailer. A common weighting system assigns 3 to very important, 2 to moderately important, 1 to slightly important, and 0 to unimportant attributes.

Fourth, each site alternative is rated in terms of each location attribute. Any number of rating scales can be constructed; one possible scale might range from 1 to 10, with 1 as very poor and 10 as highly superior. To illustrate, a site alternative located on a major thoroughfare with a high volume of traffic throughout the day might be rated a 9 or a 10; another site alternative located on a traffic artery characterized by high volumes of traffic only during the morning and evening rush hours could be rated either a 5 or a 6.

Fifth, a weighted rating is calculated for each attribute for each site alternative. The weighted rating is obtained by multiplying each attribute rating by its weight. Sixth, the weighted ratings for all attributes are added to produce an overall rating for each site alternative. Finally, all evaluated alternatives are ranked in order of their overall ratings.

Figure 10–5 illustrates the checklist method for evaluating one site alternative for a fast-food restaurant. If, for example, the numerical value of 236 is the highest of all evaluated alternatives, from the standpoint of site considerations this alternative would be rated as the retailer's first choice. The checklist method has the advantages of being (1) easy to understand, (2) simple to construct, and (3) easy to use. In addition, it gives considerable weight to the opinions of location experts who know the firm and its locational requirements.

Quantitative Methods

Although beyond the scope of this book, several quantitative models can be used to evaluate retailer sites. Two of these are analog models and regression analysis.

Analog models are used to make sales projections for new stores based on the sales performances of existing stores. The chain retailer can approach the evaluation problem by finding the best "match" between the site characteristics of new site alternatives and those of a successful existing site. This matching process usually is quantified into a statistical model.

Ease of implementation is the principal advantage of an analog approach; however, this model suffers from two important drawbacks:

> One problem is that the results are dependent on the particular stores chosen as analogs and therefore rely heavily on the analyst's ability to make judicious selection of analogous stores. . . . The second, and perhaps more important difficulty, is that the method does not directly consider the competitive environment in evaluating the sites. The competitive situation is brought into consideration only through the selection of analog stores.[37]

Regression models are a more rigorous approach to the problem of site location; hence, they offer certain advantages over checklist and analog approaches. First, a regression model allows "systematic consideration of both trading area factors as well as site-specific elements in a single framework. Further, regression models allow the analyst to identify the factors that are associated with various levels of revenues from

FIGURE 10–5
The checklist method

Evaluation Factor	Rating	Weight	Weighted Rating
Interception			
Volume of vehicular traffic	8	3	24
Quality of vehicular traffic	8	3	24
Volume of pedestrian traffic	3	3	9
Quality of pedestrian traffic	2	3	6
Cumulative attraction			
Number of attractors	4	1	4
Degree of attraction	5	1	5
Compatibility			
Type of compatibility	6	2	12
Degree of compatibility	7	1	7
Accessibility			
Number of traffic arteries	8	3	24
Number of traffic lanes	10	3	30
Directional flow of traffic	7	2	14
Number of intersections	7	2	14
Configuration of intersections	4	3	12
Type of medians	2	3	6
Speed limits of traffic arteries	5	3	15
Number/type of traffic-control devices	6	2	12
Size and shape of site	6	3	18
Overall site rating			236

*For definitions of evaluation factors, see the text discussion of site-evaluation criteria.

stores at different sites."[38] The basic multiple regression model for analyzing determinants of retail performance is expressed as a linear function (f) of location (L), store attributes (S), market attributes (M), price (P), and competition (C):

$$Y = f(L,S,M,P,C)$$

SELECTING SITE LOCATIONS

The final selection of a retail site is essentially a process of elimination. By analyzing regional and local markets, assessing retail trading areas, and appraising retail site locations, the range of choices has been narrowed to site alternatives consistent with the firm's objectives, operations, and future expectations. If markets, trading areas, and sites have all been carefully evaluated, the retailer should be able to arrive at the final location decision. Normally the retailer will select not the optimal location but a compromise location that has most of the desirable attributes.

In the end, no steps, procedures, or models can totally quantify the final site selection process. Nevertheless, with the data generated and the analysis completed in the market, trading-area, and site evaluations, the retailer has sufficient information to make a good site selection.

SUMMARY

To appraise retail site locations, the location analyst must determine each site's ability to interact with its trading area. The retailer's problem is how to identify, evaluate, and select a good site location.

The site identification process is the first step in appraising retail site locations. After identifying all potential site alternatives, the evaluator can initially screen each alternative in terms of availability, suitability, and acceptability. Retail site alternatives can be classified as either isolated or clustered. Isolated sites are retail locations geographically separated from other retail sites; normally they will not share customers with other retailers. The retailer that selects an isolated site is seeking to gain either a monopolistic or an operational advantage. Clustered sites are retail locations that are geographically adjacent to or in close proximity to one another. Normally they are capable of sharing customers with minimal effort. Two types of clustered sites exist. An unplanned retail cluster results from the natural evolutionary process of urban growth. It includes central business districts, secondary business districts, neighborhood business districts, and string/strip clusters. The planned retail cluster includes clusters such as regional, community, neighborhood, and mini-specialty shopping centers.

The second step in appraising retail site locations is site evaluation based on site evaluation principles and methods. Several principles used in the evaluation are interception, cumulative attraction, compatibility, store congestion, and accessibility. The checklist method provides the basic framework for making both subjective and objective evaluations of retail site alternatives. Quantitative site evaluation methods include analog models and regression analysis.

The final step in site appraisal is site selection. The process of elimination narrows the range of choices to site alternatives that are consistent with the firm's objectives, operations, and future expectations. Essentially the task of site selection becomes one of selecting the best location from several acceptable alternatives.

STUDENT STUDY GUIDE

Key Terms and Concepts

acceptability (p. 361)
accessibility (p. 378)
analog models (p. 381)
availability (p. 361)
central business district (CBD) (p. 363)
checklist method (p. 381)
clustered site (p. 361)
community shopping center (p. 371)
compatibility (p. 377)
cumulative attraction (p. 377)
interception (p. 375)
isolated site (p. 361)
monopolistic isolation (p. 362)
neighborhood business district (NBD) (p. 365)
neighborhood shopping center (p. 371)
operational isolation (p. 362)
power strip (p. 373)
regional shopping center (p. 366)
regression models (p. 381)
retail site (p. 361)
secondary business district (SBD) (p. 364)
specialty shopping center (p. 374)
store congestion (p. 377)
string/strip cluster (p. 365)
suitability (p. 361)
super regional shopping center (p. 366)

Review Questions

1. What three questions should the retailer ask in conducting an initial screening of site alternatives?
2. Why would a retailer select an isolated site?
3. What is the key to successfully revitalizing the central business district?
4. Compare and contrast secondary and neighborhood business districts.
5. What distinguishes a super regional from a regional shopping center?
6. Describe the four basic shopping center configurations.
7. How might a shopping center developer overcome the "tunnel" effect?
8. Compare and contrast a community and neighborhood shopping center.
9. What is a mini–specialty mall center?
10. Describe the site evaluation principle of interception.
11. Why is cumulative attraction important?
12. How does the principle of compatibility affect the evaluation of a retail site?
13. Describe the role of traffic arteries and lanes in determining the accessibility of a site.
14. What role do the number and configuration of intersections play in creating an accessible site?
15. How do the number and type of traffic control devices influence the accessibility of a retail site?
16. Describe the two quantitative methods of retail site evaluation.

Review Exam

True or False

_____ 1. A clustered site can be defined as two or more closely located retailers capable of sharing customers with minimal effort.

_____ 2. The key to successful revitalization projects is not so much the development of new and existing physical facilities as the creation of a safe and pleasant shopping atmosphere.

_____ 3. A major limitation of string/strip cluster sites is that they typically are associated with higher rents than those found in central and secondary business districts.

_____ 4. The community shopping center typically offers a wide range of both convenience and shopping goods.

_____ 5. A high degree of compatibility is more likely when pricing structures of neighboring businesses complement one another.

_____ 6. Because they have less traffic congestion, secondary streets generally provide a greater accessibility to trading areas than do major thoroughfares.

_____ 7. A retailer can substantially increase store accessibility by selecting a corner site where more than four corners exist at an intersection.

Multiple Choice

_____ 1. A retailer that uses an operational isolation strategy does so to achieve greater flexibility in
a. Site geography
b. Transportation network
c. Operating costs
d. Operating methods
e. All of the above

_____ 2. Strands of mobile home dealerships, new- or used-car lots, and side-by-side fast-food restaurants are all examples of
a. Mini-specialty malls
b. Neighborhood shopping centers
c. String/strip clusters
d. Community shopping districts
e. Neighborhood shopping districts

_____ 3. A _____ is a free-standing booth with highly specialized product lines and services located within mall areas of regional and super regional shopping centers.
a. Caboose
b. Mini-specialty center
c. Kiosk
d. Specialty court
e. Store front

_____ 4. The _____ is a planned clustered site that obtains its customers from one or a few neighborhoods within a five-minute drive of the cluster and contain five to fifteen stores.
a. Community business district
b. Neighborhood shopping center
c. Neighborhood business district
d. Community shopping center
e. Mini-specialty cluster

_____ 5. According to the principle of _____, a cluster of similar and complementary retailing activities generally will have greater drawing power than dispersed and isolated stores engaging in the same retailing activity.
a. Cumulative attraction
b. Compatibility
c. Store association
d. Store congestion
e. Accessibility

_____ 6. The principle of accessibility states that the more easily potential consumers can _____ a site, the more likely they will be to visit the site to shop.
a. Exit
b. Traverse
c. Enter
d. Approach
e. All of the above

_____ 7. The _____ method provides the evaluator with a set of procedural steps to follow in arriving at a subjective yet quantitative expression of a site's value.
a. Analog
b. Regression
c. Checklist
d. Question
e. Cluster

STUDENT APPLICATIONS MANUAL

Investigative Projects: Practice and Applications

1. Investigate the business vitality of the central business district in your community. Describe the general physical, cultural, and economic environment. What are the retailing strengths and weaknesses of your CBD? Characterize the types of consumers who shop there. What specific recommendations would you make to improve the shopping climate of your CBD?
2. Visit one super regional or regional shopping center and one community or neighborhood shopping center, and evaluate the tenant mix of each in terms of "com-

patibility." Map the type and location of each retailer in the cluster, and identify and explain examples of good and poor compatibility.

3. Select the fast-food restaurant closest to your home or school. Evaluate the physical and psychological dimensions of the restaurant's site accessibility. Provide illustrations to support your evaluation.
4. Survey your local retailing community and select three similar types of specialty clothing stores in three substantially different locations. Using the checklist method presented in Figure 10–5, assess the site location of each store. Justify your rating for each evaluation factor, and make a final decision as to which store has the best site location.

Tactical Cases: Problems and Decisions

■ CASE 10–1
The Limited, Inc.: Considering a New Location Strategy*

The Limited, Inc. has become the leading force in American retailing by offering apparel tailored to the tastes and lifestyles of fashion-conscious contemporary consumers. By positioning itself as the dominant specialist in the fashion apparel market through multiple retail formats and a state-of-the-art distribution system, The Limited has become one of the top achievers across all industries in the United States. A basic operating principle in the firm's pursuit of excellence is to offer the absolute best customer shopping experience anywhere—the best stores—the best merchandise—the best merchandise presentation—the best customer service—the best "everything" that a customer sees and experiences.

In the "quest for the best," The Limited currently is considering a new "cluster location strategy" that would group several or possibly all of its various retailing formats within one shopping mall. For example, within one shopping mall The Limited could create a store cluster composed of a (1) Limited store, (2) Limited Superstore, (3) Compagnie Internationale Express, (4) Lane Bryant, (5) Victoria's Secret, (6) Lerner store, (7) Sizes Unlimited, (8) Abercrombie & Fitch, and (9) Henri Bendel. Exhibit A profiles each of The Limited, Inc.'s retailing formats.

ASSIGNMENT

Evaluate the proposed cluster location strategies. As a location consultant, would you recommend it to the chairperson of The Limited, Inc.? Defend your recommendation. Assume the chairperson wants you to develop two different "cluster" prototypes; one for an upscale shopping mall in southern California catering to upper-income consumers and one for a typical middle-class shopping center in St. Louis. Support your prototypes.

*This case was prepared by Dale Lewison and Jon Hawes, The University of Akron.

EXHIBIT A
The Limited, Inc. retailing formats

Limited stores: Include stores in every major market, with an average store size of 4,000 square feet. The Limited specializes in medium-priced fashion apparel that complements the tastes and lifestyles of contemporary women 20 to 40 years of age.

Limited Superstores: A 10,000-to-20,000-square-foot, upsized version of a Limited store. Added to the extended assortment of women's clothing are men's and children's departments.

Compagnie Internationale Express: Offers the latest, most creative international assortment of sportswear and accessories designed to appeal to spirited men and women on the cutting edge of world fashion. Store designs and merchandise displays offer fashion-forward consumers age 15 to 25 an exciting place to shop. There are stores in most major markets, with an average size of 2,600 square feet.

Lane Bryant: With stores averaging over 4,000 square feet, Lane Bryant is the foremost retailer of women's special-size apparel—fashions for sizes 14 and up. The format's ability to supply special-size customers with attractive and fashionable sportswear, ready-to-wear, intimate apparel, and accessories has resulted in a pattern of continuous expansion.

EXHIBIT A
continued

Victoria's Secret: Offers an international lingerie collection, which provides contemporary women with imaginative, high-fashion, designer intimate apparel through retail and mail-order divisions. With stores averaging 1,900 square feet, the goal set for this division is to bring intimate apparel out of the closet and into the vanguard of fashion.

Lerner stores: Fashion-forward sportswear, coats, dresses, and accessories at popular and budget prices. With stores in every major market, and an average size in excess of 6,000 square feet, Lerner is the nation's largest specialty retailer under a single trade name.

Sizes Unlimited: Offers sportswear, dresses, and accessories, sizes 14 and up, priced below similar goods in most department and specialty stores. Offers a wide assortment of first-quality merchandise, nationally known brand labels, and private labels at prices that appeal to the value-conscious customer. The stores average 3,500 square feet and are found in most major markets.

Abercrombie & Fitch: A very traditional men's clothier with an outdoorsmen and sportsmen image. A&F is an upscale men's store with a unique fashion image.

Henri Bendel: Represents the best in international designer clothing and accessories. The store occupies a unique position at the apex of the fashion world (57th Street in Manhattan). It provides the ultrasophisticated customer with merchandise of incomparable style and quality. Henri Bendel plans to open stores in the top 40 U.S. markets.

■ CASE 10–2
Clemente Cleaners: Evaluating Site Accessibility

BACKGROUND

Clemente Cleaners had occupied the same location on the northwest corner of Johnston Avenue and Oak Park Boulevard for the last 27 years. Bart Clemente, owner and operator of Clemente Cleaners, originally selected the site because he thought it represented a convenient stop for customers commuting between Walnut Valley, a large suburb, and the central business district of Omaha. Customers could drop off their cleaning on the way to work and pick it up on the way home. The selection of the Johnston Avenue site proved to be one of the best business decisions Clemente ever made. For 27 years, Clemente Cleaners serviced the commuting public and enjoyed the benefits of a successful business.

Two years ago, the Metro Traffic Engineering Department made a complete study of the numerous traffic problems that commuters were experiencing during their weekday work trips to and from the central city. After considerable deliberation, a decision was made to convert two of the major traffic arteries into one-way streets. Washington Avenue was designated a one-way westbound artery leading into the central business district, while Johnston Avenue was designated an eastbound traffic artery out of the city (see Exhibit A).

While the realignment of traffic arteries marked the end of numerous traffic problems, it also represented the beginning of a substantial decline in revenues for Clemente Cleaners. Although the store remained reasonably profitable, many of Clemente's long-time commuter customers found it more convenient to go elsewhere.

Many of Clemente's customers from Walnut Valley frequently had commented on their satisfaction with Clemente Cleaners and expressed their potential support if Bart Clemente decided to open a second conveniently located outlet in Walnut Valley. Unfortunately, good locations are hard to find in Walnut Valley, but after a ten-month search, Clemente found a Madison Avenue site that he thought might be appropriate (see Exhibit B).

From his service records, Clemente determined that a large number of his former customers lived within one mile of the site. Most of these customers would have to pass the site on their shopping trips to Walnut Valley Mall and Eastland Shopping Center. Walnut Valley Mall was a large regional center anchored by Sears, J. C. Penney, and two large local department stores. A large discount store and a catalog showroom were the principal tenants of Eastland Shopping Center. In Clemente's mind, there was no question that the site's trading area contained sufficient business potential to support his proposed venture. What troubled him was the site itself. While the existing building was adequate for his needs, he would have to share the parking lot (eight parking spaces) with Robert's Florist. In addition, Clemente was somewhat concerned about the site's accessibility.

CURRENT SITUATION

Clemente's option on the site expires at the end of the month; hence, he has to make a decision soon. Having limited experience in site analysis, Clemente engaged the services of Professor Kristine Michaels, head of the marketing department at the local state university. Michaels agreed to investigate the site accessibility issue and make appropriate recommendations. She also agreed to address the issue of whether Clemente should exercise the rent, lease, or buy clause of his option.

ASSIGNMENT

Assume the role of Professor Michaels. First, prepare a written report on the pros and cons of the site's accessibility, and make whatever recommendations you think are appropriate. Second, prepare a report on the pros and cons of renting, leasing, and buying a location, and make a recommendation to Clemente regarding this issue. Be sure to provide adequate support and rationale for your recommendations.

*This case was prepared by Dale M. Lewison, The University of Akron, and Charles R. Patton, Pan American University.

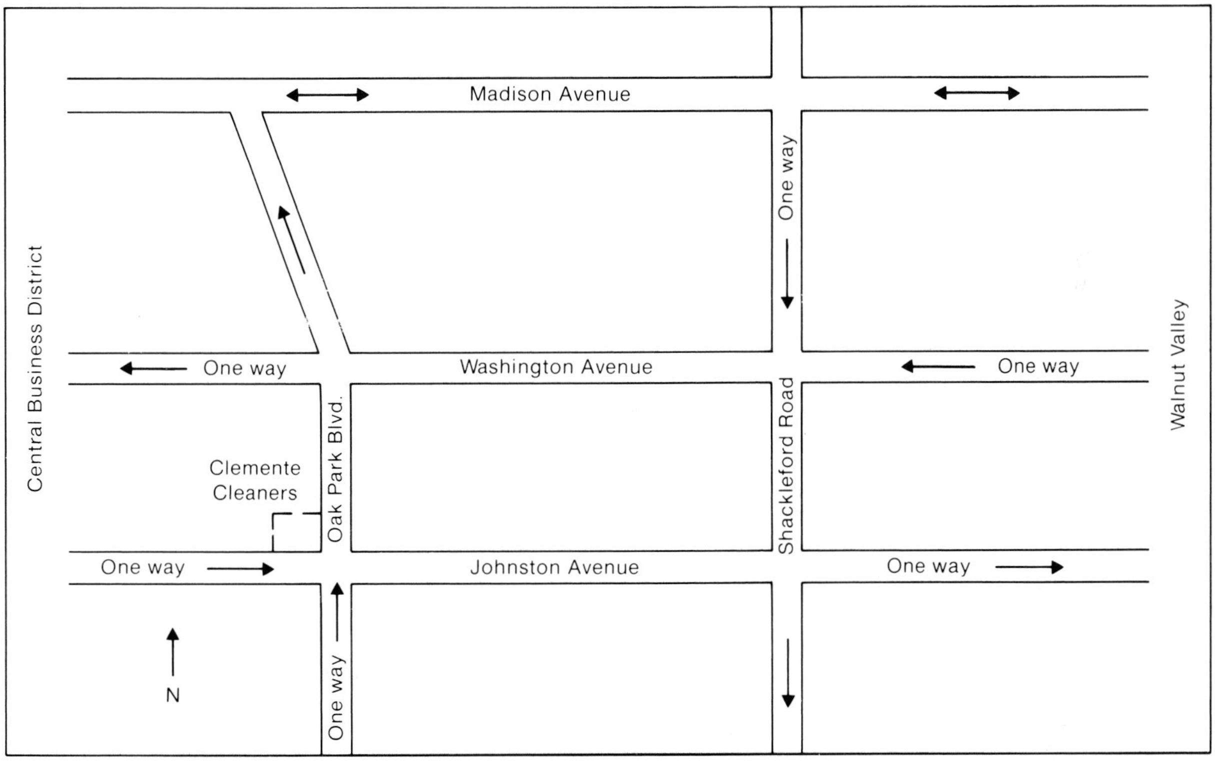

EXHIBIT A
New traffic artery pattern

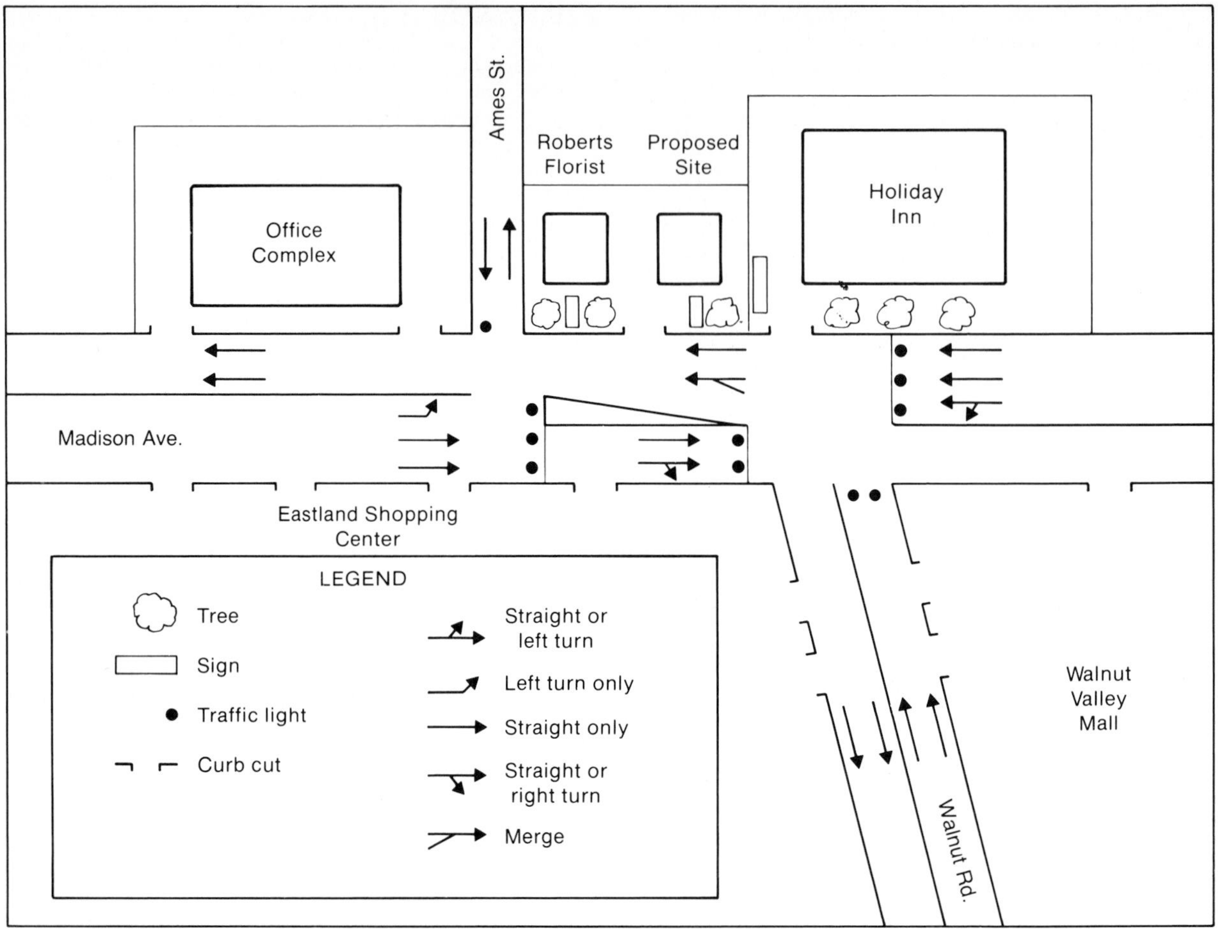

EXHIBIT B
The proposed Madison Avenue site

ENDNOTES

1. Mary Krienke, "In-Town Centers That Work," *Stores*, March 1990, 46.
2. "Entertainment Anchors: New Mall Headliners," *Chain Store Age Executive*, August 1989, 54.
3. Eric C. Peterson, "New Tools to Create An Image," *Stores*, September 1989, 42.
4. Jacquelyn Bivins, "Fun and Mall Games," *Stores*, August 1989, 35, 40–44.
5. Amy Dunkin and Scott Ticer, "Airport Shopping Gets an Upgrade to First Class," *Business Week*, March 6, 1989, 54.
6. "900 North Michigan Rises on Chicago Skyline," *Chain Store Age Executive*, April 1987, 30.
7. Joseph Weber, "Jim Rouse May Be Losing His Touch," *Business Week*, April 4, 1988, 33.
8. See Eric Peterson, "New Downtown Centers," *Stores*, July 1989, 58–60.
9. David Greising, "All That Digging and Still No Pay Dirt!", *Business Week*, April 30, 1990, 31.
10. Kate Fitzgerald, "Malls Toot Own Horns," *Advertising Age*, January 15, 1990, 57.
11. See Joshua Levine, "Lessons from Tysons Corner," *Forbes*, April 30, 1990, 186–188.
12. See Eric C. Peterson, "The 1990s: What's Ahead," *Stores*, February 1990, 73–74, 76.
13. See Eric Peterson, "MXD—Mall Excitement," *Stores*, January 1986, 144–146, 151–152; "New Focus Emerging," *Stores*, March 1987, 36–40.
14. "Building Up to the Year 2000," *Chain Store Age Executive*, May 1987, 44.

15. Ibid.
16. "Theme Centers Draw Multi-Market Customers," *Chain Store Age Executive,* May 1987, 98.
17. See Harold Carlson, "Leasing to Temporary Retail Tenants," *Journal of Property Management* (July-August 1989): 34–37.
18. See Eric C. Peterson, "Outlook on Design," *Stores,* October 1989, 23–24, 26. See also Eric C. Peterson, "Economics of Space," *Stores,* May 1989, 67–68.
19. See "Forest Fair: Super Mall!", *Stores,* April 1989, 38–39.
20. See "New Floor Enhances Mall Renovation," *Chain Store Age Executive,* March 1990, 80.
21. See "Retailers See Strips as New Options," *Chain Store Age Executive,* February 1989, 6A–7A.
22. Joan E. Primo and Howard L. Green, "To Mall or Not to Mall: Where Retail Opportunities Lie," *Marketing News,* February 15, 1988, 10.
23. See "At Issue: Over 'Power'ing The Strip," *Chain Store Age Executive,* October 1989, 29–31.
24. See Eric C. Peterson, "Power Centers! Now," *Stores,* March 1989, 61–66.
25. See Eric C. Peterson, "Strip Centers: Changing?", *Stores,* March 1990, 53–54.
26. "Wal-Mart Puts Indiana in High Gear," *Chain Store Age Executive,* March 1990, 78.
27. Kurt Anderson, "Spiffing Up the Urban Heritage," *Time,* November 23, 1987, 74.
28. Diane Schneidman, "Buildings Saved from Wrecker's Ball Enjoy Second Life as a Shopping Mall," *Marketing News,* February 15, 1988, 7.
29. Primo and Green, "To Mall or Not to Mall," 10.
30. See "Canada Centers: Overbuilt, Underanchored," *Chain Store Age Executive,* March 1990, 34.
31. "The Real Estate Connection," *Chain Store Age Executive,* January 1990, 35–39.
32. See Dorothy Sarantopoulos, "Successful Retail Site Selection," *The Real Estate Journal* (Winter 1989): 44–47.
33. "Drive-in Rental Stores a Fast Hit," *Akron Beacon Journal,* August 21, 1989, D4.
34. Richard L. Nelson, *The Selection of Retail Locations* (New York: F. W. Dodge, 1958), 66.
35. See Stephen Brown, "Retail Location Theory: The Legacy of Harold Hotelling," *Journal of Retailing* 65 (Winter 1989): 450–470.
36. See Sevgin Eroglu and Gilbert D. Harrell, "Retail Crowding: Theoretical and Strategic Implications," *Journal of Retailing* 62 (Winter 1986): 346–363.
37. C. Samuel Craig, Avijit Ghosh, and Sara McLafferty, "Models of the Retail Location Process: A Review," *Journal of Retailing* 60 (Spring 1984): 21.
38. Ibid.

OUTLINE

THE MERCHANDISING PROCESS

THE PRODUCT MIX

- Total-Product Concept
- Product-Mix Concept
- Product-Mix Decisions

PRODUCT EVALUATION

- Product Considerations
- Market Considerations
- Supply Considerations
- Brand Considerations

PRODUCT INFORMATION

- Internal Sources
- External Sources

PRODUCT-MIX STRATEGIES

- Narrow Variety/Shallow Assortment
- Wide Variety/Shallow Assortment
- Narrow Variety/Deep Assortment
- Wide Variety/Deep Assortment

PRODUCT-MIX TRENDS

- Shotgun Merchandising
- Rifle Merchandising

OBJECTIVES

- Understand tactics used in developing a merchandise mix.
- Recognize retailers' need to market all of a product's dimensions.
- Understand and make the "which" and "how many" product decisions.
- Evaluate new and existing products and their effect on merchandising decisions.
- Acquire and evaluate sources of product information.
- Define and describe the various types of product-mix strategies.
- Discuss major emerging trends in the development of product mixes.

PART IV

CHAPTER 11

PRODUCT STRATEGIES

Planning the Merchandise Mix

PRODUCTS AS INTERPRETATIONS OF CONSUMER NEEDS

In the struggle for the satisfaction of worldly desires, the acquisition of clothes plays a big part. The summit of the dress world is that of the haute couture. Its roots go back to the beginning of history. The feel of good clothes on the body and the freedom of movement given by skilled cutting are pleasures which come naturally to the well-born, and once acquired by the ambitious, are not easily abandoned.[1]

Sir Hardy Ames

The trademark was a thing I wanted to obtain. I had a signature, but I wanted to create my own trademark with this signature. That is, I wanted that name to be not only a clothing signature, I wanted it to become a recognized brand name like . . . like Coca Cola . . . a product, you know, that would stand the test of time. And that product was the trademark, and now I've really created a brand name that never goes out of style.[2]

Pierre Cardin

At Liz Claiborne, Inc., they know their customer. She's about 35 years old and probably not a perfect size 8. It may not be haute couture, but outfitting white-collar women with average figures has a lot more potential. Claiborne exploited one of the most powerful trends of our generation . . . translating fashion trends into clothes working women could wear comfortably—stylish but not too trendy. . . . Her creations weren't avant-garde, but simple, updated interpretations of classics. "I always knew I wanted to design for the busy American woman."[3]

Liz Claiborne

THE MERCHANDISING PROCESS

Consumers patronize a particular retail outlet for many different reasons: its convenient locations, friendly personnel, desirable prices, and pleasant shopping atmosphere. The reason common to all customers for visiting a particular store, however, is the expectation of finding a product or a set of products that will fulfill some present or future need. In a general sense, fulfilling customer product expectations is what retail merchandising is all about.

Merchandising is the process of developing, securing, managing, and pricing the merchandise mix to meet the firm's marketing and financial objectives. The *merchandising process*, as illustrated in Figure 11–1, consists of five stages. The first two stages are concerned with developing the merchandise mix, which is composed of product strategies and service strategies. The retailer's concern here is to determine what and how many products and services to offer. Next, the retailer must procure the products. Stage 3 deals with the problem of buying and handling the merchandise mix, from where, when, and how to get products into the store. The fourth stage in the merchandising process is managing the retailer's inventories. To ensure efficient, profitable operations, the retailer must plan and control the inventory levels. The fifth stage consists of pricing the merchandise offering. Pricing decisions must address the issue of how much to charge the final consumer in order to achieve acceptable sales levels and profit margins.

FIGURE 11–1
The merchandising process

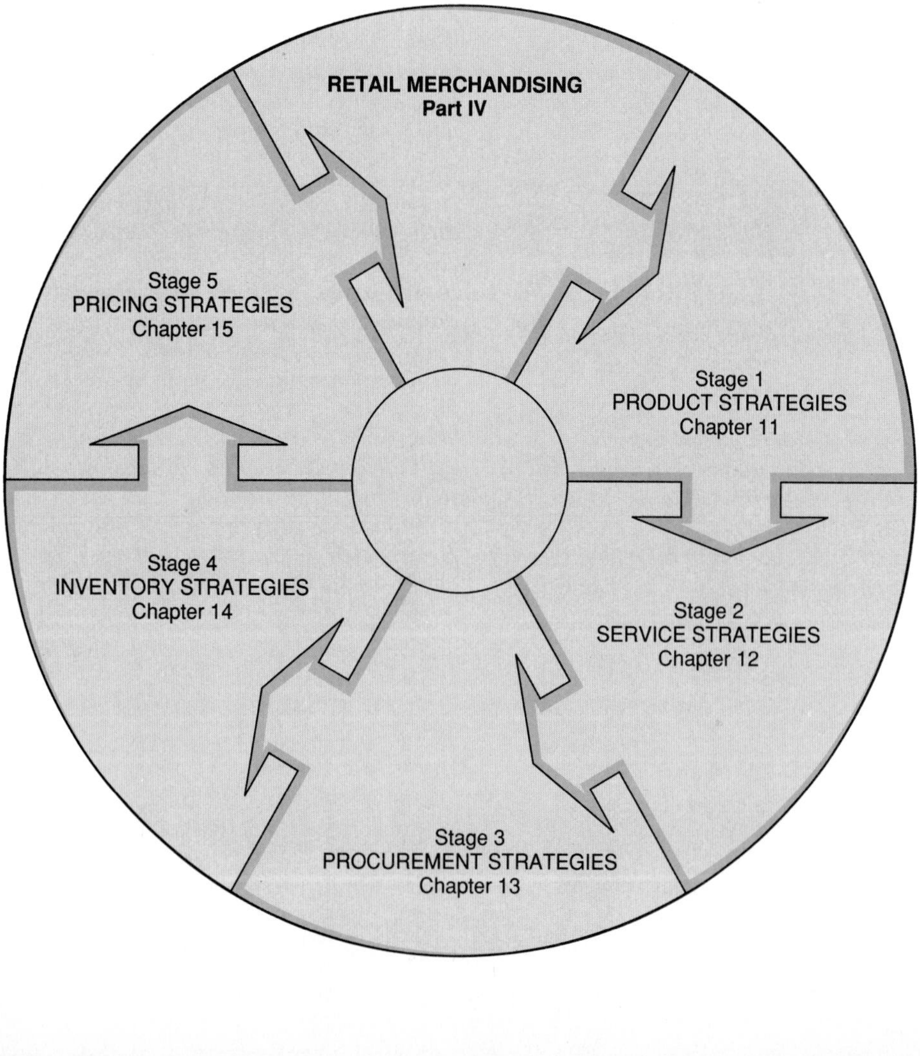

Developing the merchandise mix is a means for the retailer to segment the market and appeal to a select group of consumers. By buying, stocking, and selling a select combination of products, and by offering a certain level of services, the retailer can appeal to consumers of a particular age, sex, occupation, race, or income level, as well as to other demographic groupings. Likewise, the retailer can develop the merchandise mix to appeal to certain *lifestyles*—the "swinger," the "sophisticate," the "homebody"—or to certain *buyer-behavior patterns*—the brand-loyal consumer, the style-conscious consumer, the quality-minded consumer.

Equally important in the merchandising process is ensuring the firm's profitability. To accomplish this objective, the retailer must efficiently develop, secure, and control the merchandising process. The retailer should include in its mix products that contribute to the total profitability of the mix. To ensure profitable operations, the retailer must use a merchandise budget in which sales, stocks, reductions, purchases, markups, and margins are carefully planned. The final attempt to manage profitability is to control product inventories.

The entire merchandising process is examined in this and the next four chapters; the remainder of this chapter describes factors that affect product strategies. Chapter 12 discusses the retailer's service strategies. Problems in procuring the merchandise mix and their solutions are handled in Chapter 13. The inventory planning and control processes are treated in Chapter 14. Finally, Chapter 15 discusses the issues surrounding the establishing and adjusting of retail prices.

THE PRODUCT MIX

To develop product mix, the retailer must first understand what a product really is. The product is not simply some item of merchandise with certain physical and functional attributes; it is something much more complex. Before we discuss the concept of the product mix, let's first examine the total-product concept.

Total-Product Concept

The **total-product concept** recognizes that a product is more than just the tangible object offered for sale. Retailers that sell "things" will soon discover that there is no one to sell them to. To be successful, the retailer must act on the premise that a product is more than just the functional and aesthetic features; instead, it incorporates the various service features and psychological benefits conveyed by the product. In essence, the total-product concept acknowledges the need for retailers to market every one of a product's dimensions. The relationship among a product's many facets is illustrated in Figure 11–2.

A product's **functional features** include the tangible elements of size, shape, and weight, together with its chemical and/or biological makeup. Today, performance and fashion not only coexist, but in fact are quite dependent upon one another.[4] For example, athletic apparel must not only be fashionable but "offer benefits of qualities such as stretch, moisture-transport, and abrasion/wind-resistance . . . [and must be] lightweight, long-wearing, and easily washable."[5] Functional features are extremely important because they determine to a large extent how well the product will actually perform the functions it was designed to accomplish. If a product cannot clean and polish, or brighten and freshen, or cool and heat, then all other aspects of the product are severely diminished.

The **aesthetic features** of a product are elements that appeal to the five senses. If a product does not look, smell, feel, sound, and/or taste "right," its merchandising qualities have been substantially reduced or eliminated. Consumers have strong preconceived ideas about how a product should look, smell, feel, sound, and taste. Wendy's "Give a little nibble" advertisement, which asks the customer to taste the

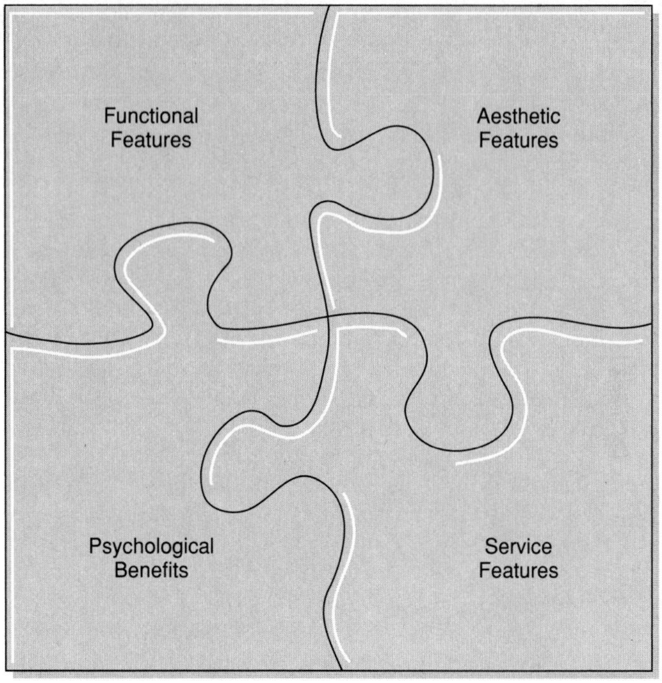

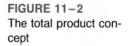

FIGURE 11–2
The total product concept

meat—Is it dry and chewy? Or hot and juicy? Is it bland or is it tasty?—is directed at enhancing the perception of Wendy's hamburger as a desirable physical product.[6] Laura Ashley, the British retailer, has made the English countryside the focus of her aesthetic appeal, "the clothes are affordable, feminine, and rural. Made of natural fabrics, they have flowing lines, wildflower prints, frills, and bows. The company sells lots of sweet dresses, high neck blouses, sailor outfits, and navy blue basics."[7]

Service features are "extras" that might include delivery, alterations, installation, repairs, warranties, returns, adjustments, wrapping, telephone and mail ordering, or any other service that consumers want for purchase satisfaction. A retailer must determine which service features are *required* for the purchase decision and which are simply *desired* by the customer as an added product dimension. These requirements and desires then are incorporated into the retailer's product-service mix. The surge in dual-income families and the corresponding rise in careerism should suggest to the retailer that time-saving conveniences are fast becoming a required, not desired, part of the total product offering. As the American family faces more stress and less time, the retailer wants to assist the customer in freeing up time by offering shopping services.[8]

When consumers buy products, they seek something more than the physical product: they expect to benefit in some way from the purchase. The expected **psychological benefits** that consumers derive from buying, using, and possessing the product are essential to the consumer's need satisfaction. Consumers buy products to be beautiful, safe, thin, comfortable, and noticed, or to gain prestige, recognition, security, independence, love, or a host of other benefits. Retailers that recognize that a product's psychological endowments are as important as, if not more important than, the product itself will have considerably more to sell to their customer than just a physical product. At Last, Inc. designs and sells sympathetically styled clothes for seriously overweight boys and girls; the firm recognizes that it is not selling clothes, rather it is selling self-esteem.[9] People don't want lawn and garden tools; they want nice-looking lawns their families can play on and their neighbors can admire. To paraphrase Charles Revson of Revlon Cosmetics: We manufacture cosmetics; in the store, women seek hope and the promise of beauty.

Product-Mix Concept

The first step in operationalizing the total-product concept is to develop the product mix. The **product-mix concept** refers to the full range or mixture of products the retailer offers to consumers. The product mix represents "appropriate combinations" of products to meet the specific needs of one or more identified target markets. The number of appropriate mixes is nearly unlimited. As such, success often depends on whether the retailer can identify and operationalize a *new and appropriate mix*. The Limited, in its new superstore format, is redefining its appropriate product mix to include children's outfits, accessories, lingerie, and higher-priced women's career wear.[10] In making product-mix decisions, the retailer must also recognize the degree of perishability of many products. What is an appropriate mix today might not be an appropriate mix tomorrow.

If the product mix represents "appropriate combinations," the obvious question becomes "appropriate combinations of what?" The answer is "appropriate combinations of product lines and product items." A **product line** is any grouping of related products. A **product item** refers to a specific product within a product line that is unique and clearly distinguishable from other products within and outside the product line.

Product Lines

Based on type and degree of relationship, product lines are often subdivided to facilitate the retailer's planning of a product mix. Products can be related in terms of (1) satisfying a particular need (e.g., health or beauty aids); (2) being used together (e.g., pieces of living room furniture); or (3) being purchased or used by a similar customer group (e.g., women's, men's, or children's apparel). The degree to which products are related also can vary greatly from a close relationship to a remote relationship. There is no single method of subdividing product lines, nor is there common terminology for subdivisions.[11] For illustration here, the product line is subdivided into three groupings: merchandise group, merchandise category, and merchandise class or classification.

A **merchandise group** is a broadly related line of products that retailers and consumers associate together according to end use. Examples of merchandise groups include such wide product combinations as furniture, appliances, home furnishings, housewares, apparel, sporting goods, food products, personal-care products, and automotive products. Single-line retailers often are identified on the basis of these broad product groupings (e.g., hardware store, clothing store). Mass merchandisers frequently use merchandise groups to identify operating divisions.

A **merchandise category** is a closely related line of products within a merchandise group. This level more clearly distinguishes consumer need, usage pattern, or behavior. Merchandise categories often correspond to the operating departments of a traditional department store and serve as a way to identify many specialty retailers (e.g., men's, women's, or children's apparel).

A **merchandise class or classification** is a specific line of products within a merchandise category; for example, sport and dress shirts within men's apparel, lipstick and eye shadow within cosmetics, and sofas and end tables within living room furniture. This subdivision is important because products within merchandise classes are directly comparable and substitutable. It is the level within a product line at which consumer *comparison shopping* occurs.

An example of a product's three subdivisions (merchandise groups, categories, and classifications) is illustrated in Figure 11–3. As shown, subdividing a product line is essentially a refinement process that helps simplify the retailer's problem of how to (1) target certain consumer groups, (2) allocate store space and locations, (3) develop efficient inventory control systems, and (4) create a unique store image.

Product Items

Within a product line, a product item is distinguishable by its brand, style, size, color, material, price, or any combination of these factors. A *brand* is a distinctive grouping of products identified by name, term, design, symbol, or any combination of these markings. Used to identify the products of a particular manufacturer or seller, brand is a common criterion in distinguishing both product lines and product items within lines. *Style* refers to the characteristic or distinctive form, outline, or shape of a product item. As a unique mode of expression or presentation, style can be the principal criterion by which consumers distinguish one product item from another (e.g., clothing). Products also come in various sizes. *Size* can refer to the product's actual size (e.g., 42-long or X-large) or to the size of its package (e.g., family size, 12-ounce bottle). The physical magnitude, extent, and bulk of a product not only are distinguishing features that influence the consumer's purchase decision, but they are also important factors in the retailer's decision to buy, stock, display, and shelve the product. *Colors, materials,* and *prices* are also important features in distinguishing one product item from another.

Product-Mix Decisions

In developing the product mix, the retailer faces two basic decisions: "Which product lines and items?" and "How many product lines and items?" A product is only "right" when it is right for all three merchandising activities of buying, stocking, and selling. If a product is easy to sell but creates extremely difficult buying and stocking problems, the retailer should seriously question whether to include it in the product mix!

This display in a men's wear department illustrates a merchandise category.

RETAIL STRATEGIES AND TACTICS

Category Management—A New Tool for Managing Product Lines

Category management is an attempt by retailers to focus their attention on product categories as opposed to individual brands. The goal is to manage a closely related line of products (category) by analyzing sales performance to see what improvements can be made in the product mix and to identify market niches not currently being reviewed by the retailer. Provigo, Inc., a Montreal grocery retailer, has realigned its buyers into a category management organization. Historically, the firm's buyers were responsible for all the products from a given manufacturer. Presently, each buyer is responsible for a specific category and works with all the vendors for the product category. Using both syndicated and scanner data, each buyer requires the vendor to forgo their own brand-specific sale objectives and merchandising plans and promotional programs that will differentiate and grow the merchandise category. Substitute sales (replacing Brand A with Brand B) is not an acceptable product strategy. Additional sales of the entire product category is the objective; the vendor that contributes the most to this objective is the vendor who is most likely to benefit the most from increased sales to the retailer.

Source: Based on Kevin T. Higgins, "Category Management: New Tool Changing Life for Manufacturers, Retailers," *Marketing News*, September 25, 1989, 2, 19.

Which Products?

No simple criteria determine whether a product line or item should be part of the product mix. The retailer must judge each product on its own merits relative to its particular situation. In considering which products, the retailer should ask the following questions:

1. Is the product consistent with our current and proposed product mix?
2. Is it consistent with the store image we want to portray?

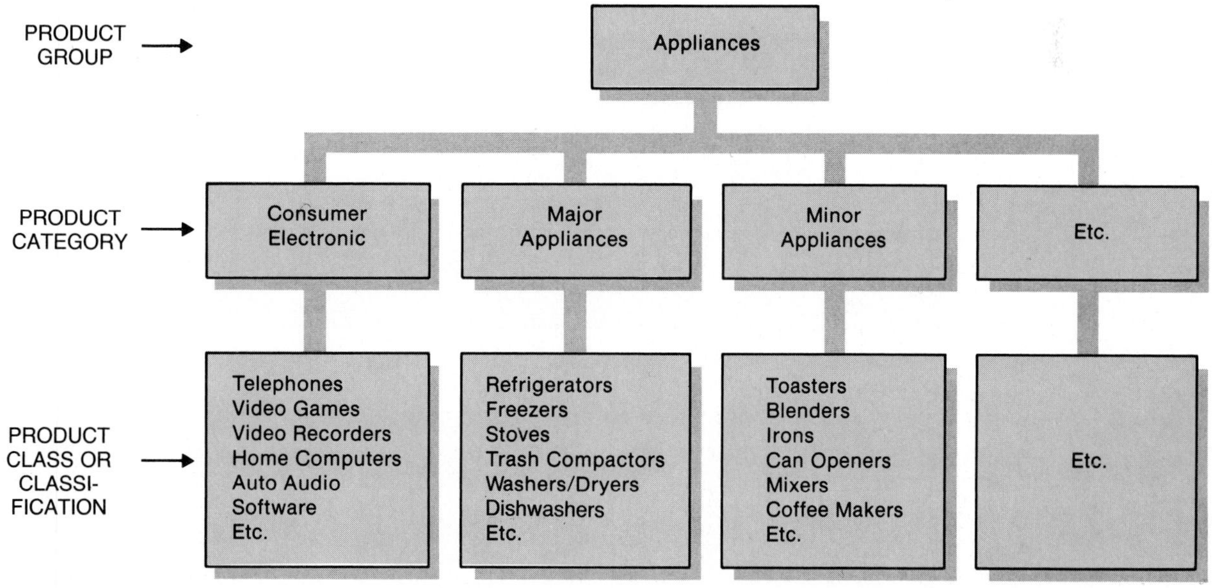

FIGURE 11–3 Product-line subdivisions

3. Will the product be appropriate to existing target markets or will it require the development and cultivation of new market segments?
4. What level of sales support does the product require in terms of personal selling, advertising, and sales promotions?
5. What is the existing market potential and what growth potential does the product have?
6. How susceptible is the product to demand cycles and the actions of competitors?
7. Does the product require new fixturing or specialized storage facilities, or can it be properly displayed and stored with existing fixtures and facilities?

How Many Products?

Another basic problem for the retailer is the number of different product lines and items to include in the product mix. The retailer should ask and attempt to answer the following questions to decide how many products.

1. Should we carry several product lines or specialize in one or a few lines?
2. How broad a selection (brands, styles, sizes) should we offer in each line?
3. How many different price lines should we offer?
4. Do we want a broad or limited market appeal?
5. Are there strong consumer preferences for certain brands and styles? If so, what are they?
6. What are the cyclical demand patterns (product, fashion, seasonal cycles) associated with the various product items?
7. What effect does an extensive or limited product offering have on inventory control and investment?

The how many products decision is two-dimensional, requiring decisions on both product variety and product assortment. **Product variety** is the number of different product lines the retailer stocks in the store. The retailer can engage in variety strategies ranging from a narrow variety of one or a few product lines to a wide variety encompassing a large number of product lines. **Product assortment** refers to the number of different product items the retailer stocks within a particular product line. Assortment strategies vary from shallow assortments of one or a few product items within each line to deep assortments having a large selection of product items within each line. The dimensions of the how many products decision are illustrated in Figure 11–4. (These variety and assortment strategies are discussed more fully later in the chapter.)

FIGURE 11–4
How many products?

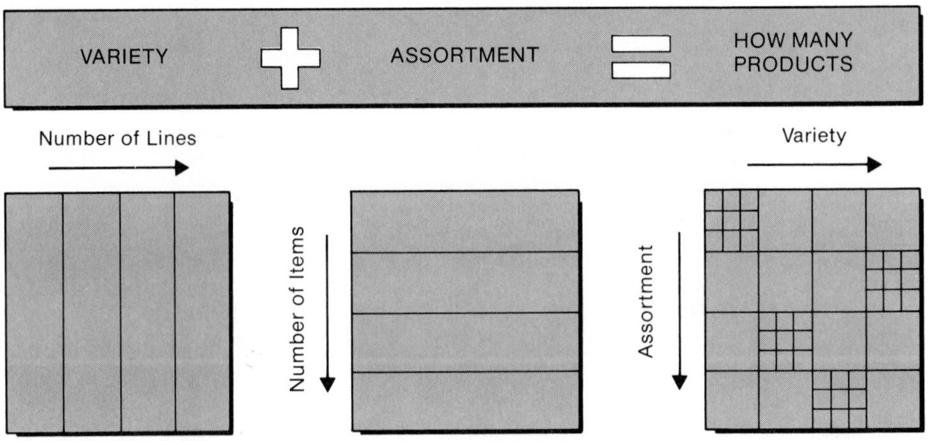

RETAIL STRATEGIES AND TACTICS

Why Liz, Not Cher, Joan, Julio, Mikhail, Herb, and Catherine—Selecting the Right Image

Why has Liz Taylor's Passion been so successful while other celebrity fragrances have failed to successfully capture the public's attention and patronage? Cher's Uninhibited, Joan Collins's Spectacular, Julio Iglesias's Only, Mikhail Baryshnikov's Miska, Herb Alpert's Listen, and Catherine Deneuve's Deneuve have images that are somehow not right for a perfume. In merchandising an intimate item, image is critical. "Elizabeth Taylor manages to evoke both awe and empathy in an audience unbounded by age, sex, or income. Taylor's struggles with weight control, substance abuse, and men have Liz more approachable and real. A strong bond is forged between Liz and women who are struggling with the same or related problems." On the other hand, Catherine Deneuve's stunning and icy beauty appears unapproachable and unreal; hence, it is not the right image for an intimate and personal product item.

Source: Adapted from Joshua Levine, "Doesn't Everyone Want to Smell Like Cher," *Forbes*, April 2, 1990, 142–44.

PRODUCT EVALUATION

Retailers continually are besieged with a barrage of "new" and "improved" products and must evaluate each of these products before making any product-mix decision. Some require more extensive evaluation than others. Retailers use three sets of criteria to aid them in making which and how many products decisions: product, market, and supply considerations.

Product Considerations

Product considerations are those criteria directly concerned with the characteristics of the product itself. The three product considerations are compatibility, attributes, and profitability.

Product Compatibility

In developing a product mix, the retailer should consider **product compatibility**—the nature of the relationship among various product lines and among various product items within them.[12] Based on the type of compatibility, retailers classify products as (1) substitutes, (2) complements, or (3) unrelated. The degree of product compatibility ranges from a perfect to a general relationship.

A **product substitute** is a product consumers use for the same general purpose as another product; it has the same basic functional attributes and meets the same basic consumer needs. A *perfect substitute* is a product consumers perceive as being essentially the same as another product. In this case, the consumer is totally indifferent about what product to buy and use. A *general substitute* is a product consumers perceive as being different from another product but that serves the same general purpose (e.g., Stove Top Stuffing instead of potatoes).

In deciding which products to sell, the retailer usually should avoid perfect substitutes. They divert sales from other products without adding anything in return. From the consumer's viewpoint, perfect substitutes do not even add the element of choice because a choice situation is unimportant. In addition, perfect substitutes complicate inventory control and increase handling costs. General substitutes present a different situation. For the homemaker whose family is tired of potatoes, the availability of a general substitute (dressing or rice) might preserve a lost sale (potatoes). General substitutes represent an increase in the selection a retailer offers consumers; as such, they can increase total sales.

The retailer must realize that many "new" products offered by manufacturers are often nothing more than "me-too" substitutes that add little, if anything, to the store's total sales. Whereas a selection of various me-too products is necessary for consumer comparison shopping, the retailer should review the product mix periodically to avoid an unprofitable proliferation of me-too merchandising.

A **product complement** is a product that is bought and used in conjunction with another product. A *perfect complement* is a product consumers must purchase because their original product purchase cannot function immediately or effectively without it (e.g., film is a perfect complement to a camera). *General complements* are products sold in conjunction with other products because they enhance or supplement the original purchase in some way. Apparel accessories that are color- and style-coordinated with a suit or dress are excellent examples of general complements. J.C. Penney's Mixit, a store-within-a-store concept, bases its strategy on general complements by featuring coordinated apparel for young women that can be mixed and matched with little effort.[13] Its Units specialty store chain, which sells one-size-fits-all separates in which every color coordinates with all other colors, is also based on the complement concept. Both perfect and general complements are highly desirable additions to the retailer's product mix because they often represent additional, unplanned sales beyond the original, planned purchase. Also, consumers tend to be less sensitive about the price of complements; hence, retailers often sell them at above-average markups. As a rule, the depth of assortment for complements is rather extensive, and the chances for additional sales increase when consumers have a great selection.

Unrelated products are neither substitutes nor complements, but retailers should seriously consider them for their product mix since they represent potential additional sales, theoretically at low risk and a reasonable profit. Some impulse goods fit this description. Normally, unrelated products are not stocked in depth; rather, retailers often follow a strategy of "creaming," stocking and selling only the best-selling items. (The process of item additions and line combinations are discussed later in this chapter.)

Product Attributes

The attributes of the product itself strongly influence which and how many products retailers stock. Four **product attributes** to consider are product bulk, standardization, service requirements, and required selling method.

Product bulk is the weight or size of a product in relation to its value. Bulky products usually require substantial space, both on the sales floor and in the stockroom, and often require special handling. If only limited space is available, the retailer may have to forgo stocking bulky products or limit the depth of selection. Furniture, appliances, lawn and garden equipment, and some home-improvement products are examples of bulky products. In addition, many bulky products typically are low in sales per square foot of floor space. In fact, some retailers have found that the space these bulky items occupy should be (and has been) turned over to more productive merchandise with higher sales per square foot.

Product standardization is the second product attribute retailers should consider in evaluating product attributes. Generally, standardized products fit into the retailer's routine operating procedures, whereas nonstandardized products often require special buying, stocking, and handling. Few products offer enough potential to the retailer to justify developing specialized merchandising skills. Unless the supplier is willing to make certain adjustments or provide considerable support, nonstandardized products should be excluded from the product mix.

Because products vary noticeably concerning *required service levels,* retailers should evaluate each product individually. If a required customer service (e.g., home delivery, home repair, or long-term credit) is not part of the retailer's normal service offering, the retailer should seriously consider the product's service requirements

Are these general or perfect complements?

before adding it to the product line. It is seldom possible for a retailer to add a new service for a new product line and expect that line to be profitable.

Required selling methods are particular selling skills needed to sell a product. Some products call for a personal selling approach, while others can be sold on a self-service basis. Generally, self-service retailers should not sell merchandise that requires personal selling. Likewise, an upscale retailer that stocks too many self-service items risks the prestige and product-quality image of the store.

Product Profitability

In determining the merits of a product, **product profitability** is one of the most important and complex criteria retailers use, since it can be expressed and measured in so many different ways. It is sufficient to state here that each product should make some contribution to profit; the contribution can be direct in the sense of per-unit profit or indirect by creating customer traffic and additional sales on other products.

Market Considerations

Retailers use market considerations as criteria to evaluate a product according to its compatibility with the retailer's markets and customers. Products should be examined relative to their life- or fashion-cycle stages, market appropriateness, lifestyle implications, and competitive positions.

Are tanning and yogurt a complementary product-service offering?

Product Life Cycle

Products pass through several stages in their lifetime, each identified by its sales performance characteristics. This series of stages is called the **product life cycle** (PLC). Knowing what stage a product is in helps the retailer judge both its existing and future sales potential. Also, the PLC stage suggests a particular retailing strategy. The four stages of the product life cycle are *introduction, growth, maturity,* and *decline*. Figure 11–5 illustrates one basic shape of the PLC as defined by sales-performance levels.

In the *introductory stage,* products are characterized by low sales and losses, high risk, and high costs. Many products never make it out of the introductory stage. Thus, the retailer's risks are high. On the other hand, when manufacturers invest heavily in advertising to gain consumer awareness and acceptance, and offer liberal returns and adjustments, the retailer's risk is substantially reduced. For many retailers, new products are essential to their avant-garde image and the necessary merchandising skill is to select only introductory products that are truly innovative.

Another consideration for retailers is that the manufacturer may decide to limit distribution of the product to a few *exclusive* or several *selective* outlets. Faced with this situation, the retailer must decide to get in at once or be shut out permanently. A retailer that stocks introductory products should limit selection to a few key items until primary demand for the product has been established.

FIGURE 11–5
The product life cycle

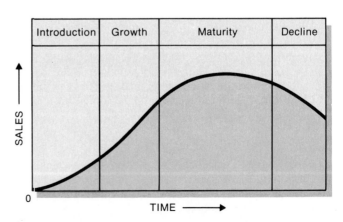

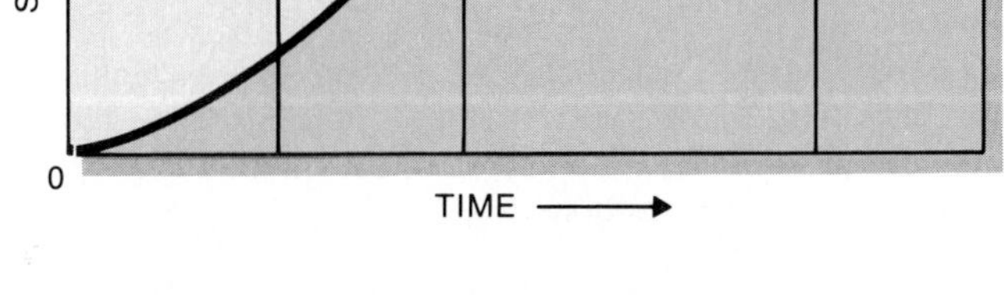

Almost without exception, the most desirable products for retailers are those in the *growth stage*. Products in the growth stage are characterized by accelerating sales, highest profit levels of any stage in the PLC, limited competitors in the market, and lower relative costs and risk. To satisfy the growing number of customers, retailers usually stock an extensive assortment of growth products. EPI Products, a company that positioned itself as a leader in unique, quality-driven products that rid women of everything from unwanted hair to tension, calluses to dental stains, has enjoyed tremendous success in getting prime space for its new product line by offering unparalleled in-store support such as videos, demonstrations, and large, contemporary point-of-purchase displays.[14]

In the *maturity stage*, sales increase at a slower rate and finally begin to level off. Characteristics of this stage are (1) a highly competitive market, (2) falling prices and margins, (3) more intensive advertising, and (4) lower profits. In most markets, video sales and rentals have already reached the mature stage of its life cycle. Mass merchants like Wal-Mart and K mart have begun ordering huge quantities of tapes . . . and selling them below $20 a tape, often as loss-leaders.[15] Most retailers should include or continue to include mature products in their product mix because consumers expect them. For example, blood-red and yellow power ties are yesterday's news; the sharp dresser today is wearing ties of eclectic patterns that look like impressionist originals.[16]

As a rule, retailers do not include *declining products* in their product mix. Normally, retailers drop these products, if they have not done so already, because products in the decline stage are high-risk items. This stage is characterized by rapidly declining sales and profits (or losses) and little, if any, manufacturer support in promotion. Retailers that continue to stock declining products should only do so in limited quantities and assortments and only if demand is sufficient to yield a reasonable profit.

Fashion Life Cycle

Style, design, and fashion are related yet different concepts. **Style** incorporates those special characteristics or specific features that distinguish one product from another of a similar type. For example, the specific style features that help to distinguish one skirt from another include length (floor, ankle, knee, short, mini), cut (wrap-around, accordion-pleated, bias-cut), and fabric (denim, gabardine, chiffon, seersucker).[17] Individual interpretations or versions of the same style are called **designs** (see Figure 11–6). Within a specific style, there can be many variations in trimmings, texture, decoration, or other details.[18] A **fashion** is a product that has distinctive attributes that are currently appropriate and represent the prevailing style. As illustrated in Figure 11–6, fashion is a style that gains some level and duration of customer acceptance.

Fashion is a sign of the times; it frequently reflects what a culture is feeling, thinking, and doing in all walks of life.[19] Figure 11–7 identifies some of the signs of the times for the last three decades. For the 1990s, designers have handed over the style reins to the general public.

> Consumers will individualize their styles, ranging from gothic to comfortable. *Vogue* says women should nix the term "aggressive" from their fashion vocabulary: "This is the new era of femininity in dress—of jackets with softer shoulders, of curvy tailoring, of a fluidity in skirts. Of dresses that show the body without grabbing it." *Vogue* also buried power dressing—"battalions of women done up like linebackers ready to rush the boardroom at Morgan Stanley." Rival fashion mag *Mirabella* also has unveiled its views on fashion in the '90s: "Relaxed uniforms are the new way to dress; mail order a great way to shop. Everything's lighter, simpler, faster."[20]

Major fashion houses frequently distinguish between their premium-priced collections, displayed at the New York and Paris fashion shows and sold to a limited number of wealthy clients (*high fashion*), and their classification merchandise, which is

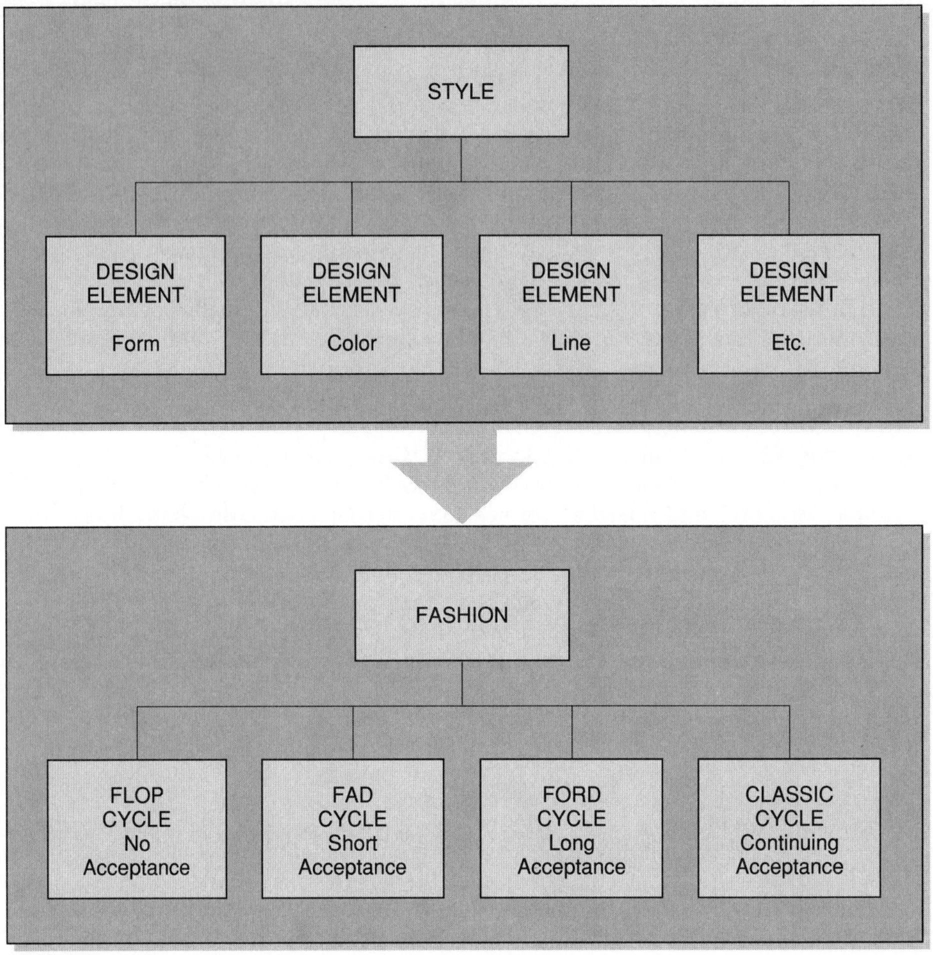

FIGURE 11–6 Relationship between style, design, and fashion

lower in price, with a broader appeal, and incorporates the features of last year's collections (*mass fashion*). Profits derived from classification sales subsidize the development of collections, which cast a premium halo over the classification merchandise, for which, in turn, a premium price can be charged.[21] Fashions represent great opportunities for retailers, but also substantial risks. Fashionable products include the following:

- High-margin items that can provide above-average profits
- Shopping and specialty goods that consumers will spend time, money, and effort to find
- Products that enhance the retailer's general image and help generate consumer traffic
- A means of distinguishing a retailer's operation from the competition

Fashion-conscious consumers may be characterized as follows:

- Oriented toward the social world
- Gregarious and likable
- Active participants in society
- Self-assertive, competitive, and venturesome
- Attention seekers and self-confident
- Aesthetic-, power-, and status-oriented individuals[22]

FIGURE 11–7
Signs of the times

1960s		
Woodstock	*2001: A Space Odyssey*	Ironed hair
Pop art	*The Sound of Music*	Nehru jackets
Psychedelics	*Bonnie and Clyde*	Love beads
The Beatles	*The Graduate*	Teased hair
Flower children	*Z*	Go-Go boots
Hair on Broadway	"Let the Sun Shine In"	Miniskirts
	"Strangers in the Night"	Dark eyes, pale lips
	"Moon River"	Pillbox hats
	"I Want to Hold Your Hand"	Prints
1970s		
Roller skating	*The Godfather*	Granny dresses
Disco	*The Great Gatsby*	Platform shoes
A *Chorus Line* on Broadway	*Annie Hall*	Message tee-shirts
	Rocky	Hot pants
	Butch Cassidy and the Sundance Kid	Designer jeans
	"Cabaret"	Punk
	"Send in the Clowns"	
	"The Way We Were"	
	"Losing My Mind"	
	"Killing Me Softly"	
1980s		
MTV	*Ghandi*	Men's wear
New wave music	*Diva*	Sweaters
Tina Turner	*Rambo*	The big shirt
Michael Jackson	*An Officer and a Gentleman*	Oversized silhouettes
Postmodern art and architecture	"Born in the U.S.A."	Stirrup pants
Cats on Broadway	"Flashdance"	Preppy
	"We Are the World"	Cropped tops
		Leggings
		Dusters

Source: Jeannette A. Jarnow, Miriam Guerreiro, and Beatrice Judelle, *Inside the Fashion Business* (New York: Macmillan Publishing Company, 1987), 47.

Like the product life cycle, the fashion life cycle is a conceptualization of the "life of a fashion." The risk associated with fashion products comes from the uncertainty surrounding both consumers' *level* of acceptance and the *duration* of their acceptance of the fashion. The fashion industry thrives on the concept of psychological obsolescence. A major driving force for consumers is the continual search for newness and the discarding of the old.[23] One management tool retailers use to reduce the risks of including fashion products in their product mix is the *fashion cycle*. During its lifetime, a fashion passes through three stages: introduction, acceptance, and decline, during which it struggles to obtain customer acceptance and customer adoptions.

Customer acceptance of fashion varies significantly according to level of acceptance (as measured by sales) and the duration of that acceptance (as measured by weeks, months, years). Based on the two acceptance factors, four types of fashion cycles occur: the flop, fad, ford, and classic (see Figure 11–8). A **flop** is a fashion cycle rejected by all consumer segments almost immediately. Other than for a few fashion innovators

FIGURE 11–8
Types of fashion cycles

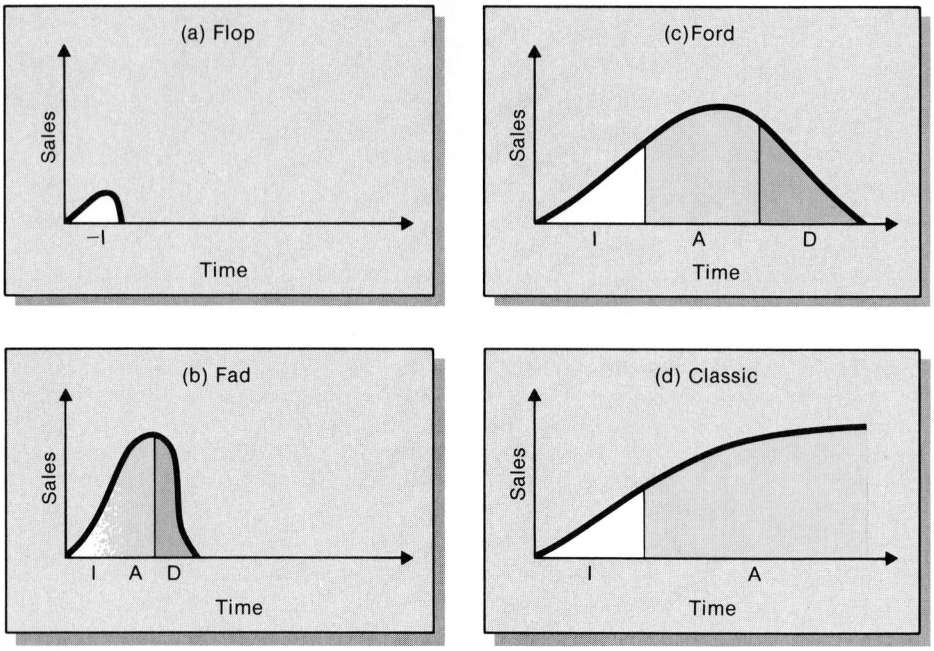

Key: I = Introductory Stage A = Acceptance Stage D = Decline Stage

who try and then discard the fashion, a flop gains neither a significant level nor duration of acceptance. Flops are fashion items most retailers hope to avoid; they not only represent the financial loss of obsolete merchandise, they also tend to tarnish the retailer's image as a fashion leader. Some flops are inevitable—they are the realization of the risks that go with fashion merchandising.

A **fad** is a fashion that obtains a relatively high level of customer acceptance for a short time. It is quickly accepted, but rejected with the same quickness (see Figure 11–9). Typically, the lifetime of a fad ranges from a few weeks to several months. Because a relatively large number of these items can be sold at substantial markups (consumers are somewhat price insensitive regarding fads) in a short period of time, fads are extremely profitable. They are also highly risky, however, because of the short duration of the cycle. To capitalize on a fad, the retailer must stock the item at the introductory or early part of the cycle. The sudden demise of acidwash jeans has been predicted ever since its odd, mottled hue first appeared in 1987; however, this fashion innovation has proven itself to be more than just a fad as it continues its status as a runner.[24]

A best-seller in fashion merchandising is referred to as a **ford**. A ford is also referred to as a "runner" or "hot item." Fords gain wide customer acceptance over extended periods of time. Because of their wide acceptance, long-term salability, and stable demand, fords usually are produced by many different manufacturers in a variety of price lines.[25] For the same reasons, nearly every retailer must include fords in the product mix or suffer loss of profits and loss of a fashion image. The miniskirt is an excellent example of a ford, lasting from 1965 to 1971; however, its reintroduction in the 1980s resulted in a fashion fad that soon flopped. Men's leisure suits are another example of a ford.

The "classic look," the "classic cut," and the "classic shape" describe a style trend that endures for many years (see Figure 11–10). The **classic** fashion has both a high level and a long duration of acceptance. Although a classic might undergo minor

FIGURE 11–9
Great fads of our time

How many do you remember? How many did you own? How long did you keep them?

Shmoos
Rubik's Cubes
Hula Hoops
Nehru jackets
Running
Pet Rocks
Puka beads
Love beads
Indian glass beads
3-D movies
The Lindy
Skateboards
Ankle bracelets
Coonskin caps
Telephone booth packing
Flubber (from the Disney flick *The Absent-Minded Professor*)
Slime (mutant son of Flubber)
Nautilus
Super Balls
Dickies
Clackers
Zoot suits
E.T.
Disco

Source: Adapted from Stephen Fried, "Summer Madness," *Philadelphia*, August 1983, p. 122.

changes, it essentially looks the same. The aging of the baby-boom generation has produced shifts in apparel demand. The fad orientation of the 1960s and early 1970s gave way to the "preppie look" in the late 1970s. This look has evolved into a new approach to dressing, consisting of classically styled pieces in updated colors and traditional items combined in innovative ways. The "layered look" and "investment dressing" are terms fashion-conscious people use to describe these classically styled items.[26] The classic, even more than the ford, is an absolute must in the retailer's product mix. The decision relative to the classic is not whether to stock it, but rather which price line to stock from which supplier with which product features. The pantsuit, introduced as a fashionable women's garment in 1966, retains a high level of acceptance in almost all market segments. It has become a classic fashion because it fits the needs and lifestyles of the modern woman, especially the working woman.

Several theories have been proposed to explain the process by which consumer groups adopt fashionable products. An understanding of this consumer adoption process provides the retailer with one more tool by which to judge the appropriateness of a fashion to the targeted market. The three basic theories of fashion follow.

1. **Trickle-down theory** hypothesizes that new innovative fashions and styles originate in the upper socioeconomic classes and are passed down through the middle class to the lower socioeconomic consumer. European designers (i.e., in Paris, London, Milan) are considered to be the usual origin for a given fashion cycle; however,

FIGURE 11–10
Trend or fad? Guidelines for assessing trends and fads

- A new product is more likely to be a trend if it is consistent with the consumer's basic values and lifestyles. New products which produce value and lifestyle conflicts are more likely to be a fad!
- A new product is more likely to be a trend if it promotes a voluntary change in behavior that is derived from customer satisfaction. Products which force a behavioral change (e.g., adoption of inexpensive products during tough economic times) tend to be more fadish in nature.
- A new product stands a better chance of becoming a trend if it can be modified or expressed in different ways by different people. Fads are more rigid (e.g., exaggerated, extreme, and impractical hairstyles).
- A new product is more likely to be a trend if it is based on a good underlying theme (e.g., physical fitness). Fadish products are often based on a specific manifestation or expression of a basic theme (e.g., fadish diet). Specific manifestations come and go and often are replaced by other expressions of a basic theme.
- A new product is more likely to be a trend if it is supported by new developments in related areas (e.g., nutrition, physical fitness, nonsmoking, and stress reduction). If a new product stands alone, it is more likely to be a fad.

Source: Adapted from "Distinguishing Fads from Trends with 6 Research Guidelines," *Marketing News,* January 21, 1983, 3, 15.

American designers are becoming the original source with greater frequency. Figure 11–11a illustrates and describes this theory.

2. **Trickle-up theory** states that some unusual fashions or styles are developed in the lower socioeconomic classes, picked up by the upper class, and finally adopted by the middle class (see Figure 11–11b). Blue jeans, the funky look, and the leather look are examples.
3. **Trickle-across theory** recognizes that a fashion or style can originate within any social class. Fashions and styles are marketed to opinion leaders within one or more social class levels; these opinion leaders are then instrumental in getting other members of the same social class to adopt the fashion or style. Hence, the fashion spreads horizontally through the population within the upper, middle, and/or lower social class.

Market Appropriateness

Retailers should evaluate new-product candidates on their chances for success in the marketplace, that is, *market appropriateness*—how well the new product matches the consumption and buying needs of targeted consumers. Several characteristics that serve as good indicators of how well a product might be received by the retailer's current and potential customers are relative advantage, affinity, trialability, observability, and complexity.

Relative advantage is the extent to which the new product is perceived to be better than existing products. A product that offers clear-cut advantages or provides a more satisfying benefit package is more likely to attract the interest and patronage of the store's customers.

Affinity is the extent to which the new product is consistent with the consumer's current buying and usage behavior. An emerging category of products are the so-called organizational goods, product items designed to tidy up the home, office, and any place else that requires organization. Hold Everything, a retail and catalog seller of organizing

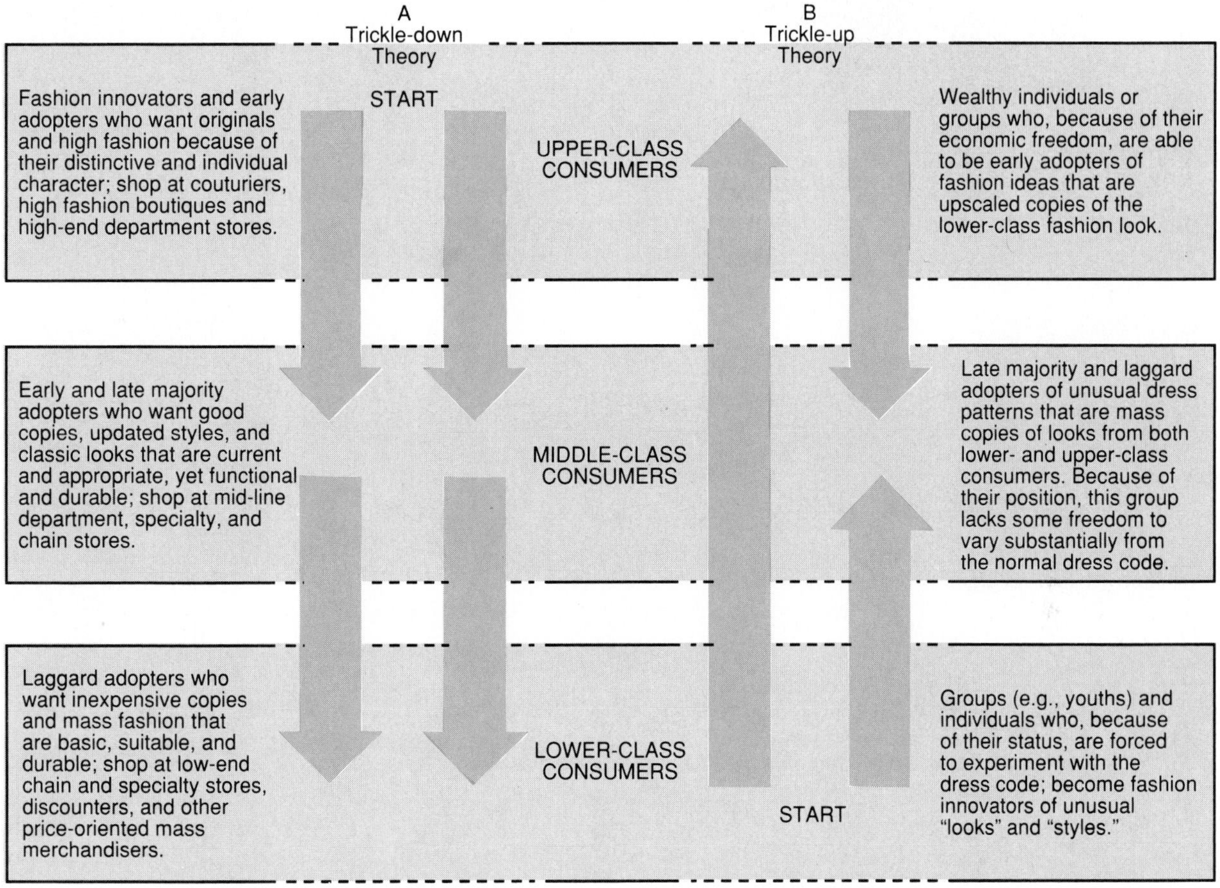
A
Trickle-down
Theory
START
B
Trickle-up
Theory
Fashion innovators and early adopters who want originals and high fashion because of their distinctive and individual character; shop at couturiers, high fashion boutiques and high-end department stores.
UPPER-CLASS CONSUMERS
Wealthy individuals or groups who, because of their economic freedom, are able to be early adopters of fashion ideas that are upscaled copies of the lower-class fashion look.
Early and late majority adopters who want good copies, updated styles, and classic looks that are current and appropriate, yet functional and durable; shop at mid-line department, specialty, and chain stores.
MIDDLE-CLASS CONSUMERS
Late majority and laggard adopters of unusual dress patterns that are mass copies of looks from both lower- and upper-class consumers. Because of their position, this group lacks some freedom to vary substantially from the normal dress code.
Laggard adopters who want inexpensive copies and mass fashion that are basic, suitable, and durable; shop at low-end chain and specialty stores, discounters, and other price-oriented mass merchandisers.
LOWER-CLASS CONSUMERS
START
Groups (e.g., youths) and individuals who, because of their status, are forced to experiment with the dress code; become fashion innovators of unusual "looks" and "styles."

FIGURE 11–11
Fashion adoption theories

goods, is enjoying rapid expansion because it appeals to the space-conscious and time-sensitive consumer who believes everything has a place and it should be in its place.[27] Products that require noticeable behavioral modification are often viewed by consumers as being incompatible with their needs. A product that is consistent with the consumer's beliefs, values, and experiences is more likely to gain customer acceptance and a faster and higher rate of adoptions.

Trialability is the extent to which a new product can be tested on a trial basis. All new-product purchases involve some risk to the purchaser. Anything that substantially reduces the risk improves the chances for initial and subsequent purchases. A product that can be physically divided into small quantities and given as free samples or sold in trial sizes benefits from good trialability. If division is not possible, demonstrations and guarantees can reduce perceived risks.

Observability is the extent to which the consumer can see a new product's favorable attributes. If relative advantages are easily visible and can be easily described to others, the new product's probability of market success is greatly enhanced.

Complexity is the extent to which a new product can be easily understood or used. Products that require the consumer to invest considerable time and effort to reap any benefits will involve greater selling efforts and a slower rate of consumer adoptions. With today's time constrained consumer, anxiety-free products without lots of fancy bells and whistles, and complex instructions are generally more appropriate. Consumers just don't want to squander their mental energy figuring out how something works.[28]

Would you categorize these fashion items as flops, fads, fords, or classics?

Lifestyles

A lifestyle is a pattern of living shaped by psychological influences, social experiences, and demographic makeup. Knowing targeted consumer's activities, interests, and opinions makes retailers better able to select products that are consistent with both the consumer's lifestyle and the retailer's image. Developing product lines in accord with consumer living patterns is referred to as **lifestyle merchandising**. This method of product evaluation requires the retailer to do the following:

1. Identify target markets based on consumers' lifestyles and their product, place, promotion, and price preferences.
2. Determine which lifestyle markets are consistent with the retailer's image and mode of doing business.
3. Evaluate which and how many products to carry based on their ability to satisfy certain lifestyle markets.

Many fashion retailers go to trade shows and producer markets looking for merchandise suited for their targeted consumers' lifestyle. One illustration of how retailers can characterize consumers' lifestyles appears in Figure 11–12. Using this lifestyle scheme and others like it, retailers can select, purchase, and stock merchandise that matches their target consumers' lifestyles.

> Looking for their roots, home has become Mother Ship for those affluent, ambitious, self-obsessed young babyboomers known as Yuppies. Homes and home furnishings are on center stage for this demographic/psychographic consumer group. Boomers who never baked a potato are buying industrial ranges with microwaves and restaurant-size freezers.[29]

"The Perfectionist"

- Age: 25–45
- Size: Misses 4–14
- A woman who is *first* in a fashion trend; has the most advanced taste of all customers—the "Fashion Leader."
- Active; worldly; career-oriented; involved; free-spirited; energy abounding.
- Inherently understands fashion . . . incorporates fashion into every aspect of her lifestyle.
- Uniqueness and individuality are her two main concerns—she depends on clothes as a means of self-expression.
- She is governed by her emotions. When in an adventurous mood, she seeks the most advanced fashions . . . always avant-garde, nonconforming, often impractical. When in a classic mood, her taste level is pure, clean, and sophisticated.
- She combines a mix of fashion looks to cover her variety of emotional and active lifestyle needs.
- She is extremely conscious of her body; chooses clothes to complement her figure.
- Demands and appreciates quality.
- Impressed by designers who style for her contemporary lifestyle.
- Not necessarily price conscious; buys what she desires.
- She is influenced by her surroundings when shopping.
- Does not respond well to markdowns or price promotions.
- Needs little salespeople attention.
- Expects new arrivals often.
- Buys impulsively.
- Loyal to a store wherever she feels her *mood runs free.*

"The Updated"

- Age: 25–60
- Size: Misses 4–16
- Desires fashion after it has been modified from its pure, advanced stages. Very often *this season's updated styles were last season's perfectionist styles.*
- Demands smart-looking items; stylish, yet not extreme.
- Working girl or woman; housewife; mother.
- Desires clothes that are functional additions to her wardrobe—multipurpose.
- Desires high degree of quality, practicality, and value for the price.
- Not necessarily label conscious.
- Will buy regular stock markdowns; responds only moderately to price promotions.
- Loyal to store that separates her look, supports her type, and puts her look together for her.
- Fastest-growing misses customer type.

"The Young Affluent"

- Age: 25–50
- Size: Misses 4–14
- Career woman, wife.
- Leads active social life; involved.
- Often attracted to designer labels.
- Ruled by current designer trends.
- Respects fine merchandise.
- Demands quality.
- Is an investment buyer; designer wardrobe builder.
- Taste level similar to updated customer, but not price conscious.

"The Traditionalist"

- Age: 26–65
- Size: Misses 8–20
- The conformist . . . likes fashion only after it is accepted.
- Less career-oriented; more job-oriented. Oftentimes office worker, teacher, housewife.
- Does not react to, or desire, fashion extremes.
- Extremely label conscious—loyal to those she has worn and liked in the past.
- Price conscious; quality aware.
- Very practical; demands ease of care.
- Very insecure about fashion in general—must have fashion put together for her.
- Fashion influenced by peers.
- Loyal to stores and professional salespeople who service her needs.
- Responds exceptionally well to price promotions and markdowns.
- Replacement customer; conservative taste.

"The Establishment"

- Age: 45+
- Size: Misses 8–20
- Older, refined woman—dignified.
- Active in community; holds prestigious position.
- An investment buyer; wardrobe builder.
- Loves fine workmanship, fabrics, and detail.
- Concerned with quality and value.
- Appreciates designer merchandise.
- Limitless buying ability.
- Seeks clothes that fill her needs.

Source: M. M. Cohn, Little Rock, AK.

FIGURE 11–12
Lifestyle merchandising

Competitive Conditions

To decide which products to include in or exclude from the product mix, the retailer must consider the competitive conditions under which the product is available. Two aspects of competitive conditions are type and degree of competition. Type of competition refers to whether the product is available to direct or indirect competitors. A **direct,** or **intratype, competitor** is one whose merchandising program is about the same as another retailer's. An **indirect,** or **intertype, competitor** is one whose merchandising program is noticeably different from that of a retailer of similar products.

A product that is available to direct competitors has no "distinctive" advantage to any retailer. In some cases, however, it might help a retailer to establish that the store's image is on par with its competitors', and therefore the retailer would want to promote comparison shopping. Adopting a product that is available to indirect competitors might either help or hurt the store's image. If upscale, indirect competitors stock the product, the retailer's image can be enhanced, but if downscale, indirect competitors stock the product, the retailer's image could be damaged.

The degree of competition refers to the number of competitors that are or will be stocking the product. **Competitive conditions** can be either **exclusive** (no competitors), **selective** (few competitors), or **intensive** (many competitors). Exclusive rights to a product offer several advantages. First, they help build an exclusive image by distinguishing the retailer's product mix from the competitors' mixes. Second, they permit greater freedom in merchandising products, since the retailer can worry less about what competitors are doing. Sears has exclusive product arrangements with the Walt Disney Co. and McDonald's, which are but two of the many exclusive arrangements Sears has initiated as it shifts emphasis from being a mass merchandiser toward a specialty retailer of exclusive products.[30] Suppliers, however, do not grant exclusive rights to their products without expecting something in return, so retailers must have a clear understanding of the requirements they must meet to handle the product exclusively.

Selective competition is generally not as desirable as an exclusive arrangement. For retailers that want some limit on competition but still need comparable products to facilitate customer comparison shopping, a selective arrangement is the best alternative. Retailers normally have little incentive to stock the product when there is intense competition; however, they are often forced to carry intensively distributed products that are readily available in competitive outlets because consumers expect them to be in stock.

The retailer's typical assortment strategy varies with competitive conditions. Retailers should carry a deep assortment of product items and a limited assortment of selective products. And, for intensively distributed products, retailers must resort to one of two strategies: (1) stock only the best-selling items to satisfy customers whose preferred item is not available and who will accept a substitute, or (2) stock a deep assortment to satisfy most customers and thereby create a store image of "complete selection."

Supply Considerations

In evaluating what and how many products to include in the product mix, the retailer should examine not only market conditions but also supply considerations, two of which are the *availability* and the *reliability* of the supplier.

Availability of Supply

Before making a decision to stock a product, the retailer should study the product's **availability of supply**. Following are four basic questions the retailer should ask:

1. Is the product readily available through the retailer's normal channels of distribution?

2. Are alternative backup sources of supply available?
3. Will the product be available on a continuing basis?
4. What are the terms and conditions of sale under which the product is available?

Ideally, for the retailer to make a positive decision on a product candidate, the product should be available from normal channels, with sufficient alternative supply sources, and under terms and conditions consistent with the product's sales and profit potential.

Reliability of Supplier

In deciding whether to include a product in the product mix, a retailer should also evaluate the **reliability of the supplier**. The ease of getting the product into the store at the *right time*, in the *right quantities*, and in *good condition* is a necessary consideration. Criteria that describe a supplier's reliability include (1) shipping on time, (2) filling orders adequately, (3) maintaining adequate stocks (avoiding stockouts), and (4) adjusting orders to meet the retailer's changing needs. (Chapters 15 and 16 regarding buying and procurement give further information for choosing the right supplier.)

Brand Considerations

What's in a name? A great deal! Most consumers rely on brand names to distinguish among the massive numbers of product offerings by competing marketers; in essence, consumers use brand names to help them define their product and store choices. Retailers depend on brand names to distinguish themselves from competing retail organizations and to develop a cadre of loyal customers. Assuming the retailers' name(s) and brand(s) are associated with positive images created by user satisfaction, the store can position itself on the consumer's quality continuum (i.e., establish a reputation). Although branding can be viewed from a number of different perspectives, this chapter examines brand considerations in terms of no-names (generics) versus name-brand labels and manufacturer (national) brands versus store (private-label) brands. Finally, this chapter examines the merchandising of licensed products.

No-Name Generics Versus Name-Brand Labels

No-name generic products are unadvertised, lower-grade, no-frill brands that are offered as low-cost alternatives to name-brand merchandise. These plain-packaged, starkly labeled products (i.e., list of contents) achieved record levels of sales during the high inflationary periods of the early 1980s. Generics are an expected part of the product mix in most supermarkets and drugstores. Therefore, the major decision is how many generic products to stock. Typically, food and drug retailers tend to increase the selection of generic products in stores located within market areas comprised of price-oriented consumers and during times of high inflation and economic recession when everyone's buying power is reduced. Given the somewhat questionable and unreliable quality of generic products, consumers tend to be more cautious with food than nonfood products; hence, the selection of nonfood generics can be increased with lower selling risks. A final consideration in developing the generic product mix is the belief of some experts that selling generics simply cannibalizes the sale of more profitable private labels and manufacturers' brands. Those who hold this viewpoint recommend keeping generic stock at "bare-bones" levels.

Manufacturer (National) Brand Versus Store (Private) Brands

Manufacturer brands are products that are produced, owned, controlled, and sometimes distributed by the manufacturer (e.g., Ford, General Electric, Kellogg, IBM, Arrow). They are referred to as national brands because many of them have countrywide recognition created through national advertising programs. The national status of these manufacturer labels creates the image of better and more consistent quality; to consumers they represent a known or a "sure thing" with little or no purchase risk.[31] Some manufacturer brands are in fact regional or local in scope and unknown outside their own area, and their quality may or may not be better than private label merchandise.

Store, or **private-label, brands** are items that are owned, controlled, merchandised, and sold through the retailer's own outlets (e.g., Kroger, Radio Shack, The Limited, and Sears). Historically, consumers often considered private labels as somewhat lower-quality, lower-status, and lower-priced merchandise, and many retailers directly or indirectly promoted this perceptional difference between house and national brands. For example, many department stores often stock the lower price points within a merchandise category with private-label items, whereas the prestige points are covered with designer labels (e.g., Christian Lacroix, Karl Lagerfeld, Geoffrey Beene, Calvin Klein, and Ralph Lauren) and bridge lines (e.g., Anne Klein II, Calvin Klein Classics, and Perry Ellis Portfolio). Brooks Brothers is the classical exception to this perception, and many department and specialty stores are emulating this traditional private-label retailer. For example, The Limited has made private-label merchandise a cornerstone of its strategy. Its private brand Forenza and Outback Red combined are the third largest in sales of women's apparel in the country.[32]

"The battle of the brands" (manufacturer vs. store) is a never-ending process. In every product category manufacturers and retailers are continually changing strategies in an attempt to find the right collection of products for their chosen markets. For example, in the cosmetic/fragrance category, national labels such as Chanel, Coty, and Revlon are expanding their retailer lists to include more chain drugs, more specialty stores, if for no other reason, to defend against the incursions into the fragrance/cosmetic business of Benetton, Victoria's Secret, and other store brands that are picking off their potential customers.[33] The which products (manufacturer or store brand) decision will vary considerably with the different retailers' individual merchandising formats; however, the retail manager should consider the pros and cons of stocking manufacturer and private-label merchandise (see Figure 11–13).

Licensed Products

A product's greatest asset is often the intangible benefits and psychological symbols associated with its name. **Licensed products** are items that are designed and sold through identification with a famous individual or corporate name, title, logo, slogan, or fictional character; the owner of the name, logo, or character develops contractual arrangements permitting licensees to use that identification on products they make and sell. Cartoon characters (Teenage Mutant Ninja Turtles), sports organizations (National Football League), corporate logos (Ford Motor Company), fashion designers (Yves St. Laurent), and celebrities (Baryshinikov Bodywear) are just a few of the licensed product categories the retailer can consider for inclusion in the product mix. Figure 11–14a illustrates total retail sales of licensed products by type of product, while Figure 11–14b portrays total retail sales by product category.

In choosing from the vast selection of licensed products, retailers and their buyers should be increasingly selective. The days of the almost guaranteed licensed product success have disappeared as the number of items has increased and their novelty has diminished.

Though licensed names with widespread media exposure can do very well, especially in the short run, most experts today recommend that a retailer evaluate licensed goods as it would any other merchandise, looking first for quality, design, price, and compatibility with current store image and consumer wants—with or without the name. If those criteria are met, sales can be greatly enhanced as a result of the extremely fast customer recognition factor and personal identification with the image

Manufacturer Brands	
Pros	**Cons**
Presold to target consumers	Lower gross margins
Lower selling costs	Selling restrictions
Attracts new customers	Pricing restrictions
Helps create assortments	Advertising restrictions
Enhances store image	Create more brand loyalty than store loyalty
Allows comparison shopping	
Private-Label Brands	
Pros	**Cons**
Greater price flexibility	Higher selling costs resulting from demand stimulation
Higher gross margins	Greater financial risk resulting from greater involvement
No advertising restrictions	Expanded buying and procuring responsibilities and costs
Enhance store and store brand loyalty	
Better product quality control through specification buying	
Promotes distinctive store and product image	
No direct brand competition	

FIGURE 11–13 Retailer's viewpoint: The pros and cons of manufacturer and private-label brands

projected by the licensed name. Thus, for example, though the licensed Coca-Cola clothing line has enjoyed enormous retail success, retail executives attribute its popularity primarily to its quality, stylishness, and reasonable price. The Coke example also illustrates the principle that retailers should look for an appropriate marriage between name and product; Coca-Cola's casual, good-times, active image, and lifestyle associations provide an exceptional match with its licensed line of beach towels, sweatshirts, and other active wear. For instance, the name Dr. Scholl's makes sense for hosiery, foot baths, or shoes, but it doesn't make sense for mugs or beach towels. On the other hand, for beach towels or coolers, and so on, it does make sense to go to a property like Coppertone.[34]

Despite retailers' best efforts to carry in their stores only the right mix of licensed lines, the enormity of the product selection and the basic uncertainty of exactly which licensed names will catch on make these choices very difficult. The desire of some image-conscious retailers to be the first in an area to merchandise hot new licenses adds additional pressure by emphasizing quick decisions. In response to these problems, some large department stores test market a licensed product or product line in a few stores before deciding whether to carry it throughout the entire chain.

Another problem to consider when choosing which licenses to carry is the often accelerated product life cycles of licensed goods. The retailer must be especially alert to timing the introduction and discontinuation of sales of a licensed product line. Many licensed products, such as designer clothing and Disney items, remain strong sellers for years, but others (e.g., those tied to currently popular celebrity names or one-time events like Halley's comet) can have sales that peak within months and then fall precipitously.

Several other licensing strategies are also available. One is called *direct licensing*, in which a retailer (usually a large chain) signs an exclusive agreement to carry licensed

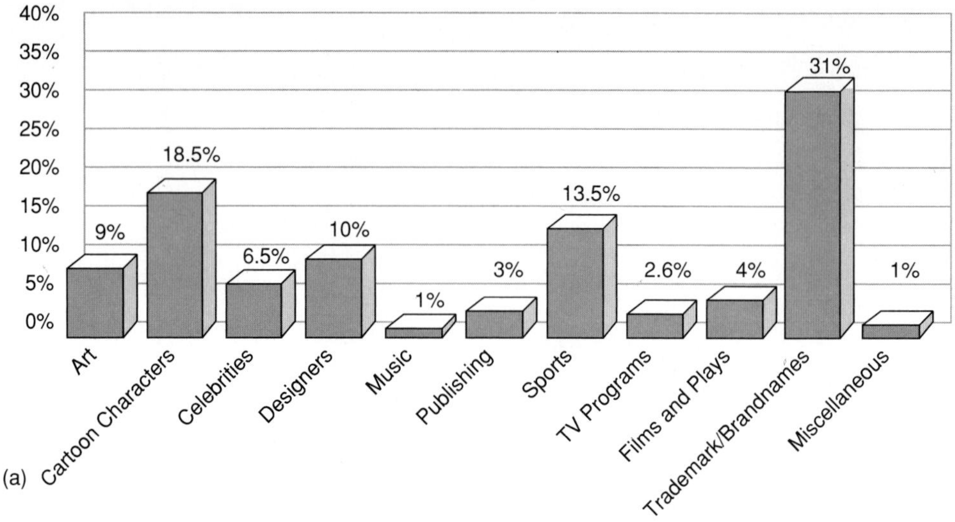

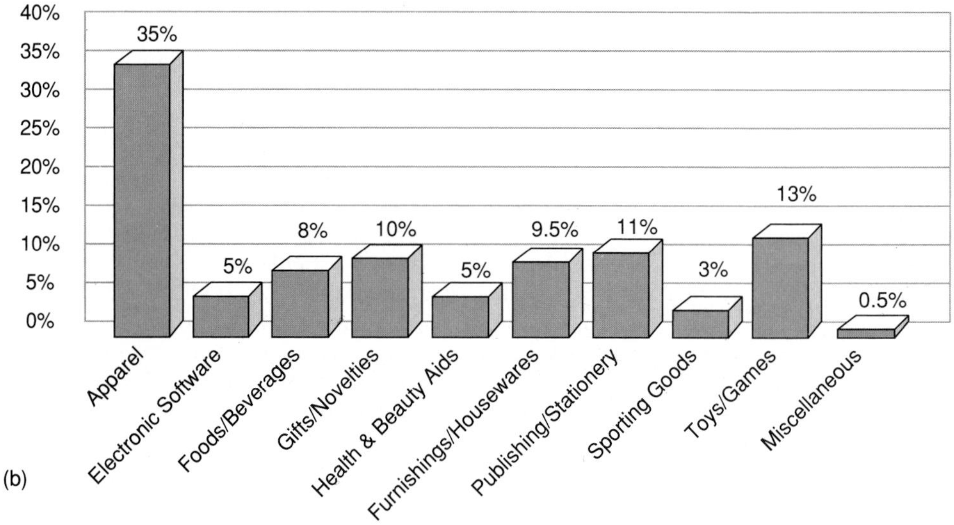

FIGURE 11–14 Retail sales of licensed products by (a) type of product and (b) product category (source: adapted from "Licensed Merchandise: $59.8 Billion and Growing. Here's How." *Stores,* June 1989, 46)

products, and often takes an active role in their design and manufacture. Sears is considered the leader in this type of venture, as exemplified by its cooperative agreement with McDonald's for merchandising the McKids' brand of children's wear. K mart's Jaclyn Smith apparel line has proved so successful that the retailer has entered into another exclusive agreement for a line of "Dirty Dancing" women's sportswear—the line is supported by the original film and its sequel; also by sweepstakes and dance contests.[35]

Another popular technique for the marketing of licensed products is through in-store *boutiques,* where all goods of a given license are merchandised together, often using innovative visual displays and special promotions. The boutique strategy can both increase sales of the licensed goods and generate store traffic. Some retailers even base entire promotion campaigns around a licensed product line, a tactic used by a group of

Clubhouse Shops: Sports Licensed Merchandise Retailing

RETAIL STRATEGIES AND TACTICS

It's a whole new ballgame in retailing—in sports licensed merchandise retailing, that is.

"It" is a growing chain of Major League Baseball Clubhouse shops, a venture of Bradley Specialty Retailing, in conjunction with Major League Baseball teams around the country. What makes the Clubhouse shops different is, first, that each is directly supported by the professional baseball team in its market. But an even more striking difference is the way they are designed and merchandised.

The shops offer a retail atmosphere that inspires the excitement of a theme park, have all the trappings to lure impulse shoppers, but promotions make it a destination store. People are driven into the stores by being constantly reminded of their association with the home team. The Clubhouse shop interiors actually replicate a ballpark, featuring a baseball diamond complete with authentic pitcher's mound and lifelike pitcher; home plate, with uniformed batter and catcher at the ready; and everything else needed to convey the realistic environment of a baseball field.

The merchandise selection is meant to be upscale. About 50 percent of the assortment is devoted to baseball, with the remainder highlighted by other licensed sports products meaningful to the region including football, basketball, hockey, soccer, NASCAR, and so on.

Team apparel—such as jackets, caps, shirts, jerseys, ranging in size from toddler to extra, extra large, is the emphasis; but in order to stand apart from other sports-oriented stores, the merchandise mix goes beyond the traditional. For instance, in the novelties category are items like a telephone built into a batter's helmet atop a wooden stand. In gifts, the stores carry goods such as high-quality pen and pencil sets and lapel pins. And for nostalgia seekers, there are items like replicas of oldtimer jerseys and caps from the Brooklyn Dodgers, New York Giants, and Philadelphia Athletics, along with autographed photos of baseball greats, and a selection of actual field memorabilia—things like broken bats, tarnished balls, and used uniforms—which are very popular and carry a pretty high price tag. Last year's jersey from a top player could sell in the $500 to $700 range.

As an added attraction to fans, the Clubhouse also sells tickets to the home team's games. The Clubhouse stores are merchandised by sport, and then by team within each sport. A separate college section is set up to feature all types of merchandise relating to the local school or schools. There is also some cross-merchandising, as in an entire cap wall featuring every cap carried in the store.

Source: Penney Gill, "Major League Licensing," *Stores* (June 1989): 48–49. Copyright © National Federation, Inc., New York, New York.

sixteen J.C. Penney stores in the New York City area. Their month-long promotion, featuring 300-square-foot Disney shops, in-store appearances of Mickey Mouse and other Disney characters, showings of classic Disney film footage in the boutiques, and widespread publicity, was considered an enormous success and on some evenings brought thousands of additional shoppers into the store.[36]

There is an increasing trend toward manufacturers licensing their trademarks and brand names. Within this category, there is increasing emphasis on the concept of

FIGURE 11–15
Selected examples of corporate licensing of brand name and trademarks

Corporation/ Licensor	Trademark/ Brand Name	Product Line	Producer/ Licensee
*Pillsbury	Doughboy Little Sprout	Kitchen Ensembles	Fieldcrest Cannon
*Campbell Soup	Campbell Kids Name	Kitchen Gadgets	Bonny Products
*Lenox China	China Patterns	Table Linen Collection	Sunweave Linen
*Corning Glass Works	Corelle Dinnerware Corning Houseware	Vinyl Tablecloths	Lintex Group
*Esprit	Fashion Design Name	Bed and Bath Linens	West Point Pepperell
*J. G. Hook	Brand Name	Acrylic and Melamine Servingware	Oneida Silversmiths

brand or line extensions, where the licensed products bear a more or less direct relationship to the licensor's original product line.[37] The licensing of corporate brand names and trademarks is particularly active in the home furnishings area. Figure 11–15 provides some selective examples. Designers such as Laura Ashley, Ralph Lauren, Christian Dior, Bill Blass, and Adrienne Villadini are all active in licensing their name and style image to this same bed-and-bath category; these designer labels are sold through licensees or through their own outlets (e.g., Ralph Lauren and Laura Ashley).

PRODUCT INFORMATION

There are excellent sources of information to help retailers make product-mix decisions. Internal sources include sales records, want books and slips, sales personnel, in-store testing, and customer returns. External sources are comparison shopping, consumer opinions and behavior, vendors, trade shows, trade publications, residential buying offices, and special reporting services.

Internal Sources

The most widely used internal source of product information must be the store's past sales for various product lines and items. Past **sales records** are especially useful for deciding about staple merchandise. As a result of the regular demand for staples, past demand often is the key to predicting future demand. On the other hand, cyclical demand patterns for fashion goods limit the usefulness of past sales for estimating future demand. The past may very well be the past for fashion goods and have little to do with what consumers want in the future. Although past sales data are useful in many situations, they are of limited or no use for new products.

Another method for determining what customers want is to record their inquiries about (1) products the retailer does not stock and (2) products the retailer carries but that currently are out of stock. Salespeople can systematically record inquiries in want books or want slips. **Want books and slips** range from simple blank notebooks and slips of paper to printed books and forms.

Sales personnel are an excellent source of information. Because they have more direct contact with consumers than anyone in the firm, salespeople are in a position to observe why and how consumers buy. Reports from sales personnel must be viewed with caution, though, since they are subjective and tend to reflect the salesperson's own biases and preferences. Nevertheless, if properly encouraged, salespeople can provide the retail manager information on how existing products are selling and insight into which products might sell in the future.

Retailers frequently use **in-store testing,** test marketing within their stores, to judge customer wants. New product introductions are both costly and risky because only about 5 percent are truly new offerings and not me-too products. Testing is often the only way to reduce the risk of a 4-out-of-5 failure rate.[38] Products are pretested by stocking a sample order and observing customer responses. If the product stimulates no interest, the retailer can dispose of the merchandise with minimal losses. If the product sells in sufficient quantities over a short period of time, the retailer can reorder a much larger quantity of the merchandise.

Sometimes it is as important to find out what customers do not want as it is to find out what they do want. Store data on **customers returns** provide valuable information on the product mix, but the retailer must try to discover why customers returned the merchandise to make the data useful.

External Sources

A good outside source of information on what consumers want is what other stores sell them. Through **comparison shopping** at both competing and noncompeting stores, a retailer can often discover missed product opportunities and also inspect the merchandising techniques that competitors are using to move certain products successfully. Comparative checks should include examining the competitor's window and store displays, advertisements, promotions, featured products, prices, shelf quantities, and product appeals. Some retailers even hire people to pose as customers to discover what methods and appeals competitive salespeople are using in merchandising their products. By learning how competitors think, the retailer can distinguish between promotions used to promote fast movers and those used to move "dogs."

For complete information on what competitors are doing, many retailers use the three-level comparison shopping strategy. This strategy calls for retailers to shop at stores operating above, at, and below their own targeted market. Shopping at all three levels gives the retailer information on what products customers might want in the near future (above), what products they are currently buying (at), and what products are dated (below). This strategy helps retailers decide what products they should *add* in the near future and those they should quickly *delete* from their product mix.

Perhaps the most effective methods for determining consumer preferences are to ask and to observe. Asking consumers their opinions and observing their behavior yield first-hand information on what products consumers want and when, where, how, and why they want them. Three common methods for soliciting consumer opinions and observing consumer behavior are **consumer surveys, consumer panels,** and **consumer counts.**

Being in contact daily with large numbers of retailers, **vendors** and their representatives have a wide range of experiences on which to base their product opinions. They are thus excellent sources of product information, although retailers must be somewhat wary of their reliability. As a rule, vendor information is accurate in a general sense; however, vendor representatives are often overly enthusiastic about their own products.

Trade shows are occasions when manufacturers get together to exhibit their merchandise in one place. Trade shows range from exhibitions of a particular line of

Trade shows offer retailers a convenient way to compare vendors and merchandise.

products to general merchandise displays. These events allow retailers to comparison shop, talk to various vendor representatives, and to inspect displayed merchandise. They also give retailers an opportunity to talk about their experiences with various products, vendors, and merchandising programs.

Trade publications are good sources of information because (1) they provide basic trade information and (2) they contain numerous advertisements of interest to the retailer. Trade publications have feature articles and special reports on topics such as new products, industry trends, merchandising tips, current developments, and legal and environmental issues.

Many retailers either rely on independent residential buyers or establish their own **residential buying offices** in major producer markets. Major producer markets (domestic) in the apparel industry, for example, are New York, Dallas, and Los Angeles. A representative in producer areas keeps the retailer abreast of which products are available and which new products are in the offering.

Retailers subscribe to numerous **specialized reporting services**. Frequently, these services offer information on certain product lines and merchandising activities (e.g., advertising, store displays, and facings). They provide retailers with information periodically (daily, weekly, monthly) in the form of newspapers, special reports, or flash reports, but the cost can be substantial. Moreover, depending on the reporting, the information can be dated.

PRODUCT-MIX STRATEGIES

The basic objective in planning product-mix strategies is to offer consumers an optimal number of product lines and an optimal number of product items within each line. The optimal number of lines and items a retailer should carry varies with the type and extent of the market served, as well as with operating capabilities. Several different optimal strategies are possible, depending on the retailer's circumstances. Figure 11–16 illustrates the four basic variety/assortment combination strategies: (1) narrow variety/shallow assortment, (2) wide variety/shallow assortment, (3) narrow variety/deep assortment, and (4) wide variety/deep assortment.

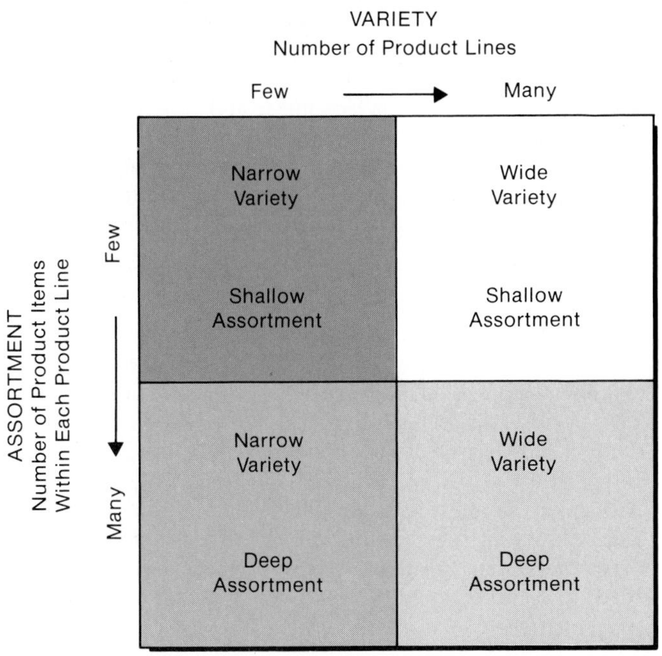

FIGURE 11–16
Product-mix strategies

Narrow Variety/Shallow Assortment

A **narrow variety/shallow assortment strategy** offers consumers the most limited product selection (lines and items) of any of the combination strategies. Retail operations characterized by narrow variety/shallow assortment are unconventional. Vending machines that hold only two or three choices of soft drinks, door-to-door sales representatives who sell only one product line with a limited number of product features, and the newsstand that offers only one or two newspapers are examples of retail institutions that use the narrow variety/shallow assortment strategy. The key to merchandising this limited product-mix strategy successfully is *place and time conveniences*. Because it offers a limited choice, the narrow variety/shallow assortment retailer must make its offering readily available where and when consumers want it. Generally, the narrow variety/shallow assortment strategy suffers from a poor image and little, if any, customer loyalty other than that generated by convenience. A limited product mix, however, does create certain benefits. It simplifies operations, makes inventory control problems insignificant, and minimizes facility requirements. A major benefit is the retailer's small investment in inventories.

Wide Variety/Shallow Assortment

The basic philosophy behind the **wide variety/shallow assortment strategy** is "stock a little of everything." The retailer offers a wide selection of different product lines but limits the selection of brands, styles, sizes, and so on within each line. Most variety stores (five and dime stores), general stores, and some discount houses follow this product-mix philosophy. McCrory, Ben Franklin, F.W. Woolworth, and M.H. Lamston are the major U.S. operators of variety stores.[39] A wide and shallow product mix offers the advantages of appealing to a broad market, satisfying the consumer in terms of product availability if not product selection, promoting one-stop shopping, and permitting reasonable control over inventories. The disadvantages of this product-mix strategy are lost sales and customer disappointment with the lack of selection within lines, low inventory turnover rate on slow-moving product lines, weak store image, and limited store loyalty. Heck's, a West Virginia discounter, lost its competitiveness by trying to carry a full line of products within limited-size stores; it failed to maintain sufficient stock levels on basic product lines and advertised merchandise. The result was Chapter 11 and eventual takeover by Jordache Enterprises.[40] A paradox of sorts can occur within the wide variety/narrow assortment strategy. A retailer that wants to project a prestige image might choose to stock many different high-priced product lines but limit the selection within each line to one or two unique items—originals or limited editions.

Narrow Variety/Deep Assortment

The "specialty" philosophy characterizes the **narrow variety/deep assortment strategy**. Some retailers try to appeal to a select group of consumers by offering only one or a few product lines with an excellent selection within each line. The baby boomlet spawned by baby boomers during the late 1980s has created a boomlet in children's specialty retailing. Kids 'R' Us, KidsMart, Little Folks Shop, McKids, and GapKids are some of the narrow variety, deep assortment retailers who are focusing on the children's markets.[41] By offering a specialized mix of products supported by specialized personnel, the narrow variety/deep assortment retailer can develop a distinct store image and a loyal customer following. Additional advantages to the retailer are as follows:

- Rare sales losses as a result of an inadequate selection of brands, styles, sizes, colors, and materials
- Greater likelihood of a high level of repeat shopping
- Greater specialization in the buying, managing, and selling of a limited line of products
- Good economies of scale in ordering large quantities of the same product

The principal limitation of a specialty strategy is that successful operations *depend solely on a single or limited line of products*. Putting all the eggs in one basket creates a high risk for the retailer that sells in a very limited market. When adverse conditions occur in the market area, the specialty retailer suffers the most.

Wide Variety/Deep Assortment

The full-line department store best typifies the **wide variety/deep assortment strategy**. One-stop shopping is the basic philosophy of this all-inclusive product-mix strategy. A large number of product lines with supporting depth in each line allows the retailer to make a broad market appeal while satisfying most of the product needs of specific target markets. Few sales are lost as a result of an inadequate variety or assortment. Generally, satisfied customers develop store loyalty, leading to a high level of repeat shopping. Although retailers generally regard a wide variety/deep assortment strategy as the most desirable strategy from the viewpoint of selling, they also recognize the problems they must encounter in store operations. The most common problems are (1) the necessarily high level of investment in inventory to support such a diverse product mix; (2) the low stock-turnover rate associated with many marginal product lines; and (3) the amount of space, fixtures, and equipment the retailer must have to merchandise properly such a wide range of products. In recent years, this strategy of trying to be most things to most people has placed the department store format in a vulnerable position as competitors attack from all directions (see Figure 11–17).

PRODUCT-MIX TRENDS

To survive in the contemporary world of retailing, product mixes must be adapted rapidly and creatively to the dynamics of the marketplace. Future winners in the field of retailing will be those that can best identify consumers' emerging unsatisfied needs

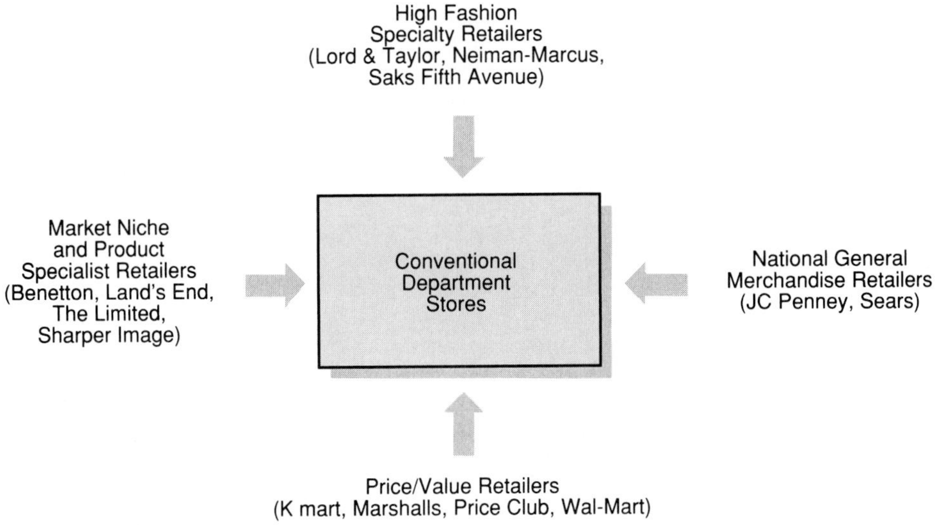

FIGURE 11–17
The vulnerable department store (source: reprinted with permission from Leonard L. Berry, "Editor's Corner," *Retailing Issues Letter* 1 [Arthur Andersen & Co. in conjunction with the Center for Retailing Studies, Texas A&M University, 1987]: 4)

and develop innovative product-mix strategies to satisfy them. Two emerging product-mix trends of particular interest are shotgun merchandising and rifle merchandising.

Shotgun Merchandising

Shotgun merchandising is the marketing strategy of broadening the retail offering to meet consumer's expanding needs. By expanding the number of product options, retailers try to increase the size of their total market by appealing to several submarkets—attempting to satisfy the specific needs of several individual market segments. In diversifying the product mix, the shotgun merchandiser attempts to develop a general-purpose mix that will satisfy the product needs of most consumers "pretty well." A retailer can either add new product items or combine major product lines to develop a general-purpose mix.

Item Addition

Item addition involves adding to one retailer's traditional product lines the more desirable product items normally associated with another type of retailer. Book, magazine, cosmetic, and apparel racks are item additions to the supermarket's primary product offerings. In the retailing industry, item addition is often referred to as *cherry picking*, because the product item additions are those retailers consider the cream of the crop, the best of the product line. Characteristics of these product items are (1) low risk because of reasonably sure sales, (2) relatively high turnover rates, (3) adequate margins for respectable profits, (4) minimal personal selling effort, (5) routine ordering and stocking procedures, and (6) relatively low per-unit prices with high levels of impulse and unplanned purchasing.

Retailers use the item-addition strategy on both a permanent and a temporary basis. Frequently, retailers add products on a trial basis to determine how well customers will receive them and whether the product additions provide sufficient profits with minimal operating difficulties. If these conditions are met, the retailer will add the product permanently. Wal-Mart, K mart, and other discounters are adding more grocery items (e.g., spaghetti sauce, canned peas, and microwavable meals) as they successfully experiment with expanded grocery sections and discover the drawing power of food.[42] "Gasoline Alley is starting to look like a shopping mall. At many of today's slick stations, you can pick up fresh doughnuts, pizza, and bread; even a real movie."[43] In other instances, some retailers engage in seasonal item-addition strategy. During Christmas, for example, retailers add "hot items" as potential gift selections, although they would not stock these items during other times of the year. Wisconsin Toy has developed a consignment operation in which it provides a toy department for retailers during the six weeks prior to Christmas.[44]

Line Combination

Line combination is the second shotgun strategy, in which the retailer combines two or more broad product lines into the store operation. The principle behind combining major merchandise lines is to provide consumers with a one-stop shopping opportunity for a wide range of products, and therefore satisfy several needs under one roof. An example of a retail organization that uses the line-combination strategy is the superstore. The superstore combines many of the standard product lines of the supermarket, drugstore, variety store, and hardware store. Holiday Plus, a Minneapolis hypermarket operation, offers an especially broad and deep sporting goods department (e.g., golf, tennis, hunting, fishing, archery, hockey, camping, softball, baseball, and exercise equipment), an extensive assortment of general merchandise (e.g., 73,000 SKUs), and a full-fledge supermarket (24,000 SKUs).[45] With consumers demanding more and more convenience and with the desire for one-stop shopping, superstores could be the wave of the future.

Rifle Merchandising

Rifle merchandising is a strategy of targeting a product offering to a select group of customers. Although the number of product lines is very selective—often only one or two lines—there is a large assortment of product items within each line. In essence, the rifle merchandiser employs a penetration strategy, concentrating product options within limited lines to serve all of the individual needs of a given market segment for a particular line of products. Burlington Coat, Linens 'n Things, Herman's World of Sporting Goods, and Tower Records are superspecialists who are narrowly defining sharply focused retail formats that exemplify the rifle merchandising approach to the marketplace.[46] Staples, Office World, Office Max, and Office Square are all office supply superstores that utilize a rifle merchandising strategy to target small and medium businesses as well as individuals who need a complete assortment of office supplies and equipment.[47] By concentrating on a limited line, the rifle merchandiser develops a specific-purpose mix that will satisfy very well all of the targeted consumers' specific needs for a given product. In creating specific-purpose mixes, the rifle merchandiser uses one of two marketing strategies: either market positioning or multiplex distribution.

Market Positioning

Market positioning is the strategy of creating a position for a store and its product mix in the minds of consumers by relating it to other stores and their mixture of products. By specializing in certain product lines and by offering a choice within those lines, the rifle retailer hopes to establish a market niche and a particular market image. Positioning helps customers know the real differences among competing products (retailers) so that they can choose the one that is of most value to them.[48] True positioning must be based on real merchandising and operating dimensions, otherwise it becomes more illusion than reality, more hype than honesty.[49] A long-time rifle merchandiser, The Gap, is repositioning itself to attract an older customer base. The Gap is changing its image from a teenaged jeans mecca to a purveyor of casual and active sportswear for middle-aged men and women. Creating an image leads the rifle merchandiser to program its entire operation so that the consumer will perceive it as occupying a unique position within a particular product category. By focusing on certain product lines and developing highly complementary price, place, and promotional strategies, the rifle merchandiser attempts to achieve a dominant position in the sales of particular product lines. To meet the desires of salaried middle-class women for mink and other furs, the Fur Vault positioned itself as the affordable and friendly salon—a clear distinction from the typical expensive, snobby, and stuffy salon.[50] This strategy positions the store in the minds of consumers as one that "has it all" in a particular class of merchandise. Baskin-Robbins Ice Cream Shops, National Shirt Shops, Radio Shacks, Dunkin' Donut Shops, Blockbuster Videos, Bookshop and Container Store are examples of multiunit retailers that have pursued a limited-line market-positioning policy. An unsuccessful positioning strategy was the attempt by the Marriott Corp. to establish a middle market position by combining its Bob's Big Boy, Allie's, and Wag's Coffee Shops into a single national chain of casual restaurants. "It was a nebulous niche that few consumers wanted. The restaurants weren't as cheap or as appealing to children as fast food. Nor could they please adults with a nice dining-out atmosphere."[51]

Multiplex Distribution

No single retailing approach is likely to be sufficient in the future simply because markets are diverging more and more with respect to wants, needs, and buying power. Therefore, a single way of doing business is unlikely to appeal to all market segments.[52] An extension of the market-positioning strategy is the **multiplex distribution strategy** (also referred to as **portfolio retailing**). In the last decade, rifle merchandisers have begun to operate multiple types of outlets with individual product mixes serving multiple market segments.[53]

In multiplex distribution, the rifle merchandiser aims at a number of different target markets. This specialized type of merchandiser accomplishes the task of serving several target markets using a "free-form" organization that permits it to develop a specialized product mix for each market segment. Williams-Sonoma, the San Francisco-based retailer, operates five different stores and catalog businesses directed at the home; the five divisions include William-Sonoma (kitchenware), Pottery Barn (housewares), Hold Everything (closet and storage), Gardener's Eden (garden equipment), and Ralph Lauren Home Collections (home furnishings).[54] K mart's portfolio of retail operations includes PACE Membership Warehouse, Pay Less Drug Stores, Walden Books, American Fare (hypermarkets), Builders Square (home centers), Office Square (office supply superstores), and Sports Authority (sporting goods superstores).[55] Operating under the assumption that no one individual store can please all consumers, the portfolio retailer simply develops individual product mixes positioned to meet the needs of a given market segment. Big names in adult fashion are "begetting shops selling miniature versions of high fashions—Benetton's 012, for kids 0 to 12 years of age; GapKids with pint-size to teen-sized jeans, . . . Laura Ashley's Mother and Child shops offering infants' and children's clothing and bedroom furnishings with the romantic look."[56] The Limited also employs the free-form concept of multiplex distribution; its individual retailing formats include Limited Stores, Limited Express, Lane Bryant, Victoria's Secret, Lerner Stores, Sizes Unlimited, Henri Bendel, and Brylane Mail Order. Another portfolio retailer is the Melville Corp.; its mix of specialty businesses includes Marshall's (off-price retailing), Thom McAn (shoe stores), CVS (health and beauty stores), KayBee (toy stores), and Chess King (young men's clothing chain).

SUMMARY

Offering the right product in the right quantities in the right place at the right time at the right price and with the right appeal constitutes the desired merchandising process. The three stages of the merchandising process are developing the merchandise mix (product and service mix), procuring the merchandising mix (buying and handling process), and managing the merchandise mix (planning and controlling process).

To develop a product mix, the retailer must first understand the total-product concept. The total product is the sum of the product's functional, aesthetic, and service features plus the psychological benefits the customer expects from buying and using the product. Product mix refers to the full range of products a retailer offers to the consumer. It is composed of product lines (any grouping of related products) and product items (specific products within a product line that are clearly distinguishable). Product lines can be subclassified into merchandise groups, classes, and categories. Product items are different brands of products, differentiated by brand name, style, size, color, material, and price.

Product-mix decisions revolve around two separate but related decisions—which and how many products to stock. Deciding which products requires determining what product types are to be included in the product mix. Deciding how many products concerns developing product variety (number of different products to stock) and product assortment (number of different product items to stock in each product line).

Retailers use several criteria to decide which and how many products to carry: product compatibility, product attributes, product profitability, product life cycles, fashion cycles, product appropriateness, and competitive conditions. The retailer must also consider the availability of needed products and the reliability of suppliers.

The retailer can consult several sources of information to evaluate the merits of a product. Internal sources consist of sales records, want books and slips, sales personnel, in-store testing, and customer returns. External sources of information are comparison shopping, consumer opinions and behavior, vendors, trade shows, trade publications, residential buying offices, and special reporting services.

Regarding product mix, a retailer can use one of four variety/assortment strategies: narrow variety/shallow assortment, wide variety/shallow assortment, narrow variety/deep assortment, and wide variety/deep assortment. Correct selection of a product-mix strategy depends on the retailer's current or proposed variety/assortment situation.

Retailers are responding to the changing marketplace by employing either a shotgun or a rifle approach to merchandising. The shotgun merchandiser appeals to a combination of market segments by broadening its product lines through either product-item addition or product-line combination. The rifle merchandiser appeals to a target-market segment by using either a market-positioning strategy or a multiplex distribution system.

STUDENT STUDY GUIDE

Key Terms and Concepts

affinity (p. 408)
availability of supply (p. 412)
classic (p. 406)
comparison shopping (p. 419)
complexity (p. 409)
design (p. 403)
direct and indirect competitors (p. 412)
exclusive, selective, and intensive competitive conditions (p. 412)
fad (p. 406)
fashion cycle (p. 403)
flop (p. 405)
ford (p. 406)
generic product (p. 413)
generics (p. 413)
in-store testing (p. 419)
item addition (p. 423)
licensed products (p. 414)
lifestyle merchandising (p. 410)
line combination (p. 424)
manufacturer brands (p. 413)
market positioning (p. 424)
merchandise category (p. 395)
merchandise class (p. 395)
merchandise group (p. 395)
merchandising (p. 392)
multiplex distribution strategy (p. 425)
narrow variety/deep assortment strategy (p. 422)
narrow variety/shallow assortment strategy (p. 421)
observability (p. 409)
product assortment (p. 398)

product attributes (p. 400)
product compatibility (p. 399)
product complement (p. 400)
product item (p. 395)
product life cycle (PLC) (p. 402)
product line (p. 395)
product-mix concept (p. 395)
product profitability (p. 401)
product substitute (p. 399)
product variety (p. 398)
relative advantage (p. 408)
reliability of supplier (p. 413)
residential buying offices (p. 420)
rifle merchandising (p. 424)
shotgun merchandising (p. 423)
specialized reporting services (p. 420)
store (private) brands (p. 414)
style (p. 403)
total-product concept (p. 393)
trade shows (p. 419)
trialability (p. 409)
trickle-across theory (p. 408)
trickle-down theory (p. 407)
trickle-up theory (p. 408)
unrelated products (p. 400)
want books and slips (p. 418)
wide variety/deep assortment strategy (p. 422)
wide variety/shallow assortment strategy (p. 421)

Review Questions

1. What is the total-product concept? Briefly describe each of the concept's components.
2. How do product lines differ from product items?
3. Describe the two basic decisions the retailer faces in developing the product mix.
4. Define product variety. How does it differ from product assortment?
5. Identify and describe the three basic classes of products based on product compatibility. Which of these classes of products should be included in the retailer's product mix?
6. How do the product attributes of bulk and standardization influence the retailer's decisions of which and how many products should be stocked?
7. What should the retailer's stocking strategy be for products in each of the four stages of the product life cycle?
8. Develop a profile of a fashion-conscious consumer.
9. Describe each of the four fashion cycles and discuss what the retailer's stock position should be relative to each cycle.
10. Which five product characteristics are used in evaluating new product offerings relative to their market appropriateness?
11. What is lifestyle merchandising?
12. What are the internal sources of product information?
13. Identify the four basic variety/assortment combination strategies used in developing a retail product mix. Briefly describe each strategy.
14. Compare and contrast the strategies of shotgun and rifle merchandising.

Review Exam

True or False

_____ 1. Aesthetic product features are extremely important because they determine to a large extent how well the product will actually perform those functions that it was designed to accomplish.

_____ 2. A product item is a specific product within a product line that is unique and clearly distinguishable from other products within and outside the product line.

_____ 3. Consumers tend to be less sensitive about the price of product complements; hence, retailers often sell complements at above-average markups.

_____ 4. Almost without exception, the most desirable products for the retailer to stock are those in the introduction stage of the product life cycle.

_____ 5. The fashion retailer's decision relative to the classic fashion is not whether to stock it, but rather what price line to stock from what supplier with what product features.

_____ 6. Retailers are often forced to carry intensively distributed products because they are so readily available in competitive outlets and consumers expect them to be in stock.

_____ 7. The superstore is a good example of a retail organization that uses the line combination strategy.

Multiple Choice

_____ 1. A broadly related line of products that retailers and consumers associate according to end use and that mass merchandisers frequently use to identify operating divisions is referred to as merchandise _____.

a. class
b. group
c. category
d. item
e. fad

_____ 2. A _____ is a product that consumers perceive as different from another product but that serves the same overall purpose.
   a. perfect substitute
   b. general substitute
   c. perfect complement
   d. general complement
   e. none of the above

_____ 3. A fashion that obtains a relatively high level of customers and whose lifetime ranges from a few weeks to several months is a _____.
   a. fad
   b. flop
   c. classic
   d. ford
   e. trend

_____ 4. Which of the following guidelines for assessing trends and fads is false?
   a. A new product is more likely to be a trend if it is consistent with the consumer's basic values and lifestyles.
   b. A new product is more likely to be a trend if it promotes a voluntary change in behavior that is derived from customer satisfaction.
   c. A new product stands a better chance of becoming a trend if it cannot be modified or altered.
   d. A new product stands a better chance of becoming a trend if it is based on a good underlying theme.
   e. All of the above statements are false.

_____ 5. Which of the following assortment strategies should the retailer use for intensively distributed products?
   a. Stock only the best-selling items to satisfy a majority of customers and hope other customers will be willing to accept these items as substitutes.
   b. Stock a deep assortment to satisfy all customers and thereby create a store image of complete selection.
   c. Avoid stocking intensively distributed products.
   d. Select strategy "A" (best-selling items) or "B" (deep assortment); either strategy is acceptable.
   e. None of the above strategies is acceptable.

_____ 6. Stocking a little bit of everything is the basic product mix philosophy associated with a _____ strategy.
   a. narrow variety/shallow assortment
   b. wide variety/shallow assortment
   c. narrow variety/deep assortment
   d. wide variety/deep assortment
   e. shallow variety/wide assortment

_____ 7. The strategy of creating a place for a store and its product mix in the minds of consumers by relating it to other stores and their mixture of products is called _____.
   a. multiplex distribution
   b. market positioning
   c. line combination
   d. item addition
   e. market development

STUDENT APPLICATIONS MANUAL

Investigative Projects: Practice and Applications

1. Identify and discuss the functional, aesthetic, service, and psychological features (the total product) of each of the following products: (1) a steak dinner, (2) a cologne, and (3) a 35-mm camera.
2. Survey your local supermarket and identify at least three examples of each of the following: (1) perfect substitutes, (2) general substitutes, (3) perfect complements, and (4) general complements. Explain your descriptions.
3. A fashion is a concept of what is currently appropriate and represents the prevailing style currently in vogue. Interview a local buyer of fashion apparel and identify and describe fashions that are currently appropriate for your area. Do local fashions differ from the prevailing styles that are in vogue nationally? How and why?
4. How exclusive is the Pierre Cardin name? Describe the product lines carrying the name and the distribution of those products.
5. Identify and describe some major special reporting services used by retailers to obtain information on products.
6. Survey retail stores in your local community and find specific examples of item addition and line combination. Do you believe these retailing strategies are being accepted by the consuming public? Why or why not?
7. Identify three limited-line stores in your community that are engaging in a market-positioning strategy. What merchandise and operating tactics are they using to establish a market niche and a particular market image in the consumer's mind?

Tactical Cases: Problems and Decisions

■ CASE 11–1
Lockner's Department Store: The Role of A Toy Department*

INTRODUCTION

For the last 40 years, Lockner's Department Store had been recognized as one of the leading retail merchandisers in the midwestern city of Plains, Iowa (1987 population, 175,000). The area is expected to continue above-average population growth for the next 20 years. During the last four decades, Lockner's had built a reputation as an upscale retailer of quality merchandise. By carefully designing the firm's total merchandising program, Lockner's management had generally been successful in appealing to both middle- and upper-class consumers. Over the last five years, sales and profit objectives for most merchandise departments were met or exceeded. The one exception to this is the toy department. For Betty Lockner, founder and president of the store, this situation was simply unacceptable.

LOCKNER'S MERCHANDISING STRATEGY

The Product-Service Mixes

Good quality, high style, and an excellent variety of brand-name merchandise were hallmarks of the firm's product mix. To help differentiate its product mix from competitive product offerings, Lockner's featured a number of top-quality private labels in several different product lines. Also, a variety of specialty and imported goods not commonly found in competitive stores were an integral part of Lockner's product strategy. To enhance its image as an upscale, full-line department store and as a one-stop shopping store, Lockner's carried a deep assortment of brands, models, styles, and colors for most product lines.

Excellent service was another key ingredient in the store's merchandising program. Lockner's offered a complete service mix with a variety of credit, delivery, and wrapping plans, and alterations, repair, and layaway services. All essential and expected services were provided free or, in a few cases, at a minimal fee.

The Promotional-Place Mixes

Lockner's promotional strategy was directed at enhancing the store's prestige image. To do so, local newspaper advertisements focused on appeals stressing product selection and quality, service offerings, and shopping atmosphere.

Product advertisements featuring a few carefully selected items were used to inform customers of new and special merchandise. The store also ran numerous institutional advertisements that attempted to communicate the message that "Lockner's is *the* place to shop." After a customer had been attracted to the store, considerable attention was given to capitalizing on the traffic, through such promotional tools as attractive and accessible displays, special effects, and promotional demonstrations.

The store was located on the newly opened Hub Mall, an open-air pedestrian mall in downtown Plains. The area featured many renovated or new specialty and more fashion-oriented shops. Lockner's was completely renovated inside and out at the same time as the mall. Both the area and the store were accessible to the area's population and offered a pleasurable and exciting shopping environment not found anywhere nearby.

THE TOY INDUSTRY

Estimates of sales in the toy industry are in the neighborhood of $2 billion annually. Department stores typically sell about 13 percent of all toys, games, and hobby items. Sales in department stores, however, indicate that they sell a higher than average share of dolls and educational and scientific toys.

Toys are product items with interesting life cycles. Both the level and duration of consumer acceptance can vary substantially from one toy line to another. Toys range from faddish product items whose life expectancy is short (several months) to classics like Monopoly and Scrabble that remain popular for decades. Frequently, the general nature of the life cycle for a particular new toy can be explained by the toy's origin. Currently, many new toy ideas originate in popular movies or television programs; hence, the life expectancy depends on the level and duration of popularity for these entertainment vehicles. For instance, Strawberry Shortcake products once enjoyed tremendous success, but since the demise of the television program, the popularity of these products has declined considerably. In contrast, Star Wars toys have enjoyed tremendous popularity for several years, and sales are expected to continue at fairly substantial levels as a result of plans to continue sequels into the 1990s.

Technologically and socially, the toy industry has undergone considerable change during the last few decades. On the technological front, toys have evolved dramatically from the cornhusk dolls of the seventeenth century. Today, computer technology has had a major impact on toys and games in the sense that many computer games and software for home computers have broadened the appeal of such "toys" to all age groups. The old rule that toys appeal only to young children no longer applies. Computer and board games offer people the opportunity to exercise their analytical prowess by making key decisions that affect the outcome of the game. For all age groups, the trend appears to be away from passive games of chance to more active games of skill and decision making.

Socially, toys have evolved with the social values and moods of the country. As exemplified by the Fisher Price line, educational values are often preeminent for parents shopping for toys for younger children. Today, motives for purchasing toys include not only entertainment value but the belief that toys can play an important role in children's mental, physical, and creative development. Contemporary social values are also reflected in the type of toys purchased. In past years, dolls only cried "Mama"; today, dolls have more extensive vocabularies, are often anatomically correct, and can perform a number of biological functions. Further, as roles of men and women are redefined, so too are toys and toy buying. Boys are increasingly accepting dolls (Star Wars figures, G.I. Joe figures, He-Man figures, Cabbage Patch dolls, etc.), and girls are increasingly becoming active in sports.

The toy industry is highly competitive; of the estimated 125,000 toy items produced each year, approximately 12,000 achieve a high level of customer acceptance. Of the 12,000 that do gain wide acceptance, only a few return to the same level of public acceptance the following year. Thus, knowing what is and what is not a hot item is vital to survival in the toy industry.

Product offerings are planned by toy manufacturers in April, and production levels are set at that time. Product competition takes several forms. Toy manufacturers compete for the rights to produce toy items that are expected to succeed (e.g., Star Wars toys), for the development of new products, and for the development of additional product features and options for existing toys. Manufacturers' representatives, printed materials, and trade shows are the major promotional vehicles for obtaining orders from wholesalers and retailers. Orders for toys are accepted from April through August and are filled on a first-come, first-served basis. Because the manufacturer produces a preset number of a given toy, it is essential that wholesalers and retailers place orders for "hot" items early. Advertising is vitally important at both local and national levels. To create product awareness and to promote product and brand preference, toy manufacturers advertise heavily on television during Saturday mornings and on other programs directed toward children. At the local level, manufacturers and retailers often run cooperative newspaper or other local advertising to inform customers about which stores have the product and their prices.

Clearly the major target market for toys is the youth market. Children with allowances and some with babysitting, yardwork, and other income represent a strong economic force. In addition, children play an "influencer" role in the family. Demand for a particular toy depends heavily on the ability of children to influence parents to purchase that item. A number of research studies show the following:

1. Children are strongly influenced by television commercials; in three out of four cases, preferred toys had recently been seen on television.
2. Peer groups are strong influences of toy preference for many children. (This influence occurs in the form of the "two-step flow of communication"—television advertisements to playmates or peers who buy the product and then influence their friends to buy it, too.)
3. Younger children attempt to influence parental purchasing more frequently than do older children.
4. The frequency of parents' giving in to a child's requests for a particular toy increases with the age of the child.
5. Parents are preferred twice as much as peers as a source of product information even by adolescent children.
6. Mothers are the general purchasing agent for most families; they therefore make the majority of actual toy purchasers.

MIKE ROGERS'S SITUATION

In February Mike Rogers, toy department manager for Lockner's Department Store, contemplated the toy department's role in the firm's overall merchandising strategy. The toy department has been used as a seasonal "leader" department; that is, its primary function was to attract consumers into the store during the Christmas season by offering an excellent selection of popular toys at competitive prices. During the rest of the year, the toy department was largely neglected both by Lockner's management and by Lockner's customers. At these times, Lockner's stocks seasonal toys plus a variety of the most popular toys. Prices are kept competitive.

Lockner's toy stock during the nonholiday seasons consists primarily of the most popular toys and dolls. Rogers had never bought many board games, European specialty toys, specialty and collectable dolls, or the more extraordinary toys. Instead, he'd chosen to stay with the basics except for the seasonal promotions.

Recently, Rogers wondered whether a new role for the toy department might be worth considering. Rogers believed it would be appropriate to review the department's overall situation with the idea of identifying strategy alternatives and making possible recommendations for a new merchandising role for the toy department.

ASSIGNMENT

1. What options are available for the future selling season?
2. Identify the merchandising role you would adopt for Lockner's toy department and justify your selection.

*This case was prepared by George Prough and Dale Lewison, The University of Akron.

■ CASE 11–2
Fredericks of Hollywood: Heading toward the Mainstream*

Fredericks of Hollywood, the California-based specialty retailer had fallen on hard times. For nearly fifty years, Fredericks' stores had been providing consumers with a vast array of "naughty" products. Originally a seller of women's intimate apparel, product offerings had been expanded to include "adult toys," explicit books, and other novelty goods.

Throughout the early 1980s, sales and profits had been on a downslide. By the end of 1986, it had become clear that Fredericks was in trouble. Profits had fallen steadily, having peaked at $4 million in 1981, plummeting to a loss of nearly $2 million in 1986. Assuming the position of chairman and CEO in 1985, George Tomson had quickly recognized that Fredericks' product strategy needed to be reformulated.

Over the years, the retailer's merchandising mix had lost a clear focus. In addition to the provocative line of intimate apparel, Fredericks' stores also carried a variety of unrelated, often unproductive, categories such as off-color novelty items, explicit reading material, sportswear, and outerwear. Product offerings ranged from wigs and costumes to earthquake-proof ceiling mirrors to musical Christmas underwear. Merchandise selections appeared to be more oriented toward providing shock value than quality or style.

In addition to carrying a confusing and cluttered array of merchandise, Fredericks had also earned the reputation of being a tacky and garish place to shop. Mannequins, looking very much like ladies-of-the-evening, sported the raciest of undergarments. Daring lingerie, predominantly in red and/or black, was scattered throughout the stores. Few pastels were to be found. Also scarce was any type of plain or simply styled lingerie. Most of the retailer's offerings sported lace, bows, metal embellishments, peek-a-boo openings, or some combination of these adornments. Stores were disorganized and unattractive, having lost any real merchandising polish amid scattered goods, many of which were not in line with the retailer's original product focus—intimate apparel.

A variety of societal trends had chipped away at Fredericks' success. The loose, free-living lifestyles of the 1960s and 1970s had been replaced by the more conservative, professionally oriented lifestyles of the 1980s. Sexuality was no longer being flaunted openly—and the mysterious aura of romance was back. As America faced the 1990s, a pronounced trend back toward the importance of home, hearth, and the family was emerging. These trends, coupled with the stigma attached to Fredericks' name, made many consumers apprehensive to even be seen walking into a Fredericks store.

Especially threatening to Fredericks was the staggering number of women entering the workplace. For these women, intimate apparel often represented their only means of self-expression underneath business suits and uniforms. Products that were attractive, yet practical and comfortable, were winning out over Fredericks' explicit underthings. Out were animal prints and metal-studded, black vinyl teddys. In were soft cottons and silks with more conservative styling and feminine detail.

In the intimate apparel market, Fredericks was faced with competition on many fronts. Over fifty percent of intimate apparel volume was accounted for by department and discount stores. Chain stores, such as Sears, J.C. Penney, and Montgomery Ward, together captured over 20 percent of retail dollars in the segment.

Fredericks was also being challenged by formidable competition within the specialty retailing segment. The Limited's Victoria's Secret was a rapidly rising star. These remarkably successful stores featured high quality, softly feminine intimate apparel, as well as an upscale, beautifully decorated store atmosphere. The chain's rapidly increasing popularity was causing even major department stores to reevaluate the merchandising strategies of their women's foundations lines. Along with Victoria's Secret, other specialty stores featuring upscale, intimate apparel included Mentionables and Knickerbox.

Faced with an outdated product line, changing consumer values, and a wide range of competitive threats, Fredericks needed to reevaluate its merchandise strategy and competitive position.

ASSIGNMENT

1. Evaluate Fredericks' product line strategy in terms of variety and assortment. Identify its shortcomings and strengths. What changes in product selection do you recommend?
2. Who are Fredericks' customers? Based on current product line and merchandising tactics, develop a lifestyle profile (attitudes, interests, and values) of the typical customer. Who *should* Fredericks' customers be? Develop a hypothetical lifestyle profile of this person.
3. How might Fredericks reformulate its product strategy to address competitive threats? Develop a product positioning strategy that would give Fredericks a competitive niche in the market.
4. In view of its relatively small size, Fredericks of Hollywood has remarkably high name recognition. What product strategies could be used to capitalize in this recognition?

*This case was prepared by Amy Morgan, The University of Akron.

Sources: Marianne Wilson, "The De-Sleazification of Frederick's" *Chain Store Age Executive,* September 1989, 94–96; Kathleen Kerwin, "Frederick's of Hollywood Trades Its X Rating for an R," *Business Week,* December 11, 1989, 64; and Pat Corwin, "Staying on Top of Daywear Trends," *Discount Merchandiser,* January 1988, 44–46.

ENDNOTES

1. Sir Hardy Ames, "A Century of Fashion," *The FIT Review* 6, Spring 1990, 15.
2. Jacques Pessis, "Pierre Cardin: An Interview by Jacques Pessis," *The FIT Review* 6, Spring 1990, 29.
3. Kathleen Deveny, "Can Ms. Fashion Bounce Back?" *Business Week,* January 16, 1989, 64.
4. Fisher A. Rhymes, "The Fashion of Performance," *The FIT Review* 4 (Spring 1988), 30.
5. Ibid., 31.
6. Bob Garfield, "Images a Plus for Wendy's," *Advertising Age,* April 13, 1987, 30.
7. Cotten Timberlake, "Laura Ashley Chain Enduring Tough Times," *Akron Beacon Journal,* December 18, 1989, C–6.
8. See Stuart Silverstein, "No Fast Explanation for Need to Save Time," *Akron Beacon Journal,* May 3, 1990, A1, A7.
9. Eugene Carlson, "A Small Business Thrives on Oversize Clothes for Kids," *The Wall Street Journal,* September 22, 1984, B–2.
10. Stephen Phillips, "It's Turnaround Time for Verna Gibson," *Business Week,* February 20, 1989, 117–118.
11. Penney Gill, "Bridge-(Wo)manship," *Stores,* October 1987, 20.
12. See Alain Bultez, Els Gijsbrechts, Philippe Naert, and Piet Vanden Abeele, "Asymmetric Cannibalism in Retail Assortments," *Journal of Retailing* 65, Summer 1989, 153–92.
13. Amy Dunkin, "The Newly Minted Penney: Where Fashion Rules," *Business Week,* April 17, 1989, 88–90.
14. Joyce Anne Olivler, "Epilady's Popularity Is a Sisterly Success Store," *Marketing News,* May 14, 1990, 8–9.
15. Peter Newcomb, "Can Video Stores Survive," *Forbes,* February 5, 1990, 39.
16. See Seth Lubove, "As the Worms Turn," *Forbes,* March 19, 1990, 76, 80, 83.
17. Jeannetta A. Jarnow, Miriam Guerreiro, and Beatrice Judelle, *Inside the Fashion Business* (New York: Macmillan Publishing Company, 1987), 28.
18. Ibid.
19. See Maryanne Smith Bohlinger, *Merchandising Buying* (Boston: Allyn and Bacon, 1990), 175–89.
20. Cyndee Miller, "Fashion Industry Adapts to New Consumer Power," *Marketing News,* February 5, 1990, 1–2.
21. John A. Quelch, "Marketing the Premium Product," *Business Horizons,* May–June 1987, 44.
22. Miriam Tatzel, "Skill and Motivation in Clothes Shopping: Fashion-Conscious, Independent, and Apathetic Consumers," *Journal of Retailing* 58 (Winter 1982), 91–92.
23. Sallie Hook, "Managers Must Know Conceptual Distinctions of Fashion Marketing," *Marketing News,* May 8, 1987, 23.
24. See Pat Corwin, "Alternatives to Acidwash: New Looks in Men's Jeans," *Discount Merchandiser,* February 1990, 60–64.
25. Miriam Tatzel, "Skill and Motivation," 56.
26. Walter J. Salmon and Karen A. Cmar, "Private Labels Are Back in Fashion," *Harvard Business Review* May–June 1987, 102.
27. See Pauline Yoshihashi, "Everything Looks in Place for Sellers of Neatness Aids," *The Wall Street Journal,* April 2, 1990, B–1, B–2.
28. Penney Gill, "WSJ Profiles Seven Shopper Types in New Study," *Stores,* November 1989, 37.
29. Faye Rice, "Yuppie Spending Gets Serious," *Fortune,* March 27, 1989, 148.
30. Scott Hume, "Sears Gains Exclusivity with Disney Contract," *Advertising Age,* November 23, 1987, 63.
31. See "Consumers: Store Brands Should Have the Same Quality as National Brands," *Marketing News,* May 8, 1989, 5.
32. Salmon and Cmar, "Private Labels," 99.
33. "Marketing Goes through Series of Profound Changes," *Drug & Cosmetic Industry,* February 1990, 24.
34. Penney Gill, "Licensing: Less Puff, More Meat," *Stores,* June 1989, 45.
35. Ela Schwartz, "A New Lease on Leasing," *Discount Merchandiser,* August 1989, 59–64.
36. "How Penney's Saluted Mickey and Friends," *Stores,* February 1987, 14.
37. Ibid., Penny Gill, "Licensing: Less Puff, More Meat."
38. Tim Hammonds, "The Price of Two Many Failures," *Progressive Grocer,* February 1990, 46, 48.
39. "McCrory: Redefining the 5 & 10," *Chain Store Age Executive,* July 1987, 15.
40. Ela Schwarts, "Heck's: Life after Chapter XI," *Discount Merchandiser,* February 1990, 24–30.
41. Muriel J. Adams, "Kids' Specialty Retailing," *Stores,* March 1990, 18–24.
42. Jennifer Pellet, "Aggressive Growth in Grocery?" *Discount Merchandiser,* April 1990, 46–48.
43. Mark Ivey, Lois Therrien, and Maria Shao, "It's Not Just a Fill-up Anymore, It's an Event," *Business Week,* June 19, 1989, 90.
44. See Ela Schwartz, "Capitalizing On Overlooked Toys," *Discount Merchandiser,* February 1990, 52, 56–57.
45. Jay L. Johnson, "Hypermarkets Thrive in Minneapolis," *Discount Merchandiser,* April 1990, 56–60.
46. "Hot Format for New Growth: Superspecialists," *Stores,* August 1987, 63.
47. See Howard Schlossberg, "Office Supply Superstores Reshape the Industry," *Marketing News,* January 22, 1990, 2. Also see "Firm That Ignited Superstore Rage Makes Plans to Stay Ahead of Pack," *Marketing News,* January 22, 1990, 2.
48. Edward DiMingo, "The Fine Art of Positioning," *The Journal of Business Strategy,* March/April 1988, 34.
49. Ibid.

50. Jeffrey A. Trachtenberg, "R.I.P. Fred the Furrier," *Forbes,* February 20, 1989, 122–123.
51. Kathleen Deveny, "Middle-Price Brands Come under Siege," *The Wall Street Journal,* March 20, 1990, B8.
52. Jagdish N. Sheth, "Emerging Trends for the Retailing Industry," *Journal of Retailing* 59 (Fall 1983), 14.
53. See Robert J. Kopp, Robert J. Eng, and Douglas J. Tigert, "A Competitive Structure and Segmentation Analysis of the Chicago Fashion Market," *Journal of Retailing* 65, Winter 1989, 496–515.
54. Mario Shao, "The King of Kitchens Heads for the Living Room," *Business Week,* February 13, 1989, 63.
55. "Reorganization at K mart Specialty Retailing," *Discount Merchandiser,* April 1990, 16.
56. Muriel J. Adams, "Hot New Retail Formats," *Stores,* February 1988, 34–35.

OUTLINE

OBJECTIVES

- Appreciate the increased importance of the retailer's service offering in providing customer satisfaction.
- Recognize the need for customer service quality in all aspects of the retailer service program.
- Describe service levels for both customer service features and customer service actions.
- Identify the principal objectives in a retail service program.
- Name and profile the major features of a customer service program.
- Discuss the five stages in creating positive customer service actions.

PART IV

SERVICE STRATEGIES

Providing Sales-Support Services

CHAPTER 12

THE SERVICE IMPERATIVE

It seems so simple. Businesses exist to serve customers and should bend over backward to satisfy their needs. But too many companies still don't get it. And in the 1990s, more customers are likely to take the opportunity to reward the ones that do.[1]

Whatever service means to each retailer, keeping shoppers happy will be ever more important. With a glut of stores and legions of smart customers, those who don't will find the decade ahead no bargain.[2]

The good news is that there is a growing awareness of the room for improvement in service quality, and more and more companies are trying to do something about it. There is also a growing realization that service quality can ultimately make or break a company and that customer satisfaction has direct bottom line implications.[3]

CUSTOMER SERVICE: DEFINITION AND DESCRIPTION

If the 1990s is the decade of the customer, then customer service is the strategy of the decade. Business futurists are subcribing to customer service—the key role in creating customer satisfaction. The enhanced role of customer service can be explained in part by the partial neutralization of some of the other elements in the retailer's strategic arsenal. Technological advances have resulted in a slew of products of similar quality; hence, product quality differentiation becomes more difficult. These same technologies have made it possible to locate, communicate, duplicate, and distribute new product concepts, thereby limiting the retailer's ability to create unique product assortments for extended periods of time. New, expanded retailer formats (e.g., super-specialty stores and mega-general merchants), with their expanded assortments, further complicate the problem of developing either a better customer-focused merchandise mix or a one-stop-shopping opportunity. Competitive pricing strategies such as sales promotional pricing, everyday low pricing, and price-matching policies have all contributed to the problem of trying to differentiate on the bases of price. Finally, many market areas are overstored; this market saturation hampers the retailer's efforts at finding trading areas and site locations that will provide a locational advantage. So, what's left? Quality customer service is the remaining merchandising area that is lacking or underdeveloped in many retail organizations. Service quality can be defined as the difference between customer expectations of service and the customer's perception of the service actually received.[4]

For both retailers selling products and pure service retailers, competitive success is now and will continue to be driven to a large extent by customer perceptions of the quality of the services provided by the retailer.[5] In order to develop a quality service program, retail management must first have an understanding of and an appreciation for the complexities of the service issue. Customer service can be defined as all the features, acts, and information that augment the customer's ability to realize the potential value of a core product or service.[6] This definition suggests a number of relationships that need to be clarified (see Figure 12–1). First, customer service is concerned with what augmenting service extras the retailer should provide.[7] *Customer service features* such as delivery and installation, alteration and repairs, wrapping and packaging, returns and adjustments, credit and layaway, parking and toting, information and complaint resolution, and store hours are all complementary services that enhance the customer's perceived value of the original purchase of a core product or service. Second, customer service is equally concerned with how or in what manner all of these extra service features are to be performed. *Customer service actions or acts* deal with

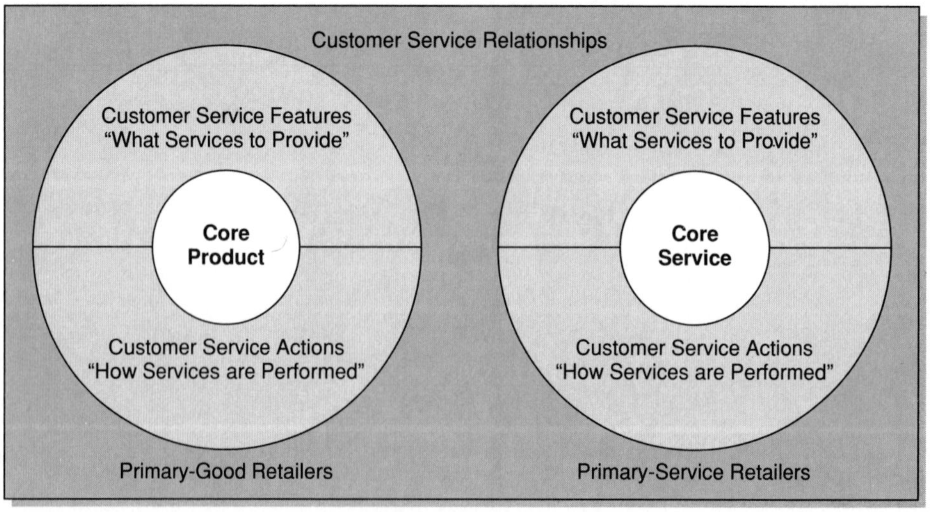

FIGURE 12–1 Customer service relationships

the issues of the friendliness, politeness, willingness, trustworthiness, dependability, reliability, security, and approachability of the service provider. Third, both the primary-good retailer, whose principal market offering is a core product (e.g., an apparel, hardware, or food retailer), and the primary-service retailer who centers on a core service (e.g., insurance agent, real estate broker, personal-care specialist) must be concerned with developing a quality service program that incorporates desired service features support by superior service actions. Finally, it is not sufficient to offer all of the required service features supported by superior service actions. The retailer must effectively communicate to the customer the extent of the service package by providing information that allows the customer to fully perceive the uniqueness and quality of the retailer's service offering.

CUSTOMER SERVICE: LEVELS AND OBJECTIVES

Service level assessment and the creation of service objectives are the initial tasks in developing a quality customer service strategy. Service level assessment determines where the retailer is in the service continuum, and identifying service objectives helps the retailer in directing the organization in doing what it ought to do.

Customer Service Levels

Retail management must establish service levels for both the types of services to be offered (service features) and the quality of the service offering (service actions). One set of dimensions and rating scales that might be used in evaluating the retailer's total service offering (customer service features and customer service actions) is shown in Figure 12–2.

Service Levels: Customer Service Features
Service levels for customer service features can be described in terms of customer expectations regarding the retailer's service offering (optional, expected, essential) or the extent of the retailer's service assortment (full-service, limited-service, or self-service). Figure 12–3 illustrates these two classification schemes.

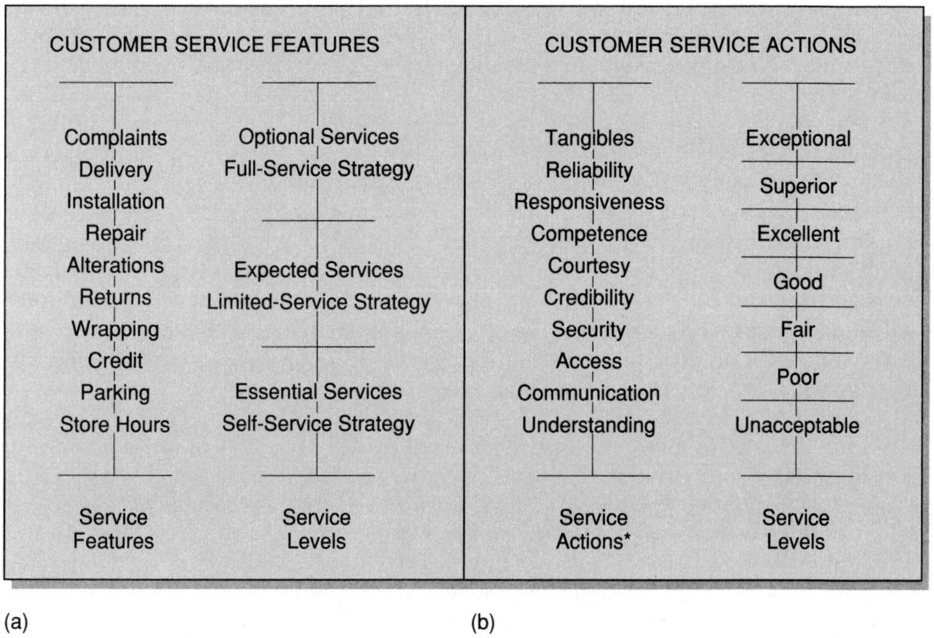

FIGURE 12–2
Service levels for customer service features and actions (source: adapted from Valarie A. Zeithaml, A. Parasuraman, and Leonard L. Berry, *Delivering Quality Service* [New York; The Free Press, 1990], 20–21)

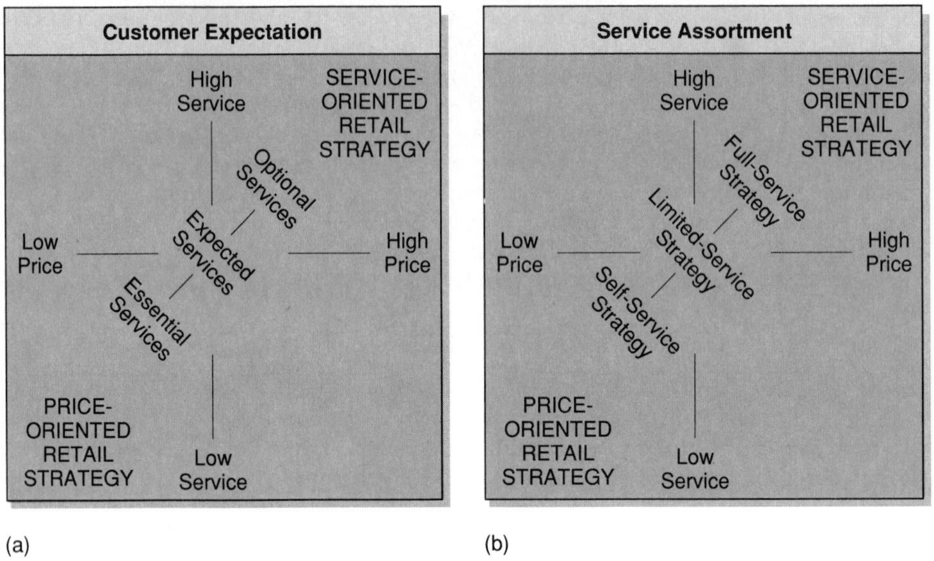

FIGURE 12–3
Service levels for customer service features (source: Reprinted by permission from BUSINESS Magazine. "How to Position for Retail Success," by George H. Lucas, Jr. and Larry G. Gresham, April-May-June 1988. Copyright © 1988 by the College of Business Administration, Georgia State University, Atlanta.)

Essential services are basic and necessary to the retailer's merchandising and operational activities; without them, the retailer could not meet the basic transactional needs of the customer. Without essential services, the retailer could not operate. Although essential services vary from one type of retail operation to another, the following services are essential to most retail formats: (1) maintaining store hours, (2) providing parking facilities, (3) supplying information and transactional assistance, (4) furnishing merchandise displays, and (5) handling customer complaints. Retailers who restrict their service offering to essential services are typically **self-service** operations that are pursuing a *price-oriented retail strategy* (see Figure 12–3b). Warehouse retailers, wholesale clubs, box supermarkets, and some discount stores selling staple merchandise are the most common proponents of this low-price, low-service strategy.

Expected services are not essential for the retailer to operate, but are expected by consumers. Failure to offer expected services is failure to meet customer expectations. Delivery, credit, and alterations are three services that consumers expect from appliance, furniture, and clothing stores, respectively. Consumer surveys and competitive analysis are the best ways to determine what's expected and what's not. Retailers who offer all essential and expected services are following a **limited-service** strategy. By offering a moderate level of service at middle-price points, this retailer targets the value-oriented consumer. Some chain stores, variety stores, and limited-line specialty retailers are the most common fence-sitters. In recent years, these middle-of-the-road operations have been caught in a competitive squeeze between high- and low-end retailers. With rising expectations for both better service and lower prices, middle-level retailers cannot compete with upscaled specialty department stores in service, and they fall short of the price levels offered by super-efficient, low-cost superstores.

Optional services are neither necessary to the retailer's operation nor expected by the customer. Nevertheless, optional services are used by retailers to develop a unique service offering and thereby distinguish themselves from other less service-intense retailers. For example, McDonald's added stock repeater boards in selected restaurants where businesspeople make up most of the morning trade.[8] The distinctive optional service mix offered by Nordstrom, the Seattle-based specialty department store, includes: (1) a no-questions-asked return policy backed by a full refund or exchange practice; (2) a formally dressed piano player in each store who provides soothing

Specialized services help to build store traffic.

background music; (3) a "personal book" on each regular customer that profiles the customer's preferences, needs, and buying history, together with important dates (birthdays) and other information that helps sales associates in providing individualized service; (4) shopping service that will find a needed product at a competitive store if it cannot be found at Nordstrom; (5) home, office, or anywhere delivery; (6) prompt and courteous service at all times under all conditions; and (7) free shopping environment that allows almost unlimited customer freedom in their involvement with the merchandise (e.g., no electronic security tags or limitations on the number of garments a customer can take into the fitting room). These important extras are in addition to the full range of services offered by other traditional department stores. With essential, expected, and optional services, the retail firm becomes a **full-service** retailer pursuing a service-oriented retail positioning strategy (see Figure 12–3). Some differentiating characteristics that separate service winners from service losers are identified in Figure 12–4.

FIGURE 12–4
Winning and losing in the retail service game

Winning Service Retailers

- Are noticeably more friendly, courteous and really care about customer satisfaction
- Go out of their way to understand customer needs
- Consider the smallest detail as critical
- Know the business exceedingly well: Its products, its services, its procedures, and how to get things done quickly and accurately
- Shine under pressure, especially in solving customer problems
- Adopt integrity as their byword
- Exhibit genuine appreciation for patronage

Losing Service Retailers

- Dehumanize the service delivery interaction by inattention or plastic professionalism
- Regard questions or service requests as interruptions or nuisances
- Often do not keep promises
- Are poor troubleshooters and unskilled in rectifying problems promptly
- Appear disorganized, inefficient, and waste the customer's time without noticeable regret
- Communicate in vague language

Source: George A. Rieder, " 'Show Me': The Secret to Building a Service-Minded Culture," *Retailing Issues Letter* (Center for Retailing Studies, Texas A&M University, June 1986), 1.

RETAIL STRATEGIES AND TACTICS

Service-Oriented Retail Strategies vs. Price-Oriented Retail Strategies

Strategic Characteristics

Management structure

Product offering

Functional emphasis areas

Location

Scale economies

Product mix

Service-Oriented Retail Strategy High Price, High Service (HPHS)	Price-Oriented Retail Strategy Low Price, Low Service (LPLS)
Decentralized. A great deal of decision-making responsibility is delegated to individuals in contact with customers.	**Centralized.** Nearly all decision-making power resides with high-level managers. Subordinates are provided with detailed guidelines for dealing with nearly all situations.
Customized. While the physical product may be similar, customer contact personnel provide various services desired by the customer (product information, comparison, assortment and so forth). In some instances (such as flower or gift shops), the salesperson may, in fact, create the physical product to the customer's specifications.	**Standardized.** The product is usually prepackaged and sold off the shelf, as is. Buying is centralized with almost no store-to-store variability within the chain. Minimal or no on-floor assistance is provided (or should be expected). Customer contact occurs largely at the checkout counter.
Marketing and store management. The major business functions are determining the most appropriate product offering (marketing research), developing the appropriate image in the customer's mind (promotion), and delivering that product at the point of sale (personal selling and store management). Buying is important and requires a high level of coordination with marketing and store management.	**Finance and buying.** The key aspect is acquiring the financial backing to buy in large quantities. Due to relatively low margins, costs must be carefully monitored to avoid moving into the red on a product category. Buyers play a key role in finding and securing large quantities of merchandise in a timely fashion. The role for marketing is communicating just how low the prices are.
Very important. Having a convenient location is one of the key services provided by the HPHS retailer. The site must minimize the "costs" of shopping at the store.	**Unimportant.** If prices are attractive enough, customers will be willing to expend effort to get to the LPLS store. Poor sites with their corresponding lower prices are just another way to keep costs down.
Very limited (if not negative). Due to the need to customize the total product offering, doing more of it is not necessarily cost effective, nor does it make it simpler. The small specialty store has a definite advantage here.	**Significant.** As the product being offered is standardized, buying and selling more of it reduces the costs associated with each transaction. Entrants in LPLS will benefit from prudent expansion of their operations.
Narrow and deep. This store is charging for assortment, so it must provide assortment. A shop specializing in a product area (such as lightbulbs) must carry a vast variety. In order to be knowledgeable and have adequate inventory in product area(s), the retailer definitely needs to limit the number of areas (widths) in which products are offered.	**Wide and shallow.** It is important to offer a vast array of merchandise, but minimal selection in a product category. Brands should be purchased only when special deals are available. Due to the self-service nature of the sales floor, each product consumes a lot of space. This reduces selection and often results in simpler decisions on the part of consumers.

Service-Oriented Retail Strategies vs. Price-Oriented Retail Strategies (continued)

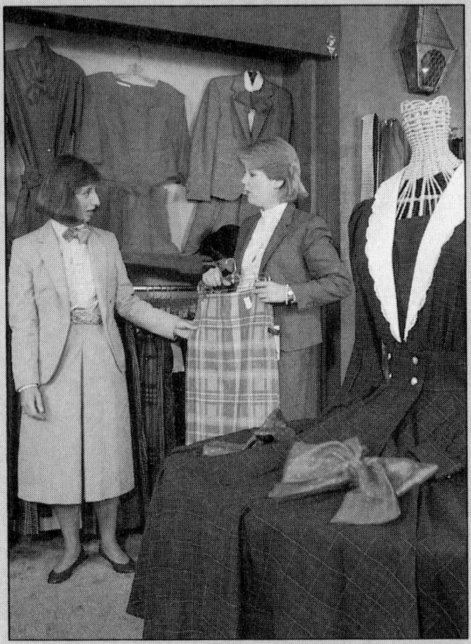

Strategic Characteristics

Stock turnover

Promotional emphasis

Orientation

Vendor relationship

Service-Oriented Retail Strategy High Price, High Service (HPHS)	Price-Oriented Retail Strategy Low Price, Low Service (LPLS)
Slow. Due to the depth of the product offering needed to provide adequate assortments, inventory turnover should be relatively slow. Profitability comes not from turnover, but from the profit margins on each item.	**Rapid.** Items that are slow movers take up space and should not be carried. Because the retailer is making only a small percentage on each item, a large number of units must be sold.
Customer service. Advertising and related promotions should stress the high service image of the retailer. Retailers should select a medium that can deliver a high service institutional message. Personal selling must deliver the promised level of service on the sales floor. The success of this approach depends on it.	**Price.** Advertisements must stress the store's major advantage—low price. Personal selling plays no role beyond the clerk at the checkout counter or the stock person removing a selected item from a high shelf. In many instances, such as Sam's Wholesale Clubs, the only promotion is word of mouth. Some deep discounters are making extensive use of direct mail.
Customer satisfaction, long run. A chief outcome from a successful HPHS strategy must be the development of a relationship with a sizable group of loyal customers. The major concern is customer satisfaction with the ability of the retailer to provide a total product that meets the customer's needs on a regular basis.	**Customer satisfaction, short run.** If the merchandise is of acceptable quality and the price is low enough, the customer will buy it and be satisfied. Low service levels can lead to repeat customers, but not to the development of true relationships.
Strong. The vendor's sales force must work closely with the retailer's buyers and salespeople to move the product through the channel. It is critical that store sales personnel have high levels of product knowledge. The vendor is the major source of this information.	**Loose.** The vendor sees the retailer primarily as a way to move volume merchandise. Margins do not cover service at any stage of the distribution channel. Once the retailer finds a lower price, the relationship will terminate.

Source: Reprinted by permission from BUSINESS Magazine. "How to Position for Retail Success," by George H. Lucas, Jr., and Larry G. Gresham, April-May-June 1988. Copyright © 1988 by the College of Business Administration, Georgia State University, Atlanta.

Service Level: Customer Service Actions

How services are performed is as important as what services are offered. For example, to have an unconditional merchandise return policy, then to hassle customers when they return merchandise is a totally inappropriate service strategy. Any service feature (e.g., delivery and installation) is only as good as the service actions (e.g., courtesy and reliability) that support it. As shown in Figure 12–2b, service level ratings for customer-service actions can range from unacceptable to exceptional. Using the seven point scale of: (1) unacceptable, (2) poor, (3) fair, (4) good, (5) excellent, (6) superior, or (7) exceptional, the retailer can evaluate any list of service actions that might be appropriate to the retail organization.[9] One such list is provided in Figure 12–5.

Customer Service Objectives

In the following discussion of customer service objectives, the focus is on primary-goods retailers and the supplementary service offering. Primary-service retailers are discussed in Chapter 20.

Increasing Form Utility

Retailers often receive products from suppliers that require final adjustments and assembly. Additional form-creating services that retailers offer include altering and tailoring for clothing products, installing appliances and home furnishings, engraving and personalizing jewelry, and assembling lawn and garden equipment. Busy, time-constrained consumers often do not have time to fool around with getting a product ready to use.

Facilitating Time Utility

For some consumers the right time is now; they want immediate gratification. Consumer credit and extended store hours are two services retailers offer to create time utility. Other consumers are more concerned with saving time; for them, retailers can add time utility to their product mix by accepting telephone and mail orders or by providing carry-out services. Layaway services also add time utility by permitting the consumer to reserve a purchase for some future time when payment is more convenient. Finally, storage service (e.g., for furs) provides consumers with safe places to keep merchandise for future use. Prompt and efficient service is fast becoming a must for the full-service retailer. "In just a few years, the standards for photoprocessing have shifted from seven days to overnight to one hour. The same thing is occurring

FIGURE 12–5
Representative list of customer-service actions

Tangibles	Physical facilities, equipment, and appearance of personnel
Reliability	Ability to perform the promised service dependably and accurately
Responsiveness	Willingness to help customers and provide prompt service
Assurance	Knowledge and courtesy of employees and their ability to inspire trust and confidence
Empathy	Caring, individualized attention the firm provides its customers

Source: A. Parasuraman, Valeria A. Zeithaml, and Leonard L. Berry, "SERVQUAL: A Multiple-Item Scale for Measuring Consumer Perceptions of Service Quality," *Journal of Retailing* 64 (Spring 1988): 23.

with mail delivery, eyeglass service, furniture delivery, automobile maintenance, and other categories."[10]

Enhancing Place Utility

The best way to add place utility to a product mix is through convenient locations. Delivery services also form an essential part of some retailers' total product. Without home deliveries, most bulky products (e.g., furniture and appliances) would have no value to consumers who have no means to transport them. Some food retailers offer catering services to enhance their products' place value.

Promoting Possession Utility

Possession utility is the satisfaction consumers receive from owning and using a product. To promote possession utility, retailers must provide consumers with information to facilitate the exchange of ownership process. Personal selling, fashion shows, information booths, complaint desks, bridal registries, and consultants are some of the informational services retailers offer. Vons, a California-based supermarket chain, is experimenting with VideOcart, a shopping cart that has a video screen capable of displaying everything from sale items in a particular aisle to ingredients for a chicken teriyaki dinner and where to find them.[11] Given that two out of three shoppers make buying decisions while in the store, providing useful information at the point-of-sale is a possession-enhancing service of considerable value to the customer. Additionally, retailers provide credit, cash personal checks, and tender itemized receipts (an itemized list of products purchased by name or brand model, size, per-unit price, number of items purchased, date and time of purchase, and basic store information).

Increasing Customer Convenience

Services that provide customer convenience and comfort include packaging, bagging, free parking, check cashing, restaurants, snack bars, restrooms, lounges, parcel checking, push carts, water fountains, and complimentary coffee. Any service that helps customers get into the store, travel around the store, and stay in the store not only enhances customers' convenience but also increases the likelihood of planned purchases as well as additional, unplanned purchases. Shoppers at California-based Lucky Stores who want to pay in cash no longer have to withdraw the money from their wallet or suffer through a time-consuming check-approval process. Instead, using a debit card, in just seven seconds customers can pay a retailer directly out of their checking accounts via an electronic funds transfer.[12] At Fred Meyer's 187,000-square-foot megastores in Portland, Oregon, customer convenience is enhanced through the use of large-scale illuminated maps and directories at each entrance. In addition, "ten interactive directories are scattered throughout the store. Printed maps are available for customers to carry. Customer service call buttons are everywhere in the store. Huge banners with department names and corresponding illustrations hang from the ceiling and can be seen at great distances."[13]

Creating a Store Image

A retailer can use the service mix to pursue one of several image strategies. By offering a *full range of services,* the retailer can promote the image of being a full-service store with quality merchandise and prestige prices. Conversely, the retailer can choose to offer only services that are essential to the exchange process, thereby creating a no-frills, low-price image. Wal-Mart is adept at striking the delicately balanced need to convince customers that its prices are low while still retaining an edge in customer service. To create its service image, Wal-Mart uses such little touches that enhance its image. For example, at Wal-Mart: (1) an aggressively friendly grandfather guards the entrance, smiling at babies and striking up conversations with shoppers; (2) a store employee follows customers to their cars to pick up their shopping carts; (3) all employees wear subdued blue vests that make it easy for customers to identify and reinforces Wal-Mart's image as a friendly, nonthreatening place to shop; and (4) all merchandise is bagged in brown paper sacks rather than plastic bags, which customers find more difficult to handle.[14]

Providing Customer Security

Restroom attendants, properly lighted stores and parking facilities, and security guards all enhance the customer's feeling of a safe and secure environment. Perhaps equally important to most customers is product security, provided by such services as warranties, return privileges, allowances, and maintenance contracts. L.L. Bean promises 100 percent satisfaction or your money back, although other catalog operations (e.g., Horchow Mail Order and Sharper Image) offer only limited guarantees on merchandise.[15] The following is another example of how to provide customer security:

> Sterling Jewelry stores offers a diamond guarantee and certificate of registration that guarantees the diamond against loss from mounting for life; will refund the full purchase price within 90 days if the customer wishes to return the stone; states that the diamond has been cut and polished by master craftsmen; offers lifetime cleaning and inspection at no charge; guarantees the mounting against manufacturer's defect; and allows the full purchase price plus an additional amount based on current market value when the ring is exchanged for a larger diamond.
>
> An ESP agreement (Extended Service Plan) gives protection for three years for a $10 charge. Under these terms Sterling guarantees to make any repairs needed, at no charge, on protected jewelry worn under normal conditions.[16]

Improving Store Traffic

Retailers frequently incorporate into their mix services intended solely to generate additional traffic through their stores. For example, some stores provide (1) rooms for public and private meetings; (2) space for various types of exhibits; (3) rental services for products that might not be related to their product mix; (4) post office, utility bill collection, and entertainment ticket facilities; (5) license bureaus; and (6) various types of professional services (e.g., tax, health, and personal care). All these services tend to draw in customers who might not otherwise be attracted. Macy's in San Francisco created its Hospitality Room for conventioneers who are visiting the city. These traffic-building services range from offering refreshments to shopping assistance.[17]

Unconditional guarantees are services that provide customer security.

Offering an on-site cooking course can help a retailer generate store traffic as well as promote sales.

Establishing Competitive Position

Retailers can use services to establish either competitive parity or to create a competitive edge. To remain competitive, retailers offer many services because they are essential to the retailer's operation, competitors offer them, or customers expect them. To gain a competitive edge, some retailers offer services that are not essential to their operations or expected by consumers. A distinctive service mix can create competitive benefits that are long lasting and reasonably difficult to imitate. Burger King's Kids Club program is directed at neutralizing McDonald's strong "kiddieland" image; membership in the program includes "bimonthly giveaways, posters, logos, personalized identification cards, and a periodic newsletter that chronicles fictional escapades of the club's animated founding members."[18] Return trade and greater store loyalty are two of the benefits of customer involvement activities. Toys 'R' Us has its kids' club, the Geoffrey Fun Club, that provides quarterly newsletters and a personalized adventure book.

Building Specific Demand

Although most services contribute either directly or indirectly to the total demand, retailers often build demand for a particular product line or item by offering services that focus consumers' attention on that product. Many cosmetic companies, including Elizabeth Arden and Shiseido, use computer simulation to provide their customers with high-tech information about skin and hair needs. Shiseido's Makeup Simulator "is able to give the customer an on-screen make-over, change hair styles, . . . and add henna or highlights without physical application of the product to the customer."[19] Because of the tremendous increase in the number of "do it yourselfers," some home centers offer instructional services and classes on how to repair plumbing, hang a light fixture, and so on to promote related product lines.

CUSTOMER SERVICE FEATURES

Customer service features include all those "extras" retailers offer to consumers to enhance the core product or service and to facilitate purchases. Key components of the service feature mix include store hours, credit plans, delivery, alterations and repairs, wrapping, and complaint resolution.

Store Hours

The retailer in today's market does not work an eight-to-five job. Because of changing consumer lifestyles, increasing competitive conditions, various legal restrictions, and additional operational requirements, the retailer must provide store hours that are convenient to the customers in its area.

Evening hours from Monday through Saturday have become commonplace for most supermarkets and other retailers of necessity goods. Many supermarkets are now open twenty-four hours a day; since many supermarkets are staffed all night with stocking personnel, around-the-clock openings can be accomplished within reasonable cost constraints.[20] Likewise, for many mass merchandisers operating in community and regional shopping centers, evening hours have become an expected service. "Regional malls across the country are opening between 9:30 and 10 A.M. and closing between 9 and 9:30 P.M. six days a week, with some regional exceptions on Saturday. Sunday hours, where permitted, are 11 or 12 to 5 or 6."[21] In part, night openings are the retailer's response to changing lifestyles of consumers who find it more convenient and enjoyable to shop at night. Evening hours not only increase the cost of doing business (labor, utilities) but also increase personnel problems (individuals who do not want to work at night) and security risks (as exemplified by the number of night robberies at convenience-food stores).[22]

The issue of **Sunday hours** is similar to night hours in all respects except for the social, religious, and legal restrictions imposed in some parts of the country. Many state and local governments have enacted laws, often referred to as "blue laws," that determine (1) whether Sunday openings are allowed, (2) what types of products can be sold on Sundays (necessities vs. nonnecessities), and (3) when and how many hours stores can be open (e.g., from 1 to 6 P.M.). In addition to legal restrictions, retailers should consider the effect Sunday hours might have on their stores' images.

Consumer Credit

"Charge it!" "Buy now, pay later!" "Easy terms available!" "Only $10 down and $10 a month!" "Financing is available!" "Four years to pay!" These notices proclaim that credit has become a basic way of life for many U.S. consumers. To a substantial majority, credit has become either an essential or an expected part of the retailer's service mix. The question for most retailers is not whether to offer credit, but what type of credit to offer.

Attitudes toward credit depend to a certain extent on social class. In a study of credit card usage, researchers found that lower classes used credit cards for installment purchase, restricted use of credit cards to purchases of durable and necessity goods, and tended to search for retailers that honored their particular credit cards. In contrast, the researchers learned that upper-class consumers view credit cards more as a convenience, use them in making luxury-goods purchases, and do not seek out stores that accept their particular credit cards.

Credit Systems

The retailer can elect one of several different credit systems: in-house credit, third-party credit, and private-label credit.

In-House Credit System. An **in-house credit system** (also referred to as proprietary credit) is owned, operated, and managed by the retail firm. Retailers offer credit services for a variety of reasons: (1) consumers expect the service, (2) store image will be enhanced, (3) many consumers cannot afford the retailer's assortment of merchandise unless they are offered credit, (4) competitors offer credit arrangements, and (5) market and economic conditions dictate the need for credit. Offering an in-house credit plan has advantages and disadvantages for most retailers.[23] Advantages include the following:

- *Customer attraction.* Stores that offer credit services tend to attract customers who are more interested in product quality, store reputation, and service offerings and less interested in prices.
- *Customer loyalty.* Credit-granting stores more easily build repeat business, since credit customers tend to be more loyal than cash customers.
- *Customer goodwill.* Credit-granting stores generally have a more personal relationship with their customers and therefore become the first place the customer shops for a particular purchase.
- *Increased sales.* Credit services increase total sales volume because credit customers tend to buy more goods and pay higher prices than customers who do not use credit.
- *Sales stabilization.* Credit sales are more evenly spread throughout the month, whereas cash sales correspond more closely with those times immediately following paydays.
- *Market information.* Credit applications provide considerable amounts of information (age, sex, income, occupation, etc.) on the credit consumer; credit records can reveal a history of what, when, and where (which department) the customer bought.
- *Promotional effort.* Because credit customers are known to be customers of the store, they are an excellent foundation on which to build a mailing or telephone list for special promotions; additionally, the monthly statement credit customers receive is an effective vehicle for promotional literature.

In addition to these advantages, retailers realize the disadvantages associated with offering credit services. The most commonly cited disadvantages are those related to increased costs:

- *Higher operating expenses* result from additional facilities, personnel, equipment, and communications expenses necessary to provide credit services.
- *Costs of fees and commissions* paid to outside credit agencies that provide part or all of the retailer's credit services.
- *Tied-up funds* diverted to accounts receivable, thereby forcing the retailer to borrow working capital.
- *Bad debts,* losses from uncollectables, are part of the risk of providing credit services.

These additional costs are acceptable if they can be covered by offsetting revenues. Some retailers realize a substantial profit from their charges for credit services; Sears, for example, makes substantial profits on its retail credit operations.

Third-Party Credit System. As an alternative to offering in-store credit services, many retailers use **third-party credit systems,** accepting one or more of the credit cards issued by outside institutions. Often referred to as third-party cards, the most common types are those issued by banks (MasterCard and VISA) and entertainment-card companies (American Express, Diner's Club, and Carte Blanche). Gasoline companies also issue credit cards that consumers can use at stations carrying their brands.

Major advantages to accepting third-party cards are that retailers (1) do not have the problems of establishing and maintaining a credit department; (2) are relieved of the unpleasant tasks of investigating credit applications, billing customers, and pursuing collections; (3) can offer credit to consumers who otherwise would not qualify (e.g., out-of-town consumers) and thereby make sales they might have lost; and (4) can maintain a steady cash flow, since financial institutions convert credit card sales quickly and regularly into cash minus agreed-on service charges. Financial institutions are making their credit cards very attractive through a number of creative bank-card enhancements; the most common enhancement is the multipurpose card that allows customers to make long distance calls, charge merchandise, use ATMs, and buy travel insurance.[24] The retailer does, however, have certain responsibilities in accepting and processing credit card sales, including filling out sales drafts properly, cooperating with financial institutions in identifying expired and stolen cards, obtaining authorization for charges over certain purchase ceilings, and submitting sales drafts to the credit agency within an agreed-on time.

The chief disadvantages for retailers that accept credit cards are the costs of the service and the depersonalization of relationships with customers. Credit agencies charge rates varying with the retailer's potential credit sales volume and several market and competitive conditions. Since the rate is negotiable, the retailer should make every effort to obtain the best possible terms. Depersonalization comes in the form of reduced store loyalty (the customer can shop anywhere the credit card is accepted) and the consumer's lost feeling of "belonging" to a store in which they have a personal account.

Private-Label System. A **private-label credit system** is one that retailers offer under their name but that a bank operates and manages. The retail firm realizes most of the benefits associated with in-house credit systems while avoiding many of the problems associated with credit management.[25] Typically, the cost of this type of system is comparable to most in-house systems, and it is an attractive option for the retailer that has had difficulty turning its credit operation into a profit center.[26]

Credit Plans

Depending on the type of credit system, one or more of three different types of credit plans will be available to the consumer: the open account, the installment plan, and revolving credit. The retailer's decision about which and how many types of credit plans to offer depends on the customer's need for a particular type of credit balanced against the retailer's need for cash for operating expenses.

Open Account. Often referred to as the "regular charge" or "open book credit," the **open-account credit** plan allows customers to buy merchandise and to pay for it within a specific time period without finance charges or interest. Usually, the customer is expected to pay the full amount within thirty days of the billing date, although some retailers extend the due date to either sixty or ninty days to promote special occasions or to distinguish their credit services from the thirty-day services their competitors

Affinity and Co-Branding Credit Cards

RETAIL STRATEGIES AND TACTICS

Affinity cards and co-branding credit cards are two additional credit systems available to the retailer. Affinity cards are based on a relationship among an affinity group or organization (e.g., American Marketing Association, Rails To Trails Conservancy, California State University), a third-party credit system (e.g., VISA, MasterCard), and the individual customer and credit user. The relationship and involvement (i.e., affinity) might be emotional (Sierra Club), professional (American Bar Association), or intellectual (Texas A&M University); hence, greater card loyalty should be forthcoming. The affinity relationship might be illustrated as follows:

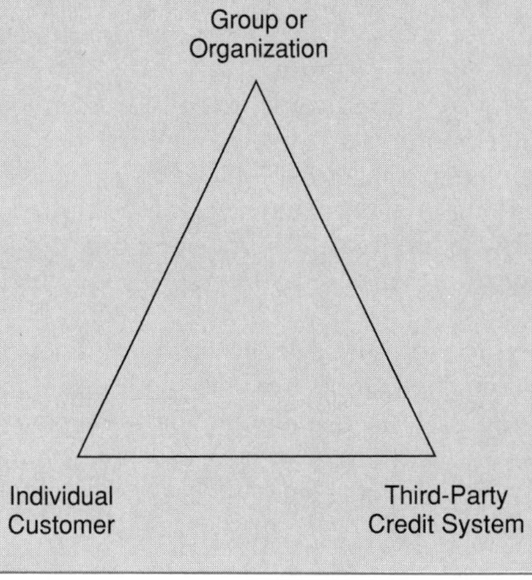

Co-branding cards involve a relationship among a retailer, a third-party credit system, and the individual customer and card user. Graphically, it might be portrayed as follows:

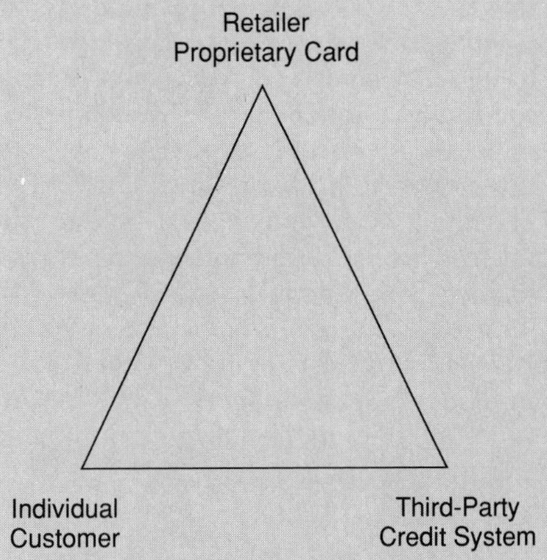

Typically, the credit card looks like the retailer's proprietary card (e.g., Younkers, May, Macy's, or Casual Corner), but has a VISA or MasterCard logo on it that allows the cardholder to use it not only in the retailer's store, but anyplace else where VISA or MasterCard are accepted. This type of an arrangement should enhance and maintain store loyalty and create greater customer convenience.

Source: Based in part on "Co-branding and Affinity Cards," *Stores,* February 1990, 20–21.

offer. This **deferred billing** is often used during the Christmas season as a sales promotion tool and as an incentive to finalize the sale of a major purchase (i.e., the appliance dealer who offers "ninety days same as cash"). Beyond the due date, if full payment is not received, the retailer can assess a finance charge. The retailer usually grants an open account without requiring the customer to make a down payment or to put up collateral to secure the purchase. Given the free nature of the service and its lack of formal security, retailers generally reduce both credit costs and risks by limiting open-account credit to customers who have established good credit records.

Installment Credit. Most customers would find it impossible to purchase large-ticket items such as automobiles, furniture, and appliances if they could not make small down payments and spread the additional payments over several months or years. The **installment-credit** plan allows consumers to pay their total purchase price (less down payment) in equal installment payments over a specified time period. Usually, equal installment payments are due monthly, although weekly and quarterly payments are optional. Retailers prefer to receive a down payment on installment purchases that equals or exceeds the initial depreciation of the product. Some retailers require only a minimal down payment or no down payment to make the sale.

Installment-credit arrangements are legal contracts between retailers and consumers. Terms and conditions include the total amount of each payment, the number of payments, and the dates the payments are due. In addition, the contract specifies financial charges (interest, service, insurance) and penalties for late or nonpayment. Retailers carry installment accounts in one of three ways: conditional sales agreements, chattel mortgages, and lease agreements. In the **conditional sales agreement,** the title of the goods passes to the consumer conditional on full payment. The retailer can repossess the product and obtain a judgment against the consumer for any lost product value and expenses resulting from repossession. Retailers prefer the conditional sales contract since it gives them the most protection from loss.

In a **chattel mortgage agreement,** title passes to the customer when the contract is signed, but the product is secured by a lien against it for the unpaid balance. **Lease agreements** are contracts in which the customer rents a product in the present with the option to buy in the future. Consumers usually pay periodic rent, which is applied toward the purchase price.

Revolving Credit. Revolving credit incorporates some of the features of both the open-account and installment plans. Of the several variations of revolving credit plans, the two most common are the fixed-term and the option-term.

The **fixed-term revolving credit** plan requires the customer to pay a fixed amount on any unpaid balance at regularly scheduled intervals (usually monthly) until the amount is paid in full. Under this plan, customers have a credit limit, such as $500, and may make credit purchases up to this limit as long as they continue to pay the agreed-on fixed payment (e.g., $50) each month. People who use fixed-term revolving accounts are usually assessed a finance charge (e.g., 1.5 percent per month, or 18 percent annually) on the unpaid balance.

Option-term revolving credit gives customers two payment options. They can either pay the full amount of the bill within a specified number of days (typically 30) and avoid any finance charges, or they can make at least a minimum payment and be assessed finance charges on the unpaid balance. As with the fixed-term account, a credit line is established and customers are free to make purchases up to the established limits.

Credit Management

A retailer that decides to offer in-store credit as part of the service mix must develop a credit-management system. Although the wide range of credit management activities is beyond the scope of this text, two activities essential to successful credit management are (1) forming sound policies for granting credit and (2) determining good procedures for collecting credit accounts.

Granting Credit. Before granting credit to individuals, retailers should first request that applicants complete a credit application. Whether the retailer personally investigates the applicant or uses one of the many credit bureaus, it should evaluate each individual on the basis of the **three C's of credit:** character, capacity, and capital.

Character in a credit sense refers to attributes that distinguish one individual from another in meeting obligations. Desirable traits include maturity and honesty—characteristics that indicate willingness to accept responsibility (to pay bills) regardless of the circumstances. Personal interviews, reference checks, and the applicant's credit history help the retailer evaluate this attribute.

Capacity is the measure of an individual's earning power and ability to pay. A credit applicant's income is important not only in deciding whether to extend credit, but also in determining how much credit to extend.

The third indication of credit worthiness is *capital* (i.e., the applicant's tangible assets). Accumulation of capital suggests that the applicant is capable of managing financial affairs and gives the retailer hope of recovering losses if it becomes necessary to sue the customer for nonpayment.

A more sophisticated system for screening credit applications is a **credit-scoring system**—the process of replacing subjective lending with scientific scoring. The procedures for developing a credit-scoring system follow:

- *Identifying* is an examination of good and bad credit accounts to identify characteristics associated with individuals who are good or poor credit risks. Figure 12–6 is one list of general characteristics that might be used in developing a credit-scoring system.
- *Weighting* is the weighting of each characteristic (by assigning point values) based on its ability to discriminate between good and poor credit risks.
- *Scoring* is the evaluation of credit applications by adding the points received on the various application characteristics to arrive at a total score.
- *Accepting/Rejecting* is accepting or rejecting a credit application based on minimum point score.
- *Limiting* is setting a credit limit based on the total points assigned to the application; the higher the score, the higher the credit limit.[27]

Credit Collections. Most credit accounts are handled through a routine, efficient billing system without any collection problems. When credit-collection problems (such as slow payment, nonpayment, or incorrect payment) occur, the retailer must have

FIGURE 12–6
Characteristics used in developing credit-scoring systems

Telephone at home	Bank savings account
Own/rent living accommodations	Bank checking account
Age	Zip code of residence
Time at home address	Age of automobile
Industry in which employed	Make and model of automobile
Time with employer	Geographic area of United States
Time with previous employer	Finance company reference
Type of employment	Debt-to-income ratio
Number of dependents	Monthly rent/mortgage payment
Types of credit reference	Family size
Income	Telephone area code
Savings and loan references	Location of relatives
Trade-union membership	Number of children
Age difference between man and wife	Number of other dependents
Telephone at work	Ownership of life insurance
Length of product being purchased	Width of product being purchased
First letter of last name	

Source: Noel A. Capon, "Credit Scoring Systems: A Critical Analysis," *Journal of Marketing* 46 (Spring 1982): 85. Reprinted from the *Journal of Marketing,* published by the American Marketing Association, Chicago, IL 60606.

policies and procedures to handle them.[28] Any credit-collection procedure entails several basic steps. First, credit accounts must be *reviewed* periodically and routinely to identify delinquent accounts. Immediate identification of delinquent accounts is critical because the more overdue the account becomes, the harder it is to collect. Second, the retailer should make every effort to *determine the reason* for the delinquency. If the customer faces unexpected financial problems, the retailer should strive to reach some mutually agreeable arrangement that will not only satisfy the debt but also preserve the debtor as a customer. On the other hand, if the customer has no intention of repaying the debt or is a poor manager of finances, the retailer should initiate actions to settle the account, either by requiring the consumer to make payments with penalties on a definite time schedule or by turning the account over to a collection agency.[29] Eventually, a retailer realizes that some customers are no longer desirable either as credit customers or cash customers (typically, a customer whose account is far overdue will avoid the store and take cash business elsewhere). Thus, in general, credit-collection methods must be flexible enough to meet specific situations.

Delivery Service

Delivery service is one of the most controversial aspects of a service mix. In general, delivery service is difficult to plan, execute, and control. Before including delivery service in the service mix, the retailer must have a clear understanding of when to offer it, what problems it entails, under which terms and conditions it can be offered, and what type of delivery system is most appropriate to the operation.

Many circumstances justify including delivery services in the service mix.

1. Delivery is practically indispensable in retailing such bulky products as furniture, appliances, building materials, and lawn products (trees and shrubs).
2. In large urban areas where customers traveling by public transportation are greatly inconvenienced by taking purchases with them, delivery is often necessary.
3. Retailers that actively solicit telephone and mail orders must provide home-delivery services.
4. Delivery services for emergency goods, such as prescription drugs, are perceived by consumers as a valuable addition to the retailer's service mix.
5. For retailers engaged in institutional sales (such as schools and hospitals), sales frequently are made and prices quoted on the basis of delivering the product to the institution's facilities.
6. Some retailers have a prestige image to protect and therefore must include delivery services in their merchandise mix.

The problems associated with delivery service are substantial. One of the most difficult problems is immediacy. When consumers purchase a product, they want immediate possession, with delivery either the same day or within a short period. It is virtually impossible for the retailer to provide immediate delivery without increasing costs. A second major problem involves "not-at-homes." Delivery personnel face a recurring problem of what to do when the customer is not at home. Some retailers attempt to reduce this problem by telephoning the customer before delivery. A third problem in offering delivery services is the variations in demand. The day-to-day, week-to-week, and month-to-month fluctuations in demand for delivery services seriously undermine management planning; to be always ready to handle peak delivery times is cost-prohibitive. Additional problems include damage in transit, inaccurate deliveries, and problems of security.

Retailers can elect to use either an in-store system or an independent system. Each has its advantages and disadvantages. **In-store delivery systems** can be either wholly owned and operated by an individual store (private store systems) or partially owned and operated with other stores (cooperative store systems). Private in-store systems offer numerous advantages. Of all the delivery systems, they give the retailer the greatest level of control over delivery operations and the greatest flexibility in adjusting services to customer needs. The retailer can personalize delivery vehicles with its name, slogan, and other messages, and the delivery personnel work for the retailer. Unfortunately, private systems are the most expensive to establish and maintain, and many retailers simply cannot afford to operate them.

Independent delivery systems are owned and operated independently from the retailer. They offer their services either on a contractual basis (consolidated systems) or on an open-to-the-general-public basis (parcel post and express services). Consolidated systems are independent firms that, for a fee, will deliver a store's packages; the fee depends on the number, size, weight, and handling characteristics of the packages. The typical consolidated operation of an independent system is to pick up the store's packages on a regularly scheduled basis, take the packages to a central facility where they are sorted for efficient routing, and deliver the packages to customers on a specific time schedule. Most consolidated delivery firms perform cash on delivery (COD) functions, make call backs, and assume full liability for damaged or lost packages. The major limitations of using consolidated services are lack of control over delivery time and inability to monitor the behavior of delivery personnel. Express services and parcel post serve the needs of the general public. Retailers can resort to these systems when the delivery destination lies outside their delivery-service area.

Alterations and Repairs

Many retailers offer alterations and repairs both as a supplement to the sale of products and as an income-producing service. Consumers expect retailers of expensive clothing to provide alteration services and retailers of appliances, television sets, automobiles, and other durable goods to provide repair services. Traditionally, retailers offered alteration services as part of a garment's sales price; in recent years, however, retailers have experimented with various types of alteration charges ranging from no charge for minor alterations to partial or full charge for major alterations. To facilitate product-related alterations and to justify their investment in workroom facilities, equipment, and personnel, some retailers have established income-producing tailoring operations. Retailers usually charge customers for repairs on durable goods according to the terms and conditions of product warranties and established store policies. Normally, consumers bear no charge (or at most a minimum charge) for repairs on products still under warranty or that occur within a prescribed period after the purchase date. After the warranty or policy date expires, the retailer charges the consumer for repairs on a profit-making basis. To increase their income from repair services, many chain retailers (such as Sears) offer maintenance contracts on a fixed-fee basis. In addition to creating revenues, maintenance contracts also aid retailers in fully using their repair and service departments.

The retailer that deems it necessary to provide alteration or repair services has two operation alternatives: in-store and out-of-store services. In-store alteration and repair services gives the retailer all of the advantages associated with direct control of such activities; however, this alternative also presents numerous management problems and requires substantial capital investments. Out-of-store alterations are subcontracted to private-service retailers specializing in tailoring services. Retailers normally use authorized, local repair services, factory repair services, and other subcontracted private-service firms to do out-of-store repairs. Disadvantages of using out-of-store repair services are lack of control, customer inconvenience, and longer service time.

Wrapping

The three basic types of wrapping services retailers perform are bagging or sacking, store wrap, and gift wrap. Most consumers expect retailers to place purchases in a bag even when the products are prepackaged. **Bagging** (1) facilitates handling (especially when multiple purchases are involved); (2) protects purchases from inclement weather; and (3) preserves the privacy of the customer purchase. Proper bagging takes into account the size, shape, weight, and strength of the bag and the goods that go into it.

Store wrap is the wrapping of customers' purchases in a standard (color and design) wrapping paper or box. Most department and specialty stores offer this service free of charge. Store wrap not only is an additional service for many retailers but also is a way to supplement their stores' advertising programs. The retailer that incorporates its prestige name with store wrap can provide additional purchase incentives for customers who either seek a prestige gift or want their gift receivers to know the present came from a prestige store.

Gift wraps normally incorporate additional wrapping features such as bows and ribbons to distinguish them clearly from store wraps. Due to increased costs of materials and labor, the customer normally is charged an additional fee for gift-wrapping services.

Wrapping services are handled on either a departmental or a centralized basis. **Department wrapping** is performed by either the salesperson who makes the sale or the department cashier and wrapper. The advantages of having the salesperson wrap the merchandise are convenience for the customer, the opportunity for the salesperson to make an extra sale, and enhancement of the store's image through personalized service. Disadvantages of department wrapping are that salespeople must leave their primary job of selling and that salespeople normally do not excel at gift wrapping. Many stores perform **centralized wrapping** at one central location, but many large stores centralize wrapping on each floor. Although more cost-efficient than department wrapping, this

Gift wrapping departments may be centralized on each floor or in one location for the whole store.

system does represent an inconvenience for customers, who must find the wrapping desk and may have to wait in line.

Complaint Resolution

In 1962, President John F. Kennedy identified four basic consumer rights: the right to safety, the right to be informed, the right to choose, and the right to be heard. Two of these rights, the right to be heard and to be informed, are key factors in the customer-complaint process. Customers expect to be informed of all operating policies that affect their patronage, and they expect to be heard when they want to register a complaint. While customer complaints typically are viewed negatively, especially if excessive in number, they also can be viewed positively. First, a customer who complains gives the retailer a chance to identify and correct a problem. Second, customer complaints serve as a major source of information regarding the retailer's products, services, and other merchandising activities. Finally, it is "notable that if a complaint is resolved quickly, the customer will tell an average of five other people about his good experience. . . . On the other hand, the cost of losing an existing customer is very high. It could cost five times as much to get a new customer as it does to keep an existing one."[30]

Causes of Complaints

Most customer complaints result from one of three general causes: product-related, service-related, and customer-related difficulties.[31] Product-related causes include the following:

1. *Poor-quality products*—inferior workmanship and materials that cause fading or bleeding colors, shrinking or stretching fabrics, and rusting or tarnishing metals
2. *Damaged products*—merchandise that is chipped, stained, soiled, ripped, spoiled, or scratched
3. *Incorrect products*—merchandise that is either mislabeled according to size and price or mismatched in terms of color and style
4. *Insufficient selection*—out-of-stock merchandise, discontinued merchandise, limited-line merchandise, and new merchandise

Service-related causes involve customer dissatisfaction with sales personnel and services such as checkout, delivery, workroom, and customer accounts. Complaints about sales personnel usually center around the salesperson's (1) *disposition* (indifferent, discourteous, unfriendly, pushy); (2) *incompetence* (lack of product knowledge, poor selling skills, lack of familiarity with store policies); (3) *dishonesty* (unfulfilled promises, false information, additional charges, incorrect change); or (4) *selling methods* (overselling customers by selling them too much of an item or by trading them up to a product they cannot afford). Complaints about delivery services include late, lost, and incorrect deliveries and untidy and unpleasant delivery personnel. Improper alterations, lengthy delays, and overcharges are the chief causes of complaints stemming from workroom services. Finally, improper handling of accounts irritates customers. Errors in billing, receipt of a bill after it has already been paid, and delays in receiving account statements are some of the more irksome problems.

Customers make mistakes; sometimes they are intentional, sometimes they are not. Customer mistakes are also a cause of customer-related complaints. For example, customers may purchase a product thinking it will match or fit another product they own. If it does not, they may want to return it. If the retailer does not issue a refund, then the customer surely will complain. A change of mind is another cause of complaint. Customers often change their minds because they later think the product is not really the style, quality, price, or color they wanted. Most consumers consider these legitimate reasons for returning goods, and they expect the retailer to make an exchange or give a refund. Questioning the customer's motives invites further customer complaints.

Alternatives for Handling Complaints

The retailer has several alternatives in handling consumer complaints.[32] They include offering returns and refunds; making product adjustments, price adjustments, and service adjustments; and practicing good customer relations.

Returns and Refunds. Policies on returning merchandise range from "no returns" or "all sales final" to "satisfaction guaranteed or your money back." A retailer that has a no-return policy should make that policy clear by posting signs, printing the policy on sales slips, verbal statements by salespeople, or a combination of these means.

Retailers that guarantee satisfaction must decide whether to refund the customer's money in the form of cash or as a credit slip. Some retailers prefer to give cash refunds because they feel this policy creates greater customer satisfaction, relieves the store of further obligation, and frees store personnel to perform more productive work. Proponents of the credit-slip refund believe this method is better because it maintains contact with the customer and ensures a future sale and at least part of the profit from the original sale. As with the no-return policy, retailers should inform customers of any conditions or restrictions on returning merchandise and receiving refunds before the purchase is made.

Product Adjustments. Complaints about incorrect products can easily be handled by allowing customers to exchange the incorrect product for a correct one. By offering to clean, repair, alter, or exchange products, retailers can satisfy most customers' complaints about damaged products.

One way to handle consumer complaints about poor-quality products is to substitute a higher-quality product for the poor-quality product. This policy is especially appropriate when the product sold was, in fact, of lower quality than the price suggested, or when the retailer wants to protect a quality product and store image. Finally, complaints concerning insufficient selection can be handled by either (1) agreeing to stock the product; (2) explaining why the product cannot be stocked, then offering an appropriate substitute; or (3) directing the customer to a store that stocks the desired product.

Price Adjustments. Price adjustments can either be given as an allowance or as a discount on the purchase price of the product. Since it is not always possible to exchange or adjust a product that has been damaged, the retailer often can satisfy customers by reducing the price of the product to compensate for the damages. Price adjustments also can include free merchandise and discount coupons. When the retailer is obviously at fault, price adjustments are generally the most effective way to show the customer that the store is making an extra effort to correct the problem.

Service Adjustments. Retailers can handle service adjustments in much the same way as price adjustments. For example, if a consumer says that a garment alteration is unsatisfactory, the retailer should make the additional alteration free of charge. If a billing error shows the customer paid a bill late, any late charges or interest penalties the retailer would normally charge should be dropped.

Customer Relations. Some situations generate customer complaints for which none of the preceding adjustments are appropriate. A rude salesperson is one example. In such cases, the customer may just want to be heard or to "blow off steam." Whether the complaint is justified or not, good customer relations dictate the retailer listen carefully and politely, reassure the customer, and apologize for the situation. Who knows? The individual might be a very good customer who simply had a bad day and was set off by a minor incident. By allowing the customer to register the complaint and by handling that complaint professionally, the retailer keeps a good customer.

Systems for Handling Complaints

Customer complaints in small stores usually are handled by the store owner or manager; large stores, however, must develop a system for handling complaints. The two alternatives are centralized or decentralized systems.

All customer complaints are referred to a central office or complaint desk under a **centralized complaint system**. This arrangement allows the retailer to use personnel who are trained in the art of handling people. Also, the retailer can implement a more uniform policy for handling complaints and making adjustments, and management receives more accurate information on complaints than if a particular department reported the complaint itself. Additional benefits of a centralized complaint system are (1) complaints are handled privately and not aired in public and (2) complaint records can be standardized, analyzed, and used by management to correct causes of complaints. Shortcomings associated with central complaint systems focus on the fact that some customers prefer to deal with the department or salesperson from whom they made their original purchase.

A **decentralized complaint system** handles customer complaints at the department level. Department salespersons usually handle minor complaints and adjustments while the department manager is responsible for major complaints. Although customers generally prefer this type of system, it has its disadvantages. First, there can be considerable variation in how complaints are handled within and between departments. Second, many complaints are not reported to central management, and much of what is reported is biased. Third, commissioned salespersons are reluctant to make certain adjustments that might affect their commissions. Finally, most departmental personnel are not trained to handle complaints or to make adjustments.

Guidelines for Handling Complaints

How a store handles a customer's complaint can, in many cases, be more important to the customer than the actual adjustment.[33] Many retailers find that if they display an immediate and sincere willingness to be fair, the customer will reciprocate by being willing to accept any reasonable adjustment. There are no absolute rules or steps for handling all complaints and all customers, but the general guidelines presented in Figure 12–7 are appropriate "do's" and "don'ts" for most situations.

1. Be pleasant to the customer.
2. Act in a businesslike manner.
3. Apologize for the inconvenience.
4. Give assurance of satisfaction.
5. Encourage the customer to talk.
6. Listen carefully.
7. Avoid interruptions.
8. Avoid arguing.
9. Display a sincere desire to please.
10. Ask for suggestions.
11. Take action quickly.
12. Thank the customer.
13. Correct the condition.

FIGURE 12–7
Guidelines for handling complaints

CUSTOMER SERVICE ACTIONS

Retailers need to develop an action plan to ensure that their customer service actions are sufficient to provide the quality of service appropriate to the retailer's operations. Superior customer service just doesn't happen—it must be planned and managed just like all other aspects of the retailer's business. The following five steps would be part of any action plan to promote quality customer service.

Research: Expectations/Desires

What do customers expect? What do customers want? The best research approach for finding the answers to these and other such questions concerning service quality is to ask them, and above all, to listen to the answers carefully. Formal customer surveys, focus group studies, complaint resolution analysis, evaluation of returns and allowances, suggestion boxes, and the recording (mental or otherwise) of informal customer comments can be used. Observation of customer reaction to the store, merchandise, promotions, and personnel can also reveal substantial useful information. There is a wealth of information within every retail store if the retailers will organize to secure and process that information.

Development: Features/Actions

Decisions regarding what services are to be offered and how they are to be performed have already been discussed. It is sufficient to say that *each* customer service feature and corresponding service action must be carefully considered in light of customer expectations and retailer resources. It is far better to provide a few high quality services than to provide a wide variety of low quality services.

Communication: Promises/Offers

Both the retailer's service mix (features) and service quality (actions) should be carefully communicated to the customer. Poor communication that leads to misunderstandings is of itself a poor service. The retailer's service offerings can be communicated through carefully posted signs, in-store announcements, information booths, informed sales associates, available managers, and printed matter such as brochures. It is extremely important that retailers do not promise or appear to promise a service or service level that they cannot live up to. Promising customers more than they can deliver can be disastrous. It is the retailer's responsibility to ensure clear and concise communication concerning the store's service offerings.

Execution: Motivate/Evaluate

Quality customer service just doesn't happen. Friendly, courteous, responsive, honest, and reliable store personnel simply do not suddenly materialize out of store fixtures. Retail employees at all levels must be motivated. While financial motivation (e.g., commissions and bonuses) is an important part of the encouragement process, the retail organization must develop a "service culture" in which all store employees recognize their responsibilities to customer service. Training sessions, motivation seminars, employee recognition programs, material and nonmaterial rewards, and many thank-yous are all part of the employee motivation program.

Management: Relationships/Partnerships

Retail managers must be accessible to customers and employees. Good customer service starts in the executive suite. If an effective customer service program is to be developed, top executives must support the program financially, operationally, and personally. But for all the inspirational efforts of CEOs, the nitty-gritty of the customer service program falls to sales associates and frontline managers. Successful service programs have typically emerged from management-employee relationships that can best be described as partnerships. When employees see themselves as partners in the organization, they become stakeholders who have an invested interest in seeing that the team succeeds. The chances that a stakeholding partner will take care of providing quality customer service is much greater than the efforts one could expect out of an employee.

SUMMARY

Quality customer service is vital to the success of any retail operation in the 1990s. Customer service involves all of the features, acts, and information that augment the customer's ability to realize the potential value of a core product or service. Service quality is the difference between customer service expectations and what service the customer actually received. Retailers must not only be concerned with what services to offer, but equally concerned with how well each service is provided.

Customer-service levels for service features (e.g., returns, deliveries) can be described as essential, expected, or optional. Low-service-level retailers (e.g., self-service) provide only essential services while high-service-level retailers (e.g., full-service) provide all three types of service—essential, expected, and optional. Customer-service actions (e.g., friendliness, reliability, etc.) can be evaluated on a rating scale of unacceptable to exceptional.

Customer service objectives direct the efforts of the retailer's service program. Some common service objectives include: increasing form, time, place, and possession utility; enhancing customer convenience and security; improving store image, traffic, and competitive positions; and building specific demand for the retailer's core products and services.

Customer service features include all those "extras" that enhance the core product and service offering. Store hours, credit, delivery, alterations and repairs, wrapping, and complaint resolution are the most common service features in most retail service programs. The five actions to ensure exceptional customer service actions are research, development, communication, execution, and management.

STUDENT STUDY GUIDE

Key Terms and Concepts

bagging (p. 455)
centralized complaint system (p. 459)
centralized wrapping system (p. 456)
chattel mortgage agreement (p. 452)
conditional sales agreement (p. 452)
credit-scoring system (p. 453)
customer service actions (p. 444)
customer service features (p. 437)
customer services (p. 436)
decentralized complaint system (p. 459)
deferred billing (p. 451)
department wrapping system (p. 456)
essential services (p. 438)
evening hours (p. 448)
expected services (p. 438)
fixed-term revolving credit (p. 452)
gift wrap (p. 456)
independent delivery system (p. 455)
in-house credit system (p. 449)
installment credit (p. 451)
in-store delivery system (p. 454)
lease agreement (p. 452)
open-account credit (p. 450)
optional services (p. 438)
option-term revolving credit (p. 452)
primary-goods retailers (p. 444)
primary-service retailers (p. 437)
private-label credit system (p. 450)
service level (p. 444)
service quality (p. 436)
Sunday hours (p. 448)
store wrap (p. 456)
third-party credit system (p. 450)
three C's of credit (p. 452)

Review Questions

1. Distinguish between a customer-service feature and customer-service action.
2. Using customer expectations and service assortments, describe the various types of service levels for customer-service features.
3. List some examples of customer service actions.
4. Identify the services the retailer should offer to increase form utility.
5. Which services might the retailer offer to promote possession utility?
6. Identify the two chief disadvantages for retailers that accept third-party credit cards.
7. Does a private-label credit system differ from in-store and third-party systems? How?
8. Briefly describe the three types of credit plans.
9. List the three C's of credit and describe each.
10. Outline the basic procedures for establishing a credit-scoring system.
11. Characterize the three basic types of wrapping services.
12. Identify the major product-, service-, and customer-related causes of complaints.
13. What are the alternative methods for handling customer complaints?

Review Exam

True or False

_____ 1. A major benefit of offering optional services is that it can aid the retailer in developing a unique service offering and thereby help to distinguish his or her store from competitive store operations.

_____ 2. Expected services are basic and necessary to a particular retail operation.

_____ 3. Consumer credit, layaway, and extended store hours are all services directed at the service objective of increasing form utility.

_____ 4. Credit-granting stores more easily build repeat business because credit customers tend to be more loyal than cash customers.

_____ 5. A major disadvantage of third-party credit card sales is that they result in tied-up funds in accounts receivable, thereby forcing the retailer to borrow working capital.

_____ 6. The immediate identification of delinquent accounts is critical because the more overdue the account becomes, the harder it is to collect.

_____ 7. One acceptable alternative for handling customer complaints about insufficient selection of merchandise is to direct the customer to a store that stocks the desired product.

Multiple Choice

_____ 1. Which of the following is not an example of a primary-goods retailer?
a. department store
b. beauty shop
c. shoe store
d. gift shop
e. hardware store

_____ 2. Customer service _____ deals with the issue of how well a retailer is providing a given service.
a. feature
b. optional
c. action
d. weapon
e. none of the above

_____ 3. Product warranties, return privileges, and maintenance contracts are all services directed at _____.
a. enhancing place utility
b. increasing form utility
c. increasing store traffic
d. facilitating time utility
e. providing customer security

_____ 4. All of the following are advantages of using a private in-store system of delivery, *except* .
a. higher degree of control over service
b. lower operating costs
c. greater degree of flexibility in adjusting service levels
d. more opportunity to prospect for new sales opportunities
e. more opportunity to personalize the service

_____ 5. The installment-credit plan _____.
a. is used for purchasing large-ticket items such as cars, furniture, and appliances
b. allows consumers to pay their total purchase price in equal installment payments over a specified time period
c. is a legal contract between retailer and customer
d. can be in the form of conditional sales agreements, chattel mortgages, or lease agreements
e. all of the above

_____ 6. Bagging the customer's purchase serves all of the following purposes, *except* it _____.
a. facilitates handling
b. increases sales
c. protects purchases
d. preserves privacy

_____ 7. Which of the following factors is *not* a disadvantage associated with a decentralized complaint system?

a. Customers generally prefer a centralized complaint system.
b. There is considerable variation in how complaints are handled within and between departments.
c. Many complaints are not reported to central management.
d. Many complaints are reported in a biased manner.
e. Most departmental personnel are not trained to handle complaints.

STUDENT APPLICATIONS MANUAL

Investigative Projects: Practice and Applications

1. Develop a comprehensive list of potential customer service features for each of the following retailers: (1) a chain discount store, (2) a supermarket, and (3) a high-fashion boutique. For each retailer and list of features, classify each service on the basis of its importance (essential, expected, or optional) to the retailer's typical customer. Justify your classifications.
2. Review the retail-service objectives; then, for each of the following retailer firms rank the objectives in order of their importance to the retailer's success: (1) a True Value hardware store, (2) a Radio Shack electronics store, (3) a 7-Eleven convenience store, and (4) a J.C. Penney department store. Justify your rankings.
3. In addition to the three C's of credit, what other criteria might a retailer consider for use as signs to indicate whether a credit applicant is a good or poor credit risk?
4. Interview three local retailers and profile their customer complaint resolution system. Compare and contrast the three systems. Which system is the most effective? Why?

Tactical Cases: Problems and Decisions

■ CASE 12–1
"Dear Manager": Coping with Consumer Complaints*

Bill Baker was having a trying morning. The dog got into the trash (again), the bakery didn't have the muffins he wanted, and traffic was backed up all the way into the city. Bill tried to shake off these annoyances as he prepared to open the store.

The morning at Rich's Friendly Appliances seemed to be going better when the mail came at 10:30. As manager, Baker had the responsibility of dealing with the various invoices, product announcements, payments, and the like as they came in each day. Rarely were there any real letters, except those from customers complaining about one thing or another. In his four years with the store, Baker could remember only one letter that complimented and thanked the store for its efforts. Today's mail was no exception. Mixed in with notices promising manufacturer support for another "truckload" sale and some booklets on Toast/Bake/ Microwave ovens were several letters from customers. These he saved for last.

After having coffee and a danish, Baker settled in to read the letters. The first was from Baltimore and came in a hand-addressed envelope (Exhibit A). "Hey lady, we all got problems," Baker thought as he read the letter. "Forget the autobiography and tell me the problem." He checked the Recent Sales file for the ticket and discovered that the washer was a relatively low-price but comparatively high-margin item. There were no notations on the delivery slip. "Well, what do you want?" Baker wondered as he finished reading the letter. "I'm certainly not going to send you a hundred bucks for this." Just then, the telephone rang and he set the letter aside until later.

After rescheduling a couple of deliveries, Baker returned to the mail. The next letter had been typed on obviously good-quality stationery with a civic group's letterhead (Exhibit B). The amount of money demanded got his attention right away. "A $265 rebate?" Baker fumed, "That's a pretty big chunk of this week's profit." As he was finishing the letter, one of the saleswomen came in and told him that she could close a sale if the store could "throw in" an icemaker. "No way," he exploded, "do you know how much those things cost us?" The saleswoman was surprised at this response but returned to the customers. She was pleased that Baker came out of the office and helped to close the sale with a half-price offer on the icemaker.

After a few more telephone calls, Baker finally read the third letter (Exhibit C). It dealt with a bottom-of-the-line microwave that sold well at a small margin. "A new glass tray will eat me up on that item," he thought. Checking the inventory, which showed ten in stock, he saw that the gross mark-up was only $17.35.

After reading the final letter, another threat to sue (Exhibit D). Baker was exhausted. He wasn't even sure

EXHIBIT A

3900 Southwestern Blvd.
Apt. 31-C
Baltimore, MD 21227

6/13/87

Rich's Appliances
Glen Burnie, MD 21220

Dear Managers,

I really didn't want to write this letter, but my sister-in-law said to. We really like the washer we bought, so that's not the problem.

With three kids, my husband and myself we do a lot of cleaning. It was bad enough carrying the stuff around here in the building. The machines kept breaking down and getting dirty. Half the time only 3 washers were working and you'd have to wait for a turn.

They finally got new machines here. But it costs $2.00 to wash and dry a load of clothes. I guess we could use the clothesline out back, but I hate to leave my stuff out there unless I'm watching it and you know I can't do that and watch the kids too.

We decided to get a washer and dryer cause they give us the hook-ups and the place. We saved up so we could put half down on the washer first. After we get that paid for we'll save up for the dryer.

When we came in, the salesgirl (Trudy was her name) was so very nice. She helped us figure out what we needed and what was a good buy. The one we got wasn't on special, but it seemed like a good price. We were so pleased that delivery and hook-up were only a little bit extra.

The people came out right on time to install the washer. (I was surprised that a woman was one of them.) They brought it in and hooked it to the water and the drain and we started a load. Everything seemed to work then and it has really worked well ever since.

I was so proud of the new washer that I asked Mrs. Webb, our manager, to come in and see it. She said it looked like a "good, basic machine." We had some coffee and store-bought cookies.

When she was leaving, Mrs. Webb saw a hole in the plaster wall and a tear in the staircase rug leading to the utility room. She told me that part of the lease was a damage deposit and we'd have to pay for repairs when we moved out unless we fixed it ourselves.

I had just cleaned that staircase the day before because I knew your men (people it turns out) were coming the next day. There wasn't a hole or a tear then, I'm sure about it. They must have happened when the washer was delivered. I didn't watch too close, as I was trying to keep Nancy, our youngest, out of the way.

When I told my sister-in-law she said to call the store. Trudy didn't know what to do about it and said you weren't in. She said to write to you because you are so busy when you are there.

I wasn't going to bother you, but Mrs. Webb said it might cost $100 to get these things fixed right. We don't plan to move anytime soon, why else would I buy a washer and dryer, but that is a lot of money for something we didn't do. I'm sure you'll take care of this.

Thank you for your help,

Mrs. F. (Christine) Albenasi

EXHIBIT B

SUNNY HEIGHTS
NEIGHBORHOOD ASSOCIATION
Potomac, MD

June 11, 1987

Rich's Friendly Appliances
Glen Burnie Mall
Glen Burnie, MD 21220

To the manager:

As a recent purchaser of a refrigerator from your store, I must vehemently protest the quality which I received. The icemaker which is installed in the QwikChill 500 simply does not keep up with my family's needs. I am therefore requesting a credit in the amount of half of the original purchase price (i.e., $265 out of $529).

Since the refrigerator was purchased and delivered in April, we have never accumulated more than a half tub of ice cubes. While we seldom run out completely, the quantity produced forces my family to constrain its use of ice. We believe this to be completely unacceptable.

This refrigerator was needed for its ice-making ability. Because it is only able to make a half tub, I feel that it is worth only half the price. In addition, I have already invested over $400 of my own time in shopping for, helping your people install, and trying to improve the performance of the refrigerator. As you can see, there is no way that I can come out even on this exchange, but I'm willing to be reasonable and settle for $265.

Please send a check, by the end of this month, to my home address:

54 Crabcake Ln.
Potomac, MD 21407

I have no desire to invest any additional time in shopping for a different refrigerator. I am convinced this is the best you can do.

Thank you,

James Flavin, President

JF:mtp

EXHIBIT C

William Baker, Manager
Rich's Friendly Appliances
Glen Burnie Mall
Glen Burnie, MD 21220

295 Forest Ave.
Dorsey, MD 21076
June 13, 1987

Dear Mr. Baker:

I'm writing to request a replacement glass tray for the microwave oven (Triton #31RS) which I purchased and which was delivered on the 10th of this month. When my husband and I opened the carton, we found the tray had a crack running through about 2/3 of its length. I also did not receive the recipe book promised in the advertisement.

I hope the items are in stock, or at least available readily in the area. If so, perhaps we can have this problem cleared up by the end of the week.

Since the oven was delivered to me, I assume that these replacement items can also be delivered. I will telephone you Friday A.M. to check on progress.

Sincerely,

Ellen Cole

EXHIBIT D

Rich's Friendly Appliances
Glen Burnie Mall
Glen Burnie, MD 21220

1313 Mockingbird Ln
Laurel, MD 21250
June 13, 1987

Sir:

What's the matter with you guys? Why can't I get any decent service. I've had it with this oven and now I want it replaced.

I bought this house early in 1986, when they were building it. Since I was living alone, my friends suggested that I have a microwave oven installed instead of a regular oven. I even came down to your fine (Ha!) store and picked one out and paid extra so the contractor would substitute.

Well, let me tell you it's been nothing but trouble. No matter how many different things I try, everything is always undercooked or overcooked. Sometimes the stuff I defrost is half-cooked before I'm ready to use it.

The builder is no longer in business, but this isn't really his fault. I want you to come out and replace this piece of junk with a real, electric oven. I also want my $100 back.

If I don't have this by the end of the month, I'm going to get a lawyer and sue you. I'll also have you shut down for selling things that don't do what they are supposed to. I'll be waiting to hear from you.

(signed) Frank Martin

how to react. He closed the office door, sat back in his chair, spread the four letters in front of him, and mused about his possible responses.

ASSIGNMENT

1. How should Bill respond to each letter?
2. Is responding to customer calls and letters an adequate way to monitor consumer satisfaction? Suggest other methods.
3. What operational changes are indicated by these letters?

*This case was prepared by Douglas Hausknecht, The University of Akron.

■ CASE 12–2
Don't Give an Inch: Handling Returns and Adjustments*

Date:	Thursday, April 6, 1989, 4:35 P.M.
Scene:	Retail sales floor, Quality Auto Service Centers
Characters:	Mike and Jackie Buckholzer, a married couple and customers; Pam Adams, Retail Sales Associate

ACTION

Mike: Let me get this straight. The four all-season, steel-belted radials are on sale for $49.95 each—or a total of $200.

Pam: About $200 plus tax, plus balancing and alignment.

Mike: What about the tire-protection plan? What does it cost?

Pam: That is $79.95.

Jackie: According to this [pointing to sign], the protection plan includes the initial alignment and wheel balance.

Pam: That's right.

Mike: So, the four tires plus the protection plan will be close to $300 with tax.

Pam: A few dollars less.

Jackie: Let's have them check and see if they can find out what's causing the rattle under the left rear side of the car.

Pam: Well, let's have the service people put it up on the rack and check it out.

Date:	Thursday, April 6, 1989, 5:08 P.M.
Scene:	Auto service floor, Quality Auto Service Centers
Characters:	Mike and Jackie Buckholzer, customers; Pam Adams, Retail Sales Associate; John Zee, Mechanic

ACTION

Pam: John, let's put this Stanza up on the rack and check it out. The Buckholzers are concerned with some noise coming from the left rear side.

John: [After inspecting the undercarriage of the car.] Look at this exhaust system. The muffler and tail pipe are all hanging loose. The exhaust system clamps have all rusted through. Two of them have already broken and another is about to. Both the muffler and the tail pipe are almost rusted through.

Mike: What's all that going to cost me?

John: Around $100, but we'll have to check the price with Tri-County Nissan. Look at this. [John demonstrates that the left front tire has some play in it.]

Jackie: What does that mean?

John: It means that you are going to have to replace the strut; sooner or later you will have trouble with it. Also, it will cause uneven wear on the new tire.

Mike: What about the other side? Does it need to be replaced also?

John: [after inspecting it] No. It's fine, see, there's no play in this wheel.

Mike: How much does a new strut cost?

John: On these smaller cars, you have to replace the whole strut assembly. I'll have to check the price tomorrow morning when Tri-County Nissan opens up, but with parts and labor, it shouldn't be more than $100.

Jackie: Well, Mike, there goes your new golf bag.

Mike: And there goes your new dress, Jackie.

Pam: Mr. Buckholzer, where can we contact you tomorrow morning? As soon as we check on the prices for the exhaust system and strut assembly, we will call you with a total estimate.

Mike: I have an early morning appointment but I should be back in my office from 9 A.M. to 11 A.M. My telephone number is 555-4646.

Pam: OK, we'll get hold of you then. The service manager will call you before we proceed.

Jackie: When will the car be ready?

Pam: Tomorrow afternoon.

Mike: Pam, we'll pick it up around 4 P.M. Well, Jackie, we planned on $250, and it's going to cost twice what we planned on.

Date:	Friday, April 7, 1989, 9:23 A.M.
Scene:	Buckholzer residence, kitchen phone
Characters:	Jackie Buckholzer, customer; Ben Reeves, Service Manager

ACTION

Jackie: Buckholzer residence.

Ben: Hello, Mrs. Buckholzer, this is Ben Reeves, Service Manager for Quality Auto Service Centers. I haven't been able to reach your husband at work. I have the estimate of the repairs that were discussed.

Jackie: Well, how much will it cost?

Ben: It'll be $490 for the exhaust system, struts, valve stems, grease seals, and labor.

Jackie: That includes everything—$490 is the total bill?

Ben: That's it.

Jackie: OK, go ahead. When can we pick it up?

Ben: Late afternoon.

Date:	Friday, April 7, 1989, 4:47 P.M.
Scene:	Auto service floor, Quality Auto Service Centers
Characters:	Mike and Jackie Buckholzer, customers; Adam, Mechanic

ACTION

Jackie: Look, there's our car. It's still up on the rack with the wheels off.

Mike: When will the Stanza be done?

Adam: In about an hour, maybe a little longer.

Jackie: We can't wait that long. We're expected for dinner.

Mike: I suppose we'll have to make another trip up here tomorrow. Can we pick it up tomorrow?

Adam: Yeah, that will give me plenty of time to get it done.

Date:	Saturday, April 8, 1989, 12:43 P.M.
Scene:	Retail sales floor, Quality Auto Service Centers
Characters:	Mike and Jackie Buckholzer, customers; Tim Harmon, Retail Sales Associate; Ben Reeves, Service Manager

ACTION

Mike: I'm here to pick up my car.

Tim: Your last name, please.

Mike: Buckholzer, Mike.

Tim: Will it be charge or cash? [Tim keys up the terminal and receives a printed invoice.] The total comes to $800.08.

Mike: There must be some mistake. The estimate was $490.

Tim: Let me check. [Tim again keys up the terminal and obtains the same results.] No. $800.08 is the total. See here.

4	R13 Z2 tires @ 49.30	197.20
1	Tire protection plan	79.95
4	New Valve Stems @ 2.00	8.00
1	LF Bearing FWD	22.60
2	Gas Strut Assembly @ 91.00	182.00
1	Repack four wheel bearings	26.00
2	Front grease seals @ 8.00	16.00
1	Muffler	200.26
	Sales Tax	36.97
	TOTAL	800.08

Jackie: I did not authorize this. The total cost for everything was $490, and that is all I authorized, and that is all we are paying.

Tim: Let me get the service manager.

Ben: Is there some problem?

Mike: Yes, there is. We had repairs completed on our car that were not authorized.

Ben: [Examining the terminal printout and the work order.] Yes, Mrs. Buckholzer, you authorized this work. You see, Mr. Buckholzer, I tried to call you at your office but couldn't reach you, so I called your wife and informed her of the charges and she authorized them.

Jackie: I authorized $490, not $800. Thursday night your mechanic told us that it would be about $500 for everything.

Ben: It is, $490 for parts and labor.

Mike: No. The $490 includes the tires plus the protection plan plus the repairs.

Ben: No, the $490 is only for the repairs. The tires are totally separate.

Jackie: That's not what you said. I asked you what the total bill was, and you said $490, including everything.

Ben: We operate the service business separate from tire sales. What you agreed to pay for the tires is a separate issue. I only deal with repair and installation services.

Mike: How is a customer to know that you treat these two businesses separately? Let me talk to the manager.

Ben: I am the manager on the weekend. The store manager is not in today.

Mike: Call him at home.

Ben: I can't do that.

Mike: I would like to talk to someone else, other than yourself. I don't believe you can be objective about this since you were involved.

Ben: You'll have to wait until Monday.

Mike: All right. But we need the car. My daughters are waiting for my wife.

Ben: I can't let you have the car unless you pay the full amount.

Jackie: It's our car, and your mistake. I have people waiting for me up at the mall.

Ben: I can't help that.

Mike: I will pay the $490 we agreed to and come in on Monday to talk to the manager.

Ben: No, you will have to pay the full amount.

Mike: Check your records. Less than six months ago I bought four new tires and a protection plan from you on my other car. I live in a new home, less than two miles from here. I'm not about to skip town over $300.

Ben: That's beside the point. I will have to have the $800 or I can't release the car.

Jackie: I need the car, and I'm taking it.

Ben: If you do, I will call the police and have you arrested.

Mike: It's our car. Is this the level of service you provide? Call the police right now. We'll let them decide.

Ben: No, I am not going to call the police unless you take the car.

Mike: Then call the manager or his boss or someone in charge.

Tim: Ben, I think you'd better call someone.

Ben: Keep out of this. I'll take care of it.

Mike: OK, I find your product and service unacceptable. Your sign says my satisfaction is guaranteed. I am not satisfied. So restore my car to its original form, and I will be on my way.

Ben: I can't do that.

Mike: What the hell can you do? You can't call a manager or anyone else. You can't restore my car. You can't quote prices or provide the services you agreed to.

Jackie: We have to pick the kids up.

Mike: I will be back on Monday to talk to the manager. When I do, I do not intend to accept anything except my car in its original form. I do not want your tires, struts, exhaust system, or anything else.

Date:	Monday, April 10, 1989, 9:21 A.M.
Scene:	Store manager's office, Quality Auto Service Centers
Characters:	Mike Buckholzer, angry customer; George Wills, Store Manager

ACTION

Mike: . . . and that is basically the problem I had with your product, service, and service manager. I want my car restored . . .

George: Mr. Buckholzer . . . .

ASSIGNMENT

Assume the role of George Wills, Store Manager.

1. How would you resolve the problem with Mr. Buckholzer? Develop various scenarios for resolving the issue, and identify the pros and cons for the store and for the customer. What would be your best offer to Mr. Buckholzer?
2. Who is right? Who is wrong? Why?
3. Evaluate Ben Reeves' performance in handling this complaint situation.
4. What suggestions would you make for improving the complaint handling process?
5. Are there other suggestions you could make for improving the store's operations?

*This case was prepared by Dale M. Lewison and Jon Hawes, The University of Akron.

ENDNOTES

1. Stephen Phillips, Amy Dunkin, James B. Treece, and Keith H. Hammond, "King Customer," *Business Week*, March 12, 1990, 94.
2. Christopher Power, Amy Dunkin, and Laura Jereski, "Slugging It Out for Survival," *Business Week*, January 8, 1990, 33.
3. Richard T. Garfein, "Guiding Principles for Improving Customer Service," *Journal of Services Marketing* 2 (Spring 1988), 37.
4. A. Parasuraman, Valeria A. Zeithaml, and Leonard L. Berry, "SERVQUAL: A Multiple-Item Scale for Measuring Customer Perceptions of Service Quality," *Journal of Retailing* 64 (Spring 1988), 12–40.
5. James M. Carman, "Consumer Perceptions of Service Quality: An Assessment of the SERVQUAL Dimensions," *Journal of Retailing* 66 (Spring 1990), 33–56.
6. William H. Davidow and Bro Uttal, *Total Customer Service—The Ultimate Weapon* (New York: Harper & Row Publishers, 1989), 22.
7. See Duane L. Davis, Joseph P. Guiltinan, and Wesley H. Jones, "Service Characteristics, Consumer Search, and the Classification of Retail Services," *Journal of Retailing* 55 (Fall 1979), 3–23.
8. Peter Geiger, "Stock Quotes Served With Hamburgers," *Akron Beacon Journal*, October 28, 1987, F–1.
9. A. Parasuraman et al., "SERVQUAL: A Multiple-Item Scale for Measuring Customer Perceptions of Service Quality."
10. Leonard L. Berry, "Market to the Perception," *American Demographics*, February 1990, 32.
11. E. A. Torriero, "Electronic Shopping 'a la cart,'" *Akron Beacon Journal*, May 2, 1990, E–1.
12. "Debit Card Systems Gain Momentum," *Chain Store Age Executive*, January 1987, 115.
13. "Fred Meyer Megastores Goes Hollywood," *Chain Store Age Executive*, March 1990, 78.
14. Francine Schwadel, "Little Touches Spur Wal-Mart

Rise," *The Wall Street Journal,* September 22, 1989, B–4.

15. Joseph Pereira, "L.L. Bean Scales Back Expansion Goals to Ensure Pride in Its Service Is Valid," *The Wall Street Journal,* July 31, 1989, B–3.
16. Denise Gallagher, "Sterling Jewelry," *Stores,* January 1989, 112.
17. Dinah Witchel, "The Store As Tourist Lure," *Stores,* May 1987, 112.
18. Bill Carlino, "Franchisees on BK Kid's Club: What Took So Long?" *Nation's Restaurant News,* March 19, 1990, 12. And Bernice Kanner, "Kids' Clubs Mean Big Money," *Cleveland Plain Dealer,* April 1, 1990, 1–E and 4–E.
19. Sandra Lee Breisch, "Cosmetic Beauty is in the Eye of the Computer," *Advertising Age,* March 2, 1987, S–12.
20. David J. Jefferson, "Southern California Supermarket Chains to Clash by Night," *Wall Street Journal,* March 23, 1988.
21. Jules Abend, "Mall Hours: How Long," *Stores,* May 1989, 70. And "Uniform Shopping Hours Coming on Strong," *Stores,* May 1989, 76–77.
22. See "Shopping Center Hours: The Long and Short of It," *Stores,* May 1989, 72.
23. See Jules Abend, "More Valuable Plastic," *Stores,* February 1988, 78-85, 88, 90, 92. Also see "Proprietary Credit," Stores, September 1989, 50, 52–53.
24. See "Bank Card Enhancement," *Stores,* September 1989, 54–55.
25. See Jules Abend, "Service: Key to Credit," *Stores,* April 1990, 38–41.
26. See "Private Label: Pros and Cons," *Stores,* September 1989, 54–55. And "The Case for Private Label Credit," *Stores,* April 1990, 43–44.
27. See Noel Capon, "Credit Scoring Systems: A Critical Analysis," *Journal of Marketing* 46 (Spring 1982), 82–91.
28. See Jules Abend, "Repair Job for Shoppers?" *Stores,* April 1988, 100–112; "Turmoil in Credit: What's Next?" *Stores,* April 1987, 86–90, 93; and "New Ways to Cut Risk," *Stores,* September 1987, 76.
29. See "Using Collection Agencies," *Stores,* April 1990, 45-46.
30. Henry Vanderleest and Shaheen Borna, "A Structured Approach to Handling Customer Complaints," *Retail Control,* October 1988, 18.
31. See Jennifer Pellet, "Keeping the Peace," *Discount Merchandiser,* September 1989, 55–56.
32. Jagdip Singh, "A Typology of Consumer Dissatisfaction Response Styles," *Journal of Retailing* 66 (Spring 1990), 57–100.
33. See Patricia Sellers, "How to Handle Customers' Gripes," *Fortune,* October 24, 1988, 88–100.

PART IV

PROCUREMENT STRATEGIES

Buying and Handling Merchandise Inventories

CHAPTER 13

OUTLINE

OBJECTIVES

- Identify alternative sources of supply and channel options for procuring the product mix.
- Explain the methods and procedures for initiating and maintaining supply contacts.
- Discuss the criteria for evaluating and methods for negotiating with sources of supply.
- Discuss the strategies for deciding how many sources of supply should be used in securing merchandise and describe the buying methods used in the actual purchasing of merchandise.
- Compare and contrast a traditional purchase order system and a quick response replenishment system.
- Design and explain an effective in-store system for receiving, checking, marking, and stocking incoming merchandise.

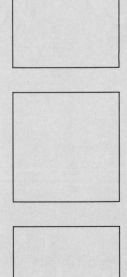

NEW RELATIONSHIPS AND TECHNOLOGIES

Manufacturers have other complaints, too. Some say retailers are increasingly using aggressive tactics to extract more money from vendors. Such methods include making payments late, charging big penalties for shipping errors, and insisting on "markdown money" for clothes not sold at full price. In addition, some retailers have severed ties with some apparel companies, replacing them with more profitable "private label" store brands. Many of the strongest manufacturers haven't been bullied by such tactics. But the relationship between retailers and vendors has become "adversarial."[1]

The buyer-seller relationship has been one-upmanship, adversarial all the way through. In fact, we have been competing against each other to the detriment of both. That time has gone. Technology no longer encompasses that program. The survivors are learning to develop partnership relationships where each one is less concerned about giving away trade secrets than about having a complete understanding as to what's needed when, and how to best accomplish it.[2]

At The Limited . . . every garment in every store is tracked on a daily basis. This results in more timely markdowns, better purchasing decisions, and more effective distribution of merchandise to different stores. Similarly, at The Home Depot, over 30,000 sku's are tracked by the computer inventory management system from the time an order is placed, to delivery to the stores, through customer check-out.[3]

THE RETAIL PROCUREMENT SYSTEM

The **retail procurement system** is composed of three processes that are essential to the retailer's quest for securing the right products in the right quantities at the right time at the right price (terms and conditions of sale). Buying, ordering, and handling merchandise are the three processes comprising the retailer's procurement system. The **merchandise buying process** involves all the activities necessary for establishing a successful relationship with various sources of supply. The **merchandise ordering process** is concerned with the efficient securing of the retailer's merchandise inventories. The **merchandise handling process** involves all the activities of physically getting the merchandise into the store and onto the shelves. The sequential activities (buying, ordering, and handling) of the retail procurement system are illustrated in Figure 13–1.

THE MERCHANDISE BUYING PROCESS

Retail buying can be viewed as the decision-making process through which the retail buyer identifies, evaluates, and selects merchandise for resale to the consumer. The **merchandise buying process** is the retailer's first step in getting merchandise into the store. Primary concerns are determining (1) what sources of supply are available and under what terms and conditions; (2) how to contact and evaluate various suppliers; and (3) how, when, and where to negotiate with and buy from alternative supply sources. The buying process should follow, in sequence, the four steps outlined in Figure 13–2. This outline will provide the structure for the first part of this chapter. To complete the buying task efficiently and in a timely way, a retailer must establish a buying organization. The major structural dimensions in developing a retail buying organization are given in Figure 13–3.

Identifying Sources of Supply

The first step in the buying process is to identify the available sources of supply. From these sources, the retailer must decide which channel to use in procuring each

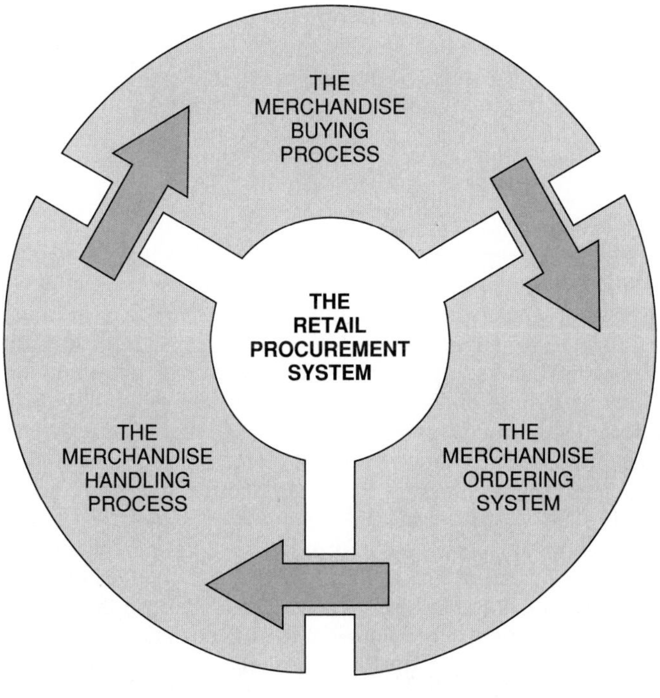

FIGURE 13–1
The retail procurement system

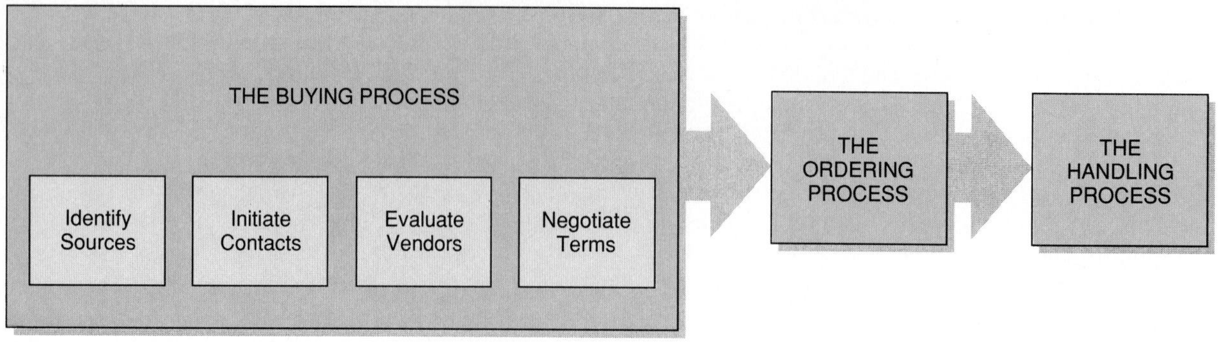

FIGURE 13–2
The merchandise buying process

merchandise line. In some cases, a direct channel to the manufacturer or original producer (e.g., farmer) is preferred. In other cases, an indirect or extended supply channel using one or more intermediaries—often referred to as *middlemen*—is desired. Specifically, the retailer can select from any one or a combination of the following sources of supply:

- Raw-resource producers
- Manufacturers
- Intermediaries
- Resident buying offices

The Raw-Resource Producer

Under certain circumstances, the retailer may elect to obtain supplies directly from the raw-resource producer. Large food retailing chains frequently bypass traditional supply sources in their efforts to secure fresh fruits and vegetables and to obtain raw materials for their private-label brands. Both large and small food retailers often secure stocks of some specialty food items (e.g., ethnic foods) directly from local producers. Buying food products directly from the raw-resource producer offers a retailer the advantages of increased speed and reduced handling, both of which are important in getting these perishables to the store fresh and with minimal damage. Other products that retailers buy directly from raw-resource producers include lumber, some construction materials, and other bulky materials that incur extra expense if handled by additional intermediaries.

The Final Manufacturer

Recently, large retailing organizations have emerged that have the volume to consider direct purchasing from manufacturers. When direct buying is available and feasible, the retailer gains several advantages. Obtaining *fresher products* is cited as one benefit of buying directly from the manufacturer. Merchandise procured from the manufacturer is frequently packaged and shipped directly from the production line. *Quicker delivery* is a second benefit. Direct channels of distribution are generally faster than indirect channels in processing initial orders, whereas wholesalers are usually faster on fill-in orders. Direct purchases are almost a necessity for highly perishable fashion and fad items. The third advantage of using the manufacturer as a source of supply is *lower price*. Eliminating the wholesaler and taking on the intermediary's functions enable the retailer to reduce certain costs and realize savings. Fourth, manufacturers can give retailers *more information* about their product lines than wholesalers do, because manufacturers' salespersons specialize in selling only their products, whereas wholesalers' salespeople sell product lines of several manufacturers.

FIGURE 13–3
Major structural dimensions of a retail buying organization

Formality

A **formal buying organization** has a separate department or division to handle the buying function and related merchandising activities. Used by large retailers, the formal structure presents a clear definition of the department's authority and permits greater use of personnel trained in the buying process. Formal buying structures, however, are generally more costly to establish and to maintain. **Informal buying organizations** incorporate the buying process into the existing organizational structure, where the task of buying is handled by existing store personnel. Because of their lower costs and greater flexibility, informal buying organizations are used mainly by smaller retailers. Shortcomings of informal buying structures include lack of clearly defined authorities and responsibilities and lack of coordination between various activities and personnel.

Centrality

In **centralized buying,** the retailer gives a central office the authority and responsibility to buy merchandise, rather than leaving the decision to each individual store in the multiunit chain. A central buying office allows the retailer to take advantage of discount structures through volume purchases, coordinate and control the buying process for the entire chain, use full-time buying specialists, gain preferential treatment from suppliers, and maintain a consistent customer image of the store's merchandise and quality. On the other hand, central buying hinders adapting to local market needs. Additional problems include information lags, time delays, and poor morale because of the distance between the buying office and the local units and the formal nature of the buying organization.

Decentralized buying is structured and conducted at the local level. Each store or group of stores within a certain geographic market is responsible for the buying process. Adaptability to local market needs is the major advantage in this type of buying organization. Lack of control, inconsistency between stores, and loss of some economies of scale in purchasing are the main shortcomings of buying structures developed around local autonomy.

Specialization

Some retailers prefer to have each buyer specialize in one or a few related merchandise lines—**specialized buying;** others find it necessary to have a few buyers secure all the merchandise lines—**generalized buying.** Higher costs are the principal disadvantage of specialized buying, whereas lower costs are the primary benefit of generalized buying. In turn, greater buying skills and product and market knowledge are associated with specialization, while less-developed skills and less knowledge are found in a generalized buying organization.

The fifth advantage of the manufacturer-to-retailer channel is *better adjustment*. Direct relationships between manufacturers and retailers lead both to more lenient adjustment policies and to quicker adjustment responses on products that the retailer's customers return. Most adjustment negotiations can be conducted more efficiently in face-to-face meetings than by going through third parties (wholesalers). Finally, direct purchases permit the retailer to order and secure goods made to its *specifications*. Many large chain operations (e.g., J.C. Penney and Sears) have a large percentage of their goods made to their specifications and identified with their names. A retailer trying to develop a product line tailored to the needs of specific target markets may see specification buying as the best alternative for meeting those needs.

The Wholesaling Intermediary

The third alternative source of supply is wholesaling intermediaries that position themselves in the distribution channel between the manufacturer and the retailer. Their role in facilitating the transfer of goods between manufacturers and retailers varies, depending on the nature of their operations as well as the functions and services they are willing to provide. Most intermediaries do not provide the full range of wholesaling functions—buying, selling, breaking bulk, assortment creation, stocking, delivery services, credit extension, information and consultation, and title transfer (see Figure 13–4). Instead, they tend to specialize in one or a limited number of these functions. Based on the number and type of functions, wholesaling intermediaries fall into several groups. Figure 13–5 identifies these groups of wholesalers. Selection of one of these types depends on the retailer's specific needs.

Merchant intermediaries are wholesalers that are directly involved in the purchase and sale of goods as they move through the channel of distribution. What distinguishes merchant intermediaries from agent intermediaries is that merchants take title to the goods they deal in, while agents do not assume ownership. As illustrated in Figure 13–5, merchant intermediaries can be classified as full-function and limited-function operations. For many small- and medium-sized retailers that do not have the volume of sales to buy directly from the manufacturer, merchant intermediaries represent the most important source of supply.

Full-function merchant intermediaries generally perform a full range of wholesaling functions. Based on the width of their product lines, three types of full-function merchant intermediaries can be identified. The **general merchandise wholesaler** handles a number of different and often unrelated product lines with no one product line being dominant (e.g., hardware, household durables, personal-care products, and automotive supplies). **Single-line wholesalers** limit their activities to one general product line (e.g., either hardware, drugs, or dry goods), while **specialty-line wholesalers** restrict their activities to one specialty line within a general line of products (e.g., frozen foods).

Limited-function merchant intermediaries limit their activities to certain wholesaling functions, in the belief that many retailers are only interested in having those functions provided and do not want to pay for services that are neither needed nor used. The **cash-and-carry wholesaler,** for example, is the discount supermarket of the wholesaling industry because the retailer must (1) go to the wholesaler's place of business, (2) select and assemble the order, (3) check out at a central station, (4) pay cash for the assembled order, and (5) load and transport the order. **Drop shippers** are wholesaling operators that normally distribute bulky products, such as lumber and building materials, that are expensive to transport and handle. The drop shipper operates out of an office, takes retail orders by phone or mail, passes the orders on to the producer, and arranges to have the order shipped directly to the retailer. The **truck distributor** operates its business out of a truck; the driver/salesperson can travel an established sales route and perform the sales and delivery functions simultaneously. The **rack jobber** operates in much the same way as the truck distributor, but the rack jobber usually furnishes the racks or shelves for displaying merchandise. In addition, the rack jobber is responsible for stocking the racks, building attractive displays, and pricing the merchandise. In return, the retailer furnishes floor or shelf space, acts as the sales agent, and collects the money from the customer.

Agent intermediaries specialize in buying and selling merchandise for others. They facilitate the exchange process between manufacturer and retailers by bringing them together. The two distinguishing characteristics of agent intermediaries are (1) they do not take title to the goods they deal in and (2) they normally provide only a limited number of functions. Also, agent intermediaries usually work on a commission basis, may have either an intermittent or continuous working relationship with clients, and normally do not represent both the buyer and seller in the same transaction.

Buying tasks. Wholesalers act as purchase agents when they anticipate the merchandise needs of retailers and their customers. By locating appropriate sources of supply and securing merchandise that is suitable to the retailer's needs, the wholesaler greatly enhances the retailer's buying and procurement processes.

Selling tasks. Wholesalers help simplify buying procedures by having salespersons calling at the retailer's place of business. Wholesaling intermediaries help reduce the retailer's cost of securing goods by: (1) eliminating some trips to the market, and (2) assuming some of the responsibilities (e.g., order follow-up, self-stocking), for getting the merchandise onto the retailer's displays.

Credit-extending tasks. Many wholesaling intermediaries finance part or all of a retailer's inventory. The most common credit extension is the setting of the date when the net price of an invoice is due in full. By providing 30, 45, 60, or more days to pay an invoice without charges, the wholesaler is in effect financing the retailer's inventory. Consignment and memorandum selling wherein the retailer does not pay for the merchandise until it is sold is still another form of extending credit. In addition, many wholesalers make available to retailers short-, intermediate-, and long-term loans that can be used as working and fixed capital.

Informing tasks. Marketing research and source information are two important functions provided by the wholesaler. Many large wholesaling operations engage in an ongoing effort to determine marketplace needs and conditions. By passing this information on, retailers have reference points for examining their market performances and adjusting their marketing programs. On the source side, the wholesaler's unique position within the channel allows him to provide useful information on products, manufacturer's programs, supply sources, and activities of competitors.

Consulting tasks. Wholesalers provide their customers with a host of various advisory services. The more common consultant services deal with accounting, advertising, personnel training, financial and legal advice, location analysis, inventory control, and facilities planning.

Title-transferring tasks. Free-and-clear title to products is essential to the exchange process. Merchant wholesalers that own the goods they deal in assume the responsibility for transfer of payments and the management of title exchange. Agent wholesalers that do not take title to the goods facilitate the exchange of title by providing or arranging for the services necessary to the title-exchange process.

Bulk-breaking tasks. A quantity gap occurs between manufacturer's need to produce and sell in larger quantities and the retailer's need to buy in smaller quantities. Wholesaling intermediaries help bridge this quantity gap by: (1) buying in car- or truck-load quantities, (2) performing break-in bulk activities, and (3) selling smaller quantities (e.g., case lots) to retailers. This bulk-breaking function helps reduce the cost of doing business by reducing inventory carrying and handling costs.

Assortment-creating tasks. An assortment gap exists between manufacturers that need (manufacturing economies of scale) to provide and sell a limited line of identical or nearly identical products and retailers that must offer the consumer a wider selection of products. Wholesalers can fill this gap by buying the limited product lines and items of many different manufacturers and combining these lines and items into appropriate assortments. The retailer's quest for either mass- or target-market appeal is greatly enhanced by the availability of diversified product assortments.

Stocking tasks. Retailers often have limited stockroom space and inventory investment capital. Wholesalers provide an invaluable service by reducing the space and capital needed for retail stock. This reduces the need for facilities and inventory carrying costs for the retailer. The local nature of wholesalers also enhances the time and place availability of products for restocking purposes.

Delivery tasks. Quick and frequent deliveries by the wholesaler help avoid or replenish stockout conditions that result in lost sales. A timely delivery system is one service a wholesaler provides that aids the retailer in holding down in-store inventories that are required to meet customer expectations. Reliable deliveries are also an integral part in reducing safety stock and the risk and investment associated with such stock.

FIGURE 13–4
Wholesaling functions

FIGURE 13–5
Types of wholesaling intermediaries

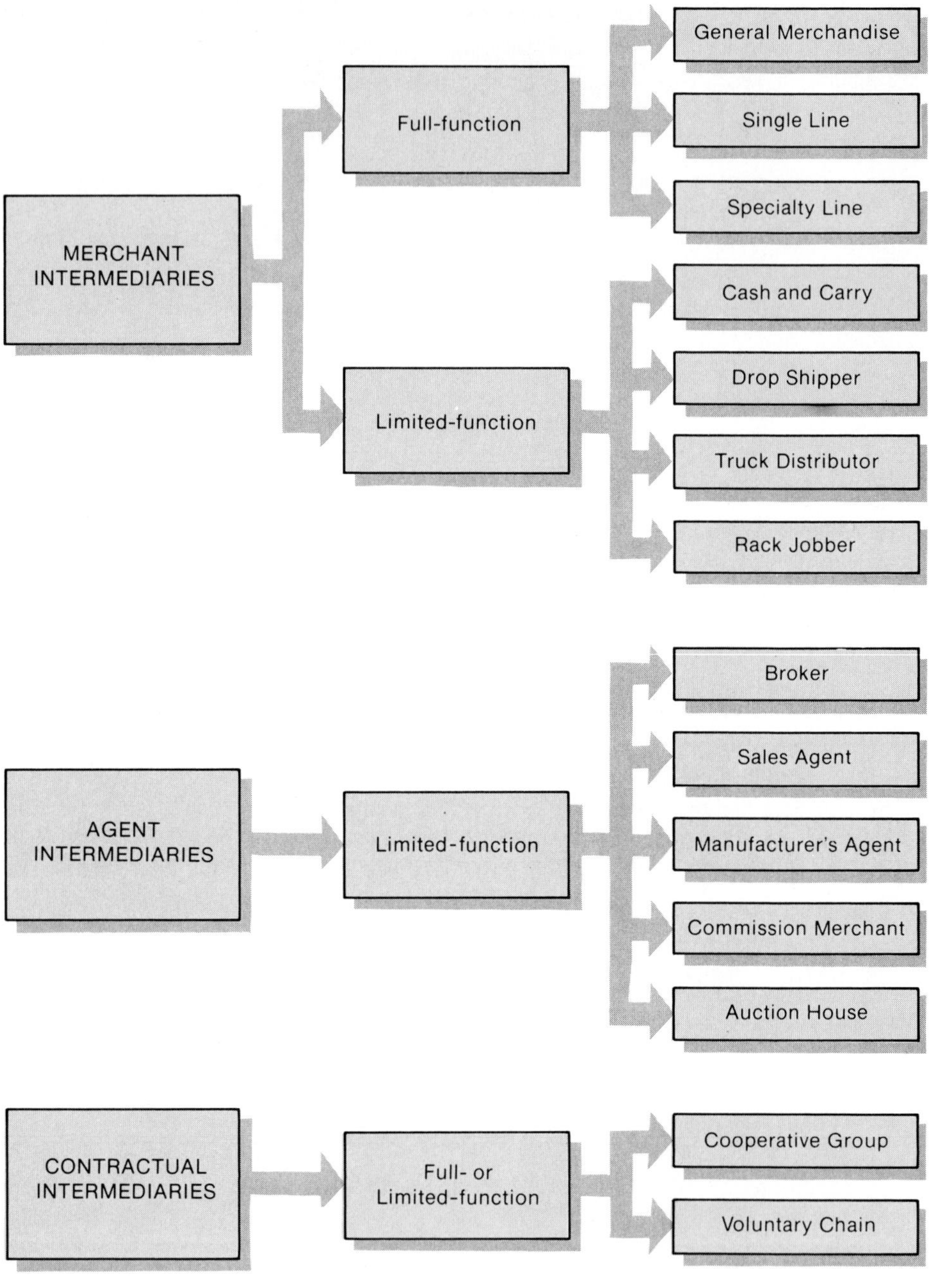

Brokers are agent intermediaries whose primary function is to bring prospective buyers and sellers together to complete a transaction. *Information* is the broker's stock-in-trade. **Sales agents** assume the entire marketing function for a manufacturer. In effect, the sales agent becomes the manufacturer's marketing department.[4] The **manufacturers' agent** is essentially the sales organization for several manufacturers within a prescribed market territory. Normally an agent carries complementary product lines from several manufacturers as opposed to product lines that compete directly. **Commission merchants** take physical possession of goods, provide storage and handling, and act as the selling agent for the producer. By providing the physical facilities for producers to display their products and retailers to inspect them, the **auction house** plays an important role in the wholesaling of used cars and agricultural products.

To combat the numerous competitive advantages of large chain organizations, many small retailers have entered into contractual arrangements with these wholesalers, known as **contractual intermediaries**. Typically, the retailer agrees to purchase a certain amount of merchandise from the wholesaler in return for lower prices and merchandising or promotional services. The two types of contractual intermediaries are **cooperative groups** and **voluntary chains** (see Chapter 2).[5]

This kind of display is typical of a wholesaler who operates as a rack jobber.

The Resident Buying Office

Resident buying offices are organizations specializing in the buying function and located in major wholesaling and producing markets.[6] Their central-market location puts the resident buyer in an excellent position to serve as the retailer's eyes and ears on supply conditions. The principal services resident buyers offer are information and buyer assistance. They provide information on (1) the availability of products; (2) the reliability of suppliers; (3) the present and future market and supply trends; and (4) the special deals, prices, promotions, and services that various suppliers offer. Buyer-assistance services include locating sources of supply, making initial contact with suppliers, aiding in sales negotiations by using their clout as representatives of several retailers, arranging delivery and payment schedules, and following up on orders to ensure the fast and timely arrival of merchandise at the retailer's store.[7]

The two general types of buying offices are the **store-owned buying office** and the **independent buying office**. Although resident buying offices are most commonly associated with the central apparel markets of New York, Dallas, and Los Angeles, other central markets are also populated with resident buyers; for example, because High Point, North Carolina, is the capital of the U.S. furniture industry, several resident buying offices are located there. San Francisco has recently entered into the fashion mart business with its 740,000 square foot Fashion Center.[8]

International Sourcing

Amalfi shoes, Louis Vuitton handbags, Lowenbrau beer, Outback Red sportswear, Yves St. Laurent fragrances, Esprit de Corp clothing, Cafe au Chocolat coffee, Yellow Cab. Co. apparel—are they American or foreign? Brand names are often misleading; nevertheless, international sources of supply are an integral part of most buying programs. There is hardly a product category that some retailer does not secure from some foreign source. The complexity of issues surrounding foreign goods and international sourcing is beyond the scope of this discussion; however, retailers often cite numerous advantages in support of overseas buying. First, foreign markets offer opportunities to discover and obtain unique and distinctive products (styling, materials, workmanship, and handcrafting) that will help retailers establish a differentiated advantage in merchandise assortments. Second, in most product categories, cost structures (goods, handling, and transportation) are equal to and often better than domestic sources. Third, foreign vendors are more willing and able to adjust their production to retailers' market and operating needs; domestic sources are often hampered by labor, governmental, and other restrictions in adjusting the production schedule. This greater flexibility is considered by many fashion retailers to be more significant than many of the price-structure benefits associated with foreign sources. Finally, in many product categories, foreign products have a real or imaginary status of quality and prestige; upscaled wearing apparel, wines, home electronics, and automobiles are a few examples.

There are potential risks associated with international sourcing, including (1) higher buying costs resulting from travel expenses, (2) legal complications caused by export/import regulations, (3) financial risks caused by foreign currency exchange rates, (4) supply continuency risks in some foreign areas where governmental and political environments are unstable or should the U.S. government become more protective, and (5) social risk in the form of a "Buy America" backlash when the domestic economy turns down. Wal-Mart's "bring it home to the USA" program is a buy-American program designed to build loyal Wal-Mart shoppers and to help avoid any consumer backlash.[9]

A retailer can obtain foreign merchandise through an **importer**—a U.S.-based commission wholesaler who represents retailers in the buying process. They provide services ranging from simply handling import dues to acting as a complete buying organization. Retailers can also use **commissionaires**, who operate full and limited buying offices within one or more foreign countries. Some retailers have "taken things into their own hands." The Limited and Charming Shoppes have developed *international programmed sourcing*—an international buying organization consisting of a network of foreign suppliers who are contracted to produce merchandise against specific orders from their parent company, as well as from other buyers. Mast Industries, a commercial division of The Limited, employs a worldwide network of 150 contract-production facilities to supply customers of The Limited and its many different retailing formats.[10] "Somewhere on this earth, no matter what the hour, there are associates of Mast inspecting quality, explaining specifications, or working at any one of the dozens—a multitude—of separate tasks that enabled them to grow to a global sourcing network."[11]

Contacting Sources of Supply

The second step in the buying process is to contact the potential sources of supply. Although most retailers have preferred sources, each retailer should strive to maintain as many supply-source contacts as possible. Contacts for a potential sales transaction can be initiated by either the vendor or the retailer.

Vendor-Initiated Contacts

Vendor-initiated contacts include store visits by sales representatives and telephone and mail-order solicitations.

Sales calls at the retailer's place of business represent the most common method of selling staple merchandise. Store visits are also used to sell some fashion goods to medium-sized and small retailers, which usually lack the resources to go to the market. From the retailer's viewpoint, store visits by supplier representatives offer the benefits of (1) saving time and money traveling to the market, (2) avoiding the strenuous market-search process, (3) allowing easy in-store access to inventory and sales records for reference purposes, and (4) permitting consultation with other store personnel before placing an order. Some vendors use telephone and mail contacts to prospect for customers, to make appointments for store visits, to follow up on orders, and to check on the needs of existing accounts.

Retailer-Initiated Contacts

Like vendors, retailers make initial contacts for products they need. Visiting central markets and resident buying offices, attending merchandise shows, and making telephone and mail inquiries are the four ways retailers seek vendors' products and services. Within **central markets** are concentrated the selling offices and merchandise showrooms of a large number of suppliers. In one visit the retailer can review and compare the merchandise offerings of several suppliers. Frequently, suppliers help retailers in their review and comparisons by setting up permanent displays in a central facility. The furniture mart in Chicago and the apparel mart in Dallas are examples of

A New Image in Retail Buying

J.C. Penney Company, Inc., . . . has been using the Sony Still Image System. . . . The Still Image System allows the transmission of accurate, highly detailed color pictures between Dallas (headquarters) and each of our overseas offices in only four minutes.

This means that when our Hong Kong office, for example, sources a particular garment and wants to show it to the Dallas office, they send it through Still Image System. . . . The pictures are transmitted within minutes and can even be plugged into our DBS (Direct Broadcast System) satellite network for broadcast to our stores. Going the other way, when a buyer in Dallas sees a new style or competitor's product, and wants to explore the possibility of importing it, a picture of that product can be instantly transmitted to the appropriate overseas office anywhere in the world.

Source: "Image Technology: A New Retail Vision," *Discount Merchandiser,* March 1990, 54.

WORLD OF RETAILING

Retail Technology

these types of facilities. Associated with central markets are resident buying offices discussed previously.

Merchandise shows or **trade fairs** are periodic displays of many suppliers' merchandise lines in one place at one time. Usually, a group of suppliers gets together and stages a show at a hotel or some other central facility such as a merchandise mart or convention facility. Merchandise showings can be either national, regional, or local. Retailers use **telephone** and **mail** contacts to make initial inquiries on the availability of and to place last-minute orders, reorders, and orders for fill-in merchandise. When the retailer is familiar with the supplier and the merchandise, telephone and mail contacts are efficient and relatively safe.

A central market, like this Gift Mart, allows retailers to see and compare many suppliers' merchandise.

Evaluating Sources of Supply

After identifying and contacting several sources of supply, the retailer must then evaluate each supplier to determine how consistent its operating characteristics are.[12] This third step of the buying process requires evaluation criteria and methods to rank the relative capabilities of each supply alternative to serve the retailer's needs.[13]

Evaluation Criteria

Criteria for evaluating potential suppliers are merchandise criteria, distribution criteria, price criteria, promotion criteria, and service criteria.

Merchandise Criteria. The first consideration in evaluating alternative sources of supply is what merchandise the supplier offers. The suitability, availability, and adaptability of the suppliers' merchandise lines are three common merchandise criteria. *Suitability* refers to how well the merchandise fits the needs of the retailer's customers. Suitability can be judged on the basis of assortment factors such as brand, style, and price, as well as individual factors such as uniqueness, originality, and durability. Suitable merchandise is also judged according to aesthetics (e.g., fabric, color, and print) and quality (e.g., construction, fit, and crafting).

To determine *availability*, the buyer must first find out whether the supplier will accept an order. If so, will the merchandise be available in the appropriate quantities, sizes, styles, and colors? Merchandise availability may in fact be based on the size of the order; for example, many suppliers establish minimum quantities that retailers must order to purchase merchandise from them.

The third merchandise criterion is *adaptability*—the supplier's willingness to make necessary changes in the product to meet the needs of the retailer and its customers. Adaptability may involve (1) producing products to the retailer's specifications, (2) placing the retailer's private label on the product, and (3) adjusting production (color, sizes, styles) to take advantage of fast-moving items or incorporating new trends into existing merchandise lines.

Distribution Criteria. Because delivery delays are a concern to all retailers, an important evaluation criterion is how well suppliers perform their *distribution* and *delivery* functions. Past performance is usually a good indication of future performance. Also of interest to most retailers is the degree of *exclusiveness* the supplier offers in particular lines of merchandise—whether the product is offered on an exclusive (one retailer per market), selective (few retailers per market), or intensive (many retailers per market) basis. Additional distribution and delivery policies the retailer should consider for potential suppliers are (1) whether delivery services are offered, (2) terms and conditions of the delivery service, (3) order size and assortment constraints, (4) initial-order processing time, (5) reorder processing time, and (6) ease and flexibility of placing an order. Figure 13–6 lists more criteria that could be used to evaluate a supplier's distribution performance.

Price Criteria. Price criteria center around two considerations: price to the consumer and price to the retailer. Regarding the price to the consumer, the major issues the retailer should evaluate are price appropriateness and price maintenance. The retail selling price must be appropriate to the retailer's target market. Price *appropriateness* should be measured in terms of value (i.e., offering the consumer the best quality at the best price). Price *maintenance* is the supplier's policy of maintaining the retail selling price at or above a certain level. Some suppliers insist that retailers sell their merchandise at a suggested retail price. For a high-volume discounter that relies heavily

FIGURE 13–6
Supplier evaluation: Using distribution criteria

Major Category	Subcategory
Product availability	Line item availability Product group availability Invoice fill Cases/units
Order cycle time	Order entry Order processing Total cycle time
Consistency	In order cycle time In shipment dispatch In transit time In arrival time In warehouse handling
Response time	Order status Order tracing Backorder status Order confirmation Product substitution Order shortages Product information requests
Error rates	Shipment delays Order errors Picking & packing errors Shipping & labeling errors Paperwork errors
Product/shipment related malfunction	Damaged merchandise Merchandise refusals Claims Returned goods Customer complaints
Special handling	Transshipment Expedited orders Expedited transportation Special packaging Customer backhauls

Source: Louis W. Stern and Adel I. El-Ansary, *Marketing Channels,* 2d ed. (Englewood Cliffs, NJ: Prentice-Hall, 1983), 161.

on price appeal substantiated by price comparisons, price-maintenance policies are simply unacceptable in most cases.

The second group of price considerations concerns what price the retailer must pay for the merchandise. Perhaps the most important consideration is whether the price will permit the retailer to take a sufficient markup to cover expenses, make a profit, and still be competitive in the marketplace. (Price negotiation will be discussed shortly.)

Promotional Criteria. Many merchandise lines require a considerable amount of promotional support to be successfully marketed. The *type* and *amount* of promotional assistance the retailer can expect from a supplier are therefore important evaluation criteria. Promotional assistance assumes many different forms, including advertising allowances, cooperative advertising, in-store demonstrations, free display materials, and various consumer inducements such as premiums, coupons, contests, and samples. Also, the extent to which the supplier supports the sale of merchandise through national and/or local advertising is an important factor. Ultimately, the essential question for the retailer is, "Does the supplier help me sell?"

Service Criteria. Besides the various types of merchandise, distribution, price, and promotional supports, some suppliers provide some or all of the following supplementary services:

- Financing and credit services
- Return privileges
- Warranty and repair services
- Sales force training
- Accounting services
- Inventory planning and control
- Prepackaging, prelabeling, and preticketing
- Markdown insurance
- Display units, fixtures, and signs
- Store facilities design services

The extent to which the retailer might consider some of these services in evaluating supply sources depends on its need for them. While any one of these services can help the retailer reduce either operating expenses or capital investment, they also make the retailer more dependent on the supplier who furnishes the service. Care must be taken to determine what strings are attached.

Evaluation Methods

To effectively evaluate alternative sources of supply, retailers must systematically assess each store using objective methods. Three methods are the weighted-rating method, the single-most-important criterion method, and the minimum-cutoff method.

The **weighted-rating method** is a procedure for evaluating supply alternatives by assigning weighted values to each of a set of evaluation criteria. Although several weighted-rating procedures have been devised, the decision matrix approach to vendor selection developed by John S. Berens illustrates the method.[14]

- **Step 1: Criteria selection**. This step entails selecting criteria to evaluate sources of supply that are most relevant to the retailer and its relationship to potential suppliers.
- **Step 2: Criteria weighting**. Predetermined weights (or levels of importance) are assigned to each evaluation criterion. Frequently, this weighting process is accomplished by simply rank-ordering all criteria from most to least important and assigning the highest value to the criterion deemed most important and subsequent lower values to those that are less important.
- **Step 3: Supplier selection**. This is a procedure for choosing which potential suppliers to include in the evaluation.
- **Step 4: Supplier rating**. In this step, each of the selected suppliers is rated on the basis of each evaluation criterion. By comparing each supplier to all other suppliers for each criterion, the retailer can assign a minimal rating to each supplier.
- **Step 5: Weighted rating**. Each supplier's rating is multiplied on each evaluation criterion (step 4) by the criterion weight (step 2) to obtain the weighted rating for each supplier. To obtain the overall weighted rating for each supplier, simply add the weighted rating of each criterion.

Vendor Technology Manages Retail Industry

WORLD OF RETAILING

Retail Technology

Hosiery might be a highly profitable item for the retailer, but Hanes sensed that most salespeople didn't care to put much time or effort into pushing panty hose. They simply are not a big-ticket item.

So Hanes Hosiery Inc., Winston-Salem, N.C., decided to take things into its own hands and fight back with technology. . . . Members of the Hanes sales staff periodically visit each store, straighten the stock, fill in displays, and make sure there's an adequate supply of product on hand. Before leaving, they even take an inventory and create a replenishment order.

Reps used handheld Telxon computers equipped with UPC-reading wands. When they complete the inventory, they use a lightweight Kodak Diconix 150 printer to create a full report. Both battery-powered units fit in a single carrying case and are ready for use in a few minutes.

After comparing the inventory report against the store's target stock level, reps use a Grid laptop computer to generate a new order, and electronically transmit it to Hanes' main office.

In some cases, reps will transmit the current inventory level to Hanes' mill, where, based on the targeted stock level, a replenishment order is calculated on the host computer. In either case, the store manager has a hard copy of the order.

The system drastically cuts down the time needed for restocking the store . . . before computerization, orders took seven days or more to reach the company's mill. Now, orders are in the queue immediately.

And you're assured of accuracy. . . . Orders can be checked by the computers before the reps communicate with the company's Digital VAX mainframe.

Source: Cyndee Miller, "Hanes Takes the Snags out of Maintaining Hosiery Inventory," *Marketing News* (May 14, 1990): vol. 24, p. 23. Reprinted from *Marketing News*, published by the American Marketing Association, Chicago, IL 60606.

The retailer starts by selecting the source that received the highest weighted rating and attempts to secure the necessary commitments from that supplier. If more than one source is needed or if the highest-rated source is not available, the retailer simply proceeds down the weighted-rating list until all the needed supply sources are secured. Figure 13–7 illustrates Berens' weighted-rating method.

As the name implies, some retailers evaluate and select suppliers on the basis of the **single-most-important criterion**. This method is similar to the weighted-rating method in that the retailer completes the criteria-selection, criteria-weighting, and supplier-selection steps, then compares suppliers and judges one superior according to the single-most-important criterion. If no supplier is judged superior on the basis of this criterion, then the evaluation procedure continues to the second-most-important criterion, the third, and so on, until one supplier emerges as superior.

The **minimum-cutoff method** recognizes that it is not always possible to determine the precise importance of each criterion. It is usually possible, however, to establish some minimum standard or cutoff point for each evaluation criterion. Using this method, the retailer (1) selects the criteria for inclusion in the evaluation, (2) establishes a minimum-cutoff standard for each criterion, (3) compares each supplier to the minimum cutoff on each criterion, (4) eliminates all suppliers that fall below the minimum-cutoff standard on any criterion, and (5) chooses among suppliers that have exceeded the minimum cutoff on all criteria. This method can be combined with the single-most-important criterion method to produce an even more exacting supplier-evaluation technique.

FIGURE 13–7
Decision matrix approach to supplier selection (source: John S. Berens, "A Decision Matrix Approach to Supplier Selection," *Journal of Retailing,* 47, no. 4[Winter 1971–1972]; 52)

	Criteria Weight (Step 2)	Supplier A	Supplier B	Supplier C	Supplier D	Supplier E
Criterion 1: Supplier Can Fill Reorders	6	3 / 18	2 / 12	4 / 24	1 / 6	0 / 0
Criterion 2: Markup Is Adequate	4	2 / 8	4 / 16	3 / 12	0 / 0	1 / 4
Criterion 3: Customers Ask for the Line	1	1 / 1	2 / 2	4 / 4	3 / 3	0 / 0
Criterion 4: Supplier's Line Has Significant Changes from Season to Season	2	3 / 6	4 / 8	2 / 4	1 / 2	0 / 0
Criterion 5: Supplier's Line Contributes to Fashion Leadership	5	2 / 10	1 / 5	0 / 0	3 / 15	4 / 20
Criterion 6: Supplier's Line is Cut to Fit Customers Well	2	1 / 2	0 / 0	3 / 6	4 / 8	2 / 4
Criterion 7: Supplier Advertises Line in Local Media	1	0 / 0	1 / 1	2 / 2	4 / 4	3 / 3
Supplier TOTAL SCORES		45	44	52	38	31

Negotiating with Sources of Supply

The fourth step in the buying process is active negotiation with suppliers identified in the evaluation step as potentially suitable sources. In the retailer-supplier relationship, the three most common issues subject to negotiation are *price, logistics,* and *service*. In negotiating, retailers must not fall into the supply-side mentality trap; that is, basing buying decisions on suppliers' deals and promotions rather than on consumer needs and expectations.[15]

Negotiating the Price

The price the retailer pays for the same merchandise is usually subject to negotiation. While any number of factors could conceivably influence the price the retailer pays, three factors play dominant roles: (1) list price, (2) discount and allowance terms, and (3) transportation and handling terms.

Price negotiations usually start with the supplier's basic price list. For administrative convenience, most suppliers establish their pricing structures around basic **list prices** that they use for an extended time period. By adjusting their list prices upward or downward using various types of "add-ons" and "discounts," suppliers can avoid publishing frequently revised price lists, and at the same time they can make necessary price accommodations for individual retail customers.

As the starting point for negotiation, the basic list price is a crucial element in estimating the supplier's "final" price to the retailer. Since some suppliers publish what are, in effect, inflated list prices, substantial differences in the final price can result because of large variations in discounts and allowances as well as transportation and handling terms.

Discount and Allowance Terms. The final selling price to the retailer is the difference between the supplier's list price and the negotiated discounts and allowances. The principal types of discounts are trade, quantity, seasonal and cash discounts, and promotional allowances.

A **trade discount** is a form of compensation that the buyer may receive for performing certain services (functions) for the supplier. Also referred to as a functional discount, the trade discount is usually used by suppliers selling merchandise through catalogs and is based on a quoted list price. The supplier offers one price to all potential buyers and makes price changes simply by adjusting the amount of the trade discount offered to any given buyer. The size of the trade discount depends on the type, quantity, and quality of the services the potential buyer is willing to provide. Therefore, variations in trade discounts are legally justifiable on the basis of the different costs associated with doing business with different buyers. If the buyer is instrumental in helping the supplier realize certain savings, part of those savings are passed along to the buyer in the form of larger trade discounts.

Trade discounts come in single and chain forms. The **single trade discount** is expressed as a single percentage adjustment (e.g., 50 percent) to the supplier's list price. For example, a product with a list price of $200 less a 40 percent trade discount (which would amount to an $80 trade discount) costs the retailer $120 ($200 × .40 = $80; $200 − $80 = $120). A trade discount can also be calculated by using a chain of discounts. Expressed as a series of percentages (e.g., 40 percent, 20 percent, 10 percent), the **chain trade discount** is applied to the list price in successive order. The first percentage discount is calculated on the original list price, the second percentage discount is calculated on the value resulting from the first calculation, and so on until each percentage discount is taken into account. A product listed at $300 less a 40/20/10 percent discount costs the retailer $129.60, since altogether that represents a discount of 56.8 percent. To illustrate this calculation of a chain trade discount; for example:

list price =	$300.00	($300 × 40% = $120)
	−120.00	
	180.00	($180 × 20% = $ 36)
	− 36.00	
	144.00	($144 × 10% = $ 14.40)
	− 14.40	
retailer's price =	$129.60	

The purpose of expressing the trade discount in the form of a chain is to facilitate offering different discounts to different buyers. The buyer that performs many services for the supplier receives the entire discount chain (40 percent, 20 percent, 10 percent), while the buyer that performs a limited number of services is offered only part of the chain (40 percent, 20 percent, or possibly only 40 percent).

Suppliers offer **quantity discounts** to retailers as an inducement to buy large quantities of merchandise. Large order quantities help reduce the supplier's selling, handling, billing, transporting, and inventory costs. Some of the cost savings are passed along to the buyer in the form of quantity discounts. However, buying large quantities normally increases the retailer's operating expenses, ties up operating capital, and creates additional inventory-control problems. The retail buyer must also be aware of the potential risk of overbuying and then having to mark down the overstocked merchandise.

Quantity discounts can be expressed and calculated in several different ways. They can be based on either the dollar value of the total order or on the number of units (or cases) in the order. Quantity discounts can also be handled as a percentage reduction from list price or simply expressed in some form of a schedule with unit or dollar sales corresponding to a particular dollar discount amount. A different approach to quantity discounts is to quote a carload or truckload price. Any order less than a carload or a truckload is adjusted by a system of add-ons; for example, a retailer placing a less-than-carload order is quoted the carload unit price, plus a certain percentage (e.g., 6 percent) of that price as an add-on. Given the numerous methods for calculating quantity discounts, the retailer should take the time to verify exactly what type and how much of a quantity discount the supplier is offering.

Three types of quantity discounts—noncumulative, cumulative, and free merchandise—are common. A **noncumulative quantity single discount** is based on a single order or shipment. The supplier uses this type of discount to encourage the retailer to increase the size of an order—the bigger the order, the bigger the absolute discount. Quantity discounts that apply to several orders or shipments placed with the supplier over an extended period (usually a year) are referred to as **cumulative quantity discounts**. Not only do these discounts apply to several orders, but usually the amount of the discount increases as the total (accumulated) order size increases. The supplier's purpose for applying cumulative discounts is to encourage return trade by reducing the price of merchandise on subsequent orders. *Free merchandise* is also a form of quantity discount. The "13" dozen, whereby the supplier offers one free dozen for every 12 dozen ordered, is a common way to give the retailer free merchandise instead of a price reduction or a cash payment.

Seasonal discounts are price reductions given to buyers who are willing to order, receive, and pay for goods during the "off season." Although the retailer can realize a savings in the cost of the merchandise by taking seasonal discounts, the savings must be viewed in light of (1) additional inventory costs and problems; (2) greater risks resulting from price changes, style changes, and merchandise depreciation; and (3) restricted use of investment capital already tied up in the merchandise.

A **cash discount** is one given for making prompt payment. To encourage retailers to pay their bills before the due date, the supplier sometimes permits the retailer to deduct a certain percentage discount from the net invoice price. When negotiating cash discounts and related payment terms, the retailer needs to consider three factors: net invoice price, discount amount, and dating terms.

The first consideration in negotiating cash discounts is to establish what constitutes the net invoice price. As the base for calculating cash discounts, the net invoice price is crucial in determining the dollar amount of the discount. The **net invoice price** is the net value of the invoice or the total invoice minus all other discounts (trade, quantity, seasonal, etc.). An exception may occur when the supplier allows the transportation charges to be included in the net invoice figure. Depending on trade practices, the inclusion of transportation charges may be open for negotiation; if so, it is obviously to the retailer's advantage to have them included.

The second factor the retailer must consider is the **discount amount**. While a 2 percent cash discount is common in many trades, the rate ranges from no cash discounts to whatever the supplier is willing to allow. The amount of the cash discount is standardized in some industry trades, and both the retailer and supplier are generally bound by the trade standards. In other trades, the cash discount amount is totally negotiable. Some retailers insist on a cash discount and automatically deduct a standard discount if payment is made within a specific time period (usually ten days). They take the discount regardless of the terms expressed in the supplier's invoice.

Dating terms are as significant in negotiating cash discounts and payment conditions as the net invoice price and the discount amount. The importance of dating terms is that they (1) determine the cash discount period or the amount of time the retailer has to take advantage of the cash discount, and (2) provide the invoice due date or the amount of time the retailer has to pay the net invoice price in full. Ten days is the most common cash discount period, while 30 days from the dating of the invoice is a fairly standard invoice due date. Both cash-discount periods and invoice due dates vary, however, depending on the particular situation and on the retailer's ability to negotiate dating terms.

The two general classes of dating terms are immediate and future. Sometimes suppliers insist on **immediate dating**, allowing no time for the cash discount or extra time for the invoice payment. Prepayment and cash on delivery (COD) are two examples of immediate dating. **Prepayment dating** means the retailer must make payment when the order is placed. Suppliers use prepayment terms when two circumstances occur simultaneously: (1) the retailer is either unknown or unreliable (bad credit rating) and (2) the merchandise is customized or highly perishable. **Cash on delivery** terms are enforced when the retailer is either unknown or unreliable, but when the merchandise can be easily sold if returned to the supplier.

Future dating is the practice of allowing the retailer more time to take advantage of the cash discount or to pay the net amount of the invoice. In essence, it encourages the retailer to delay payment and helps in short-term financing of inventory. Figure 13–8 describes several types of future dating.

One additional negotiating issue regarding cash discounts is *anticipation,* or an extra cash discount for paying the net invoice *before the cash-discount period expires.* It is an amount the retailer may take in addition to the cash discount. The anticipation amount depends on the number of days the invoice is paid before the last day of the discount period; for example, paying the invoice on the fourth day of a ten-day cash-discount period entitles the retailer to deduct six days of anticipation at a previously agreed-on daily discount rate. Large retailers, as well as those with surplus cash available, use anticipation extensively.

Most experts recommend that retailers take every cash discount available, because most cash discounts yield an equivalent annual interest rate far in excess of the yield most other investments produce. Also, the yield on most cash discounts is more than

FUTURE DATING TERMS	SELECTED EXAMPLES	EXPLANATION OF EXAMPLES	
		Cash Discount Terms	Net Invoice Terms
Net	Net, 30	no cash discount allowed	net amount due within 30 days of invoice date
Date of Invoice (DOI)	2/10, net 30	2-percent discount within 10 days of invoice date	net amount due within 30 days of invoice date
End of Month (EOM)	2/10, net 60, EOM	2-percent discount within 10 days of the first day of the month following the invoice date	net amount due within 60 days of the first day of the month following the invoice date
Receipt of Goods (ROG)	4/10, net 45, ROG	4-percent discount within 10 days after receiving the goods at the retailer's place of business	net amount due within 45 days after receiving the goods at the retailer's place of business
Extra	3/10-60 extra, net 90	3-percent discount within 70 days of invoice date	net amount due within 90 days of invoice date

FIGURE 13–8
Types of future-dating terms

enough to cover the interest on funds borrowed to meet the time requirement of the cash-discount period.

Promotional Allowances. To gain the retailer's cooperation in promotional activities, the supplier frequently offers a promotional allowance. **Promotional allowances,** which reduce the price retailers pay suppliers for merchandise, include advertising allowances, preferred selling space, free display materials, and merchandise deals. *Advertising allowances* are discounts retailers earn by advertising the supplier's products in the local media. In essence, the retailer assumes part or all of the supplier's local advertising function and is compensated by the supplier for money spent and services performed in the form of an advertising allowance. Retailers give vendors *preferred selling space* in return for a price reduction. A variation of this type of space consideration is the "slotting allowance"—admission fees paid by manufacturers to get their product on crowded shelves.[16] Preferred sales areas include (1) a freestanding display in a high-traffic aisle, (2) an end-of-aisle display, (3) a high-exposure area near a checkout counter, or (4) a special window display. In some cases, the more preferred the selling space, the greater the allowance. Retailers also use *free display materials* in the form of counter, window, and floor displays, signs, banners, and shelf strips, as well as various types of giveaways. These materials help to increase sales, reduce selling costs, and earn allowances from suppliers. Promotional allowances also can take the form of *merchandise deals* in which the supplier substitutes free merchandise for monetary allowances as compensation for performing promotional functions. As with all other discounts, promotional allowances must be judged on a cost-benefit basis.

Negotiating the Logistics

The retailer's actual laid-in cost of merchandise also depends on which party assumes the transportation charges and handling responsibilities. In negotiating logistic (transportation and handling) terms, the retailer must consider all of these issues: Who pays transportation charges? Who bears transportation charges? Where does the title exchange hands? Who is responsible for filing claims? The payer and the bearer of transportation charges may or may not be the same person; for example, to facilitate delivery speed, the supplier may pay transportation charges when the goods are loaded at the factory but charge them back to the retailer on the invoice. In such cases the retailer ultimately bears the cost of transportation.

Equally important is the point at which title to the merchandise is transferred from the supplier to the retailer. The party that has title while the goods are in transit is responsible for bearing any insurance costs that might be needed above the liability of the carrier to cover loss. The location where title exchange occurs also influences which party is responsible for filing and collecting any damage claims against the carrier. Damage claims not only can be expensive to collect in some cases but can also occupy a considerable amount of the retailer's time. Figure 13–9 illustrates the six most common expressions of transportation and handling terms. As a note of caution, however, transportation terms are characterized by a variety of expressions (e.g., the terms *plant* or *factory* are often substituted for *origin; store* or *retailer* may be used instead of *destination*). Therefore, retailers should not hesitate to ask for clarification of any expression they do not fully understand.

Negotiating the Service

In addition to price, the various types and levels of services the supplier provides also are subject to negotiation. In some cases, a service is fairly standard with only minor adjustments allowed; in other cases, certain services are totally negotiable. The discussion on evaluating sources of supply identified ten different supplier services. Although services may be available, the retailer may not receive some or any of them

Handling Merchandise...

for effective product distribution.

The merchandise handling process involves all of the activities of physically getting the merchandise into the store and onto the shelves. Receiving, checking, marking and stocking are all key elements in the retailer's merchandise handling system.

Electronic technologies are rapidly becoming an integral part of the procurement systems necessary for effective and efficient processing of merchandise inventories.

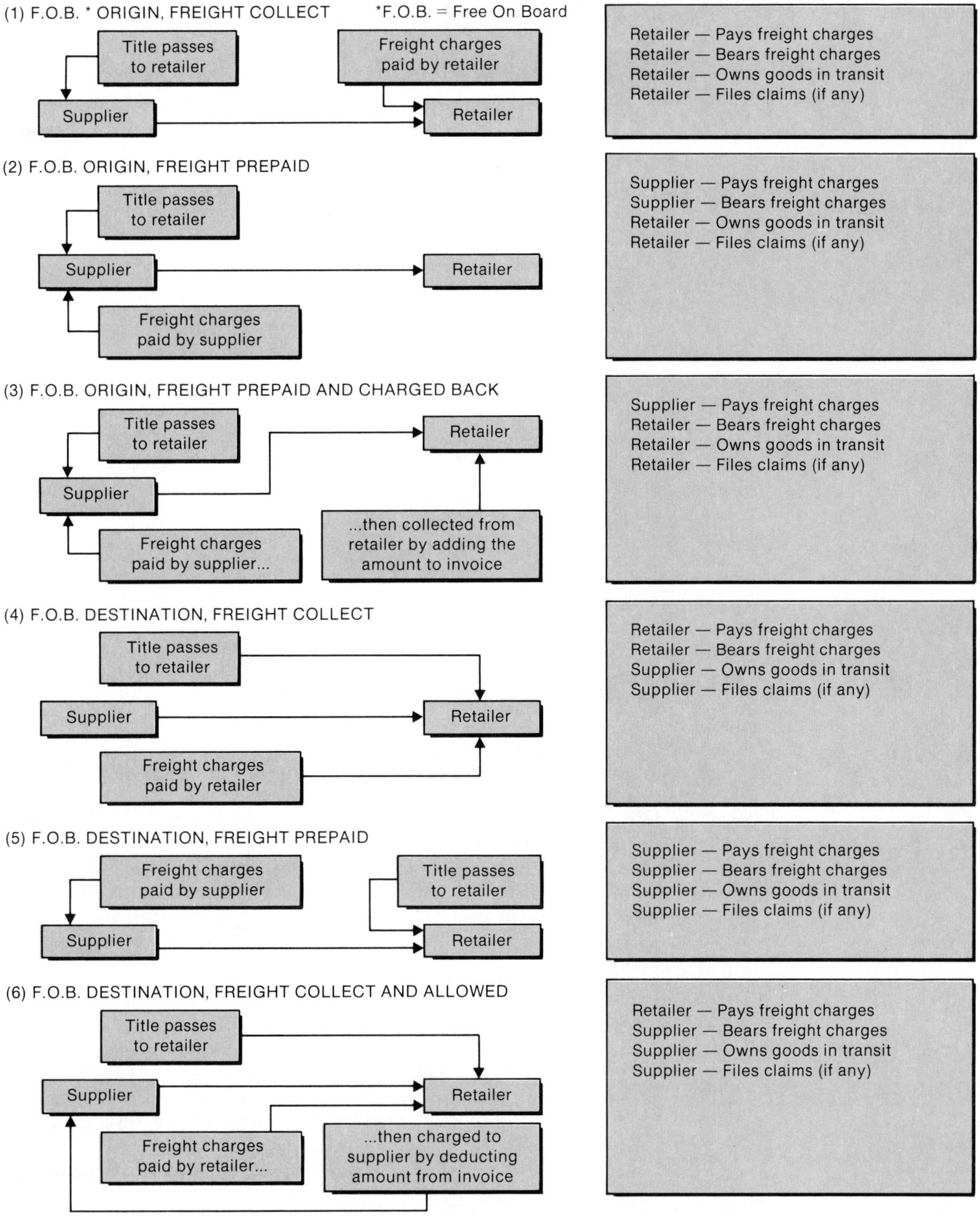

FIGURE 13–9
Transportation terms and conditions (source: adapted from Murray Krieger, *Practical Merchandising Math for Everyday Use* [New York: National Retail Merchants Association, 1980], 4)

without actively seeking them as part of the buying process. The terms and conditions for any one of these ten services must be detailed before purchase if the retailer expects the supplier to provide them.

THE MERCHANDISE ORDERING PROCESS

Once the negotiation stage is completed, the retailer is then in a position to initiate ordering process. As seen in Figure 13–10, the **merchandise ordering process** is the logical extension of the buying process, and is concerned with three issues: (1) should purchase orders be concentrated with a few vendors or spread out among many suppliers—buying strategies; (2) what type of buying procedures should be used under what type of circumstances—buying methods; (3) what type of vendor relationships and order processing arrangements should the retailer establish or become involved in—traditional purchase-order systems and/or quick response replenishment systems.

Retail Buying Strategies

In deciding how many different sources of supply to use in securing the store's merchandise, the retailer can elect to pursue one of two buying strategies: concentrated or dispersed. With a **concentration strategy,** the retailer decides to use a limited number of suppliers, believing it leads to lower total costs and preferential treatment. By concentrating purchases, the retailer can lower the laid-in cost of the merchandise by taking advantage of quantity discounts and lower transportation rates. Operating expenses can be lower, since ordering, receiving, and processing of merchandise are more efficient with fewer suppliers. Equally important, many retailers believe that if they become a preferred customer by concentrating their purchases, they can expect to receive special considerations for merchandise and supplier services. Using tight operational controls, May Department Stores use as few suppliers as possible; then, by giving them large orders, it can exert the leverage to wring better deals. May often gets quicker deliveries of goods than its rivals. Sometimes it is able to negotiate bigger concessions from suppliers to cover markdowns it is forced to take.[17]

Proponents of the **dispersion strategy** believe that concentrated buying is concentrated risk, because it is dangerous to put all your eggs in a few baskets. By spreading orders over many suppliers, these retailers believe they can (1) obtain a greater variety of merchandise, (2) be made aware of "hot" items, (3) ensure backup sources of supply, and (4) promote competitive services from different supply sources. Retailers must make the decision to use a concentration or a dispersion strategy in light of their individual situations. Generally, retailers of staple merchandise tend to

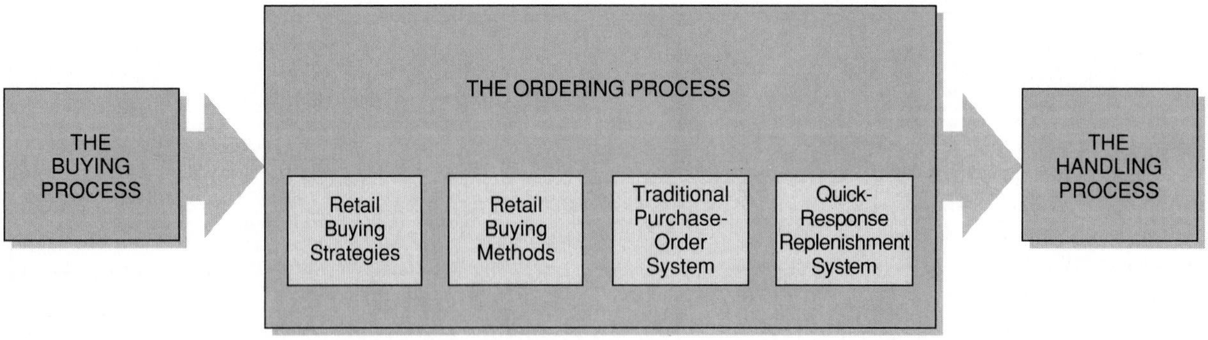

FIGURE 13–10
The merchandising ordering process

concentrate their purchases, whereas retailers of fashion merchandise usually elect a less-concentrated approach.

Retail Buying Methods

Retailers use several buying methods, depending on their circumstances. They include regular, consignment, memorandum, approval, and specification buying. Retailers use regular buying to secure the vast majority of their merchandise lines. **Regular buying** involves the systematic cutting and issuing of purchase orders and reorders. The entire buying process is conducted in conjunction with the merchandise budget and the inventory-control process. Purchases are mechanical and automatic. Most staple goods and many fashion goods can be handled by this method.

Consignment buying is an arrangement whereby the supplier retains ownership of the merchandise shipped to the retailer, and the retailer (1) displays the merchandise, (2) sells it to the final consumer, (3) deducts an agreed-on percentage commission, and (4) remits the remainder to the supplier. Merchandise not sold within a prescribed time is returned to the supplier. This method of buying is usually used when the merchandise is expensive, new, or of such a high-risk nature that the extent and duration of demand are relatively unknown.

Memorandum buying is essentially a variation of consignment buying. The main difference is that the title to the merchandise exchanges hands when it is shipped to the retailer. The retailer retains the right to return to the supplier any unsold merchandise and to pay for the merchandise after it has been sold. The retailer's purpose for assuming title is to gain more control in setting the selling price to the final consumer.

When merchandise is shipped to the retailer's store before the final purchase decision has been made, the retailer is buying on approval. Before the retailer can sell the merchandise it must secure ownership. **Approval buying** allows the retailer to inspect the merchandise before making the purchase decision and to postpone any purchase until physical possession has been secured. Postponing possession can result in lower inventory carrying costs, more time to take advantage of cash discounts, and more time to prepare a merchandising program for the goods.

Many large retail organizations want some of their merchandise made to their specifications. Specifications can range from minor changes in existing lines of merchandise to complete specifications covering raw materials, design, quality, labeling, and packaging. Through **specification buying,** the retailer can acquire merchandise that is unique and distinctive from that of competitors and that is thus personalized. Usually, specification buying involves considerable negotiation between retailer and supplier, and ordering lead times are quite long.

Traditional Purchase-Order System

While a certain level of cooperation and coordination is a necessary part of any distribution system, the interaction between buyers and sellers in a traditional purchase-order system is essentially an adversarial relationship. In this traditional system both the vendor and the retailer attempt to secure the best possible terms and conditions for their organization during each purchase transaction. Strong negotiation skills are vital in this adversary relationship if the retailer is securing desired merchandise under favorable terms. The basic dimensions of a traditional purchase-order system are shown in Figure 13–11. As illustrated, this system is composed of a series of functions within each organization (receiving, selling, and buying for the retailer and sales, production, and distribution for the vendor), and between organizations (ordering and delivery).

A traditional purchase-order system starts with the retailer obtaining sales data via manual (e.g., point-of-sale tallies and price-ticket or cash register stubs) or automatic

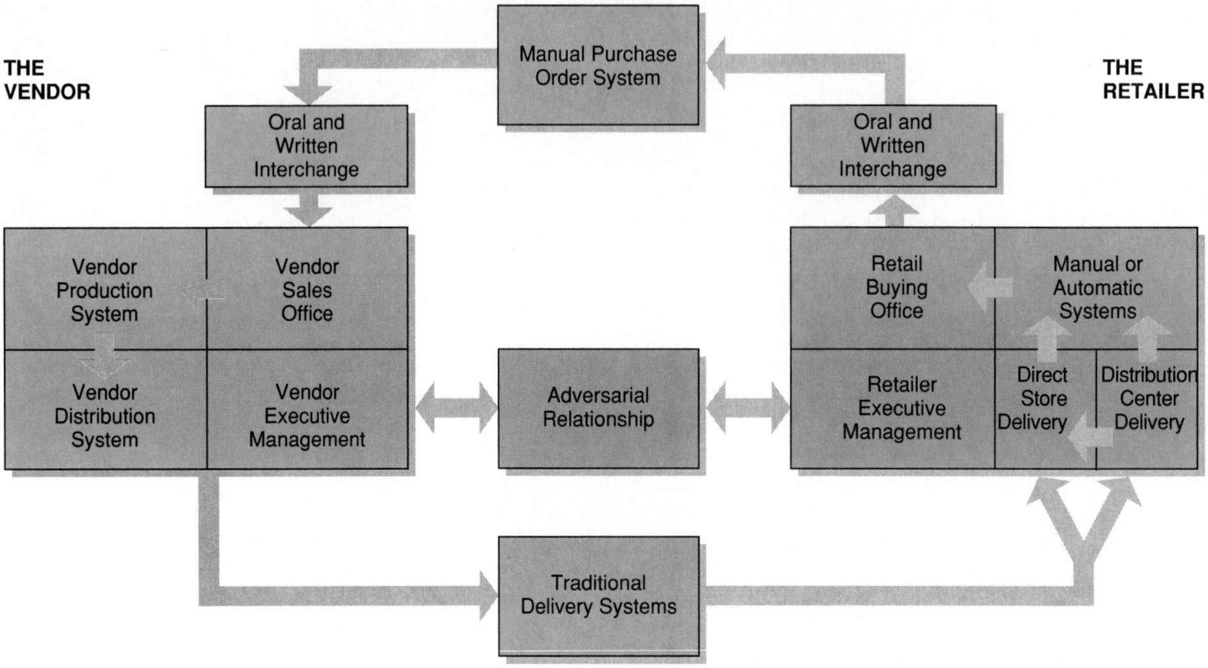

FIGURE 13–11
Traditional purchase-order system

(e.g., point-of-sale terminal keys) inventory information systems. The sales data are then provided to the retailer's buying office, which uses the information in preparing buying plans and purchase orders. The buyer often faces a variety of circumstances that determine which of many different types of orders must be placed. Ordering procedures might involve placing orders (1) with different suppliers at different levels in the channel of distribution; (2) at different times to accommodate past, present, and future needs; (3) for either regular or special merchandise; and (4) with complete or partial specification of terms and conditions of sale. Figure 13–12 identifies and briefly describes seven types of orders that might be placed depending on the circumstances.

Retailers can place merchandise orders orally or in writing. Because oral agreements in some states are legally binding only up to some stated limit and are subject to vastly different interpretations, retailers should have them accurately transcribed into written form at the earliest possible time. When placing a written order, the buyer can use a form provided by the vendor or one provided by the retailer. It is generally recommended that retailers use their own forms whenever possible.

The **order form,** a legally binding contract when signed by both parties, specifies the terms and conditions under which the transaction is to be conducted. These terms and conditions usually are stated on both the front and back of the order form. The front of the order form usually contains standard information on the terms and conditions of sale. The back side of the retailer's order form usually contains a standardized statement of the general conditions under which the supplier will be held legally responsible if it accepts the order.

To be sure the right order is received in the right place at the right time, the retailer needs follow-up procedures. Following up an order is also necessary to make a purchase contract legally binding. In most cases, the original copy of the purchase order, which is sent to the vendor, constitutes a legal *offer to buy*. No purchase contract exists, however, until the seller *accepts* the buyer's offer. Therefore, the first step in following up an order is to determine whether the supplier has accepted the order. The retailer should maintain adequate records, including the supplier's formal notification of

Regular orders:	Orders placed by the buyer directly with the vendor. Involves ordering regular stock items with complete specifications as to terms and conditions of sale and delivery.
Reorders:	Orders placed with existing supplier for previously purchased goods, usually under terms and conditions specified by the original order.
Advance orders:	Orders placed in advance of both the normal buying season and the immediate needs of the retailer. Involves ordering regular stock items in anticipation of receiving preferred treatment.
Back orders:	Orders placed by the buyer for merchandise that was ordered but not received on time. Involves orders that the supplier intends to ship as soon as goods are available.
Blanket orders:	Orders placed with suppliers for merchandise for all or part of a season. Involves ordering merchandise without specifying such assortment details as sizes, colors, and styles and such delivery details as when and how much to ship. Requisitions against the blanket order will be placed as the need for the merchandise arises.
Open orders:	Orders placed with central market representatives (e.g. resident buyers) to be filled by whatever supplier the representative considers best suited to fill the order.
Special orders:	Orders placed with suppliers for merchandise not normally carried in stock or for specially manufactured merchandise. May involve specification buying.

FIGURE 13–12
Types of orders

acceptance for each order. Follow-up procedures also include checking the supplier's acceptance to determine whether the supplier has made any changes in the order. Retailers use both routine and special procedures in following up an order.

Routine follow-up procedures are used to check for order acceptance and discrepancies between the retailer's original order and the supplier's acceptance. Various types of filing systems are used to flag purchase orders that have not been checked. The buyer manually or electronically reviews the files frequently to determine which orders require additional attention. The buyer routinely sends either a postcard, a personal letter, or a telegram, or, if circumstances are urgent, makes a telephone call. There are **special follow-up** procedures if the importance of the order merits them. These special procedures usually involve the use of a field expediter (e.g., resident buyer) who personally visits the vendor.

Once the order has been received and verified by the vendor's sales office, it is then processed through production according to purchase-order specifications. Final delivery of the merchandise is handled by the vendor's distribution system according to the terms and conditions set forth in the purchase order. Scheduled deliveries can be made to either the retailer's individual store outlets or a centralized distribution center (see Figure 13–11).

Quick Response Replenishment System

Quick response (QR) is a short cycle merchandise replenishment (reorder) system that involves an automatic restocking of the retailer's inventories within a matter of days; this shorter cycle is in contrast to the more extended restocking cycles (e.g., weeks or months) associated with traditional purchase-order systems. The goals of a QR system include: (1) higher inventory turnover rates, (2) lower inventory carrying costs, (3) fewer out-of-stock situations, (4) reduced storage space requirements, and (5) better customer service through more finely tuned merchandise assortments.[18]

While the basic organizational structure of a quick response system is essentially the same as a traditional purchase order system (compare Figure 13–11 and Figure 13–13), the QR system possesses four operating characteristics not commonly associated with a more traditional ordering system:[19]

1. A nonadversarial partnership between the retailer and the vendor
2. A point-of-sale (POS) system that is capable of realizing the full benefits of UPC scanning
3. An electronic data interchange (EDI) system that permits the use of electronic purchase orders (EPO)
4. A just-in-time (JIT) delivery system that allows direct-store-delivery (DSD).

Nonadversarial Partnership

The quick response system demands a high level of cooperation and trust between the participating parties. For the QR system to work, a great deal of proprietary information must be shared and used for the benefit of both parties. Management for both the retailer and the vendor must view the relationship as a partnership; one in which each transaction is a win-win situation for both partners. Rose Stores, a southeastern discounter, was able to cut its replenishment cycle for Rubbermaid products from eight weeks to two days through a "cooperative spirit of working together."[20] Wal-Mart is altering its buying practices to accommodate quick response programs. As described by

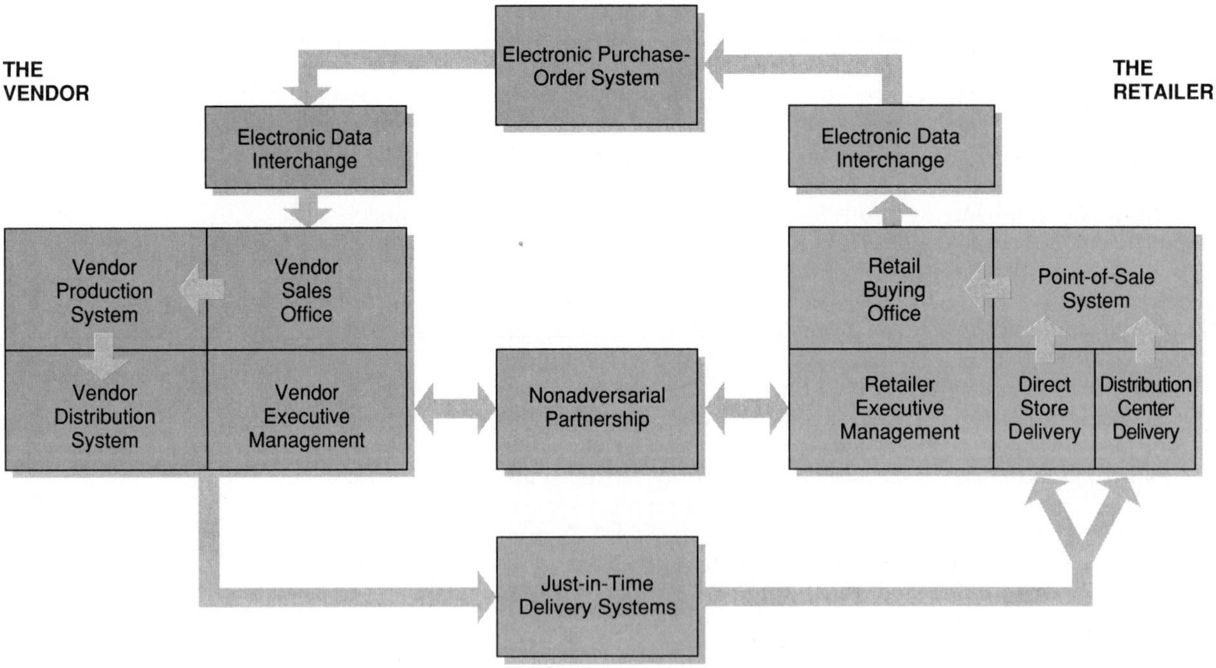

FIGURE 13–13
Quick response replenishment system

Wal-Mart management: "We want to win at everything we do, and it has been ingrained in our buyers that we want to buy as well as possible."[21] However, with Procter & Gamble, Rubbermaid, and General Electric, "Wal-Mart is trying a nonadversarial approach in which it shares sales projection data through computer links, hoping the vendor can anticipate needs."[22]

Point-of-Sale System

Technological advancements in electronic (computer-controlled) equipment have generated a wave of new marking procedures that are compatible with various **point-of-sale** (POS) systems. **Electronic marking** devices can code prices onto tickets and tags that can be quickly and automatically read and processed by optical scanning equipment or **optical character recognition** (OCR) systems. Optical scanners usually are employed at checkout counters, where they read all information on the ticket or tag and transmit it to the store's computer system for further processing (e.g., for inventory control and accounting records). While the checkout counter wand is the most common type of optical scanner used in general merchandise retailing, fixed-slot scanners (checkout counters with built-in laser beams that read tags as the merchandise is passed over the beam) are the predominate system used in the supermarket industry. Scanning provides both the retailer and consumer with faster, more accurate information than any other form of checking.[23] Scanning is simply the most effective method of data collection. A bar-coding scanner is 300% to 1000% faster than key entry. Plus, key entry produces an error in every 300 keystrokes.[24] Kroger Supermarkets are currently experimenting with a checkout system that allows consumers to scan their own purchases; Figure 13–14 describes the system.

With the installation of optical scanners, many retailers have elected to use a standardized marking system. These universal vendor marking (UVM) systems involve coding merchandise tags with a machine-readable code that is sponsored by one or

FIGURE 13–14
The ultimate in self-service: Self-service scanning

The Check-Robot utilizes a flat-top scanner, a touch-sensitive video display monitor, a conveyor belt, and a sensing mechanism used for security purposes.

The consumer scans each item in her shopping basket and then places it on a conveyor belt which is activated by the scanner. Overhead on the monitor, the product identification and price are displayed for the last five items scanned, scrolling upward as more items are added. The groceries move down the conveyor belt through a metal archway to a bagging area where a Kroger bagger is stationed.

After all items have been scanned, the consumer brings the receipt to a nearby payment station and tenders her bill.

At the consumer's disposal are all the functions a cashier would enjoy on a traditional POS terminal, but instead, on the touch-sensitive screen. There is a subtotal button and a button that allows the option of voicing the prices.

If a consumer comes up against a bar code that won't scan, she merely presses the numbers of the code into the video monitor, just as a cashier would do on a POS terminal. The product description and price are displayed just as if the item were scanned.

Coupons are accommodated in a rather simple way. "There's a button right beside the price [on the screen] that says 'coupon'." "When you touch that, it highlights that item on the screen and puts an asterisk next to the item on the receipt. This helps the cashier verify the product was purchased; the amount of the coupon is subtracted at the time payment is made."

Source: Reprinted by permission from "The Ultimate in Self-Service: Scan Your Own," *Chain Store Age Executive* (June 1987), p. 53. Copyright © Lebhar-Friedman Inc. 425 Park Avenue, New York, NY 10022.

more trade associations. In the past, the National Retail Federation, Inc. (NRFI) sponsored the **optical character recognition-font A** (OCR-A) code, which is equally human and machine readable. The second standardized code in common use is the **universal product code** (UPC). Used largely within the supermarket industry, the UPC is a bar code system that identifies both the product and the manufacturer (see Chapter 5). Recently, there has been a tremendous increase in the acceptance and popularity of UPC; as a result, the NRFI endorses it as the preferred marking system for all merchandise.[25] "No UPC. No PO" (purchase order) is a sign that is posted at Toys 'R' Us headquarters.[26]

The net result of using a scanner type bar code system is the tremendous amount of detailed information (e.g., brand style, size, model, and color of item) that is available to the retailer's buying office and that can be shared with the product item's vendor. By electronically sharing this POS product information, quick response starts to become a reality.

Electronic Data Interchange

Electronic data interchange (EDI) (the share of data between retailer and vendor electronically) is an important technological development for improving purchase-order management via computer linkages (see Chapter 5). Using EDI systems, retail managers now have a variety of options for structuring their electronic purchase-order (EPO) systems. Figure 13–15 illustrates the most common structures retailers and vendors use in exchanging electronic purchase-orders and invoice data. The options follow.

Mail Linkages. Purchase-order and invoice data are transcribed onto magnetic tape or diskettes and transmitted between retailers and vendors via the mail. This is a practical option for communicating a large volume of information when time is not critical.

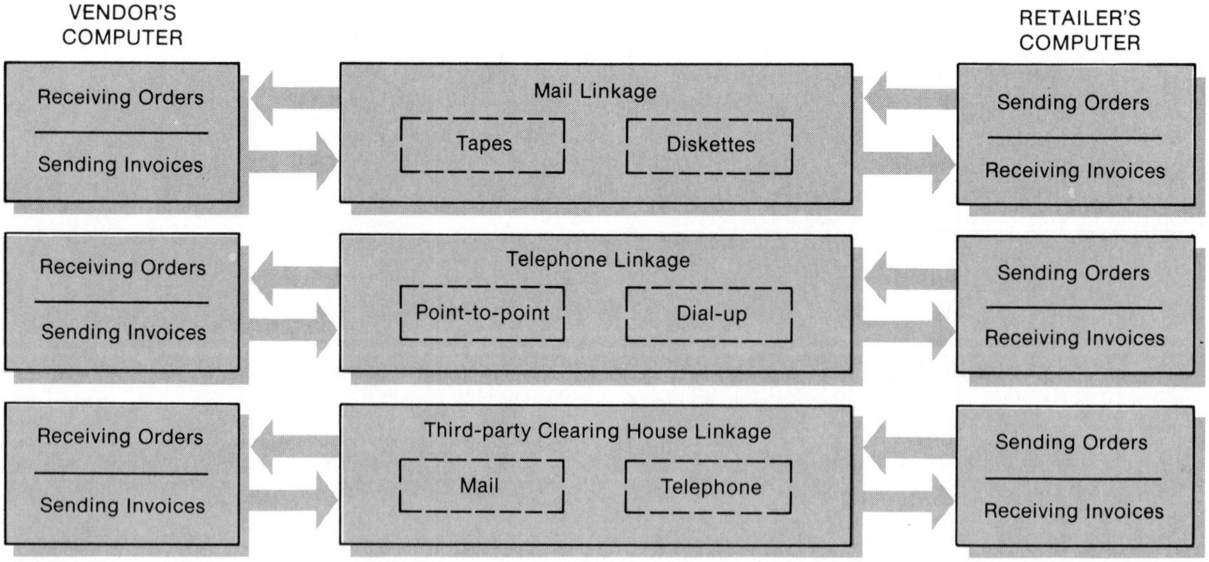

FIGURE 13–15
Electronic purchase-order systems

Telephone Linkages. Purchase-order and invoice data are communicated between the retailer's computer and the vendor's computer via the telephone. The *point-to-point* option involves arranging transmission schedules and common protocols to allow direct computer-to-computer interchange of data.[27] The *dial-up* option involves the storage of retailer orders and vendor invoices in on-line files and allowing each party dial-up access to these files. K mart's dial-up system works something like this: (1) store manager electronically sends purchase orders to K mart headquarters; (2) store order is "homogenized" in the ordering system; (3) consolidated purchase orders for each store are available each morning; and (4) each vendor has an assigned path and time slot for calling K mart headquarters to obtain orders.[28]

Third-Party Clearing Houses. A third-party data processing company makes arrangements to (1) receive orders and invoices, (2) sort them by addressees, (3) store them on-line, and (4) allow subsequent access by authorized addressees. This method allows use of a standardized machine language to establish a bridge for common communication, thereby eliminating the need for separate and distinct methodologies among various vendors and retailers.

To the retailer, the advantages of the EPO system include more effective inventory management, more effective open-to-buy systems, and reduction of ordering lead times, thereby improving in-stock positions and stock turnovers while reducing inventory carrying costs.

Just-in-Time Delivery System

The just-in-time (JIT) delivery system involves scheduling merchandise delivery dates to the retailer that coincide exactly with the day (just-in-time) inventory levels reach a critical stage. By shipping smaller quantities on a more frequent basis, the vendor is able to help reduce a retailer's average stock on hand, thereby increasing inventory turns while reducing inventory costs. The JIT delivery system is the retailer's payback for providing real-time POS data via the electronic purchase orders. A further enhancement of the quick response system is the ability to utilize *direct store delivery* (DSD) or *distribution center delivery* (DCD).[29] Depending on the nature of the retailer's merchandise handling process (see next section), efficiencies of distribution can be realized by either having merchandise delivered directly to the store or the distribution center. Standard bar code shipping container marking and electronic shipment notification are two technological and operational advancements that are contributing to the further development and acceptance of JIT systems.[30]

THE MERCHANDISE HANDLING PROCESS

The **merchandise handling process** deals with the physical processing of incoming merchandise. Efficient processing of incoming shipments is necessary to ensure their timely arrival on the sales floor. Figure 13–16 identifies the four processing concerns when handling incoming goods: receiving, checking, marking, and stocking merchandise. The specific tasks to be accomplished by the in-store handling system are illustrated in Figure 13–17.

Receiving Merchandise

Receiving is the actual physical exchange of goods between the retailer and the supplier's transporting agent. It is the point at which the retailer takes physical possession of the goods. Retailers can receive merchandise shipments through either the front door (customer entrance) or the back door. Generally, the retailer should avoid front-door receiving. The typical back-door receiving operation consists of an unloading area and a receiving area. The area devoted to unloading should permit easy maneuverability and facilitate careful handling. The receiving area should be large

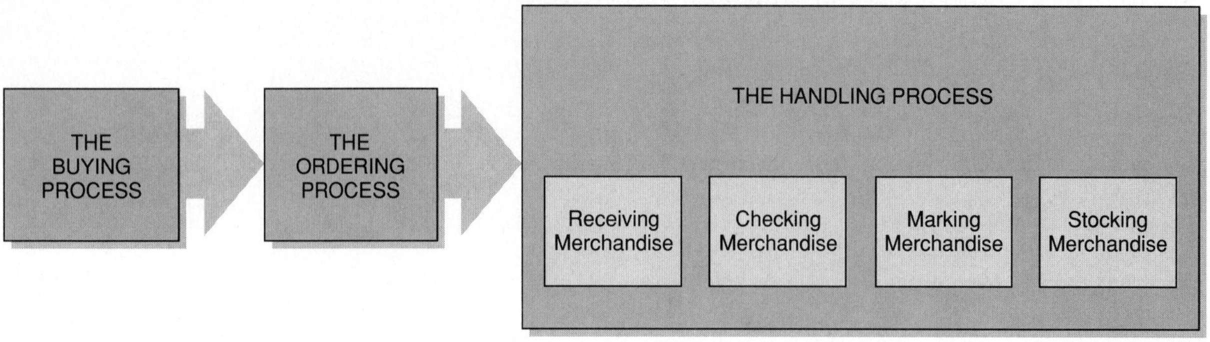

FIGURE 13–16
The merchandise handling process

enough to allow inspection of incoming shipments, and to act as a holding area for merchandise awaiting transfer to the checking room. Proper processing involves inspecting, verifying, and logging incoming shipments.

Inspecting Shipments. The first step in inspecting incoming merchandise is a visual inspection of the exterior of each package to determine whether the package has been damaged (crushed, punctured) or opened (broken seal). If a package has been badly damaged or opened, the receiving clerk should refuse to accept the shipment unless the carrier's employee agrees to witness the visual inspection of the contents of the package. Packages that are slightly damaged may be accepted, but before signing for the shipment, the receiving clerk should make a notation of the damage on all transportation and receiving documents.

Verifying Shipments. After inspecting the shipment for visual damage, the receiving clerk should make several verifications. First, the clerk must verify that the shipment was ordered by consulting the receiving department's file of purchase orders or a log (schedule) of incoming shipments. Second, the completeness of the shipment must be verified; sometimes suppliers ship only partial orders. Third, the receiving clerk should verify that the actual makeup of the shipment is the same as that described on the *bill of lading* (a transportation document between the shipper and carrier that serves as a receipt for the goods tendered to the carrier). The number of cartons in the shipment and the weight of each carton should also be checked. Fourth, freight charges are verified by comparing the total weight of the shipment with various rate schedules. Finally, additional verification might include recording the name and address of the supplier and the carrier, the name of the person making the delivery, and the delivery date.

Logging Shipments. To facilitate and organize the processing of incoming shipments, each shipment is logged in a receiving record and assigned a receiving number. The **receiving record** and number follow the shipment through the checking, marking, and stocking steps of the handling process and serve as a quick reference should problems arise. The accounting department also uses the record to verify shipment before invoices are paid.

Checking Merchandise

Checking is the process of determining whether the supplier has shipped what the retailer ordered and whether the shipment has arrived in good condition.

Checking involves opening each package, removing the merchandise, and examining it. The retailer can make three checks to ensure it has received what was

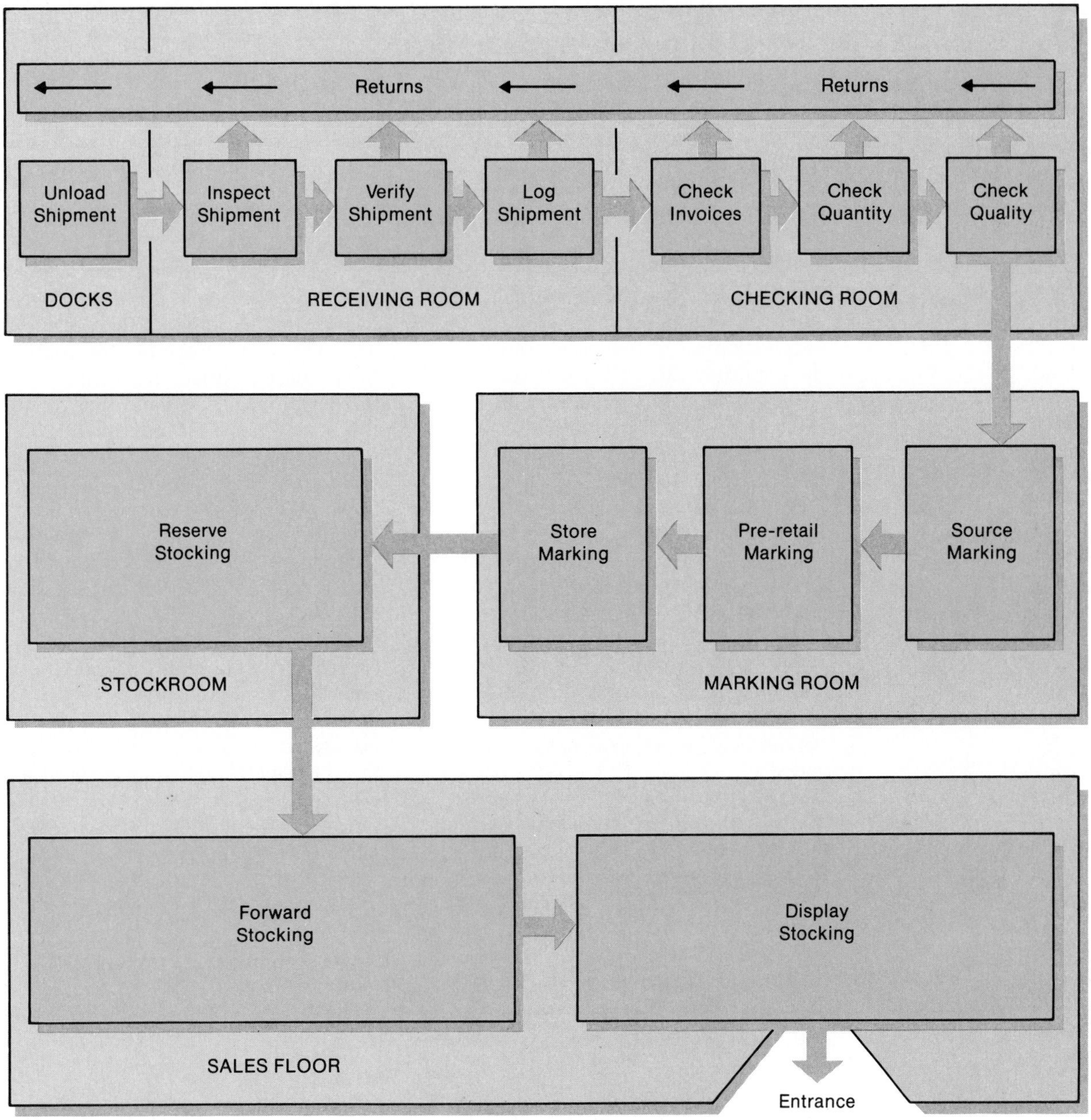

FIGURE 13–17
The in-store merchandise-handling process

ordered: an invoice, a quantity, or a quality check. In the **invoice check**, the retailer compares the invoice with the purchase order. The invoice is the supplier's bill and is the document that itemizes particulars of the shipment in terms of merchandise assortment, quantity, and price. It also identifies the terms of the sale, delivery terms, and the amount due for payment. Checking personnel must determine whether the retailer's purchase order exactly matches the supplier's invoice.

During the **quantity check**, the checking personnel unpack and sort each package to check the actual physical contents of each package against the purchase order, the invoice, or both. Essentially, the checker sorts each package by style, size, and color (or other assortment factors) and makes a physical count to determine whether the package contains the same number of units as listed on the invoice and purchase order. Any

WORLD OF RETAILING

Retail Technology

Price Chopper Supermarkets Direct Store Delivery System

The system works as follows: a vendor representative making his delivery first goes into the store's back room and plugs his hand-held computer into an outlet known as a DEX port. Through this outlet an electronic invoice of delivery information is transmitted to Price Chopper's in-store computer.

The vendor may use any hand-held computer of his choosing so long as the information it transmits conforms to the published DEX/UCS standards.

As the delivery is physically unloaded into the backroom, the store's receiving agent plugs his own hand-held computer into the DEX port, and uses it to view the invoice item by item. As he does this, he counts the amount of product being unloaded and enters the numbers into the hand-held for verification.

If a number does not match the amount called for in the invoice, the hand-held beeps and asks for a recount. If the same count is entered a second time, an adjustment is recorded and sent.

When the receiver finishes checking the invoice, the system asks if there are items to be added. If there are, the receiver enters or scans the pertinent UPC codes and enters the quantity of each item.

At the end of the process, the final invoice and totals are displayed and then stored for later transmittal to Price Chopper's headquarters computer, which polls stores for transaction data nightly.

If the invoice differs from the initial transmission, the vendor representative plugs his hand-held back into the DEX port to receive the updated invoice, which he later transmits to his company's main system.

This is reinforced at Price Chopper headquarters, where any transactions inconsistent with the product data-base are flagged and relayed to the appropriate merchandisers or buyers. . . . the check-in process with each vendor is quick (about 5–10 minutes) and it is possible to accept delivery from more than one vendor at a time.

Moreover, Price Chopper's computer is equipped with monitoring capabilities which can flag vendors who consistently come in with correct quantities and clean invoices.

For a few vendors who have proven highly reliable in their invoicing during a period of at least three months, a detailed review of their deliveries may not always be deemed necessary. "For those reliable vendors, we might just do a spot check once in a while. With other vendors, however, we do a detailed check-in every time."

Source: Reprinted by permission from "Price Chopper Quiets Backroom Chaos," *Chain Store Age Executive* (January 1990) 76–77. Copyright © Lebhar-Friedman, Inc., 425 Park Avenue, New York, NY 10022.

shortages, overages, or substitutions are noted and reported to the buyer or merchandise manager.

The **quality check** actually involves two separate checks. First, the merchandise is examined for any damage that is obviously the result of shipping. This kind of damage is the responsibility of the carrier and the insurer of the shipment. The second check is for imperfections in the merchandise and for lesser-quality merchandise than the retailer ordered.

The retailer can use one of three methods to check the quantity of incoming shipments: the direct check, the blind check, or the semiblind check. In the **direct check,** the retailer checks off from the invoice, which lists all the ordered and shipped items, each group of items as they are counted. Speed and simplicity are the principal advantages of the direct check. The **blind check** is a procedure in which the checker

Retailers have four possible methods for checking quantities of incoming shipments.

lists and describes each merchandise group on a blank form and then counts and records the number of items in each group. Next, a comparison is made between the checker's list and descriptions with the invoice or purchase order to determine whether there are any discrepancies. Generally, the blind method is the most accurate for checking incoming shipments, but it is also the most expensive because of the additional time and labor involved. The **semiblind check** is a checking technique that provides the checker with a list and description of each merchandise group in the shipment but not the quantities for each group. The checker must physically count and record the number of items in each merchandise group. The semiblind method has the advantage of being both reasonably fast and accurate.

Marking Merchandise

Marking is affixing to merchandise the information necessary for stocking, controlling, and selling. Customers want information on the price, size, and color of merchandise before they are willing to buy, and the retailer needs to know when and from where the merchandise was secured, its cost, and where it goes to maintain proper inventory and record controls. The facilities, equipment, procedures, and personnel for marking merchandise should be tailored to the volume and type of merchandise. Hand and mechanically operated marking systems usually are sufficient for most small retail operations. More sophisticated mechanical and electronic systems are more appropriate for large retailing organizations with sufficient merchandise volume to justify the expense.

The three most common marking systems are source marking, preretailing, and store marking. **Source marking** is the system by which the retailer authorizes the manufacturer or supplier to mark the merchandise before shipping it to the store. The merchandise is marked either with preprinted tickets sent to the supplier by the retailer or with tickets printed by the manufacturer. Source marking reduces both in-store marking expenses and the time it takes to get the merchandise onto the sales floor. A standard tag code and format enable the retailer to make very effective use of electronic data processing equipment. **Preretailing** is a retail buying practice of deciding the selling price of merchandise before it is purchased and recording that price on the store's copy of the purchase order so the store's "markers" can put the selling price on the merchandise as soon as it comes through the doors. **Store marking** is the practice of having store personnel mark all merchandise after the store has received it. It also is used to complete the marking process initiated in the preretailing system.

Merchandise should be marked before it reaches the sales floor. Merchandise can be marked by means of hand, mechanical, or electronic equipment. **Hand marking** is accomplished by using grease pencils, ink stamps, and pens to directly mark the merchandise, package, label, tag, or ticket. **Mechanical equipment** can produce tags and tickets in both printed (human-readable language) and punched (machine-readable language) forms.

Retailers frequently elect to use bulk marking on merchandise that is characterized by low unit value, high turnover, and suitable size and shape for bin, rack, or table displays. Individual marking is too expensive for many hardware items, variety goods, candies, and toiletries. **Bulk marking** involves simply placing similar merchandise with the same price in a display and attaching one price card to the display. It can save time in marking and speed the delivery of merchandise to the sales floor. Technology is also coming to bulk-marking procedures—**electronically programmable shelf labels** involve small liquid crystal display (LCD) labels that are attached on the edge of the shelf and can display new prices instantly on command (see Figure 13–18).[31]

Stocking Merchandise

Once the merchandise has been marked, the retailer must decide where to stock the merchandise. **Stocking** includes all the activities associated with in-store and between-store distribution of merchandise. Stocking may involve moving merchandise to the sales floor for display or to the reserve or stocking rooms for storage. The retailer can use an in-store or warehouse stocking plan or some combination of the two plans.

The primary goal in stocking is to move the merchandise as close as possible to its selling point. To accomplish this goal, most retailers follow the policy of **in-store stocking,** maximizing the amount of display and forward stock and minimizing the amount of stock in reserve. **Display stock** is stock placed on various display fixtures that customers can directly examine. **Forward stock** is backup stock that is temporarily stored on the sales floor near its selling department. Forward stock may be carried in perimeter storage areas around the department or in drawers or cupboards beneath the sales floor display fixtures. **Reserve stock** is backup stock held in reserve, usually in a central stockroom. Reserve stocks are converted to forward or display stocks as quickly as possible.

Warehouse stocking is used for certain types of merchandise or under certain operating conditions. Bulky products such as furniture and appliances usually require warehouse stocking, because the retailer must limit the amount of display stock on the

FIGURE 13–18
Electronically programmable shelf label

Prices of more than 500 items will change today at Bauersfeld's supermarket in Topeka, Kan., but the clerks won't have to peel outdated labels off the shelves.

Instead, they will change the prices electronically, plugging a hand-held computer into programmable labels clipped to the store's shelves. The computer sends a signal to a microchip in the molded plastic label, which then displays the new price in half-inch-high liquid crystal numerals.

Such devices are part of the grocery industry's continuing effort to reduce overhead with technology. Already more than half of the nation's supermarkets have electronic scanners at checkouts to ring up prices of bar-coded packages. Programmable shelf labeling promises to trim labor costs further and allow quicker price changes than are now possible.

Source: from Richard Gibson, "Electronic Price Labels Tested in Supermarkets," *The Wall Street Journal,* 31 March 1988. Reprinted by permission of *The Wall Street Journal* © Dow Jones & Company 1988. All rights reserved.

This kind of stocking fixture maximizes the amount of display and forward stock.

sales floor. Forward stocking is generally prohibitive for such products. Disassembled products that are sold in their cartons are usually picked up by the consumer at a warehouse delivery door or delivered to the customer's home. Seasonal products typically are held in warehouses until the appropriate selling season.

Many retailers prefer using central warehouse and distribution centers that serve several stores because of the operating conditions associated with chain store operations.[32] The receiving, checking, marking, and stocking functions are initially accomplished at these regional facilities, then the merchandise is distributed to individual stores. Central facilities often are more efficient, based on the economies of scale that large retailers can realize in ordering, transporting, and processing incoming merchandise and in using modern, expensive facilities and equipment. The key to an effective distribution center is to move merchandise, not store it.[33]

Retailers are increasingly using outside companies for the distribution function. **Contract warehousing** involves contracting with third-party warehouse companies to take care of all or part of the retailer's distribution needs. Services provided range from pick-up and consolidation of vendor shipments to delivery to the distribution center.[34] Store delivery, checking, marking, and other receiving functions are also handled by the contract warehouse.

SUMMARY

The retail procurement system incorporates three processes—merchandise buying, ordering, and handling. In the merchandise buying process, the retailer establishes the procedures for identifying, contacting, evaluating, and negotiating with sources of supply.

In identifying sources of supply, the retailer must decide what type of channel to use in procuring each merchandise line; the retailer has several options including various types of raw-resource producers, manufacturers, intermediaries, resident buying offices, and international sourcing. Contacting sources of supply is the second step in the buying process. Contacts can be initiated by either the vendor or the retailer. Vendor-initiated contacts include store visits by vendor salespersons or mail and telephone solicitations. Retailers contact sources of supply by visiting central markets, using resident buying offices, attending merchandise shows, and making telephone and mail inquiries.

The third step in the buying process is evaluating various alternative suppliers. Suppliers can be evaluated on the basis of (1) the suitability, availability, and adaptability of the merchandise they offer; (2) the exclusiveness and policies associated with the supplier's distribution system; (3) the appropriateness of the supplier's price and policies regarding price maintenance; (4) the type and amount of promotional assistance; and (5) the type and amount of supplementary services. Three methods for evaluating supply sources are the weighted-rating method, the single-most-important criterion method, and the minimum-cutoff method. Negotiating with sources of supply is the final step in the buying process. Negotiation involves discussing various issues of concern to both the retailer and the supplier. The three most common issues subject to negotiation are price, logistics, and service. Price negotiations start with the supplier's list price and those discounts and allowances taken to adjust the list price. The most common price adjustments are trade, quantity, seasonal, and cash discounts, along with promotional allowances. Logistic negotiations are concerned with various transportation and handling terms that affect the retailer's laid-in cost of the new merchandise.

The merchandise ordering system involves four decisions—what types of buying strategy and method to use and deciding to use a traditional purchase order system or a quick response replenishment system, or both. In deciding what buying strategy to use, the retailer can elect to concentrate purchases with a few suppliers or disperse them among many suppliers. In selecting the actual buying method, the retailer can buy merchandise using a regular, consignment, memorandum, approval, or specification method of buying.

Traditional purchase-order systems are essential adversarial relationships that require the retailer to use effective negotiations in order to secure the best possible deal. Traditional systems are based on the manual cutting and processing of purchase order forms supported by routine and special follow-up procedures. Quick response replenishment systems are short cycle merchandise reorder systems that involve an automatic restocking of the retailer's inventories within a matter of days. Quick response systems rely on computer-based electronic technologies and a nonadversarial partnership between retailers and vendors in order to realize considerable efficiencies in order processing and inventory management.

The handling process includes all of the physical operations associated with getting merchandise into the store and onto the shelves. The four basic steps in handling are receiving, checking, marking, and stocking.

Receiving is the physical exchange of goods between the retailer and the supplier's transporting agent. Retailers must plan facilities and procedures for receiving, inspecting, verifying, and logging incoming shipments. Checking is the process of determining whether the supplier has shipped what the retailer ordered and whether it has arrived in good condition. Personnel are trained to know what and how to check merchandise.

Marking is affixing to the merchandise the information necessary for stocking, controlling, and selling it. Marking systems that retailers use include source marking, preretailing, and store marking. Retailers mark merchandise by hand, mechanically, and electronically. Stocking includes the activities associated with in-store and between-store distribution of merchandise. The primary goal of stocking is to move the merchandise as close as possible to its selling point.

STUDENT STUDY GUIDE

Key Terms and Concepts

agent intermediary (p. 476)
approval buying (p. 493)
auction house (p. 479)
blind check (p. 502)
broker (p. 478)
bulk marking (p. 504)
cash-and-carry wholesaler (p. 476)
cash discount (p. 488)
cash on delivery (COD) (p. 489)
centralized buying (p. 475)
chain trade discount (p. 487)
checking (p. 500)
commissionaire (p. 480)
commission merchant (p. 478)
concentration strategy (p. 492)
consignment buying (p. 493)
contractual intermediary (p. 479)
cooperative group (p. 479)
cumulative quantity discount (p. 488)
dating terms (p. 488)
decentralized buying (p. 475)
direct check (p. 502)
direct store delivery (p. 499)
discount amount (p. 488)
dispersion strategy (p. 492)
display stock (p. 504)
distribution center delivery (p. 499)
drop shipper (p. 476)
electronic data interchange (p. 498)
electronic purchase-order (EPO) system (p. 496)
formal buying organization (p. 475)
forward stock (p. 504)
full-function merchant intermediaries (p. 476)
future dating (p. 489)
generalized buying (p. 475)
general merchandise wholesaler (p. 476)
immediate dating (p. 489)
importer (p. 480)
informal buying organization (p. 475)
in-store stocking (p. 504)
invoice check (p. 501)
limited-function merchant intermediaries (p. 476)
list price (p. 486)
manufacturers' agent (p. 478)
marking (p. 503)
memorandum buying (p. 493)
merchant intermediaries (p. 476)
minimum-cutoff method (p. 485)
net invoice price (p. 488)
noncumulative quantity single discount (p. 488)
optical character recognition-font A (OCR-A) (p. 498)
order form (p. 494)
point-of-sale (POS) (p. 497)
prepayment dating (p. 489)
preretailing (p. 503)
promotional allowances (p. 490)
quality check (p. 502)
quantity check (p. 501)
quick response replenishment system (p. 495)
rack jobber (p. 476)
receiving (p. 499)
regular buying (p. 493)
reserve stock (p. 504)
resident buying office (p. 479)
routine follow-up (p. 495)
sales agent (p. 478)
seasonal discount (p. 488)
semiblind check (p. 503)
single-line wholesaler (p. 476)
single-most-important criterion method (p. 485)
single trade discount (p. 487)
source marking (p. 503)
special follow-up (p. 495)
specialized buying (p. 475)
specialty-line wholesaler (p. 476)
specification buying (p. 493)
stocking (p. 504)
store marking (p. 503)
traditional purchase-order system (p. 493)
truck distributor (p. 476)
universal product code (UPC) (p. 498)
voluntary chain (p. 479)
warehouse stocking (p. 504)
weighted-rating method (p. 484)

Review Questions

1. Why might the retailers buy directly from the manufacturer?
2. How are full-function merchant wholesalers distinguished from one another?
3. Identify and describe the four types of limited-function merchant wholesalers.
4. What types of information and buyer assistance services does the resident buying office provide?
5. How can the retailer evaluate the merchandise offered by a given supplier? Identify and discuss the evaluation criteria.
6. What distribution and delivery policies and standards should the retailer consider when evaluating a particular supplier?
7. What would be the retailer's price if a product had a list price of $40 and a trade discount structure of 30/20/5?
8. How does a cumulative quantity discount differ from a noncumulative discount?
9. What are two general classes of dating terms? Discuss each class.

10. What are promotional allowances? Describe their four common forms.
11. What issues should the retailer consider when negotiating transportation and handling terms?
12. Identify and briefly describe the five buying methods a retailer might use.
13. What options do retailers have in structuring their electronic purchase-order system?
14. What is a just-in-time delivery system?
15. The retailer makes three checks to see that it has received what was ordered. What are the three checks?
16. How might the retailer check quantities of incoming shipments?
17. Discuss the options a retailer has for in-store stocking.

Review Exam

True or False

_____ 1. Merchant middlemen are wholesale sources of supply that do not take title to the goods they deal in but that are directly involved in the purchase and sale of goods as they move through the channel of distribution.

_____ 2. Central markets are periodic displays of the merchandise lines of many suppliers in one place at one time.

_____ 3. The purpose for expressing the trade discount in the form of a chain (e.g., 40, 30, 10) is to facilitate the process of offering different discounts to different buyers.

_____ 4. In memorandum buying, the retailer retains the right to return to the supplier any unsold merchandise.

_____ 5. The dial-up telephone linkage option is an electronic purchase order system that involves arranging transmission schedules and common protocols to allow direct computer-to-computer interchange of data.

_____ 6. The blind check method is generally the most accurate method for checking incoming shipments.

_____ 7. Forward stock is backup stock held in reserve, usually in a central stockroom.

Multiple Choice

_____ 1. Which of the following is *not* one of the advantages of centralized buying?
a. better volume discounts
b. greater adaptability to local markets
c. better control of the buying process
d. greater likelihood of preferred treatment from suppliers

_____ 2. Gary George has assumed the responsibility for all of the marketing functions (selling, pricing, promoting, and distributing) for a manufacturer of home furnishings. In effect, he has become the marketing department for the manufacturer. Gary is a _____.
a. commission merchant
b. manufacturer's agent
c. sales agent
d. drop shipper
e. agent wholesaler

_____ 3. A product has a list price of $20. If the retailer is granted a chain grade discount of 30, 20, 10 percent, what would the product cost the retailer?
a. $10.08
b. $11.20
c. $ 8.00
d. $14.00
e. $20.00

_____ 4. Which of the following is *not* an example of promotion allowance?
a. advertising allowance
b. preferred selling space
c. free display materials
d. merchandise deals
e. all of the above are promotion allowances

_____ 5. A _____ is an electronic purchase-order system that is a practical option for a large volume of information when time is not a critical element.
a. road express connection
b. third-party clearing house
c. telephone linkage
d. mail linkage
e. satellite linkage

_____ 6. The _____ check involves checking off from the invoice each group of items as they are counted.
a. blind
b. semi-blind
c. direct
d. combination
e. blank

_____ 7. _____ is the retail buying practice of deciding on the selling price of merchandise before it is purchased and recording that price on the store's copy of the purchase order so that store markers can put the selling price on the merchandise as soon as it comes through the door.
a. Postretailing
b. Store marking
c. Source marking
d. Preretailing
e. Hand marking

STUDENT APPLICATIONS MANUAL

Investigative Projects: Practice and Applications

1. Visiting central markets is a principal method used by retailers to initiate contacts with suppliers. However, many retailers are not well versed in how a central market operates, nor are they accustomed to the hectic atmosphere surrounding central markets; the next result often is buying mistakes. Interview several retail buyers and identify the potential problems they face in making central market visits. Then, develop a set of general guidelines that the retail buyer should follow during a buying trip to a central market.
2. Developing and maintaining good supplier relationships is extremely important if the retailer expects to initiate new and keep old reliable sources of supply. Develop a list of rules that a retailer should observe in establishing and/or maintaining good relationships with vendors and suppliers.
3. Consignment buying, memorandum buying, approval buying, and specification buying are all special buying methods used by retailers under various conditions. Interview a merchandise manager for a department store or specialty store; determine under what conditions each of these special buying methods is used and why.
4. Gain the cooperation of a local retailer and evaluate his or her receiving and checking system. Analyze the facilities and procedures used in receiving and checking. Determine the strengths and weaknesses of the system. What recommendations would you make for improving the system?
5. From the viewpoint of the consumer, what are the principal objections to the use of optical scanning systems that require code marking systems (e.g., universal product code)?
6. By contacting suppliers of store fixtures, obtain information (catalogs, brochures, etc.) on the types of fixtures and equipment that are available for in-store stocking of display and forward stock. Assume that you are going to be the manager of a small (20 feet wide and 50 feet deep) new exclusive men's clothing store with no separate storage room. What fixtures and equipment would you select for display and forward stock? Justify your selection.

Tactical Cases: Problems and Decisions

■ CASE 13–1
Apex Stores: A Buy-American Campaign*

Alexander Ferris, president and chief executive officer of Apex Stores, Inc., was preparing for the 10:00 meeting he had called of top executives in each of the corporation's four divisions. Each division represented one of the four retail store chains owned by Apex.

1. Fashion Works is a chain of 26 stores throughout Ohio, Michigan, Indiana, and Illinois that carry low- to medium-priced apparel for men and women.
2. Style Corner is an 18-store division featuring higher-priced women's fashions in the same Midwest market served by Fashion Works.
3. Minerva's is an upscale, fashionable chain of 21 women's clothing stores located along the West Coast.
4. Cray's is a midpriced department store chain consisting of 16 units primarily operating in the Midwest, although there were plans for expansion into Pennsylvania, New York, and Maryland. Cray's carries a full line of men's and women's clothing, cosmetics, home electronics, furniture, appliances, housewares, and toys.

When the executives were all assembled in his office at Apex's Chicago headquarters, Ferris outlined his new plan that he was considering for all four of the company's divisions. He wanted to institute a policy of buying the goods sold in Apex's stores from American manufacturers whenever possible, whereas in the past, purchases had always been made without regard to country of origin.

"In recent years, I've noticed a rising percentage of our overall purchases have been from foreign suppliers," Ferris said. "I think this is a trend that needs to be stopped. Concern about the U.S. trade deficit with foreign countries is growing, and I believe we have some responsibility to do our part to reduce imports."

But Ferris admitted that his idea was not driven solely by patriotic fervor. He thought that American consumers were increasingly sensitive to a product's country of origin and that they would react quite favorably to Apex's campaign to sell as many American-made goods as possible. Ferris was also confident that this move by Apex would take advantage of other national efforts to promote products made in America.

One promotion effort, sponsored primarily by the U.S. textile industry, was launched in the mid-1980s under the auspices of the Crafted with Pride in the USA Council. The council developed an extensive ad campaign using celebrity spokespersons—working for free—proclaiming, "It matters to me," and pointing to made-in-America labels on their clothing. Another independent group leads the Buy American Campaign, a nonprofit, grass-roots organization that uses its annual advertising budget of several million dollars to tout American-made goods in general. In addition, several other store chains and manufacturers had recently adopted "buy-American" promotions or policies.

"I think the time is right for us to have a Buy American policy of our own," Ferris told the executives. "I believe we should make a public promise to buy American-manufactured goods whenever we can, and set some target, such as 75 percent of total purchases, to be reached in some chosen time period, such as one year. I'm open to negotiation on the specific details, but I'm convinced that we must take a step in this direction. Please do some research on how this will affect your divisions, and report back to me with your analysis and recommendations in two weeks."

The division presidents didn't speak as they left the office and headed down the hallway to the elevator. Once inside, however, they immediately began to discuss their boss's idea. "I was certainly not expecting that," said Erin Dietrick, head of Fashion Works. "I was just reading the other day that the National Retail Merchants Association has been lobbying Congress to keep international trade as open as possible, for the benefit of consumers."

"Yes, that's true, but several large chains, like K mart, Wal-Mart, and The Limited, have recently adopted buy-American campaigns of one sort or another," noted Jayne Hardin, the Style Corner's president. Responded Richard Bellows of Cray's Department Stores, "I don't care what anyone else is doing. This will certainly make my buyers jobs a heck of a lot tougher, whatever the specifics turn out to be."

All of them agreed that whatever decision was made, it needed to be based on sound business principles, not just emotion. The question they faced was whether a buy-American campaign was really a good idea for Apex Stores, Inc.

ASSIGNMENT

1. As mentioned in the case, several large retailers have developed buy-American purchasing policies in the past several years. What do you see as the advantages and disadvantages of these strategies?
2. From a retail buyer's point of view, how would you feel about your company decision to announce a percentage of purchases that will be made from American suppliers within a year. How might it affect your job? Your career?
3. If a buy-American policy is chosen for Apex Stores, should it be the same for all four divisions? What arguments can you offer in favor of employing a different strategy for each chain?

*This case was prepared by Daniel Gilmore, The University of Akron.

■ CASE 13–2
Showcase Gallery: Exploring Supplier Relationships*

BACKGROUND

Frank Smith just finalized a deal for a store facility that would become the future Showcase Gallery. Smith had always wanted to open his own furniture store in the community and had the opportunity to do so when the previous owner of a home furnishings store retired. The investment involved a 14,000-square-foot facility in a growing, high-income suburban area. He financed the venture through previous savings and investments by his family.

Smith had a working knowledge of the furniture trade, having been employed for eleven years as a manufacturer's representative in the industry. He brought to the venture a knowledge of case goods and upholstery and experience in interior design—a level of knowledge not often found among retail personnel.

The opportunity to work for himself, to be his own boss, had always been Smith's dream. Consequently, he placed great importance on operational autonomy. Having experienced the other half of the dealer-supplier relationship, however, Smith recognized that his autonomy might have to be tempered somewhat to achieve benefits possible only through mutual cooperation.

CURRENT SITUATION

With the purchase of the retail facility, Smith first had to decide which type of dealer-supplier arrangement would be most appropriate for his needs and the firm's future success. He had three alternatives: conventional arrangements, programmed merchandising, or business-format franchising. As he examined each option, Smith realized that his decision not only would have significance in developing trade relations but also could have a major impact on his performance as a dealer. Smith mentally reviewed the implications of each dealer-supplier arrangement.

Conventional Arrangement

With a conventional arrangement, Smith would deal with many suppliers. The highly fragmented furniture industry consists of many dealers and manufacturers, and dependence of any one firm or another is accordingly low. Consequently, a conventional arrangement tended to involve a relatively less enduring, loosely aligned relationship. Smith had observed that dealers were often suspicious of suppliers and did not cooperate fully for fear of becoming locked into a relationship.

Despite the potential problems, some dealers felt this arrangement gave them greater operational flexibility in serving their customers. They were not confined to particular styles or price points offered by a particular manufacturer; instead, they were able to adapt quickly to the changing needs of the community by working with a large number of suppliers to provide an appropriate product assortment that would have broad appeal to various customer groups.

Programmed Merchandising

Programmed merchandising arrangements are a second alternative. This type of relationship would require Smith to establish several formal or implied licensing agreements with a select number of primary suppliers. These supplier-developed arrangements are tailor-made programs designed to generate greater dealer commitment for one or more of the supplier's product lines. To encourage strong dealer commitment, the supplier offers selected retailers customized programs such as in-store merchandising assistance, advertising allowances, discount structures, and sales promotional support.

In return for the right to handle the supplier's merchandise line and to benefit from the privileges of the supplier's programs, Smith would be expected to limit his involvements with competitive products and to commit significant resources to support each of the supplier's merchandise lines. Support requirements include maintaining a minimum level of inventory investment in each line of merchandise and committing a minimum amount of floor space to permanent display of the supplier's products. Smith also would be expected to cooperate in supplier-initiated programs such as factory-authorized sales and other special sales promotions.

Business-Format Franchise

Colony House, a business-format franchise, was the third alternative that Frank investigated. This option involved a tightly knit dealer-supplier arrangement in which Colony House (the franchisor) would provide Frank (the franchisee) with a patterned way of doing business. Colony House would provide a total store concept. This concept included a plan for store layout and design, a complete line of merchandise, a comprehensive merchandising program, and a detailed operations manual. Colony House's total store concept was highly coordinated to achieve a sharply focused image that appeals to a targeted group of consumers. Product assortments included early and traditional American furniture and home accessory items. In contrast to the industry's frequent style changes, Colony's continuity of established merchandise lines enabled customers to purchase coordinated furniture pieces over an extended period.

The initial investment for a standard 12,000-square-foot operation would be approximately $250,000. Because Frank already had an existing facility, Colony House would require that he alter the exterior and interior of the building to make it consistent with the Colony House image. In return, Colony would provide architectural plans, training, and merchandising backup. Although no franchise fee was required, an annual fee (5 percent of sales) would be charged for promotional support.

Colony House believed that strong commitment was necessary for the formulated concept to succeed. Consequently, it screened retail applicants closely to determine their compatibility with Colony House. It reviewed each applicant's background, personality, and business philosophy. Franchisees, although independent businesses, were expected to adhere very closely to Colony's recommendations regarding store operations and merchandising.

ASSIGNMENT

1. Outline the advantages and disadvantages of each supplier-dealer arrangement.
2. Recommend the most suitable supplier-dealer arrangement for Frank Smith and explain the rationale for your recommendation.
3. Advise Smith as to how your recommendation will influence his trade relations and store performance.

*This case was prepared by Jeffrey Dilts, The University of Akron.

ENDNOTES

1. Teri Agins, "Clothing Makers Don Retailers' Garb," *The Wall Street Journal,* July 1989, B1.
2. Jay L. Johnson, "Are We Ready for Big Changes," *Discount Merchandiser,* August 1989, 53.
3. Robert F. Lusch, "Retail Control Systems for the 1990's," *Retailing Newsletter* 2 (Published by Arthur Andersen & Co. in conjunction with the Center for Retailing Studies, Texas A&M University), January 1990, 1.
4. See Renee D. Howerton and Teresa A. Summers, "Apparel Sales Representatives: Perceptions of Their Roles and Functions," *The FIT Review* 4 (Spring 1988), 10–18.
5. See Kenneth G. Hardy and Allan J. Magrath, "Buying Groups: Clout for Small Businesses," *Harvard Business Review* (September–October 1987), 16–23.
6. See Jacquelyn Bivins, "Buying Office Status Reports," *Stores,* May 1989, 54–56, 60–61.
7. See "What Is the Proper Role of a Buying Office," *Stores,* May 1989, 54–55.
8. See Cyndee Miller, "Fashion Center Touted As 'Mecca' for Retail Buyers," *Marketing News,* Feb. 5, 1990, 2, 21.
9. "Strategies for the New Century," *Chain Store Age Executive,* January 1990, 28.
10. Roger D. Blackwell and W. Wayne Talarzyk, "Life-style Retailing: Competitive Strategies," *Journal of Retailing* 59 (Winter 1983), 14.
11. The Limited, promotional brochure.
12. See Gary Robins, "Vendor Role: Changing," *Stores,* May 1990, 81–83, 86.
13. See Janet Wagner, Richard Ettenson, and Jean Par-

rish, "Vendor Selection among Retail Buyers: An Analysis of Merchandise Division," *Journal of Retailing* 65 (Spring 1989), 58–79.

14. John S. Berens, "A Decision Matrix Approach to Suppliers' Selection," *Journal of Retailing* 47 (Winter 1971), 52.
15. John Freeh, "Supermarkets Find New Ways to Lure More Shoppers," *Cleveland Plain Dealer,* April 1, 1990, 1–E, 4–E.
16. Laurie Freeman and Janet Meyers, "Grocer 'Fee' Hampers New Product Launches," *Advertising Age,* August 3, 1987, 1, 60. Also see Steve Weinstein, "New Deal: Out of the Case and into the Street," *Progressive Grocers,* February 1990, 39–48 and Lois Therrien, "Want Shelf Space at the Supermarket? Ante Up," *Business Week,* August 7, 1989, 60–61.
17. Francine Schwadel, "Minding the Store," *The Wall Street Journal,* January 19, 1990, A–1, A–5.
18. See Gary Robins, "New Support for Quick Response," *Stores,* May 1990, 86–88. And "Logistics and Benchmarking," *Stores,* April 1990, 26. And Gary Robins, "New Role for the Buyer," *Stores,* December 1989, 34–37.
19. See "Quick Response: The Right Thing," *Chain Store Age Executive,* March 1990, 49–53.
20. See Jay L. Johnson, "Rose's: Fighting Back," *Discount Merchandiser,* April 1990, 21–28.
21. John Huey, "Wal-Mart, Will I Take over the World?" *Fortune,* January 30, 1989, 58.
22. Ibid.
23. Richard Weizel, "The Price Is Right? Debate Goes on over Grocery Price Scanners," *Akron Beacon Journal,* February 26, 1990, D1, D3.
24. "Penney Move Heralds the Era of the Bar Code," *Chain Store Age Executive,* January 1990, 74. Also see "Bar Coding Adds Speed, Accuracy," *Purchasing World,* February 1989, 29–30.
25. See "Goal for PLG: Pre-Ticketing with UPC," *Stores* (March 1988), 30–32 and Jules Abend, "Tracking UPC Growth," *Stores* (September 1987), 52, 57–64, 70.
26. Judith Graham, "Bar Codes Becoming Universal," *Advertising Age,* April 18, 1988, 36.
27. See Gary Robins, "EDI: Closing the Loop," *Stores,* April 1988, 53–62.
28. See "At K-Mart: Nearly 200 Vendors Now on a Direct Electronic Purchase Order System: How It Is Working," *Stores,* May, 1981, 50–52.
29. See Gary Robins, "New Role for the DC?" *Stores,* April 1989, 29–33. And "Direct Store Delivery on the Move," *Discount Merchandiser,* August 1989, 57–59. And Warren Thayer, "*Perishables Management:* We Need a Traffic Cop," *Progressive Grocer,* February 1990, 30–36.
30. See Al D. McCready, "Paperless Retailing," *Retail Control,* December 1989, 17–21.
31. Warren Thayer, "Electronic Shelf Labels: How They Stack Up," *Progressive Grocer,* January 1990, 61–66. And "Technology Hits Shelf Pricing," *Discount Merchandiser,* September 1989, 72–74.
32. See Gary Robins, "Logistics And the DC," *Stores,* April 1990, 19–22.
33. See Jules Abend, "Moving Goods Faster," *Stores,* October 1987, 60–69.
34. "Contract Warehousing Catches On," *Chain Store Age Executive,* October 1989, 108.

PART IV

INVENTORY STRATEGIES

Planning and Controlling Merchandise Inventories

CHAPTER 14

OUTLINE

MERCHANDISE PLANNING

DOLLAR PLANNING: MERCHANDISE BUDGETS

- Planning Sales
- Planning Stock Levels
- Planning Reductions
- Planning Purchases
- Planning Profit Margins

UNIT PLANNING: MERCHANDISE LISTS

- Basic Stock List
- Model Stock List
- Never-Out List

MERCHANDISE CONTROL

INVENTORY-INFORMATION SYSTEMS

- Inventory Information
- Inventory Systems
- Inventory Valuation

INVENTORY-ANALYSIS SYSTEM

- Stock Turnover
- Return on Inventory Investment
- Direct Product Profit
- Open-to-Buy

OBJECTIVES

- Discuss the need for merchandise planning as an essential tool in ensuring that both the customer's merchandise needs and the retailer's financial requirements are satisfied.
- Plan an acceptable balance between merchandise inventories and sales.
- Devise and use a merchandise budget in the dollar planning of the retailer's investment in merchandise inventory.
- Devise and use a merchandise list in the unit planning of the retailer's merchandise assortment and support.
- Describe the need for merchandise control in maintaining a planned balance between the retailer's merchandise inventory and sales.
- Outline the method for collecting and procedures for processing merchandise data.
- Discuss the methods and procedures for valuing the retailer's inventories.
- Explain the methods and procedures for evaluating past merchandising performances.
- Identify the methods and procedures for making future merchandise decisions.

PLAN, PLAN, PLAN—CONTROL, CONTROL, CONTROL

A sound policy for managing merchandise inventories is essential to enable the retailer to offer the right product in the right place at the right time in the right quantities and at the right price. **Merchandise management** focuses on planning and controlling the retailer's inventories. **Merchandise planning** consists of establishing objectives and devising plans for obtaining those objectives. The planning process normally includes both dollar planning in terms of merchandise budgets and unit planning in terms of merchandise lists. **Merchandise control** involves designing dollar and unit inventory information and analysis systems for collecting, recording, analyzing, and using merchandise data to determine whether the stated objectives have been achieved. Planning is the process of establishing performance guidelines, whereas control is the process of checking on how well management is following those guidelines (see Figure 14–1). This chapter is devoted to a discussion of planning and controlling the retailer's merchandise inventories.

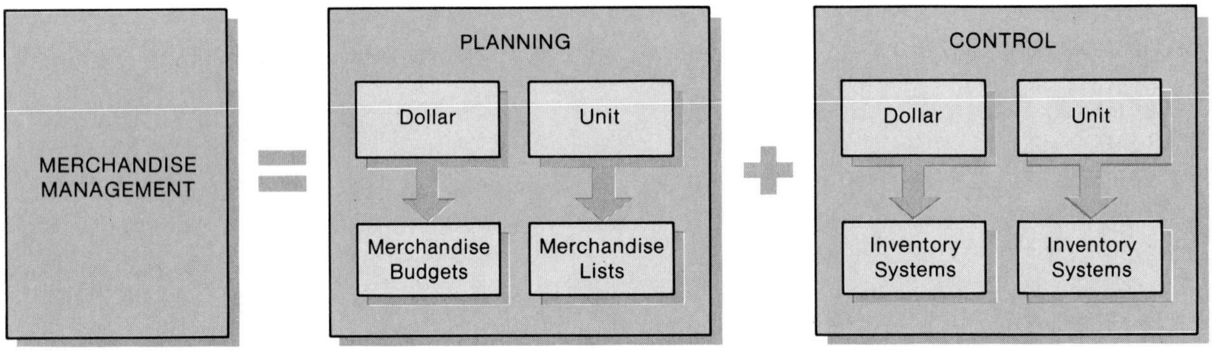

FIGURE 14–1
The merchandise-management process

MERCHANDISE PLANNING

The overall objective of merchandise planning is to satisfy both the customer's merchandise needs and the retailer's financial requirements.[1] To accomplish that objective, the retailer must devise merchandise plans that create an acceptable balance between merchandise inventories and sales. This inventory-to-sales balance requires the retailer to plan each merchandise category carefully regarding (1) inventory investment, (2) inventory assortment, and (3) inventory support.

Inventory investment involves planning the total dollar investment in merchandise inventory so that the firm can realize its financial objectives. **Inventory assortment** is planning the number of different product items (brand, style, size, color, material, and price combinations) the retailer should stock within a particular product line and determining whether this assortment is adequate to meet the merchandise-selection needs of the firm's targeted consumers.[2] **Inventory support** refers to planning the number of units the retailer should have on hand for each product item to meet sales estimates (e.g., stocking 100 six-packs of Coca-Cola in the 12-ounce can). By carefully planning the investment, assortment, and support aspects of merchandise inventories, the retailer can take a major step toward the merchandising objective of customer satisfaction at a profit. Both dollar and unit planning are essential if the retailer expects to balance inventory investment, assortment, and support. Inventory investment is the focus for dollar planning, whereas unit planning centers on the retailer's inventory assortment and support.

DOLLAR PLANNING: MERCHANDISE BUDGETS

Dollar planning is largely a financial-management tool that retailers use to plan the amount of total value (dollars) inventory they should carry. It answers the inventory question of how much the retailer should invest in merchandise during any specified period. Dollar planning is accomplished through a **merchandise budget**—a financial plan for managing merchandise inventory investments. The merchandise budget consists of five stages:

1. Planning sales
2. Planning stock levels
3. Planning reductions
4. Planning purchases
5. Planning profit margins

To facilitate merchandise planning and the preparation of the merchandise budget, most retailers use a form that summarizes basic budgetary information for a given merchandise grouping during a specified time period. Figure 14–2 illustrates a common form for preparing the merchandise budget.

Planning Sales

The starting point in developing the merchandise budget is sales planning. It is absolutely necessary to accurately forecast future sales; if future sales are incorrectly estimated during this initial stage, then all other aspects of the merchandise budget (stock levels, reductions, purchases, profit margins) will reflect this initial error and will require the retailer to adjust the budget throughout its application.

Before making sales estimates, the retailer must select the control unit for which the projections will be made. The **control unit** is the merchandise grouping that serves as the basic reporting unit for various types of information (e.g., past, current, and future sales). The retailer can elect to estimate future sales for an entire store, for a merchandise division or department, or for an individual product line or item. Using merchandise categories (specific lines of products that are directly comparable and substitutable, such as blenders) as the basic control unit is recommended because it is generally much easier to aggregate information (summing merchandise categories into

FIGURE 14–2
Form for preparing a merchandise budget (BOM, beginning-of-the-month stock)

SIX-MONTH MERCHANDISE BUDGET

Date ____________ Department ____________

		Aug.	Sept.	Oct.	Nov.	Dec.	Jan.	Total
Sales	Last Year							
	Planned							
	Adjusted							
	Actual							
BOM Stock Levels	Last Year							
	Planned							
	Adjusted							
	Actual							
Reductions	Last Year							
	Planned							
	Adjusted							
	Actual							
Purchases	Last Year							
	Planned							
	Adjusted							
	Actual							
Initial Markup %	Last Year							
	Planned							
	Adjusted							
	Actual							

merchandise classes and groups) than it is to disaggregate information (breaking down merchandise groups into classes and categories).

Annual Sales Estimates

An examination of the retailer's past sales records is the starting point for making sales forecasts for each merchandise category (control unit). By plotting the actual sales for each control unit over the past few years, the retailer can identify past sales patterns and gain some insight into possible future sales trends. This approach to sales estimates is generally referred to as *time-series forecasting*. It represents a simple, inexpensive, and widely used method for obtaining reasonably reliable estimates of sales in the near future. Time-series forecasting is generally quite appropriate for staple merchandise, somewhat less appropriate for fashionable merchandise (those fashions in a ford or classic life cycle), and totally inappropriate for faddish merchandise.

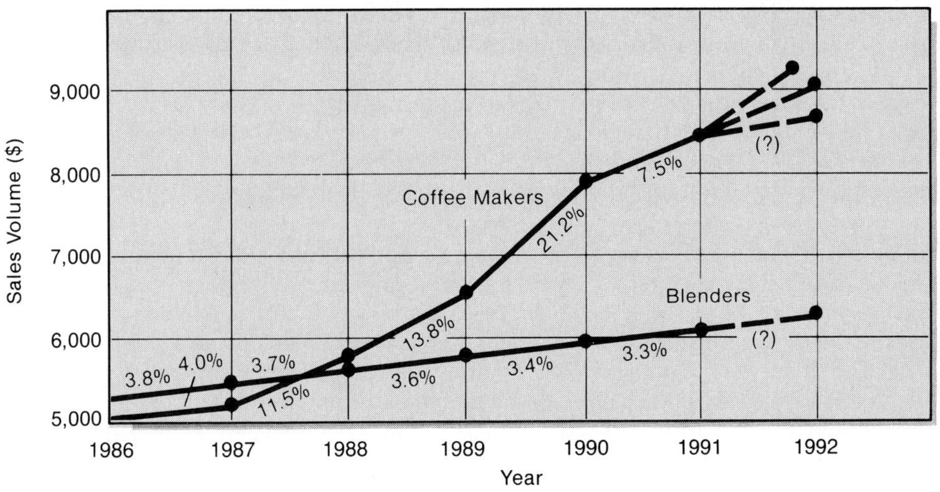

FIGURE 14–3
Six-year sales record for automatic-drip coffee makers and electric blenders

For purposes of illustration, Figure 14–3 presents a department store's six-year sales experience (1986 to 1992) with automatic-drip coffee makers and electric blenders. Past sales for these two merchandise categories reveal some interesting patterns. While both have experienced sales increases, the amount and stability of the increases are noticeably different. The store's past blender sales reveal a small yet steady increase in dollar sales. Looking at changes in the percentage increase in sales per year, we see that sales are increasing but at a decreasing rate. These figures suggest that the blender is in the maturity stage of its product life cycle and that sales are fairly stable and predictable, at least in the near future. The past sales pattern for coffee makers shows both large and small dollar and percentage increases, together with drastic changes from one year to the next. Viewing the overall pattern of coffee maker sales, the retailer could conclude that this product has passed through the growth stage of its product life cycle and done so fairly erratically at that. (Look at the percentage increase in sales. Sales increasing at an increasing rate are indicative of a product in the growth stage of the product life cycle.) In 1991, however, sales of coffee makers began to show increasing sales at a decreasing rate—a possible sign that the product is entering its maturity stage. Thus, because of the erratic changes in the rate of sales of coffee makers and the data's suggestion that the product *might* be entering its maturity stage, the retailer's 1992 sales estimates for coffee makers are very likely to be much less accurate than sales estimates for blenders.

Annual sales estimates for each merchandise category are estimated largely by judgmental or qualitative methods. Two such methods are the fixed and variable adjustment procedures.

Fixed Adjustment Method. With the fixed adjustment method, the retailer adjusts last year's sales by some fixed percentage to estimate the coming year's sales. The direction (plus or minus) and the size (the exact percentage) of the adjustment are based on the retailer's past sales experience with each merchandise category. For example, based on the past sales trend for electric blenders shown in Figure 14–3, the department store's forecaster might well expect a 3.2 percent increase in sales for 1992 in the absence of extenuating circumstances that might strongly influence the sale of blenders. The fixed adjustment method usually works reasonably well in estimating future sales if a clear and stable sales trend has been established. When past sales patterns are erratic, however, a fixed percentage adjustment is inappropriate.

Equally inappropriate is the "beat last year's sales" approach for calculating next year's sales estimates. Some retailers simply estimate future sales by using a fixed percentage (e.g., 4, 6, 8 percent) that will yield sales estimates above last year's sales performance. This approach does not recognize that various merchandise categories are in different stages of their product life cycles. While some are in the growth stage (accelerated sales growth), others may be in the maturity (declining sales growth) or decline (decreased sales) stages of the cycle. Beating last year's sales may be an appropriate sales goal for the store as a whole, but it is not an appropriate sales-estimating method for an individual category of merchandise.

Variable Adjustment Method. The second method for estimating annual sales is the variable adjustment method. As with the fixed adjustment method, the forecaster usually starts with an examination of the past sales history of the merchandise category. Based on the sales history, the forecaster determines a percentage change (e.g., 6 percent) that appears reasonable. The figure is then adjusted upward or downward by a degree that depends on the nature of the merchandise and its exposure and sensitivity to environmental influences. To make these adjustments, the retailer might consider the following external environmental factors: (1) the general prosperity of local and national markets; (2) rate of inflation; (3) chances for recessionary developments; (4) discernable trends (growth or decline) in the size of the target market population; (5) changes in the demographic makeup of the population (e.g., age, income, family structure, etc.); (6) developing legal and/or social restrictions; (7) changing patterns of competition (e.g., type, size, and merchandising strategies); and (8) changing consumer preferences and lifestyles. Internal factors to consider in adjusting annual sales estimates include (1) changes in the amount and location of shelf or floor space devoted to the merchandise category; (2) changes in the amount and type of planned promotional support; and (3) changes in basic operating policies (e.g., longer store hours or higher levels of service).

In summary, the **annual sales estimate** for a particular merchandise category equals the previous year's sales plus or minus a fixed or variable percentage adjustment. The adjustment factor is a blend of forecaster judgment, experience, and analytical skill. Figure 14–4 provides a four-stage recap of how to conduct a judgment forecast.

Monthly Sales Estimates

Retail planning periods typically are based on one-month or several-month periods; for example, some retailers estimate sales for products for the three-month winter season or the six-month fall/winter season.[3] The best operational estimate for budgetary planning purposes is **monthly sales estimates**. Estimating monthly sales involves three steps: (1) making annual sales estimates; (2) determining estimated monthly sales; and (3) adjusting monthly sales estimates using a monthly sales index.

- **Step 1: Making annual sales estimates**. To make monthly sales estimates, the forecaster starts with annual sales estimates, as discussed.
- **Step 2: Determining average estimated monthly sales**. The second step in estimating monthly sales is to allocate the annual sales estimate derived in step 1 on a monthly basis. One way to make this allocation is to determine average estimated monthly sales by dividing the annual sales estimate by the number of months in a year (12). This figure would be a reasonably reliable estimate of monthly sales if we could assume that sales were evenly distributed over the 12 months of the year.
- **Step 3: Adjusting average estimated monthly sales**. Average estimated monthly sales are adjusted according to a *monthly sales index* based on past monthly sales records. The purpose of this adjustment is to obtain a *planned monthly sales figure,* the final estimate of each month's sales that the retailer will use throughout the budgetary process. By indexing past monthly sales, the forecaster can establish a sales norm for an "average month" by which all other monthly sales can be judged. The average month is represented by an index value of 100. Any month with an index below 100 represents monthly sales below the norm; above-average sales are

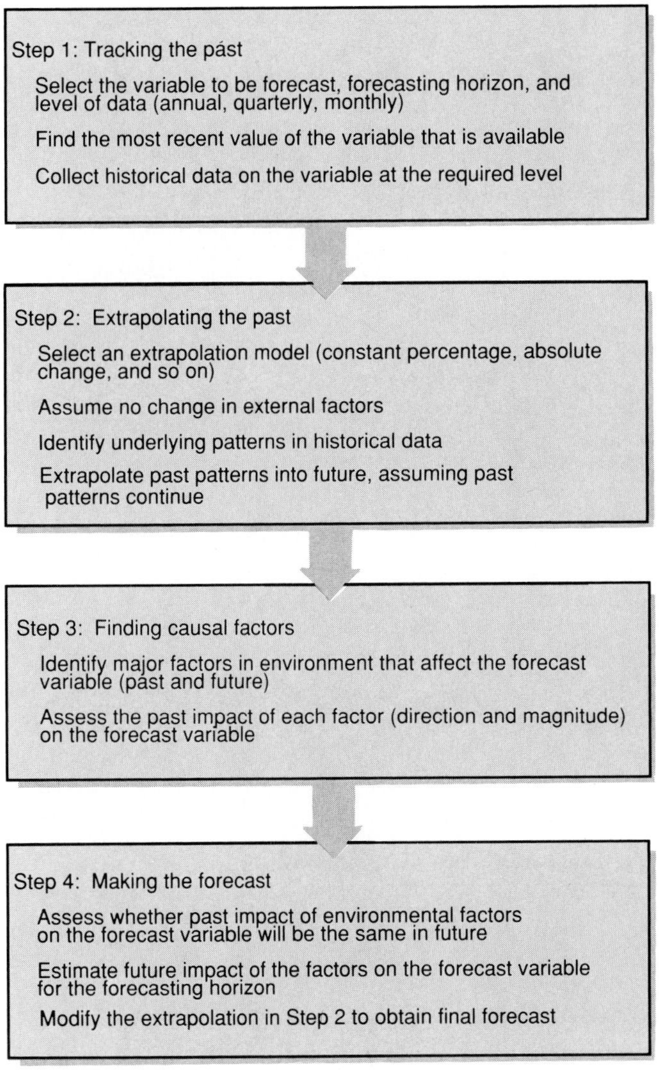
Step 1: Tracking the past
Select the variable to be forecast, forecasting horizon, and level of data (annual, quarterly, monthly)
Find the most recent value of the variable that is available
Collect historical data on the variable at the required level
Step 2: Extrapolating the past
Select an extrapolation model (constant percentage, absolute change, and so on)
Assume no change in external factors
Identify underlying patterns in historical data
Extrapolate past patterns into future, assuming past patterns continue
Step 3: Finding causal factors
Identify major factors in environment that affect the forecast variable (past and future)
Assess the past impact of each factor (direction and magnitude) on the forecast variable
Step 4: Making the forecast
Assess whether past impact of environmental factors on the forecast variable will be the same in future
Estimate future impact of the factors on the forecast variable for the forecasting horizon
Modify the extrapolation in Step 2 to obtain final forecast

FIGURE 14–4
Four-step judgmental forecasting process (source: Reprinted with permission from Steven W. Hartley and William Rudelius, "How Data Format and Problem Structure Affect Judgmental Sales Forecasts: An Experiment," *1986 AMA Educator's Proceedings,* published by the American Marketing Association, Chicago, IL 60606.

represented by index values exceeding 100. For example, a monthly sales index of 76 indicates that sales for that month are 24 (100 − 76) percent below the average. An index value of 181 denotes an above-average sales performance of 81 (181 − 100) percent.

Procedures for calculating the monthly sales index are shown in Figure 14–5. The monthly sales index is obtained by dividing the actual monthly sales by average monthly sales and multiplying by 100. An example of calculating the monthly sales index is presented in Figure 14–6. We see that the actual monthly sales for men's and women's watches is highly seasonal; the sales peaks correspond to the May/June graduation and December holiday seasons. Average monthly sales are obtained by dividing the total annual sales by 12 (months in a year); in the example, $168,000 divided by 12 equals $14,000. January's monthly sales index of 24 was calculated by dividing $3,400 (actual monthly sales) by $14,000 (average monthly sales) and multiplying by 100. The

FIGURE 14–5
Procedures for calculating the monthly sales index

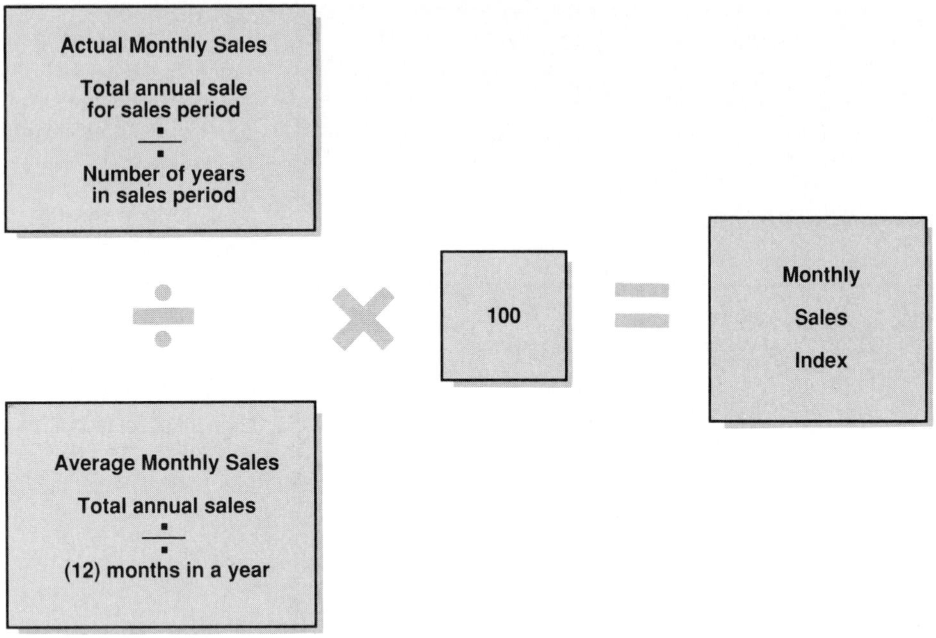

FIGURE 14–6
Example of calculating the monthly sales index (men's and women's watches)

Month	Actual Monthly Sales ($)	Monthly Sales Index[a]
January	3,400	24
February	3,600	26
March	6,800	49
April	7,000	50
May	23,800	170
June	27,200	194
July	6,600	47
August	7,200	51
September	10,600	76
October	8,800	63
November	25,400	181
December	41,400	296
Total annual sales	168,000	
Average monthly sales	14,000	
Average monthly index		100

[a] $= \frac{\text{actual monthly sales}}{\text{average monthly sales}} \times 100$

remaining eleven monthly sales indexes were calculated in the same manner. Once the monthly sales index has been calculated, it can be used to adjust future (estimated) annual and average monthly sales to obtain planned monthly sales—a basic element in all the stock planning methods to be discussed next. *Planned monthly sales* are obtained by multiplying the *average estimated monthly sales* (see step 2) by the *monthly sales index* (see step 3).

Planning Stock Levels

The second stage in developing a merchandise budget involves planning appropriate stock levels for a specific sales period. Ideally the retailer's stock plan should (1) meet sales expectations, (2) avoid out-of-stock conditions, (3) guard against overstock conditions, and (4) keep inventory investment at an acceptable level. Although it is extremely difficult to devise a plan to achieve all these objectives, four methods can serve the retailer in planning stock requirements. They are the basic stock method, the percentage variation method, the week's supply method, and the stock/sales ratio method.

The Basic Stock Method

The **basic stock method** is designed to meet sales expectations and avoid out-of-stock conditions by beginning each month with stock levels that equal the estimated sales for that month plus an additional basic stock amount that serves as a cushion or safety stock in the event that actual sales exceed estimated sales. The safety stock also protects the retailer against stockouts if future shipments of merchandise are delayed or arrive damaged and must be returned to the vendor. On the negative side, safety stock means that the retailer has a larger investment in inventory and greater inventory carrying costs. Retailers that use the basic stock method want to ensure minimum stock levels for a particular merchandise category. Generally, retailers that operate stores and departments with low inventory turnover are most likely to use this method.

The basic stock method involves calculating the beginning-of-the-month stock (BOM stock) for each month of the sales period. The BOM stock is computed by adding a basic stock amount to each of the planned monthly sales as determined in the sales-planning stage of the budgetary process. For example, let's assume that the department manager for the jewelry department of Selmer's Department Store is in the process of planning stocks for the upcoming Christmas season (October, November, and December). Using the basic stock method, the department manager would plan the BOM stock for each of the three months (sales period) using the procedures outlined in Figure 14–7.

To illustrate the basic stock method, we continue with the watch example; Figure 14–8 reconstructs the three-month Christmas sales period of October, November, and December. Based on past sales records, the retailer knows that the turnover rate (number of times the average stock on hand is sold during a given time period) for watches during this three-month sales period has averaged about two. Using the information in Figure 14–8, BOM stock is determined for the month of October in the following manner:

average monthly sales for
October, November, December = \$81,000 ÷ 3 = \$27,000
average stock for October,
November, December = \$81,000 ÷ 2 = \$40,500
basic stock = \$40,500 − \$27,000 = \$13,500
BOM stock for October = \$9,450 + \$13,500 = \$22,950

As shown, a basic or safety stock of \$13,500 is added to each month's planned sales to arrive at the BOM stock. The BOM stocks for November and December are shown in

BOM Stock for Month X = Planned Monthly Sales for Month X + Basic Stock

Basic Stock = Average Stock for Sales Period − Average Monthly Sales for Sales Period

Average Stock for Sales Period = Total Planned Sales for Sales Period ÷ Estimated Inventory Turnover Rate for Sales Period

Average Monthly Sales for Sales Period = Total Planned Sales for Sales Period ÷ Number of Months in Sales Period

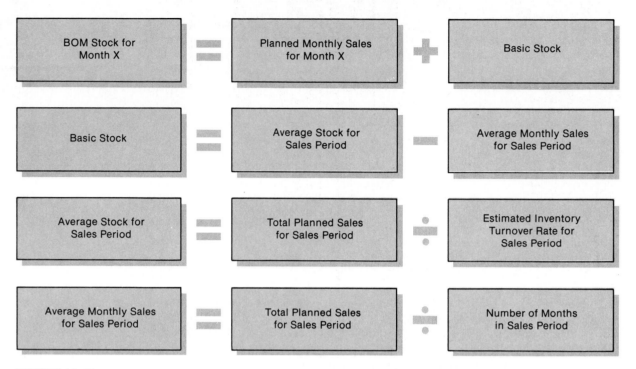

FIGURE 14–7
The basic stock method for determining BOM stock

Figure 14–8. When actual sales either exceed or fall short of planned sales for a given month, the retailer can easily adjust the amount of overage or shortfall to bring the next month's BOM stock back to its calculated level (in this case, $13,500).

The Percentage Variation Method

The **percentage variation method** uses a procedure that attempts to adjust stock levels in accordance with actual variations in sales. BOM stock is increased or decreased from average stock for the sales period by one half of the percentage variation in planned monthly sales for that month from the average monthly sales for the sales period. The calculating procedures for the percentage variation method are shown in Figure 14–9.

$$\text{BOM stock for October} = \$40{,}500 \times \frac{1}{2}\left(1 + \frac{\$9{,}450}{\$27{,}000}\right) = \$27{,}337.50$$

The BOM stocks for November and December have been calculated and are shown along with the October BOM stock in Figure 14–8.

FIGURE 14–8
BOM stock for men's and women's watches (jewelry department, Selmer's Department Store)

Sales Period	Planned Monthly Sales ($)[1]	BOM Stock Using Basic Stock Method ($)	BOM Stock Using Percentage Variation Method ($)
Oct.	9,450	22,950	27,337.50
Nov.	27,150	40,650	40,905.00
Dec.	44,400	57,900	53,460.00
Total	81,000	—	—

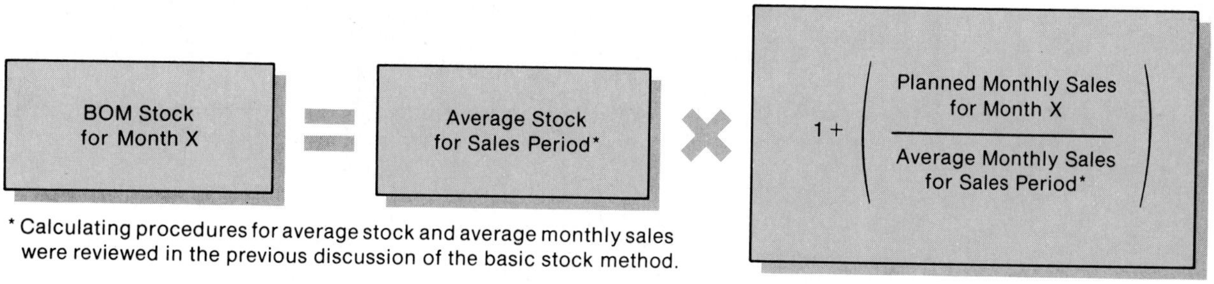

FIGURE 14–9
The percentage variation method for determining BOM stock

Retailers prefer to use the percentage variation method with merchandise categories characterized by a high turnover rate (usually exceeding six times per year) because it results in less stock fluctuation than use of the basic stock method.

The Week's Supply Method

The **week's supply method** is a stocking plan that determines stock levels in direct proportion to sales. As a means to plan stocks on a weekly basis, this method uses a desired annual stock turnover rate to establish the amount of stock necessary to cover a predetermined number of weeks. If the manager of Selmer's jewelry department thinks an annual stock turnover rate of eight is both desirable and feasible, determining stock for the start of the Christmas sales period (October) would be done as shown in Figure 14–10. Using the data in Figure 14–8,

number of weeks to be stocked	=	52 ÷ 8 = 6.5 weeks
average weekly sales	=	$180,000 ÷ 52 = $3,462
BOM stock for October	=	$3,462 × 6.5 = $22,503

Having determined the number of weeks' supply to stock (6.5 weeks) and the average weekly sales ($3,462), stock levels can be replenished frequently and regularly (e.g., weekly or biweekly) before stock shortages occur. The principal limitation of this method is that during weeks with a slow stock turn (below annual rate), there will be an excessive accumulation of stock. Therefore, this method is most appropriate for retailers whose merchandise categories show stable sales and stable stock turnover rates.

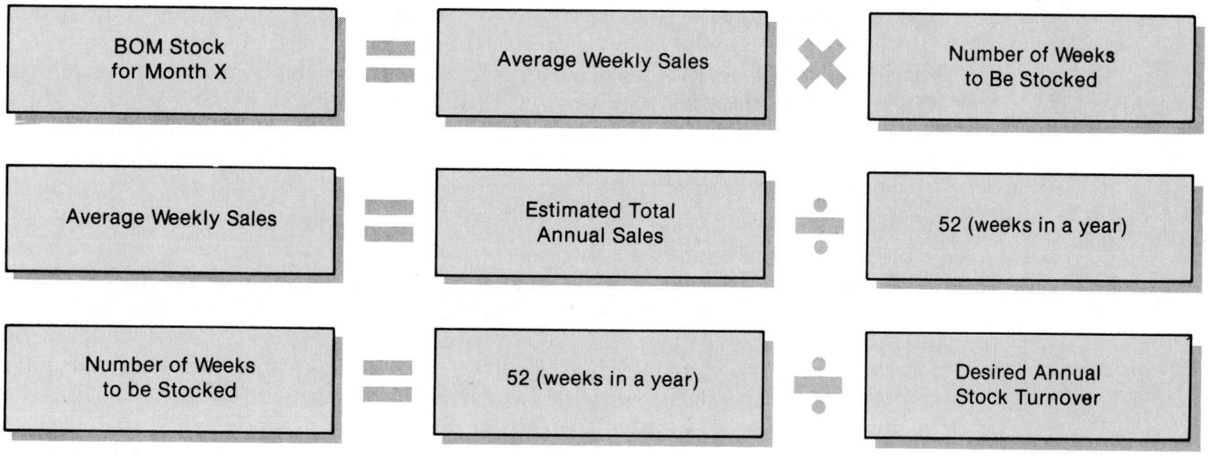

FIGURE 14–10
The week's supply method of determining BOM stock

FIGURE 14–11
Stock/sales ratio method of determining BOM stock

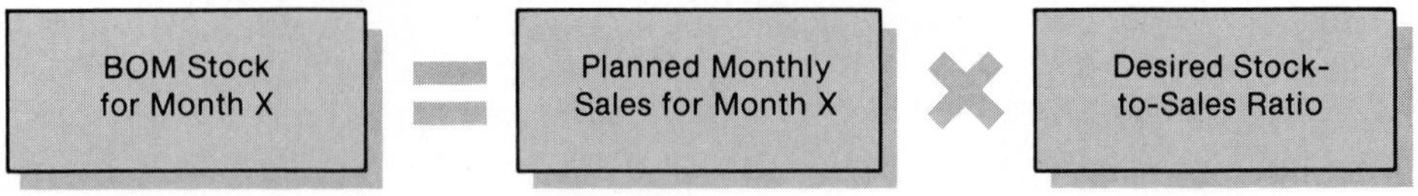

The Stock/Sales Ratio Method

The **stock/sales ratio method** is another method retailers use to determine BOM levels. The assumption behind this method is that the retailer should maintain a certain ratio of goods on hand to planned monthly sales. This ratio could be 2:1, 3:1, or any other appropriate relationship. A stock/sales ratio of 2:1 means the planned monthly sales of \$5,000 would require \$10,000 of stock. The key to using this method is finding a dependable stock/sales ratio, for which the best source is the retailer's own past record—provided that it has been kept in sufficient detail over a reasonable length of time. Stock/sales ratios also can be obtained from various trade sources, such as the National Retail Federation, Inc.'s annual publication, *Department Merchandising and Operating Results of Department and Specialty Stores.*

To illustrate this method, let's assume that past sales records for Selmer's jewelry department reveal that a 2:1 stock/sales ratio is desirable. Based on the planned monthly sales cited in Figure 14–8, the BOM stock for October would be calculated as shown in Figure 14–11.

$$\text{BOM stock for October} = \$9{,}450 \times 2 = \$18{,}900$$

Using the same procedures, the BOM stock for November would be \$54,000, while December's BOM stock would be \$88,800.

Planning Reductions

The third stage in developing the merchandise budget is to plan reductions. **Retail reductions** can be defined as the difference between the merchandise item's original retail value and the actual final sales value. This difference is the result of three factors: markdowns, discounts, and shortages. **Markdowns** are reductions in the original retail price for the purpose of stimulating the sale of merchandise. The amount of markdown can vary considerably depending on the type of merchandise and the conditions under which it is sold. Figure 14–12 provides some typical markdown percentages for department store operation. **Discounts** are reductions in the original retail price that are granted to store employees as special fringe benefits and to special customers (e.g., clergy, senior citizens, disadvantaged consumers) in recognition of their special status. **Shortages** are reductions in the total value of the retailer's inventory as a result of shoplifting, pilfering, and merchandise being damaged and misplaced. Department store shortages range from one percent for cosmetics and drugs to 2.9 percent for female accessories (see Figure 14–12).

Planning reductions essentially involves making a percentage-of-sales (dollars) estimate for each of the three major reduction factors: markdowns, discounts, and shortages. These percentage estimates are made on the basis of past experience or obtained from trade sources. To be consistent with sales and stock-level planning, reduction estimates should be made in retail dollars on a monthly basis for a particular merchandise category. Continuing our watch example, if the retailer's past records reveal that for the month of October men's and women's watches experienced average monthly markdowns of 6 percent and discounts and shortages averaged 1.5 percent and 2.5 percent, respectively, then the total planned reductions for October would be 10 percent of planned monthly sales, or \$945 (see Figure 14–8).

Product Category	Markdowns (%)	Stock Shortage (%)
Female apparel	29.4	2.5
Female accessories	15.6	2.9
Men's and boy's apparel and accessories	21.8	1.9
Infant and children's clothing and accessories	23.7	1.6
Shoes	25.0	0.6
Cosmetics and drugs	2.2	1.0
Recreation	14.6	1.7
Home furnishings	14.9	1.3
All other merchandise	13.8	2.3

FIGURE 14–12
Markdown and stock shortages for department stores, 1988

Source: David P. Schulz, "New MOR Data for 1988," *Stores* (November 1989), 53. Copyright © National Retail Federation, Inc., New York, New York.

Planning Purchases

Planning purchases constitutes the fourth stage in developing a merchandise budget. In this stage, the retailer plans the dollar amount of merchandise that must be purchased for a given time period (e.g., a month or a season) in view of planned sales and reductions for that period as well as the planned stock levels at the beginning of the period and the desired stock levels at the end of the period. (The ending stock usually equals the beginning stock for the next period.) The format for calculating planned purchases for a monthly planning period is as follows:

  planned monthly sales
+ planned monthly reductions
+ desired end-of-the-month stock
= total stock needs for the month
− planned beginning-of-month stock
= planned monthly purchases

For illustration purposes, let's assume that the manager of Selmer's jewelry department is planning the October purchases of men's and women's watches. From our previous discussions we have the following information concerning October: (1) planned monthly sales estimated at $9,450 (see Figure 14–8); (2) planned monthly reductions, estimated at 10 percent of sales, of $945; (3) desired end-of-the-month stock of $40,650 (the beginning-of-the-month stock for November—see Figure 14–8); and (4) planned beginning-of-the-month stock of $22,500 (see Figure 14–8). Given this information, the planned purchases for the month of October are

	planned monthly sales	$ 9,450
+	planned monthly reductions	$ 945
+	desired end-of-the-month stock	$40,650
=	total stock needs for the month	$51,045
−	planned beginning-of-the-month stock	$22,500
=	planned monthly purchases	$28,545

The planned monthly purchases of $28,545 were computed in terms of retail prices. To find out what the manager must spend in terms of cost prices, the retailer must multiply the retail value ($28,545) by the cost equivalent (the percentage of the retail price that is the manager's cost). For example, if merchandise costs are 60 percent of the retail price, then the manager can plan to make purchases totaling $17,127 at cost prices ($28,545 × .60). The planned monthly purchase value represents the retailer's additional merchandise needs for that month—how much merchandise must be purchased and made available during that month.

Planning Profit Margins

An integral part of developing the merchandise budget is to allow for a reasonable profit by ensuring an adequate dollar **gross margin**—the difference between cost of goods sold and net sales. An adequate dollar gross margin must cover the operating expenses associated with buying, stocking, and selling the merchandise, as well as produce an acceptable operating profit. The procedures for determining dollar gross margin and operating profit are as follows:

$$\begin{array}{rl} & \text{net sales (\$)} \\ - & \underline{\text{cost of goods sold (\$)}} \\ = & \text{gross margin (\$)} \\ - & \underline{\text{operating expenses (\$)}} \\ = & \text{operating profit (\$)} \end{array}$$

Retailers attempt to achieve an adequate gross margin and operating profit by planning an **initial markup percentage**—the percentage difference between the cost of the merchandise and its original retail price—that will cover expenses, profits, and reductions. The formula for calculating the initial markup percentage is shown in Figure 14–13.

Sales and reduction estimates are obtained from the sales and reduction planning stages of the merchandise budget. Expense estimates are based on past experience as revealed by expense records. After making sales, reduction, and expense estimates, the retailer can then establish a realistic profit objective. To facilitate easy planning, reductions, expenses, and profits are estimated as a *percentage of sales*. For example, in planning the required initial markup percentage on men's and women's watches for the coming year (1990), the manager of Selmer's jewelry department has estimated total annual sales of \$180,000, reductions at 10 percent of sales, or \$18,000, and anticipated expenses at 20 percent of sales, or \$36,000. Further, assuming that the manager desires a profit objective of 12 percent of sales or \$21,600, which is considered both feasible and acceptable, the manager calculates the required initial markup on watches:

$$\text{required initial markup percentage} = \frac{\$36{,}000 + \$21{,}600 + \$18{,}000}{\$180{,}000 + \$18{,}000} = 38.2\%$$

The same formula can be used when expenses, profits, reductions, and sales are expressed in percentage terms (sales equals 100 percent). For example,

$$\text{required initial markup percentage} = \frac{20\% + 12\% + 10\%}{100\% + 10\%} = 38.2\%$$

This required initial markup percentage represents an overall average for a merchandise category (e.g., watches). As long as this category average is maintained, the actual initial markup on any individual merchandise item (a watch of a particular brand, style, and price) may vary from the average to adjust to different demand conditions, competitive circumstances, and other external and internal merchandising factors.

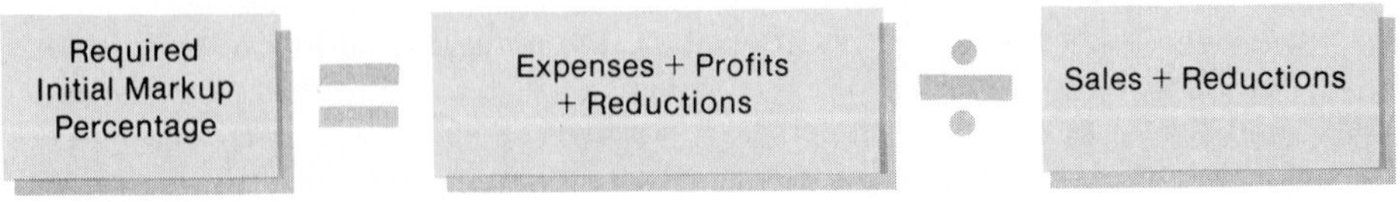

FIGURE 14–13
Procedure for calculating required initial markup percentage

UNIT PLANNING: MERCHANDISE LISTS

Unit planning is an operational management tool to plan the merchandise assortment and support. It is directed at determining the amount of inventory the retailer should carry by item and by units and answers the inventory questions of how many product items (assortment) and how many units of each item (support) to stock. Unit planning involves the use of several *merchandise lists*—a set of operational plans for managing total selection of merchandise. Based on the type of merchandise the retailer carries, one or more of the following three merchandise lists will apply.

1. Basic stock list—for planning staple merchandise
2. Model stock list—for planning fashion merchandise
3. Never-out list—for planning key items and best sellers

Merchandise lists essentially represent the ideal stock for meeting the consumer's merchandise needs in terms of assortment and support.

Basic Stock List

The **basic stock list** is a planning instrument retailers use to determine the assortment and support for staple merchandise. **Staples** are product items for which sales are either very stable or highly variable but very predictable. In either case, estimates of the required assortment of merchandise items and the number of support units for each item can be made with a relatively high degree of accuracy. Thus, in planning for staple merchandise, the retailer can develop a very specific stocking plan. The basic stock list is a schedule or listing of "stock-keeping units" (SKUs) for staple merchandise. A **stock-keeping unit** is a merchandise category for which separate records (sales and stock) are maintained; an SKU can consist of a single merchandise item or a group of items. The basic stock list usually identifies each SKU in precise terms. A retailer can use the following product characteristics to distinguish clearly an SKU of staple merchandise: (1) brand name, (2) style or model number, (3) product or package size, (4) product color or material, (5) retail and/or cost price of the product, and (6) manufacturer's name and identification number. In addition to a complete listing of SKUs, the basic stock list also contains a detailed description of the stock position for each SKU by stock levels (merchandise support, or the total number of units). Also, this description of stock support normally identifies (1) a minimum stock level to be on hand, (2) actual stock on hand, (3) amount of stock on order, (4) planned sales, and (5) actual sales. Stock support information is recorded on a standardized form at regular and frequent intervals (e.g., quarterly or monthly). Figure 14–14 illustrates one of several possible forms for recording the information contained in a basic stock list.

The importance of carefully maintaining a basic stock list cannot be overstated. Most merchandise departments, including those that are fashion oriented, contain at least some product items that are basic staples. Examples are black nylon socks and white cotton briefs in the men's wear department. Given the "essential" character of staple merchandise in the consumer's buying behavior patterns, close supervision over the stock position of staples is absolutely necessary. The simple fact that consumers expect an adequate supply of staple merchandise makes it all the more important to have an adequate supply. Many staple items have no totally satisfactory substitutes for many consumers. A stockout of a particular staple forces the consumer to look elsewhere for the item. By being unable to meet the consumer's need for a basic staple, the retailer not only loses the sale but also damages the store's assortment image and strains the customer's goodwill. Additionally, the customer, in the process of looking elsewhere, may decide to switch to a competitor whose stock of staples is well maintained.

Stock Keeping Unit		Vendor Description			Merchandise Description						Stock Description				
Number	Name	Manuf. Name	Manuf. I.D.	Brand	Style/ Model	Material	Color	Size	Price			Quarters			
									R	C		1	2	3	4
											MS				
											PS				
											AS				
											OH				
											OO				
											MS				
											PS				
											AS				
											OH				
											OO				
											MS				
											PS				
											AS				
											OH				
											OO				
											MS				
											PS				
											AS				
											OH				
											OO				

Key: R = Retail Price; C = Cost Price; MS = Minimum Stock; PS = Planned Sales; AS = Actual Sales; OH = Stock on Hand; OO = Stock on Order

FIGURE 14–14
A basic stock list form

Model Stock List

Stock planning for fashion merchandise is accomplished through use of the **model stock list**—a schedule or listing of SKUs for fashion merchandise. The model stock list differs from the basic stock list because it defines each SKU in general rather than precise terms. Common criteria in identifying a model SKU are *general price lines* ("better dresses" at \$100, \$150, and \$200 or "moderate dresses" at \$40, \$60, and \$80); *distribution of sizes* (misses 8, 10, 12, 14, and 16); *certain basic colors* (black cocktail dresses or navy-blue blazers); *general style features* (long and short sleeve dresses or crew neck, v-neck, and turtleneck sweaters); and *product materials* (wool, cotton, and polyester dresses). The more general character of each SKU in a model stock plan reflects the transience of fashion merchandise, which represents only the currently prevailing style. The likelihood of style changes within a short period and the high probability that market demand (sales) will fluctuate considerably within any selling season require a more general approach to stock planning. If the model stock list calls for 300 "better dresses" equally distributed among the \$100, \$150, and \$200 price lines, the retailer is still free to adapt to specific fashion trends that are currently stylish. In the initial planning of model stock lists, desired support quantities for each SKU are established on the basis of past sales experience. The exact distribution of those quantities among the various assortment features (e.g., colors, styles, and materials) is left to the buyer's judgment about what is and will be appropriate for the store's customers. In essence, the model stock list provides general guidelines on the size and composition of an ideal stock of fashion merchandise, without specifying the exact nature of the merchandise assortment or support.

The form used to plan the model stock list differs somewhat from the basic stock list form. First, the vendor description is usually absent or abbreviated. Second, the merchandise description is more generalized. Finally, the stock description is frequently more detailed, breaking down each season (quarter) into desired stock levels at various times within the season: beginning of the season, seasonal peak, and end of the season.

Never-Out List

The **never-out list** is a specially created list of merchandise items that are identified as key items or best-sellers for which the retailer wants extra protection against the possibility of a stockout. As a result of the high level of demand for these items, many retailers establish rigid stock requirements. For example, a retailer might specify that 99 percent of all items on the never-out list must be on hand and on display at all times. Stockouts of these key items result in permanent loss of sales. Typically, the consumer will simply not wait to purchase best-sellers. Never-out lists can include fast-selling staples, key seasonal items, and best-selling fashion merchandise. The integrity of the never-out list is preserved through regular and frequent revision. The importance of the never-out list is underscored by the fact that many chain organizations expect individual store managers to have a near-perfect record in maintaining the stock levels for merchandise on the list. Even a moderate number of stockouts of merchandise on the list is considered an indication of poor management.

MERCHANDISE CONTROL

Merchandise control is the process of designing and maintaining inventory systems for controlling the planned balance between inventory and sales. Inventory control provides the necessary parameters to the planning process.[4] Merchandise control can be viewed as the sum of two types of inventory systems: an inventory-information system and an inventory-analysis system. The **inventory-information system** is the set of methods and procedures for collecting and processing merchandise data pertinent to the planning and control of merchandise inventories. The **inventory-analysis system** includes methods for evaluating the retailer's past merchandising performance and decision-making tools for controlling future merchandising activities. As with merchandise planning, merchandise control relies on the retailer's inventory information and analysis systems to control inventory investment as well as inventory assortment and support.

The retailer's merchandise controls must be able to supplement the basic merchandising decisions of buying, stocking, and selling. A well-conceived merchandise-control system can aid in the merchandise decision-making process by providing essential information and analysis on both the right amount (dollars) and the right quantity (units) to buy, stock, and sell. It also provides a better position to (1) prevent stockouts, which result in lower profits resulting from lost sales and reduced store loyalty because of customer dissatisfaction, and (2) avoid overstocks, which lower profits because of higher inventory carrying costs and greater risks of markdowns.

INVENTORY-INFORMATION SYSTEMS

To control their inventories effectively, retailers must have an efficient means of obtaining information on the inventories' past and current status. An adequate inventory-information system is a prerequisite to planning and controlling future merchandising activities. Before examining the major types of inventory-information systems, let's consider the kinds of information retailers need for controlling inventories sources for that information.

Inventory Information

Kinds of Information

Merchandise investment and merchandise assortment and support are the principal elements the retailer wants to control. To complement merchandise planning, the retailer's inventory-information system must be capable of providing both dollar control and unit control. **Dollar control** considers the "value" of merchandise and attempts to identify the dollar amount of investment in merchandise. Dollar control requires the retailer to collect, record, and analyze merchandise data in terms of dollars. **Unit control** deals with the number of different product items (assortment) and the number of units stocked within each item (support). It is the number of physical units (sales, purchases, and stock levels) recorded and analyzed. Both dollar and unit control are essential for the retailer who needs investment information for profit control and assortment information for stock control.

Sources of Information

The retailer's source of inventory information is the inventory system. Inventory systems differ depending on when (perpetually or periodically) inventory is taken and how (book or physical) it is taken. Based on these two factors, inventory procedures can be classified as either perpetual book inventory systems or periodic physical inventory systems.

A **perpetual book inventory** refers to a system of inventory taking and information gathering on a continuous or ongoing basis using various accounting records to compute stock on hand at any given time. The purchase, sales, and markdown figures needed to calculate stock on hand are derived from internal accounting records that must be kept current if the computed book inventory is to correctly reflect the retailer's true stock position. In summary, a perpetual book inventory represents an up-to-the-minute, -day, or -week accounting system in which all transactions that affect inventory are considered as they occur or shortly thereafter. Its major advantage is that the retailer can determine stock on hand as required by operating conditions and the need for inventory information.

A **periodic physical inventory** refers to a system of gathering stock information intermittently (usually once or twice a year) using an actual physical count and inspection of the merchandise items to compute sales for the period since the last physical inventory. Limitations of a periodic physical inventory system are the time-consuming process of making an actual, physical count of each merchandise item and the fact that most retailers have faster, easier, and more time-saving methods for obtaining sales information. Nevertheless, a physical inventory must be taken at least once a year for income tax reporting purposes. A physical count of the retailer's inventory also is necessary to determine stock shortages (book inventory minus physical inventory). Finally, for the small retailer that can afford neither the electronic data processing equipment nor the accounting personnel to maintain a sophisticated accounting system, a periodic physical inventory is the only alternative.

Inventory Systems

The major types of inventory-information systems used in merchandise control are (1) dollar/perpetual/book, (2) dollar/periodic/physical, (3) unit/perpetual/book, and (4) unit/periodic/physical. These four systems are based on the kinds of information the retailer needs and the methods and sources for obtaining that information.

Dollar/Perpetual/Book

Dollar control using a **dollar/perpetual/book inventory** system provides the retailer with continual information on the amount of inventory (dollars) that should be on hand at any given time as determined by internal accounting records. The basic procedures for calculating a perpetual book inventory in dollars are as follows:

	beginning stock on hand
+	purchases
=	total stock handled
−	sales
−	markdowns
=	ending stock on hand

Dollar control systems express values either in terms of retail prices or cost prices. To simplify the discussion of dollar control, all values are considered at retail price.

In the preceding formulation, the beginning stock-on-hand value is the ending stock-on-hand value from the preceding accounting period. Merchandise data concerning purchases, sales, and markdowns are obtained from the appropriate internal accounting records. The computed ending stock on hand is the dollar value of the retailer's inventory, provided no shortages have occurred as a result of customer shoplifting, employee pilfering, or other causes that would reduce the value of the merchandise on hand. To determine actual stock shortages, the retailer would have to check the book inventory by taking a physical inventory. Many retailers use an estimated shortage percentage (e.g., 2 percent) based on past experience to adjust the ending stock-on-hand value perpetually. A final adjustment is then made at the end of the season or year by conducting a physical count and valuation of the merchandise.

Dollar/Periodic/Physical

A **dollar/periodic/physical inventory** system for dollar control provides the retailer with periodic information on the amount of inventory (dollars) actually on hand at a given time as determined by a physical count and valuation of the merchandise. It permits the retailer to compute the dollar amount of sales since the last physical count. A periodic physical inventory usually is computed at designated intervals (monthly, quarterly, or semiannually) using the following basic procedure:

	beginning stock on hand
+	purchases
=	total stock handled
−	ending stock on hand
=	sales and markdowns
−	markdowns
=	sales

The beginning stock on hand is the value of the ending stock on hand brought forward from the previous accounting period. Internal purchases and markdown records are used to determine the dollar amount of purchases and markdowns since the last accounting. The ending stock-on-hand figure is derived from a physical count and valuation of the merchandise inventory. The sales figure is computed as shown and incorporates the value of whatever shortages have occurred. Most retailers have easier and more timely means to obtain sales information.

Unit/Perpetual/Book

A perpetual book inventory system for unit control—a **unit/perpetual/book system**—involves continual recording of all transactions (e.g., number of units sold or purchased), which changes the unit status of the retailer's merchandise inventory. Each unit transaction is posted as it occurs or shortly thereafter (e.g., on a daily basis). Perpetual unit control provides a running total of the number of units of a given type that are flowing into and out of the store or department and helps the retailer continually control the balance between units on hand and unit sales. Perpetual unit control systems are maintained manually or through various automatic recording systems.

Manual Systems. A manual system of perpetual unit control is maintained by the retailer's accounting personnel, who continually record merchandise data on standard forms. To determine stock on hand, the accountant simply adds the number of units received during the accounting period and subtracts the number of units sold. The number of units received into stock is obtained from records furnished by the receiving department or clerk. Information on the number of units sold can be gathered by means of a number of manual systems, such as (1) *point-of-sale-tallies* (sales personnel keep track of the number of units sold by making a tally mark on a merchandise list after each sale); (2) *price-ticket stubs* (sales personnel remove information stubs from price tickets when the merchandise is sold and collect, sort, and tally the number of units sold); and (3) *cash-register stubs* (sales personnel remove information stubs from receipts before giving them to customers; these stubs are then used to determine the number of units sold).

Automatic Systems. Computer-based electronic data processing equipment allows the retailer to automatically convert merchandise data on sales, purchases, and stocks into useful information for planning and controlling merchandise assortment and support. Several automatic systems are available including tag, card, and point-of-sale systems. A *tag system* uses prepunched merchandise tags containing basic assortment information that are attached to each merchandise item. These tags are collected when the item is sold and sent to a data processing facility where the information is fed into the computer. *Card systems* are similar to tag systems, except sales personnel record assortment information directly onto punch cards or scanner cards, which are then fed into the data processing system and used for unit control purposes. *Point-of-sale (POS) systems* use cash registers or terminals capable of transmitting assortment information (e.g., style, price, color, material) directly to the central data processing facility as the sale is being recorded. A number of different methods can be used to record sales and assortment information in a point-of-sale system. Two common methods are (1) *optical scanners,* which read codes (e.g., Universal Product Code) that have been premarked or imprinted on the merchandise item or package, and (2) *terminal keys,* which transmit data directly to the computer when sales personnel depress them. Point-of-sale systems are becoming the dominant form of gathering merchandise information.[5]

Unit/Periodic/Physical

Unit control also can be achieved by making a periodic physical check on the status of the retailer's inventory—**unit/periodic/physical inventory**. Stock levels are monitored by a visual inspection or a physical count.

For a visual inspection, stock-control personnel visually examine the stock of each item to determine whether sales have depleted the stock to the point of reordering. Several methods can determine at a glance the general condition of the stock; for example, display or storage bins can be divided into quarters, with each quarter having the capacity to hold a certain number of units. When a designated number of quarters (e.g., two) are empty, the person responsible for stock control reorders merchandise to refill the bin. Another example of visual stock control is placing merchandise (e.g., hardware items) on a sequentially numbered pegboard (e.g., 1 to 25). When the stock reaches a certain level, say 10, then 15 units are reordered.

The second method of monitoring stock levels and determining unit sales is a physical count—actually counting and recording the number of units on hand at regular intervals. The retailer attempts to determine the number of units sold since the last physical count by adding purchases during the intervening period to the beginning stock on hand and then subtracting the ending stock on hand obtained from the current physical count. A physical counting system is considerably more time-consuming and expensive than the visual inspection method.

Inventory Valuation

A major financial concern of every retailer is determining the actual worth of the inventory on hand. How the retailer establishes the value of the inventory can have a profound effect on the outcome of various financial statements (e.g., the income statement and the balance sheet). Retailers can value their inventories at cost (what they paid for the merchandise) or at retail (what they can sell the merchandise for). This section examines the cost and retail methods of inventory valuation and reviews the relative strengths and weaknesses of each method.

The Cost Method

Small retailers generally prefer the **cost method of inventory valuation** because it is easy to understand, easy to implement, and requires a limited amount of record keeping. The retailer simply values merchandise inventory at the original cost to the store each time a physical inventory is taken. One of two procedures typically is used in computing the cost value of merchandise items. First, the original cost can be coded on the price tag or merchandise container. The second procedure retailers use is to imprint a serialized reference number on each price tag corresponding to an itemized merchandise stock-control list containing the per-unit cost of each item.

A major problem of the cost method occurs when the retailer procures various shipments at different times during inflationary periods. If the wholesale price of an inventory item remained constant, the retailer's costs for various shipments of the same product would be identical. Unfortunately, constant wholesale prices are the exception, and fluctuating wholesale prices are usually the rule. Although the rate of inflation can vary significantly, the mere fact that inflation exists creates a problem (the extent of the problem depends on the rate of inflation), with different shipments of identical products being purchased at different wholesale prices (cost to retailer). The retailer then must decide which cost value to use. FIFO (first-in, first-out) and LIFO (last-in, first-out) are two inventory costing methods used to resolve this dilemma.

The **FIFO (first-in, first-out) method** assumes that merchandise items are sold in the order in which they are purchased; that is, older stock is sold before newer stock that was purchased at a later date. The cost of the oldest units in stock determines the retailer's cost of goods sold. From an operational viewpoint of maintaining the freshness of merchandise in stock, FIFO makes good sense and is the operating practice of most retailers. From a financial accounting viewpoint, however, during inflationary periods the FIFO method results in an overstatement of profits, thereby increasing the firm's tax liability.

Under **LIFO—the last-in, first-out method**—recent acquisition costs are used to price inventory (even though in actuality, the inventory bought last is not sold first). The cost of the newest units in stock determines the retailer's cost of goods sold.

Although the cost method is simple, it does have several disadvantages. First, a cost valuation of inventory requires a physical count of the merchandise, and the need to count and decode prices is both time-consuming and costly. Second, the cost method does not provide a book inventory of what merchandise ought to be on hand. Therefore, the retailer has no means to determine shortages. (Remember, shortages equal book inventory minus physical inventory.) Finally, the cost method is often untimely, because physical inventory is usually taken only once or twice a year. As a result, the retailer cannot prepare weekly, monthly, and quarterly financial statements. Semiannual or annual financial statements are inadequate for effective planning and control for many retailers. The disadvantages of the cost method can be largely overcome if the retailer elects to employ the retail method of inventory valuation.

The Retail Method

The **retail method of inventory valuation** allows the retailer to estimate the cost value of an ending inventory for a particular accounting period without taking a physical inventory. Essentially, the retail method is a book inventory system whereby the cost value for each group of related merchandise (e.g., a department) is based on its retail value (selling price). By determining the percentage relationship between the total cost and the total retail value of the merchandise available for sale during an accounting period, the retailer can obtain a reliable estimate of the ending inventory value at cost. To use the retail method, the retailer must make the following calculations: (1) the total merchandise available for sale, (2) the cost complement, (3) the total retail deductions, and (4) the ending inventory at retail and cost values.

Total Merchandise Available. The total merchandise available for sale is illustrated in the following example:

		Cost($)	Retail($)
	beginning inventory	120,000	200,000
+	net purchases	80,000	140,000
+	additional markons	—	2,000
+	freight charges	4,000	—
=	total merchandise available	204,000	342,000

As shown, beginning inventory and purchase figures are kept both at cost and at retail values. The beginning inventory is the ending inventory brought forward from the previous accounting period, obtained from the stock ledger that the accounting department maintains. Net purchases represent all purchases the retailer made during the accounting period minus any returns to the vendor. A purchase journal is used to record all purchase transactions. Any additional markons taken since setting the original retail price are added to the retail value of the inventory to reflect the market value of the merchandise. A price-change journal is maintained to keep track of additional markons as well as markdowns and other changes in the original retail selling price. Finally, freight charges, obtained from the purchase journal, are added to portray the true cost of the merchandise correctly.

Cost Complement. The cost complement is the average relationship of cost to retail value for all merchandise available for sale during an accounting period. In essence, it is the complement of the cumulative markup percentage. The cost complement is computed as follows:

$$\text{cost complement} = \frac{\text{cost value of inventory}}{\text{retail value of inventory}}$$

Using the previous example in which the value of the total merchandise available for sale equaled \$204,000 at cost and \$342,000 at retail, then

$$\text{cost complement} = \frac{\$204{,}000}{\$342{,}000} = .5965$$

In this example, the retailer's merchandise cost is, on the average, equal to 59.65 percent of the retail value of the merchandise.

Retail Deductions. The third step in the retail method of inventory valuation is to determine the total merchandise available for sale. Retail deductions include merchandise that has been sold, marked down, discounted, stolen, and lost. Total retail deductions are obtained by adding all the deductions, reducing the retail value of the merchandise that was available for sale. To continue our illustration,

	sales for period	$160,000
+	markdowns	30,000
+	discounts	10,000
+	shortages (estimated)	2,000
=	total retail deductions	$202,000

The sales figure for the accounting period represents both cash and credit sales and is obtained from the retailer's sales journal. The amount of markdowns taken during the accounting period and the amount of the discounts granted to employees and special customers can be secured from the price-change journal. Because shortages resulting from shoplifting, employee pilfering, and lost merchandise cannot be determined without a physical inventory, the retailer usually estimates the shortage figure based on past experience.

Ending Inventory Value. The final step in implementing the retail method is to determine the value of ending inventory at retail and at cost. The retail value of ending inventory is computed by subtracting total retail deductions from total merchandise available for sale at retail. In our example,

	total merchandise available at retail	$342,000
−	total retail deductions	202,000
=	ending inventory at retail	$140,000

The cost value of ending inventory is calculated by multiplying the ending inventory at retail by the cost complement in the following manner:

ending inventory at cost = ending inventory at retail × cost complement
ending inventory at cost = $140,000 × .5965 = $83,510

Although the figure $83,510 is only an estimate of the true cost value of the ending inventory, it is sufficiently reliable to allow the retailer to estimate both the cost of goods sold and gross margin for the accounting period. To complete our example:

	total merchandise available at retail	$204,000
−	ending inventory at retail	83,510
=	cost of goods sold	$120,490

	sales for the period	$160,000
−	cost of goods sold	120,490
=	gross margin	$ 39,510

Although the retail method has the disadvantages of requiring the retailer to keep more records (stock ledger and sales, purchases, and price-change journals) and use averages to estimate cost values, its advantages are numerous. The retail method forces the retailer to "think retail," in that it highlights both retail and cost figures. Second, frequent and regular calculations of various financial and operating statements are possible as a result of the availability of cost and retail information. These statements are essential to good financial planning and control and allow the retailer to adjust more quickly to changing market conditions. Third, when the retail method is used, physical inventories are taken in retail prices, thereby eliminating the costly, time-consuming job of decoding cost prices. Recording physical inventory in retail prices greatly simplifies the process and encourages a more frequent physical count of stock. Fourth, the retail method facilitates planning and control on a departmental basis. Sales, purchases, inventories, and price-change information are recorded by department and can be used to evaluate each department's performance. Fifth, by providing a book figure on what inventory should be on hand, the retail method allows the retailer to determine shortages each time a physical inventory is taken. Sixth, the retail method facilitates planning for insurance coverage and collecting insurance claims by providing an up-to-date valuation of inventory.

Given the many advantages of the retail method of inventory valuation, it is not surprising that it is used extensively by large departmentalized and chain store retailers to gain tighter control over their various operating units.

INVENTORY-ANALYSIS SYSTEM

Inventory information is only useful when it provides the retailer with insights into past mistakes and with foresight for future planning. Merchandise data collected and processed by the inventory-information system can be used to evaluate past performances and to plan future actions. A determination of stock turnover return on inventory investment and direct product profit are the principal methods for evaluating the retailer's past performance in controlling merchandise inventories. The dollar and unit open-to-buy methods are two of the more important tools for controlling future merchandising activities.

Stock Turnover

Stock turnover is the rate at which the retailer depletes and replenishes stock. Specifically, stock turnover is defined as the number of times during a specific period (usually annual) that the average stock on hand is sold.

Stock turnover rates can be calculated in both dollars (at retail or at cost) and units. The formulas for figuring stock turnover rates are shown in Figure 14–15. (Data on net sales, cost of goods sold, and number of units sold are obtained from the inventory-information system.) **Average stock** on hand for any time period is defined as the sum of the stock on hand at the beginning of the period, at each intervening period, and at the end of the period divided by the number of stock listings. For example, the average stock at retail for the summer season of June, July, and August would be calculated as follows:

FIGURE 14–15
Computing stock turnover rates

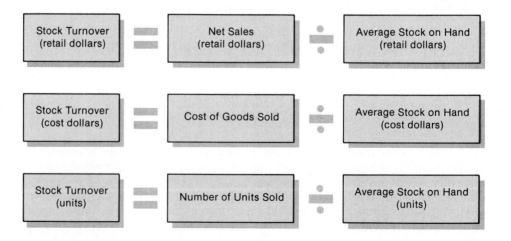

Stock Turnover (retail dollars) = Net Sales (retail dollars) ÷ Average Stock on Hand (retail dollars)

Stock Turnover (cost dollars) = Cost of Goods Sold ÷ Average Stock on Hand (cost dollars)

Stock Turnover (units) = Number of Units Sold ÷ Average Stock on Hand (units)

June 1	\$ 60,000
July 1	\$ 40,000
August 1	\$ 50,000
August 31	\$ 35,000
total inventory	\$185,000

$$\text{average stock} = \frac{\text{total inventory}}{\text{number of listings}}$$

$$\text{average stock (June–August)} = \frac{\$185{,}000}{4} = \$46{,}250$$

If the net sales (retail dollars) for the three-month summer season were \$220,000, then the stock turnover rate at retail would be

$$\text{stock turnover at retail} = \frac{\text{net sales}}{\text{average stock on hand}}$$

$$\text{stock turnover at retail (June–August)} = \frac{\$220{,}000}{\$\ 46{,}250} = 4.76$$

Benefits of High Turnover

High stock turnover rates generally reflect good merchandise planning and control. Several benefits accrue to retailers with a high rate of stock turnover, including (1) *fresher merchandise:* With a rapid stock turnover there is more frequent replacement of merchandise and, therefore, a continuous flow of new and fresh merchandise into the store; (2) *fewer markdowns and less depreciation:* A fast stock turnover is associated with a faster rate of sales and, therefore, reduced losses resulting from style or fashion obsolescence and soiled or damaged merchandise; (3) *lower expense:* A quick stock turnover helps to reduce inventories and, therefore, reduce such inventory expenses as interest and insurance payments, storage costs, and taxes on inventory; it also helps to reduce promotional costs, since a new and fresh selection of merchandise tends to more easily sell itself; (4) *greater sales:* A rapid stock turnover allows the retailer to adjust the merchandise assortment according to the changing needs of the target market and, therefore, to generate more customer interest and a greater sales volume; and (5) *higher returns:* A rapid stock turnover resulting in an increase in sales and a corresponding decrease in stocks will generate a higher return on inventory investment, hence, a more productive and efficient use of the retailer's capital.

Increasing the rate of stock turnover requires the retailer to control the size and content of its inventory. The retailer must carefully balance inventory investment for greater profit with inventory assortment and support for adequate customer selection. Strategies for increasing stock turnover include (1) limiting merchandise assortment to the most popular brands, styles, sizes, colors, and price lines; (2) reducing merchandise support by maintaining a minimum reserve or safety stock; (3) clearing out slow-moving stock through price reductions; and (4) increasing the promotional effort in an attempt to increase sales.

Limitations of High Turnover

A high rate of stock turnover is not without its problems. Excessively high stock turns can mean the retailer is buying in too-small quantities. If so, then the retailer is (1) not taking full advantage of available quantity discounts; (2) adding to the costs of transportation and handling; and (3) increasing accounting costs by processing too many orders. Another potential problem with high stock turnover is the danger of losing sales because of stockouts.

FIGURE 14–16
Computing return on inventory investment

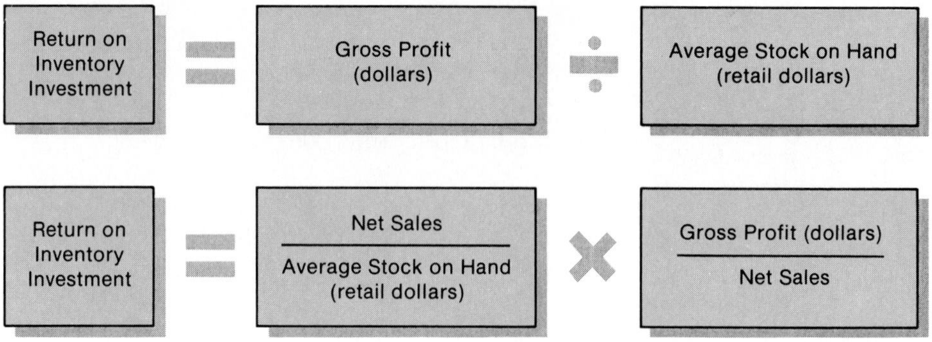

Return on Inventory Investment

The second method for evaluating past performance in controlling merchandise inventories is **gross margin return on inventory** (GMROI)—the ratio of gross margin dollars to the average stock on hand. This ratio tells the retailer the dollar investment in inventory needed to achieve a desired gross profit (gross margin dollars).[6] Specifically, return on inventory investment can be expressed as shown in Figure 14–16. Essentially, return on inventory investment concerns the relationship between stock turnover and profitability. The importance of this ratio is that it allows the retailer to evaluate past and future effects of turnover on a store's (or department's) profitability. Before initiating plans to increase the stock turnover rate, the retailer should first determine how a higher stock turnover rate might affect profitability.

Direct Product Profit

The final analytical tool used by retailers for evaluating their past performance in controlling merchandise inventories is direct product profit. First used in the supermarket industry, **direct product profit** (DPP) allows the retailer to calculate the profitability of a merchandise category as well as a particular product item (SKU). The advantage of using DPP is that the retailer assigns direct product costs to a specific merchandise item rather than use a gross margin figure with its associated average costs for all products within a category of merchandise. If carefully determined, direct product profit is simply a more accurate reflection of a product item's true profit contribution. Because products have different cost structures, DPP provides a means for making meaningful comparisons. Using modern computer technology and spreadsheet programs, DPP is finding more widespread application within the retailing industry. As seen in Figure 14–17, direct product profit is being used to assist the retailer in making decisions regarding promotional and price strategies, stocking and display decisions, and operating procedures.

Direct product profit equals gross margin dollars plus earned discounts and allowances (e.g., payment discounts and merchandise plus backhaul allowances) minus direct product costs (all variable or direct costs associated with merchandising the product item—promotion, selling, transportation, warehousing, and handling). Figure 14–18 provides a sample calculation of DPP. The most difficult problem with determining DPP is obtaining accurate expense figures. The usefulness of DPP can be further enhanced by determining direct product profits per square foot, or some other space measurement.

Open-to-Buy

Open-to-buy is one of the retailer's most important tools for controlling future merchandise inventories. This tool helps the retailer decide how much to buy.

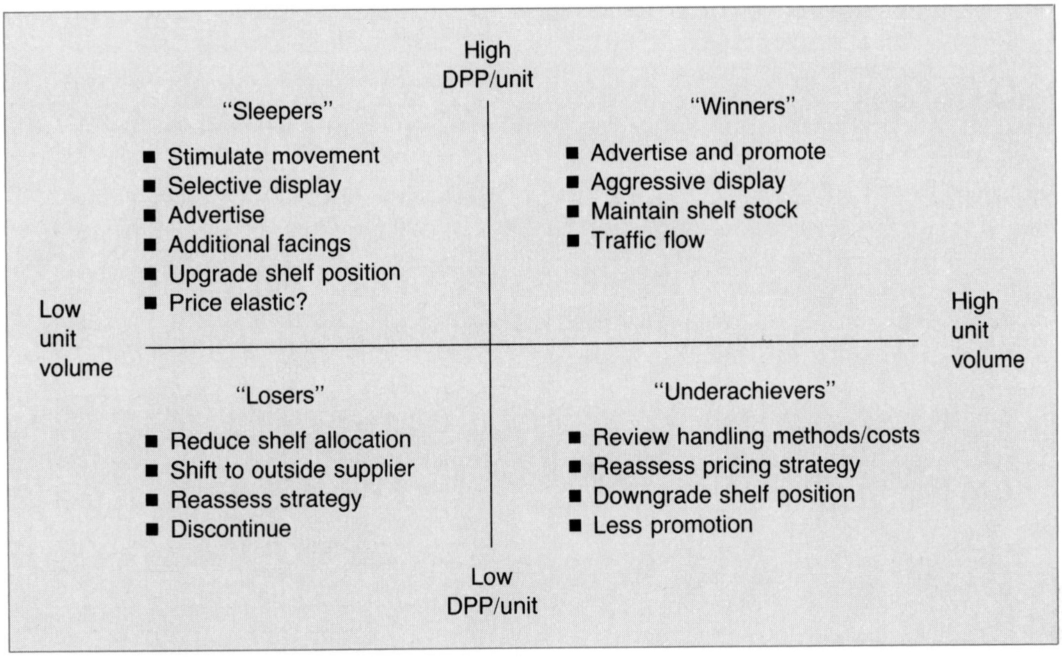

Source: *Retail and Distribution Management,* April 1987, p. 12.

FIGURE 14–17
Merchandising decisions and direct product profit

Open-to-buy is the amount of new merchandise the retailer can buy during a specific time period without exceeding the planned purchases for that period. Open-to-buy represents the difference between what the retailer plans to buy and what it has already bought—planned purchases minus purchase commitments. Open-to-buy applies to both dollar and unit control. Dollar open-to-buy sets a financial constraint on the retailer's buying activities, whereas unit open-to-buy controls assortment and support in the buying process.

Open-to-buy is a versatile control tool. The retailer can use it to control purchase activities on a daily, weekly, or monthly basis. Also, open-to-buy can help control purchases of any classification or subclassification of merchandise. As a control tool, it allows the retailer to allocate purchases so stocks are maintained at predetermined levels by either the merchandise budget (dollar planning and control) or a merchandise list (unit planning and control).

Dollar Open-to-Buy

Dollar open-to-buy is used to determine the amount of money the retailer has to spend for new merchandise at any given time. It can be calculated and recorded at both retail and cost prices. To calculate **dollar open-to-buy at retail** prices for any day of a monthly period, the buyer starts with planned monthly purchases and subtracts purchase commitments already made during the month. Figure 14–18 shows the steps for determining dollar open-to-buy at retail. To obtain **dollar open-to-buy at cost**, the buyer simply multiplies open-to-buy at retail by the complement of the initial markup percentage. Figure 14–19 shows the formula for determining open-to-buy at cost.

To illustrate, a buyer for a women's apparel department is planning a trip to the market on April 15 and wants to know how much she can buy without exceeding the budget. Examination of the merchandise budget for April reveals that planned sales for the month were $70,000, while reductions (shortages, markdowns, and discounts) were $4,000. Inventory records reveal that the store started the month with $60,000 worth of inventory, and plans call for an ending inventory of $50,000. A review of purchase orders indicates that the department has made purchase commitments of $14,000 since

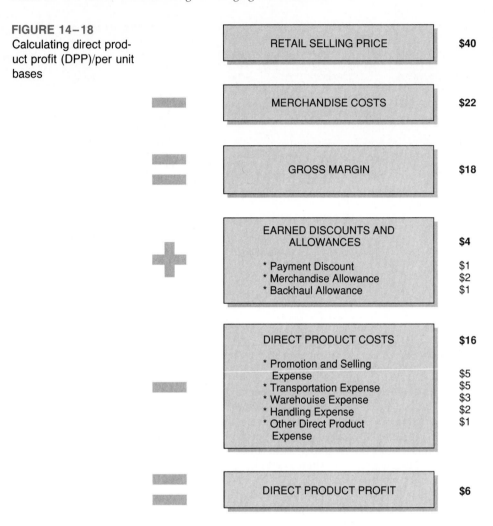

FIGURE 14–18
Calculating direct product profit (DPP)/per unit bases

	RETAIL SELLING PRICE	**$40**
−	MERCHANDISE COSTS	**$22**
=	GROSS MARGIN	**$18**
+	EARNED DISCOUNTS AND ALLOWANCES	**$4**
	* Payment Discount	$1
	* Merchandise Allowance	$2
	* Backhaul Allowance	$1
−	DIRECT PRODUCT COSTS	**$16**
	* Promotion and Selling Expense	$5
	* Transportation Expense	$5
	* Warehouise Expense	$3
	* Handling Expense	$2
	* Other Direct Product Expense	$1
=	DIRECT PRODUCT PROFIT	**$6**

the beginning of the month. Given an initial markup percentage of 50 percent on retail, the buyer calculates the dollar open-to-buy to be $50,000 at retail and $25,000 at cost. These figures were obtained by first calculating planned purchases for April ($70,000 + $4,000 + $50,000 − $60,000 = $64,000), then subtracting all purchase commitments ($14,000) made through the 15th of the month.

Unit Open-to-Buy

For the retailer engaged in unit control, unit open-to-buy is a successful and necessary tool in preventing stockouts and overstocking. Unit open-to-buy is most frequently used to control inventories of staple merchandise. This method lends itself to formal and systematic procedures for reordering merchandise that has well-established and predictable sales trends. **Unit open-to-buy** calculations involve two steps: (1) determining maximum inventory and (2) computing the unit open-to-buy quantity.

- **Step 1: Determine maximum inventory. Maximum inventory** is the number of merchandise units the retailer needs to cover expected sales during the reorder and delivery periods plus a safety stock for either unexpected sales or problems in securing the merchandise. The formula for determining maximum inventory is shown in Figure 14–20.

Planned Monthly Sales + Planned Monthly Reductions + Desired End-of-the-Month Stock = Total Stock Needs for the Month

Total Stock Needs for the Month − Beginning-of-the-Month Stock − Purchase Commitments = Open-to-buy (at retail)

Open-to-buy (at retail) × 100%—Initial Markup % = Open-to-buy (at cost)

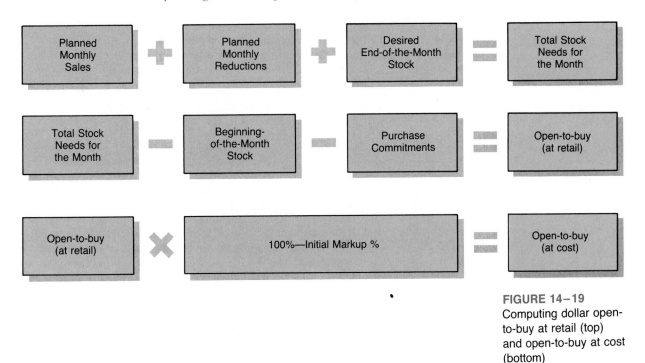

FIGURE 14–19
Computing dollar open-to-buy at retail (top) and open-to-buy at cost (bottom)

Maximum Inventory (MI) = [Reorder Period (RP) + Delivery Period (DP)] × Rate of Sales (RS) + Safety Stock (SS)

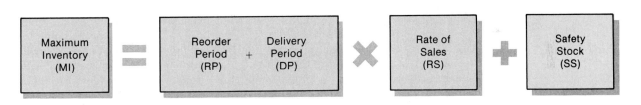

Where RP = the time interval between the scheduled place of orders (e.g., number of weeks)
DP = the amount of time between placement of an order and its arrival in stock ready to be sold (e.g. number of weeks)
RS = the number of units expected to be sold during a specified time period (e.g., on a weekly basis)
SS = the number of reserve units needed to cover any unexpected sales or delivery delays (e.g., a three-week supply)

Unit Open-to-buy = Maximum Inventory − Stock on Hand + Stock on Order

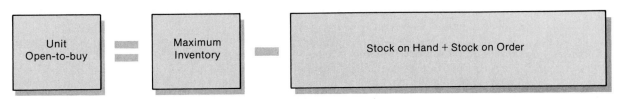

FIGURE 14–20
Computing unit open-to-buy

As an illustration, a hardware retailer reorders a staple item of merchandise every six weeks, expecting that delivery will take three weeks. Based on past experience, the hardware retailer expects to sell approximately 40 units a week and considers a two-week safety stock necessary. The maximum inventory (MI) for the merchandise is 440 units. It is calculated as follows:

$$\begin{aligned} MI &= (6 \text{ weeks} + 3 \text{ weeks}) \times 40 \text{ units} + 80 \text{ units} \\ &= (9 \text{ weeks}) \times 40 \text{ units} + 80 \text{ units} \\ &= 360 \text{ units} + 80 \text{ units} \\ &= 440 \text{ units} \end{aligned}$$

The hardware retailer therefore must stock 440 units to cover the reorder period and delivery period and to ensure a safety stock capable of covering two weeks' sales if the reorder is delayed or sales are higher than expected.

Step 2: Compute unit open-to-buy. Maximum inventory represents the number of merchandise units the retailer is open-to-buy if there is no stock on hand or stock on order. Unit open-to-buy is defined as maximum inventory minus stock on hand and stock on order. The computation formula is shown in Figure 14–20. Suppose our hardware dealer determines that it had 210 units on hand (obtained from the inventory-information system) and 90 units on order (obtained from purchase orders). Then,

$$\text{open-to-buy} = 440 - (210 + 90) \text{ (or 140 units)}$$

The systematic nature of unit open-to-buy permits easy computerization of this control tool.

SUMMARY

The merchandise management process focuses on planning and controlling the retailer's inventories. Establishing merchandise objectives and devising tactics for obtaining these objectives are the focal points for merchandise planning. The planning process includes both dollar planning, in terms of merchandise budgets, and unit planning, as accomplished through the use of merchandise lists. Satisfying consumers' needs and ensuring retailers' profits are the principal reasons for planning the merchandise mix. The retailer must carefully plan inventory investment (the total dollar amount invested in merchandise), inventory assortment (the number of different products stocked within a particular product line), and inventory support (the number of units to be stocked for each product item).

Dollar planning is accomplished by means of a merchandise budget—a financial plan for managing merchandise inventory investments—that requires the retailer to consider (1) sales, (2) stock levels, (3) reductions, (4) purchases, and (5) profit margins. The retailer uses unit planning to determine the amount of inventory to carry in terms of items (assortment) and units (support). A merchandise list—a set of operational plans for managing the retailer's total selection of merchandise—is used in unit planning. Based on the type of merchandise the retailer carries, one or more of the following lists are appropriate: basic stock list (for planning staple merchandise), model stock list (for planning fashion merchandise), and never-out list (for planning key items and best-sellers).

Merchandise control involves designing dollar- and unit-inventory-information and -analysis systems for collecting, recording, analyzing, and using merchandise data to control the planned balance between the retailer's merchandise inventory and sales. Merchandise control is the necessary complement to merchandise planning.

An inventory-information system is a set of methods and procedures for collecting and processing merchandise data that are pertinent to planning and controlling merchandise inventories. Depending on the kind of information needed and the available sources of that information, the retailer can elect to use a (1) dollar/perpetual/book system, (2) dollar/periodic/physical system, (3) unit/perpetual/book system, or (4) unit/periodic/physical system. An essential element in dollar control is knowing the true value of inventories. The two methods of inventory valuation are the cost method and the retail method. The cost method is simpler, whereas the retail method provides more timely and useful information.

The inventory-analysis system includes methods for evaluating the retailer's past merchandising performance as well as the decision-making tools available for controlling future merchandising activities. Stock turnover analysis, return on inventory investment ratios, and direct product profit figures are used to evaluate the retailer's past performance. Dollar and unit open-to-buy are key methods of controlling future inventories.

STUDENT STUDY GUIDE

Key Terms and Concepts

annual sales estimates (p. 518)
average stock (p. 536)
basic stock list (p. 527)
basic stock method (p. 521)
control unit (p. 515)
cost method of inventory valuation (p. 533)
direct product profit (p. 538)
discounts (p. 524)
dollar control (p. 530)
dollar open-to-buy at cost (p. 539)
dollar open-to-buy at retail (p. 539)
dollar/periodic/physical inventory (p. 531)
dollar/perpetual/book inventory (p. 531)
dollar planning (p. 515)
first-in, first-out (FIFO) method of costing inventories (p. 533)
gross margin (p. 526)
gross margin return on inventory (GMROI) (p. 538)
initial markup percentage (p. 526)
inventory-analysis system (p. 529)
inventory assortment (p. 515)
inventory-information system (p. 529)
inventory investment (p. 515)
inventory support (p. 515)
last-in, first-out (LIFO) method of costing inventories (p. 533)
markdowns (p. 524)
maximum inventory (p. 540)
merchandise budget (p. 515)
merchandise control (p. 514)
merchandise management (p. 514)
merchandise planning (p. 514)
model stock list (p. 528)
monthly sales estimates (p. 518)
never-out list (p. 529)
open-to-buy (p. 539)
percentage variation method (p. 522)
periodic physical inventory (p. 530)
perpetual book inventory (p. 530)
retail method of inventory valuation (p. 534)
retail reductions (p. 524)
shortages (p. 524)
staples (p. 527)
stock-keeping unit (SKU) (p. 527)
stock/sales ratio method (p. 524)
stock turnover at cost (p. 536)
stock turnover at retail (p. 536)
stock turnover in units (p. 536)
unit control (p. 530)
unit open-to-buy (p. 540)
unit/periodic/physical inventory (p. 532)
unit/perpetual/book inventory (p. 531)
week's supply method (p. 523)

Review Questions

1. Distinguish among the three concepts of inventory investment, assortment, and support.
2. What is a merchandise budget? Identify the five stages in developing a merchandise budget.
3. How does the variable adjustment method differ from the fixed adjustment method of estimating annual sales?
4. Gina Lewis is the department manager of the "better dresses" department. Having estimated planned monthly sales for the upcoming year, Gina must now plan the appropriate stock levels for the fall season. To obtain a better idea of the stock that will be needed, Gina has decided to calculate BOM stock for each month using both basic stock and percentage variation methods. Using an estimated inventory turnover rate of two, calculate the BOM stock for each month using both methods.

Planned Monthly Sales	
August	$32,000
Sept.	$18,000
Oct.	$10,000

5. A hardware retailer estimates its total annual sales for plumbing equipment to be $72,000 and hopes to achieve an annual stock turnover rate of six. Using the week's supply method, calculate the BOM stock for January.

6. What are retail reductions? Identify and describe their cause.
7. How are planned monthly purchases determined?
8. Given the following information, calculate the required initial markup percentage.

1. Sales	$240,000
2. Expenses	22 percent of sales
3. Reduction	8 percent of sales
4. Desired profit	14 percent of sales

9. What is an SKU? How are SKUs distinguished from one another?
10. Basic stock lists are used as a planning instrument for what type of merchandise?
11. What is a model stock list? What criteria are used in identifying a model stock-keeping unit?
12. What are never-out lists used for?
13. What distinguishes perpetual book inventory from periodic physical inventory?
14. What types of manual and automatic systems are used to gather information on the number of units sold?
15. How are stock levels monitored in a unit/periodic/physical inventory system? Briefly describe each method.
16. Describe the FIFO and LIFO methods of costing inventories.
17. List the advantages of the retail method of inventory valuation.
18. What are the benefits and limitations of high stock turnover rates?
19. Why is the return on inventory investment ratio important?
20. What is direct product profit? How is it determined?
21. What are the procedural steps for determining dollar open-to-buy?
22. What is maximum inventory? How is it computed? What role does it have in determining unit open-to-buy?

Review Exam

True or False

_____ 1. Inventory assortment and support is the focus for dollar planning.

_____ 2. The fixed adjustment method usually works reasonably well in estimating future sales if a clear and stable sales trend has been established.

_____ 3. The stock-to-sales ratio method of planning inventory levels requires the retailer use a 2 stock units to 1 sales unit ratio.

_____ 4. The model stock list is used for planning inventory assortment and support for staple merchandise.

_____ 5. For most retailers, a periodic physical inventory is the fastest, easiest, and most time-saving method they have for obtaining sales information.

_____ 6. When the LIFO method of inventory costing is used, the cost of the oldest unit in stock determines the retailer's cost of goods sold.

_____ 7. Excessively high stock turnover rates could mean that the retailer is buying in too small quantities.

Multiple Choice

_____ 1. Planning the number of different product items the retailer should stock within a particular product line is concerned with planning the retailer's inventory _____.
a. investment
b. assortment
c. variety
d. support
e. width

_____ 2. The merchandise budget consists of the following stages of planning:
a. sales, stock levels, reductions, purchases, and promotions
b. sales, stock levels, reductions, purchases, and profit margins
c. sales, prices, stock levels, promotions, and purchases
d. locations, products, prices, services, and promotions
e. sales, stock levels, prices, promotions, and purchases

_____ 3. The _____ method begins each month with stock levels that equal the estimated sales for that month plus a safety stock in the event that actual sales exceed estimated sales.
a. basic stock
b. percentage variation
c. weeks' supply
d. stock-to-sales ratio
e. variable adjustment

_____ 4. The model stock list is used for the unit planning of _____ items.
a. key
b. staple
c. fashion
d. best selling
e. hot

_____ 5. A _____ inventory refers to a system whereby inventory is taken and information is gathered on a continual or ongoing basis using various accounting records to compute stock-on-hand at any given time.
a. perpetual book
b. perpetual physical
c. periodic book

d. periodic physical
e. dollar unit

_____ 6. Using the _____ method of inventory valuation, the retailer assumes that merchandise items are sold in the order in which they are purchased.
a. cost complement
b. LIFO
c. retail
d. FIFO
e. average

_____ 7. All of the following strategies are used by retailers to increase stock turnover rates, *except* _____.
a. limiting merchandise assortment
b. increasing promotions
c. increasing prices
d. limiting safety stock
e. stocking only popular brands

_____ 8. Unit open-to-buy equals maximum inventory _____ stock-on-hand _____ stock-on-order.
a. plus . . . plus
b. plus . . . minus
c. minus . . . plus
d. minus . . . times
e. minus . . . minus

STUDENT APPLICATIONS MANUAL

Investigative Projects: Practice and Applications

1. A number of general approaches and methods can be used to make sales estimates. The fixed and variable adjustment methods of forecasting were discussed in this chapter. Identify and discuss two additional sales estimating techniques. From the viewpoint of the retailer, what are the advantages and disadvantages of each? Under what circumstances is each method appropriate for estimating retail sales?
2. Gain the cooperation of a local independent retailer and develop a complete merchandising budget for a given product line utilizing the format discussed in the text. What difficulties did you encounter in developing the budget? How did you overcome these difficulties? What format changes would you recommend for improving the budgetary process as outlined in the text?
3. Secure an interview with a local department or specialty store buyer. Determine what product lines or items are included on the store's never-out list and why those products are on the list. Using the information gathered in the interview, develop a set of criteria and guidelines for determining what products should be included on the never-out list.
4. By making a visual survey of several hardware, variety, and sporting goods stores, identify and describe several examples of the visual inspection method used in a unit/periodic/physical inventory information system.
5. Retailers can calculate stock turnover in retail dollars, cost dollars, and units. Describe the circumstances and reasons why a retailer would employ each of these methods for calculating stock turnover.
6. Identify and explain several causes for low stock turnover rate.
7. What is the June dollar open-to-buy at retail for the sporting goods department, given the following information as of June 1:

Planned sales for June	$42,000
Planned reductions for June	$ 1,000
Planned stock for June 30	$50,000
Actual stock on June 1	$30,000
Existing purchase commitments	$ 4,000

   What is the June dollar open-to-buy at cost, assuming a 44 percent initial markup on retail?
8. From past experience, John Rogers knows that sales for men's underwear are characterized by a well-established pattern. Therefore, he expects to sell approximately 180 units per week. To guard against unexpected sales or delivery delays, John plans to maintain a four-week safety stock. Normally, John places reorders every eight weeks and allows four weeks for delivery. By checking the stock and purchase records, John determines that he has 600 units on hand and 200 units on order. What is John's unit open-to-buy?

Tactical Cases: Problems and Decisions

■ CASE 14–1
Value Shoes—Planning Monthly Sales and Stock Levels*

Value Shoes is a price-oriented family shoe store located in a community shopping center. Catering to the lower-income shopper, Value Shoes is a low-margin operation that requires careful attention to planning and controlling inventory. As owner and operator of Value Shoes, Tom Nelson strives to incorporate all the objective inventory control procedures he learned from attending several Small Business Administration seminars.

Today's task is to develop sales and stock plans for the children's shoe department. Given the sales seasonality of children's shoes, developing sales estimates and monthly stock plans can be challenging. Using the variable adjustment method, Tom arrived at an annual sales estimate of $9,000 for 1989. Tom now faces the tasks of calculating the planned monthly sales for each month and the beginning-of-the-month (BOM) stock for each month of the first quarter. If the annual turnover rate of four turns and the monthly sales pattern (see Exhibit A) hold true for 1989, then the task should not be too difficult.

ASSIGNMENT

Assume the role of Tom Nelson and complete the tasks of calculating the planned monthly sales and the BOM stock for January, February, and March.

*This case was prepared by Dale Lewison and John Thanopoulos, The University of Akron.

EXHIBIT A
Value Shoe Store: Monthly sales record, children's shoes*

	1984	1985	1986	1987	1988
January	400	400	500	600	600
February	300	400	400	500	700
March	300	400	500	600	800
April	800	800	900	1000	1200
May	700	700	800	800	900
June	400	500	600	500	700
July	200	300	300	500	700
August	600	600	600	700	800
September	900	1100	1400	1500	1800
October	500	700	600	700	800
November	400	500	500	600	700
December	700	800	900	1000	1200

*rounded to the nearest hundred

■ CASE 14–2
Baker's Mowers: Avoid Getting Trimmed*

It was the end of December 1990 and Tom Baker, the owner of Baker's Mowers, had some serious work set out before him. During the year his mower supplier had constantly raised prices until they had reached a cost of $150 per unit in the last shipment. Recently though, Tom had found another supplier of the same mower whose initial order unit price was $150 but would give Tom cumulative 10 percent discounts with each successive order during the year. The bottomed discount price was $120 and shipments as small as 25 units could be sent quarterly with the first one arriving on the first of April. Tom decided he would use this new supplier because the former supplier foresaw no price reductions in the future and Tom wanted to keep up his profits without raising the $300 retail price on his mowers.

Having researched as much as he could about next year's economic forecast, taking into consideration the area's tremendous housing growth, and seeing his nearest competitor close up, Tom Baker was predicting his mower sales to increase by $19,200. This figure didn't seem at all unreasonable considering the growth Baker's Mowers had achieved over the last two years.

As Tom began looking over the 1990 records, he was startled by the high ending inventory. He knew he was wasting money by tying up his funds in so much inventory and vowed that next year's ending inventory would be ten units. To help him plan his stock levels for each month, Tom was going to heed the advice in the *National Hardware Retailers* magazine and keep a 1.5 inventory to sales ratio.

The records also revealed that Tom always ended up with about 5 percent in reductions for the typical year: 3 percent due to markdowns, and 1 percent in discounts to friends, relatives, and landscapers. The really bad news though was that no matter how hard Tom tried, Baker's Mowers would have losses of one percent due either to theft or damage.

Armed with three years' worth of monthly sales figures (Exhibit A), Tom Baker reached for his calculator to begin some serious number crunching. His favorite basketball team, the Wildcats, would be on TV in three hours. Tom was determined to figure out next year's monthly sales estimates, how much to order from his new supplier, and be home before the game's opening tip off.

	1988	1989	1990
January	$1500	$1800	$ 2100
February	1500	1800	2100
March	3000	3300	3600
April	4500	4800	5100
May	6000	7200	8400
June	7500	8100	10500
July	4500	5100	7500
August	1500	3000	4500
September	1500	2100	2700
October	1500	1800	2100
November	600	1500	2400
December	300	1500	1800

EXHIBIT A
Baker's Mowers: Monthly sales figures (1988–1990)

ASSIGNMENT

Using the numbers in Exhibit A, determine the following:

1. Develop next year's monthly sales estimates.
2. Find the beginning of the month stock for each month in 1991.
3. Assuming that everything will go according to plan, determine the monthly purchases for Baker's Mowers.

*This case prepared by Jim Connell, The University of Akron.

ENDNOTES

1. See Gary Robins, "New Planning Systems," *Stores,* July 1989, 61–66.
2. "Planning for Size/Color," *Stores,* July 1989, 66.
3. See Stephen Bennett, "Selling Ideas for Spring," *Progressive Grocer,* January 1990, 13–18. And "Selling Ideas for Summer," *Progressive Grocer,* March 1990, 15–18.
4. William L. Clarke, "Integrating the Logistics of Merchandise Management," *Retail Control* (June/July 1987), 26.
5. See "NRMA's New POS Study," *Stores* (April 1987), 67–74.
6. See Daniel J. Sweeney, "Improving the Profitability of Retail Merchandising Decisions," *Journal of Marketing* 37 (January 1973), 60–68.

OUTLINE

OBJECTIVES

- Set specific, measurable price objectives consistent with the needs of both the consumer and the retailer.
- Assess the impact of demand, competition, cost, product, and legal considerations on the retailer's price-setting activities.
- Describe the methods by which retailers set their prices.
- Differentiate the numerous policies supplementing and modifying retail price-setting methods.
- Explain the need to adapt prices to the changing external and internal environmental conditions of the retail firm.
- Differentiate among the three basic types of price adjustments.
- Identify the necessities of price markdowns and explain the factors that determine when and how great a price markdown should be taken.

PART IV

PRICE STRATEGIES

Establishing and Adjusting the Retail Price

CHAPTER 15

GETTING OFF THE SALES TREADMILL

The best way to bring customers flocking into any retail store? Textbook answer: a major promotion with heavily advertised price cuts of 30%, 40%, or more. Just one problem. It doesn't work so well anymore. "You advertise 25% off these days and most customers just sneeze at it and wait for the 'real' sale."[1]

Bargain hunters, beware. Retailers are starting to do away with something that gets your juices flowing; the sale. In what is shaping up as a major shift in retail marketing, many big chains are scaling back regular prices and abandoning sales as their primary promotional weapon. Stirring in their usual dose of hype, the retailers call this new strategy "everyday low pricing."[2]

But industry sources believe most retailers continue to play the markdown game because customers have come to expect discounts on everything. "Once you start doing this, you're on a treadmill."[3]

The right price is one that consumers are willing and able to pay and willing to accept in exchange for merchandise and services. The right price allows the retailer to make a fair profit while providing the consumer with value satisfaction before, during, and after the sale. From the consumer's viewpoint, price can act as a forceful attraction or as an absolute repellent in the consumer's store-selection process. It can also serve as either an incentive or a deterrent in the decision to buy. Some consumers consider price the most important criterion in selecting stores and products; others are far less sensitive to price. Retailers view prices in terms of (1) profitability, or how much they will have left after covering the merchandise cost and operating expenses; (2) sales volume, or how many merchandise units they can sell at various prices; (3) consumer traffic, or how many consumers they can attract to the store using various price levels or strategies; and (4) store image, or what type of image they will project to consumers through different price levels, policies, and strategies.

This chapter examines price-setting objectives, determinants, methods, and policies as well as the various means of adjusting retail prices: discounts, markons, and markdowns. Figure 15–1 illustrates the pricing concerns of the retail manager.

FIGURE 15–1
The retailer's pricing concerns

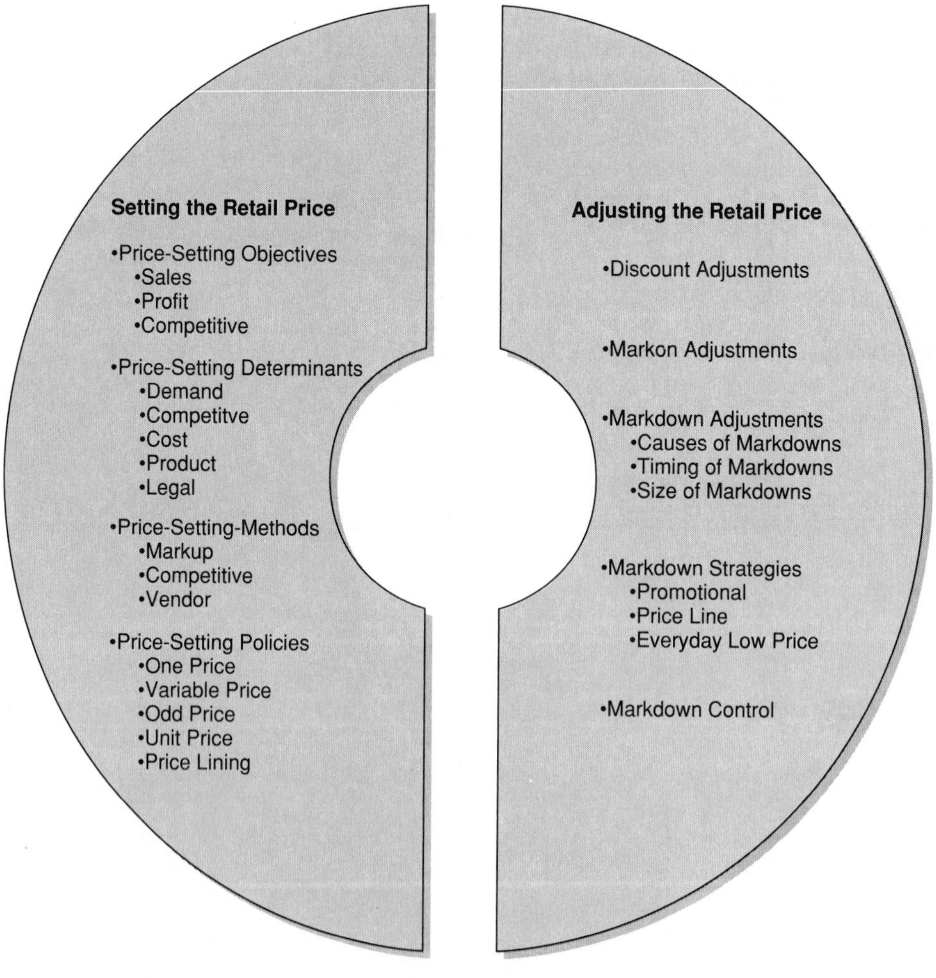

SETTING THE RETAIL PRICE

Price-Setting Objectives

In any decision-making process, the decision maker should establish objectives. Price setting is no exception. Before the retailer can effectively establish prices consistent both with the firm's requirements and the consumer's expectations, it should set specific, measurable objectives based on well-thought-out pricing guidelines. Retail price objectives are generally categorized in three groups: sales objectives, profit objectives, and competitive objectives.

Sales Objectives

Retailers usually state sales objectives in terms of either sales volume or market share. The primary reason for **setting sales-volume objectives** is to achieve future sales growth or to maintain current sales levels. Sales growth in the form of "beating last year's sales" by some percentage is a common objective for many retailers. How appropriate this kind of pricing objective is ultimately depends on its effect on profits.

Market-share objectives are price-setting goals that retailers set to increase or maintain their share of the total market. Market share is a measure of the retailer's sales position relative to all competitors in the same trading area, in terms of percentage share of total sales for that trading area. If *market-share growth* is the principal objective in setting prices, the retailer must realize that any increase in percentage share of the market must come at the expense of one or more of its competitors. Therefore, some type of aggressive action and retaliatory pricing actions should be anticipated from competitors seeking to protect their share of the market. As a pricing objective, market-share growth may be a preferred goal for a new and expanding product market rather than for an older one, because many competitors in the former situation are more interested in increasing their sales as opposed to their market share. In mature and stable product markets, however, *market-share maintenance* is generally the more accepted pricing objective. Price-cutting activities in mature markets will force competitors to meet the new price, lowering profit margins for all concerned.

Profit Objectives

Profit maximization and target return on investment and on net sales are the three most-cited profit objectives for guiding price-setting decisions. **Profit-maximization objectives** seek the highest possible profit through pricing and other merchandising activities. In practice, a profit-maximization objective is at the expense of wholesalers, manufacturers, and consumers. Such activities will lead to conflict, thereby jeopardizing the retailer's source of supply and damaging the retailer's customer image.

Target return objectives are profit objectives for guiding price-setting decisions. Target returns are usually expressed as a certain percentage return on either capital investment or net sales. *Return on investment* (ROI) is a ratio of profits to capital investments (facilities, fixtures, equipment, inventory, etc.). ROI is a measure of how efficiently a retailer is in using investment to generate profits. *Return on net sales* (ROS) is the percentage value derived by dividing dollar profit by net sales. To achieve this targeted return, retailers set prices by using markup percentages large enough to cover all appropriate operating expenses (payroll, rent, utilities, professional services, etc.), plus the desired dollar profit per unit needed to generate the targeted percentage return on net sales.

Competitive Objectives

Competitive price objectives also take several forms, including (1) meeting competition, (2) preventing competition, and (3) nonprice competition.[4] Some retailers simply follow the leader in their price-setting activities; their price objectives can be best described as meeting their major competitor's price. Certain retailers within a given trade area act as price leaders for some product lines. The price followers simply adjust their prices accordingly. Other retailers take preventing competition as their pricing objective and set their prices low enough to discourage additional competitors from entering the market. Other retailers prefer to avoid price competition; they would rather compete on the basis of better product or service offerings, better locations and facilities, greater promotional efforts, or any other merchandising activities except price.

Price-Setting Determinants

Each retailer faces several considerations in trying to establish a selling price that will both sell the merchandise and offer a profitable return. The retailer should examine demand, competitive, cost, product, and legal factors.

Demand Considerations

Consumers' perceptions of and reactions to different prices must be taken into account before making price-setting decisions. Some consumers' buying behavior closely reflects the **law of demand**; consumers will buy more products at lower prices than at higher prices. The retailer must consider the effects of different price levels on consumer demand.[5] This effect is called **price elasticity of demand**—a measure of the effect a price change has on consumer demand (i.e., the number of units sold). Demand elasticity describes the relationship between a percentage change in price and a percentage change in quantity sold. *Elastic demand* is a condition in which a change in price strongly influences consumer demand.[6] For example, consumer demand is more elastic for stock-up items (nonperishable goods like soap, toothpaste, canned foods, etc.) then for nonstock-up items (perishables and low usage rate goods).[7] *Inelastic demand* occurs when a change in price has little or no influence on consumer demand. A good way to remember the difference between elastic demand and inelastic demand is to consider the consumer's degree of *sensitivity* to the price change. Inelastic demand means that consumers are relatively insensitive to the change in price, whereas under elastic demand conditions they are sensitive to price changes.[8]

In some cases, changing the price of a merchandise item will change the demand for not only that item but also a different item. *Cross-elasticity of demand* occurs when a change in the price of one product results in a change in demand for another product. For example, the demand for a complementary product (e.g., film) may decrease as a result of increased prices and reduced demand for the product it complements (e.g., cameras). A different result can occur between "substitute" products. In this situation, cross-elasticity of demand might produce an increased demand for tea as the price of coffee rises. Retailers must watch the price-demand interplay among products closely so as to avoid costly pricing errors. Although it would be virtually impossible to formally determine the price elasticity of demand for each merchandise line carried, the retailer should develop a feel for which products are highly sensitive to changes in price.

Competitive Considerations

It is imperative to consider competitors' pricing actions in setting prices. Although prices need not equal those of competitors, the retailer should provide consumers with a price difference they can accept and justify based on differences in service, location, and product-mix factors. In response to tough competition from T.J. Maxx stores and Hit or Miss shops, Marshalls discount apparel stores fought back by selling more lower-priced goods; the result of this strategy was that customers believed quality was deteriorating. Marshalls is trying to re-establish its image by emphasizing its name brands, renovating stores, and redesigning merchandise displays.[9]

Excessive price competition among retailers in the form of pricing "wars" usually does not benefit any of the parties, and retailers must realize that price competition is one of the least distinctive forms of competition. A retailer's price cuts can be instantaneously offset by competitors that easily match the lower price. Given the relative brevity of price competition (because of the high likelihood of precipitating price reprisals), retailers must consider alternative forms of competition (product, service, promotion, and so on) before engaging in aggressive price-setting activities.[10]

The freedom a retailer enjoys in setting prices depends on estimates of its competitive position. A retailer that judges its competitive position as strong because of a distinctive retail mix, highly loyal consumers, or a unique store image has greater freedom in price-setting decisions. On the other hand, "me-too" retailers that lack distinctiveness in the nonprice areas of their operations are restricted to a me-too pricing strategy. Finally, the retailer must recognize that the competitor's price is more important for some merchandise items than for others. First, the retailer must closely consider products that consumers purchase frequently and the supplier distributes intensively because consumers can easily make price comparisons. Second, for products with high unit value—big-ticket items—retailers need to seriously consider competitors' prices. The retailer can set prices for these kinds of products below, with, or above those of competitors, depending on the type of price image desired.[11]

Cost Considerations

A major determinant in any price-setting decision is the cost the retailer must pay for merchandise. In defining merchandise cost, it is important to include not only the actual cost of the merchandise but also all costs incurred in getting the merchandise into the store and preparing it for sale. Retailers determine merchandise costs by following the procedure outlined in Figure 15–2. Calculating merchandise cost this way gives the retailer a more accurate picture of the true cost. For many retailers, merchandise cost is both a reference and starting point for price-setting decisions. Their approach to the pricing problem is cost-oriented; they set the retail selling price of a product at a level high enough to cover not only the cost of the merchandise but also the fixed and variable expenses associated with merchandising the product plus an additional profit margin.

Product Considerations

Retailers should not make price-setting decisions without considering the product's characteristics. Different products can command different prices at different times and in different locations.

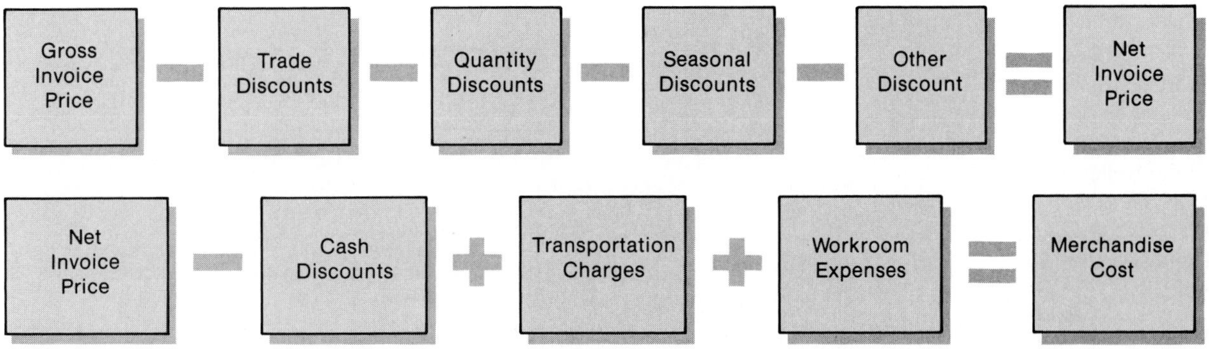

FIGURE 15–2
Determining merchandise cost

Retailers must consider *product perishability* and its associated risks. Perishable products often require higher initial prices to cover markdowns that become necessary as the product loses its marketability. Product perishability takes several forms:

- *Physical perishability*—loss of marketability resulting from physical damage or deterioration of the product
- *Style or fashion perishability*—a loss of marketability as a result of style, fashion, or model obsolescence (as in being "out of style" or "the old model")
- *Seasonal perishability*—loss of marketability because the product is out of season

It is also worth noting that a retailer may decide to set a lower initial price on some highly perishable products to move them out before a loss in marketability occurs; for example, a retailer might place a low price on a quart of fresh strawberries during the strawberry-picking season.

Product quality, whether perceived or real, is another major product determinant the retailer should examine before setting a price. For example, few cars actually need premium gas but ads often warn that lesser brands may cause engine damage. The tactic is working: Premium now accounts for 28 percent of the market. Quality is the big motivation today.[12] Depending on the price/quality image the retailer wants to project, one of several possible pricing strategies can be used. Figure 15–3 illustrates nine possible pricing strategies based on product quality. From this figure, we see that the retailer can assume quite a number of roles in offering a particular product-quality level at various price levels.

Product uniqueness is a characteristic that retailers can exploit to realize a premium price. Consumers who seek something different tend to be insensitive to price and therefore willing to pay higher prices for products that exhibit originality.[13]

Legal Considerations

Price-setting decisions are subject to numerous legal constraints. According to law, any pricing activity that any governmental agency considers to be a present or probable restraint on trade or an unfair trade practice can be illegal. Price setting is perhaps the most regulated aspect of the retailer's business.

Price-Setting Methods

Price-setting decisions are both an art and a science. A policy of setting low prices might well produce high sales volumes, but result in inadequate profit margins. High prices usually allow for excellent profit margins; however, the merchandise must be sold before those profits can be realized. Knowing when a price is too high or too low is an

FIGURE 15–3
Product-quality considerations in price-setting decisions (source: Phillip Kotler, *Principles of Marketing* [Englewood Cliffs, NJ: Prentice-Hall, 1980], 402)

PRODUCT QUALITY \ PRODUCT PRICE	High	Medium	Low
High	Premium Strategy	Penetration Strategy	Superbargain Strategy
Medium	Overpricing Strategy	Average-Quality Strategy	Bargain Strategy
Low	Hit-and-run Strategy	Shoddy-Goods Strategy	Cheap-Goods Strategy

art that comes with the experience of being in the business. Nevertheless, certain price-setting methods blend the art of experience with the science of retail mathematics.

Markup Method of Pricing

Markup is the difference between the cost of the merchandise and its retail price. Although markup appears to be a relatively simple concept, it incorporates several complex relationships expressed in a variety of ways.

Dollar markup is a cost-oriented approach to setting prices wherein the retailer adds to the cost of the merchandise a dollar amount large enough to cover related operating expenses and to provide a given dollar profit. Dollar markup is most frequent for big-ticket items (e.g., jewelry) because dollar values simply appear more real. However, dollar markup can be deceptive when one compares different types of merchandise.

Percentage markups are calculated to facilitate the process of setting prices and to permit comparisons between merchandise lines and departments. In calculating percentage markups, the retailer must first determine the markup base. Markups can be calculated on the cost of the merchandise or on the retail selling price. Formulas for calculating percentage markups are illustrated in Figure 15–4. Suppose, for example, that a hardware retailer pays $80 for a power lawnmower that sells at retail for $150. The retailer's percentage markup on cost would be 87.5 percent, whereas on retail it is 46.7 percent. The calculations are as follows:

$$\text{markup percentage at cost} = \frac{\$150 - \$80}{\$80} = 87.5\%$$

$$\text{markup percentage at retail} = \frac{\$150 - \$80}{\$150} = 46.7\%$$

In practice, retailers prefer to compute markups on the retail base. Given its popularity, we will focus on retail-based markups for the remainder of our discussion.

Retailers find a **cumulative markup** on a group of merchandise items (e.g., a product line) useful in daily operations. This cumulative markup cannot be computed by averaging the individual markups on each merchandise item in the group; instead, the retailer must calculate cumulative markup based on the weight each item contributes to the total markup of all the items in the merchandise group. To illustrate, the buyer for the men's department of a large specialty store wants to determine the

$$\text{Markup Percentage (at cost)} = \text{Retail Selling Price} - \text{Cost of Merchandise} \div \text{Cost of Merchandise}$$

$$\text{Markup Percentage (at retail)} = \text{Retail Selling Price} - \text{Cost of Merchandise} \div \text{Retail Selling Price}$$

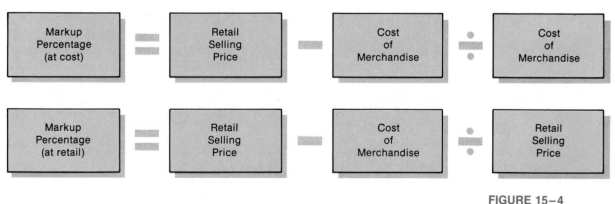

FIGURE 15–4
Determining markup percentage (at cost or at retail)

cumulative markup on a stock of men's summer suits. A check of inventory and purchase records for the month of June reveals that the month started with an inventory costing $20,000 that retails for $40,000. Additional purchases costing $16,000 and retailing for $30,000 have been added since the beginning of the month. The total cost and retail value of the merchandise follows:

	Cost	Retail
beginning stock	$20,000	$40,000
additional purchases	+$16,000	+$30,000
total stock	$36,000	$70,000

The cumulative markup percentage at retail is computed as

$$\text{markup percentage at retail} = \frac{\text{retail (\$)} - \text{cost (\$)}}{\text{retail}}$$

$$= \frac{\$70{,}000 - \$36{,}000}{\$70{,}000} = 48.6\%$$

Using the cumulative markup percentage, the retailer can adjust markup plans throughout the merchandising season.

Up to this point, we have discussed markup in general terms as the difference between the cost of merchandise and its retail price; however, we must now distinguish among three kinds of markup: the initial markup, the maintained markup, and the gross margin.

Initial markup refers to the difference between merchandise cost and the original retail price. Stated differently, it represents the first markup placed on a merchandise item. Rarely, however, does the retailer receive the initial markup for each item within a merchandise line because of the retail reductions that decrease the original retail price set for the item. Retail reductions take the form of shortages, discounts, and markdowns.

A **maintained markup** is the difference between gross merchandise cost and actual selling price. Stated differently, maintained markup equals initial markup minus all retail reductions; that is, initial markup is what the retailer originally hoped to receive, and maintained markup is what the retailer actually received. Although retailers do not usually expect to gain the full initial markup on merchandise sales, they still need to use initial markup as a profit-margin planning tool.

The **initial markup percentage** is the key element in guiding the retailer's price-setting decisions. Essentially, this pricing strategy establishes the initial markup percentage—and therefore the retail price—to achieve a specified target profit. The basic formula for calculating the initial markup percentage is shown in Figure 15–5. As shown, the initial markup percentage equals the sum of the operating expenses, operating profit, alterations cost, and retail reduction, divided by the sum of the net sales and retail reduction. The initial markup must be large enough to cover store operating expenses and retail reductions as well as to provide a profit and to cover any alteration costs. Alteration costs (e.g., hemming trousers, assembling products, etc.) are added because they represent a legitimate expense the retailer incurs in making the merchandise more marketable.

As a brief illustration of the initial markup percentage formula, consider the following problem. A sporting goods retailer wants to know the appropriate initial markup percentage on a new line of tennis rackets. Planning records reveal the figures: (1) estimated operating expenses of 28 percent, (2) planned operating profit of 12 percent, (3) estimated alteration cost (e.g., stringing rackets) of 4 percent, (4) expected shortages of 2 percent, (5) planned markdowns of 4 percent, and (6) estimated

$$\text{Initial Markup }\% = \frac{\text{Operating Expenses }\% + \text{Operating Profit }\% - \text{Cash Discounts }\% + \text{Alterations Costs }\% + \text{Retail Reduction }\%}{\text{Net Sales }100\% + \text{Retail Reductions }\%}$$

$$\text{Initial Markup }\% = \frac{\text{Maintained Markup }\% + \text{Retail Reduction }\%}{\text{Net Sales }100\% + \text{Retail Reductions }\%}$$

$$\text{Maintained Markup }\% = \text{Initial Markup }\% - \left(\text{Retail Reduction }\% \times 100\%\text{—Initial Markup }\%\right)$$

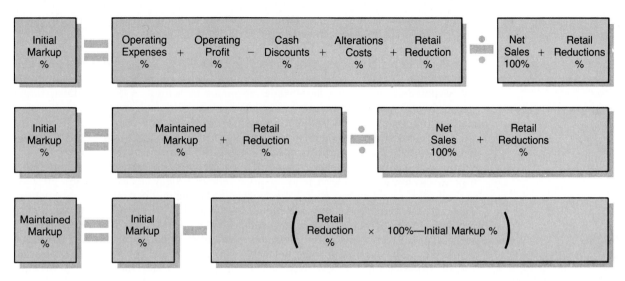

FIGURE 15–5
Computing the initial and maintained markup percentage

employee discounts of 1 percent. Using the preceding formula, the initial markup percentage should be as follows:

$$\text{initial markup }\% = \frac{28\% + 12\% + 4\% + 7\%}{100\% + 7\%}$$
$$= \frac{51}{107} = 47.7\%$$

To determine the actual percentage markup realized after the foregoing computations have been completed, the retailer can use the maintained markup percentage formula expressed in Figure 15–5. For example, the retailer had originally planned for an initial markup of 40 percent, and retail reductions amounting to 8 percent actually occurred:

$$\text{maintained markup }\% = .40 - [.08(1.00 - .40)]$$
$$= .352 \text{ or } 35.2\%$$

The retail reduction percentage is adjusted because it was based on net sales, while the initial markup percentage was based on the original retail price.

Gross margin refers to the difference between net sales and total merchandise costs. As such, it is closely related to maintained markup (net sales minus gross merchandise costs). The differences between gross margin and maintained markup or between total merchandise cost and gross merchandise costs are adjustments for cash discounts and alteration costs. This difference can be illustrated as follows:

gross margin = maintained markup + cash discounts − alteration costs
maintained markup = gross margin − cash discounts + alteration costs

If there were no cash discounts or alteration costs, then gross margin would equal maintained markup.

Competitive Pricing Method

A competitive pricing method means the retailer sets prices in relation to competitors' prices. It is largely a judgmental price-setting method whereby the retailer uses competitive prices as reference points for price-setting decisions. Competitive price setting is popular among some retailers because it is simple to administer; the basic decision rules are to price either below, at, or above competitors' price levels.

One price-setting alternative is **pricing below the competition**. Mass merchandisers, such as hypermarkets, superstores, and discounters, engage in pricing strategies that attempt to undersell competitors. Pricing below competition is a price-setting policy aimed at generating large dollar revenues to achieve a desired dollar target return. In other words, these retailers practice a low-price, high-volume, high-turnover pricing strategy.

To successfully sell merchandise at low prices and still generate sufficient profit margins calls for certain merchandising strategies. To price below competition, the retailer not only must secure merchandise at a lower cost, but must also keep operating expenses as low as possible. The lower-price retailer usually stocks and sells "presold" or "self-sold" merchandise, thereby reducing advertising and personal selling expenses. Typically, these retailers sell name brands at the lowest prices to build traffic and to promote a low-price image. Low-price retailers stock private brands of many standard items that consumers cannot easily compare with other retailers' private brands and on which they can receive high margins at the lower prices. These retailers keep their service offerings at the minimum levels necessary to sell the merchandise; any nonessential services they offer carry a separate, additional charge. Their physical facilities are spartan and project an austere image. In addition, the structure of the store's management organization is generally flat (the number and specialization of managers are minimal and general). Generally speaking, the profit strategy of the retailer that elects to price below competition is to keep expenses low to keep prices low; this in turn attracts consumers and generates a profitable sales level through rapid inventory turnover rates.

The second alternative method of competitive price setting open to the retailer is selling a merchandise item at the "going" or traditional price within the store's general trading area. **Pricing with the competition** implies that the retailer has, in general, elected to de-emphasize the price factor as a major merchandising tool, and instead decided to compete on a location, product, service, and promotion basis. Competitive price parity does not necessarily imply that the retailer matches every price exactly. Usually, this policy involves setting prices that are within an acceptable range of the competitive standard. Small price discrepancies, especially if they reflect proportional variances in service levels, either go unnoticed or are accepted by consumers. In selecting this middle-of-the-road strategy, retailers should recognize that in recent years being mainstream is to be mundane. "Solid middle-of-the-road names such as Sears, Holiday Inn, and Smirnoff, are struggling against a slew of new competitors that strike from two sides above and below. . . . Getting stuck in the middle is a terrible fate. . . . It's the phenomenon of being a mass brand as the market splinters."[14]

Some retailers attempt to differentiate themselves by setting prices above the going trade-area price. Although the higher-priced stores do not expect to achieve the turnover rates of their lower-priced competitors, they do expect their products to make a substantially *greater per-unit profit* than the lower-priced retailer's products. Strategically, if the retailer chooses **pricing above the competition**, then it must include several of these consumer benefits: (1) many free services, (2) higher-quality merchandise, (3) exclusive merchandise, (4) personalized sales attention, (5) plusher shopping atmosphere, (6) full staffing in all functional areas of store operations, (7) prestige image, (8) superconvenient locations, and (9) longer store hours. In other words, the retailer of higher-priced merchandise must provide consumers with a total product having functional, aesthetic, and service features that give consumers the psychological benefits they expect from buying, using, and possessing the product. Many exclusive specialty shops and some department stores engage in price-setting strategies that establish prices above those of less-prestigious competitors.

Vendor Pricing Method

A third price-setting alternative is to let the manufacturer or wholesaler determine the retail price. This type of price setting assumes the form of a "suggested retail price." Vendors suggest retail prices by supplying the retailer with a price list, printing the price on the package, or affixing a price tag to the merchandise. While they are not legally required to use the suggested retail price, many retailers think it represents a fair estimate of the going market price for certain products. Although the vendor method of setting prices does relieve the retailer of that difficult task, it is not appropriate for many products and many retailers. As guidelines for retailers, the vendor's suggested price is not appropriate when (1) it fails to provide a sufficient margin to cover merchandise costs, store operating expenses, and an adequate profit; (2) it fails to stimulate sufficient sales; (3) it simply is not competitive with merchandise of a similar quality; or (4) it fails to provide the retailer's customers with the value they deserve.

Price-Setting Policies

Retailers are also guided by a number of price-setting policies that supplement and modify price-setting methods. For example, a retailer may set prices by using the markup method. The established retail price (e.g., $40) is then modified to accommodate an odd-pricing policy (e.g., $39.95). This section discusses several price-setting policies: the one-price policy, the variable-price policy, the multiple-price policy, odd-pricing, unit pricing, and price lining.

Most U.S. retailers follow a **one-price policy**, charging *all* customers the same price for the same product under similar circumstances. In contrast to many foreign consumers, most U.S. consumers are accustomed to paying the established price marked on the merchandise. Price "haggling" or "bargaining" is usually limited to big-ticket items, such as automobiles and appliances, and to used merchandise. Bargaining over the price for big-ticket items often centers on the allowance the customer can receive for a trade-in. A one-price policy facilitates the speed at which each transaction can be made, helps simplify the retailer's various accounting records, reduces the retailer's need for sales personnel, and makes a self-service strategy possible. Some retailers have carried the one-price concept to the ultimate limit; that is, all products in the store are priced at one or a few set prices. One Price Clothing Stores offer their merchandise for six dollars. Simply $6 is another chain that follows suit.[15]

A **variable-price policy** allows the customer to negotiate the final selling price. The best bargainers receive the lowest prices. Retailers that use variable pricing deal in merchandise with one or more of the following characteristics: (1) high initial markups, (2) need for personal selling, (3) unstandardized or specialized product features, (4) service requirements, and (5) infrequent purchase rates. Variable pricing gives the retailer price flexibility and increases its ability to adjust to the consumer's purchase motivations, but it can increase the retailer's labor costs, selling time, and dissatisfaction among any customers who were unable to negotiate the same low price as some other customers.

A **multiple-price policy** attempts to increase both unit and dollar sales volume. This pricing strategy gives customers a discount for making quantity purchases; that is, the retailer offers a reduced price if consumers are willing to purchase several units at the multiple-unit price. For example, the retailer can price a can of peas at $.50 each or three for $1.37. Essentially, multiple-unit pricing is a form of psychological pricing, in that many consumers have been conditioned to expect a bargain price if they buy in multiple quantities. Retailers commonly use multiple-unit pricing with products purchased regularly and frequently and characterized by a low per-unit price.

Odd pricing is the strategy of setting prices that end in odd numbers (e.g., $.49, $1.99, $9.95, and $29.50). By setting prices below even-dollar amounts, the retailer is

WORLD OF RETAILING

Business Ethics

An Effective Pricing Tactic or A Questionable Business Ethic?

It seems as though it should be good news for shoppers: Big retailers increasingly are promising to match the lowest advertised price a shopper can find.

But there's a cloud in all this silver lining. The marketing pitches are largely a boon to the stores, drawing customers by giving them what can be a false sense of security.

When a store pledges to match a competitor's advertised prices, it isn't promising that all its prices are the lowest in town. What's more, such stores expect only a small percentage of shoppers to try to collect on price-matching promises.

"Retailers have gone into the business of selling price insurance," says Leo J. Shapiro, a market researcher in Chicago. A price-matching pledge, he adds, amounts to "an insurance policy that shoppers won't feel foolish."

Benefits for a Select Few

Critics question the fairness of the policies, which allow merchants to cut special deals with only the most conscientious comparison shoppers. "That's the deceptive part," says Robert Kahn, an industry consultant and newsletter publisher who often criticizes retailing practices. "Retailers don't really have an intent to sell for lower prices [than competitors] or they would meet that price for everybody."

Ivan Png, a pricing specialist at the Graduate School of Management at the University of California at Los Angeles, says price-matching policies actually give merchants "a way to keep prices a little higher for the loyal customers while giving a lower price to new customers the store is trying to attract. It's a way to make more money," he adds.

Price-matching pledges proliferated in the early 1980s, as retailers responded to heavier competition and a growing bargain consciousness among shoppers. The tactic was first used in the cutthroat consumer-electronics, auto-supply, and general discount-store businesses, but it spread. So many stores began using the policies as a marketing pitch that mainstream merchants had little choice but to start making the claim, too.

Late last year, Montgomery Ward & Co. expanded its price-matching policy

relying on a psychological ploy in which consumers perceive odd prices as substantially below even prices (e.g., $2.95 is perceived to be considerably less than $3.00). The theory is that consumers will think of a $2.95 price in terms of $2.00 rather than $3.00.

The strategy of odd pricing varies with the general price level of the product. Products with low per-unit prices (under $5) are odd priced at one or two cents below an even price (e.g., $.49, $1.99, and $3.98). As the per-unit price increases, products are priced at odd values that represent a greater reduction from even prices. For example, products ranging in price from $10 to $20 tend to be odd priced at $9.95 or $19.95—a five-cent differential. Nine- and five-dollar odd endings are common among big-ticket items (e.g., $199 and $495). While nine and five are the most common odd-price endings, retailers also use three and seven to project a bargain-price image.

Given the multiplicity of package sizes and shapes together with the diversity of price tags and product labels, many consumers cannot determine which purchase is the best value for the money. As a result, some retailers have initiated a unit-pricing system to eliminate this uncertainty. **Unit pricing** is the retailing practice of posting prices on a per-unit-measurement basis. By stating the price per ounce, pound, quart, or yard for each brand, the retailer helps the consumer compare prices among products of different sizes, shapes, and quantities. Per-unit price tags are usually posted on shelf facings from its electronics and auto-supply departments to all items in its stores. And on March 1, Sears, Roebuck & Co., the nation's largest retailer, instituted a similar pledge as part of its move to a competitive policy called "everyday low pricing."

"We think it would be uncompetitive not to have a price-matching policy when many of our competitors do," says Thomas E. Morris, vice president of marketing at Sear's merchandise group. Sears, he says, considers its pledge a way "to communicate to the customer a confidence that the prices are good throughout the store."

Price-matching policies typically require shoppers to produce a competitor's ad showing a lower price for an identical item. Most stores also offer to match or beat their competitors' advertised prices for 30 days after a purchase.

Retailers say they are responding to the fact that consumers nowadays compare prices more often than in the past and wait for sales to make purchases, particularly with big ticket items. Offering to match a competitor's price gives merchants "a way of intercepting these shoppers," says Sid Doolittle, a partner in the Chicago retail consulting firm of McMillan Doolittle. "It's an important sale-closer."

But retail-industry executives and consultants readily concede that few shoppers actually bother to collect on the price guarantees.

Some companies claim that this is because their prices are truly competitive. But others acknowledge that most shoppers simply don't want to go to the trouble of doing the necessary research to get what they believe will be only a small price differential. I don't think the average person has the time to go out seeing if they got the very lowest price in town. . . . Price-matching policies are also more limited than they first appear because they usually apply only to "identical" items. Appliances and electronic goods are among the best merchandise to compare. But clothing and household goods often carry private labels, meaning they are made exclusively for one store. Sears, for example, still sells mostly house brands, though it is adding national brands at a furious pace.

Source: Francine Schwadel, "Who Wins with Price-Matching Plans." Reproduced with permission from *The Wall Street Journal,* January 16, 1989, p. B1.

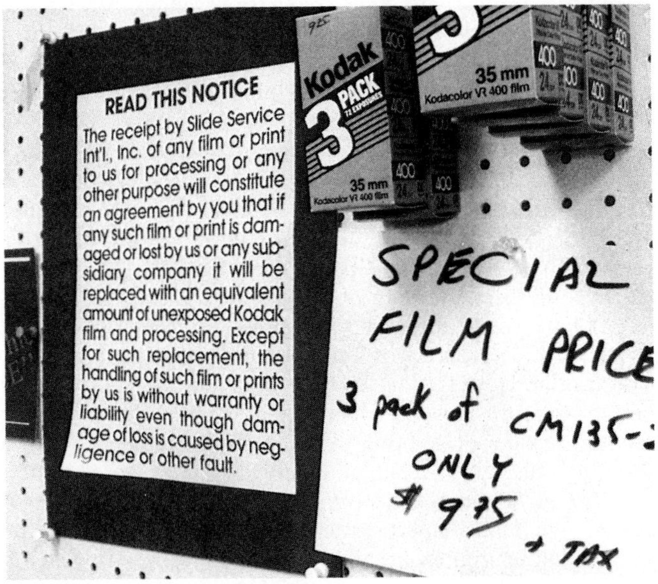

Multiple pricing suggests that the consumer is getting a bargain by buying in quantity, which may not always be true.

Odd pricing leads the consumer to perceive an item's cost as substantially lower than it would be at an even price.

directly above or below the product. Maintaining a unit price system usually means that the retailer will incur additional time, labor, equipment, and material expenses.

The objective of a **price-lining** policy is to direct retail prices at a targeted consumer group. To accomplish this objective, the retailer must perform two tasks. First, the retailer must identify the appropriate pricing zone for each targeted consumer group. A **pricing zone** is a range of prices that appeals to a particular group of consumers either for *demographic reasons* (e.g., income or occupation); *psychographic reasons* (e.g., lifestyle or personality); *product usage reasons* (e.g., heavy or light users); or *product benefit reasons* (e.g., economy, function, or sociability). Usually, retailers identify price zones in broad terms; for example, economy price range, intermediate or family price range, and prestige or luxury price range. Although most retailers tend to focus on one broadly defined price range, some retailers try to cover more than one range (e.g., middle-to-high). but they rarely try to appeal to all three ranges. Attempting to cover the entire price range would defeat the target-marketing objective of a price-lining strategy.

Pricing lines are *specific pricing* **points** established within pricing zones. Assume, for example, that a specialty store retailer has identified three pricing zones for men's suits: (1) the low-range suit (under $100), (2) the middle-range suit ($100 to $200), and (3) the high-range suit (above $200). Also suppose the retailer has targeted the middle-price-range consumer as the one to whom it wishes to appeal. Then, the retailer might establish price lines at $119.95, $159.95, and $189.95. The use of price lines is commonly associated with shopping goods and in particular with wearing apparel. Figure 15–6 illustrates one hypothesized example of the potential range of pricing zones and points within the fashion apparel industry for department store operations.

A price-lining policy has several advantages for both consumer and retailer. Advantages for the consumer are that (1) it facilitates comparison among merchandise items, and (2) it reduces shopping confusion and frustration and helps the consumer make purchase decisions. For the retailer, price lining (1) simplifies the personal selling effort, (2) makes advertising and sales promotion more effective, (3) increases the chances of trading up the customer to the next price, (4) creates an image of good merchandise depth and support, and (5) simplifies the buying process, because the buyer secures only merchandise that can be profitably priced at a given pricing point.

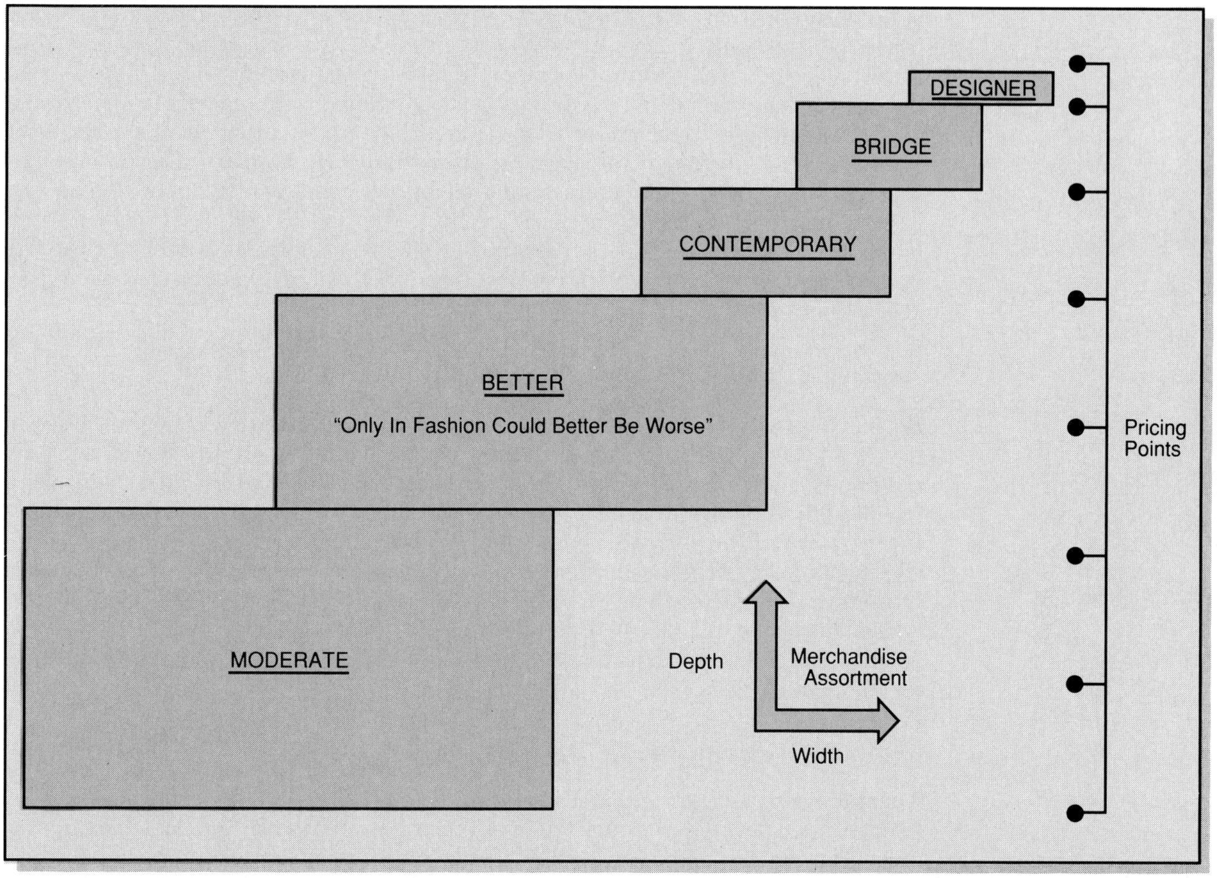

*Michael Gross, fashion writer for the *New York Times*.

FIGURE 15–6
Conceptualization of various pricing zones and pricing points for fashion apparel within a department store product mix

A price-lining policy also creates some difficulties. If the retailer does not carefully establish pricing points, it is likely to project to consumers an image of inadequate merchandise assortment and consequently eliminate customers who are either above or below the price lines they seek. A second potential problem is that retailers find it extremely difficult to reduce one line without reducing all lines. To do so destroys the carefully planned spread among all price lines. Price lining also makes it easier for competitors to develop successful competitive-pricing strategies. A limited number of price lines might well aid competitors in planning counter-price strategies. Finally, during times of rising costs, it is difficult to maintain price lines without reducing product quality.

ADJUSTING THE RETAIL PRICE

Price adjustments are one means for the retailer to adapt to changing external and internal environmental conditions. Retailers often find it necessary to adjust prices either upward or downward. The three basic types of adjustment are discounts, markons, and markdowns.

Discount Adjustments

In the previous discussion on developing the merchandise budget, we examined the role of markdowns, discounts, and shortages in planning retail reductions. **Discounts** were defined as reductions in the original retail price, granted to store employees as special fringe benefits and to special customers (e.g., clergy, senior citizens, and some disadvantaged consumers) in recognition of their special circumstances. Regardless of the reason for granting the discount, each discount given represents a downward adjustment in price, and as such has a direct impact on profit margins. Employee discounts are a customary privilege in many retail organizations. They represent a supplementary means of compensating employees and are frequently used as a motivational tool. Customer discounts are granted to special consumer segments for a number of reasons. Drugstores frequently give "golden-agers" discounts to customers over the age of 65. Sales to other business or professional organizations are often made at a discount price.

Markon Adjustments

Retailers use the term *markon* in a variety of ways. Here, however, **markon** refers to markups taken after the initial selling price has been established. In essence, a markon represents an additional markup and an upward adjustment in the initial selling price. Upward adjustments are needed to cover increases in wholesale prices and operating expenses as well as to correct consumers' quality perceptions of merchandise. When consumers believe the quality of a product is questionable because of its low price, retailers sometimes can correct this misconception by increasing the price, thereby taking advantage of the perceived price-quality relationship. Retailers also take additional markons when the demand for an item is high and consumer price sensitivity for the item is low.

Markdown Adjustments

A **markdown** is a downward adjustment in the original selling price of a merchandise item. A markdown represents the difference between what the merchandise was originally valued at and what it actually sells for. Markdowns, together with shortages and employee and customer discounts, are the three major factors retailers consider in planning retail reductions. Retailers use both dollars and percentages to express markdowns. "All men's slacks reduced $5!" is a typical dollar markdown expression. Per-unit **markdown percentages** are computed as a percentage of the reduced selling price or as a percentage of the original selling price. The latter expression is generally referred to as the off-retail markdown percentage.

The formula used for computing per-unit markdowns as a percentage of the reduced price is shown in Figure 15–7. For example, a dress originally priced at $30 is reduced to $20; the markdown as a percentage of the reduced price would be ($30 − $10)/$20 or 50 percent. This procedure is generally preferred for expressing reduced prices. The **off-retail markdown percentage** formula is also shown in Figure 15–7. The off-retail markdown percentage on the same dress would be 33.33 percent or ($30 − $20)/$30.

Causes of Markdowns

Retailers must take markdowns for a number of reasons, some of which are beyond the retailer's control. In other cases, markdowns are caused by errors in the retailer's judgment. Markdown causes can be categorized as buying, selling, and operational related.

Buying-Related Causes

Many markdowns result from retailers' errors in buying or procuring merchandise. Price reductions are often necessary to adjust for errors in the assortment, support, and

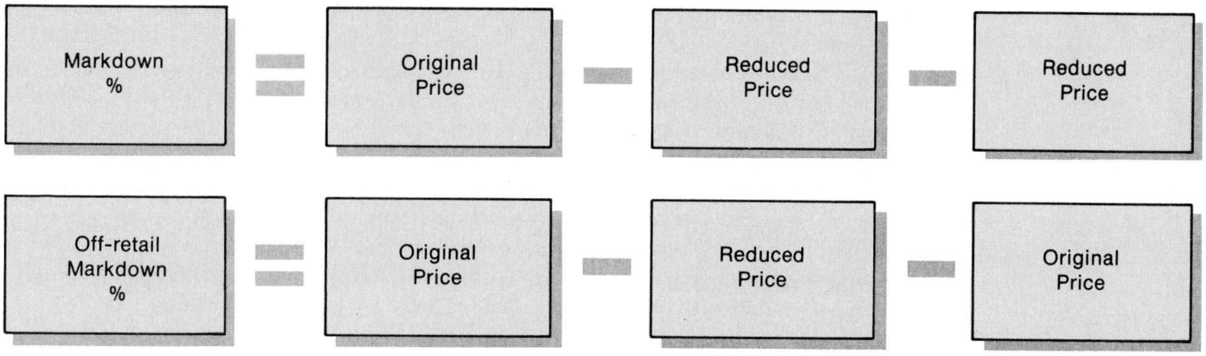

FIGURE 15–7
Determining markdown percentage

quality of merchandise the retailer purchased, as well as for mistakes in timing of purchases and selection of suppliers.

Assortment errors occur when the retailer buys brands, styles, models, sizes, colors, and materials that do not match what consumers want to buy. Assortment errors are serious not only because they necessitate markdowns, but also because they can require major price reductions to move the merchandise. Very attractive prices are typically the only way to sell merchandise the consumer does not really want.

Support errors are quantity errors that result when the retailer buys too much merchandise. Overbuying and overstocking certain merchandise items cause the retailer to tie up capital that could be invested in more profitable merchandise. Support errors occur when the retailer fails to plan sales, stocks, and purchases adequately or fails to execute the plans outlined on the merchandise budget and merchandise list.

Timing errors occur when retailers secure merchandise at the wrong time; they fail to match retail inventories with what their consumers want when they want it. In these cases, markdowns become necessary because the retailer faces surplus merchandise at the end of a selling season. Reordering at the height of a selling season and late shipments are two common causes for surplus merchandise.

Misjudging the quality of merchandise consumers expect is another reason retailers take markdowns. To move merchandise with unacceptable materials or workmanship, retailers must reduce prices.

The final buying-related cause of markdowns is the retailer's *selection of suppliers*. The retailer should evaluate the service-performance levels of each supplier. Late, incorrect, and damaged shipments all contribute to the retailer's need to take price reductions.

Selling-Related Causes. Even buying and securing the right merchandise in the right quantity at the right time are not enough to avoid unplanned price reductions; retailers must also control their selling activities. Selling-related causes of markdowns include errors in pricing, attempts to stimulate sales or to gain competitive price parity, and various policies and practices relating to the sale of merchandise.

A *pricing error* is any set price that does not create customer interest in the merchandise. Initial prices can be set too high or too low. High prices result in lost sales because consumers' perceptions of value are not satisfied. Low prices result in customer concern over quality. In either case, price adjustments are needed to match customers' perceptions of value and quality.

Retailers frequently use markdowns to *stimulate* sales. They may use this purposeful reduction of prices to attract additional consumer traffic into the store, to introduce a new line of merchandise, to boost customer interest during a slack sales period, to reduce inventories on slow-moving merchandise, or for a host of other reasons. Sales-stimulation markdowns can take the form of loss or low-price leaders, special or promotional prices, a multi-unit pricing scheme, or the use of coupons and premiums.

Sometimes retailers use markdowns to achieve *competitive parity*. Direct and indirect competitors that sell the same (or similar) merchandise at lower prices have a comparative shopping advantage over other retailers in their trading areas. Retailers take markdowns to achieve competitive price parity when they cannot justify the price differential on the basis of additional customer services, unique store-image characteristics, or general convenience factors such as time and place utility.

Selling policies also can create conditions that lead to markdowns. A policy of "aggressive selling" (e.g., trading the customer up to higher-priced merchandise, selling the customer more than is desired, making false or misleading claims about product performance) can lead to an above-average rate of merchandise returns. It may be late in the selling season by the time the merchandise makes it back to the sales floor, and the retailer must reduce prices to clear the merchandise out by the end of the season. Some retailers engage in "umbrella merchandising"—stocking a limited number of high-fashion merchandise items, such as designer clothing and limited editions, to display merchandise that creates or enhances the store's contemporary image. Retailers often stock this promotional merchandise knowing that much of it will require drastic price reductions to be sold. Another policy that leads to markdowns is "assortment maintenance"—the image-building policy of carrying a complete selection until late into the selling season—that requires markdowns in the form of clearance sales. Finally, a selling policy that encourages customers to take home merchandise and is supported by a liberal return policy increases the likelihood of taking markdowns.

Operationally Related Causes. In a retail store's day-to-day operations, both internal and external circumstances arise that create the need for some type of corrective action in the form of a price reduction. Two such circumstances are market shifts and distressed merchandise.

Market shifts are changes in demand levels for a particular merchandise line. Faddish and fashion merchandise often have fast and sometimes unexpected changes in both the level and duration of customer acceptance. Introduction of a new product or a new brand can have unsettling effects on the demand for existing products already in stock. The demand for seasonal merchandise is highly dependent on having near-average climatic conditions. A mild winter, for example, can seriously reduce the demand for winter sporting equipment.

By its very nature, *distressed merchandise* requires price reductions. Merchandise that becomes damaged, dirty, or shopworn must be marked down to compensate the purchaser for the obvious reduction in value. Odd lots (e.g., a set with one or more pieces missing) also require markdowns.

Timing of Markdowns

An important issue for every retailer is when to take markdowns.[16] Opinions differ; some retailers prefer to take early markdowns, but others feel that a policy of late markdowns is the more profitable strategy.

Early Markdowns. **Early markdowns** reduce the selling price of a merchandise item when either of two conditions is present: (1) there is a notable slack in the rate of sales for that item or (2) the item has been in stock for a specific time period (e.g., six weeks). Proponents of early markdowns cite a number of advantages: (1) *fresher stock:* Early markdowns help make room for new merchandise by weeding out slow movers, thereby freeing investment capital and selling and storage space; (2) *smaller markdowns:* Early markdowns reduce the size of the markdown required to sell the merchandise because some demand for the item still remains, and because the chances of the item's becoming shopworn are substantially reduced; (3) *reduced selling expenses:* Early markdowns promote rapid clearance of merchandise without the additional advertising and personal selling expenses that are normally associated with major sale promotion campaigns; (4) *increased customer traffic:* Early markdowns encourage customers to take advantage of reduced prices (both advertised and unadvertised specials) because of the continuous availability of marked-down merchandise; (5) *reduced selling risks:* Early markdowns permit sufficient time to take a second and possibly a third price reduction in one selling season if they become necessary to move the merchandise; (6) *heightened market appropriateness:* Early markdowns prevent repetitive showing of dated merchandise at regular prices. Market appropriateness is extremely important in selling fashion merchandise. Many fashion-oriented consumers are willing to buy only new arrivals at full prices, and they expect a continual influx of new merchandise. Other fashion-oriented consumers are willing to buy fashion merchandise that is well along in the fashion cycle only if the price has been reduced.

Early markdowns are most frequent among large department stores and medium-priced specialty retailers who are very promotion oriented.

Some retailers have an early-markdown policy that takes markdowns on a routine basis. **Automatic markdown** policies reduce prices by a fixed percentage at regular intervals. Automatic markdowns are generally taken without regard to how well the merchandise is selling. Waldenbooks is experimenting with an automatic markdown program that operates as follows:

> The books will be discounted in three steps. When a book has been in the store for 60 days, the price will be reduced. After another 30 days, the price will be reduced again. Depending on the original price of the book, there will be a third reduction 120 days after the book entered the store. As prices are reduced, the books will be moved from one area of the store to another.[17]

Late Markdowns. **Late markdowns** maintain the original selling price until late in the selling season, at which time a major clearance sale is held. A policy of taking late markdowns is most common with smaller specialty retailers and the more prestige- or status-oriented stores. Late-markdown advocates stress these advantages: (1) *They preserve exclusive image.* Late markdowns help prestige retailers preserve a store image of high quality and exclusiveness by not mixing sale-priced goods with regular-priced merchandise and by not mixing regular, prestige-oriented customers with bargain-seekers during the normal course of the selling season. (2) *They encourage creative selling.* Late markdowns allow sufficient time for the retailer to experiment with different selling approaches. By displaying the merchandise in different places and ways, the retailer can often influence the demand for that item. (3) *They allow "late bloomers."* Late markdowns allow each merchandise line a trial sales period of sufficient duration to realize the line's full potential. Some lines of merchandise simply take longer to catch on. (4) *They reduce purchase postponement.* Late markdowns discourage customers from waiting until the merchandise item is placed on sale before making a purchase. (5) *They create the "big event."* Late markdowns allow the retailer to accumulate large quantities of regularly stocked merchandise for a major clearance sale. Because of its infrequency and the fact that the clearance sale incorporates regularly stocked merchandise, the potential promotional impact is great enough to create the "big event."

Size of Markdowns

The purpose of a markdown is to increase the customer's incentive to buy the merchandise. Each markdown, therefore, should be large enough to attract customers' attention and induce them to buy. At the same time, unnecessarily deep markdowns will adversely affect the retailer's profit margins. There are no hard and fast rules for determining the size of a markdown. Some retailers believe in making the first "bath" count; that is, they take deep initial markdowns, thereby reducing the need for later, more drastic markdowns. Other retailers think taking several shallow markdowns is the best approach to clearing merchandise with the least-negative impact on profit margins. Some retailers are making more extensive use of the "straw man" policy schemes—a phony regular price that is quickly lowered, the sale price that is what the retailer actually expects to sell at, and deeper markdowns, as necessary, to clear the merchandise out.[18]

The degree of physical, fashion, or seasonal perishability strongly influences the size of the markdown. Highly perishable merchandise (e.g., a particular fashion near the end of its fashion cycle or a seasonal product approaching the end of the season) typically requires substantial markdowns as part of the clearance effort. Fashionable and seasonal items often require initial markdowns of 25 to 50 percent, whereas 10 to 15-percent markdowns on staple merchandise usually are sufficient to create customer interest.

The original retail selling price of the merchandise influences the size of the markdown needed to generate customer interest. For example, a $5 markdown on a $100 item would hardly be sufficient to attract additional buyers. On the other hand, that same $5 markdown on a $20 item is perhaps more than enough to clear the item out of stock. On average, the retailer must reduce the price at least 15 percent to create customer attention.

The amount of markdown the retailer takes also depends on the time in the selling season. Early in the selling season the retailer can take smaller markdowns knowing that, if the merchandise fails to sell at the reduced price, there is still time to take additional markdowns. Late markdowns must usually be deeper to stimulate sales.

Several additional factors determine the size of the markdown. For example, the need for substantial markdowns often depends on the number of units in stock that require clearance, the need for space (storage and selling), and the need for investment capital. A retailer facing a drastic overstock may decide that the only way to correct the situation is to take drastic markdowns. A continual flow of incoming merchandise means that the retailer must have adequate storage and selling space. Finally, old merchandise represents a major source of funds for many retailers. To gain immediate use of these funds, the retailer will need to take substantial markdowns.

Markdown Strategies

Retailers use many pricing strategies that incorporate markdowns either directly or indirectly. Clearance sales are examples of direct markdowns. Indirect price reductions are best exemplified by the retailer's use of coupons, premiums, and trading stamps. The following discussion examines some of the more common pricing strategies that either directly or indirectly incorporate the markdown concept.

Promotional Pricing Strategies

All promotional pricing strategies have at least one thing in common: They are designed to draw consumers into the store where, it is hoped, they will purchase not only reduced merchandise but also regularly priced merchandise. To this end, retailers use a variety of promotional pricing strategies. Typical are sale prices, prices with coupons and premiums, leader prices, and special-purchase prices.

"**Sales**" are an everyday occurrence in most retail markets. Retailers cite a variety of reasons for holding sales, such as clearances, liquidations, and closeouts. Overuse of sales is making "it increasingly difficult for retailers to get off the price-cutting merry-go-round. . . . Retailers unwittingly are teaching consumers that they shouldn't buy something until it's placed on sale unless they absolutely, desperately need it."[19]

Coupons are sales promotion devices in the form of redeemable cards (e.g., direct mail) or cut-outs (e.g., newspapers) that allow the customer to purchase specific merchandise at a reduced price. Coupons issued by the manufacturer do not represent a markdown for the retailer; however, coupons issued by the retailer do represent markdowns because the retailer bears the cost of the difference between the original and reduced selling price. **Premiums** include free merchandise or merchandise that has been drastically reduced. Retailers normally offer premiums to consumers after they have completed some requirement (such as test driving an automobile, filling out a form, or buying a certain dollar amount of merchandise).

Leader pricing is the strategy of selling key merchandise items below their normal markup or in some cases, even below the retailer's merchandise costs (negative markup). As with other promotional prices, the main objective of leader pricing is to attract consumers to the store in the hope that they also will purchase other merchandise that has normal markups.[20] Although leader merchandise contributes very little profit on a per-unit basis, its indirect contribution to total dollar profit can be substantial if the retailer makes anticipated additional sales on high-profit items. In using a leader price strategy, the retailer aims to make money on the mix of products, not on every single item in the mix. To be effective, leader merchandise should include well-known (frequently national brands), widely used items priced low enough to attract most income groups, and to be easily recognized as a bargain.[21] Supermarkets, in

Coupons the retailer issues represent a markdown, whereas retailers are reimbursed for manufacturers' coupons.

weekly advertised specials, often use meat, dairy, and bakery products as leader merchandise. Leader pricing strategies differ depending on the extent of the markdown and the retailer's purpose in attracting the potential customer. The three types of leader pricing strategies are low-leaders, loss-leaders, and bait-leaders.

Low-leaders are prices set below the customary selling price but above the retailer's actual cost of the merchandise. Customer attraction is the principal objective of the low-leader strategy. Low-leaders also generate some gross profit, thereby contributing to operating expenses and possibly to the retailer's operating profit. **Loss-leaders** are prices reduced to or below the retailer's cost of the merchandise. Such drastic price cuts aim to improve substantially the store's customer traffic. To make loss-leaders work, sales of regular-priced merchandise must be great enough to more than offset the losses generated by the sale of loss-leaders.

A **bait-leader** is an extremely attractive advertised price on merchandise that the retailer does not intend to sell; the attractive advertised price is "bait" to get the customer into the store. Having accomplished this, the retailer attempts to switch the customer from the merchandise featured in the advertisement to merchandise priced at full markup—hence the common description for this pricing strategy as "bait and switch." Retailers use numerous ploys to switch the customer to more expensive merchandise. In the first step, called the *trade-off,* the retailer tries to disinterest the customer in the advertised bait merchandise. The trade-off can be handled by (1) *persuasion* (convincing the customers that the bait merchandise is of extremely inferior quality and a poor value even at the sharply reduced price); (2) *refusal* (refusing to sell the merchandise on the grounds that it is unsafe, unhealthy, or unsupported [e.g., warranties] by either the retailer or the manufacturer); and (3) *stockouts* (informing the customer that the advertised merchandise was in very short supply and all units were sold before the customer's visit). The second task is trading up the customer to more expensive merchandise by stressing the higher quality of the substitute merchandise, the better services the customer will receive (delivery, installation, wrapping, repairs, etc.), the easy availability of credit, and any other appeal judged to be effective in convincing the baited customer. (The legal nature of bait and switch was discussed in Chapter 4.)

A **special-purchase price** is a low advertised price on merchandise the retailer has purchased at reduced prices. Because these promotional prices are initially set below the retailer's customary price for such merchandise, indirectly they represent a markdown pricing strategy. The purpose for special-purchase pricing is the same as for most promotional pricing: to generate customer traffic. The legalities of *first* establishing a going market price is the most commonly cited reason for not directly advertising special purchases as reduced in price. Special-purchase pricing is most often associated with large chain-store retailers that enjoy buying economies of scale.

Price-Line Adjustment Strategies

For the retailer whose original price-setting strategies included pricing zones (a range of prices) and pricing lines (at specific pricing points), markdown adjustments create a slightly different price-reduction problem. Shallow markdowns usually involve reducing the price of an item from one pricing point within a pricing zone to a lower pricing point within the same zone, and may be adequate for small clearance sales to dispose of a limited number of units. Deep markdowns are taken by moving a merchandise line from a pricing point in one zone to a pricing point in a lower pricing zone. Deep markdowns become necessary when the retailer considers the merchandise inappropriate for the targeted customer within the original pricing zone.

The second issue in making price-line adjustments is whether to inform the customer that a markdown adjustment has been made. The retailer may decide to drop a merchandise item from one price point to a lower pricing point without informing the customers of the item's markdown condition simply by replacing the old price tag with a new one. If the retailer believes it is beneficial for the customer to know about the price reduction, there are two ways to communicate the information: re-mark the old price tag so that the reduction is shown on the original tag or mark the merchandise down to an "off" pricing point. For example, a merchandise item can be reduced from its original pricing point of $29.95 to $24.00 rather than to the next lower pricing point of $19.95. Consumers perceive the even-ending pricing point as a reduced price.

Everyday Low Pricing Strategies

Everyday low pricing is the pricing policy of maintaining price points at the same low level year-round. By avoiding the price yo-yo of markups and markdowns, the retailer establishes greater price credibility through a more consistent and understandable price program.[22] Adoption of the everyday low price policy involves cutting prices 20 to 40 percent; in other words, dropping prices permanently to or near the retailer's former sale and promotional prices.[23] It represents a permanent markdown.

The success of this type of price policy has been clearly established by such retail success stories as Wal-Mart, Toys 'R' Us, and Circuit City. Montgomery Ward, Workbench, Inc., Target, and Dillard's Department Stores have all initiated some form of this low-price tactic. However, everyday low pricing is not for every retailer. Cut rate outlets such as warehouse clubs at the low end and fancier department stores that emphasize fashion, service, or upper-crust niceties, for example, will not embrace it. Pricing is just one facet of offering value to the customer, but you can also offer it through service, assortment, convenience, location, and other ways.[24]

The popularity of everyday low pricing is an outgrowth of customer frustrations with sale and promotional pricing. Customers have lost the ability to judge whether or not a sale price is a real bargain or a fictitious high price so that a future sale might be justified.[25] In general, many customers are fed up with constantly changing prices; it is hard for them to recognize a fair deal, let alone a good deal. New pricing tactics were necessary because the word "sale" has lost most of its meaning.

Everyday low pricing requires that the retailer be able to achieve everyday low costs. Cost reductions are possible due to (1) fewer employees for ticketing and reticketing merchandise, (2) less labor for display setup and maintenance, (3) reduced advertising and other promotional costs, and (4) fewer merchandise returns and subsequent markdowns. Additional benefits associated with this type of pricing policy include less ill-will resulting from stockout of sale items, higher perceived price credibility, improved image due to fair value pricing, and reduced customer haggling, resulting in freed-up clerks for providing other customer services.

Markdown Control

Some markdowns are inevitable, the natural result of the risks retailers assume going into business. An extremely low markdown percentage could indicate that the retailer is not assuming sufficient risks to take advantage of emerging market opportunities. On the other hand, excessive markdowns are often indicative of poor planning and control procedures. One expert estimates that 49 percent of the merchandise purchased at a department store is price-slashed; the result is the continual eroding of margins.[26] By carefully planning sales, stock levels, purchases, and profit margins, the retailer can control to a reasonable extent both the amount and the timing of markdowns. To facilitate **markdown control** many retailers require their buyers to maintain records on the causes or reasons for taking markdowns on a particular merchandise item. Careful analysis of these records allows the retailer to take corrective action when necessary and to detect excessive markdowns.

RETAIL STRATEGIES AND TACTICS

Will Sears Succeed with Everyday Low Pricing?

In March 1989, Sears officially switched over to its "everyday low pricing" retailing strategy. Sears mostly abandoned its traditional weekly sales and set new prices that were between its old "regular and sale" prices. Sears also vowed to resort far less often to running sales to attract customers. "The sale that never ends" served as the slogan for the advertising blitz that introduced the new price policy. While retail experts roundly applaud Sears' new found chutzpa, the risks are numerous and considerable. While everyday low pricing will save money on sales promotions and labor, the policy squeezes margins and makes cutting Sears' high costs a pressing issue. Everyday low pricing requires efficient operations to maintain profit margins; only low-cost players can succeed with this type of pricing. Sears could have a big problem: its selling and administrative expenses are among the highest in general-merchandise retailing. Compared with Wal-Mart and K mart, Sears' operating expenses are at least 50 percent higher. Adding to Sears' problems are claims that its new pricing tactics are misleading. The New York state Attorney General accused Sears of creating the false impression that its everyday low prices represent substantial discounts from the former prices when it actually has offered consumers no significant savings. The fact that Sears sold 55 to 60 percent of its merchandise on sale lends some credibility to the concern. Given these cost and legal concerns, Sears might modify their policy somewhat; an everyday value price could be a more realistic pricing position for the "big store."

Sources: Based on James E. Ellis, Brian Bremner, and Michael Oneal, "Will the Big Markdowns Get the Big Store Moving Again?" *Business Week*, March 13, 1989, 110, 114. Brian Bremner and Michael Oneal, "The Big Store's Big Trauma," *Business Week*, July 10, 1989, 50–51, 54–55. Francine Schwadel, "Sears Calls It 'Low Prices,' New York Calls It Misleading," *The Wall Street Journal*, January 22, 1989, B1, B4; and Steve Weiner, "Its Not Over Until It's Over," *Forbes*, May 28, 1990, 58, 60, 64.

SUMMARY

Retailers view prices in terms of their ability to generate profits, sales, and consumer traffic, as well as how they affect the store's image. In setting retail prices, the retailer can elect to be guided by profit, sales, or competitive objectives. A number of factors influence the retailer's price-setting decisions, including demand, competitive, cost, product, and legal considerations.

Retail price-setting methods include those that are cost oriented (markups), competition oriented, and vendor oriented. Retailers often use numerous different pricing policies in refining their price-setting tactics. For example, retailers can use a one-price policy, a variable-price policy, a multiple-unit policy, odd pricing, unit pricing, and price lining guidelines for their stores' prices.

Retailers use price adjustments as adaptive mechanisms to accommodate changing market conditions and operating requirements. Both upward and downward adjustments are needed from time to time to adapt to the dynamic retailing environment. Three common types of price adjustments are discounts, markons, and markdowns.

The three general causes for markdowns are buying related (e.g., assortment, support, and timing errors as well as misjudgment of merchandise quality and problems associated with suppliers); selling related (e.g., attempts to stimulate sales, to achieve competitive parity, and to correct improper selling policies); and operational related (e.g., market shifts and distressed merchandise). Some retailers prefer to take early markdowns, whereas others believe late markdowns are more profitable. The size of the markdown depends on the type of merchandise, the price of the item, and the time in the selling season. Markdown pricing strategies include promotional strategies (sales, coupons, premiums, price leaders, and special-purchase prices) and price-line adjustment tactics. To avoid excessive and unnecessary markdowns, the retailer must establish markdown control policies.

STUDENT STUDY GUIDE

Key Terms and Concepts

automatic markdown (p. 567)
bait-leader (p. 570)
competitive price objectives (p. 551)
cumulative markup (p. 555)
discounts (p. 563)
dollar markup (p. 555)
early markdowns (p. 566)
gross margin (p. 557)
initial markup (p. 556)
initial markup percentage (p. 556)
late markdowns (p. 567)
leader pricing (p. 569)
loss-leader (p. 570)
low-leader (p. 570)
maintained markup (p. 556)
markdown control (p. 571)
markdown percentage (p. 564)
markdowns (p. 564)
market-share objectives (p. 551)
markons (p. 564)
multiple-price policy (p. 559)
odd pricing (p. 559)
off-retail markdown percentage (p. 564)
one-price policy (p. 559)
percentage markup (p. 555)
price elasticity of demand (p. 552)
price lining (p. 562)
pricing above competition (p. 558)
pricing below competition (p. 558)
pricing line (p. 562)
pricing with competition (p. 558)
pricing zone (p. 562)
profit-maximization objectives (p. 551)
sales-volume objectives (p. 551)
special-purchase pricing (p. 570)
target return objectives (p. 551)
unit pricing (p. 560)
variable-price policy (p. 559)

Review Questions

1. When might the retailer prefer a market-share maintenance objective over a market-share growth objective?
2. How are two target return-pricing objectives expressed? Explain each expression.
3. What does price elasticity of demand measure?
4. From a product perspective, when are competitive price levels a more important pricing consideration?
5. Discuss how merchandising costs are determined.
6. Identify and discuss the several forms of product perishability.
7. Identify the formulas for calculating percentage markup at retail and at cost.
8. Compare and contrast the initial and maintained markups.
9. Which merchandising strategies are essential to a successful below-competition pricing strategy?
10. When is the vendor's suggested selling price not appropriate?
11. Distinguish pricing zones and pricing lines. Discuss each.
12. What are the advantages to the consumer and to the retailer of a price-lining policy?
13. What is a markon? When are markons applied?
14. Describe the two methods for computing markdowns.
15. Briefly describe the four selling-related causes of markdowns.
16. What are the advantages of early markdowns?
17. What size markdown should the retailer take?
18. Describe typical promotional pricing strategies used by the retailer.
19. Differentiate among low-, loss-, and bait-leaders.

Review Exam

True or False

_____ 1. Market-share growth is an appropriate pricing objective in expanding product markets.
_____ 2. Price competition is one of the least distinctive forms of competition.
_____ 3. Maintained markup equals initial markup minus all retail reductions.
_____ 4. Pricing lining makes it easier for competitors to develop successful competitive pricing strategies.
_____ 5. A liberal return policy is one method a retailer should use to help reduce the need for taking price markdowns.

_____ 6. A policy of late markdowns usually means the retailer must take deep markdowns to stimulate sales.

_____ 7. Loss-leaders are prices set below the retailer's customary selling price but above the retailer's actual merchandise cost.

Multiple Choice

_____ 1. The competitor's price is more important for some merchandise items than for others. In particular, the competitor's price is an important consideration for which of the following product groups?
a. products that consumers purchase frequently
b. products that retailers distribute intensively
c. products with high value
d. all of the above
e. none of the above

_____ 2. An appliance dealer purchases a toaster for $14 and sells it for $24. What is the retailer's percentage markup on cost?
a. 71.43
b. 58.33
c. 41.66
d. 171.42
e. 100.00

_____ 3. The difference between gross merchandise cost and the actual selling price of the merchandise is referred to as _____.
a. initial markup
b. cumulative markup
c. gross margin
d. maintained markup
e. markdown

_____ 4. What pricing policy is directed at giving the customer a discount for making quantity purchases?
a. one-price
b. variable-price
c. multiple-price
d. odd-pricing
e. unit-pricing

_____ 5. What odd price ending(s) is(are) most commonly used by retailers?
a. 9
b. 1
c. 5
d. 3
e. a and c

_____ 6. The practice of _____ will often lead to additional markdowns because the retailer knowingly stocks for display image purposes a limited number of high-fashion merchandise items that are unlikely to sell at their full markup prices.
a. aggressive selling
b. assortment maintenance
c. umbrella merchandising
d. support maintenance
e. none of the above

_____ 7. Advantages of late markdowns include all of the following, *except* _____.
a. preserving exclusive images
b. encouraging creative selling
c. reducing selling risks
d. allowing late bloomers
e. creating the big event

STUDENT APPLICATIONS MANUAL

Investigative Projects: Practice and Applications

1. Are retailers "free" to set whatever prices they feel are necessary to make a profit? Explain your answer.
2. If a retailer elects to use sales volume objectives in setting retail prices, how will it affect merchandising decisions regarding location, store facilities, product mix, and promotional strategies?
3. Some retailers prefer to avoid price competition; they prefer to engage in nonprice competition. Why?
4. Under what market conditions should a retailer consider "meeting competition" as a pricing objective?
5. Why do many small retailers prefer to compute percentage markups at cost rather than at retail?
6. Visit the following types of retailers and observe what price-setting policies are employed: (1) a major chain department store (e.g., Sears), (2) a major discount chain (e.g., K mart), (3) a franchised fast-food restaurant chain (e.g., Pizza Hut), and (4) a major shoe chain (e.g., Kinney). Provide specific examples.
7. "An automatic markdown policy is generally a good policy for all apparel retailers." Do you agree or disagree with the preceding statement? Justify and explain your answer. From the retailer's viewpoint, discuss the pros and cons of increasing the price (markons) of existing stock as soon as increases in wholesale prices are announced.
8. Develop a set of guidelines that all retailers should adhere to when advertising reduced prices, regardless of what markdown strategy is used.

Tactical Cases: Problems and Decisions

■ CASE 15–1
Free Bacon or Only $1.49: Testing Price Offerings*

The fast-food industry usually confronts a sales slump during the first quarter of each year. During this period, when the frequency of customer visits declines, competitors in the hamburger segment of the industry attempt to boost total sales, to improve customer counts, and to increase average sales by offering reduced prices on their smaller-size, lower-price hamburgers.

In planning for this predictable downturn in sales, Wendy's International, the fourth largest hamburger chain, decided one year to try a different competitive product strategy by offering a "quality sale," that is, a create-a-meal deal that involved a more upscaled product item, the bacon cheeseburger. The intended target market was adult males, 18 to 25 years of age, and known to be heavy fast-food users. The problem was how to express and portray the sales terms to the consumer. Should the meal deal be expressed as a value-enhancement offer or a price-reduction offer? Wendy's management wanted to test the two price expressions in the following manner. The value enhancement offer was to be expressed as follows:

"FREE BACON"—Order a Bacon Cheeseburger
and Get the Bacon Free

The rationale behind this offer was that *free* would enhance readership of Wendy's ads and would be perceived more favorably because the total value of the offer would appear to be worth more than the actual savings as a result of the consumer belief of getting something for nothing.

The price-reduction offer was to be expressed as:

ONLY $1.49—Get Our Bacon Cheeseburger
Special for Only $1.49

The belief that the customers would find a concrete dollar amount easier to relate to than a free offer was the basic premise for this kind of offer.

ASSIGNMENT

Assume the role of an account manager for Wendy's sales promotion agency.

1. Develop a hypothesis as to which of the two price offers will be most effective in achieving a favorable customer response. Support your hypothesis with a complete rationale for your beliefs.
2. Develop and conduct a market test of the two sales promotion offers suggested by Wendy's management to determine which is the most effective. Report your findings and analysis.
3. Identify two variations for each of the price expressions—value enhancement and price reductions. Conduct a market test on your suggestions and report your results.

*This case was prepared by Dale M. Lewison and Douglas Hausknecht, The University of Akron.

■ CASE 15–2
Burger Barn Breakfast Muffins*

As the burger wars progress, the largest national hamburger chains have increased competition across dayparts. The fiercest battles have been over the breakfast market. Every form of breakfast food is being tried—McDonald's is testing cold cereal in some outlets.

The struggle has trickled down to smaller chains and individual outlets. Burger Barn, a regional U.S. chain, has served a basic breakfast for some time. They are now considering the addition of bran, oatbran, and other muffins to the line. The assumption is that these will appeal to those customers who don't want the usual eggs, bacon, or sausage to start the day.

When the company added bacon and eggs to the menu, it did not require an equipment change. The stoves and grills could accommodate the new products. Muffins will require some form of baking or open heat. Tests of prebaked muffins have shown that none had acceptable quality (i.e., microwave and heat'n'serve versions).

Burger Barn is considering two alternatives. One is to mix a batter and bake the muffins in the store. The other alternative also requires in-store baking, but the mix is prefrozen into disposable muffin trays. Company taste tests have found no significant preference for either product over the other.

In order to add the product, an oven must be added to each store. Ovens that are adequate for this purpose can be acquired in quantity for $900. They can accommodate 2 dozen muffins at a time and can be run for as little as $.085 per hour for electricity. These are small and have an estimated useful life of three years.

The other costs for muffin making depend on which alternative is selected (see Exhibit A). The product may be tested in a limited number of stores. If introduced, however, the product must be carried by all. This will require a promotional campaign to effectively introduce the item. The best estimate of the cost of this campaign averages to $1000 per store for the first year.

The breakfast trade has not been doing too badly. On average, 22 people are served during breakfast hours. This compares with 142 during lunch and 44 during dinner. Almost 30 percent of the lunch and dinner crowds opt for the salad offerings rather than the burgers or other sandwiches.

Most of Burger Barns's products are priced slightly

above the major national competition. Management feels that the quality and portion size justify this premium. Surveys among loyal Burger Barn customers support this contention. At present, the average price of competing muffins is $.95.

ASSIGNMENT

1. Under each plan, what is the variable (direct) cost per muffin? How much should Burger Barn allow for waste (muffins that cannot be sold on the day baked)? Does this vary or remain the same between the plans?
2. The first year is important for any product. How much is the fixed cost of producing muffins in the first year? Is this based on out-of-pocket cost or standard retail accounting practice?
3. If Burger Barn sets the price at the same level as the competition, how much is profit per muffin? At that rate, how many muffins must be sold in the first year to pay off the fixed costs? How many muffins per day is that? Does this seem like a reasonable number to sell?
4. Under normal production practices, Burger Barn can only produce batches of muffins. One batch is 24 muffins. This can be considered a fixed (step) cost. If you assume that each store makes one batch of muffins per day, how many must be sold from that batch to break even for the day? Is this a feasible sales level? Remember that more than one variety is being considered.
5. We assumed that price was to be set based on the competition. What other bases for price should be considered? Recommend a price for Burger Barn.
6. Should Burger Barn mix the batter in store or use frozen muffins? What other considerations are important? Are other production options possible?

*This case was prepared by Douglas Hausknecht, The University of Akron.

EXHIBIT A
Muffin costs

	Plan A	Plan B
Ingredients	$.14/muffin	$7.20/tray of muffins
Package	.04/muffin	.04/muffin
Preparation	20 minutes	none
Cleanup	10 minutes	none
Baking time	30 minutes	45 minutes

ENDNOTES

1. Steve Weiner, "Price Is the Object," *Forbes*, February 20, 1989, 123.
2. Francine Schwadel, "The 'Sale' Is Fading As a Retailing Tactic," *The Wall Street Journal*, March 1, 1989, B1.
3. Teri Agins, "As Retailers' Sales Crop Up Everywhere, Regulators Wonder if the Price Is Right," *The Wall Street Journal*, February 13, 1990, B–5.
4. See James S. Murphy, "Nonprice Competition Hurts Small Retailer," *Marketing News*, October 23, 1989, 4–5.
5. See Ruth N. Bolton, "The Robustness of Retail-Level Price Elasticity Estimates," *Journal of Retailing* 65 (Summer 1989), 193–219.
6. See Rosalind Wells, "Apparel Prices Affect Consumer Demand," *Retail Control*, January 1989, 2–11.
7. David S. Lituack, Roger J. Calantone, and Paul R. Warshaw, "An Examination of Short-term Retail Grocery Price Effects," *Journal of Retailing* 61 (Fall 1985), 10.
8. See Roger J. Calantone, Cornelia Droge, David S. Lituack, and C. Anthony DiBenedetto, "Flanking in a Price War," *Interfaces* 19 (March–April 1989), 1–12.
9. Frank McCoy, "Melville's New Crew Aims to Get Back to Speed," *Business Week*, July 13, 1987), 94.
10. See Robin T. Peterson, "Price Cutting Can't Be Sole Strategy," *Marketing News*, October 23, 1987, 10,12.
11. See Francine Schwadel, "Ferocious Competition Tests the Pricing Skills of a Retail Manager," *The Wall Street Journal*, December 18, 1989, B1, B4.
12. Mark Ivey, Lois Therrien, and Maria Shao, "It's Not Just a Fill-Up Anymore—It's An Event," *Business Week*, June 19, 1989, 90, 92.
13. Thomas T. Nagle, *The Strategy of Tactics of Pricing* (Englewood Cliffs, NJ: Prentice-Hall, 1987), 59.
14. Kathleen Deveny, "Middle-Price Brands Come Under Seige," *The Wall Street Journal*, March 20, 1990, B–1.
15. Pat Corwin, "Finessing the One-Price Strategy," *Discount Merchandiser*, April 1990, 66–68, 72.
16. See Michael Levy, "How to Determine When to Take Markdowns and How Much They Should Be," *Retail Control* (January 1987), 35–48.
17. Cynthia Crossen, "Waldenbooks to Cut Some Book Prices in Stages in Test of New Selling Tactic," *The Wall Street Journal*, March 29, 1988, 30.
18. Leonard L. Berry, "Multidimensional Strategies Can Combat Price Wars," *Marketing News*, January 31, 1986, 10.
19. Ibid.

20. See Rockney G. Walters and Heikki J. Rinne, "An Empirical Investigation into the Impact of Price Promotions on Retail Store Performance," *Journal of Retailing* 62 (Fall 1986); 237–66.
21. See Gerard J. Tellis, "Beyond the Many Faces of Price: An Integration of Pricing Strategies," *Journal of Marketing* 50 (October 1986), 146–60.
22. Ibid., Francine Schwadel, "The 'Sale' Is Fading As a Retailing Tactic."
23. Ibid., Steve Weiner, "Price Is the Object."
24. Ibid.
25. Ibid., Teri Agins, "As Retailers' Sales Crop Up Everywhere, Regulators Wonder if the Price is Right."
26. See "Are Department Stores the Leading Off-Pricer?" *Discount Merchandiser,* April 1990, 79.

OUTLINE

OBJECTIVES

- Describe the communication process and discuss its impact on retail promotions.
- Identify and define the five major components of the retailer's promotion mix.
- Discern the role of retail advertising in attracting, informing, and motivating consumers.
- Specify and analyze the components necessary for planning a successful retail advertising program.
- Delineate the organizational structures and the advertising functions necessary for accomplishing an effective advertising program.
- Discuss the instruments and methodologies for evaluating advertising effectiveness.

PART V

ADVERTISING STRATEGIES

Creating and Directing the Advertising Function

CHAPTER 16

STERLING JEWELRY—AVOIDING THE CLUTTER

The key to Sterling's advertising program is continuity. The company has initiated a series of radio ads that are not only unique because of their personality voices, but also because of their theme. "We have built the current radio campaign on 'trust' and chosen spokespeople who convey this idea to the listener." Some of the personalities representing Sterling in the commercials are television stars Jill Eikenberry and husband Michael Tucker. Their commercial has a Stiller-and-Meara style that talks about "great relationships being built on trust." In the same vein, football coach Don Shula and his wife, and singing star Tammy Wynette and her husband, do similar radio spots, building the Sterling image of trust.

Sterling believes in reinforcing the continuity of radio ads with famous names. When it comes to print advertising the stress is on continuity also. Full-color catalogs are fielded eight times a year; ROP inserts, numbering 30 million, are printed rotogravure in several locations and drop shipped. This massive advertising clout keeps the jewelry chain's name before the public at holiday and gift giving times, as well as several other times a year. Plans may include TV, perhaps in major markets. "But TV would be a trade-off. It would have to be a grabber. We don't want to be part of the clutter of advertising. Our idea is to stay out of the clutter and create our own image."

For that reason, most Sterling stores do not participate in mall advertising, except where required by lease. "We prefer to use our advertising monies to better advantage." Currently Sterling spends 6% of sales on advertising and promotions.[1]

Unlike most other businesses, retailers do not generally take their product to market. Instead, they rely on consumers to take the initiative of visiting their stores or placing an order by phone or mail. Most consumers will not take this initiative unless they are in some way motivated to do so. Before consumers will visit a particular store, however, they must be aware of its existence, know its location, and have some idea of what is available inside. They also may want information about prices they must pay, the terms of sale they can expect, services available, and store hours. In addition, consumers need to be persuaded that a particular retailer's offering is most suited to their needs. Effective retailers supply this information and persuasion, generally through their retail promotional efforts.

RETAIL PROMOTIONS

The fourth element in the retail mix is promotion. **Promotion** involves both providing the consumer information regarding the retailer's store and its product-service offering, as well as influencing consumer perceptions, attitudes, and behavior toward the store and what it has to offer. As implied in the definition, promotion is both an informative and persuasive communication process; therefore, it is useful to view the retailer's promotional efforts from the standpoint of the communication process. For example, Consolidated Stores Corp., operators of Odd Lots and Big Lots closeout stores, uses newspaper ads that stress its good prices (persuasive communications) "but instead of just listing merchandise and prices, the ads tell exactly why the manufacturer closed out the goods. That way, customers won't suspect that the products are irregular, damaged, or counterfeit" (informative communications).[2]

The Communication Process

The **communication process** involves transmitting meaningful messages between senders (i.e., retailers) and receivers (i.e., target consumers). Figure 16–1 illustrates the communication process and its participants (senders and receivers), processes (encoding and decoding), and acts (transmission and feedback).

The *source* of the communication process is the **sender**—a retailer that wants to inform or persuade a select group of consumers (**receivers**) about the benefits of an idea (e.g., lower prices, quality merchandise, high fashion, fast service, or contemporary image). To be effective, the message must be **encoded** into messages using signs and symbols (e.g., words, displays, pictures, or gestures) that (1) promote understanding of the idea, (2) attract attention of the intended audiences, (3) stimulate needs felt by intended audiences, and (4) suggest a course of action for need satisfaction. Having developed an effective message, the sender must then select the most appropriate communication channel or *medium* (e.g., salespeople, newspapers, magazines, radio, television, direct mail, in-store displays, and sales promotions) for **transmitting** the message to consumers targeted as the most suitable **recipients** of the message. The receiver or target audience is the intended destination of the sender's message and the object of the sender's promotional efforts (e.g., creating awareness, generating interest, and initiating behavioral change).

Upon reception of the message, the receiver **decodes** it and interprets its meaning either correctly or incorrectly, depending on how well the message was encoded and the decoder's experience and skill with the communication process. After the decoding process has been completed, the receiver may or may not react (e.g., visit the store, phone in an order, or do nothing). The nature of the receiver's *response* or lack of it is then communicated back to the sender as **feedback**. The information gained through the feedback mechanism is vital in developing and encoding new ideas for future promotions. A final element in the communication process is **noise**, anything that occurs during the communication process that distracts senders or receivers, interferes with

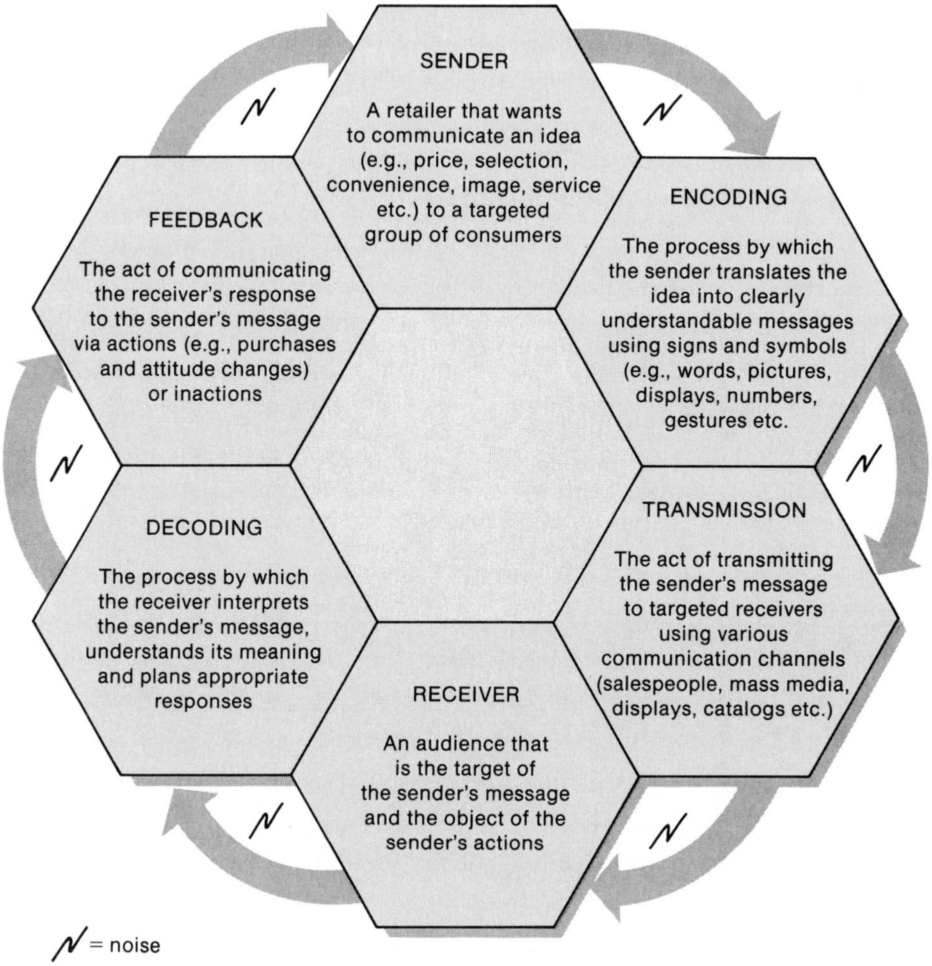

FIGURE 16–1
The communication process

the encoding and decoding activity, or interrupts the transmission or feedback process (see Figure 16–1).

The Promotion Mix

The retailer's promotion mix compromises various combinations of the five basic promotional elements: advertising, personal selling, store displays, sales promotions, and publicity. The remainder of this chapter looks at the advertising function. Chapter 17 discusses personal selling, sales promotions, and publicity. Store displays were discussed in Chapter 8.

To develop and implement the promotion mix, retailers use some combination of these elements:

- **Advertising**—indirect, impersonal communication carried by a mass medium and paid for by an identified retailer
- **Personal selling**—direct, face-to-face communication between a retail salesperson and a retail consumer

- **Store displays**—direct, impersonal in-store presentations and exhibitions of merchandise together with related information
- **Sales promotions**—direct and indirect impersonal inducements that offer an extra value to consumers
- **Publicity**—indirect, impersonal communication (positive or negative) carried by a mass medium that is neither paid for nor credited to an identified sponsor

Figure 16–2 compares the general characteristics of each type of promotion.

RETAIL ADVERTISING

Retail advertising includes all paid forms of nonpersonal communications about stores, merchandise, service, or ideas by an identified retailer. Its purpose is to favorably influence consumers' attitudes and perceptions about the store, its merchandise, and its activities and to induce sales directly or indirectly. To distinguish it from publicity, advertising is described as a *paid* form of communication. Advertising is impersonal because the message is delivered through the public medium to many consumers simultaneously, which distinguishes it from personal selling (see Figure 16–2).

Functionally, advertising has three basic purposes: to inform, persuade, and remind target audiences of the retailer's total offering. For the retailer to be effective,

PROMOTION TYPE / CHARACTERISTIC	ADVERTISING	PERSONAL SELLING	STORE DISPLAY	SALES PROMOTION	PUBLICITY
MODE OF COMMUNICATION	Indirect Nonpersonal	Direct Face-to-face	Direct Nonpersonal	Indirect Nonpersonal	Indirect Nonpersonal
REGULARITY OF ACTIVITY	Regular	Regular	Regular	Irregular	Irregular
FLEXIBILITY OF MESSAGE	Unvarying Uniform	Personalized Tailored	Unvarying Uniform	Unvarying Uniform	Beyond Retailer's Control
DIRECTNESS OF FEEDBACK	Indirect Feedback	Direct Feedback	Indirect Feedback	Indirect Feedback	Indirect Feedback
CONTROL OF MESSAGE CONTENT	Controllable	Controllable	Controllable	Controllable	Uncontrollable
IDENTITY OF SPONSOR	Identified	Identified	Identified	Identified	Unidentified
COST PER CONTACT	Low to Moderate	High	Varies	Varies	No Cost

FIGURE 16–2
Characteristic profile of types of promotion (source: adapted from William Zikmund and Michael d'Amico, *Marketing* [New York: John Wiley & Sons, 1984], 494)

consumers must have sufficient information as to what and who the retailer is. Informative advertising provides necessary information on the retailer's product mix, operating characteristics, and pricing strategies. Persuasive advertising is directed at convincing the consumer that the retailer has the right offer; that it, in fact, is the best alternative in meeting the consumer's individual needs. Finally, it is not only important to inform and persuade the consumer the retailer has got what the consumer needs, it is equally important that the retailer's offering has been and will continue to be the most appropriate solution to the consumer's shopping needs.

Understanding How Advertising Works

Consumers go through a series of steps, at varying rates, before they are motivated to accept something such as a store or a product and to take the action to patronize the business or buy the product they have accepted. Communications theorists have proposed several models of this personal "adoption" process, most of which are similar. The model presented here is known as **DAGMAR** (defining advertising goals for measured advertising results). Developed by Russell Colley, the model describes a sequence of steps through which prospective customers move from total unawareness of a store and its offering to store patronage and purchase (action).

As Figure 16–3 illustrates, several steps intervene between unawareness and action (or store selection). Through advertising, the retailer can help consumers move to *awareness* of the store and its offerings; to *comprehension* or understanding of the store and its image, price structure, services, and so on; to *conviction* or favorable attitudes toward the store. To build awareness and comprehension, each time Wal-Mart enters a new market, they precede the opening with a "pre-awareness campaign" using TV and print advertisements one month before the doors open. When an outlet opens, Wal-Mart does monthly direct mailings and weekly newspaper inserts to obtain continuing favorable consumer response.[3] Although advertising cannot accomplish this

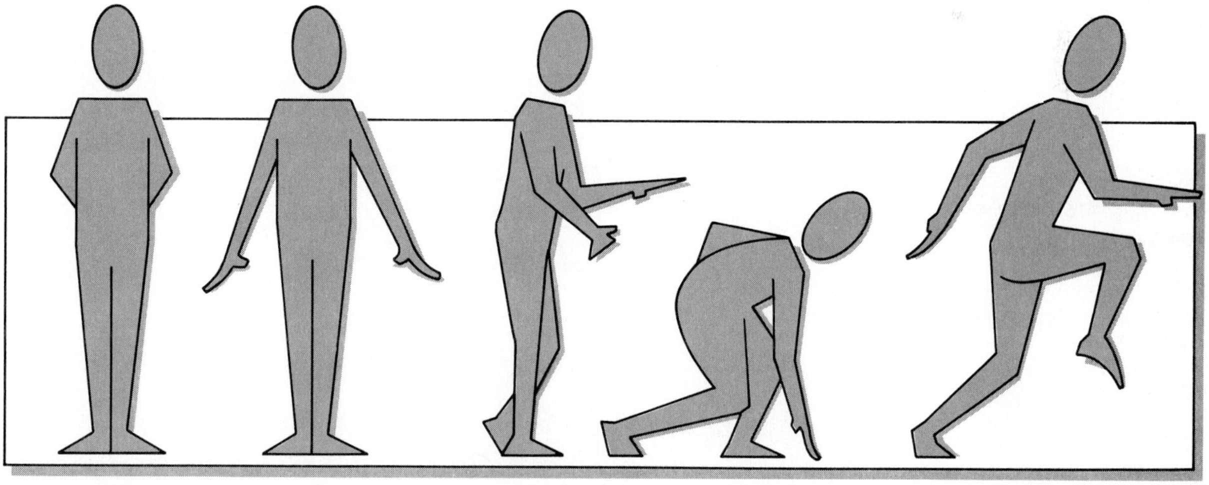

FIGURE 16–3
The DAGMAR consumer-adoption model (source: adapted from Russell H. Colley, *Defining Advertising Goals for Measured Advertising Results* [New York: Association for National Advertisers, Inc., 1961], 46–69)

process alone (other aspects of the retailer's marketing mix also play important roles in moving customers through this behavioral sequence), it plays a major role, particularly in the awareness and comprehension steps.

Advertising affects a large number of people simultaneously with a single message because of the mass media it uses. Although it is itself a mass form of communication (and therefore impersonal), the ultimate effects of advertising are often magnified by personal communications among consumers. This phenomenon, known as the **two-step flow of communications**, is illustrated in Figure 16–4.

The first step in the process is the communications flow from the media to opinion leaders. (**Opinion leaders** are persons whose attitudes, opinions, preferences, and actions affect others.) The second step is word-of-mouth communications from opinion leaders to others (followers). This communication may occur through personal conversations (a "fashionable" woman tells her friends where she bought her new coat) or through nonverbal personal communications (the friends notice the label in her coat). Regardless of how the second step takes place, it is crucial to the influence advertising has on consumers.

An obvious implication of the two-step flow theory is that retail advertising should reach opinion leaders. Unfortunately, this is not an easy task, because opinion leaders are not easy to locate. A retailer may be able to locate opinion leaders through observation; for example, a women's fashion retailer may read in the newspaper the names of the sponsors and participants in style shows put on by a women's club, then write or call these potential opinion leaders and invite them to select some merchandise. If they are satisfied, the retailer would ask them to "pass the word." Other methods of working with opinion leaders include the following: (1) create opinion leaders out of certain persons by supplying them with free merchandise and information; (2) work through influential persons in the community, such as disc jockeys, television personalities, and class presidents; and (3) create advertising that depicts people having conversations about one's store or products.

Identifying Types of Advertising

Retail advertising has two basic purposes: to get customers into the store and to contribute to the store's image. The first purpose is immediate: Today's advertising brings buyers into the store tomorrow, tomorrow's advertising brings them the next day, and so on. To accomplish this, the store must give buyers some specific reasons to come

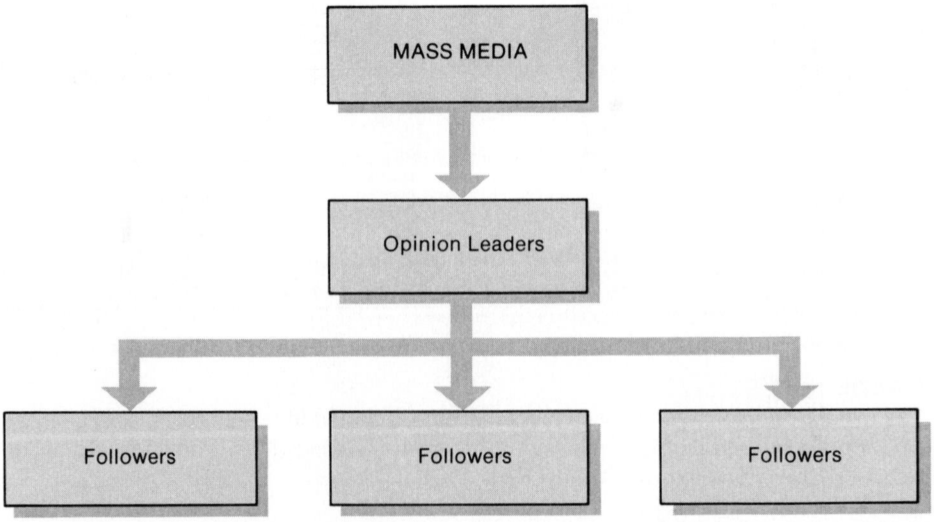

FIGURE 16–4
Two-step flow model of communications

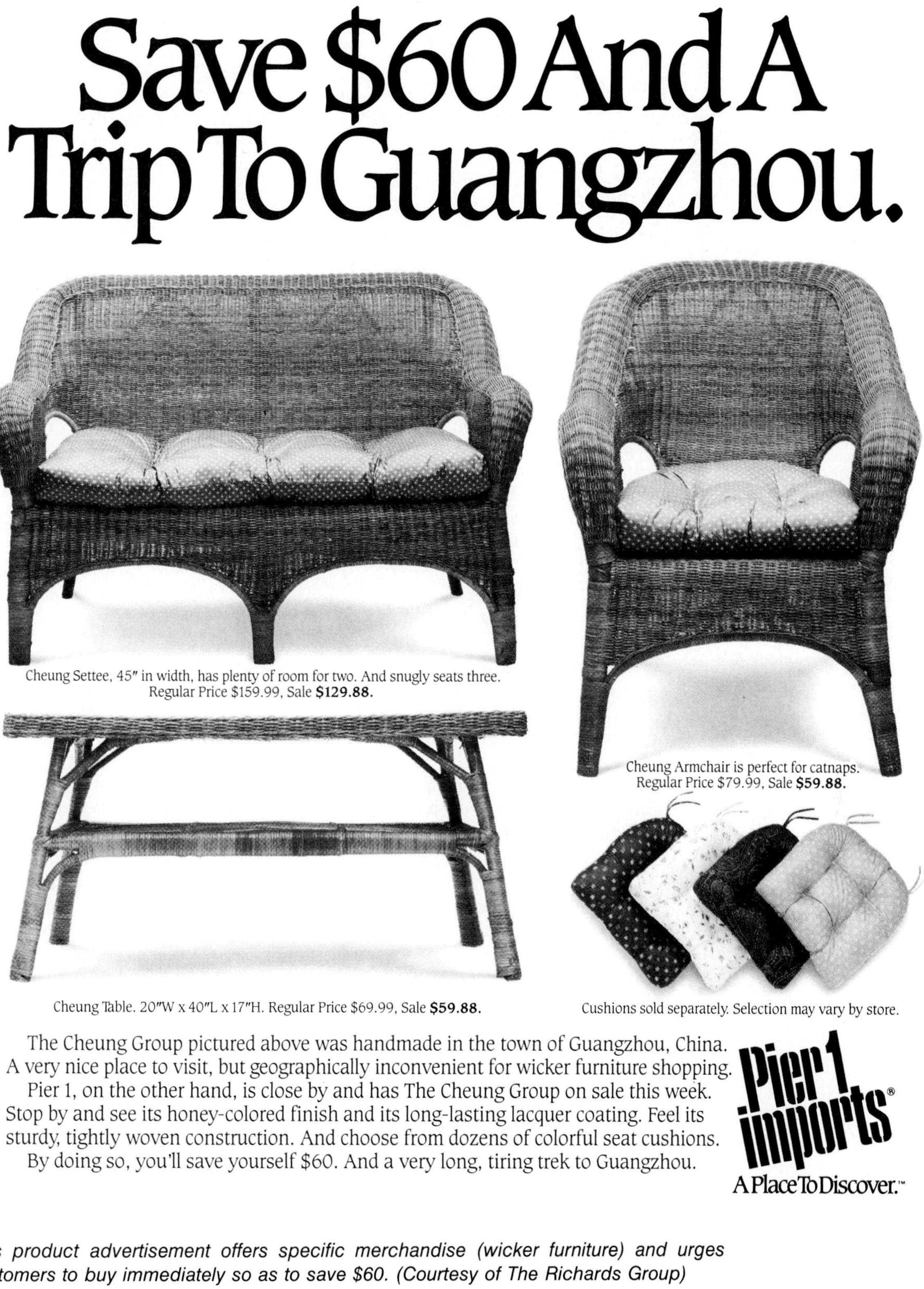
Save $60 And A Trip To Guangzhou.
Cheung Settee, 45″ in width, has plenty of room for two. And snugly seats three. Regular Price $159.99, Sale **$129.88.**
Cheung Armchair is perfect for catnaps. Regular Price $79.99, Sale **$59.88.**
Cheung Table. 20″W x 40″L x 17″H. Regular Price $69.99, Sale **$59.88.**
Cushions sold separately. Selection may vary by store.
The Cheung Group pictured above was handmade in the town of Guangzhou, China. A very nice place to visit, but geographically inconvenient for wicker furniture shopping.
Pier 1, on the other hand, is close by and has The Cheung Group on sale this week. Stop by and see its honey-colored finish and its long-lasting lacquer coating. Feel its sturdy, tightly woven construction. And choose from dozens of colorful seat cushions.
By doing so, you'll save yourself $60. And a very long, tiring trek to Guangzhou.
Pier 1 imports®
A Place To Discover.™

This product advertisement offers specific merchandise (wicker furniture) and urges customers to buy immediately so as to save $60. (Courtesy of The Richards Group)

WORLD OF RETAILING

International Retailing

Word of Mouth Not Enough

The Frenchmen figured that since they'd gotten their original inspiration in America, their hypermarket would be a natural in this country. Carrefour opened its first U.S. hypermarket this past February in northeast Philadelphia. And though it is the only one of its kind in that part of the country, sales at the store have been disappointingly sluggish and profits nonexistent. Carrefour is learning the hard way that what makes good marketing sense in Europe and Latin America doesn't necessarily translate in the U.S. . . . So why no profits? Because too few shoppers even know the store is there. Carrefour invested $5 million in equipment, hiring and training and other costs, but almost nothing on promoting the store when it opened.

A major blunder. Quiet store openings are customary in France, not here. "We wanted to spread the hypermarket concept slowly, by word of mouth," says Carrefour U.S.A. President Girard de Ganay. Compare Carrefour's approach to that of Hypermart U.S.A., a division of Wal-Mart. Hypermart U.S.A.'s three superstores in Texas and Kansas are so busy that shoppers complain about overcrowding. A fourth will open in Kansas City, Kansas this year. But when Wal-Mart opens a new hypermarket, it makes sure shoppers for miles around know about it, through advertising for several weeks in local newspapers, on TV and with mailbox stuffers. Other hypermarket operators include Auchan, another French retailer, which opened a store in Houston this past October, also amidst heavy promotion.

Source: Diana Fong, "Cherchez la Store," *Forbes*, Jan. 9, 1989, 311, 314.

to the store now. Retailers also want long-run, or delayed, results from advertising. They want customers to know "who" the store is in relation to competitors and the community as a whole. They also want customers to be favorably inclined to shop at the store because of its image. Accordingly, retailers undertake two kinds of advertising: product and institutional.

Product advertising presents specific merchandise for sale and urges customers to come to the store immediately to buy. This indirect form of advertising helps to create and maintain the store's reputation through its merchandise. Product advertising themes center around promoting merchandise that is new, exclusive, and of superior quality and design as well as around themes relating to complete assortments and merchandise events. Announcements of sales, special promotions, or other immediate-purpose advertising are other types of product advertising. T.J. Maxx, the off-price retailer, in an attempt to change consumer perceptions has "shifted away from its long-running general advertising, which had the slogan, 'The Maximum for Minimum at T.J. Maxx' to a more direct approach. The new T.J. Maxx ads showcase individual items. One ad has a lineup of feet wearing 'brand name' athletic shoes, with the discount prices listed."[4]

Institutional advertising sells the store generally as an enjoyable place to shop. Lands' End has spent millions to build a brand identity for the term Lands' End. Their advertisements rarely feature a product; rather, they "sell Lands' End itself as a quality image, as a good neighbor, as a company that you would want to do business with."[5] Through institutional advertising, the store helps to establish its image as a fashion leader, price leader, leader in offering wide merchandise selection, superior service, or quality, or whatever image the store chooses to cultivate. To "neutralize" the junk food misconception about its food, McDonald's ran a series of magazine ads stressing the nutritional value of its food.[6] (The FDA later required McDonald's to curb these ads.) In reality, practically all of a store's product advertising should communicate its

RETAILING IN THE 90's

Institutional Advertising...

presenting messages to enhance the retailer's image.

Institutional advertising is designed to create, enhance, and/or maintain a retailer's image relative to targeted consumer groups. It is used to supplement the retailer's public relations efforts by building goodwill and developing favorable perceptions among noncustomer publics, as well as reinforce favorable perceptions held by current store patrons.

T
he tropical
floral collection, and
other fabulous nightwear for the nineties.
Now available at most Sears stores.
SEARS
Now something for everybody.

Institutional advertisements attempt to sell the store, not the product. Its purpose is to promote the store as an enjoyable, interesting, exciting, relaxing, and prestigious place to shop.

LIFE IS HA
NBO is e
Easy salespeople. Easy selection. Easy parking. Easy alterations. Easy locations. And, at 30% to 60% off retail, easy to afford. NBO is easy. So easy.

Product Advertising...

promoting product items to gain consumer reactions.

Product advertising is directed at selling specifically identified goods stocked by the store or services offered by the retailer. The focus of product advertising is on promoting product features (e.g., three speeds), product benefits (e.g., faster and safer), and product usage (e.g., indoor or outdoor).

RETAILING IN THE 90's

Cooperative Advertising…

sharing promotional costs between vendor and retailer.

Cooperative advertising involves the vendor paying part of the advertising cost incurred by the retailer in promoting the vendor's product within the retailer's local market area. Cooperative advertisements allow both vendors and retailers to make more efficient use of promotional budgets.

institutional image as well. The art, copy, typography, and logotype of product advertising all help to convey store image.

Another way a retailer might undertake product advertising economically is to take advantage of **cooperative advertising**. Manufacturers prepare print and broadcast advertising material of their own products and allow the retailer to insert its store name and address in the ad, then manufacturer and retailer split the cost of media space or time to run the ad. Usually the cost split is 50:50, although the percentages vary. Some manufacturers also make direct-mail advertising of their products available to retailers to distribute to their customers.[7] Sometimes the material is free to the retailer, or the manufacturer may charge a nominal fee.

Developing an Advertising Strategy

Like all other retail mix operations, advertising, to be effective, must be done within the framework of an overall plan. A comprehensive advertising program, like any other well-managed project, must be systematically planned, organized, executed, and controlled. In other words, the retailer must (1) determine what it wishes to accomplish with advertising, (2) establish the organizational structure necessary for implementing objectives, (3) develop a means for reaching these objectives, and (4) measure the degree to which it met the objectives. At the minimum, an advertising strategy should consist of the four stages shown in Figure 16–5.

PLANNING THE ADVERTISING FUNCTION

Planning the advertising function involves (1) a statement of objectives and (2) developing a budget.

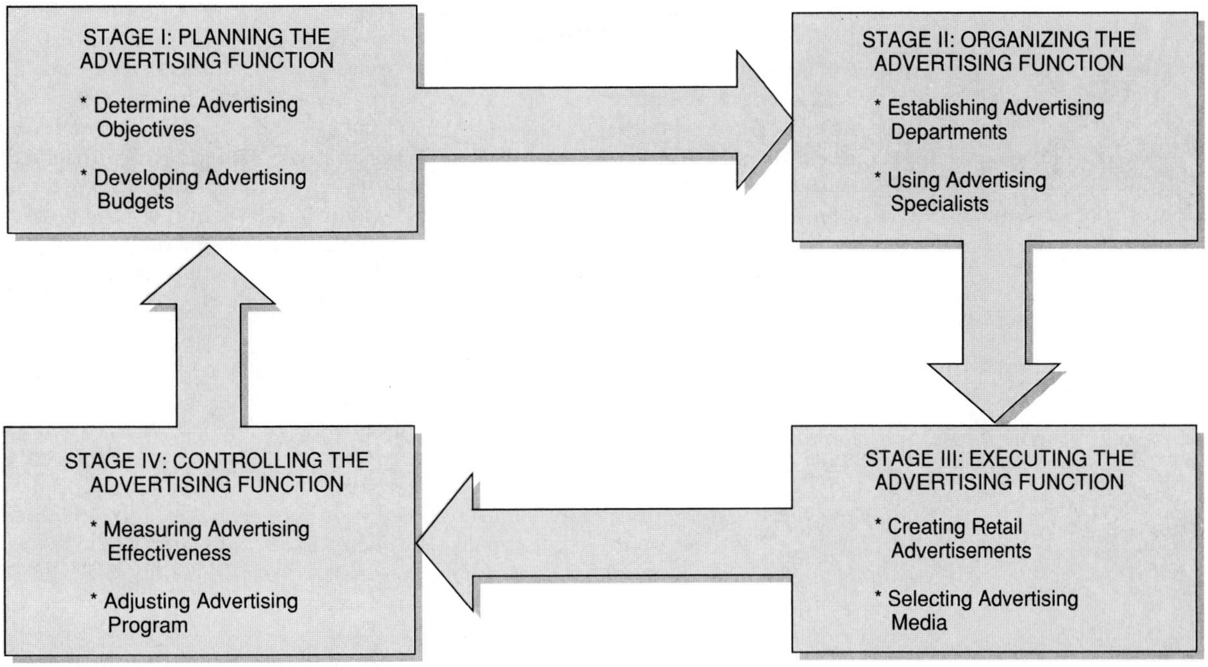

FIGURE 16–5
Retail advertising strategy

Determining Advertising Objectives

Objectives—statements of results the retailer wishes to achieve—are the most essential requirement for effective advertising planning. Effective planning is next to impossible without established goals of desired end results.

Store Image. To acquire and keep regular customers, every store needs to be thought of as unique in some way by its target market. The retailer may wish to establish an image by size (large), merchandise specialization (Early American furniture store), clientele ("designer" lines for "discriminating" shoppers), fashion leadership or merchandise quality (always presenting fashion "news"), or by price levels (not being undersold on products with well-known prices). Frequently, department stores use "fashion umbrella ads," in which they illustrate the latest or newest fashion merchandise. The purpose of the ads is not to sell a particular number of units but to show that the store is first with something, such as a style, an item or a concept.[8]

Store Positioning. *Positioning* is a term advertisers use in reference to attempts to get the market to think of the store in a certain way in relation to its competition.[9] In an attempt to position itself as the fast-food restaurant that treated customers as individuals, Burger King developed the advertising slogan "sometimes you've gotta break the rules." The slogan has been judged by some experts as ill-focused and ineffective because (1) many customers don't understand it, (2) it does not differentiate Burger King from arch rival McDonald's, and (3) it might suggest inappropriate behavior to younger consumers.[10]

Traffic Generation. *Traffic* refers to the number of people who visit the store and the frequency with which they visit. In general, the more consumers who visit the store, the greater the store's sales. Retailers can generate traffic in many ways. One of the surest methods is to provide customers with a special purpose for visiting, which can be achieved through sales, "theme" promotions (such as bridal seminars), special-merchandise showings, demonstrations, and so forth, each of which must be advertised. Price advertisement is another method for generating customer traffic. However, one very successful car dealer never advertises new cars on price; rather, its advertisement touts the dealer location, inventory, and service. "Price leader advertising is a great way to draw customers but it always creates a conflict when you tell them that the one they want has already been sold. This type of advertising creates an adversarial relationship, so we stay away from it."[11] The retailer can measure the results of efforts to produce traffic by actually counting the number of people who enter the store.

Special Events. Sales-promotional events are planned in advance, oriented around some theme, and coordinated through merchandising, store decoration, and advertising. One of retailing's most famous special events is Dallas's Nieman Marcus annual "Fortnight," a two-week fall happening featuring a unique theme. For example, the store may create an exotic atmosphere of some foreign country complete with displays and sales of rare and exclusive merchandise. The event induces many customers to visit the store out of curiosity, many of whom make purchases totally unrelated to the special advertised event. Measurable objectives might be evaluated by head counts or average number of purchases during the course of the promotion.

Increasing Average Purchases. Many retailers believe the most fruitful method for expanding sales is to induce present customers to buy more. Retailers can identify present customers through charge account records, by asking them to register, by recording names and addresses from personalized checks, and in other ways. These

A GERMAN FORTNIGHT
OCTOBER 17-NOVEMBER 5. CELEBRATING 300 YEARS OF GERMAN IMMIGRATION IN NORTH AMERICA.
Succumb to the outrageous luxury of Baden-Baden. ■ Where Napoleon III and the Kaiser along with their courts summered and "took the cure" — the legendary waters of the river Oos. ■■ We've recaptured the famous spa in Cosmetics. ■ With its own Lancaster Beauty Farm with lotions, scrubs, masques and massage creams to cleanse and purify body and facial skin. ■ And Ralph Lauren makeup artists to make a healthy glow more glowing. ■■ Ah, what wonders these waters work. ■ Complimentary makeovers by Ralph Lauren and Lancaster teams, daily. ■■■ Lancaster facials, 30.00.
Make your appointment: 741-6911, ext. 2101, First Floor, Downtown.
Neiman-Marcus

A special-event advertisement. (Mind and Body © 1973 by Avedis Baghsarian. Reprinted by permission.)

people have already demonstrated a measure of favor toward the store by buying, so concentrated efforts to induce them to buy more may be one of the greatest potential payoffs to advertising. Most retailers attempt to accomplish this objective by direct-mail invitations to sales or by new-merchandise showings.

Sales. Advertising is intended to contribute to expanded sales. Some retailers therefore express advertising objectives in terms of sales (e.g., increase average monthly sales for the shoe department by 10 percent over last year). The major limitation of such a broad sales objective for advertising is that many factors (e.g., prices, merchandise quality) affect sales besides advertising.

Developing Advertising Budgets

Executing the advertising campaign requires spending money. Therefore, determining the advertising appropriation is the next step in developing a comprehensive advertising plan. Although many retailers use the terms *appropriation* and *budget* synonymously, *appropriation* refers to the total expenditure for advertising undertaken in a time period, whereas *budget* refers to the allocation of the total expenditure across departments, merchandise lines, advertising media, and planning periods such as weeks, months, and seasons.

Advertising budget allocations are made on the basis of departments, merchandise lines, media, and time periods. At different times, the store will want to feature different items in its product line and deemphasize promotion of other items. Some stores choose to promote high-markup, low-turnover items heavily and deemphasize lower-markup, higher-turnover items. Others may elect either to introduce a new line or achieve a higher market penetration in a given line. Retailers can select from among several different advertising media, depending on their objectives and strategies. The retailer must determine how much of the total advertising appropriation to devote to each of the media (e.g., radio, newspapers) to make those expenditures more efficient. Finally, most retailers advertise more at certain times and less at others. Some advertise extensively before and during heavy buying periods, while others attempt to offset slack periods with heavier advertising.

Retailers use many methods to determine their advertising budgets. These range in sophistication from little more than guesswork to highly sophisticated techniques.

Some small sole proprietors depend on intuition and practical experience to develop an advertising budget—the **educated-guess method**. The retailer simply looks at last year's sales and advertising expenditures, determines what it hopes to accomplish this year, considers other necessary expenditures, and chooses an amount to spend on advertising next year. This method is little better than no method at all, because more sophisticated methods are available that are not much more difficult.

One of the most widely used methods of determining the advertising appropriation is the **percentage-of-sales method**. To develop a budget with this method, the retailer takes a predetermined percentage of either the previous sales or the estimated sales for the coming year to calculate how much to spend on advertising. The percentage figure is based on either the "traditional" figure the company has taken in the past, personal "insight," or an industry average. After determining the total advertising budget, the retailer then allocates the budget according to sales by departments, merchandise lines, and time periods. The percentage-of-sales method is popular among retailers because it is simple; unfortunately, it has no logical tie-in with achieving advertising objectives.

Competitive Parity Method. Some retailers set their advertising appropriation at the amount they estimate their most important competitors are spending—the **competitive parity method**. By monitoring the amount of advertising Retailer B is doing and estimating its costs, Retailer A may determine its appropriation and even allocate the appropriation across time periods, media, and merchandise in the same proportions as B. There are three basic problems with the competitive parity method. First, Retailer A is estimating the amount Retailer B has spent in the *past* to estimate how much to spend in the *future*. In general, little relationship could be expected between how much one store spent for advertising *last* year and how much another should spend *next* year. Second, Retailer B may not allocate its total promotional dollars in the same way as A. B may deemphasize advertising and emphasize in-store personal selling. If A bases its advertising appropriation on B's expenditures, it may underadvertise without compensating for B's in-store effort. Third, A has no way of knowing whether B's allocation method is appropriate for B, much less for A, and B's advertising expenditures certainly bear little direct relation to A's sales, profit objectives, market position, or share of the market.

Objective and Task Method. One of the most logical methods of advertising appropriation and budgeting is the **objective and task method**, by which retailers follow a four-step process:

1. Establish the objectives for advertising.
2. Determine the type and amounts of advertising necessary to accomplish these objectives.
3. Determine the overall cost of the advertisement.
4. Schedule the advertisements day by day.

The last step allows for budgeting the total appropriation across media, product lines, and time periods.

As an example, assume that one of the retailer's advertising objectives is as follows: "By November 30 of this year, 50 percent of all women in our trading area who are 25 or older and who have household incomes over $25,000 will give our store name when asked 'Which store in town sells the best women's coats?' " To reach this objective, the retailer must perform certain tasks, such as producing advertisements, selecting the necessary media for reaching the stated target market, determining how many ads to run in each medium selected, and when (time of month, week, day) to run the ads. After establishing all the tasks necessary to meet the objective(s), the retailer adds the cost to perform each task. This sum is the retailer's advertising budget.

ORGANIZING THE ADVERTISING FUNCTION

Day-to-day advertising functions include deciding which products to promote, developing copy and artwork, and scheduling and placing ads in the media. How the store is organized to execute these functions depends on its size and the funds available for specialized personnel to perform the functions.

Retail Advertising Departments

The owner-manager or one of the partners in small sole proprietorships and partnerships must handle the advertising function. With so many other store duties to perform, it is unlikely that this person will be an expert in advertising production. Thus, the main function is to establish advertising objectives, appropriations, and budgets and to work with outside advertising specialists—usually freelancers, media representatives, and advertising agencies.

Large stores have small advertising departments with an advertising manager who supervises a few artists, copywriters, and production specialists. The manager usually is responsible for establishing objectives, appropriations, budgets, and scheduling and for working with store merchandise managers and other managers to determine what will be promoted and how. This is usually the person who interacts with outside specialists in agencies and the media. Because most retailers advertise primarily in newspapers, the artists and copywriters spend most of their time developing newspaper copy.

The largest stores are likely to have a complete advertising and sales-promotion department. A **sales promotion director** usually is responsible for supervising and coordinating the activities of an advertising manager, a display manager, and a special events, publicity, or public relations coordinator. The **advertising manager** performs all the advertising activities described and supervises an art director, copy chief, and production manager. The **sales promotion manager** works with merchandise managers to develop and coordinate advertising, promotion, and displays with sales and special promotions. Even in the largest stores, in-house advertising production is likely to be print oriented; however, large stores often use the services of an advertising agency for broadcast production and scheduling.

Outside Advertising Specialists

Freelancers, advertising agencies, and media representatives are the three principal advertising specialists available to the retailer. An **advertising freelancer** might be an artist, copywriter, or photographer who produces advertising on a part-time basis. Freelancers usually operate alone, but sometimes have a small staff, charge a fee or an hourly rate for work, and work on their own premises or at the retailer's store. **Media representatives** are the employees of newspapers and radio or television stations whose principal job is to sell advertising space and time. These specialists also can arrange to produce the retailer's advertisements. Usually, newspapers do not charge for production and take compensation only for the space they sell. Radio stations normally do not charge for production, only for time, but charge a production fee for the tapes they make if they are broadcast on other stations. Television stations generally charge a fee for producing commercials in addition to the air time. Although **advertising agencies** produce the majority of national advertising, most retailers do not use them.

EXECUTING THE ADVERTISING FUNCTION

Few retailers become directly involved in creating advertising. Nonetheless, all must be able to distinguish good, effective advertising from poor, ineffective advertising. This section introduces the basic process of creating advertising. For simplicity, we limit our discussion to newspaper advertising, the most common kind of retail advertising.

Creating Retail Advertisements

There are as many processes for creating ads as there are creators of ads. In general, though, the creator of an advertisement must take into account the following steps in developing an effective ad:

1. Determine the purpose of the advertisement.
2. Decide on the basic message.
3. Select the communications approach.
4. Develop the total advertisement, part by part.

The Purpose of the Advertisement

An individual advertisement can have one or more purposes, such as promoting the store as a whole, making customers aware of a special event, focusing on a single product, or highlighting several products. Regardless of the purpose for a single advertisement, all advertising has some degree of "institutional" content as well. To achieve the double benefit of special-purpose advertising and institutional advertising, the retailer should select a special theme, product, or combination of products to feature, but should always maintain the same style in advertisements.

MY, MY. THE CLIENT'S REALLY LOOKING FORWARD TO YOUR PRESENTATION.
Maybe this time, just once, he'll have an open mind. But then again, well, he's always been one to make snap judgements.
To sell that proposal, your staff is going to need every slight advantage, every bit of confidence. Who knows? Maybe they need Juster's.
We offer an unique Corporate Clothing Program that can make their business wardrobes work harder. You know, give them that little extra edge. Help them wrestle with those unnerving corporate situations. And come out on top.
When your company participates, your employees receive a seminar on proper business dressing, personal consultation, special tailoring services, plus other valuable incentives. Call us at 333-1431, and ask how this exclusive program can work for you.
Juster's. We can give your employees' clothing the right kind of bite.
SURVIVAL OF THE FITTEST Juster's
Nicollet Mall, Southdale, Brookdale, Ridgedale, Rosedale, Highland Village.

Targeting customers' wants and needs and showing how a product can satisfy wants and needs combine to create an advertisement's appeal. (Courtesy of Miller Meester/DBK & O)

The Basic Message

Two basic elements in persuasive communications such as advertising are *what is said* and *how it is said*—substance and style. Too many advertisers concentrate on style and forget about substance, but the substance must be clear before advertising can be effective. Stipulating the basic **advertisement message** is determining what to say. Most retail advertising messages are quite simple: "Ours is a high-fashion store"; "Our women's coats are of highest quality"; "Our meat selection is the best in town." But the message should not be pulled out of thin air. Instead, it should be based on the target customer's wants and needs and the ability of the advertised product to *satisfy* those wants and needs. The combination of these two is the advertising *appeal*. If, for example, the advertiser thinks its target customers are concerned not with the quality of a coat but with its social acceptability, then the basic appeal of the message should be "Fashionable women wear this coat," not "This coat will last for five years." Note that both messages stress the *benefit* consumers derive from buying, and not the *features* of the coat from which they derive the benefit. Although the retailer's advertisement can point out that a coat has a double-stitched lining (a product feature), the resulting benefit (the lining is unlikely to separate from the coat) is the basic message the retailer should stress.

The Communications Approach

In determining the **communications approach**, the advertiser turns attention from *what* to say to *how* to say it. Most messages can be effectively communicated by either a rational or an emotional approach. The *rational* approach uses facts, narrative, and logical reasoning to persuade the consumer. The *emotional* approach appeals to the consumer's sense of aesthetics, ego, or feelings. For example, a tire dealer may effectively use a rational approach to promote snow tires ("You can get there on time—even if you wake up to snow") or it may arouse a husband's fear and protective instincts by depicting a solemn wife and two wide-eyed children under the headline, "Are you sure they'll get home tonight?" Although both approaches can be effective, advertising practitioners believe the emotional approach is more effective.

The Total Advertisement

After the retailer determines the message and approach, it must then develop the total advertisement. The **total advertisement** consists of several components: headline, illustration, copy, logotype or "signature," and layout (the visual arrangement). Although each component has a specific purpose, they work together to accomplish the ad's basic purpose: *to motivate the consumer to action*. An advertisement's layout, illustration, and headline all work to capture the consumer's attention and to create *awareness*.

Layout. The principal purpose of an ad's **layout** is to capture attention and guide consumers through all parts of the advertisement. Several other layout considerations merit attention. For example, one old advertising rule of thumb is that the principal focal point of the layout should fall five eighths from the top. Sparse illustrations with lots of white space suggest quality and prestige, whereas cluttered ads suggest discounting and a price appeal.

Headline. An ad's **headline** performs several functions besides getting attention. It should motivate the reader to review the remainder of the ad by providing news ("Blatt's Biggest Sale Ever!"), selecting readers ("Now You Can Get Organized"), and arousing curiosity ("Color TV for a Dollar a Day? Want to Know More?"). In general, the more original the headline, the better. The headline must be coordinated, however, with the remainder of the advertisement's basic message. In fact, the headline condenses the basic advertising message, telling the reader essentially what is to come.

Walt Frazier, 1955
Even as a kid I had an eye for colors and style. Even my cool demeanor was evident. But things are not always the way they seem, and it was many years later before I felt cool and confident in front of a camera.
Walt Frazier
Bloomingdale's has been serving cool customers for 100 years.
bloomingdale's
It wouldn't be the same without you.

This advertisement promotes the store's image as a long-established business that remains up to date ("serving cool customers for 100 years"). (Courtesy of Fallon McElligott)

Illustration. **Illustrations** help build consumer comprehension. The most common illustration is a drawing or a photograph of the product. The illustration can depict the product alone, isolate certain product features or details, show the product in context (such as illustrating a sofa in a completely furnished living room), depict the product in use, or illustrate how a consumer can derive a benefit from the product.

Copy. The **copy**—what is actually said in the advertisement—helps develop consumer comprehension, conviction, and action. In brief, good advertising copy should be simple and readable, yet vivid in word selection; it should be conversational in tone, interesting, enthusiastic, informative, point out benefits, and suggest action. Effective copy can be either brief or lengthy; however, the chance that anyone will read long copy is remote.

Logotype. The **logotype,** or *logo* in common usage, is the store's distinctive "signature" that appears in all advertising. It usually is coordinated with the store's sign, point-of-purchase advertising, labels, shopping bags, and so forth. Done in a distinctive style, script, or type, the logo identifies the store in the consumer's mind in much the same way that a trademark identifies a product or company. The store's logo should be carefully designed, since it may have a significant impact on consumers. Most retailers use the same logo for all their advertising, although some stores will vary their logos depending on the products they advertise. A logo is effective when it suggests the store's "character" or the nature of the retailer's merchandise. For example, a women's sportswear store might use a "lazy" script for a logotype, whereas an early-American furniture store might choose an antique type of script. A good logo communicates the store's personality and product offerings.

Selecting Advertising Media

The retailer's advertising message must be carried to the market by some communications vehicle, called advertising *media*. The retailer can select from among *print media,* such as newspapers, shopping publications, and magazines; *broadcast media,* such as radio and television; *sign media,* such as outdoor and transit; and *miscellaneous media,* including point-of-purchase media and advertising specialties, such as calendars or ashtrays. The retailer also can choose to become its own medium and use direct advertising to the consumer through mailed or hand-delivered letters, circulars, and catalogs.

Selecting advertising media is not easy. The retailer must choose the medium or media that will best communicate the advertising message to the greatest number of consumers in the retailer's target market at the lowest cost. To accomplish these tasks, large retailers usually employ several media over a given time and must select the best media for their purposes based on an understanding of the strengths and weaknesses of each medium. Different media have different abilities to accomplish various communication tasks. One shopping mall manager uses a combination of media: "TV gets the image of the mall across, print gets dates, times, and location of events out, and radio creates the excitement that gets people into the mall."[12]

Media Characteristics

There are many characteristics to consider in choosing advertising media. Some media are costly, some are inexpensive; some communicate a given message well, others poorly; some present the message continually, others are instantaneous.

Communication effectiveness refers to a medium's ability to deliver the desired impact to the target market. Print media show consumers pictures and words they can see and read. With radio, consumers can only listen to the message, whereas television allows them to both see and hear the retailer's communication. The print media are

Effective Advertising Requires Target Marketing

RETAIL STRATEGIES AND TACTICS

How did the shopping get so rich at Tysons Corner? . . . The answer in part: superior marketing. Tysons knows its customers. The average mall customer earns $36,000 a year. Tysons' shoppers earn $62,000 on average, and are younger and far less likely to have children than the average mall shopper. Only 10% of Tysons' customers are in their mid-to-late teens.

Knowing its customers means tailoring events to them. These are free-spending shoppers who manipulate computer data in nearby offices by day and sleep in the manicured suburbs of McLean and Springfield by night. That means, for example, print ads with pretentious playfulness, rather than a blatant hard sell. "The joy of cooking. The joy of sex. What's left? The joy of shopping," ran one newspaper ad. Tysons also spends over $500,000 annually on local TV commercials, rare for malls, which normally fend for themselves. One of Tysons' TV spots mimics the old Connie Francis hit song "Where the Boys Are," changing the words to "Where the stores are." As recent surveys have shown, many Americans now put shopping ahead of sex on their list of favorite pastimes.

Source: Joshua Levine, "Lessons From Tysons Corner," *Forbes*, April 30, 1990, 186, 188.

generally thought to be effective with an intelligent audience, whereas the broadcast media are more effective with a less intelligent audience. Newspapers and radio stimulate quick attention to a retailer's current offering, whereas television and magazines create long-term images in the consumer's mind.

Geographic selectivity is a medium's ability to "home in" on a specific geographic area such as a city and its surrounding area. This is an important media characteristic to a retailer, because most customers live in the local area. A medium that delivers the message to many people outside the retailer's market has a high degree of "wastage" circulation, viewership, or listenership, since these people are unlikely to buy from that retailer. Of the major media, local newspapers and local radio and television stations offer the retailer reasonably good geographic selectivity.

Audience selectivity refers to the medium's ability to present the message to a certain target audience within a population. Most magazines appeal to people with special interests, such as antique collectors, golfers, and electronics hobbyists. Radio stations also have a high degree of audience selectivity because their programming formats (e.g., country and western music, classical music, rock) appeal to distinct groups of consumers.[13] Television also can be highly selective when individual programs are considered. On the whole, people who watch "Monday Night Football" have different interests from those who watch "Days of Our Lives." Newspapers, on the other hand, do not have a selective audience; they appeal to groups with a wide array of interests and socioeconomic profiles. Audience selectivity can be increased by placing ads in strategic locations *within* a newspaper (for example, an ad for a sporting goods store in the sports section).

Flexibility refers to the number of different things the advertiser can do in the medium. Direct mail, for example, allows the advertiser to enclose money, coupons, pencils, postage-paid envelopes—in fact, practically anything, limited only by the advertiser's ingenuity. Radio, on the other hand, can provide words, music, and sound, but nothing more.

Impact refers to how well a medium stimulates particular behavioral responses within the target market. Television and magazines are better than other media in building store images, for example, whereas newspapers and the yellow pages of a telephone directory are better at generating immediate purchase behavior.

Prestige is the amount of status consumers attach to a medium. In general, consumers attribute more prestige to advertising in print media than broadcast media.

Naturally, the prestige of print media varies with the individual publication (e.g., the *New Yorker* versus *Mad* magazine). Broadcast media are thought to be less prestigious in general because of the typically "lowbrow" nature of most programming.

Immediacy is the medium's ability to present a timely or newsworthy message. Radio announcements, for example, can be prepared today and aired tomorrow, whereas magazines require one to three months notice in advance of the issue date. Newspapers also need very little lead time (usually 24 hours) to place a retailer's ad. If a snow or ice storm hits a city one day, knocking out electrical power, retailers can advertise oil lamps and butane-burning stoves the next day. A medium's ability to deliver a retailer's message *immediately* helps the retailer when external events present instant opportunities to the business.

Life means the length of time the announcement continues to sell. Broadcast announcements are gone in an instant and must be repeated to be effective, but a newspaper ad may "live" for several hours while people read the paper. Ads in magazines, which people read leisurely, may continue to live for several weeks, since consumers leave them in their homes and reexpose themselves to them over a long period of time.

Coverage refers to the percentage of a given market that a medium reaches. A newspaper might be read by 70 to 90 percent of adults in a certain city, whereas only a fraction of the same market may be reached by a "hard rock" FM radio station. Although coverage is often an important criterion in reaching a market, it must be considered in light of audience selectivity.

Cost should be viewed in both absolute and relative terms. Absolute cost is the amount of money a retailer must pay to run an advertisement in a medium; for example, the cost of a full-page ad in a newspaper might be $2,000 for one day. Relative cost is the number of dollars the retailer spends to reach a specific number of people; for example, if the full-page newspaper ad reaches 300,000 people, then the relative cost is $6.67 per 1,000 readers. If, on the other hand, the retailer spends $250 on a radio ad, much less money is spent in absolute terms, but if the message is heard by only 25,000 people, then the relative cost would be $10.00 per 1,000 listeners. Therefore, retailers should compare relative costs as well as absolute costs in selecting media. Once again, audience selectivity and wastage are among the criteria to consider in making final media selections.

Frequency refers to the number of times the same viewer or reader may be exposed to the same advertisement. A consumer might pass an outdoor poster twice daily for 90 days, whereas a radio spot might be broadcast a dozen times before a person hears it once. Similarly, consumers are likely to read newspapers only once per day, but see a magazine ad in one issue several times.

Newspaper Advertising

Newspapers have always made up the bulk of retail advertising, probably because their local nature fits the retailer's desire for geographic coverage, prestige, and immediacy.[14] Retailers spent 36 percent and 17 percent of their overall 1990 ad budget on newspaper run-of-press and inserts, respectively.[15] In addition, newspapers are a "participative" medium that people read partly for the advertising; in fact, many consumers use newspapers as a shopping guide. As mentioned, retailers gain some measure of audience selectivity by advertising in specific sections of the paper, such as the sports, society, and financial sections. The cost of **newspaper advertising** is neither the highest nor the lowest of the available media.

By size and format, newspapers are classified as either standard or tabloid. Most large newspapers are standard; that is, they are about 23.5 inches deep and eight columns wide, with each column about 2 inches wide. Tabloid newspapers are smaller "booklet" papers, five columns wide by about 14 inches deep, or about half the size of standard newspapers.

Newspapers can also be classified as dailies or weeklies, metropolitan, community, or shopping newspapers. Metropolitan newspapers are circulated over an entire metropolitan area (e.g., the *New York Times*), whereas community newspapers are published for a portion of a city or a suburb (e.g., *Newsday,* the Long Island newspaper). Shopping newspapers are comprised mostly of retail and classified advertising.

Newspapers sell two kinds of advertising space: *classified* and *display*. Classified advertising is carried in a special section and used only by certain kinds of retailers, such as automobile dealers. Most retailers, however, use display advertising, which is spread throughout the newspaper. The basic unit of space the retailer buys from the newspaper is *agate line* (or "line" in common use). An agate line is one column wide and 1/14 of an inch deep. Fourteen lines of space thus equals one *column inch,* the basic space unit for smaller papers. One full page of advertising equals about 2,400 lines or approximately 172 column inches, depending on the size of the paper.

Newspapers publish their rates on *rate cards* that they make available to customers. A retailer that buys newspaper space one time with no stipulations would pay the paper's *open rate*. Few retailers, however, actually pay the open rate, since the cost of newspaper space generally decreases with the quantity bought and increases as the retailer improves the "quality" of its advertising by specifying a particular position in the paper or by using color.

Most retailers that advertise regularly make *space contracts* with the newspaper, by which the retailer agrees to use a certain amount of space over the year and pay a certain amount per line that is lower than the paper's open rate for the same space. The lower rate is simply a quantity discount. A retailer that advertises heavily in a newspaper can receive up to 40 percent off the open rate in a large space contract. Unless otherwise specified, newspaper rates are ROP (run of the paper), meaning the paper will put the ad wherever it sees fit in composing the paper. This is not necessarily undesirable, because newspapers, like other businesses, want to satisfy their customers. They, therefore, do the best they can to make up an attractive paper and place advertising where it fits best. A retailer who is willing to pay a premium called a *position charge* can, however, specify a position in the paper. The retailer can then specify the first three pages, the sports, society, or financial section, or even a specific page. Some retailers even rent a certain space permanently. For ROP ads, newspapers generally place larger ads closer to the front of a section and smaller ads nearer the back.

Most newspapers can print in color, and color advertising is becoming more common. Needless to say, the retailer pays more for color, and the more color used, the more the retailer pays. Many newspapers also can insert preprinted color advertisements.

Newspaper rate structures are determined by circulation: The greater the circulation, the higher the rates, and vice versa. A paper's paid and unpaid circulation is audited by the Audit Bureau of Circulations, which publishes a report of circulations throughout the paper's city and its retail trading zone, the area beyond the city proper for which the city is a trade center. To compare newspapers' advertising rates, which vary widely, advertisers commonly use a calculation called the *milline rate,* which is the paper's cost of getting a line of advertising to a million people. The formula for the milline rate follows:

$$\text{milline rate} = \frac{\text{line rate} \times 1{,}000{,}000}{\text{circulation}}$$

Magazine Advertising

Few retailers advertise in consumer magazines. Although magazines do offer a high degree of prestige, audience selectivity, and impact (when used correctly), they generally lack geographic selectivity, which is what the vast majority of retailers require. Because magazines' advertising rates, like newspapers', are based on total circulation, a retailer that places an ad must pay for wasted circulation outside its trading area. Thus, a Kansas City retailer that advertises in a nationally circulated magazine pays to advertise not only to Kansas City residents but also to readers in Maine and Louisiana. To offset this disadvantage, many magazines publish regional editions (same editorial matter, different advertising) for certain geographic areas (e.g., Southwest) and major cities (e.g., New York). City and regional magazines have grown in both number and circulation, and the greater geographic selection of these magazines makes them a more feasible advertising medium for some retailers.

Magazines also require a considerable period of time between publication date and the date advertising materials must be available. Magazines therefore do not accommodate the immediate-response advertising that makes up the majority of retail business. Most retailers that use magazines are either nationwide chains or stores with branches in several nearby cities.

Magazine advertising usually is bought in pages and fractions, such as half page, one-third page, or two-thirds page. Generally, the only premium positions are inside the front cover, the inside and outside of the back cover, opposite the table of contents, and the center spread. Magazine rates, like newspaper rates, are based on circulations, and the rate structures, circulations, facts of publication, and publication requirements are published in *Standard Rate and Data Service*. Magazines' rates are compared by a calculation known as cost per thousand (CPM). As briefly described earlier, it is computed as follows:

$$\text{CPM} = \frac{\text{cost of page} \times 1{,}000}{\text{circulation}}$$

If a full-page black and white advertisement in a magazine costs \$5,000 and the circulation is 750,000, then CPM = \$5,000 × 1,000/750,000 = \$6.67. As with newspapers, one magazine may have a higher cost per page but a lower CPM than another, depending on their relative circulations.

Radio Advertising

Americans own about five radio receivers per household, and American retailers have used radio extensively almost since its inception. Among its advantages are low cost and a high degree of geographic and audience selectivity. Although radio broadcasters claim otherwise, sound alone is not a very good communications medium. Therefore, advertisers should stick with a simple message, make it easy to remember (hence the radio "jingle"), and repeat the message frequently.

Like other media advertising rates, radio rates are based on audience sizes. *Coverage* is the geographic area over which the station's signal can be heard; *audience* refers to the number of people who actually listen. Some 50,000-watt "clear-channel" radio stations broadcast over a geographic area, including many areas outside the retailer's market area. *Regional* stations cover smaller geographic areas that are much larger than a typical city. *Local* stations (1,000 watts or less) broadcast a signal that usually does not carry further than about 25 miles, and most listeners are clearly in the retailer's market area.

Radio stations appeal to highly specialized audiences because of their programming: rock and roll stations, easy-listening stations, classical music stations, all-news stations, or talk-show stations. Moreover, radio listeners are much more station-loyal than television viewers, who switch freely from one channel to another. Radio is particularly important to drivers, who have their radios tuned in about 62 percent of their drive time; peak drive times are 7 to 9 A.M. and 4 to 6 P.M.

Radio advertising is sold as either *network* radio (buying from several stations that air joint programming) or *spot* radio (bought from individual stations). Because most retailers want to advertise in one city only, most buy spot radio announcements. Stations divide their total air time into classes, usually labeled as AAA, AA, A, B, and C, with the best times being early morning (6 to 10 A.M.) and late afternoon (3 to 7 P.M.). Generally, the fewest people listen at night, so this time is the cheapest. Spot announcements usually are sold in 1-minute, 30-second, and 10-second periods for a certain number of repetitions (e.g., 15, 50, or 150 times). Retailers often buy weekly package plans for a number of repetitions of a message of a certain duration over a certain time class; for example, retailers can select twenty 30-second announcements in class AA time for a week. They also can buy joint sponsorship of certain programs, such as the daily stock market report. *Standard Rate and Data Service* lists radio stations' packages and rates and describes their programming.

Radio rates are based on audience size. Estimates of the number and characteristics of listeners at certain times of the day are made by companies like The Pulse, Inc. and American Research Bureau. These statistics are sold to radio stations, which in turn make them available to potential advertisers. The retailer, as an advertiser, can write its own radio copy and have the station produce it—provide the announcer and develop a musical background and whatever sound effects are needed. Normally, the station does not charge for this service if the retailer runs the message on the producing station.

Television Advertising

Television is the most glamorous and conspicuous advertising medium in this country. Reaching about 99 percent of all U.S. homes, this medium garners a large amount of advertising dollars, but not from retailers. Typically, only the larger chain organizations have the budgets to support **television advertising** (see Figure 16–6).

Although television is an excellent communications medium, its high cost constraints eliminate all but the largest retailers from using it regularly. Moreover, preparing television commercials requires expertise that store advertising departments do not usually have, so most retailers depend on advertising agencies to produce and place their television commercials. Television stations also will produce commercials for a fee.

Like radio time, television time is sold as network or spot time. Unlike radio, the majority of television programming originates from the networks. Since most retailers' markets are localized again, only the largest nationwide chains can buy network television time. Most retailers buy spot announcements from local stations. In contrast to the number of radio stations, only a few television stations operate in most cities.

Television time rate structures and measurements of audience size on which rates are based are quite complex. A complete discussion is beyond the scope of this book; the reader is referred to any standard advertising text. In general, television stations divide their time into classes based on size of audience at a given time. The larger the audience, the higher the cost of advertising time. *Prime time,* when most people watch television, is 7:30 to 11 P.M. on the East and West coasts and 6:30 to 10 P.M. in the Midwest. *Fringe time* comprises the hours immediately preceding and following prime time. *Daytime* and *late nighttime,* the least expensive times, are when the fewest people watch television. Advertising rates, therefore, are lowest during the times with few viewers and highest during prime time, which normally attracts the most viewers.

Local stations sell spot announcements in and around programming at certain times, as well as packages of announcements much like radio packages. As in almost all media, television stations allow advertisers a quantity discount; the greater the number of repetitions, the lower the cost per repetition. The retailer can buy 1-minute, 30-second, and 10-second spots (or combinations of these), or it may buy partial sponsorship of the station's local programming.

FIGURE 16–6
The best TV commercials of 1987: As picked by editors of *Advertising Age*

McDonald's "Mac Tonight" (Davis, Johnson, Mogul & Colombatto; Ian Leach): The idea was to stress dinner. The method in this :30 was to adapt the foot-tapping music of "Mack the Knife" to McDonald's lyrics and have it played by a smiling figure with a half-moon head seated at the piano. Festive amusement park background is replete with McDonald's and Coke signs and a giant rotating mock-up of a McD.L.T. McDonald's regional operators' agency handled this one, and its West Coast success led to spot going national. Third-quarter earnings up 14%, which the company credited partly to the spot. AA's adWatch ranked it No. 1 in recall for September.

McDonald's "Daddy's Little Girl" (Leo Burnett USA; Steve Horn Productions): Dad, after picking up young daughter and friends after the dance, is persuaded to take them to McDonald's because "all the cute boys" will be there. As father follows girls into entrance, daughter stops: "Dad! You're not coming in?" 'Course not, says Pop. He eats his burger in the station wagon. Daughter, sipping Coke, waves to him surreptitiously through window. A story designed, says McD., to strengthen the emotional bond with the public.

McDonald's "The New Kids" (Leo Burnett USA; Harmony Pictures): It's a tender tale of a senior citizen's first day of work at McDonald's. The young crew, taken aback at his age, is soon impressed with his prowess: "Sure you've never done this before?" On returning home, wife asks him how it went. Reply: "Don't know how they got along without me." For McDonald's, one planned recruitment result: A flood of senior-citizen job applications.

Southland Corp.'s 7-Eleven "Dabney/-Chicken" (W.B. Doner & Co.; Elite Films): Actor Dabney Coleman has some good-natured fun positioning 7-Eleven as the store for key commodities like eggs, milk and soft drinks. Opens with Dabney in henhouse selling merits of eggs. As cackling grows loud, he angrily shouts, "Quiet!" Silence, as camera freezes on hens. At end, he apologizes to hen for "getting a little emotional." Slogan: At 7-Eleven, "Even good prices come easy." So does Dabney.

Frederick & Nelson department store (R, Seattle) "Great Department Store" (Cole & Weber; Paul Hopkins/Sue Mowrer): "What makes a great department store?" asks voice-over as a colorful, appealing array of products parades past—perfume to designer fashion to furniture. Contributing mightily to the atmosphere is the Gershwin music, in vogue for other advertisers, too, in 1987 (United Airlines among them). Screen and voice-over sew it up: "One of the great department stores—Frederick & Nelson."

Amoco Silver gasoline "Lone Ranger-Prospector" (DMB&B; Yarbrough & Co.): Launching a new midgrade unleaded gas, Amoco uses Lone Ranger and reference to his horse, Silver, to associate with the product name. It's a lighthearted spoof of the Lone Ranger as, after gassing up, he rides off into the sunset in his Jeep, shouting, "Hi-yo, Silver, awa-a-y." With all that aging and nostalgic audience, awareness of the new gas hit 62%.

Source: Merle Kingman, "Music is the Magic for Most of the Best." Reprinted with permission from the March 14, 1988 issue of *Advertising Age*, p. 5–8. Copyright © by Crain Communications, Inc.

The sizes of local stations' television audiences are measured by firms such as the A.C. Nielsen Company and the American Research Bureau. By means of diaries, electronic recording devices, and interviews, these companies estimate the number of people in the station's market area watching various television programs. With these figures, station managers can compute a CPM figure in much the same way that newspapers compute their CPMs. Television and radio stations have a special problem, however; viewership and listenership figures vary with the same program on a day-to-day and week-to-week basis and also vary from one program to another. Thus, for any one program, it is sensible to calculate an average audience size. A way to calculate CPM for a television station is shown here:

$$\text{CPM} = \frac{\text{average cost of a minute's advertising} \times 1{,}000}{\text{average audience size}}$$

Sign Advertising

Retailers use outdoor advertising media extensively, especially posters, bulletins, and spectaculars. **Sign advertising** gives retailers impact, coverage, frequency, geographic selectivity, and a long life for a relatively low CPM. As described by experts, "out-of-home scores well in segmentation. . . . [I]t permits geographic targeting of specific groups. And it has the added advantage not only of reaching target audiences but also frequently exposing them to the ad message . . . [and it] has the lowest cost-per-thousand impressions of any medium."[16] Outdoor signs, however, are good for presenting only a short reminder message, perhaps the store name, an illustration, and a few words of copy.

Outdoor signs are owned or leased by local plant operators that install the advertisers' messages and are responsible for maintaining the signs and the surrounding areas. The three basic outdoor signs are the 30-sheet, 12- by 25-foot *poster* that most

Sign advertising can be effective and relatively inexpensive.

people call a "billboard," *painted bulletins,* and outdoor *spectaculars*. Painted bulletins are signs approximately 14 by 48 feet on which the advertising message is actually painted in sections by an artist working from a miniature. When the advertisement is painted in sections, the advertiser can move the message to another location. Outdoor spectaculars are nonstandardized, custom-made signs that use elaborate lighting, falling water, rising steam, billowing smoke, and other techniques to attract consumers' attention. Although these signs have higher attention value, they are quite costly to produce.

Outdoor signs usually are bought in "showings" for periods of time of 90 days and up. A number 100 showing is the number of signs sufficient for a daily exposure of the message to a population equal to that of the market area. Other showing sizes are number 75, 50, 25, and 150; a showing size of 75, for example, means that the number of signs will expose the advertiser's message to 75 percent of the market area. The number of signs in a showing is not fixed. Fewer signs are necessary if they are exposed to heavy traffic, whereas more signs are needed if they are exposed to light-traffic areas. The Traffic Audit Bureau, Inc. audits, by markets, the "circulation" of posters and bulletins (the amount of traffic passing by) and publishes the results in *The Audited Circulation Values of Outdoor Advertising*. The medium's prices are based on these circulation figures. The CPM of outdoor advertising can be computed as follows:

$$\text{CPM} = \frac{\text{rental of all showings bought per month} \times 1{,}000}{\text{number of cars passing by in a month} \times \text{average number of passengers in the car (the "auto load factor")}}$$

Transit advertising includes car cards, exterior displays, and station posters. *Car cards* are the posters (usually 11 by 28 inches) displayed on interior wall racks in buses, subway trains, and the cars of rapid transit systems. *Exterior displays,* which vary in size, are the advertisements shown on the outside of buses, cars, and taxis. *Station posters* are signs displayed in the interiors of subway, railroad, and rapid-transit stations.

Advertisers buy transit advertising from transit-advertising companies, also known as *operators,* which function much the same as outdoor plant operators. Car cards normally are sold in *runs*. A full run is two cards in every bus, car, and so forth in the market. Half runs and quarter runs are also possible. The rate structure in transit advertising is similar to that of outdoor advertising, because it is based on the volume of traffic passing through bus and train routes. The rates for exterior or traveling displays and station posters are not standardized but, as for outdoor showings, are based on the number of people who view them. The CPM for transit advertising is calculated in the same way as for outdoor media. Like outdoor advertising, transit advertising is relatively inexpensive.

Direct Advertising

Direct advertising is a medium that retailers use extensively to communicate their product offerings to a select group of consumers. The retailer creates an advertisement and distributes it directly to consumers either through the mail or through the personal distribution of circulars, handbills, and other printed matter. Although direct advertising is expensive in terms of CPM, it is the most selective medium, since the ads are read only by people the retailer selects. It also is a personal form of advertising and extremely flexible. Direct advertising can include pictures, letters, records, pencils, coins, coupons, premiums, samples, and any other gifts the retailer chooses to include.

Retailers may choose to distribute direct advertising to their charge customers or other known or potential customers, or they may buy a mailing list from mailing-list houses, which sell lists for a certain charge per thousand names. The variety of these

WORLD OF RETAILING

Business Ethics

Check Your Check

Around the country, direct-mail promotions that look like checks, government documents, legal notices, and urgent telegrams are used to market automobiles, vacation resorts and other products and services. The advertising typically comes in envelopes that bear no indication they contain promotional material. Instead, the envelopes often have a window displaying a document resembling a check made out to the recipient. They often carry an official-looking return address, sometimes accompanied by a government-style emblem, such as an eagle or the Statue of Liberty.

The envelopes sometimes mimic the brown Social Security checks, or have a message encouraging people to buy U.S. Savings Bonds and directions to the postmaster on procedures to handle the mail, quoting sections of postal regulations.

Some promotions around the country use threats to get consumers to open envelopes they might otherwise throw away. A 1987 promotion for the Fountains Resort near Palm Springs, Calif., was sent in an envelope bearing an eagle, a return address of "Department of F.B.I." and, in bold, capital letters, the words: "Notice of attempt to serve warrant of appearance." In lighter type, it read: "Notice to claim cash and/or merchandise." Inside the envelope was a letter from "Fountains Bureau of Invitations."

Outdoor World Inc. of Bushkill, Penn., mailed campground promotions in envelopes bearing the words "notice of audit" and a return address to the Division of Adjustments and Disbursements, Washington, D.C. In February, as part of a settlement of a lawsuit brought by the Massachusetts attorney general over Outdoor World's business practices, the company agreed that it no longer would use government look-alike documents.

Source: Anthony Giorgianni, "Direct-Mail Gimmicks under First," *The Plain Dealer,* April 29, 1990, B3.

lists is astonishing, ranging from magazine subscribers to professional groups to hobbyists to owners of certain products. The retailer never sees these lists; instead, advertising pieces are sent to the mailing-list house, which addresses and mails them. Some retailers prepare their own direct advertising, whereas others choose agencies to prepare it and arrange for distribution. The cost of direct-mail advertising is also measured by the CPM criterion:

$$\text{CPM} = \frac{\text{cost of preparing and distributing advertising} \times 1{,}000}{\text{total number of recipients}}$$

Unlike most other advertising media, the effectiveness of direct advertising can be directly measured if the advertisement calls for a response or an order. By dividing the total sales resulting from customer responses by the total cost of preparing and distributing the direct-advertising materials, the retailer can establish a measure of the cost per sale or response for this promotion.

CONTROLLING THE ADVERTISING FUNCTION

To establish some measure of control over its advertising effort, the retailer must evaluate the effects of advertising. The retailer must first establish specific, measurable advertising objectives, then acquire or develop instruments and methodologies to determine whether those objectives were met. As mentioned, advertising objectives can be stated in terms of either sales or communications levels. Because sales are affected by factors both internal and external to the retailer's operations, meaningful measurements of **advertising effectiveness** are difficult to make, especially in the long run. Short-run advertising objectives can be measured broadly, however, if we assume very few changes occur in the short run (one day to a week). If noticeable changes do occur in this short run, then the retailer must temper its evaluation of advertising effectiveness in light of this information or consider the evaluation a failure. Given that external and internal factors remain relatively stable, the retailer can make a gross measurement of its advertising's sales effectiveness in two ways. (1) For all advertising messages designed to stimulate immediate sales (such as coupons, half-price sales, etc.), the retailer can measure dollar sales increases, increases in number of purchases, increases in store traffic, and so on against those for a comparable period (e.g., last year at the same time or last week). (2) For any direct-advertising campaign, the retailer can

FIGURE 16–7
The effectiveness of advertising (source: Irwin Broh, "Measure Success of Promotions with In-Store Customer Surveys," *Marketing News,* 13 May 1983, 17)

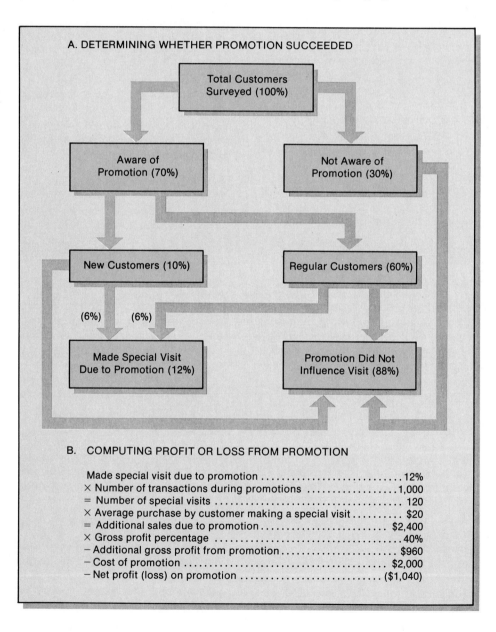

A. DETERMINING WHETHER PROMOTION SUCCEEDED

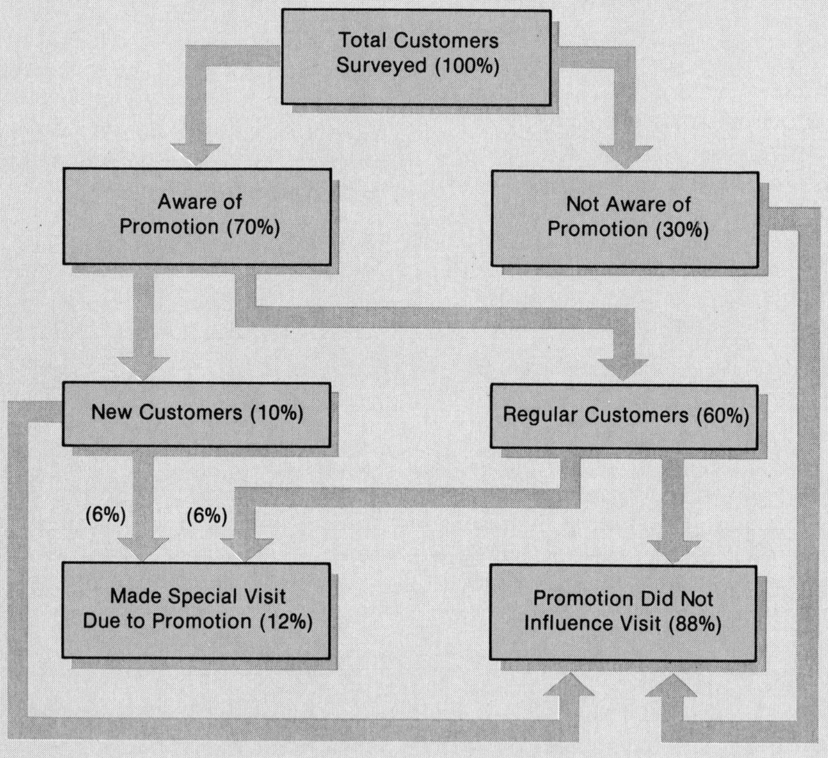

B. COMPUTING PROFIT OR LOSS FROM PROMOTION

Made special visit due to promotion	12%
× Number of transactions during promotions	1,000
= Number of special visits	120
× Average purchase by customer making a special visit	$20
= Additional sales due to promotion	$2,400
× Gross profit percentage	40%
– Additional gross profit from promotion	$960
– Cost of promotion	$2,000
– Net profit (loss) on promotion	($1,040)

measure in-store and out-of-store inquiries, sales increases, or traffic increases. Increases in sales, consumer traffic, and number of purchases are all important success measurements for advertising. An even more appropriate measure of the success of a retail promotion, though, is to compare the gross profits from additional sales generated by the promotion to the cost of the promotion.[17] One method for obtaining this measurement is shown in Figure 16–7.

Advertising designed to achieve communications objectives should be measured over the long run. Changes in customer awareness, attitudes, perceptions, and behavioral intentions toward the store should be measured either by personal interviews or mail surveys. In this case, the retailer must use both pretest and posttest measurements to establish possible changes in consumers' opinions of the store.

SUMMARY

Promotion is the fourth element in the retail mix. It involves providing consumers with information about the retailer's store and its offering and influencing their perceptions, attitudes, and behavior. Promotion is also closely related to the communication process, because transmitting meaningful messages through the retailer's promotion mix involves the five major components of advertising, personal selling, store displays, sales promotion, and publicity. Managing the retail advertising function consists of planning, organizing, executing, and controlling advertising strategies. Advertising works for the retailer by prompting individual consumers to move through the adoption process and by stimulating the two-step flow of mass communications.

In developing advertising plans, the retailer sets advertising objectives, identifies the types of advertising it must conduct, and develops advertising appropriations and budgets. Retail advertising takes the form of product advertising, institutional advertising, or some combination of the two. The advertising appropriation is the total amount spent on advertising, whereas the budget is the allocation of this appropriation across departments or across merchandise lines, time periods, and advertising media. Advertising appropriation and budgeting methods include the educated-guess method, the percentage-of-sales method, the competitive parity method, and the objective and task method.

Organizing and executing the advertising function depends heavily on store size and available funds. Small stores rely heavily on outside advertising specialists, whereas large stores normally have a sales promotion and advertising manager to supervise artists, copywriters, publicity directors, and display managers. In addition, this manager works with store merchandise managers and outside advertising specialists.

Executing the advertising function consists of creating advertisements and selecting advertising media. The retailer must determine the purpose of the advertisement, create the basic message, develop the communications approach, and finalize the total advertisement. The total print advertisement consists of layout, headline, illustration, copy, and logotype. Retailers use newspapers, consumer magazines, radio, television, sign media, direct advertising, and numerous other media.

Advertising control, the job of evaluating advertising effectiveness, consists of determining what to measure and how to measure it. The retailer may choose either sales or communications measures and from among numerous methods of measuring advertising effectiveness.

STUDENT STUDY GUIDE

Key Terms and Concepts

advertisement message (p. 594)
advertising (p. 581)
advertising agencies (p. 592)
advertising budgets (p. 590)
advertising effectiveness (p. 606)
advertising freelancer (p. 592)

advertising manager (p. 592)
audience selectivity (p. 597)
communication effectiveness (p. 596)
communication process (p. 580)
communications approach (p. 594)
competitive parity method (p. 590)
cooperative advertising (p. 587)
copy (p. 596)
cost (p. 598)
coverage (p. 598)
DAGMAR (p. 583)
decoding (p. 580)
direct advertising (p. 604)
educated-guess method (p. 590)
encoding (p. 580)
feedback (p. 580)
flexibility (p. 597)
frequency (p. 598)
geographic selectivity (p. 597)
headline (p. 594)
illustration (p. 596)
immediacy (p. 598)
impact (p. 597)
institutional advertising (p. 585)
layout (p. 594)
life (p. 598)
logotype (p. 596)
magazine advertising (p. 600)
media representative (p. 592)
newspaper advertising (p. 598)
noise (p. 580)
objective and task method (p. 591)
opinion leaders (p. 584)
percentage-of-sales method (p. 590)
personal selling (p. 581)
prestige (p. 597)
product advertising (p. 585)
promotion (p. 580)
publicity (p. 582)
radio advertising (p. 600)
receivers (p. 580)
sales promotion (p. 582)
sales promotion director (p. 592)
sales promotion manager (p. 592)
senders (p. 580)
sign advertising (p. 603)
store displays (p. 582)
television advertising (p. 601)
total advertisement (p. 594)
transmission (p. 580)
two-step flow of communications (p. 584)

Review Questions

1. Identify and briefly describe the various participants, processes, and acts of the communication process.
2. List the five elements of the promotion mix. Define each element.
3. How is product advertising different from institutional advertising?
4. What is the purpose of an advertising objective aimed at store positioning?
5. What considerations should the retailer take into account when allocating advertising budgets?
6. Describe the four-step objective and task method of determining the retailer's advertising budget.
7. In developing the basic advertising message, the retailer is concerned with which two issues?
8. List the five components of a total advertisement and define each component.
9. Which media characteristics do retailers consider when selecting the most appropriate types of media for communicating with their consumers?
10. Newspapers sell two kinds of advertising space. What are they? How is newspaper space measured?
11. Explain the following newspaper advertising concepts: open rate, space contract, ROP, and position charge.
12. How are newspaper rate structures determined?
13. Identify the positive and negative aspects of magazine advertising from the retailer's viewpoint.
14. How is radio advertising sold?
15. From the retailer's perspective, what are the positive and negative characteristics of television advertising?
16. What are the three types of outdoor advertising? Describe each type.

Review Exam

True or False

_____ 1. The difference between advertising and publicity is that advertising refers to television media and publicity refers to print media.

_____ 2. In cooperative advertising, the retailer and the manufacturer split the cost of media space.

_____ 3. The "percentage of sale" method of setting advertising expenditures is generally accepted as the best means to determine an advertising budget.

_____ 4. Copy is the store's distinct signature, which appears in all advertising.

_____ 5. Radio advertising is characterized by greater immediacy than magazine advertising.

_____ 6. Television advertising is the most important advertising medium for retailers as defined by total advertising expenditures.

_____ 7. Direct advertising is one of the least expensive methods of advertising.

Multiple Choice

_____ 1. The order in which the communication process occurs is _____.

a. transmitting, sending, encoding, decoding, receiving, and feedback
b. sending, encoding, decoding, transmitting, receiving, and feedback
c. sending, encoding, transmitting, receiving, decoding, and feedback
d. encoding, sending, decoding, receiving, feedback, and transmitting
e. none of the above

_____ 2. Establishing favorable attitudes toward the store is an achievement that is associated with the _____ stage of the DAGMAR model.
a. unawareness
b. awareness
c. comprehension
d. conviction
e. action

_____ 3. The communications approach focuses on _____.
a. what the retailer is saying
b. how the message is conveyed
c. to whom the message is directed
d. the choice of media to convey the message
e. the cost of the message

_____ 4. A lot of white space in an advertisement suggests _____.
a. quality and prestige
b. limited product line
c. discounting and a price appeal
d. the retailer wanted to minimize costs of the ad
e. none of the above

_____ 5. Retailers that wish to purchase a specific area in the paper will pay a(n) _____.
a. position charge
b. open rate
c. short rate
d. ROP rate
e. space rate

_____ 6. A medium's ability to present a timely or newsworthy message is referred to as _____.
a. geographic selectivity
b. audience selectivity
c. impact
d. immediacy
e. life

_____ 7. A measurement of the success of a retail promotion is _____.
a. an increase in sales
b. to compare the gross profits from additional sales generated by the promotion to the cost of the promotion
c. an increase in consumer traffic
d. an increase in the number of purchases
e. all of the above

STUDENT APPLICATIONS MANUAL

Investigative Projects: Practice and Applications

1. To benefit from the "two-step flow of communication process," the retailer must identify, reach, and work with opinion leaders. For specific products and/or stores in your community, identify potential opinion leaders, describe how the retailer might secure their cooperation, and discuss some specific examples of how retailers and opinion leaders might work together to create greater consumer awareness of the retailer, to enhance store image, and to promote store traffic.
2. By surveying your local newspaper, identify advertisements directed toward the objectives of (1) building store image, (2) positioning the store in the market, (3) generating store traffic, and (4) creating special events. Which of your advertisements is most effective in accomplishing its objective? Why?
3. Discuss the pros and cons of participating in cooperative advertising. Under what circumstances should a retailer agree to cooperative advertising?
4. Discuss why a retailer might elect to heavily promote high-markup, low-turnover products and to deemphasize or eliminate the promotion of low-markup, high-turnover products.
5. Assume the following retailers have budgeted 3 percent of their estimated $600,000 sales volume for advertising: (1) a record and tape store, (2) a campus book store, and (3) a children's shoe store. Identify and describe the major media and time considerations they need to bear in mind in allocating their advertising budgets. Develop a media and time allocation plan for their advertising budgets. Develop a media and time allocation plan for each store and justify each plan.
6. Identify two retailers in your community that currently do not have a logo. For each retailer, develop a distinctive logo that they could use with their advertising. Be creative!
7. List four major radio stations that serve your community. Interview each station manager and determine the audience selectivity of each station. Identify the types of retailers that would best be served by each station. Explain.

Exhibit A

THE JAMES DEAN GALLERY

FAIRMOUNT, INDIANA
THE HOMETOWN OF JAMES DEAN

"The James Dean Gallery" houses the world's largest collection of memorabilia and archives dealing with the short life and career of one of the most remembered personalities in film history.

The exhibit includes thousands of items including clothing from his films, high school yearbooks, a rare Warner Brothers life-mask, and hundreds of original movie posters, books, and magazines from over twenty different countries from around the world. Also included are hundreds of tribute and novelty items that have been produced since the 50's, such as plates, mugs, busts, puzzles, and gum cards.

James Dean graduated from Fairmount High School in 1949 and moved to California where he got bit parts in a few films. Discouraged, he left for New York, where he appeared in over two dozen television dramas and two Broadway plays. On Broadway he was spotted by director Elia Kazan who whisked him to Hollywood to star in his first major role in *"East of Eden"*. Dean made only two more films, *"Rebel Without A Cause"* and *"Giant"*, before his tragic death at age 24 in a California highway accident on September 30, 1955.

"The James Dean Gallery" gives visitors an opportunity to view many of the items which have helped to keep the memory of the famous Indiana native alive.

Memorabilia on display at "The James Dean Gallery".

Other points of interest in the small Indiana town include, Dean's gravesite, old "Fairmount High School", and "The Fairmount Historical Museum", which also offers an impressive display of James Dean memorabilia.

Artwork from original painting by
Kenneth Kendall

Open to visitors:
Daily 10:00 a.m. - 5:00 p.m.
Admission:
$2.00

From Indianapolis, take I-465 to I-69 N then to exit 55, SR 26. Go west on SR 26 4 miles to Fairmount. **From Ft. Wayne** go south on I-69 to exit 55, SR 26, go west on SR 26 to Fairmount. Go south on Main Street 3 blocks.

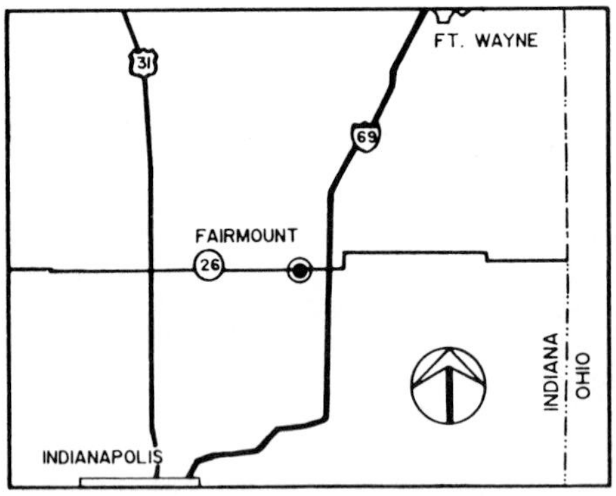

THE JAMES DEAN GALLERY
and GIFT SHOP
425 N. Main Street
Fairmount, Indiana 46928
(317) 948-3326

Tactical Cases: Problems and Decisions

■ CASE 16–1
The James Dean Gallery*

America's countryside is dotted with little museums devoted to its folk heroes. Among these museums is the James Dean Gallery in Fairmount, Indiana. The gallery was established in 1988 to preserve the memory of the life and career of a young film star. As with most such museums, the gallery contains personal artifacts and memorabilia. Since James Dean's death in 1955 there has been a profusion of novelty items and other commemoratives issued. Many of these are on display and/or for sale.

The gallery's chief revenue sources are admissions ($2.00 per person) and the sale of books and memorabilia. The first years have been a struggle, but the business is stabilizing. The gallery operator, James Dean archivist David Loehr, is now planning for the future. He is looking over 1989 business results to make some projections for the rest of 1990.

The gallery recorded approximately 6,000 visitors over the course of the year. Approximately 20 percent of these came during Fairmount's Museum Days weekend. The Museum Days event is held at the end of every September, in commemoration of Dean's death. Visitors come to see the town, Dean's home, the Fairmount Historical Museum, and the gallery. There is also a classic car and street rod show held at the same time. These events draw large crowds to Fairmount and the largest neighboring city, Marion.

Sales receipts from the museum shop for 1989 show $13,500 in retail sales. The average markup on retail price is 60 percent. Even with admission revenues, the gallery is operating at a loss. Dave expects to have the gallery self-sustaining in a year or two.

Virtually all of the gallery's operating costs are fixed. In 1989, the costs came to about $23,000 including $7,000 spent on advertising and promotion. Dave had 10,000 advertising cards printed at a cost of $350.00 to be distributed at highway rest areas, tourist hotels, and the like (Exhibit A). The cards were included in a mailing to Dave's list of visitors and others who have expressed interest in the gallery. At present, that list numbers 2,500. Each receives two three-page mailings each year to keep apprised of new items on display and for sale. Some of these people order merchandise by mail, but these sales are recorded with the wholesale side of the business.

The only other advertising that is done consists of occasional display advertisements in the newspapers in Marion and Muncie. These are placed just before Museum Days and in holiday editions. The gallery's ads are typically 4 inches × 2 columns; the costs for these are shown in Exhibit B.

Dave is expecting revenues to increase by about 20 percent in 1990. James Dean's greatest appeal remains with females 14–22 and males and females 35–49. The gallery draws heavily from these groups. In addition, Dean fans from all over make special trips to see Fairmount and visit the gallery while there. Some foreign fans

EXHIBIT B
Advertising costs

	Page Rate	Circulation
Newspapers		
Marion Chronicle Tribune	$ 2100	25000
Muncie Star Press	3200	35000
Indianapolis Star News	18000	350000
Fort Wayne Journal Gazette	6400	120000
Toledo (OH) Blade	6600	150000
Magazines		
Movie Fan	15000	270000
Seventeen	27000	1400000
People	43000	13500000
	30 Second Anytime	**Audience**
Radio (Top 40)		
Marion	$ 25	1900
Muncie	47	4000
Indianapolis	250	12000
Direct mail		
Bulk rate is $.132 per ounce, presorted.		

come to the United States for this reason only. The rest of the visitors are travelers who happen by on U.S. 69 and stop in out of curiosity. Dave would like to determine how best to contact the various audiences. He has collected some advertising rate information (Exhibit B), but is unsure whether the vehicles are sufficient. In addition, he wonders whether additional media types should be included. Last year's advertising seemed to help, but he doesn't know whether the money was spent efficiently.

ASSIGNMENT

Advise Dave on advertising plans for 1990 and beyond. How should the budget be determined? What media should he use? Which vehicles within those media? Is the direct mail going to the correct audience? How should advertising be distributed across the year? You may wish to consider alternatives beyond just advertising the gallery (e.g., sales promotions or cooperative advertising).

*This case was prepared by Douglas Hausknecht and Kevin Casper, The University of Akron. The data have been disguised.

■ CASE 16–2
Anderson's Old-Fashioned Gourmet Hamburgers Discovers the Yellow Pages and Other Facts of Life*

Stan Anderson is a young man in his early thirties with dreams of success in the restaurant business. A marketing major from the University of Texas at El Paso, Stan is currently the manager for a large gift shop in the city's newest shopping mall. Although his career with the gift shop has been successful, he longs for the excitement and financial reward that can come from being an independent entrepreneur.

Stan believes that El Paso is ripe for a restaurant specializing in "gourmet" hamburgers (à la Fuddrucker's). Stan has secured what appears to be a prime location on the prosperous west side of town, only three blocks from the above-mentioned shopping mall. The restaurant is on a heavily traveled street with excellent traffic counts. The restaurant itself is a very stylish building only four years old. (The former restaurant appeared quite popular, but suddenly closed. Although rumors have speculated as to the cause for the demise, the problems seem to have been strictly internal and in no way attributable to the site itself.)

The owner of the property has been quite selective with respect to tenants, and that, coupled with the rather high cost of the property, has kept the property vacant for nearly a year. Using family contacts as an introduction, Stan was able to secure the favor of the owner, and has obtained a one-year lease with option to renew. Although Stan has never managed a restaurant, he was the assistant manager at a country club and part of his duties included overseeing the food service operation. As a result of that experience, plus his management position at the mall, plus his marketing education, Stan feels confident that he can make the restaurant a success.

As with most business ventures, a somewhat substantial amount of investment in equipment, fixtures, remodeling, carpeting, signs, and so forth had to be made. Stan had only a small amount of savings, so almost all of these expenditures were paid for using a loan, co-signed by his father. All total, Stan borrowed $38,000 at 16 percent, which he has promised to repay in monthly installments over three years. As part of the business plan which Stan submitted in his effort to secure the loan he developed the following pro forma income (P&L) Statement:

Pro Forma Profit and Loss Statement		
Gross Sales		$ 300,000
Variable Costs		
Food (40%)	−120,000	
Labor (20%)	−60,000	
	−180,000	−180,000
		120,000
Fixed Costs		
Rent ($2400 × 12)	−28,800	
Loan ($1334 × 12)	−16,000	
Insurance ($900 × 12)	−10,800	
Utilities ($600 × 12)	−7,200	
Supplies ($400 × 12)	−4,800	
Advertising	−6,300	
Professional Help		
CPA ($125 (24 + 6))	−3,750	
Bk/sec ($10 (4 × 52))	−2,080	
Legal ($150 × 12)	−1,800	
Salaries		
Asst Mgr	−18,500	
Stan draw ($1500 × 12)	−18,000	
	−118,030	−118,030
Net Profit before Taxes		1,970
Income Taxes		985
Net Profit after Taxes		985

Admittedly, the projected profits are not exactly huge, and the salary draw that Stan will be getting is less than his current salary. However, the loan will be paid off in just three years, and should the sales grow, that would increase profits even more. Stan has tried to be conservative in his estimate of sales and honest in his estimates of expenses so he feels that the income statement is a fair assessment.

ADVERTISING EXPENDITURES

Stan figured the advertising allocation by applying the restaurant industry average of 2.1 percent of sales to the gross sales estimate of $300,000. Knowing the importance of promotion, and especially so at the beginning, Stan had hoped to spend more than the $6,300 allocation; however, the income statement does not appear to leave much room for expansion. Stan was looking over the following media/promotion alternatives as suggested in his collegiate strategic marketing text, along with current prices for El Paso, Texas.

Newspaper	
(2 columns ×4 inches)	$311.20/per insertion (aft & morn)
Television	
(30-second spot on evening news)	$300/per spot
Radio	
(30-second spot on KLAQ)	$ 60/per spot
(30-second spot on KFOX)	$ 35/per spot
Billboard on Freeway	
(excellent location near the restaurant)	$1,500/month

Stan has been considering the following schedule: The newspaper deal he is considering will provide him an insertion in the special entertainment section that the papers run before every weekend. The $311.20 would provide for one insertion in both the afternoon paper and the morning paper. To run the ad for a month would cost $1,245. After two weeks he would run a series of television spots. He wanted to run two spots a week, for two weeks, on each of the three local stations. Then two weeks later he would do his radio schedule, two spots a day, for two weeks on the two stations he had selected.

However, after Stan contacted the media reps, his plan to use "textbook" media began to unravel. The billboard company insisted on a minimum commitment of four months. That would be $6,000 right there. Shorter commitments could be obtained, but they required a "painting" surcharge of $800.

The TV schedule would consume $3,600 within the space of just two weeks (2×2×3×$300 = $3,600). The radio schedule would also consume the advertising budget at an alarming rate (2×14×$60 = $1,680 plus 2×14×$35 = $980) for a total of $2,660. To make matters even worse, all of the radio and TV sales reps emphasized the fact that the key to success in electronic media is repetition, and the schedule that Stan had outlined really did not seem to have enough repetition to be successful. Of course, it would be the objective of any salesperson to increase the number of spots, but Stan got the distinct impression that the media reps were honestly concerned that with such a small number of reps the campaign might have no discernible effect, thereby souring Stan on electronic media forever.

Yet even the modest advertising schedule he had outlined appears too expensive for Stan. One month of billboard, one month of newspaper, plus the radio and TV would be $9,805 ($2,300 + $1,245 + $3,600 + $2,660). Not only would this exceed the entire year's allocation by over 50 percent, but it would do so in the first month! When he first began working on his pro forma income statement an allocation of $500/month for advertising had seemed quite substantial. After finding how much media $500 would buy, it did not seem substantial at all; rather, it appeared dreadfully puny.

His strategic marketing text had said virtually nothing about any types of promotion other than those major media discussed above. But obviously Stan was going to have to find some less expensive promotional vehicles. He called a small company that handles bus bench advertising. They charge a $30 set-up fee for each bench, and then a monthly charge of $28 a month per bench (minimum six-month contract). There are eight locations that would appear suitable ((8×$30) + (8×$28×6) = $1,584).

Stan is also considering direct mail. A local company delivers packets of coupons to selected homes at a delivered cost (including printing) of only 4 cents apiece. There are two delivery areas in west El Paso, which include 10,000 and 15,000 homes, respectively. The mailing cost to both areas would be an even $1,000. (The $1,000 represents only the cost of the mailing. Most firms using the packets offer some type of discount. Since he has no information regarding redemption rates, the effect of the discount on profit margins is currently unknown. Should Stan decide to use the mailings, he intends to carefully monitor the redemption rate as well as the total dinner ticket to determine the overall profitability of the mailing.) At any rate, Stan figures he could try two or three mailings for the cost of the two week TV schedule. In addition, the coupons in the mailings can be precisely monitored and tracked, whereas the effectiveness of media advertising is virtually impossible to assess.

Although Stan wishes to spend the bulk of his yearly allocation early in the year in order to get an aggressive start, he is also toying with the idea of some kind of special promotional event in the summer. (Opening day is to be February 14. Stan was originally planning some type of Valentine's Day promotion to go along with the opening, but his budget would not seem adequate for that.) Stan had also been considering a radio station "remote" (cost = $1,200) maybe in conjunction with a hot-air balloon (cost = $600) sometime in the summer.

ENTER THE YELLOW PAGES SALESMAN

Stan was still mulling these various possibilities when he was visited by a salesman for the Yellow Pages. The restaurant was not yet open for business, but Stan was in the building overseeing the remodeling. The salesman said that it was really fortunate that he caught Stan when he did because the directory was "closing" at the end of next week. Once the directory is closed, there is no chance to be in the Yellow Pages until the next directory a year later.

Truth to tell, Stan had never given the Yellow Pages a moment's thought. But then, evidently he is not the only one to overlook this multibillion dollar promotional medium. Stan checked his trusty strategic marketing text . . . nary a word. He checked his old retailing text; likewise, not a word. In fact, Stan checked a number of texts and SBA publications and none of them gave the Yellow Pages any more than a passing mention, with most of them ignoring the Yellow Pages completely. This lack of attention is even more startling when you consider the statistics concerning promotional expenditures. For the year 1988, *Direct Marketing* magazine gives the following estimates:

Local Newspaper	$27.5 billion
Television	$25.8 billion
Direct Mail	$21.2 billion
YELLOW PAGES	$ 7.8 BILLION
Radio	$ 7.7 billion
Consumer Magazines	$ 6.0 billion
Cable Television	$ 1.1 billion
Outdoor	$ 1.1 billion

In addition, the salesman reeled off a host of eye-catching statistics. He claimed that research done in Westfield, New Jersey, by Statistical Research Incorporated found that more people use the Yellow Pages to make their buying decisions than any other media. According to their study, an average of individual results for 24 product and service categories revealed that:

28% utilized Yellow Pages
25% utilized Newspapers
12% utilized Television
7% utilized Radio

The study also showed that 32 percent of all dollars spent on the products came from those who referred to the Yellow Pages prior to purchase. Other statistics claim that 80 percent of adults who refer to the Yellow Pages follow up with a call and that 50 percent make a purchase within 48 hours. Of special importance to Stan, according to Statistical Research Incorporated's 1985–1986 Usage Study Report, the category of "Restaurants" was the most frequently referenced heading.

DETERMINING POSITION IN THE YELLOW PAGES

With statistics such as these, Stan obviously wanted to be in the Yellow Pages. And since his restaurant was so new, he wanted to have a large, eye-catching display ad positioned toward the beginning of the restaurant section.

The placement of display ads within a given category heading is determined by three factors. First, and most important, is size. All of the half-page ads will run before any of the quarter-page ads; all of the quarter-page ads will run before any of the eighth-pages ads, and so on. Within a given size, longevity is the next factor considered, with "old" customers taking precedence over "newer" customers. And finally, ads are run in the order in which the contracts are received.

Stan felt that his ad would need to be at least a half page in size in order to stand out from the other submissions. He was relieved when he was told that a half-page ad would cost a mere $320.80. As you no doubt remember from the discussions above, even with some of the cheaper promotions such as bus bench ads ($1,584) and one direct mailing ($1,000) along with two weeks on the most appropriate radio station ($1,680) and two weeks of newspaper ($622), Stan would have spent $4,886 of his $6,300 budget. Thus the Yellow Page cost of only $320 would still leave him with over $1,000.

Stan was ready to sign the contract when he came to a shocking realization. The figure that the Yellow Page salesman was quoting was the *monthly* charge. The bill for a half-page for a year would be $3,850. (And unlike some of the other media, you have to sign up for a full year; you can't tell them to remove your name from all of the books after six months.) Although the Yellow Page salesman was quite insistent that Stan make a decision quickly to get in the book before it closed, Stan was in no condition to sign anything. In fact, it was all he could do to keep from swooning. He quickly turned his attention to some paint that the painters were getting on the new carpet (yes, the walls should have been painted before the carpet was laid, but the carpet layers were a week early and the painters were two weeks late). Stan took the salesman's card and promised that he would get back to him within the week. Sales rep's hype notwithstanding, telephone books do come out in the spring and Stan knew that the deadline for getting in this year's book would be fast approaching. At the same time, however, the prospect of spending over 60 percent of his ad budget on Yellow Pages alone seemed downright frightening. It was obvious that he was going to have to totally rethink his entire advertising budget.

ENTER THE "REAL" YELLOW PAGES SALESMAN

Stan had a hard time sleeping that night thinking about the adjustments that he was going to have to make in his advertising budget in order to incorporate the Yellow Pages. Imagine his surprise the next day when another "Yellow Pages" salesman arrived. Stan quickly informed the salesman that he had already had the salespitch from Jim, the Yellow Pages representative.

The new Yellow Pages salesman curtly informed Stan that they did not have any salesmen named "Jim" working for their company. Stan was confused. Were not the "Yellow Pages" the "Yellow Pages"? You know, those ads printed on yellow pages in the back of your telephone book?

The answer, to Stan's amazement, was "no." For reasons unknown, the Bell System did not trademark either the name "Yellow Pages," nor the familiar "walking fingers" logo, and as a result, anyone can produce a "Yellow Pages" directory incorporating the various yellow pages logos. The first salesman that had called upon Stan represented one of these "independent" directories, as opposed to the "telephone company" directory, AKA "Telco" or "utility" directory. (It could have been worse for Stan. El Paso has just three "yellow pages" directories . . . the greater Los Angeles metropolitan area is served by 168 directories including directories for specific neighborhoods, for designated ethnic groups, and for selected demographic segments.)

Being the traditionalist that he is, Stan was relieved that the "real" Yellow Pages representative had contacted him before he had signed the contract with that "other" directory. Stan would have been mighty upset if his restaurant had not been in the telephone book when the new directories were published. Now he would get his half-page ad in the right directory!

Unfortunately, Stan was in for another rude surprise. The telephone company Yellow Pages are considerably more expensive than the independent directories. A half-page ad in the Telco book costs $691.75/month or $8,301 for a year.

Stan was in shock. He had no idea that Yellow Page advertising was so expensive. Even a quarter-page ad would run over $4,000 for the year. Shown below are the rates for various size ads in the Telco directory vs. the independent directory. (Note: The independent directory has three columns per page, hence the use of one-third of a page. The Telco directory has four columns per page, hence the use of one-eighth and one-sixteenth.) Once again, Stan needed time to think.

Size	Telco/per year	Independent/year
1/2 page	$8,301	$3,850
3/8 page	$6,261	na
1/3 page	na	$2,321
1/4 page	$4,221	$1,760
3/16 page	$3,201	na
1/6 page	na	$1,199
1/8 page	$2,181	na
1/12	na	$ 619
1/16 page (2″ × 2″)	$1,161	na

Note: A "plain" listing in the Telco Yellow Pages is free with a business phone. A "bold" listing can be obtained for $156/year.
na—not applicable.

HOW RESTAURANTS USE THE YELLOW PAGES

Having discovered how incredibly expensive the Yellow Pages can be, Stan did a bit of investigating. He was curious as to how the Yellow Pages fit within the promotional budget of independent restaurants similar to his. There were 59 restaurants using display advertising in the utility Yellow Pages. Reassuming his collegiate personna and masquerading as a student doing a class project, Stan canvassed these 59 restaurants asking them how they divided their promotional budget. As shown in the figures below, the Yellow Pages was their primary promotional outlet.

Promotion	Percent of Budget
Yellow Pages	59.9%
Newspapers	20.5
Radio	8.5
Flyers	5.2
Direct Mail	3.4
Billboards	1.8
Magazine	0.7

Stan was also curious as to how these restaurants evaluated the effectiveness of their Yellow Pages advertising. Not a single owner was able to provide any advice. None of the owners made any attempt whatsoever to track the effectiveness of their Yellow Page advertising, with nearly 80 percent voicing the opinion that it would be an impossible task so there was no reason to even try.

Despite the absence of any hard data, evidently they felt that the advertising was helpful. Comparing their current display ad in with their ad from the previous year, 12 increased the size of their ad, 44 kept it the same size, and only 3 opted for a smaller ad. When asked why they chose the size ad they did, the majority simply shrugged and said that was what they could afford. If the restaurant had a good year and they had a little extra money in the budget they would take out a bigger ad. If the restaurant had a bad year and the budget was lean, they would cut back.

The restaurant owners provided Stan with little in the way of help, and the closing date for the book was indeed right around the corner. Far from an afterthought, Stan's decision on the Yellow Pages would be the major determinant in the allocation of his entire advertising budget.

ASSIGNMENT

1. If you were Stan, how would you allocate the advertising budget? Defend your decision.

2. The use of the Yellow Pages varies markedly between different types of business. Look at the Yellow page listings under plumbers vs. the listings for grocery stores. What do you think accounts for that difference?
3. The use of the Yellow Pages also differs between independent restaurants vs. franchise restaurants. What accounts for that difference?
4. Because his dad was a friend of the owner, Stan was able to lease the restaurant considerably below market value. The owner suggested that Stan's lease be $2,400/month the first year, $4,800/month the second year, and $7,200/month the third year, which would bring the property up to market value. After that the lease would be adjusted according to the CPI. Assuming that other costs remain fixed, what would Stan's break-even sales figure for the second and third year?

*This case was prepared by Wilke English, The University of Texas at El Paso.

ENDNOTES

1. Denise Gallagher, "Sterling Jewelry," *Stores,* January 1989, 112.
2. Stephen Phillips, "Can the Closeout King Unload Its Woes?" *Business Week,* Dec. 7, 1987, 94.
3. Laurie Freeman, "Wal-Mart Blankets Wisconsin," *Advertising Age,* Aug. 17, 1987, 26MW.
4. Teri Agins, "Discount Clothing Stores, Facing Squeeze, Aim to Fashion a More Rounded Image," *The Wall Street Journal,* March 15, 1990, B1.
5. Ronit Addis, "Big Picture Strategy," *Forbes,* Jan. 9, 1989, 70.
6. Scott Hume, "McDonald's Heavy in Print for Nutrition," *Advertising Age,* Jan. 19, 1987, 2.
7. See Jay L. Johnson, "Winds of Change at Hills," *Discount Merchandiser,* April 1990, 32, 37.
8. "Ad Effectiveness: Can It Be Calculated?" *Chain Store Age Executive* (September 1987), 66.
9. See Jennifer Pellet, "Ad Campaign to Reposition Bradlees," *Discount Merchandiser,* July 1989, 48–52.
10. Mark Landler and Gail DeGeorge, "Tempers Are Sizzling over Burger King's New Ads," *Business Week,* Feb. 12, 1990, 33.
11. Marc Beauchamp, "I Never Learned Anything from Another Car Dealer Except What to Do Wrong," *Forbes,* June 26, 1989, 150.
12. Kate Fitzgerald, "Malls Toot Own Horns," *Advertising Age,* Jan. 15, 1990, 37.
13. See Joshua Levine, "Drive Time," *Forbes,* March 19, 1990, 144–46.
14. See Janet Meyers, "Retailers Press Papers for Targeted Buys," *Advertising Age,* Jan. 15, 1990, 6.
15. Alison Fahey, "Burned by '89, Retailers Pare Ad Hikes: Survey," *Advertising Age,* March 19, 1990, 46.
16. Richard Edel, "Segmentation Attracts New Product Categories," *Advertising Age,* May 12, 1986, S–1.
17. Irwin Broh, "Measure Success of Promotions with In-Store Customer Surveys," *Marketing News,* May 13, 1983, 17.

PART V

PROMOTION STRATEGIES

Managing and Implementing Personal Selling, Sales Incentive, and Public Relations Efforts

CHAPTER 17

OUTLINE

OBJECTIVES

- Explain why the basis for personal selling is good communications.
- Identify the traits and skills of a good salesperson.
- Name and discuss the seven steps of the retail selling process.
- Describe how sales incentives attract customers and stimulate consumer purchases.
- Explain how publicity affects retail operations.

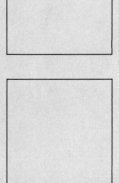

FAT BUSTERS

Millions of Americans share a bond: a desire to lose weight. National Nutrition Month, sponsored by the Chicago-based American Dietetic Association, is a perfect opportunity for retailers to help customers shed pounds.

Last year, Shaw's Supermarkets, a 60-store chain based in East Bridgewater, Mass., teamed up with the Massachusetts Dietetic Association and the New England Dairy and Food Council to observe Nutrition Month and hold "Fat Busters Day."

Shaw's distributed a Fat Busters pamphlet to shoppers in all of its stores. Titled, "Get Started Tips," the pamphlet featured 12 suggestions "to get the most nutrition you can for your calories and less fat from your daily food choices." Each of the tips in the pamphlet was illustrated with a cartoon. Items recommended in the pamphlet—bagels, for example—were displayed in stores.

Fat Busters Day, a three-hour promotional event, was held at a Shaw's store in Brockton, Mass., and featured sampling of such items as whole grain bread, yogurt-based dip, and fresh fruit.

Registered dieticians wearing buttons that read, "Professional Fat Busters," were stationed throughout the store to answer shoppers' questions. Local radio show hosts broadcast over the public address system. "Carrot Man," a registered dietitian, gave nutrition tips. Children tested their skills in a hula-hoop contest, a juggling competition, and at bubble gum blowing—using sugar free gum, of course.[1]

THE PERSONAL SELLING EFFORT

Personal selling is, perhaps, the most important element in the store image-creating process. Salespeople are usually the first people in the store to interact with customers on a face-to-face basis; thus, they have tremendous influence on how consumers perceive a store. In sum, salespeople are a significant factor in enhancing or detracting from the consumer's total impressions of a retail store.

This section covers personal selling as a communication process, the characteristics of a good salesperson, and the steps in the retail selling process.

The remainder of the retailer's promotion mix is discussed in this chapter. Retail selling is a special kind of selling whereby the customer comes to the store with a general or specific need in mind. To supplement the store's advertising and personal selling efforts, retailers must offer in-store sales incentives that encourage customer purchases and capitalize on public events that affect the store and its personnel. Personal selling, customer sales incentives, and publicity are the focal points of this chapter.

The basis for *all* personal selling is personal communications. Communication is *not* something you do *to* someone, but something you do *with* someone. **Personal communications** is the process of exchanging ideas and meanings with other people. Although one person is listening, even that person is active, not passive, in every communications situation. Figure 17–1 shows the basic elements of the communications interaction between a customer and a salesperson.

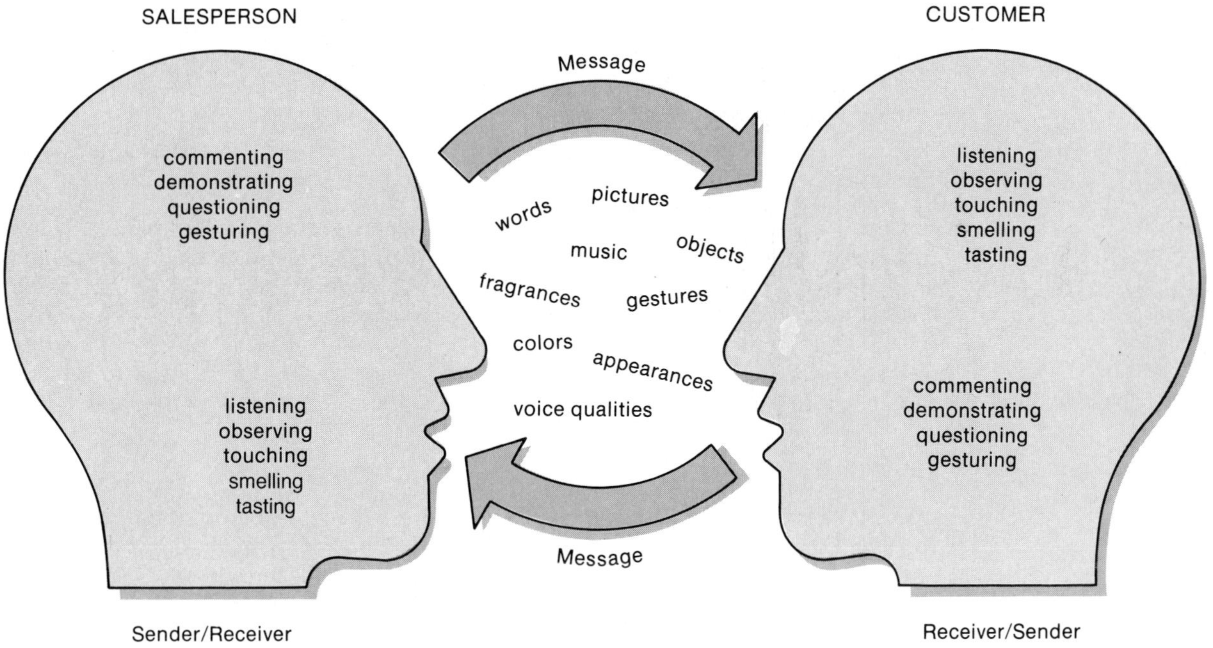

FIGURE 17–1
A communications model of the customer–salesperson interaction (a partial adaptation from Robert F. Spohn and Robert Y. Allen, *Retailing* [Reston, VA: Reston Publishing, 1977], 236)

The model also illustrates that both customer and salesperson are simultaneously sending and receiving information. The transmission and reception of information comes in many forms, such as words, objects, fragrances, colors, gestures, appearances, music, and voice qualities, to name but a few. With all of these communications channels occurring at the same time, a good salesperson must be a good listener and observer and adapt quickly to each moment in the selling situation.

THE EFFECTIVE SALESPERSON

Whether a salesperson is an "order getter" or an "order taker," certain qualities or characteristics are needed to be effective. **Order getters** are sales personnel who are actively involved in the selling process; they play a key role in obtaining a buy decision from the customer. They must persuade customers that what they are selling is best for them. **Order takers** simply comply with customers' requests for certain types of merchandise. They are more involved with simply handling a transaction (e.g., ringing up the sale and bagging the merchandise); nevertheless, their role as efficient service providers should not be undervalued. The more difficult job (and more rewarding) is order getting. Although most of the characteristics described in this section apply more to the order getter, they are traits that can also help order takers to be successful. Characteristics of an effective salesperson fall into four categories: physical traits, personality traits, individual skills, and message-presentation skills.

Physical Traits

Although there may be a fine line between **physical traits**, such as personal grooming and hygiene, and personality traits, they are sufficiently different to discuss separately. Clean clothing, shined shoes, clean, well-groomed hair, clean teeth and fresh breath, a well-shaven, clean-smelling body, and a pleasant smile are essential. Of course, these physical features can quickly be negated by an unpleasant personality.

Personality Traits

Personality traits are individual characteristics people acquire over a lifetime. These traits become an inherent part of a person through prior learning. Good salespeople have developed personality traits of sociability, curiosity, imagination, creativity, enthusiasm, sincerity, ambition, and reliability. Good salespeople get along with people, want to know, want to try new ways, want to do something different, have great interest in their work, are honest about their work and dealings with others, want to achieve certain self-imposed objectives, and state the truth about the product they sell.

Individual Skills

One can develop **individual selling skills** if one is willing to work on them. Based on research, several skills an individual can acquire are (1) perceived expertise, (2) perceived credibility, (3) positive attitude, (4) good listenership, (5) salesperson-customer similarity, and (6) adaptability.

Expertise

Salespeople whom customers **perceive as expert** have a much greater chance of making a sale than salespeople whom customers perceive as having less expertise. People who are high in expertise are those who are more qualified than others to speak on a particular topic. Salespeople with special education or training, information, and knowledge to talk about the product they sell have the expertise to be effective at their job. The key word in this discussion, however, is *perceived*. No matter how expert the salesperson, selling effectiveness depends on whether the customer *perceives* the person as an expert. Studies suggest that expertise must be communicated to each customer to effectively increase sales.

Credibility

Similarly, how effective a salesperson will be in making a sale depends partly on how **credible the customer perceives** the person to be. The more credible a salesperson is perceived to be, the more sales are likely to be made. A credible salesperson is believable, trustworthy, and honest in dealing with customers. Research in this area shows strong evidence of the persuasive powers of people who are perceived as credible.

Attitude

A salesperson is more effective with a positive rather than a negative attitude toward himself or herself, the message (and product), and the customer.[2] A **positive attitude** means self-confidence, not arrogance. Successful salespeople have confidence in their abilities to do their job. A salesperson also must have a positive attitude toward the product and what is said about it. If the salesperson does not believe in the product, why should the customer? Finally, a salesperson must have a positive attitude toward customers, demonstrated by paying careful attention to what the customer says, showing respect for the customer, and not talking down to the customer.

Listening Skills

Salespeople too often overlook **listening skills**. Some sales clerks are so busy talking and listening to themselves that they fail to listen to their customers. Failure to be a good listener can lead to lost sales. If they do not listen carefully, salespeople cannot determine customers' needs, wants, or preferences. Good listening skills not only improve the salesperson's chances of making a sale but also can provide feedback through the salesperson to top management about changes that might be made in store policies, merchandise lines, and a variety of other aspects of store operations. Figure 17–2 presents some guidelines for developing good listening skills.

FIGURE 17–2
Guidelines for developing good listening skills

1. Do not only listen to the words themselves, but also watch carefully for nonverbal cues to the real intentions of the customer.
2. Practice being interested in what customers have to say. Remember you are not always the most interesting person around.
3. Be sensitive to the customer's personal pronouns, such as "I", "we", "you", "us" and "our". These are cues to things that really interest the customer.
4. Do not be distracted by peculiarities in the speech of the customer.
5. Establish eye contact with customer.
6. Ask clarifying questions to test your understanding of a message.
7. Shut up and listen when the customer wants to talk.
8. Relax. Try not to give the customer the impression that you are just waiting to jump in and start talking.
9. Do not assume you understand the customer's problem or need. Keep listening while they keep talking.
10. Listen for ideas, not just words.

Source: Ronald B. Marks, *Personal Selling,* 2d ed. (Boston: Allyn and Bacon, Inc., 1985), 130–31.

Similarity

"People are persuaded more by a communicator they perceive to be similar to themselves," one expert pointed out. Salespersons who can quickly discover a **salesperson-customer similarity** can capitalize on this common characteristic to enhance their chances of making the sale. A salesperson can detect similarities by asking questions, listening, and observing. For example, if the customer is accompanied by children and the salesperson is a parent, the subject can be brought up in conversation. Or, if through conversation one learns that the customer is a student, professor, or staff member at the local university, the salesperson should mention the fact—if it is true—that he or she buys season tickets to all the games, attends the plays, supports the university, or whatever. The more specific the similarities, the better. *Perceived similarity* can be based on personality, dress, race, skin color, religion, politics, interests, group affiliations, and many more attributes. Clever salespersons quickly determine similarities between themselves and their customers and use them in casual talk.

Adaptability

Good salespeople demonstrate adaptability to differences in customer types. Figure 17–3 shows the types of customers that salespeople will encounter and suggests how they should react to each customer type. Salespeople must learn to identify customer types and adapt accordingly, without losing their own identity.

Message-Presentation Skills

Through training, salespeople can develop **skills in message presentation** that will help them become more persuasive and increase sales.

Message Strategy

Salespeople can present merchandise to customers either by explaining only the product's strengths and benefits (one-sided message) or by describing the product's

A perceived salesperson–customer similarity enhances the chance of making a sale.

Basic Types of Customer	Basic Characteristic	Secondary Characteristic	Other Characteristics	What Salesperson Should Say or Do
Arguer	Takes issue with each statement of salesperson	Disbelieves claims, tries to catch salesperson in error	Cautious, slow to decide	Demonstrate; show product knowledge; use "Yes, but . . ."
Chip on shoulder	Definitely in a bad mood	Indignation; angry at slight provocation	Acts as if being deliberately baited	Avoid argument; stick to basic facts; show good assortment
Decisive	Knows what is wanted	Customer confident choice is right	Not interested in another opinion—respects sales person's brevity	Win sale—not argument; sell self; tactfully inject opinion
Doubting Thomas	Doesn't trust sales talk	Hates to be managed	Arrives at decision cautiously	Back up merchandise statements by manufacturers' tags, labels; demonstrate merchandise; let customer handle merchandise
Fact-finder	Interested in factual information—detailed	Alert to sales person's errors in description	Looks for actual tags and labels	Emphasize label and manufacturer's facts; volunteer care information
Hesitant	Ill at ease—sensitive	Shopping at unaccustomed price range	Unsure of own judgment	Make customer comfortable; use friendliness and respect
Impulsive	Quick to decide or select	Impatience	Liable to break off sale abruptly	Close rapidly; avoid oversell, overtalk; note key points
Look around	Little ability to make own decisions	Anxious—fearful of making a mistake	Wants sales person's aid in decision—wants adviser—wants to do "right thing"	Emphasize merits of product and service, "zeroing" in on customer-expressed needs and doubts
Procrastinator	I'll wait 'til tomorrow	Lacks confidence in own judgment	Insecure	Reinforce customers' judgments
Silent	Not talking—but thinking!	Appears indifferent but truly listening	Appears nonchalant	Ask direct questions—straightforward approach
Think it over	Refers to need to consult someone	Looking for another adviser	Not sure of own uncertainty	Get agreement on small points; draw out opinions; use points agreed upon for close

Source: C. Winston Borgen, *Learning Experiences in Retailing* (Santa Monica, CA: Goodyear Publishing), 293.

FIGURE 17–3
Customer types and what salespersons should say or do

weaknesses as well as strengths (two-sided message). Although it might sound strange to mention a product's weaknesses to customers (or the strength of competitors' products), this strategy works under certain circumstances. When consumers are not knowledgeable about a product, however, the general rule is to present a one-sided message; that is, to be more persuasive and produce more sales, it is better to tell them only about the benefits, advantages, and strengths. When customers lack product knowledge, they are unable to comprehend product weaknesses and will become confused if the salesperson tries to explain them. Therefore, to this audience, *sell only the strong points of the product*.

On the other hand, if the salesperson is presenting a product to a customer who is very knowledgeable about the product, the best strategy is either to explain the product's strengths as well as its weaknesses or to describe both the product's strengths and the competing products' strengths. Since the customer is knowledgeable about the product, he or she will have already recognized the weakness in the merchandise or the strengths of other retailers' products. Do not, therefore, insult the customer's product knowledge or intelligence. Instead, salespeople should admit to *minor* weaknesses in a brand or *minor* strengths in those of competitors. Customers will respect the salesperson's honesty, therefore he or she will be more credible to them. When using the two-sided message, one's own merchandise "wins"—there are fewer weaknesses in one's merchandise or fewer strengths in competitors' brands.

Message Positioning

Salespeople should place their strongest selling points at the beginning (opening) and the end (closing) of the message, *never* in the middle. Psychologists tell us that people remember the beginning and ending of a message better than the middle. Salespeople, therefore, should always capture the customer's attention with strong points of the merchandise at the beginning of the sales presentation and summarize those points in the closing.

Customer Conclusions

The general selling rule is to draw a conclusion in the sales presentation, summarizing reasons the product is right for the customer. Unfortunately, many customers cannot add together the logical statements they hear as to why they should purchase the merchandise. Therefore, the salesperson should do it for them by quickly summarizing major points and telling them (in conclusion) why they should buy. The exception to this rule is when one encounters highly intelligent people who can easily draw conclusions for themselves, and drawing a conclusion insults the intelligence of the prospective buyer.

Customer Participation

Salespeople are more likely to sell a product when they can get the prospective buyer to try it as they explain its benefits. Psychologists tell us that *active participation* not only helps consumers learn the benefits of a product but also helps persuade them to purchase it. The rule in retail selling is to let customers touch, feel, smell, taste, and hear the product. Get them to take a test drive, taste the sausage, smell the ham, feel the power as they maneuver the dials, play the video game, see how the diamond ring looks on the hand. Customers' active involvement and participation with the product in the store is a powerful selling technique—perhaps the most effective way to present the message.

Message Appeals

All people have emotions, and the heart often rules the mind. Salespeople must recognize and use their customers' emotions to good advantage. We all would like to

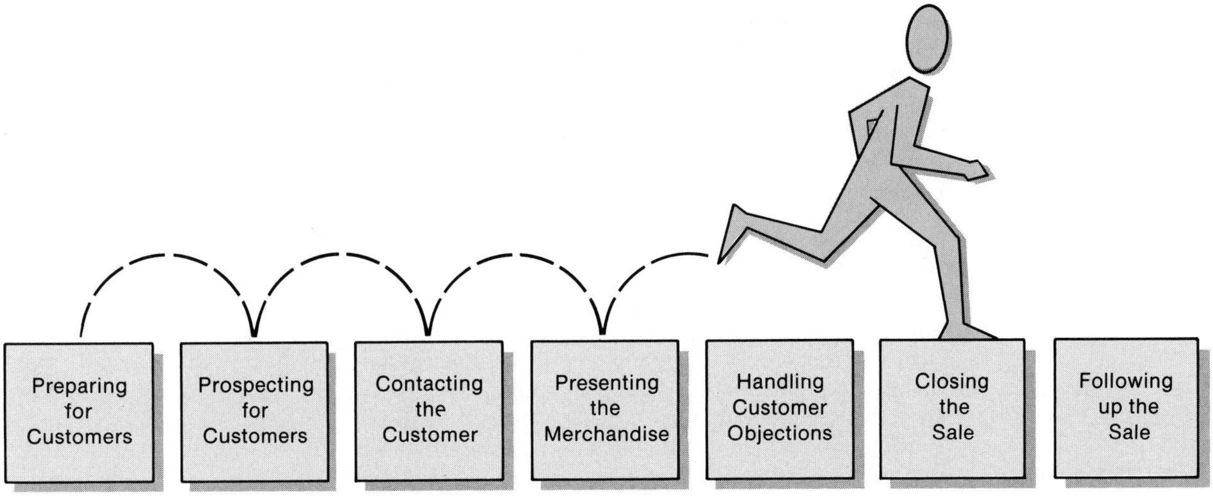

FIGURE 17–4
The seven steps of the retail selling process

believe we make buying decisions rationally and logically, but usually we do not. Instead, we purchase most products largely on an emotional basis. Given these emotional aspects of purchase behavior, salespeople should acquire the skill of describing their merchandise in emotional terms.

THE RETAIL SELLING PROCESS

Several basic steps occur in every selling situation. The length of time that a salesperson takes in each step depends on the product, the customer, and the selling situation. The seven steps of the retail selling process appear in Figure 17–4.

Preparing for Customers

Preparing for the customer is the first step in the selling process. In this stage, the salesperson does the *preliminary* work necessary for effective interaction with the customer. This stage can be subdivided into long-run preparation and short-run preparation.

In long-run preparation, the salesperson learns store policies and procedures and gains knowledge about the merchandise. These learning activities include becoming familiar with store operating procedures, return policies, and guarantees; learning to operate merchandise that the store (or department) sells; and knowing manufacturer warranties—to name but a few. Short-term preparations are daily and weekly activities, including learning what merchandise is currently in stock; which items are on sale; recent changes in store policies and operating procedures; changes that have occurred in new styles, fashions, and models of merchandise; and dozens of other day-to-day store happenings.

Prospecting for Customers

Prospecting is the process of finding people who are *willing* to buy the merchandise a store has to offer and are *able* to pay for that merchandise. Salespeople learn through experience how to spot good prospects. Good prospects generally display more intense interest in the merchandise than poor prospects who are just browsing. A variety of behavioral cues set good prospects apart from the poor prospects; for example, carrying several bags of merchandise from other stores is often a clue to a shopper's interest in making additional purchases.

Prospecting is particularly important when the store is full of customers. An alert salesperson will single out prime prospects and not waste time with browsers. When the store is not busy, salespeople should attend to everyone, including weak prospects to build possible future business and enhance the store's image of having concern for its customers.

Contacting the Customer

Initial impressions are important determinants in successfully making a sale. A warm smile and an appearance of genuine interest in customers and their needs are parts of a good initial impression. Sam Walton asks all Wal-Mart associates to make the following pledge: "From this day forward, I solemnly promise and declare that every customer that comes within ten feet of me, I will smile, look them in the eye, and greet them, so help me Sam."[3] At the beginning of the contact, the salesperson should make an opening comment that quickly captures the buyer's attention and arouses interest. Further, the first words should be positive and should stimulate any needs the customer might be displaying. If a woman is holding up a blouse to examine, the salesperson might open by saying, "That blouse certainly would look nice on you. Would you like to try it on?" This opening compliments the woman's taste in clothing, stimulates her need to "look nice," and requests her to take an *action* (try it on). A simple "May I help you?" is a routine, worn-out phrase that almost invites the customer to turn down the request.

Openings should be original and appropriate to the situation. Consider the following examples of customer situations and potential salesperson responses.

Situation 1: Customer looking at a home video game.

- *Preferred opening* Salesperson: "Press this button like this [salesperson turns game on], and the game's all set to go. Why don't you try your luck?"
- *Nonpreferred opening* Salesperson: "Do you need some help in how to operate this thing?" Customer: [Gads, he thinks I'm stupid or something.] "No, I was just looking."

Situation 2: Woman looking at a coat in an exclusive, high-fashion women's clothing store.

- *Preferred opening* "That's 100-percent mink. Please let me help you on with it to see how it looks and feels."
- *Nonpreferred opening* "Want some help?" Customer: [She thinks I don't know how to put on a coat!] "No, thank you."

Situation 3: Shopper looking at a telephone in a phone center store.

- *Preferred opening* "That phone will make a call for you if simply one button is pressed. Look how easy it is to operate."
- *Nonpreferred opening* "Are you interested in a phone?"

In summary, a salesperson's opening statement at the point of initial contact can determine whether conversation will continue and, therefore, whether the sale can be made. A good opening should attract the customer's attention, arouse interest, stimulate a customer need, and be original to the situation. A poor opening is generally one that can be answered with a yes or a no. In a selling situation, a good beginning is usually necessary for a happy ending (the sale).

Presenting the Merchandise

After making initial contact, the salesperson is in a position to present the merchandise and the sales message. How the salesperson should present the merchandise depends on the customer. Because customers are not identical, the salesperson's presentations should not be identical; instead, they should be tailored to the individual circumstances. Toyota trains its sales associates to tailor a presentation to the customer's specific interest—or "hot button"—for example, aerodynamics and styling.[4] Some basic guidelines can help the salesperson make a good presentation. Remember, however, that salespeople must continually exercise their creativity to adapt to particular customers and circumstances.

Learn the Customer's Needs and Wants

To know what merchandise to show, the salesperson must learn what the customer needs and wants. Asking key questions and listening attentively help the salesperson to determine what merchandise the store has that might meet those needs and wants. When questions are asked at the right time and the right place, they are powerful tools for raising a customer response level.[5] Questions allow the salesperson to (1) discover important information that is useful in closing the sale, (2) demonstrate genuine interest in the customer, (3) move the customer toward active involvement in the sales process, (4) correct any misconceptions about the product or the store, and (5) develop rapport with the customer.[6] Figure 17–5 provides guidelines in how to ask questions. The pay in selling is far greater for asking the right questions than for knowing the right answer—a closed mouth gathers no foot.[7] At this point, the salesperson must closely observe the customer's reactions to each piece of merchandise shown to determine the level of product interest; that is, whether the product is a "must have," "should have," or "would be nice to have" item. The salesperson can also, in this initial presentation, determine whether to try trading up—attempting to sell higher-quality, higher-priced merchandise or to sell a larger quantity than the customer originally intended to buy. The salesperson may believe that the customer would be better satisfied with more durable, stronger, lighter, heavier, bigger, or softer materials or may think the customer

FIGURE 17–5
Guidelines on how to ask questions

1. Start with broad questions and move toward narrower questions. Broad, open-ended questions are less threatening than narrow, specific questions.
2. Listen to everything the customer says.
3. Keep questions simple and focused. Use one idea at a time.
4. Ask sensitive questions in a nonthreatening way (e.g., "How much were you planning to spend?" not "How much can you afford?"). If you must ask a very personal question, always explain why.
5. Always ask questions that are easy to answer! Studies show that people would rather answer a question when they agree than voice their objections.
6. Turn the statements your customer makes into questions to clarify or reinforce feelings. "So, Tuesday would be best for you, is that right?"
7. Use questions to develop the presentation! "You mentioned that your present car needs repairs. What types of repairs does it need?" Explain the advantages of a new car.
8. Use caution when leading clients with questions. Always respect the intelligence of your prospect.
9. Use questions to give information. "Are you aware of our 90-days same as cash policy?"

Source: Nido R. Quebein, "The Power of Asking Questions." *Personal Selling Power* (January/February 1988): 20–21.

needs a larger quantity to complete the job or to save money. Because customer need satisfaction is a goal of the retailer, then determining customer needs and wants is a logical first step in presenting and selling merchandise.

Reduce Customers' Perceived Risk

Customers run the risk that the product they buy might not perform correctly, might fall apart or break down, might embarrass them in a social setting (a "gold" necklace chain turns the neck green), or might be unsafe. These concerns are particularly strong for high-cost items; refrigerators, washers, cars, sets of tires, houses, and television sets represent substantial outlays of money and therefore risk. Perceived risk takes the form of financial, physical, or social risk. Therefore, products with high perceived risk must be accompanied by assurances of satisfactory performance. The salesperson should stress the manufacturer's warranty, the retailer's money-back guarantee, the retailer's in-house repair facilities, the dependable brand name, and so on. This selling situation might also be an opportunity for the salesperson to trade up the customer to higher-quality merchandise to reduce perceived risk and thus make the sale.

Demonstrate the Product

Some products lend themselves to demonstration better than others, but virtually all products can be demonstrated somehow. Demonstrating the merchandise means the customer sees the product in action—its features, benefits, and possible advantages. To enhance product demonstration, specialty retailers are increasingly holding **trunk shows**, keenly aware that no store salesperson can present an outfit as deftly as the designer or manufacturer. Retailers are even extending them to mid-priced clothing brands, jewelry, nuts, and shoes.[8] While demonstrating the product, the salesperson should point out the unique features and benefits to reinforce what the customer is seeing. A product can often sell itself, particularly if the salesperson helps a little. Demonstrations can also help reduce some customers' perceived risk in purchasing the product. BMW is currently experimenting with saving prospective buyers time by dropping off demonstrator cars for test drives at the prospect's home or office.[9]

Actively Involve the Customer

Get customers actively involved with the product! Have them touch, smell, taste, hear, and feel it. "Push the accelerator and feel the power, *experience* its smooth ride, *listen* to the quiet of the engine and the outside air, *touch* the soft velour seats," a car salesperson might say while the customer is actually using, controlling, and experiencing the product.

Chances of persuading customers to buy a product improve greatly when they actively interact with it. A good salesperson points out how the product affects the customer's five senses ("Smell the manly scent of this cologne." "Taste the rich flavor of this coffee." "Feel the softness of this sweater.") The more of the customer's senses a salesperson can stimulate, the greater the chance of a sale.

Sell Product Benefits, Not the Product

"In the factory we produce cosmetics; in the store we sell the promise and hope of beauty!" "We don't sell the steak, we sell the sizzle." What all manufacturers, retailers, and salespeople must realize is that they don't sell physical products, but the physical, social, and psychological *benefits* they provide consumers. People don't buy lawn mowers, they buy trim lawns. People don't buy ¼-inch drill bits, they buy ¼-inch holes. Customers buy, in effect, the end result (the benefit), not the product for the product's sake. Therefore, salespeople should sell benefits. Encyclopedia sales representatives learned this idea a long time ago—"We provide your children with *educational* materials, not encyclopedias. Don't you think your child's education is important?"

Successful retail sales representatives demonstrate the product and actively involve the customer.

Make the Message Simple

Too often salespeople present merchandise in *technical* terms and phrases that the average customer does not understand. As a result, many customers are frightened off or confused and a sale is lost. Good salespeople present the product message in words that are clear and understandable to the customer. The salesperson must be ready to adapt quickly to each consumer's level of understanding and sophistication. Sometimes the salesperson must use analogies and speak simply; for other customers, the salesperson might engage in technical conversation. The sales-message level should be geared to the customer's product-knowledge level. Thus a golden rule is to *communicate the message at the customer's level of understanding and knowledge.* Salespeople should not talk over their customers' heads or insult their intelligence by speaking too simply.

Handling Objections

Consumers who do not purchase a product immediately after the merchandise presentation are likely to have perceived stumbling blocks, objections to buying the product. A salesperson must anticipate objections and know how to handle each type. Figure 17–6 summarizes techniques of handling customer objections. Customer objections are of five kinds: product, price, place (store), timing, and salesperson.

Some consumers think the *product* is just not right for them. It is too big, too small, too heavy, too light, does not look right on them, is too simple, too complex, or one of a host of other objections. The salesperson must be creative and adaptable in handling objections. If the customer says "This doesn't look right on me," it probably means "My friends (family, co-workers, boss, etc.) wouldn't like it." A creative salesperson counters with reasons why the customer's reference groups might well approve of this merchandise. This approach reinforces the customer's self-image and gives supporting approval from others for making the purchase. In other cases, customers may object to the product by saying they are not sure it will perform as it should, to which the salesperson should reiterate the proven record of the product, its warranties, and store guarantees.

Price is a common customer objection that takes two forms. First, the customer really wants the product but doesn't have the cash to pay for it. In this case, the salesperson can emphasize the store's easy credit terms ("You can buy this washing machine for only $10 a month."). In other cases, the customer does not consider the product worth the price; for these customers, the salesperson must emphasize the

FIGURE 17–6
Summary of objection-handling techniques

Method	When to Use	How to Use
Head-on	With objections arising from incorrect information	Salespeople directly, but politely, deny the truth of the objection; to avoid alienating prospects, it is helpful to offer proof
Indirect denial	With objections arising from incorrect information	Salespeople never directly tell prospects that they are wrong, but still manage to correct the mistaken impression
Compensation	With valid objections, but where compensating factors are present	Salespeople agree with prospects initially, but then proceed to point out factors that outweigh or compensate for the objection (for this reason, it is often called the "yes, but" technique)
"Feel, felt, found"	With emotional objections, especially when prospects have retreated from their adult ego states, and when the prospect fails to see the value of a particular feature and benefit	Salespeople express their understanding for how prospects feel, indicate that they are okay since others have also felt that way, but have found their fears to be without substance
Boomerang	When the objection can be turned into a positive factor	Salespeople take the objection and turn it into a reason for buying
Forestalling	With any type of objection	From prior experience, salespeople anticipate an objection and incorporate an answer into the presentation itself, hoping to forestall the objection from ever coming up

Source: Ronald B. Marks, *Personal Selling* (Boston: Allyn and Bacon, Inc., 1985), 326.

product value, perhaps by mentioning that competitors' prices are about the same even though their products do not have comparable features, warranties, or guarantees.

Customers might not like the *store* itself. An advertisement or a display caught their eye, they came into the store and saw something they liked, but they usually don't shop in this store or "a store like this," and therefore feel uncomfortable buying here. To meet this kind of objection, the salesperson must assure customers of the integrity of the store, its management, and its merchandise.

Putting the purchase off (*timing*) is another objection salespeople frequently encounter. Customers might not know exactly why they don't want to buy now; they just don't. Customers usually use the timing objection to conceal their real objections. Thus, this type of objection is difficult for salespeople to handle, since they do not understand its underlying motives. Handling this objection is groping in the dark. Nevertheless, the salesperson can emphasize the need to buy immediately ("The sale ends today at this extraordinarily low price" or "There are only a few left in stock."). Any statement indicating the urgency to buy now might overcome this objection.

One last possible customer objection can be to the *salesperson*. Shifty eyes, long hair, short hair, conservative dress, wild dress, garlic on the breath, or any number of other "faults" may turn away a customer. Whatever the reason, the salesperson is often unlikely to detect it. If the salesperson guesses that this is the objection, he or she should direct the customer's attention to the product—its benefits, its advantages, or its need-fulfilling capacities—or turn the sale over to another salesperson.

Closing the Sale

Closing the sale (suggesting that the customer make the purchase) is the natural conclusion to the selling process. *Timing* in the closing stage, however, is critical. Customers often provide verbal or physical (body language) cues that suggest they might be ready to make a purchase. Figure 17–7 identifies several physical and verbal cues for potential closing opportunities. In timing the closing, the salesperson must adapt to the individual customer and circumstances. Some customers do not want to be rushed into making the final decision; others don't want to wait too long to have the salesperson begin to close. Still other customers do not know how to make the decision or won't make the decision without help. In this latter situation, the salesperson must *tell* them to make the purchase. These people need someone to make decisions for them. In other cases, customers definitely make up their own minds and don't want to be pushed. In dealing with customers like these, the salesperson can remind them of their need and of how the merchandise meets that need, restate the advantages and benefits of the merchandise, and explain why they must buy now and not put off the decision.

Skilled salespeople have developed several closing techniques that move the customer toward the purchase decision. After the customer has examined several pieces of merchandise, for example, the salesperson usually can determine which one or two

FIGURE 17–7
Spotting closing cues

Physical cues provided by customers

1. The customer closely reexamines the merchandise under consideration.
2. The customer reaches for his billfold or opens her purse.
3. The customer samples the product for the second or third time.
4. The customer is nodding in agreement as the terms and conditions of sale are explained.
5. The customer is smiling and appears excited as he or she admires the merchandise.
6. The customer intensely studies the service contract.

Verbal cues provided by customers

1. The customer asks "Do you offer free home delivery?"
2. The customer remarks "I always wanted a pair of Porsche sunglasses."
3. The customer inquires "Do you have this item in red?"
4. The customer states "This ring is a real bargain."
5. The customer exclaims "I feel like a million bucks in this outfit!"
6. The customer requests "Can you complete the installation by Friday?"

merchandise items the customer prefers. To avoid confusing the customer and to aid in the final decision, the salesperson should put away the less-preferred items. If the customer has tried on seven rings, the five or six least-preferred rings should be put back in their cases. "I can tell this is the one you really like the most," the salesperson might say. "May I wrap this for you? Will this be cash or charge?" Figure 17–8 identifies seven of the more common closing techniques.

Another aspect of closing a sale is to show customers other merchandise that complements the item they are going to buy. This technique is called **suggestive selling**. If the customer is buying a sport coat, the salesperson can suggest a shirt and tie that are a "perfect" match for the coat. Suggestive selling is a service to customers who might not have thought of purchasing complementary items to enhance the appearance

Technique	Definition	Example
Direct close	The salesperson asks the customer directly for the order	"Can I write this order up for you?"
Assumptive close	The salesperson assumes the customer is going to buy and proceeds with completing the sales transaction	"Would you like to have this gift wrapped?"
Alternative close	The salesperson asks the customer to make a choice in which either alternative is favorable to the retailer	'Will this be cash or charge?"
Summary/agreement close	The salesperson closes by summarizing the major features, benefits, and advantages of the product and obtains an affirmative agreement from the customer on each point	"This dishwasher has the features you were looking for"—YES "You want free home delivery"—YES "It is in your price range"—YES "Let's write up the sale."
Balance-sheet close	The salesperson starts by listing the advantages and disadvantages of making the purchase and closes by pointing out how the advantages outweigh the disadvantages	"This dishwasher is on sale; it has all the features you asked for, you have 90 days to pay for it without any financial charges, and we will deliver it free. Even though we can not deliver it until next week, now is the time to buy."
Emotional close	The salesperson attempts to close the sale by appealing to the customer's emotions (love, fear, acceptance, recognition)	"The safety of your children could well depend on this smoke alarm. Now is the time to get it installed."
Standing-room-only close	The salesperson tries to get the customer to act immediately by stressing that the offer is limited	"The sale ends today." "This is the last one we have in stock."

FIGURE 17–8
Types of closing techniques

or use of their intended purchase. Both customers and salespeople can benefit from suggestive selling when the additional items represent true benefits for the customer.

Next, the salesperson must perform several *administrative* tasks in closing the sale, such as ringing up the sale on the cash register, checking the accuracy of the address and other parts of the check that the customer may present, verifying the customer's credit card, and boxing, bagging, or wrapping the merchandise. Finally, closing the sale is not complete until the salesperson has said thank you, asked the customer to come back, and has said good-bye. This phrase in closing the sale is called *developing good will,* and repeat business depends on it!

A good salesperson continues to sell the customer *after* the sale. The sale is not over once the customer has walked out the door. Many customers are happy about their purchases at the time they buy them, but later begin to doubt the wisdom of their buying decision. The doubt phase usually affects consumers who have made a substantial investment of time, effort, and money. A salesperson might follow up the sale by assuring customers they have made the right decision, the merchandise is of good quality, their friends and relatives will approve, and the store and manufacturer back the merchandise. Salespeople have three ways to follow up a sale: (1) writing a letter to the customer, (2) telephoning the customer, and (3) personally visiting the customer. A personal visit is out of the question for most salespeople because it involves so much time away from work, so with certain exceptions, telephone calls or letters are the best options for following up a sale. Letters are more effective in reducing a postpurchase doubt because customers can read letters at their convenience. Therefore, the rule on sales follow-up is to send the customer a letter.

THE CUSTOMER SALES INCENTIVE PROGRAM

Retailers use the term *sales incentive* in many different ways. A common usage includes all promotional activities other than advertising, personal selling, and publicity as sales incentives or sales promotions. This text defines **sale incentive** as any direct or indirect nonpersonal inducement that offers extra value to the consumers. Retailers use these extras to supplement advertising, personal selling, and other merchandising activities. Typically, sales incentives are temporary offers extended to the customer to stimulate an immediate response—the purchase of a good or service. Sales incentives are targeting activities in that they are directed at triggering particular customer actions.

Coupons

Coupons are manufacturer or retailer certificates that give consumers a price reduction on specific kinds of merchandise. Consumers obtain coupons from newspapers, magazines, mail, on and in packages, door-to-door, and in-store advertising supplements. Couponing attracts customers to the store. Shoppers come into the store to purchase the "bargain" but usually end up buying other merchandise as well.

"Optical card coupons" are currently being tested in a number of stores. Consumers receive optical cards that contain "cents-off" coupons by mail. When consumers buy featured items, they present optical cards at checkstands. Cents-off offers that are specified on the card are matched with purchase data obtained by scanners. When validated, savings are deducted from the bill and the cents-off offer is marked as used.[10]

Couponing is popular with consumers and is a relatively low-cost sales incentive program; however, it also has its problems. First, everyone is into the act. With billions of coupons distributed each year, it becomes more difficult to gain customer attention and to get "one up" on competitors. A second problem is in coupon distribution. In-pack coupons create repurchases by current users, not new users. Frequent coupon redeemers use coupons for brands they already use, hence, few new sales. Third, misredemption (illegal redemption) is a major problem. Fourth, complex coupons (e.g.,

Coupons are sales incentives used by retailers to stimulate an immediate consumer response.

self-destruct, sticky, multiple purchase, and size-specification coupons) add significantly to handling time and create customer confusion.

Sampling

Sampling involves giving the customer a free trial or sample of the product; it gets the customer involved with the product through hands-on experience. Trial use invites active participation, which can quickly lead to a customer purchase decision; however, only some products should be sampled. The kinds of products retailers can sample have low unit cost, are small in size, and are subject to high repeat sales. Supermarkets hand out samples of sausage; bakeries provide sample pastries; Hickory Farms places cheese and crackers at convenient points throughout its stores so customers can sample them. Sampling is generally quite expensive, but because it gives customers direct experience and involvement with the product, it is thus a powerful tool to induce purchases.

Premiums

A premium is a merchandise item given to the consumer free of charge or at a substantial price reduction as an inducement to purchase another product or to participate in an activity, or both. Essentially, a premium is an extra bonus or gift given to a qualified customer. A customer purchase is the most common way to qualify for a premium; however, premiums are sometimes given for visiting the store or participating in an activity (e.g., taste-testing a new product). Store visits and participation events are often referred to as "traffic-building premiums." Several types of premiums involve retailers with manufacturers in this kind of effort to create sales incentives: self-liquidating, direct or value pack, mail-in, and continuing premiums.

Self-liquidating premiums require the consumer to pay something for the premium; typically, the consumer must pay an amount sufficient to cover the costs associated with the premium. Successful self-liquidating premiums are merchandise

Electronic Couponing—No More Accordion Boxes

WORLD OF RETAILING

Retail Technology

Electronic couponing is the next step in the ongoing courtship by supermarkets of frequent customers. Marketers use the information consumers generate to give them automatic discounts while they collect information about consumer spending habits. If electronic rebates catch on, as industry experts predict, supermarkets will be able to advertise directly to their customers without having to flood local newspapers with coupons. . . . Consumers like electronic couponing because it frees them from clipping coupons. UPC-coded cards automatically credit customers with existing coupons at the checkout line. "It relieves the customer of looking for coupons, clipping coupons, keeping them in those silly accordion boxes."

Supermarkets should gain as well. Customers who apply for the cards are asked to fill out a questionnaire detailing such facts as age, occupation, and the number of people in their household. When customers present their card to a cashier for an electronic rebate, a computer tracks their purchases. "You can tell exactly what each person buys." . . . Tracking an individual's buying habits helps supermarkets determine which products sell and what they need to stock so that the customer will keep coming back for more. Customers come back for more because they don't have to clip coupons to save money.

Source: Jan Larson, "Farewell to Coupons," *American Demographics*, February 1990, 14, 16.

items that usually cannot be obtained elsewhere, and their uniqueness makes them valued gifts that consumers perceive to be worth considerably more than what they have to pay for them. The cosmetic industry in concert with many department and specialty store retailers provides an excellent example of self-liquidating premium offers. These offers take the form of purchase with purchase (PWP) and gift with purchase (GWP) premiums, which account for a large percentage of cosmetic and fragrance sales. These PWP and GWP premiums might consist of garment bags, overnight totes, sunglasses, billfolds, ties, and other apparel items complete with the insignias of the company or designer (e.g., Calvin Klein, Ralph Lauren, and others). Creating and maintaining customer sales and return trade was the goal of McDonald's offer of "Garfield" coffee cups for $.99 each time a customer purchased a breakfast item. The customer had to make several trips to McDonald's to get a full set of cups because a different cup was available each week for four weeks.

Direct premiums or value packs are free gifts given to the customer at the time of purchase. The gift can be (1) attached to the product package, "on packs"; (2) contained in the product package, "in packs"; (3) found adjacent to the product package, "near packs"; or (4) provided in special decorator packages with the product, "container-packs." To the extent that these direct premiums generate store traffic and ensure rapid product turnover, they are desirable additions to both the retailers' and manufacturers' sales incentive program. When direct premiums require additional shelf space, however (e.g., near-packs), special handling (e.g., on-packs), or result in other cost-generating activities, the retailer must closely evaluate the cost-benefit aspects.

Mail-in premiums require the customer to send in a proof-of-purchase to receive a free gift. This type of premium encourages first-time or repeat purchases; however, given the extra effort required of the customer, it has limited acceptance on the part of the general consuming public. But if the retailer does not have to get involved with processing and handling the mail-in offer, this type of premium is still another weapon in a successful sales incentive arsenal.

Continuity premiums require the customer to make repeat purchases of products and services to benefit from the premium offer. This kind of premium is offered as part of a continual, ongoing sales incentive program. The customer's length and degree of involvement usually determines the value of the gift; longer and greater involvement results in bigger and better gifts. The most common type of continuity premiums are trading stamps. Sperry and Hutchinson (S&H) Green stamps and Quality Stamp Company are two organizations that are working to revive this once important sales incentive tool that enjoyed peak popularity in the 1960s.[11] Pressure-sensitive stamps, more convenient stamp collection books, and better gift selection catalogs are some of the improvements for enhancing the image of this form of inducement and convincing both retailers and consumers to return to trading stamps as a buyer reward system.

Competing with trading stamps is a new type of continuity premium—the frequent buyer program.[12] This format gives customers bonus points for each purchase, with the number of points corresponding to the amount of purchase. Tom Thumb, the Dallas-based supermarket chain, is using scanner cards in a frequent-shopper program called Tom Thumb's Promise Club. Customers receive a Promise Card that entitles them to accumulate Promise Points each time they shop at Tom Thumb. Club members also are eligible for discounts on 125 different items each month.[13] A newsletter informs customers of specials, a monthly statement informs them how many promise points they have earned, and a money voucher is given to use toward future grocery purchases.[14] Sears is also experimenting with its version of a frequent buyer program; Bonus Club shoppers can get incentives ranging from $5 gift certificates to automobiles.[15]

Contests and Sweepstakes

Contests and **sweepstakes** are theme-based sales incentive programs designed to create a special event that generates customer involvement with the store and its merchandise. Contests are promotional activities in which participants compete for rewards; successful participants are selected on the basis of their skill in completing a particular task (e.g., designing a store advertisement or completing a puzzle).

Sweepstakes are promotions in which customers win prizes based on chance. For the sweepstakes to be legal, however, the customer cannot be required to risk money for a chance; the major requirement is that the customer fill out an entry form to have a chance to win. Sweepstakes involve pure chance and minimal effort for entrants. Because of relaxation in games of chance laws, more retailers are turning to sweepstakes in their sales promotion programs. Sweepstakes are conducted under a variety of formats, including: (1) *straight sweepstakes*—winning entry is randomly pulled out of a container holding all entries; (2) *matching sweepstakes*—a winning number or symbol must match a preselected number or symbol; (3) *instant win sweepstakes*—a winning number(s) or symbol(s) are revealed by rubbing off or washing off a covering; and (4) *programmed learning sweepstakes*—the winning entry is selected from a group of entries that have information correctly provided from the sponsor's label, package, or ad.

Specialty Advertising

The Specialty Advertising Association defines **specialty** advertising as a useful article of merchandise that is imprinted with an advertisement and given to the customer without obligation. Specialty items can range from inexpensive key chains to expensive travel bags. To be successful, a specialty should be useful, fashionable, and appropriate for the targeted consumer. A good rule for the retailer to remember about a specialty item is that the store's name will be on the item; hence, the item should be consistent with the store's image.

Sweepstakes are promotions in which customers win prizes based on chance.

Tie-ins

Sales incentive **tie-ins** are another approach to attracting attention to a store's offerings. Burger King has replaced its house salad dressing with actor Paul Newman's name brand.[16] Successful tie-ins can generate excitement, enthusiasm, and sales (e.g., Ghostbusters), but if the tie-in (such as a movie) bombs, the retailer can suffer (e.g., Ghostbusters II). Tie-ins assume a variety of forms. Macy's created a Batman boutique while K mart developed a whole line of clothing around the movie Dirty Dancing and its sequel.[17] Besides a tie-in with an entertainment event, tie-ins can occur in conjunction with national holidays, special occasions, sporting events, local celebrations, annual conventions, unusual events, and other products, to name but a few ways. The purpose of tie-ins is to capitalize on the excitement generated by momentary trends or events (e.g., Teenage Mutant Ninja Turtles).[18] They are by definition transient—how many people today would buy a coffee mug with a bicentennial decal (1776–1976) on it?

Tie-ins of complementary merchandise have several advantages:

- *Increased awareness*. By promoting two or more compatible pieces of merchandise, the retailer can attract more attention than by promoting a single piece of merchandise.
- *Increased readership*. Readership of advertising sales promotion literature will increase, particularly if there is a logical tie-in with the merchandise.
- *Reinforced image*. Where there are natural "go-togethers," the image of the store's merchandise can be reinforced because of the combined benefits the consumer will derive from using both pieces of merchandise together.
- *Cross brand trial*. If customers are loyal to one brand of a store's merchandise, they are likely to try the complementary merchandise because of the promotional marriage.
- *Cost efficiency*. Retailers can save money by promoting tie-ins; that is, two or more pieces of merchandise can be promoted together, achieving a synergistic effect.

WORLD OF RETAILING

■■■

Business Ethics

McDonald's and the Environment—A Win-Win Situation

McDonald's might add another principle to the list: Educate your customers incessantly. Faced with growing protests over the volume of waste it generates, especially the polystyrene foam packaging used for hot food, the restaurant giant has taken major steps to reduce waste at the source, to recycle what's left, and to explain what it is doing. Just by making its drinking straws 20% lighter, the chain eliminated one million pounds of waste per year. All napkins in U.S. stores are now made from recycled paper, as are carry-out drink trays and office paper at headquarters.

McDonald's, a long-time supporter of polystyrene foam packaging, will phase out foam packaging in all of its U.S. restaurants. Working in partnership with the Washington-based Environmental Defense Fund, this phase-out is part of McDonald's broad pro-environmental initiative. Initially, the foam hamburger boxes will be replaced with biodegradable wrappers similar to those currently used with its small hamburgers. While paper wrappers take up 90% less space than foam when discarded and broken down in landfills, paper wrappers do have the negative factor of requiring the cutting down of trees.

With increased interest on the part of ecology-minded customers, McDonald's is developing and testing various paper-recycling techniques. To make customers aware of its strong environmental positions, McDonald's is describing its efforts and explaining recycling on the paper liners on customers' trays, in advertising, in brochures it hands out in stores, and in mailings to school teachers. That's a lot of describing and explaining: McDonald's serves 18 million customers in the U.S. each day, making its tray liners alone one of the largest of the nation's mass media.

Source: David Kirkpatrick, "Environmentalism," *Fortune,* February 12, 1990, 50–51. © 1990 The Time Inc., Magazine Company. All rights reserved; "A Burger to Go—Hold the Plastic," *Time,* November 12, 1990, 111.

THE PUBLIC RELATIONS PROGRAM

Publicity is one of the tools of public relations. It can be defined as positive or negative communication that is indirect, nonpersonal, is carried by a mass medium, and is neither paid for nor credited to an identified sponsor. A key concern to the retailer regarding publicity is that the firm has no control over *what* is said (the message), *how* it is said (the presentation), *to whom* it is said (the audience), and *how often* it is said (the message frequency). Nevertheless, publicity plays an important supportive role in enhancing and augmenting product and store advertising. Hence, it behooves the retailer to appreciate both the positive and negative results of good and bad publicity. Domino's Pizza has been dogged by bad publicity. Consumer groups and state safety officials want to halt the company's 30-minute delivery guarantee because of dozens of serious accidents involving Domino's drivers. And the National Organization for Women urged a Domino's boycott becuase of Monaghan's (company founder) financial support of abortion opponents.[19] A positive story can greatly enhance the retailer's image; on the other hand, that positive image can be negated by one incident of negative publicity. Although retailers cannot control publicity, they can take steps to gain favorable publicity and to lessen the impact of negative publicity.

Publicity can be either planned or unplanned. **Planned publicity** means the retailer exercises some control over the news item. Regarding **unplanned publicity**, the retailer simply responds to the uncontrollable events as they occur. Planned publicity includes press releases, press conferences, photographs, letters to the editor, editorials, and special events. Large retailers will typically send out dozens of news releases about their stores and activities. Further, they use press conferences to describe major new events that might be of interest to the public. Pictures and drawings are useful devices for showing store-expansion plans, new equipment to better serve customers, and so forth; these are generally newsworthy items that bring attention to the retailer. These approaches to gaining favorable publicity are subject to the whims of the news media, because they select what they consider newsworthy. The media, however, do have space or time to fill, and persistence and continually disseminated media releases increase the likelihood of favorable coverage.

To develop a publicity story, the retailer first must identify the *kinds* of stories the media accepts and the *criteria* they use to make decisions. This step gives retailers basic ideas on which to develop stories.

Stories that depict new and unusual events, store innovations, improvements in working conditions, new store openings, and stories that are currently important to the public often attract the interest of the news media. Publicity must also be newsworthy, somewhat unusual, appeal to a broad cross section of the public, and must be truthful. Publicity stories are more effective if they are dramatic or emotional and if they show action or human interest through photographs and illustrations.

SUMMARY

Personal selling is a communication process between salesperson and customer. Communication is a two-way process in which both members actively exchange ideas and meanings. The characteristics of a good salesperson generally can be divided into physical traits, personality traits, individual skills, and message-presentation skills.

Steps in the retail selling process are (1) preparing for the customer, (2) prospecting for customers, (3) contacting the customer, (4) presenting the merchandise, (5) handling objections, (6) closing the sale, and (7) following up the sale. A good salesperson prepares well for the sale even before greeting the customer, then adapts throughout the sale to each customer and set of store circumstances as they arise.

Coupons, sampling, premiums, contests, sweepstakes, specialties, and tie-ins are among the many devices retailers use to communicate with customers about their store and their merchandise. Sales incentive approaches are limited only by the retailer's imagination. With ongoing technological innovations, businesses are creating growing numbers of sales incentive tools to stimulate customer interest in their merchandise.

Publicity is an important part of a retailer's public relations program. Good publicity can bring attention to a retailer and its merchandise and help build a good store reputation and sales. Bad publicity can ruin a retailer. A retailer therefore must learn how to manage its publicity.

STUDENT STUDY GUIDE

Key Terms and Concepts

adaptability of salesperson (p. 622)
alternative close technique (p. 632)
assumptive close technique (p. 632)
balance-sheet close technique (p. 632)
boomerang method (p. 630)
compensation method (p. 630)
contests (p. 636)
continuity premiums (p. 636)
couponing (p. 633)
direct close technique (p. 632)
direct premiums (p. 635)
emotional close technique (p. 632)
feel, felt, found method (p. 630)
forestalling method (p. 630)
head-on method (p. 630)
indirect denial method (p. 630)
individual selling skills (p. 620)
listening skills (p. 621)
mail-in premiums (p. 635)
message-presentation skills (p. 622)
order getter (p. 620)
order taker (p. 620)
perceived credibility (p. 621)
perceived expertise (p. 620)
personal communication (p. 619)
personality traits (p. 620)

personal selling (p. 619)
physical traits (p. 620)
positive attitude (p. 621)
premiums (p. 634)
publicity (p. 638)
sales incentives (p. 633)
sampling (p. 634)
salesperson-customer similarity (p. 622)
self-liquidating premiums (p. 634)
specialties (p. 636)
standing-room-only close technique (p. 632)
suggestive selling (p. 632)
summary/agreement close technique (p. 632)
sweepstakes (p. 636)
tie-ins (p. 637)
trading up (p. 627)

Review Questions

1. How are personal selling and personal communications related?
2. What are some of the personality traits of a good salesperson?
3. Describe the role of salesperson expertise and credibility in the selling process.
4. How can a salesperson improve listening skills?
5. Does salesperson-customer similarity affect the selling process? How?
6. When should a salesperson use a one-sided sales message? When is a two-sided sales message appropriate?
7. Where should the strongest selling points be positioned within a sales message?
8. Should the salesperson draw conclusions for the customer? Are there any exceptions?
9. How can salespeople integrate emotional terms into a sales presentation?
10. What should the salesperson determine in prospecting for customers?
11. Describe the sales practice of trading-up the customer.
12. What should the retail salesperson sell?
13. What are the most common methods for handling customer objections? Give an original (nontextbook) example of each technique.
14. When should a salesperson attempt to close a sale?
15. Describe the various types of closing techniques available to the salesperson. Give an original example of each technique.
16. What is the best option for following up a sale? Why?
17. What is a sales incentive?
18. What is the primary purpose of sampling?
19. Compare and contrast the various types of premiums.
20. Identify the advantages of tie-in promotions.
21. What doesn't the retailer control in publicity-related stories?

Review Exam

True or False

_____ 1. Customers are persuaded more by a salesperson they perceive to be similar to themselves.
_____ 2. When consumers are not knowledgeable about the product, the general rule is to present them with a two-sided message.
_____ 3. "May I help you" is a well-established opening that any retail salesperson can use successfully in contacting the potential customer.
_____ 4. The forestalling method of handling objections can be used with any type of objection.
_____ 5. "The sale ends today" is a good example of the standing-room-only close.
_____ 6. McDonald's "Garfield" coffee cups are a good example of direct premiums.
_____ 7. Sweepstakes are sales incentives that involve pure chance and a minimal effort on the part of the customer.
_____ 8. One advantage of publicity is that the public perceives news stories as having higher credibility than advertising.

Multiple Choice

_____ 1. Close rapidly, avoid oversell, avoid overtalk, and noting key points is what salespersons should say or do when dealing with a(n) _____.
a. doubting Thomas
b. look around
c. impulsive
d. procrastinator
e. hesitant

_____ 2. In selling merchandise, salespeople should place their strongest selling points at the _____.
a. beginning
b. middle
c. end
d. a and b
e. a and c

_____ 3. When a retail salesperson stresses the manufacturer's warranty, the retailer's money-back guarantee, and the product's dependable brand, the salesperson is attempting to _____.

a. learn the customer's needs and wants
b. reduce the customer's perceived risk of buying
c. demonstrate the product's physical features
d. actively involve the customer in the sales presentation
e. make the sales message simple

_____ 4. Retail salespeople should use the indirect denial method for handling objections _____.
a. arising from incorrect information
b. arising from valid objections but where compensation factors are present
c. that can be turned into a positive factor
d. that are largely emotional
e. of any type

_____ 5. In following up a sale, the more effective method in reducing a customer's postpurchase doubt is _____.
a. writing a letter to the customer
b. telephoning the customer
c. making a personal visit to the customer
d. all of the above are equally effective

_____ 6. The _____ type of sweepstakes are those in which the entrant is required to give back some information from a label, package, or advertisement, with winners chosen from the correct entries.
a. straight
b. matching
c. instant winner
d. programmed learning
e. contest

STUDENT APPLICATIONS MANUAL

Investigative Projects: Practice and Applications

1. One of the most effective ways to obtain information about any aspect of the retailer's operation is to ask consumers what they think. Review the characteristics of a good salesperson; then, develop a form that can be used by consumers to evaluate the performance of store salespeople.
2. Salespeople can make a sales presentation using either a one- or two-sided message. Select a specific product (i.e., a specific brand, style, model, and size), and develop a sales presentation using a two-sided message.
3. Customers often have hidden objections and are reluctant to express their concerns. In other cases, customers often state a false objection because they do not want to tell the true reasons (e.g., cannot afford the product) for their lack of willingness to make a purchase commitment. Nevertheless, the hidden and false objection can kill the sale. Conduct a literature search or interview experienced salespeople to ascertain methods for discovering and overcoming these hidden or false objections.
4. Discuss the statement, "Retail selling is essentially a problem-solving situation; that is, customers are looking for solutions to problems, not products." If this problem-solving theory of retail selling is true, how should a retail salesperson approach the selling situation?
5. Strangely enough, coupons work best with older, more affluent, better educated, urban consumers and married consumers than with consumers who need the savings more—the less affluent, young, single, and less educated. Explain why.
6. Sampling is generally used in association with products characterized by low per-unit cost. What actions might the retailer take to allow the consumer to sample high per-unit-cost products?
7. The effectiveness of any sales incentive tool varies according to the operational and merchandising characteristics of a given type of retailer. Identify the most and least effective sales incentive tools for each of the following retailers: (1) a small gift shop; (2) a hardware store; (3) a fast food restaurant; and (4) a cosmetic department. Explain your selection.

Tactical Cases: Problems and Decisions

■ CASE 17–1

Selling Furniture at Retail: Probe, Listen, Explain, and Close*

"Chip, our couch did not survive the move. We need a new one. In fact, we could use all new living room furniture."

Molly and Chip Halpin had just been transferred to Chicago from Providence, Rhode Island. They were both 37 with three kids, aged 10 (girl), 6 (boy), and 6 months (girl).

"Whoa there! All new living room furniture? We can't afford that. We just bought a new minivan. You're right about the couch though; it looks bad and sinks to the floor when you sit on it. Find out where the good deals are, honey, and next weekend we'll go shopping for a couch," said Chip.

"OK, but we'll have to probably bring the kids with us. I don't have a babysitter yet."

After a preliminary search, Molly found two stores that advertised good brands of sofas at discounted prices. First they went to a traditional furniture store. The selection of contemporary styles wasn't quite as good, but delivery was free. They weren't in the store for 30 seconds when a salesperson approached them.

"Hello folks, my name is Lucretia Griffith. What a fine looking family you have. Oh, a baby, how precious. She's a doll, how old is she?"

"Six months," beamed Molly.

"What room are you decorating?" said Lucretia.

"Oh, we're not decorating a whole room. We're just in the market for a new couch," said Chip.

"Well, we have an excellent selection of top name brand sofas, chairs, tables, and accessories. And, as you can see, we discount all products. No one sells these higher-end brands for prices as low as Best Furniture," explained Lucretia.

"We'd just like to look around for a while," said Molly.

"Fine. If you need some help, I'll be on this floor," replied Lucretia.

Molly and Chip rummaged through the store looking at sofas for the next 45 minutes. The baby was good but the older children were bored and a constant distraction.

"Hey Chip, this striped couch is really sharp. The overstuffed stripe is the latest look. Isn't it comfortable. How much is it? Twelve hundred dollars, ugh, more than we were thinking of spending."

"Yeah, it is really comfortable. I like the look, too."

"Find something you like, folks?" inquired Lucretia. "This manufacturer offers one of our best values. This sofa has coil springs, kiln-dried wood frame, and high-quality, long staple cotton stuffing. At $1,200 it is a heck of a buy and I can further discount it to $1,099 for you."

"Do you think it will hold up to the kids? The blue stripe and white background will show all the dirt," said a suddenly worried Molly.

"Well, we can put a treatment on the sofa but frankly, if you have three children perhaps you should be considering other fabrics, like Herculon, that wear like iron," said Lucretia.

"You're right, do you have this sofa in Herculon?" asked Chip.

"No, a pattern like this cannot be made in Herculon," replied Lucretia. "Here are some Herculon sofas."

"Phew, these are ugly. They have no style, they belong in a motel," said Chip. "Molly, why don't we just keep the kids off the sofa. They have their own toy room where they spend most of their time. When they watch TV in the living room, we'll have them sit in their own 'special' chairs."

"How will this sofa fit with the rest of your furnishings?" inquired Lucretia.

"OK, I guess. We really don't have good furniture in the living room right now. We have one decent cream-colored chair, with a very subdued small scale pattern. The tables are beat-up pine. We really need all new living room furniture," said Molly.

"Yes, that's the way to buy furniture. I really try to encourage customers to buy a room full of furniture at a time and carefully coordinate the pieces so that the room makes a statement and fits together. When you buy furniture one piece at a time, you typically end up with a hodgepodge that looks unprofessional. I am a certified interior designer and can work closely with you, in creating a beautiful room. I will come to your house, look at the room, and consult with you about your style preferences, all at no charge," said Lucretia.

"Gee, that sounds wonderful. I hate to admit it, but I've never been any good at decorating. I don't even like doing it," said Molly.

Chip's mouth dropped and the color drained from his face. "Redecorate the whole living room! You've gotta be kiddin'! That'd be $5,000 in a heartbeat. There's no way we have that kind of money right now. What's wrong with just buying a couch? I don't want to make a statement. I just want a decent couch to sit in that's not an embarrassment. Isn't the hodgepodge approach a style all its own . . . the eclectic style or something."

"You're right, we can't afford that," sighed Molly.

Chip looked at his watch. "Molly, we've got to go. I want to mow the lawn before it gets dark. Come on kids, we're going. Thank you for your time, Lucretia."

"Here's my card. Call me if you need anything," said Lucretia.

On the way home Chip and Molly decided to try the second store tomorrow.

ASSIGNMENT

1. Critique the sales presentation of Lucretia Griffith. What, if anything, should Lucretia have done differently.
2. Molly and Chip are going to another furniture store tomorrow. What would be your approach to selling them living room furniture?

*This case was prepared by James T. Strong, The University of Akron.

■ CASE 17–2
Nordies: Motivation or Intimidation?*

THE SUCCESS OF NORDSTROM, INC.

In the extremely competitive retail department-store industry, Nordstrom Inc. of Seattle, Washington, has been astonishingly successful. Nordstrom has 58 stores and 30,000 employees. The chain focuses on upscale baby boomers and has, until recently, located stores in the Pacific Northwest and California. The foundation of Nordstrom's success is unparalleled customer service. Nordstrom achieves this through a decentralized management structure, empowering local store and department managers with unheard of decision responsibility. Decentralized merchandise buying allows Nordstrom to capitalize on regional differences in taste and style. Promotion from within and their own management training school, "Nordstrom University," increases the loyalty and competence of their managerial ranks. The firm also benefits from closely held family ownership and has avoided the high levels of debt that plague many of its competitors who overextended themselves in bloody takeover battles.

The statistics reveal Nordstrom's success. For example, in 1988 its sales per square foot rose to $380, nearly double the department-store industry average. Perhaps more impressively, in 1988 when many large retailers were struggling, Nordstrom rang up a 21 percent sales gain to $2.3 billion. In fact, so many of Nordstrom management practices are being copied by other department stores that some industry analysts are referring to the "Nordstromization" of the industry.

Nordstrom's success in providing extremely high levels of customer service, reminiscent of earlier eras of retailing, is attributable in large part to their sales force. To promote service, salespeople are given the freedom to do almost anything to satisfy shoppers. For example, Billie Burns, a former men's clothing department manager, once got a call from a regular customer who was racing to the airport and needed some clothes. Mr. Burns selected some blazers, slacks, and underwear, charged them to the customer's account and met the man's car outside the store. Service like that creates loyal customers. Consequently, Nordstrom is able to lower advertising and rely on word-of-mouth for promotion. This service inspired loyalty also allows the firm to maintain high margins on its merchandise.

HIGH PERFORMANCE–HIGH COMMISSION

What motivates Nordstrom's retail clerks to provide this level of service in an age when many times consumers search in vain for retail sales assistance? Two key factors are high pay and commission compensation. In an attempt to implement a management-by-objective program, the firm sets specific sales quotas for each salesperson, to focus effort and determine compensation. Commissions are only paid if sales quotas are hit and repeated failure to reach quota results in termination.

Many of Nordstrom's salespeople thrive in this high commission, high pressure selling environment. For example, Pat McCarthy, a salesman in the flagship Seattle store is one of thousands of Nordstrom salespeople who have been very successful. Pat has worked for over 20 years in the men's clothing department and has generated yearly commissions of over $80,000. "It's really a people job, which I love," says Mr. McCarthy. "Every year my sales have gotten progressively better." Other salespeople feel Nordstrom allows them great freedom "to get the job done." Doris Quiros, a salesperson in San Francisco, states that other retailers "give you a big book of rules; when I came here, Nordstrom gave me one with only one rule: Use your best judgment. That's because they want me to be my own boss."

Salespeople at Nordstrom call themselves "Nordies" and many have a fanatical devotion to the firm. At a typical department store 90 percent of a salesperson's compensation is simply based on being there, at Nordstrom it's just the opposite. Nordstrom attracts career-oriented college graduates due to higher compensation levels and good opportunities for advancement. They pay, in combination with a base pay rate of as high as $10 per hour, commissions ranging from 5 percent to 10 percent, after salespeople meet volume quotas. The average Nordstrom salesperson earns around $25,000 per year compared to the national average of $12,000.

The company requires most employees to start their career on the sales floor, as did the owners (Bruce, John, and Jim Nordstrom). As an incentive for loyalty, however, Nordstrom promotes entirely from within. This creates many advancement opportunities because the firm is growing rapidly.

MOTIVATING THE TROOPS

Management improves salesperson performance with frequent motivation seminars and meetings. Salespeople are encouraged to write and repeat upbeat statements called "affirmations." Examples of affirmations are: "I feel proud being a Pacesetter," "I only sell multiples," "Do it for Nordstrom." At pep rallies blond bathing beauties prance on stage, chanting "Vol-ume! Vol-ume!"

Salespeople are also motivated by management's close attention to performance. In each store salespeople are ranked by sales per hour and those who fall below minimum standards face termination. The company frequently employs contests to reward and recognize strong performers. For example, "Who looks more Nordstrom" contests encourage employees to shop at Nordstrom. Smile contests are also frequent occurrences. Pictures of winning "smilers" are hung in the lunchroom. Top sales performers are awarded prestigious "Pacesetter" titles. Good customer service is rewarded with cheers at company meetings, occasional $5, $10, and $100 bonuses or "All Star" honors.

To further ensure that salespeople are providing the required high level of customer service "secret shoppers" impersonate consumers and report on performance. Salespeople are also required to write daily quotas of thank-you letters to customers and fill monthly customer-service "books" with letters from grateful customers.

These management techniques have been very successful for Nordstrom. Sales have increased from just over $900,000 in 1985 to $2.3 billion in 1989. More importantly net income during the same period rose from over $40 million to $123.3 million.

CLOUDS ON THE HORIZON?

However, not all is bright at Nordstrom. In the first quarter of 1990 the firm faced markdowns, bloated inventories, and a major setback in a labor dispute with their vaunted sales force. These problems led to an expected decrease in profits, which has not occurred since the firm went public in 1971. Industry analysts expect the reduction to be about 5 percent.

Perhaps even more troublesome is a negative decision by the Washington (state) Department of Labor and Industries. Observers speculate that the decision could diminish Nordstroms' ability to continue to provide high levels of customer service that has been the backbone of its success. The agency states that Nordstrom failed to pay salespeople for providing some of the extra services for which the chain is famous. The company has been ordered to properly compensate employees for all hours worked and to pay back wages. Apparently at some stores time clocks were continually "broken" or salespeople were instructed to clock out and they were not compensated for performing non-selling tasks such as stock work, personal delivery, and writing customer thank-you notes. Managers justified this to employees by stressing the need to keep sales per hour ratios high.

"We're looking at what is likely to be the highest wage claim in the history of the state," says Mark McDermott, the agency's assistant director for employment standards. "These are employment-practice patterns the company engaged in, not isolated incidents."

Joe Peterson, president of United Food and Commercial Workers Local 1001, which represents Nordstrom employees in the Seattle area, speculates that the Nordstrom corporate culture will have to change completely. The present culture provides high levels of customer service but salespeople are expected to work many hours without pay in an environment of constant pressure and harassment according to 500 complaints filed with the union. At present, only 1,500 of the firm's 30,000 employees are unionized. The union claims that $2.1 million in back pay claims have already been paid and future claims could total $30 to $40 million.

However, company owner Bruce Nordstrom dismisses the issue as a bookkeeping problem and states that the company's policy has always been to compensate workers for all work performed. He said in a statement after the agency's decision that complying "will not alter our culture or affect our continued commitment to customer service." Co-owner, Jim Nordstrom dismisses the union's stack of claims as a "bargaining ploy" and states that if employees are working without pay, breaks or days off, it is "isolated" or by "choice." He argues that "a lot of employees want to work every day and as many people thank us for letting them work all these hours as complain." Jim Nordstrom thinks salespeople should work harder. "I think people don't put in enough hours during the busy time. We need to work harder." He explains that salespeople are expected to perform many tasks, such as taking out the trash because stock people are constantly being cut back. "It may have happened that some people were asked to pitch in" and carry out the trash. "That would be great if that happened. If people don't want to, then obviously some people don't want to work hard."

Some former salespeople disagree. Cherie Validi compares Nordstrom to a cult and competitors claim Nordstrom's sales force is "brainwashed." Petra Rousau, a 10-year sales veteran recalls "I'd be up 'til 3 A.M. doing my letters, and doing my manager's books. Before you know it your whole life is Nordstrom. But you couldn't complain, because then your manager would schedule you for the bad hours, your sales per hour would fall and next thing you know you're out the door."

Pat Bemis joined Nordstrom on the promise of greater income and the status of being a "Nordie." She soon found herself working harder, making less, and being subject to constant threats from management. "The managers were these little tin gods, always grilling you about your sales. You felt like your job was constantly in jeopardy. They'd write you up for anything, being sick, the way you dressed." Ms. Bemis was consistently a top seller but some years she made only $18,000, far below her expectations. Ms. Bemis recalls that "working off the clock was just standard," crucial to elevating sales per hour. "In the end, really serving the customer, being an All-Star meant nothing; if you had low sales per hour, you were forced out."

MOTIVATED TO SELL OR TO "SHARK"?

The behavior motivated by commission compensation does not always lead to the desired result. "Sharking" sales seems to be a common problem for Nordstrom. Some salespeople hog the register to boost their sales while others give kickbacks to the few noncommissioned cashiers on the floor. In the case of Cindy Nelson competition for sales cost a salesperson her job. Apparently, the sales colleagues of Ms. Nelson were jealous of her success as the number one salesperson in her store. She had won two Pacesetter awards and was about to win a third when five of her fellow salespeople, lead by numbers two and three, accused her of "stealing" their sales. She was fired and her manager refused to let her examine the sales receipts in question. "I was totally stunned," recalls Ms. Nelson. "This whole time I thought I was going to be this great Nordstrom person and now I was nothing, a nobody. I became an emotional wreck." In October of 1988 a Seattle court award her $180,000 in damages and she settled with the company out of court for an undisclosed sum.

These chinks in the armor of Nordstrom come at a time when the highly successful retailer plans to add 15 more stores to the 58-store chain and enter major Midwestern and Eastern markets, such as New York, Chicago, Minneapolis, and Baltimore. Industry observers speculate that maintaining success will be harder and harder for the family controlled business as it grows and leaves its traditional area of the Pacific Northwest.

ASSIGNMENT

1. Does Nordstrom have a significant problem with its sales force or is this an example of isolated cases and gripers?
2. Is Nordstrom taking unfair advantage of its sales force

or simply demanding performance? Would you change anything?

3. Can commission compensation work with retail salespeople? How should it be structured?
4. Will Nordstrom have to change its corporate culture and sacrifice its competitive advantage of high customer service to avoid sales force unionization? Will Nordstrom's present culture be effective as it moves toward becoming a national chain?

*This case was prepared by James T. Strong, The University of Akron.

Sources: Francine Schwadel, "Courting Shoppers: Nordstrom's Push East Will Test Its Renown for the Best in Service," *The Wall Street Journal,* August 1, 1989, p. A1, A4 and Susan Faludl, "Sales Job: At Nordstrom Stores, Service Comes First—But at a Big Price," *The Wall Street Journal,* February 20, 1990, p. A1, A12.

ENDNOTES

1. Stephen Bennett, "Selling Ideas for Spring," *Progressive Grocer,* January 1990, 43. Copyright © Progressive Grocer Magazine a division of Maclean Hunter Media, Inc., Stamford, Connecticut.
2. See William Weitzel, Albert B. Schwarzkopf, and E. Brian Peach, "The Influence of Employee Perceptions of Customer Service or Retail Store Sales," *Journal of Retailing,* 65, Spring 1989, 27–39.
3. John Huey, "Wal-Mart, Will It Take over the World," *Fortune,* January 30, 1989, 58.
4. Wendy Zellner, "Two Days in Boot Camp—Learning to Love Lexus," *Business Week,* September 4, 1989, 87.
5. Nido R. Quebein, "The Power of Asking Questions," *Personal Selling Power* (January/February 1988), 20–21.
6. Ibid.
7. See Dottie Enrico, "GWP and PWP: Pros and Cons," *Stores* (September 1986), 63–68.
8. Teri Agins, "Clothing Stores Let Designers Hawk Clothes," *The Wall Street Journal,* March 14, 1989, B–1.
9. Bruce Hager and John Templeman, "Now They're Selling BMWs Door-to-Door-Almost," *Business Week,* May 14, 1990, 65.
10. James G. Hertel, Jr., "Consumer Marketing Opportunities for the Optical Memory Card Industry," *Optical Information Systems,* January–February 1989, 21.
11. Diane Schneidman, "Trading Stamps Face Redemption as Viable Marketing Tool," *Marketing News,* February 13, 1987, 1, 28.
12. See David Scholes, "Targeting Frequent Users," *Direct Marketing,* March 1989, 56–58.
13. Jan Larson, "Farewell to Coupons?" *American Demographics,* February 1990, 16.
14. Ibid.
15. Francine Schwadel, "Sears Plans to Offer Promotional Prizes to Frequent Buyers," *Wall Street Journal,* March 1, 1988. Also see "Electronic Marketing—Learning from America's Largest Retailers," *Supermarket Business,* October 1988, 13–15.
16. Richard Gibson, "Burger King Senses Rebound Around Corner," *The Wall Street Journal,* April 6, 1990, B1.
17. Ela Schwartz, "A New Lease on Licensing," *Discount Merchandiser,* August 1989, 64.
18. See Joshua Hammer and Annetta Miller, "Ninja Turtle Power," *Newsweek,* April 16, 1990, 60–61.
19. Wendy Zellner, "Why the Pizza King May Abdicate the Throne," *Business Week,* September 25. 1989, 46.

OUTLINE

OBJECTIVES

- Appreciate the need for strategic retail management and planning.
- Develop an organizational mission statement that can serve as a focus for the firm's current and future activities.
- Construct the organizational objectives for achieving the organization's mission.
- Conduct a portfolio analysis and classify different business units on the basis of their market and cash flow positions.
- Identify the various types of growth and performance opportunities and evaluate the appropriate strategies associated with each type of opportunity.

PART VI

STRATEGIC RETAIL MANAGEMENT

Current Strategies and Tactics

CHAPTER 18

BACK TO STRATEGIC MANAGEMENT

After 10 years of managing retail businesses to maximize cash flow in the very short term, the retail industry will return, by the end of the 1990s, to a more fundamental and longer term strategic management perspective.

Decision making will return to longer time frames; strategy will refocus on customers and competition; executives will re-examine soft investments for strategic capital; and performance will be measured not merely in terms of next quarter's cash flow but, more importantly, in terms of long range profitability and earnings growth.

Concentration on strategic management is clearly one of the common attributes of almost all High Performance Retailers.[1]

STRATEGIC RETAIL MANAGEMENT

Planning is essential if the retail organization is to survive and prosper in the competitive environment associated with consumer markets. **Strategic retail management** is the process of planning the organization, implementation, and control of all the firm's activities. It involves making both strategic and tactical decisions for different levels within an organization. The strategic management process consists of two major components: the strategic plan and the retailing plan.

Before discussing each of these plans, it is instructive to examine the issue of strategic versus tactical planning as it relates to the various levels (corporate, strategic business unit, store, department, and product line) within the retail organization. *Corporate planning* is conducted by the corporate headquarters management team and is directed at developing an overall plan for the entire organization. The corporate planning process is strategic because it establishes the general framework for the firm's actions over an extended period of time. As a broad statement based on experience, intuition, and analytical judgment, the corporate plan outlines the organization's general business intent. *Business planning* involves developing a course of action for each of the **strategic business units** (SBUs) within the retail organization. An SBU is a business division with a clearly identifiable merchandise strategy (retail format) that targets a market segment (customer focus) within a defined competitive environment (market position). Business planning identifies the role of each SBU in the overall corporate strategy.

The planning process continues with the development of plans for each store, department, and product line within each SBU. *Store, department,* and *product line planning* is more tactical than strategic. It focuses more on current problems and decisions faced in implementing SBU and corporate strategy.

Figure 18–1 presents planning levels for a large retail organization. Planning at the corporate level is conducted by upper-level management for The May Department Stores Company in their corporate headquarters in St. Louis. Corporate plans set the parameters for the business plans developed by each of the firm's SBUs (business segments and operating divisions). Using the corporate and business plans as guidelines, store, merchandise, and department managers develop tactical plans for each store, department, and product line. In a small retail organization such as a local chain or independent retail operator, the entire planning process may be conducted by one or a small group of individuals in a single location.

Keeping in mind that planning can be both strategic and tactical and occurs at several levels within the organization, we now turn our attention to a more comprehensive examination of the retailer's strategic plan.

Strategic planning aims to develop a long-term course of action that will provide an overall sense of direction for a retail organization's business activities. The **strategic plan** is a grand design or blueprint for ensuring success in all of the organization's business endeavors. A strategic plan is directed at achieving a strategic fit between the organization's capabilities (present and future) and its environmental opportunities (present and future). A good fit enables the organization to sustain competitive assets and overcome competitive liabilities, as well as to anticipate external environmental changes and identify needed internal organizational adjustments.

The development of an organization's strategic plan is a process that consists of (1) establishing the organization's mission, (2) identifying the organization's objectives, (3) evaluating the organization's portfolio of SBUs, and (4) assessing the organization's opportunities. Figure 18–2 illustrates the process of developing a strategic plan.

ORGANIZATIONAL MISSION

The **mission statement** is a generalized yet meaningful expression of the organization's future direction. It is a commitment to future actions. As a statement of intended future actions, the organizational mission has numerous tasks to perform.

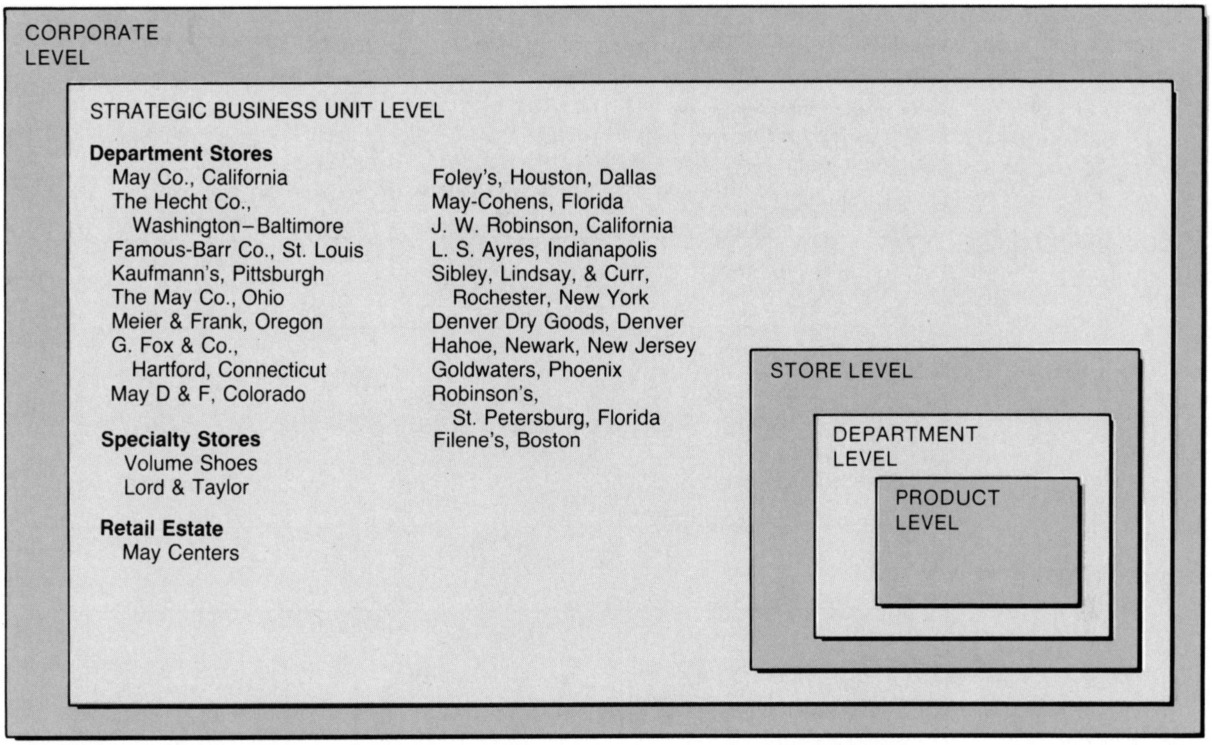

CORPORATE LEVEL
STRATEGIC BUSINESS UNIT LEVEL
Department Stores
May Co., California
The Hecht Co., Washington–Baltimore
Famous-Barr Co., St. Louis
Kaufmann's, Pittsburgh
The May Co., Ohio
Meier & Frank, Oregon
G. Fox & Co., Hartford, Connecticut
May D & F, Colorado
Foley's, Houston, Dallas
May-Cohens, Florida
J. W. Robinson, California
L. S. Ayres, Indianapolis
Sibley, Lindsay, & Curr, Rochester, New York
Denver Dry Goods, Denver
Hahoe, Newark, New Jersey
Goldwaters, Phoenix
Robinson's, St. Petersburg, Florida
Filene's, Boston
Specialty Stores
Volume Shoes
Lord & Taylor
Retail Estate
May Centers
STORE LEVEL
DEPARTMENT LEVEL
PRODUCT LEVEL

FIGURE 18–1
Business planning levels: The May Department Stores Co.

First, a mission statement identifies both the business and customer domains wherein the organization operates or plans to operate. A well-defined mission will answer such business domain questions as "What *is* our business?" "What *will* our business be?" and "What *should* our business be?" Corresponding questions in the customer domain are "Who *is* our customer?" "Who *will* our customer be?" and "Who *should* our customer be?" As Figure 18–3 illustrates, strategic gaps grow between each of these business and customer domain questions as one moves from the present to the future. These gaps represent the difference between current, expected, and desired performances, and as such, they indicate the possible need for changing the strategic plan of the organization.

Second, a mission statement identifies the organization's responsibilities toward the people with whom it interacts. Retailing has been described as a people business, and the mission statement should recognize this orientation. In its mission statement, the Dayton Hudson Department Store Co. reaffirmed its commitment to people through (1) serving *customers* by offering better service than competitors; (2) serving *communities* by contributing to a strong, healthy environment; (3) serving *shareholders* by providing a superior return on their investment; and (4) serving *employees* by offering rewarding careers.

Third, a mission statement provides a general blueprint for accomplishing the organizational mission. The May Department Stores Co.'s mission statement used a symbol for communicating its mission of excellence in retailing by meeting its general objective: "top quartile performance" as measured by "return on common stockholders' investment." The May mission symbol is a pyramid whose base is formed by the associates who make up the organization. The May Co. said it plans to achieve its general mission and objective by "building a strong organization and setting clear strategy."[2] The organizational foundation of the firm's pyramid is directed at developing

FIGURE 18–2
The strategic plan

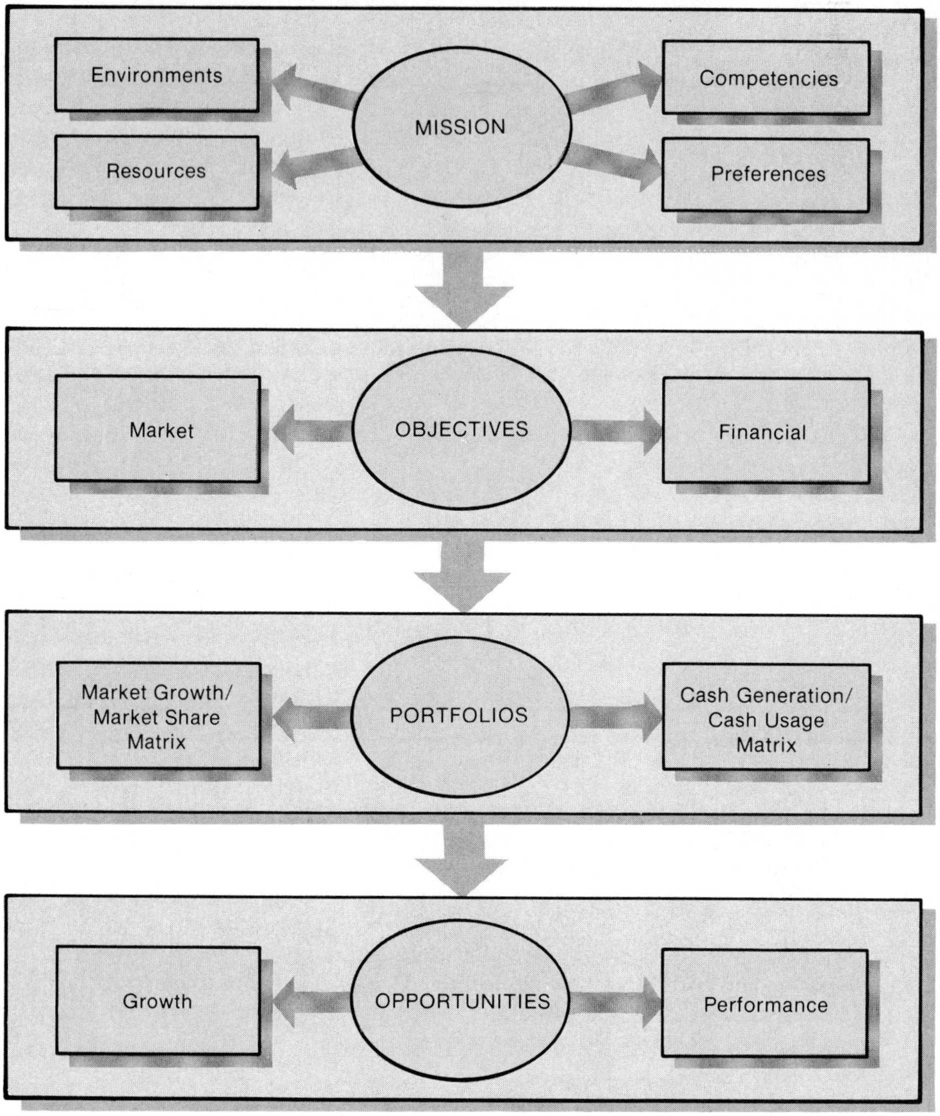

a superior general management, cultivating an innovative corporate culture, and securing the best talent in retailing.[3] The strategy focus of the firm will be on productivity, merchandise impact, genuine customer service, sound pricing practices, vital sales promotions, visually exciting stores, and efficient systems (see Figure 18–4).

The statement of the organizational mission is developed by taking several factors into account. These factors include environmental considerations, resource considerations, distinctive competencies, and managerial preferences.

Environmental Considerations

The retail organization must accommodate and react to several different environments that present both opportunities and threats. Some of the major components of an organization's environment are suppliers, marketing intermediaries, customers, competitors, and the public (see Figure 18–5).

RETAIL STRATEGIES AND TACTICS

Is It a Strategy or Is It a Tactic?

A tactic is a singular idea or angle. A strategy has many elements, all of which are focused on the tactic.

A tactic is independent of time and relatively constant. A strategy unfolds over a period of time. A sale is a tactic used at one time or another by most of the retailers in America. A store that has a sale every day is a discount store, which is a strategy.

Some retailers have sharpened this tactic into a powerful strategy. Syms is a highly successful discount clothing store in the New York area. "At Syms," say the television commercials, "you'll never hear the word sale. An educated consumer is our best consumer."

A tactic is a competitive advantage. A strategy is designed to maintain that competitive advantage.

A tactic is external to the product, service, or company. It may not even be a product the company makes. A strategy is internal. (Strategies often require a great deal of internal reorganization.)

A tactic is communications-oriented. A strategy is product-, service-, or company-oriented.

The principle of bottom-up marketing is simple: You work from the specific to the general, from the short term to the long term.

Find a tactic that will work and then build it into a strategy. Find one tactic, not two or three or four.

Most managers think in terms of strategy and tactics. That is, they search for a strategy they can express in terms of many different tactics. The emphasis in traditional marketing is expanding sideways into different markets using a number of tactics. The corporate strategy then gets more and more general to encompass a profusion of tactics.

Most generals do not like to focus on tactics. It takes the fun out of the process. Most generals like to generalize. It's more in keeping with the prerogatives of higher office to work on the "mission and values" statement than it is to eat a Whopper at a Burger King. When you get to be a high priest of business, you feel the overwhelming urge to pontificate.

When you get to the top, you like to be "free." Free of all those messy tactical details of the business. Free to participate in the fun side of marketing, the development of the grand strategy.

Source: Al Ries & Jack Trout, "Tactic versus Strategy," *Bottom-Up Marketing:* 12–14. Reprinted by permission from McGraw-Hill Book Company, New York, New York © 1988.

As a marketing intermediary, the retail organization has an internal environment within which the daily operation of the firm must be successfully completed. The strengths and weaknesses of the organization's structure and personnel must be accounted for when developing mission statements. The planning process should involve all levels of the organization to ensure a full commitment from all affected parties. Plank No. 13 of K mart's mission statement is "Retailing is a people business; therefore K mart believes that people should be rewarded and encouraged to be more entrepreneurial."[4]

As a team member in the marketing channel of distribution, the mission statement must also address the needs of suppliers and customers. The retailer's mission should recognize the need for a coordinated effort and a cooperative spirit in conducting channel affairs. Retail organizations that have adopted the marketing concept (customer satisfaction at a profit) will, as a matter of course, consider the expectations of their targeted markets and make provisions within the mission statement for gaining buyer acceptance of the firm's programs.

FIGURE 18–3
Fundamental mission statement questions

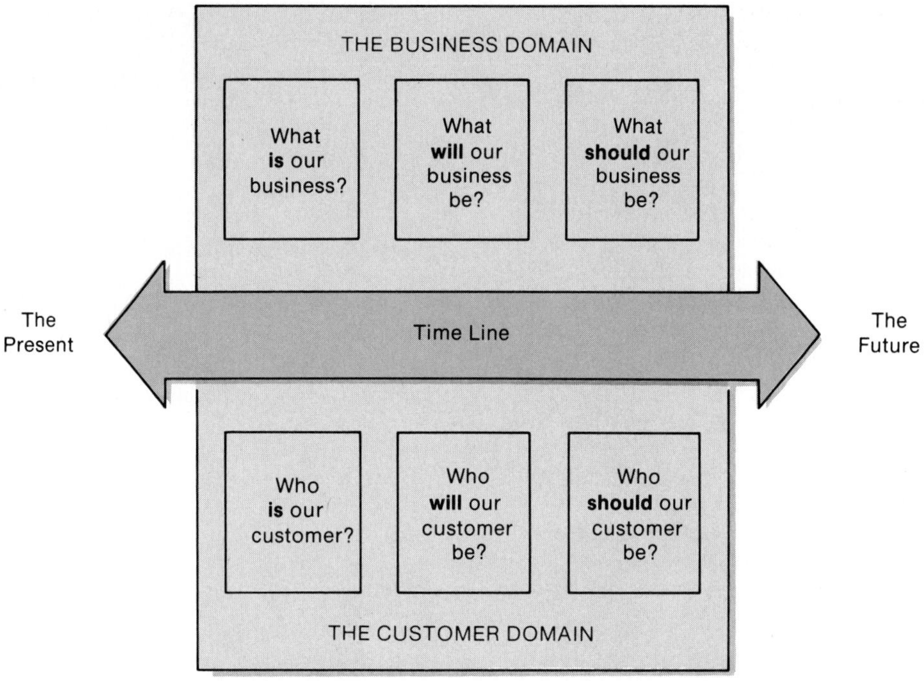

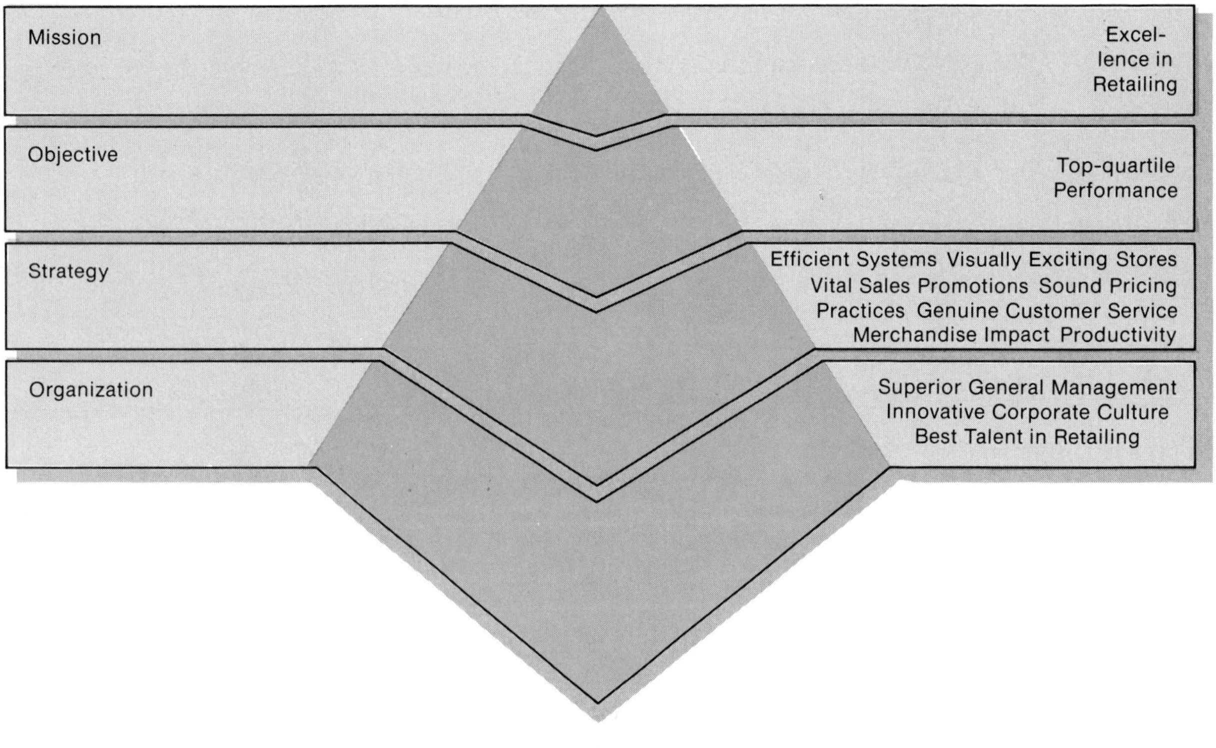

FIGURE 18–4
The mission pyramid of The May Department Stores Co. (source: The May Department Stores Co. annual report, 1983)

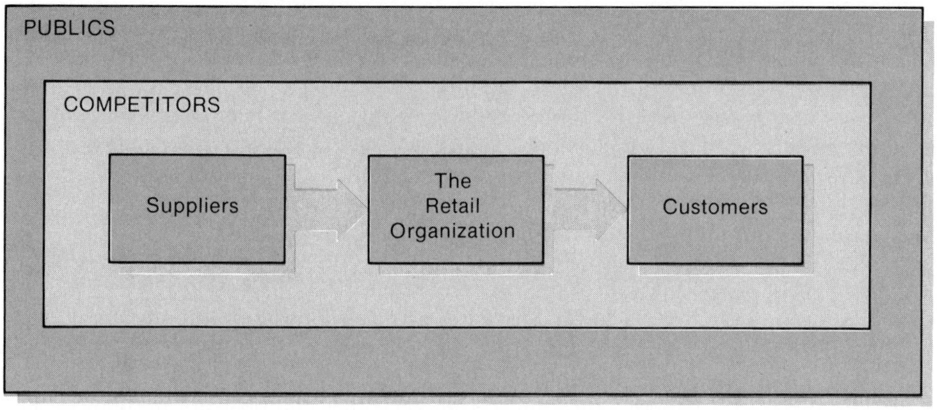

FIGURE 18–5
The environments to be considered in developing organizational missions

Retailing activities are not conducted within a vacuum; the mission statement therefore must recognize the existence of competitors and the expectations of the general public. The strategic planning process must devote considerable attention to positioning the retail organization relative to competition. The general public's perception of the retail organization is also vital to acceptance of the firm's activities. The goal of serving the public need by being a responsive corporate citizen meeting its social responsibilities also needs to be addressed within the mission statement. The mission statement of Kings Supermarkets in New Jersey emphasizes brotherhood as part of the firm's mission; orientation and training emphasizes that one doesn't have to love other associates, but one has to learn to live with them and respect them.[5]

Resource Considerations

The mission statement must be realistic. The extent of that realism depends on the resources available to the retail organization. Because resources are essential to implement the firm's current and future strategies, the mission statement should recognize the problems associated with acquiring, maintaining, and using resources. The resource base to consider in developing the mission statement consists of (1) the financial assets and liabilities of the firm, (2) the organizational composition and structure of the management team, (3) the human resource component in terms of supporting personnel, and (4) the physical plant—store facilities, fixtures, and equipment.

Distinctive Competencies

A careful assessment of practically any retail organization will reveal certain merchandising and operating capabilities that distinguish it from competing organizations. Distinctive competencies might occur in such areas as visual merchandising, exclusive supplier relationships, customer communications and sales promotions, unique store imagery, inventory planning and control systems, organization integration, product assortments, market coverage, or store atmospheres. The list of possible distinctive competencies is almost endless. Consolidated Stores Corp., operators of Big Lots and Odd Lots stores, had as its distinctive competencies the buying of close-out merchandise. Recently, however, the firm has grown so fast that it has outdistanced its abilities and resources to sustain its growth rate without revamping its strategies and tactics.[6] The Walt Disney Company locates its Disney stores in tourist locations (i.e., distinctive competency) like San Francisco's Pier 39 and Cleveland's Terminal Tower Mall. In any case, distinctive competencies are solid foundations for suggesting future strategies in a mission statement.

Managerial Preferences

Additional considerations in developing a mission statement include the merchandising and operating preferences of the organization's cadre of managers. The type and extent of managerial expertise (e.g., mass merchandise vs. specialty retailing) will vary among retail organizations; therefore, it is both logical and practical to consider management strengths when planning the organization's future directions. In addition, managerial intuition should not be overlooked when plotting a new and innovative course of action and finding unique methods of strategy implementation.

ORGANIZATIONAL OBJECTIVES

An **organizational objective** can be defined as a strategic position to be attained or a purpose to be achieved by the retail organization and/or one of its strategic business units. It is an aim or end-of-action statement toward which the retail organization's efforts are directed. Chapter 1 introduced the concept of the scales of retailing—the desirability of striking a balance between satisfying the customer's merchandising needs and meeting the retailer's need of a satisfactory financial performance. The two major categories of organizational objectives reflect this balance: the market objectives of customer patronage and competitive position and the financial objectives of profitability and productivity. Figure 18–6 presents a typology of organizational objectives.

Market Objectives

Market objectives are aimed at securing customer patronage and achieving competitive positions within the general marketplace. Market objectives are realized by carefully planned merchandising programs that can satisfy the consumer's psychological, social, and personal needs.

Sales Volume. Sales volume increases are a commonly identified objective. A sales growth objective is typically expressed as a certain percentage increase (e.g., 15 percent) for a particular strategic business unit (e.g., a store) over a defined time period (e.g., next year). It is an expansion objective that involves additional commitment of the organization's resources and the forgoing of short-term profits for long-term gains. Increases in total sales volume might be achieved by (1) adding new operating units, (2) increasing advertising expenditures, (3) improving a product/service offering, (4) lowering prices, or (5) making other merchandising adjustments (e.g., added convenience) that can increase customer satisfaction.

Another type of sales volume objective is to increase the average customer sale. Increasing the total amount spent by each customer during a store visit should have a direct and positive effect on total sales. Kinney Shoes, a subsidiary of F.W. Woolworth Co., repositioned its women's shoes to appeal to working women who are willing and able to spend more on fashionable dress shoes; the goal was to increase the average sale by 10 to 15 percent.[7] Personal selling and various sales promotion methods are used to increase the amount of the average sale.

Customer Traffic. Many retailers believe that if they can attract customers into the store, then they can obtain desired sales through customer exposure to the direct merchandising efforts of the organization. Their objectives are thus to increase (1) the total number of customers visiting the store during a specific time period; (2) the total complement of various types of customers attracted into the store (e.g., low-, middle-, and upper-income consumers); and/or (3) the magnitude of specific customer groups targeted for special attention (e.g., professional women). Safeway, for example, by offering the added convenience of in-store banking to its present and potential

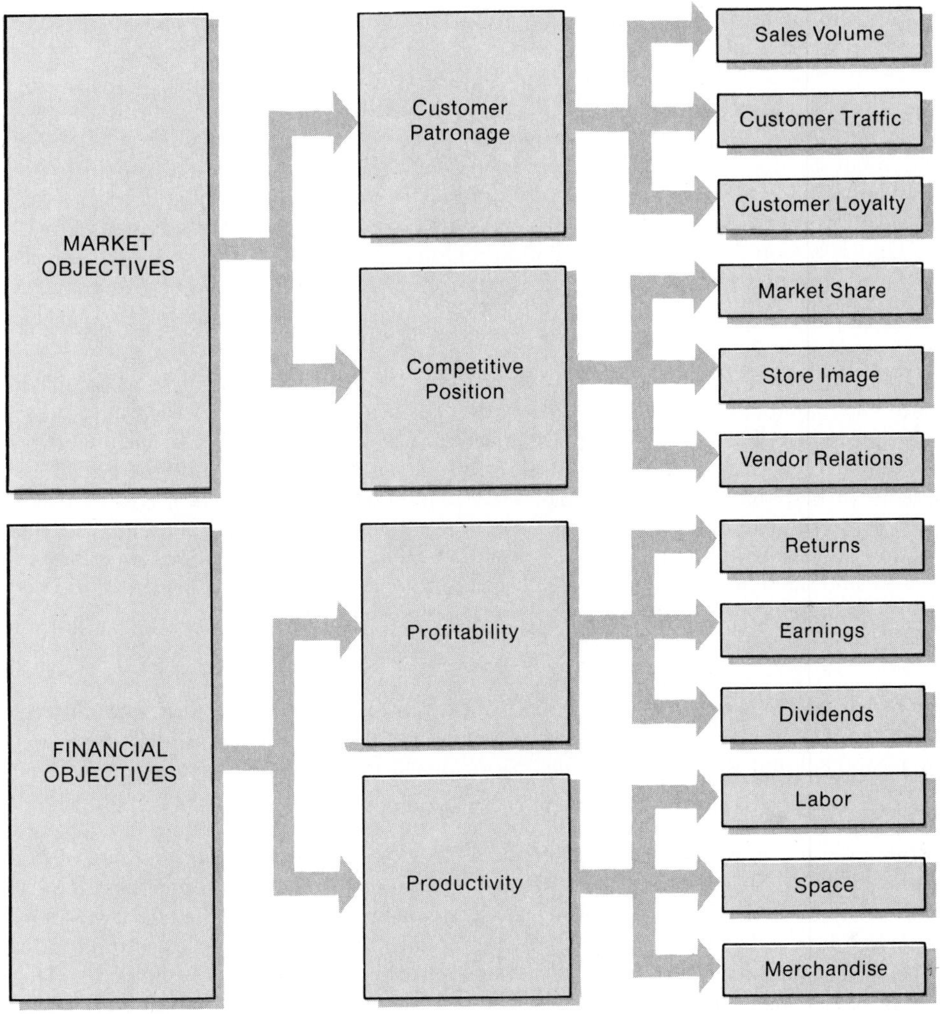

FIGURE 18–6
A typology of organizational objectives

customers, enhances its prospects of increased store traffic and customer patronage (market penetration).[8] Possible strategies to increase the total number of customer visits include additional mass advertising, sales promotions, and special-event merchandising. Offering a range of pricing points and a wider selection of merchandise are two means by which the firm can expand its appeal to a more extensive customer base. Offering unique services, specialty merchandise lines, and personal selling from sales representatives who have appropriate expertise can increase the traffic of targeted customer groups. Walgreen Co. has become the nation's leading drug store chain; a key ingredient in its success is the use of high-margin prescription drugs as traffic builders and excellent service as the cornerstone for return trade.[9]

Customer Loyalty. A customer loyalty objective is aimed at improving return trade. Repeat business is essential to almost any retail operation because for many it represents store loyalty. The average number of store visits or purchases during a defined time period is one means of measuring return trade. Ideally, a worthy objective is to develop a high preference level for the organization and its merchandising programs. Obviously, the key to store loyalty is customer satisfaction. Retailers should understand the realities of customer loyalty—it is something the retailer has to earn and keep on earning.

The type and quality of services provided to the customer are important strategic considerations in developing customer loyalty. A retail organization often develops strategies based on the *completeness* of the service offering: essential services (basic to the retailer's operation) and expected services ("extras" that help distinguish the retailer's service mix). Service quality is generally expressed in terms of the service levels offered by competitors—better transactional efficiency, better service availability, and less trouble in service execution. "Don't get caught in the trap of being an upscaled store with low-end service," is one expert's advice. "Today's customers want and expect good service because their time is limited and more valuable."[10]

Market Share. Market share objectives are the most commonly used form of expressing competitive position. **Market share** is a measure of a retail organization's sales position relative to all competitors within the same market. It is calculated by dividing a retail organization's total sales by total market sales for a defined business type or product line category. In expanding market areas, *market share growth* could well be an appropriate objective (e.g., increase market share by 6 percent over the duration of this planning period). On the other hand, retail organizations operating in mature and stable market areas generally call for the more moderate objective of *market share maintenance* (e.g., protect our current market share against the aggressive actions of all competitors).

Store Image. An *image* is the mental conception of something held in common by members of a group. **Store image** is the mental picture of a retail organization as viewed by customers and the general public. Store image includes both the "functional" or physical properties of the store as well as its "psychological attributes"—a sense of belonging or a feeling of friendliness.[11] Because the term "store" is used here in its most generalized meaning, to the consumer, store image is a symbolic representation of the basic attributes, orientations, and activities of the organization. Originally, Pier 1 Imports appealed to the hippies or beatniks; its image suggested you had to drive a VW or wear a tie-dyed shirt to get into the store. Today, the firm has upscaled the business format to appeal to customers whose tastes have become more sophisticated.[12] The stores are well stocked with merchandise, offer few markdowns, and swamp shoppers with service.[13] Retailers establish image objectives because they realize that consumers tend to categorize people, places, and things in relative terms (e.g., bigger, better, faster, easier, and sooner). By offering wider product selections, higher quality products, better price values, more convenient locations, easier credit terms, and faster service, retailers can competitively position themselves in the minds of consumers. By careful planning it is possible to position the organization in an imagery niche that clearly distinguishes it from its competitors. Limited, Inc. has enhanced its image and retained its leadership role in specialty apparel retailing by creating a more fresh, upscale look through new store fixtures, expanded store size, greater product assortment, and higher service levels.[14]

Vendor Relations. Carving out a viable competitive position includes a supply side that a retail organization's statement of objectives should also recognize. Prudent retail organizations strive to ensure that they are well positioned with respect to both established vendors (e.g., to be considered a preferred account by desired vendors) and new emerging sources (e.g., to engage in a systematic search for suppliers of new and innovative products). Retailers also must cooperate and coordinate their activities with other members of the marketing channel of distribution.

The "functional" properties and "psychological attributes" of these restaurants give each a different store image.

Financial Objectives

Financial objectives try to ensure that the retail organization operates profitably and productively. Financial objectives provide quantifiable standards by which the organization's performance will be judged. Targeted returns, earnings, and dividends are three common profitability goals. The three most critical resources to be managed in a traditional retail enterprise are merchandise, space, and labor.[15]

Returns. The monetary return the retail organization desires can be stated in terms of return on sales or assets. These profit-based objectives reflect what management expects in return for its efforts. A *return on sales* (net profit divided by net sales)

Rank	Company	Per employee ($000) Profits	Sales	(rank)	Assets	(rank)	Employees (000)
RETAILING—APPAREL							
1	**Limited**	5.8	77.7	(2)	40.4	(2)	59.9
2	**Gap**	4.6	74.1	(4)	27.1	(6)	21.4
3	**Nordstrom**	4.3	100.8	(1)	64.4	(1)	26.5
4	**Melville**	4.0	76.7	(3)	30.8	(5)	98.5
5	**TJX Cos**	3.0	74.1	(4)	37.8	(4)	29.0
6	**Petrie Stores**	1.4	55.9	(7)	39.0	(3)	22.5
7	**Brown Group**	1.2	62.8	(6)	24.6	(8)	29.0
8	**US Shoe**	1.1	54.2	(8)	26.0	(7)	46.0
	Industry medians	**3.5**	**74.1**		**34.3**		
RETAILING—DEPARTMENT STORES							
1	**General Cinema**	37.7	79.3	(7)	118.4	(3)	25.1
2	**Mercantile Stores**	5.9	105.1	(4)	70.4	(5)	22.0
3	**Dillard Dept Stores**	5.6	115.9	(2)	94.9	(4)	26.3
4	**Equitable of Iowa**	5.0	143.2	(1)	703.7	(1)	4.1
5	**JC Penney**	4.1	83.0	(5)	65.5	(6)	194.0
6	**May Dept. Stores**	4.0	76.8	(8)	62.4	(7)	125.0
7	**Sears, Roebuck**	3.0	105.5	(3)	170.5	(2)	510.0
8	**Carter Hawley Hale**	0.2	79.5	(6)	60.1	(8)	36.0
	Industry medians	**4.6**	**94.1**		**82.7**		
RETAILING—DRUG & DISCOUNT							
1	**Longs Drug Stores**	4.6	158.7	(1)	42.6	(5)	13.3
2	**Wal-Mart Stores**	4.4	104.9	(5)	33.2	(9)	247.0
3	**Rite Aid**	3.6	108.6	(4)	53.1	(1)	28.9
4	**Walgreen**	3.3	117.3	(2)	38.2	(6)	47.4
5	**Dayton Hudson**	2.9	95.1	(6)	46.6	(2)	143.4
6	**K mart**	0.9	82.8	(8)	36.5	(8)	360.0
7	**Rose's Stores**	0.4	71.8	(9)	23.6	(10)	21.0
8	**Ames Dept Stores**	0.0	88.3	(7)	44.0	(4)	60.0
8	**Hills Dept Stores**	0.0	71.4	(10)	44.6	(3)	27.0
10	**Fred Meyer**	−0.3	108.8	(3)	38.0	(7)	21.0
	Industry medians	**1.9**	**100.0**		**40.4**		

FIGURE 18–7
Comparison of labor productivity by various types of retailers

Rank	Company	Per employee ($000) Profits	Sales	(rank)	Assets	(rank)	Employees (000)
RETAILING—SPECIALTY							
1	**Price Co**	10.4	436.1	(1)	113.5	(2)	11.8
2	**Toys 'R' Us**	9.0	133.6	(9)	85.8	(5)	35.9
3	**Circuit City Stores**	8.2	222.5	(3)	96.8	(4)	8.9
4	**Tandy**	8.1	114.2	(11)	85.2	(6)	37.5
5	**Spiegel**	7.6	175.5	(6)	147.4	(1)	9.7
6	**Home Depot**	6.9	169.8	(7)	68.8	(10)	16.3
7	**Sherwin-Williams**	6.5	127.4	(10)	82.5	(8)	16.7
8	**Lowe's Cos**	5.0	176.4	(5)	76.4	(9)	15.0
9	**Blockbuster**	4.2	38.0	(13)	39.4	(12)	10.6
10	**Costco Wholesale**	3.9	414.6	(2)	99.2	(3)	7.9
11	**Service Merchandise**	3.6	165.5	(8)	83.3	(7)	20.0
12	**Waban**	2.6	182.8	(4)	47.7	(11)	11.3
13	**Woolworth**	2.5	66.8	(12)	29.6	(13)	132.0
	Industry medians	**6.5**	**169.8**		**83.3**		
RETAILING—SUPERMARKETS & CONVENIENCE							
1	**Weis Markets**	6.0	85.5	(14)	45.2	(6)	14.5
2	**Giant Food**	4.3	127.7	(5)	42.5	(8)	25.5
3	**McDonald's**	4.1	34.5	(15)	52.1	(4)	176.0
4	**Albertson's**	3.7	141.4	(3)	35.5	(10)	52.5
4	**Food Lion**	3.7	123.7	(8)	33.6	(12)	38.1
6	**Bruno's**	3.0	125.5	(6)	37.8	(9)	18.1
7	**Hannaford Bros**	2.8	112.6	(11)	34.8	(11)	13.5
8	**Smith's Food & Drug**	1.9	125.1	(7)	52.6	(3)	13.8
9	**Great A&P Tea**	1.6	121.2	(10)	31.2	(13)	92.0
9	**Winn-Dixie Stores**	1.6	106.7	(13)	18.4	(15)	88.9
11	**American Stores**	0.7	131.2	(4)	44.1	(7)	167.7
12	**Kroger**	−0.1	110.8	(12)	25.0	(14)	170.0
13	**Circle K**	−0.3	144.0	(2)	76.1	(1)	25.9
14	**Vons Cos**	−0.7	149.2	(1)	47.3	(5)	35.0
15	**Penn Traffic**	−1.0	122.7	(9)	54.9	(2)	22.0
	Industry medians	**1.9**	**123.7**				

Source: "The Forbes 500's—Jobs and Productivity," pp. 282, 284–285. Reprinted by permission of *Forbes* magazine, April 30, 1990. © Forbes, Inc., 1990.

FIGURE 18.7
(continued)

objective identifies what percentage of the average sales dollars should be profit. For example, an objective of 20 percent could be the targeted net profit return on net sales. To realize a fair return on the organization's asset investment, a *return on assets* (net profit divided by total assets) objective is frequently included in the organization's statement of objectives. The Woolworth Corporation has a minimum overall goal of 13 percent return on investment for each of its specialty store operations.[16]

Earnings. Objectives should also reflect the performance of the organization relative to stockholders' interests. A targeted *earnings per share* of common stock can be established as an objective to show the amount of earnings available to the owners of common stock. A desired objective of $4 per share of common stock could be the targeted earnings/share ratio.

Dividends. A designated proportion of the earnings that will actually be allocated to stockholders can also serve as an objective. **Dividends** are a measure of the return to common stock owners on their investment (this statement does not reflect any increase or decrease in the market value of the common stock). For example, a retailer could set as its objective a $2 dividend yield on each share of common stock.

Labor. The productivity of the organization's labor pool can be measured by dividing net sales by the total number of employees or by dividing net sales by the total number of worker hours of labor; the latter measure would take into account the productivity of both full- and part-time employees. Another view of labor productivity can be obtained by examining and comparing profits and assets on a per-employee basis (see Figure 18–7). Retailing can be a labor-intensive business; hence, the contribution of human resources must be recognized and productivity performance standards established. Many retailers also recognize that turnover adversely affects labor productivity, and therefore strive to reduce this phenomenon by setting employee satisfaction objectives aimed at increasing employee retention. On the other hand, Food Lion, the Atlantic states' supermarket chain, has developed their expansion strategy to target smaller communities where: (1) alternative employment options are limited; (2) unemployment is higher; (3) antipathy to unions is present; and (4) part-time jobs are needed.[17]

Space. One of the retailer's most important resources is the merchandising and operating space available. Most retail organizations attempt in their plans to maximize their selling space and its productivity. Sales/productivity ratios are established for stores as well as for individual department and product line areas. Space productivity is measured by dividing net sales or gross margin by the most appropriate expression of area. Some examples of sales/space or margin/space productivity ratios are (1) net sales per square foot of floor space, (2) net sales per cubic foot of display area, (3) net sales per linear foot of shelf space, and (4) gross margin dollars per square foot. By having a monopoly location at many airport terminals, Duty Free Shops pull in a hefty $2100 in annual sales per square foot compared with the $400 average for most specialty retailers.[18]

Merchandise. *Inventory turnover* is the most widely used criterion for measuring the productivity of merchandise; it can be defined as the number of times (e.g., four times) during a specific time period (e.g., a year) that the average stock on hand is sold. The desired objective is to achieve the highest possible inventory turnover rate for the type of merchandise being sold and the additional resources that must be used to improve turnover rates. Obviously, convenience goods will have higher stock turns than specialty goods; therefore, an annual turnover objective of three turns for specialty goods could be considered as productive as 15 yearly turns for convenience goods. Stock turnover rates for specialty stores averaged about 2.62 turns in 1988; during the same year, department stores averaged 2.87 turns.[19] An objective of increasing the turnover rate by increasing advertising or adding more sales personnel may prove productive if increased expenditures do not exceed the additional profits derived from such a strategy.

Other Objectives

In addition to market and financial objectives, retail organizations often identify many objectives that relate to their social responsibilities. Such social objectives include supporting charitable causes, providing educational opportunities, assuming an equitable tax burden, and participating in professional and social organizations and events.

ORGANIZATIONAL PORTFOLIO

The third stage in developing a strategic plan is to review the organization's portfolio of strategic business units. An **organizational portfolio** is the collection of strategic business units held and managed by a retail organization. The portfolio approach to retail planning is becoming an increasingly important method used by the diversified retail organization. Portfolio analysis is appealing because it suggests, but does not dictate, specific courses of action to achieve a balanced mix of businesses that will provide the maximum long-run benefits from scarce cash and managerial resources.[20] Portfolio analysis is not in and of itself a strategy, however; rather, it is an analytical tool to provide perspective on the organization's current situation (where it is now) and to suggest possible courses of action for the future (where it wants to be). A commonly used portfolio approach is the growth/share matrix developed by the Boston Consulting Group (BCG).

BCG Portfolio Approach

The **BCG portfolio approach** is best illustrated by the use of two matrices: the market growth/market share matrix (see Figure 18–8) and the cash generation/cash usage

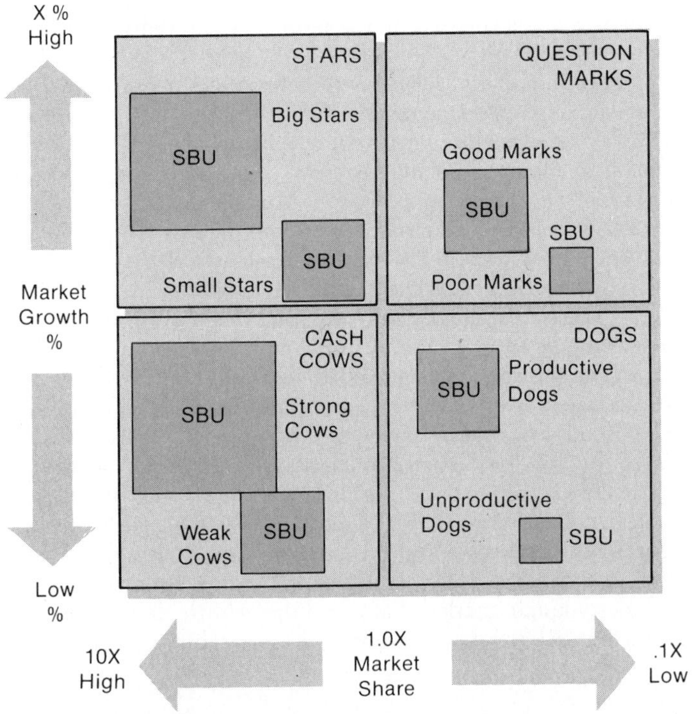

FIGURE 18–8 Market growth/market share matrix

FIGURE 18–9
Cash generation/cash usage matrix

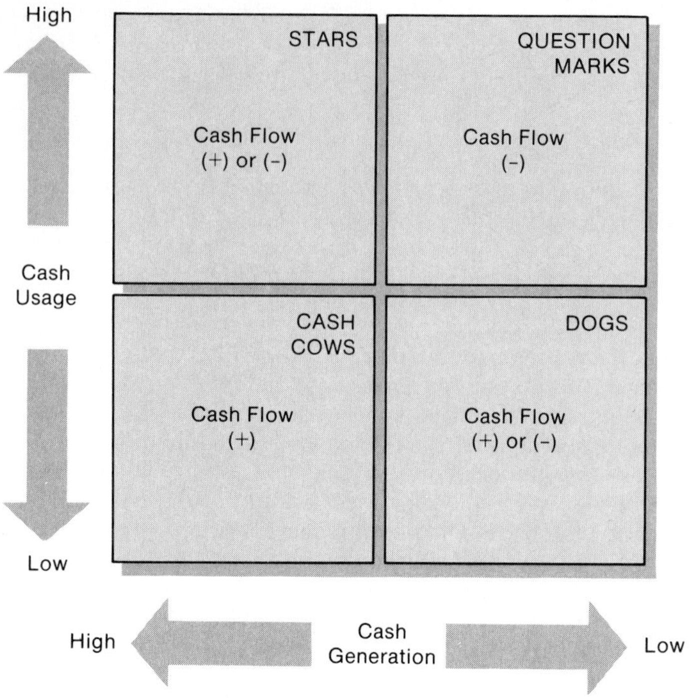

matrix (see Figure 18–9). The former is used to illustrate current market positions of each strategic business unit, whereas the latter identifies each SBU's net cash flow position.

Market Growth/Market Share Matrix. In Figure 18–8, the vertical axis identifies the annual growth rate (percentage) of each SBU's operating market. The logic of including market growth rate in such an analysis is based on the benefits to be derived from the experience curve. As the organization gains more experience, it can reduce costs and realize greater business unit profits. The sales growth rate ranges from a low of 0 percent to a high of whatever percentage is appropriate (e.g., 25 percent). A rate of 8 to 12 percent is generally considered to be quite good in most industries.

The horizontal axis indicates the relative market share of the SBU, a ratio of SBU share of the market to that of the largest competitor. Market share is considered important, based on research indicating that profitability of an SBU is directly related to its market share. The size of each square in the matrix shows each SBU's dollar sales, and the location of each SBU square indicates its competitive market share position for various growth-rate markets. The size and location of each SBU square simply suggest different financial and marketing needs.

To facilitate analysis of the growth/share matrix, it is arbitrarily divided into four quadrants classifying SBUs as one of four different types of businesses: stars, cash cows, question marks, or dogs. **Stars** are SBUs having a high market share within a high-growth market. These businesses are market leaders within their respective industries. As Figure 18–8 shows, stars can be big or small, depending on the sales volume and share of the market. **Cash cows** are SBUs having a high market share within a low-growth market. Like stars, cash cows also have a dominant or leader position; unfortunately, this position occurs in a less desirable market. Some cows are stronger than others, based on the sales volume, market share, and the growth characteristics of their market (see Figure 18–8). SBUs with a low market share in a high-growth market are classified as **question marks**. These are often also called *problem children* because they offer considerable promise if given the attention they need. Depending on the amount of promise it shows, an SBU might be considered a good mark (reasonable chance for increasing market share and sales volume with an acceptable resource investment) or a poor mark (market share and sales volume increases are unlikely within acceptable resources commitments). **Dogs** are SBUs that have a low market share within a low-growth market. Their prospects for the future are dim; nevertheless, dogs can be productive if they find a market niche and produce an acceptable profit level.

Cash Generation/Cash Usage Matrix. The net cash flow situation for stars, cash cows, question marks, and dogs is shown in Figure 18–9. The vertical axis shows cash usage (low to high) and the horizontal axis portrays cash generation (low to high). Stars are both high users and generators of cash, but their net cash flow tends to be negative because they require considerable cash to expand with their growing market and maintain or improve their market share. Cash cows are the key to the organization's cash flow problems. Given the low market growth rate, fewer expenditures are needed to maintain market position; cash cows therefore tend to be net cash generators. The SBU cash cow provides the bulk of the cash to finance stars' and question marks' marketing operations. Question marks typically use more cash than they produce. If the organization decides that a question mark is capable of becoming a star, then it must provide the cash needed to capture additional market share. Dogs can produce either a positive or negative net cash flow. Properly niched within a secure market segment, some dogs can provide some cash that can be used to finance stars and question marks. Other dogs are unproductive because of their vulnerable position in no-growth markets; in such cases, they can become cash traps and a lost cause. George Day, a highly regarded professor and consultant, described an overall strategy for this type of portfolio analysis:

> The long-run health of the corporation depends on having some businesses that *generate* cash (and provide acceptable reported profits), and others that *use* cash to support growth. Among the indicators of overall health are the size and vulnerability of the "Cash Cows" (and the prospects for the "Stars," if any), and the number of "Problem Children" and "Dogs." Particular attention must be paid to those businesses with large cash appetites. Unless the company has abundant cash flow, it cannot afford to sponsor many such businesses at one time. If resources (including debt capacity) are spread too thin, the company simply will wind up with too many marginal businesses and suffer a reduced capacity to finance promising new business entries or acquisitions in the future.[21]

Resource Allocation Matrix. The combined information provided in the market/growth share matrix and the cash generation/usage matrix suggests ways to allocate financial resources. As Figure 18–10 illustrates, for each different category of SBU (stars, cash cows, question marks, and dogs), two or more of five following possible allocation alternatives are suggested:

1. *Building* involves increasing an SBU's market share. The decision to build an SBU typically requires cash infusion. The building alternative is used to expand smaller stars into bigger stars and to transform promising question marks into stars.
2. *Holding* involves maintaining an SBU's market share. The decision to hold is a defensive posture by which the organization will protect and reinforce its current market share. The goal is to make big stars productive in terms of positive net cash flow and to keep strong cash cows producing a large cash flow.
3. *Harvesting* involves milking an SBU of its cash to finance other SBU alternatives that seem to have a brighter future. This cash extraction is often at the expense of the long-run survival of the SBU being harvested. Given the drastic nature of this

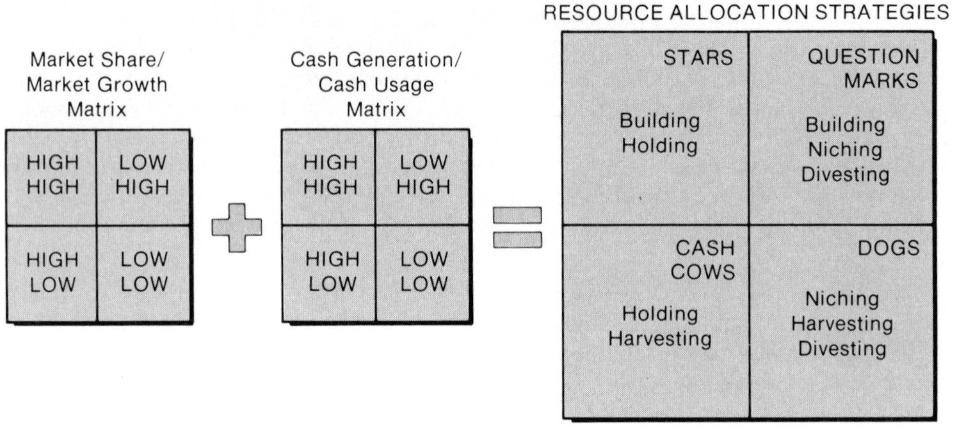

FIGURE 18–10
Strategies for allocating organizational resources

alternative, it should be used only for weaker cash cows and dogs whose futures are extremely dim with little hope of maintenance or survival and where additional resource investment is unjustifiable.

4. *Niching* involves moving an SBU into a market niche (segment) in which the fit between resource requirements and available resources is more acceptable. The goal is to find a market niche where the SBU is reasonably protected from the actions of competitors while allowing it to generate sufficient long-term sales volumes and profits to justify the repositioning costs. Niching is used for some question marks and dogs that demonstrate the potential for a unique and limited market appeal.
5. *Divesting* involves disposing of SBUs that offer little or no hope of improving either their market share or cash flow position. Divestment can be accomplished by selling or liquidating the SBU. Unproductive dogs and poor question marks are both candidates for divestiture. May Department Stores approaches each acquisition with an accountant's eye rather than a merchant's. Rather than trying to revive weak stores, May closes them and concentrates their resources on more promising opportunities.[22]

ORGANIZATIONAL OPPORTUNITIES

Portfolio analysis allows the retail organization to assess its current situation (what its business is) and to identify possible future courses of action (what its business should be) for various strategic business units. After completion of the portfolio analysis, the decision to target some SBUs for extinction (harvesting) or replacement (divesting) while others are targeted for maintenance (holding) and growth (building) often leaves a strategic gap between the current and desired performance of the retail organization; in other words, projected sales will fall short of desired sales (see Figure 18–11). To fill this strategic gap, retail management must take advantage of any opportunities for better growth and/or improved performance. In the department store industry, opportunities for new stores in different cities are limited now. So, expansion-minded chains are forced to seek market share and sales growth by acquiring existing stores in other cities.[23]

Growth Opportunities

Kotler identified three types of growth opportunities: intensive, integrative, and diversification. Figure 18–12 illustrates these opportunities and identifies the appropriate strategies to be used in pursuing a particular type of opportunity.

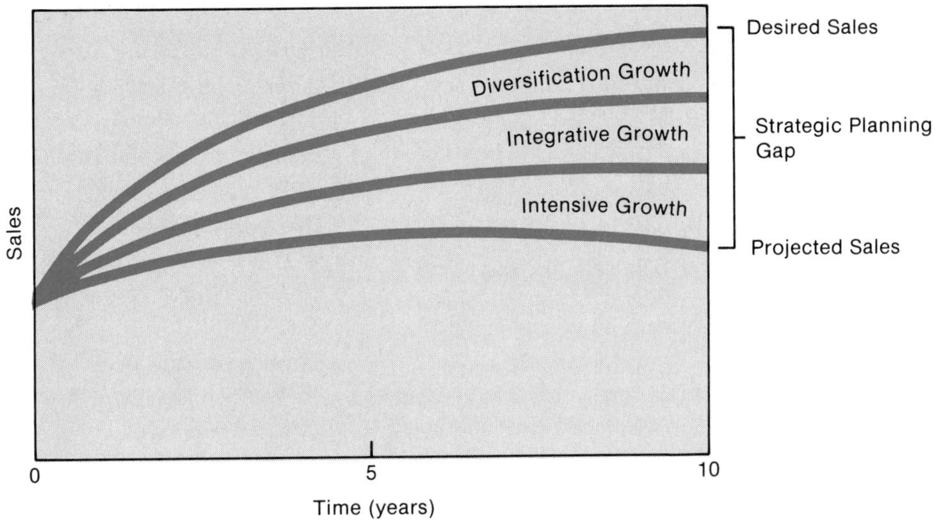

FIGURE 18–11
The strategic planning gap (source: Phillip Kotler, *Marketing Management: Analysis, Planning, and Control,* 5th ed. © 1984, p. 57. Reprinted by permission of Prentice-Hall, Englewood Cliffs, NJ.)

Intensive Growth

Opportunities found within the organization's current portfolio of businesses are referred to as **intensive growth** opportunities. As shown in Figure 18–12, three possible strategies can improve the performance of existing SBUs: **market penetration, market development,**[24] and **product development.**[25] Figure 18–13 outlines the objective for each of these intensive growth strategies and identifies some of the tactics and methods retailers use in implementing these strategies.

Integrative Growth

Opportunities can take the form of backward, forward, or horizontal integration. For integrative growth, the organization's efforts focus on building or acquiring SBUs related to the organization's current portfolio of SBUs.[26] An **integration strategy** aims to increase sales by incorporating one or more levels of the marketing channel of

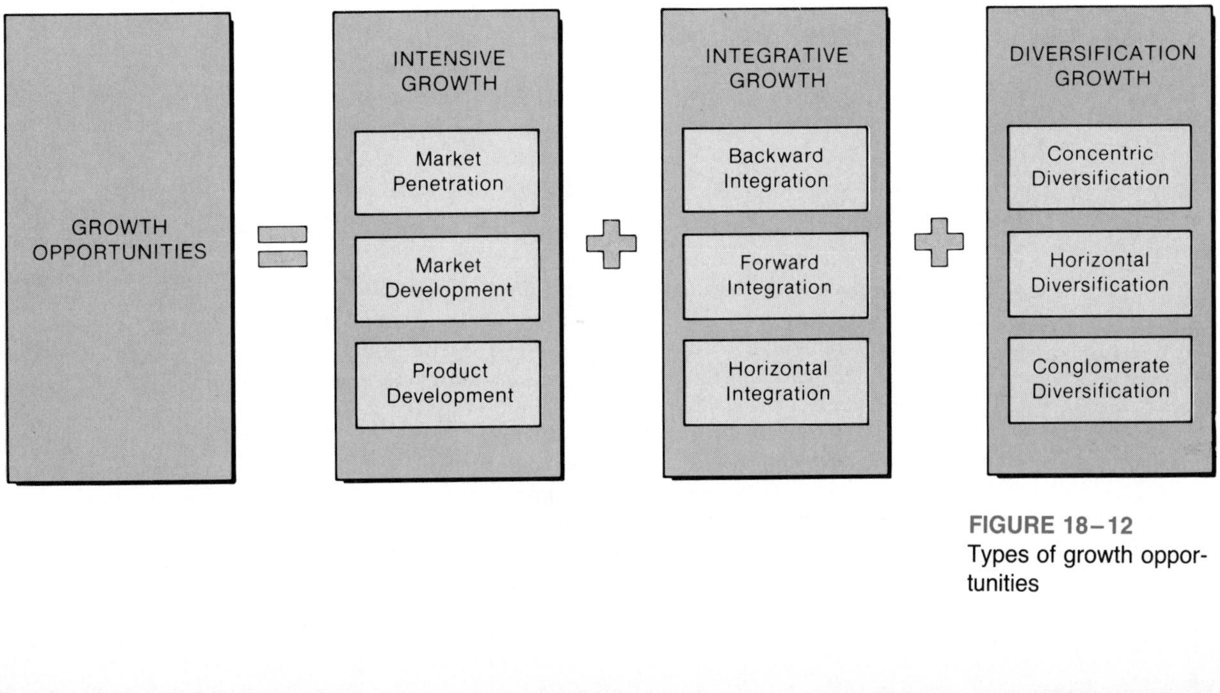

FIGURE 18–12
Types of growth opportunities

Strategy	Objective	Tactics	Methods
Market penetration	To increase the sales productivity of current SBU stores within existing markets	Increase patronage level of current customers by increasing the frequency of store visits and the amount of the average sale per customer visit Stimulate trial visits among nonpatrons who reside in existing trading areas Entice customers who currently patronize competing outlets with existing trading areas	Increase advertising and sales promotion activities Expand product and service mix Use suggestive selling techniques Engage in trade-up selling techniques Develop special event merchandising programs Offer lower prices
Market development	To increase sales by expanding existing store operations into new markets	Open new geographic markets Appeal to new market segments Expand into new market levels	Locate and develop new store sites within new trading areas Develop new product, service, price, and image programs that appeal to different consumer groups Offer products and services to wholesaling and manufacturing organizations
Product development	To increase sales within existing markets by developing new product/service mixes	Increase sales by replacing old product lines with new product lines Increase sales by adding new product lines and items	Adjust product variety and assortment to create a more differentiated product mix Add the more desirable product items that are normally associated with another type of retailer Develop general-purpose product mix by combining two or more broad product lines

FIGURE 18–13
Intensive growth strategies

distribution into the organization's operations. **Backward integration** involves seeking ownership and/or control of supply systems (e.g., a retailer acquiring a wholesaler or manufacturer). **Horizontal integration** is achieved by seeking ownership and/or control of competitors at the same level within the marketing channel. Ames Department Stores bought the Zayre discount chain in the belief it could turn around the ailing chain; instead, this unsuccessful horizontal integration attempt resulted in Ames seeking protection under Chapter 11.[27] Another example of horizontal integration is the purchase of Marshall Field's Department Stores of Chicago by the Dayton Hudson Corp. of Minneapolis.[28] The once-ailing A&P has been transformed into one of the nation's strongest supermarket chains through a total revamping of its operations as well as a carefully executed horizontal integration growth policy. A&P's regional acquisitions include Kohl's Food Stores (Milwaukee), Dominion Stores (Ontario), Shopwell (New York), Waldbaum (New York), and Borman's (Detroit).[29]

RETAIL STRATEGIES AND TACTICS

Specialization or Conglomeration

While maintaining a single focus seems to be a pervasive trait among excellent retailers, the practices of a few excellent retailers are a clear departure from this norm. A good example of "sticking to the knitting" is McDonald's exclusive focus on fast-food retailing. Similarly, Toys 'R' Us' successful inroads into the apparel business through its Kids 'R' Us chain is illustrative of diversification into a related area. Many retailers have been unsuccessful when they attempted to diversify into radically different retailing niches.

Only a few retailers have been quite successful in applying the principles of conglomeration to retailing. Melville is a diverse group of merchandising operations under one corporate umbrella. It is one of the country's top off-price, brand-name apparel retailers (Marshall's), it leases and operates footwear departments in discount stores (Meldisco), runs chains of health and beauty aid stores (CVS), shoe stores (Thom McAn), toy stores (Kay-Bee), and young men's clothing stores (Chess King). Its other off-price and regular price chains include Linens 'n Things, Wilsons Suede & Leather and Open Country. The diversification strategy of Melville is not entirely in the spirit of "sticking to the knitting," yet is highly successful.

Source: P. "Rajan" Varadarajan, "Pathways to Corporate Excellence in Retailing," *Retailing Issues Letter* (Published by Arthur Andersen & Co. in conjunction with the Center for Retailing Studies, Texas A&M University, 1989), 2.

Many manufacturers (Sherwin-Williams) and wholesalers (True Value Hardware) have engaged in **forward integration** by developing or acquiring retail businesses and operating them as part of their strategic marketing efforts. Esprit de Corp. is building a network of franchised and company-owned retail stores; this funky fashion design company is changing its channels of distribution. Jordache Enterprises, the blue jean manufacturer, has entered the retailing field by its acquisition of Heck's Inc., the West Virginia-based discount chain.[30]

Diversification Growth. When the retail organization adds attractive SBUs whose business nature and format are dissimilar to current SBUs, the company is engaged in **diversification growth**. For example, Investcorp International Inc., a low-profile partnership of Arabian investors, represents a diversified conglomerate whose portfolio includes Saks Fifth Avenue (upscale apparel), Color Tile Inc. (floor coverings), Carvel Corp. (ice cream), Sports & Recreation Inc. (sporting goods), and Gucci (upscale apparel and leather goods).[31] Concentric, horizontal, and conglomerate diversification are three different diversifying strategies for increasing sales. **Concentric diversification** tries to attract new customers by adding businesses having technological or marketing similarities with existing businesses. K mart's venture into home centers (Builders Square) and office supply superstores (Office Square) are examples of concentric diversification.[32] The objective of **horizontal diversification** is to increase sales by adding SBUs that appeal to the organization's current customers even though they are not technologically related to its current businesses. The joint venture of IBM and Sears in developing a videotex service is a good example of concentric diversification: computer and information processing by IBM and retailing and merchandising by Sears. Finally, the retail organization can diversify by adding new businesses that are totally unrelated to its current SBUs in hopes of appealing to entirely new markets. Sears is one example of a retailer who has engaged in **conglomerate diversification**. Sears, for example, has diversified extensively into the area of financial services with insurance (Allstate), real estate (Coldwell Banker), and stock brokerage

Liz Claiborne is engaging in forward integration by developing company-owned retail stores.

(Dean Witter Reynolds).[33] Because of the complexities of managing many different types of businesses, conglomerate diversification can be very risky. For example, Kinder-Care, Inc., the nation's largest day-care chain, had diversified into an odd assortment of side businesses including two Florida thrifts, a specialty retail chain, and a deer-hunter's magazine called *Buckmasters*.[34] Management difficulties resulting from this conglomeration of businesses has forced Kinder-Care to restructure its organization and to pursue a less diversified course of action.

Performance Opportunities

A number of opportunities exist for improving the organization's profits and productivity through more efficient usage of organizational resources—financial, human, and facilities. The previous discussion on organizational objectives identified the need to achieve acceptable performance in (1) return on sales and assets, (2) earnings per share, (3) labor and space productivity, and (4) inventory turnover. Improved operational and managerial efficiencies are the key to achieving desired performance standards. Toys 'R' Us, The Limited, Wal-Mart, and May Department Stores are among an elite group of national retailers whose size, market clout, and efficiency have positioned them to succeed. These "power retailers" are fast and focused and have been on the cutting edge of merchandising and operating developments.[35]

The value of strategic planning is that it provides a systematic method for analyzing the economic and competitive prospects for the retail organization and for charting a long-term course of action. The retail organization, however, must guard against having the strategic planning process become less of a creative thinking exercise

Woolworth Corporation: A Concentric Diversification Success Story

For Woolworth Corporation, America's shopping malls are like hundreds of laboratories, for it is within the shopping clusters that the company test markets merchandising ideas to create national specialty store chains with a merchandise focus that ranges from costume jewelry to kids' clothing to sporting equipment.

The retailer once known for dowdy dime stores that sell trinkets and doodads has become the owner of an unusually wide variety of stores. It isn't just the owner of variety stores. . . . What Woolworth seems to excel at is devising its own concepts or spinning strings of small stores by linking existing chains. New free-standing shops are evolved from individual departments in its variety stores.

Today, Woolworth Corporation does business through 43 successful retail chains and operates over 8,000 stores. The powerhouses of the Woolworth's diversification strategy include the following retailing formats:

- Foot Locker—running shoes and sportswear
- Kinney Shoes—family shoes
- Afterthoughts—costume jewelry, handbags, and accessories
- Champs Sports—athletic merchandise
- The Rx Place—deep-discount drugs
- Kid's Mart—children's clothing
- Woolworth Express—down-sized variety stores

In addition to these specialty retail operations, Woolworth is growing other niche specialists in both domestic and international markets. Domestic operations include Lady Foot Locker, Kids Foot Locker, Athletic X-Press, Northern Reflections, Herald Square Party Shop, and Susie's. Woolco-Canada, Mathers-Australia, and Rubin-Germany are part of Woolworth's international retail operations.

Currently, Woolworth Corporation's specialty store strategy represents one of the nation's most successful examples of a concentric diversification growth strategy. As described by Woolworth management,

One of the reasons for this dramatic growth is unusual responsiveness to ever-changing consumer tastes. Giving people exactly what they need and want has made us the world's largest specialty retailer, and assures the continued vitality of our general merchandise stores. And it's exactly how we intend to keep on growing—no matter what our customers are going to call us.

Source: Based in part on Marybeth Nibley, "Woolworth Focusing on the Small Picture," *Akron Beacon Journal,* March 5, 1990, D7; and "Our Customers Call Us All Sorts of Names," a Woolworth Corporation advertisement appearing in *The Wall Street Journal,* Oct. 5, 1989, B-3.

RETAIL STRATEGIES AND TACTICS

and more of a bureaucratic process. Retail management should not confuse strategy with planning and implementation. Without safeguards, the strategic planning process can lose contact with the external world of customers and competitors and the internal world of line managers who must implement designated strategies. The key to a successful strategic plan is the implementation of the retailing plan.

SUMMARY

Strategic retail management is the process of planning the organization's survival and growth. Planning is conducted at corporate, SBU, store, department, and product-line levels of the organization. The retail organization's strategic plan is an overall business plan developed for the entire firm that involves (1) identifying the organizational mission, (2) establishing organizational objectives, (3) conducting an organizational portfolio analysis, and (4) evaluating organizational opportunities.

The mission statement is a generalized yet meaningful expression of the organization's future direction. Its three tasks are to identify (1) the business and customer domains within which the organization operates, (2) the organization's responsibilities toward the people with whom it interacts, and (3) the blueprint for accomplishing the organizational mission. Mission statements are developed according to environmental and resource considerations, distinctive competencies, and managerial preferences.

Organizational objectives identify the specific purposes the firm is to achieve. Most retail organizations identify two general sets of objectives: market and financial. Market objectives aim at securing customer patronage (sales volume, customer traffic, and customer service objectives) and achieving competitive positions within the general marketplace (market share, store image, and vendor relations objectives). Financial objectives establish goals for profitability (returns, earnings, and dividends) and productivity (labor, space, and merchandise).

Organizational portfolio analysis involves reviewing the SBUs that comprise the total business interests of a diversified retail organization. The most commonly used portfolio approach is the market growth/market share matrix developed by the BCG. A portfolio analysis allows the retail organization to assess its current situation (what its business is) and to identify possible future courses of action (what the business should be).

The final step in developing a strategic plan is to identify and evaluate potential opportunities for continued organizational growth and improved organizational performance. Growth opportunities can be identified as intensive (market penetration, market development, and product development), integrative (backward, forward, and horizontal integration), and diversifying (concentric, horizontal, and conglomerate diversification). Performance opportunities include more efficient use of financial, human, and facility resources.

STUDENT STUDY GUIDE

Key Terms and Concepts

backward integration (p. 666)
Boston Consulting Group (BCG) portfolio approach (p. 661)
cash cows (p. 662)
concentric diversification (p. 667)
conglomerate diversification (p. 667)
diversification growth (p. 667)
dogs (p. 663)
financial objectives (p. 657)
forward integration (p. 667)
horizontal diversification (p. 667)
horizontal integration (p. 666)
integration strategy (p. 665)
intensive growth (p. 665)
market development (p. 665)
market objectives (p. 654)
market penetration (p. 665)
market share (p. 656)
mission statement (p. 648)
organizational objectives (p. 654)
organizational portfolio (p. 661)
product development (p. 665)
question marks (p. 663)
stars (p. 662)
store image (p. 656)
strategic business unit (SBU) (p. 648)
strategic plan (p. 648)
strategic retail management (p. 648)

Review Questions

1. What is strategic retail management? Describe its two major components. Define each.
2. At what level does strategic and tactical planning occur? How is each planning level different from the others?
3. Characterize a strategic plan. Describe its purposes.
4. What are the four elements of the strategic planning process? Define each.
5. Describe the three tasks of an organizational mission.
6. Identify the factors to be considered in developing an organizational mission. Briefly describe each factor.

7. There are six types of market objectives. Provide a brief description and example of each.
8. List the six types of financial objectives. Provide a brief description and example of each.
9. Describe the BCG market growth/market share matrix approach to portfolio analysis.
10. What are the five possible alternatives for the allocation of financial resources as identified in the BCG portfolio approach? Discuss each alternative.
11. What three strategies are associated with integrative growth opportunities? Briefly describe each.
12. Compare and contrast concentric diversification, horizontal diversification, and conglomerate diversification.

Review Exam

True or False

_____ 1. Store, department, and product line planning is more tactical than strategic in nature.

_____ 2. The mission statement is expressed in very specific terms in order to clearly identify specific actions to be taken.

_____ 3. A portfolio analysis is an analytical tool to provide perspective on the organization's current situation (where it is now) and suggesting possible courses of action for the future (where it wants to be).

_____ 4. Dogs always produce a negative cash flow.

_____ 5. Building involves expanding small stars into big stars and transforming promising question marks into stars.

_____ 6. Increasing the patronage level of current customers is one tactic used by retailers as part of their market development strategy.

Multiple Choice

_____ 1. A strategic plan is directed at achieving a strategic fit between _____.
a. the organization's present capabilities and its present environment opportunities
b. the organization's future capabilities and its future environment opportunities
c. the organization's present capabilities and its future environment opportunities
d. all of the above relationships
e. none of the above relationships

_____ 2. _____ is an organizational objective aimed at improving return trade and increasing repeat business
a. Sales volume
b. Customer traffic
c. Customer loyalty
d. Market share
e. Earnings

_____ 3. Gross margin dollars per square foot is a _____ objective.
a. market share
b. labor productivity
c. space productivity
d. dividends
e. customer traffic

_____ 4. _____ provide the bulk of the cash to finance the expansion of other SBUs.
a. Question marks
b. Dogs
c. Problem children
d. Good children
e. None of the above

_____ 5. The goal of _____ is to find a market wherein the SBU is reasonably protected from the actions of competitors.
a. building
b. holding
c. harvesting
d. niching
e. divesting

_____ 6. _____ diversification is accomplished by adding new businesses that have technological or marketing synergies with existing businesses.
a. Horizontal
b. Concentric
c. Backward
d. Conglomerate
e. Elliptical

_____ 7. To increase the sales productivity of current SBU stores within existing markets is the objective of _____.
a. product development
b. horizontal integration
c. market development
d. conglomerate diversification
e. product extention

STUDENT APPLICATIONS MANUAL

Investigative Projects: Practices and Applications

1. Strategic distinction in terms of a unique merchandising and/or operating characteristic is essential for success in the 1990s. Choose five of the following retailers from your region and identify the strategies that distinguishes them from their competitors now or in the past. (1) Domino's Pizza, (2) The Limited, (3) Toys 'R'

Us, (4) Wal-Mart, (5) McDonald's, (6) Circuit City, (7) Food Lion, (8) Pier 1, (9) Marshall's, (10) Nordstrom, (11) L.L. Bean, (12) Foot Locker, (13) Bloomingdale's, (14) Dillards Department Stores, (15) Disney Stores.
2. Many experts believe that innovation is an integral part of any good strategic plan. How might retail management encourage employees to be innovative?
3. Develop six specific statements (goals) concerning social responsibility that retailers might include in their mission statement.
4. Develop one specific organizational objective (nontext example) for each of the six types of market objectives and the six types of financial objectives.
5. By conducting a literature review in the library, identify current examples of each of the following growth opportunities: (1) market penetration, (2) market development, (3) product development, (4) backward integration, (5) forward integration, and (6) horizontal integration.

Tactical Cases: Problems and Decisions

■ CASE 18–1
Ray's Super: Responding to Competitive Threats*

BACKGROUND

"We can't make money on groceries," Ray Henry said, reacting to the recent price war that had turned the grocery business upside down. Henry was a manager of a moderate-sized (20,000 square feet) supermarket operation located in a middle- to upper-income suburban area of the community. Until recently, the operation had managed to generate a reasonable return. New competition had begun to squeeze profits, however.

The area's economy was recovering from a recession that had reduced the population by 7 percent as a result of job layoffs. Decreased volume placed greater importance on price competition. "Almost every trick of the trade was employed," Henry said, "including double and triple coupon redemptions." As a result, increases in area food prices were substantially below the national norm.

In the face of high labor costs, grocery chains attempted to negotiate wage concessions to improve profitability. Unsuccessful in this endeavor, National Groceries pulled out of the market, closing eight stores—including three large-scale superstores that had opened during the past two years.

Sav-More, a regional grocery wholesale operation, responded by opening three of the former National superstores and converting five of its existing area stores to a super discount warehouse format. An "Every Day Low Prices" policy on all items replaced weekly specials and double- and triple-coupons promotions. Sav-More advertising claimed price cuts on approximately 8,000 items, with the biggest cuts in packaged foods and paper goods.

Competitors, for the most part, responded in kind by cutting prices across the board. Overnight, the cost of a basket of 30 commonly purchased items had been reduced by an average of $7.89 in a majority of area stores.

CURRENT SITUATION

Concerned about the turn of events, Henry noted that "if this continues, I won't be able to stay in business." He suspected that the average purchase made in his store had declined, largely as a result of reduced volume for packaged goods. Revenues generated by perimeter departments, such as the deli and produce, appeared to be maintaining their previous levels.

Henry was not at a loss for alternatives; his personnel had recommended various solutions. He had to determine which strategy would help maintain customer patronage and build sales.

Mary Walle, assistant manager and part owner, had suggested an immediate price cut across the board to regain volume. Alice Dunlap, produce manager, disagreed because she thought such action would adversely affect profitability. Based on her previous management experience with a national chain, Dunlap argued that the size of the present store was not sufficient to generate the volumes necessary to be profitable at the lower margins suggested. Alternatively, she recommended that the operation build on its strengths in perishables and personal service.

Ray Nader, head butcher, agreed that the operation could differentiate itself from competitors by employing service departments. "The main attraction of warehouse operations is price, not service," he commented. Accordingly, he recommended expanding the service areas to include a specialty fish department, based on customer suggestions. "The margin on specialty items and perishables can make up for the volume lost on low-margin packaged groceries," Nader pointed out.

ASSIGNMENT

1. Evaluate the strategies described in this situation. Under what conditions would one strategy be more appropriate than another?
2. What strategies and tactics would you recommend that Ray Henry follow? Explain.

*This case was prepared by Jeffrey Dilts, The University of Akron.

■ CASE 18–2
James Travel

After starting James Travel in 1974, Leron James was concerned about the direction he should take with his agency. Back then the agency business had been a lot more fun. James had felt much closer to his customers, and he'd known many by name. He also liked the personal interaction, the chance to get to know people and provide them with quality travel services. This preference had always guided his methods of doing business, and he'd tried to make his agency and the travel agents who worked there more conscious of service to customers, of advising them of the many options available, not just acting to write them tickets. A number of other travel agencies in town seemed to be just ticketing agencies, writing up tickets requested by their customers but providing little else in the way of advice or the full range of services that an agent could provide.

INDUSTRY CHANGES

Numerous changes had occurred in the travel industry, significantly influencing the nature of the travel agency business. The airlines were deregulated in 1978, and in the years that followed, major changes occurred regarding air travel. More people were traveling now than ever before, partly because of the periodic airfare wars, frequent flyer programs, and other similar incentives. For many of these people, however, the role of the travel agent was simply that of a ticketer. These people called the agent with a specific flight schedule in mind (and only that) and asked for the lowest fare. The agent had almost no interaction with the individual and could offer little in the way of advice. In addition, the amount of money or commission made by the travel agent on booking a discount airline ticket was very low. In fact, on some of the real supersaver fares, James and other agents claimed they actually lost money. Because many of these travelers shop around for the lowest fare, the chances of James Travel gaining any degree of store loyalty from such customers was quite low.

One other effect of airline deregulation was an increase in the number of ticketing options. Many airlines now compete for the most profitable routes, so competition in these areas is intense. Other airlines have attempted to carve out particular niches for themselves. Overbooking in this situation is a common problem. The travel agent facing this will find not only many alternatives available but also a dramatic number of daily changes in the form of canceled flights, flight changes, flight delays, and the like, all of which have made dealings with the airlines hectic indeed.

Another significant change occurred in 1985, when the effects of the Competitive Marketing Case began to be felt. This case brought an end to the Civil Aeronautics Board (CAB) and resulted in deregulation of the sale of airline tickets. This meant that instead of dealing only with travel agents, airlines could now deal with any retail organization that adhered to that carrier's standards. After nearly 40 years worth of exclusivity, agents were now faced with newer forms of competition, including such possibilities as banks, hotels, retail chain stores, Ticketron and other ticketing outlets, vending machine-type distribution, and others. Not only were these competitors new to the travel agency business, but they also brought with them newer and often unusual methods of competing. As a result, travel agents have been undergoing a period of great confusion and uncertainty regarding the new competitive forces from their suppliers (air and other carriers) and from their markets as well.

As has been true with other deregulated industries, the travel agency business has seen a shift in emphasis in the size of travel agencies. As was seen in the banking and financial industry following its deregulation, the travel agency business has been undergoing a period of merger, acquisition, and reformulation of strategies. The June 1986 special Louis Harris survey issue of *Travel Weekly*, the major weekly newspaper of the travel industry, reported that the market was being increasingly dominated by either small, specialized agencies or large agency networks, (mega-agencies). Small agencies often have prospered because of their local nature or because they have acquired some strong (though small) defensible specialized niche in the market. On the other extreme, large mega-agencies have been acquiring many medium-sized agencies, while other medium-sized agencies have been forming networks or consortia to give them buying power and market clout in the form of standardized marketing and advertising efforts around the country as well as the ability to make appeals to very large corporate and other clients. This posed a problem for many medium-sized agencies such as James Travel that were caught in the middle of all this. The overall share of the travel market for medium-sized agencies (those with annual sales of between $2 million and $5 million) declined from 43 percent in 1983 to 38 percent in 1986.

THE TYPICAL TRAVEL AGENT

The Louis Harris survey of travel agents conducted in 1986 and included in the special June issue of *Travel Weekly* reported the following facts about the typical travel agency:

Annual sales volume was $1.9 million.
Business travel (including combined business-pleasure travel) accounted for 53 percent of all bookings, and purely personal-pleasure travel was 47 percent.
Of total bookings, air represents 62 percent; cruises (the fastest growing category), 14 percent; hotel bookings, 10 percent; car rentals, 7 percent; rail travel, 3 percent; and motorcoach and miscellaneous bookings, 4 percent.

Travel agents such as James Travel act as retailers of tickets for travel and as counselors of the various options available to the traveler. They can provide services ranging from simply issuing tickets to assembling a complete itinerary related to travel (including nearly all aspects of the travel plans). They generate sales revenues on the commissions they receive when ticketing the various components of the travel plans or when charging fees for particular services.

THE SITUATION FACING JAMES TRAVEL

James Travel was located in an urban area of nearly 900,000 people in the northeastern United States. The area had grown lately at about the same pace as the national average, and the demographic and economic makeup of the area were about typical in terms of the demographics, and slightly upscale in terms of the socioeconomic characteristics.

By reading the trade publications available to many travel agents, James and his son Shaun had become more aware of the recent changes facing travel agents around the country. In May of 1988 they attended a series of workshops on strategic planning in the travel industry and returned with great enthusiasm to begin developing plans for their agency. During that summer, they studied the performance of James Travel over the prior ten years. Of special significance were the following findings:

1. Growth in agency bookings increased dramatically during the early years, but lately had slowed to a pace parallel to that of the industry and also parallel to that being experienced in general in their market.
2. Sales in 1987 were $2.3 million, giving James Travel a market share in their target area of 2.1 percent. This puts them slightly above average in terms of share in the area they served. Though James Travel served a wider community than the surrounding community at large, James and his son estimate that the surrounding community contains a total of approximately 70 travel agents.
3. In 1977, James Travel's business/pleasure ratio was approximately 51 to 49 percent. Although this was somewhat below the national level, it was not troublesome, because this had not been a focus. In 1987, this figure had dropped to 47 to 53 percent, in part reflecting the loss of business travelers to the larger mega-agencies and the networks that had made special attempts to gather such business.
4. Ten-year performance figures show some changes in the makeup of James Travel's business. These are shown in Exhibit A.

Because of deregulation and the changes in competition, James felt that it would be difficult to predict activities of the near future with any certainty. He did have some information, however. And always an optimist, he'd generally been pleased with his progress. He'd put a lot of himself into this business. Although the long hours away from home may have cost him his marriage (his wife had divorced him four years previously), he'd seen his agency grow and prosper. He wanted to continue to make things happen.

Last year, one of the local agencies with whom James Travel had been competing had signed an agreement with Travel World, a huge national mega-agency that provides management, marketing, and promotional assistance for its local members. Now under the Travel World name, that agency had been running big local ads featuring Travel World's excellent graphics and strong bargain-oriented copy. Partly in response to this strong marketing effort, the travelers who want discount airfares seemed to be going to this agency in significant numbers. Their airfare bookings were up nearly 15 percent over the prior year's figures. James estimated that he'd lost some business to this agency but not too much. He'd never tried too hard to appeal to the discount traveler and suspected that a lot of the growth in Travel World's sales came from infrequent travelers and from the other agencies in town who specialized more in discounted air fares.

THE DECISION FACING THE JAMESES

James and his son both felt that some strategic decisions should be made regarding the direction James Travel should take. They were too aggressive and too proud of their agency to let it sit still. Competition had increased dramatically, especially in the area of discount air travel. With Travel World's strong resources, high visibility, and obvious focus in the area of discounting, James and his son both did not think that the discount airfare market would change much except to continue moving toward Travel World. With the newer forms of competition likely to make inroads into the travel agency business, there was further incentive to make significant changes and to make

EXHIBIT A
James Travel percentage of sales, 1977 to 1987

Sales Sources	1977 percent	1987 percent
Air Travel	68	53
Cruise	8	18
Hotel	10	11
Car Rentals	5	6
Rail	4	5
Motorcoach and Misc.	5	7
Total	100	100

those changes before the competitive situation became too clouded.

The Jameses thought that James Travel might be able to join forces with some other larger mega-agency such as Travel World or some other consortium of agencies. This would increase James Travel's market clout. But they would then have to give up some autonomy and might have to change their name and identity to satisfy the requirements of the association.

Alternatively they thought that James Travel could focus its marketing on some specific niche or on a differentiating aspect of their agency to establish it with a position of strong defense against the newer forms of competition. And there may be other options that James and his son hadn't yet considered.

ASSIGNMENT

What strategic direction do you think is appropriate for James Travel? Support your decision.

*This case was prepared by George Prough and Jeffrey Dilts, The University of Akron.

ENDNOTES

1. "Strategies for the New Century—High Performance Retailers Plan for the Year 2000," *Chain Store Age Executive,* January 1990, 29.
2. The May Department Stores Co. Annual Report.
3. See Francine Schwadel, "Minding the Store: As Retailing's Chic and Indebted Stumble, Bland May Co. Thrives," *The Wall Street Journal,* January 19, 1990, A1, A5. Also see Brian Bremner, "If May Stores Are Plain Janes, Who Needs Flash?" *Business Week,* January 22, 1990, 32.
4. Jackie Bivins, "Corporate Cultures," *Stores,* February 1989, 11.
5. Steve Weinstein, "Education, Bigotry, and Substance Abuse," *Progressive Grocer,* February 1990, 24.
6. Michael Selz, "Consolidated Stores Discovers Bigger Isn't Always Better," *The Wall Street Journal,* January 18, 1990, B2.
7. Teri Agins, "Kinney Polishing Image for Its Line of Women's Shoes," *The Wall Street Journal,* March 30, 1988.
8. P. "Rajan" Varadarajan and Daniel Rajaratnam, "Symbiotic Marketing Revisited," *Journal of Marketing* 50 (January 1986), 11.
9. Rick Reiff, "Convenience with a Difference,"*Forbes,* June 11, 1990.
10. Sallie Hook, "Retailers Turn to Narrowcasting to Survive," *Marketing News,* February 15, 1988, 9.
11. David Mazursky and Jacob Jacoby, "Exploring the Development of Store Images," *Journal of Retailing* 62 (Summer 1986), 146–47.
12. Shannon Thurmond, "Pier 1 Sets Its Course,"*Advertising Age,* February 22, 1988, 30.
13. Susan Caminiti, "What Ails Retailing," *Fortune,* January 30, 1989, 64.
14. See Carol Hymowitz, "Upscale Look for Limited Puts Retailer Back on Track," *The Wall Street Journal,* February 24, 1989, B1, B4.
15. Robert F. Lusch, "The New Algebra of High Performance Retail Management," *Retail Control* (September 1986), 15–16.
16. Marybeth Nibley, "Woolworth Focusing on the Small Picture," *Akron Beacon Journal,* March 5, 1990, D7.
17. Thomas B. Mechling, "Food Lion: Cut-rate Prices, Cut-throat Practices," *Business and Society Review,* Winter 1990, 40.
18. Lisa Driscoll, "It's Taking Off with Jet-Lagged Shoppers," *Business Week,* May 21, 1990, 108.
19. David P. Schulz, "NRMA's New 1988 FOR," *Stores,* December 1989, 31.
20. George S. Day, "Diagnosing the Product Portfolio," *Journal of Marketing* 41 (April 1977), 29.
21. Ibid., 31.
22. Charles Siler, "Milking the Cow, Hard," *Forbes,* February 6, 1989, 49–50.
23. Michael Totty, "Expansion-Minded Dillards Is Catching Some Attention," *The Wall Street Journal,* March 16, 1988.
24. See Lisa Gubernick, "So Where Are the Overcoats," *Forbes,* June 11, 1990, 178–79.
25. See Lawrence H. Wortzel, "Retailing Strategies for Today's Mature Marketplace," *Journal of Business,* Spring 1987, 45–56.
26. See Christopher Power, "Macy's Buyout Loses A Lot of Its Luster," *Business Week,* March 19, 1990, 40. Also see Donald Stone, "Mergers and Acquisitions in Retailing—Good and Bad News," and Alan Gilman, "Who Was Minding the Store?" *Retailing Issues Letter* (Published by Arthur Andersen & Co. in conjunction with the Center for Retailing Studies, Texas A&M University, 1990), 1–5. And Todd Mason, Amy Dunkin, Michele Galen, Leah J. Nathans, and Stephen Phillips, "It'll Be a Hard Sell," *Business Week,* January 29, 1990, 30–31.
27. Joseph Pereira, "Ames Seeks Protection under Chapter 11 After Retailers' Talks with Lenders Stall," *The Wall Street Journal,* April 27, 1990, A3, A7. Also see Christopher Tucker, "How Ames Is Digestings Its 'Whale,'" *Business Week,* September 11, 1989, 62. And Subrata N. Chakravarty, "James Harmon's Two Hats," *Forbes,* May 28, 1990, 43–44.
28. Francine Schwadel, "Dayton Hudson Agrees to Buy Marshall Field's," *The Wall Street Journal,* April 20, 1990, A2, A5. Also see Russell Mitchell, "From Punching Bag to Retailing Black Belt," *Business Week,* November 20, 1989, 62, 66.
29. Andrea Rothman, "A&P Is Thriving So Why Is James

Wood Still Round," *Business Week,* April 10, 1989, 90–91.

30. Peter Pae, "Heck's Inc. to Sell 55 Retail Stores to Clothing Maker," *The Wall Street Journal,* January 2, 1990, B–4. Also see Kerry Pechter "Jordache's Purchase of Heck's Puzzles Many in Retail Field," *The Wall Street Journal,* January 4, 1990, B3.
31. Jeffrey A. Trachtenberg, "Arab Group to Buy Saks for $1.5 Billion in Gamble on the U.S. Retailing Industry," *The Wall Street Journal,* April 26, 1990, B1, B5.
32. See Howard Schlossberg, "Office Supply Superstores Reshape the Industry," *Marketing News,* January 22, 1990, 2.
33. See Steve Weiner, "It's Not Over until It's Over," *Forbes,* May 28, 1990, 58, 60, 64.
34. Dean Foust, "Has This Problem Child Learned Its Lesson?" *Business Week,* June 22, 1989, 28.
35. Amy Dunkin and Michael Oneal, "Power Retailers," *Business Week,* December 21, 1987, 86.

PART VI

RETAILING DYNAMICS

Future Trends and Directions

CHAPTER 19

OUTLINE

THE DYNAMICS OF RETAILING IN THE NINETIES

THE CHANGING RETAIL MARKETPLACE

- Time: The Currency of the Nineties
- Earth: We Have Seen The Enemy—And It Is Us
- Neotraditionalism: Coming Back Home to the Good Life
- Boomers: Twentysomething, Thirtysomething, Fortysomething
- Wellness: In The Land of Non
- Income: The Bifurcation of the Marketplace
- Consumers: Growth Targets Within a Mature Market

THE ADAPTING RETAIL ORGANIZATION

- Vendor Relationships: Fostering Partnerships and Creating Alliances
- Micro Merchandising: Individualism and Mass Customization
- Store Image: An Identity Crisis in a Cookie Cutter World
- Store Size: How Big Is Too Big?
- Market Positioning: The Polarization of Retailing

OBJECTIVES

- Recognize the dynamic character of the retail environment and the consumer marketplace.
- Understand the retailer's need to adjust to a changing environment.
- Identify some of the key shifts in the consumption and behavioral patterns of retail consumers now and in the future.
- Describe some of the adaptive strategies and tactics utilized by retail organizations in their bid for future survival and growth.
- Appreciate the challenges and opportunities to be found in the nineties.

A RETURN TO CUSTOMER SATISFACTION

We are entering a decade of a strong individualist consumer society that Alvin Toffler, of Future Shock *fame, identifies as a "segmented consumer." First and foremost, retailers must recognize the strong implications of a "buyer's market." Customers are being offered a wide choice of shopping experiences, but no one operation can capture them all. Therefore, it is incumbent upon management to define their target market and direct their energies toward solving that market's problems.*[1]

Trying to describe the retail environment in the last decade of the 21st century . . . is a difficult task. Everything has changed, and changed in ways that will reshape an industry created and built during the height of American materialism. Technology, demographics, consumer attitudes, and the advent of global economy are all conspiring to rewrite the rules for success. . . . Success in the next decade will depend upon the level of understanding retailers have about the new values, expectations, and needs of the customer.[2]

THE DYNAMICS OF RETAILING IN THE NINETIES

The 1980s was an era of upheaval and turmoil as well as growth and progress in the nation's retail industry. The economy advanced, then declined, and advanced again; the decade ended with a slower economic pace. In this roller coaster economy, retailers had to cope as best they could. Technological advancements forced new business practices like never before. The pace of life increased and consumers demanded that retailers keep up. But the struggle isn't over. It's just beginning.[3] A financial calm will appear after a decade of stormy mergers and acquisitions; however, the winds of change will continue to blow in the technological, operational, and organizational structures of retail businesses. Application of existing technology and the further development of new technological assets will continue to revolutionalize retail operations and practices. People power in the form of customers, employees, shareholders, and stakeholders will play an expanded role in the retail organization. The winners in the 1990s will be retailers who listen to the consumer, as well as all other constituents who have a stake in the business. If not mean, then lean, will be the watchword for the retailer's organizational structure.

The chapter title, "Retailing Dynamics—Future Trends and Directions," adequately identifies the focus of the discussion in this chapter (see Figure 19–1). Seven dynamic changes in the retail marketplace are examined in light of their affect on retail merchandising practices and operational policies. Next, five major retail organizational adaptations are discussed in relationship to finding a successful retailing format for the 1990s. While the following discussion is not an exhaustive review of retailing trends and directions, it does provide a representative feel for the dynamism of the retailing world.

THE CHANGING RETAIL MARKETPLACE

The importance of personal time and mother earth, the return to traditional and healthy lifestyles, and the changing demographic makeup of the nation's population are central marketplace themes that will have an affect on all retailers during the 1990s. Each of the trends are examined.

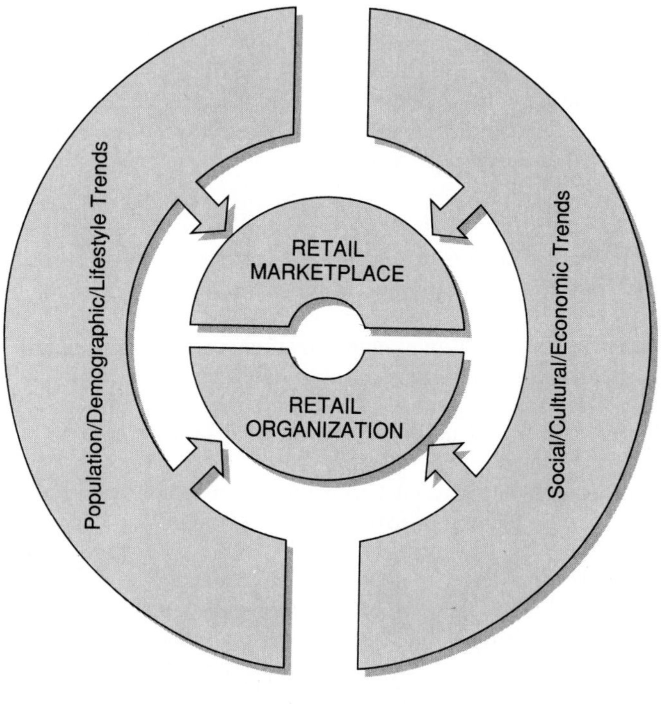

FIGURE 19–1
The dynamics of retailing

Time: The Currency of the Nineties

Time squeeze, time compression, time poverty, and time control are but a few of the expressions used by various writers to communicate the consumer's growing concern over the lack of personal free time. For most of the past century, America was driven by a common set of attitudes and beliefs that caused us to trade time for money and both for material possessions. Increasingly, people of all ages are moving away from this toward a perspective that defines one's progress and success through one's experiences.[4] Personal time is becoming a precious asset; consumers are increasingly willing to do or pay anything to conserve "their time." One writer describes time as "the currency of the nineties";[5] people will be as concerned with time exchanges as they are with monetary transactions.

The scarcity of free time is the outcome of a number of factors that have worked together to consume a substantial proportion of the consumer's free time. The more common factors include: (1) the increasing number of two-career, dual-income families whose work schedules often conflict with one another; (2) lifestyles and consumption levels that create the financial demand for working overtime or getting a second job; (3) upwardly mobile career expectations that demand greater time commitments and investments; (4) long commute times between suburban homes and inner-city jobs; and (5) time requirements needed to maintain homes and personal possessions, to care for spouse and children, to meet social and professional obligations, and to manage personal and financial affairs. For the future, all of these time pressures are expected to continue throughout the nineties.[6]

Time is increasingly becoming a premium commodity. American consumers are constantly seeking to gain greater control over their time usage by allocating it more efficiently and by creating more discretionary, leisure hours. The desire for time control is more than just a quest for convenience . . . it reflects a new determination among consumers to tailor daily schedules to *their* needs rather than having schedules imposed on them.[7] As consumers seek to overcome time pressures, convenience will take on a whole new meaning as technology continues to reshape expectations about how much time needs to be allotted to various activities. Whether it is in the preparation of meals, the commute to work, the processing of information, or the purchase of goods, people will place strong emphasis on accomplishing these things with as little wasted time as possible.[8] Success in the 1990s will require the retailer to assist, not hinder, the consumer's quest for time expenditure control. Time savers and convenience enhancers will need to be developed to ensure maximum merchandising and operating efficiency.

Actions currently being used or developed by retailers to assist consumers include offering:

- Better organized stores that feature layouts, displays, signs, directories, information booths, and people who assist the consumer in locating and comparing desired merchandise.
- Faster transaction time by providing additional centralized checkout lanes, departmental express checkout stations, and do-it-yourself automated checkout terminals, each being supported by state-of-the-art, point-of-sale systems that feature itemized receipts, price lookup, check and credit card verification, and other transactional efficiencies.
- Greater time convenience, as delivered by such offerings as multiple or branch locations, home delivery and service calls, and drive-up, drive-through, and carry-out services.
- Easier shopping formats via home shopping networks, video catalogs, mail-order retailing, telephone orders, and interactive computer shopping systems; no in-store effort can provide consumers as time efficient shopping as does from-home shopping.[9]

- Greater selection of products and services that reduces both the risk and time it takes a customer to select (large assortment of name-brand merchandise), buy (product warranties and maintenance contracts), use (microwaveable or preassembled).
- Fairer pricing programs that reduce the need for the customer to engage in time-consuming price comparison activities; everyday-low-prices is a pricing program that is suited to the stressed consumer who does not have time to price shop.
- Instant rebates, electronic coupons, and simpler promotional programs that are informative and allow for easier participation are more conducive to the time-strapped consumer than either mail-in rebates or the clipping and redeeming of coupons.

Earth: We Have Seen The Enemy—And It Is Us

The hottest issue of the 1990s could well be a born-again environmental movement that should gather righteous steam as the nation moves toward the next millenium.[10] As environmental issues gather momentum, the power of local and national environment groups (e.g., Sierra Club and the National Wildlife Federation) could well become an important external force having a direct impact on both the retailer's merchandising and operating practices. Awareness of and interest in how consumer products and shopping habits affect the environment are no longer the causes of a few zealots, they are concerns of mainstream American consumers.

At the local level, consumers are increasingly recognizing that they are the cause of environmental problems—discarded packaging and disposable products are clogging landfills; aerosol cans and personal care products are polluting the air; auto exhaust and incinerator plants are creating summer smog alerts; detergents and pesticides are spoiling groundwater; and trash and garbage are littering streams, lakes, and lands.[11] What is so significant about this revitalized environmentalism is that it is a local, grassroots movement in which the participants don't see themselves as protecting the environment—they're protecting their homes and communities. As Americans cope with issues close to home, they will increasingly confront questions about their own lifestyles.[12] According to a Gallup survey, nine out of ten consumers state they are willing to make a special effort to buy environment-friendly products, to sacrifice some conveniences (e.g., disposability) to protect the environment, and to pay more for products that are in harmony with nature.[13] Americans are beginning to recognize and accept the real cost of a cleaner and safer environment.

As a member of the local community, retailers will be expected to become actively involved with the green revolution; their involvement must be taken seriously as a social responsibility and not as a marketing fad to be exploited. McDonald's, which produces hundreds of millions of pounds of paper and plastic waste annually, has become a crusading proponent of recycling, and aims to become one of America's leading educators about environmental issues.[14] For Wal-Mart's senior management, environmentalism is a cause and not a marketing scheme.[15] It has requested that its suppliers provide more recycled products or products that are capable of being recycled. Environment-friendly products are highlighted with signs (printed on recycled paper) on shelves explaining why they're better for the environment than some other choices. L.L. Bean compiled a list of conservation organizations needing outdoor volunteers and sends the information to customers who request it via a toll-free number.[16] Major department stores are supporting an anti-ivory campaign. Other retailers have joined the fur boycott.

Several western supermarket chains, including Ralph's Grocery Co. in California, have a Green Cross labeling program: Strict standards developed by a private consultant will promote recycling and reduce confusion over misleading claims. Products and packaging will have to contain at least 50 percent recycled consumer waste to receive a recycling seal. To win a Green Cross environmental seal, products must fulfill recycling requirements and the manufacturing process must not emit any known

RETAIL STRATEGIES AND TACTICS

Body Shop—An Environment-Friendly Retailer

The London-based Body Shop, with 14 outlets in the U.S., puts environmental concerns at its core and in the process finds its way to the green in customers' pockets. The skin- and hair-care stores display literature on ozone depletion next to sunscreens and fill their windows with information on issues like global warming. Every employee is assigned to spend half a day each week on activist work. Customers get discounts if they bring their old bottles back to the store for recycling. In 1988 the chain collected over a million signatures in Britain on a petition asking Brazil's president to save the rain forests. In 13 years the Body Shop has opened 420 stores in 38 countries. Sales for the year ended February 1989 were over $90 million with pretax profits of about 20%.

Source: "Leading the Crusade into Consumer Marketing," *Fortune,* February 1990, 50.

carcinogens or chemicals causing birth defects, or violate pollution laws.[17] Other supermarkets are offering consumers the choice of biodegradable plastic bags or recycled paper bags in which to carry groceries home. In New York, some supermarkets offer a plastic grocery bag—Earth Sack—that will begin degrading within 3 days of being exposed to ultraviolet light.[18] There is a potential public relations problem with making such biodegradable claims; these claims can be viewed as misleading because of the very limited amount of ultraviolet light that degradable plastics get in a landfill. Environmentalism is also having its effect on service retailers. Back to nature in the form of nature walks, rock-climbing expeditions, white-water rafting trips, cross-country bike tours, and other low-environmental–impact travel and recreation activities (i.e., ecotourism) are giving rise to whole new industries.

Neotraditionalism: Coming Back Home to the Good Life

The late eighties saw a shift toward a neotraditional lifestyle that placed greater emphasis on family, home, religious beliefs, and traditional values and attitudes.[19] Coming back home completes a national lifecycle that started in the sixties when people left home in search of a more nontraditional, nonconforming value system. While these rediscovered traditional values will reflect past beliefs, the home-oriented lifestyle of the 1990s will exhibit significant differences from the past—a reinvention of the 1950s in a 1990s framework.[20]

The reemergence of the home as the focal point of people's lives is the direct result of their need to gain and maintain control over the personal, family, social, and work relationships. The home is a personal habitat wherein the individual can feel in control, therefore safe and secure. The ideal home of the 1990s will be both communal and private; it will provide the principal setting for family and social activities, as well as meet the individual's need for a personal life and perhaps a home work station. The nineties home will offer the visible warmth and comfort of traditional architecture and decor while providing its inhabitants the invisible support of technology.[21] The "home fortress" will make staying at home more fun, convenient, comfortable, and secure. Figure 19–2 describes some of the shifting values in the creation of a personalized environment for simple pleasures.

Smart televisions, smart appliances, and even smart houses will become technological, and to a lesser extent, economical realities. With a "smart house," a call from your car phone on the way home from work could activate the following scenario: The refrigerator defrosts a pie and tells the oven to start the roast; the range signals the microwave oven to heat the souffle; and 102-degree water fills the bath tub. As you drive

Up	Down
Traditional	Trendy
Quality	Quantity
Casual	Formal
Comforting Country	Hard Edged Modern
Personal Choice	Style Dictates
Clean	Clutter
Working Women	Housewives
Household Automation	Household Help
Substance	Pretense
Personal Media	Mass Media
Idealism	Materialism

Source: Valerie Free, "The Homing of America," *Marketing Insights,* April 1990, 16.

FIGURE 19–2
Shifting values affecting home creation

under the automatic garage door, the lights switch on, the heat fires up, the security system turns off, and music plays from a compact disc.[22] While the total automated smart house will be out of the reach of most Americans, some version of the smart television will find its way into most homes by the end of the decade. "Smart televisions," or communication control centers, will be able to read the TV listings and record programs for later viewing after it has edited out the commercials. At the same time, it will scan databases for information of interest, answer the telephone, select and play music, and run other appliances that have been integrated into the system.[23]

Home office automation will make "homework" a viable option for secretaries, typists, data processors, programmers, analysts, and a variety of professionals (e.g., researchers). Personal computers, fax machines, and other telecommunication technologies (e.g., electronic imaging) will permit easy interaction between the home and the workplace (i.e., local, national, or international). The 1990s will see the rebirth of the "cottage industry" tradition—high-tech style.

For the retailer in the nineties, home will become mother-ship for a vast majority of consumers. Home-focused retailing formats will prosper; consistently experts cite home goods and services retailing as the growth industry of the future. Home entertainment, home shopping, home furnishings, home decorating, home maintenance and repair, home office supplies, home delivery, and lawncare services are but a few of the "in-home" goods and services that should prosper if properly merchandised. The nineties consumer is springing for oversized bathrooms with whirlpool tubs and other gadgets that exercise, relax, and medicate the body, lavish entertainment centers or rooms packed with CD players, tape decks, VCRs, stereo TVs and electronic diaries, and kitchens that bristle with automatic breadmakers, pasta machines, food processors, and contraptions that dispense cappucino.[24] Perhaps the best way to describe retailers who are targeting this emerging homebody is to refer to them as being in the environmental operation and enhancement industry.

Boomers: Twentysomething, Thirtysomething, Fortysomething

As the millenium nears, no demographic trend holds more importance to the retailer than the middle-aging of 75 million baby boomers who were born between 1946 and 1964.[25] Figure 19–3 identifies the aging pattern of the baby boom generation from 1985 to 2000. Boomers between the ages of 35 and 44 will increase by 36.7 percent; 45- to 54-year-old boomers will increase by 65.2 percent during the 15-year period between 1985 and 2000. As baby boomers enter their peak earning years, this age wave will have a profound impact on all aspects of retailing. The clear and unmistakable implication is

FIGURE 19–3
The aging of the baby boom generation

Population by Age: 1985–2000 (in thousands)

	1985	1990	1995	2000	% Change
+ All ages	238,631	249,657	259,559	267,955	12.3%
Under 15	51,861	54,582	56,724	55,903	7.8
15–24	39,717	35,548	34,110	36,088	−9.1
25–34	**41,788**	**43,529**	40,520	36,415	−12.9
35–44	**32,004**	**37,847**	**41,997**	**43,743**	**36.7**
45–54	22,464	25,402	**31,397**	**37,119**	**65.2**
55–64	22,188	21,051	20,923	23,767	7.1
65+	28,609	31,697	33,888	34,921	22.1

Source: U.S. Census Bureau.

that retailers will have to respond to this powerful mass of mature consumers throughout the nineties and beyond.

Like all generations, baby boomers present a collection of many different marketing segments; it would be a serious mistake for retailers to think of them as one targetable consumer group that can be reached by one or a few mass merchandising programs. As seen in Figure 19–3, there is within-group variance between mature-, middle-, and young-boomers in their lifestyles and buying behavior. Also evident in Figure 19–4 is the variance in lifestyles and buying behavior between boomer consumers and preboomer babies and postboomer busters. Nevertheless, the one theme that is or will be central to the baby boom generation is middle age; all boomers will either enter, occupy, and/or exit the middle-age years during the 1990s. For that reason, this discussion will focus on the concerns and behaviors that characterize the middle years.

In one extensive study of middle age consumers from the baby boom generation, the following eight psychological and social characteristics were identified as being a significant force in driving the marketplace in the next decade.[26]

- Middle-aged consumers will defy the age markets traditionally associated with maturity. Extended longevity has greatly altered the what, when, where, or how boomer consumers get married, raise children, buy a home, decide to retire, go to college, rest from work, and try to relax. Mid-life consumers should well experience several varying mini–life cycles instead of one generally defined pattern of living.
- Middle-aged consumers will seek ways to balance work, family, and recreation. Dominant themes in the nineties will be raising families, quality-of-life, and productive work; each will play an important part in the boomer's concept of the good life. They will be looking at product technologies and personal services to assist them in obtaining and maintaining a balanced lifestyle.
- Middle-aged consumers will become increasingly concerned with health and wellness. Age and predisposition will converge to heighten interest in health (e.g., avoiding high blood pressure or caring for an injury) and wellness (e.g., nutrition and exercise). Due to the skeptic nature and high educational level of boomers, they will assume an assertive role in maintaining their health. As charter members of the youth society, boomers will redefine what middle-age means—it will be more vigorous, more active, more casual, more attractive—in short, more youthful.
- Middle-aged men and women will become increasingly similar in the marketplace. Retailers will have to adapt to the converged attitudes, expectations, and buying habits of a more androgenous male/female. Women will be just as an important a factor in the workplace as men, and men will assume equally important roles in the home and life of the family.

Babies	Boomers	Busters & Boomlets
■ **World War I Babies** (born 1910–1919)—representing 5.3% of the U.S. population in 1990, 2.6% in 2000. Due to the impact of the Stock Market Crash and Great Depression, they remain overly cautious about spending money on all but basic necessities. ■ **Roaring '20s Babies** (1920–1929)—representing 8.2% of population in 1990, 5.7% in 2000. Experiences take priority over possessions, with spending on travel, entertainment, friends, and family remaining high and spending on personal apparel declining. ■ **Depression Babies** (1930–1939)—representing 8.8% of population in 1990, 7.3% in 2000. Spending today is on children's college, upgraded home furnishings, big domestic cars, and travel and entertainment as well as other luxuries; but during the next decade, focus will shift dramatically from status spending on husband's career to status spending on retirement. ■ **World War II Babies** (1940–1945)—representing 6.5% of population in 1990, 5.9% in 2000. Polarized between traditional, achievement—oriented households that have remained intact, and those whose dreams slipped away (often divorced females), spending now is on kids, upgraded home furnishings, travel and entertainment and autos.	■ **Mature Boomers** (1946–1950)—representing 7.1% of population in 1990, 6.5% in 2000. Ambivalent toward materialism, they feel guilty about spending, but like nice things, indulging their own children as they were once indulged. During the coming years, their spending will shift toward maintaining their fantasies. ■ **Mid-Boomers** (1951–1957)—representing 11.6% of population in 1990, 10.7% in 2000. Less ambivalent about material goods, the women in this cohort know they deserve nice things, especially when they work hard for their money, and spend more than any other cohort's females on apparel. In contrast, many men in this group could care less about making a fashion statement and prefer practial, functional apparel. During the next decade, spending will shift from individual to family needs; and consumers will become more price-conscious while still demanding quality. ■ **Young Boomers** (1958–1964)—representing 12.4% of population in 1990, 11.6% in 2000. Dramatically different from their older siblings, they are today focused on making money and spending it on themselves, buying "apartment furniture," home entertainment products and selected luxuries. During the next decade, their spending will accelerate along with their incomes, as they buy career wear and buy and furnish homes.	■ **Mature Busters** (1965–1970)—representing 9.1% of population in 1990, 8.8% in 2000. Largely peer-driven and highly media-impacted, their spending will increase dramatically with their first "real" job earnings. In the coming years, they will spend on furnishing apartments, on children, on sporting goods, and on work-related items like wardrobes, transportation, and PCs. ■ **Young Busters** (1971–1976)—representing 8.3% of population in 1990, 7.9% in 2000. Still in their key developmental years, they spend not only what they earn, typically from part-time work, but also influence family spending. In the next decade, they will spend on first cars, apartment furnishings, entry-level work clothes, and electronic gadgets. ■ **Mature Boomlets** (1977–1982)—representing 8.5% of population in 1990, 8.2% in 2000. Highly indulged by their Boomer parents, and typically children of dual working parents, this cohort has more money, more responsibilities, and more influence on household spending than previous cohorts had at comparable ages. By 2000, many will still influence family spending, and will spend on tuition and books, consumer electronics, food and personal items. Apparel expenditures will still be geared toward leisure wear.

Source: "Cohorts Study: Age Matters," *Stores* (November 1989): 36. Copyright © National Retail Federation, Inc., New York, New York.

FIGURE 19–4
DuPont's consumer cohorts

- Middle-aged consumers will be experienced shoppers with considerable buying experience and product information. Boomers will seek, demand, and expect product and service quality; experience has taught them to recognize and value this quality. Boomers will also be less inclined to follow fads or buy on impulse; rather, they will be aggressive evaluators of products and services.
- Middle-aged consumers will place greater emphasis on convenience and comfort. Convenience is essential to time conservation and time is very important to the boomer who might be experiencing a "mid-life crisis." Comfort in terms of both physical and psychological dimensions are important to the consumer who might be seeking a warm, safe, and hassle-free environment. Time and place convenience together with quality form utility will continue to be extremely important patronage reasons to be considered by retailers.
- Middle-aged consumers will be looking for ways to increase their sense of control. With middle age comes a sense of vulnerability and heightened awareness of risks. Diminished physical capacities, impending retirements, and loss of loved ones are all occurrences that contribute to feelings that one has a loss of control over events that shape one's life. Risk reduction goods and services that give the consumer a sense of control over physical and financial affairs will flourish in the nineties.
- Middle-aged consumers will be increasingly interested in purchasing experiences rather than things. The age of accumulation will be replaced by the age of involvement. Products and services will be judged on the basis of how well they create a desirable experience or enrich the quality of the consumer's life. The quest for vivid experiences should be one focus of the retailer's merchandising efforts.

Wellness: In The Land of Non

Wellness is an individual's state of physical and mental health; it suggests a soundness of mind and body. As a broad concept, wellness incorporates the notion of a stable and balanced lifestyle. The nineties generation will attempt to achieve a state of wellness through abstinence, exercise, and nutrition.

Abstinence will be a sign of the times, for the nineties consumer; it will represent a sense of control—if not control over one's environment, at least control over one's self. Yesterday's glamour of conspicuous consumption is becoming today's stigma of no self-control. "Non" will become more than a prefix, it will become a lifestyle.

> It is the dinner bell: non-fat ice cream, non-dairy spread, non-caffeine cola, non-alcoholic beer.
>
> It is the mating call: "Non-smoking, non-drinking prince seeks sober princess."
>
> The red circle with the slash has become the country's all-purpose problem buster.
>
> Membership in the "Anons"—12-step programs that include Alcoholics Anonymous, Overeaters Anonymous, Narcotics Anonymous, Gamblers Anonymous, Sexaholics Anonymous, Workaholics Anonymous, and dozens more—has doubled in the last decade.[27]

One trendsetting lifestyle group of the 1990s could well be the "Nones"—those individuals who want none of this and none of that. Their motto could well be "Just Say No."

The fitness fanaticism of the eighties—a trend that at times showed all the zeal and kindly tolerance of a secular Spanish Inquisition—will mellow considerably during the nineties.[28] Last decade's fitness craze for external youthfulness will be replaced by this decade's search for everlasting wellness. As the ranks of the middle-age bulge swell with recruits from the boomer generation, a kinder and more gentle physical fitness program will prevail. The fitness market is becoming more segmented—the mass jogging market is becoming the niche markets of the jogger, hiker, and walker while the aerobics market is being segmented into high-impact, non-impact, and aquatic aerobics.[29] Recreational exercise (e.g., tennis, golf, bowling, dancing, etc.) will also enjoy substantial growth through the rest of this century.

Consumers are not just eating better; they're eating different. A key trend for tomorrow's food and restaurant industry is the growth of the diversified diet, incorporating a wide variety of ingredients and cuisines.[30] The globalization of the American dinner table will result in increased popularity of poultry, fish, and seafood at the expense of beef products. Ethnic foods that offer convenience, nutrition, and low cost will find expanded markets. Faddish health-food crazes (e.g., calcium, oatbran), based on real and imaginary health problems and solutions, will also continue to find markets. Good nutrition will be a merchandising appeal that works with consumers who are experiencing age-related problems.

Products and services for slowing down (e.g., anti-aging products for hair and skin, and facelifts) and covering up (cosmetics and hair replacement) the aging process should enjoy a boom decade. Figure 19–5 identifies additional product and service opportunities for meeting consumer wellness needs.

Income: The Bifurcation of the Marketplace

The polarization between the "haves" and the "have-nots" in America has widened and is perhaps the most troubling legacy of the 1980s and the greatest challenge of the 1990s. After adjusting for inflation, the increase in income inequality becomes evident by the fact that average family income of the poorest 20 percent actually declined during the last decade—they have less purchasing power today than at the beginning of the eighties. In contrast, the typical family in the top 20 percent has enjoyed a substantial increase in real earnings during the 1980s.[31] Looking at the problem in another way, the richest 5 percent of American families captured fully 16.9 percent of aggregate income in the United States. The poorest fifth of American families—a group four times the size of the richest group just described—earned 4.6 percent of the national income in 1987.[32]

The income gap between the haves and the have-nots is most pronounced between black and white households and young and old Americans. Black households earned about 56 percent of the median household income for whites; a decade earlier, black income was 60 percent of white income. In 1970, 24.6 percent of persons over the age of 65 lived below the poverty line while 14.9 percent of those under 18 lived in poverty. By 1987, they had switched places. The proportion of the elderly living in poverty had dropped to 12.2 percent, while that of young had leaped to 20 percent.[33] Living just above the poverty line are 45 million lower-middle class (i.e., the "have-somes") consumers who also feel the gap between themselves and the more affluent upper-middle class counterparts (i.e, the "have-alots").[34]

Abstinence	Exercise	Nutrition
Non-Dairy	Sporting Goods/Services	Light Foods/Drinks
Non-Fat	Recreational Goods/Services	Low Foods/Drinks
Non-Sugar	Exercise Goods/Services	Diet Foods/Drinks
Non-Salt	Health Goods/Services	Lean Foods/Drinks
Non-Caffeine	Fitness Goods/Services	Health Foods/Drinks
Non-Alcoholic	Weight Control Goods/Services	Natural Foods/Drinks
Non-Caloric	Therapy Goods/Services	Organic Foods/Drinks
Water	Stress Control Goods/Services	Vitamins and Minerals
Air	Self-Improvement Goods/Services	Pharmaceuticals

FIGURE 19–5
Consumer wellness goods and services

The bifurcation of the marketplace should further exacerbate the polarization of retailers into the upscale, focused retail formats that target the affluent consumer and the lower-priced, discount merchants who direct their efforts at attracting the less affluent, low-end buyer. Market bifurcation also suggests that general merchant retailers who are neither competitively priced nor particularly individualistic could be at a competitive disadvantage due to their middle-ground position—serving the middle market with a middle-of-the-road retailing format.[35]

The affluent consumer will expect, demand, and get better quality products, more unique merchandise, higher quality service, better shopping atmospherics, more convenient store locations, and store images that support their quest of status and recognition. The competition in the high-end market is intense and will continue to intensify throughout the 1990s as specialty boutiques, department stores, and focused catalog retailers scramble to build and hold loyal customer followings.

As the upscale market begins to mature, the downscaled market of regular folks will stage something of a comeback. Unlike the catered-to, high-end consumer, the somewhat-overlooked, low-end buyer represents a market that will require some attention in this last decade of the twentieth century. Boostered by the success of Homer Simpson (of the "Simpsons") and Roseanne Barr (of the ABC series), blue collar and other nonprofessional lifestyles are receiving increased attention from some members of the retailing industry.[36] With eroding real incomes, many of these traditionally loyal shoppers (e.g., Sears) are becoming comparative shoppers and bargain hunters. To regain and retain their loyalty, price-oriented retailers will need to offer branded merchandise at competitive and easy-to-understand prices. Everyday low prices on quality branded products will remain strong customer appeals as low-end consumers seek to reduce the risks and hassles of buying.

Consumers: Growth Targets within a Mature Market

During the 1990s, the nation's overall economic growth is expected to be quite modest; the U.S. retail market has reached maturity. A mature market will require retailers to carefully search for specific market segments that have growth potential. Population increases supported by greater income levels have propelled the maturity and kiddie segments into the limelight as markets that have strong potential for growth throughout the 1990s and beyond. Both of these expanding markets will receive greater attention from retailers as they seek to survive and prosper during the nineties.

Maturity Market: The Young and the Restless

The mature, 50-plus market is large (over 60 million) and is getting larger; Figure 19–6 illustrates the growth of the market. By 1995, mature consumers will account for 1 out of every 4 consumers; by the year 2010, that ratio will stand at 1 consumer out of 3. While increased numbers is certainly a major factor in the growth potential of the mature market, an even more significant factor is the fact that people over 50 already control 75 percent of the nation's wealth and half the discretionary income. Today's 50-plus consumers aren't behaving like their parents and grandparents. They're wealthier, healthier, and better educated.[37] Mature consumers exhibit heavy expenditure patterns in the following product and service categories:

- Leisure travel and home entertainment
- Second homes and home furnishings
- Luxury and domestic automobiles
- Cosmetics and bath products
- Lawn and garden products
- Clothing and accessories
- Stocks, bonds, and mutual funds
- Recreation and sporting goods

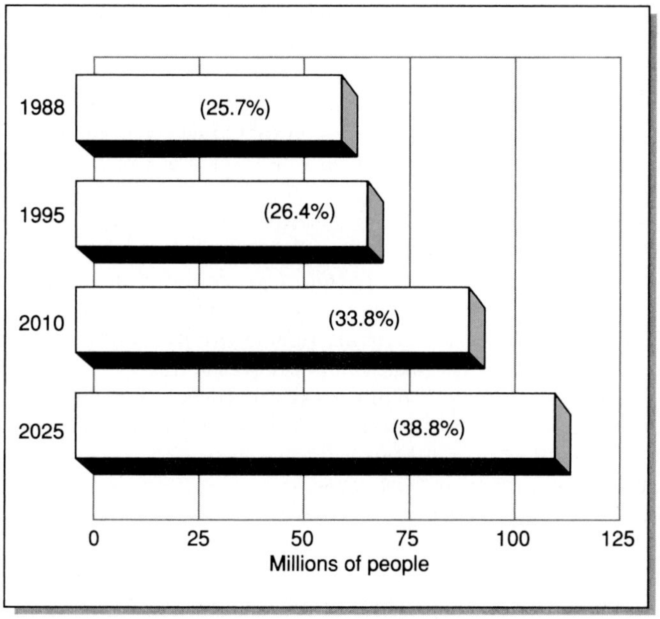

FIGURE 19–6
Growth of the 50-plus market, by total population and percent of U.S. population (source: Bureau of the Census)

- Health clubs and health foods
- Medicines and medical supplies

In reality, mature consumers have needs in just about all product/service classifications and categories. What they require is modest product/service modifications (e.g., larger print books, more fully cut apparel, and more leisurely paced activities). As shoppers, the 50-plus market demands quality in what it buys, and courteous, efficient, informed service when it buys. The older consumer opts for quality over all other attributes, tends to buy fewer items of a higher quality, and is not so much price-sensitive as value-sensitive. The consumers expect to get what they pay for, whether the absolute price is higher or lower.[38]

Kiddie Market: The Young and the Privileged

The baby boomlet spawned by the baby-boom generation during the late 1980s will continue throughout the decade of the nineties; as a result, children's specialty retailing will also experience continued growth.[39] Spending on kids is one of the fastest-growing sectors of America's economy—spending on and spending by children 4 to 12 years old is likely to remain robust for some years. The kiddie, 12-minus market is estimated to be about 2 percent of the entire U.S. economy.[40] The robustness of this preteen market can be attributed to the following five factors:

- More and more boomlets are being added to the market as more and more boomers start their families,
- Thirtysomething parents have more money to spend and to give to their children in a quest to build an even better baby.[41]
- The well-equipped kid has become something of a status symbol in some social circles.[42]
- Working parents are trying to compensate for the lack of quality time with the children by providing an abundance of quality products.
- Well-heeled, gift-giving grandparents add greatly to the market—they account for about 30 percent of the children's buying.[43]

RETAIL STRATEGIES AND TACTICS

Riding the Silver Streak

So you want to ride the Silver Streak into the future? Here's how:

- *Focus on quality*. Silver Streakers want it, know it, and will demand it. Furnish them with the information that will help them make their decisions—in your advertising, and in your store. Contrary to long-held prejudices, they are more than willing to try new products, services, and experiences . . . if that trial is justified. Moreover, the definition of quality itself has evolved: It doesn't mean "fancier"; it means "more elegant." It doesn't mean elaboration; it does mean simplicity. And above all, it means ease of use.
- *Provide outstanding service*. In every retail study of this group, poor customer service is the Silver Streaker's number one gripe. This means more than a customer's being able to find someone to ring up the sale and not having to spend more time in line than shopping. It also means retailers being willing to stand behind what they sell, making sure that return/exchange policies are liberal and uncomplicated, providing delivery and on-premise alteration services, making phone and mail shopping easy, and having informed, helpful, efficient salespeople. Any personalized service that makes shopping easier and more pleasant will be welcomed by the older shopper.
- *Make the store user friendly*. Silver Streakers see no reason why shopping can't be made more congenial in its particulars: places to rest and refresh; more convenient—and safer!—parking facilities; good signage to help you find what you want, good lighting so you can see the merchandise when you find it, and easy-to-read tags and shelf-talkers.

Silver Streakers are buy people, with more money than time or patience, and there is a very real opportunity for retailers to create innovative versions of "one-stop shopping"—as important a concept for a department or specialty store as for the local 200,000-sq.-ft. mass marketer.

Source: Stephani Cook, "Riding the Silver Streak," *Arthur Anderson Retailing Issues Letter* vol. 2, no. 4, Center for Retailing Studies, Texas A&M University, September, 1989.

The kiddie market has attracted a wide variety of specialty store formats; from large chains with a general market appeal (e.g., Kids 'R' Us) to the superspecialist targeting a well-defined market niche (e.g., Benetton 012); children's specialty retailers will continue to define and target new market opportunities. The potential growth opportunities are suggested by the number of major retail organizations that have developed new retail chains targeted to this segment: Kids 'R' Us by Toys 'R' Us, Kids Mart and Little Folks Shop by F.W. Woolworth, McKids by Sears and McDonald's, Limited Too by The Limited, EspritKids by Esprit, Mother and Child by Laura Ashley, GapKids by The Gap, and The Kids Store by Montgomery Wards.

Kids' retailers are increasingly directing more of their merchandising effort at children as opposed to their parents. McKids, for example, design stores having a child-friendly environment, with tropical fish, a toy kitchenette, interactive activities, and large-screen video monitors to involve kids in the shopping experience. They even have a separate pint-sized entrance of their own. And the fact that children can play in a controlled setting has obvious appeal to parents.[44]

THE ADAPTING RETAIL ORGANIZATION

As suggested by the Theory of Natural Selection (see Chapter 2), retailers who want to survive must be both willing and able to change and adapt to the environmental conditions under which they operate. This section examines some of the many merchandising and operational adaptations retailers will need to consider in order to prosper and grow during the nineties.

Vendor Relationships: Fostering Partnerships and Creating Alliances

The bottom line for many retailers in the 1990s will be measured by the strength of the relationships they are able to build with their vendors. High performance retailing in the year 2000 will mean increasing not only individual company performance but also the company's alliance with suppliers and providers of other resources. Managing these extra-corporate alliances and leveraging their impact on a company's market and financial performance will be a key aspect of the successful retail company of the coming decade.[45] New partnerships and alliances with vendor resources will play an integral part in creating the competitive vertical marketing systems of the future.

Strong retailer/vendor relationships are beneficial to both parties. With a wealth of information from scanning, retailers will take a more active role in the manufacturers' product development, research, and planning process.[46] The reduced risks associated with new product introduction and old product modification should be considerable for both parties; customer satisfaction should also be greatly enhanced. Value-added partnerships are also essential to the effective use of electronic transmission of purchase orders, invoices, and advanced orders, as well as the full utilization of quick response and just-in-time inventory systems.[47] Adversarial relationships within channels of distribution will be replaced by a cooperative spirit so essential to the totally coordinated distribution system. The alternative to retailer/vendor cooperation could well be retailer/vendor competition. In the past, vendors cooperated because they lacked direct access to the market; today, the best of class resources/designers (Lauren, Claiborne, Coach, Waterford/Wedgewood, Esprit) are opening their own retail chains to ensure their growth, create the type of POS environment they seek, and/or gain greater control over their distribution.[48]

Micro Merchandising: Individualism and Mass Customization

Consumer markets are becoming more segmented. The individualism of consumer tastes and preferences that emerged as a significant marketing force in the 1980s is expected to continue into the nineties. Target markets become more defined as market segments become market niches, which in turn are becoming individual markets. The ultimate in target marketing and customer satisfaction might well become a customized product supported by a micro-merchandising effort that is carefully tailored to the buyer's expectations. Customized products typically involve **mass customization** wherein computer-assisted operational and merchandising practices are used to individually shape traditional mass-market products.[49] Mass customization is often achieved through modularization—a point of sale customizing wherein standardized parts and components are used to customize a product at the end of the distribution chain (i.e., retail store). For example, a customer might buy one manufacturer's turntable, another's amplifier, and speakers from a third vendor; the final stereo system is tailored to one individual's specific needs but the parts are standard mass product components.[50] IKEA, the Swedish furniture company, allows customization of some of its products (e.g., couches) by providing fabric choices and pillow styles.[51] Services can also be mass customized. Rocky Aoki, founder of Benihana of Tokyo restaurants, has started a seafood chain that utilizes (a version of) this new concept. Serving an average of fifteen different fresh fish daily, customers can have their choice stir-fried (Cantonese, Szechuan, Shanghai, or Thai style), broiled (California, Japanese, or French style), steamed or poached (Chinese or Norwegian style), sautéed (Grecian, Parisienne, Florida Indian River, or Louisiana blackened style), char-grilled (Key West, Nouvelle Cuisine, or Roman style), or deep-fried (Tempura, Cajun, or Italian style). The result, with an average inventory, an assembly-line kitchen, and an easy-to-read menu, is 285 different dinners to choose from—about one for every seat in the restaurant.[52]

RETAIL STRATEGIES AND TACTICS

What's in Store: Analysts Sort out the Survivors

So, you think Sears is pretty smart, pushing that everyday-low-price strategy? And you figure Campeau Corp. will help build Lazarus and Abraham & Straus into retailing powerhouses in the 1990s?

Well, you are wrong—at least according to the 10 leading retail analysts *Advertising Age* asked to point to the next decade's big winners and losers.

The following excerpts reflect the analysts' opinions.

LOSERS

Sears Roebuck & Co.—New everyday-low-price strategy does too little too late for mega-retailer. Its unwieldy administrative apparatus and huge overhead cost structure are likely to cause continued problems.

Lazarus—Campeau Corp. unit tries to pump up sales with short-term promotional tactics. But it has lost its merchandise focus and become a slave to the number crunchers. Lazarus represents a strong sell-off candidate for Campeau.

Ames Department Stores—Despite strong management, the chain could fail in its attempt to turn around troubled Zayre Corp. division, which it acquired last year.

Casual Corner—This specialty apparel merchant has lost sight of its customers. It is behind the fashion times with an approach that offers neither novelty nor excitement.

American Fare—Merchandise featured at this hypermarket joint venture of K mart Corp. and Bruno's is overpriced. The format is in need of substantial fine-tuning if it is to become a magnet for customers traveling significant distances.

Carrefour—The French retailer has not been able to adapt European hypermarket formula to the U.S. market.

Abraham & Straus—Abraham & Straus is under significant and potentially damaging financial pressure from highly leveraged parent Campeau Corp. Sale of the department store is a distinct possibility.

The Federated Group—Mismanagement is a major problem for Federated, especially as other worthy competitors saturate the consumer electronics market.

Rose's Stores—This regional discounter is at serious risk of being overrun by Wal-Mart Stores.

For successful retailers in the nineties, product assortment planning will incorporate mass customization. Competition and the search for new markets will force retail companies to develop and manage product assortments at the smallest level of aggregation—be it small groups of highly homogeneous customers or a single individual consumer. Thus, a specific retail format will be needed to service each specific segment. If retailers want to serve a total market, they will do it with a portfolio of store formats.[53]

Store Image: An Identity Crisis in a Cookie Cutter World

Just as the individualization of consumer tastes and preferences will necessitate the customization of the product/service offering (see above), this same market phenomenon will promote the customization of store images. Stores that clearly communicate well-established and understandable identities in the 1990s will have the best chance of

Bradlees—Troubled management and insufficient capital support from its parent Stop & Shop Cos. place this discounter at significant risk.

WINNERS

Wal-Mart Stores—The customer is king in this retail empire built on everyday low prices. Its ability to control costs is uncanny.

K mart Corp.—The retailer has a broad-based diversification strategy that strengthens its presence in important niche markets.

Dillard Department Stores—Dillard provides affordable and quality fashion alternatives to middle America. Its excellent centralized management and operations are backed by state-of-the-art information systems.

Nordstrom—It is tops in service and offers an extensive assortment of fashionable apparel at reasonable prices. Outstanding corporate culture.

The Limited—Chain has unparalleled marketing and merchandising savvy. Top-notch distribution systems shorten order times and keep this specialty merchant on the cutting edge of fashion.

Toys 'R' Us—Toy category juggernaut knows what is hot or not sooner than anyone else. Its huge low-priced assortment is supported by strong marketing that clearly focuses on the ultimate consumers of its products—children.

Pier 1 Imports Inc.—Pier 1 consistently turns up original and unique merchandise. Chain is well positioned as consumers focus on making the home into a refuge.

Montgomery Ward & Co.—Streamlining into power specialty departments has worked for the national merchant. A legacy of consumer goodwill is activated by strong marketing and responsive merchandising.

Spiegel Inc.—Catalog retailer is extremely sophisticated in identifying and appealing to multiple market segments; offers both fashion and convenience.

Home Shopping Network—HSN has survived the shakeout period in this industry, and is starting to read its markets more effectively. The consumer's desire for convenience will be critical to its long-term appeal.

Source: Special Report. Reprinted with permission from the April 24, 1989, issue of *Advertising Age,* p. S–2. Copyright © by Grain Communications, Inc.

meeting the expectations of consumers. In the 1990s, customers will be demanding that you provide focus, that you edit for them, that you create a point of view that tells them simply and honestly what you stand for and why they should shop with you.[54] The age of the cookie cutter store is over. The 1990s will force retailers to throw their cookie cutters away and to develop individualist store formats that project a unique and appropriate image. Retailer identity is best created by the use of theme marketing—the use of a theme as a focal point for the retailer's merchandising effort. Theme marketing uses all forms of communication with strong emphasis or store atmospherics and merchandise presentation. Selling the theme rather than the merchandise can be a powerful force in attracting consumer attention and patronage. Ralph Lauren Polo Shops, Benetton's United Colors, Banana Republic's Safari Motif, Bloomingdale's urban chic, and Macy's Cellar are all examples of retailers who have successfully employed a theme marketing approach to the image identification problem.[55] Experiences, not merchandise, will be the hot seller or in-product of the nineties.

Therefore, marketing skills, not merchandising practices, will be the tools of preference.[56] Winners will be recognized for their identities, losers will go unrecognized for the lack of it.

Store Size: How Big Is Too Big?

Is there a limit to how big a store should be? While stores may get somewhat larger by the year 2000 due to the broader variety of products and services that will be required to meet consumer preferences, the mass in mass merchandising could well peak out in the 1990s. Larger stores at all levels (e.g., supermarket to the hypermarket) are receiving mixed reviews.[57]

From a consumer perspective, larger store formats offer greater one-stop shopping opportunities with certain price advantages. However, even for the original "shop till you drop" consumer, the multi-hour shopping trip is simply too long. As sizes increase (e.g., the 200,000+-square-foot hypermarkets), the massiveness of such stores create tremendous hurdles for the time-constrained consumer who seeks conveniences of time and place. For other customers, the mega-store environment is too overwhelming in terms of both its vertical and horizontal space. The mature consumer and the parent/child shopper also find the vastness to be a barrier to an enjoyable and comfortable shopping experience. Crowded parking lots, long checkout lines, packed shopping aisles, and overtaxed service desks are additional problems associated with huge facilities that dampen the advantages of the one-stop shop.

From the retailer's perspective, increased store sizes offer the potential for economies of scale that come with a large operation. Actual operating results within the U.S. market have been somewhat disappointing; this is especially true within the hypermarket industry. Wal-Mart has suspended its plans for building any more hypermarkets in favor of its super-center concept (combination of discount department stores and grocery stores). This action represents a downsizing of its big store concept from 225,000 to 150,000 square feet.[58] The move away from hypermarkets for Wal-Mart, as well as the limited plans for expansion of the jumbo store concept by other hypermarket operators, suggests that the large retail formats are still in the development stage of their life cycle. Operational problems that are part of a large-store operation include: (1) finding and recruiting enough qualified workers in a scarce labor market, (2) maintaining a secure operation in a sea of merchandise, (3) operating a low margin business (i.e., 15 to 18 percent) with high fixed costs, (4) maintaining a huge physical plant—basic housekeeping chores of cleaning, servicing, and repairing store equipment, and (5) keeping the store shelves stocked and organized.

Are bigger stores better? Retailers at all levels and sizes are finding that more space is not necessarily the answer to greater profitability. As a result, the 1990s could bring some downsizing or at the very least, the maintenance of store size at current levels. Growth in store space will be highly selective.

Market-Positioning: The Polarization of Retailing

The 1980s witnessed a polarization of retailing as growth industries evolved around either the specialty store format or formats that employed mass merchandising techniques within a large store facility. The general merchant who occupied the competitive middle ground experienced slow or no growth and a decline of market share. Profitability of **polar retailers** was quite rewarding while **middle merchandisers** turned in a disappointing profit performance.

During the 1990s polarization will continue to be an important competitive positioning strategy as retailers struggle to service appropriate markets. As illustrated in Figure 19–7, to the mega and mass merchandiser, polar retailing involves developing merchandising programs and operational practices that are effective and efficient in

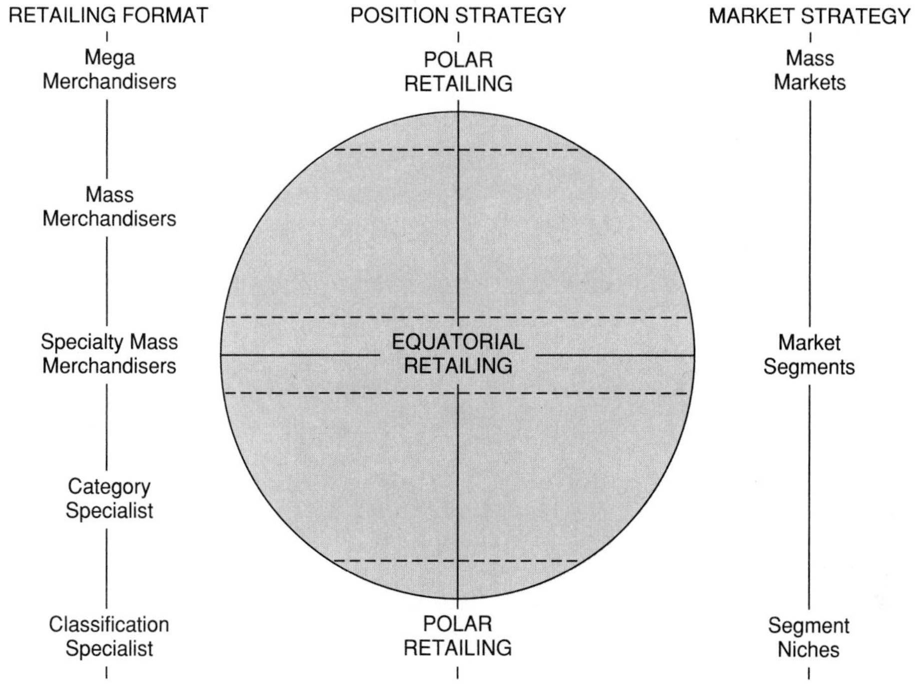

FIGURE 19–7
The polarization of retailing

servicing the mass markets. On the other hand, polar retailing for the category and classification specialist necessitates the development of a highly focused merchandise mix capable of reaching narrowly defined market segment niches. **Equatorial retailing** is the competitive middle position between the polar extremes; it involves a combination of the two polar formats (i.e., specialty mass merchandiser) designed to target more broadly defined market segments.

The polarization of retailing is not just limited to the mass merchandiser-specialist dichotomy. Retail analyst Walter Loeb predicts a major polarization for the 1990s between commodity retailing and fashion retailing—with both types evolving into either convenience or distribution outlets. Nordstrom's and Bloomingdale's are cited as fashion destination stores while Price Club and Wal-Mart's Hypermarket U.S.A. typifies the commodity destination store.[59] Consultant Nina Gruen states that "retailers can only survive and profit in this competitive environment if they adopt one of two polar strategies. They can offer 'excitement and bargains' (the Price Store model) or 'excitement, service, and education' (the Nordstrom's and Home Depot models)."[60] In today's highly fragmented retail environment, one writer suggests that "apparel retailers are likely to polarize on high-end versus low-end merchandise, with little in between. . . . The role of brands will be strong in both segments."[61]

For the most part, the 1990s will be a decade of refining, restructuring, and exploiting the specialty and mass merchandising concept; new format development will typically be extensions of existing polar formats. Customer services, store size and atmospherics, product selection and presentation, and store locations are just four additional dimensions that some experts identify as being used to extend polarization and to establish a defensible competitive market position.

As in the past, the key to success in the nineties will be retailing formats that meet customer needs (satisfaction) while achieving organizational goals (performance). Strategies and tactics for successful marketing and merchandising must be matched with equally viable operational and financial programs. Figure 19–8 identifies the major strategical and tactical elements that have helped polar retailers in their attempts to

FIGURE 19–8 Strategical and tactical descriptions of polar retailers

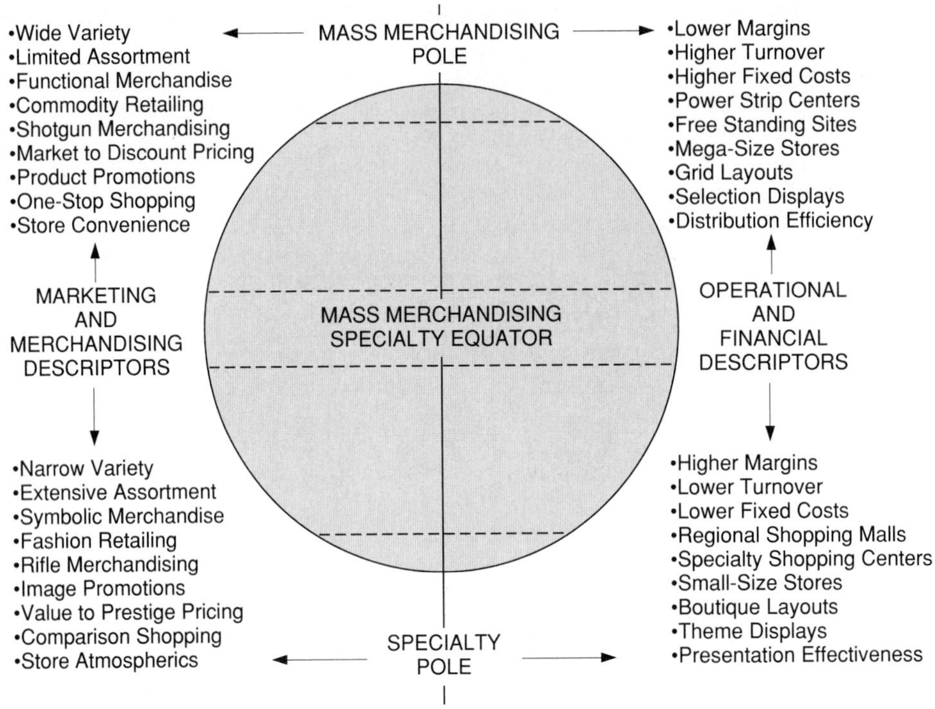

establish a defined position within the marketplace. At both the mass merchandising pole and the specialty pole, retailers are putting together a large number of unique and competitive retail formats using various combinations of and emphases on the marketing/merchandising and operational/financial elements identified in Figure 19–8. Repositioning can be accomplished by changing the combination of elements or shifting the emphasis from one element to another.

The emergence of polarized mass-and-specialty retailing, the upheaval and turmoil in the department store industry as a result of mergers and acquisitions, and the merchandising and operational vulnerability of outdated chain store operations, has led to much speculation and proclamation concerning the future of the equatorial mid-merchandiser. If a retail store falls between the two polar strategies, it is unlikely to survive in the competitive 1990s.[62] Department store retailing as we knew it is no more.[63] The days when the retail giants—Sears, K mart, J.C. Penney—could open a store, stock the shelves, offer reasonable pricing and service, and wait for the customers to roll in ended in the 1970s.[64] So, what is the future of these general merchants who occupy a place within the equatorial zone? Like so many intermediaries, success depends on finding an innovative compromise between two polar extremes.

Historically, institutional change is evolutionary, not revolutionary—it does not happen all at once and out of the blue.[65] Nevertheless, the last two decades have probably witnessed more evolutionary development than any other period in retailing history; the result has been a richness of retailing concepts and formats ranging from hypermarkets to discount department stores to office supply power formats to the super-specialist.[66] The opportunity for evolutionary growth may be waning, however. It is hard to identify a product category in which at least some form of specialty super store does not exist. Similarly, most of the categories in which warehouse operations make economic sense have already been developed. It may be time for the next retail revolution.[67]

While the next retail revolution may involve a number of scenario changes, the scenario being followed by most equatorial retailers is that of a combinatory nature. General merchants are exhibiting considerable adaptive behavior in developing new integrative retailing formats that incorporate various strategical and tactical features of both the mass merchandiser and the retail specialist. Figure 19–9 illustrates the world of retailing as it relates to the continuum of retailing formats. At the north pole, the dominant retailers are hypermarkets and super-centers, together with warehouse and discount retailers. Polar retailing at the south pole ranges from the single-line specialist to the very narrowly focused niche and super-specialist. In and around the equator are six different retailing formats that have or are in the process of developing some type of specialist/mass merchandise combination. These integrative formats include:

- *Discount Department Store*—a compromise of the discount store and the department store. The disadvantages of discount retailing that are achieved through mass

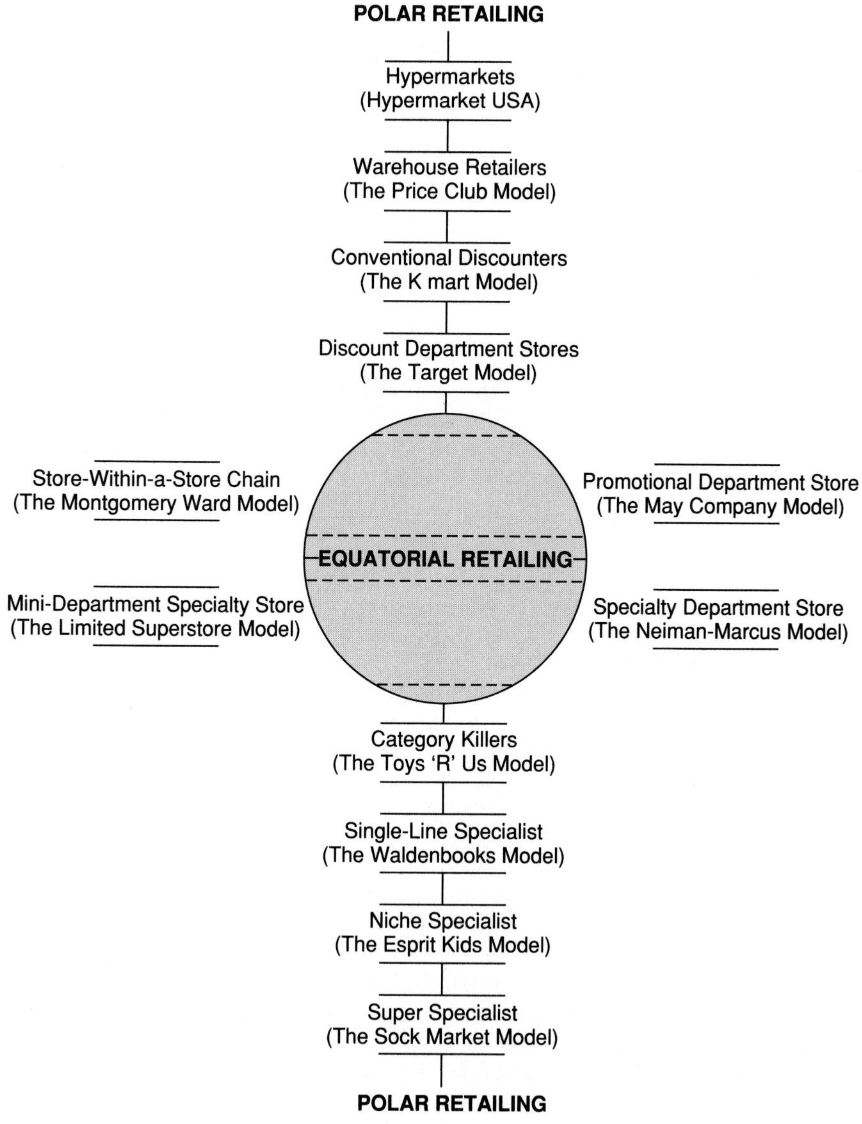

FIGURE 19–9
The world of retailing

merchandising is supported by the benefits of specialization that results from store departmentalization. Target, a division of Dayton Hudson, typifies this type of format.

- *Promotional Department Store*—a combination of a traditional department store with an aggressive advertising and sales effort supported by highly efficient, technologically based centralized management that maintains tight control over all organizational operations. May Department Stores Company is the principal proponent of this retailing concept.
- *Store-Within-a-Store*—a mall-without-walls concept that incorporates both company-operated stores (e.g., Electronic Avenue) and leased specialty stores (e.g., Toys 'R' Us) under one roof. The store has both a general store identification (Montgomery Wards) and individual store identities. Sears is a convert to this format.
- *Specialty Department Store*—a department store that has narrowed its assortment by eliminating all or most hardlines. This format retained the departmental structure of the department store while narrowing its product focus by concentrating on fashion apparel and related merchandise. Neiman Marcus, Nordstrom, and Saks Fifth Avenue all typify this strategy of boutiquing the department store.
- *Mini-Department Specialty Store*—a specialty retailer that engages in line extension by adding boutique departments that are logical and tested extensions of existing merchandise lines. The Limited Super Store concept is an example of this specialty store format that is becoming more departmentalized.
- *Category Killer*—a specialty retailer who utilizes such mass merchandising techniques as huge stores, large selection displays, competitive prices, warehouse stocking, centralized checkout and customer service, and computer-based technologies to gain market dominance in a single product category. Killers and would-be killers include Toys 'R' Us, Circuit City, and Office Square.

With every trend there are countertrends; hence, it is not surprising that as more and more effort was focused on the polar extremes of retailing, someone would rediscover the old but changed opportunities that occupied the middle. Where discrepancies or gaps occur, opportunities emerge; middle-ground opportunities will continue to materialize throughout the nineties. The 1990s will truly be dynamic as retailers continue to scrabble to position themselves within the world of retailing (see Figure 19–9).

SUMMARY

The 1980s was a decade of change for all retailers; the 1990s promise to be equally dynamic. The retail marketplace and the consumers that comprise it will undergo many changes. Some of the more significant changes having an impact on both merchandising practices and operational policies include: (1) consumer's poverty of time and the need to gain greater control over their usage of time; (2) the revitalized interest in environmental issues and a renewed commitment to the earth's welfare; (3) a shift toward a neotraditional lifestyle and an increased emphasis on family, home, religious beliefs, and traditional values and attitudes; (4) the middle-aging of the baby boom generation; (5) the search for a state of wellness through abstinence, exercise, and nutrition; (6) the bifurcation of the marketplace into the "have" and "have-not" consumers; and (7) the growth of the maturity and kiddie markets.

In response to changes in the marketplace, retail organizations will have to adapt in order to prosper and grow. While a host of adaptations will be necessary, the following are key survival changes. First, retailers will have to foster partnerships and create alliances with vendors in order to develop competitive vertical marketing systems. Second, product customization supported by a micro-merchandising effort will be needed to meet the individual needs of highly segmented markets. Third, retailers will need a clear identity and a unique image in order to stand out in a world of me-too retailing. Fourth, the right size for a store in the future may not always mean something bigger; store size must be right for both target consumers and retailer operations. Finally, competition in the nineties will involve a wide array of retailing formats; successful retail operations will find ways to establish a competitive position within the market.

STUDENT STUDY GUIDE

Key Terms and Concepts

boomers (p. 683)
busters (p. 684)
environment friendly (p. 681)
equatorial retailing (p. 695)
kiddie market (p. 689)
market bifurcation (p. 687)
market positioning (p. 694)
mass customization (p. 691)
mass merchandisers (p. 695)
maturity market (p. 688)
micro merchandising (p. 691)
middle merchants (p. 694)
neotraditionalism (p. 682)
polarization of retailing (p. 694)
polar retailers (p. 694)
specialty retailers (p. 696)
store image (p. 692)
time control (p. 680)
time poverty (p. 680)
vendor partnerships (p. 691)
wellness (p. 686)

Review Questions

1. Why are consumers pressed for time? Identify the key factors in the creation of the time squeeze.
2. Identify specific actions that retailers can take to assist consumers in their quest for more free time.
3. Describe how the environmental movement will affect retail businesses. Provide examples.
4. What is neotraditionalism? Which retailers are most likely to benefit from this movement?
5. Who are the boomers? Why are they important to retailing?
6. How will wellness be defined by the nineties generation? How will the wellness movement affect retailers?
7. What does market bifurcation entail? What impact does this process have on retailers?
8. How should retailers ride the "silver streak" into the future?
9. Describe the benefits that retailers receive from a closer relationship with vendors.
10. Discuss mass customization and its role in creating customer satisfaction.
11. How is retailer identity created?
12. Are bigger stores better?
13. Describe the polarization of retailing and its relationship to market positioning.
14. Who are the polar retailers? Provide nontext examples. Who are the equatorial retailers? Provide nontext examples.

Review Exam

True or False

_____ 1. Neotraditionalism is a 1990s movement in which consumers are leaving home in search of a more nontraditional, nonconforming value system and lifestyle.

_____ 2. No demographic trend holds more importance to the retailer during the 1990s than the middle-aging of the baby boomers who were born between 1946 and 1964.

_____ 3. The income gap between the "haves" and "have-nots" is increasing.

_____ 4. With the aging of the U.S. population, the kiddie market will continue to decline in both size and buying power until it bottoms out in the late 1990s.

_____ 5. Adversarial relationships between retailers and vendors is a health situation because it promotes competition and is essential in the development of vertical marketing systems.

_____ 6. Bigger stores are not always better stores.

Multiple Choice

_____ 1. Which of the following actions is *not* a practice retailers should use in aiding consumers in their quest for time control?

a. better organized stores
b. faster transaction time
c. easier shopping formats
d. reduced product selection
e. simpler promotional programs

_____ 2. Which of the following statements about middle-age boomer consumers is false? Middle-aged consumers will _____.
a. seek ways to balance work, family, and recreation
b. become increasingly concerned with health and wellness
c. be experienced shoppers with considerable buying experiences
d. place greater emphasis on convenience and control
e. be increasingly interested in purchasing things rather than experiences

_____ 3. The 1990s generation will attempt to achieve a state of wellness through _____.
a. drugs
b. abstinence
c. exercise
d. nutrition
e. a, c, and d above
f. b, c, and d above

_____ 4. Mature consumers are defined as _____ consumers.
a. 50-plus
b. 60-plus
c. 65-plus
d. 75-plus
e. none of the above

_____ 5. A customer who buys one manufacturer's turntable, another's amplifier, and speakers from a third vendor is engaging in _____.
a. bifurcation
b. assortment planning
c. mass merchandising
d. mass customization
e. mass confusion

_____ 6. _____ are specialty retailers that engage in line extension by adding boutique departments that are logical and tested extensions of existing merchandise lines.
a. Category killers
b. Mini-department specialty stores
c. Specialty department stores
d. Store-within-stores
e. Promotional department stores

STUDENT APPLICATIONS MANUAL

Investigative Projects: Practice and Application

1. Conduct a survey of the literature and identify three additional marketplace trends that could have major effects on retailers. Briefly discuss each trend and provide specific examples of how the trend will negatively and/or positively affect retail operations.
2. Conduct in-store surveys and identify five merchandising examples of retailers that are effectively utilizing a wellness theme to target health-conscious consumers. Describe the effectiveness of your examples.
3. By surveying print advertisements (newspapers and magazines), identify three good examples and three bad examples of retailers who are communicating a clear identity and a unique image. Be specific and support your analysis.
4. Review Chapter 2, then position the following retailers in the world of retailing as shown in Figure 19–9. What is the relative market position of the following retailers: (1) off-price retailer, (2) convenience store, (3) conventional supermarket, (4) food and drug combo supermarket, (5) catalog showroom, and (6) a vending machine.

Tactical Cases: Problems and Decisions

■ CASE 19–1
The "Greening" of Shop 'n Save*

THREATS AND OPPORTUNITIES CREATED BY THE ENVIRONMENTAL CRISIS

Robert Bradley, the CEO of Shop 'n Save supermarkets, was becoming increasingly concerned about the impact environmentalism may have on his firm. Shop 'n Save operated a chain of 32 supermarkets in the New England area. The company was profitable but margins were eroding and operating costs continued to climb.

Bradley had begun reading more about the environmental problems facing the United States, partly due to his own personal worries about pollution but also as a businessman concerned about how pollution regulation may negatively effect his chain. He also noted that some retailers were using "green" marketing, portraying themselves as environmental advocates, and he wondered if Shop 'n Save should do the same. A recent staff report revealed the several facts that may forecast changing consumer behavior thereby necessitating a change in Shop 'n Save's marketing strategy and tactics.

Americans are worried about the environment. The large demonstrations and massive publicity surrounding Earth Day, on April 22, 1990, reveal that concern. The National Anxiety Center included nuclear waste, the ozone layer, air pollution, water pollution, and garbage on its top-10 "worry" list. Roper polls indicate that 62 percent of Americans call pollution a very serious threat to their health and the environment. Only 44 percent felt this way in 1984.

Federal and state governments have recently become more involved in reducing pollution, after the laxity of the Reagan administration. Indictments and convictions for violating federal pollution laws nearly doubled in 1989 over 1988, and the $13 million in criminal fines levied during fiscal 1989 was an 80 percent increase over 1988. California leads the way, with some experts suggesting that internal combustion engines may be prohibited in the Los Angeles basin by the mid-1990s.

Bradley felt one of the more alarming items in the report was the finding in the Roper study that 75 percent of the respondents felt that businesses should handle the environmental cleanup job but only 36 percent think business is doing a good cleanup job. This seemed to predict more governmental regulation, something Bradley viewed with disdain. Bradley wondered if enough consumers were sufficiently sensitive to pollution issues to buy from companies they felt were environmentally friendly and boycott firms perceived unfriendly? The fact that one research report stated that 60 percent of consumers surveyed are involved with recycling surprised Bradley; at least, this indicated consumers are willing to change behavior to help cleanup. For Bradley, the main issue is if the environmental movement continues to build, will retailers who did not position themselves as environmentally friendly and practice "green" marketing would be at a competitive disadvantage.

Bradley assigned one of his staff members, Steve Caraccia, to develop a list of feasible ways Shop 'n Save could incorporate environmentalism into their marketing strategy. The report (Exhibit A) was sent to top management, and a strategy meeting was set to discuss the issues.

STRATEGY SESSION—OPPOSITION TO CHANGE

The strategy meeting began with Caraccia reviewing his suggestions to position Shop 'n Save as an environmentally friendly company. The discussion began.

Don Morgan, Chief Operating Officer, spoke first. "Steve, these are some interesting ideas. But are you sure consumers are really willing to put hard cash to support

EXHIBIT A
Alternatives for Shop 'n Save to adapt to the environmental crisis

1. Assign a top executive responsibility for integrating environmentalism into the marketing strategy. This executive would be responsible for becoming knowledgeable about the environmental movement and capable of separating "myths" from realities. Outside consultants who have expertise on how businesses, especially retailers, should deal with environmental issues could provide valuable assistance.
2. Educate buyers regarding the differences between environmentally friendly products (e.g. cloth diapers) and damaging products (e.g. chlorine bleach) and encourage them to promote friendly products when possible.
3. Educate and encourage suppliers to produce and distribute products that are not harmful to the environment.
4. Educate consumers about environmental issues. Provide literature in the stores regarding the major threats to the environment and ways in which the average family can help.
5. Advertise and promote environmentally safe products and position Shop 'n Save as a store that is committed to reducing pollution. A few examples of "green" products are a line of 100 percent recycled paper products, organically grown produce, and phosphate-free laundry detergent. Possibly, Shop 'n Save could develop a private label line of environment- and body-friendly products.
6. Stop environmentally unsound operational practices. For example, recycle waste, use recycled paper, use biodegradable shopping bags, do not spray fruits and vegetables with chemicals to improve appearance or shelf-life, and offer consumers discounts if they bring in previously used containers.
7. Provide convenient recycling facilities in store parking lots. This may prove to be unnecessary in those communities where recycling is mandatory.

their pro-environment sentiments? We've been burned too many times by research that shows consumers want low-fat, low-calorie products. We stock these products and our customers ignore them and continue to buy the unhealthy stuff! There's a big difference between what people say they will do and their actual behavior. Let's face it, who's going to say they're not for the environment in a public opinion poll? I'd hate to spend big bucks making Shop 'n Save a 'green' retailer only to find out our customers won't change their old buying patterns. Our role is to provide goods and services that people want. Convincing them to change their habits is too hard and too expensive. Let the government force them to change through legislation."

"I agree with Don, let's not get too far ahead of our customers. I read where Loblaw's, a Canadian supermarket chain, spent $5 million on their environmental programs. Our margins are eroding now, where will we get $5 million to spend on being environmentally friendly?" said Jeff Schmidt V.P. of Marketing.

"Nobody said anything about spending $5 million, Jeff. We're just discussing the issue," interjected Bradley.

"Bob, I'm all for the environment but I really think we should move carefully in this area. None of us knows very much about the environmental problem and how a food retailer should adapt. Maybe this is a fad, like oat bran. Those companies that overpromoted oat bran cereals are now catching a lot of flak for misleading advertising. I could just see us promoting some kind of 'green' product that turns out to be harmful to the environment," said Morgan.

"That's a good point. I read where biodegradable products are not an answer to our landfill problems because landfills are built so products will not degrade and leak into the ground water. Thus promotions about biodegradable products are a sham," offered Schmidt.

"Gentlemen, there are a number of experts who feel that fundamental changes in societal values are occurring in support of the environment. Shouldn't we be proactive and take advantage of these changes rather than wait until change is forced upon us by governmental regulation?" said Caraccia.

"I still have serious reservations. So what if we wait for government regulation. It might not affect us that much and at least all our competitors would be in the same boat. As a relatively small firm whatever we do isn't going to affect whether regulation is increased or not. Somehow the idea of trying to make a buck off the pollution problem doesn't sit well with me. We're a food retailer, not the Sierra Club. People don't expect us to be advocates for the environment, they may perceive us as manipulative if we try to benefit from this problem," said Morgan.

Bradley had not anticipated so many objections nor the complexity of the issue. He wanted his firm to do something to support the environment and wondered how to proceed.

QUESTIONS:

1. How should Bradley proceed in trying to adapt his firm's marketing strategy to environmental issues? Should the firm take action or wait and see how competitors react?
2. Do you think retailers have an ethical and social responsibility to promote and operate in an environmentally friendly fashion?
3. Will consumers voluntarily pay more money to live in a safer environment?
4. Is it government's role to legislate environmental standards or can the business community be counted on to step forward and raise standards voluntarily?

*This case was prepared by James T. Strong, University of Akron.

Sources: The factual information in this case about the environment was taken from the following articles: Howard Schlossberg, " 'Greening' of America Awaits Green Light from Leaders, Consumers," *Marketing News,* March 19, 1990, 24, 6, 1, 16; Ela Schwartz, "Down-to-Earth Retailing," *Discount Merchandiser,* March 1990, 30, 3, 48–52; and Emily T. Smith, Vicki Cahan, Naomi Freundlich, James Ellis, and Joseph Weber, "The Greening of Corporate America," *Business Week,* April 23, 1990, 96–103.

■ CASE 19–2
Sears, Roebuck, and Company: Retail Survival Strategies*

From its beginnings as a catalog operation bringing previously unobtainable goods to the rural peoples of the United States, Sears, Roebuck, and Company made a business of catering to the merchandise needs of the American middle market. Throughout most of the twentieth century, Sears grew and prospered with the nation. By the 1960s, Sears had become as much a leader in the retailing world as the United States was in the global world. However, the turbulence of the late 1960s, 1970s, and 1980s heralded an era of change for the giant retailer.

As Sears, Roebuck, and Company approached the 1990s, management was faced with a cumbersome task. "The Place America Shops" was in danger of becoming "A Place America Shopped Once upon a Time." Long the most trusted name in American retailing, Sears had been slipping further and further from the winning track for the last two decades. Struggling throughout most of the seventies and eighties, Sears Merchandise Group, the unquestioned heart of the company's business, was in need of revitalization.

The retail giant's earnings were erratic, domestic market share was declining, and revenue growth was below the industry average. The only figures on the rise for Sears were its operating costs, which represented some of the highest in the retailing industry.

Burdened by a cumbersome bureaucracy, Sears was incapable of facing the challenges presented by the fast-paced retailing world of the eighties. One apparent problem was the mindset of the typical Sears' employee: They had been indoctrinated with the notion that they were untouchable as members of the world's largest, most trusted retailing team. So many years of success had bred an arrogance and an internal focus that caused the company to be slow in reacting to changes in the retailing environment. Recognizing the need for drastic action, management embarked on a variety of changes that included a revamping of the firm's organizational structure, product mix, pricing program, and advertising strategy. The goal of this restructuring was to revitalize the management team, cut costs, improve decision-making capabilities, and develop a more attractive product, price, and promotional mix.

REVAMPING THE ORGANIZATIONAL STRUCTURE

Summer 1988 was a time of drastic change for Sears' management. Eight thousand of these employees were moved from the Sears Tower to less auspicious offices, an early retirement program was introduced, and random job shifts were implemented. Merchandise buyers also felt the winds of change. Once noted for its large, extremely specialized buying organization, Sears began streamlining the department in order to heighten its efficiency. Stores concentrated solely on inventory management of the specific merchandise category and became directly accountable for the performance of the merchandise in their charge.

EXPANDING THE MERCHANDISE OFFERING

Recognizing the need to provide consumers with more diverse product offerings, Sears introduced a new strategy aimed at using name brand merchandise to attract customers and boost sales. The plan involved increasing Sears' national brand percentage from 15 percent to 40 percent. It was hoped that the retailer would be able to turn itself into a "Store of Superstores" featuring name brand items and a more exciting atmosphere. Sears' premiere national brand effort was in the creation of Brand Central, an appliance and home electronics store-within-a-store that features over 60 national brands, plus Sears' own private labels. The size of these "power format" departments ranges from 10,000 to 14,000 square feet, depending on the potential of the local market.

Brand Central features such brand names as General Electric, Magnavox, JennAir, and Sony, in addition to a mix of the retailer's own labels—Sears and Kenmore. A careful analysis of each product segment was done in order to decide where to add national brands and where to continue to rely on private labels. Several name brand additions were needed in the home electronics segment, traditionally a weak spot for Sears.

Similar concepts to the Brand Central format were tested for many of the retailer's product groups including automotive goods, hardware, lawn and garden products, home fashions, and especially men's and women's apparel—an area in which Sears acutely felt the competitive crunch of discounters and specialty goods retailers.

For years, the focus of Sears' apparel strategy involved private-label, strictly middle-market goods. Clothing lines endorsed by persons well past the height of their celebrity were filled with dated, unexciting apparel. Sears was unable to improve its fashion image because of a lack of support from big name manufacturers, and conversely, was unable to attract national labels due to its poor fashion image. Status and style have become the keys to profitability in the mass market clothing business. Having failed to capitalize on these new requisites for success in apparel merchandising, Sears lagged well behind its rivals in providing consumers with contemporary apparel. Sales of commodity items, such as robes, pantyhose, and underwear—long one of Sears' merchandise strengths, were being captured in increasingly large quantities by downscale discounters.

In an effort to regain consumer interest, Sears rolled out several new apparel concepts such as the Mainframe juniors' department and its joint venture with McDonald's, McKids children's clothing. Throughout all apparel departments, the move was to a more fashion-oriented look including more stylish clothing and more natural fibers, supported by trendier displays and fixtures.

PRICING

An October 31, 1988, announcement by Sears' management marked the beginning of the retail giant's most radical attempt to regain price parity with the discounters and specialty stores that were luring away large numbers of Sears' core customer base. The plan involved "everyday low prices" and the elimination of the retailers' frequent barrage of sales promotions. Sears had relied on a strategy of running merchandise at relatively high regular prices, then periodically reducing prices to a "sale" level on as many as 9,000 items per month. Out-of-step with industry trends, these expensive tactics were hurting the company in terms of high operating costs and a loss of market share.

Implementation of everyday low pricing was projected to save nearly $200 million of the costs associated with a frequent sales promotion strategy. These savings were to be realized from reduced headquarters management, a reduction in sales floor time needed to plan, mark, and remark sale items, lower distribution expenses, and elimination of inventory duplication. The new pricing program would require fewer models at varying prices than were required by Sears' previous policy. Inventory costs would be lessened as the number of items in many lines of merchandise would be reduced.

ADVERTISING

Both Brand Central and everyday low pricing were promoted by Sears in an uncharacteristically aggressive way. The original television spot for Brand Central marked the first departure from Sears' longstanding practice of avoiding comparison advertising. The company decided to launch a strong attack on the competition in its attempt to boost revenues by shedding is bland, private-label image. The multimillion dollar campaign promoting the retailer's new pricing policy included a barrage of both newspaper and television ads. As part of this media campaign, Sears boldly promised to meet or beat competitor's advertised prices on identical items. Advertisements heralded the new policy as Sears' biggest change in its more than one hundred years of retailing. Consumers were promised that every time they shopped a Sears store, the atmosphere would be one of a never-ending sale.

CURRENT SITUATION

Sears entered the 1990s with little evidence of radical improvement in performance. Several problems arose from the national brand strategy and everyday low pricing. The cost burden brought about by changes in brand strategy made it very difficult for Sears to match competitors' prices on identical and similar merchandise. The array of brands now being carried was much more difficult to buy, distribute, and manage than Sears' traditional dedicated lines. Even more troublesome was the unimpressive response to everyday low pricing. Initially, the program realized an increase in patronage due to consumers' eagerness to see what changes had been made. However, a consistent increase in sales did not materialize. Instead, Sears reverted to advertisements which closely resembled "sale" ads. These sale-like promotions have created concern among industry experts that rather than attracting more customers, Sears was instead confusing them. Sears maintained that its intention was never to eliminate all sales, only to eliminate constant weekly advertised specials. They fully intended to continue running sales for traditional reasons such as season-end clearances or one-time deals with suppliers. Sears also stated that it would occasionally adjust prices on well-recognized items in order to be competitive.

While Sears' circulars no longer made use of the word "sale," items were still being advertised with such statements as "prices good through . . . ," "reduced prices until . . . ," and "good for one week only." These types of phrases led to accusations that Sears was merely playing word games with the American public. The extensive advertising of the new pricing policy made it very difficult to explain the softening of the retailers' position. Sears' advertising had only mentioned once that stores would continue to offer special buys; rather, it advised customers to think of shopping at Sears as going to a sale that never ends.

Sears remains in a precarious position; the new strategies aimed at revitalizing the chain for the 1990s had not met with resounding success. Instead, sales were still declining and the retailer's everyday low pricing policy was generating both legal and ethical questions. Unfortunately, these new policies were not the survival strategies they had been heralded to be.

ASSIGNMENT

1. Has Sears effectively identified a target market? If so, who are they? If not, who should they be?
2. What are the pros and cons of Sears' strategies for combatting competition from specialty stores and discount retailers?
3. Discuss the pros and cons of national brand and private label brand strategies.
4. What are the legal and ethical ramifications of Sears' everyday low pricing strategy?
5. Recommend ways in which the advertising for everyday low pricing could be improved.

*This case was prepared by Amy Morgan and Dale Lewison, The University of Akron.

Sources: Murray Forseter, "Master Plan to Revitalize Sears Still Under Scrutiny," *Chain Store Age Executive;* July 1989, 38 and 40; Jay L. Johnson, "Sears Succumbs to National Brands," *Discount Merchandiser,* November 1988, 44 and 46; Michael Oneal, "Sears Faces a Tall Task," *Business Week,* November 14, 1988, 54–55; Michael Oneal, "Shaking Sears Right Down to its Work Boots," *Business Week,* October 17, 1988, 84 and 87; Francine Schwadel, "What Looks Like a Sale, but Isn't a Sale?" *The Wall Street Journal,* April 26, 1989, B–1; and Patricia Sellers, "Why Bigger is Badder at Sears," *Fortune,* December 5, 1988, 79–80.

ENDNOTES

1. Joseph B. Siegel, "Retailing: Back to Fundamentals," *Retail Control,* February 1990, 24.
2. Jeffrey J. Hallett, "Retailing in the 1990's: Love Your Customer or Lose Them," *Retail Control,* February 1990, 8.
3. "Strategies for the New Century," *Chain Store Age Executive,* January 1990, 27.
4. Jeffrey J. Hallett, "Retailing in the 1990's: Love Your Customer or Lose Them," *Retail Control,* February 1990, 10.
5. Anne B. Fisher, "What Consumers Want in the 1990's," *Fortune,* January 29, 1990, 108.
6. See John P. Robinson, "The Time Squeeze," *American Demographics,* February 1990, 30, 32–33.
7. "31 Major Trends Shaping the Future of American Business," *The Public Pulse* (New York: The Roper Organization Inc., 1988), 1.
8. Jeffrey J. Hallett, "Retailing in the 1990's: Love Your Customer or Lose Them," ibid.

9. Eleanor G. May, "A Retail Odyssey," *Journal of Retailing,* 65, Fall 1989, 365.
10. Penelope Wang, "What's Hot," *Money,* March 1990, 114.
11. Mark K. Solheim, Melynda Dovel Wilcox, and Sarah Young, "A Cleaner Environment—What to Buy," *Changing Times,* February 1990, 29.
12. Elizabeth Ehrlich, John Hoerr, Michael J. Mandel, David Castellon, Antonio N. Fins, and Todd Mason, "How the Next Decade Will Differ," *Business Week,* September 25, 1989, 156.
13. See Mark K. Solheim et al., ibid.
14. David Kirkpatrick, *"Environmentalism," Fortune,* February 12, 1990, 44.
15. "Leading The Crusade Into Consumer Marketing," *Fortune,* February 12, 1990, 50.
16. Francine Schwadel, "Retailers Latch on to the Environment," *The Wall Street Journal,* November 13, 1989. B1.
17. Randolph B. Smith, "Rush to Endorse 'Environmental' Goods Sparks Worry about Shopper Confusion," *The Wall Street Journal,* April 16, 1990, B1.
18. "Leading the Crusade into Consumer Marketing," ibid.
19. See Nina Gruen, "The Retail Battleground, Solutions for Today's Shifting Marketplace," *Journal of Property Management,* 54, July/August 1989, 14–17.
20. Ibid.
21. Valerie Free, "The Homing of America," *Marketing Insights,* April 1990, 16.
22. Ibid., 20.
23. Fisher, "What Consumers Want in the 1990's," 112.
24. Faye Rice, "Yuppie Spending Gets Serious," *Fortune,* March 27, 1989, 148.
25. Elizabeth Ehrlich et al., "How the Next Decade Will Differ," 142.
26. This discussion is taken from Ken Dychtwald and Greg Gable, "Portrait of a Changing Consumer," *Business Horizon,* January/February 1990, 62–73.
27. Molly O'Neill, "In The Land of Non," *Akron Beacon Journal,* June 3, 1990, E1.
28. Anne B. Fisher, "What Consumers Want in the 1990s," *Fortune,* January 29, 1990, 110.
29. Ibid., "31 Major Trends Shaping the Future of American Business," 3.
30. Ibid.
31. Aaron Bernstein, "America's Income Gap: The Closer You Look, The Worse It Gets," *Business Week,* April 17, 1989, 78.
32. Karen Pennar, "The Free Market Has Triumphed, But What about the Losers?" *Business Week,* September 25, 1989, 178.
33. Ibid., 179.
34. Joe Mandese, "Who Are the Targets?" *Marketing & Media Decisions,* July 1989, 31.
35. Ibid., "31 Major Trends Shaping the Future of American Business," 3.
36. Kathleen Deveny, "Downscale Consumers, Long Neglected Start to Get Some Respect From Marketers," *The Wall Street Journal,* May 31, 1990, B1.
37. Waleaa Konrad and Gail DeGeorge, "U.S. Companies Go for the Gray," *Business Week,* April 3, 1989, 64.
38. Stephani Cook, "Riding the Silver Streak," *Retailing Issues Letter* (Published by Arthur Andersen & Co. in conjunction with the Center for Retailing Studies, Texas A&M University, September 1989), 2.
39. Muriel J. Adams, "Kids' Specialty Retailing," *Stores,* March 1990, 18.
40. Peter Newcomb, "Hey, Dude, Let's Consume," *Forbes,* June 11, 1990, 126.
41. Peter Newcomb, ibid., 128.
42. Ibid.
43. Muriel J. Adams, "The Children's Place," *Stores,* March 1990, 10.
44. Lynn G. Coleman, "Right Now, Kids Are Very Hot," *Marketing News,* June 25, 1990, 1.
45. "Strategies for the New Century," *Chain Store Age Executive* (January 1990), 28.
46. Jackie Bivins, "Corporate Cultures," *Stores,* February 1989, 12.
47. Thomas R. Rauh, "Strategies for the 1990s," *Discount Merchandiser,* July 1989, 54.
48. Walter K. Levy, "The End of an Era: A Time for Retail Perestroika," *Journal of Retailing* 65, Fall 1989, 397.
49. Knut Rostad, "Kotler: Take Advantage of 'Superabundant' 90s," *Marketing News,* May 14, 1990, 5.
50. Stanley M. Davis, "From 'Future Perfect': Mass Customizing," *Planning Review,* March/April 1989, 18.
51. Ibid.
52. Ibid., 19.
53. Frederick W. Langrehr, "10 Trends in Retailing," *Exchange,* Fall 1988, 12.
54. Judith Graham, "A Crash Course in Surviving '90s," *Advertising Age,* April 24, 1990, S-1.
55. R. Fulton Macdonald, "Capitalizing on the Coming Revolution," *Retail Control,* January 1990, 26.
56. See Walter J. Salmon, "Retailing in the Age of Execution," *Journal of Retailing* 65, Fall 1989, 368–378.
57. See Steve Weinstein, "Are Bigger Stores Better," *Progressive Grocer,* May 1990, 141–146.
58. Kevin Kelly and Amy Dunkin, "Wal-Mart Gets Lost in the Vegetable Aisle," *Business Week,* May 28, 1990, 48.
59. Penney Gill, "Know Your Customer," *Stores,* November 1989, 31.
60. Nina Gruen, "The Retail Battleground: Solutions for Today's Shifting Marketplace," *Journal of Property Management,* July/August 1989, 14.
61. John Byington, "Retailing in the Nineties," *Discount Merchandiser,* May 1990, 20.
62. Nina Gruen, "The Retail Battleground: Solutions for Today's Shifting Marketplace," ibid.
63. Howard Schlossberg, "Retailing in the '90s: How It

Got Here from There," *Marketing News*, June 25, 1990, 14.
64. Robert F. Lusch, "Retail Control Systems for the 1990's," *Retailing Issues Letter* (Published by Arthur Andersen & Co. in conjunction with the Center for Retailing Studies, Texas A&M University, January 1990), 1.
65. Ronald Savitt, "Looking Back to See Ahead: Writing the History of American Retailing," *Journal of Retailing* 65, Fall 1989, 337.
66. Albert D. Bates, "The Extended Specialty Store: A Strategic Opportunity for the 1990s," *Journal of Retailing* 65, Fall 1989, 383.
67. Ibid.

PART VI

SERVICE RETAILERS

Exploring Growth Opportunities

CHAPTER 20

OUTLINE

THE NATURE OF SERVICE RETAILING

THE IMPORTANCE OF SERVICES

THE TYPES OF SERVICE RETAILERS

- Services Offered
- Operating Characteristics

THE RIGHT SERVICE BLEND

- Offering the Right Service: Add Tangibility
- In the Right Way: Control Variability
- In the Right Place: Bridge Inseparability
- At the Right Time: Overcome Perishability
- At the Right Price: Enhance Profitability
- By the Right Appeal: Increase Communicability

THE RIGHT SERVICE STRATEGY

OBJECTIVES

- Identify the unique characteristics that distinguish service retailers from goods retailers.
- Describe the importance of service retailers in our nation's economy.
- Discern and discuss the various types of service retailers and their operations.
- Explain the factors involved in offering the right service in the right way in the right place at the right time at the right price by the right appeal.
- Use the strategic service vision to integrate both the service retailers' external (customer) and internal (employee) functions.

THE EMERGING SERVICE ECONOMY

That prophet of capitalism, Adam Smith, had little use for what we call the service economy. He dismissed the labors of tutors, shopkeepers, and household servants as backward or worse. A visionary in other ways, Smith could not foresee that service enterprises ultimately would become high-powered global competitors, every bit as cosmopolitan and as technologically advanced as manufacturers.[1]

Services are the growth sector of a modern society. They are larger, more powerful, and above all more important than they once were. Today, more than three out of five workers are employed in such service industries as banking, insurance, retailing, airlines, hotels, and health care.[2]

The service sector of U.S. business displays bold paradoxes. It is the engine powering growth in the economy, yet ofttimes it is a wheezer in delivering profits. It is a world of ferocious rivalry in which competitive advantages can disappear overnight. But it is also a world in which innovative and flexible companies can outshine the field for years.[3]

The retailing of services involves most of the same problems and decisions associated with the retailing of goods. Many of the merchandising and operating strategies and tactics discussed in the previous 19 chapters therefore are equally applicable to service retailers, with appropriate modifications. This chapter describes the nature and types of service retailing, identifies its distinguishing characteristics, and discusses the issues surrounding the development of appropriate service blends and the integration of marketing and operating strategies.

THE NATURE OF SERVICE RETAILING

What is a **service**? The definition of service is rather illusive because of the concept's multifaceted nature. Depending on the environmental and temporal context, a service could be many different activities to different people at different times. There is no standard or commonly accepted definition of service within the context of business or retailing operations. Nevertheless, Figure 20–1 attempts to illustrate the multifaceted nature and complex, interactive character of retail services. As shown, a retail service can be any of the following:

- An intangible process that is provided to inform a client (e.g., a lawyer's advice on what and what not to say in court)
- A variable performance that is orchestrated to entertain a patron or fan (e.g., a concert by The Boss, Bruce Springsteen)
- An inseparable procedure that is provided to benefit a patient (e.g., a cardiovascular surgeon who performs open-heart surgery)
- A perishable event that is created to amuse a customer (e.g., a water slide at an amusement park)
- A profitable task that is developed to satisfy a traveler (e.g., a slot machine in the lobby of a hotel)
- A communicable act that is produced to educate a student (e.g., an interesting lecture by your professor)
- A host of any other combination of elements and examples that you might think of

It is obvious, then, that retail services can be defined and characterized along many different dimensions.

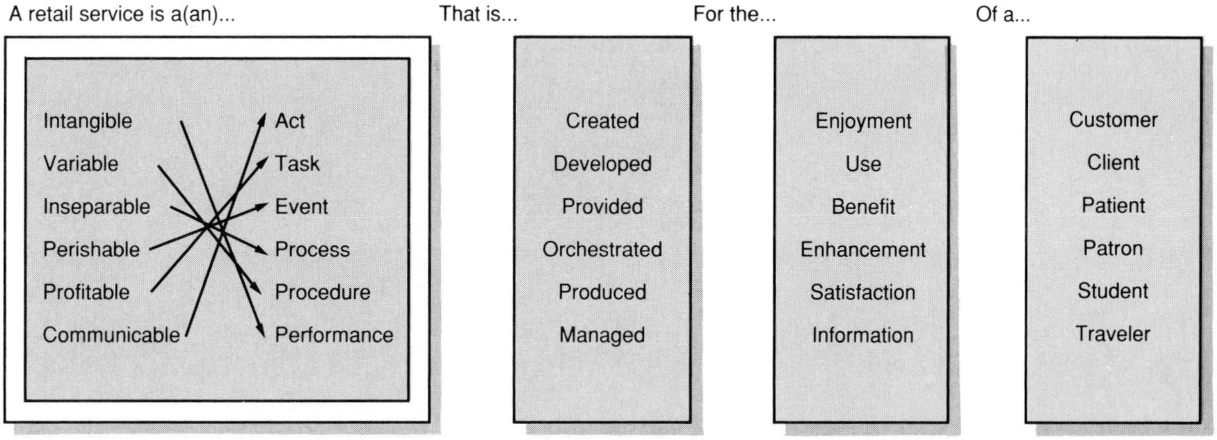

FIGURE 20–1
What is a service?

Who provides services? Individuals, groups, and organizations are all service providers. Although we tend to think of services as face-to-face interactions between individuals (e.g., doctor–patient, consultant–client, student–tutor), some services are essentially the collective efforts of a group (e.g., jazz quartet, car wash attendants, basketball team) or an organization (hospital, museum, employment agency). The customer's particular situation and need determines whether an individual or collective effort is required to develop the service package.

How do *service retailers* differ from *goods retailers?* Goods retailers emphasize physical objects; service retailers emphasize people, ideas, and information instead of things.[4] There is no clear distinction between goods and service retailers; rather, "it is generally accepted that there is a continuous spectrum running from a pure good to a pure service. Many goods companies are building service-related benefits into their projects, and many service companies deliver goods as part of the bundle of benefits they provide to consumers."[5] Figure 20–2 illustrates the goods–services continuum for the ultimate consumer.

On the **pure goods** end of the continuum are retailers who provide no services whatsoever. One example might be the roadside vegetable stand that doesn't even provide a formal parking area; another example is the farmer's market that requires customers to bring their own containers and harvest their own products. As a point of fact, even retailers who emphasize goods retailing usually provide essential services necessary to the successful operation of business (e.g., parking, bagging, and store hours).

At the other end of the continuum are **primary-service retailers,** which concentrate on rendering a service; the core of the business is a service. Like goods retailers, primary-service retailers often supplement their core-service offering with both complementary services and goods (e.g., a psychiatrist who provides medication for the patient and bills the patient at the end of the month).

At the midpoint of the continuum (see Figure 20–2) are retail businesses that have an equal or near-equal emphasis on goods and services. A special dining occasion is special because of the quality and presentation of the food, the attentiveness and courtesy of the waiter, and the atmospherics and comfort of the room and table. When an individual patronizes a fast-food restaurant like McDonald's, is it for good food or fast

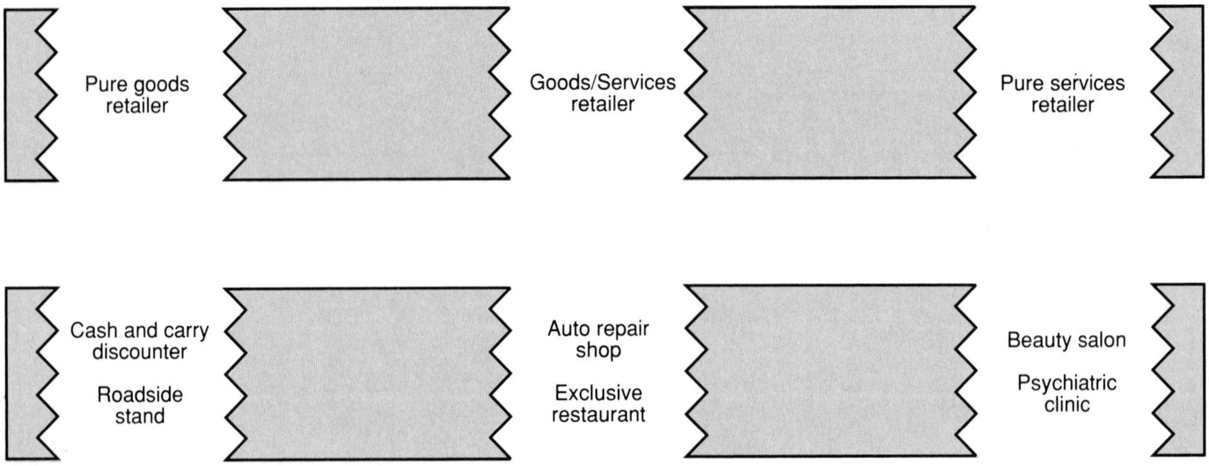

FIGURE 20–2
The goods–service continuum for ultimate consumers

service? It depends on the circumstances—with or without children, seeking a quick lunch or a leisure dinner.

THE IMPORTANCE OF SERVICES

How important are services? In many respects, services represent the most important part of our nation's economy. "Service is no longer an industrial by-product, a sector that generates no wealth but 'simply moves money around' as some economists have scoffed. Service has become a powerful economic engine in its own right—the fast track of the new American economy."[6] More than 60 million Americans are employed in one of the many service sectors; by 1995, total service sector employment will be 75 million. Nine out of 10 jobs created between now and 1995 are expected to be in services.[7] When one considers that the combined total output of all the various service sectors accounts for nearly 70 percent of the gross national product, the importance of services becomes quite obvious.[8] The United States has become the first nation to have a predominantly service-oriented economy, and there is every reason to believe the boom in the service economy will continue. Supporting this conclusion are such demographic trends as dual-income families, an aging population, and a more educated population.[9]

THE TYPES OF SERVICE RETAILERS

The complex, multifaceted nature of services allows an equally complex, multifaceted classification system. Like goods retailers, service retailers can be classified according to the character of the service, its organizational structure and operating characteristics, the type of channel relationships and the level of integration, the firm's size and ownership arrangements, and the type and degree of customer contact. By whatever criterion we group and identify service retailers, a mutually exclusive classification system is impossible. For our purposes, this chapter examines two of the more common schemes based on the character of the service offered and the operating characteristics.

Services Offered

The U.S. Department of Commerce, through the Bureau of Census, classifies services-oriented activities into four major categories: (1) transportation, communication, and public utilities; (2) finance, insurance, and real estate; (3) public administration; and (4) services. The first three categories are self-explanatory, but the services category requires further explanation; it is broken down as follows:

- *Lodging places*—hotels, motels, rooming and boarding houses, sporting and recreational camps, trailer parks and camp sites
- *Personal services*—laundry and dry cleaners, linen and diaper service, carpet and upholstery cleaning, photographic studios, beauty and barber shops, shoe repair, funeral homes and crematoriums, reducing salons and health clubs, tax services, and other personal services
- *Business services*—advertising, credit reporting and collections, blueprinting and photocopying, commercial photography, art and graphics, cleaning and maintenance services, employment agencies, computer, data processing, research and development, management and administrative, public relations, security services, equipment rental or leasing, testing laboratories, and other business services
- *Automotive services*—car, truck, trailer and recreational vehicle rentals, auto and truck repairs, parking facilities, car washes
- *Repair services*—radio, TV, appliances, and furniture repair, farm machinery, lawn and garden equipment, and watch, clock, and jewelry repair
- *Motion pictures*—motion picture production and distribution
- *Amusement and recreation services*—dance group halls and studios, live theaters, radio and TV production, symphony orchestras, opera companies, music organiza-

tions and presentations, sporting establishments and clubs, golf courses and amusement parks, carnivals and circuses, museums and art galleries, and other entertainment and attractions

- *Health services*—offices of health professionals, medical and dental labs, and outpatient care facilities
- *Legal services*—offices of lawyers and other legal aid services
- *Educational services*—libraries, business and vocational schools, schools, and other educational services
- *Social services*—job training and rehabilitation, child day-care, residential care, and individual and family social services
- *Noncommercial institutions*—noncommercial museums, art galleries, and botanical and zoological gardens
- *Membership organizations*—business, professional, civic, social, and fraternal organizations
- *Miscellaneous services*—architectural, engineering, surveying, accounting, auditing, scientific, and research organizations

For a more detailed description and classification of the service categories, check the most recent *Census of Service Industries* in your local school library.

Operating Characteristics

Service retailers can be classified on their degree of reliance on equipment in performing the service and on the level of skill required by the service provider.[10] As seen in Figure 20–3, *equipment-based service retailers* rely heavily on equipment, and skill levels range from a totally automated service provider (e.g., automatic teller machines) to highly skilled airline pilots. *People-based service retailers* are highly

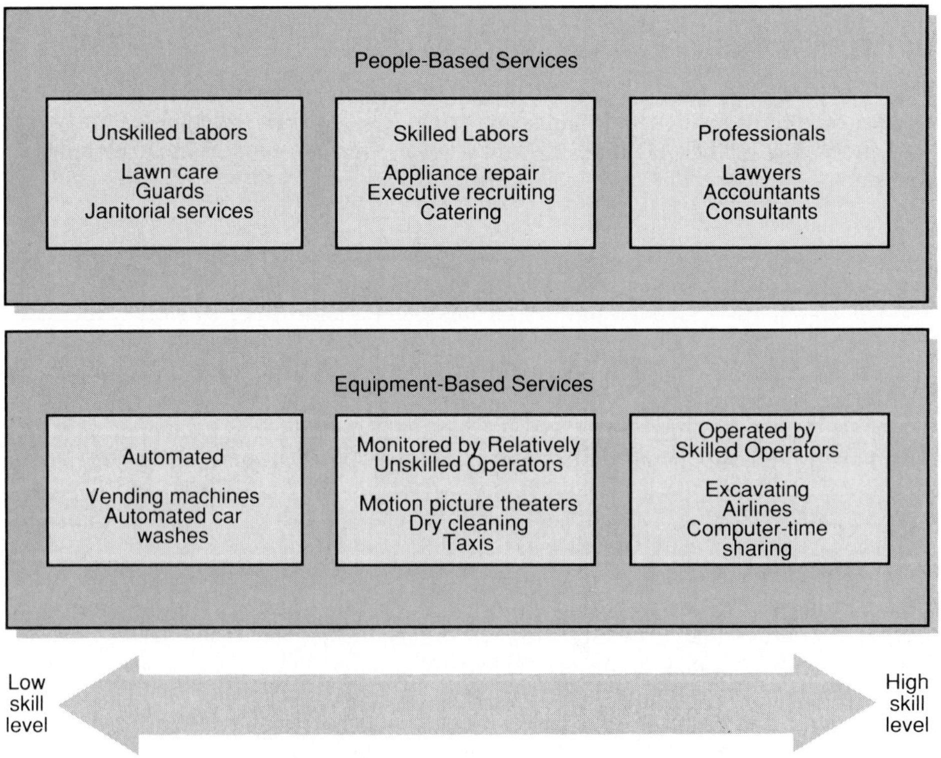

FIGURE 20–3 Classifying service retailers: Based on operating characteristics (Reprinted by permission of *Harvard Business Review.* An exhibit from "Strategy Is Different in Service Businesses" by Dan R. E. Thomas, July/August 1978. Copyright © 1978 by the President and Fellows of Harvard College; all rights reserved.)

dependent on an individual to perform the service; that individual may be an unskilled provider (e.g., janitor) or a highly skilled professional (e.g., surgeon).

THE RIGHT SERVICE BLEND

Understanding the unique characteristics inherent in services is a prerequisite to developing successful marketing plans. As is the case with goods and the right merchandising blend (see Chapter 1), service retailers must develop a service blend that is right for their customers. Figure 20–4 identifies the six ingredients of the **right service** blend and the major goal of each ingredient. This discussion reviews the major issues facing the service retailer and includes examples of unique and successful applications within the service industry.

Offering the Right Service: Add Tangibility

If you can see, hear, smell, touch, and taste what you have purchased, it is more good than service; if you cannot see, hear, smell, touch, and taste your purchase, it is more a service than a good. "It is whether the essence of what is being bought is tangible or intangible that determines its classification as a good or a service."[11] Physical features (size, shape, workmanship, etc.) determine to a considerable extent how well a good will function; one can evaluate these features before making a purchase. A service is not distinguished by physical features; hence, consumers have a difficult time judging the service before making the purchase, and in many cases, they have little or no tangible evidence to take away with them to show they have made a purchase or gained something of ongoing utility. Memories from a concert, ideas from a lecture, impressions from a funeral, and excitement from a game are not tangible. Thus a major marketing problem for every service retailer is to add a greater degree of **tangibility** to the firm's services.

At the center of every demand for a service is the core benefit or benefits sought by the consumer. In the financial investments industry, for example, the investor at any one time might be looking for investment security, opportunity, direction, convenience, or special treatment (see Figure 20–5). Whatever the benefit sought, the service provider must find some way to "tangibilize" the offer—to help the customer visualize and mentally grasp the core service concept. The service offering can be made tangible by (1) providing representations of the service, (2) creating physical and mental symbols for the service, (3) developing name or brand recognition for businesses or service lines, and (4) adding extra peripheral services or supplementary goods.

A *visual representation* of the service and its positive attributes (benefits) can notably enhance the tangibility of the service offer. An architect who provides a scale model of the proposed building or facility has created a tangible substitution for design

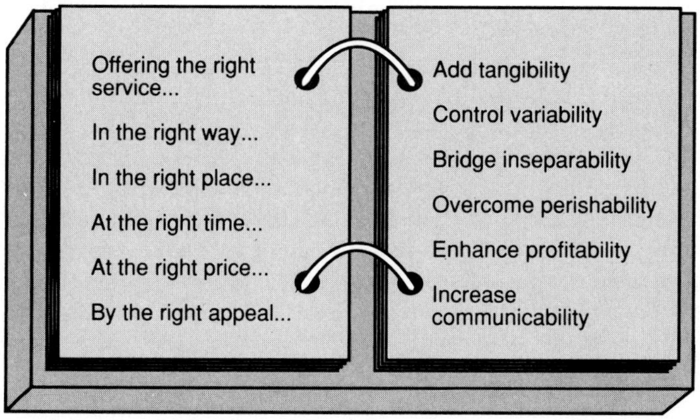

FIGURE 20–4
The right service blend —ingredients and goals

FIGURE 20–5
The core service benefit

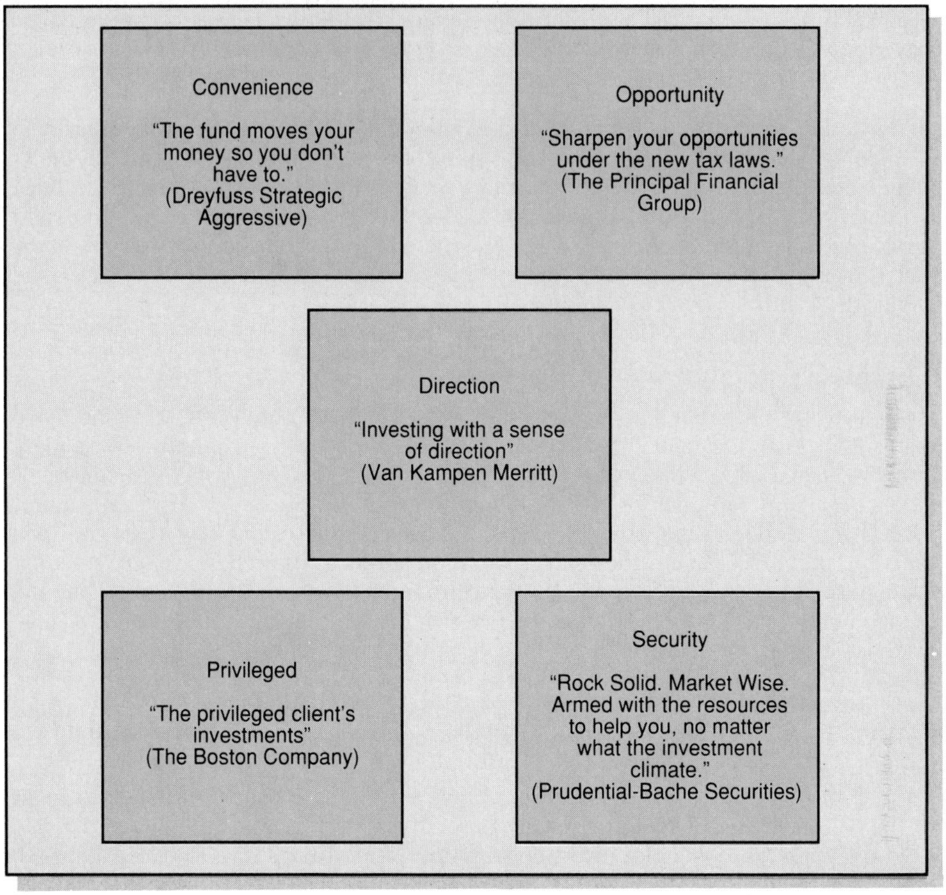

ideas and concepts that might not otherwise be appreciated or understood. When that same architect provides a complete set of architectural plans and specifications, the consumer has available sufficient information to make a good judgment and correct decisions before, during, and after the purchase. Examples of visual concept representations are (1) an information systems analyst's schematic drawing of a proposed information flow, (2) a management consultant's organization chart demonstrating the reporting relationships (line and staff) within an organization, (3) an interior design specialist's sketches illustrating a room layout, and (4) a professor's diagram (handout) portraying a concept or idea. These examples not only are visual, but they also provide the customer with something to hold.

Symbols, both *physical* and *mental,* can be used to show the tangibility of a service and its benefits.[12] A classic example of physical symbolization is the "plastic credit card"; it represents credit (i.e., money and purchasing power) and a whole lot more (*status*—plain, silver, gold cards; *convenience*—cash, check, charge cards; and *security*—limited liability and cashless crime target). Mental symbols can be equally effective in creating service-offering tangibility. "Hands (Allstate), rocks (Prudential), umbrellas (Traveler's), and blankets (Nationwide) are used to more effectively communicate what insurance can provide people; they are devices used to make the service more easily grasped mentally."[13] The American eagle, the Christian cross, and the scales of justice are three examples of symbols that may be associated with both physical and mental imagery. Oasis Laundries of San Jose, California, runs billboard ads

Service Retailing...

operating an intangible, variable, inseparable, and perishable business.

C U N A R D
AT PLAY WITH CUNARD, CIRCA 1903
For more information on Cunard sailings to Europe, The Caribbean, Alaska, The Orient, South Pacific, and around the world call your travel agent. Or, for a free brochure or $8.95 videotape depicting life aboard one of our top-rated ships, call 1-800-221-8200.
CUNARD
SINCE 1840
CUNARD
AT PLAY WITH CUNARD, 1990
Registries: QE2-Great Britain, Sagafjord, Vistafjord-Bahamas, Sea Goddess I & II-Norway © 1990 Cunard
WE'RE NOT THE BEST BECAUSE WE'RE THE OLDEST. WE'RE THE OLDEST BECAUSE WE'RE THE BEST.
QUEEN ELIZABETH 2 • SAGAFJORD • VISTAFJORD • SEA GODDESS I • SEA GODDESS II

Retail services lack tangibility—you have a hard time seeing, hearing, smelling, touching, and tasting them. Service retailers can add a sense of tangibility by providing representations of the service, by creating physical and mental symbols for the service, by developing name or brand recognition for the service, and by adding supplementary goods that support the service concept.

Retail services are highly variable due to the people-oriented nature of the service offering. To consistently provide customers with top quality services, the service retailers must first ensure employee satisfaction through a high level of motivation and a constructive training program.

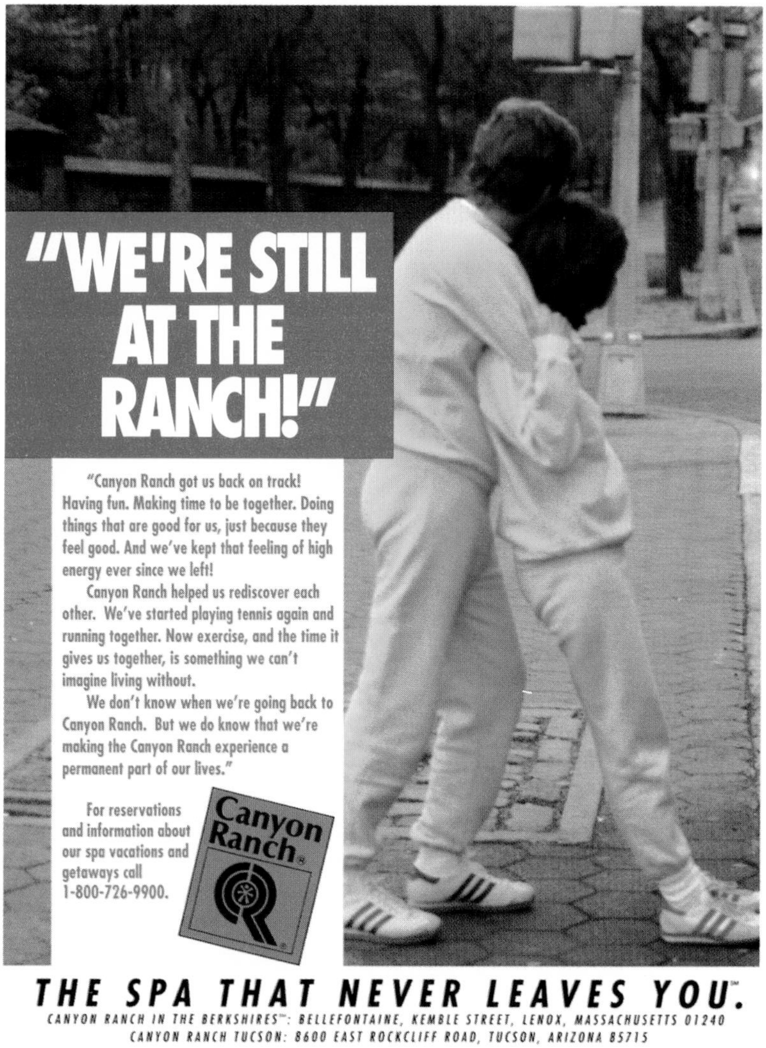

Retail services typically involve simultaneous production and consumption of a service; the service provider is inseparable from the service consumer. The inseparability of the exchange process within the service industry requires that service delivery systems be developed carefully.

Services are perishable in that they often cannot be stored and carried as inventory. Because service demand and service supply do not often match up, service retailers must find ways to synchronize the demand for services with the supply of services.

showing a hospital operating room with the headline "It's almost as clean as our Laundromats."[14] Duds 'n Suds, another chain of laundromats, uses the slogan "Good Clean Fun" to symbolize its efficiently run homelike laundromats that provide entertainment and other amenities to its clientele.[15]

Service identification and differentiation often depend on linking a specific image or concept with a specific brand name. Adding tangibility through *name association* is the focus of this tactic. Names can be associated with service type, quality, convenience, cost (price), status, and a host of other identities. Consider the associations with these service names and brands: child care (Kinder-Care and LaPetite Academy), auto care (Jiffy Lube and Grease Monkey), home care (Molly Maid and Tailor-Maid), health care (MetLife and Kaiser-Permanente), emergency health care (Rapid Response and Med Center), car rental (Budget and Nationwide), automatic teller machines (Green Machine and Money Station), air travel (American Airlines and Trans World Airlines), freight transportation (Overnite and Roadway)—the potential list of service branding examples is almost endless. A variation of the service branding strategy is to offer new services in association with a well-known name. Sears, for example, has created a financial services conglomerate in association with its retail operations. Sears has also branched into insurance (Allstate), real estate (Coldwell Banker), stock brokerage (Dean Witter Reynolds), and a credit card (Discover). Bank One, a large financial institution in Ohio, is experimenting with a financial services superstore that includes full-range banking, insurance, real estate, and brokerage services.

A more tangible service can be created through *service-line extensions*—adding extra peripheral services or supplementary goods. SAS advertises itself as "the business airline" with a focus on transcontinental flights to Europe. In an advertisement in *Business Week,* SAS has made tangible its basic service, air transportation, using both extra services and goods. The ad copy reads as follows:

> SAS EuroClass. It's the intercontinental business class with a style all its own. In the interest of everyone's comfort, we've removed a whole row of seats. Our cabins are smaller and more intimate, but you get more space, more legroom and seats that recline 33% further. And, for the first time, you get a choice. You can either enjoy the best traditional service—with a leisurely meal, a movie and plenty of attention. Or you can opt for a new way of flying in our secluded sleep/work class cabin. By night, it's almost like home. After we've served you a quick meal, we'll bed you down with proper sheets. Home comforts, indeed. We do everything short of singing you a lullaby. (That might disturb the peace.) There's no smoking in this cabin. And no movie. We won't even bother you with breakfast unless you ask for it. By day, the cabin is an "office in the sky." We'll give you what you need to do some work—everything from overhead film to typewriters. We'll even give you peace and quiet. If you need something we'll be there. Otherwise, we won't bother you. We believe that this kind of choice is the future of long-distance flying. So why not enjoy tomorrow's way of flying today? And tonight, too, for that matter.

In the Right Way: Control Variability

Services tend to be people-oriented activities on both the production and consumption sides of the service-exchange process. As a result of the people-intensive nature of this process, service providers have considerable latitude in deciding and providing various service levels; services can range from totally standardized to totally customized activities. For example, a college course in business administration can range from the totally customized independent study to the highly standardized mass classroom lecture (see Figure 20–6). Whatever level of service is selected, the service retailer must offer service in the **right way**—it must control the process to ensure that the level of service matches the value of the service. Which is most valuable as an educational experience: a mass lecture, a seminar, or an independent course? What does each course cost the

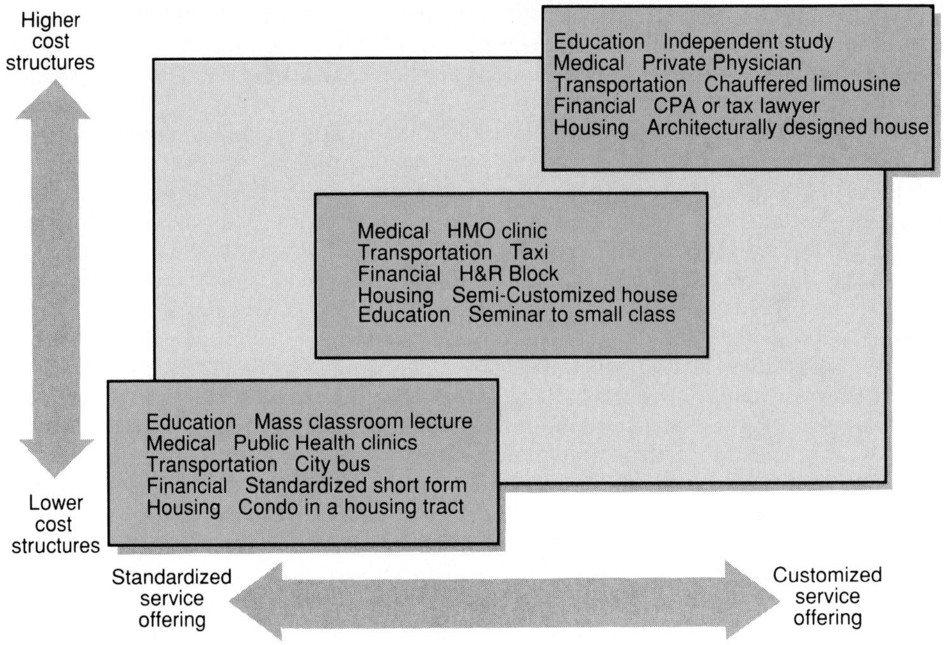

FIGURE 20–6 Customer service levels and cost structures

student? Does the service level equal the value level? In these cases, controlling **variability** means finding a match between customer service levels and customer cost structures.

The quality and consistency of services can also vary considerably because of the various skill levels and degrees of automation employed in the production and delivery of a service. Adding to the degree of variability are the personal attributes and attitudes of the service provider and how these are conducted in providing service (e.g., the doctor's bedside manner, the courtesy of the hotel bell captain, or the efficiency of the bank teller). Controlling service variability in this case requires that management ensure customer satisfaction by first ensuring employee satisfaction through high motivation and constructive training. Good personnel management is critical to successful retail service operations. (This issue is elaborated on in the last section of this chapter.)

In the Right Place: Bridge Inseparability

Inseparability is the typical exchange mode in the service industry; that is, under typical conditions a service is produced and consumed simultaneously (e.g., a lecture by a professor, a cleaning by a dental hygienist, and an actress's live performance)—the right place is anywhere the provider and consumer are together. Day-care services tend to be local mom-and-pop businesses. The reason is that parents value a provider's personal involvement with their child.[16] Simultaneous production and consumption means that the service provider is often physically present when consumption occurs.[17] In cases where service production and consumption can be separated, intermediaries (service agents) can facilitate the exchange process. Depending on the degree of inseparability of production and consumption, service retailers can use either a direct- or indirect-channel delivery system. Service-delivery system options are shown in Figure 20–7.

The *direct-channel delivery system* is a one-on-one relationship between service producer and service consumer. It is used when the service cannot be separated from

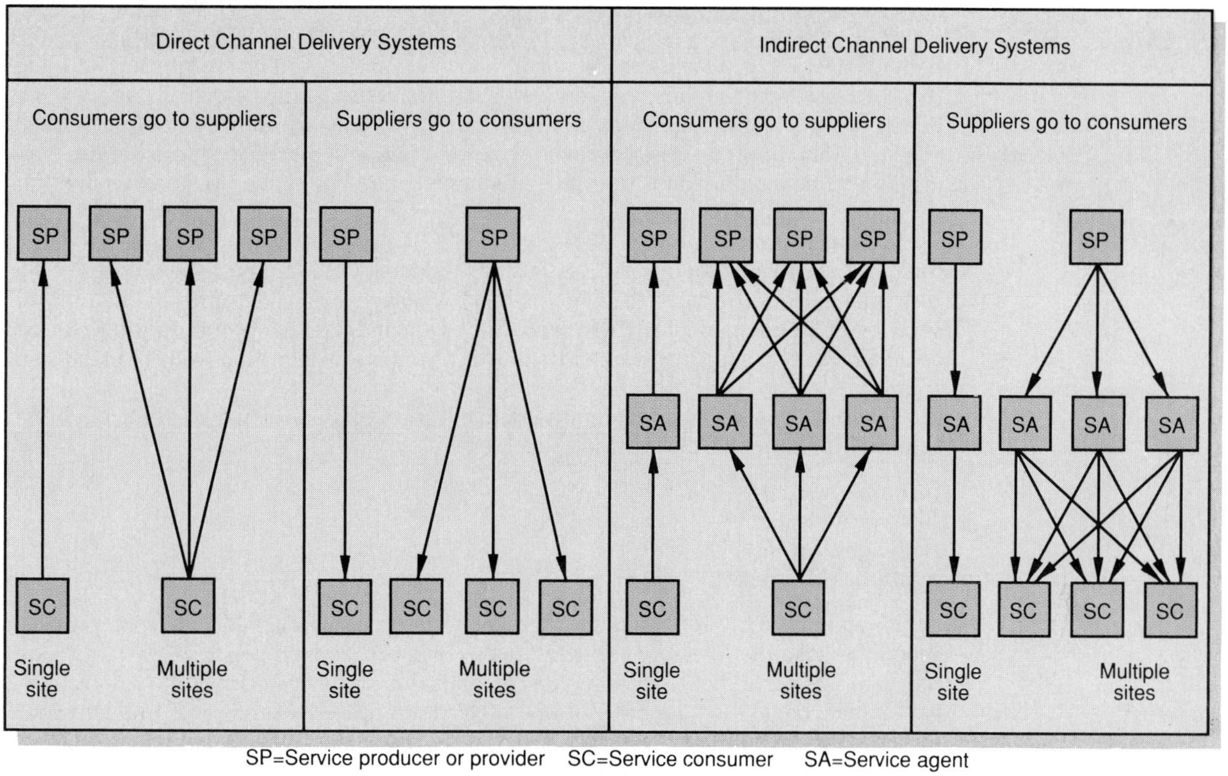

FIGURE 20–7
Types of service delivery systems

the producer. Direct-channel delivery options (see Figure 20–7) include consumer to supplier and supplier to consumer channels.

The *consumer to supplier channel* (1) requires the consumer to go to a single site for the service (e.g., hospital for surgery) or (2) allows the consumer to select one of several sites (e.g., emergency medical care chain). The *supplier to consumer channel* (1) delivers the service to a single site (e.g., home lawn care) or (2) provides the service at any one of several locations (e.g., tailoring service at home, office, or club). As an inexpensive way to expand their reach, many banks are putting branches in grocery stores and other retail establishments that provide customers with both time and place convenience.[18]

The *indirect channel delivery system* involves a facilitating agent between producer and consumer. For example, Sotheby's, the auction house, acts as a facilitator between buyers and sellers of high quality art pieces.[19] It is used when the service can be separated from the producer. Like direct channels, the service-exchange process can be initiated by the consumer's going to the producer or the producer's going to the consumer (see Figure 20–7); single and multiple outlets also are found within the indirect channel option. A representative sample of common service intermediaries associated with indirect delivery systems would include travel, ticket, and employment agents and stock, real estate, and insurance brokers. A travel agent with a single location may have only one option in selecting an airline (e.g., a feeder airline) when booking a flight from one small airport to another. The same agent or an agent with several locations has multiple options (airlines), however, when booking flights between New York and Chicago. A service supplier (local symphony orchestra) may elect to sell tickets through (1) an exclusive ticket sales agent with one (e.g., downtown) location, (2) an exclusive ticket sales agent with several ticket outlets, or (3) several ticket sales agents who may have one or more outlets.

At the Right Time: Overcome Perishability

Neither time nor a service can be put into storage and carried as inventory. The value (revenue-producing abilities) of services is defined temporally; a service is offered at a particular time. After that **right time** has passed without the service being used, the value of that service is lost forever. Classic examples of service **perishability** are described this way: "What is the value of an empty airplane seat on yesterday's flight or the unused appointment time because of a no-show?" Fluctuating demand is a key contributing factor to the high degree of service perishability; when demand stabilizes, the perishable character of services is greatly reduced. Offering the right services at the right time requires service retailers to strive to balance and synchronize their supply of services to the demand for their services.[20] Demand-supply synchronization can be accomplished by adjusting demand, adjusting supply, or adjusting both demand and supply.

Adjusting and synchronizing the demand for a service retailer's output might be achieved by means of the following:

Incentive systems
Reservation systems
Reminder systems
Punishment systems

Incentive systems can shift demand from peak times to off-peak periods. Incentives take the form of (1) lower prices for lower demand periods (e.g., afternoon movie or late-night flight); (2) quantity discounts for patronage during off periods (e.g., two-nights' lodging for the price of one night during the weekend); (3) product extras for off-peak service (e.g., complimentary dessert for the early-bird dinner); and (4) service extras to reshape demand patterns (free late-fall cleanup with each annual summer lawn-care program). *Reservation systems* can schedule supply to meet customer demand to maximize the service provider's output and to minimize customer uncertainty and confusion. Doctors, dentists, hair stylists, and auto care centers are but a few examples of service retailers who schedule their time carefully and fully. *Reminder systems* are used to contact customers immediately before scheduled service time to verify day and time of appointment and to avoid any perishable down time for the service retailer. Reminders usually are conducted the day before the appointment. *Punishment systems* charge customers for missed appointments or appointments that were canceled too late for rescheduling the service-provider's time. Full and partial charges might be levied.

There are several tactics for altering supply capacities to better match demand patterns. One service-retailing expert recommends the following:

- Use part-time employees and perform only essential tasks during peak demand periods.
- Train employees to perform multiple jobs so they can switch from one to another as demand dictates.
- Use paraprofessionals so that professionals can concentrate on duties requiring their expertise (e.g., parabankers who do legwork, solve routine problems, and handle clerical duties).
- Substitute equipment for human labor to make the service system more productive (e.g., automated car washes and computer-prepared income tax returns).[21]

At the Right Price: Enhance Profitability

Service providers often are divided into profit and nonprofit enterprises. Nonprofit businesses (e.g., educational, religious, charitable, and civic organizations) strive to meet social and public interest goals while services-for-profit retailers seek financial gain.[22] Our concern in this discussion is limited to the for-profit service retailer.

Managing labor, equipment, and facility costs while obtaining the **right price** are the key elements in the service retailer's **profitability** equation. Unlike the goods retailer, "cost-of-goods-sold" is not a major profit determinant. Controlling labor cost is usually the single most important contribution the labor-intensive service-retailer can make to ensure satisfactory profits.

The service-retailer's price is often not a price; rather, price is expressed in terms of a fee, charge, rent, tariff, contribution, commission, admission, donation, tuition, interest, rate, offering, or retainer. Regardless of what it is called, the service retailer's price is important because it takes on greater emphasis as a result of the intangibility of the service offering. Correctly or incorrectly, price is often used as the most important indicator of the quality of the service.

Price determinants and price-setting methods for service retailers are similar to those of goods retailers. Depending on the circumstances, the service retailer might use demand-based, cost-plus, and/or competitive-oriented pricing strategies and tactics. (A review of these strategies and tactics, discussed in Chapter 15, would be helpful.)

By the Right Appeal: Increase Communicability

Creating the **right appeal** is the same for service retailers as it is for goods retailers; it involves the three-step process of presenting the *right message* to the *right audience* through the *right media,* which add up to **communicability**.

The right message addresses the concerns of the targeted consumer. Service retailers can make a service, patronage, or price appeal. *Service appeals* emphasize the rightness of the service offering in meeting the consumer's needs. Unfortunately, as a result of the intangible nature of most service offerings, it is often quite difficult to communicate the exact nature, the true value, the extra dimensions, the full benefit, and a host of other attributes that comprise a service offering. The persuasive and informative communication process becomes quite challenging when the object of the promotion is an idea, task, event, process, procedure, or performance. Developing a service appeal usually centers on building name-brand recognition and creating an image the customer can visualize. *Patronage appeals* are somewhat more tangible messages; they emphasize the rightness of the service provider's facilities, location, and operating hours.[23] *Price appeals* are a major promotional element for some service retailers. For example, an advertised competitive price is essential to the success of auto repair, home cleaning, lawn care, travel, recreational, and entertainment firms. In the professional services field (medical, dental, and legal), price appeals were (and in some cases still are) considered unprofessional, unethical, and/or low class.[24] These restrictions on price advertising are rapidly disappearing as more and more professional services firms become market-oriented chain organizations (e.g., Hyatt Legal Services or The Dental Center at Sears). Service retailers use both "logical" (a factual presentation) and "emotional" (an appeal to feelings) approaches to presenting their message in the right way.

The highly intangible, variable, personal, and perishable nature of most services requires that service retailers target their promotional appeals. The *right audience* is the individual or targeted group of individuals who can use a particular type of service at a particular time. Few service concepts (e.g., freedom, health, salvation, security) can be effectively targeted and promoted to a mass audience. Although general demand for a service concept might be created through promotional appeals to mass markets, specific demand for a particular provider's service must be created through tailored appeals to targeted audiences.

THE RIGHT SERVICE STRATEGY

People, customers, and employees should be the focal point of all strategic planning for service retailers. In the retail service industry, customer satisfaction at a profit often equates to employee satisfaction through high motivation. High-contact service

FIGURE 20–8
Externally oriented strategic service vision

Target market segments	Positioning	Service concept	Value-cost leveraging	Operating strategy	Strategy-systems integration	Service delivery system
What are common characteristics of important market segments? What dimensions can be used to segment the market? Demographic? Psychographic? How important are various segments? What needs does each have? How well are these needs being served? In what manner? By whom?	How does the service concept propose to meet customer needs? How do competitors meet these needs? How is the proposed service differentiated from competition? How important are these differences? What is good service? Does the proposed service concept provide it? What efforts are required to bring customer expectations and service capabilities into alignment?	What are important elements of the service to be provided, stated in terms of results produced for customers? How are these elements supposed to be perceived by the target market segment? By the market in general? By employees as a whole? How do customers perceive the service concept? What efforts does this suggest in terms of the manner in which the service is: Designed? Delivered? Marketed?	To what extent are differences between perceived value and cost of service maximized by: Standardization of certain elements? Customization of certain elements? Emphasizing easily leveraged services? Management of supply and demand? Control and quality through– Rewards? Appeal to pride? Visibility and supervision? Peer group control? Involving the customer? Effective use of data? To what extent does this effort create barriers to entry by potential competition?	What are important elements of the strategy? Operations? Financing? Marketing? Organization? Human resources? Control? On which will the most effort be concentrated? Where will investments be made? How will quality and cost be controlled? Measured? Incentives? Rewards? What results will be expected versus competition in terms of: Quality of service? Cost profile? Productivity? Morale and loyalty of servers?	To what extent are the strategy and delivery system internally consistent? Can needs of the strategy be met by the delivery system? If not, what changes must be made in: The operating strategy? The service delivery system? To what extent does the coordination of operating strategy and service delivery system ensure: High quality? High productivity? Low cost? High morale and loyalty of servers? To what extent does this integration provide barriers to entry to competition?	What are important features of the service delivery system, including: The role of people? Technology? Equipment? Layout? Procedures? What capacity does it provide? Normally? At peak levels? To what extent does it: Help ensure quality standards? Differentiate the service from competition? Provide barriers to entry by competitors?

Source: Reprinted by permission of *Harvard Business Review.* An exhibit from "Lessons in the Service Sector" by James L. Heskett, March/April 1987.

Basic element (dark shading)   Integrative element (light shading)

FIGURE 20–9
Internally oriented strategic service vision

Target employee group	Positioning	Service concept	Value-cost leveraging	Operating strategy	Strategy-systems integration	Service delivery system
What are common characteristics of important employee groups? What dimensions can be used to describe these employee groups? Demographic? Psychographic? How important are each of these groups to the delivery of the service? What needs does each group have? How well are these needs being served? In what manner? By whom?	How does the service concept propose to meet employee needs? How do competitors meet such needs? How are relationships with employees differentiated from those between competitors and their employees? How important are these differences? What is "good service" to employees? Does the proposed service concept provide it? What efforts are required to bring employee expectations and service capabilities into alignment?	What are important elements of the service to be provided, stated in terms of results produced for employees and the company? How are these elements supposed to be perceived by the targeted employee group? How are these elements perceived? What further efforts does this suggest in terms of the manner in which the service is: Designed? Delivered?	To what extent are differences between returns to employees and the level of effort they put forth maximized by: The design of the service concept? The design of the elements of the operating strategy? Job design? The leveraging of scarce skills with a support system? The management of supply and demand? Control of quality through– Rewards? Appeal to pride? Visibility? Supervision? Peer group control? Involving the customer in the delivery of the service? Effective use of data?	How important is direct human contact in this provision of the service? To what extent have employees been involved in the design of the service concept and operating strategy? How desirable is it to: Increase employee satisfaction? Increase employee productivity? What incentives are provided for: Quality? Productivity? Cost? How does the strategy address employee needs for: Selection? Assignment? Development? Evaluation? Compensation? Association?	To what extent are the strategy and the delivery system for serving important employee groups internally consistent? To what extent does the integration of operating strategy and service delivery system ensure: High quality? High productivity? Low cost? High morale and "bonding" of the target employee group?	What are important features of the service delivery system, including: The role of people? Technology? Equipment? Layout? Procedures? What does it require of target employee groups? Normally? At peak periods of activity? To what extent does it help employees: Meet quality standards? Differentiate their service from competitors? Achieve expectations about the quality of their work life?

Source: Reprinted by permission of *Harvard Business Review*. An exhibit from "Lessons in the Service Sector" by James L. Heskett, March/April 1987.

Basic element | Integrative element

business activities require highly integrated marketing and operating functions. It is not enough to strike some type of a balance between the customer's service needs and the service retailer's operating requirements; these two functional areas must be coordinated and integrated into a single strategic plan. One such plan was developed by Professor James Heskett of the Harvard Business School. His plan has two parts: the externally oriented strategic service vision and the internally oriented strategic vision.[25]

The **externally oriented strategic service vision** is directed at planning and integrating the service provider's marketing and operating functions for the benefit of the service consumer. As identified in Figure 20–8, the externally oriented strategic service vision model consists of the basic elements to be integrated and the integrative links that bridge the various marketing and operating elements. Professor Heskett describes the *strategic service vision* as follows:

> The need of most service organizations to plan as well as to direct marketing and operations as one function has led to the formation in leading companies of what I call a *strategic service vision*. Its elements consist of identification of a target market segment, development of a service concept to address targeted customers' needs, codification of an operating strategy to support the service concept, and design of a service delivery system to support the operating strategy. . . . A company naturally tries to position itself in relation to both the target market and the competition. The links between the service concept and the operating strategies are those policies and procedures by which the company seeks to maximize the difference between the value of the service to customers (the service concept) and the cost of providing it. This difference, of course, is a primary determinant of profit. And the link between the *operating strategy* and the *service delivery system* is the integration achieved in the design of both.[26]

Integrating customer-oriented functions is not enough to ensure success. Employees also must be fully integrated into the process. To repeat, most services are people-based on both the consumption and production sides of the exchange process; hence, the service retailer must also have an **internally oriented strategic service vision**. "High-performance service companies have gained their status in large measure by turning the strategic service vision inward by targeting groups of employees as well as customers."[27] This inner-directed vision is shown in Figure 20–9. It differs from the outer-directed vision mainly in that the focus of planning and integrating is on the firm's employees and not its customers.

The integrative elements in Figures 20–8 and 20–9 are guidelines for planning, implementing, and directing a strategic plan that will ensure a service team effort in targeting various markets.

SUMMARY

A service is a multifaceted concept involving several activities performed by an individual or group of individuals for the benefit of a customer or group of customers. Service retailers differ from goods retailers in that the former emphasize people, ideas, and information, and the latter focus on physical things and objects. The nation's service industry is the most important sector of the economy; it is the principal employer of the nation's workforce and accounts for nearly 70 percent of the gross national product.

Service retailers are classified by the Department of Commerce into four major categories: (1) transportation, communications, and public utilities, (2) finance, insurance, and real estate, (3) public administration, and (4) services (lodging, personal, business, automotive, repair, motion pictures, amusement and recreation, health, legal, educational, social, and various miscellaneous groupings). Services also can be classified according to operating characteristics, such as equipment-based and people-based service retailers.

The right service blend consists of six ingredients. The ingredients and their associated goals include offering the right service (add tangibility) in the right way (control variability) in the right place (bridge inseparability) at the right time (overcome perishability) at the right price (enhance profitability) by the right appeal (increase communicability).

The right service strategy requires that the service retailer plan and integrate the marketing and operations functions for both the firm's customers and its employees. The inner- and outer-directed strategic service vision provide the necessary guidelines for developing the service retailer's strategic plans.

STUDENT STUDY GUIDE

Key Terms and Concepts

communicability (p. 719)
externally oriented strategic service vision (p. 722)
goods/services retailer (p. 710)
inseparability (p. 716)
internally oriented strategic service vision (p. 722)
perishability (p. 718)
primary-service retailer (p. 710)
profitability (p. 719)
pure goods retailer (p. 710)
right appeal (p. 719)
right place (p. 716)
right price (p. 719)
right service (p. 713)
right time (p. 718)
right way (p. 715)
service (p. 709)
tangibility (p. 713)
variability (p. 716)

Review Questions

1. Develop three original definitions and examples of a retail service.
2. Who provides services?
3. Distinguish service retailers from goods retailers. Give an original example of a pure-goods and a pure-service retailer.
4. Identify two additional examples for each of the various types of equipment-based and people-based service retailers.
5. Outline the issues of concern in offering the right service and adding tangibility.
6. Give additional original examples of physical and mental symbols of service organizations.
7. Discuss the problem of service variability and how the service retailer might control this problem.
8. Describe the channel delivery system operations available to the service retailer.
9. Why are services perishable? Cite three examples.
10. Identify and describe the systems service retailers use to synchronize demand and supply.
11. Express the concept of price in other terms or language.
12. What is typically the most important factor in determining the price of a service?
13. Describe the process of increasing communicability by the right appeal.
14. Why is it important to integrate both the marketing and operating functions internally and externally?

Review Exam

True or False

_____ 1. All services are conducted as face-to-face interaction between one individual and another.

_____ 2. The United States has become the first nation to have a predominantly service-oriented economy.

_____ 3. An important marketing principle is that services are distinguished by their physical attributes, which should be fully used in service retailers' merchandising strategies.

_____ 4. A professor who utilizes a diagram to portray a concept or idea to his or her students is using a visual representation to add tangibility to his or her service offering.

_____ 5. The "good hands" of Allstate Insurance is an example of using mental symbols to tangibilize a service offering.

_____ 6. Because of the variability in the personal attributes and attitudes of the individual service provided, controlling this variability requires that service managers first ensure employee satisfaction through motivation and training before attempting to provide customer satisfaction.

Multiple Choice

_____ 1. Of the following operations, which is *not* a good example of a pure services retailer?
a. psychiatric clinic
b. employment agency

c. exclusive restaurant
d. massage parlor
e. management consultant

_____ 2. Tangibilizing the service offering can be accomplished by _____.
a. providing representation of the service
b. creating physical and mental symbols for the service
c. developing name or brand recognition for businesses or service lines
d. adding extra peripheral services or supplementary goods
e. all of the above

_____ 3. A chain of medical emergency care centers is a good example of a(n) _____.
a. direct consumer to supplier channel
b. direct supplier to consumer channel
c. indirect consumer to supplier channel
d. indirect supplier to consumer channel
e. none of the above

_____ 4. An empty airplane seat on yesterday's flight best represents the _____ problem of a service retailer's offering.
a. perishability
b. communicability
c. variability
d. normalization
e. none of the above

_____ 5. There are several tactics for altering supply capacities to better match service demand patterns. Which of the following actions is *not* one of those tactics?
a. using part-time employees
b. training employees to perform multiple jobs
c. charging customers for missed or canceled appointments
d. using paraprofessionals as partial substitutes for professionals
e. substituting equipment for human labor

_____ 6. The service retailer's price is expressed in terms of a(n) _____.
a. fee
b. commission
c. admission
d. retainer
e. all of the above

STUDENT APPLICATIONS MANUAL

Investigative Projects: Practice and Applications

1. Using the multi-definitional model in Figure 20–1, provide a specific service industry example for ten different definitions of a retail service. For example, a concert by the Dallas Symphony Orchestra is a perishable event that is orchestrated for the enjoyment of a patron.
2. Identify five nontext examples of physical or mental symbols used by service retailers to add tangibility to their service offering.
3. Do you think punishment systems for demand-supply synchronization is fair? Why or why not?
4. By surveying magazines and other print media, find three examples of service retailers who are using a service appeal, a patronage appeal, and a price appeal in an attempt to increase communicability by using the right appeal.

Tactical Cases: Problems and Decisions

■ CASE 20–1
Nutri/System Inc.: The Fat's in the Fire*

The diet industry has enjoyed record growth for several years; it has expanded at a rate of 15 percent a year with total industry revenues exceeding $3 billion. A host of environmental factors have contributed to the growth of the diet industry, including: (1) an aging population concerned with health issues; (2) a cultural trait that thin is appealing and heavy is unattractive; (3) an increasing income level capable of supporting special diet programs; and (4) a greater interest in wellness problems and solutions. An additional boost to the diet industry came about with the announcement by talk-show queen Oprah Winfrey that she had shed 67 pounds using a diet powder called Optifast. The five heavyweights in the diet industry include Weight Watchers International, Nutri/System Inc., Diet Center Inc., Thompson Medical Co. (Slim-Fast powder), and Sandoz Nutrition Corp. (Optifast powder). In addition to these five firms, a large number of companies market a wide range of weight-control devices (pills, programs, powders, supplements, etc.).

Nutri/System Inc. is enjoying great success in the growing diet industry in large part due to its effective marketing programs that create a professional medical image for this storefront chain of weight-loss centers. This professionalism is an extremely important patronage factor in attracting and retaining the often insecure and overweight client. The professional image starts at the front door with weight-loss centers that look like medical offices. On entering the center, the client is processed by a staff of professional-looking weight-loss consultants in white lab coats. A sophisticated-looking computer called the Nutri/Data computer identifies the ideal weight of the client; then the client is informed that the Nutri/System program meets the guidelines of leading national health organizations. A final touch of medical professionalism is added when the client is asked to complete a psychological questionnaire concerning job, family, and other relationships; this information obtained from the questionnaire is useful in analyzing behavior characteristics that affect eating behavior.

The Nutri/System program requires the client to pay an upfront fee based on the amount of weight the client wants to lose. For example, a client wishing to lose 30 pounds might be charged a fee of $700; the exact fee varies somewhat with the location of the center. The client incurs additional costs ($50 to $65 per week) through the required purchases of Nutri/System foods—an 1,100 to 1,500 calorie-a-day diet. The company's Weight Maintenance Reward program allows clients to recoup up to half their upfront fee by maintaining their target weight for one year. The cost of this program to Nutri/System is self-liquidating in that the client is required to buy two days' worth of Nutri/System food per week for one year. Clients visit the Nutri/System Center on a weekly basis with each visit consisting of: (1) weigh-in and recording progress toward weight-loss goal; (2) meeting with a personal Nutri/System nutritional specialist who helps plan each week's menu; and (3) group therapy session in which everyday food problems are discussed.

A key part of the Nutri/System program is their foods. Outside food manufacturers produce, package, and label the ever-changing assortment of foods that include pizza, tacos, and Polynesian-style chicken. Each item is easy and quick to prepare. Responding to preferences of overweight people for food with more texture and flavor, NuSystem foods tend to be chewy and spicy. All packages are premeasured for easy recording of calorie intake. With a 100 percent markup, the sales of Nutri/System food accounts for 70 percent of Nutri/System revenues.

Perhaps the most effective part of the Nutri/System marketing program is the firm's promotional strategies. The first strategy involves an old time-honored print ad technique—a "before" shot of a client in an unflattering view in black and white is positioned along side a flattering "after" shot of a client who has lost a great deal of weight; the "after" photo is often in color with the client wearing attractive clothing in an interesting pose. The second promotional strategy involves the buying of local radio time with radio station deejays being offered free Nutri/System diet programs. The advertisement typically consists of the deejays talking about the progress they are making on their programs and the positive results of the weight-loss effort (e.g., buying new, smaller clothing).

For Nutri/System and the other four major players in the diet industry, a number of legal, ethical, and health issues have surfaced that could dampen the current diet boom. The industry is under government scrutiny for questionable marketing practices and misleading advertisements. Congress is investigating complaints from former diet-center clients who have claimed to experience health problems from dropping too much weight too quickly. Many experts believe that obesity and overweight conditions are serious health problems that should only be treated by extensively trained medical personnel. Although Nutri/System food is FDA regulated, other diets which rely primarily on powders, drinks, and pills do not require FDA approval as do most drugs; hence, there is often no effective regulation of significant segments of the diet industry. Ethical issues revolve around the question of whether or not most dieters gain back either all or most of the weight they lost by reduced-caloric-intake diets. For medical reasons, dieters cannot live indefinitely on 1,100 to 1,500 calories per day; hence, with any program that requires this, they become depressed and irritable, which leads to overeating. Critics claim that none of the diet programs are successful because they do not effectively teach clients how to change their eating behavior and how to adapt to long-term necessary lifestyle changes.

ASSIGNMENT

Investigate the legal, ethical, and health issues associated with the diet industry. Are they real? Carefully identify and describe the specific problems relative to each issue. Then, develop a list of recommendations and corresponding action plans for dealing with each problem. Assume you were directing your report to the management of Nutri/System Inc.

*This case was prepared by Dale Lewison, John Thanopoulos, and Jon Hawes, The University of Akron.

Source: Material for this case was adapted from Matthew Schifrin, "Living Off the Fat of the Land," *Forbes*, November 13, 1989, 186–187, 192, 194, 196 and Joseph Weber, "The Diet Business Takes It on the Chins," *Business Week*, April 16, 1990, 86, 88.

■ CASE 20–2

Metro Bank: Adapting Consumer Services to Consumer Behavior Patterns*

The Metro Bank of Capital City was chartered in 1920 and was the second largest commercial bank (in total deposits) in the state. The bank's facilities consisted of a central bank and 27 outlets. The central bank served as the center of banking operations and was located in the downtown area. Metro's statewide facilities consisted of a centrally located outlet in each of the state's 18 principal cities (populations ranging from 32,000 to 280,000).

In its early years, the bank's management philosophies were quite conservative under its now-retired founder, J.P. Homestead. Although the board chairman, Arthur B. King, and the president, Malcom S. Hargrave, followed a somewhat more aggressive management philosophy, Homestead's conservative influence was still prevalent in many of the major policy decisions. Several of the bank's top managers felt that Homestead's conservative influence helped Metro avoid the recent problem of overextending on high-risk loans, which had led to the collapse of several banks.

Metro's current operating philosophy was described accurately by one competitor as "progress through discretion." In past years, Metro's management had adopted banking innovations when sufficient evidence demonstrated that the innovation was in the best interest of the bank and its customers. These policies had created a consumer image of reliability, an image most managers felt was one of the bank's strongest assets. Recently, however, some of the bank's younger managers had exerted considerable pressure to initiate more progressive policies. Janet F. Peterson, vice president of marketing and research, felt that the bank's management should be more receptive to banking innovations. Peterson believed that increasing competition, in terms of new competitors and new competitive marketing strategies, would require early adoption of new technologies and approaches if Metro were to maintain or increase its present growth. The trend in recent years has been toward greater competition among commercial banks as well as intensified competition with other financial institutions. This competition extends across all facets of the banking business.

Commercial banks offer a wide array of financial services to individuals, firms, institutions, government, and other organizations. These services include storage of funds in interest-bearing accounts (savings accounts) and in interest and noninterest-bearing accounts (checking accounts) for day-to-day transactions; loans for a variety of purposes; trust services; safe deposit boxes for valuable personal items; financial planning; and investment counseling. While commercial banks offer a wide range of services to both commercial and retail consumers, not all banks offer all services. The product-service offering of each bank facility is shown in Exhibit A.

The general state of the economy affects the level of checking and savings deposits, the demand for personal and commercial loans, and the costs of resources. Banking operations are affected by cultural and social factors such as attitudes toward the use of credit, attitudes toward women as customers, pressure for greater social responsibility, and the continuing redistribution of the population into the suburbs.

As a quasi-utility, the banking industry has been subject to a high degree of government control and regulation. Regulatory agencies include the Federal Reserve Board, the Federal Deposit Insurance Corporation, the Comptroller of the Currency, and state banking authorities. As an example, national banks must obtain approval from the Comptroller of the Currency for the location of new branch banks.

Major technological changes affect the competitive environment of the banking industry. Electronic Funds Transfer System (EFTS) is an example. The EFTS is an electromechanical method of transferring value, partially replacing the method of paper transfer of value (i.e., cash and checks).

One of these EFTS components has been classified as customer-bank communication terminals (CBCT) by the Comptroller. These terminals may be located on the site of an existing banking office or off-site such as in a shopping center. They can be staffed (operated by a bank employee) or unstaffed (operated by the customer), on-line (connected directly to the bank's central computer) or off-line (self-contained). One type of CBCT is the automated teller machine (ATM), which typically allows customers to make deposits, withdraw cash, pay on loans, and make account transfers. Another type of CBCT is the point-of-sale (POS) terminal, which can be used at checkout counters in supermarkets, department stores, and other business establishments. Retailers use POS for check or credit card authorization and for debit-card authorization, which allows immediate transfer of funds from the purchaser's account to the store's account.

METRO'S CURRENT SITUATION

In recent months Metro's top management had devoted considerable discussion to the need for additional banking outlets. The management consensus was that potentially profitable sites existed in the rapidly expanding suburban areas of Capital City. Moreover, management felt that additional profit potential existed in several of the state's 18 other principal cities and in smaller cities (10,000 to 30,000 people). Although senior management generally agreed that expansion was necessary to increase market share, they disagreed considerably as to what form the expansion should take.

The need for a decision on the expansion issue had acquired greater importance in recent weeks. Two of Metro's competitors, First Central Bank (the state's largest) and First Farmers' Bank (the fourth largest), had expanded their service offerings through the use of ATMs in conjunction with their existing branch facilities. Just recently, Peterson learned that First Farmers' intended to limit further construction of traditional brick-and-mortar branches and embark on an ambitious expansion program of off-site ATMs in shopping centers, employment centers, and other major activity centers. Its expansion program was based on the belief that banking services are primarily convenience goods; therefore, banking facilities should have the greatest possible geographical distribution. Since ATMs were available to customers 24 hours a day, 7 days a week, the marketing strategy appeared to be one of creating greater spatial and time convenience.

Metro's senior management was concerned about a recent report showing that market share of deposits peaked in 1980 and had declined slowly since then. Management's assumption was that market share of deposits was correlated closely with share of the total number of branches. Metro's share of branches, however, continued to increase in 1984 and 1985 while share of deposits decreased. Many of the larger banks in the state experienced a similar trend. The exceptions to this trend were First Central and First Farmers', which experienced substantial growth.

One of Metro's stated goals was to maximize market shares subject to a rate of return of at least 15 percent. In 1985, the market share fell to 19.5 percent, under 20 per-

EXHIBIT A
Product-service offering by facility

Services	Full-Service Bank	Limited-Service Bank	Automated Teller Machine	Point-of-Sale Terminal
Open accounts	x	x		
Make loans	x			
Cash withdrawals	x	x	x	
Deposits	x	x	x	
Transfers	x	x	x	
Loan payments	x	x	x	
Credit card payments	x	x	x	
Other bill payments	x	x	x	
Determine current balance	x	x	x	
Trust services	x			
Safe deposit boxes	x	x	x	
Financial counseling	x			
Cash third-party checks	x	x		
Purchase traveler's checks	x	x		
Purchase cashier's checks	x	x		
Purchase money orders	x	x		
Check authorization	x	x		x
Credit card authorization	x	x		x
Debit card authorization (to allow immediate transfer of funds from buyer's to seller's account)	x	x		x

cent for the first time since 1977, although the rate of return remained slightly above 15 percent.

In light of the situation, Hargrave asked Peterson to develop and evaluate alternative expansion plans that would increase Metro's market share and rate of return. In addition, Hargrave instructed Peterson to consider the following issues:

1. Construction of a brick-and-mortar branch would cost a minimum of about $250,000, or about five times as much as the cost of an ATM.
2. The chairman of the board had expressed repeatedly the opinion that ATMs cannot be cost justified in terms of the profits they generate, an opinion shared by some experts.
3. Several of Metro's large commercial accounts had expressed a wide range of views as to the desirability of the EFTS.
4. At the recent conference of the National Association of Bank Managers, several experts expressed strong feelings concerning the problems of fraud, security, and malfunctioning of ATMs.
5. Recent consumer surveys showed considerable mixed reactions to the use of ATMs.
6. Several of Metro's senior bank officials were concerned that any radical departure from current modes of operation might have considerable negative effects on the bank's image.
7. Pricing concepts in the banking industry were under-

going significant changes; whereas most banks sought to make each application of each service profitable, some banks would adopt pricing strategies based on the profitability of the total customers and/or a total class of customers.
8. Point-of-sale terminals were in use at checkout counters in retail stores and generally were installed with one terminal per checkout counter, or anywhere from 1 to 20 terminals per store.

In her initial meeting with the bank's marketing research department, Peterson outlined the major issues of the problem as presented in the previous discussion. She expressed the following opinion:

"Innovative expansion is the key to regaining and increasing the bank's market share. For any expansion program to meet the bank's market-share goals, we must develop expansion alternatives incorporating product-service mixes that not only satisfy the needs of our existing customers, but also provide the opportunities for attracting new customers. In my opinion, the only way to attract large numbers of new customers is to create the image of a modern, progressive bank. This type of image requires fresh and imaginative marketing programs. Today's banking customer chooses and continues to patronize a bank for many different reasons; however, all of these reasons are strongly related to today's modern lifestyles. What I need from this department are innovative alternatives for expansion that not only are conducive to the consumer's modern way of life but will be acceptable to the dated gentlemen upstairs.

"I believe that our current research files" (see Exhibits B to G) "are sufficient for the initial development of these alternatives. We can always collect additional data later that would be more suited to whatever alternative we come up with. If you have any ideas about additional information that might be required, or if there are any specific aspects to the problem you feel should be drawn to my attention, submit them to me in writing by the end of the week. Otherwise, within the next six weeks, I expect from the department recommendations as to the most feasible expansion alternatives. Now, are there any questions?"

Bob Sidewood: How many alternatives do you want?

Peterson: I'll leave that up to you.

Sidewood: Are there any specific issues you wish us to consider?

Peterson: I think I have at least mentioned most of the issues pertinent to the problem. Again, I would think that consumer needs and responses might serve as the focal point in developing the alternatives. But you shouldn't overlook all of the other issues I've noted. Also, I'm sure that there are additional issues that you might consider.

Sidewood: One last question. How extensive an area should we consider?

Peterson: The entire state.

Cheryl Armstrong: As a resident of this state for 55 years and a banker for 27, I feel that I know the people of this state and the customers who bank with us. Although we want to think progressively, let's not forget that this state's population is quite conservative. These people are bound in tradition. It has taken this long for them to trust dealing with us. How long will it take to get them to trust dealing with a machine?

Peterson: You have a point. But people have changed. We have an influx of people from all parts of the country into this state. The newcomers don't have the same lifestyles.

Doug Robeson: As research analyst, I have data that support both of your contentions. People in this state have been slow to adopt banking in general and innovative banking practices in particular. The population's composition, however, has changed in the states' major cities. Out-of-state companies have opened major branches of their businesses here and have relocated many of their personnel as well. Although they represent a small percentage of the state's population, these outsiders have learned the advantages of using the new technologies in banking.

Peterson: Well, it is true that these people have been exposed to new banking techniques and do adapt to change more rapidly, but they are a minority. I think we should consider educating the rest of the population to the advantages of new banking technology. Just look at the strides First Central and First Farmers' have made.

Greg Lucas: Ms. Peterson, it is true that those banks have increased their market shares, but I agree with Ms. Armstrong. The people of this state are staunch conservatives, and particularly the customers who bank with us. If we try to become 'progressive,' as you call it, we will lose the solid image we have built with our loyal customers and they'll go elsewhere. People are reliable and trustworthy; machines are nothing but metal and electrical circuits.

Peterson: But people of this state are changing, and people from out of state with more progressive views are coming in. We cannot continue to manufacture the horse-drawn carriage! Does anyone have any final comments before we adjourn?

Robeson: If I may make one last comment, let me say once again that I can see both sides to this question. As I view it, we are concerned with several issues. Each must be analyzed. We must consider changing lifestyles of bank consumers in this state. On the whole, are consumers changing rapidly enough to accept modern banking techniques in the near future? Second, what image do we convey and to whom? Third, can we educate people to accept and use machines? Their prior learning habits may not be easy to change. I don't presently have answers to these questions.

Peterson: You've raised some good questions, Mr. Robeson. And as project director, I know you will have answered these in the report I expect from this department.

EXHIBIT B
Bank patronage reasons: Retail and commercial consumers

Patronage Reason	Importance (%)						
	First	Second	Third	Fourth	Fifth	Sixth	Totals
Location	42	5	19	25	3	6	100
Hours	34	4	22	20	10	10	100
Services	10	43	15	13	11	8	100
Personnel	7	20	9	17	22	25	100
Reputation	5	7	10	6	21	51	100
Facilities	2	21	25	19	33	0	100
Totals	100	100	100	100	100	100	

Source: Statewide Consumer Survey, Marketing Research Department, Metro Bank.

EXHIBIT C
Consumer banking trip behavior: Retail and commercial consumers

Shopping Characteristics	Type of Consumer (%)	
	Retail Consumer	Commercial Consumer
Type of trip: I conduct my banking business in connection with:		
Trips between home and work	32	10
Special trips from home	30	8
Special trips from work	17	57
Shopping trips	18	—
Business trips	2	23
Other	1	2
Total	100	100
Trip frequency: I visit the bank:		
Less than once a month	1	—
Once a month	8	—
More than once a month (less than weekly)	21	—
Once a week	51	1
More than once a week (less than daily)	19	11
Once a day (weekday)	—	69
More than once a day	—	19
Total	100	100

Source: Statewide Consumer Survey, Marketing Research Department, Metro Bank.

EXHIBIT D
Demographic characteristics of automated equipment users and nonusers

Demographic Characteristics	Nonuser(%)	Infrequent User (%)	Frequent User (%)	Total User (%)
Sex				
Male	53.9	64.0	64.9	59.1
Female	46.1	36.0	35.1	40.9
Age				
21–34	36.8	49.3	54.5	43.4
35–49	47.4	44.0	39.0	43.4
50 and over	15.8	6.7	6.5	13.1
Social class				
Upper-middle	27.6	14.7	33.8	23.7
Lower-middle	38.2	53.3	39.0	45.6
Upper-lower	34.2	32.0	27.3	30.7
Marital status				
Married	86.8	85.3	87.0	86.9
Single	7.9	10.7	9.1	8.4
Widowed, divorced	5.3	4.0	3.9	4.7
Education				
Postgraduate	13.2	13.3	14.3	12.8
College graduate	23.7	32.0	29.9	27.7
Some college	28.9	32.0	28.6	30.3
Subtotal	65.8	77.3	72.8	70.8
High school graduate	25.0	17.3	19.5	22.6
Some high school	6.6	5.3	6.5	5.5
Eighth grade or less	2.6	—	1.3	1.1
Income				
Under $5,000	2.6	4.0	2.6	2.9
$5,000–$7,999	3.9	6.7	2.6	5.1
$8,000–$10,999	21.1	22.7	10.4	17.2
$11,000–$13,999	19.7	24.0	15.6	20.1
$14,000–$17,999	13.2	10.7	18.2	16.1
$18,000 and over	34.2	22.7	44.2	32.8
Refused	5.3	9.3	6.5	5.8

Source: Statewide Consumer Survey, Marketing Research Department, Metro Bank.

EXHIBIT E
Consumer bank selection criteria

Selection Criteria	Customer Type and Importance Rank(%)					
	Retail Consumers			Commercial Consumers		
	First	Second	Third	First	Second	Third
Recommendation of friends and relatives	3	4	8	—	—	2
Recommendation of a professional acquaintance	2	6	1	11	9	8
Good reputation	4	3	—	9	8	14
Located near where I shop	10	8	3	—	—	—
Located near where I work	11	10	14	16	10	10
Located near where I live	18	16	10	—	1	1
Offers full service	11	13	11	29	22	13
Helpful personnel	8	7	4	6	15	10
Open during the evening hours	5	7	4	11	6	8
Open on Saturdays	7	4	6	4	12	6
Attractive facilities	—	6	3	—	—	—
Convenient automatic services	5	6	12	4	5	11
Interest charges on loans	1	—	1	6	7	9
Interest paid on savings	3	3	3	—	—	1
Availability of credit	—	1	—	4	5	5
Overdraft privileges on checking accounts	3	4	6	—	—	—
Premiums or gifts for new accounts	7	2	9	—	—	—
Convenient parking	1	—	2	—	—	1
Convenient entrance/exit	1	—	3	—	—	1

Source: Statewide Consumer Survey, Market Research Department, Metro Bank.

EXHIBIT F
Likelihood of using automated teller equipment

Characteristics	Very Likely (%)	Somewhat Likely (%)	Somewhat Unlikely (%)	Very Unlikely (%)
Age				
18–34	34.1	21.7	11.2	29.2
35–49	33.2	18.6	11.3	33.2
50–64	19.8	12.5	14.7	49.6
65 and over	10.9	7.8	14.7	51.9
Income				
Under $7,500	15.2	11.0	11.0	51.7
$7,500–$10,000	25.8	20.0	11.9	37.7
$10,000–$15,000	34.8	17.4	12.1	32.6
$15,000–$20,000	34.1	20.3	14.8	26.8
Over $20,000	28.9	12.3	15.8	41.2
Sex				
Male	26.8	16.7	15.0	37.0
Female	28.0	16.2	10.5	40.0

Source: Statewide Consumer Survey, Market Research Department, Metro Bank.

EXHIBIT G
Automated teller equipment: Advantages versus disadvantages

Characteristics	Advantages Outweigh (%)	About Equal (%)	Disadvantages Outweigh (%)	Advantages Outweigh Plus Equal (%)
Occupation				
White collar	31.6	38.6	29.8	70.2
Blue collar	25.4	12.8	61.7	38.3
Professional	12.9	45.2	42.0	58.0
Housewife	23.6	31.1	45.3	54.7
Retired	23.5	5.9	70.6	29.4
Other	41.2	35.3	23.5	76.5
Age				
18–23	40.0	40.0	20.0	80.0
24–34	27.5	25.8	46.7	56.3
35–44	16.7	33.3	50.0	50.0
45–55	20.3	29.7	50.0	50.0
56–64	16.7	16.7	66.7	33.3
65 and over	33.4	13.3	53.4	46.6
Income				
Under $5,000	12.5	25.0	62.5	37.5
$5,000–$10,000	32.6	30.2	32.3	62.7
$10,000–$15,000	38.2	21.8	40.0	60.0
$15,000–$20,000	25.0	36.5	38.5	61.5
Over $20,000	29.2	33.3	37.5	62.5
Refused	17.1	31.4	51.4	38.6

Source: Statewide Consumer Survey, Market Research Department, Metro Bank.

ANALYTICAL PROBLEM

As director of the project, prepare an appropriate expansion plan that identifies and evaluates the most feasible alternatives for Metro Bank. As stated by Peterson, that plan must be predicated on meeting existing customers' needs as well as attracting new customers.

What are the possible effects of your recommended alternatives on the bank's (1) internal operations, (2) promotional programs, (3) product-service mix, and (4) pricing strategy?

*This case was revised and updated by Dale M. Lewison and Kenneth E. Mast, University of Akron, as adapted from Dale M. Lewison and Roger Cannaday, "The Second National Bank of Capital City: The Adoption of Service Innovations," in *Retailing: Cases and Applications*, D. M. Lewison and M. W. DeLozier, eds. (Columbus, OH: Merrill, 1982); 49–60.

ENDNOTES

1. Sylvia Nasar, "America Still Reigns in Services," *Fortune*, June 5, 1985, 64.
2. Glenn DeSouza, "Now Service Businesses Must Manage Quality," *The Journal of Business Strategy*, May/June 1989, 21.
3. Carol J. Loomis, "Stars of the Service 500," *Fortune*, June 5, 1989, 55.
4. James L. Heskett, "Lessons in the Service Sector," *Harvard Business Review* (March–April 1987), 126.
5. John E.G. Bateson, "Retailing and Services Marketing: Friends or Foes?" *Journal of Retailing* 61 (Winter 1985), 11.
6. Steven K. Beckner, "The Boom That Won't Quit," *Nation's Business* 74 (April 1986), 27.
7. Ibid.
8. Ibid.
9. See Judith Waldrop, "Spending by Degree," *American Demographics*, February 1990, 23–26.
10. See Christopher H. Lovelock, "Classifying Services to Gain Strategic Marketing Insights," *Journal of Marketing* (Summer 1983), 9–20.
11. Leonard L. Berry, "Services Marketing is Different," *Business* (May–June 1980), 25.
12. See Sak Onkvisit and John J. Shaw, "Service Marketing: Image, Branding, and Competition," *Business Horizons* 32, January/February 1989, 13–18.
13. Berry, "Services marketing," 27.
14. Cyndee Miller, "An Oasis for Hip Consumers," *Marketing News*, February 19, 1990, 2.
15. John W. Schouten and James H. McAlexander, "A Company Study–Positioning Services for Competitive Advantage: The Case of Duds 'n Suds," *Journal of Service Marketing*, Spring 1989, 73.
16. Joseph Weber, "Why Day Care is Mostly Mom and Pop," *Business Week*, July 10, 1989, 65.
17. Berry, "Service Marketing," 27.
18. See "Supermarketing Can Be Super Marketing," *ABA Banking Journal*, September 1989, 49–53.
19. See Judith H. Dobrzynski, "A Bigger Canvas for Sotheby's," *Business Week*, May 21, 1990, 134–36.
20. See Richard L. Cohen, "Saturday Banking Explodes Throughout California," *Intangibles*, June 1989, 10–13.
21. Berry, "Service Marketing," 28.
22. See John A. Byrne, "Profiting from the Nonprofits," *Business Week*, March 26, 1990, 66–70, 72, 74.
23. See Seth Luboue, "The Disney Touch," *Forbes*, April 16, 1990, 90–91.
24. See Judy E. Pickens, "What's Hot, What's Not in Legal Marketing," *Intangibles*, June 1989, 7–9.
25. See James L. Heskett, "Lessons in the Service Sector," *Harvard Business Review* (March–April 1987), 118–126.
26. Ibid., 119.
27. Ibid., 119–20.

APPENDIX A
Supplementary Cases

■ CASE 1
Tony Cironi Learns How to Deal with Troublesome Customers*

Tony Cironi, owner and manager of Cironi's Sewing Center, was in a reflective mood. For the first time since the start of his business, he felt optimistic. He had started out as a small Singer sewing machine dealer. Within the space of four years, Cironi's Sewing Center had grown to one of the largest sewing centers in Akron, Ohio. He now carried more than 7 brands of sewing machines, a full line of attachments and parts, and a line of miscellaneous sewing accessories. Profits were good; sales were growing. Overall, he felt good about his business. The only thorn on the rosebush, so to speak, was *dealing with customers!*

In the beginning, Tony had blindly followed the simple dictum, "The customer is always right." Over time, however, a number of disturbing incidents involving customers had occurred that could not be resolved with such a simple philosophy. Moreover, many of these incidents were sufficiently similar as to fall into categories of behavior. In Tony's opinion, the time had come to formulate a few policies regarding certain types of customer behavior. Although satisfied customers were the key to his success, he could not and would not let them run his business.

Upon further reflection, Tony decided that such policies should address specific customer types: time wasters, price shoppers, and chronically unsatisfied customers. He began to jot down some notes as he recalled both recent and typical behaviors in each of these categories. Perhaps an in-depth, analytical examination of these incidents would provide direction to the formulation of some useful policies.

TIME WASTERS

A typical incident of this sort happened only yesterday. A husband and wife came into the store looking for a sewing machine cabinet. Tony was the only one in the store that day and could not get to them immediately since he was on the phone when they came in. By the time he broke loose and approached them, they were looking through the brochures on sewing machine cabinets. Tony introduced himself and said, "I see you're looking for a cabinet. We have a few of these cabinets on the floor but we can order anything you want. Did you have anything particular in mind?"

Although Tony had addressed both husband and wife, he had expected the wife to answer. Based on past experience, the wife was usually the decision maker in this type of purchase. However, she glanced at her husband and sort of sidled off to look at notions. Her husband cleared his throat nervously, and said, "Well, we're just looking. We have a sewing machine and would like to get a nice cabinet for it."

Tony: What kind of machine do you have?

Husband: A Sears.

Tony: What type of cabinet are you looking for?

Husband: Well, we've actually seen a cabinet we like at another store and just wanted to see what you have.

Tony: Do you remember the make and model number?

Husband: No, but it had an electric lift and a—(pause)—hutch.

At this point the husband waved his wife over and asked her if she remembered the make and model number of the cabinet at the other store. She shook her head negatively and glanced over at the cabinet models on display.

Tony: Good, that gives us something to go on. Not too many manufacturers make that type of cabinet—only Singer and Parsons. Which store did you see it in?

Husband: It was a fabric store.

Tony: Jo Ann Fabrics?

Husband: I think so.

Tony: OK, then the cabinet you saw was a Parsons. We have their brochure here and one of their models on the floor. Not the one you want, but you can get some idea of the type of wood and quality of construction of a Parsons. We can order the model you want and have it here within ten days. Our price on that particular cabinet model is $799. I will need the model number of your Sears machine, though, because you will need a special insert for installation. I would want to order the insert at the same time as we order the cabinet. Do you know the model number of your Sears machine?

The husband glanced nervously at his wife and asked, "Mary, do you know the model number of your Sears machine?" The wife looked very noncommittally at her husband and shook her head.

Tony: Well, that's no problem. We can write the order now. You can put down the required 10 percent of list price and call in the model number of your Sears machine later today.

The husband and wife simply looked at one another, and the wife began to examine a Bernina sewing machine. At this point, Tony noticed a lady who must have entered the store earlier and who now was looking at a very expensive Bernina electronic sewing machine. Tony recognized her because she had been in the store before. He knew that she was in the market for a top-of-the-line sewing machine. So Tony thought quickly and said, "I'd like to sell you this cabinet today. We can offer you free delivery and installation. I would also be happy to tune up your Sears machine at the same time. We usually charge $40 for a tune-up, but I'll do it for free if you buy the cabinet from me."

Wife: I don't know. (She looked at her husband.) We just can't make up our mind about what we want.

Husband: We sort of want to wait until we get our income tax return.

Tony: That's understandable. Why don't you give me your name and phone number. I'll check with you later this month. The sales rep for Parsons might come by before you're ready to buy. If so, I'll give you a call. You might be able to come in while he is here.

Wife: I don't know.

She glanced at her husband. He looked at her for a minute and said, "I guess we would rather wait. If we make up our mind, we'll come back."

Tony: OK. I'd be glad to help you whenever you decide.

As the couple turned to go, Tony looked around for the other customer and found that she was leaving the store. He thought to himself that he had just made a very bad mistake. The other customer might have bought today. The couple he just spent so much time with will probably never be back. He could kick himself.

PRICE SHOPPERS

"Price shoppers! They create all kinds of problems for me," exclaimed Tony. One particular incident that happened last month still rankled. A lady came into the store on a very busy day and spent close to 3 hours with Sandy (Tony's part-time salesperson) on a demonstration of an electronic model Pfaff sewing machine. Apparently, Sandy had gone through an extensive demonstration, including program instructions on how to execute fancy stitches (buttonholes, decorative stitching, etc.) and hands-on use of the machine. Throughout this time, Tony had been tied up with other customers and did not get a chance to "close the sale." However, Sandy assured him that she had tried hard to close the sale, but the lady just would not commit.

After a couple of days, Tony followed up by telephone but the customer was still undecided. He followed up again after a week and at that time, the customer said that she had purchased a Pfaff machine, identical to the one which had been demonstrated by Sandy, in a nearby town for $500 less than Tony's price! Since his price quote was $1499 on a list price of $1799, Tony had been momentarily puzzled. How could she get such a good price? In response to that question, she admitted that she had managed to buy this particular Pfaff model from a dealer who was going out of business! At this point, Tony simply said to himself, "Well, win some, lose some!—but the next time I see Sandy giving a demonstration lasting over an hour to the same customer, I'll take the time to go over, end the demonstration, and try to close the sale."

The typical price shopper scenario would have ended here. In the case of this particular customer, though, Tony was faced with a situation that seemed to call for some sort of policy on his part. The real problem developed several days ago when this same customer attended a sewing machine seminar sponsored by Cironi's Sewing Center. The seminar featured a sales representative from Pfaff who put on a comprehensive demonstration of the Pfaff electronic sewing machine. During the seminar, Sandy recognized the lady and overheard her ask the sales rep about after-sale service availability for the machine she just bought. The sales rep told her that she could have her Pfaff machine serviced at any Pfaff dealer nationwide. After the demonstration, the lady came up to Tony and said, "Mr. Cironi, my new Pfaff is not working right. I bought it to make drapes for my living room and after making the first pair, it started stitching crazy-like. The thread bunches under the fabric and the machine jams up. I hope you can fix it. It's still under warranty so you should fix it for free. Do you come out to my house or what?"

Instantly, Tony knew what was wrong. This woman had damaged the hook that goes down into the bottom of the bobbin case. It was a $100 part and would take at least $50 in labor to repair the machine. Although Pfaff would cover the cost of the part, the labor cost would be eaten by the dealer—him, if he was dumb enough to go along with this!

Because of the seminar and the presence of the sales rep, Tony was noncommittal. He simply told the lady to give him a call, and he would discuss the problem with her then. However, he seethed inwardly, "Why should I bear the cost of after-sale service to this customer? She actually shopped in my store, was quoted a good price, and then she deliberately bought the product at dealer cost from a dealer she knew was going out of business!" On a more rational level, Tony well understood his real dilemma. He was a full-service dealer, and his price had to cover after-sale service. Should he allow customers and area dealers to use him as an after-sale service provider? On the other hand, failure to fulfill the dealer service and instruction obligations outlined in his Pfaff franchise agreement could lead to termination of his Pfaff franchise. Specifically stated in the contract was the following provision:

> In connection with the Pfaff Limited Warranty, each dealer shall, at its own expense, provide complete service (parts and labor) free of charge, in accordance with the warranty card, for one year following the purchase date of a Pfaff sewing machine for all customers located in his sales territory. The dealer shall receive credit or exchange parts at our discretion for replacing defective parts after such parts are received and inspected by us.

Tony felt that he must decide how to handle this problem *and soon*. The seminar was over, and he was expecting a call from Lady X at any moment.

UNSATISFIED CUSTOMERS

Over time, Tony had had any number of customers who simply did not like the sewing machine and/or cabinet that they purchased. In these situations, customers would want to return or exchange the product(s). In some cases, exchange or return did not cause too many problems. However, if the product(s) had been specially ordered (e.g., cabinet), or if the customer had used the product(s) for any length of time, exchange or return drastically reduced his margin on the deal. Although several recent incidents had caused him a lot of grief, the case of Mrs. Lucille Kroner stood out in his memory as the perfect reason for a policy regarding return or exchange of a product due to customer dissatisfaction with their own choice rather than with any problem due to the product's performance or manufacture (e.g., defect).

Mrs. Lucille Kroner walked into his store shortly after he opened his dealership. She bought a bottom-of-the-line Elna sewing machine and cabinet for around $350. Tony agreed to deliver the machine and cabinet and to move her old machine from a second floor room to the basement. On delivery, he showed her how to raise and lower the head. Because Elna was a free-arm machine, the cabinet mechanism for raising or lowering the machine was a little different from the usual cabinet. But Tony demonstrated the mechanism until she was able to do it properly—about 8 to 10 times.

The first sign of trouble cropped up a month later. Mrs. Kroner came back to the store and complained about the cabinet. She couldn't get the machine to "drop away" correctly and wanted to exchange the cabinet for one that Tony already had in the store. After listening to her problem, Tony agreed to the exchange if Lucille paid the retail price difference between the two cabinets—approximately $100. At the same time, Lucille bought a chair for $70 to use with the cabinet.

When Tony delivered the cabinet and chair, Lucille appeared to be satisfied. However, within a week she called Tony and complained about the chair—either the cabinet wasn't high enough or the chair wasn't low enough because her legs were hitting the cabinet while trying to use the machine. She suggested that Tony either cut the legs off the cabinet or cut the legs off the chair a little bit. The upshot of this problem was that Tony picked up the chair, arranged to have 2 inches of the legs cut off, and redelivered it to her.

Several months later, Tony got another phone call from Lucille. Now she didn't like the second cabinet! At this point, Tony began to get very irritated. As far as he could tell, Lucille had the very same complaint as she had with the first cabinet. But when he refused to consider any further adjustment, Lucille became hysterical. As a result, Tony agreed to consider the possibility of another exchange. About a week later, she came to the store and picked out a more expensive credenza style cabinet. Once again Lucille only paid the retail price difference between the two cabinets, or $280.

The delivery of the third cabinet was not pleasant. In his own words, Tony felt like a "chump." He would have to sell the second cabinet as a "used" product, so most of the profit associated with selling a sewing machine and cabinet to Lucille would be wiped out. If the cost of his time was considered, he had actually lost money on the deal.

Consequently, when Lucille showed up a month later wanting to exchange the third cabinet plus chair for a fourth cabinet and new chair, Tony blew up. "Mrs. Kroner, you picked out that cabinet and chair. You're the one who wanted to exchange those cabinets. I had nothing to do with those decisions. In fact, I have taken a beating on all those exchanges. Every time I take back something from you, I have to sell it at less than full price. I cannot make any more exchanges for you." Lucille responded by screaming that he had cheated her, that the cabinet did not match the chair, and that he had charged her too much money for everything.

When she calmed down a little, Tony made a quick decision. He told her that he would be out to her house the very next day to pick up the machine, cabinet, and chair, and that he would give her a check for $844—exactly what she had paid for it all.

The next day Tony drove out to Lucille's house for the last time. As he left the house, Lucille started to say something, but Tony cut her off. He handed her the check and said, "Lady, I never intend to do business with you again. Don't even think about buying anything else from me—*ever!*"

QUESTIONS

1. Does Tony Cironi have a decision problem in each of the described incidents? If so, at what point should he recognize the problem? Formulate a statement of each decision problem.
2. What alternative solutions do you see for each decision problem defined in Question 1? What criteria would you use to evaluate alternatives? Evaluate the alternatives using your criteria.
3. On the basis of these incidents, should Tony formulate one or more store policies? If so, what types of policies and specific statements of policy do you recommend?

*This case was prepared by J. B. Wilkinson, Youngstown State University, and Douglas R. Hausknecht, University of Akron. The authors thank Bob Barnes, owner of Barnes Sewing Center in Akron, Ohio, for factual information regarding customers.

■ CASE 2
IKEA: A Global Retailer*

IKEA, an acronym created from the name Ingvar Kamprad (IKEA's founder), Elm Taryd (his family farm), and Agunngryd (his home village), had its conception in 1949 as a mail order catalog firm for furniture. Four years later, Ingvar Kamprad opened his first IKEA store in Almhult, Sweden. Today, worldwide operation now encompasses 77 stores in 18 countries around the world.

This ready-to-assemble retailer, recognized for its trendy and distinctive merchandising concepts, operates high volume warehouse outlets offering high quality furniture at large discounts. IKEA promises champagne dining on a beer budget.

IKEA has been so successful in selling its lifestyle furniture concept that sales reached $2.6 billion in 1988. IKEA is particularly successful in West Germany, where it has 18 stores accounting for over one-third of its total sales.

Percent of Sales

West Germany	32.4
Scandinavia	27.9
Rest of Europe	26.9
Rest of World	12.8

In North America, IKEA is growing rapidly. There are currently nine IKEA stores in Canada and five stores in the United States located in Pittsburgh, Penn., Plymouth Meeting, Penn., Baltimore, Md., Washington D.C., and Elizabeth, N.J. All of these stores are served by one warehouse located in Philadelphia. These east coast locations are heavily populated and are relatively easy to ship from Sweden, allowing for lower transportation costs. Transportation costs are also reduced because ready-to-assemble furniture is cheaper to ship than fully assembled furniture. Sales in 1988 totaled $93.0 million, making IKEA the leading manufacturer and retailer of lifestyle furniture in the United States. By 1992, it plans to open 31 more stores throughout the United States. In addition, mail-order will soon be available, making IKEA accessible nationwide.

The company organizes all of its business into four basic operative functions: product, purchasing, distribution service, and retailing. All other functions, such as finance and accounting, support these four major areas.

FURNITURE INDUSTRY

The two leading indicators of consumer demand for furniture and home furnishings are the residential housing market and the remodeling market. Studies have shown that when housing sales decline, furniture sales will usually follow. Increases in mortgage rates and fears of a recession and inflation have caused this cyclical industry to worry about future sales. Market forecasts for the early nineties call for a decline in sales with housing starts declining and the sale of existing homes falling.

Despite these housing sales predictions, there is good news in the home remodeling sector. The Department of Commerce has estimated that the remodeling market will continue to grow throughout the nineties. As more people remodel their homes, furniture sales should increase. According to a *Home Magazine* survey, 82.0 percent of those involved in remodeling had plans to buy new furniture. This strength in the remodeling and refurbishing sectors should help offset the softness of the housing market.

PRODUCT

The company offers a very large and widely varied product line with 9,000 items in the United States and 12,000 items worldwide. Of these items, three-quarters are furniture and the remaining quarter are home furnishings, such as textiles, housewares, floor coverings, accessories, and plants. The best sellers are the bookcases and the storage products.

IKEA offers two ways to meet its customers' needs: self-service and full-service. One-half of IKEA's products are self-service items that are flat-packed in a rectangular box and are to be taken home for assembly. Each one of these items comes with a leaflet that includes a detailed description of the components, schematic diagrams, assembly directions, and even an allen wrench. The full-service items are products (such as sofas) that are too large and bulky to be flattened for storage.

Although IKEA's regional managers are permitted to vary their product line somewhat, all stores must carry the same core products. This Scandinavian furniture is modern in design and appearance. It is simple, light, colorful, aesthetic, and user friendly. Color and presentation play a major role in selling IKEA's merchandise. Although the demand is high for Scandinavian furniture in the United States, there have been complaints from many American consumers regarding the comfort of the upholstered goods. Furniture that is considered comfortable in Scandinavia may not be comfortable in other cultures.

IKEA also offers other attractions to entice the consumer to shop at these stores. IKEA's goal is to have a relaxed, inviting atmosphere that will make the customer stay longer, and therefore, spend more. Consequently, many family-oriented events and features such as bands, clowns, baby-changing rooms, supervised children's play areas, and a Swedish restaurant are offered.

IKEA's rapid growth has created supply and distribution problems. Demand for their products is so great that the stores are continuously experiencing stockouts on various items. Even the largest stores are inadequately stocked to meet the demand. Part of the problem is due to IKEA's policy of buying a whole year's supply of goods in advance in order to keep prices down. This practice requires accurate sales forecasting. The problem is further accentuated by having difficulty in staging shipments from Europe, which presently supplies 93.0 percent of IKEA's merchandise.

IKEA's Suppliers (percent)

Scandinavia	52.0
Eastern Europe	20.0
Rest of Europe	21.0
Rest of World	7.0

Stock shortages are estimated to be costing the company close to $500 million in lost sales per year.

MARKETING AND PROMOTION

One of IKEA's major marketing strategies is to promote the fact that their furniture is aesthetic, functional, and a good value. Another key strategy is to establish a European concept in the United States by informing Americans about Scandinavian furniture and IKEA's retailing format. The firm does not adapt their stores to American tastes.

IKEA doesn't rely on sales to increase business. In fact, it has only one sale per year, offering discounts of up to 70 percent. Instead, they concentrate on such promotions as huge store openings that are highly visible and draw tremendous traffic. IKEA has spent approximately $2 million on each of the U.S. store openings. Radio, newspaper, and television advertisements are used frequently to promote the stores. However, their full-colored 196-page catalog is their strongest promotional tool. The catalog is produced each year in ten different languages. One-half of the company's promotional budget is spent on the production and distribution of this catalog.

PRICES

IKEA's stores are developed on the concept of offering competitive low prices on high-quality merchandise. Customers are attracted to the stores because the unassembled products sell for 30 to 50 percent lower than for finished furniture of comparable quality at other stores. This low-pricing structure is attributable to no special orders and no home delivery costs. The merchandise is displayed with tags that include self-service information such as the cost of the product, what it's made of, how to put it together, and where to pick it up in the warehouse. Self-service alleviates the need for salespeople, thereby reducing overhead. IKEA mass produces its furniture lines, which cuts costs further. Also, the flat-packed, disassembled merchandise cuts warehouse costs and transportation costs.

Because IKEA buys merchandise in large quantities direct from the manufacturer, costs are reduced through volume discounts. Large volume purchases from suppliers also reduce shipping costs. In addition, prices are lower because stores are located near major highways outside of city limits where real estate costs are somewhat reduced.

COMPETITION

There are over 2,000 retailers that sell furniture. However, because of a vast array of furniture designs and market niches, IKEA has only four main competitors: Levitz, Workbench, Habitat, and Stor. Of these, Habitat and Stor pose the most serious threat. Habitat, with headquarters in New York, competes both in the United States and European markets, and is the only other large multinational furniture retailer besides IKEA. Stor, based in California, borrowed many of IKEA's merchandising and marketing ideas and modified them to appeal to the California consumer. It also offers Scandinavian-styled furniture that is boxed for home assembly. Stor currently has three stores and plans to open 30 more in 13 western states. Stor is the largest retailer of lifestyle furniture on the west coast.

CUSTOMERS

IKEA attracts 53,300,000 customers each year. In the United States, approximately 40,000 people shop at these stores each week. The fact that 30 to 40 percent of all IKEA shoppers come from out of state indicates that IKEA has a much larger trading area than most other furniture retailers. A shopper will spend an average of two hours in the store during one visit. Thus, IKEA seems to be successful in its strategy of creating a relaxed atmosphere that encourages the customer to shop longer, making the shopping experience a day outing for the family.

TARGET MARKET

IKEA targets the 25- to 44-age group who are college-educated, have a professional or managerial job, and earn over $30,000 a year. In addition, this group is married, has children, and own their own home. This group, often referred to as the "yuppies," tends to prefer this type of furniture because it represents good value for the money, is very stylish, and can be taken home immediately, allowing for instant gratification.

The 25- to 44-year-old segment makes up one-third of the total population (43.5 million people) and is the fastest growing demographic segment. Because of its large size and high level of discretionary income, this group is considered the most significant market for furniture. The future outlook for furniture purchasing for this age group looks very promising. As this group ages and starts families, it is becoming more home oriented. Many are new home buyers who will spend more on furniture now than at any other time in their lives.

QUESTIONS

1. Is IKEA correct in their decision to not adapt their merchandise to different regional markets?
2. How can IKEA alleviate their distribution and out-of-stock problems?
3. Do you think it is wise to focus on the "yuppie" segment? As this target market ages, do you see any potential problems?
4. How does IKEA maintain its growth?
5. Discuss the pros and cons of IKEA's promotional strategy. In particular, is one sale per year viable? Is too much emphasis and money being placed on the catalog as a means to market IKEA?

*This case was prepared by James T. Strong and Jeannie Latona, The University of Akron.

■ CASE 3
Mary Kay Cosmetics, Inc.: Corporate Planning in an Era of Uncertainty*

Mary Kay Cosmetics, Inc. of Dallas, Texas, is an international manufacturer and distributor of skin care products, makeup items, toiletry items, accessories, and hair care products. Founded in 1963 by Mary Kay Ash, a highly motivated entrepreneur, the firm experienced spectacular sales growth in its early years. As a direct-selling organization, much of its success was based on motivating and constantly replenishing its more than 170,000-member sales force. Mary Kay had planned to become "the finest and largest skin care teaching organization in the world."

Senior management recognized in early 1989 that the firm was suffering from some of the same problems that were affecting the whole direct-sales industry. The company was suddenly having problems attracting new recruits who would become "beauty consultants" and "sales directors" as well as consumers of the firm's product line. Management was evaluating a corporate strategy that had been developed by the firm's founder. The organization was repositioning itself for future growth. The question was now, "What do we need to do to get us where we want to go, to reach the kind of customer we want to reach, to recruit the kind of consultant we want to recruit?"

BACKGROUND INFORMATION

Mary Kay Cosmetics was founded on September 13, 1963, in Dallas, Texas, by Mary Kay (now Mary Kay Ash). The company had an initial working capital of $5,000, the right to use a skin care formula that had been created by a hide tanner, and nine saleswomen. The first headquarters was a 500-square-foot storefront in Exchange Park, a large bank and office building complex in Dallas.

The first basic line of cosmetics was manufactured to specification under the label of "Beauty by Mary Kay" by another firm. It included what was called the "Basic Skin Care Set." It consisted of a limited number of basic items that, when used as the company suggested, provided a balanced program of skin care. The firm also sold custom wigs. Wigs were styled at the headquarters location and at skin care shows and were originally used as a traffic generator. They were discontinued in 1965. Management believed that it could achieve corporate success in direct sales by establishing a "dream company" that would be based on the personal philosophies of the founder. The Mary Kay philosophy suggested that every person associated with the company, from the chairman of the board to the newest recruit, live by the golden rule, "Do unto others as you would have them do unto you," and the priorities of God first, family second, and career third.

Initial corporate strategies included heavy emphasis on personal relationships, opportunities for women to fully utilize their skills and talents, no geographical restrictions on sales territories, and a sales presentation in the home for no more than five or six women. Merchandise was available for immediate delivery from stock. All products were sold on a cash basis. Every Mary Kay representative was considered an independent businessperson to be remunerated in the form of commission. Pink was selected as the corporate color.

By 1989, Mary Kay Cosmetics, Inc. had again become a private corporation after going public in 1968. It had sales in 1988 of $405,730,000, a sales staff of 170,000 beauty consultants and sales directors, a compensation structure to allow women to earn commensurate with their individual abilities and efforts, and total brand awareness of 90 percent of all women. Mary Kay was ranked by *The Wall Street Journal* as an industry leader in basic skin care research and in product development. The company had a new production facility, a new warehouse, and a new corporate headquarters in Dallas, all of which were internally financed. The product line was distributed throughout the United States and through wholly owned subsidiaries in Australia, Canada, Argentina, and West Germany. The average number of beauty consult-

EXHIBIT A
Analysis of Mary Kay independent beauty consultants—1984–1988

Year	Average Number of Consultants	Average Productivity	Net Sales ($000)
1988	170,316	$2,382	$405,730
1987	148,080	$2,199	$325,647
1986	141,113	$1,807	$255,016
1985	145,493	$1,711	$248,970
1984	173,101	$1,603	$277,500

ants, their average productivity, and net sales for the years 1984 through 1988 are shown in Exhibit A.

THE MARY KAY MYSTIQUE

Much of the initial and continuing success of the firm was attributed to the entrepreneurial spirit of its founder and chairman emeritus, Mary Kay Ash. Mary Kay traced her strong-willed, competitive spirit to the constant, positive reinforcement her mother gave her while growing up in Texas. "I was taught to put my best effort into everything I did, and I can honestly say that I've always done that," Mary Kay said. "I competed with myself and strove to excel." Her "you can do it" philosophy guided the company through the challenges and setbacks of its early years.

Mary Kay spent 13 years of her professional direct-sales career with Stanley Home Products, Inc. She became one of the firm's leading salespersons and was promoted to management. She also worked for another 11 years in a similar position with a company in Houston called World Gift. After becoming its national training director for 43 states, she left the organization. Later, upon deciding that retirement did not satisfy her, she developed a strategy and philosophy that was to become Mary Kay Cosmetics. She became its first president. A son, Richard Rogers, joined her on the death of her second husband. Another son, Ben, and a daughter, Marilyn, eventually became part of the organization.

As president, Mary Kay became a walking showcase for the company's products. Her values and motivational incentives became the basis for the firm's marketing program. Her definitions of happiness brought women to the firm as beauty consultants, sales directors, and users of the product line. "Under her 'frills and lace' is a high-powered businesswoman who has built a skin care empire, and in a pioneering style," suggested *Marketing and Media Decisions*, a trade magazine. The color pink, her "favorite" color, was found in her attire, her office, her home, and every facet of corporate life.

A unique and idealistic individual, Mary Kay Ash was called "one of the most influential and respected personalities in business and philanthropic circles" by *Executive Female*, a respected magazine among entrepreneurs. She also received many of the most distinguished cosmetic, direct sales, and professional awards, including "Cosmetic Career Woman of the Year," "Direct Selling Hall of Fame," and the 1978 "Horatio Alger Award." She was the cover feature on several magazines, including the *Saturday Evening Post; Business Week* named her one of America's top corporate women, and *Time* cited her in its economy and business section. She also appeared on such television shows as "Sixty Minutes," "Phil Donahue," and "Good Morning America."

"Far from being an employer," indicated Nicole Woolsey Biggart in a recent book on direct-selling organization leadership, "Mary Kay Ash . . . is mother, sister, guardian angel, and patron saint to the women who sell her products." In this context, a national sales director maintained, "We don't adore Mary Kay, we admire her, and we would want to emulate her." In the belief that "adore" versus "admire" was a good distinction, management felt that Mary Kay had positioned the company for the day when "she no longer would be here." As president, Mary Kay had maintained, "Although Mary Kay Cosmetics was created as the dream of one woman, it has long since achieved independent existence. And because our company is grounded in a solid foundation of specific values and principles, its continuance no longer depends upon any single person."

A number of programs were in place to cushion the eventual departure of Mary Kay from active management. Initially, her philosophy was captured on film, in books, and in articles written about her. Also, a national sales director program, made up of the firm's top saleswomen, was established to emphasize continuing the Mary Kay spirit in the company. Mary Kay was developed as an entity as opposed to an individual by perpetuating all of the ideas that she felt should be part of her "dream company." "This is important," indicated Richard C. Bartlett, the current president, in an interview. "Here we are talking about philosophical beliefs which traditionally, in business and religion and other organizations, do continue on if the organization is imbued with them."

On November 10, 1987, Mary Kay Ash was named chairman emeritus. Richard R. Rogers, her son, was named chairman. Richard C. Bartlett, whose initial experience in direct selling was with Tupperware and later as vice president of marketing at Mary Kay, was named president and chief operating officer. "I plan to remain active in the firm on a continuing basis, working with salespeople," indicated Mary Kay. "Our sales force now consists of tens of thousands of skilled sales professionals, and they are supported by an experienced management team."

THE CORPORATE CONCEPT

The original corporate strategy of the firm was based on the "Mary Kay Marketing Plan." In the plan the sales force or "beauty consultants" sold the company's skin care products at home demonstration shows. They were supervised and motivated by "sales directors" who also were responsible for replenishing the sales force on a continuing basis with new recruits. The plan was a corporate strategy designed to include the best features and avoid the mistakes Mary Kay had previously encountered in her 20 years with direct-selling companies.

As a part of the plan, the marketing program was intended to foster retail sales to ultimate consumers. Commissions were earned by beauty consultants on products sold at retail prices to ultimate consumers. All products were purchased directly from the company and were based on the same discount schedule. All sales directors were once beauty consultants, thus avoiding the multilevel practice of selling franchises or distributorships.

In the plan there were no territories to limit where consultants could sell or recruit. The consultant was required to purchase a "showcase" of basic products and carry an inventory. Consultants were encouraged to sell only Mary Kay products during their skin care classes to avoid creating trademark confusion and divided effort.

Consultants were considered to be self-employed. The marketing plan was intended to support the independent contractor status. At the corporate level, management was expected to manufacture quality cosmetics, plan product and market development, provide for discounts and commissions, advertise, plan for working capital for corporate growth, and offer incentive awards and prizes for beauty consultants who excelled in sales, recruiting, or leadership.

One of the most special aspects of the marketing plan was the use of national and regional seminars, career conferences, and management conferences that individuals could attend on a voluntary basis for inspiration, training, and general professional upgrading. At the national level, this strategy manifested itself annually in what the company called "Seminar." Seminar was an elaborately produced series of four consecutive three-day sessions that attracted a total of 24,000 sales participants to the Dallas Convention Center.

The highly motivational event had a tradition of recognition, education, and entertainment. It included hours of classes on product knowledge, marketing and sales techniques, and other business management topics. It culminated in an awards night in which thousands of glamorous, elegantly dressed, bejeweled women received extravagant recognition as achievers in the organization. Mary Kay traditionally presided over the event. She appeared on stage, sometimes emerging at the top of a series of lighted stairs, sometimes arriving in a carriage drawn by white horses and surrounded by footmen.

Typically, participants would proceed to the stage to claim expensive prizes such as mink coats, gold and diamond jewelry, trips to places like Acapulco, and use of new pale-pink Cadillacs, Buicks, and Oldsmobiles. "So in our company, we eliminated practical gifts," indicated Mary Kay, "I would try to choose prizes that would excite and thrill the recipient. I thought that the best prizes were things a woman wanted but probably wouldn't buy for herself." The legendary pink Cadillac for many became a symbol of Mary Kay Cosmetics and its incentive programs.

THE CHANGING EXTERNAL ENVIRONMENT

All of the firm's products were sold on the principal bases of price and quality in highly competitive markets. On the basis of information available to it from industry sources, management believed there were some 13,000 companies (including both direct sales and manufacturing companies) that had products that competed with Mary Kay. The firm competed directly with direct-sales companies in sales of cosmetics products and indirectly with firms that manufactured cosmetics and toiletry items that were sold in retail or department stores. It also competed in the recruiting of independent sales persons from other direct-selling organizations whose product lines may or may not have competed with those of Mary Kay.

The direct-selling industry consisted of a few well-established companies and many smaller firms that sold about every product imaginable including toys, animal food, plant care products, clothing, computer software, and financial services. Among the dominant companies were Avon (cosmetics), Amway Corp. (home cleaning products), Shaklee Corp. (vitamins and health foods), Encyclopedia Britannica, Tupperware (plastic dishes and food containers), Consolidated Foods' Electrolux (vacuum cleaners), and the Fuller Brush Co. (household products). Avon Products, Inc. was substantially larger than Mary Kay in terms of total independent sales people, sales volume, and resources. Several other competitors such as Revlon, Inc., a firm that sold cosmetics primarily through retail stores, were larger than Mary Kay in terms of sales and had more resources.

By the late 1980s, corporate management at Mary Kay considered the direct-selling industry and the cosmetics industry to be at maturity. The spectacular sales growth characteristic of the 1960s and 1970s had given way to a pattern of stagnant revenue and profit growth. The industry was having difficulty attracting new sales people who generated much of its sales growth and provided a return to sales directors. Competition for the customer was great as there were not as many users coming into the market. Industry problems were blamed on a number of factors: the increasing number of working women, which cut into both the number of available recruits and sales targets; the improvement in the economy, which encouraged women to avoid involvement in part-time sales and to shop for more expensive beauty products; shorter product life cycles, which forced new products, new innovations, and twists of existing products that were getting old; and the growing competition from firms selling similar products. There were also hostile takeovers, such as the 1989 bid of Amway Corporation for Avon Products, Inc. and leveraged buyouts, such as the December, 1985, LBO of Mary Kay by its founders. According to President Bartlett, senior management would have to "react by being much more flexible, by being able to come out with new products, by introducing new innovations, and by developing new strategies for existing products that were getting old."

Industry research had identified Avon, a direct competitor, as having products that were used by older people who wanted a less expensive product. Noxell, the manufacturer of Cover Girl products, was viewed as the creator of a moderately upscale product line that appealed to a younger market. Estee Lauder was a product line that was more upscale and appealed to an older market segment. In product image, Estee Lauder had been historically in an envious position. The firm cultivated this in all of its literature, all of its packaging, and in all of its product formulas. Revlon, whose image varied by product line, was sold through department stores and mass merchandisers. It built a multi-billion dollar business by buying out old established lines like Max Factor, Charles of the Ritz, Germain Monte, Diane Von Furstenberg, and Almae.

Although maturity was sometimes looked on with disfavor, Mary Kay executives felt that this did not mean a lack of opportunity for increased profitability or lack of opportunity to increase sales. The changing nature of competition in the cosmetics market was identified as one of the strategic concerns in the design of the Mary Kay product line. Both the mass market and upscale segments of the skin care marketplace were perceived to be changing rapidly. In both cases a plethora of new entries emerged, some from well-established American firms such as S.C. Johnson and some from European or Japanese firms. One example was an entry from L'Oreal, a European firm. The skin care line, Plentitude, was sold through mass market outlets. An example of a Japanese firm was the Kao Safina line, which was introduced through Kao's American acquisition, Jergens Skin Care.

The changing nature of science and technology was also identified as a strategic concern in an analysis of the external environment. Management felt that the period of the late 1980s and the early 1990s would see the debut of several new "cosmeceuticals": products marketed as drugs and capable of making drug claims, but with wide impact on the pharmaceutical and cosmetics markets. Upjohn's Rogaine and Ortho Laboratories' Retin-A, treatments for acne that doubled as anti-wrinkle creams, were predicted to become over-the-counter drugs within the next two to three years. New drug applications for six to eight other retinoids were known to be under way with anti-aging claims. At the same time, greater understanding of skin physiology enabled the development of more advanced traditional skin care products, including those that could legitimately make counterirritant claims and those that could protect users from environmental damage, such as from the sun.

The 1980s also saw a proliferation of regulatory activity affecting the cosmetics industry. In the United States such activity was seen from the Food and Drug Administration (FDA), the Federal Trade Commission (FTC), Congress, and various state legislatures. At the same time, cosmetics regulations were changing in the European Economic Community (EEC) countries and Argentina, Canada, and Australia. Prospects for expansion into Mexico and Thailand presented the challenge of learning to deal with regulations in markets that were new to Mary Kay. It was clear that a new wave of regulatory activity affecting the industry had commenced. Ingredients, claims, packaging, testing, advertising, and other activities of the cosmetics industry were being closely scrutinized by regulators and legislators with a view toward regulatory control. A series of hearings held by Congressman Ron Wyden, D-OR, during 1988 were predicted to produce new cosmetics legislation in Congress.

Corporate research revealed that the Mary Kay customer was primarily identified by its beauty consultants. The company did very little direct customer prospecting. Beauty consultants found their customers one by one or in small groups through referrals, and through holding skin care classes where they might know one person but not the other members of the group. The typical Mary Kay customer was a female, in her late thirties, married, and Caucasian. Geographically, she lived in all 50 states as well as in those countries where Mary Kay had operations. Most customers were rural and suburban as opposed to urban. The Mary Kay method of selling was perceived by management to be more disposed to the woman who might not have easy access to a store and also appeared to lend itself on the supply side to mobility by automobile. By occupation, customers were white collar professionals with moderate incomes and a high school education with some college. In practice, the upper and lower ends of a market segmented by social stratification variables tended to be neglected. Consultants were perceived to be slightly more upscale than their typical customer and customarily sold down to lower levels of social stratification.

The Senior Vice President of Mary Kay, Ms. Barbara Beasley, had hoped to expand the customer base through greater penetration in three key segments: blacks, Hispanics, and mature women. In a corporate analysis of the changing consumer, she concluded that because of greater education and disposable income, many more women were becoming regular users of product lines used previously by only a few consumers. Increased consumer sophistication meant that high performance products would be required that had meaningful claims and would fit within the Mary Kay context of a teaching orientation. The market was identified as becoming increasingly segmented by usage as consumers gravitated toward brand positions such as those formulated for sensitive skin, for contact lens wearers, for mature skin, and for ethnic consumers.

MARKETING STRATEGIES

Several marketing strategies emerged as the result of an overall reexamination of existing corporate strategies. The area receiving initial attention was the product line. The lines, as reviewed in Exhibit B, consisted of skin care products for women and for men, glamour items, toiletry items for women and for men, accessories and hair care products. Skin care products, in various formulas related to skin type, included cleansers, skin fresheners, facial masks, moisturizers, and foundation makeup, and were sold in sets as a five-step beauty program. Glamour items or cosmetics included lip and eye colors, mascaras, blushers, eye liners, face powder and lip gloss. Toiletry items included hand and body lotions, bath products, and colognes. Hair care products consisted of shampoo, conditioners, and hair spray. Accessories such as samples, makeup mirrors, cosmetics bags, and travel kits were sold primarily as hostess gifts, business supplies, or sales aids.

THE PRODUCT LINES

There had been no significant additions to the product line in the first 13 years of the company. Mary Kay had purchased the rights to a line that she had been using personally for about ten years. Initially, the line consisted of only ten products focused on skin care. Although management evaluated the product line on an ongoing basis, adjustments were kept to a minimum. Corporate policy had been to purposely limit the line to a minimum number of essential skin care and glamour items. Each company consultant was encouraged to carry a basic inventory. With a product line of no more than 50 items, inventory and product information could be kept at a manageable level and products could be delivered immediately.

The Mary Kay product strategy was to offer "preeminent" products to customers. According to management definition, each product sold was "to be outstanding; to stand above others; to have paramount rank, dignity or importance." This was to mean products would be of excellent quality, be competitively priced, and be safe to use. As the product line was limited, compared to competition, each individual product had to appeal to a reasonably large segment of consumers. New product introductions were made in the cosmetics, skin care, fragrances, and toiletries markets. The five-year product plan was to focus on three major areas: (1) update, enhance, and improve current product lines, formulations, and packaging; (2) introduce significant new products in the treatment/skin care category; and (3) introduce a completely updated glamour line that would include a new system for recommending and using color, new product formulations, new packaging, and updated shades. The value added provided by the consultant would be enhanced by offering consumer-oriented videos, brochures, profiles, packaging inserts, and other educational material.

The Mary Kay Color Awareness program was introduced to update the glamour line. Its intent was to simplify the selection of glamour makeup shades by guiding women in their own color decisions and was based on three key principles: skin tone, personal preference, and wardrobe. With the program, the sales force had the ability to help customers make color choices in these areas. A line of color-coordinated eye shadows, lip colors, and blushers was introduced to support the program.

A reformulated skin care line specifically designed for men was introduced in 1987 as part of the strategy to update the skin care line. It consisted of a cleansing bar, toner, facial conditioner and oil absorber, sunscreen, moisturizer, and shave cream. It replaced a product the company called Mr. K skin care, which was the women's products repackaged in brown tubes. Management made its appeal to women who bought the product for men by saying, "Don't you care about your husband's skin? Look what it did for you. Look what it can do for him." Man-

EXHIBIT B
Product line by sales percentage

	Year Ended December 31,			
	1988	1987	1986	1985
Skin care products for women	38	40	46	41
Skin care products for men	1	2	1	1
Glamour items	28	32	24	31
Nail care products	7	—	—	—
Toiletry items for women	13	13	15	13
Toiletry items for men	3	3	3	2
Hair care products	1	1	2	2
Accessories	9	9	9	10
Total	100	100	100	100

agement predicted that this would be a growth area as more and more men started to care about their skin.

A skin care program called "skin wellness" was introduced as an education program for consumers on awareness of the factors that would affect the skin, particularly sunlight. It was considered a natural fit for Mary Kay because of the teaching orientation of the sales process. It educated the consumer on how to identify certain kinds of skin cancers in the early stages. It advised a monthly program of skin self-examination in which the consumer would literally look over her body from head to toe in a mirror. Irregularities would be checked again in a month to see if they had changed. There was no mention of Mary Kay products in the program. Although perceived as a consumer-affairs, goodwill, and trust-building program, the consumer could buy products from Mary Kay that would help with protection from the sun.

PACKAGING

Pink was selected as the corporate color because Mary Kay thought that attractive pink packages would be left out on display in the white bathrooms in vogue in 1963. The entire product line, however, had recently been repackaged. Every item was changed to make graphics consistent, to be up-to-date, and to have individual identity but still look like it was part of the Mary Kay family of products. A new corporate logo, a mix of gold and hot yellow to symbolize the heat of the sun and its eclipse, was featured on the new packages. A new shade of pink, one that was more mauve and less yellow, was selected to compliment the logo. It was considered to be more subtle, more current, more upscale than the shade of pink that had become the corporate color. It was part of the quality and value image that the company wanted to convey. The new pink would ultimately find its way onto company trucks, uniforms, promotional material, and ultimately, the Cadillacs.

ADVERTISING AND PROMOTION

In the early 1980s, when the company was growing at a very fast rate, management experimented with consumer advertising. The program was initiated in the sales division, not marketing. The advertising campaign involved magazines as well as television advertisements. Although no great change in consumer demand was documented, the reaction from the sales force was very positive. Management had concluded that if it were to use advertising in the future, it would want to impart a message to the consumer that would improve the corporate image and support the field sales force in the form of recognition and compensation.

Management justified its lack of interest in consumer advertising by claiming that it spent what its competitors spent on advertising in compensating the sales force. About 33 percent of total dollar income of the firm was estimated to go back to the field sales force in terms of commission and rewards. Promotional efforts were concentrated on rewarding the field sales force for their accomplishments. In Seminar, for example, thousands of consultants and sales directors were presented with more than $5 million in selected prizes for their outstanding performance.

The firm had an active public relations and publicity program that centered on Mary Kay Ash, launching new products in fashion magazines, and publicizing the activities and accomplishments of the field sales force. Press releases in the form of corporate publicity and financial information were a part of this program.

DIRECT SUPPORT

A direct-support program was introduced as part of a program to "build a company of substance, to create a product line of high quality and to provide a service of value to the consumer." The program involved direct mail. Consultants sent the names of their customers to corporate headquarters. Management then did a mailing to the customer that appeared to come from the beauty consultant. An upscale, four-color brochure plus a personal letter was included that identified both the consultant and consumer by name. The beauty consultant would then follow up by telephone to the consumer to inquire if the information had been received. Initially, the program created some suspicion from the field sales force. Sales people thought that management was going to take these customer names and create a house account and service customers directly. "So we worked on that for a while," contended Ms. Barbara Beasley, senior vice president of marketing, "and I think we were able to prove to them that our objective was not to bypass the consultant in starting up this direct mail program, but rather to support the consultant, which is why it's called direct support." The direct-support program was based on the consultant's contacts. If the consultant did not make the follow-up telephone call, if the consultant didn't deliver the products to the consumer, then no sale was ever made. All products were sold through the sales force.

Beauty consultants were offered products at wholesale discounts from suggested retail prices, for resale to retail customers. At retail, the Mary Kay product line was priced competitively, just below brands that were distributed through department stores and generally well above direct retail store/mass-distributed brands. Company literature included suggested retail prices, but the ultimate retail price was determined by the consultant who could charge less than the suggested retail by running her own promotions. "She can ultimately set the retail," said Ms. Curran Croskeys, vice president of product marketing at Mary Kay. "She buys it at a discount off retail, so it's up to her as to how much profit she wants to make."

PLANNING IN A MARKETING-ORIENTED FIRM

Philosophically, corporate planning at Mary Kay Cosmetics was based on the golden rule, "Do unto others as you would have them do unto you," and the priorities of God first, family second, and career third. Mary Kay maintained, "I've found when you just let go and place yourself in God's hands, everything in your life goes right. I believe we have success because God has led us all the way." In this context, she identified her son, Richard Rogers, chairman of the board and chief executive officer, as a "brilliant administrator and outstanding corporate planner [who] is recognized as one of today's bright, young financial geniuses." "Yet," she noted, "not even he can look at computer printouts or market surveys and truly predict the future."

On a more operational basis, the management team was led by Mr. Bartlett as president and chief operating officer. The organization, in Mr. Bartlett's experience, was really focused on celebrating the achievements of the sales force. In a typical organization chart, he maintained, the board chairman, the president, vice presidents, and managers were ordered down to the sales organization. At Mary Kay, the situation was thought of in the reverse. The sales force was perceived to be at the top. The president's job was to support the executive team, who in turn supported other people, who in turn supported the sales force. "The program was based upon," as Mr. Bartlett suggested, "loyalty to the people involved, loyalty to the product, and loyalty to the plan." There was a loyalty to the people, such as the director who brought the consultant into the business. There was product brand loyalty built up because the company found that it's a rare woman who could effectively sell the company's products that didn't believe in them. And there was loyalty to the plan in the form of compensation, recognition, and incentive contests that recognized sales people as individuals for their achievements.

The mission statement of the firm, as illustrated in Exhibit C, summarized the attitudes of management toward people in field sales as well as customers. It was considered an all-inclusive statement of what the company wanted to be. As President Bartlett indicated, "We used to have financial goals as part of the mission statement, and we have gone away from that. That didn't work as well for us." Having a flexible, philosophically oriented statement yielded some clearly delineated objectives for the corporation. Division and department objectives supported the mission statement.

To emphasize the importance of the corporate mission statement, President Bartlett had it printed up on small tent cards. These were distributed to all of the employees to remind them of the fundamental social and economic purpose of the firm. On the other side of the tent card were three words: "listen, listen, listen."

Manufacturing was emphasized in the first statement of preeminence because management felt that consumer-driven organizations needed to have competitive products and excellence in manufacturing to survive. As part of the changing focus at Mary Kay, the senior vice president of research and development/quality assurance reported directly to the president. Previously, the R&D and quality assurance programs had reported inside the manufacturing group. "I wanted, frankly," indicated President Bartlett, "to draw the manufacturing group into this mission so that they were not feeling separate from it; they are a part of it."

The use of the phrase *personal care products* in the mission statement was a revision of an older mission statement that included the phrase: "being the leading teaching-oriented skin care cosmetic company." This was a narrow statement that tended to focus on skin care only. The personalized service phrase was a continuation of what the firm had done well for 25 years. Management did not want this area to be neglected by other changes in the mission. Convenience was included because the strength of the firm was thought to be in the consultant. When the customer lost the consultant, it became inconvenient to buy Mary Kay products. Included was the phrase, "through our independent sales force." The sales force was thought to "drive" the objectives of the company.

There was no formal planning department at Mary Kay Cosmetics. The emphasis was placed on having a corporate mission that would be flexible and could be looked back on from time to time, as opposed to a strategy that said the firm was expected to reach certain goals in a specific year. Management felt that, as a basic strategy, a team of flexible, hard-hitting, and adaptable executives would be better able to handle the major changes that were occurring in the external environment. A recent appointment of Dr. Myra Barker as senior vice president of research and development/quality assurance and chief scientific officer reflected this strategy. "This reflects our concern for being in harmony with what might hit us scientifically in the cosmetic marketing world," indicated President Bartlett. "Good strategy is implementation strategy—where you don't get off with a planning group

EXHIBIT C
The Mary Kay mission

To achieve preeminence in the manufacturing and marketing of personal care products by providing personalized service, value and convenience to Mary Kay customers through our independent sales force.
Richard C. Bartlett, President

and say, 'This is where we're going to arrive at an X time in the future.' . . . But you're flexible enough, and you have the intellectual muscle to adapt to change."

"I fear a rigidly in-place plan" and "I fear formal planning departments" were responses of President Bartlett when asked in his Dallas office if Mary Kay Cosmetics had a formal plan for looking ahead. Bartlett had concluded that "we have an overriding mission which we can look back on, and I'd rather view the mission we have, as opposed to a locked-in concrete strategy that says we will come out at such and such a place in the year 2000. While I say that," he maintained, "there is no way that we can really anticipate all the major changes coming at us now, the geometric progression of information, governmental interference, regulation and all the myriad of factors that we have to face."

Although there was not a formal strategic planning department at Mary Kay Cosmetics, the product line was planned out for five years. Each year key executives, such as the president, department heads, directors, and all who might be involved in implementing the strategy, would meet to brainstorm sociological, consumer, industry, and scientific trends. Out of this meeting would emerge a product plan. For three years out it was very detailed, showing what the firm was doing every month. President Bartlett felt that such planning was necessary to anticipate the changes that they knew were going to happen. "You gain flexibility by having this type of plan," suggested Ms. Curran Croskeys, vice president of product marketing. "By having a track to follow, you accomplish the plan in a routine way. You use brain power and other resources to change if you have to."

THE CONTEMPORARY CHALLENGE

One era ended and another began when Mary Kay Cosmetics experienced its first sales decline in 1984. The early era is a case study in entrepreneurship. The latter era is a study in the efforts of an established organization attempting to achieve its objectives in a changed business environment. Mary Kay's initial objective was "to establish a company that would give unlimited opportunity to women." In the late 1980s there was an increase in full-time job opportunities for women elsewhere. Not only were they not available to sell the product, but they were not at home to buy it.

Mary Kay Cosmetics, Inc. had for over 25 years focused on celebrating the achievements of its sales force. Much of the forward momentum in that sales force had come from the entrepreneurial spirit of Mary Kay Ash, the founder of the company. Mary Kay had been elevated to the position of chairman emeritus. A new management team was in place. The firm had repositioned itself to meet the challenges of a new decade. The question was now, could the firm accomplish its corporate mission and objectives in this changing environment?

DISCUSSION QUESTIONS

1. Evaluate and justify the personal selling strategy of Mary Kay Cosmetics. What factors should a manufacturer consider before choosing to include personal selling as a form of promotion in the marketing mix?
2. What evidence is there to conclude that the marketing concept is understood and applied by Mary Kay management?
3. Evaluate the strategies that Mary Kay management has introduced as part of its positioning strategy. How much impact will these strategies have in the competitive environment as the firm seeks profitable growth in the marketplace?
4. How important is a mission statement in giving direction to strategy development in a marketing-oriented organization?
5. How much importance is placed on the planning function at Mary Kay Cosmetics?
6. What conclusions can you draw from a review of the financial performance of Mary Kay Cosmetics, Inc. from the years 1978 through 1988?
7. Discuss the importance of changes in the external environment. How much impact do they have on strategic planning in organizations like Mary Kay Cosmetics?
8. How much impact is the "retirement" of Mary Kay Ash likely to have on the forward momentum of the organization? What decisions and actions should be undertaken to continue Mary Kay Ash's formula for success?

°This case was prepared by James W. Camerius of Northern Michigan University and is intended to be used as a basis for class discussion rather than to illustrate either effective or ineffective handling of an administrative situation.

Presented to the Midwest Society for Case Research Workshop, 1989.

EXHIBIT D
Mary Kay corporation consolidated balance sheets—December 31, 1988 and 1987

Assets

	1988	1987
Current assets:		
Cash and cash equivalents	$ 15,039,000	$ 11,500,000
Accounts receivable	5,345,000	3,330,000
Inventories:		
Raw materials	15,172,000	11,206,000
Finished goods	34,567,000	22,865,000
	49,739,000	34,071,000
Notes receivable	—	17,267,000
Deferred income tax benefit	3,790,000	695,000
Other current assets	3,482,000	2,587,000
Total current assets	77,395,000	69,450,000
Property, plant and equipment, at cost:		
Land	4,932,000	2,950,000
Buildings and improvements	16,268,000	12,483,000
Furniture, fixtures and equip.	49,459,000	40,046,000
Construction in progress	3,385,000	605,000
	74,044,000	56,084,000
Less accumulated depreciation	(28,296,000)	(16,878,000)
	45,748,000	39,206,000
Assets held for sale	10,000,000	9,215,000
Identified intangible assets	103,820,000	108,558,000
Goodwill	31,205,000	32,624,000
Long-term investment at market	13,630,000	—
Other assets	7,245,000	2,515,000
	$289,043,000	$261,568,000

Source: Annual Report

EXHIBIT D
continued

Liabilities and Capital Deficiency

	1988	1987
Current liabilities:		
Accounts payable	$ 15,513,000	$ 12,529,000
Accrued liabilities	45,097,000	34,876,000
Deferred sales	7,685,000	4,567,000
Current port. of long-term debt	18,000,000	31,000,000
Total current liabilities	86,295,000	82,972,000
Long-term debt	81,035,000	75,000,000
Debentures	124,258,000	106,765,000
Notes payable to related parties	73,231,000	73,231,000
Deferred income taxes	333,000	1,665,000
Other liabilities	24,648,000	12,259,000
Commitments		
Capital deficiency:		
$4.50 Class A noncumulative part. con. pref. stock, $1.00 par value 730,000 shares authorized, 529,945 shares issued and outstanding	530,000	530,000
Common stock, $1.00 par value; 1,100,000 shares authorized, 365,963 shares issued and outstanding	366,000	366,000
Capital in excess of par value	5,335,000	5,335,000
Accumulated deficit	(36,902,000)	(28,380,000)
Investment valuation allowance	(1,911,000)	—
Less amount not "pushed down" to equity of subsidiary	(68,175,000)	(68,175,000)
Total capital deficiency	(100,757,000)	(90,324,000)
	$ 289,043,000	$261,568,000

EXHIBIT D
continued

Consolidated Statements of Operations
Years Ended December 31, 1988 and 1987

	1988	1987
Net sales	$405,730,000	$325,647,000
Cost of sales	104,503,000	86,501,000
Selling, gen. and admin. exp.	262,797,000	207,359,000
Operating income	38,430,000	31,787,000
Insurance proceeds	—	—
Write down of assets	(11,000,000)	(4,696,000)
Interest and other income, net	3,137,000	3,884,000
Interest expenses	(37,248,000)	(40,391,000)
Loss before income taxes and extraordinary items	(6,681,000)	(9,416,000)
Provision for income taxes	1,495,000	5,876,000
Loss before extraordinary items	(8,176,000)	(15,292,000)
Extraordinary expenses, net of related income tax benefit of $423,000 in 1988 and $5,327,000 1987	822,000	5,596,000
Net loss	$ (8,998,000)	$ (20,888,000)

Consolidated Statements of Cash Flows
Years Ended December 31, 1988 and 1987

	1988	1987
Cash flows from operating activities:		
Net loss	$ (8,998,000)	$ (20,888,000)
Adjustments to reconcile net loss to net cash provided by operating activities:		
Depreciation	8,288,000	9,180,000
Amortization	6,410,000	7,052,000
Defined benefit retirement program expense	3,598,000	—
Accretion expense	17,493,000	14,834,000
Deferred tax provision	(7,522,000)	(106,000)
Write down of assets	11,000,000	4,696,000
Loss on disposition of assets	27,000	325,000
Extraordinary expenses	1,245,000	10,923,000
Changes in assets and liabilities:		
Decrease (increase) in:		
Accounts receivable	(1,806,000)	(125,000)
Inventories	(15,870,000)	(12,767,000)
Income tax receivable	—	6,206,000
Other current assets	(895,000)	(464,000)
Goodwill	—	—
Other assets	(392,000)	(195,000)
Increase (decrease) in:		
Accounts payable	2,984,000	589,000
Accrued liabilities	11,283,000	8,817,000
Deferred sales	1,858,000	(1,996,000)
Other liabilities	(458,000)	(343,000)
Federal income tax refund	3,986,000	10,164,000
Other, net	729,000	754,000

EXHIBIT D
continued

Net cash provided by operating act.	32,960,000	36,656,000
Cash flows from investing activities:		
Purchase of investment	(15,541,000)	—
Capital expenditures	(6,025,000)	(2,576,000)
Proceeds from sales of assets	383,000	1,130,000
Net cash provided by (used in) investing activities	(21,183,000)	(1,446,000)
Cash flows from financing activities:		
Principal payment of long-term debt	(90,000,000)	(125,733,000)
Increase in long-term debt	(82,535,000)	90,000,000
Cost of refinancing debt	(1,569,000)	(8,596,000)
Proceeds from loans from life insurance policies	796,000	—
Net cash used in financing act.	(8,238,000)	(44,329,000)
Net increase (decrease) in cash and cash equivalents	3,539,000	(9,119,000)
Cash and cash equivalents at beginning of year	11,500,000	20,619,000
Cash and cash equivalents at end of year	$ 15,039,000	$ 11,500,000
Additional information:		
Cash payments (refunds) for:		
Interest (net of amounts capitalized)	17,290,000	29,107,000
Income taxes	4,755,000	(15,235,000)
Noncash financing activities:		
Restructuring an existing note receivable:		
Decrease in note receivable	$ 17,267,000	—
Decrease in accounts receivable	1,000,000	—
Increase in note receivable	(11,000,000)	—
Increase in assets held for sale	(10,000,000)	—
Increase in deferred taxes	2,733,000	—
Restructuring an existing note payable:		
Decrease in long-term debt	(16,000,000)	—
Decrease in accrued liabilities	(862,000)	—
Increase in long-term debt	16,500,000	—
Increase in deferred taxes	362,000	—

EXHIBIT E
Mary Kay Cosmetics, Inc., Dallas, TX—Financial performance, 1978–1988

Year	Net Sales (000)	Net Profit (000)	Total Assets (000)	Net Worth (000)
1988	$ 405,730	$ (8,998)	$289,043	$(100,757)
1987	325,647	(20,888)	261,568	(90,324)
1986	255,016	(55,502)	284,180	(69,351)
1985	13,457[(1)]	(1,306)[(1)]	328,922[(1)]	(13,647)[(1)]
	235,513[(2)]	21,286[(2)]	272,166[(2)]	183,304[(2)]
1984	277,500	33,781	217,554	163,746
1983	323,758	36,654	180,683	131,725
1982	304,275	35,372	152,457	95,316
1981	235,296	24,155	100,976	61,952
1980	166,938	15,135	74,431	38,633
1979	91,400	9,632	50,916	24,618
1978	53,746	4,873	36,305	25,947

Source: Company Annual Reports

[(1)]Period from December 5 to December 31, 1985
[(2)]Period ended December 4, 1985

EXHIBIT F
Mary Kay Cosmetics, Inc., Dallas, TX—Financial performance, 1978–1988

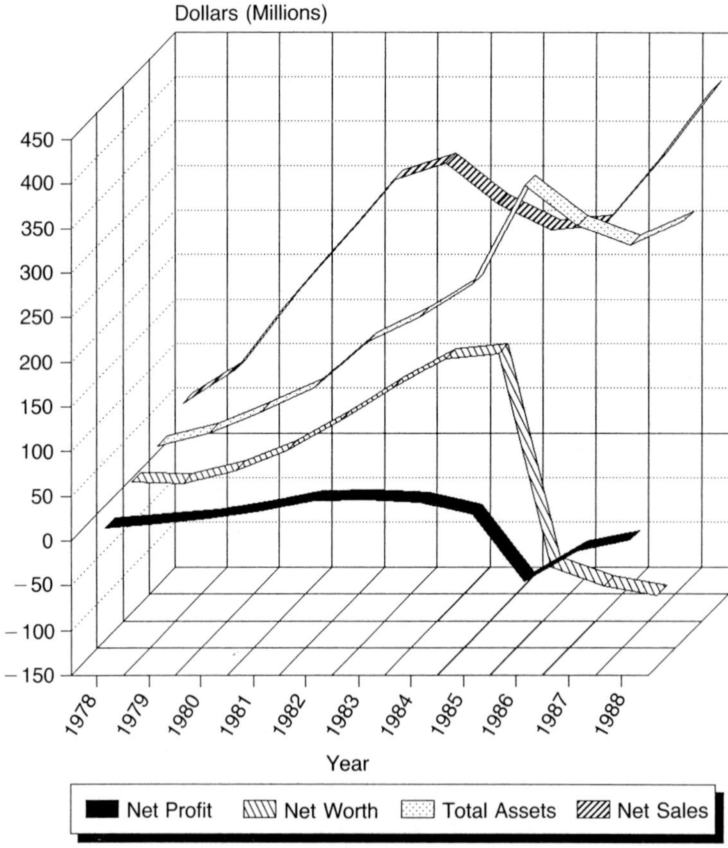

Year	Net Sales (000)	Net Profit (000)	Total Assets (000)	Net Worth (000)
1986	$2,883.10	$158.70	$2,296.30	$ 681.30
1985	2,470.10	(59.90)	2,289.00	926.40
1984	2,605.30	181.70	2,287.50	1,157.10
1983	2,607.60	172.90	2,256.80	1,273.10
1982	2,710.10	186.60	2,227.60	1,245.10
1981	2,725.20	216.50	1,611.90	930.50
1980	2,569.10	242.10	1,583.10	928.30
1979	2,377.50	244.00	1,417.00	866.30
1978	2,086.30	233.60	1,282.40	770.70

Source: Company Annual Reports

EXHIBIT G
Avon Products Inc., NY—Financial performance, 1978–1986

Year	Net Sales (000)	Net Profit (000)	Total Assets (000)	Net Worth (000)
1986	$398,030	$59,123	$344,214	$233,904
1985	406,043	13,016	277,161	164,276
1984	459,115	13,207	260,660	154,451
1983	538,729	35,145	261,795	151,125
1982	471,876	24,008	222,074	120,758
1981	454,522	24,543	191,670	105,601
1980	411,331	12,071	173,191	86,979
1979	314,149	21,288	164,707	78,859
1978	275,369	19,294	112,991	61,691

Source: Company Annual Reports

EXHIBIT H
Shaklee Corporation, San Francisco, CA—Financial performance, 1978–1986

Year	Retail Sales (000)	Salespeople
1988	$9,695,556	3,996,000
1987	8,789,415	3,614,000
1986	N/A	N/A
1985	8,360,000	5,129,994
1984	8,640,000	5,808,928
1983	8,575,000	5,114,276
1982	8,500,000	4,933,413
1981	N/A	N/A
1980	7,500,000	4,908,947

Source: Direct Selling Association—1988

EXHIBIT I
Direct selling industry, 1980–1988

REFERENCES

Ash, Mary Kay. *Mary Kay* (Revised Edition). New York: Harper & Row, 1986.

Ash, Mary Kay. *Mary Kay on People Management*. New York: Warner Books, 1984.

Ballen Kate. "Get Ready for Shopping at Work." *Fortune* (February 15, 1988), p. 95, 98.

Barker, Myra. Interview with Senior Vice President of R&D/QA, Mary Kay Cosmetics, Inc. (January 31, 1989). Dallas, Texas.

Barmash, Isadore. *More Than They Bargained For: The Rise and Fall of Korvettes*. New York: New American Library, 1981.
Bartlett, Richard C. Interview with President, Mary Kay Cosmetics, Inc. (January 31, 1989). Dallas, Texas.
Beasley, Ms. Barbara. Interview with Senior Vice President of Marketing, Mary Kay Cosmetics, Inc. (January 31, 1989). Dallas, Texas.
Biggart, Nicole Woolsey. *Charismatic Capitalism: Direct Selling Organizations in America*. Chicago: University of Chicago Press, 1989.

Chase, Marilyn. "At the Shaklee Corp., Selling Is Believing." *Wall Street Journal* (March 9, 1989), p. B8.
Chase, Marilyn. "Looking for Miracles, Young and Old Flock to Purchase Retin-A," *Wall Street Journal* (February 12, 1988), p. 1, 7.
Coughlin, Marilyn. "Making a Business of Belief: Sociologist Examines the Direct-Selling Industry in America." *The Chronicle of Higher Education* (July 19, 1989), p. A5–A6.
Croskeys, Curran. Interview with Vice President of Product Management, Mary Kay Cosmetics, Inc. (January 31, 1989). Dallas, Texas.

"Direct Marketers Adapt to New Lifestyles." *Marketing News* (June 19, 1989), p. 7.
Direct Selling Association. *A Statistical Study of the Direct Selling Industry in the United States: 1980–1985* A Report Prepared by the Direct Selling Association, Washington, D.C.: Direct Selling Association, October 1986.
Direct Selling Association, *The 1988 Direct Selling Industry Survey*. A report prepared by the Direct Selling Association, Washington, D.C.: Direct Selling Association, July 1989.
Dolan, Carrie. "Entrepreneurs Often Fail as Managers." *Wall Street Journal* (May 15, 1989), p. B1.
Dunkin, A., and C. Ducas. "How Cosmetics Makers Are Touching Up Their Strategies." *Business Week* (September 23, 1985), p. 66–68, 73.

Fannin, Rebecca. "The Beauty of Being Mary Kay." *Marketing & Media Decisions* (December 1982), p. 58–61.
"Flight of the Bumblebee," *Forbes* (August 12, 1985), p. 12.

Hattwick, Richard E. "Mary Kay Ash." *The Journal of Business Leadership* (Spring 1988), p. 21–40.
Hilder, David B., and Jeffrey A. Trachtenberg. "Avon Stock Sags on Withdrawal of Amway Bid." *Wall Street Journal* (May 19, 1989), p. A4.

Kingan, Adele. "Entrepreneur's Corner: Mary Kay Ash, Founder and Chairman of the Board, Mary Kay Cosmetics, Inc." *Executive Female* (November–December 1982), p. 12–14.

"Mary Kay Board Approves New Bid by Firm's Founder." *Wall Street Journal* (July 1, 1985), p. 16.
"Mary Kay Cosmetics, Inc. Business Brief." *Wall Street Journal* (February 11, 1985), p. 28.
"Mary Kay Cosmetics, Inc. Business Brief." *Wall Street Journal* (December 4, 1985), p. 59.
"Mary Kay Cosmetics Gets Buyout Offer From Managers, Valued at $280 Million." *Wall Street Journal* (May 31, 1985), p. 4.
"Mary Kay Cosmetics: Looking Beyond Direct Sales to Keep the Party Going." *Business Week* (March 28, 1983), p. 130.
"Mary Kay Cosmetics Picks Rogers As Its Chairman," *Wall Street Journal* (November 10, 1987), p. 42.
"More Than a Cosmetic Success, 1920." *Wall Street Journal* (March 28, 1989), p. B1.

Nissen, Beth. "Woman to Woman: Mary Kay Sales Agents Zero In on Prospects in Their Living Rooms." *Wall Street Journal* (September 28, 1978), p. 1, 24.

Olive, David. "All the Way with Mary Kay," *Canadian Business* (November 1984), p. 77–81.

Rinefort, Foster. Interview with management consultant. (July 31, 1989). Eastern Illinois University, Charleston.
Rothbart, Dean, and Laurie P. Cohen. "About Face: The Party at Mary Kay Isn't Quite So Lively, As Recruiting Falls Off." *Wall Street Journal* (October 28, 1983), p. 1, 12.
Rothman, Andrea. "For James Preston, It's Still Avon Calling." *Wall Street Journal* (December 9, 1988), p. B13.

Schifrin, Matthew. "Peeking inside LBO's." *Forbes* (June 13, 1988), p. 66, 68.
Sloan, Pat. "Mary Kay, Jafra Show Dramatic Growth." *Advertising Age* (August 23, 1982), p. 22.
Sloan, Stanley H. "Avon Calling: Cosmetics Firm Makes a Strong Comeback from a Recession Dip." *Wall Street Journal* (April 6, 1977), p. 1, 17.

Trachtenberg, Jeffrey A. "Sallie Cook is One of a Million Reasons Amway Liked Avon." *Wall Street Journal* (May 19, 1989), p. A1, A4.

■ CASE 4
K mart Corporation: Corporate Strategy at the Crossroads*

K mart Inc. in 1990 included a number of retail formats including discount department stores, warehouse clubs, sporting goods stores, home improvement centers, and specialty shops in the United States and several foreign countries, including Canada, Australia, China, and Puerto Rico. Measured in sales volume, it was the second largest retailer and largest discount department store chain in the United States.

By the late 1980s, the discount department store industry was perceived to have reached maturity. K mart, as part of that industry, had a retail management strategy that was developed in the late 1950s. The firm was at the crossroads, in terms of corporate strategy. The problem was what to do over the next 20 years.

THE EARLY YEARS

K mart was the outgrowth of an organization founded in 1899 in Detroit by Sebastian S. Kresge. The first S. S. Kresge store represented a new type of retailing that featured low-priced merchandise for cash in low-budget, relatively small (4,000- to 6,000-square-foot) buildings with sparse furnishings. The adoption of the "5 cents and 10 cents" or "variety store" concept, pioneered by F. W. Woolworth Company in 1879, led to rapid and profitable development of what was then the S. S. Kresge Company.

Kresge believed it could substantially increase its retail business through centralized buying and control, developing standardized store operating procedures, and expanding with new stores in heavy traffic areas. In 1917, the firm was incorporated. It had 150 stores and, next to Woolworth, was the largest variety chain in the world. Over the next 40 years, the firm experimented with mail order catalogs, full-line department stores, self-service, a variety of price lines, and the opening of stores in planned shopping centers.

By 1957, corporate management became aware that the development of supermarkets and the expansion of drug store chains into general merchandise lines had made inroads into market categories previously dominated by variety stores. It also became clear that a new form of store with a discount merchandising strategy was emerging.

THE CUNNINGHAM CONNECTION

In an effort to regain its competitiveness in 1957 and possibly save the company, Frank Williams, then president of the S. S. Kresge Company, nominated Harry B. Cunningham as general vice president. This maneuver was undertaken to free Mr. Cunningham, who had worked his way up the ranks in the organization, from operating responsibility. He was being groomed for the presidency and was given the assignment to study existing retailing business and recommend marketing changes.

In his visits to Kresge stores and those of the competition, Cunningham became interested in discounting—particularly a new operation in Garden City, Long Island. Eugene Ferkauf had recently opened large discount stores called E. J. Korvette. They had a discount mass-merchandising emphasis that featured low prices and margins, high turnover, large free-standing departmentalized units, ample parking space, and a location typically in the suburbs.

Cunningham was impressed with the discount concept, but he knew he had to first convince the board of directors, whose support would be necessary for any new strategy to succeed. He studied the company for two years and presented it with the following recommendation:

> We can't beat the discounters operating under the physical constraints and the self-imposed merchandise limitations of variety stores. We can join them—and not only join them, but with our people, procedures, and organization, we can become a leader in the discount industry.

In a speech delivered at the University of Michigan, Cunningham made his management approach clear by concluding with an admonition from the British author, Sir Hugh Walpole: "Don't play for safety, it's the most dangerous game in the world."

The board of directors had a difficult job. Change is never easy, especially when the company has a proud heritage. Before the first presentation to the board could be made, rumors were circulating that one shocked senior executive had said:

> We have been in the variety business for 60 years—we know everything there is to know about it, and we're not doing very well in that, and you want to get us into a business we don't know anything about.

The board of directors accepted H. B. Cunningham's recommendations. When President Frank Williams retired, Cunningham became the new president and chief executive officer, and was directed to proceed with his recommendations.

THE BIRTH OF K MART

Management conceived the original K mart as a conveniently located one-stop shopping unit where customers could buy a wide variety of quality merchandise at discount prices. The typical K mart had 75,000 square feet, all on one floor. It generally stood by itself in a high-traffic, suburban area, with plenty of parking space, and with a floor plan common to other units in the organization.

The firm made an $80 million commitment in leases and merchandise for 33 stores before the first K mart opened in 1962 in Garden City, Michigan. As part of this strategy, management decided to rely on the strengths and abilities of its own people to make decisions rather than employing outside experts for advice.

The original variety store operation was characterized by low gross margins, high turnover, and concentration on return on investment. The main difference in the K mart strategy would be the offering of a much wider merchandise mix.

The company had the knowledge and ability to merchandise 50 percent of the departments in the planned K mart merchandise mix, and it contracted for operation of the remaining departments. In the following years, K mart took over most of those departments originally contracted to licensees. Eventually all departments, except shoes, were operated by K mart.

THE MATURATION OF K MART

For retailers, the end of the 1980s was considered a very unstable period. Campeau Corporation with its Federated and Allied Department Store Divisions was in bankruptcy. The Bloomingdale specialty store division of Federated Stores was offered for sale and then withdrawn. To avert a takeover attempt, the British B.A.T. Industries sold Marshall Field department stores to Dayton Hudson Corporation, and offered for sale the Saks Fifth Avenue specialty store division. L. J. Hooker Corporation tried to raise cash by selling its Bonwit Teller and Sakowitz stores; it liquidated the B. Altman chain as well as parts of Bonwit after fruitless sale efforts. May Department Stores sold its Caldor and Venture discount divisions, each with annual sales of more than $1 billion. After decades of development work, Dayton Hudson Corporation sold Lechmere, its appliance and electronics retail unit.

Corporate management at K mart considered the concept of a discount department store to be a mature idea. K mart itself was the largest discount department store organization, with 2,194 stores. The industry was characterized by a reduced number of store openings, reduced expansion of square feet of floor space, and similar product offerings by competitors. Although maturity was sometimes looked on with disfavor, K mart executives felt that this did not mean a lack of profitability or a lack of opportunity to increase sales. The industry was perceived as being reborn. It was in this context that a series of new marketing programs, designed to upgrade the K mart image, were developed.

By the late 1980s, the discount department store industry had gone through a series of fundamental changes. Nearly a dozen firms like E. J. Korvette, W. T. Grant, Arlans, Atlantic Mills, and Ames passed into bankruptcy or reorganization. Many historically regional firms such as Wal-Mart Stores, Target Stores, and Shop Ko Stores began carrying more fashionable merchandise in more attractive facilities and shifted their emphasis to more national markets. Wal-Mart, based in Bentonville, Arkansas, was especially growth oriented and emerged as the second largest discount chain in sales volume. Specialty discounters such as Toys 'R' Us were making big inroads in toys, sporting goods, paint and other lines. The so-called superstores of drug and food chains were rapidly discounting increasing amounts of general merchandise. Some firms like Woolworth (Woolco Division) had withdrawn from the field entirely after years of disappointment.

Many retailers such as Target, which adopted the discount concept, attempted to go generally after an upscale customer. The upscale customer tended to have household income of $25,000 to $44,000 annually. Other pockets of population were being served by firms like Zayre, which served consumers in the inner city, and Wal-Mart, which served the needs of the more rural consumer in secondary markets. Senior management at K mart felt that all firms in the industry were facing the same situation. First, they were very successful five or ten years ago but were not changing and, therefore, were becoming somewhat dated. Management that had a historically successful formula, particularly in retailing, was perceived as having difficulty adapting to change, especially at the peak of success. Management would wait too long and then would have to scramble to regain competitiveness.

K mart executives found that discount department stores were being challenged by several new retail formats. Some retailers were assortment oriented, with a much greater depth of assortment within a given product category. To illustrate, Toys 'R' Us was an example of a firm that operated 20,000-square-foot toy supermarkets. Toys 'R' Us prices were very competitive within an industry that was very competitive. When the consumers entered a Toys 'R' Us facility, there was usually no doubt in their minds that if the product wasn't there, no one else had it.

Other retailers were experimenting with the off-price apparel concept where name brands and designer goods were sold at 20- to 70-percent discounts; home improvement centers that were warehouse-style stores with a wide range of hard-line merchandise for both do-it-yourselfers and professionals; and drug supermarkets that offered a wide variety of high turnover merchandise in a convenient location. In these cases, competition was becoming more risk oriented by putting $3 or $4 million in merchandise at retail value in an 80,000-square-foot facility and offering genuinely low prices. The F&M stores in the Detroit market, Drug Emporium in the midwest, and a series of independents were examples of organizations employing the entirely new concept of the drug supermarket.

Competition was offering something that was new and different in terms of depth of assortment, competitive price image, and format. K mart management perceived this as a threat because these were viable businesses and hindered the firm in its ability to improve and maintain share of market in specific merchandise categories.

Corporate research revealed that on the basis of convenience, K mart served 80 percent of the population. One study concluded that 1 out of every 2 adults in the United States shopped at a K mart at least once a month. Despite this popular appeal, strategies that had allowed the firm to have something for everybody were no longer felt to be appropriate for the 1990s. K mart found that it had a broad customer base because it operated on a national basis. Its strategies had assumed the firm was serving everyone in the markets where it was established.

K mart was often perceived as aiming at the low-income consumer. The financial community believed the K mart customer was blue collar, low income, and upper-lower class. The market served, however, was more professional and middle class because K mart stores were initially in suburban communities where the growth was occurring.

Although K mart has made a major commitment in more recent years to secondary or rural markets, these were areas that had previously not been cultivated. The firm, in its initial strategies, perceived the rural consumer as different from the urban or suburban customer. In readdressing the situation, it discovered that its assortments in rural areas were too limited and there were too many preconceived notions regarding what the Nebraska farmer really wanted. The firm discovered that the rural consumer didn't always shop for bib overalls and shovels but shopped for microwave ovens and all the things everyone else did.

The goal was not to attract more customers but to get the customer coming in the door to spend more. Once in the store the customer was thought to demonstrate more divergent tastes. The upper-income consumer would buy more health and beauty aids, cameras, and sporting goods. The lower-income consumer would buy health and beauty aids, toys, and clothing.

In the process of trying to capture a larger share of the market and get people to spend more, the firm began to recognize a market that was more upscale. When consumer research was conducted and management examined the profile of the trade area and the profile of the person who shopped at K mart in the past month, they were found to be identical. K mart was predominantly serving the suburban consumer in suburban locations.

In "lifestyle" research in markets served by the firm, K mart determined there were more two-income families, families were having fewer children, there were more working wives, and customers tended to be homeowners. Customers were very careful how they spent their money and were perceived as wanting quality. This was a distinct contrast to the 1960s and early 1970s, which tended to have the orientation of a "throw away" society. The customer had said, "What we want is products that will last longer. We'll have to pay more for them but we will still want them and at the lowest price possible." Customers wanted better quality products but still demanded competitive prices. According to a K mart Annual Report, "Consumers today are well educated and informed. They want good value and they know it when they see it. Price remains a key consideration, but the consumer's new definition of value includes quality as well as price."

MARKETING STRATEGIES

Several new marketing strategies emerged as the result of an overall reexamination of existing corporate strategies. This new marketing program included: accelerated store expansion and refurbishing, capitalizing on dominant lifestyle departments, centralized merchandising, more capital investment in retail automation, an aggressive and focused advertising program, and continued growth through new specialty retail formats.

In February 1990, K mart announced a five-year, $2.3 billion new store opening, enlargement, relocation, and refurbishment program. This program involved virtually all U.S. K mart discount stores. There would be approximately 250 new full-size K mart stores, 620 enlargements, 280 relocations, and 30 closings. In addition, 1,260 stores would be refurbished to bring their layout and fixturing up to new store standards. The new look featured a broad poppy red and gold bank around interior walls as a horizon; new round, square, and honeycombed racks that displayed the full garment; relocation of jewelry and women's apparel to areas closer to the entrance; and redesigning of counters to make them look more upscale and hold more merchandise.

One area receiving initial attention was improvement in the way products were displayed. The traditional K mart layout was by product category. Often these locations for departments were holdovers from the variety store past. Many departments would now give up prime locations. As part of the new marketing strategy, the shop concept was introduced. Management recognized that it had a sizable "do-it-yourself" store. As planning management discussed the issue, "nobody was aware of the opportunity. The hardware department was right smack in the center of the store because it was always there. The paint department was over here and the electrical department was over there." "All we had to do," management contended, "was put them all in one spot and everyone could see that we had a very respectable 'do-it-yourself' department." The concept resulted in a variety of new departments such as "Soft Goods for the Home," "Kitchen Korners," and "Home Electronic Centers." The goal behind each department was to sell an entire lifestyle-oriented concept to consumers, making goods complementary so shoppers would want to buy several interrelated products rather than just one item.

Name brands were added in soft and hard goods as management recognized that the customer transferred the product quality of branded goods to perceptions of private label merchandise. In the eyes of K mart management, "if you sell Wrangler, there is good quality. Then the private label must be good quality."

Additional programs emphasized the quality image. In a joint venture with *McCall's*, a new magazine called *Betsy McCall*, aimed at girls ages 6 to 12, was launched. Pro golfer Fuzzy Zoeller was engaged to promote golf equipment and other associated products. Mario Andretti, who races in the Championship Auto Racing Teams' Indy car series, agreed to co-sponsorship of his car with associated promotion. Dusty Lenscap, an animated marketing character, was introduced to promote photo developing equipment.

K mart hired Martha Stewart, an upscale Connecticut author of lavish best-selling books on cooking and home entertaining, as its lifestyle spokesperson and consultant. Martha Stewart was featured as a corporate symbol for housewares and associated products in advertising and in-store displays. Management visualized her as the next Betty Crocker, a fictional character created some years ago by General Mills, Inc., and a representative of its interest in lifestyle trends. A separate division was established to manage strategy for all Martha Stewart label goods and programs. Merchandise was featured in the redesigned once-a-week K mart newspaper circular that now carried the advertising theme: "The quality you need, the price you want."

Several thousand prices were reduced in 1989 to maintain price leadership across America. As management noted, "it is absolutely essential that we provide our customers with good value—quality products at low prices." Although lowering of prices hurt margins and contributed importantly to an earnings decline, management felt that unit turnover of items with lowered prices increased significantly to "enable K mart to maintain its pricing leadership which will have a most positive impact on our business in the years ahead."

A centralized merchandising system was introduced to improve communication. A computerized, highly automated replenishment system tracked how quickly merchandise sold and just as quickly put fast moving products back on the shelves. Satellite capability and a point-of-sale (POS) scanning system were introduced as part of the program. Regular, live satellite communication from K mart headquarters to the stores would allow senior management to communicate with store managers and allow for questions and answers. The POS scanning system allowed the record of every sale and transmission of the data to headquarters. This enabled K mart to respond quickly to what's new, what's in demand, and what would keep customers coming back.

In the mid 1970s and throughout the 1980s, K mart became involved in the acquisition or development of several smaller new operations. K mart Insurance Services, Inc., acquired as Planned Marketing Associates in 1974, offered a full line of life, health, and accident insurance centers located in 27 K mart stores primarily in the South and Southwest.

In 1982, K mart initiated its own off-price specialty apparel concept called Designer Depot. A total of 28 Designer Depot stores were opened in 1982, to appeal to customers who wanted quality upscale clothing at a budget price. A variation of this concept, called Garment Rack, was opened to sell apparel that normally would not be sold in Designer Depot. A distribution center was added in 1983, to supplement both of the above ventures. K mart attempted an unsuccessful joint venture with the Hechinger Company of Washington, D.C., a warehouse home center retailer. However, after much deliberation, K mart chose instead to acquire Home Centers of America of San Antonio, Texas. The division would be building 80,000-square-foot warehouse home centers named Builders Square. It would capitalize on K mart's real estate, construction, and management expertise, and Home Centers of America's merchandising expertise.

Waldenbooks, a chain of 877 book stores, was acquired from Carter Hawley Hale, Inc. in 1984. It was part of a strategy to capture a greater share of the market with a product category that K mart already had in its stores. K mart had been interested in the book business for some time and took advantage of an opportunity in the marketplace to build on its common knowledge base.

The Bruno's Inc. joint venture in 1987 formed a partnership to develop large combination grocery and general merchandise stores, or "hypermarkets." The giant, one-stop-shopping facilities of 225,000 square feet would trade on the grocery expertise of Bruno's and the general merchandise of K mart to offer a wide selection of products and services at discount prices.

In 1988, the company acquired a controlling interest in Makro Inc., a Cincinnati-based operator of warehouse "club" stores. Makro, with annual sales of about $300 million, operated member-only stores that were stocked with low-priced fresh and frozen groceries, apparel, and durable goods in suburbs of Atlanta, Cincinnati, Washington, and Philadelphia. Pace Membership Warehouse, Inc., a similar operation, was acquired in 1989.

The company's specialty retail group included Builders Square, warehouse home improvement stores; Pay Less Shoes; Northwest, Inc., super drug stores; the Walden Book Company, specialty book stores; and Bargain Harold's Discount Limited, Canadian mini variety stores. K mart Canada also included K mart discount stores and Kresge and Jupiter variety stores.

On April 6, 1987, K mart Corporation announced that it agreed to sell most of its 55 Kresge and Jupiter variety stores in the United States to McCory Corporation, a unit of the closely held Rapid American Corporation of New York. The move left the firm with approximately 4,000 retail units in the various divisions.

THE PLANNING FUNCTION

Corporate planning at K mart was the result of executives, primarily the senior executive, recognizing change. The role played by the senior executive was to get others to recognize that nothing is good forever. Good planning was perceived as the result of those who recognized that at some point they would have to get involved. Poor planning was done by those who didn't recognize the need for it. When they did, it was too late to survive. Good planning, if done on a regular and timely basis, was assumed to result in improved performance. K mart's director of planning and research contended, "planning, as we like to stress, is making decisions now to improve performance tomorrow. Everyone looks at what may happen tomorrow, but the planners are the ones who make decisions today. That's where I think too many firms go wrong. They think they are planning because they are writing reports and are aware of changes. They don't say, 'because of this, we must decide today to spend this money to do this to accomplish this goal in the future.'"

The director of planning and research of K mart believed that K mart had been very successful in the area of strategic planning. "When it became necessary to make significant changes in the way we were doing business," he suggested, "that was accomplished on a fairly timely basis." When the organization made the change in the 1960s, it recognized there was a very powerful investment opportunity and capitalized on it—far beyond what anyone else would have done. "We just opened stores," he continued, "at a great, great pace. Management, when confronted with a crisis, would state, 'it's the economy, or it's this, or that, but it's not the essential way we are doing business.'" He continued, "Suddenly management would recognize that the economy may stay like this forever. We need to improve the situation and then do it." Strategic planning was thought to arise out of some difficult times for the organization.

EXHIBIT A
continued

Consolidated Balance Sheets
($ Millions)

Assets	January 31, 1990	January 25, 1989
Current assets:		
Cash (includes temporary investments of $35 and $594, respectively)	$ 353	$ 948
Merchandise inventories	6,933	5,671
Accounts receivable and other current assets	698	527
Total current assets	7,984	7,146
Investments in affiliated retail companies	512	506
Property and equipment-net	3,850	3,896
Other assets and deferred charges	799	578
	$13,145	$12,126
Liabilities and Shareholders' Equity		
Current liabilities:		
Long-term debt due within one year	11	1
Notes payable	601	—
Accounts payable-trade	2,319	2,334
Accrued payrolls and other liabilities	830	649
Taxes other than income taxes	322	282
Income taxes	216	226
Total current liabilities	4,299	3,492
Capital lease obligations	1,549	1,588
Long-term debt	1,480	1,358
Other long-term liabilities including K mart restructuring obligations	745	459
Deferred income taxes	100	220
Shareholders' equity:		
Common stock, 500,000,000 shares authorized; shares issued 204,918,993 and 204,293,757, respectively	205	204
Capital in excess of par value	602	588
Restricted stock deferred compensation	(1)	—
Retained earnings	4,341	4,345
Treasury shares	(146)	(131)
Foreign currency translation adjustment	(29)	(3)
Total shareholders' equity	4,972	5,009
	$13,145	$12,126

EXHIBIT A
continued

Consolidated Statements of Cash Flows

(Millions)	Fiscal Year Ended January 31, 1990	January 25, 1989	January 27, 1988
Cash provided by (used for):			
Operations			
Net income	$ 323	$ 803	$ 692
Noncash charges (credits) to earnings:			
Depreciation and amortization	461	437	401
Restructuring of K mart stores and other charges	582	—	—
Deferred income taxes	(164)	8	12
Undistributed equity income	(35)	(42)	(36)
Increase in other long-term liabilities	22	97	67
Other-net	29	53	56
Cash provided by (used for) current assets and current liabilities:			
(Increase) in inventories	(1,042)	(86)	(418)
Increase (decrease) in accounts payable	(216)	19	102
Other-net	(76)	(73)	90
Total provided by (used for) discontinuing retail operations	(116)	1,216	966
Total provided by (used for) discontinued operations	13	(5)	(58)
Net cash provided by (used for) operations	(103)	1,211	908
Investing			
Additions to owned property	(631)	(570)	(542)
Acquisition of Pace	(268)	—	—
Proceeds from the sale of property	147	117	30
Other-net	(53)	(52)	(27)

EXHIBIT A
continued

Consolidated Statements of Cash Flows (Millions)	Fiscal Year Ended January 31, 1990	January 25, 1989	January 27, 1988
Net cash used for investing	(805)	(505)	(539)
Financing			
Proceeds from issuance of long-term debt and notes payable	718	346	200
Reduction in long-term debt and notes payable	(1)	(184)	(318)
Reduction in capital lease obligations	(92)	(96)	(83)
Common stock issued	14	16	46
Reissuance of treasury shares	—	—	14
Purchase of treasury shares	(15)	(33)	(75)
Dividends paid	(311)	(256)	(225)
Net cash provided by (used for) financing	313	(207)	(441)
Net increase (decrease) in cash and equivalents	(595)	499	(72)
Cash and equivalents at beginning of year	948	449	521
Cash and equivalents at end of year	353	948	449

EXHIBIT B
K mart/S. S. Kresge Company—Financial performance, 1960–1983

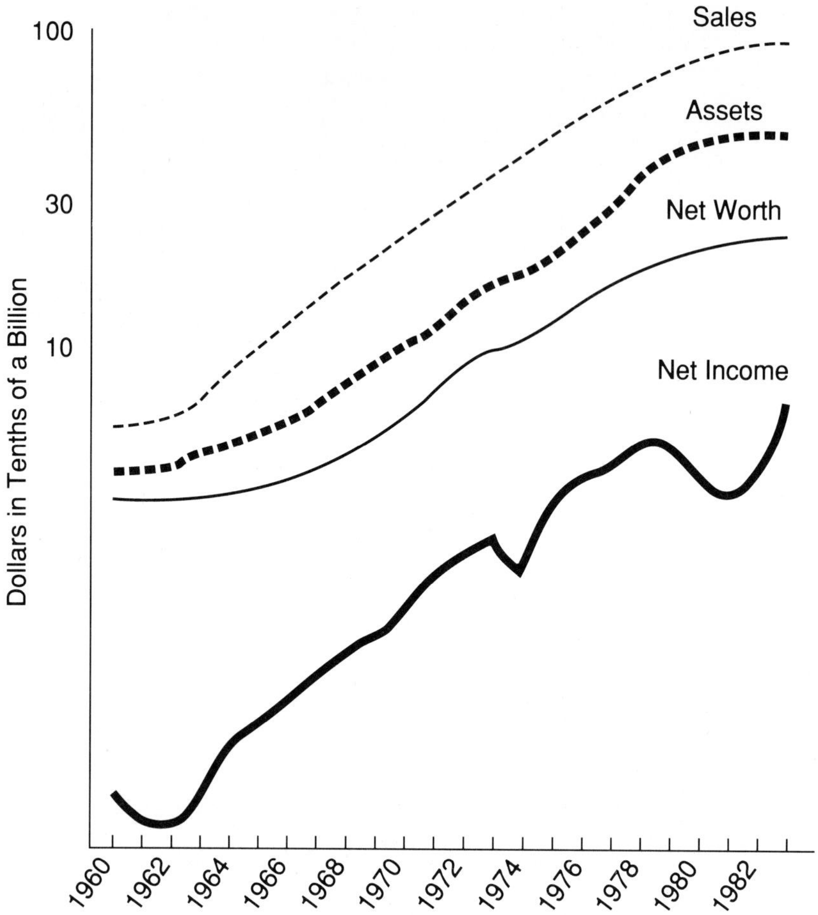

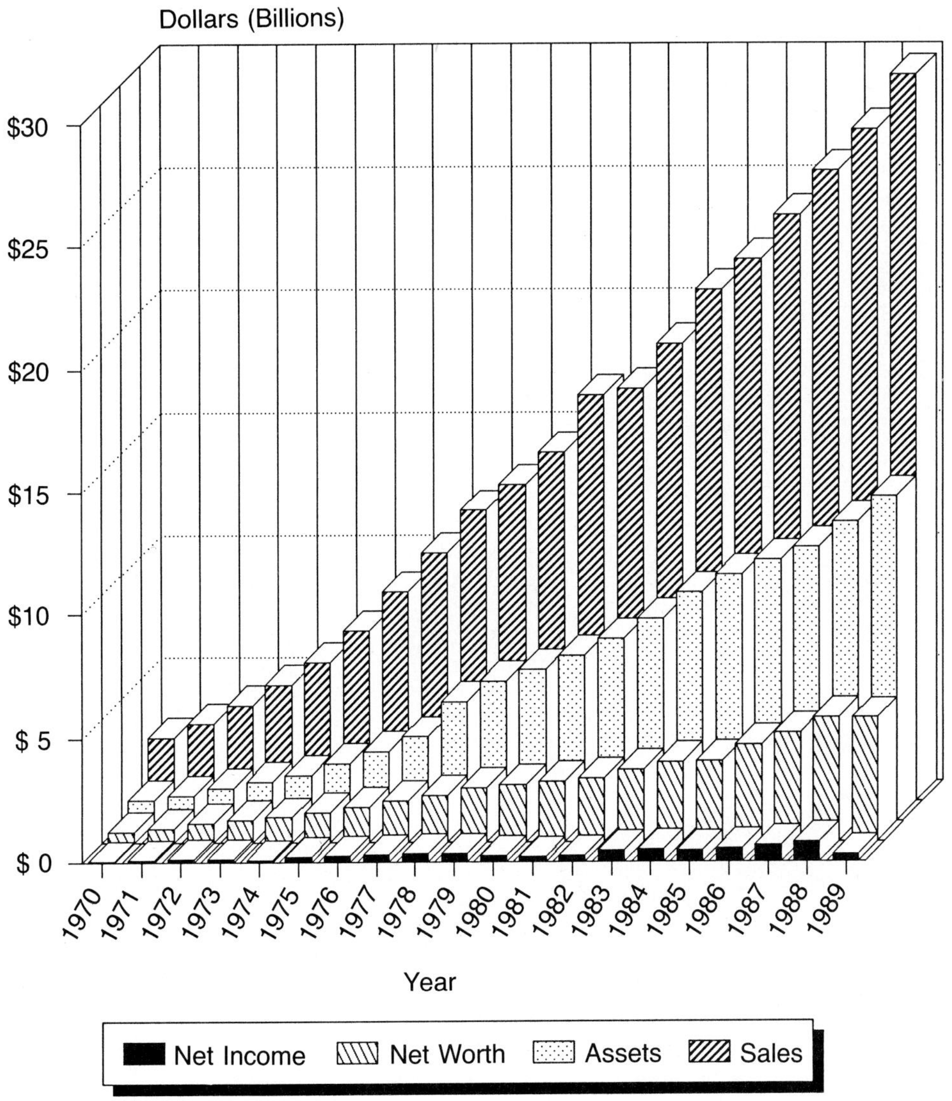

EXHIBIT C
K mart/S. S. Kresge Company—Financial performance, 1970–1989

EXHIBIT D
K mart/S. S. Kresge Company—Financial performance, 1970–1989

Year	Sales (000)	Assets (000)	Net Income (000)	Net Worth (000)
1970	2,595,155	926,227	66,994	456,761
1971	3,139,653	1,095,948	96,116	548,469
1972	3,875,183	1,383,439	114,674	779,726
1973	4,702,504	1,652,773	138,251	924,512
1974	5,612,071	1,896,110	104,772	1,016,000
1975	6,883,613	2,377,541	200,832	1,197,825
1976	8,483,603	2,865,572	266,574	1,441,793
1977	10,064,457	3,428,110	302,919	1,687,817
1978	11,812,810	4,836,260	343,706	1,915,666
1979	12,858,585	5,642,439	357,999	2,185,192
1980	14,204,381	6,102,462	260,527	2,343,172
1981	16,527,012	6,673,004	220,251	2,455,594
1982	16,772,166	7,343,665	261,821	2,601,272
1983	18,597,900	8,183,100	492,300	2,940,100
1984	20,762,000	9,262,000	503,000	3,234,000
1985	22,035,000	9,991,000	472,000	3,273,000
1986	23,812,000	10,578,000	570,000	3,939,000
1987	25,627,000	11,106,000	692,000	4,409,000
1988	27,301,000	12,126,000	803,000	5,009,000
1989	29,533,000	13,145,000	323,000	4,972,000

After taxes and extraordinary credit or charges
Source: *Fortune* Financial Analysis and Annual Reports

EXHIBIT E
Wal-Mart Stores, Inc.—Financial performance, 1980–1989

Year	Sales (000)	Assets (000)	Net Income (000)	Net Worth (000)
1980	$ 1,248,176	$ 475,879	$ 41,151	$ 164,844
1981	1,643,199	592,345	55,682	248,309
1982	2,444,997	937,513	82,794	323,942
1983	3,376,252	1,187,448	124,140	488,109
1984	4,666,909	1,652,254	196,244	737,503
1985	6,400,861	2,205,229	270,767	984,672
1986	8,451,489	3,103,645	327,473	1,277,659
1987	11,909,076	4,049,092	450,086	1,690,493
1988	15,959,255	5,131,809	627,643	2,257,267
1989	20,649,001	6,359,668	837,221	3,007,909

Source: Wal-Mart Annual Reports

REFERENCES

Business Week. "Where K mart Goes Next Now That It's No. 2" (June 2, 1980), 109–10, 114.

Bussey, John. "K mart Is Set to Sell Many of Its Roots to Rapid-American Corp's McCory" *Wall Street Journal* (April 6, 1987), 24.

Carruth, Eleanore. "K mart Has to Open Some New Doors on the Future." *Fortune* (July 1977), 143–50, 153–54.

Chain Store Executive. "Why Chains Enter New Areas" (December 1976), 22, 24.

Chain Store Executive. "It's Kresge . . . Again" (November 1975), 16.

Dewar, Robert E. "The Kresge Company and the Retail Revolution" *University of Michigan Business Review* (July 2, 1975), 2.

Guiles, Melinda G. "Attention, Shoppers: Stop That Browsing and Get Aggressive" *Wall Street Journal* (June 16, 1987), 1, 21.
Guiles, Melinda G. "K mart, Bruno's Join to Develop 'Hypermarkets'." *Wall Street Journal* (September 8, 1987), 17.
Ingrassia, Paul. "Attention Non K mart Shoppers: A Blue-Light Special Just for You." *Wall Street Journal* (October 6, 1987), 42.
Key, Janet. "K mart Plan: Diversify, Conquer: Second Largest Retailer Out To Woo Big Spenders." *Chicago Tribune* (November 11, 1984), 1–2.
Main, Jerry. "K mart's Plan to Be Born Again." *Fortune* (September 21, 1981), 74–77, 84–85.
Mitchell, Russell. "How They're Knocking the Rust Off Two Old Chains." *Business Week* (September 8, 1986), 44–48.
Rice, Faye. "Why K mart has Stalled." *Fortune* (October 9, 1989), 79.
Schwadel, Francine. "Attention K mart Shoppers: Style Coming to This Isle." *Wall Street Journal* (August 9, 1988), 6.
Sellers, Patricia. "Attention, K mart Shoppers." *Fortune* (January 2, 1989), 41.
Stavro, Barry. "Mass Appeal." *Forbes* (May 5, 1986), 128, 130.
Sternad, Patricia. "K mart's Antonini Moves Far Beyond Retail 'Junk' Image." *Advertising Age* (July 25,1988), 1, 67.
Wellman, Michael. Interview with Director of Planning and Research (August 6, 1984), K mart Corporation.
Woodruff, David. "Will K mart Ever Be a Silk Purse?" *Business Week* (January 22, 1990), 46.

APPENDIX B
Retailing Careers

So you want to consider being a retailer? Or at least you might want to consider entering the retailing field? This appendix provides a glimpse of what it is like to be in retailing. You will discover some of the joys and, yes, also some of the frustrations involved in the retailing field. You will learn that people must have special characteristics to be successful retailers. You will read about employment opportunities, ownership opportunities, employment features in a retailing career, and the personal attributes of retailers. After you have read this appendix, you can decide—is retailing for you?

RETAILER ATTRIBUTES AND PERSONALITIES

Whether a neophyte or a veteran, an independent entrepreneur or a chain store employee, the individual engaged in retailing must have certain personality traits and attributes to succeed in the marketplace. Some of the more successful retailer personality types include the people pleaser, the risk taker, the problem solver, the decision maker, and the retail entrepreneur.

The People Pleaser

The retailer is in the people business. No other type of business deals so directly with so many people in such a variety of ways. Successful retailers have a genuine interest in and general liking for *people*. **People-pleasing retailers** can appreciate their customers, empathize with them, and recognize their motives. Thus, people pleasers are retailers who understand people, recognize their problems, know their goals, and try to satisfy their needs. To be a successful retailer, a person must be able and willing to please people.

The Risk Taker

Risks are an inherent part of any business, and retailing is no exception. There are risks in deciding what merchandise to stock, where to locate, how many and which markets to serve, how extensive a product line to offer, and which and how many services to provide. Because no retailer can precisely determine what every customer wants or match everything that competitors are doing better, risks are simply unavoidable in retailing. The **risk taker** not only is willing to assume the inherent chances of going into business but is able to tell a good merchandising risk from a bad one. A successful risk taker can reduce risk by gathering and analyzing pertinent information.

The Problem Solver

Retailers not only *understand* retailing problem situations but enjoy solving them—they are active **problem solvers**. A typical retail operation faces a great diversity of problems, ranging from the physical problems of getting the merchandise into the store and onto the shelves to the mental and emotional problems of handling dissatisfied and vocal customers. Regardless of the situation, the retailer must be prepared to solve not only routine problems but also unusual ones. What's more, the retailer should enjoy it!

The Decision Maker

Of the large number of managerial decisions a retailer faces, the range of possible choices in each decision can be equally broad. Retailers must make daily decisions about locations, facilities, merchandise, prices, promotions, and service, and they must make periodic decisions about staff, suppliers, and investors. Not everyone is willing or able to make these decisions under pressures of time and with limited knowledge. To the **decision maker,** making choices under adverse and uncertain conditions is natural. The decision maker must understand and adapt daily to a changing marketplace.

The Retail Entrepreneur

A retail **entrepreneur** organizes, manages, and assumes the responsibilities of running a retail business. Although the term *entrepreneur* generally refers to an individual, the concept of entrepreneurship is actually appropriate to all retail organizations, since entrepreneurial skills are needed in all successful retailing careers. Like most skills, entrepreneurship exists in degrees. The following ten entrepreneurial attributes are important in creating an organizational culture that enhances the retailer's chances for success:

- Take risks but always be careful to minimize exposure. Take reasonable risks based on a clear evaluation of the expected and unexpected.
- Focus on opportunities rather than on problems, and make the primary focus customer needs rather than internal interests or limitations.
- Constantly seek improvement. It is the keystone of productivity, profitability, and customer satisfaction.
- Keep a clear head when it comes to your perception of reality. Be impressed with productivity and not appearances.
- Emphasize personal contact. Stay in touch with employees at all levels. Recognize the importance of your own example, emphasizing an open-door policy and personal contact as a leadership style.
- Keep things simple. Complex solutions in themselves don't necessarily produce incremental profits but often reduce opportunities.
- Allow for some level of ambiguity. Everything need not be tightly wrapped in a neat package or carefully explained in a manual.
- Court both change and flexibility to find improved service opportunities and increased efficiencies. Understand that every opportunity has an elusive life and is a moving target.
- Discourage focus on the negative, which will tend to produce a fear of failure and squelch the entrepreneurial spirit.
- Be purposeful and communicate the vision. The entrepreneurial spirit feeds off purposeful pursuit. There is a driving passion to make each opportunity work when everyone understands the corporate direction and the focus on consumers.[1]

No single measurement is appropriate for all individuals, and no one test measures all the attributes a retailer needs to be successful in retailing. Two psychologists, however, have developed what they deem indicators of what makes a successful retailing entrepreneur. A summary of this test of entrepreneurial mental skills and attitudes is shown in Figure B–1.[2]

The entrepreneurial skills of people-pleasing, decision-making, problem-solving, and risk-taking people, together with the abilities for organizing and managing, can be acquired to some degree in a formal learning situation, such as a college classroom, or in an informal learning situation, such as a work setting. Most people learn entrepreneurial skills in both ways.

The ideas in this book have built on and expanded whatever entrepreneurial skills you have and given you new insights into the world of retailing and the entrepreneurial spirit that people need to launch prosperous retailing careers.

EMPLOYMENT ASPECTS OF A RETAILING CAREER

To judge career opportunities in different fields, one should investigate the employment features for each career path. We will discuss several key aspects of a retailing career: employment security, employee compensation, working conditions, career advancement, and job satisfaction.

Employment Security

Employment in the retail sector offers the capable individual a high level of job security. Several factors account for this security. First, although all economic sectors suffer during a recession, the decline in retail employment is notably less than employment losses in either the manufacturing or wholesaling sectors. Second, the large number of employment opportunities in retailing creates a high level of job mobility, and increased mobility generally results in increased job security. The third factor accounting for the high level of job security in retailing is transferability of skills. Good merchandising skills can easily be transferred from one department to another within a firm, from one type of retailer to a different retailing operation, and even from retailing firms to wholesaling and manufacturing companies. This transferability of skills is essentially an extension of the mobility factor. Because skill transferability increases the number of employment opportunities, it thereby increases present job security.

Employee Compensation

Retail salaries vary considerably, ranging from minimum wage for lower-echelon, part-time employees to competitive salaries for upper-echelon managers. Where starting retail salaries are somewhat lower than those in other industries, the multitude of managerial levels within most retailing organizations provide opportunities for rapid advancement and can often result in a higher salary for the retail manager in just a few years. Equally important, retailing is a geographically dispersed industry in which a large number of middle- and upper-level managerial positions offer very attractive salaries and benefits. Also, for the prospective employee with limited formal education, entry to higher-salaried positions in retailing is not education oriented but productivity oriented (e.g., based on ability to generate profits or sales). Finally, there is the opportunity for self-employment. (The potential returns for owning and operating one's own businesses are discussed later in this appendix.)

Working Conditions

Retail working conditions have their pluses and minuses. On the plus side, the retail employee enjoys the benefits of a variety of work assignments, a number of pleasant work environments, and a host of people-oriented work relationships. If variety is the spice of life, then the prospective employee should find a retailing career very attractive. The natural progression in training retail manage-

Your psychological makeup can play a strong role in making your business a success or a failure. Here are some questions based on ideas supplied by Richard Boyatzis and David Winter, two psychologists who have studied the entrepreneurial character. The questions are designed to reveal whether you have entrepreneurial attitudes. Even if no answer fits your feelings precisely, choose the one that comes closest. (The answers to these questions are provided on page 784.)

1. If you have a free evening, would you most likely (a) watch TV, (b) visit a friend, (c) work on a hobby?
2. In your daydreams, would you most likely appear as (a) a millionaire floating on a yacht, (b) a detective who has solved a difficult case, (c) a politician giving an election night victory speech?
3. To exercise, would you rather (a) join an athletic club, (b) join a neighborhood team, (c) do some jogging at your own pace?
4. When asked to work with others on a team, which would you anticipate with most pleasure? (a) Other people coming up with good ideas, (b) cooperating with others, (c) getting other people to do what you want.
5. Which game would you rather play? (a) Monopoly, (b) roulette, (c) bingo.
6. Your employer asks you to take over a company project that is failing. Would you tell him that you will (a) take it, (b) won't take it because you're up to your gills in work, (c) give him an answer in a couple of days when you have more information?
7. In school, were you more likely to choose courses emphasizing (a) fieldwork, (b) papers, (c) exams?
8. In buying a refrigerator, would you (a) stay with an established, well-known brand, (b) ask your friends what they bought, (c) compare thoroughly the advantages of different brands?
9. While on a business trip in Europe, you are late for an appointment with a client in a neighboring town. Your train has been delayed indefinitely. Would you (a) rent a car to get there, (b) wait for the next scheduled train, (c) reschedule the appointment?
10. Do you believe people you know who have succeeded in business (a) have connections, (b) are more clever than you are, (c) are about the same as you but maybe work a little harder?
11. An employee who is your friend is not doing his job. Would you (a) take him out for a drink, hint broadly that things are not going right and hope he gets the message, (b) leave him alone and hope he straightens out, (c) give him a strong warning and fire him if he doesn't shape up?
12. You come home to spend a relaxing evening and find that your toilet has just overflowed. Would you (a) study your home repair book to see if you can fix it yourself, (b) persuade a handy friend to fix it for you, (c) call a plumber?
13. Do you enjoy playing cards most when you (a) play with good friends, (b) play with people who challenge you, (c) play for high stakes?
14. You operate a small office-cleaning business. A close friend and competitor suddenly dies of a heart attack. Would you (a) reassure his wife that you will never try to take away any customers, (b) propose a merger, (c) go to your former competitor's customers and offer them a better deal?

Source: Marlys Harris, "The Entrepreneur—Do You Have What It Takes?" *Money* 7 (March, 1978), 52. Reprinted from *MONEY* magazine by special permission; copyright 1990 The Time Inc. Magazine Company.

FIGURE B–1
Testing the entrepreneurial you

ment personnel requires that the employee gain experience with all aspects of the business. Typical retail training programs involve experiences with merchandising (e.g., buying and selling responsibilities); operations management (e.g., inventory planning and control responsibilities); sales promotion (e.g., advertising and retail display responsibilities); and personnel management (e.g., recruiting and training store personnel). Figure B–2 illustrates these programs.

The pleasant work environment is the result of the retailer's efforts to create a *buying atmosphere*. Contrasted with the sterile atmosphere of most offices, the opportunity to work in an exciting and stimulating physical store environment is a definite plus of retail employment. Many individuals find that the "action is where the people are." Given the people-oriented nature of the retailing business, individuals who crave action should find a retailing career very rewarding.

FIGURE B–2
Retail training programs: A variety of work experiences—the Sears model (source: *Retail Management Careers,* Sears Merchandise Group, company brochure, 9)

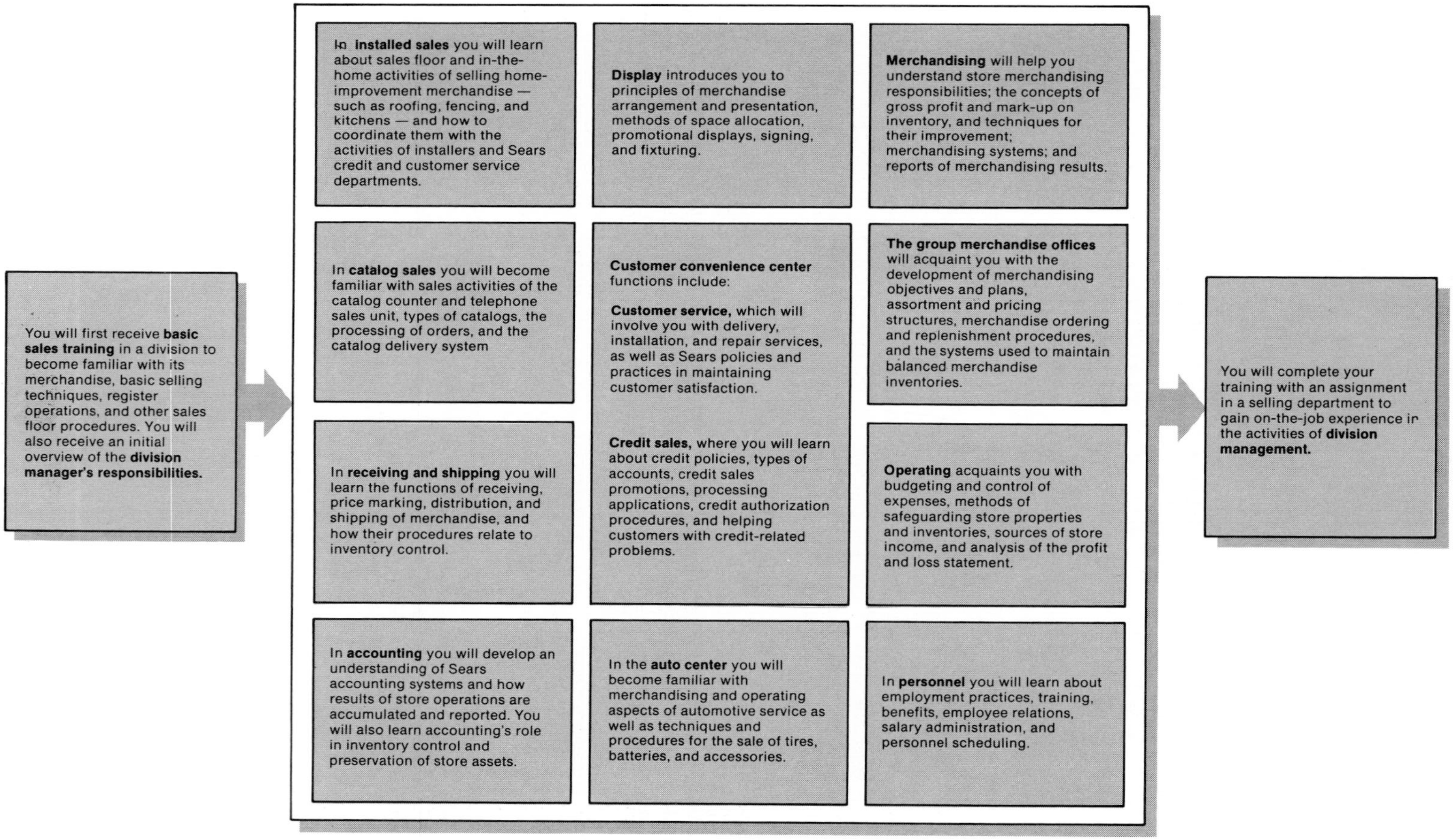
You will first receive basic sales training in a division to become familiar with its merchandise, basic selling techniques, register operations, and other sales floor procedures. You will also receive an initial overview of the division manager's responsibilities.
In installed sales you will learn about sales floor and in-the-home activities of selling home-improvement merchandise — such as roofing, fencing, and kitchens — and how to coordinate them with the activities of installers and Sears credit and customer service departments.
Display introduces you to principles of merchandise arrangement and presentation, methods of space allocation, promotional displays, signing, and fixturing.
Merchandising will help you understand store merchandising responsibilities; the concepts of gross profit and mark-up on inventory, and techniques for their improvement; merchandising systems; and reports of merchandising results.
In catalog sales you will become familiar with sales activities of the catalog counter and telephone sales unit, types of catalogs, the processing of orders, and the catalog delivery system
Customer convenience center functions include:
Customer service, which will involve you with delivery, installation, and repair services, as well as Sears policies and practices in maintaining customer satisfaction.
Credit sales, where you will learn about credit policies, types of accounts, credit sales promotions, processing applications, credit authorization procedures, and helping customers with credit-related problems.
The group merchandise offices will acquaint you with the development of merchandising objectives and plans, assortment and pricing structures, merchandise ordering and replenishment procedures, and the systems used to maintain balanced merchandise inventories.
In receiving and shipping you will learn the functions of receiving, price marking, distribution, and shipping of merchandise, and how their procedures relate to inventory control.
Operating acquaints you with budgeting and control of expenses, methods of safeguarding store properties and inventories, sources of store income, and analysis of the profit and loss statement.
In accounting you will develop an understanding of Sears accounting systems and how results of store operations are accumulated and reported. You will also learn accounting's role in inventory control and preservation of store assets.
In the auto center you will become familiar with merchandising and operating aspects of automotive service as well as techniques and procedures for the sale of tires, batteries, and accessories.
In personnel you will learn about employment practices, training, benefits, employee relations, salary administration, and personnel scheduling.
You will complete your training with an assignment in a selling department to gain on-the-job experience in the activities of division management.

The most commonly cited minuses of a retailing career concern working hours. Of particular concern are the questions of how long and when employees work. While lower-echelon positions have a "normal" work week of 40 hours, the aspiring management trainee should expect to work considerably longer. Compared with the hours expected at lower-level managerial positions in other businesses, however, the retail manager's work week is reasonable. The longer retail store hours of recent years have resulted in more supervision during nonstandard working times. Because of these extended hours, both management and nonmanagement personnel are expected to work off-hours (such as evenings), off-days (such as weekends), and some off-times (such as holidays).

Career Advancement

The opportunities for rapid advancement in retailing result from several interacting factors: the number of retail establishments, the diversity of retailing positions, and the number of managerial levels. The number of retail establishments is large and expanding. As a result, managerial positions abound. For the ambitious and talented, finding potential positions for career advancement is not difficult. Equally important in finding a career environment in which rapid advancement is possible is a job market characterized by a diversity of positions. Retailing has enough diversity to allow all individuals to seek and to foster a career niche best suited to their talents (see Figure B–3). Additionally, upward mobility need not be hampered by an individual's getting locked into a particular type of job that suits neither one's talents nor one's aspirations.

The third factor contributing to an accelerated rate of advancement is the typical retail organization's large number of managerial levels. Consider, for example, the managerial levels one might find in a department store chain: assistant department manager, department manager, assistant merchandise and/or promotions manager, assistant store manager, store manager—and upward into the various district, regional, and national managerial positions. The aspiring retail manager does not have to wait for a chance at the one big career break. Making small yet steady career advancements gives the retail manager greater control over future opportunities and greater satisfaction from current job responsibilities.

Consider a final note: Retailing offers women some of the best opportunities for professional advancement in the business world. These opportunities arise in part from women's power as the majority of customers at many stores. The belief that women managers have both a greater understanding of female shoppers' needs and greater ability for developing meaningful relationships with this group of customers has created a career path for women in retailing that can definitely be characterized by rapid advancement.

Job Satisfaction

Many aspects of a retailing career can provide job satisfaction. Some of the aspects already mentioned are the diversity of job responsibilities, potential for rapid advancement, opportunities to work with people, challenges of a continually changing environment, and competitive levels of compensation. Others features are the freedom to use one's initiative, quick recognition of one's abilities, and continuous opportunities to demonstrate leadership.

The nature of a retail store's operating and merchandising activities gives employees and managers a considerable degree of independence. The opportunity for motivated individuals to use their initiative in assuming responsibilities and making meaningful decisions is rewarding and tends to promote considerable job satisfaction. Retailing careers provide many opportunities for people who want the freedom to "do their thing." Most store managers, for example, are responsible for running their own show. Their responsibilities extend to all facets of the business: merchandising, operations, personnel, promotions, and finance.

Retailing offers ample opportunities to demonstrate one's talents and abilities and have those talents and abilities recognized. Most people need feedback before they can judge how satisfied they are with their performance. Where else can one get a daily rating of job performance? Large retailing organizations compute sales, expense, and profit figures daily, by means of electronic data processing systems, for each operating unit. In smaller retailing organizations, the relative sales and profit positions of various operating units are usually known through more informal means. In either case, this timely feedback affords career-minded people opportunities to demonstrate their abilities and to communicate their successes to their superiors who are directly responsible for career advancements.

The opportunity to assume a leadership role is a key factor to job satisfaction for some individuals. The people-intensive nature of retailing offers unlimited occasions for leadership-minded people to stand out rather than fit in.

Finally, many people relate job satisfaction at least in some degree to the status or image of their field of endeavor within the general business community. In recent years, as retailers have become a dominant force in the marketing and distribution of goods, their status has reached parity with other business careers. Successful retailing requires the same professional skills as any other business, a fact now widely recognized throughout the business community.

EMPLOYMENT OPPORTUNITIES

Employment choices are among the most important decisions people make and represent long-term commitments with profound effects on professional, personal, and family lives as well as general lifestyles. Therefore, it behooves anyone to approach an employment choice with the utmost preparation. The first step in planning for employment is to assess one's personal strengths and weaknesses, hopes and aspirations, and career goals and objectives. Each prospective employee needs to make a life audit and a career audit before engaging in an employment search.

FIGURE B–3
Retail management: A diversity of career paths—the R. H. Macy & Co. model (source: *Your Career Planning Workbook,* R. H. Macy & Co., Inc.)

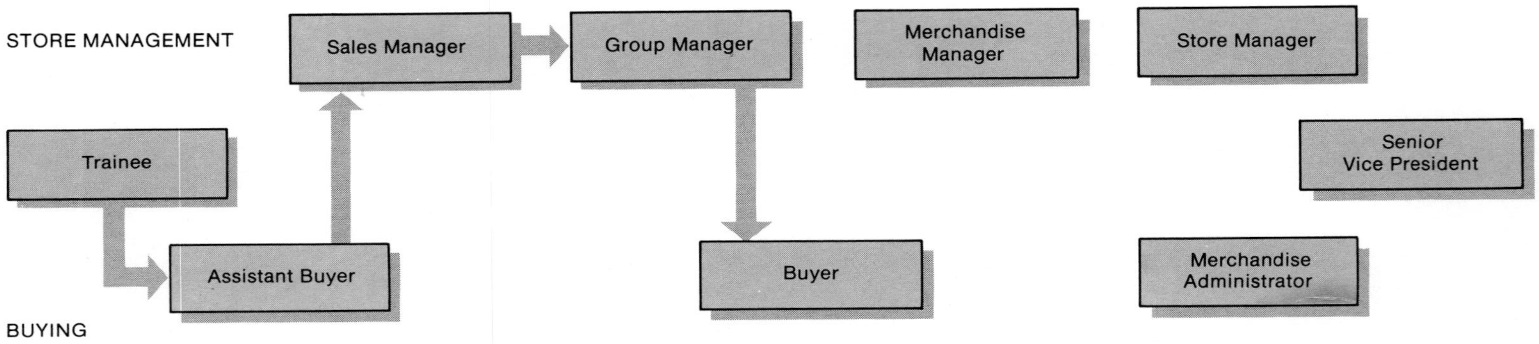

Trainee
General orientation to the retailing industry and the specifics of our operations through both classroom work and extensive on-the-job experience.

Sales Manager
Responsible for running a complete selling area in a store, including merchandise presentation, supervision of sales personnel, customer service, inventory control, and all other aspects of running a business.

Assistant Buyer
Learning to be a Buyer through assisting a Buyer in planning, acquiring, pricing, distributing, and promoting a category of merchandise for all stores of a division.

Group Manager
Responsible for executing merchandising plans for several departments in a store and reaching sales goals; supervises, trains, and develops sales managers.

Buyer
Responsible for planning, selecting, acquiring, pricing, distributing, and promoting merchandise for all stores of a division. With experience, buying responsibilities increase.

Merchandise Manager
Similar to Group Manager's position but with responsibility for expanded merchandise categories; coordinates the efforts among differerent departments; acts as major liaison between store executives and buyers.

Store Manager
Responsible for the total operation of a store, including merchandising, operations, and personnel; responsible for community relations, overall image of the store, and providing leadership in planning and goal setting.

Merchandise
Administrator responsible for conceptualizing and planning overall buying in several related merchandise classifications for a division; coordinates, develops, and evaluates the work of buyers, with responsibility for profits.

Senior Vice President for Merchandising
Responsible for developing and overseeing divisional objectives and policies in buying, merchandise planning, advertising, promotion, and systems for large sectors of the business; direct responsibility for the overall profitability of those sectors.

Making a Personal Assessment

The Life Audit. For understandable reasons, no one has your best interest at heart as much as you do. No one can know and understand you or your abilities, interests, and aspirations as well as you. Unfortunately, many individuals do not really know themselves well because they have never taken the time to assess what they want and expect out of life. A **life audit** is an attempt to seek insight into one's true feelings about one's abilities and aspirations. A form of self-analysis, a life audit involves simply answering truthfully a series of questions about one's expectations. No prescribed set of questions is appropriate for every life audit; however, the audit should include questions regarding family issues, personal values, general attitudes, basic beliefs, and personal goals and objectives. A life audit gives people a better self-understanding and helps them decide whether they might be successful and happy in the world of retailing.

The Career Audit. To start and maintain a successful career, you need a career plan that includes necessary strategies and tactics for success. To develop a career plan, you should first conduct a **career audit**. Figure B–4 illustrates a career audit, a set of twenty questions that many executive recruiters believe will help you discover yourself and your career aspirations. These questions not only are useful in developing initial career plans, but also can serve as guidelines to continually evaluate career assets and liabilities. One of the most difficult aspects of a job search, especially for recent college graduates, is determining what job function is most interesting to them.[3]

Securing a Retail Position

After you have completed a personal assessment, you are then ready to secure a retail position—the **employment-search process**. Because of the many and various employment opportunities in retailing, the strategies and tactics of a search for a retail position must be systematic and comprehensive. This discussion covers how to identify prospective employers, obtain a personal interview, prepare for an interview, and participate in the interview.

Identifying Prospective Employers. Prospective employer identification is a process of organizing opportunities. The four steps include listing employment criteria, ranking employment criteria, scaling employment preferences, and matching job preferences with prospective employers.

- **Step 1: Listing employment criteria.** In the initial stages of an employment search, you must determine the general conditions under which you are willing to accept a job, that is, your **employment criteria**. Although the particulars of any job (e.g., salary) are determined during actual employment negotiation, you may have certain preconditions regarding employment. Common preconditions involve location, organization, and position. For personal, professional, and many other reasons, you may prefer or need to work in a particular part of the country or in a particular state or city. You should also list any preconditions regarding

1. Do I work better in a large or small corporation?
2. How important is geographic location to me? To my family?
3. Am I a loner, or do I work better as a member of a group?
4. Am I more comfortable following than leading?
5. Do I analyze better than I execute?
6. Am I an innovator?
7. Do I work more successfully under pressure?
8. Am I a good planner?
9. Am I a good listener?
10. Do I think well on my feet?
11. Do I express myself well orally? In writing?
12. What characteristics do I admire in others?
13. Which function of my job do I perform most effectively?
14. Which do I perform least effectively?
15. What do I enjoy doing most?
16. In the past six months, what accomplishment has most satisfied me? Which has been the most difficult?
17. What have I done to correct my shortcomings?
18. What level of responsibility do I aspire to in five years?
19. What should I be earning then?
20. How will I achieve these levels?

Source: Robert Ankerson, "Marketing a New Product," *MBA: Master in Business Administration* (October, 1975), 28.

FIGURE B–4
Twenty questions to ask in making a career audit

the kind of organization for which you are willing to work. Representative organizational preconditions might include the size of the firm, the type of organization (e.g., independent vs. chain organization), and nature of the operation (e.g., department, specialty, or discount organization). Finally, you should include a list of any preconditions regarding positions you are willing or unwilling to accept. For example, you should consider your interest (or lack of interest) in accepting a position in such areas as merchandising, operations management, sales promotion, or personnel.

- **Step 2: Ranking employment criteria**. Not all the criteria identified in step 1 will necessarily be equally important to you. Step 2 of the prospective employer-identification process requires that you rank each of the employment criteria according to importance. You may judge some criteria extremely important or essential (e.g., for family reasons you must find a job in the greater Chicago area); others might be preferences but not absolutely essential (e.g., you prefer to work in the merchandising area of a large department store). Finally, you might view other criteria as not important but a definite plus (e.g., the opportunity to work in a particular merchandising department—women's apparel). By ranking employment criteria, you develop a concrete means of judging employment opportunities.
- **Step 3: Scaling employment preferences**. The third step in identifying prospective employers is to develop a preference scale of employment opportunities. This step requires developing general job descriptions for first, second, and third preference levels. For example, your most-preferred job description might be an assistant manager of a women's apparel department in a major Chicago metro-area department store, preferably somewhere in the northwest part of the city. On the other end of the scale your least-preferred job description might be the same type of job in an out-of-state location. After you have developed two or three general job descriptions for each of the three preference levels, you will be ready for the final stage of your employer-identification process.
- **Step 4: Matching job preferences with prospective employers**. Now that you have listed, ranked, and scaled your preferences, the final step in the employer-identification process is to match those preferences with prospective employers. The matching process consists of compiling a list of jobs and screening that list of prospective employers according to your scaled preferences.

It will be to your benefit to explore all possible sources in compiling a **jobs list**. The campus placement office is a logical starting point, as it represents one of the most fruitful sources for good leads for potential employment. It also provides a number of services (e.g., setting up personal interviews) that can greatly facilitate your employment-search process. By checking with your placement office frequently and regularly, you will be able to keep your jobs list updated. You also need to systematically check the employment sections of local and national newspapers as well as trade and professional journals, magazines, and newspapers. Federal equal employment opportunity requirements have made these publications a good source for locating employment opportunities. Commercial employment agencies are still another source. Before making any commitments to one of these agencies, however, be sure you fully understand what services they provide and under what conditions and terms. You can obtain additional job leads by sending inquiries to the personnel departments of retail firms you believe have the potential to offer the kind of employment you desire. Finally, some of the best leads to employment opportunities come through personal contacts. Professors, friends, relatives, and social and professional acquaintances often provide an inside track to opportunities.

Screening a jobs list is a fairly routine procedure if you have carefully completed the previous step in the employment-search process—scaling employment preferences. Jobs-list screening involves (1) reducing your jobs list to employment opportunities that meet your minimum requirements for employment and then (2) rank ordering the remaining jobs on the list according to your preferences. This screening results in a list of available and acceptable employment opportunities rank ordered from most- to least-desirable.

Obtaining a Personal Interview. Personal interviews are a way for retailers to question and observe job applicants in a face-to-face situation. Most retailers consider interviews essential to hiring. One short interview with the store's personnel manager is usually all that is necessary for lower-echelon positions. By contacting the personnel department and completing an application form, qualified applicants normally will be granted a personal interview.

The **personal interview process** for most managerial positions is much more involved. Typically, it involves a series of personal interviews with various managers at different levels. Although it is necessary to be successful at each of these interviews, getting the *initial* interview is the most crucial step because without it nothing else happens. Obtaining the initial interview can be quite simple or extremely difficult. The method you use to get the first interview depends on the circumstances surrounding the job (e.g., type and level of the position) and the firm's employment practices (e.g., where and how they recruit). There are several methods for obtaining the initial interview with retailing firms. They include (1) obtaining an on-campus interview schedule from the school placement office and scheduling an interview through that office; (2) contacting the store's personnel office and making arrangements for the initial interview; (3) asking personal contacts to set up a personal interview; and (4) writing brief letters and making telephone calls and personal visits to one or more of the firm's managers to discuss possible employment opportunities.

Preparing for a Personal Interview. Lack of preparation is perhaps the most common error applicants make in the personal-interview process. It is foolish for anyone to spend several years in college preparing for a career and then fail to spend several hours preparing for the key interview that could very well launch a career with the right firm. Preparing for a personal interview involves getting to know something about the firm interviewing you and helping the firm in its efforts to get to know you.

Before the interview, you should do some research on the firm. Your ability to talk knowledgeably about the firm and its activities will pay substantial dividends during the actual interview. Preparation not only will make a favorable impression on the interviewer, but will also allow you to answer and ask meaningful questions. Your information search on the firm should help you to discuss the firm's organizational structure, market positions, merchandising strategies, financial positions, and future prospects. Examining various trade magazines, industrial directories, and other reference books can provide a good general picture of the firm and its operations.

To help the firm get to know you, you will need to prepare a resume, which should include (1) a brief statement of personal data (e.g., name, address, telephone number, marital status, date of birth, health status, and physical condition); (2) a brief outline of educational experience (i.e., type of degree, name of school, date of graduation, major and minor fields of study, class ranking, scholarships, honors, awards, and extracurricular activities); (3) a short history of work experience (i.e., a list of jobs, positions and responsibilities, names of employers, and dates of employment); and (4) a summary of other activities, interests, and skills that support your professional credentials. Also, you might wish to include a list of references and a short statement of your career objectives. In preparing a resume, the following guidelines are helpful:

1. *Be concise.* The purpose of a resume is to stimulate the interviewer's interest and not to tell your life story. A one-page resume is sufficient to create this interest. If interviewers want to know more, they will ask for more information and clarification.
2. *Be factual.* Experienced interviewers will recognize resume "puffery" and generally take a dim view of it. A statement of a few real accomplishments is received much more favorably than a list of artificial ones.
3. *Be professional.* A well-organized, neatly produced resume is an excellent "scene setter" for your personal interview. A poorly organized resume with confusing layout, typographical errors, misspellings, and blurred or messy photocopying make a definite statement about your abilities to organize and to produce good work.

As a final note, you must recognize that it is your responsibility to establish and verify the time and place for each interview. Missing or being late to an interview is rarely excusable, regardless of the reason. You should therefore plan for unforeseen delays to ensure getting to your interview on time.

Taking a Personal Interview. The interview situation varies according to the interviewer's personal preferences. Some interview situations are conducted formally in a structured question-and-answer format. Other interview situations are informal, conducted without any apparent structure. Figure B–5 outlines the typical stages and topics of an initial interview. Whether the interview is formal or informal, your ability to read the interview situation and to react accordingly will determine your success. All interviews, formal or informal, usually have four parts: (1) rapport building—few minutes of chit-chat to open the interview; (2) questions and answers—information exchange; (3) the sell—applicant outlines what he or she can do for the retailer while the retailer explains the opportunities available with the organization; and (4) the close—each party, if favorably impressed, tries to end the interview on a positive note.[4] No absolute rules apply in taking a personal interview, but the guidelines that follow are useful in most situations.

- **Dress appropriately.** The job or position for which you are interviewing will provide you with cues on how to dress. Do not overdress or underdress for the occasion.
- **Be prepared for openers.** Many interviewers like to open their interviews with broad questions such as "What do you expect out of life?" "Why do you want to work for our firm?" "Where do you want to be in your career ten years from now?" or "What do you think you can do for our company?"
- **Be relaxed.** Interviewers expect a reasonable amount of nervousness; however, excessive nervousness may well suggest to the interviewer that you are unable to handle pressure situations. Avoid nervous gestures. On the other hand, avoid appearing so relaxed or "laid back" that you give the impression of being disinterested in the interview or the job.
- **Listen carefully.** Let the interviewer guide the interview, at least during the initial stages. Interviewers provide cues as to how they want to conduct the interview and what they want to talk about. Also, by listening carefully, you will be able to fully understand the nature of the questions and thus give better responses.
- **Ask questions.** If you want a job with the interviewer's company, you should be able to show your interest by asking intelligent questions about the firm.
- **Be informative.** You should answer the interviewer's questions fully and quickly but avoid talking too much or too fast. Most of the interviewer's questions will require more than a yes or no answer; however, you should avoid telling your life story, boasting about your accomplishments, and complaining about your problems.
- **Be somewhat aggressive.** It is better to be perceived as a little too aggressive rather than too passive. In terms of aggressiveness, the right impression to portray might be that you are a "mover," but not a "shaker."
- **Be honest.** Answer questions as truthfully as you can. Interviewers recognize that everyone has strengths and weaknesses. Frankly admitting a weakness adds credi-

Stages	Interviewer Topics	Interviewer Looks for
1. First impressions	Introduction and greeting Small talk about traffic conditions, the weather, the record of the basketball team	Firm handshake, eye contact Appearance and dress appropriate to the business, not campus, setting
2. Your record	*Education* Reasons for choice of school and major Grades: effort required for them Special areas of interest Courses enjoyed most and least, reasons Special achievements, toughest problems Value of education as career preparation Reaction to teachers High school record, SAT scores *Work Experience* Nature of jobs held Why undertaken Level of responsibility reached Duties liked most and least Supervisory experience Relations with others *Activities and Interests* Role in extracurricular, athletic, community, and social service activities Personal interests—hobbies, cultural interests, sports	Intellectual abilities Breadth and depth of knowledge Relevance of course work to career interests Special or general interest Value placed on achievement Willingness to work hard Relation between ability and achievement Reaction to authority Ability to cope with problems Sensible use of resources (time, energy, money) High energy level, vitality, enthusiasm Leadership ability; interest in responsibility Willingness to follow directions Ability to get along with others Seriousness of purpose Ability to motivate oneself, to make things happen Positive "can do" attitude Diversity of interests Awareness of world outside the laboratory Social conscience; good citizenship

FIGURE B–5
Stages and topics covered during the initial interview (stages 2 and 3 are the most important parts of the interview)

bility to the statements you make about your strengths. Admitting a weakness also makes you appear more trustworthy to the interviewer.

Following these guidelines greatly improves one's chances for a successful interview. One last point: If you can make the interviewer feel comfortable and at ease, then you have gone a long way toward getting a second interview and possibly a position with that company.

OWNERSHIP OPPORTUNITIES

Regardless of their income, many people who work for others feel they are living a hand-to-mouth, paycheck-to-paycheck existence. According to one old adage, the only way to get ahead is to get other people to work for you or to get money working for you—the idea is that income and perhaps job satisfaction are limited when you work for someone else. Many people find that self-employment is the answer to a better income, greater independence, a more rewarding career, and an improved lifestyle. Many people think that going into business for themselves is the only way they can fully realize their hopes and aspirations. To have a chance at realizing their personal, career, and life goals, these individuals are willing to assume the considerable burdens and risks of owning and operating their own businesses.

The preceding chapters fully discussed the factors necessary for a successful retail operation. With that background in mind, consider whether *you* are the kind of

Stages	Interviewer Topics	Interviewer Looks for
3. Your career goals	Type of work desired Immediate objectives Long-term objectives Interest in this company Other companies being considered Desire for further education/training Geographical preferences and limitations Attitude toward relocation Health factors that might affect job performance	Realistic knowledge of strengths and weaknesses Preparation for employment Knowledge of opportunities Seriousness of purpose; career-oriented rather than job-oriented Knowledge of the company Real interest in the company Work interests in line with talents Company's chance to get and keep you
4. The company	Company opportunities Where you might fit Current and future projects Major divisions and departments Training programs, educational and other benefits	Informed and relevant questions Indications of interest in answers Appropriate but not undue interest in salary or benefits
5. Conclusion	Further steps you should take (application form, transcript, references) Further steps company will take, outline how application handled, to which departments it will be sent, time of notification of decision Cordial farewell	Candidate's attention to information as a sign of continued interest

Source: Reprinted with permission from *Peterson's Business and Management Jobs 1985,* © 1984 by Peterson's Guides, Inc., P.O. Box 2123, Princeton, New Jersey 08540. Current edition available at bookstores or direct from the publisher.

FIGURE B–5
continued

person who could succeed as an independent retailer. To help assess this possibility, take the self-evaluation test in Figure B–6; it should give you some insight into whether you have the personal attributes to become an independent retailer. If, after taking the self-evaluation test, you decide that you do have what it takes to be an independent retailer, three options are open to you: (1) starting a new business; (2) buying an existing business; or (3) securing a franchise. Each option has its advantages and disadvantages that you should fully explore. Figure B–7 compares issues surrounding the decision to start a new business or buy an existing one. The principal concerns associated with securing a franchise are outlined in Figure B–8.

FIGURE B–6
Do you have what it takes to be an independent retailer?

Under each question, check the answer that says what you feel or comes closest to it. Be honest with yourself.

Are you a self-starter?

- ☐ I do things on my own. Nobody has to tell me to get going.
- ☐ If someone gets me started, I keep going all right.
- ☐ Easy does it, man. I don't put myself out until I have to.

How do you feel about other people?

- ☐ I like people. I can get along with just about anybody.
- ☐ I have plenty of friends—I don't need anyone else.
- ☐ Most people bug me.

Can you lead others?

- ☐ I can get most people to go along when I start something.
- ☐ I can give the orders if someone tells me what we should do.
- ☐ I let someone else get things moving. Then I go along if I feel like it.

Can you take responsibility?

- ☐ I like to take charge of things and see them through.
- ☐ I'll take over if I have to, but I'd rather let someone else be responsible.
- ☐ There's always some eager beaver around wanting to show how smart he is. I say let him.

How good an organizer are you?

- ☐ I like to have a plan before I start. I'm usually the one to get things lined up when the gang wants to do something.
- ☐ I do all right unless things get too goofed up. Then I cop out.
- ☐ You get all set and then something comes along and blows the whole bag. So I just take things as they come.

How good a worker are you?

- ☐ I can keep going as long as I need to. I don't mind working hard for something I want.
- ☐ I'll work hard for a while, but when I've had enough, that's it, man!
- ☐ I can't see that hard work gets you anywhere.

FIGURE B–6
(continued)

Can you make decisions?

☐ I can make up my mind in a hurry if I have to. It usually turns out O.K., too.
☐ I can if I have plenty of time. If I have to make up my mind fast, I think later I should have decided the other way.
☐ I don't like to be the one who has to decide things. I'd probably blow it.

Can people trust what you say?

☐ You bet they can. I don't say things I don't mean.
☐ I try to be on the level most of the time, but sometimes I just say what's easiest.
☐ What's the sweat if the other fellow doesn't know the difference?

Can you stick with it?

☐ If I make up my mind to do something, I don't let *anything* stop me.
☐ I usually finish what I start—if it doesn't get fouled up.
☐ If it doesn't go right away, I turn off. Why beat your brains out?

How good is your health?

☐ Man, I *never* run down!
☐ I have enough energy for most things I want to do.
☐ I run out of juice sooner than most of my friends seem to.

Now count the checks you made.

How many checks are there beside the *first* answer to each question? ______
How many checks are there beside the *second* answer to each question? ______
How many checks are there beside the *third* answer to each question? ______

If most of your checks are beside the first answer, you probably have what it takes to run a business. If not, you're likely to have more trouble than you can handle by yourself. Better find a partner who is strong on the points you're weak on. If many checks are beside the third answer, not even a good partner will be able to shore you up.

Source: *Checklist for Going into Business,* Small Marketers Aids No. 71, Small Business Administration (October, 1976), 4–5.

Should I start my own business from scratch or should I purchase an existing business? These are the two alternatives facing the potential small business manager. If the business is started fresh, there are these advantages:

1. You can create a business in your own image. The business is not a made-over version of someone else's place, but it is formed the way you think it should be.
2. You do not run the risk of purchasing a business with a poor reputation that you would inherit.
3. The concept you have for the business is so unusual that only a new business is possible.

The creation of a new business also has some substantial drawbacks. Some of the disadvantages include:

1. Too small a market for your product or service.
2. High cost of new equipment.
3. Lack of a source of advice on how things are done and who can be trusted.
4. Lack of name recognition. It may take a long time to persuade customers to give your business a try.

Buying an existing business also has advantages and disadvantages. The major advantages are:

1. A successful business may provide the buyer with an immediate source of income.
2. An existing business may already be in the best location.
3. An existing business already has employees who are trained and suppliers who have established ties to the business.
4. Equipment is already installed and the productive capacity of the business is known.
5. Inventories are in place, and suppliers have extended trade credit which can be continued.
6. There is no loss of momentum. The business is already operating.
7. You have the opportunity to obtain advice and counsel from the previous owner.
8. Often, you can purchase the business you want at a price much lower than the cost of starting the same business from scratch.

Purchasing an existing business can have some real drawbacks, such as the following:

1. You can be misled, and end up with a business that is a "dog."
2. The business could have been so poorly managed by the previous owner that you inherit a great deal of ill will.
3. A poorly managed business may have employees who are unsuited to the business or poorly trained.
4. The location of the business may have become, or is becoming, unsuitable.
5. The equipment may have been poorly maintained or even be obsolete.
6. Change can be difficult to introduce in an established business.
7. Inventory may be out of date, damaged, or obsolete.
8. You can pay too much for the business.

To avoid buying a business that cannot be made profitable, investigate six critical areas:

1. Why does the owner wish to sell? Look for the real reason and do not simply accept what you are told.
2. Determine the physical condition of the business. Consider the building and its location.
3. Conduct a thorough analysis of the market for your products or services. Who are your present and potential customers? You cannot know too much about your customers. Conduct an equally thorough analysis of your competitors, both direct and indirect. How do they operate and why do customers prefer them?
4. Consider all of the legal factors which might constrain the expansion and growth of the business. Become familiar with zoning restrictions.
5. Identify the actual owner of the business and all liens that might exist.
6. Using the material covered in previous chapters, analyze the financial condition of the business.

The business can be evaluated on the basis of its assets, its future earnings, or a combination of both. Don't confuse the value of a business with its price. Price is determined through negotiation. The bargaining zone represents that area within which agreement can be reached.

Source: Norman M. Scarborough and Thomas W. Zimmerer, *Effective Small Business Management* (Columbus: Merrill Publishing Co., 1984), 130–31.

FIGURE B–7
To start or buy?

FIGURE B–8
A retail franchise: Is it for you?

The Franchisor and the Franchise

1. Is the potential market for the product or service adequate to support your franchise? Will the prices you charge be in line with the market?
2. Is the market's population growing, remaining static, or shrinking? Is the demand for your product or service growing, remaining static, or shrinking?
3. Is the product or service safe and reputable?
4. What will the competition, direct or indirect, be in your sales territory? Do any other franchisees operate in this general area?
5. Is the franchise international, national, regional, or local in scope? Does it involve full- or part-time involvement?
6. How many years has the franchisor been in operation? Does it have a sound reputation for honest dealings with franchisees?
7. How many franchise outlets now exist? How many will there be a year from now? How many outlets are company-owned?
8. How many franchisees have failed? Why?
9. What services and assistance will the franchisor provide? Training programs? Advertising assistance? Financial aid? Are these one-time programs or are they continuous in nature?
10. Will the firm perform a location analysis to help you find a suitable site?
11. Will the franchisor offer you exclusive distribution rights for the length of the agreement, or may it sell to other franchises in this area?
12. What facilities and equipment are required for the franchise? Who pays for construction? Is there a lease agreement?
13. What is the total cost of the franchise? What are the initial capital requirements? Will the franchisor provide financial assistance? Of what nature? What is the interest rate? Is the franchisor financially sound enough to fulfill all its promises?
14. How much is the franchise fee? **Exactly** what does it cover? Are there any continuing fees? What additional fees are there?
15. Does the franchisor provide an estimate of expenses and income? Are they reasonable for your particular area? Are they sufficiently documented?
16. Does the franchisor offer a written contract which covers all the details of the agreement? Have your attorney and your accountant studied its terms and approved it? Do **you** understand the implications of the contract?
17. What is the length of the franchise agreement? Under what circumstances can it be terminated? If you terminate the contract, what are the costs to you? What are the terms and costs of renewal?
18. Are you allowed to sell the franchise to a third party? If so, will you receive the proceeds?
19. Is there a national advertising program? How is it financed? What media are used? What help is provided for local advertising?

The Franchisee—You

20. Are you qualified to operate a franchise successfully? Do you have adequate drive, skills, experience, education, patience, and financial capacity? Are you prepared to work hard?
21. Are you willing to sacrifice some autonomy in operating a business to own a franchise?
22. Can you tolerate the financial risk?
23. Are you genuinely interested in the product or service you will be selling?
24. Has the franchisor investigated your background thoroughly enough to decide you are qualified to operate the franchise?
25. What can this franchisor do for you that you cannot do for yourself?

Source: Norman M. Scarborough and Thomas W. Zimmerer, *Effective Small Business Management* (Columbus: Merrill Publishing Co., 1984), 101–2

ENDNOTES

1. Donald Zale, "The Need to Rekindle the Entrepreneurial Spirit," *Retailing Issues Letter* (Center for Retailing Studies, Texas A&M University, September 1986), 2.
2. Figure B–1 showed some of the indicators of entrepreneurial attitudes. (Note: The best answers to these questions are [1] c, [2] b, [3] c, [4] a, [5] a, [6] c, [7] a, [8] c, [9] a, [10] c, [11] c, [12] a, [13] b, and [14] c. Score one point for each correct answer. Questions 1, 2, 3, 7, 9, and 12 suggest whether you are a realistic problem solver who can run a business without constant help from others. Questions 5, 6, and 8 probe whether you take calculated risks and seek information before you act. Questions 4, 10, 13, and 14 show whether you, like the classic entrepreneur, find other people satisfying when they help fulfill your need to win. Question 11 reveals whether you take responsibility for your destiny—and your business. If you score between 11 and 14 points, you could have a good chance to succeed. If you score from 7 to 10 points, you'd better have a superb business idea or a lot of money to help you out. If you score 7 or less, stay where you are.)
3. Susan Bernard, "Your Job Search Countdown," *Business Week's Careers* 3 (October/Winter Preview 1985), 96.
4. Marilyn M. Kennedy, "How to Win the Interview Game," *Business Week's Careers* 5 (September 1987), 17.

GLOSSARY

ABC markets. Based on their sales volume potential, urban centers are classified in descending order as either A, B, or C markets.

account. A record of the increases and decreases in one type of asset, liability, capital, income, or expense.

achievement tests. Questionnaires designed to measure a person's basic knowledge and skills.

advertising. Indirect, impersonal communication carried by a mass medium and paid for by an identified retailer.

advertising budget. Allocation of advertising dollars made on the basis of departments, merchandise lines, media, and time periods.

advertising cost. The amount of money a retailer must pay to run an advertisement in a medium (absolute); the number of dollars the retailer spends to reach a specific number of people (relative).

advertising effectiveness. Establishing specific, measurable advertising objectives; then acquiring or developing instruments and methodologies to determine whether those objectives were met.

advertising freelancer. An artist, copywriter, or photographer who produces advertising on a part-time basis.

advertising frequency. The number of times the same viewer or reader may be exposed to the same advertisement.

advertising manager. Performs all the advertising activities described and supervises an art director, copy chief, and production manager.

aesthetic features. Elements of a product that appeal to the five senses of hearing, seeing, tasting, feeling, and smelling.

affective component. The emotions a consumer feels about an object.

affinity. The extent to which the new product is consistent with the consumer's current buying and usage behavior.

agent intermediaries. Specialists in buying and selling that facilitate the exchange process between manufacturer and retailer by bringing them together.

analog models. Used to make sales projections for new stores based on the sales performance of existing stores.

analytical models. Various statistical and quantitative methods that researchers use internally to generate primary information.

angled-front configuration. Positioning the store's front at a slight angle to the traffic arteries.

annex approach. Locates all nonselling activities away from the sales floor in a sales support annex.

annual sales estimates. The previous year's sales plus or minus a fixed or variable percentage adjustment.

anticompetitive leasing arrangements. Limits the type and amount of competition a particular retailer faces within a given area.

antitrust legislation. A set of laws directed at preventing unreasonable "restraints on trade" and "unfair trade practices" to foster a competitive environment.

approval buying. Allows the retailer to inspect the merchandise before making the purchase decision and to postpone any purchase until physical possession has been secured.

arcade front configuration. Characterized by several recessed windows and/or entrances.

asset turnover. Net sales divided by total assets.

assets. Anything of value that is owned by a retailer.

at-home retailing. The market approach of making personal contacts and sales in the consumers' homes.

attitude. An evaluative mental orientation that provides a predisposition to respond in a certain fashion.

audience selectivity. The medium's ability to present a promotional message to a certain target audience within a population.

audiovisual displays. Making a video display by applying current technology to stimulate consumer purchases (visual merchandising, audio merchandising, and audiovisual merchandising). A combination of sound and videotape or slides to present the product's story.

augmenting extras. Auxiliary product dimensions that provide supplementary benefits to the customer.

Automatic Identification System. A group of several interacting technologies that enables machines to recognize and enter data into a computer system.

automatic markdown. Reduce prices by a fixed percentage at a regular interval.

average stock. The sum of the stock on hand at the beginning of the period, at each intervening period, and at the end of the period divided by the number of stock listings.

backward integration. The process of gaining ownership and/or control of supply systems.

bait and switch. The "bait" is an advertised low price on a product that the retailer does not really intend to sell; the "switch" involves personal selling techniques that induce the customer to buy a higher-priced product that will provide the retailer with greater profits.

bait-leader. An extremely attractive advertised price on merchandise that the retailer does not intend to sell; the attractive advertised price is "bait" to get the customer into the store.

balance sheet. A picture of the firm's assets, liabilities, and net worth on a given date which summarizes the basic accounting equation of assets equal liabilities plus net worth.

bar code. A series of light and dark bars that constitute a symbol that is typically attached to a product package or shipping carton.

basic stock list. A planning instrument retailers use to determine the assortment and support for staple merchandise.

basic stock method. Beginning each month with stock levels that equal the estimated sales for that month plus an additional basic stock amount that serves as a "cushion" or "safety stock" in the event that actual sales exceed estimated sales.

batch processing. Waiting until a considerable amount of data has been collected and then processing the entire batch at one time.

Bayesian Analysis. A technique that attempts to combine managerial judgment and objective information to assess dollar-and-cents consequences of alternative decisions.

BCG portfolio approach. A matrix model used to illustrate the current positions of an organization's strategic business units.

behavior component. The predisposition to respond in a certain way based on one's beliefs and feelings.

blind check. A procedure in which the checker (1) lists and describes each merchandise group on a blank form, (2) counts and records the number of items in each group and (3) compares with the invoice or purchase order.

blocker. One member of a team that stands between the salesperson and a shoplifting partner.

blue laws. Local laws which regulate everything from operating hours and days to operating locations.

booster. A shoplifter who shoves merchandise into concealed areas of parcels and/or clothing.

borrowed capital. Money the firm has obtained from outside sources.

boutique layout. Arranges the sales floor into individual, semiseparate areas, each built around a particular shopping theme.

brand. A distinctive grouping of products identified by name, term, design, symbol, or any combination of these markings.

brochure. This form of mail-order retailing involves preparation of a small booklet or leaflet that is mailed to potential consumers.

brokers. Agent intermediaries whose primary function is to bring prospective buyers and sellers together to complete a transaction.

building. Increasing an SBU's market share.

bulk marking. Placing similar merchandise with the same price in a display and attaching one price card to the display.

burglary. Any unlawful entry to commit a felony or a theft, even though no force is used to gain entrance.

buying behavior. The manner in which consumers act, function, and react to various situations involving the purchase of a good or service or the acceptance of an idea.

buying center. A basic unit of consumption that engages in the buying process.

buying power. The financial resources that are available to the consumer for making purchases.

buying scene. The actual place where consumers complete a purchase transaction.

carrier. A shoplifter that walks in, picks up a large piece of merchandise, removes the tags, affixes a fake sales slip, and walks out.

cash cows. SBUs having a high market share within a low-growth market.

cash discount. A discount given for making prompt payment.

catalog. Operations involve the use of specially prepared catalogs that present the retailer's merchandise both visually and verbally.

catalog showroom. A warehouse retailer featuring hard goods such as housewares, small appliances, jewelry, watches, toys, sporting goods, lawn and garden equipment, luggage, stereos, televisions, and other electronic equipment at a discount; a merchandise catalog is combined with the showroom and an adjacent warehouse as part of the retailer's operation.

category killers. Retail chains that want to achieve merchandise dominance in their respective category by creating narrowly-focused, jumbo-size stores.

census markets. Markets corresponding to the nine census regions as defined by the U.S. Census Bureau.

Central Business District (CBD). A downtown retailing cluster.

central market. An area with a concentration of selling offices and merchandise showrooms of a large number of suppliers.

centralization. The concentration of policy and decision making in one location (central headquarters or home office).

centralized complaint system. All customer complaints are referred to a central office or complaint desk.

chain store. Any retail organization that operates multiple outlets, offers a standardized merchandise mix, and utilizes a centralized form of ownership and control.

chain trade discount. A series of percentage discounts applied to the list price in successive order.

channel integration. The process of incorporating all channel members into one channel system and uniting them under one leadership and one set of goals.

chattel mortgage agreement. The title of the goods passes to the customer when the contract is signed, but the product is secured by a lien against it for the unpaid balance.

checking. The process of determining whether the supplier has shipped what the retailer ordered and whether the shipment has arrived in good condition.

checklist method. The evaluator enumerates the general factors usually considered in any site evaluation; for each general factor, the evaluation identifies several attribute measurements reflecting location needs of the proposed retail operation; each location attribute receives a subjective weight based on relative importance to the retailer; each site alternative is rated in terms of each location attribute; and a weighted rating is calculated for each attribute for each site alternative.

clash. Visual conflict among the many parts of any display, layout, or physical arrangement.

class selectivity. The ability of a medium to target specific kinds of people who share certain common characteristics.

classic. A fashion that has both a high level and a long duration of acceptance.

close-out store. An outlet that specializes in the retailing of a wide variety of merchandise obtained through close-outs, retail liquidations, and bankruptcy proceedings.

clustered sites. Retail locations that are either next to each other or in close proximity.

coercive buying. The retailer's use of financial, distribution, marketing, and other powers to gain lower prices from sellers.

cognitive component. What the consumer believes about an object based on available information and knowledge.

commission agents. Take physical possession of goods, provide storage and handling, and act as the selling agent for the producer.

commissionaires. Operators of full and limited buying offices within one or more foreign countries.

communication effectiveness. A medium's ability to deliver the desired impact to the target market.

communication markets. Markets identified on the basis of various types of media coverage.

communication process. Transmitting meaningful messages between senders.

communications approach. How a message is presented; facts, narrative, and logical reasoning to persuade (rational); appealing to the consumer's sense of aesthetics, ego, or feelings (emotional).

community shopping center. A shopping center serving a composite of many neighborhoods within a 10- to 15-minute drive from the center.

comparison shopping. When a customer compares and/or substitutes products within merchandise classes.

competitive audit. An arbitrary, composite rating of each competitor's product, service, price, place, and promotional mixes.

competitive conditions. (1) *exclusive* (no competitors); (2) *selective* (few competitors); (3)*intensive* (many competitors).

competitive parity method. Setting the advertising appropriation at the amount the firm estimates their most important competitors are spending.

competitive price objectives. Meeting the major competitor's price.

complexity. The extent to which a new product can be easily understood or used.

composite trading area. A set of trading areas, each of which is structured according to the type of goods the retailer sells.

concentric diversification. Adding businesses to a firm's portfolio that have technological or marketing similarities with existing businesses.

conditional sales agreement. The title of the goods passes to the consumer conditional on full payment.

conglomerate diversification. Adding new businesses that are totally unrelated to an organization's current SBUs in order to appeal to entirely new markets.

consignment buying. An arrangement whereby the supplier retains ownership of the merchandise shipped to the retailer, and the retailer sells the merchandise, deducts an agreed-upon percentage commission, and remits the remainder to the supplier.

consumer buying process. The sum total of the sequential parts of problem recognition, information search, alternative evaluation, purchase decision, and post-purchase evaluation.

consumer markets. Composed of individuals and/or households who are the ultimate consumers of goods or services.

contests. Promotional activities in which participants compete for rewards.

continuity premiums. Require the customer to make repeat purchases of products and services to benefit from the premium offer.

contract warehousing. Contracting with third-party warehouse companies to take care of all or part of the retailer's distribution needs.

contrast. Visual diversity among the many parts of any display, layout, or physical arrangement.

control unit. The merchandise grouping that serves as the basic reporting unit for various types of information.

controllable expenses. Those expenses over which the firm has direct control.

convenience products. Those products that the consumer is not willing to spend time, money, and effort in locating, evaluating, and procuring.

convenience store. Offers customers a convenient place to shop—time convenience (e.g., open longer and during early morning and late-night hours); and place convenience (e.g., small, compact, fast-service operations close to consumers' homes and places of business).

conventional marketing channel. A loosely aligned, independently owned and operated channel team.

cooperative advertising. Manufacturers prepare print and broadcast advertising material of their own products and allow the retailer to insert its store name and address in the ad, then manufacturer and retailer split the cost of media space or time to run the ad.

copy. What is actually said in the advertisement.

core approach. Locating all nonselling areas within a central core area surrounded by selling areas.

corollary data method. A method used to estimate trading-area sales that assumes that an identifiable relationship exists between sales for a particular class of goods and one or more trading-area characteristics.

corporation. A legal business entity authorized by state law to operate as a single person even though it may consist of many persons.

cost-justification defense. Makes it lawful to charge retailers different prices if the supplier can justify those price differences on the basis of its cost of doing business with each competing retailer.

cost method of inventory valuation. Valuing merchandise inventory at the original cost to the store each time a physical inventory is taken.

cost of goods sold. The value of the merchandise sold during any given accounting period.

coupon. This form of mail-order retailing involves using magazine and newspaper advertisements; manufacturer or retailer certificates that give consumers a price reduction on specific kinds of merchandise.

coverage. The percentage of a given market that a medium reaches.

credit. The borrowing power of a consumer, an amount of money that is placed at a consumer's disposal by a financial or other institution, and the time allowed for payment for goods and services sold on trust.

credit scoring system. The process of replacing subjective lending with scientific scoring.

cross-elasticity of demand. When a change in the price of one product results in a change in demand for another product.

cues. External stimuli that direct consumers toward specific objects that can satisfy basic needs and reduce drives.

culture. The sum total of knowledge, attitudes, symbols, and patterns of behavior that are shared by a group of people and transmitted from one generation to the next.

cumulative markup. The markup placed on an item which is based on the weight each item contributes to the total markup of all the items in the merchandise group.

cumulative quantity discounts. Discounts applying to several orders or shipments placed with the supplier over an extended period of time.

current assets. All items of value that can be easily converted into cash within a relatively short time.

current liabilities. Short-term debts that must be paid during the current fiscal year.

current ratio. Is computed by dividing current assets by current liabilities; represents the firm's ability to meet current debt with current assets.

customer service levels. The types of services to be offered and the quality of the service offering.

DAGMAR (defining advertising goals for measured advertising results). A sequence of steps through which prospective customers move from total unawareness of a store and its offering to store patronage and purchase.

debit card. An electronic checkbook that allows the retailer to automatically subtract payments from a customer's checking account at the time of sale.

debt ratio. Is computed by dividing total debt by total assets.

decentralized complaint system. Customer complaints are handled at the department level.

deceptive brokerage activities. Involve the establishment and use of "dummy" brokerage firms to secure a brokerage allowance from suppliers, giving retailers an unfair purchase-price advantage.

deceptive price advertising. Price information used to mislead consumers into believing that they are receiving a better price or a larger discount than is actually being offered.

deceptive product advertising. Making a false or misleading claim about the physical makeup of the product, the appropriate uses for the product, or the benefits from using the product, as well as using packages and labels that tend to mislead the customer about the exact contents, quality, or quantity of the package.

decoding. Receiving a message and interpreting its meaning either correctly or incorrectly, depending on how well the message was encoded and the decoder's experience and skill with the communication process.

demography. The study of statistics that are used to describe a population.

department store. A large retailing institution that carries a wide variety of merchandise lines with a reasonably good selection within each line.

department wrapping. Performed by either the salesperson who makes the sale or the department cashier and wrapper.

departmentalization. When tasks and employees are grouped together into departments to achieve the operating efficiencies of specialization for a group performing similar tasks.

design. Individual interpretations or versions of the same style.

desires. Conscious impulses toward objects or experiences that hold promise of enjoyment in their attainment.

dialectic process. A "melting pot" theory of retail institutional change in which two substantially different competitive forms of retailing merge together into a new retailing institution, a composite of the original two forms.

dichotomous questions. Limit a respondent's answer to only one of two choices.

dipper. The store employee who steals money by dipping into the cash register or mishandles cash in some other way, such as making short rings, fraudulent refunds, or false employee discounts.

direct-action messages. Urging the consumer to come to the store now to take advantage of a promotion.

direct advertising. A medium that retailers use extensively to communicate their product offerings to a select group of consumers.

direct channel. The producer eliminates both retailer and wholesaler and markets directly to the final consumer.

direct expenses. Those expenses directly attributable to the operations of a department or some other defined operating unit.

direct (intratype) competitor. One whose merchandising program is about the same as another retailer's.

direct premiums. Free gifts given to the customer at the time of purchase.

direct product profit (DPP). Allows the retailer to calculate the profitability of a merchandise category as well as a particular product item.

discounter. An employee who gives unauthorized discounts to friends and relatives.

discounts. Reductions in the original retail price that are granted to store employees as special fringe benefits and to special customers in recognition of their special status.

discretionary income. That portion of an individual's or family's disposable income that remains after purchasing the basic necessities of life—food, clothing, and shelter.

display stock. Stock placed on various display fixtures that customers can directly examine.

disposable income. The income that remains after taxes and other required payments have been deducted from total income.

dissatisfiers. Employment factors that make workers unhappy with their job, leading to high turnover and weak performance.

diversification growth. An organization's adding of SBUs whose business nature and format are dissimilar to the current SBUs held by the firm.

diverter. One member of a team of shoplifters who attempts to divert the attention of the store's personnel while a partner shoplifts.

divesting. Disposing of SBUs that offer little or no hope of improving either their market share or cash flow position.

dogs. SBUs that have a low market share within a low-growth market.

dollar control. Collecting, recording, and analyzing merchandise data in terms of dollars.

dollar markup. A cost-oriented approach to setting prices wherein the retailer adds to the cost of the merchandise a dollar amount large enough to cover related operating expenses and to provide a given dollar profit.

dollar open-to-buy at cost. The buyer multiplies open-to-buy at retail by the complement of the initial markup percentage.

dollar open-to-buy at retail. The buyer starts with planned monthly purchases and subtracts purchase commitments already made during the month.

dollar-periodic physical inventory system. Provides periodic information on the amount of inventory (dollars) actually on hand at a given time as determined by a physical count and valuation of the merchandise.

dollar/perpetual/book inventory system. Provides the retailer with continuous information on the amount of inventory (dollars) that should be on hand at any given time as determined by internal accounting records.

dollar planning. A financial management tool used to plan the amount of total value (dollars) inventory a retailer should carry.

drawing power. The area from which a shopping center could expect to derive as much as 85 percent of its total volume.

drive. Whatever impels behavior; it arises from a strongly felt inner need that requires action.

durables. Products that are capable of surviving many uses.

eater. The employee who samples the retailer's food and beverage lines or supplements lunch with a soft drink or dessert.

educated-guess budgeting method. The use of intuition and practical experience to develop an advertising budget.

elastic demand. A condition in which a change in price strongly influences consumer demand.

electronic data interchange. A communication system that allows buyers and suppliers to conduct business transactions electronically.

electronic data processing. A computer-based system of processing information.

electronic retailing. This form of retailing via electronic and video systems is in the innovation stage of the retail life cycle.

electronically programmable shelf labels. Small liquid crystal display labels that are attached on the edge of the shelf and can display new prices instantly on command.

elevated windows. Display windows with floors of varying heights.

embezzler. A highly trusted employee who takes advantage of that trust to divert the retailer's funds for either permanent or temporary use.

emotional approach. A presentation that appeals to consumers' feelings.

encoding. Using signs and symbols that promote understanding of the idea, attract attention of the intended audiences, stimulate needs felt by intended audiences, and suggest a course of action for need satisfaction.

equal-store organization. Emphasizes centralization of authority and responsibility.

equity capital. What the firm owns.

essential services. Those services basic and necessary to the retailer's merchandising and operational activities.

esteem needs. Aspirations involving prestige, recognition, admiration, self-respect, success, and achievement.

ethics. A system or code of conduct based on universal moral duties and obligations which indicate how one should behave.

exclusive dealings. Arrangements between retailers and suppliers in which the retailer agrees to handle only the supplier's products or no other products that pose direct competition.

exclusive market coverage. Using one location to serve either an entire market area or some major segment of that market.

exclusive territories. Agreements under which a supplier grants a retailer the exclusive right to sell its products within a defined geographic area.

executive training programs (ETPs). Educational sessions directed at supervisors, managers, and executives.

expected services. Services not essential for the retailer to operate but expected by customers.

expense budget. A plan or a set of guidelines that a firm uses to control operating expenses.

experimentation. A technique that researchers use to determine a cause-and-effect relationship between two or more factors.

expert systems. Computer programs that have knowledge bases contributed by experts in a particular field and are used to aid in decision making and problem solving.

expressed warranties. Written and oral statements that the seller makes to consumers about a product and performance and that the retailer is legally obligated to honor.

extended channel. Marketing through both wholesalers and retailers.

external information. Information obtained from outside the firm.

externally oriented strategic service vision. Planning and integrating the service provider's marketing and operating function for the benefit of the service consumer.

factory outlet (direct manufacturers' outlets). Sell their own seconds, overruns, and pack-aways from last season.

fad. A fashion that obtains a relatively high level of customer acceptance for a short time.

fan arrangements. Spread up and out from a small base.

fashion. A product that has distinctive attributes that are currently appropriate and represent the prevailing style.

fashion cycle. The three stages a fashion passes through—introduction, acceptance, and decline.

feedback. The nature of the receiver's response or lack of it communicated back to the sender.

financial objectives. A strategic position directed at ensuring that the organization operates profitably and productively.

financial leverage. Total assets divided by net worth.

financial ratios. Mathematical relationships between elements in the balance sheet or between a balance sheet element and an income statement element to determine a firm's financial performance.

first-in, first-out (FIFO) method of costing inventories. Merchandise items are sold in the order in which they are purchased; older stock is sold before newer stock that was purchased at a later date.

fixed assets. Assets that require a significant length of time to convert into cash, usually more than one year.

fixed-based budgeting. Each expense is budgeted to a specific dollar amount.

fixed capital. Money needed to purchase physical facilities.

fixed expenses. Are usually fixed for a given period of time and remain the same regardless of the sales volume.

fixed-term revolving credit plan. Requires the customer to pay a fixed amount on any unpaid balance at regularly scheduled intervals until the amount is paid in full.

flat organizational structure. Used by firms that limit the number of organizational levels to one or two levels.

flexibility. The number of different "things" the advertiser can do in the medium.

flop. A fashion rejected by all consumer segments almost immediately.

ford. A best-seller in fashion merchandising.

formal objective employee evaluation. Include performance records and management-by-objectives procedures.

formal subjective employee evaluation. Rating scales and checklists used to identify and list several criteria.

forward integration. Developing or acquiring retail businesses and operating them as part of the firm's strategic marketing effort.

forward stock. Backup stock that is temporarily stored on the sales floor near its selling department.

4-3-2-1 rule. The decline in value of store space from front to back of the shop is expressed by assigning 40 percent of a store's rental cost to the front quarter of the shop; 30 percent to the second quarter; 20 percent to the third quarter; and 10 percent to the final quarter.

franchising. A continuing relationship in which the franchisor provides a licensed privilege to do business, plus assistance in organizing, training, merchandising, and management in return for a consideration from the franchisee.

free-form layout. Arrangment of displays and aisles in a free-flowing pattern.

fringe trading zone. That area from which the retailer occasionally draws customers and representing 5 to 10 percent of total sales.

full-function merchant intermediaries. Performers of a full range of wholesaling functions; based on the width of their product lines, they can be identified as either general merchandise wholesalers, single-line wholesalers, or specialty-line wholesalers.

full-line discount store. A retailing institution that sells a wide variety of merchandise (full-line) at less than traditional retail prices.

full-line forcing. The supplier requires the retailer to carry the supplier's full line of products if the retailer wishes to carry any part of that line.

full-service retailer. The retailer who provides essential, expected, and optional services.

functional approach to organizational structure. The retailer groups tasks and classifies jobs according to such functional areas as store operations, buying and selling merchandise, promotional activities, or recruiting and training store personnel.

functional features. Include the tangible elements of size, shape, and weight, together with a product's chemical and/or biological makeup.

functional objectives. Specific task objectives that identify a specific function and how it is to be accomplished.

functional training. A program that develops and expands the basic skills and knowledge employees need to perform their jobs successfully.

future dating. Allowing the buyer more time to take advantage of the cash discount or to pay the net amount of the invoice.

general business license. A registration fee to operate a business.

general partnership. All partners take part in the control and operation of the partnership; hence, all partners can be held jointly and severally liable for the debts of the partnership.

generic products. Unadvertised, lower-grade, no-frill brands offered as low-cost alternatives to name-brand merchandise.

geographic approach to organizational structure. The retailer organizes tasks and assigns jobs on the basis of where those tasks and jobs are performed.

geographic selectivity. A medium's ability to "home in" on a specific geographic area such as a city and its surrounding area.

gift wraps. Incorporate additional wrapping features such as bows and ribbons to distinguish them clearly from store wraps.

good-faith defense. Makes it lawful for a seller to discriminate in price if such action is done in good faith to meet an equally low price of a competitor.

goods. Tangible items defined by their size, shape, and weight together with their chemical and/or biological makeup.

goods retailers. Retailers who sell a tangible product.

grid layout. A rectangular arrangement of displays and aisles that generally run parallel to one another.

gross adequacy. The ability of a trading area to support a retail operation without any consideration of retail competition.

gross margin. The difference between net sales and total merchandise costs.

gross margin return on inventory (GMROI). The ratio of gross margin dollars to the average stock on hand.

gross sales. The total dollar revenues received from the sale of merchandise and services.

group training methods. Involve the simultaneous training of several employees through lectures, demonstrations, case studies, role-playing activities, computer simulations, and interactive videos.

hand marking. Using grease pencils, ink stamps, and pens to directly mark, package, label, tag, or ticket the merchandise.

harmony. Visual agreement among the many parts of any display, layout, or physical arrangement.

harvesting. Milking an SBU of its cash to finance other SBU alternatives.

headline. Condenses the basic advertising message, telling the reader essentially what is to come.

heavy-handed approach to supervision. Assumes employees are lazy, passive, self-centered, and irresponsible; maintains that employers must closely supervise and control their employees to motivate them to work toward company goals and to assume responsibilities (McGregor's Theory X).

holding. Maintaining an SBU's market share.

home center. Combines the traditional hardware store and lumber yard with a self-service home-improvement center.

horizontal diversification. Adding SBUs that appeal to the organization's current customers even though they are not technologically related to its current businesses.

horizontal integration. A firm's gaining ownership and/or control of competitors at the same level within the marketing channel.

hypermarkets. Huge combination stores with square footages that average 220,000 square feet.

illegal pricing. When different prices are offered or received under similar circumstances, or when similar prices are offered or received under different circumstances.

illustrations. A drawing or a photograph of the product.

immediacy. A medium's ability to present a timely or newsworthy message.

immediate dating. Allowing no time for the cash discount or extra time for the invoice payment.

impact. How well a medium stimulates particular behavioral responses within the target market.

implied warranties. The seller's implied or "intended" promises of product performance, even though not actually expressed in either written or oral form.

importer. A domestically based commission wholesaler who represents retailers in the buying process.

income measurements. Different expressions of the monetary gain the retailer realizes from retailing activities.

income modifications. Monetary additions or reductions applied to one income measurement to calculate another measurement of income.

income statement. A picture of the retailer's profits or losses over a period of time that summarizes the firm's income and expenses.

independent delivery systems. A delivery system owned and operated independently from the retailer.

Index of Retail Saturation (IRS). A measure of potential sales per square foot of store space for a given product line within a particular market area. It expresses a relationship between a trading area's ability to consume and its ability to retail.

indirect-action messages. Attempting to change consumers' attitudes toward the retailer by cultivating its image as the "right" place for the consumer to buy.

indirect expenses. Those expenses that cannot be directly attributed to the operations of a department.

indirect (intertype) competitor. One whose merchandising program is noticeably different from that of a retailer of similar products.

individual training method. Employees "train" themselves; the individual is put on the job and expected to learn by trial and error, observation, and asking questions.

inelastic demand. When a change in price has little or no influence on consumer demand.

informal objective employee evaluation. Employment of professional or mystery shoppers to evaluate employee performance.

informal subjective employee evaluation. Have no structure and rely heavily on the supervisor's intuition.

information flow. The two-way communication of useful data between channel participants.

in-house credit system. A credit system that is owned, operated, and managed by the retail firm.

initial markup. The difference between merchandise cost and the original retail price.

initial markup percentage. The sum of the operating expenses, operating profit, alterations cost, and retail reduction, divided by the sum of the net sales and retail reduction.

installment-credit plan. Allows consumers to pay their total purchase price (less down payment) in equal installment payments over a specified time period.

institutional advertising. Selling the store generally as an enjoyable place to shop.

in-store delivery systems. Delivery systems that can be either wholly owned and operated by an individual store or partially owned and operated with other stores.

in-store testing. Test marketing products within a store, to judge customer wants.

integration strategy. A strategy developed to increase sales by incorporating one or more levels of the marketing channel of distribution into the organization's operations.

intensive growth opportunities. Opportunities found within the organization's current portfolio of businesses.

intensive market coverage. Selecting and utilizing as many retail outlets as are justified to obtain blanket market coverage or an entire market area.

intermediate-term credit. Money that can be borrowed for a term greater than one year but less than five years.

internal information. Information found within the firm.

internally-oriented strategic service vision. Fully integrating employees into the service provider's marketing and operating functions.

intertype competition. Competition between two or more retailers using different types of business formats to sell the same type of merchandise.

intratype competition. Competition between two or more retailers using the same type of business format.

intraurban market. A heterogeneous grouping of people and activities within an urban area.

inventory-analysis system. Methods for evaluating the retailer's past merchandising performance and decision-making tools for controlling future merchandising activities.

inventory assortment. Planning the number of different product items the retailer should stock within a particular product line and determining whether this assortment is adequate to meet the merchandise-selection needs of the firm's targeted consumers.

inventory-information system. The set of methods and procedures for collecting and processing merchandise data pertinent to the planning and control of merchandise inventories.

inventory investment. Planning the total dollar investment in merchandise inventory so that the firm can realize its financial objectives.

inventory support. Planning the number of units the retailer should have on hand for each product item to meet sales estimates.

invoice check. Comparing the invoice with the purchase order.

island windows. Four-sided display windows isolated from the rest of the store.

isolated sites. Retail locations that are geographically separated from other retailing sites.

item addition. Adding to one retailer's traditional product lines the more desirable product items normally associated with another type of retailer.

job description. The first step in the staffing process; contains the following items: (1) job title; (2) job location; (3) job position and relationships; (4) job description.

job specification. The minimum qualifications a person must have to obtain the job applied for.

last-in, first-out (LIFO) method of costing inventories. Recent acquisition costs are used to price inventory (even though in actuality, the inventory bought last is not sold first).

late markdown. Maintain the original selling price until late in the selling season, at which time a major clearance sale is held.

layout. Capturing attention and guiding consumers through all parts of the advertisement.

leader pricing. The strategy of selling key merchandise items below their normal markup or in some cases, even below the retailer's merchandise costs.

learning. The process of acquiring knowledge through past experiences.

lease agreements. Contracts in which the customer rents a product in the present with the option to buy in the future.

leased departments. Retailers that operate departments (usually in specialized lines of merchandise) under contractual arrangements with conventional retail stores.

ledger. A book or file in which a number of accounts are kept together.

leverage ratios. Measure the relative contributions of owners and creditors in the financing of the firm's operations.

licensed products. Items that are designed and sold through identification with a famous individual or corporate name, title, logo, slogan, or fictional character.

life. The length of time an advertisement continues to "sell."

life cycle. A description of the changes that occur in an individual's demographic, psychographic, and behavioristic profile while progressing through a series of stages during his or her lifetime.

life-style. A patterned style of living that stems from the individual's needs, perceptions, and attitudes.

life-style merchandising. Developing product lines in accordance with consumer living patterns.

light-handed supervision. Assumes that providing employees with a favorable work environment can create a situation in which employees will obtain job satisfaction and their personal goals by directing their efforts toward the firm's needs; close supervision and control are unnecessary (McGregor's Theory Y).

Likert's Summated Rating Scale. Measures attitudes and opinions by asking respondents to indicate their extent of agreement or disagreement with a list of statements concerning the issue being studied.

limited channel. A marketing channel that eliminates wholesalers and uses only retailers to reach the final consumer.

limited-function merchant intermediaries. Wholesalers that limit their services offered. Examples include cash-and-carry wholesalers, drop shippers, truck distributors, and rack jobbers.

limited partnership. A legal form of organization with one or more members of the partnership contributing capital to the formation and running of the partnership, but these limited partners do not take part in managing the firm's retail operations.

limited-service strategy. Retailers who offer all essential and expected services.

line combination. The retailer combines two or more broad product lines into the store operation.

line relationships. Affiliations among managers at different organizational levels or between a manager and a subordinate within the same level who are directly responsible for achieving the firm's strategic, operational, and/or functional objectives.

lines of authority and responsibility. Organizational principles that each store employee (managerial and nonmanagerial) should be given the authority to accomplish whatever responsibilities have been assigned to that individual.

liquid capital. Money held in reserve for emergency situations.

liquidity ratios. Answer the question of the firm's solvency; the two most common ratios used are the quick ratio and current ratio.

logical approach. A factual presentation about a merchandise offering.

logotype. The store's distinctive "signature" that appears in all advertising.

long-term credit. Loans secured for periods greater than five years.

long-term liabilities. Indebtedness that is due at some time after the current year.

loss-leaders. Prices reduced to or below the retailer's cost of the merchandise in order to attract consumers to the store.

low-leaders. Prices set below the customary selling price but above the retailer's actual cost of the merchandise.

machine vision. Using video cameras to read bar codes or identify a product through its signature.

magazine advertising. Bought in pages and fractions; usually inside the front cover, the inside and outside of the back cover, opposite the table of contents, and the center spread.

mail-in premiums. Require the customer to send in a proof-of-purchase to receive a free gift.

mail-order retailers. Business formats that contact prospective customers by mail, receive their orders by mail, and/or make their deliveries by mail.

main-store organization. The parent organization (the main store) exercises control over branch stores.

maintained markup. The difference between gross merchandise cost and actual selling price.

manufacturer brands. Products that are produced, owned, controlled, and sometimes distributed by the manufacturer.

manufacturer's agent. The sales agent for several manufacturers within a prescribed market territory.

markdown. A downward adjustment in the original selling price of a merchandise item.

markdown control. Maintaining records on the causes or reasons for taking markdowns on a particular merchandise item.

markdown percentages. A percentage of the reduced selling price or as a percentage of the original selling price.

market. A geographic area where buyers and sellers meet to exchange money for products and services.

market development. A strategy employed by a firm to increase sales of current products through new product uses or selling in new markets.

market objectives. A strategic position aimed at securing customer patronage and achieving competitive positions within the general marketplace.

market penetration. A strategy employed by a firm to increase sales of current products in a current market.

market positioning. The strategy of creating a "position" for a store and its product mix in the minds of consumers by relating it to other stores and their mixture of products.

market potential. A market's total capacity to consume a given good, service, or idea.

market potential approach. The firm selects criteria that reflect the amount of support that a geographic area will provide a given retail operation.

market share. A measure of an organization's sales position relative to all competitors within the same market.

marketing channel. A team of marketing institutions that directs flow of goods or services from the producer to the final consumer.

marketing concept. The philosophy that the overall goal of every business organization is to satisfy consumer needs at a profit.

market-share objectives. Marketing goals that retailers set to increase or maintain their share of the total market.

marking. Affixing to merchandise the information necessary for stocking, controlling, and selling.

markons. The markups taken after the initial selling price has been established.

mathematical programming. The use of mathematics to find optimal solutions to problems.

maximum inventory. The number of merchandise units the retailer needs to cover expected sales during the reorder and delivery periods plus a safety stock for either unexpected sales or problems in securing the merchandise.

Mazur Plan. Divides the retail organization into four functional divisions: finance, merchandising, promotion, and operations.

media coverage. The number of people an advertising medium reaches in a given market area.

media representatives. Employees of newspapers and radio or television stations whose principal job is to sell advertising space and time.

memorandum buying. A variation of consignment buying where title to the merchandise exchanges hands when it is shipped to the retailer but the retailer retains the right to return to the supplier any unsold merchandise and to pay for the merchandise after it has been sold.

merchandise budget. A financial plan for managing merchandise inventory investments.

merchandise buying process. The activities necessary for establishing a successful relationship with various sources of supply.

merchandise category. A closely related line of products within a merchandise group.

merchandise class (classification). A specific line of products within a merchandise category.

merchandise compatibility. The degree of relationship between various merchandise groups.

merchandise control. Designing dollar and unit inventory information and analysis systems for collecting, recording, analyzing, and using merchandise data to determine whether the stated objectives have been achieved.

merchandise group. A broadly related line of products that retailers and consumers associate together according to end use.

merchandise handling process. The activities of physically getting the merchandise into the store and onto the shelves.

merchandise management. Planning and controlling the retailer's inventories.

merchandise ordering process. The efficient securing of the retailer's merchandise inventories.

merchandise planning. Establishing objectives and devising plans for obtaining those objectives.

merchandising. The process of developing, securing, managing, and pricing the merchandise mix to meet the firm's marketing and financial objectives.

merchandising blend. Matches the ingredients of the retailer's merchandising program with the buying decisions the consumer faces.

merchandising utilities. The benefits the consumer seeks in buying, using, and possessing a product.

merchant intermediaries. Wholesalers that are directly involved in the purchase and sale of goods as they move through the channel of distribution.

mergers. When one firm acquires the stocks or assets of another firm and operates as one organization.

middle-aged market. Persons between the ages of thirty-five to sixty-four.

mini-department specialty retailers. "Power format" that utilizes their size, merchandising muscle, and operational efficiency to either dominate the market for a product category or assume at least a market leader position within the product category.

minimum-cutoff method. Establishes a minimum standard or cutoff point for each evaluation criterion; choices are made from alternatives that have exceeded the minimum cutoff on all criteria.

mission statement. A generalized yet meaningful expression of the organization's future direction.

model stock list. A schedule or listing of SKUs for fashion merchandise.

monopolistic isolation. A site that affords the retailer a uniquely convenient and accessible location to serve consumers.

monthly sales estimates. Involves three steps: (1) making annual sales estimates; (2) determining estimated monthly sales; and (3) adjusting monthly sales estimates using a monthly sales index.

motivation. The process by which consumers are moved or incited to action.

multiple-price policy. Gives customers a discount for making quantity purchases; the retailer offers a reduced price if consumers are willing to purchase several units at the multiple-unit price.

multiplex distribution strategy. Serving several target markets using a "free-form" organization that permits it to develop a specialized product mix for each market segment.

narrative projection test. Respondents are given a descriptive situation and are asked to write a paragraph in response.

narrow variety/deep assortment strategy. "Specialty" philosophy which appeals to a select group of consumers by offering only one or a few product lines with an excellent selection within each line.

narrow variety/shallow assortment strategy. Offers consumers the most limited product selection (lines and items).

natural selection. Survival of the fittest.

needs. Essential physiological and psychological requirements necessary to the general physical and mental welfare of the consumer.

Neighborhood Business District (NBD). A small retailing cluster that serves primarily one or two residential areas.

neighborhood shopping center. A shopping center that obtains its customers from one or a few neighborhoods within the immediate vicinity.

net adequacy. The ability of a trading area to provide support for a retailer after competition has been taken into account.

net invoice price. The net value of the invoice or the total invoice minus all other discounts.

net profit. The sum of operating profit and other income minus other expenses.

net sales. The income measurement that results when returns and allowances are subtracted from gross sales.

net worth. The owner's equity in the business.

never-out list. A specially created list of merchandise items that are identified as key items or best-sellers for which the retailer wants extra protection against the possibility of a stockout.

newspaper advertising. Advertising in specific sections of the paper, such as the sports, society, and financial sections.

niche specialist. Retailers who are targeting a market with carefully selected merchandise and appropriately designed stores.

niching. Moving an SBU into a market niche in which the fit between resource requirements and available resources is more acceptable.

noise. Anything that occurs during the communication process that distracts senders or receivers, interferes with the encoding and decoding activity, or interrupts the transmission or feedback process.

nondurables. Perishable products that are used up in one or a few uses.

nonprobability sample. Each individual in the total population does not have a known and equal chance of being selected.

nonstore retailing. Retailers that do not use conventional store facilities as part of their standard mode of operation.

objective and task method. Establishing the objectives for advertising; determining the type and amounts of advertising necessary to accomplish these objectives; determining the overall cost of the advertisement; and scheduling the advertisements day by day.

observability. The extent to which the consumer can see a new product's favorable attributes.

observation method. Gathering primary information by recording some aspect of consumers' overt behavior by either personal or mechanical means.

odd pricing. Setting prices that end in odd numbers.

off-price retailers. Specialty retailers that sell both soft goods and/or hard goods at price levels (20 to 60 percent) below regular retail prices.

off-retail markdown percentage formula. Original price minus reduced price divided by the original price.

off-the-job training. Conducted in centralized training-classrooms away from the employees' work environment.

one-price policy. Charging all customers the same price for the same product under similar circumstances.

one-price retailer. Stores that offer all merchandise (e.g., overruns, odd lots, cancelled orders, and closeouts) at a single, fixed price.

on-the-job training. A decentralized approach that occurs on the sales floor, in the stockroom, or in some other work environment where employees are performing their jobs.

open-account credit plan. Allows customers to buy merchandise and to pay for it within a specific time period without finance charges or interest.

open-to-buy. The amount of new merchandise the retailer can buy during a specific time period without exceeding the planned purchases for that period.

operating expense. Those expenses incurred in operating a business.

operating profit. The difference between gross margin and operating expenses.

operating ratios. Mathematical relationships between elements in the income statement used to determine a firm's operating performance.

operational objectives. General, long-term operational requirements necessary to achieve a strategic objective.

opinion leaders. Persons whose attitudes, opinions, preferences, and actions affect others.

optional services. Services neither necessary to the retailer's operation nor expected by the customer.

option-term revolving credit. Gives customers two payment options: (1) they can pay the full amount of the bill within a specified number of days and avoid any finance charges, or (2) they can make at least a minimum payment and be assessed finance charges on the unpaid balance.

order form. A legally binding contract when signed by both parties, specifying the terms and conditions under which the transaction is to be conducted.

order getters. Sales personnel who are actively involved in the selling process.

order takers. Sales personnel who simply comply with the customer's requests for certain types of merchandise.

organization orientation. A program that either initiates new employees or updates old employees on the general organizational structure of the firm and its policies, rules, and regulations.

organizational markets. Composed of industrial firms, resellers, and governments who represent intermediate consumers of goods and services.

organizational objective. A strategic position to be attained or a purpose to be achieved by the organization and/or one of its strategic business units.

organizational portfolio. The collection of strategic business units held and managed by an organization.

outshopper analysis. A method to estimate total expected sales by subtracting outshopping sales from the trading area's gross sales to arrive at a more realistic sales volume for the trading area.

overstored market areas. Those in which the capacity to retail exceeds the capacity to consume.

ownership flow. Transferring title from one channel participant to another.

participation. The active involvement in the learning process.

partner. A store employee who does not actually pilfer the merchandise or money, but who supplies outside individuals with information or devices that increase the likelihood of successful theft.

partnership. When two or more persons form a business without incorporating.

patronage appeal. Emphasizing the rightness of the store, location, and hours.

patronage probability. The area from which potential customers come who have a probability greater than zero of purchasing a given class of products or services that either a retailer or group of retailers offers for sale.

payment flow. The transfer of monies from one channel participant to another as compensation for services rendered and/or goods delivered.

per capita sales method. Estimates trading-area sales for a general product line and is a function of the per capita expenditures for that product line times the total population of that trading area.

percentage markup. Calculated to facilitate the process of setting prices and to permit comparisons between merchandise lines and departments.

percentage-of-sales method. Taking a predetermined percentage of either the previous sales or the estimated sales for the coming year to calculate how much to spend on advertising.

percentage variation method. A procedure that attempts to adjust stock levels in accordance with actual variations in sales.

perception. The process by which consumers attach meaning to incoming stimuli by forming mental pictures of persons, places, and objects.

periodic physical inventory. A system of gathering stock information intermittently, using an actual physical count and inspection of the merchandise items to compute sales for the period since the last physical inventory.

peripheral approach. Locates sales support areas around the exterior of the store or floor.

perishability. An offering which loses its qualities or meaning within a short period of time.

perpetual book inventory. A system of inventory taking and information gathering on a continuous or ongoing basis using various accounting records to compute stock on hand at any given time.

personal communications. The process of exchanging ideas and meanings with other people.

personal discrimination. When the personal biases of an individual in authority enter the decision-making process in employment matters to the detriment of applicants or employees.

personal selling. Direct, face-to-face communication between a retail salesperson and a retail consumer.

personality. A general response pattern used by individuals in coping with their environment.

personality traits. Individual characteristics people acquire over a lifetime.

physical flow. The actual movement of a physical product from one channel participant to another.

physiological needs. Life-sustaining and creature comforts that need to be reasonably satisfied before the search for fulfillment of higher-order needs.

pilferers. Shoplifters.

planned cluster site. A purposeful cluster of retail and service establishments at a location designed to serve a specific geographic, demographic, and psychographic market segment.

planned publicity. Publicity over which the retailer exercises some control.

point-of-purchase (POP) display. Designed to attract customer attention and interest, reinforce the store's creative theme, and fit in with the store's interior decoration.

population density. The number of persons living within a delineated geographic area.

predatory pricing. A pricing tactic whereby the retailer charges customers different prices for the same merchandise in different markets to eliminate competition in one or more of those markets.

premium. A merchandise item given to the consumer free of charge or at a substantial price reduction as an inducement to purchase another product or to participate in an activity, or both.

prepayment dating. Making payment when the order is placed.

preretailing. A retail buying practice of deciding the selling price of merchandise before it is purchased and recording that price on the store's copy of the purchase order so the store's "markers" can put the selling price on the merchandise as soon as it arrives.

prestige. The amount of status consumers attach to a medium.

price changer. Pays for the merchandise but only after a shoplifter's reduction by altering or switching the store's price tag or by removing the store tag and substituting a realistic fake.

price discrimination. Covers a number of situations involving pricing arrangements under various buying or selling circumstances; can be legally justified when different prices are offered or received under different circumstances.

price elasticity of demand. A measure of the effect a price change has on consumer demand (i.e., the number of units sold).

price fixing. An illegal pricing activity in which several retailers establish a fixed retail selling price for a particular product line within a market area.

price-lining. Directing retail prices at a targeted consumer group.

pricing above the competition. When the products make a substantially greater per-unit profit than the lower-priced retailer's products.

pricing below the competition. Securing merchandise at a lower cost and keeping operating expenses as low as possible.

pricing lines. Specific pricing points established within pricing zones.

pricing with the competition. The retailer has elected to de-emphasize the price factor as a major merchandising tool and instead decided to compete on a location, product, service, and promotion basis.

pricing zone. A range of prices that appeals to a particular group of consumers either for demographic reasons, psychographic reasons, product usage reasons, or product benefit reasons.

primary information. New information the retailer collects for a specific purpose tailored to its needs.

primary trading zone. The area around which a retailer can expect to attract 50 to 70 percent of its business.

principle of accessibility. The more easily potential consumers can approach, enter, traverse, and exit a site, the more likely they will visit the site to shop.

principle of cumulative attraction. A cluster of similar and complementary retailing activities will generally have greater drawing power than dispersed and isolated stores engaging in the same retailing activities.

principle of interception. A site's positional qualities that determine its ability to intercept customers as they travel from one place to another.

principle of store congestion. As store locations become more saturated with stores, other business activities, and people, they become less attractive to additional shopping traffic.

private-label credit system. A credit system that retailers offer under their name but that a bank operates and manages.

probability sample. Each individual in the total population has a known chance of being selected.

problem recognition. A felt discrepancy between an ideal state of affairs and the actual state of affairs.

product advertising. Presenting specific merchandise for sale and urging customers to come to the store immediately to buy.

product appeal. Emphasizing the rightness of a product for consumers.

product approach to retail organizational structure. The retailer organizes the store by product line.

product assortment. The number of different product items the retailer stocks within a particular product line.

product attributes. Attributes of a product which influence which and how many products retailers stock.

product compatibility. The nature of the relationship between various product lines and between various product items within them.

product complement. A product that is bought and used in conjunction with another product.

product development. Modifying current products or developing new products that appeal to current markets.

product guarantees. Policy statements by retailers expressing their general responsibility for the products they sell.

product item. A specific product within a product line that is unique and clearly distinguishable from other products within and outside the product line.

product liability. Can result from either failing to inform the customer of the dangers associated with using the product; misrepresenting the product as to how, when, and where it should be used; or selling a product that results in injury as a result of its failure to meet warranty standards.

product life cycle (PLC). A series of stages a product passes through: introduction, growth, maturity, and decline.

product line. Any grouping of related products.

product-mix concept. The full range or mixture of products the retailer offers to consumers.

product profitability. Contribution of a product directed in the sense of per-unit profit or indirect by creating customer traffic and additional sales on other products.

product substitute. A product consumers use for the same general purpose as another product; it has the same basic functional attributes and meets the same basic consumer needs.

product variety. The number of different product lines the retailer stocks in the store.

productivity-based budgeting. A series of expense budgets are prepared to correspond to various sales levels.

products. Bundles of benefits capable of satisfying consumer wants and needs.

profit margin. Net profit after taxes divided by net sales.

profit-maximization objectives. The highest possible profit through pricing and other merchandising activities.

programmed learning. (1) Employees study a unit of material; (2) they respond to a series of questions on the material they read; (3) they receive immediate feedback on their performance in answering the questions; (4) they continue to repeat the first three steps until they master the material.

promotion. Providing the consumer information regarding the retailer's store and its product-service offering as well as influencing consumer perceptions, attitudes, and behavior toward the store and what it has to offer.

promotion flow. The flow of persuasive communication directed at influencing the decisions of consumers and other channel participants.

promotional allowances. Reductions in the price retailers pay suppliers for merchandise. These include advertising allowances, preferred selling space, free display materials, and merchandise deals.

proportional trading area. An area based on the distance customers are from the store and their likelihood of patronage.

psychological benefits. Benefits derived from buying, using, and possessing the product.

psychological tests. Instruments designed to measure an applicant's personality, intelligence, aptitudes, interests, and supervisory skills.

publicity. Indirect, impersonal communication carried by a mass medium that is neither paid for nor credited to an identified sponsor.

purchase intercept technique. An in-store information-gathering technique consisting of observing customer in-store shopping behavior, recording pertinent shopping behavior information, and interviewing customers immediately about their purchase or shopping behavior.

pure goods retailer. Retailers that provide no services whatsoever.

pyramid arrangements. Triangular displays of merchandise in vertical (stacked) or horizontal (unstacked) form.

quality check. Examining merchandise for damage and imperfections.

quantity check. Checking the actual physical contents of each package against the purchase order, the invoice, or both.

quantity discounts. Discounts given by suppliers to buyers of large quantities of merchandise.

question marks. SBUs with a low market share in a high-growth market.

quick ratio. Computed by dividing current assets minus inventory by current liabilities; measures the firm's ability to meet current payments with assets that can be immediately converted to cash.

quick response replenishment system. A short cycle merchandise replenishment system that involves an automatic restocking of the retailer's inventories within a matter of days.

radio advertising. Sold as either network radio (buying from several stations that air joint programming) or spot radio (bought from individual stations).

radio frequency data communication. The transmitting of data through the airwaves between a hand-held data collection device and a host computer.

ramped windows. Standard display windows having a display floor higher in back than in front.

rank-ordered question. The respondent is asked to rank a list of factors in order of their importance.

ratio analysis. An examination of the relationship between elements in the income statement and/or balance sheet.

real-time processing. Continuous feeding of data from input devices connected directly to a computer.

receiving. The actual physical exchange of goods between the retailer and the supplier's transporting agent.

records search. All methods used in gathering internal secondary information.

reference group. A group that serves as a model or standard for an individual's behavior and attitudes.

regional shopping center. A shopping center built around one or two full-line department stores.

regression models. Models using linear or multiple regression equations to analyze determinants of retail performance.

regular buying. The systematic cutting and issuing of purchase orders and reorders.

reinforcement. The comparing of anticipated results with the actual results experienced from a chosen response.

related groupings. Ensemble displays that present accessory items along with the featured merchandise.

relative advantage. The extent to which the new product is perceived to be better than existing products.

reliability of the supplier. Criteria to be considered in including a product in the product mix.

repetition. The act of repeating a past experience, or the number of times a consumer is exposed to an advertisement.

resale price maintenance. Commonly referred to as "fair-trade laws"; was designed to permit manufacturers and wholesalers to set retail prices by requiring retailers to sign contracts agreeing to sell their products at the "suggested" prices.

reserve stock. Backup stock held in reserve, usually in a central stockroom.

resident buying offices. Organizations specializing in the buying function and located in major wholesaling and producing markets.

residential buying offices. Keeps the retailer abreast of which products are available and which new products are in the offing.

responses. The actions taken to reduce a cue-stimulated drive.

retail accordion. (also known as the general-specific-general process). Based on the premise that the changing character of retail competition stems from strategies that alter the width (selection) of the merchandise mix.

retail compatibility. The degree to which two businesses interchange customers.

retail competition. The actions of one retailer against other retailers in securing resources and the patronage of consumers.

retail displays. Nonperson, in-store presentations and exhibitions of merchandise together with related information.

retail gravitation concept. Provides a measure of the potential interaction between various locations by determining the relative drawing power of each location.

retail intelligence. Any method or combination of methods used to obtain external secondary information.

retail life cycle. The stages of this identifiable life-cycle pattern are innovation, accelerated development, maturity, and decline.

retail method of inventory valuation. Method of estimating the cost value of an ending inventory for a particular accounting period without taking a physical inventory.

retail operations approach. The area from which either a marketing unit or group can operate economically, depending on volume, cost to operate, and cost to sell and/or deliver a good or service.

retail procurement system. Comprised of the buying, ordering, and handling processes.

retail reductions. The difference between the merchandise item's original retail value and the actual final sales value.

retail research. The use of a set of scientific procedures to gather external primary information from consumers, suppliers, and competitors.

retail site. The actual physical location from which a retail business operates.

retail trading area. That area from which a store attracts its customers or obtains its business.

retailer. Any business establishment that directs its marketing effort toward the final consumer for the purpose of selling goods or services.

retailer-sponsored cooperative group. A contractual organization formed by many small independent retailers and usually involving the common ownership of a wholesaler; allows the small independent to realize economies of scale by making large-quantity group purchases.

retailing. The business activity of selling goods or services to the final consumer.

retailing information system. An interacting organization of people, machines, and methods designed to produce a regular, continuous, and orderly flow of information necessary for the retailer's problem-solving and decision-making activities.

return on assets. Net profit after taxes divided by total assets.

return on net worth. Net profit after taxes divided by net worth.

revolving credit. An incorporation of features from both the open-account and installment plans.

rifle merchandising. A strategy of targeting a product offering to a select group of customers.

right appeal. The right message, the right audience, and the right media.

right message. The right thing to say presented in the right manner.

right price. The amount consumers are willing to pay and retailers are willing to accept in exchange for merchandise and services.

right quantity. The exact match between the consumer's buying and using needs and the retailer's buying and selling needs.

robbery. Stealing or taking anything of value by force, or violence, or by use of fear.

safety needs. Feelings of security and stability.

salary plus bonus plan. A straight monthly salary supplemented by either semiannual or annual bonuses for exceeding performance goals.

salary plus commission plan. Provides employees with a salary and a commission.

Sales Activity Index (SAI). Measures an area's per capita retail sales compared to those of the nation as a whole.

sales agents. People independent of the manufacturer that assume the entire marketing function for a manufacturer.

sales incentive. Any direct or indirect nonpersonal inducement that offers extra value to customers.

sales per square foot method. The retailer computes a ratio of each retailer's floor space devoted to a specific product category to the total of all retail floor space for the product category in the trading area.

sales promotion director. Responsible for supervising and coordinating the activities of an advertising manager, a display manager, and a special events, publicity, or public relations coordinator.

sales promotion manager. Works with merchandise managers to develop and coordinate advertising, promotion, and displays with sales and special promotions.

sales promotions. Direct and indirect impersonal inducements that offer an extra value to consumers.

sales-volume objectives. Sales objectives in terms of either sales volume or market share.

sample. Some portion of a predefined population.

sampling. A sales incentive which involves giving the customer a free trial or sample of the product.

sandwich approach. Using one floor of a multilevel store for sales support activities.

satisfiers. Employment factors that produce pleasurable reactions within people's work lives.

saturated market area. An area in which the capacity to retail equals the capacity of buyers to consume a product line.

scent appeal. Process of creating an atmosphere that encourages buying through pleasant scents.

scientific method. A set of procedures that allows the retailer to gather and analyze data in a systematic, controlled fashion.

seasonal discounts. Price reductions given to buyers who are willing to order, receive, and pay for goods during the "off season."

Secondary Business Districts (SBDs). Retailing clusters located at the intersections of major traffic arteries.

secondary information. Existing information that has been collected for another purpose and that is often published.

secondary trading zone. An area surrounding the primary zone and generally representing 20 to 30 percent of a retailer's total sales volume.

selection displays. Occupy rows of stationary aisle and wall units designed to expose the complete assortment of merchandise to the consumer.

selective distortion. The act of misinterpreting incoming stimuli to make them consistent with the individual's beliefs and attitudes.

selective exposure. The act of limiting the type and amount of stimuli that is received and admitted to awareness.

selective market coverage. Choosing enough locations to ensure adequate coverage of selected target markets.

selective retention. The act of remembering only the information that the individual wants to remember.

self-actualization. The desire to reach one's full potential as an individual.

self-concept. The set of perceptions that people have of themselves within a social context.

self-liquidating premiums. Require the consumer to pay something for the premium.

self-service operation. Retailers who restrict their service offering to essential services.

self-wrappers. Shoplifters that use their own wrapping paper to wrap store merchandise before removing it from the store.

Semantic Differential Rating Scale. A set of seven-point, bipolar scales that measure the meanings and attitudes that people have regarding some object.

sender. A retailer that wants to inform or persuade a select group of consumers about the benefits of an idea.

separate-store organization. Treats each branch as an independent operation with its own organizational structure of managers, buyers, and sales personnel.

service features. "Extras" that might include delivery, alterations, installation, repairs, warranties, returns, adjustments, wrapping, telephone and mail ordering, or any other service that consumers want for purchase satisfaction.

service retailers. Retailers who sell a product that emphasizes people, ideas, and information instead of a tangible object.

services. Largely intangible activities that typically involve the application of human skills within a consumer problem-solving context.

shadow box windows. Small, box-like display windows set at eye-level heights.

shoplifting. The act of pilfering merchandise from a store display by customers and individuals posing as customers.

shopping products. Products for which consumers want to make price, quality, suitability, and/or style comparisons.

shortages. Reductions in the total value of the retailer's inventory as a result of shoplifting, pilfering, and merchandise being damaged and misplaced.

short counts. Delivering fewer items than were listed on the purchase order and signed for on the invoice.

short-term credit. Money that can be borrowed for less than one year.

shotgun merchandising. The marketing strategy of broadening the retail offering to meet consumers' expanding needs.

sight appeal. The process of imparting stimuli, resulting in perceived visual relationships.

sign advertising. Outdoor advertising (posters, bulletins, and spectaculars); good for presenting only a short reminder message (store name, an illustration, and a few words of copy).

silent witness program. Rewards employees with cash for anonymous tips on theft activities of other employees.

simulation. The use of mathematics to develop models of situations and to provide solutions by utilizing various parameter values and observing results.

single-most-important criterion. Comparing alternatives and judging one superior according to the single-most-important criterion.

single trade discount. A single percentage adjustment to the supplier's list price.

site compatibility. Fitting the store to the natural lay of the land and the natural habitat.

site geography. Site alternatives that meet the size, shape, and terrain requirements of the retailer's operation.

smart cards. An identification card that has a small microprocessor embedded in a plastic card.

smuggler. The employee who takes merchandise out of the store by whatever means available.

social needs. The desire for love, belongingness, affection, and friendship.

sole proprietorship. A business owned and managed by a single individual.

sound appeal. Process of creating an atmosphere that encourages buying through music, etc.

source marking. The system by which the retailer authorizes the manufacturer or supplier to mark the merchandise before shipping it to the store.

span of control. Sets guidelines for the number of subordinates a superior should control, depending on the level within the organization and the nature of the tasks being performed.

special business license. Applies to either the sale of certain types of products or the operation of a particular type of retail organization.

special display. A notable presentation of merchandise designed to attract special attention and make a lasting impression on the consumer.

specialization. A distinguishing feature of chain store organizations whereby employees specialize by task and function.

specialized reporting services. Offer information on certain product lines and merchandising activities; provide retailers with information periodically in the form of newspapers, special reports, or flash reports; cost can be substantial.

special-purchase price. A low advertised price on merchandise the retailer has purchased at reduced prices.

specialties. A useful article of merchandise that is imprinted with an advertisement and given to the customer without obligation.

specialty products. Those products in which the consumer's buying behavior is directed at securing a particular good, service, or idea without regard to time, effort, or expense.

specialty shopping center. A cluster of specialty retailers that tends to be more focused on its target market.

specialty store. Specializes in the merchandise it offers a consumer; vary according to (1) the type, selection, and quality of merchandise; (2) the range of price lines; and (3) the size, design, and location of stores.

specification buying. The retailer acquires merchandise that is unique and distinctive from that of competitors and is thus personalized.

spoiler. An individual who purposely damages merchandise, then takes it up to the store manager in order to obtain a markdown.

sponsor method of training. Uses an experienced employee to assume part or all of the responsibility for training a new employee.

spotting techniques. Methods by which a retailer attempts to "spot" customer origins on a map.

staff relationships. Advisory or supportive relationships appearing on organizational charts as broken lines.

staples. Product items for which sales are either very stable or highly variable but very predictable.

stars. SBUs having a high market share within a high-growth market.

stasher. The store employee who hides merchandise in a secure place inside the store.

statistical inferences. Used to make interpretations from a sample about the total population under study.

step arrangements. A series of steps beginning at a low point on one side of a display area and progressing directly to a higher point on the opposite side of that area.

stock-keeping unit (SKU). A merchandise category for which separate records (sales and stock) are maintained.

stocking. All the activities associated with in-store and between-store distribution of merchandise.

stock/sales ratio method. Maintaining a certain ratio of goods on hand to planned monthly sales.

stock turnover. The rate at which the retailer depletes and replenishes stock.

store (private-label) brands. Items owned, controlled, merchandised, and sold through the retailer's own outlets.

store displays. Direct, impersonal in-store presentations and exhibitions of merchandise together with related information.

store image. A mental picture that forms in the human mind as a result of many different stimuli.

store marking. The practice of having store personnel mark all merchandise after the store has received it.

store visibility. The consumer's mental map of where to shop for a certain product or service.

store wrap. The wrapping of customers' purchases in a standard wrapping paper or box.

straight-commission plan. A store employee receives a percentage of what he or she sells; either fixed or variable.

straight front configuration. A store configuration that runs parallel to the sidewalk, street, mall, or parking lot.

straight-salary plan. A fixed amount of compensation for a specified work period; offers the advantages of easy administration and a high level of employer control.

strategic business unit. A business division with a clearly identifiable merchandise strategy that targets a market segment within a defined competitive environment.

strategic objectives. General, long-term goals that the retail firm intends to pursue.

strategic plan. A grand design or blueprint for ensuring success in all of the organization's business endeavors.

strategic retail management. The process of planning the organization, implementation, and control of all the firm's activities.

string/strip cluster. A retailing cluster developed along a major thoroughfare and depending upon the consumption activity of people who travel these busy thoroughfares.

style. The characteristic or distinctive form, outline, or shape of a product item.

suggestive selling. A closing technique in which the salesperson shows the customer other merchandise that complements the item they are going to buy.

supercenters. Large combination supermarket/discount stores that typically range in size from 100,000 to 130,000 square feet.

supermarket. No commonly accepted definition exists because of the wide range of business formulas used in this industry.

super regional shopping center. A shopping center built around at least three and often four major department stores.

super specialist. Retailers who present a single, narrowly defined classification of merchandise with an extensive assortment of brands, sizes, colors, materials, styles, and prices.

superstore retailers. Huge combination supermarkets and discount general merchandise stores that stock and sell a complete selection of food products together with a wide variety of hard and soft goods at deep discount prices.

supervision. The process of directing, coordinating, and inspecting the efforts of store employees to attain both company and individual goals.

survey method. The systematic gathering of information directly from the appropriate respondents.

Survey of Buying Power. An annual publication compiled by the editors of *Sales and Marketing Management* magazine.

sweeper. A shoplifter who simply brushes merchandise off the counter into a shopping bag or some other type of container.

sweepstakes. Promotions in which customers win prizes based on chance.

systematic discrimination. The unintentional and inadvertent discrimination resulting from policies, practices, and decision-making criteria that negatively affect protected classes.

systems competition. Competition between two or more vertical marketing systems.

tangibility. Possessing qualities capable of being perceived or precisely identified or realized by the customer's mind.

target return objectives. Profit objectives for guiding price-setting decisions.

taste appeal. Providing potential customers with a sample of an edible product under clean and sanitary conditions.

technological environment. The various improvements in the technical processes that increase the productivity and efficiency of machines and that eliminate or reduce manual operations.

telemarketing. The selling of goods and services through telephone contact.

television advertising. Time sold as network or spot time.

Thematic Apperception Test. Respondents are shown a cartoon, drawing, or picture and then asked to put themselves into the situation and tell a story about what is happening or what they should do.

theme appeal. Ideas centered around natural and holiday seasons, historical periods, current issues, and special events to provide a focus on planning physical facilities.

theme groupings. Display merchandise according to a central theme or setting.

third-party credit systems. The acceptance of one or more credit cards issued by outside institutions.

three C's of credit. Character, capacity, and capital.

tie-ins. An approach to attract attention to a store's offering by associating the offering with an entertainment event, a character, or person's name.

total advertisement. The headline, illustration, copy, logotype, and layout of an ad.

total assets. The sum of current assets and fixed assets.

total population. The total number of persons or organizations within an area at a given time.

total-product concept. Acknowledges the need for retailers to market every one of a product's dimensions.

total sales method. The retailer allocates an equal share of the trading area's total sales for a specific product category to each competing retailer.

touch appeal. Process of creating an atmosphere that encourages buying through providing the ability to touch the product.

trade discount. A form of compensation that the buyer may receive for performing certain functions for the supplier.

trade fairs. Periodic displays of many suppliers' merchandise lines in one place at one time.

trade shows. Occasions when manufacturers get together to exhibit their merchandise in one place.

trading-area adequacy. The ability of a trading area to support proposed and existing retail operations.

trading-area potential. The predicted ability of a trading area to provide acceptable support levels for a retailer in the future.

transmission. Process of sending the message to those consumers targeted as the most suitable recipients of the message.

trialability. The extent to which a new product can be tested on a trial basis.

trickle-across theory. Recognizes that a fashion or style can originate within any social class.

trickle-down theory. Hypothesizes that new innovative fashions and styles originate in the upper socioeconomic classes and are passed down through the middle class to the lower socioeconomic consumer.

trickle-up theory. States that some unusual fashions or styles are developed in the lower socioeconomic classes, picked up by the upper class, and finally adopted by the middle class.

trunk show. Merchandise demonstrations by the designer or manufacturer within the retailer's store.

two-step flow of communications. The ultimate effects of advertising magnified by personal communications among consumers.

tying contracts. Conditional selling arrangements between retailers and suppliers in which a supplier agrees to sell a retailer a highly sought-after line of products if the retailer will agree to buy additional product lines from the same supplier.

ultimate consumers. Individuals who purchase goods and services for their own personal use or for use by members of their household.

uncontrollable expenses. Expenses over which the firm has no control and cannot adjust to current operating needs in the short run.

undercover shoppers. Persons hired to pose as customers to observe the activities and performance of employees.

understored market areas. Those in which the capacity to consume exceeds the capacity to retail.

unemployment compensation. A tax levied by the state on each retailer's payroll; employees who are either laid off or fired usually qualify for benefits; employees who simply quit usually do not qualify.

unfair trade practice acts. Regulate the right of retailers to sell either below cost or at cost plus some minimum markup.

unit control. Deals with the number of different product items and the number of units stocked within each item.

unit groupings. Highlight a separate category of product items; contain merchandise that is almost identical or closely related.

unit open-to-buy. Determining maximum inventory and computing the unit open-to-buy quantity.

unit/periodic/physical inventory. Making a periodic physical check on the status of the retailer's inventory through visual observation or actual product counts.

unit/perpetual/book system. Involves continuous recording of all transactions, which changes the unit status of the retailer's merchandise inventory.

unit pricing. Posting prices on a per-unit-measurement basis.

unity of command. States that the organizational structure of the retail firm should ensure that each store employee be directly accountable to only one immediate supervisor at any one time for any given task.

Universal Product Code (UPC). A bar code system that identifies both the product and the manufacturer.

unlimited liability. The sole proprietor assumes total responsibility for all debts stemming from the business; that responsibility extends to current and future personal as well as business assets.

unplanned publicity. Publicity over which the retailer simply responds to the uncontrollable events as they occur.

unrelated products. Neither substitutes nor complements, but retailers seriously consider them for their product mix since they represent potential additional sales, theoretically at low risk and a reasonable profit.

utilitarianism. Judges not the act itself but the consequences of the act.

values. Core beliefs or desires which guide or motivate attitudes and actions.

variable expenses. Expenses that vary with the volume of sales.

variable-price policy. Allows the customer to negotiate the final selling price.

vending machine retailing. Similar to convenience store retailing in that it usually serves to meet the "fill-in," "emergency," and "after- or off-hour" needs of consumers.

vertical competition. Competition between a retailer and a wholesaler or producer that is attempting to make retail sales to the retailer's customers.

vertical integration. The merger of two organizations from different levels within a channel of distribution.

vertical marketing system. A distribution arrangement that integrates the marketing channel to achieve operating economies and common objectives.

vertical (or tall) organizational structure. Many layers of supervisor-subordinate relationships; a large number of levels separate top management from employees at the bottom of the organization.

voice recognition. Computers responding to the human voice for data input or operating commands.

walker. Usually a woman; capable of carrying, in a completely natural way, both small items such as jewelry and large items such as small appliances out of the store.

want books and slips. Range from simple blank notebooks and slips of paper to printed books and forms.

warehouse clubs. Huge outlets which cater to customers who have joined the club in order to secure merchandise at 20 to 40 percent below prices at supermarkets and discount stores.

warehouse showroom. A single-line, hard-goods retailer that stocks merchandise such as furniture, appliances, or carpeting.

warranty. A specific statement by the seller of the quality or performance capabilities of the product and the exact terms under which the seller will take action to correct product deficiencies.

wearer. A shoplifter that tries on merchandise, then wears it out of the store.

week's supply method. A stock plan that determines stock levels in direct proportion to sales.

weighted-rating method. A procedure for evaluating alternatives by assigning weighted values to each of a set of evaluation criteria.

wheel of retailing. Most widely recognized theory of retail institutional change involving the entry phase, the trading-up phase, and the vulnerability phase.

wholesaler-sponsored voluntary chain. Contractual arrangement in which a wholesaler develops a merchandising program that independent retailers voluntarily join.

wide variety/deep assortment strategy. A large number of product lines with supporting depth in each line.

wide variety/shallow assortment strategy. A wide selection of different product lines but limited selection of brands, styles, sizes, etc., within each line.

word-association test. A set of words or phrases to which respondents must give their immediate reactions.

workers' compensation. An employee accident and disability insurance program required under various state laws; covers the employee who is accidentally injured while working or who is unable to work as a result of a disease associated with a particular occupation.

working capital. Money needed to meet day-to-day operating expenses.

zero-based budgeting. A budgeting process in which each operating department starts with no allocated expenses; to secure operating funds, each department must justify its need for each expense item on the budget.

zig-zag arrangements. Modified pyramids that zig and zag their way to the apex of the display.

zoning ordinances. Controls that local governments place on land use by regulating the types of activities and buildings located in certain areas.

NAME INDEX

SUBJECT INDEX